JEAN DUNAND

HIS LIFE AND WORKS

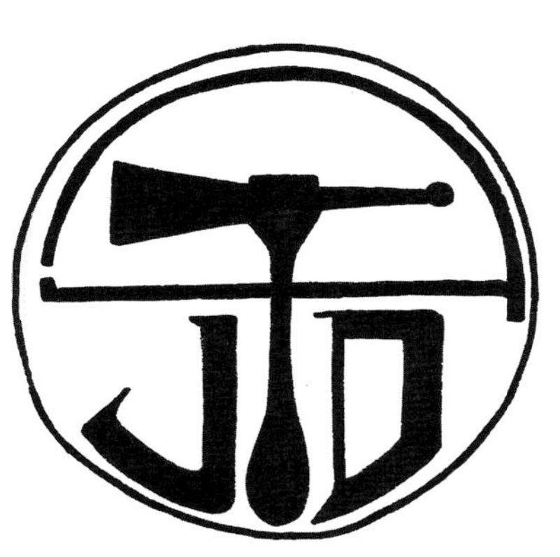

Foreword by Bernard Dunand

*with a comprehensive oeuvre catalogue
and sections devoted to
Jean Dunand's sons and collaborators,
Bernard and Pierre*

HARRY N. ABRAMS, INC., PUBLISHERS,
NEW YORK

JEAN DUNAND

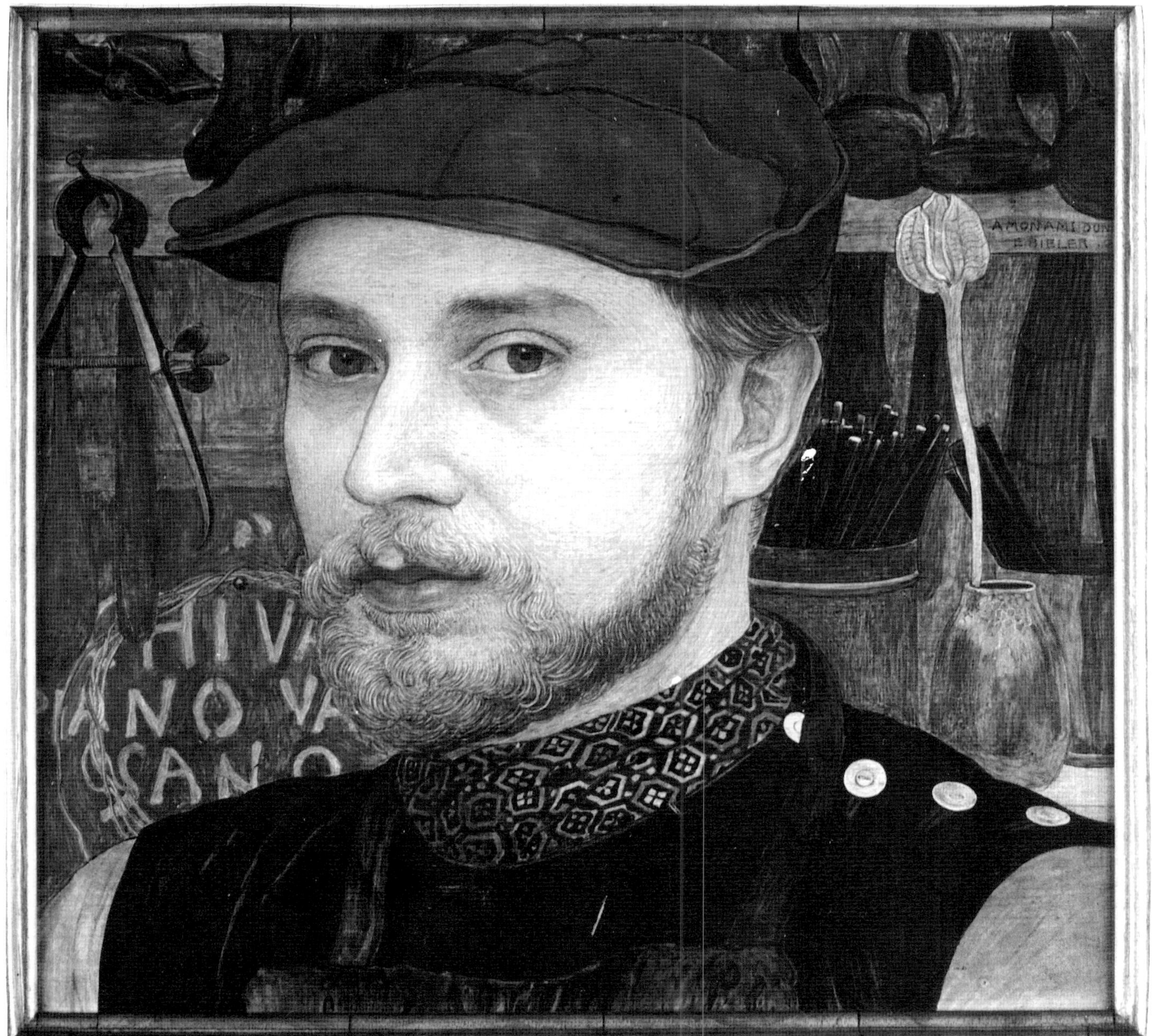

HIS LIFE AND WORKS

By

FÉLIX MARCILHAC

To the four surviving sons and daughters of Jean Dunand and to the memory of Jean-Louis and Robert Dunand

Page 1: Jean Dunand's stamp as used on dinanderie pieces made by the master-craftsman.
Page 3 (title page): Portrait of Jean Dunand by Ernest Biéler, oil on panel, 1909.

Translated and adapted from the original French

Library of Congress Cataloging-in-Publication Data

Marcilhac, Félix.
Jean Dunand: his life and works/Félix Marcilhac; foreword by Bernard Dunand; with a comprehensive oeuvre catalogue and appendices devoted to Jean Dunand's sons and collaborators, Bernard and Pierre.
p. cm.
Includes bibliographical references (p.
ISBN 0–8109–3202–4
1. Dunand, Jean, 1877–1942. 2. Artists–France–Biography.
3. Dunand, Jean, 1877–1942–Catalogues raisonnés. 4. Art deco–France. I. Title.
N6853.D855M37 1990
709'.2–dc20 89–18584
CIP

Published in 1991 by Harry N. Abrams, Incorporated, New York

A Times Mirror Company

Printed and bound in Japan

CONTENTS

The Dunand family: a brief chronology

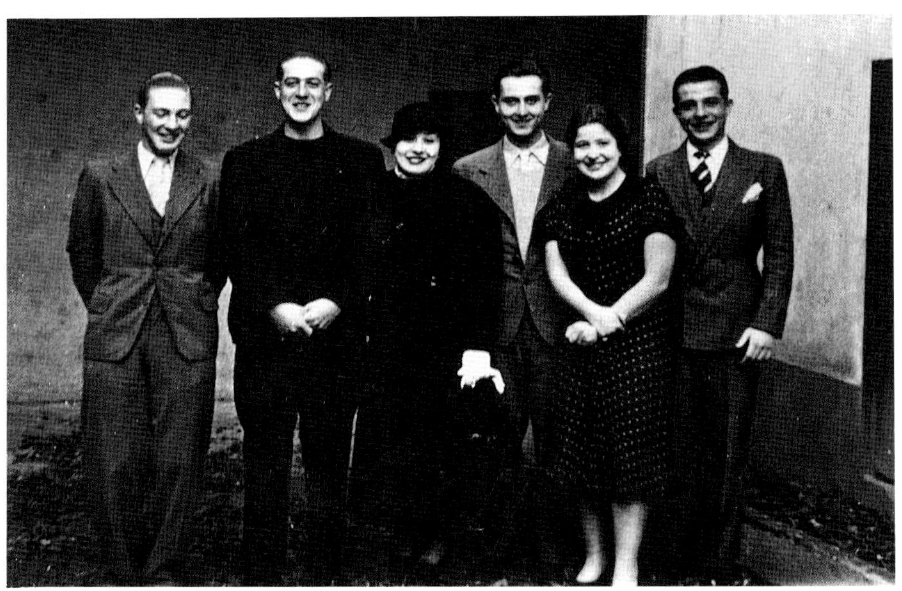

The six children of Jean Dunand photographed *c.* 1937: (from left to right) Robert, Pierre, Alix, Bernard, Suzy and Jean-Louis.

1877 Jules John Dunand born in Lancy, near Geneva, Switzerland, on 20 May, the son of Jean-Eugène Dunand and his wife Jeanne Amélie (*née* Götschi); in 1909 he decides to change his name to Jean.

1902 Dunand meets Marguerite Marie-Louise Antoinette Léonie Moutardier while on holiday in Touraine; they will be married four years later.
Dunand's mother dies in Paris.

1906 Dunand and Marguerite Moutardier are married on 18 April. The couple establish their first home at 74 Rue Hallé, Paris, where Dunand also has his studio-workshops.
They will eventually have six children:
Bernard Louis Paul *born* 13 June 1908
Louise Amélie ('Alix') *born* 24 May 1912
Pierre Philippe Alphonse *born* 31 May 1914
Jean-Louis }
Suzanne } twins *born* 26 January 1918
Robert *born* 30 April 1921
Jean-Louis was killed in action in 1940 and Robert died in 1983.

1910 Dunand's father dies in Geneva on 28 April.
On 22 November Jean Dunand and his family move to 48 Rue d'Alésia, Paris.

1919 On acquiring new premises at 68/70 Rue Hallé, the Dunand family make their home at No. 68.

1942 Jean Dunand dies in Paris on 7 June.

1966 Dunand's widow dies on 29 September.

FOREWORD

IT IS ONLY RIGHT to begin this foreword by evoking the memory of my late colleague and friend Roger Armand-Weigert, whose doctoral thesis, completed in 1937, on the subject of the official designer to Louis XIV, Jean I Bérain, led to his becoming a curator in the Department of Prints and Drawings at the Bibliothèque Nationale in Paris. He knew my father and it had been agreed that he would undertake the present volume, but he became ill and died before the task could be completed. Then, in 1981, Félix Marcilhac offered to continue the task of collecting illustrations and preparing the accompanying texts, which he has dedicated to all Jean Dunand's surviving sons and daughters. On their behalf I take this opportunity to extend my thanks to M. Marcilhac.

Directly or indirectly, my two brothers, my two sisters and I have allowed the present author to consult our family records and have shared our memories with him. Félix Marcilhac's understanding and enthusiasm led me to describe to him my personal experiences as Jean Dunand's eldest son and partner, and to this fund of personal knowledge he has applied the objectivity and practical skill of an art historian. But who exactly was this man – my father – as seen from within the family circle?

The first thing one noticed was his imposing bearing, the solid build of the typical mountain dweller. His way of walking was somehow a spontaneous reflection of his skills and achievements. The manner of his welcome, so simple and so openly cordial, conveyed a sense of humility that contrasted with his otherwise commanding presence. His face was wreathed in a kindly smile, and his eyes twinkled with wit and good humour. We retain childhood memories of the softness of his beard, that symbol of a strong character sustained by a sense of purpose. His anger, both at home and in the workshops, was feared the more for being so rare.

This strength of character, with its evenness of temper, was matched by a corresponding capacity for hard work. Father never hurried, he persevered. This 'true temperament of a self-willed and resolute man', as Félix Marcilhac describes it, was an integral part of the authority he wielded. His wide-ranging artistic abilities ensured that to this personal authority were added the esteem of his fellow artists, the respect of all who worked with him and the admiration of those who bought the objects he made. I am reminded of my brother Pierre who, while still a small child, hummed away to himself as he tried his hand at hammering, 'I'm as clever as Papa, I can make much nicer vases.' Thanks to our mother's endless devotion, we six children formed a close-knit family, devoted to our father and the example he set.

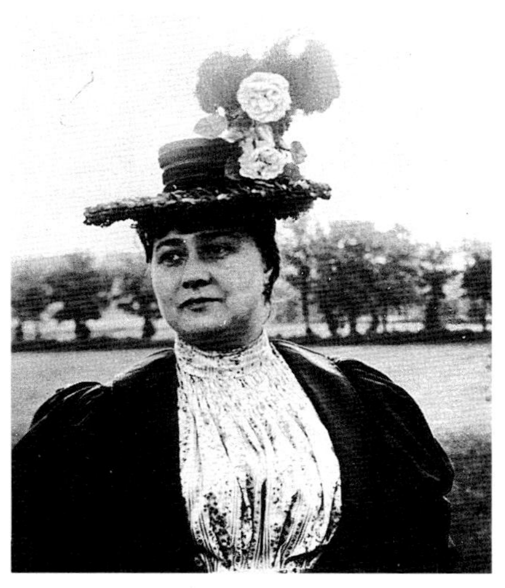

Madame Jeanne Amélie Dunand (*née* Götschi), mother of Jean Dunand.

It was at Le Gué du Roy in Touraine, the country estate of his mentor, the sculptor Jean Dampt, that my father first met the young Marguerite Moutardier, who after losing her mother in childbirth, was then being brought up by aunts on her mother's side, one living in Grenoble and the other in the village of Chemillé-sur-Dême in Touraine, both solidly Catholic middle-class households. When they became engaged, it was agreed between them that any children of the marriage would be brought up in the Protestant faith to which Jean Dunand belonged. The opinion which our friends held concerning our mother was well expressed by people such as Madeleine Vionnet, Gaston Louis Vuitton and the silk merchant Johan Colcombet, who considered her a 'grande dame' who combined kindness and dignity in equal measure.

At home we were always ready to welcome last-minute guests at mealtimes, for my father was in the habit of bringing to our table anybody who happened to be on his premises. I also remember how, at the end of the First World War, my father came across a group of Africans sitting on benches opposite a hostel for wounded foreign soldiers in the Avenue du Maine and how he brought them all home to dine with us, even though he had never seen them in his life before.

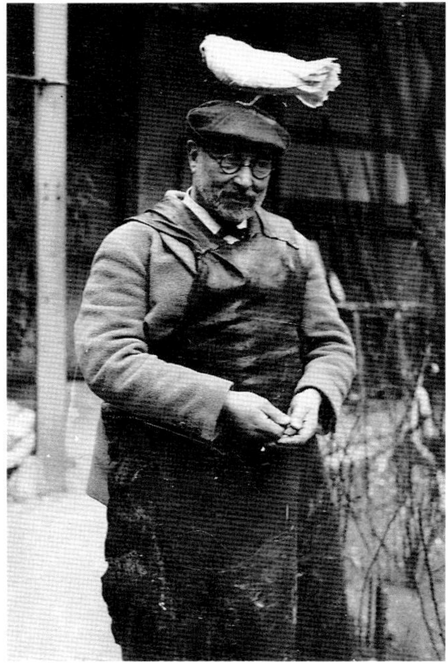

Jean Dunand photographed in the courtyard of his Paris workshops; behind him is the pigeon-loft.

Visitors to my father's workshop would find him attired in a huge leather apron with enamelled hooks, and wearing spectacles and a Brueghelesque cap. Their hands would be swallowed up by his, a firm yet sensitive hand adapted equally to the roughest smithying and to working with delicate jewels. Whenever we received visitors such as Jean Goulden, Paul Jouve and François-Louis Schmied, with the president of their group, a curator at the Louvre, Jean Guiffrey, or the directors of various shipping companies, my father would personally prepare a Swiss fondue or lobster à l'armoricaine. What couldn't he do? The late son of François-Louis Schmied, Théo, who was eight years my senior, once told me that on one occasion when my parents were staying near an isolated village in Touraine, my father helped deliver a peasant woman's child one night because there was no one else available to assist.

His ingenuity was particularly evident in the various novel gadgets which he invented and made as and when he needed them to facilitate his work in the different areas of craftsmanship he espoused. This aptitude for solving practical problems with such manifest ease always amazed his colleagues and ensured their unquestioning trust.

What was that meaning attributed to human existence which, even without their realizing it, informed my parents' attitudes and conduct? What were the hopes that sustained them? My mother prayed regularly. Throughout the recurrent difficulties that beset her husband's artistic career, and throughout the worries of two World Wars, my mother would always turn to the Almighty. Some benefit must have resulted from this, as evidenced by the care and devoted attention we received, as she sought to ease our sorrows, fears and sufferings.

As for my father, immediately upon his arrival in Paris, at the age of twenty, in 1897, he joined the Association des Etudiants Protestants in the Rue Vaugirard. He became friendly with Pastor Edouard Maury, a music lover who was later to become the father-in-law of Charles Munch, as well as with Pastor Jean Monnier, the author of the first important article to be written in France on Jean Dunand's metalwork. We also received occasional visits from the minister of the local church, the Temple de Plaisance, where we were taught religious knowledge in the tradition of liberal Protestant theology.

In my thoughts and feelings as well as in my work, I felt a remarkable affinity with my father. I accompanied him to concerts and museums the length and breadth of Europe, and his enthusiasm and well-informed comments were a source of great joy to me. I became his disciple, his 'private secretary' and his collaborator in our workshops, where I was at pains to ensure that his ideas were faithfully realized. I shared with him the regular routine tasks of keeping the workshop busy, paying the wages and settling the monthly bills.

Of course, there were times when we were busier than usual, preparing exhibitions. The events of 1925, 1931 and 1937 were particularly memorable in this respect, as were those organized by the Dunand-Goulden-Jouve-Schmied group, when we would always produce a large-scale interior. After having spent long evenings in the workshop with our assistants and following the official preview, my father would take me to dine at Prunier's, where we would eat together, on our own.

During the short spring holidays, my father and I would go off into the country and paint gouache landscapes as preliminary sketches for lacquer screens. We would set off in the evening on the overnight sleeper from Paris with our rucksacks and bicycles; at first light the next day, after drinking a bowl of milk straight from the cow, we would freewheel downhill in the valleys of the Lot and the Dordogne.

As is clear not only from Félix Marcilhac's study but from the illustrations that accompany it, my father was in no way 'doctrinaire'. He was never attracted by the absolute values of some clique or other. With him, there were no sudden, passing interests, but rather a slow, inward cultivation of beauty.

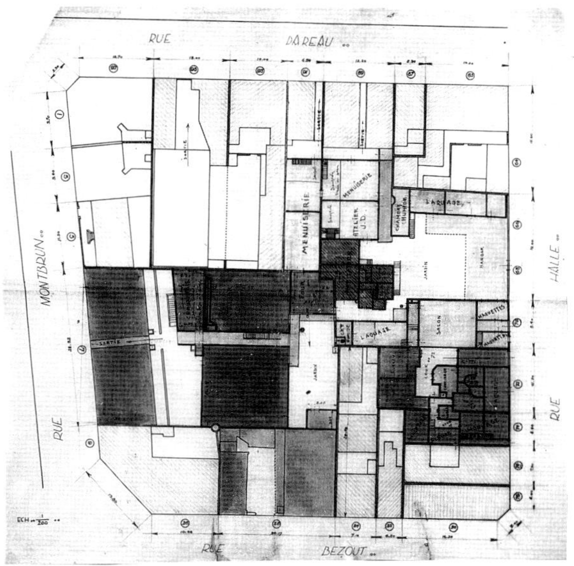

General plan of Dunand's workshop premises *c.* 1935, showing areas devoted to various processes.

wonderment at the beauties of nature? The section devoted to Dunand's Was not a feeling of gratitude towards God reflected in his constant work as a sculptor takes implicit account of this desire on his part to be true to nature. The reader will see how, at the beginning of the century, my father, like so many of his fellow artists, borrowed directly but sparingly from the world of plants, using these motifs in the *repoussé* and chased decoration of his earliest pieces in metal. Then, the better to capture the spirit of steel or brass, of pewter or lead, he transformed these plant motifs with a well-developed understanding of natural forms, into tactile and vigorous shapes conforming to those of nature herself. Finally, when investing his vases and screens with a sense of geometry, he did so not without a sense of order, but rather without any rigid system, so that – unlike certain other contemporary exponents of Cubism – his own more random approach to the use of the geometrical style remained closely bound up with that freedom of movement which typifies creation itself.

His working methods were essentially of a practical nature. The spontaneous deployment of those gifts with which he had been endowed, from patience to perseverance, left their mark on his whole career. His thinking and his imagination implied handiwork from start to finish: it was truer of Jean Dunand than of anyone else that 'things got done by being done'. In his hands craftsmanship became an art, thanks to the artistic sensibility with which he endowed it.

Professional demands obliged my godfather, the illustrator François-Louis Schmied, to spend more of his time reading than was the case with my father. In their time they had gone to the theatre together to hear the Mounet brothers in their classical repertory. Schmied himself liked to read aloud, and his friendship helped my father appreciate the uplifting qualities of all good writers, and it was with Schmied, too, that we found relaxation, attending concerts. Finally, there were the sketches and notes which my father made in museums or in the outside world, surrounded by the wonders of creation, and which, used in his studio, helped maintain a sense of reality complementing his inner emotions as an artist.

As Félix Marcilhac emphasizes elsewhere in this volume, my father gained direct experience of all the crafts of his choice, first practising them with his own hands and only after mastering each technique surrounding himself with the helpers he needed to expand production. The reader will see how, in a career lasting less than forty years, Jean Dunand mastered the arts of metalwork, woodwork and lacquerwork and how, in a small area of Paris, bounded by four streets, he built up a business employing several dozen assistants in each of these various crafts.

Enterprise and boldness typify the successive expansion of each of his different workshops. When he prevailed upon us one year to prepare a large-scale panel for the Salon des Artistes Décorateurs, I felt a certain disquiet at the unlikely prospect of the piece being sold. But was not this method of asserting his artistic stature at public exhibitions a contributory factor in confirming his suitability for the monumental schemes he was commissioned to undertake for France's ocean-going liners in the 1930s? This aptitude stemmed from his sense of space and proportion, as Félix Marcilhac points out. Thus my father forged ahead with the serenity born of a boundless confidence. It allowed him, through good times and bad, to bring up six children, while successfully carrying through, with ever-present calmness, the design and execution of a sizable number of highly accomplished works.

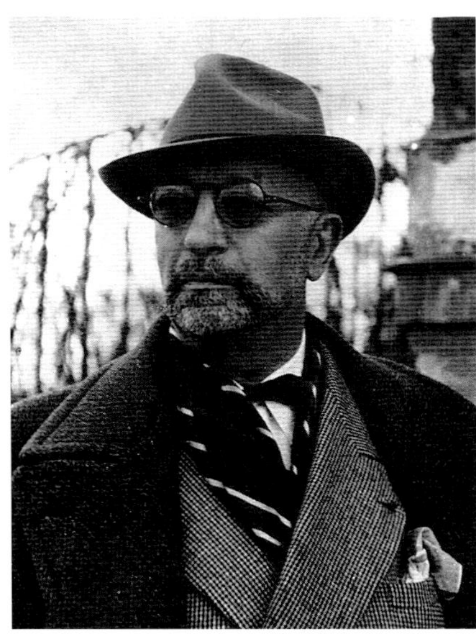

François-Louis Schmied, *c.* 1930.

In the workshops we were all fully occupied for more than a year in the preparation of the 1,200 m^2 (1,400 square yards) of murals required for the liner *Normandie*, completed in 1935. In order to give my father time to carve the six large bas-relief panels, I had to take on responsibility for dealing with the architects and the shipbuilding yard and, back in the workshops, helped by my brother Pierre, for overseeing the completion of each item of lacquered and gilded stucco within the time allowed. In this way Jean Dunand was able

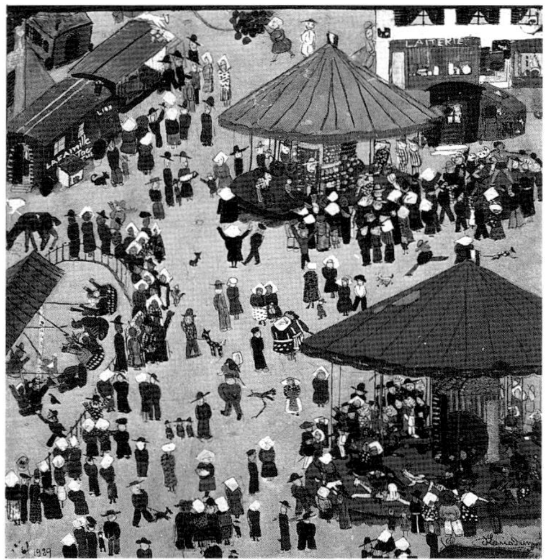

Fairground Scene, gouache sketch for a projected panel by Jean-Louis Dunand, September 1930.

to devote his full attention to the task of carving these vast panels. Kept going by coffee, he worked alone for days on end, continuing well into the evenings – a labour which in the end undermined his health.

But how did we all react 'under the eyes of death', to quote Pierre Chaunu? My father had witnessed suffering at close quarters when, as an ambulance driver in the First World War, he drove through the combat zone to rescue wounded soldiers. And his features were dark and drawn when, after I was called up in 1939, he accompanied me to Saint-Germain-en-Laye, where my regiment was assembling. Three of his sons had been called up simultaneously, the fourth, Robert, not yet old enough for military service, was later threatened with forced labour in Germany, and my mother was suffering from an acute form of asthma. In addition, my sister Alix had a son to look after and had taken him to Morocco when she went there to continue her work in *haute couture*. Finally, there was my sister Suzanne, a volunteer nurse with the Red Cross, who looked after our mother and, with all the devotion of her faith, shared in duties which were soon to involve her in no little danger.

Earlier, Jean Dunand had continued to expand his workshops as the size of his family had grown. He took me on in 1924, when preparations were already in hand for the major exhibition of 1925, the Exposition Internationale des Arts Décoratifs et Industriels Modernes. My brother Pierre joined us in 1930; a period of military service followed, after which he returned to the workshops, remaining there until he was called up in 1939 to serve in the Navy. Demobilized in July 1940, he returned to Paris to help our father and support the family at a time when I myself was still a prisoner-of-war. Our brother Jean-Louis had been killed in action in June 1940 while defending the town of Saumur, with the result that Pierre was now the only one of four sons left in Paris when our father died in 1942. He himself described the shock as resembling 'a kick up the backside'. Like Robert, Pierre had inherited our father's gifts of pragmatism and enterprise. Through a great effort of will, he was able to keep the workshop open, and it was thanks to him that I could return to Paris after the country's liberation to find our studio still in operation.

Robert had at first helped restore the production of helmets and visors for the army, but had then been obliged to leave for the provinces in order to avoid forced labour for the Germans. As a result, he contracted a lung complaint which, for a time, threatened his life. The long-term consequences of this illness led to his death at the age of sixty-two in 1983, leaving a widow and son. His publicity work in the town where he lived had gained widespread notice and appreciation for the family's artistic standards.

As for Jean-Louis, before the outbreak of war he had enrolled to study architecture at the Ecole des Beaux-Arts; he was quite clearly the most gifted of us all, as can be seen from his isometric views of village crowds painted in gouache which he began to produce from the age of eleven. My father once told me that he foresaw Jean-Louis practising as an architect and generating work for his brothers in each of the different branches of our little empire in the Rue Hallé. Tragically, however, Jean-Louis was killed at the age of only twenty-two.

As for me, I was a reserve officer in the armoured division which had been sent to Belgium to face the German armies. It was here that I was taken prisoner. During my captivity I read the Bible and, though previously a non-believer, began to develop a personal faith in Christ, as is clear from the letters which I wrote to my father. Jean Dunand was sixty-five at the time of his death in 1942. No doubt the light of God's love eventually found its way into my father's heart in the final months of his life, and I look forward to the joy of eternal reunion.

August 1987 Bernard Dunand

JEAN DUNAND: HIS LIFE AND CAREER

THE OUTSTANDING artist-craftsman Jean Dunand, born on 20 May 1877, was a native of Lancy, in the Swiss canton of Geneva. He was baptized Jules John, but after settling in Paris he adopted the name Jean in 1909. In some previous publications dealing with Jean Dunand it has been suggested that his forebears were Protestants who had fled to safety after the Edict of Nantes was revoked in 1685; family documents and official cantonal records show, however, that this was not the case.

The artist's great-grandfather, Joseph François Dunant, was born into a French Catholic family at Chapareillan (Isère) on 23 May 1777. The family subsequently moved to Lancy, then in France (the canton of Geneva was ceded to Switzerland in 1816 following the downfall of Napoleon) and a son, Jean-Eugène, was born there on 14 December 1811 and baptized a Catholic eight days later. On 14 February 1831 Jean-Eugène Dunant was granted citizenship of the canton of Geneva. His son, also named Jean-Eugène, was born at Lancy on 31 December 1854 and he too was doubtless baptized a Catholic; the registration of his birth provides the first official record of the change of spelling of the family name from Dunant to Dunand. The younger Jean-Eugène later became a gold-smelter in the clockmaking industry. He married Jeanne Amélie Götschi, who was born on 18 January 1860 in Soleure, a German-speaking, Catholic town at the foot of the Jura mountains. Their son Jules John is the subject of this book.

An uncle of the young Dunand who worked for the Post Office and who was anxious to help him suggested that his nephew should follow a similar career in the public services, but Madame Dunand's awareness of her son's artistic abilities caused the family to move to the nearby city of Geneva and thus enable him to enrol at the School of Industrial Art. This was in 1891, when he was only fourteen. The family lived in a modest apartment at 38 Rue de Lausanne. During his first year in Geneva, Dunand studied sculpture with the Paris-born Jules Hugues Salmson. Although officially enrolled in the sculpture class, Dunand seized the opportunity to attend other courses in order to learn how to handle all the various craft tools used to fashion stone, wood, bronze and gold. Throughout the next two years Dunand studied with Cagniez, an academic sculptor, and at the end of the course was awarded first prize. In 1894 he was awarded a silver medal by Geneva's municipal schools. The following year, he studied for his second diploma with a teacher called Jerdelet, and once again won first prize.

Dunand completed his studies in 1896, graduating with a diploma in sculpture and design. While a student, he had become friendly with François-Louis Schmied, who specialized in woodcuts, and with Carl Albert Angst, a sculptor like himself. On completing his course, Dunand made a plaster model of a Louis XV bracket clock based on an example by Jacquet-Droz in the Musée de l'Horlogerie in Neuchâtel. He entered his work in an interdisciplinary exhibition of clockmaking, the Concours Galland, in June 1897 and won a prize of 1,500 Swiss francs.

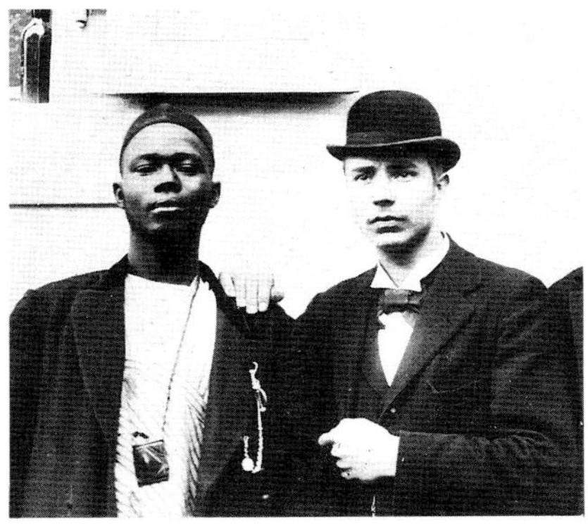

Dunand posing with Abdou Faye at the School of Industrial Art, Geneva, in 1896.

Also in 1896, the Geneva city authorities invited the inhabitants of a Senegalese village to participate in an international art exhibition there. Among the visitors was a young jeweller called Abdou Faye. Dunand became friendly with him and invited him to the college studio to model for him. He made a series of busts in plaster highlighted in colours, and sold them, with enormous success, on the Pont de l'Arve. Chancing one day in the early 1980s to enter a Geneva antique dealer's, I was surprised and amused to discover, perched on top of a column in the purest Second Empire tradition, one of these busts signed 'John Dunand'

In 1897 the city fathers of Geneva awarded Dunand a scholarship to continue his studies in Paris. This bursary happily supplemented the money that Dunand had earned by selling his statuettes, and so he set off for Paris, all the more pleased to be rejoining his friend Carl Angst, who had gone to

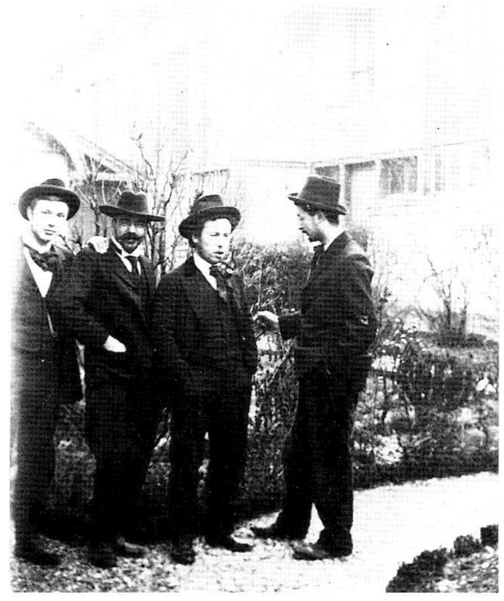

Four young Swiss artists in Paris in 1899, seen here in the courtyard of the studio in the Rue Denfert-Rochereau: (from left to right) Dunand, Bocquet, Angst and Schmied.

live there the previous year, together with another fellow student from Geneva, Théodore David. Dunand arrived in the French capital in October 1897, and an entry in the enrolment register for foreigners at the Préfecture de Police dated 22 January 1898 (no. 1250, folio 99) gives his profession as '*ciselure* craftsman'.

At that time he lodged with a relative called Peynot at 8 Boulevard Chauvelot, off the Rue de Vouillé, in the 15th *arrondissement*. Peynot owned a business dealing in building materials, and he took the young man on as an apprentice. Dunand never forgot his stay, and years later would recall, not without amusement, how his relative used to have a vine growing in the garden that abutted his workshop and how, every year, it would yield enough grapes for him to make a barrel of wine, which he was then obliged to declare at the customs house, taking it there in person on a wheelbarrow.

While apprenticed to this workshop Dunand helped to execute and put the finishing touches to the sculptures of *Fame* and the *Winged Horses* which Fremiet and Gallet had designed for the Pont Alexandre III. For this task he used a *ciselure* technique, while the figures representing the rivers Seine and Neva on the superstructure and parapet of the bridge involved him in *repoussé* work. It was at this point that he first made the acquaintance of Paul Jouve who, like him, was training to become a sculptor and working in similar circumstances.

On 1 February 1898, Dunand registered for an evening class in sculpture run by Jean Dampt at the Ecole Nationale des Arts Décoratifs (card no. 59,377), and it was with Dampt that he perfected his skills both in sculpture and in other fields. Here, too, he encountered his friend Carl Angst, who had been studying there for a year.

Jean Dampt was one of the leading figures in Paris art circles at that time. He had worked on the sculpted decorations on the new Hôtel de Ville, and although he exhibited in the regular Paris Salons every year, he also belonged to a group of independent artists including architects, painters, ceramicists and sculptors. The group was called 'L'Art dans Tout' and the aim was to design homogeneous ensembles that would invest the modern art of the time with a pleasing style devoid of any excess.

In Dampt's studio Dunand got to know several models, one of whom, a young man called Sabato Martelli, posed for him frequently, including sitting for a strikingly vigorous bust. Among the girls was an Italian, Alice Benichi, who later married François-Louis Schmied, who had himself arrived in Paris in 1898. Like Dunand, Schmied had very little money and was happy to accept Peynot's offer of accommodation in the Boulevard Chauvelot, before finding work with an engraver called Aubert.

During vacation periods Dunand would return each summer to Switzerland to visit his father and mother, and it was during one of these visits that he was initiated into the techniques of dinanderie (domestic brass and copperware), working as an apprentice with a local craftsman called Danhaver who made beaten copper bowls, basins and jugs in his studio in the Rue des Chaudronniers, Geneva.

In 1899 we find Dunand, with his friends Angst and Schmied, as a founder member of the Association des Artistes Suisses in Paris. He and Schmied shared the ground floor of Théodore David's studio in the Avenue Denfert-Rochereau, where Carl Angst also worked.

Dunand had been with Dampt for almost three years at the latter's studio at 141 Boulevard Saint-Michel when his mentor decided to operate a more rigorous selection procedure and retain as pupils only those three who he considered would gain most from his teaching and who would go on to develop a personal style in art: Dunand and Angst were in this select group. They set themselves up in the Rue Campagne-Première in Montparnasse, and during the summer they joined their teacher in Touraine, where the latter had a house called Le Gué du Roy. Here they practised their skills in sculpture and carving, and, under Dampt's watchful eye, carved pieces of furniture, for which they first shaped the separate elements individually. It was during one

Model in costume seen in front of the building in the Rue Denfert-Rochereau where Angst and David had their studio and worked with Dunand.

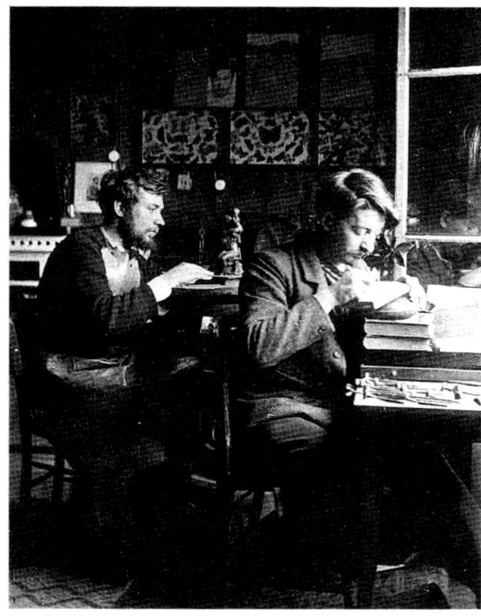

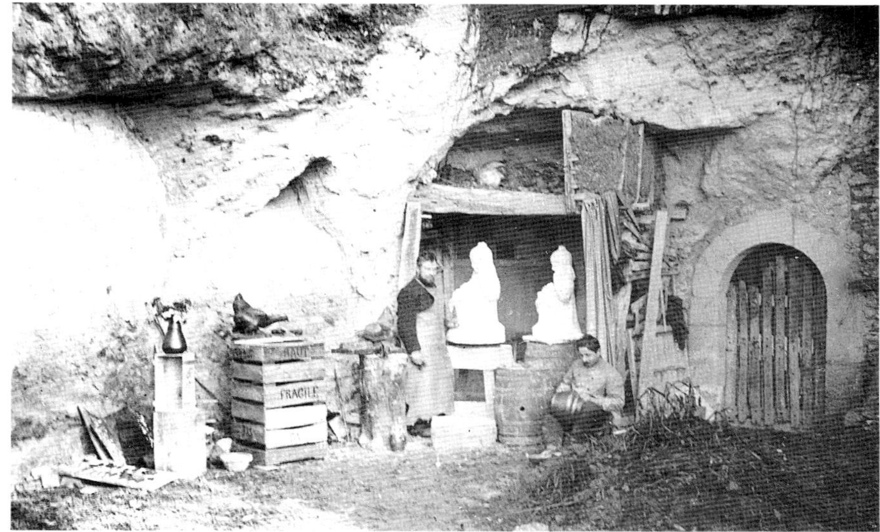

(Above) Dunand in the apartment in the Rue Michelet which he left in 1904; he is sculpting a figure of a *Mother and Child* (cat. no. 795), while his friend Schmied is working on an engraving.

(Above right) Dunand at work in 1905 on his limestone figure, *Child and Young Goat* (cat. no. 793), based on a full-size model in wood; his *Hen and Chicks* group (cat. no. 790) of 1904 can also be seen on top of a crate to his left. Photograph taken in Touraine during one of Dunand's regular summer visits.

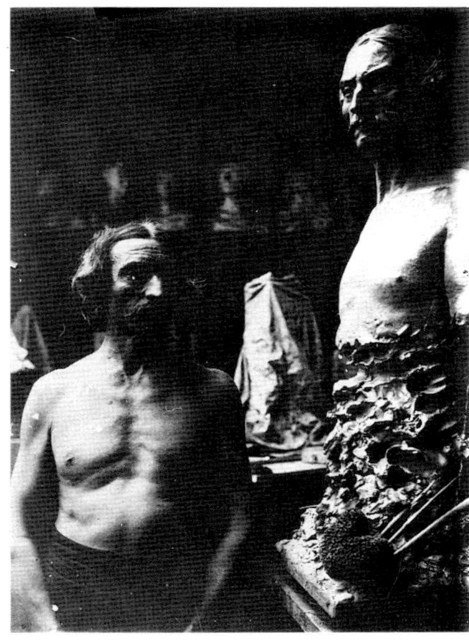

Model posing by Dunand's unfinished sculpture *Quo Vadis* (cat. no. 779) in the studio in the Rue Denfert-Rochereau, 1900.

of these visits to Touraine that Dunand first met, in the summer of 1902, the 19-year-old Marguerite Moutardier, who was holidaying locally with one of her aunts. She and Dunand would be married four years later.

Meanwhile, in 1900, Dunand's mother had decided that her presence was required in Paris to look after her son and so, leaving her husband behind in Geneva, she travelled to the French capital, where, on 22 May, she and Dunand moved into rooms at 13 Rue Michelet. There they were joined by François-Louis Schmied.

Dunand took part in the Exposition Universelle held in Paris in 1900, exhibiting as a Swiss artist in Class 9 (card no. 836). His magnificent bronze, *Quo Vadis*, depicting an old man, won him a gold medal. In the same year he exhibited for the first time at the Salon de la Société Nationale des Beaux-Arts (often simply called the Salon de la Nationale). Of his two exhibits one was a beautiful bust depicting one of his friends, Maurice Dieterlin; the other was a bust of a girl, the only surviving record of which is a poor-quality photograph.

In a letter dated 22 September 1900, the board of directors of the Musée d'Art et d'Histoire de Genève accepted a gift from John Dunand. It was the first version, in coloured plaster, of his bronze *The Child and Butterfly*. The following year, 1901, he exhibited *The Child and Butterfly* and a bronze bust of 'Mademoiselle E.K.' in the section for foreign artists at the Salon de la Nationale. This bust was acquired in 1902 by the Swiss nation for its collection in the Musée Cantonal des Beaux-Arts, Lausanne, the Palais de Rumine.

While nursing her son's friend Théodore David, who shortly died from tuberculosis, Dunand's mother contracted galloping consumption, from which she in turn died in 1902. She was buried in the cemetery at Gentilly on the outskirts of Paris. Her husband survived her by eight years; he died in Geneva on 28 April 1910.

In 1903 Dunand collaborated with Dampt on the interior decoration of the salon in the Comtesse de Béarn's house on the corner of Avenue Bosquet and Rue Saint-Dominique in Paris. He carved some of the wood panelling, door frames and furniture. As was made clear by the art critic Charles Moreau-Vauthier in a comprehensive article published in *Art et décoration* in 1906, Dunand, together with Angst, Fraysse and Collet, worked, under Dampt's supervision, on an ensemble in which the stucco on the ceilings and mouldings 'was in perfect harmony with the beautiful varieties of wood, and in which the wrought iron, ivory and gold blended with a quiet and restrained opulence.'

As a direct result of this experience, Dunand gradually turned his attention to the decorative arts. In 1903, he wrote in a letter that, 'through being pushed in this direction by my master [Dampt], who believes a sculptor

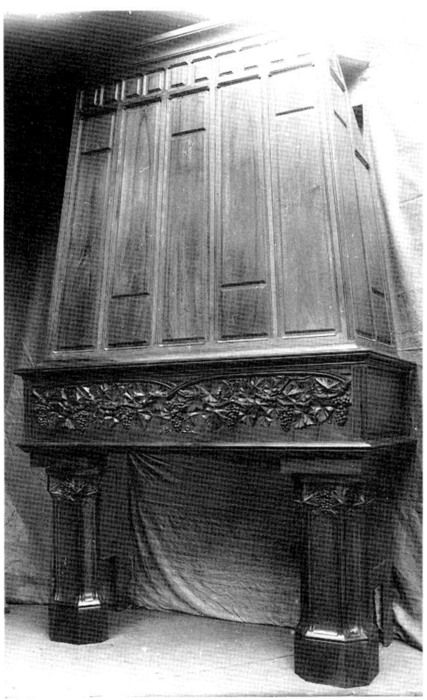

Wooden chimney-piece with carved decoration designed by Dampt, in the execution of which Dunand was also involved.

should also be a craftsman, I am turning towards the decorative arts and exhibiting a carved wooden bread-tray at the 1903 Salon.' In fact, Dunand had already realized that, as a career, sculpture would be fraught with difficulties and unlikely to bring quick rewards, hence he hoped to find a ready and more lucrative market in the field of the decorative arts. Even so, a final decision had yet to be taken.

In 1904, Théodore David's mother offered Angst, Schmied and Dunand – as a commemorative gesture to her late son – a free trip to Italy. They visited Pisa, San Gimignano, Siena, Florence, Rome, Naples and Venice. The sculptures which Dunand executed on his return showed clearly the influence of Donatello. He reworked the bust, in Burgundy stone, of his young cousin Marguerite Vercelli (*née* Vachoux), which he had begun in Lausanne in 1902 and which he now completed.

On 10 April 1904, Dunand moved to 74 Rue Hallé, in a part of Paris known as 'Little Montrouge', so called after a neighbouring district beyond the Porte d'Orléans. He occupied a small two-room apartment on the first floor, the whole of the ground floor being given over to the sculpture and dinanderie studio.

At the first Salon de la Société des Artistes Décorateurs in 1904, Dunand exhibited the recently completed bust of his cousin Marguerite Vercelli, together with a large marble sculpture of a young girl, entitled *The Awakening*, and a group depicting a hen with its chicks carved from a solid piece of walnut. Elsewhere, in the section devoted to the decorative arts at the Salon de la Nationale, he exhibited some examples of his work in copper and brass which he had made in Danhaver's studio during his visits to Geneva. Together these pieces were sufficient to secure Dunand's election as an associate member of the Société Nationale des Beaux-Arts, and from now on his name would appear regularly in catalogue listings.

From August to September examples of Dunand's work were included in the Exposition Nationale des Beaux-Arts in Lausanne, where he exhibited a new subject in a carving depicting a cat, a work which bore witness to his talent for detailed observation. Also shown on this occasion was a bronze version of his *Bust of a Young Girl.* A letter written from Berne on 1 October 1904 indicates that the work was purchased by the Musée Cantonal des Beaux-Arts de Lausanne on this date. Earlier, the reviewer of the *Gazette de Lausanne*, M. Le Diol, writing in the issue of 25 August 1904, had noted that 'This bronze, with its admirable patina, vibrates with life, its creator M. Dunand, has retained a charming sense of chasteness while depicting the figure almost nude.' This particular sale realized some 1,500 Swiss francs and was a real encouragement for Dunand at the time. At this stage, Dunand's work had already attracted the attention of Daniel Baud-Bovy, President of the Federal Fine Arts Commission in Berne and an ardent protagonist of modern art. He became a sort of private patron for Dunand. Also on show at this exhibition were works by Dunand's fellow student Louis Gallet, like him an associate member of the Société Nationale des Beaux-Arts.

In 1905 Dunand became firmly committed to a career in the decorative arts. Some years later, the French art critic Maximilien Gauthier published in *La Renaissance politique, littéraire et artistique*, under the title 'Vingt Minutes avec M. Jean Dunand' ('Twenty Minutes with M. Jean Dunand'), an interview in which he reported the artist as saying, 'The desire to earn my living certainly played a part in my decision to renounce what is known as great art ... in this way I have been able to devote myself entirely to the profession that I love, freed from the need to beg for official commissions or from having to take on work simply in order to survive.'

In fact, it was largely the success of his work in copper and brass, exhibited at the Salon de la Nationale in 1905, which, more than any other single factor, persuaded him to turn to the decorative arts, not least because the Union Centrale des Arts Décoratifs bought a very attractive copper vase inlaid with gold which he had shown in his exhibition. It is clear, moreover, that Dampt, his true mentor, had been able to detect in his forceful character

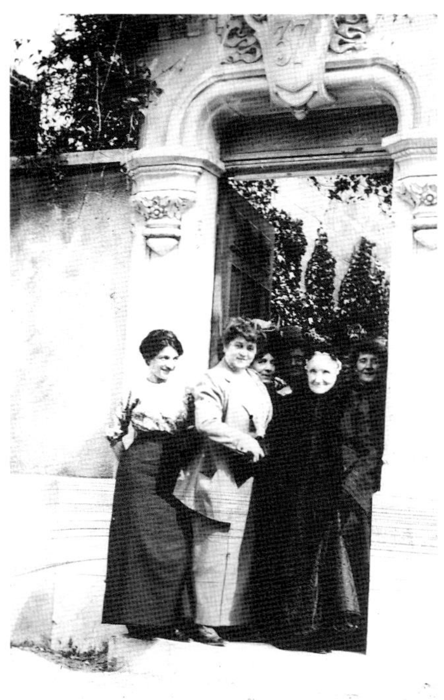

Outside the home of Madame Paul Chaix in Grenoble, *c.* 1900; on the left is Marguerite Moutardier, Dunand's future wife.

a streak of real originality, on which basis he urged his pupil to devote his energies to the applied arts rather than to sculpture, a field in which, it must be admitted, his talent was somewhat classical and lacking in originality.

In the field of dinanderie, however, the pieces he exhibited – long, slender bottles of beaten copper and gold-studded bronze – attracted the attention of reviewers. The critics were unanimous in hailing the event and in recognizing in this consummate coppersmith an artist who had successfully applied himself to the challenge of investigating various materials and realizing their potential in highly personal ways. If the forms remained traditional, the suppleness of their lines and the rightness of their ornamentation singled Dunand out as a true innovator. The Paris correspondent of the *Journal du collectionneur* of Geneva emphasized this aspect of Dunand's work in a highly complimentary article published in June 1905: 'On this occasion we are unreserved in our admiration of M. Dunand's three vases. This brilliant artist seems to have drawn from copper all that this metal has to offer by way of full and subtle forms and punching processes that are held in high esteem today, M. Dunand has elected to work entirely with a hammer. This courageous effort has produced three vases that are utterly exquisite in their feeling, wholly imbued with the artist's soul.'

On 18 April 1906, Dunand married Marguerite Marie-Rose Antoinette Léonie Moutardier, aged 23. Her father, a native of the Marseilles region, had settled in Évian, working first as clerk of works with the French Railways, later becoming the owner of a general store. He was a widower, his wife having died in childbirth. He had remarried several years later, and his only daughter had been brought up by her aunt, Mme Paul Chaix (*née* Léonie Dutey), known as Nonie, who lived at 37 Rue de Turenne, Grenoble. In this well-to-do milieu (Aunt Nonie's husband was a local glover) she pursued her studies and was successful in obtaining her higher school certificate. For several years she spent her holidays working as a sort of tutor with an aristocratic German family in order to achieve financial independence. Of an artistic temperament, she later spent each summer with another of her aunts, Mme Ferdinand de Meurs, at Chemillé-sur-Dême in Touraine. Together with her aunt, she often visited Dampt, who was a family friend, and it was during one of these visits that she had first made the acquaintance of Jean Dunand.

The newly-weds set up home in Paris at 74 Rue Hallé. Having family responsibilities, Dunand was aware that he had to provide financial stability, which was why he relegated sculpture to a position of secondary importance and cleared out his studio in order to give classes in carving and metalworking at home. He would teach up to six students at a time.

That same year he exhibited his work at the International Exhibition held in Milan, entering as a Swiss artist in the decorative arts section. His work in copper and brass earned him a gold medal. Nonetheless, and in spite of his success in Italy, his chief interest lay in oriental art, and more especially in early Chinese and Japanese bronzes. His new sculptural language was well adapted to reflect this current interest, but, in contrast to the stylization that was typical of art at this time, he developed animal and plant-like ornamentation that was increasingly realistic.

On 16 February 1906, an exhibition organized by the Cercle des Étudiants Protestants opened in the Rue de Vaugirard. Dunand exhibited a number of vases, while Schmied's contribution was a series of woodcuts, including a portrait of Jean Monnier, a Protestant pastor of Swiss origin and a friend of Dunand's family. Monnier proved a staunch moral, social and financial support for the two friends in these early years of their professional careers. At this exhibition Schmied showed an extraordinary engraved bookplate made for the Lausanne Seminary and featuring a magnificent cockerel of the Houdan breed. The delicacy and technical skill displayed here catapulted Schmied into the forefront of contemporary wood-engravers. Another of Dampt's pupils, Henri Valette, exhibited various sculptures on animal themes.

In March 1907, the first exhibition of work by members of the

Association des Artistes Suisses was put on by the Cercle International des Arts in the Boulevard Raspail. The catalogue contained a preface by the famous Swiss writer Edouard Rod. He mentioned Böcklin and Hodler, whom he held out as the spiritual leaders of this whole new generation of Swiss artists. The list of exhibitors certainly reveals the extraordinary cultural contacts that then existed between the French-speaking part of Switzerland and France; among such artists were Angst, Crotte, Grasset, Sandoz, Schmied, Steiner, Vibert and, of course, Dunand himself. In the course of the next fifty years, each would leave his mark in his chosen field, be it painting, sculpture, engraving or the applied arts. Dunand was still exhibiting as a sculptor, the two works in question being a *Bust of a Young Girl* in plaster and a reduced-scale bronze version of *The Child and Butterfly*. The latter was so pure in design and so perfectly articulated in its volumes that, despite its smaller size, it inevitably recalled Renaissance sculptures. Another cabinet contained objects in copper, steel and bronze, notable for their taste and delicacy. Among these pieces, two large vases in particular stood out, notable as much for their size as for the quality of their execution. One, of steel, was engraved with boldly executed lines, its polished surface more than ever calculated to throw into relief the dazzling white of its satin-flower design. Mother-of-pearl floral motifs were inlaid in the neck of the vase to enhance the sense of contrast.

In May 1907, Dunand exhibited at the Salon de la Nationale four superb pieces in different metals. Once again, one of his exhibits was acquired for the Musée des Arts Décoratifs. One writer, reporting on the exhibition, drew particular attention to the beauty of a plant-pot holder 'whose sombre patina is of great beauty, underlining as it does the extent to which even a somewhat rough material can harmonize superbly well with the character and function of the piece in question.' The author of the article, Maurice Pillard Verneuil, discovered here an evident application of the decorative rules which, in the tradition of Eugène Grasset and Viollet-le-Duc, he had been advocating for decades. What struck him even more, however, was a bronze vase decorated with water-lily leaves and buds, while frogs, depicted in high relief on the leaves at the base of the vase 'turn their menacing eyes to follow the flight of tiny insects', referring to gold and silver flies which Dunand had dotted around the top of the neck. 'This vase is richly executed, and the artist seems to be playing with the problems posed by *repoussé* work on metal, making those problems appear deceptively simple.' A bronze version was also made. In the issue of the journal *Architecture* of 16 June 1907, a certain Gauthier noted, moreover, that 'It is only right that we extend our highest praise to the masterly exhibits of M. Dunand, vases in copper, vases in bronze, vases in beaten steel, silver sauceboats. These objects reveal scholarly research, more especially the large vase in the middle, on which the concentrated decoration of its upper section, executed in *repoussé* work and chasing, gives the delightful impression of a flower opening up, a rare effect indeed.'

It was at this time that Dunand first came to prominence as an outstanding technician and as one of the most skilled and original of designers. Since he did not have facilities for casting metal, his bronze vases and other objects were cast by a craftsman called Groult, whose foundry was situated in the Rue des Pastourelles. Groult would send Dunand the rough castings, and it was then left to him to finish and chase them, and to inlay the precious metals. Even if, as time passed, certain of his vases tended to look crude or lacking refinement of form, the boldness and delicacy of their workmanship still made them robust and refined examples of his art. 'Their ornamentation, *repoussé* and chased and sometimes inlaid in the body of the vase, depicts friezes and corbeils of plant-like scrolls, young shoots and new leaves freshly ribbed and semi-curled, while the colour of the metal – steel, copper or bronze – is warm and shaded, but always beautiful. M. Dunand knows how to enhance the decoration with ingenuity and an exquisite sense of taste,' declared Monod in an article published in *Art et décoration* in March 1907.

Plates 1–11
PORTRAITS

OPPOSITE
1 ***Madame Dunand***, 1925
(*catalogue 134*)

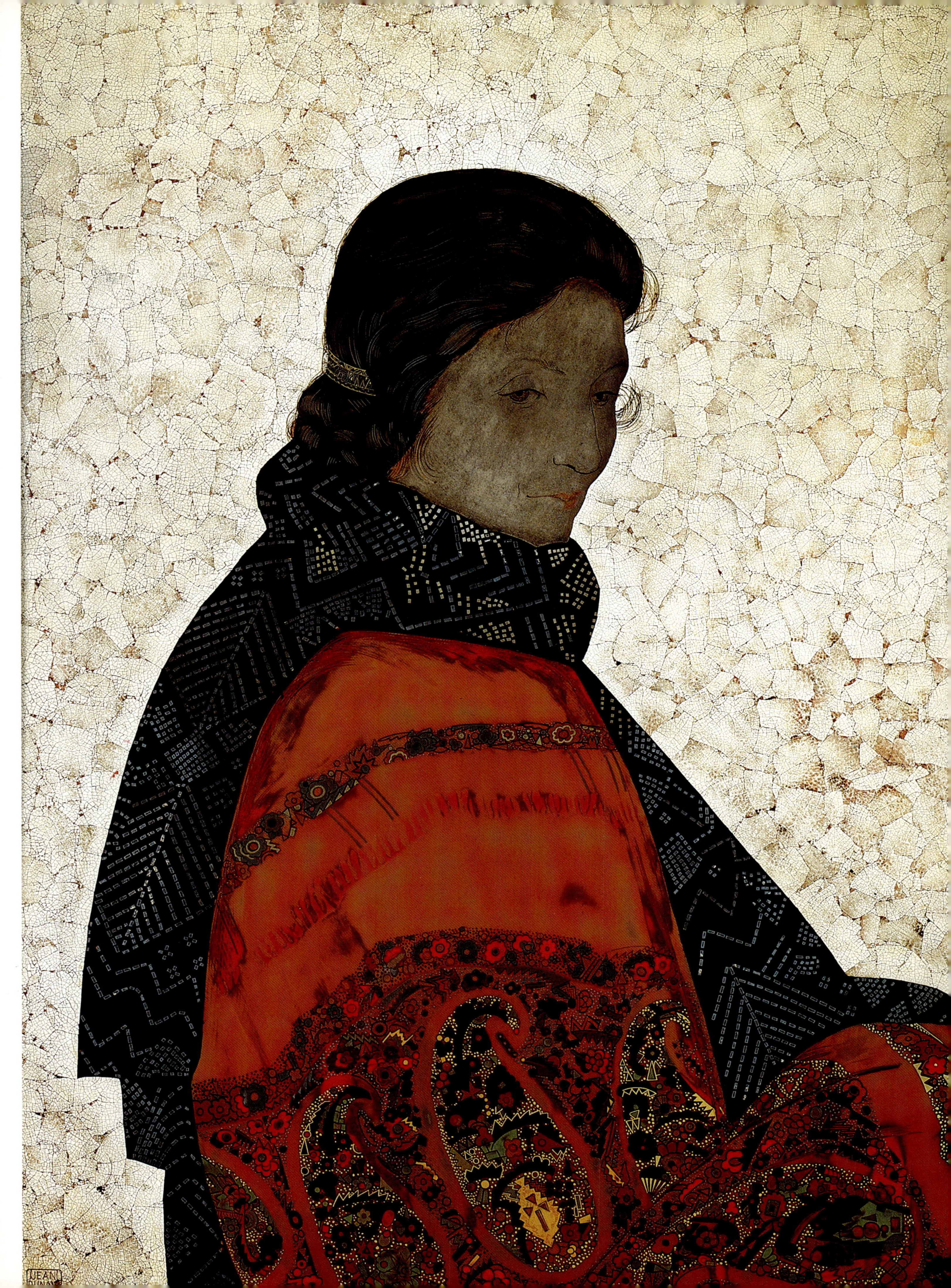
JEAN

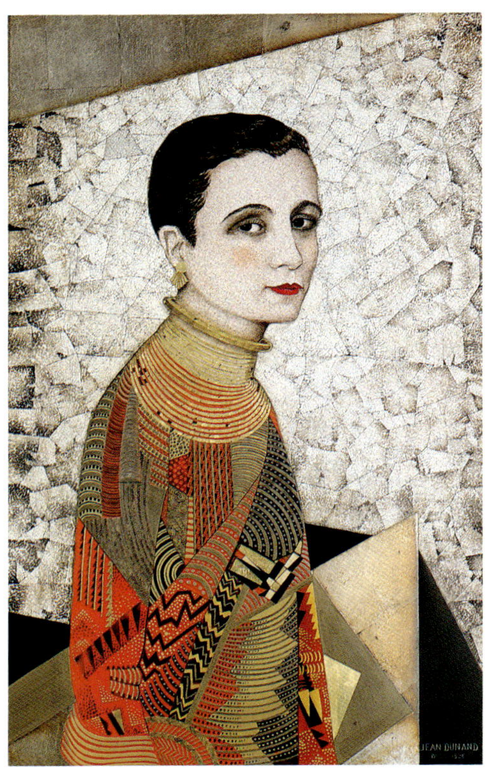

2 **Madame Agnès**, 1926
(*catalogue 137*)

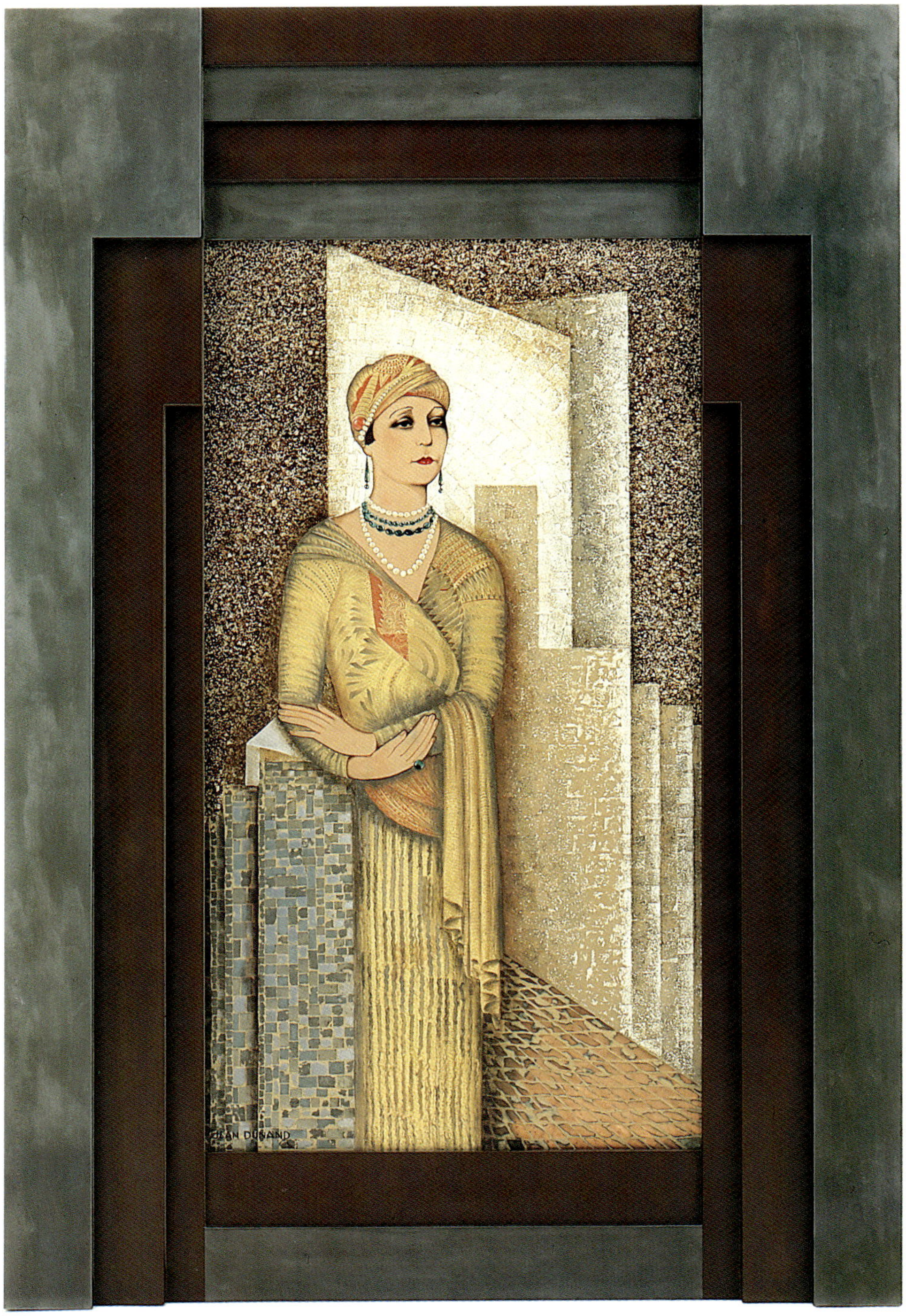

3 **Madame Jenny Sacerdote**, 1930
(*catalogue 172*)

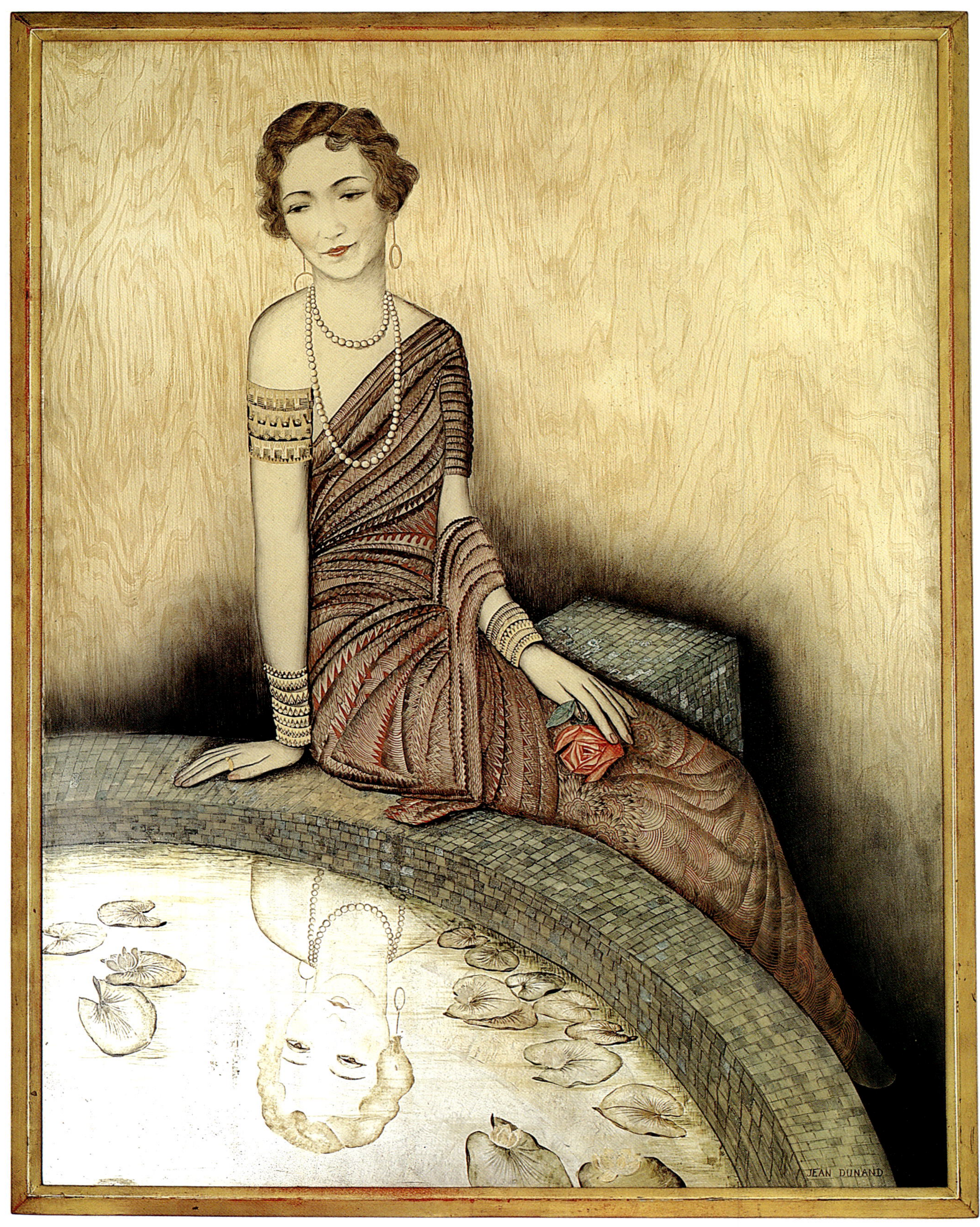

4 ***Madame Paravicini***, 1928
(*catalogue 170*)

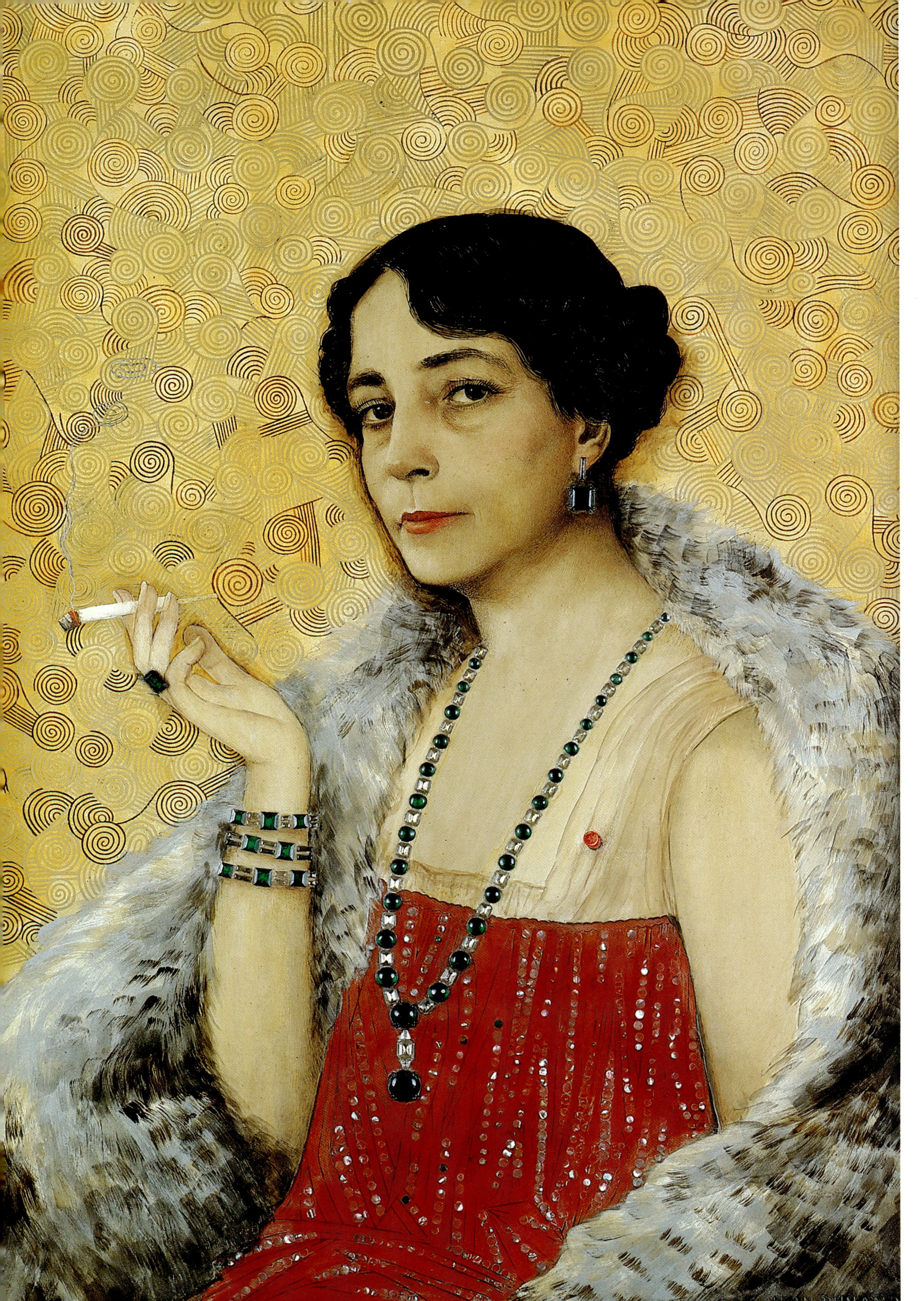

5 ***Madame Florence Blumenthal***, 1927
(*catalogue 151*)

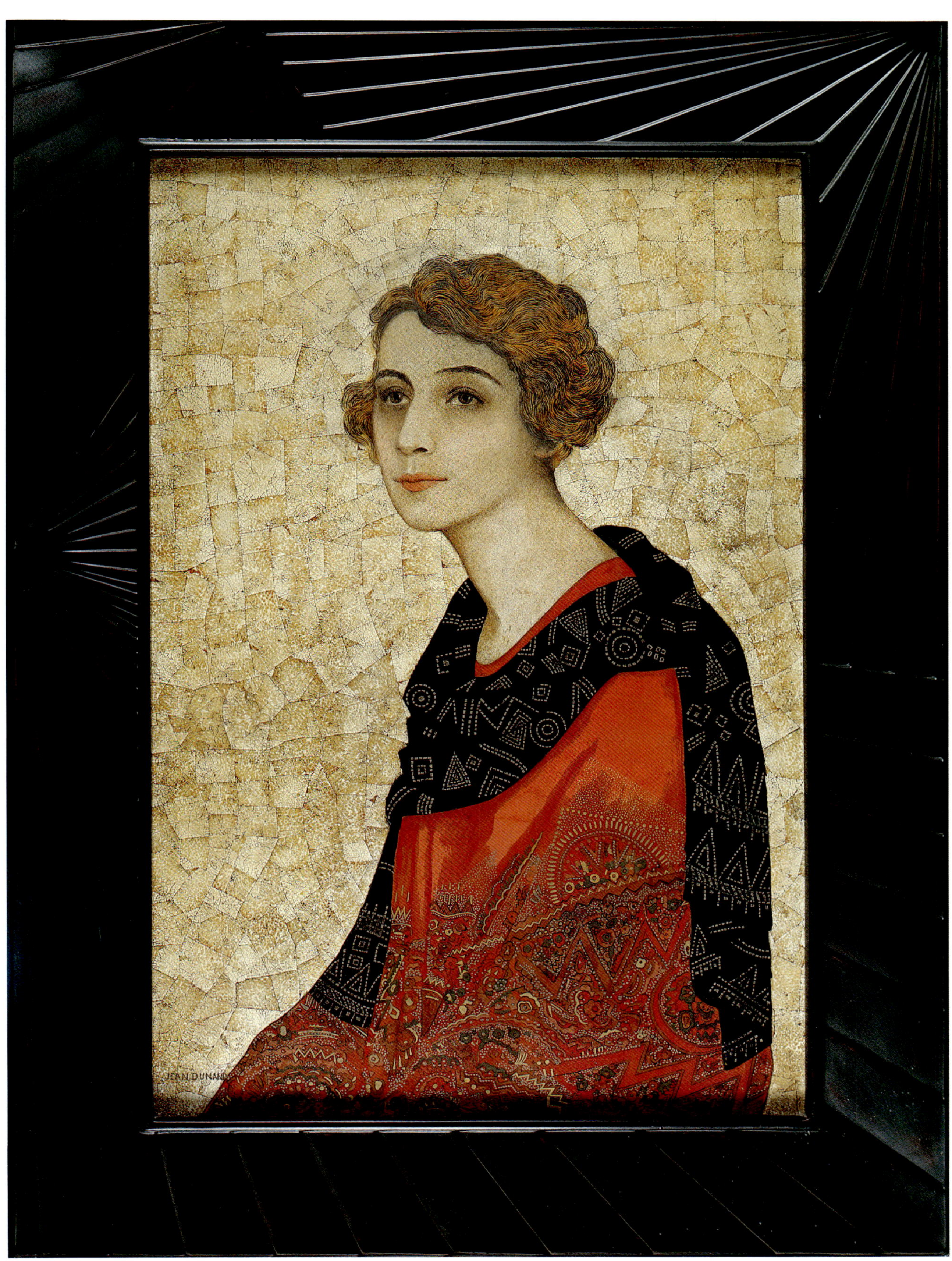

6 ***Madame Bourdillon***, 1926
(*catalogue 144*)

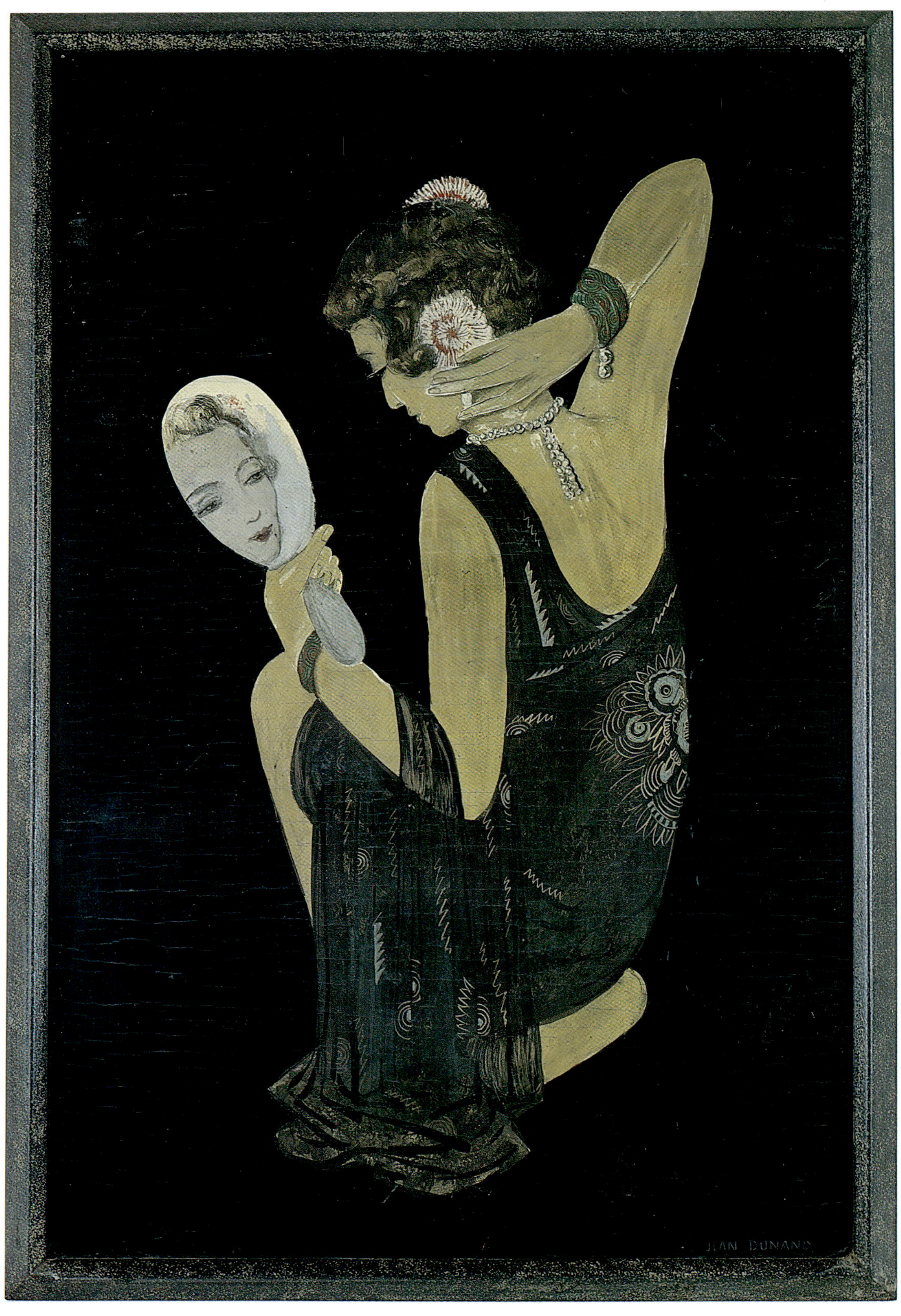

7 ***Unidentified***, *c*. 1930
(*catalogue 176*)

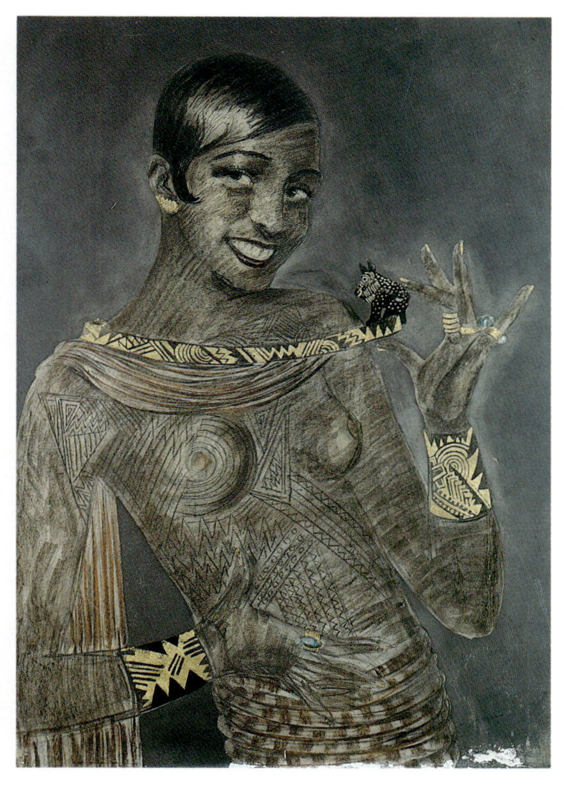

8 ***Josephine Baker***, 1926
(*catalogue 146*)

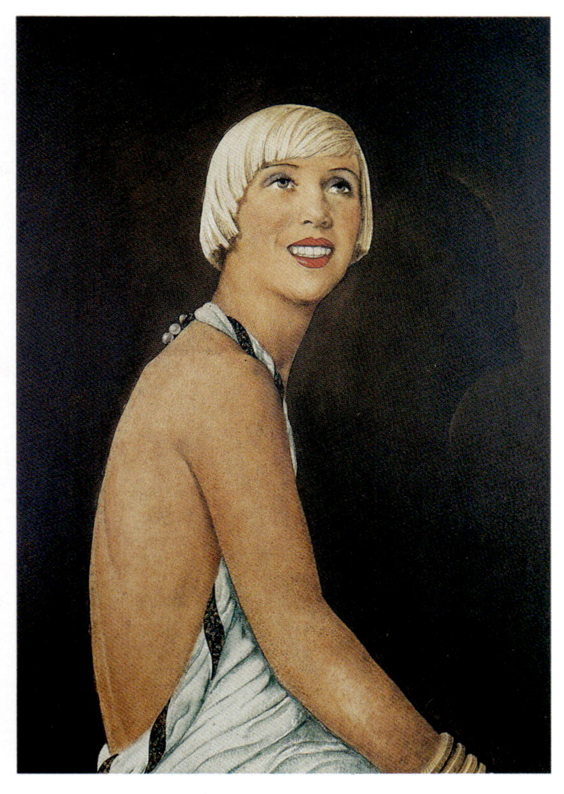

9 ***Suzy Solidor***, *c.* 1939
(*catalogue 202*)

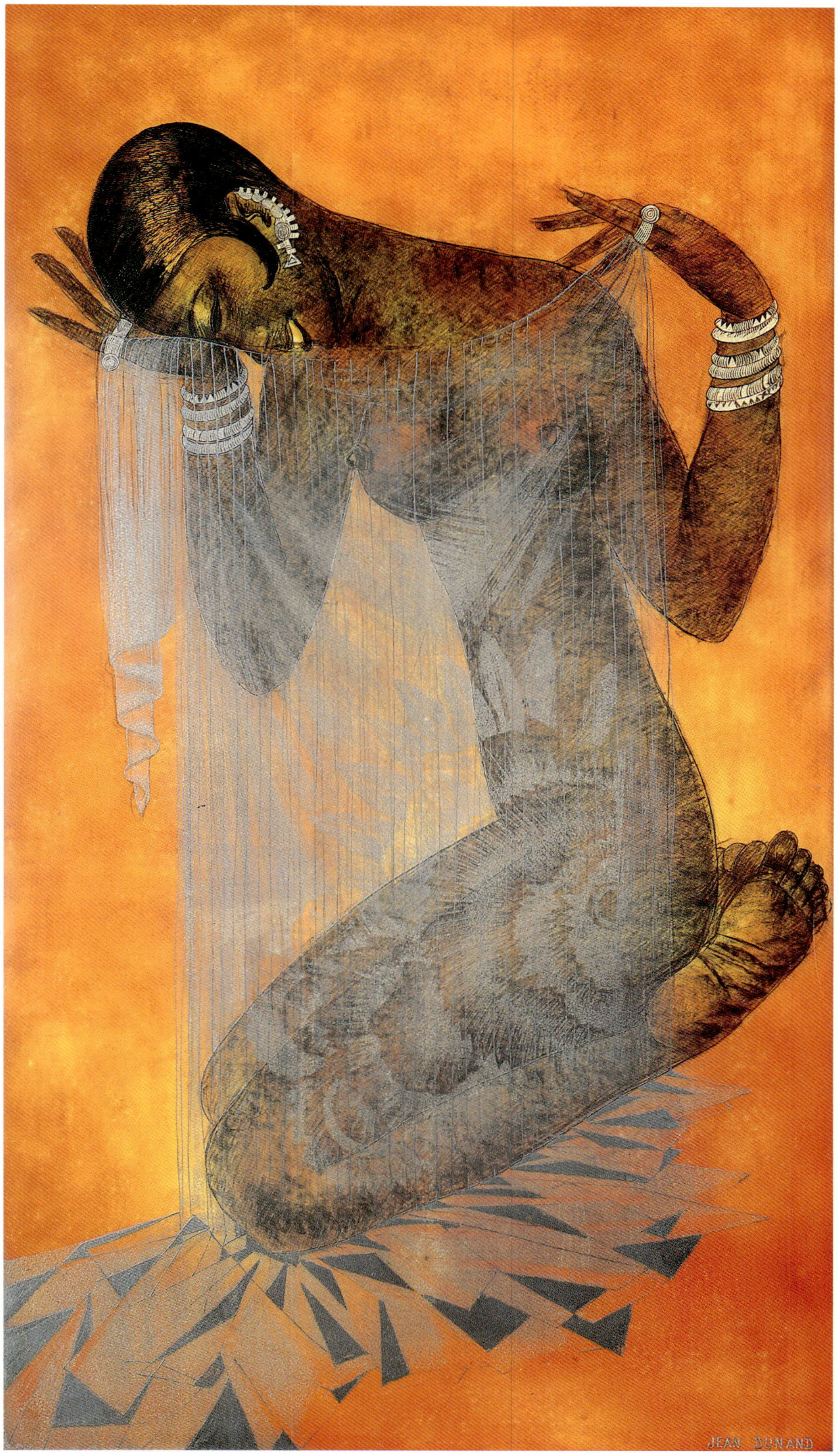

10 ***Josephine veiled***, 1927
(*catalogue 153*)

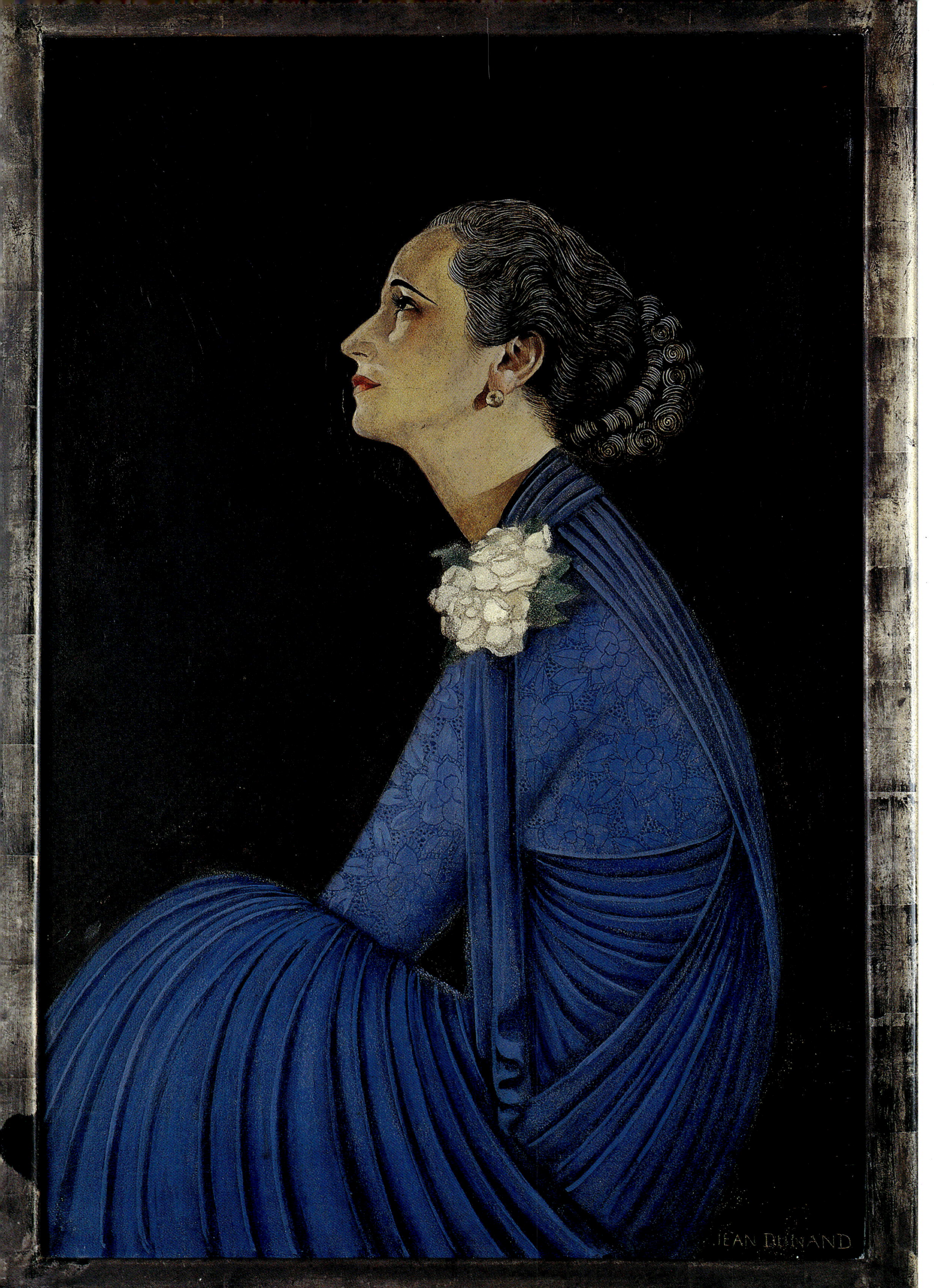
JEAN DUNAND

In September, Dunand again participated in the annual Salon National des Beaux-Arts in Geneva, exhibiting a bronze bust of a young man, yet another piece which drew comment on its vigour. It had already been shown in Paris the previous spring at the Cercle International des Arts. He also showed his new version of *The Child and Butterfly*, the graceful charm of which was admired by the local reviewers. Other works by Dunand filled a large display cabinet. Here, once again, was the immensely successful 'Frog' vase, as well as the 'Satin-flower' vase, occupying a place of honour at the centre of the display. On this occasion two of Dunand's vases (including the 'Satin-flower' vase) were purchased by the Geneva Museum aided by the generous proceeds of a trust fund established by Colonel Charles Rigaud. The first of these was described in a newspaper as 'a small steel vase with *repoussé* work and a quadrilobate bronze lap-joint and an inner receptacle, the second, a beautiful piece made of *repoussé* steel with wrought-iron handles highlighting the basic form of the vase. It was, moreover, discreetly and lightly decorated at the base, swelling out at the centre and highlighting the simple mother-of-pearl ornamentation around the neck where the iridescent orient of satin-flowers stands out against the silver thread that serves as their setting.' If the somewhat pretentious nature of the description seems rather unusual, it nevertheless reflects the general enthusiasm felt for Dunand's work. If we compare his work at this time with that of others in the field of dinanderie, we can see how extremely original his language is and that it was not mere chance that led critics and museum curators alike to praise the very same pieces.

In the context of this exhibition, a report by Hantz in the *Journal de Genève* of 2 November 1907 noted that, 'What is so striking and attractive about Dunand's work and what so many find inexplicable is its unity. It is precisely because, having conceived his form in the air, so to speak, he then becomes its craftsman, striving, with hammer in hand, to turn his conception into the form which he elaborates, a form which is born beneath his hammer blows and modelled on this initial idea. Decoration is added only as a logical complement, an element of luxury which must never detract from the object's logical appearance.'

In December 1907, Dunand took part, together with Angst and Gallet, in a sculpture exhibition at the Künstlerhaus in Zurich. Among the works he exhibited was a preliminary coloured plaster version of the bronze *Bust of a Young Girl* that had previously been acquired for the Lausanne Museum. Critics were pleased to find this charming subject shown again, noting its freshness, suggestive of *quattrocento* Florentine statuary, its naturalistic charm and its lively character. Beside this piece Dunand exhibited a bust of Sabato Martelli, who had modelled for him in Dampt's studio. It is a powerful and remarkable piece whose athletic structure is grandly and freely developed, while the head, regular and symmetrical, rests upon a massive neck. This piece was also purchased by the City of Geneva and was put on display in the Musée d'Art et d'Histoire in January 1908.

The year 1908 was to be an eventful one for Dunand, marked as it was by the birth on 13 June of his first child, a son, who was named Bernard Louis Paul. The first name was chosen by Mme Dunand's relatives, the second was to honour François-Louis Schmied (the boy's godfather), Jean Dunand's friend since childhood, and the third was a gesture of deference to the husband of Aunt Nonie, who had brought up Madame Dunand. This was also the year in which Jean Dunand first had occasion to enlarge his premises by building a studio at 72 Rue Hallé, the neighbouring property.

After successfully exhibiting works at the Musée Galliéra and the Société des Artistes Décorateurs in Paris, between 5 May and 5 June, Dunand participated in the fourth exhibition of the Galerie de l'Art Contemporain at 3 Rue Tronchet. Other Swiss exhibitors included the sculptors Angst and Gallet, the painter Ernest Biéler and the wood-engraver Schmied. Following this exhibition the Swiss Minister of Education appointed Dunand Officier d'Académie (for services to education).

OPPOSITE
11 ***Madame Agnès***, 1932
(*catalogue 188*)

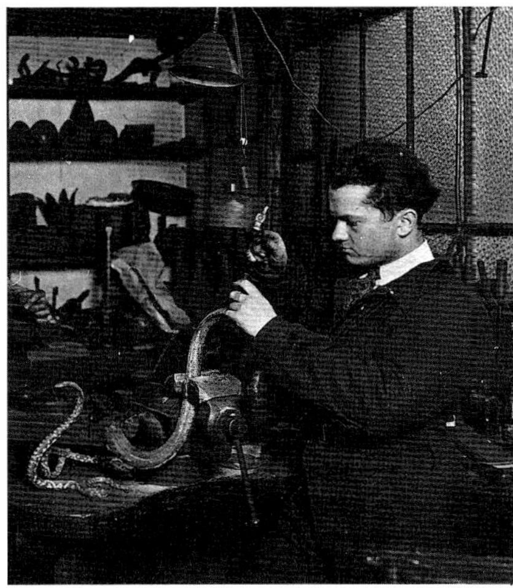

Dunand's assistant Kéco chasing a bronze snake after assembling the various parts cast separately at an outside foundry.

At the Salon de la Nationale, a lead vase by Dunand was bought by the French State for its collections at the Musée du Luxembourg, a purchase accompanied by Dunand's promotion from associate member to full member of the Société Nationale des Beaux-Arts. His fellow members now decided to invite him to sit on the jury that awarded the prizes in the decorative arts section at the annual Salon.

Dunand also exhibited his work – still in his capacity as a Swiss artist – at the 1908 Milan International Exhibition, as attested by his exhibitor's card (no. 13,581) preserved in the family archives.

In February 1909, he undertook a second, brief, visit to Italy, where he met a young orphan, twelve or thirteen years old, Francesco Zambon. They returned to Paris together on 8 February, and Zambon quickly earned himself the nickname Kéco and a job as an apprentice in Dunand's studio. Kéco was to remain in the studio throughout virtually the whole of his career, becoming the 'Best Craftsman in France' and helping Dunand's sons Bernard and Pierre in executing their work following the death of their father. Kéco died in Paris in 1952.

Another notable event of 1909 was Dunand's appearance at the first exhibition of a group calling itself 'La Cimaise' (literally, 'The Dado') which he himself had helped to found and which brought together many artists then specializing in the decorative arts. It may be noted here that the general enthusiasm for the applied arts, together with the rivalries of foreign schools, led many contemporary artists in Paris to form such groups in order to obtain greater recognition, establish their ideas and popularize their work.

It was at this point that Jules John Dunand decided to call himself Jean Dunand. (On his wedding invitation in 1906 he had modified his given names, from Jules John to Jean-John.) From 1909 onwards he would appear in the list of members of the Salon des Artistes Décorateurs as Jean Dunand.

The *Journal des débats* of 17 April 1909 drew attention to a portrait of Dunand by the Swiss artist Ernest Biéler in Room 10 at the Salon de la Nationale. Dunand was depicted in his working attire, and the painting was said to be 'very clearly composed, in bright colours . . .'. It is reproduced here as a title-page frontispiece.

In August, Dunand took part in an exhibition in Basle, where the decorative arts were somewhat sparsely represented. The following month, on 13 September, a further exhibition opened in Switzerland, this time in Lausanne, devoted to works by Biéler and Dunand. It was held in one of the rooms of the former Musée Arlaud and included 170 oils, watercolours and drawings by Biéler celebrating life in Saviese and the countryside of Valais, while Dunand's exhibits, dotted around the staircase and entrance hall or placed in display cabinets, comprised some forty hand-beaten vases, cups, flower-pot holders, boxes and buckles in various metals. The catalogue also mentions a steel vase (no. 41) owned by the City of Geneva, while several other items were presented as unique pieces. Biéler's portrait of Dunand was included among the exhibits as no. 169. An article published in the *Gazette de Lausanne* of 13 September and signed with the initials 'J.El.D.' speaks for the first time of pieces said to have been covered with lacquer in order to prevent them from rusting. According to Dunand, these early attempts were comparatively rare, and it is curious that here the reviewer has, so to speak, anticipated an experiment in which the artist was not to achieve any success until several years later. At all events, the success of the exhibition was such that, instead of lasting two weeks as planned, it was extended until 17 October. Dunand and Biéler were delighted with the whole experience and adopted this same principle of each complementing the other's work in later joint exhibitions.

On 14 December, the second Salon of the so-called 'Société Eclectique', a group of artists whose honorary president was the famous writer Anatole France, opened in Paris at the Galerie des Artistes Modernes at 15 Rue Caumartin, Paris. In its turn, this exhibition proved such a success that it was extended until Christmas. Alongside popular and provincial works by sculptors such as Louis-Henri Bouchard and Raymond Bigot, there were paintings by Bussières, Bellery-Desfontaines, Brachet and Paul Jouve. A large section had been set aside for the decorative arts, and Dunand's dinanderie exhibits were in the best company with pieces by Dammouse, Feuillâtre, Rivaud, Coudyser, Robert and Bigot. The critics singled out for special attention some silver plates with decorative motifs borrowed from nature, including Virginia creeper and hops, branches of oak or pine, and wild flowers or thistles. On all these pieces the ornamentation subtly conformed to the overall shape, arranged in a garland or gathered in posies. The catalogue listed 32 items under Dunand's name, numbered 100 to 131. Barely had the exhibition opened before several of his silver-plated copper dishes, including the thistle- and hop-motif plates, were bought by M. Dujardin-Beaumetz, Under-Secretary of State with responsibility for the Arts. They are now part of the collection at the Musée d'Orsay.

A few months later, the Artistes Décorateurs held their own exhibition in the Pavillon de Marsan. It was opened on 4 March 1910 by M. Dujardin-Beaumetz, who added to his earlier acquisitions by purchasing a copper vase for the Musée du Luxembourg. Measuring 70 cm (27½ in.) in height and 50 cm (19¾ in.) in diameter, it was notable for its 'ample and simple architecture and for a warm patina which commanded admiration from the very first moment'. Now in the Musée d'Orsay, this piece was the largest that Dunand had made to date.

The following May, at the Salon de la Nationale, the decorative arts began to supplant painting and sculpture, both in the qualitative importance of the works exhibited and in their numbers which continued to increase from one exhibition to the next. On this occasion Dunand exhibited a vase even larger than the one displayed at the Pavillon de Marsan in March. Made of copper with *repoussé* and chased decoration, it stood 1 metre (3 ft 3 in.) high – 'A size to dismay the beater', noted one journalist, apparently familiar with the technique involved.

In August, at the Zurich Exhibition, the decorative arts occupied no more than a modest space, only enamel, ceramics, jewellery and metalwork being represented there. Dunand exhibited twenty-three vases and cups in various metals. An editorial published in the *Journal de Genève* of 11 August 1910 noted that the beauty of Dunand's vases 'came from the subtle harmony of natural elements and geometric forms. By studying them closely, one can discover the source of a particular curve; whether it derives from a watermelon, from a warty gourd, from a pine-cone, from the calyx of a flower, or from a grain of seed, it will merely be a larger or smaller copy. The interpretation and the choice of such numerous elements never cease to influence him in his forms and their ornamentation, in his choice of metals and their different combinations, in the choice of patina, hammering and engraving, and the thousand and one ways of giving metals their sumptuous beauty. And yet the metal never loses its individual character.'

It was probably at this time that, faced with an increase in work, Dunand sought the help of a second *dinandier*, a certain Tambourino, like Kéco of Italian origin, who remained with him until, with the outbreak of war, he returned to Italy for good.

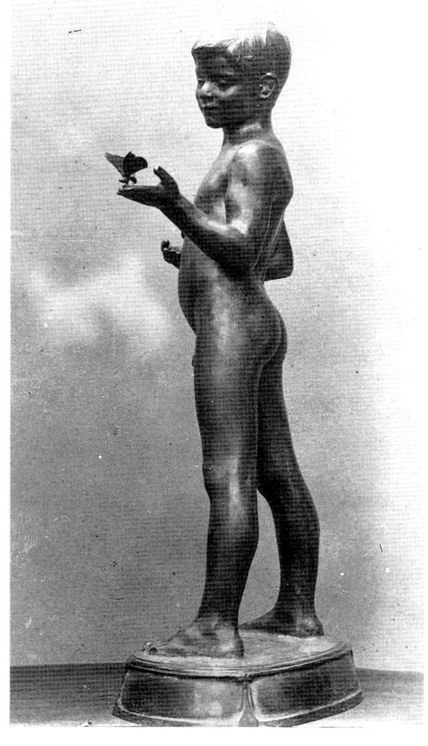

The Child and Butterflly, 1900, in its second version (cat. no. 783) in patinated plaster of Paris.

Between 10 September and 15 October, Dunand and Biéler repeated their collaborative venture of the previous year, when they jointly exhibited a collection of paintings and art metals at the Salles Léopold Robert in Neuchâtel. Biéler's chief contribution consisted of 155 paintings of the Valais countryside with 'gaunt lines and harsh colours', while Dunand limited his contribution to a handful of artistically wrought metal vases, including the 'Frog' vase, as delectable as a fable by Jean de La Fontaine, and the graceful bronze statuette *The Child and Butterfly*.

That same year – 1910 – saw Dunand's election to membership of the Salon d'Automne in Paris, while a number of his works were exhibited at the International Exhibition in Buenos Aires.

Since he needed to enlarge his studios, Dunand and his family vacated their first-floor apartment at 74 Rue Hallé and on 22 November moved to a small sixth-floor flat at 48 Rue d'Alésia, a modest apartment block owned by Girard, the creator of La Floréine beauty products.

In December Dunand was invited by the city council of Lucerne to decorate the municipal banqueting hall. The hall was built in a former farmhouse and its large ceilings with their arches and recesses had been preserved. Dunand placed panelling around the walls, so that he could add a copper frieze at head height with leaves and flowers representing the seasons of the year. Unfortunately, his work appears not to have survived.

The 1911 Salon de la Nationale provided Dunand with an opportunity to demonstrate his versatility when he made a pair of large andirons in wrought iron and copper with a decorative element based on a sunflower design. One of his exhibits was associated with a famous actress at the Comédie Française – a small gold vase with the label 'Property of Madame Barbet'. Studded with stars, it featured *repoussé* decoration depicting purple and red enamel columbines, this being the favourite flower of Madame Barbet. Between them was inscribed in elegant capital letters, the actress's motto 'Occulta redolens' ('redolent of hidden things'), an expression which admirably symbolized the mysterious fragrance of this doyenne of the French stage.

In July, a new exhibition was staged by the 'Société Eclectique', and Dunand participated by entering several vases, including a large engraved and patinated brass amphora with *repoussé* decoration. Although somewhat rustic in style, it was elegant in shape, its body highlighted with a frieze featuring the leaves and fruit of a mountain ash in relief. A small silver-plated copper dish with a clover motif was purchased by the State. A further group exhibition opened on 11 November at the Galerie Teitlinger, situated at 12 Rue La Boétie. Among Dunand's fellow exhibitors on this occasion were Decoeur, Bastard, Dammouse, Coudyser and Bouchard.

Dunand now realized the limitations of his work, and wanted to explore new avenues for his skills. From this point of view, the year 1912 was of major importance and constituted the second great turning-point in his career. On 18 February, an exhibition devoted to the decorative arts opened in Paris at the Galerie Manzi-Joyant, 15 Rue de la Ville-l'Evêque. Dunand's exhibits included two cabinets full of copperware, placed alongside the design sketch by the Catalan artist José-Maria Sert for a huge ceiling intended for the town house of the Comtesse de Béarn. In the meantime, however, Dunand, the practically minded craftsman, had arranged a meeting with a master of Japanese lacquerwork. Dunand had already worked in lacquer, albeit in a limited way and only employing it as a form of protective layer, rather like a varnish, its soole purpose being to prevent his metal vases from oxidizing.

Having glimpsed the possibilities of using lacquer for artistic ends in his own work, he sought to initiate himself into the mysteries of this centuries-old art. Several years later, in an interview with Maximilien Gauthier, Dunand explained the particular circumstances which led him to develop his interest in a skill which was little practised at that time in France: 'One day, when I was looking very closely at certain Japanese vases which I had been asked to restore, I noticed that the Japanese coppersmiths enhanced the magnificence of their work by using lacquer, the secret of which I sought in vain to discover.' He invited several of Paris's lacquerers to visit his studios and was astonished to find that in reality they were simply varnishers. The name 'lacquerer' put people on the wrong scent: it seemed as though the secret of traditional lacquerwork had been lost in France. In this interview Dunand went on to explain that, 'fortunately the Japanese themselves were interested in my copperwork and had a number of questions of a technical nature which they wanted to ask me. I took advantage of this to suggest an exchange, and agreed to reveal my secrets only to the extent that they told me theirs.' It so happened that the Japanese artist who was particularly interested in Dunand's metalwork techniques was Seizo Sugawara, who had arrived in 1990 with the national delegation to the Paris Exposition Universelle and who, having fallen in love with the country, decided to remain in France

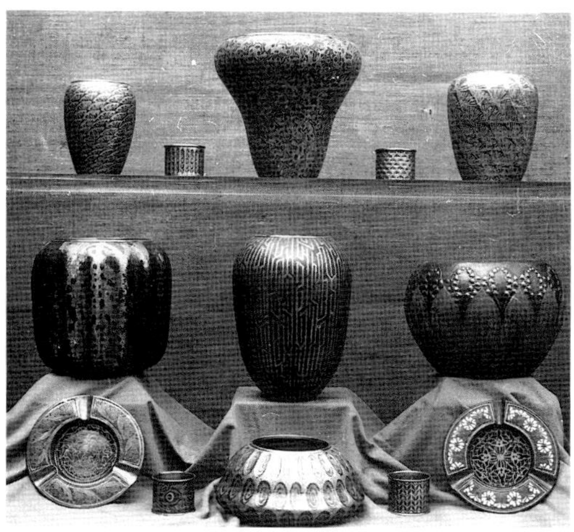

A group of metal objects shown at the Paris home of Comtesse Greffuhle in 1912 (see cat. no. 921).

when the exhibition came to an end. He began by working for a handful of art lovers, producing works which were marked by a synthesis of traditional Japanese craftsmanship and modern Western forms, enlarging on traditional non-figurative motifs and experimenting with the effects of high-quality materials.

This first meeting was followed by a series of thirteen lessons, in the course of which, contrary to all Dunand's expectations, Sugawara initiated him into the ancient and traditional procedures of oriental lacquerwork. The first lesson was held on 16 May 1912. In a small school notebook Dunand noted down the rudiments of lacquerwork as explained to him by Sugawara – the material to use, the instruments to choose, and the particular techniques to apply in pursuit of the desired aim. He had five lessons in May and eight in the course of June and July. The notebook ends with this thirteenth lesson. The two men even produced a sample together, in addition to a sort of reference table showing all the intermediate stages involved in producing a beautiful lacquer finish on wood. It is clear that Dunand did not become a lacquer artist with these few lessons but that, having properly assimilated the rudiments of the art, he no doubt felt that he could continue to work on his own, helped, if need be, by craftsmen from French colonies in Indo-China. Bernard Dunand recalls how, as a child, he admired a small ivory and gold sculpture of Joan of Arc in the family home in the Rue Hallé. It had been modelled by Jean Dampt, and Sugawara and Jean Dunand had used the piece to practise their lacquering technique and thus enhance the natural material.

Dunand's personal experiments allowed him to make progress in this new direction, although he was not convinced that the time was yet right for the results of that research to be made available to a wider public. Considering himself insufficiently prepared, he continued to exhibit his sumptuous metal vases without applying lacquer to their ornamentation.

The Protestant pastor Maury, who was a family friend and a sort of patron for Schmied and Dunand at the beginning of their careers, organized an exhibition on his estate at Villefavart in Limousin. Swiss in origin, and a major shareholder in Nestlé's, he gave regular dinner parties at his town house in Paris's 16th *arrondissement*, at which Schmied and Dunand were very pleased to be present.

For the Salon de la Nationale of 1912 Dunand produced a vase large enough to be placed at the entrance to the exhibition. Admirable in its simplicity, beautiful in its material and outline, it was highly thought of by the art critics who seem to have passed over in silence the pieces of dinanderie of more modest size which were displayed in two cabinets at the entrance to the first-floor rooms.

During the spring, Dunand took part in a group exhibition at the Bon Marché department store and also exhibited a number of pieces at a private exhibition organized by Comtesse Greffulhe in Paris. Without being really a fashionable artist, Dunand was nevertheless able to take advantage of the opportunities that came his way to develop contacts in high society in Paris. A relentless worker, determined to succeed, he left no stone unturned in his efforts to make a name for himself. Thus it was that he accepted the idea of a sort of retrospective organized by a gallery in Rheims which was quite well known in its day; as a result, he found buyers for a number of his pieces among well-to-do members of the region's champagne growers.

At the Salon d'Automne in October 1912 critics drew special attention to a marvellous plate in copper and silver depicting a snake coiled around itself, a piece displaying an extraordinarily three-dimensional quality.

On 15 October Dunand again exhibited examples of his work in Neuchâtel, while in the following month there was the third group exhibition put on by the 'Société Eclectique'. Dunand remained faithful to this group and lent his support to the gallery in the Rue Caumartin which had arranged these collective exhibitions to encourage interest in the decorative arts. In order to meet the demands of all these exhibitions, Dunand was obliged to repeat some of his models several times, more especially if they had proved

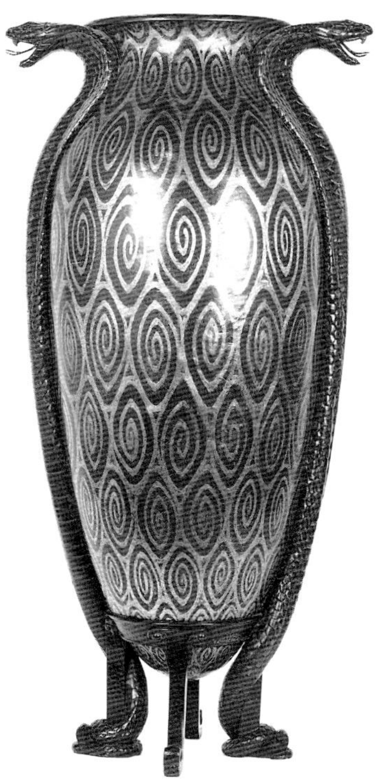

'Snake' vase, 1913, one of Dunand's largest dinanderie pieces, with an overall height of 128 cm (50½ in.); see cat. no. 934.

successful in the past. It was not unusual for an original model to enter a public collection while copies were bought by private collectors.

In February 1913, Raymond Poincaré, President of the French Republic, honoured with his presence the official opening of the eighth Salon des Artistes Décorateurs in the Pavillon de Marsan. On entering the exhibition, he encountered a monumental vase by Dunand; 128 cm (50½ in.) in height and ovoid in shape, made of brass and inlaid with silver, it stood on a wrought-iron base, its body decorated with two serpents rearing up to extend over its whole height. The bronze was finely chased and the reptiles' flattened heads formed the vase's handles. Dunand seems to have been fascinated by snakes. The gently sinuous undulation of their bodies was ideally suited to his metalwork technique. He employed the motif on many occasions, adapting it to suit boxes or singling it out for decorative elements of every size, for example on andirons for household grates. As a result, a certain M. Blot had the task of taking moulds of Dunand's works, which were then taken to a foundry for casting. In the studio Kéco would solder the different parts together and then take charge of the chased decoration.

At this exhibition Poincaré was also able to admire other, equally outstanding vases displayed in one of the cabinets. One such vase was decorated with a peacock-feather motif, while another, identical in shape, was adorned with ferns. Embossed motifs reflected each other on the various vases, in perfect harmony with the object's general shape in the form of a sort of elongated colocynth.

The copper and brass objects which Dunand made in 1913 may be justly regarded as the most beautiful pieces he ever created. The 'Snake' vase – to name but one – is a masterpiece of metalwork not only in the elegance of its curves and originality of its conception, but also in the stark simplicity of its style.

In this pre-war period, art exhibitions followed hard on each other's heels, and works by Dunand were to be seen at exhibitions in São Paulo, Munich, on the liner *France*, in Ghent and in Zurich, as well as in Paris at the Galerie Manzi, at the Théâtre des Champs-Elysées in the Avenue Montaigne and at the Château de Bagatelle in the Bois de Boulogne. Notwithstanding his growing reputation and status as an established artist, Dunand remained loyal to the Cercle des Etudiants Protestants in Paris, participating in this body's seventh exhibition, held in March that year.

In May his work was again to be seen at the Salon de la Nationale, with a large selection of 'very finely developed' vases in various metals. The famous 'Caduceus' clock, made for the couturier Jean-Philippe Worth, also dates from this year. Dunand and Schmied were among the great designer's regular guests. Every Friday evening they would dine together at Worth's house overlooking the Champ-de-Mars, and it was at his request that Dunand designed this extravagant clock in chased bronze, inlaid with gold and silver, its niello dial adorned with two hands in the shape of snakes with rhinestone eyes. The couturier's nephew, Jean-Charles Worth, who took over the business after the First World War, owned a large house in Neuilly which he wanted refurbished. The shutters of sand-blasted oak were lacquered by Dunand, a detail which was, to say the least, picturesque, matching the quality of the other examples of Dunand's work which Worth owned.

At the Salon d'Automne Dunand exhibited a cast copper chandelier made with the help of Coudyser, and the year ended with an exhibition at the Ecole des Beaux-Arts on the Quai Malaquais, when the numerous works of art which the State had bought in the preceding years were put on show. Among the pieces displayed, which included official commissions such as Monet's *Water Lilies*, critics singled out a number of works by Dunand, drawing special attention to his famous coiled-snake plate acquired at the 1912 Salon d'Automne.

At the official opening of the Salon des Artistes Décorateurs on 27 February 1914, the President of the society commended Dunand's work in the most emphatic terms. His exhibits were a fairly accurate reflection of the

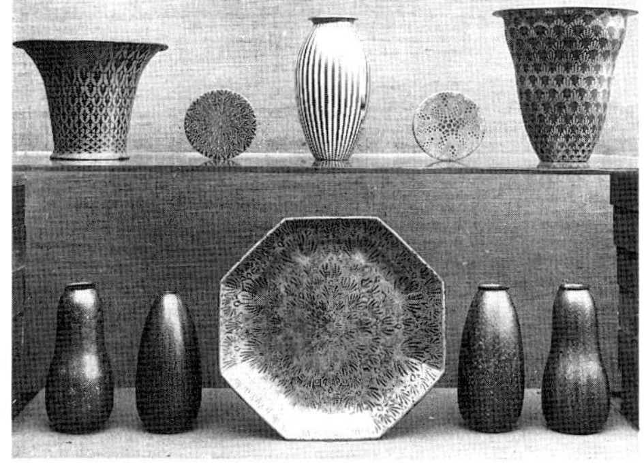

A group of works by Dunand shown at the Salon des Artistes Décorateurs in 1913; see cat. no. 962.

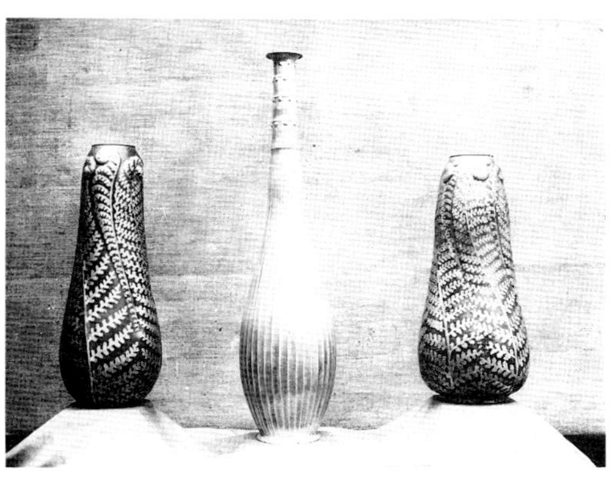

'Fern' vases and a bottle by Dunand exhibited on board the liner *France* in 1914; see cat. no. 944.

current state of his researches, with vases in various kinds of metal, delicate patinas, and plant-like ornamentation representative of an elegantly stylized naturalist art. Dunand exhibited once more the 'Caduceus' clock he had made for Jean-Philippe Worth. So spectacular was his modelling of snakes that critics compared the clock with certain sculptures from classical antiquity, an impression reinforced by the fact that the reverse side of the dial, in *repoussé* copper, revealed an extraordinary Gorgon's head worthy of the pediment of some Greek temple. A labradorite plinth underlined the sumptuousness of the whole.

In April, Dunand exhibited at Léonce Rosenberg's Galerie de l'Effort Moderne, at 21 Rue La Boétie. This was the gallery which later carried the torch of Cubist art and was second only to Daniel-Henry Kahnweiler's gallery in its encouragement of the artists of that particular movement. The following month, Dunand presented his latest work at an exhibition held in the Galerie Georges Rouard at 34 Avenue de l'Opéra. Intended to promote modern decorative art, the exhibition brought together the work of numerous artists under the title 'Les Artisans Français Contemporains', and to demonstrate its importance it was opened by François Carnot, President of the Union Centrale des Arts Décoratifs (U.C.A.D.).

In 1914 an exhibition of wares made by French craftsmen working in the luxury trades was held on board the liner *France*. The 'vitriniers', as they were called at the time, occupied practically all the rooms, while the so-called 'ensembliers', relatively few in number, exhibited furniture.

The First World War

When war was declared, Jean Dunand, although still a citizen of neutral Switzerland, contributed to the Allied cause from August 1914 to January 1916, by volunteering to work for the French Red Cross. He was appointed an ambulance driver for auxiliary hospital No. 152, opened by his friend the courturier Jean-Philippe Worth in the latter's salons and workshop at 7 Rue de la Paix.

His voluntary wartime work notwithstanding, Dunand still found time to exhibit his art, not least in the hope that people would continue to buy his works and ensure his family's livelihood. Thus, for example, he took part in the first Salon de l'Art Précieux in December 1914. During the war years his workshops were largely idle and Dunand attempted to make good the lack of manual labour by using a mechanically operated wheel and die-stamping process. This simplification of his method and the use of such a technique by so accomplished a craftsman could have led him into a whole new area of production. Quite the opposite occurred, however, for he soon realized that he could never succeed in investing the metal with life by this 'mechanical process of mass-production' which robbed his work of all suppleness and life, and abandoned it.

Dunand driving his ambulance (a converted car owned by the couturier Jean-Charles Worth) in Paris, *c.* 1916, and (right) Jean-Charles Worth visiting a wounded soldier recovering in the auxiliary hospital set up in his salon, *c.* 1917.

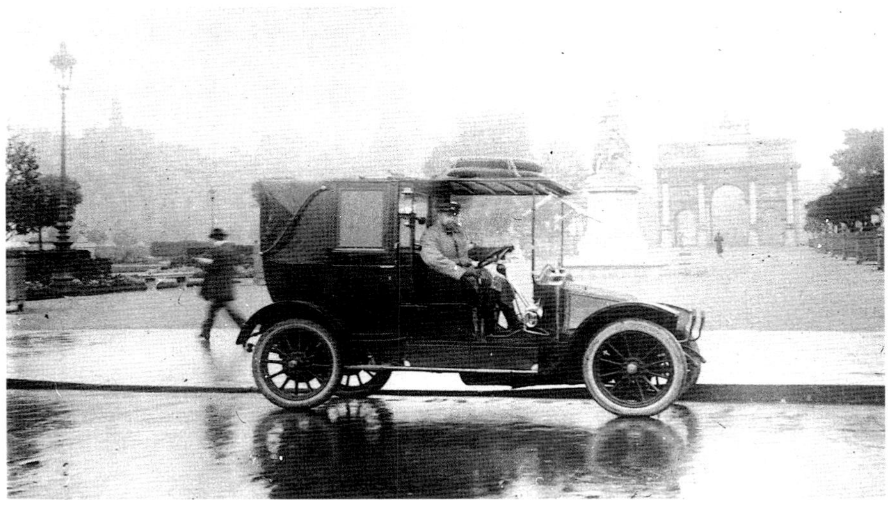

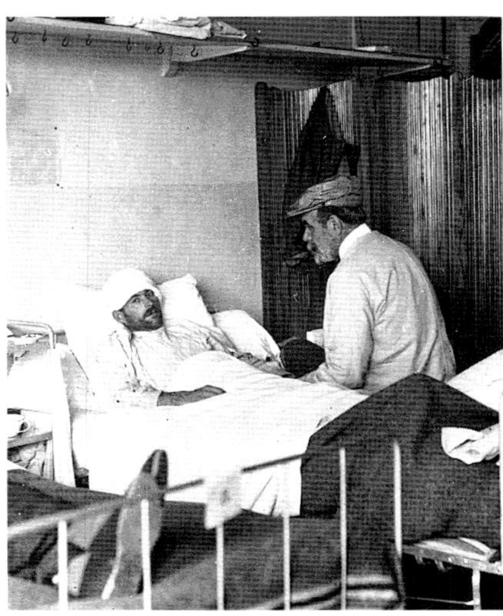

During the earliest days of trench warfare, François-Louis Schmied was gravely wounded and lost the use of an eye. His period of convalescence was spent at Trestiniel in the *département* of Côtes-du-Nord, where Jean Dunand and his son Bernard went to visit him. As a result of this injury – caused by an exploding shell – Dunand set about solving the problem of developing an 'efficient means of protecting the eyes during trench warfare.' He studied a new type of helmet with a raisable and detachable visor incorporating a wire-mesh opening made in such a way that the wearer could still have a clear view. Three thousand such visors were fitted to regulation army helmets before Dunand perfected the first manganese-steel helmet, the stronger for being cold-stamped out of a single piece of sheet metal. After countless setbacks and disappointments, Dunand succeeded in producing an initial run of a thousand helmets, manufactured by the Compagnie des Compteurs and delivered to the Army on 24 January 1917. In an article published in *Le Carnet des Artistes* on 1 May 1917, the journalist André Maurel reported that Dunand had gone to the war front 'in order to observe experiments being conducted on his invention'.

Dunand's helmet was copied, imitated and plagiarized by an unscrupulous business rival. However, thanks to the efforts of J.-L. Breton and Gaston Menier, two officials at the War Ministry, the scheme was foiled. All the competent authorities then agreed in recognizing the advantages and the effectiveness of Dunand's invention in protecting the wearer against flame throwers, shrapnel and other missiles.

The post-war era

With the end of hostilities, the menfolk began to be demobilized or were freed from captivity. In 1919, exhibitions and artistic events gradually started to gather pace, and members of pre-war groups began to reassemble. Meanwhile, on 3 January, Madame Dunand had noted in her private diary that 'Jean is dreaming of lacquer.' This obsession had led Dunand to intensify his researches and experiments to the point where he succeeded in developing a process as perfect as that of his oriental predecessors. His determination and constant need to strike out in new directions motivated Dunand to produce his most individual and most personal work of this period, rich as it already was in artistic creations. His lacquer studio, which dates from this time, was situated on the ground floor at 74 Rue Hallé. He was assisted here by a M. Bibal, a talented but by no means original painter of Basque origin, whom Dunand taught the art of lacquerwork based on his own designs. (It was this same M. Bibal who made a large gold-lacquer helmet for a tragic actress of the day, a commissioned piece which had been ordered through the good offices of Jean-Philippe Worth.) The work was carried out according to a strict formula – the final layers of lacquer being applied and the surfaces of previously lacquered objects being polished to highlight the patinas – all in a dust-free atmosphere.

In January, the Galerie Devambez in the Rue de Lisbonne broke new ground by devoting part of its display area to a permanent exhibition of applied art having a metallic theme; including gold- and silverware, dinanderie, ironware and numismatics. Dunand took part, exhibiting a number of items of household ware – teapots, trays, gongs and vases in decorated metals – just as he did the following month at an exhibition devoted to the decorative arts held at the Musée Galliéra.

At its tenth Salon, held in March 1919 at the Pavillon de Marsan, the Société des Artistes Décorateurs paid tribute to former members killed during the Great War, assembling examples of their work in several large display cabinets. In another part of the exhibition, the survivors presented their latest work as proof of their renewed activity. A reporter for *L'Eclair* noted in his article on the exhibition that Dunand's display offered 'the most beautiful of marvels, his vases in hammered and *repoussé* bronze are of an incomparable grandeur. The colour and ornamentation obtained by the "mokume" process gives the collection a warm and vibrant sense of harmony, the secret of which was once the preserve of oriental artists.' At this stage Dunand was still using lacquer to camouflage and protect the metal, or to modify its appearance, by a sort of modern alchemy, to the point of rendering it unrecognizable.

At this Salon, according to an anonymous reporter writing in the *Journal du peuple* of 6 April, 'The precious and virtually unknown manufacture of lacquerwork seems on the point of blossoming afresh. Degaine and Brugier among others, and Miss Eileen Gray, are achieving miracles in this direction.' The presence of these other artists working with lacquer was bound to stimulate Dunand himself, the more so since the work done by Eileen Gray proved that it was possible to Westernize the use of lacquer by applying it to the decoration of contemporary furniture. He, too, began to dream of matching furniture and decor, but in order to realize such a vision, he needed to enlarge his premises and diversify his workshops.

A chance to do so arose in 1919 with the ending of the order of sequestration affecting the property of a small German manufacturer named Heinsius, who lived close by at 66/70 Rue Hallé. Before the war he had worked as a mechanic and used the property as his repair shop. Dunand now took advantage of the opportunity to acquire the lease and install additional workshop facilities. No. 68 Rue Hallé was a charming private house, which Dunand and his family were able to make their new home.

Following the creation of the Blumenthal Foundation, an American organization intended to support the cause of French art after the privations of war, Dunand was appointed a member of the jury whose task it was to choose deserving artists as recipients of an annual prize. It was no doubt at this stage that, on learning of the American system of patronage and its artistic background, Dunand was given an opportunity to exhibit his work at Duwin's in New York. The gallery, at 720 Fifth Avenue, published a small descriptive catalogue listing the thirty-six objects he had put forward, including vases, trays, cups, paperweights, snakes and ashtrays. Dunand's first venture into the American continent was not without a degree of success and would be followed by many others; as a result of the acclaim his work received, he came to be viewed as an artist of international standing.

As the annual rhythm of art exhibitions resumed, Dunand participated in May in the Salon de la Société Nationale des Beaux-Arts, where a special section was devoted to the applied arts. The following month, in company with other painters and sculptors, he helped in setting up the so-called 'Nouveau Groupe' ('New Group'), which drew its members both from the Société Internationale de Peintures et de Sculptures and from the former Société Nouvelle, of which Auguste Rodin had until then been president. The group included Auburtin, Guillonnet, Karbowsky, Laparra, Charreton, Lebasque, Lebourg, Van Rysselberghe, Dufrène and Landowsky, Maurice Denis having shied away. The nucleus of the section given over to the decorative arts comprised Dunand (dinanderie), Decoeur and Lenoble (ceramics) and Bastard (inlaid ware). When this 'New Group' (yet another to use this description) exhibited its work at the Galerie Georges Petit at the end of the year, Dunand's brass- and copperware was highly commended, the individual pieces being described as 'marvels of decorative ingenuity' and even as 'museum pieces'.

The September edition of *Art et décoration* included a long article on Dunand, the text being accompanied by numerous illustrations. The writer was an eminent art critic, Emile Sedeyn, who emphasized not only the historical aspect of Dunand's career, but his technical and innovatory development. The evolution of his style was plain to see. If the forms he still used were ample and spacious with a great deal of suppleness, his ornamentation showed a clear development from a somewhat stylized approach towards an increasingly systematic use of geometry, ears of wheat, vine leaves and hop flowers giving way to rosette circles and radiating motifs. Nonetheless, Dunand retained a clear love of nature and continued, not without touches of humour, to make vases in the shape of gourds and warty colocynths.

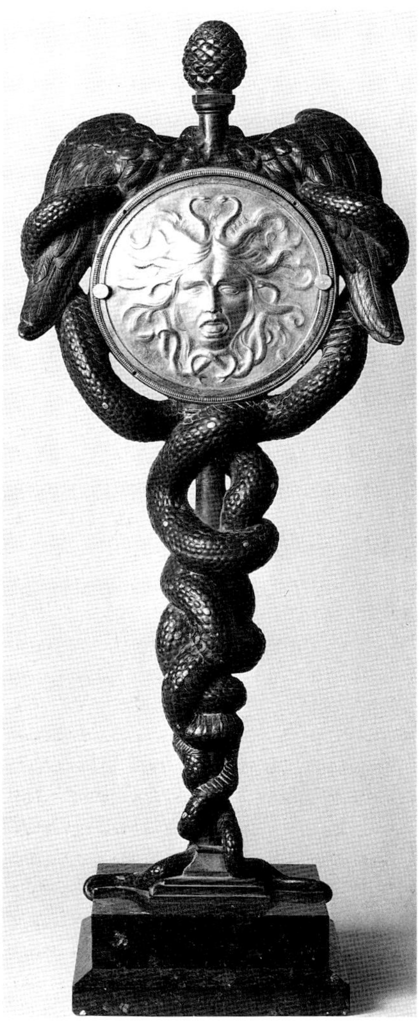

The reverse of the 'Caduceus' clock of 1913, showing Gorgon's head; see cat. no. 649 and colour plates 92, 93.

Sedeyn's article allows us to take stock of all the techniques that Dunand employed (see pp. 164 ff.): *repoussé* decoration, chasing, inlay work, and *champlevé* and *cloisonné* enamelling. It also reveals the existence of a veritable 'master-craftsman's studio', somewhat in the style of the Renaissance, with apprentices, students and disciples all working under the supervision and direction of Jean Dunand. A colour plate – extremely rare in such publications at this date – was also included and served to underline the rich variety and nuances which Dunand obtained in working his chosen materials.

By the same token, the objects shown at the Salon d'Automne were not only numerous, but displayed a high degree of skill and intelligence, confirming critical opinion that Dunand's work was of a superior quality both aesthetically and technically, thus placing him in the category of those artists whose latest works were awaited with genuine eagerness.

On 1 November 1919, Dunand was appointed a Chevalier de la Légion d'Honneur (official seal 23,627) by the Minister of Foreign Affairs, this honour having been recommended by the Minister of War 'for services rendered during the war'. Dunand's appointment served as a reward for all the vexations he had suffered when designing his new helmet for the Army. All the same, the fact that the nomination came not from M. Laferre, the Arts Minister, but from Stephen Pichon, the Minister of Foreign Affairs, created a minor scandal in artistic circles in post-war Paris.

After a somewhat tentative exhibition in 1919, the Société des Artistes Décorateurs put on its eleventh Salon in 1920 at the Pavillon de Marsan and provided all its exhibitors with a chance to develop the concept of modernity and to expand in every direction: a sort of stylistic unity was revealed in spite of the participants' different training. As a result, visitors to the exhibition could choose not only furniture to suit their own preferences but also *objets d'art* to grace their homes. Variety within an overall design scheme was no longer disconcerting, and general taste was finally evolving in the direction of modern art.

In June an exhibition was held in the Musée Galliéra with the title 'Pendules, cartels et pendulettes' ('Clocks, Wall Clocks and Travelling Clocks'). The variety of materials proved once again – if proof were needed – that there was no lack of creative activity in this immediate post-war period. The misfortunes of the past were forgotten as people began to look to the future. Engravers, wood-carvers, sculptors in marble, goldsmiths and jewellers, enamellers and glass-blowers all showed off the resources of their respective techniques in terms of their application to modern art. René Lalique exhibited afresh models of clocks, large and small, made of moulded and enamelled glass, while Dunand, for his part, re-exhibited the fabulous bronze 'Caduceus' clock of 1913. He also exhibited a series of extremely flat watch-cases with geometrical ornamentation, the perfection of which vied with the warmth of their patina. Reviving the techniques of damascening and *azziminia* which the artists of the Renaissance had borrowed from the Persians, Dunand carved out a reputation for himself as a uniquely versatile artist.

Dunand's contributions to the Salon de la Nationale of 1920 was welcomed by critics, who made particular mention of the radiating decorative motifs that gave infinite variety to the ornamentation of his pieces. In an article published in *L'Amour de l'art* in June 1920, Yvanhoé Rambosson drew a comparison between Dunand's innovations and the startling schematic creations of Elamite Susa in the eighth century BC. For other writers, one piece approaches 'the splendour of the setting sun', while of another it was even said that 'the poetry of a moonlit night restores the artist's forms to their numerical and geometrical point of departure' [*sic*].

In September, Emmanuel de Thubert, who had paid an extended wartime visit to Dunand's workshop in January 1917, wrote a major article in *L'Art et les artistes*, in which he described Dunand as an artist who had revived the art and craft of metalwork 'in the face of an industry which, with the aid of mandrels and casting techniques, has attempted to displace that art, demanding that the machine produce what the hand of man had formerly created with such consummate skill.' Here, too, the new pieces shown as illustrations reveal that lacquer was being used only as a protective covering or finish, not as an integral part of the decoration. This approach was confirmed, moreover, by the pieces which Dunand sent to the Salon d'Automne in 1920.

Ever since the war, Dunand had been dreaming of extending the use of lacquering techniques to the actual decoration of objects. On the one hand, he hoped to work in lacquer in the way that a painter works with oils; on the other, he imagined lacquering furniture in the way he had seen certain of his fellow artists do it. Unfortunately, the technical constraints specific to lacquer obliged him to revise his sculptural language completely, and, above all, to design furniture in such a way that an entire piece could be lacquered after its component parts had been assembled, without the joints being visible beneath the lacquer. He had already experimented on certain forms still found in China and Japan – low tables with rounded edges but without mouldings or recesses that would prevent the lacquer being polished uniformly.

At the 1921 Salon des Artistes Décorateurs Dunand exhibited a large panel covered in lacquer, thus tackling large plane surfaces for the first time. The panel had been commissioned by a painter friend of his, Henry de Waroquier, who wanted to see him use lacquer in his own works, and his sketch, which served Dunand as a model, represented fishing boats, their sails set to windward, seen against a backdrop of mountains. The painter's sombre, richly coloured palette was excellently suited to the available shades of lacquer. Dunand was well satisfied and felt that he had found a new sense of direction in his experiments. Lacquer now became an integral element of coloured decoration. It was no longer a question of using the material to create an effect, but rather of creating a kind of modern painting. Every type of geometrical design that he had painstakingly perfected for his brass- and copperware decoration was now transposed, without the least difficulty, to the medium of lacquer, and he was by now sufficiently in control to be able to use lacquer with ease. On the body of his vases, the effect of the geometrical compositions was one of surprising richness. What he had achieved was aesthetic perfection. He decided to explore this field in greater depth and to extend the possibilities of lacquer by applying it to Western furniture of simple design.

Dunand was appointed, successively, a member of the jury of the Société d'Encouragement à l'Art et à l'Industrie, a member of the Conseil de Perfectionnement at the Ecole des Arts Appliqués in the Rue Dupetit-Thouars, and president of the dinanderie class at the Exposition Nationale du Travail.

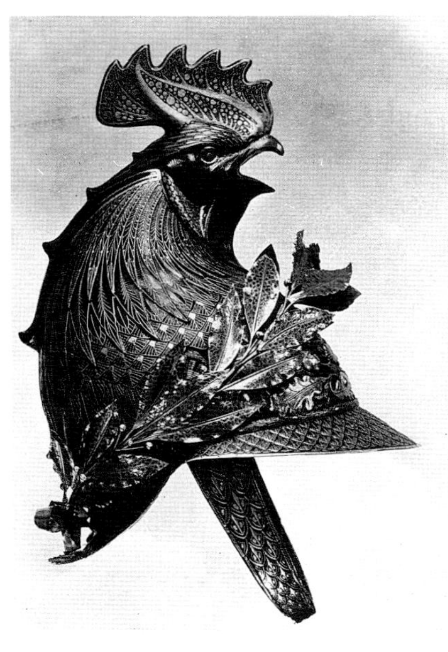

The ornate 'Victory Helmet' presented to Marshal Foch, 1921.

An exhibition of watches held in June 1921 provided Dunand with a further opportunity to demonstrate his great dexterity and technical skills. His watch-cases were becoming increasingly flat and lightweight, and their ornamentation appeared to have been taken to the ultimate stage of expressiveness. Visitors to the exhibition – art lovers, dealers and critics alike – took pleasure in the artist's spirit of inventiveness combined with an enquiring mind that had led him to revive an old procedure which involved making dovetail grooves in the metal, inserting lengths of silver wire and finally hammering and filing them flat.

In the autumn of 1921, a group of American admirers of Marshal Ferdinand Foch presented this outstanding leader in the Great War with a helmet made of steel with *repoussé* decoration, and encircled and inlaid with gold and silver, by Dunand. The 'Victory Helmet' (see pp. 176, 185) was brought from Paris to the United States by Mrs Mackay Bennett, the daughter of the principal donor. The crossing was made on board the liner *France*, a twofold symbol calculated to appeal to the Marshal, who was presented with his helmet in New York. The special presentation casket was covered with black lacquer, its top section decorated with a motif of exploding shells in metals of various shades, while the base was surrounded by a frieze depicting barbed-wire entanglements, the volutes of which enclosed the words from the *Marseillaise*, 'Le jour de gloire est arrivé'.

In December, an exhibition opened in Paris at the Galerie Georges Petit, 8 Rue de Sèze. This might be better termed a 'Salon' in view of the number of pieces displayed and the variety of disciplines represented. It brought together works by Jean Dunand, Jean Goulden, Paul Jouve and François-Louis Schmied, four artists who shared not only a common love of ostentation and spectacular display, but also a constant concern to develop ideas and a systematic search for technical perfection. In addition, they all knew each other well. Dunand first proposed forming this new group, which exhibited under the names of all four artists.

Dunand's first dealings with the Galerie Georges Petit dated from 1919, when he had taken part in the first exhibition of the 'Nouveau Groupe'. He considered it a perfect venue, but felt that a group exhibition would be much more memorable if the number of participants were reduced and if, above all, each artist's work were of a complementary nature. He was, moreover, well aware that the regular clients who frequented this gallery were the very ones whom he hoped to convince of the quality of his work. The system of exhibiting work at the Galerie Georges Petit was fairly simple, since exhibitors would hire whichever room met their space requirements and the gallery subsequently deducted commission from the proceeds of all sales. The money thus raised was used to cover the gallery's costs, including paying the assistants, one of whom was the young Jacques Dubourg, who was adept at advising customers and selling the works on display. He later specialized in modern painting and gained an international reputation in the field.

Dunand had got to know Goulden through a mutual friend, Jean Guiffrey, curator at the Louvre, whom Goulden had met in Salonika during the war. Goulden was a doctor and a member of a Protestant farming family, formerly from Alsace, but now living in the *département* of Meuse. Of an artistic temperament, he had chosen to take up painting on his return to France, having previously discovered Byzantine art in all its richness when working on Mount Athos with a restoration team sent to Greece to repair wartime damage. The relatively well-to-do Goulden acted as intermediary in obtaining commissions for Dunand, thus making it possible for the latter to enlarge his premises and employ assistants of Indo-Chinese origin to help him with his lacquerwork. It also seems likely that money was put up by Goulden to enable the four artists to hire space at the Galerie Georges Petit. He appears, therefore, to have been a sort of leading figure for the group from the time of its inception.

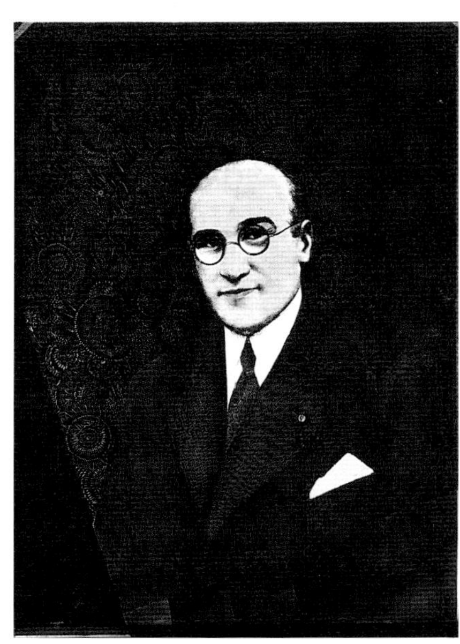

Jean Guiffrey, lacquer portrait by Dunand, 1930 (cat. no. 173).

As for Paul Jouve, Schmied was the first to make his acquaintance in 1910. Jouve had provided the illustrations for a special edition of Rudyard Kipling's *The Jungle Book* to be published by a bibliophile society, Le Livre Contemporain. The original intention had been to include coloured etchings, but since Jouve had little experience of this technique at the time, he decided to ask Schmied to prepare wood-engravings; for various reasons, however, the book was not completed until 1917 and not distributed to subscribers until 1919.

Jean Guiffrey was urged to become the group's president, and his established reputation helped the four friends immensely. The secretary was Charles Terrasse, son of the composer Claude Terrasse and nephew of the painter Pierre Bonnard. Such was the success of this mutually supportive association that the group's activities continued until 1933.

The group's first exhibition opened on 15 December 1921. Madame Dunand noted in her diary that it had been a 'great success'. Indeed, contemporary photographs show the whole affair to have been extraordinarily spectacular. Most of the objects were sold soon after the exhibition opened, and numerous orders were placed. Alongside his dinanderie, Dunand exhibited lacquered panels, including one, based on a sketch by Jouve, that

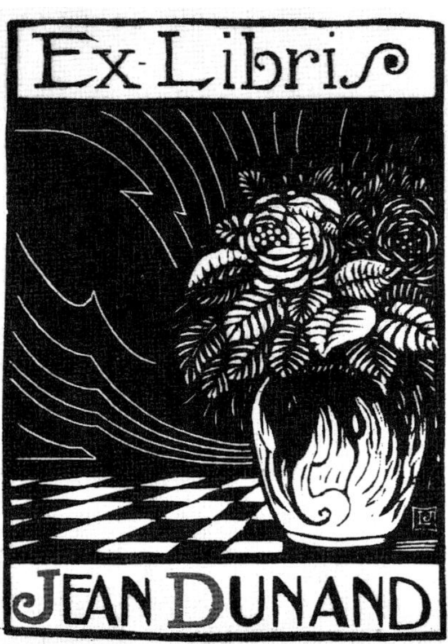

Book-plate with design by the wood-engraver Paul Jouve.

depicted an impressive panther; a cypress-studded landscape in Macedonia, was executed after a sketch by Goulden; a third, based on an earlier sketch by Waroquier, featured fishing boats. Several of Dunand's two-, four- or six-leaf lacquered screens on show had been designed in collaboration with Jean Lambert-Rucki. Two other screens were particularly admired, one with a jaguar motif based on a sketch by Goulden. A number of low tables in plain red or black lacquer and a stool, with a matching red-lacquer chest of drawers, completed the ensemble. The chest of drawers was based on a design by Goulden and decorated with a landscape in a highly simplified manner which could be said to herald abstract art. A shellac bookcase with decoration featuring a plant-like motif was a commission by Jean Berque, a painter and illustrator who collaborated on books with the Tharaud brothers. The large 'Snake' vase of 1913 and the 'Caduceus' clock of the same year completed the list of Dunand's exhibits.

The wooden frames of all these pieces of furniture had been made by a Paris cabinet-maker named Chollet. As for the panels of the screens that were shown at this first exhibition, the woodwork was prepared by Philomin Vidal, a carpenter in Dunand's workshop. They were mostly of mahogany and very dry, having previously served as counters at the Bon Marché department store, a large part of which had been destroyed by fire; they had subsequently been sold off by the firm of Boucicaut, owners of Bon Marché.

The reason for the interest aroused by this first exhibition lay in the fact that, independently of the talents of each member of the group, a new concept of luxury and quality was on offer here. After the wartime restrictions and attendant social upheaval, this surge of unusual colours and objects could not fail to win public enthusiasm. As well as suggesting the formation of the group, Dunand was also its most versatile member and its driving force. When the exhibition closed on 31 December, it was the general opinion of the art critics of the day that it had been a resounding success for all concerned.

On 29 May 1922, Jean Dunand acquired French citizenship. Although, thanks to his voluntary service during the war, this was a mere formality, his application was endorsed by Louis Barthou, a politician and bibliophile. Any foreign artist who had enlisted in France as a volunteer following the declaration of hostilities was granted French nationality on demand. Others who took advantage of this privilege included François-Louis Schmied, Gustave Miklos and Jean Lambert-Rucki.

In April the City of Geneva held an exhibition of decorative art by foreign artists at the Musée d'Art et d'Histoire, with the aim of introducing local artists to contemporary trends, especially in France. The chosen theme was metalwork, which of course embraced wrought iron as well as brass and copper, the section in which Dunand exhibited his work. Critics were unanimous in welcoming Dunand back to his native Switzerland, and showed a marked sense of pride in the fame which he now enjoyed. The French presence was organized under the aegis of the Société des Artistes Décorateurs. Their combined contribution amounted to fifty-nine pieces, including works by Capon, Linossier, Brandt, Subes, Szabo, Schenck, Maclès and others, their scope ranging from a radiator cover to ornamental wrought-iron panels and decorative art objects.

The following month, the Société des Artistes Décorateurs put on an exhibition of applied art at the Grand Palais in Paris in the context of the Salon des Artistes Français. Two large metal amphoras by Dunand with *appliqué* silver decoration were placed beneath the portico, one on each side of the main entrance in the northern section of the vast exhibition hall, while two other bowls in beaten copper were strategically placed in the colonnade leading to the entrance.

The galleries housed forty-four stands, each attesting in its own way to the resurgence of the decorative arts in France. In an article published in *Mobilier et décoration*, André Fréchet observed that this was 'an extremely important exhibition which could be considered a dress-rehearsal for the international exhibition of decorative arts which will be taking place shortly.'

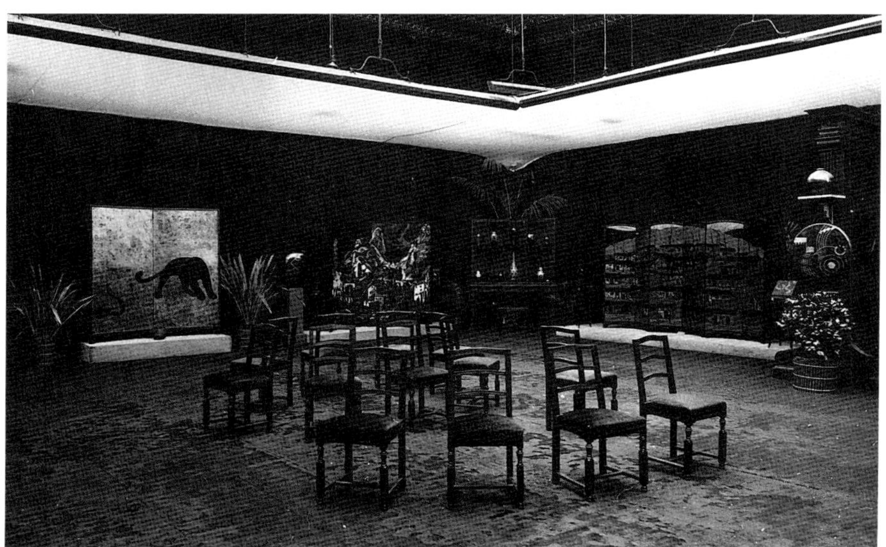

The main exhibition hall at the Galerie Georges Pétit, December 1922; the *Leopard and Cobra* screen (cat. no. 2) is seen on the left.

That exhibition was not in fact held until 1925. In another article, published in *France Libre* on 19 March 1922, Léonce Rosenthal noted that, under the pretext of being traditional, certain artists were merely copying earlier pieces, while others were elaborating existing techniques. 'Dunand is no longer content to hammer bronze and copper, to chase and inlay metals, he no longer restricts himself to patinating vases, but covers them with lacquer, sometimes including fragments of crushed eggshell, producing marvellous effects.'

In October 1922, Hébrard, the famous art publisher, put on an exhibition of works by Claudius Linossier. This Lyons-born *dinandier* had begun his career in Paris by working for Dunand for several months in 1920. Dunand's work, however, is very different, Linossier's being indisputably original, even if, at the date in question, it owed more to traditional silversmithing than it did to dinanderie, at least in the sense that Dunand understood the term.

That same autumn, a travelling exhibition of works by the Groupe Dunand-Goulden-Jouve-Schmied opened in The Hague under the sponsorship of the Comité France-Hollande. It transferred, with great commercial success, to Amsterdam and Rotterdam before being seen in Paris.

The second annual exhibition by the group of four opened at the Galerie Georges Petit on 18 December and was an immediate success, confirming the aptness of their collaboration. Once again, Dunand reiterated the principle of joint endeavour, showing works that were wholly his own, as well as others made with the help of fellow artists. One example of the latter was a lacquered screen made up of two panels and depicting a cobra rearing up in front of a leopard, the design of which was based on a sketch by Paul Jouve. Another screen, with four panels, owed its inspiration to Henry de Waroquier and showed the village of Moustiers-Ste Marie in the *département* of Alpes de Haute-Provence. A further group of pieces had been made in collaboration with Jean Lambert-Rucki. Dunand ensured that in every instance the names of his collaborators were listed in the catalogue; it was only at a later date and for personal reasons that Lambert-Rucki chose not to have his name publicly associated with Dunand's work, which he found too 'decorative'. He even arranged to enter Dunand's studio via a back door giving on to the narrow Rue Dareau behind the studio; being thus unobserved, he could not be reproached for betraying 'great art'. Nonetheless, even if in later years Dunand no longer spoke of his collaboration with Lambert-Rucki, those pieces which owed their existence to the latter's designs remain readily identifiable. At least as far as his figurative compositions are concerned, there is a note of humour and even mockery which distinguishes Lambert-Rucki's work from Dunand's. On the other hand, Schmied never mentioned his collaboration with Gustave Miklos, a little-known artist at the time, although in practice they worked together on several book-plate illustrations. A number of bibliophiles later expressed astonishment that an artist who had lost the use of one eye could achieve such accomplished results, but nothing was said.

The exhibition, which lasted until 31 December, was extremely well attended by the general public and art lovers alike (their interest no doubt whetted by the success of the previous year's exhibition), and it proved a notable commercial success. Dunand's own copy of the catalogue contains, alongside a sketch of each of the pieces exhibited, a price in code. He also noted: 'Bring other pieces to replace the ones sold.'

The following year, 1923, geometric designs became increasingly evident in Dunand's decorative work. This is particularly noticeable in a series of low tables and in gongs made in traditional dinanderie. Their surfaces are decorated with concentric circles and arcs, but disjointed by the superimposition of diagonal lines suggestive of ripples on the surface of a pond. Dunand's geometric style is even more apparent in the ornamentation of lacquered vases. Indeed, whether it be a question of a *bonbonnière* or a tray, all manner of combinations were employed and systematically developed as variations. The decoration is thus seen as an integral part of an object's overall form, in the case of vases encircling the belly, clinging to the neck or cutting cleanly and neatly across the surface in a bold diagonal stripe. In other examples the vase has the appearance of having been crudely re-assembled from broken shards. Such prismatic treatment of the decorated surface is of course further

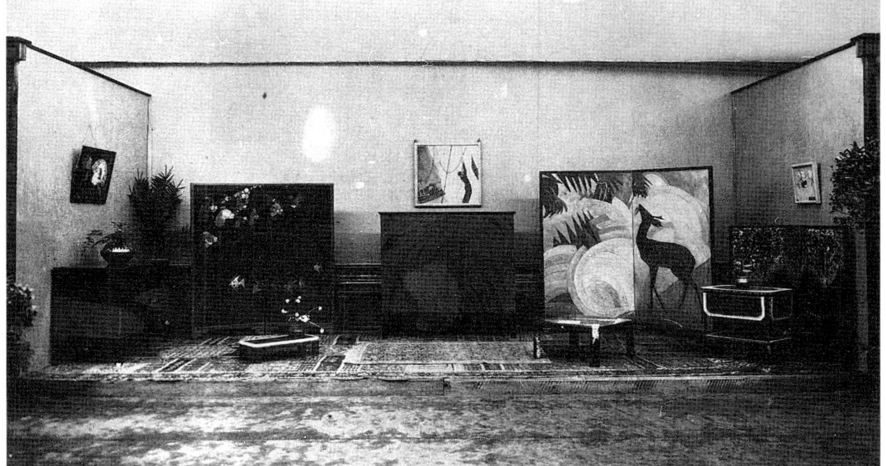

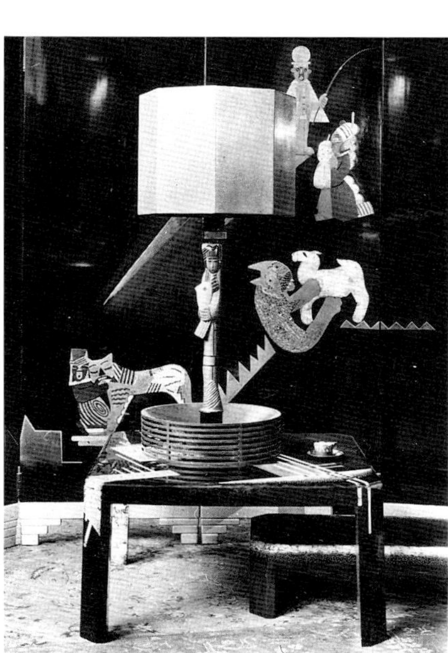

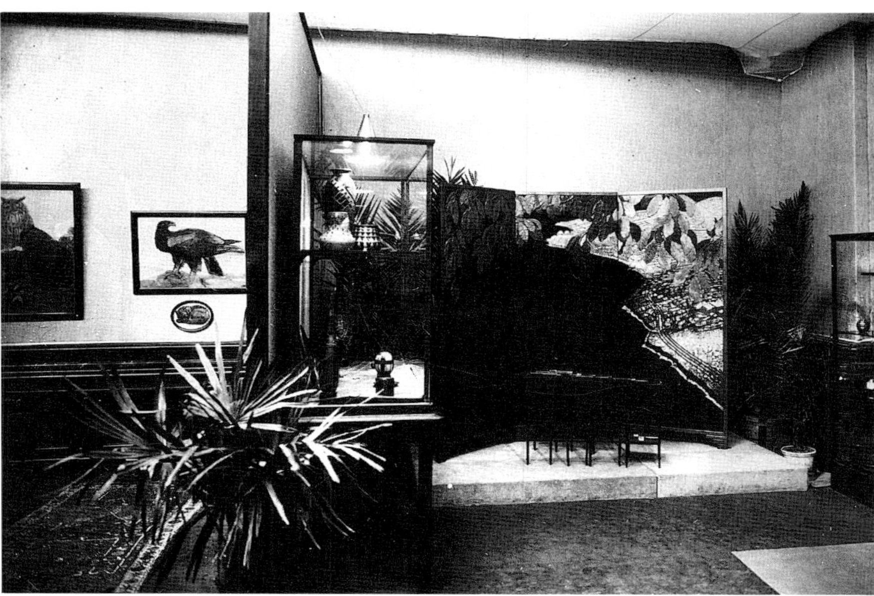

The Galerie Georges Petit, December 1923. Among the works seen in these photographs are: (above) the table lamp (cat. no. 590) and screen *Encounters* (cat. no. 13), both executed in association with Jean Lambert-Rucki; (right, above) the screens *Fish* (cat. no. 10) and *Deer* (cat. no. 8); and (right) works by Paul Jouve, together with vases and the screen *The Shores of Lake Geneva* (cat. no. 14) by Dunand.

accentuated by the effective use of bright contrasting colours, Japanese red in conjunction with black, gold or silver, or with white eggshell. On receiving a piece he had ordered from Dunand, Robert de Rothschild wrote in his letter of thanks of 6 August 1923, 'All the fish of Deauville will assuredly turn green with envy at this one, which is bound to meet with widespread acclaim.' There is no denying that from this date onwards Dunand's compositions gained in force and power of expression. Screens, vases and household items alike were adorned with extraordinary designs.

The work Dunand sent to the various annual Salons was awaited with ever greater anticipation and more and more remarked on, while his one-man shows provided guaranteed financial success for the galleries that presented them. In February 1923, a small exhibition of Dunand's work was held at the Hôtel de La Rochefoucauld in the Rue Visconti; it took place within the framework of a tribute to Swiss artists in the heart of the old Huguenot quarter of Paris once known as 'la Petite Genève'.

At the Salon des Artistes Décorateurs, Dunand again exhibited the snake and leopard screen previously seen at the Galerie Georges Petit, while Waroquier's screen design once more provided a focus of attention for visitors to the Salon d'Automne. On each occasion the response was one of praise and admiration, Dunand's warm, dark lacquers being considered triumphs of good taste and technical perfection. His clientèle grew to encompass increasingly well-to-do circles, and commissions fulfilled led in turn to further orders. Dunand was recognized as an artist in undisputed command of every technique he employed.

In October 1923, a panel decorated with large silver-scaled fish drew special comment when it was shown at the Galerie Devambez. Its 'fantastical' aspect was fairly unusual. It appears that its design was based on one of the few that Gustave Miklos was invited to submit, though the latter's name did not appear in the catalogue. Critics admired the rich and mysterious effect which the artist was able to create by depicting bubbles of air escaping from the mouths of the fish and growing larger as they rose to the surface. One reviewer even wrote that 'What we see here is a beautiful, virile art which strikes the imagination and flatters good taste, and can only serve to contribute harmoniously to enhancing the beauty of life.'

The year ended with the third Dunand-Goulden-Jouve-Schmied group exhibition held at the Galerie Georges Petit, from 13 to 31 December. Dunand's display cases contained the usual selection of vases, trays, *jardinières*, perfume burners, boxes, *bonbonnières*, gongs, ashtrays, cups and small dishes; on this occasion, however, there was also a book-binding plate in silver and black metal specially made for a well-known bibliophile, Dr Amédée Baumgartner. Elsewhere, there were screens with decorative motifs, including Japanese fish, partridges and deer, on a geometrical background; low tables, tea tables and nests of tables; decorative panels, fire-guards and small screens. A gold lacquer bas-relief, based on a sculpture by Angst, depicted Dunand's twins, Jean-Louis and Suzanne (born in 1918), its classical style in curious contrast to an extraordinary lamp of lacquered wood standing on a low table like some African fetish. This was a special commission carved by Lambert-Rucki and intended to grace the apartment of a lady with an interest in Negro art.

Once again, Dunand acknowledged the contributions of his fellow artists. Lambert-Rucki was credited with the designs for two four-panel screens, together with a firescreen and the aforementioned African-style lamp, while Biéler had provided the sketch for a screen depicting the shores of Lake Geneva. In the section devoted to Jean Goulden, a special entry described the pieces of furniture, listed as items 35 to 40, that he had made in collaboration with Dunand. They consisted of a sideboard, a chest of drawers, a cabinet of lacquered steel, a bureau decorated with eggshell, an occasional table and a *chiffonnier* (tallboy). Here, too, one notes the almost systematic geometricality of the different types of decoration. On each piece of furniture, the names of both artists figured jointly.

Plates 12–49
DECORATIVE SCREENS AND PANELS

OPPOSITE
12 ***Samples of decorative lacquer finishes***
(cf. pl. 145)

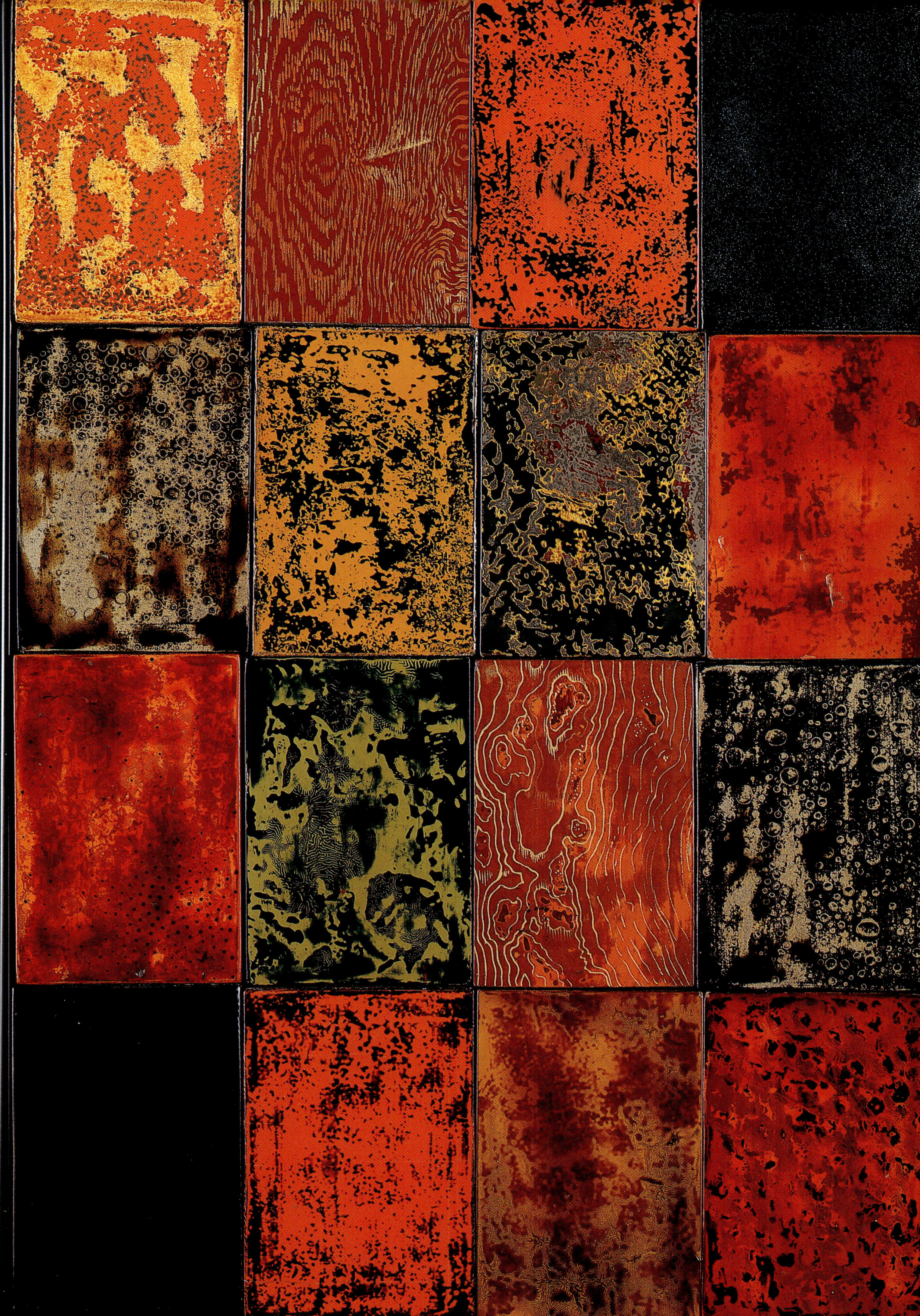

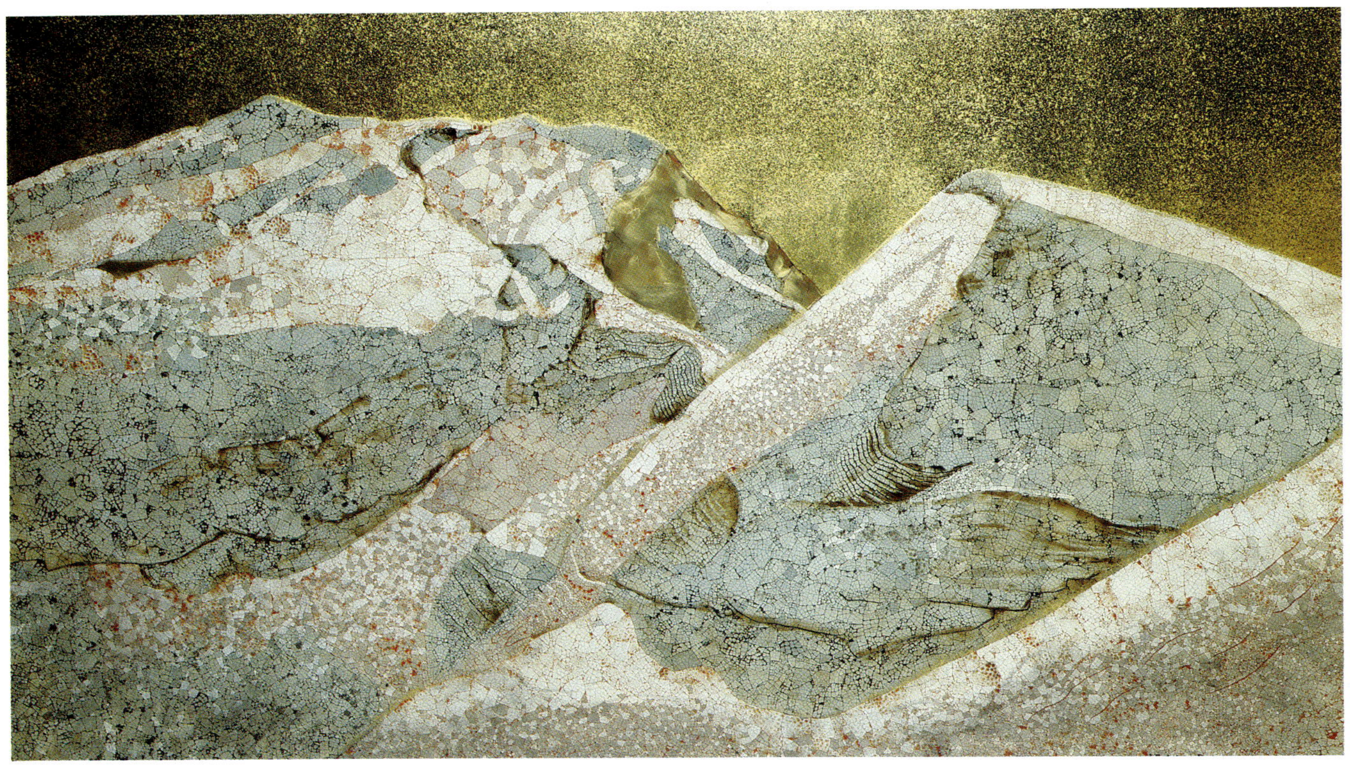

13 ***Mountain Landscape***, 1925
(*catalogue 298*)

14 ***Brittany***, 1926
(*catalogue 32*)

OPPOSITE
15 ***Saint-Cernin***, *c.* 1935
(*detail of catalogue 100*)

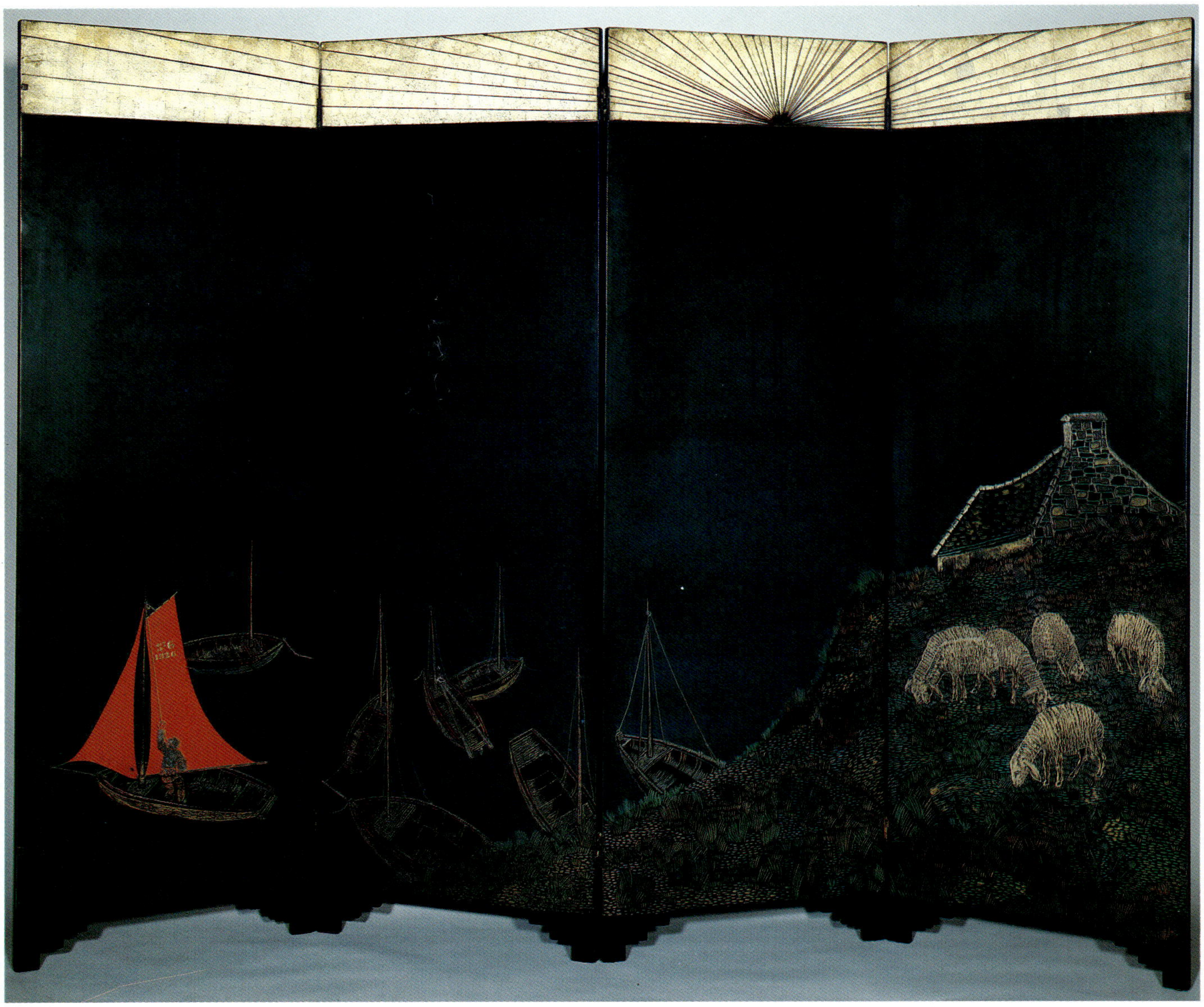

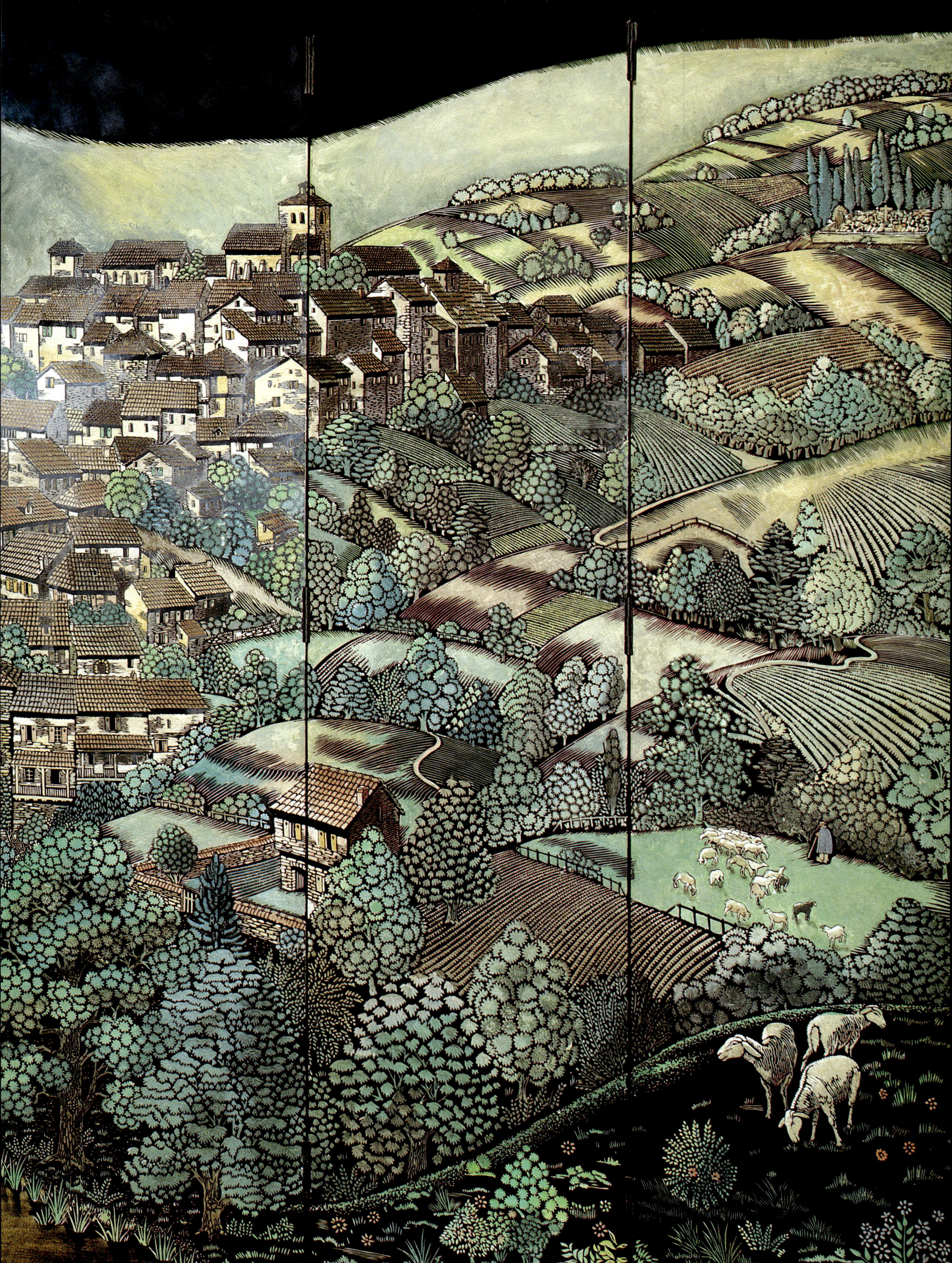

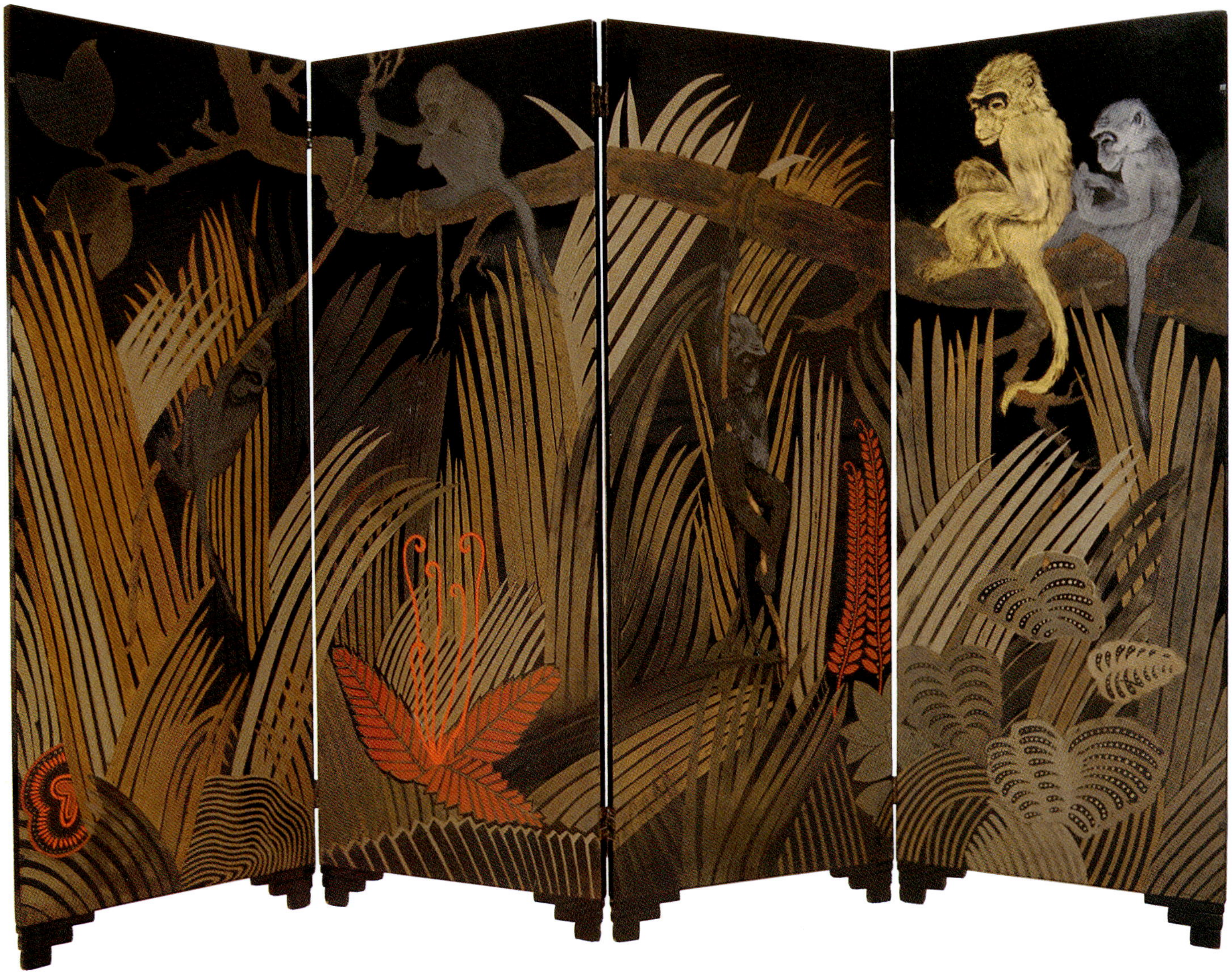

16 **Monkeys**, 1928
(*catalogue 57*)

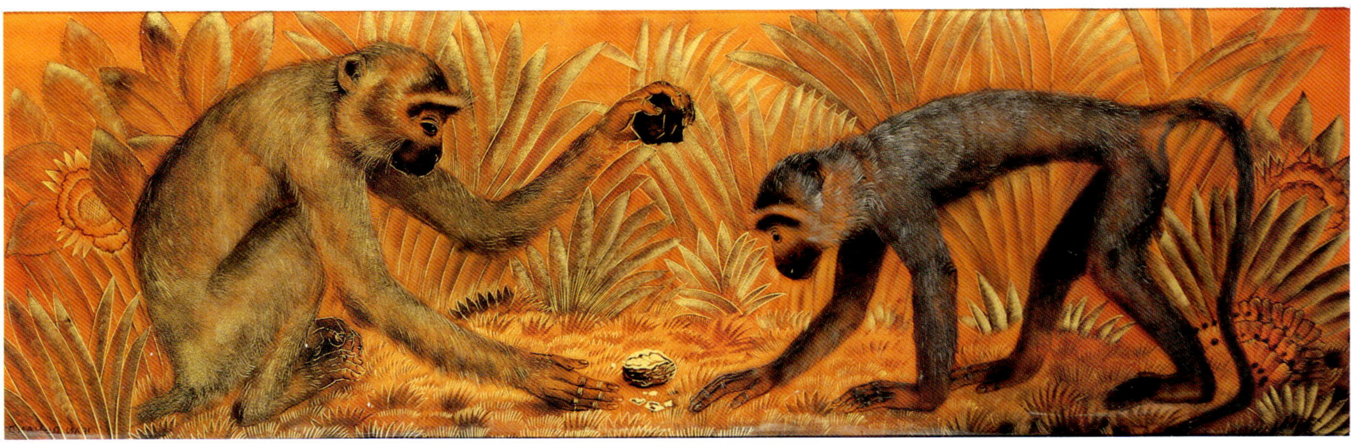

17 **Monkeys**, 1927
(*catalogue 331*)

OPPOSITE
18 **Monkey**, *c.* 1927
(*catalogue 333*)

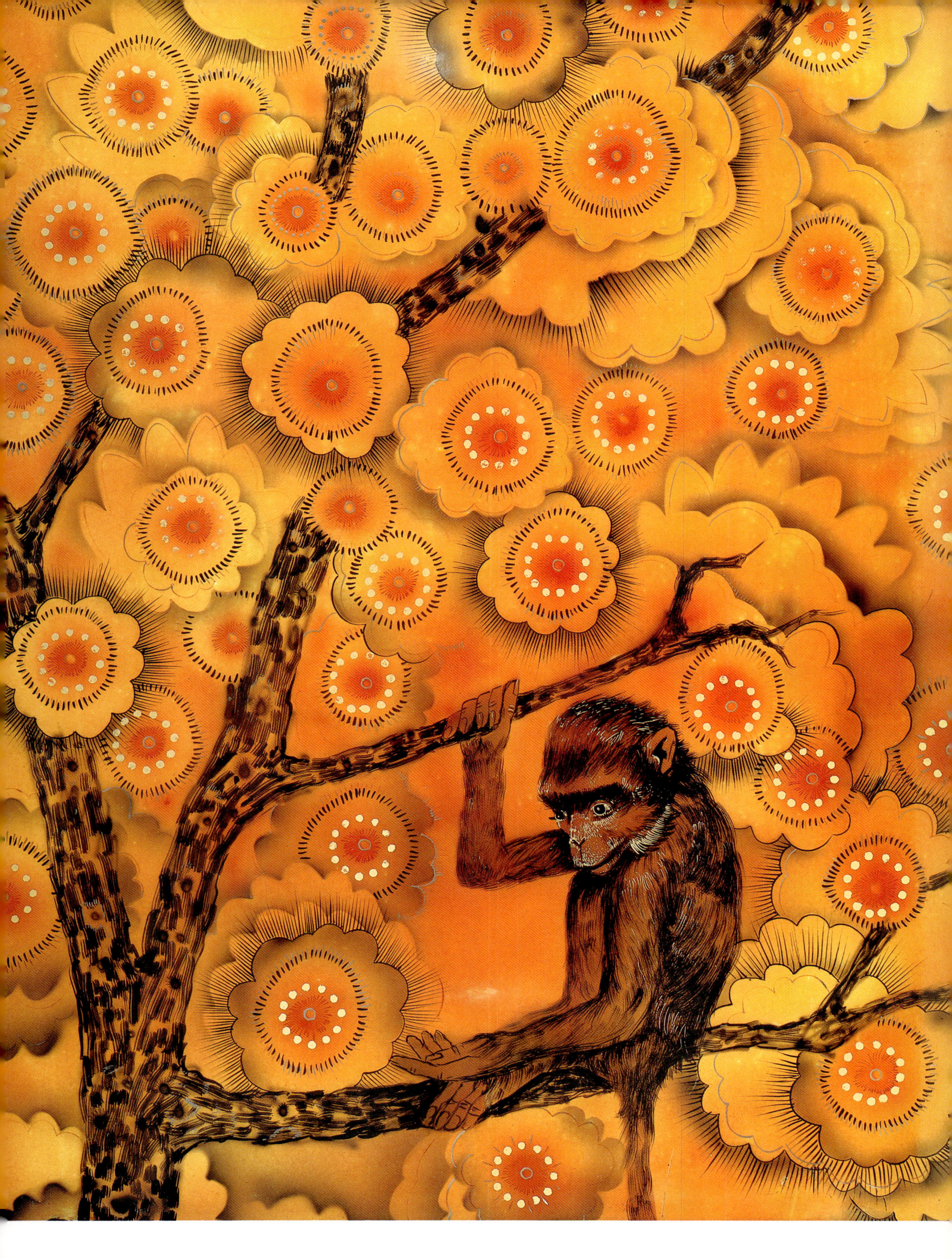

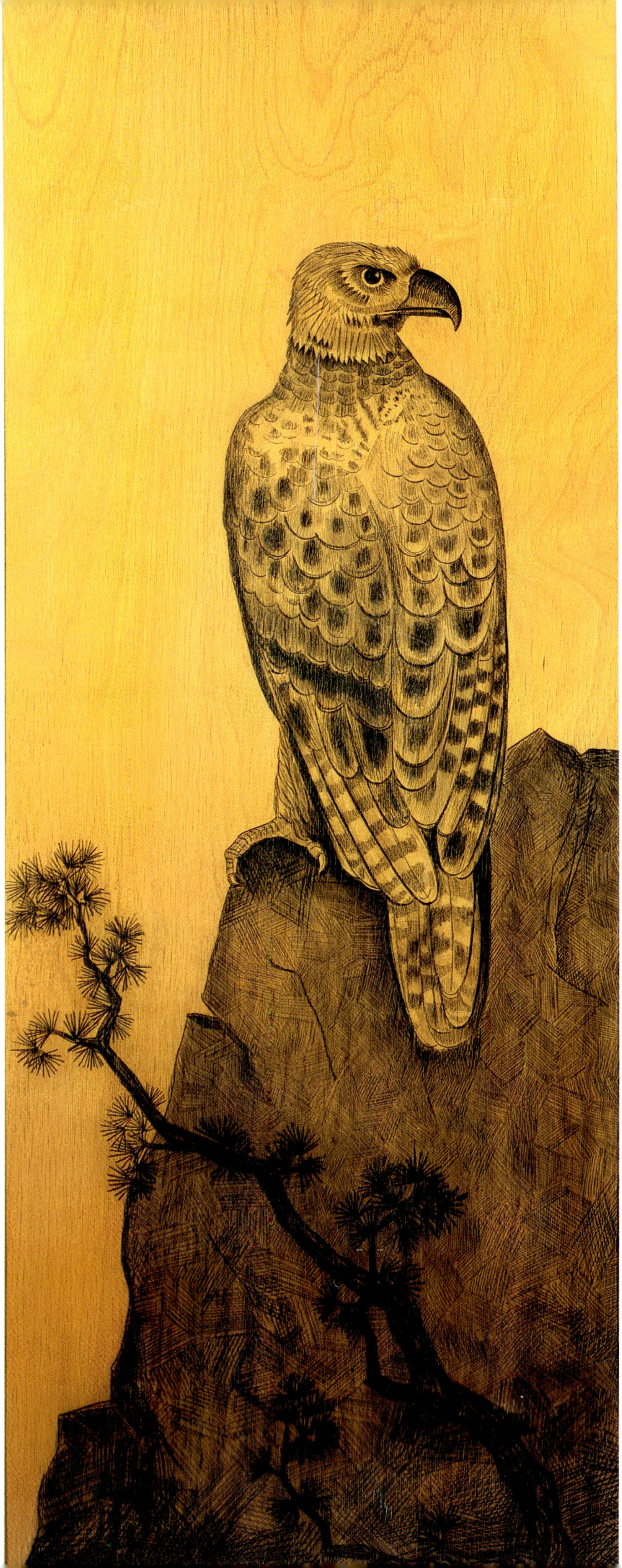

19 **Eagle**, *c.* 1925
(*catalogue 318*)

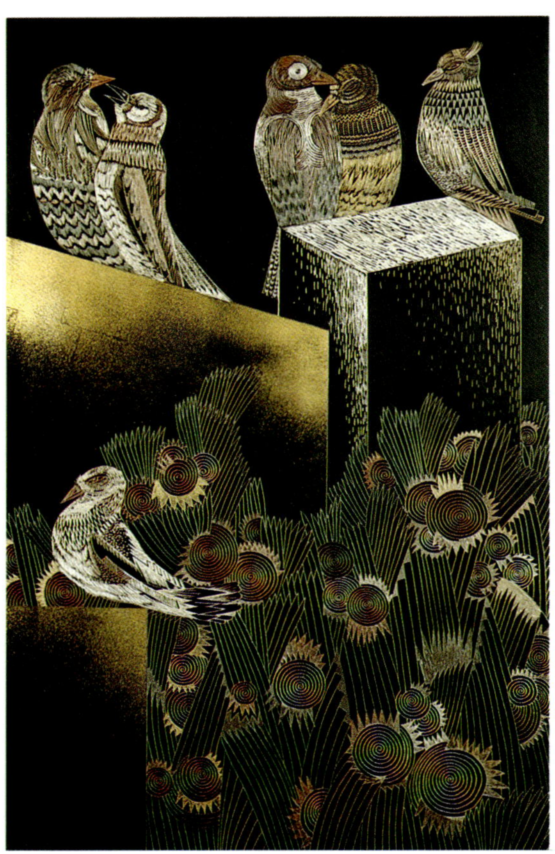

20 **Pigeons**, 1929
(*catalogue 350*)

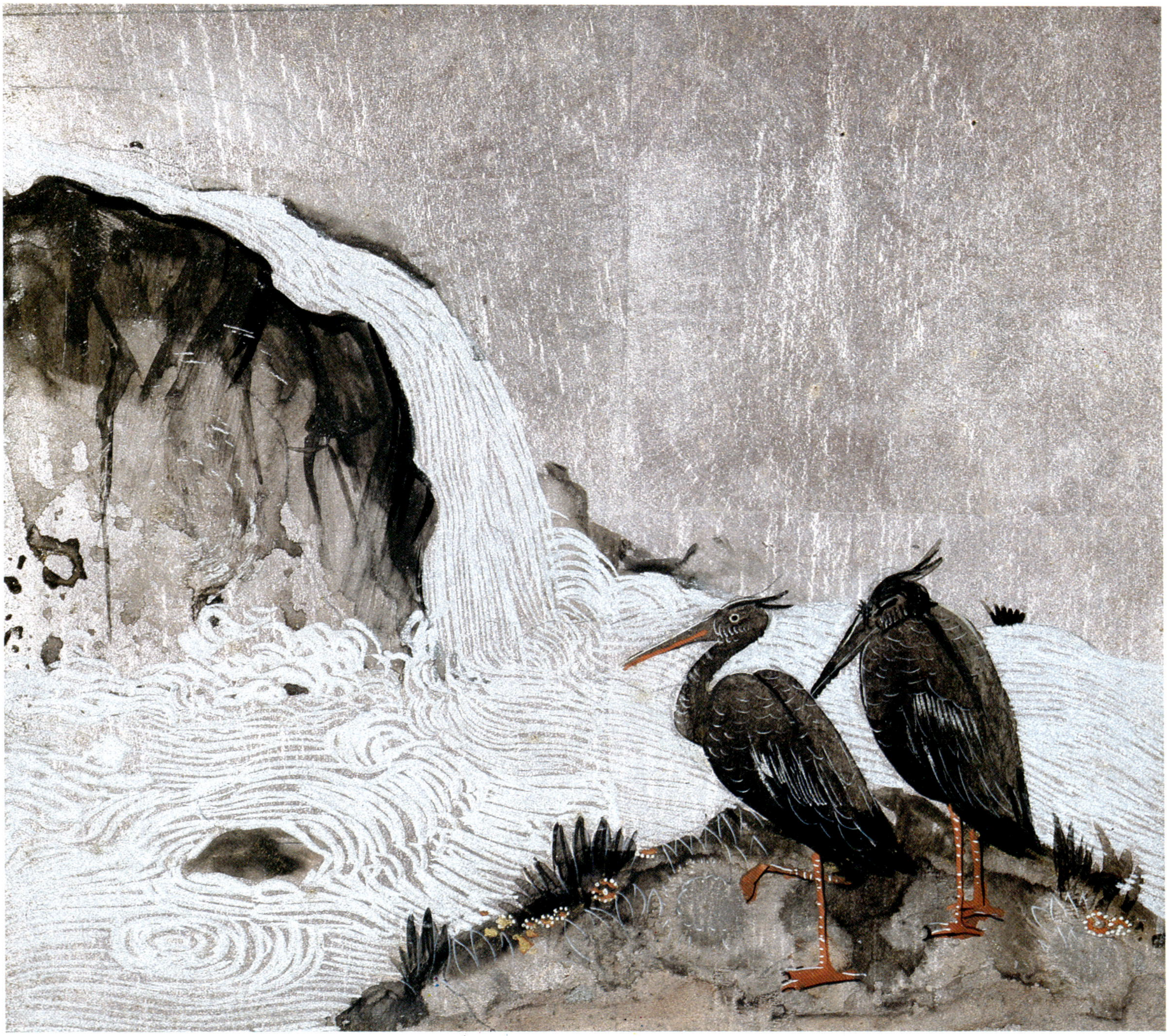

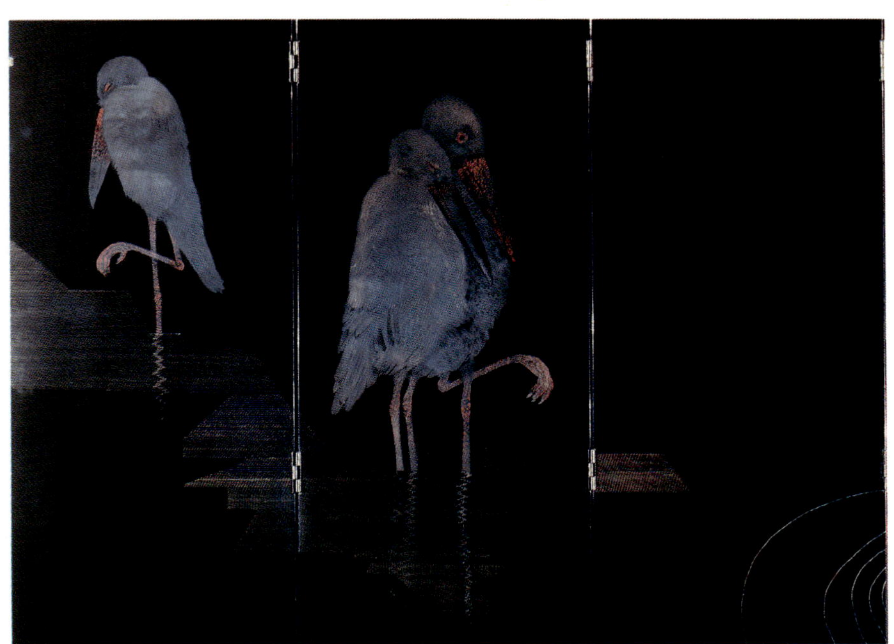

21 **Herons**, 1930
(*catalogue 374*)

22 **Herons and Frog**, *c.* 1927
(*detail of catalogue 51*)

23 ***Pigeons***, 1923
(*catalogue 308*)

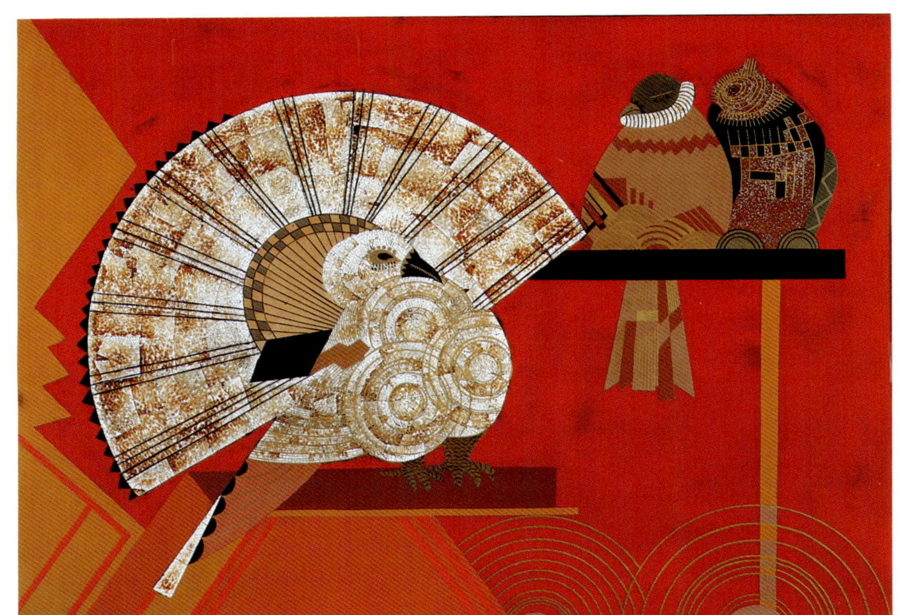

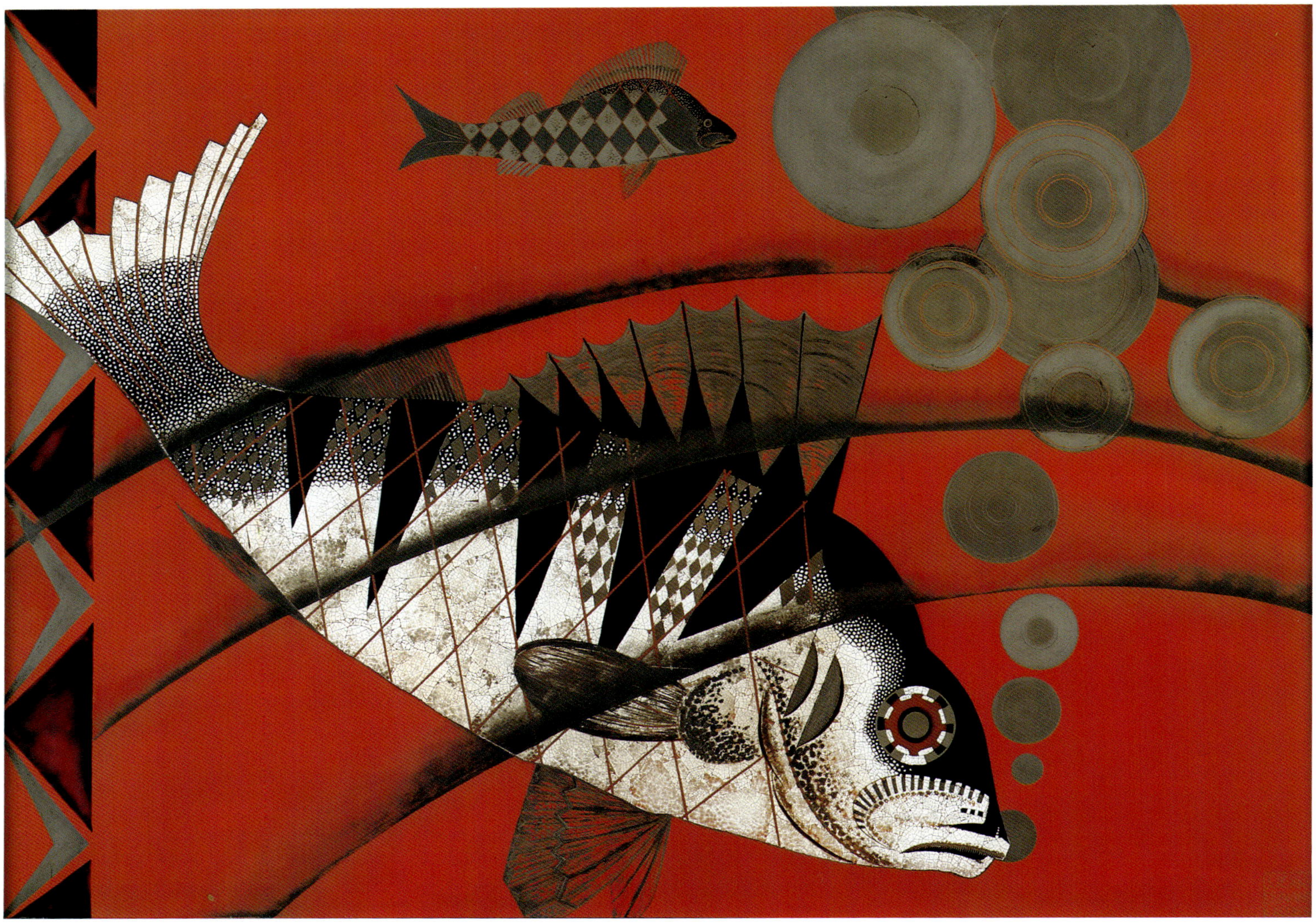

24 ***Fish***, 1925
(*catalogue 311*)

OPPOSITE
25 ***Japanese Fish***, *c.* 1925
(*catalogue 324*)

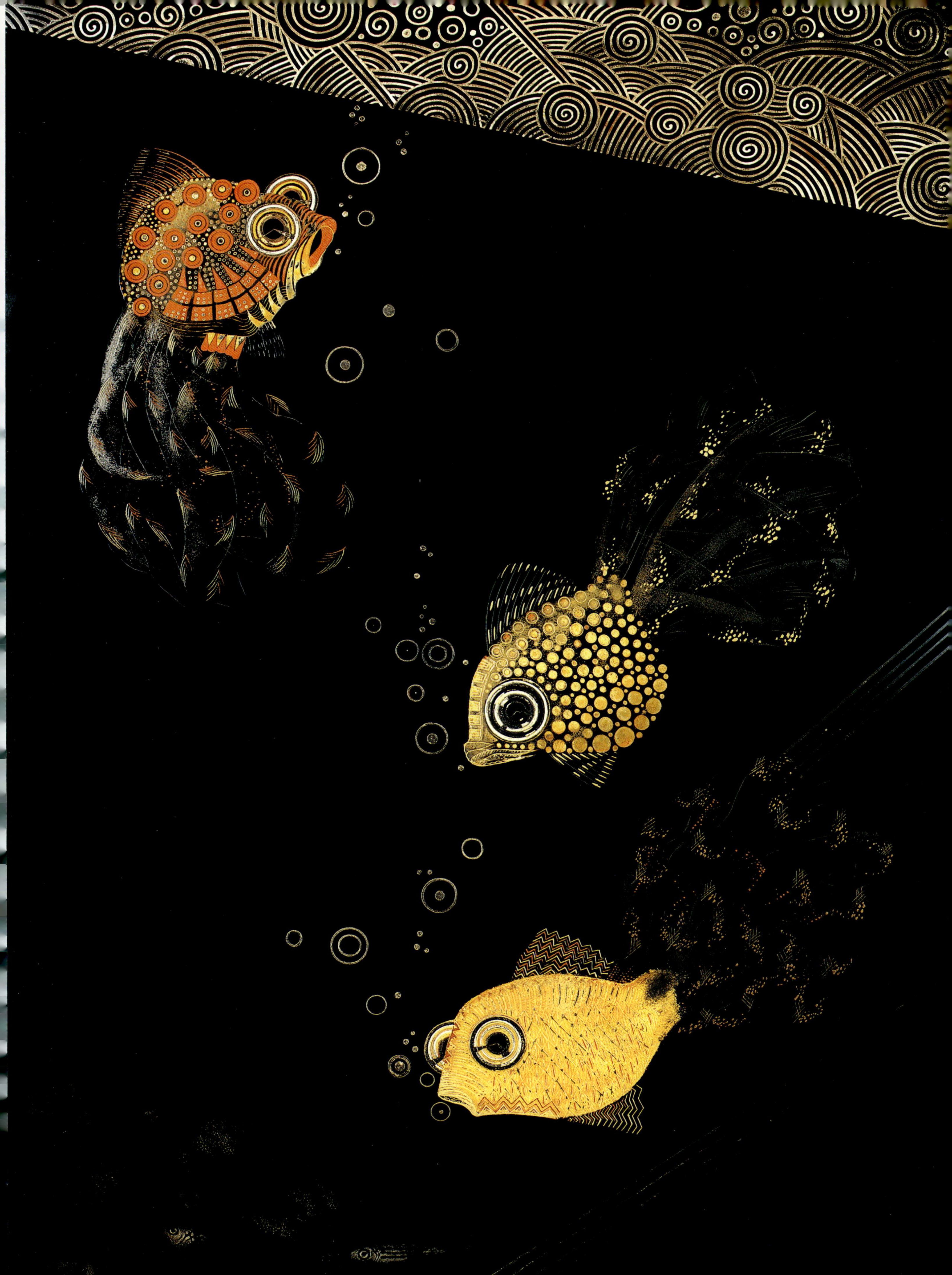

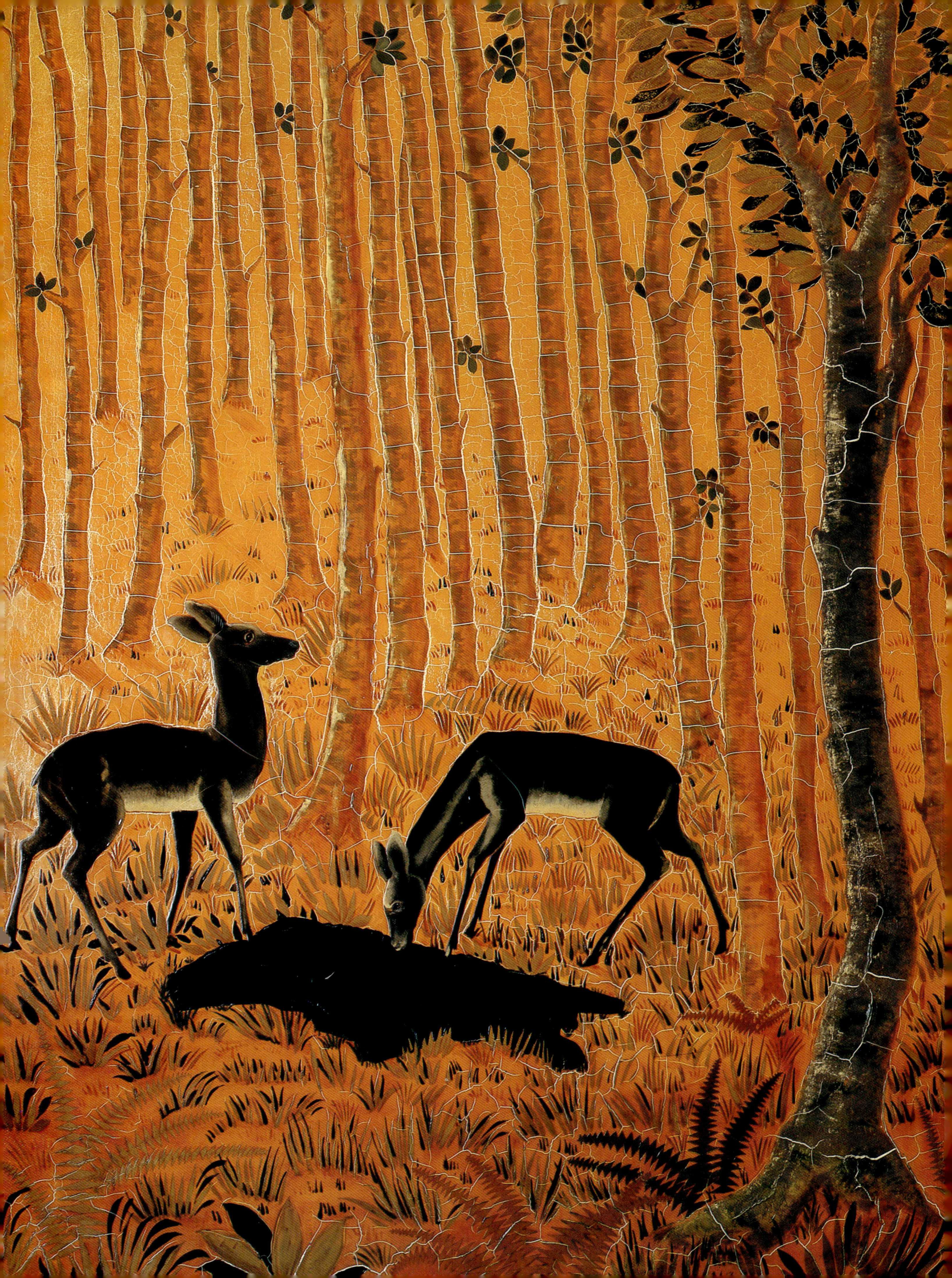

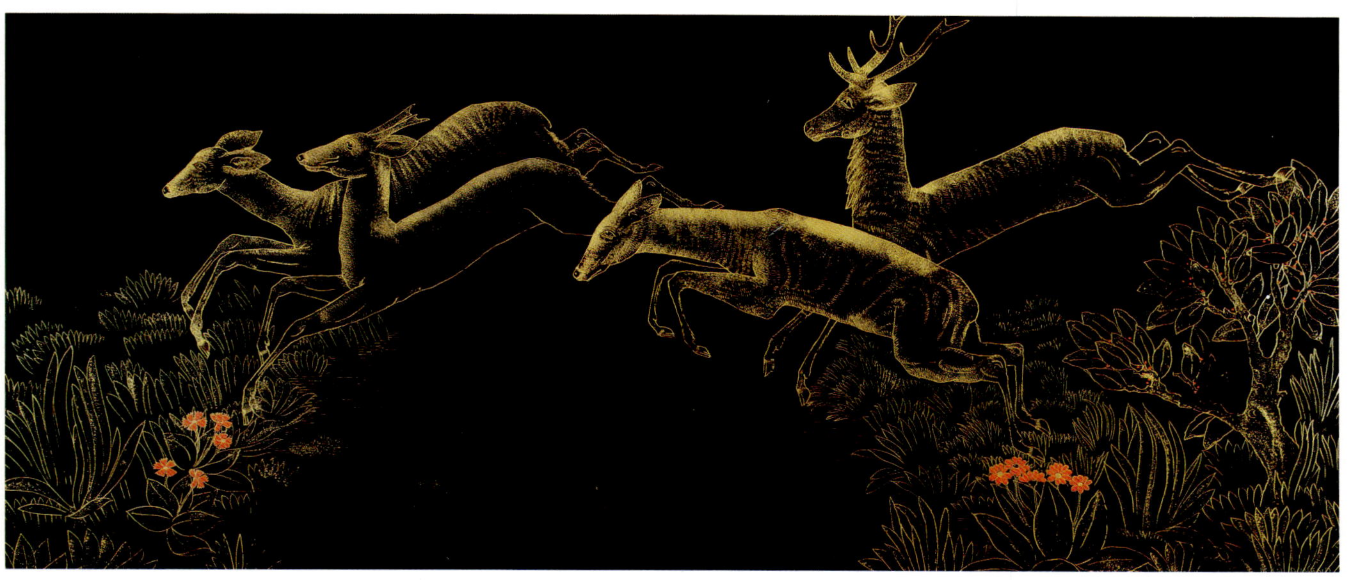

27 **The Ford**, *c.* 1930
(*catalogue 373*)

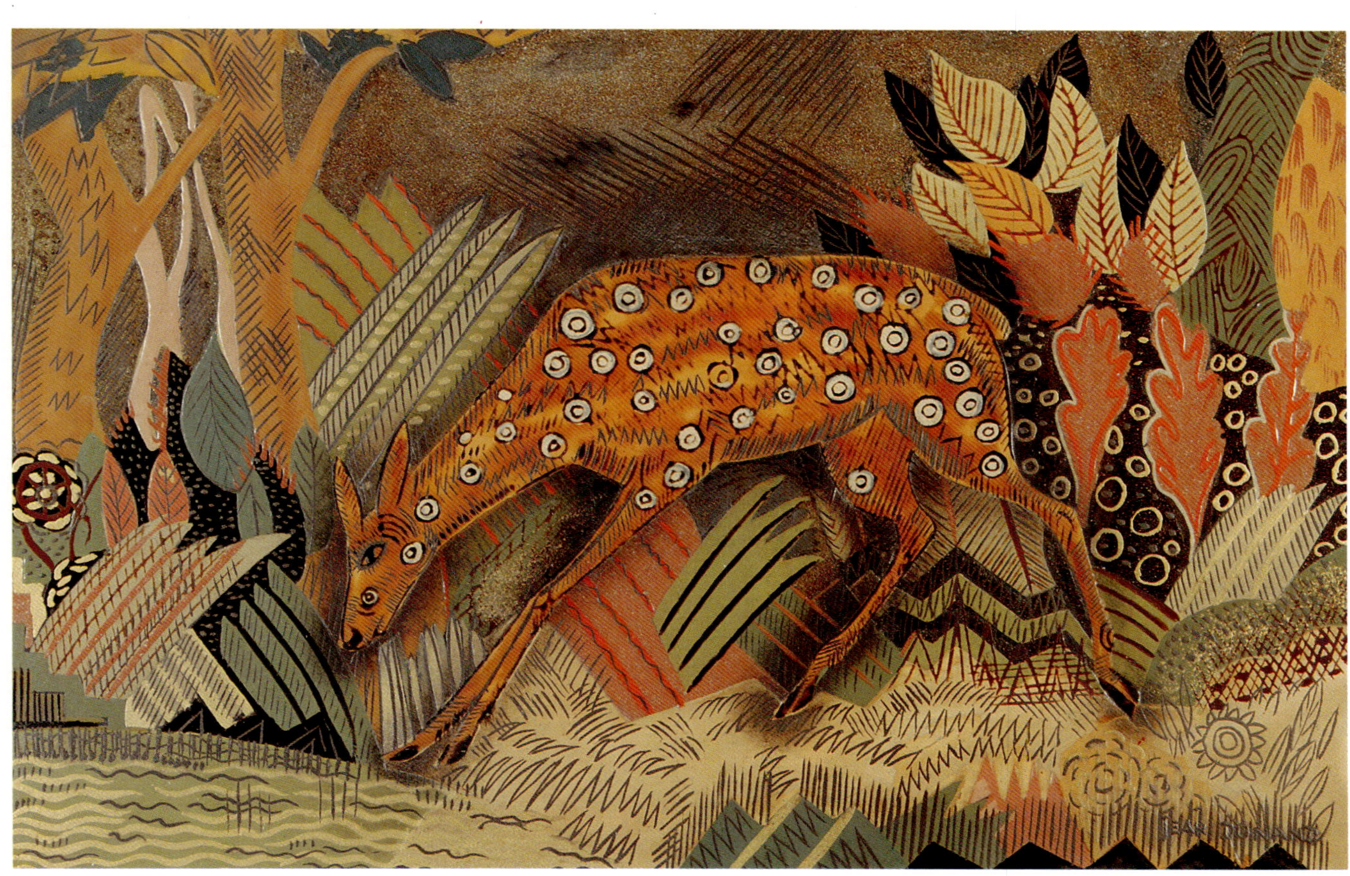

28 **Deer**, *c.* 1925
(*catalogue 312*)

OPPOSITE
26 **Deer**, *c.* 1932
(*detail of catalogue 396*)

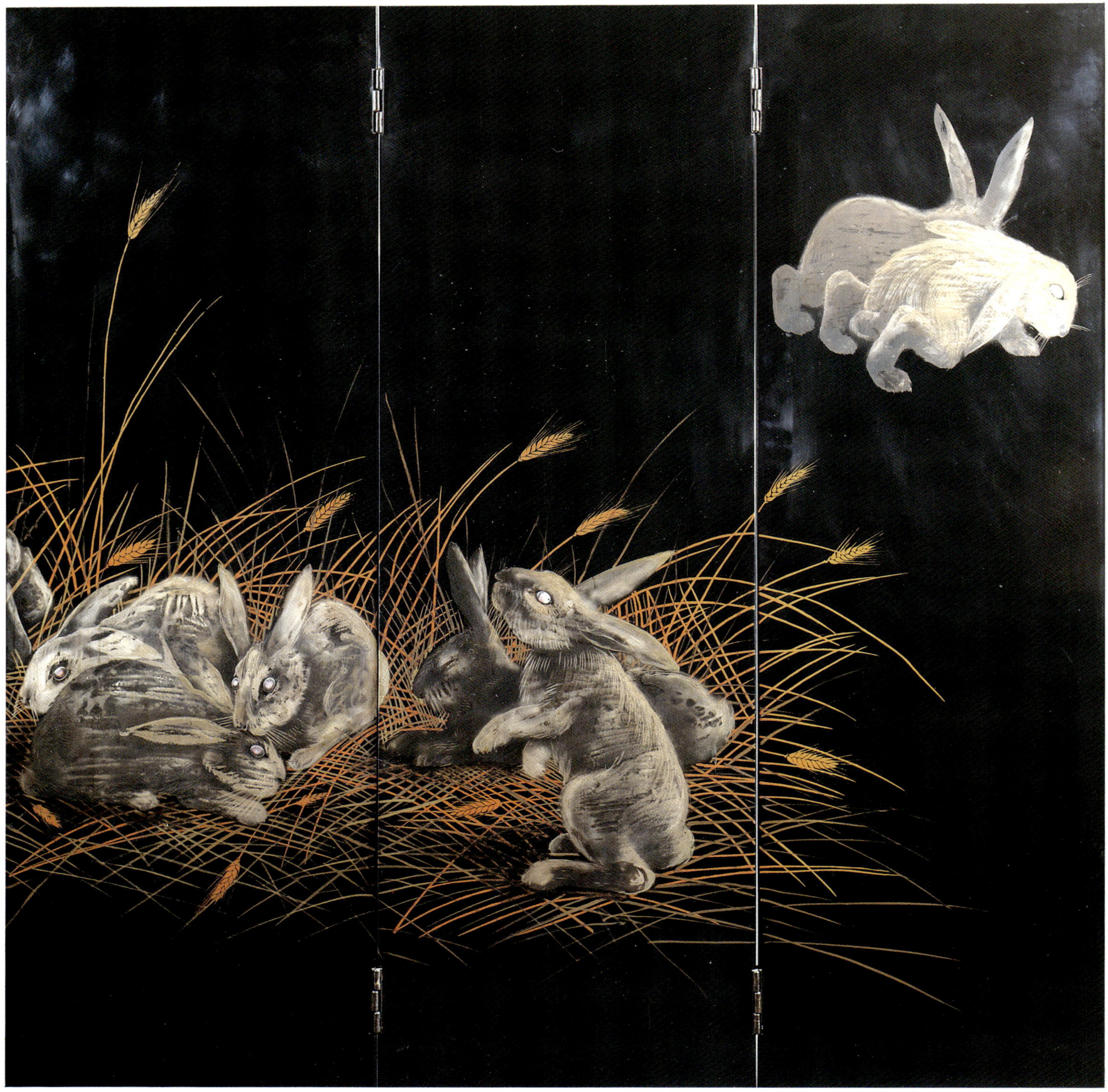

29 **Rabbits**, 1926
(*detail of catalogue 26*)

OPPOSITE
30 **Herons**, 1930
(*detail of catalogue 74*)

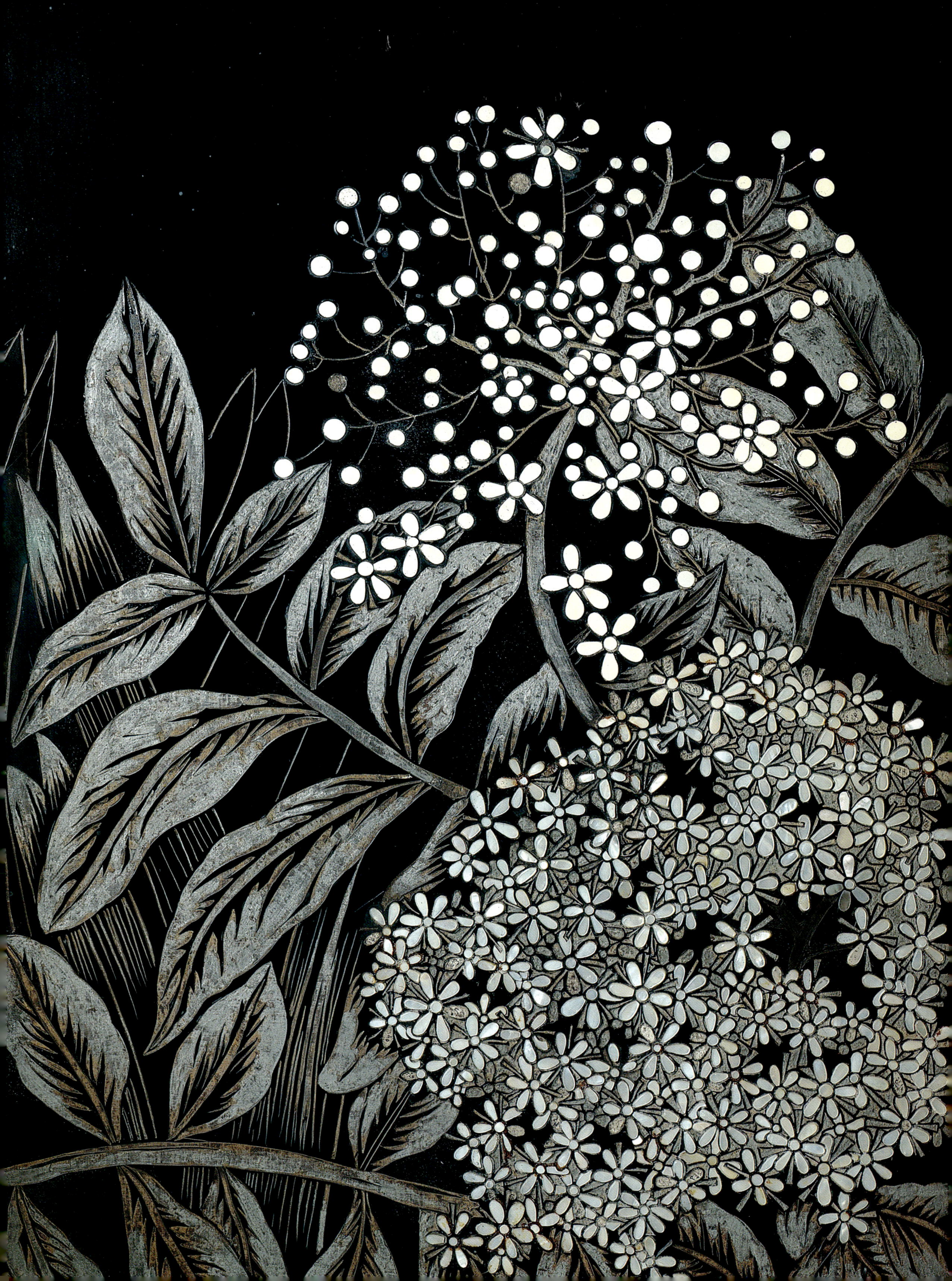

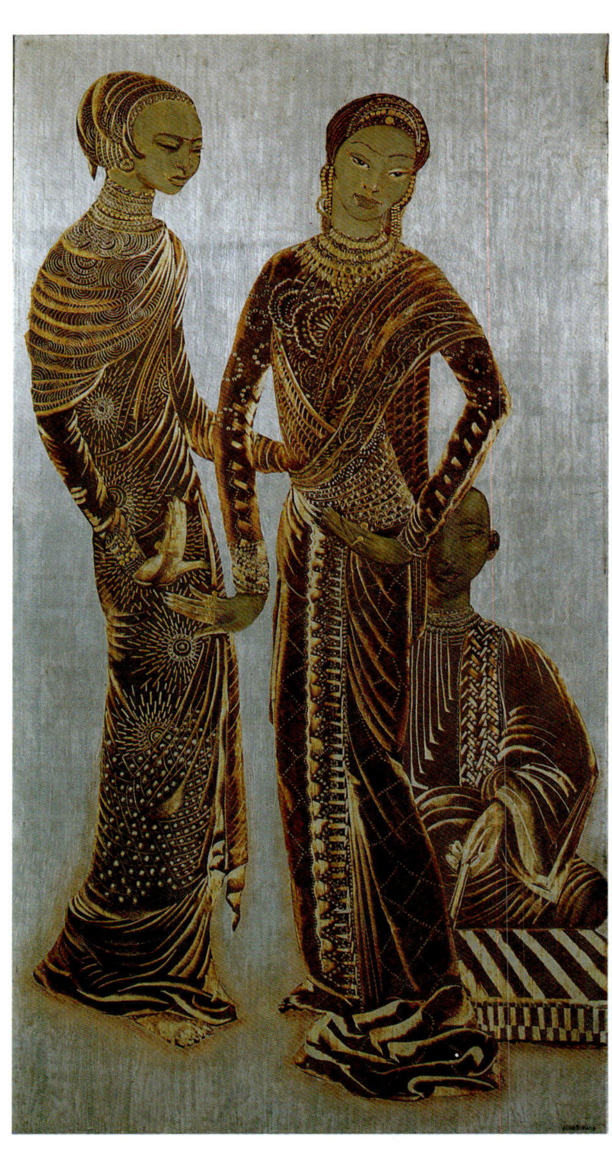

31 ***Women of Asia***, 1930
(*catalogue 1216*)

32 ***The Forest*** or ***Wild Animal at a Watering Place***, 1930
(*catalogue 1213*)

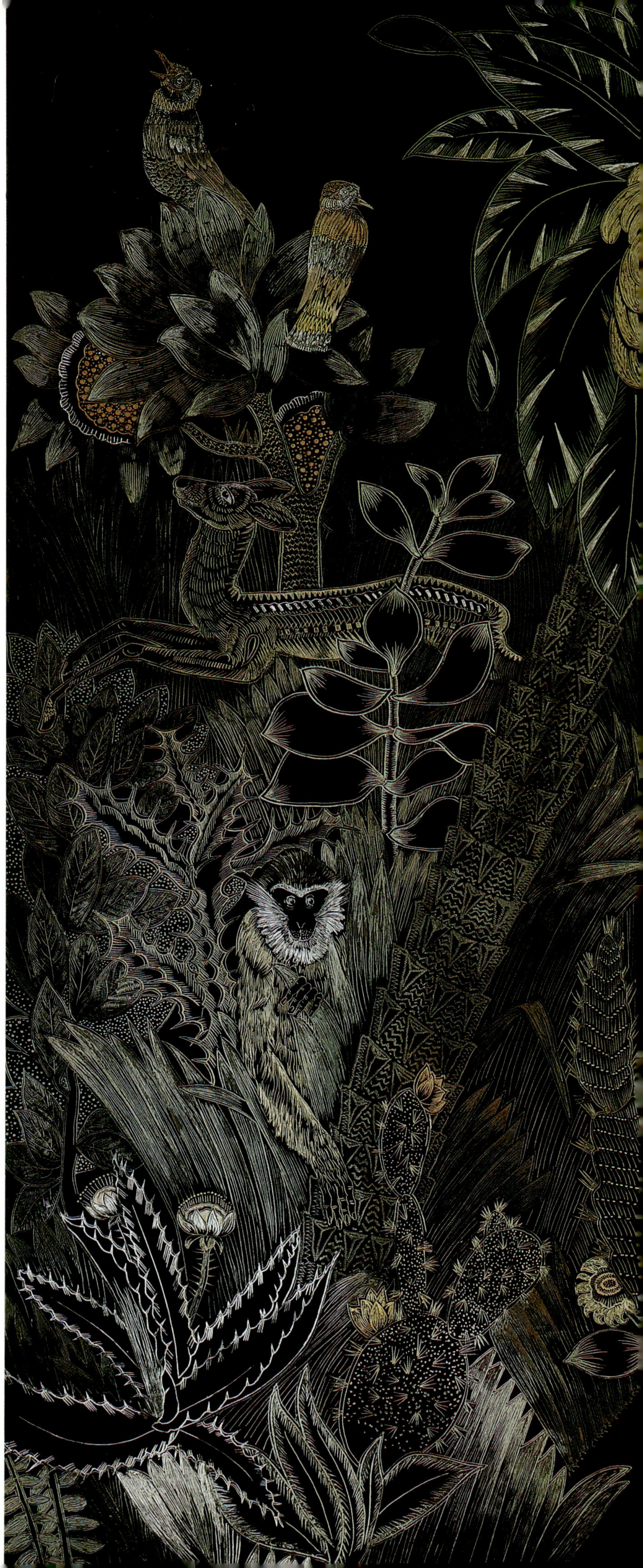

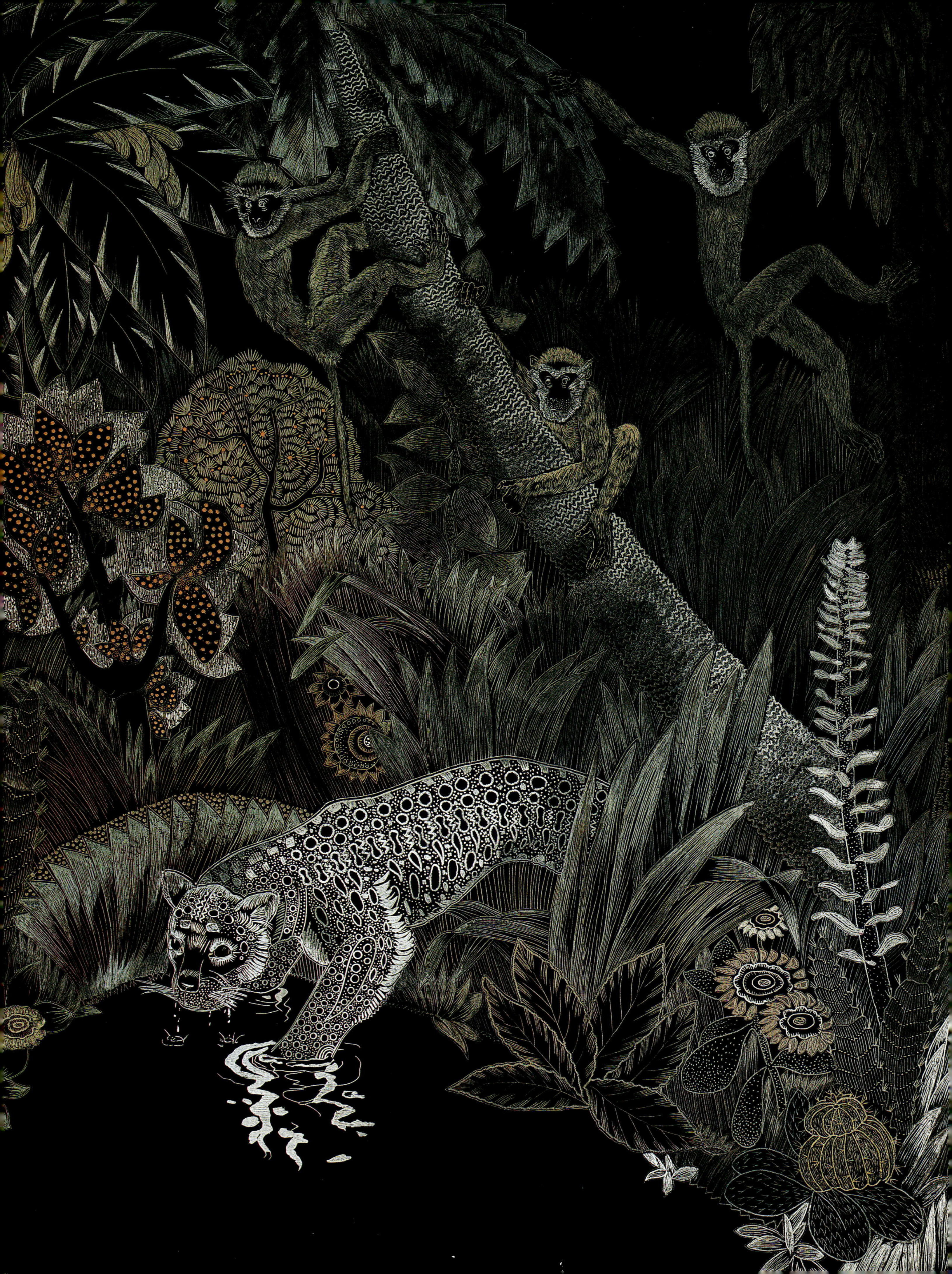

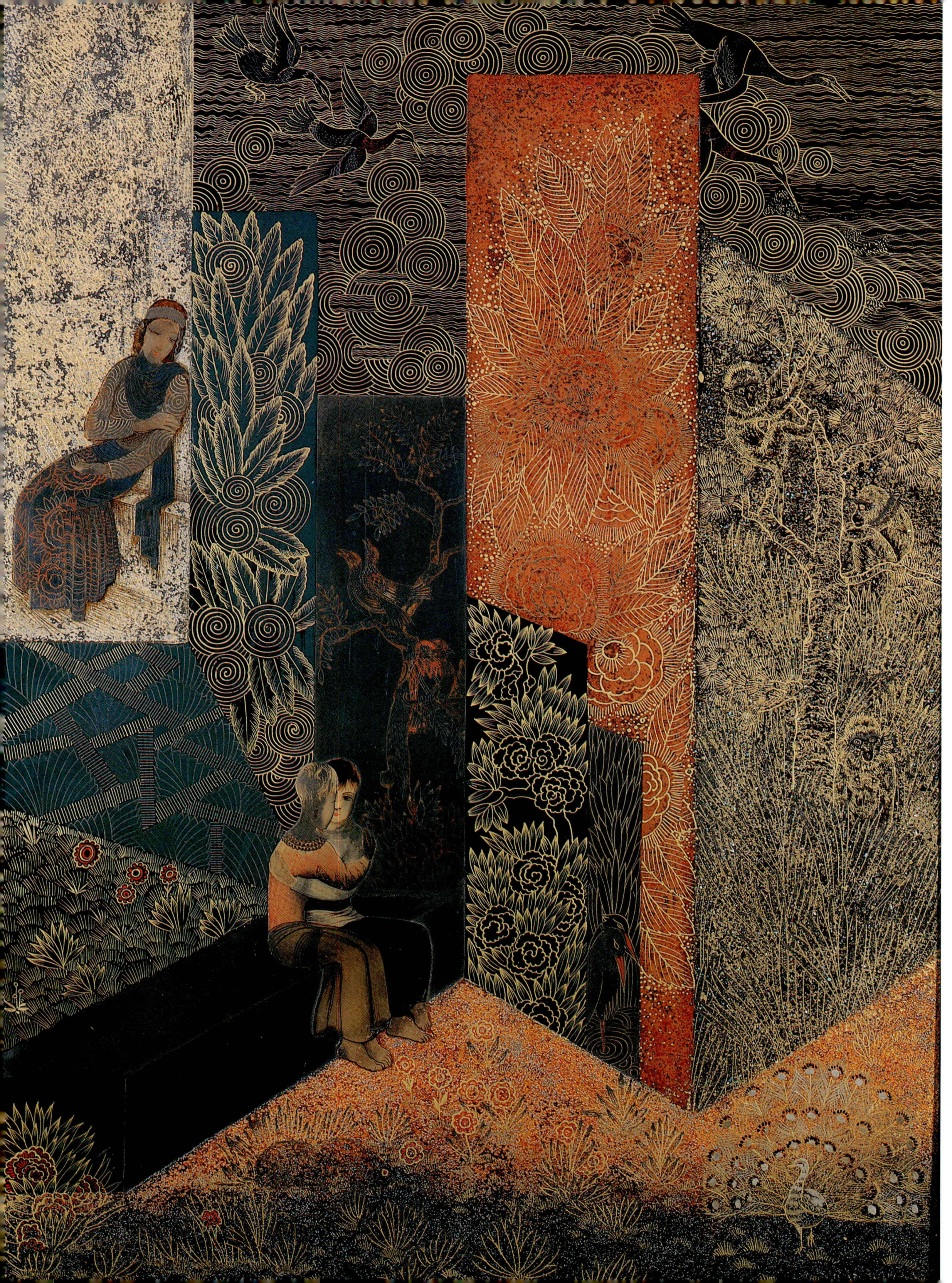

OPPOSITE
33 ***'Miniature' panel***, 1930
(*catalogue 281*)

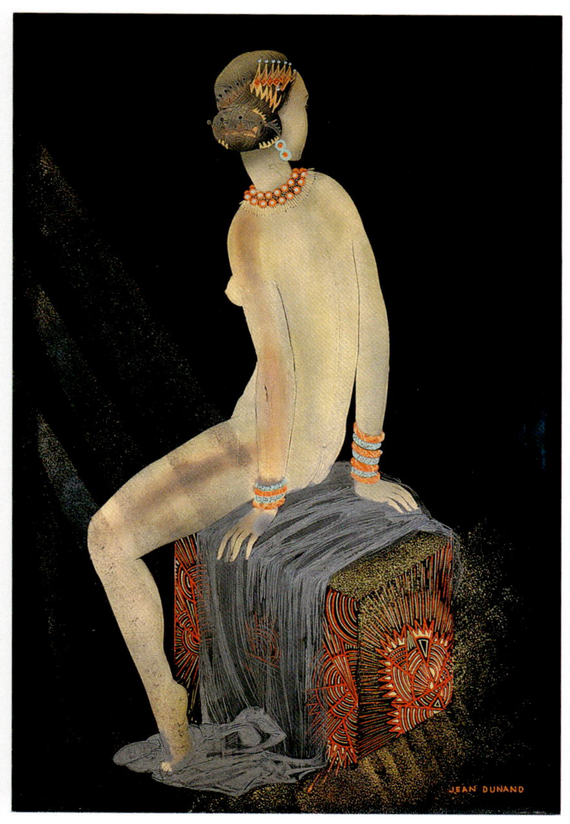

34 ***Nude, back view***, *c.* 1929
(*catalogue 267*)

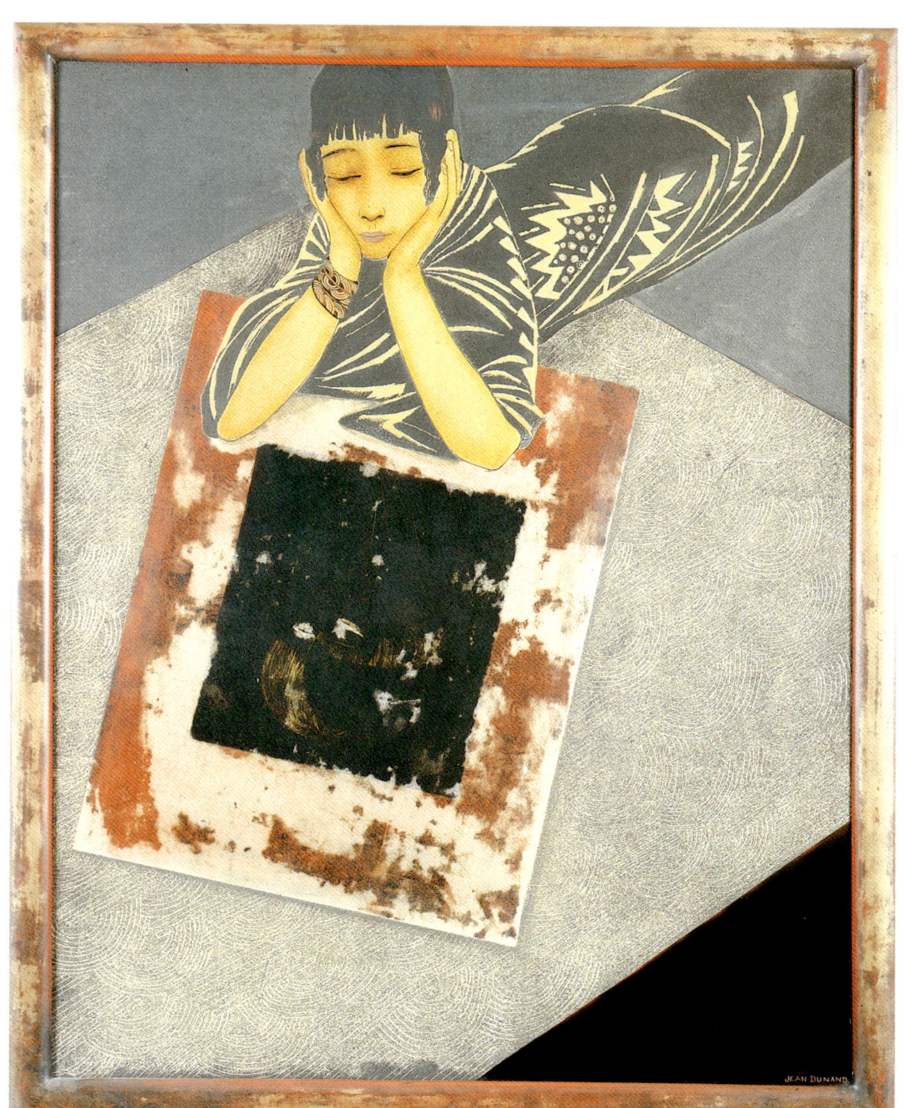

35 ***The Portrait***, 1929
(*catalogue 275*)

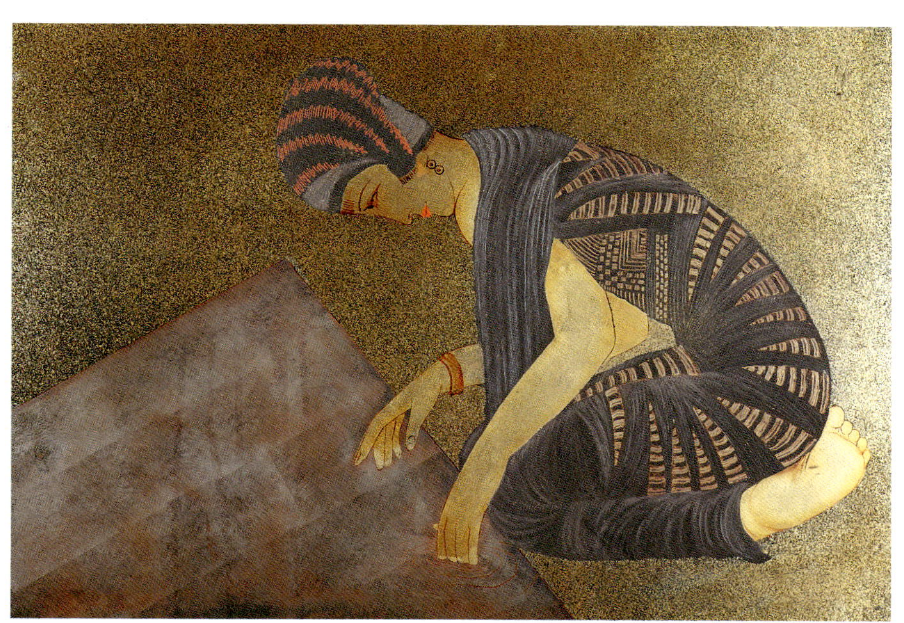

36 ***Prayer***, 1928
(*catalogue 240*)

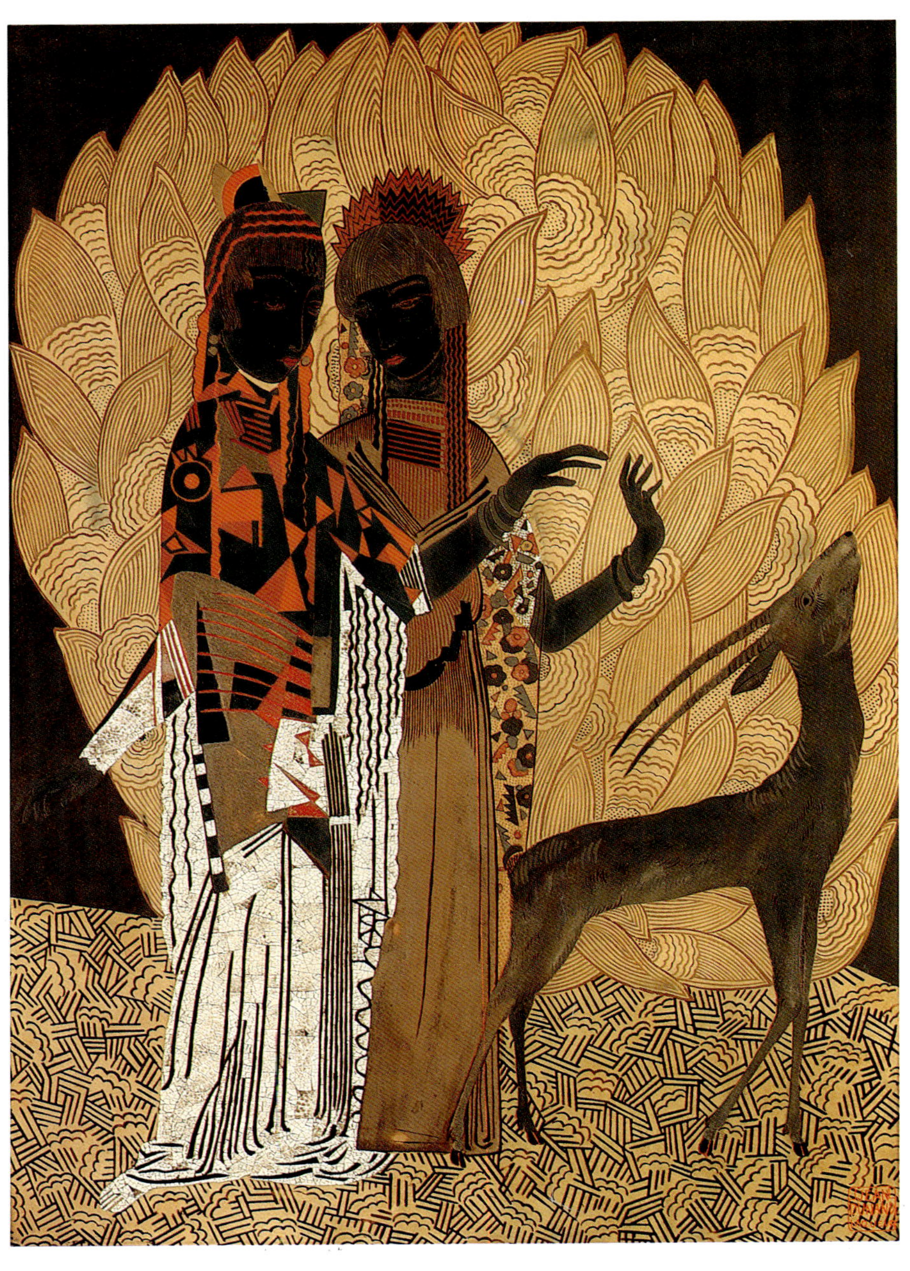

37 **Two Figures with Deer**, 1925
(*catalogue 225*)

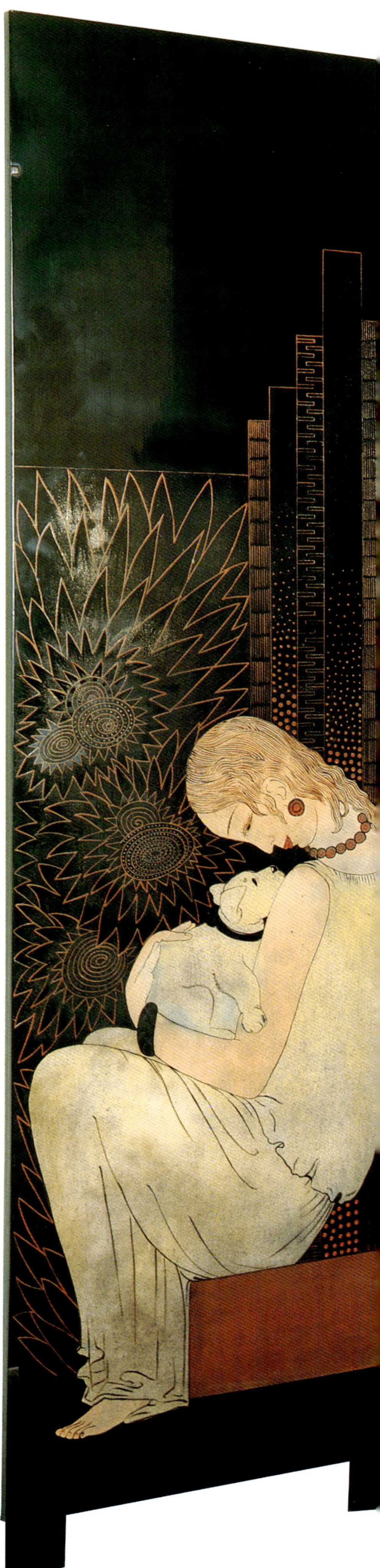

38 **Four Figures**, 1929
(*catalogue 72*)

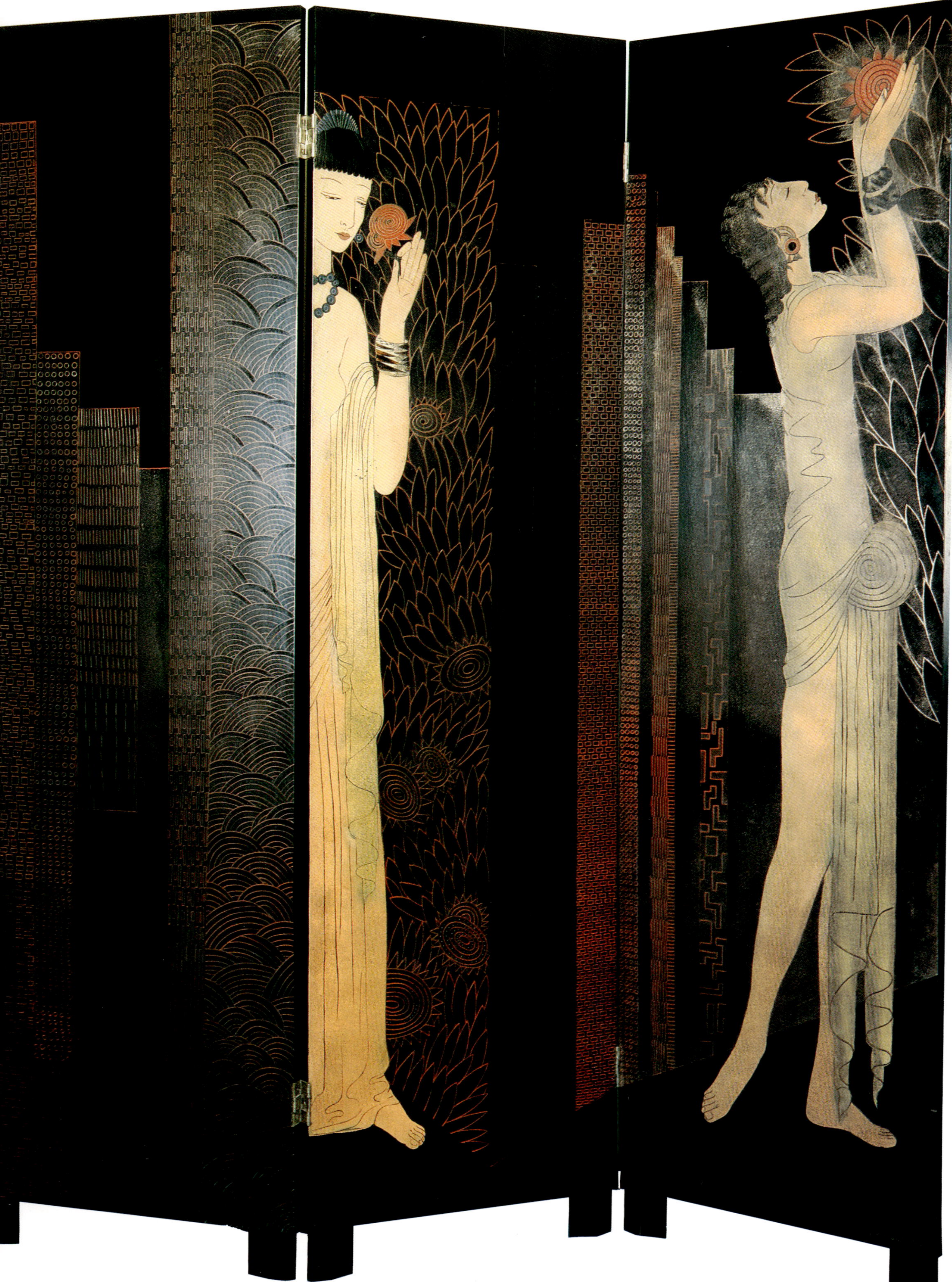

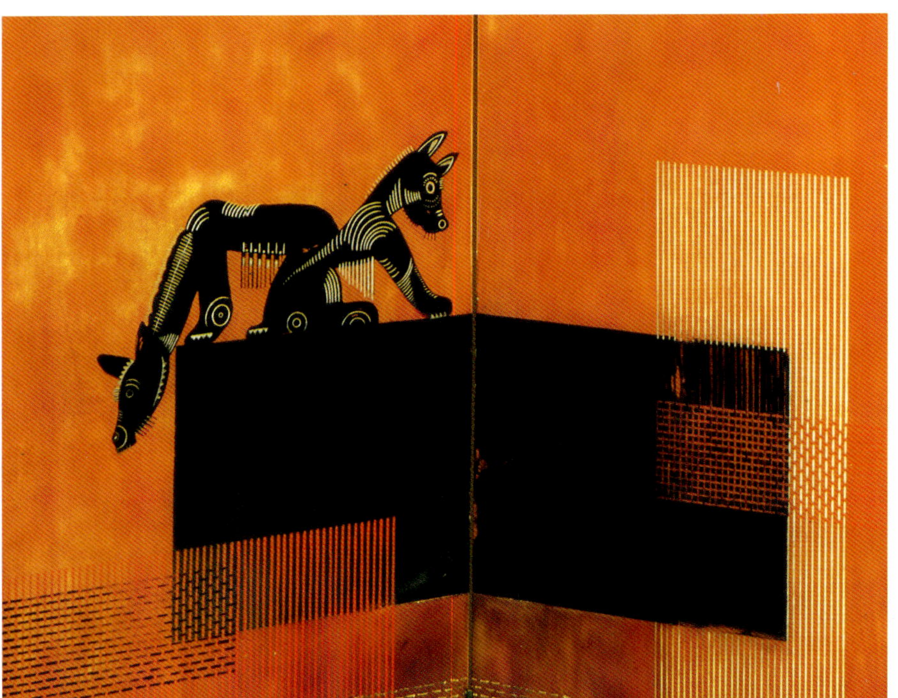

39 ***Black Animals***, 1926
(*detail of catalogue 34*)

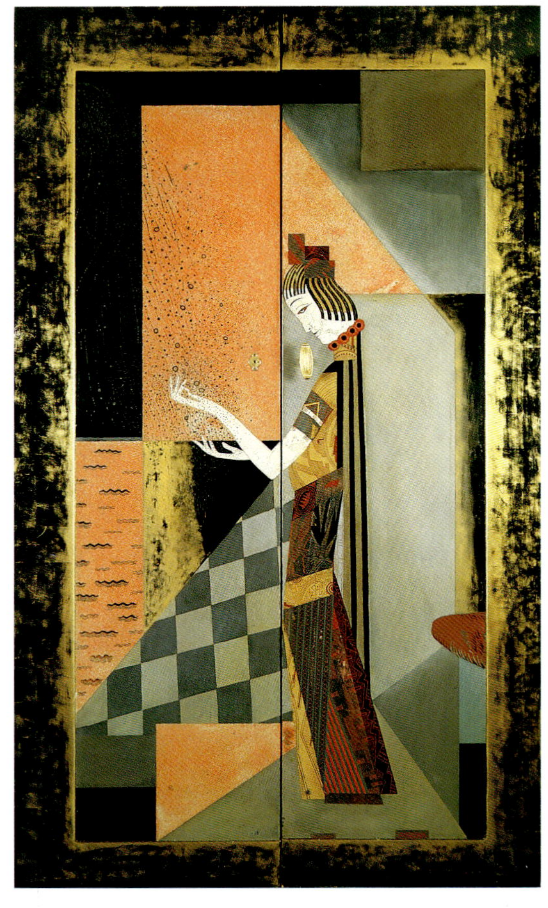

41 ***Young Woman***,
folding door, 1926
(*catalogue 563*)

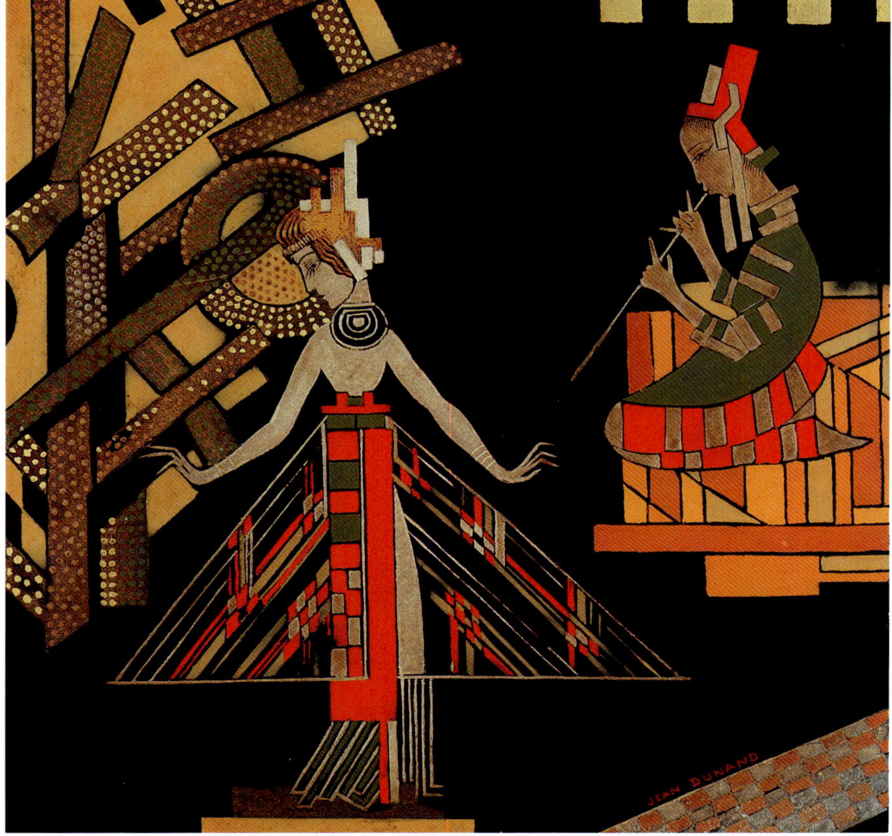

40 ***Oriental Dancer***, *c.* 1923–5
(*catalogue 223*)

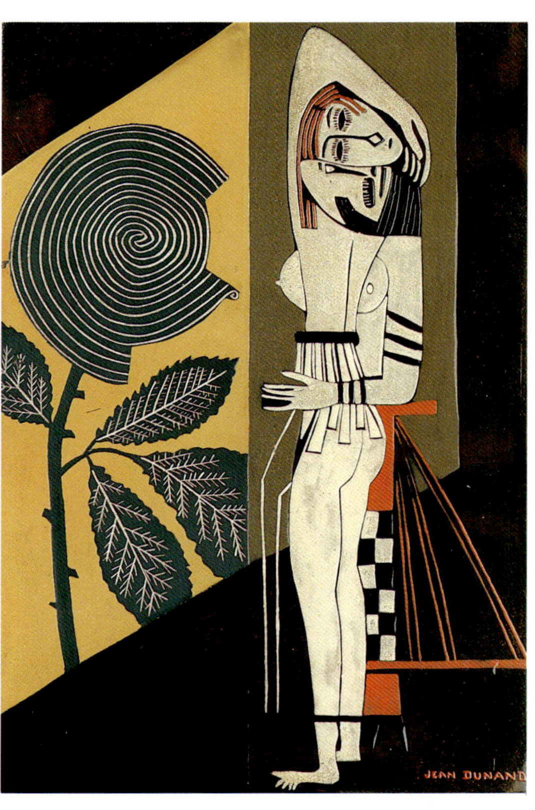

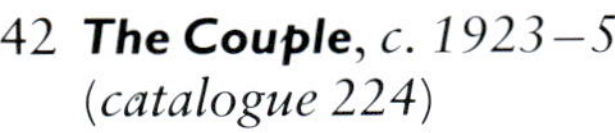

42 ***The Couple***, *c.* 1923–5
(*catalogue 224*)

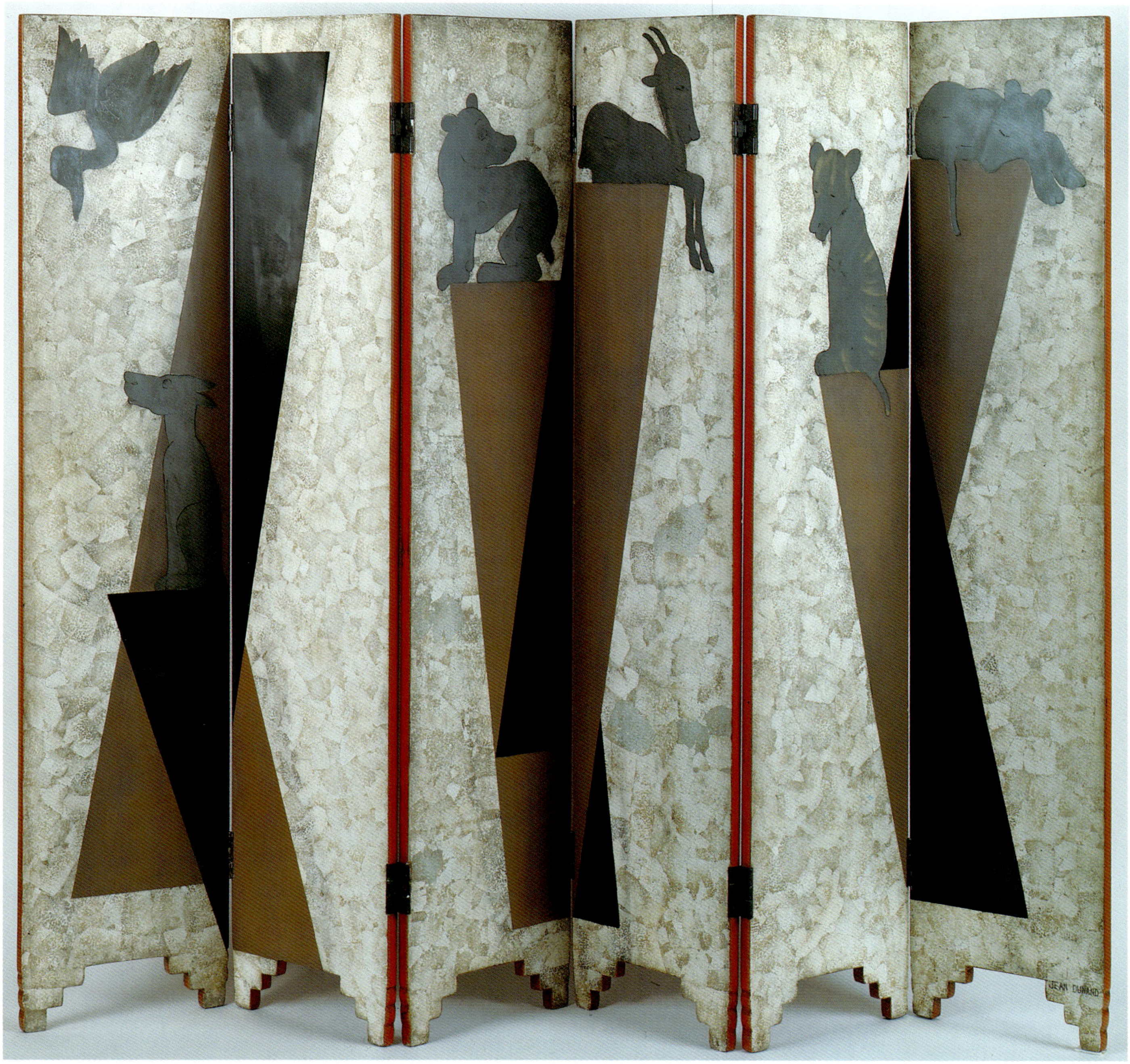

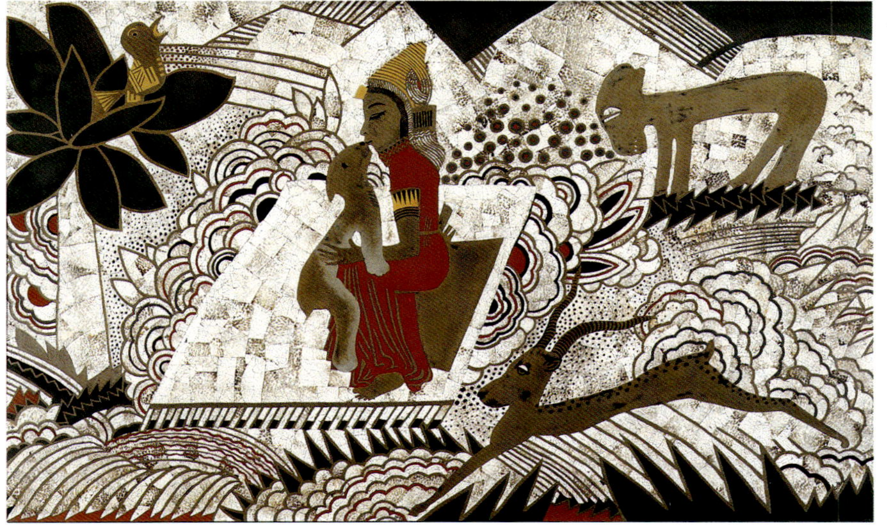

43 ***Animals***, 1927
(*catalogue 43*)

44 ***Seated Figure Stroking an Animal***, *c.* 1924–6
(*catalogue 227*)

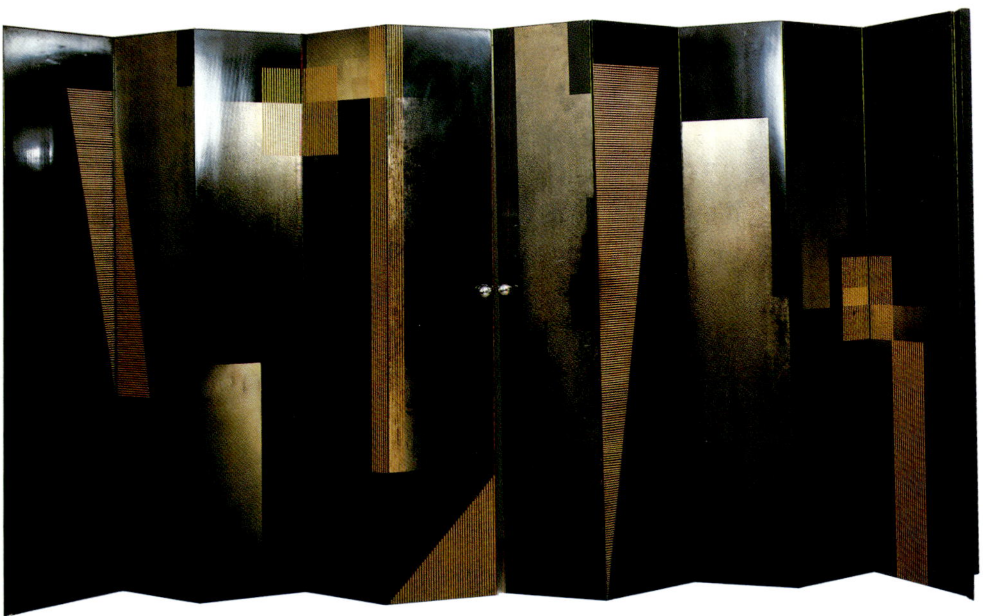

45 **Contrasting Forms**, *c*. 1930
(*catalogue 97*)

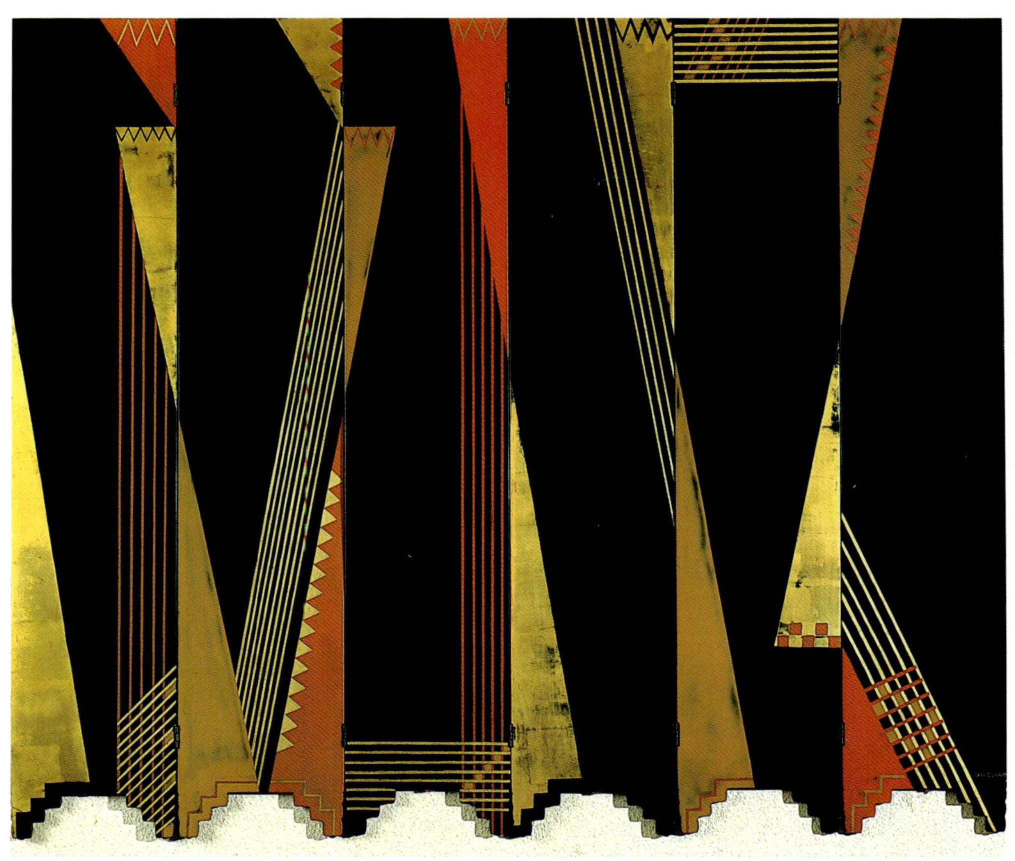

46 **Geometric Decor**, 1926
(*catalogue 21*)

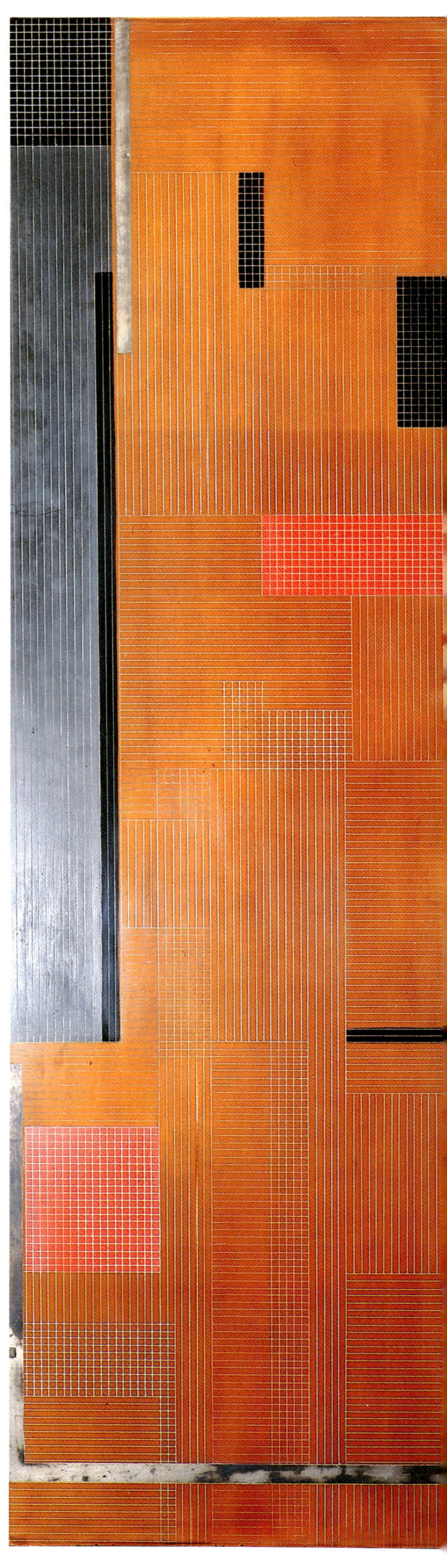

47 **Geometric**, *c*. 1927
(*catalogue 93*)

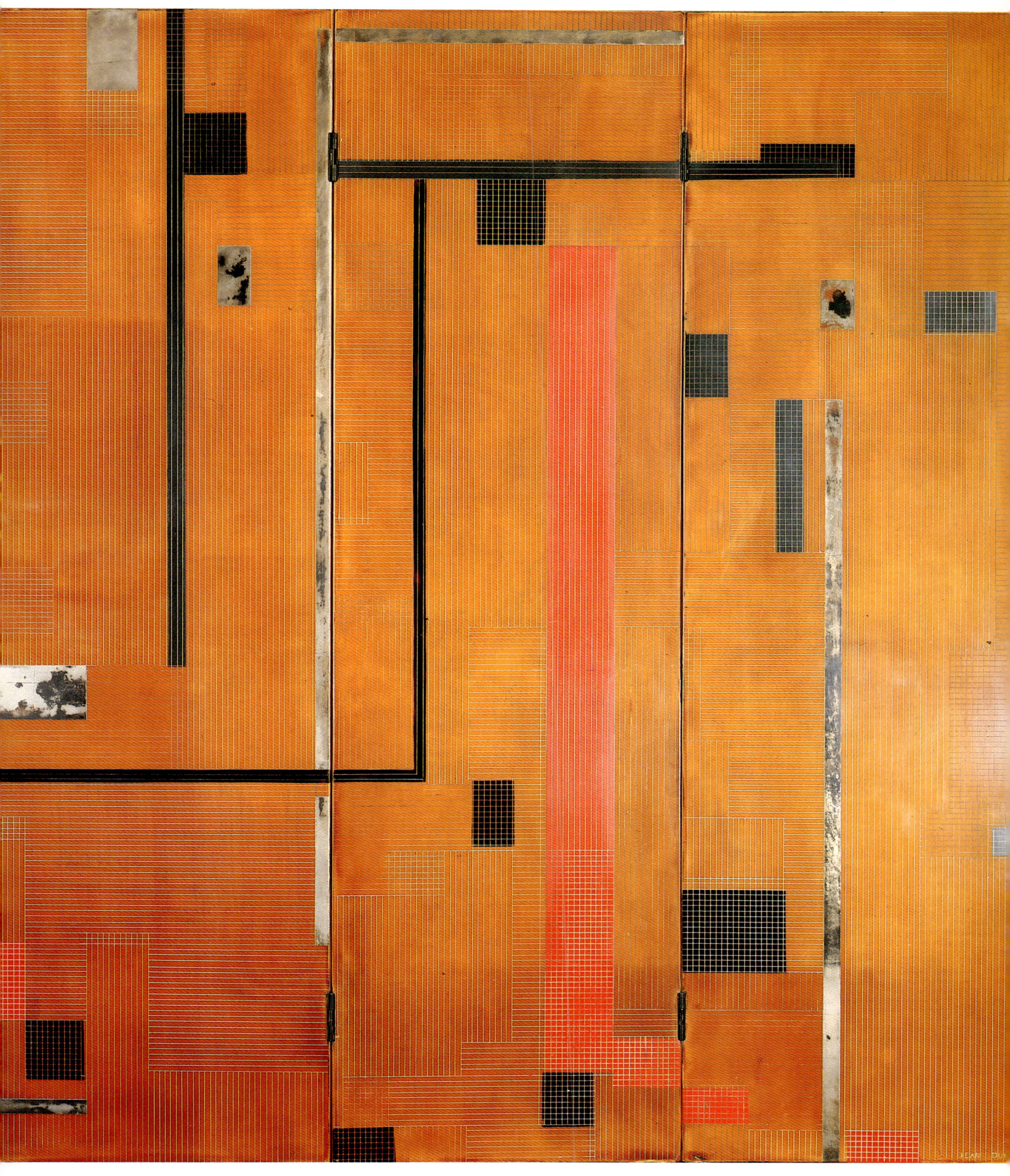

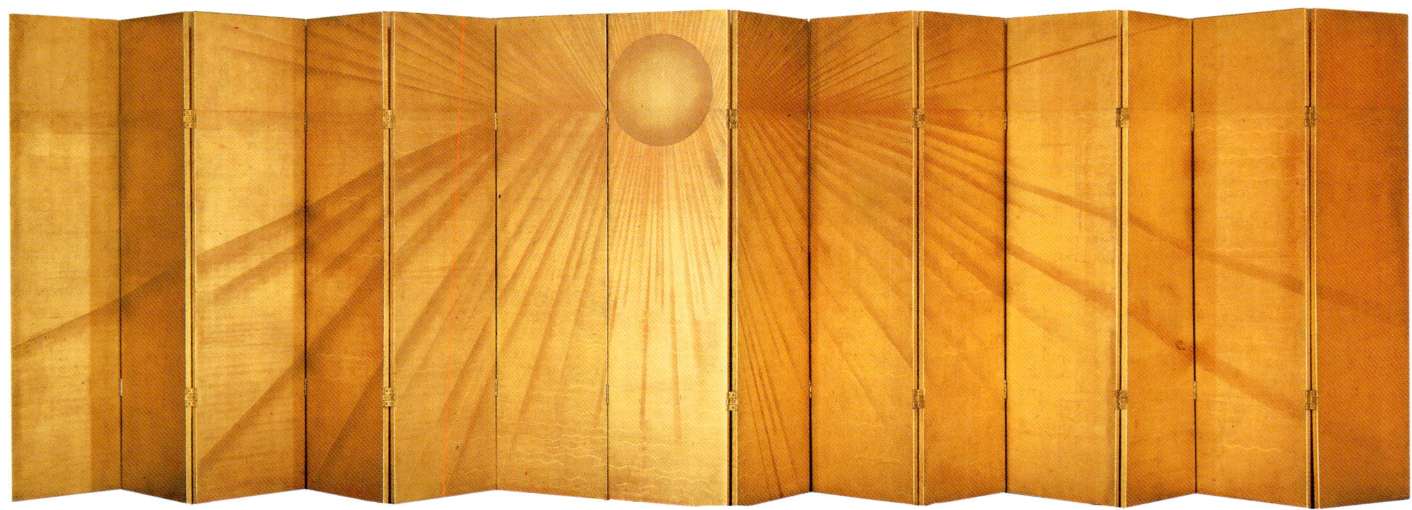

48 ***Sunrise***, *c.* 1930
(*catalogue* 96)

49 ***Grass***
(*catalogue* 109)

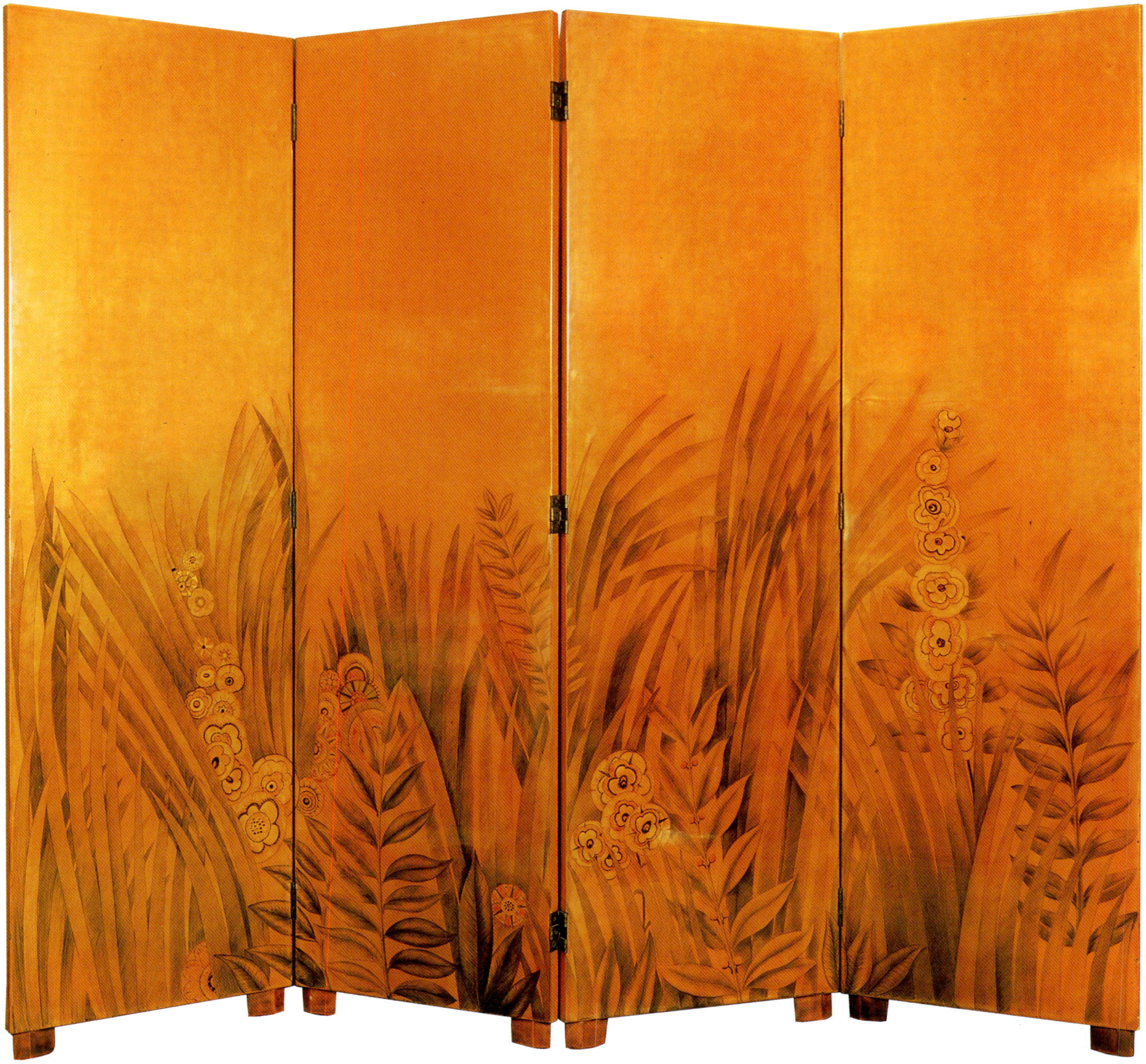

The following year – 1924 – marked Dunand's entry into the world of fashion. Of course, his earliest clients had included several couturiers (Jean-Philippe Worth, Jeanne Lanvin and Madeleine Vionnet), and he also knew other designers such as Charlotte Revil and the milliner Madame Agnès, for whom he would later create sumptuous interior designs. One must remember that by now Dunand was in charge of a large workshop with around sixty assistants (the figure would rise to more than a hundred in the 1930s at the time of his work on the liner *Normandie*), and he owed it to himself to find work for them all by opening up new outlets. Fashion is a realm in which ostentation and sophistication are in complete accord with the meticulous work carried out in the artist's studio, whether in lacquer or gold. Dunand now designed various parures and executed his first commercial jewellery – bracelets and cuff-links – which he decorated with geometric motifs. In gold and silver, galalith and oroide, they harmonized with each other and could be worn together in fanciful and extravagant combinations. Necklaces consisting of several rows, their edges nicked like notched wheels, recalled jewellery worn by the women of certain African tribes. The same was true of ear-rings that resembled Cubist sculptures. Dunand had already made his first essays in jewellery well before 1924, but what he had produced earlier had remained in an experimental stage, the pieces being intended only for his wife or for family friends.

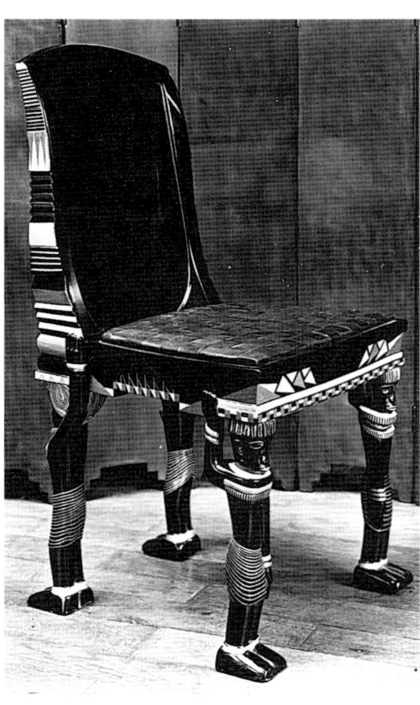

The African-style chair made by Dunand in collaboration with Lambert-Rucki, 1924; see cat. no. 1147.

So successful were these experiments that he resolved to show a whole series of buckles and clips that could be worn on shoes, hats and belts, at an exhibition devoted to fashion, fabrics and clothes organized by the Musée des Arts Décoratifs at the Pavillon de Marsan in February and March 1924. The pieces were intended to highlight the clothes designed by Louise Boulanger, Elsa Schiaparelli, Jenny Sacerdote and Jeanne Lanvin. Made of metal inlaid with silver or eggshell motifs, they were of every shape and every colour, not least because some were lacquered. For Dunand, this world now became a sort of refreshing haven where he could give free rein to his imagination, creating ornaments for lapels and brooches which invited comparison with the work of Futurist artists.

The lavish interiors of some of the automobiles made at this time also inspired Dunand to design lacquered metal boxes with smoker's sets, small hanging vases, interior panels and ornamental beading. At this same exhibition he made the acquaintance of Labourdette, the famous coachbuilder who, at the Exposition Internationale des Arts Décoratifs et Industriels held the following year, exhibited vehicles whose interiors included features specially executed by Dunand. Dunand was also in charge of designing Labourdette's private apartment, where he combined the lamp exhibited in 1923 at the Galerie Georges Petit with fanciful murals and his famous (but now vanished) African-style chair, a piece made in collaboration with Lambert-Rucki, although the latter never wanted this fact to be known. In the same room was also displayed an exceptional chimneybreast with a geometrical design decorated in lacquer and eggshell. In the neighbouring room was displayed Mme Labourdette's desk, designed by Eileen Gray.

In every sense the artists of the day felt that 1924 offered the last real opportunity to perfect their individual works before they appeared the following year at the great Exposition Internationale des Arts Décoratifs et Industriels Modernes.

The items which Dunand sent to the Salon de la Nationale in March were little more than a re-run of pieces previously seen at the Galerie Georges Petit. This was certainly true of the screen based on a design by Lambert-Rucki: here the artist's use of Cubist decorative motifs had resulted in a vast composition that bore witness to Dunand's expertise, with fantastic flowers and animals epitomizing all his earlier experiments. Even so, there were also several novelties, evidence of the artist's quest for constant self-renewal and technical perfection. One of these pieces was a small high-framed table, the top of which had the appearance of a Cubist painting made up of straight lines, squares and rectangles overlapping each other, all in shimmering harmonies of red and black lacquer, highlighted with white eggshell. A large ovoid vase also featured this decorative scheme, developed on two sides in complementary colours. These two twentieth-century masterpieces of decorative art demonstrated once again that in the case of genuine talent, the dividing line between fine art and decorative art becomes merely a question of perception. At this exhibition Dunand also presented a large, highly decorative lacquered panel, featuring a monkey motif, and a large double screen in silver lacquer and decorated with palm trees in varying shades. In the latter the variation of colour was obtained by techniques that had been little used hitherto, including scumbling, sand-papering and polishing or dulling the surface. Against this background stood a large hind, made from a single sheet of lead hammered, engraved and inlaid with other materials and paint.

On 12 June 1924, the President of the French Bar, Maître Henri-Robert, was elected to the Académie Française. His colleagues clubbed together to present him with the traditional Academician's ceremonial sword, and on Louis Barthou's recommendation they commissioned Dunand to make it. The sword was made of steel and inlaid with gold and silver, with a lacquered scabbard, while the pommel was lacquered and inlaid with mother-of-pearl. As the newspapers were at pains to point out, alongside a photograph of the newly elected member proudly displaying Dunand's sword, its execution represented a notable technical achievement.

The following month, Dunand's reputation was once more confirmed at the Salon des Tuileries, held in wooden buildings specially designed for the occasion by the well-known architects Perret Frères, who before the First World War had designed the Théâtre des Champs-Elysées and the parking garage in the Rue de Ponthieu. This 'wooden palace' was widely praised by exhibitors and visitors alike, especially as the rooms were of different sizes and excellently suited to match the scale of each individual collection of exhibits, all of which could be viewed, moreover, under ideal lighting conditions, a point underlined by Yvanhoé Rambosson in an article published in *Comoedia* on 8 July 1924. In discussing Dunand's geometric designs, Rambosson noted that 'a sort of linear musicality issues from certain objects whose conception, increasingly thoughtful, once more demonstrates his perfect mastery with metal and lacquer, surpassing the skill of the Orientals in this respect.'

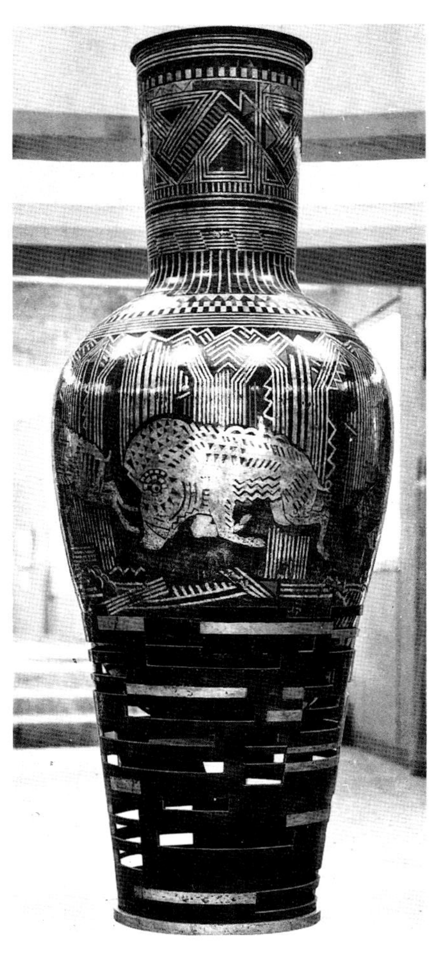

Monumental vase with decoration depicting wild boar, 1924 (cat. no. 994).

The fifteenth Salon des Artistes Décorateurs held in 1924 provided an opportunity for Dunand to exhibit, besides the Lake Geneva screen based on Biéler's sketch seen the previous December, an exceptional new work. This was a monumental vase with an ovoid body and a straight neck, a piece admired as much for its size as for its ornamentation. The vase was placed in the centre of the courtyard designed by Sézille and Rapin; conceived to suit the proportions of its surroundings, it underlined the grandeur of the courtyard setting. On the sides of the vase was depicted a herd of wild boar, the apparent movement of the animals being emphasized by the base on which the vase stood. The base was made of wrought-iron slats mounted in criss-cross layers in an arrangement that underlined the dynamism of the composition. One journalist reported that David Weil, a famous collector of old silver, had bought a wooden box decorated with eggshell and red lacquer for his house in the Rue de Chézy, Neuilly. One critic noted that Dunand's exhibits at this Salon showed ever greater refinement: 'In his lacquers he evinces a marked advance on the taste and technical skill of his earlier works, and the fish screen which the State has just bought can stand comparison with the rarest and most perfect inventions of Japan and China.'

The year was rounded off with the eagerly awaited fourth Dunand-Goulden-Jouve-Schmied group exhibition, held a little earlier than usual, from 18 November to 15 December, at the Galerie Georges Petit. Dunand exhibited his customary array of screens, panels and decorative objects. The ceremonial sword made for Maître Henri-Robert was also on display, as was a portrait study by Dunand, depicting the artist's wife. It was not until the

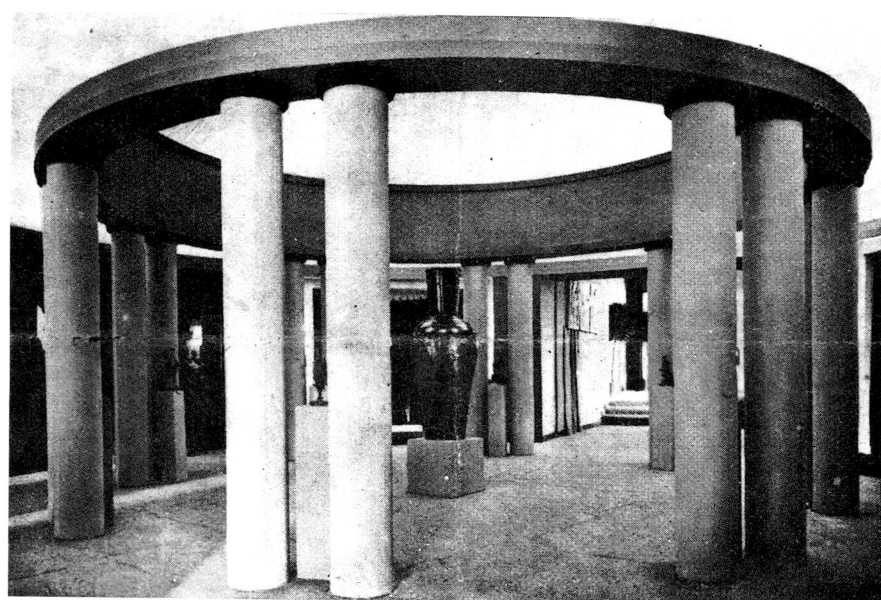

The rotunda by Sézille and Rapin at the Salon de la Société des Artistes Décorateurs, December 1924; in the centre stands the monumental 'Wild Boars' vase by Dunand (cat. no. 991).

following year that he undertook a definitive version, an extremely accomplished use of eggshell and lacquers of the most extraordinary shades. The sitter wore a richly decorated dress and scarf, the graphic realization of the garments being a technical *tour de force*. In the furniture section Dunand exhibited a large cabinet designed by Goulden, its folding doors adorned with an exotic landscape. The pieces of furniture which Dunand decorated were becoming ever more simple in form. He used elements which could be taken apart and which, having no recesses, grooves or mouldings, were easy to lacquer and rub down. Once again, the exhibition received highly complimentary reports published in specialist journals.

In December, Dunand also participated in the eighth exhibition of the Artistes Français Contemporains at the Galerie Georges Rouard, an exhibition which combined 'a selection of luxury works of distinction'. Dunand was the first to suggest the idea of smokers' accessories lacquered and inlaid with eggshell. Such articles were so much in fashion between 1923 and 1926 that many of the Indo-Chinese craftsmen employed in Dunand's workshop were enticed by rivals to work for them. Thus, Dunand noticed that certain of his employees were stealing lacquer and eggshell to work in secret at home during the evenings, using their kitchen stoves to harden the lacquer and achieving excellent results on small objects. It even appears that, probably without his realizing it, the noted jeweller Jean Fouquet had recourse to this somewhat unconventional procedure when having some of his own creations lacquered. By contrast, from this time onwards, articles sold by the firm of Dunhill were lacquered in Japan and shipped to Paris via London.

The Exposition Internationale des Arts Décoratifs et Industriels Modernes (1925)

This international Exhibition of Modern Industrial and Decorative Art, held in Paris in the grounds of Les Invalides, was the most important artistic event of 1925. The programme provided for the inclusion of every aspect of contemporary art, excepting only copies or reinterpretations of older styles. In other words, the exhibition set out to be completely modern in its approach, and on more than one count the results lived up to expectations. The exhibition provided graphic proof of the new concern with precise and clear-cut volumes. Without being truly 'modernist', its intention was to be in the vanguard of artistic development. Geometry was everywhere to be seen – even to the point of excess. Nevertheless – and despite the fact that the exhibition opened late and in a field of mud, as the press was not slow to report – the event proved a huge success with the general public.

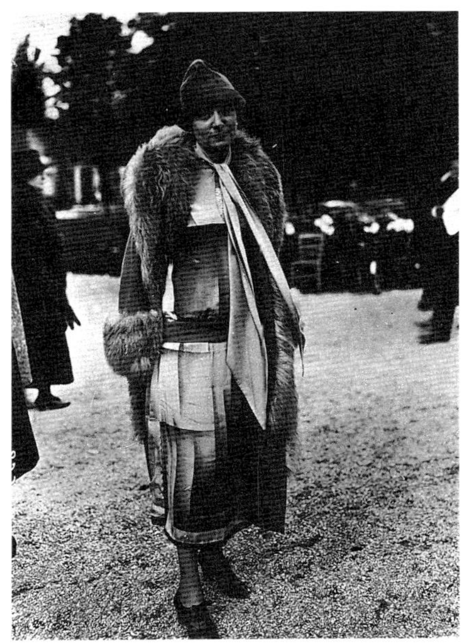

Madame Agnès in the grounds of Les Invalides during the Exposition Internationale des Arts Décoratifs et Industriels Modernes, Paris, 1925.

Dunand's involvement was of course inevitable. As an innovatory artist in brass- and copperware, he had been appointed vice-president of the metalwork class, and the organizers had invited him to make four monumental vases to decorate the inner court of the pavilion for industrial arts and crafts. Dunand chose a somewhat pot-bellied baluster-shape vaguely reminiscent of ancient Cretan vases of the type displayed in the Louvre. Each was beaten from a single sheet of copper. A tiered pedestal was added afterwards and soldered to the base. Each vase was differently decorated, geometric motifs made up of triangles, squares and chevrons being combined with undulating and vertical lines. Executed in red and yellow lacquer highlighted with gold and silver, their designs stood out against a plain black-lacquer background. Owing to their being treated as architectonic elements, something of their imposing size was lost and they contrasted strangely with the decor of the peristyle. It is certainly true that these vases would have gained from being displayed in a room more suited to show off their size and in surroundings as refined as the vases themselves. Although the architectural design of this pavilion was conceived as a whole by Charles Plumet, the general effect of the interior was scarcely calculated to be one of harmony, featuring as it did a central sculpture and bas-reliefs by Poisson, wrought-iron gates by Szabo (much admired by Dunand), and the peristyle decorated with paintings by Guillonnet, Rapin and Marret. In a display cabinet in the hall, near the 'Lady's Boudoir', a further series of Dunand's vases with sober, elegant lines were on show.

For the large salon in the Collector's House, designed by the architect Pierre Patout, Emile-Jacques Ruhlmann had planned a large cupboard, a sort of sideboard with fluted side-sections, the whole piece being mounted on castors. He invited Dunand to lacquer it in black and then to decorate it. Owing to pressure of work, Dunand had relied on Lambert-Rucki to design the ornamentation, asking only that he eschew the comic and rustic characters which he tended to introduce into any decorative subject. Lambert-Rucki evidently felt that he was being asked to 'imitate Dunand', as he himself put it, and preferred his name not to appear. All the same, his composition, depicting a dog and hedgehog against a geometric background, was one of his most spectacular and successful creations. The critics certainly paid tribute to its designer, though without naming him. The contours of the composition were finely engraved and highlighted with silver, and, as a whole, the piece had a certain elegance despite its monumentalism. The exhibition guide also mentioned a further piece, a lacquered screen in the main hall, made jointly by Dunand and Ruhlmann. In fact, however, it seems that this piece was never executed, for it does not appear in any of the photograhic records of the time, nor has it been possible to find any trace of such a screen in the family archives. Whether the project was not realized through lack of time, or whether the catalogue entry was simply at fault, cannot be determined.

Alive to the resolutely novel qualities of Dunand's work, the President of the Société des Artistes Décorateurs, Maurice Bokanowski, had entrusted Dunand with the task of designing one entire room in a group project with the theme 'A French Embassy Abroad'. Dunand elected to design a smoking room in the ambassador's private apartments. It faced the 'ambassador's salon', furnished somewhat lugubriously by Maurice Dufrène, and Dunand had the good sense to design the square chamber as a special area decorated throughout in red and black lacquer. This 'barbarous and magnificent' colour scheme did not appeal to all the critics, one of whom described the room, not without a touch of humour, as 'funereal, an imagined retreat for hypochondriac smokers'.

Although the room was a little cramped, with large and heavy square chairs, this was offset by a high recessed ceiling, cleverly designed to allow for smoke extraction and ventilation. The design was entirely Dunand's and although its realization was intended to be carried out in collaboration with Charles Hairon and Léon Jallot, in practice they do not appear to have had a

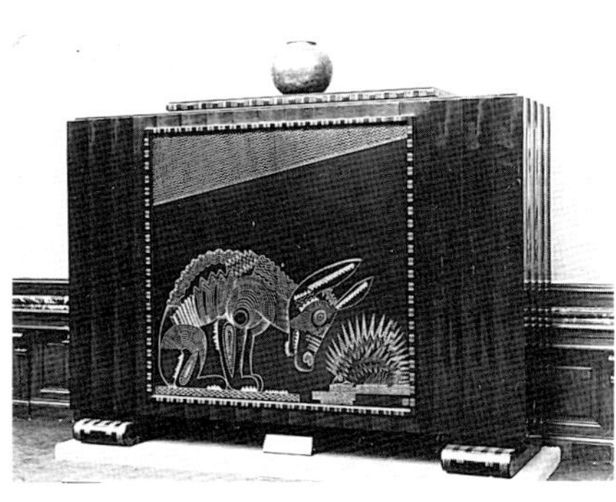

Large cupboard by Ruhlmann with lacquer decoration by Dunand after Lambert-Rucki, 1925; see cat. no. 1196 and colour plate 57.

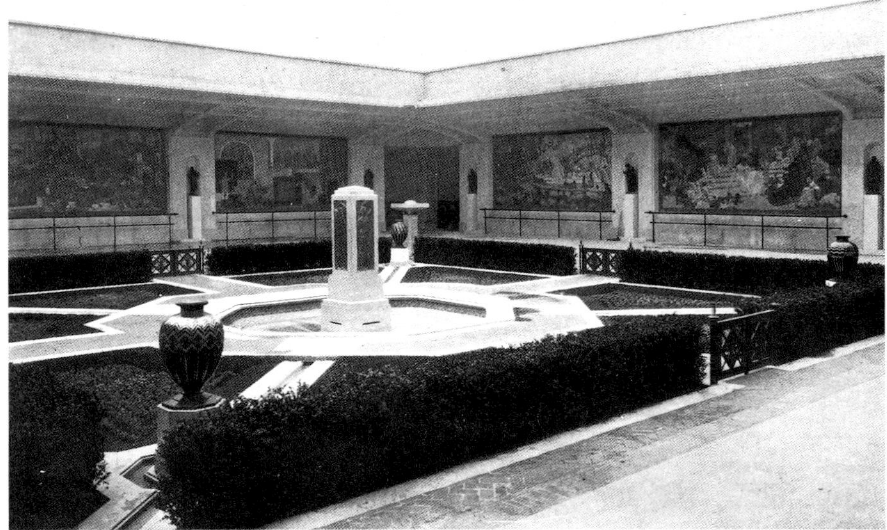

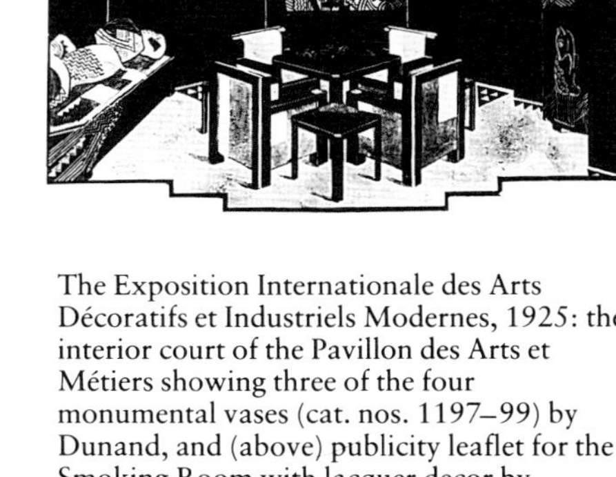

The Exposition Internationale des Arts Décoratifs et Industriels Modernes, 1925: the interior court of the Pavillon des Arts et Métiers showing three of the four monumental vases (cat. nos. 1197–99) by Dunand, and (above) publicity leaflet for the Smoking Room with lacquer decor by Dunand.

hand in it. Dunand had wanted the result to be Japanese in feeling, both in terms of its use of red and black and in the way that the volumes were handled. Many visitors considered Dunand's smoking room the best-integrated and most successful design of any in the exhibition. The room was displayed with the whole of one wall left open. Each of the side-panels, in plain black lacquer, included a sort of alcove suitable for conversation. To the left a black-lacquered couch, upholstered in lacquered leather decorated with a silver-grey geometric design, was recessed into the wall. Its black-lacquer base was engraved with zigzag lines. At the front of the stand on each side were alcoves, one containing a variety of objects, the other a decorative panel, based on a design by Lambert-Rucki. On this occasion the artist's highly individual composition depicted a mocking figure, cigarette in mouth, appearing to eavesdrop on the conversation.

On the other side of the room stood an upright piece of furniture with cut-off corners; it too was finished in black lacquer and its doors were decorated with an engraved motif, again the work of Lambert-Rucki. It is clear that, even though he preferred to enter Dunand's studio unobserved from the Rue Dareau, Lambert-Rucki did not fail to let his name be mentioned when it suited him. The design depicted puppies yapping at each other; it was engraved in simple outline and heightened with silver, as was the design on Ruhlmann's cupboard door, where an identical puppy yelped with pain as it rubbed against the quills of a hedgehog.

At the centre of the room stood a square table with cut-off corners. Likewise in black lacquer, it was positioned diagonally, with four grey-leather armchairs arranged around it. At each of the table's corners, between the armrests of the chairs, Dunand had placed four low square tables which could serve as stools or as surfaces for glasses and ashtrays during a game of cards.

The far wall was decorated with a further panel of red and silver lacquer set off with a geometric motif (the same as that used on all the cornices), the broken lines arranged with the sole intention of producing a pleasing, rhythmically structured decorative scheme.

The lacquered panels forming the walls were 3 m (10 ft) high, and the ceiling, lit indirectly, resembled a kind of stepped pyramid. Covered in silver *laque arrachée* and enlivened in the corners with red motifs, the ceiling's surface reflected a pleasant and gentle light. A beautiful, perfectly proportioned ovoid vase stood on the right-hand cupboard. 'Although the whole is small in size, the overall impression was truly of exceptional quality, and everyone could be proud of this choice and congratulate Jean Dunand on having been able to extract the secret of these beautiful lacquers from oriental artists and on having been able to apply that secret so felicitously to our

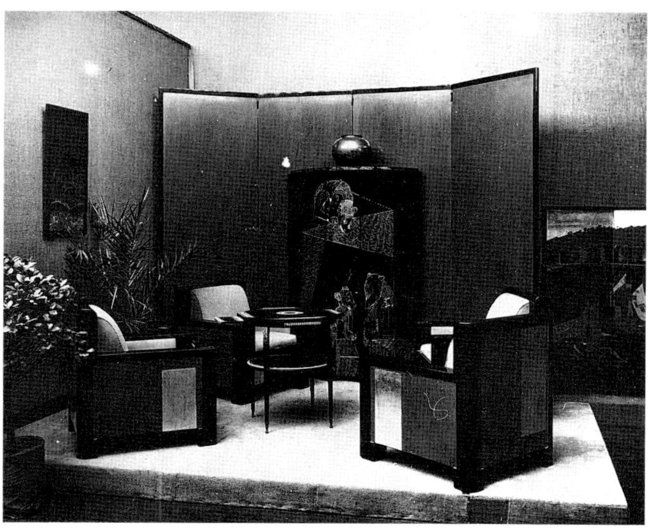

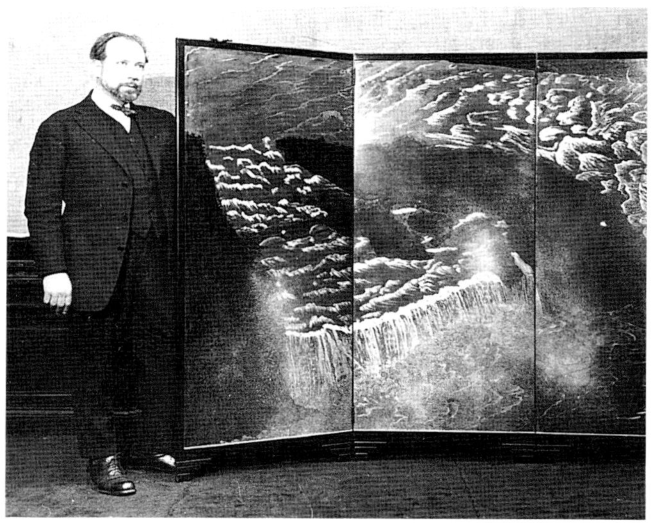

The exhibition at the Galerie Georges Petit, December 1925: (above) the lacquered armchairs seen earlier in the year in the Smoking Room at the Exposition des Arts Décoratifs; and (above right) Dunand posing beside his screen *Niagara Falls* (cat. no. 18).

modern Western civilization,' wrote Henri Clouzot in *La Renaissance de l'art français* in July 1925.

After visiting the exhibition, the couturier and art patron Jacques Doucet wrote to Dunand on 31 July, 'I have always admired your work, but what I saw today showed complete mastery and confirmed in every way your greatness as an artist.' This warm tribute summed up the general fascination with Dunand's spectacular works in the wake of this exhibition.

In the same 'Embassy', in the reception room designed by the architect Boileau, a cabinet containing works by Goulden and Dunand stood next to a desk-cum-bookcase designed by Pierre Chareau. A little further on, in the 'Hall des Collections', designed by the architect and interior designer Michel Roux-Spitz, examples of brass- and copperware and lacquered objects appeared side by side with illustrations by François-Louis Schmied. The background was a silk tapestry based on designs by Henry de Waroquier. Opposite, in the art gallery, were screens and panels by Dunand, and a number of vases decorated with geometric patterns. A further cabinet containing dinanderie was located in the large reception room in the pavilion of the Société des Artistes Décorateurs.

Dunand was of course vice-president of the society, and one can well believe that certain people were happy to think that he deserved such prominence. In fact, it would be more true to say that Dunand's style and the quality of his work, with its unprecedented luxury, exactly matched the mood of the time. This interpretation certainly appears to receive support from his contributions to other sections of the exhibition, which, if less spectacular, were equally significant. First and foremost was the Pavillon de l'Elégance, decorated and furnished by Armand-Albert Rateau, in which a number of vases had been borrowed from Dunand to embellish the stand of the milliner Madame Agnès. And in the section devoted to 'Means of Transport', Dunand's lacquerwork was displayed with glassware by René Lalique in a luxury suite conceived by Nelson and designed by the architect Bouwens de Boijen for the shipowners Compagnie Générale Transatlantique (C.G.T.). Also included in this section were Dunand's contributions to the interior design of cars, shown by the firm of Saint-Didier and the coachbuilder Binder. The section given over to suites of matching furniture, the architect of which was Pierre Selmersheim, was located on the forecourt of Les Invalides. On stand 56 the Maison Bernaux presented a dining-room scheme designed by A. Levard, its double door based on a sketch by Lucien Lévy-Dhurmer and lacquered by Dunand. It was destined for an apartment belonging to a Mme Gompel, overlooking the Seine. A little further on, by Lucie Renaudot's stand, which was designed by Maurice Dufrène, a small studio by Dumas included several vases by Dunand in its interior design. Elsewhere, in the Pavillon des Artisans Français Contemporains, a number of pieces of brass-

and copperware were on display. In Class 8, which included objects made from wood and leather, Dunand exhibited a screen (unidentified) based upon a design by Germaine Gloria. In Class 9, embracing fancy goods and leather, cabinet 33, entered by A. Cohn et Cie, contained a number of matching outfits, handbags, purses and fashion accessories with modern decorative designs by Dunand.

This major exhibition was naturally a time of intense activity, and Bernard Dunand recalls how, as a young man, he had to run last-minute errands, taking a panel to one stand, some vases to another, and a screen to a third. On that occasion, in 1925, friends and acquaintances were keen to be associated with is father's work.

Other events in the 1920s

On 20 June 1925, the President of the Société des Gens de Lettres, Georges Lecomte, was presented with a ceremonial sword as a new member of the Académie Française. Since there were some thousand subscribers, including friends and other members of the Académie, the presentation was made in the setting of the former home of Salomon de Rothschild. Very modern in design, the sword was made by Dunand in steel inlaid with gold and silver, the steel scabbard being covered with black lacquer and inlaid with eggshell. The hilt was decorated with white mother-of-pearl and burgaudine, and the dedication was engraved on the back of the blade. The decision to ask Dunand to make the sword had been influenced by articles written by the recipient on the subject of modern decorative art, which Lecomte had striven to defend and to present to a wider public as something to be universally accepted.

For the next Salon which followed, after the 1925 exhibition at Les Invalides had closed, Dunand appears to have made a panelled bed for Berne-Bellecour, a fellow designer. Its decoration, painted on a grey-lacquer background, depicted pink and white macaws fluttering between delicately patinated creeping vines. Dunand used the same motif at a later date when decorating a grand piano, a commission which no doubt he also received from Berne-Bellecour.

The year ended with the annual group exhibition at the Galerie Georges Petit. It was all the more successful on this occasion since the summer's main exhibition had created a genuine climate of interest in modern art. The pieces shown were chosen with special care and included only works of the highest quality presented with the utmost taste. The principal items had already been exhibited during the summer, but were now shown in a more luxurious setting; among such objects were Ruhlmann's large black-lacquer cupboard and the embassy smoking-room furniture with its square table, grey-leather armchairs, and corner stools. There were a handful of lacquer portraits, including the now finished likeness of Madame Dunand, and those of the fashion designers Charlotte Revil and Madame Agnès. The ensemble was completed by five large screens, one of which depicted the town of Honfleur in Normandy nestling at the foot of the cliffs, the narrow houses reflected in the calm waters. A similar anecdotal virtuosity featured in a second example, this time depicting Saint-Gildas-de-Rhuis, a village on the coast of Brittany, opposite Belle Ile, where Dunand and his family spent their holidays, while a third portrayed the Niagara Falls, and the theme of a further panel was 'Waves'. Each of these pieces confirmed the emergence of a new style – spare, almost austere, yet technically perfect. A further screen with six panels depicted exotic Japanese fish with huge diaphanous tails swimming around amidst bubbles of air and pencils of light made of metal spangles and mother-of-pearl. The bodies of the fish were made up of geometric and linear motifs and recalled the disciplined beauty of Dunand's hammered metal and silver-encrusted vases. 'To borrow this aquarium theme from the Japanese and to treat it in so novel a spirit is a real *tour de force*', wrote one art critic in the January 1926 issue of *Beaux-Arts*.

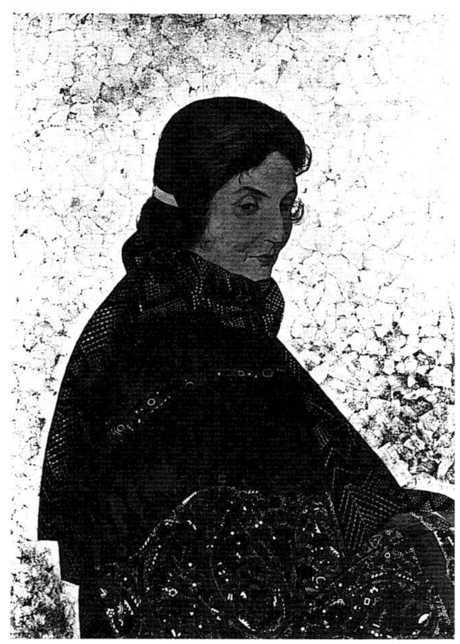

Madame Dunand, lacquer portrait, 1925; see cat. no. 134 and colour plate 1.

A number of cabinets contained beautiful vases in hammered metal, sober and with a purity of line, with lacquered decoration, cast silver or gold ornaments, or better still, bare surfaces with nothing more than a beautiful shaded patina. The ceremonial swords of the two recently elected members of the Académie, Maître Henri-Robert and Georges Lecomte, were also shown, displayed side by side. Dunand revived another oriental tradition, that of lacquered ceramic wares, with a large stoneware vase entirely covered with eggshell and black lacquer in a superb geometric pattern. Although this experiment was an unqualified success, Dunand repeated it – for reasons which cannot be established with certainty – only rarely.

In another display case a new realm of lacquer decoration was revealed, magnificent bookbinding boards lacquered and inlaid with mother-of-pearl, burgaudine and eggshell; these were made for François-Louis Schmied's bibliophile clients. Most of the designs, even if not credited in the catalogue, were by Gustave Miklos. Those presented in this display were intended for books that formed part of a subscription series and included *Les Climats, Le Cantique des Cantiques* and *L'Histoire charmante de l'adolescente Sucre d'Amour*. Designed to match the books' illustrations, these bindings satisfied the requirements of the most demanding of clients.

In March 1926, the Union Centrale des Arts Décoratifs repeated the ingenious system it had attempted for the first time the previous year, when items of furniture and other objects of feminine interest had been presented in an appropriate interior setting. Within an oval salon, embellished with lacquered tables inlaid with eggshell, Dunand submitted his previously exhibited silver-lacquer screen with its motif of tall palm trees, and another screen made in collaboration with Jean Lambert-Rucki also drew comment from the critics.

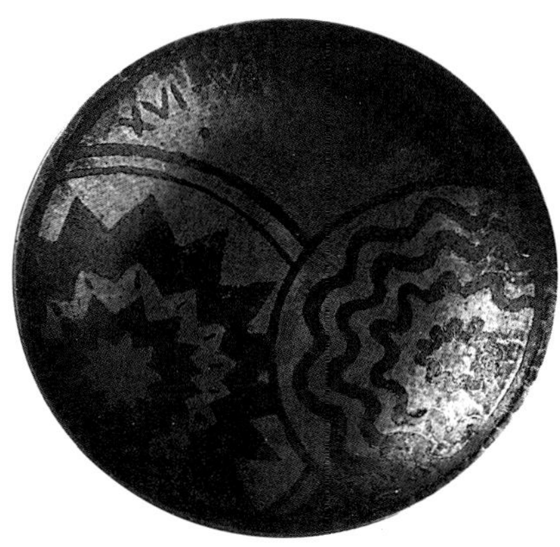

Ashtray in brass with silver inlay, one of the group specially made by Dunand for each of those present at dinner on 16 June 1926, when Dunand and François-Louis Schmied were entertained by friends and admirers at Laru's.

At the beginning of May, the Salon des Tuileries opened; here Dunand presented a number of large lacquered metal vases, tea and coffee services in copper and brass, and cigarette-cases speckled with crushed eggshell. The tiny fragments were distributed in such a way as to evoke the impression of the sky at night.

On 22 May, on the recommendation of the Minister of Trade and Industry, Dunand was promoted from Chevalier to Officier de la Légion d'Honneur for services rendered at the time of the major 1925 Exhibition, and François-Louis Schmied was similarly honoured. Dunand was now 49 years old, and some twenty friends and admirers together entertained both artists at a formal dinner at Laru's. On the evening in question, each place setting was provided with a wood-engraved menu highlighted in colours as well as gold and silver, and giving the name of the person for whom it was intended as a gesture of thanks. Schmied had designed and made them in two days and a night. Not to be outdone, Dunand produced metal ashtrays, each engraved with the date '16 June 1926', to be placed beside individual place settings.

Shortly before, on 20 May, an exhibition had opened at the Palais de Rumine in Lausanne, where the curator of the Musée Cantonal des Beaux-Arts had assembled, for a few days only, all the objects acquired for the museum at the time of 1925 Exhibition in Paris; among them several pieces by Dunand were given pride of place.

It was no doubt with great modesty, though not without a touch of mischievous humour, that Dunand took part in an exhibition of French decorative art held in Japan. Plainly aware of his hosts' delightful manner of complimenting foreign guests, Dunand was gratified to learn that his work had not displeased them. All the same, he had the good sense not to accept their invitation to give a series of lectures which would have involved revealing to his audiences technical secrets of his own discoveries. The invitation to participate came via M. Morita, the sales representative of a Japanese glass factory who was in contact with the St-Gobain glass company in France. He was based in Paris and his brother taught at the School of Fine Arts in Tokyo.

Plates 50–75
FURNITURE

OPPOSITE
50 **Cabinet** with dinanderie doors, 1934
(*catalogue 543*)

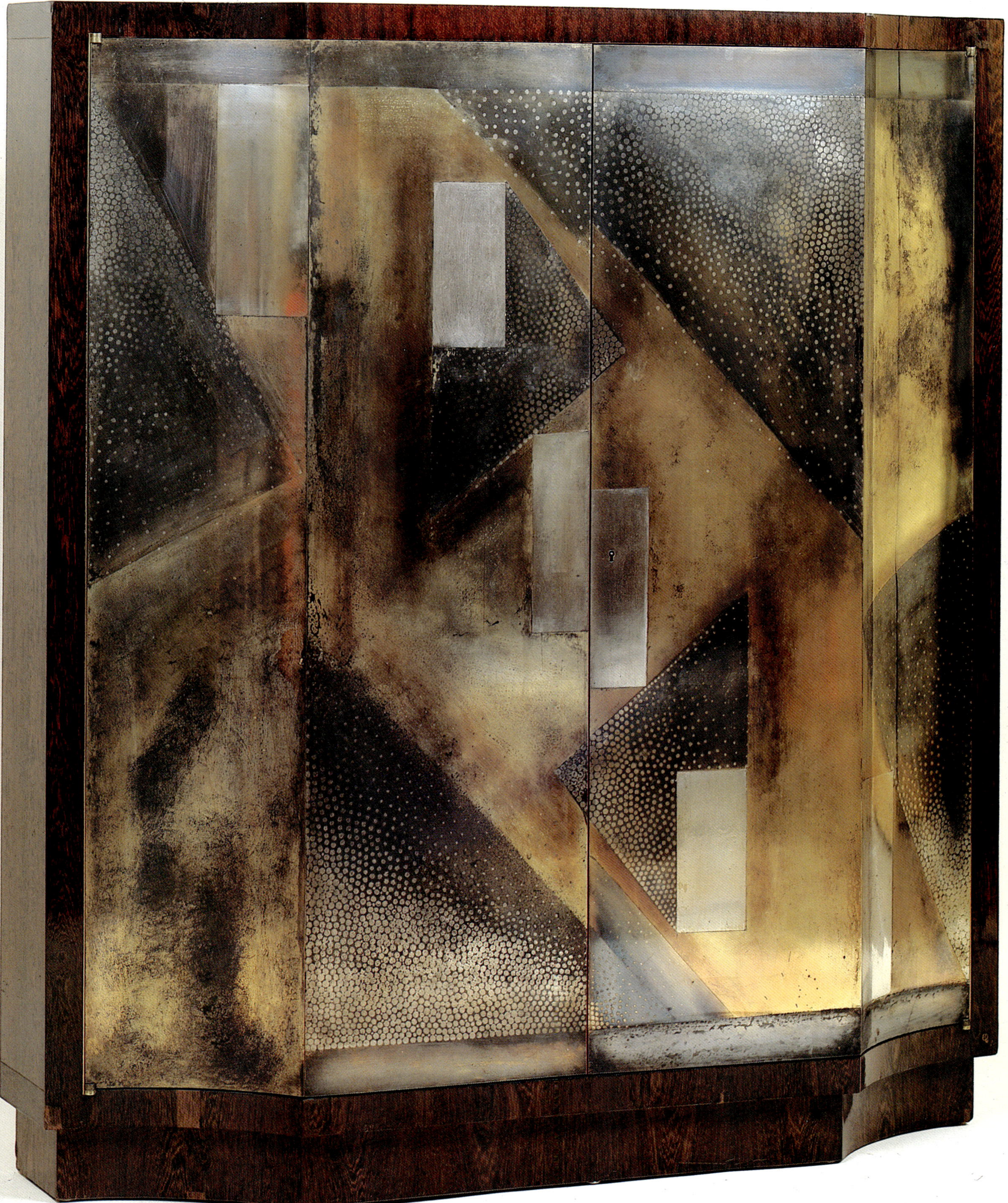

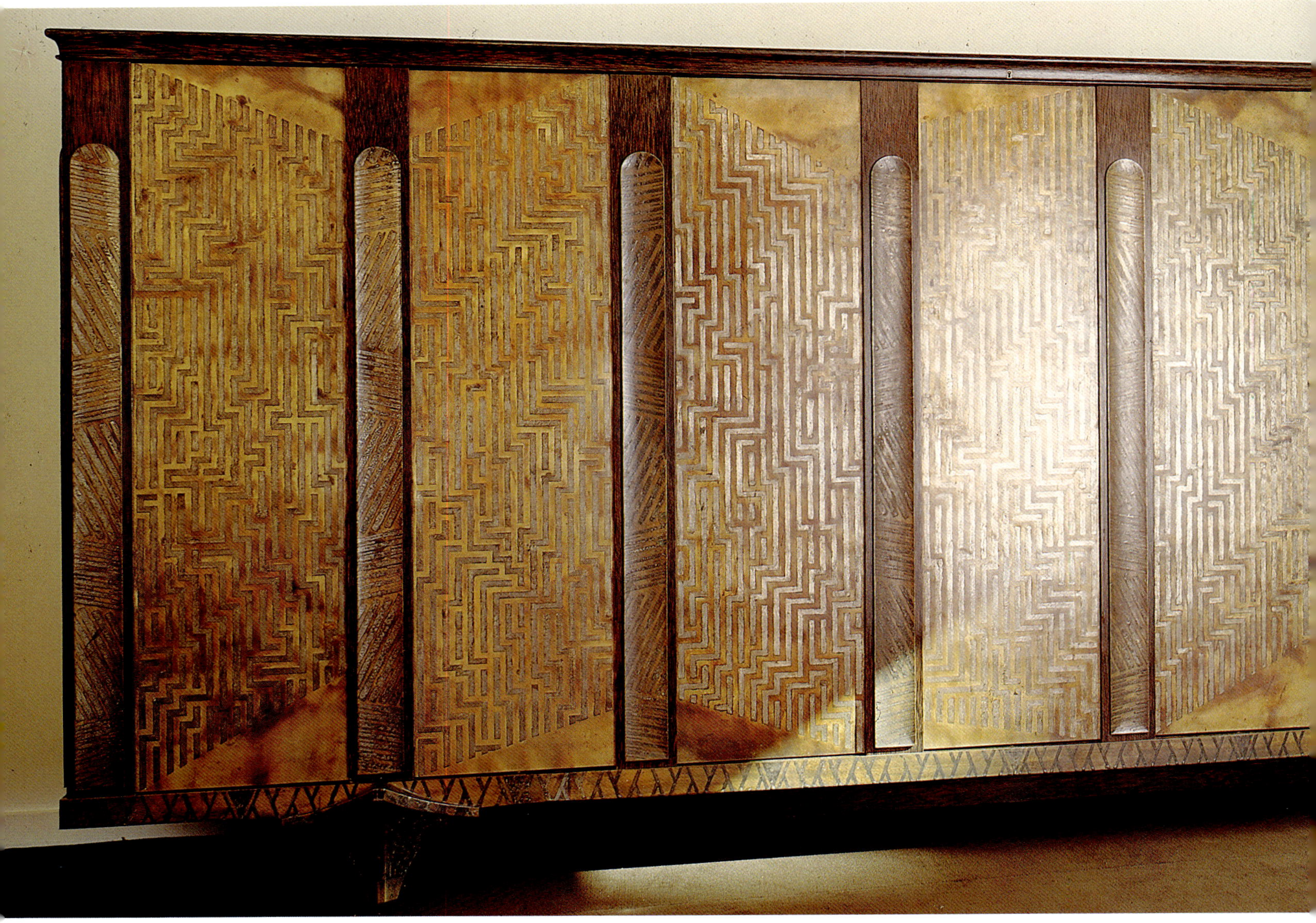

51 **Bookcase with revolving sections** designed by Jean Dunand and realized by Pierre Dunand, *c.* 1937. (*catalogue 545*)

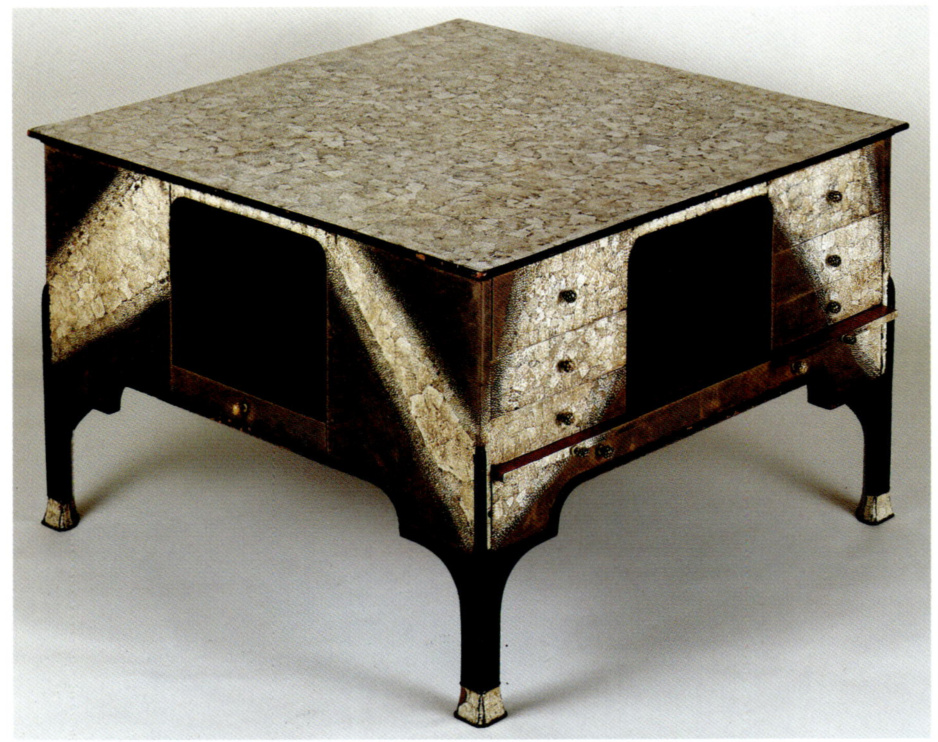

52 **Occasional table with drawers** designed by Jean Goulden, made in 1923 (*catalogue 531*)

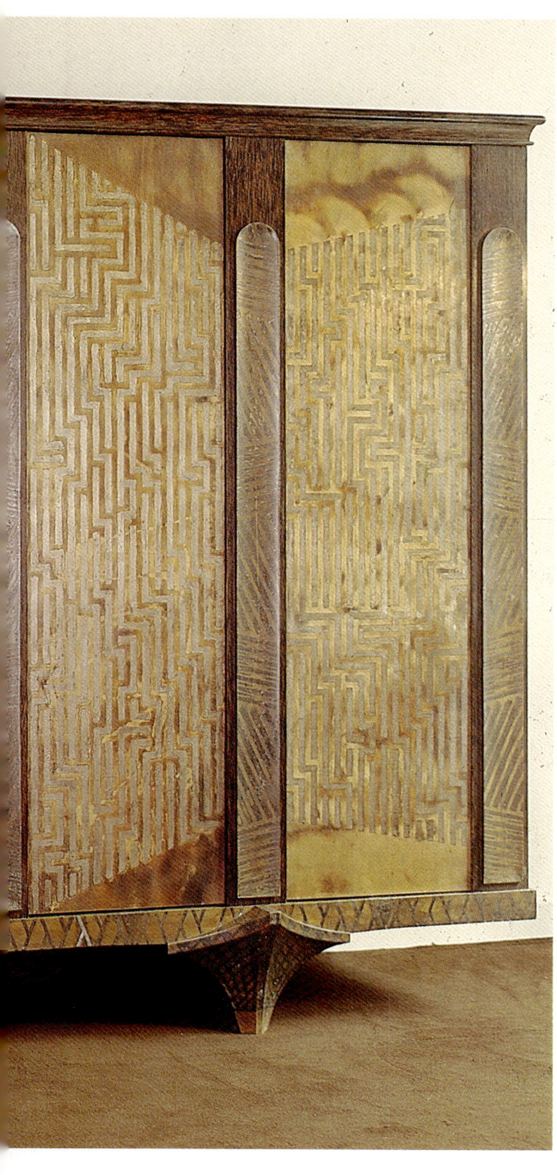

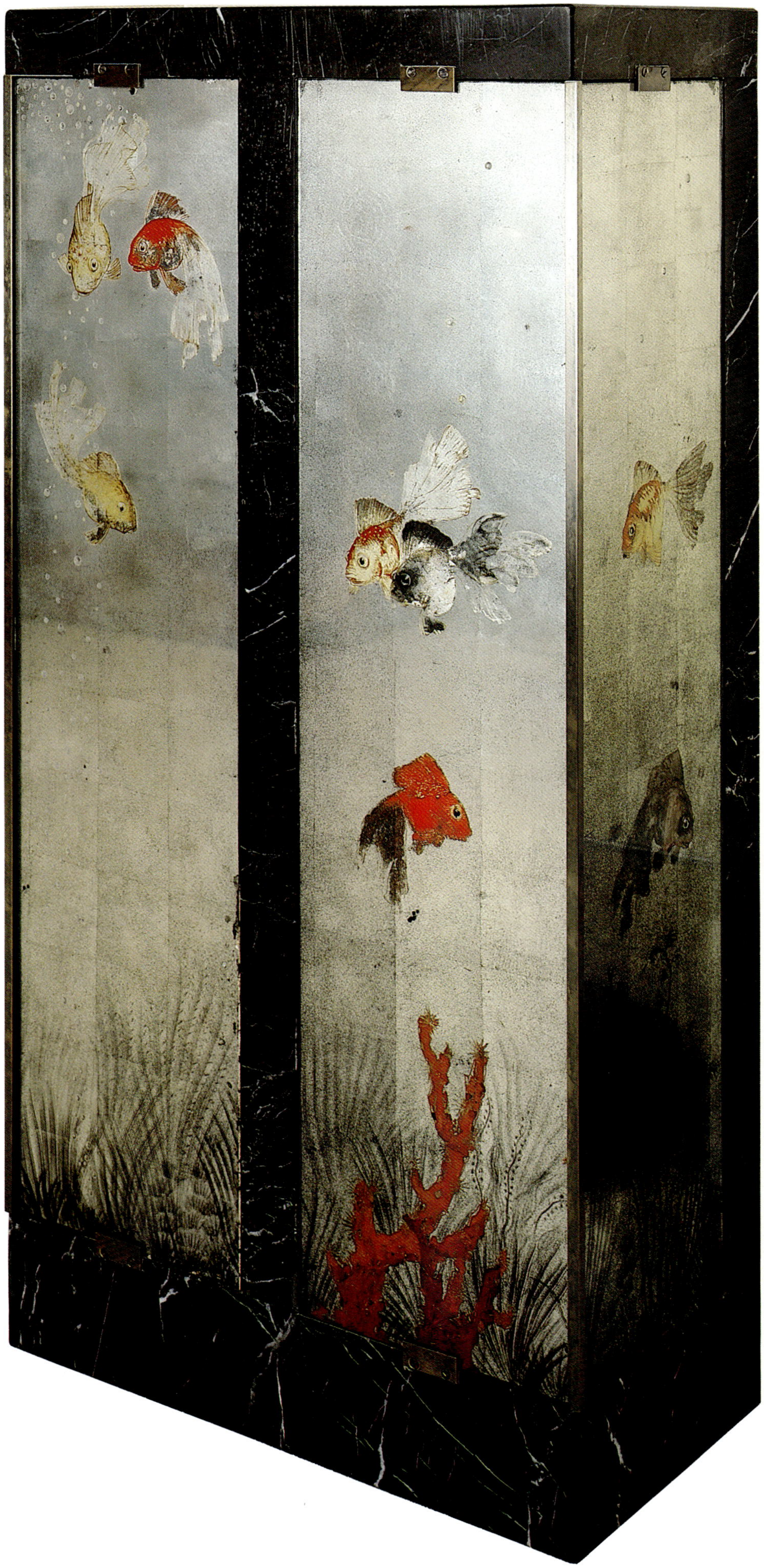

53 **Free-standing unit**
(one of a pair), *c.* 1925
(*catalogue* 486)

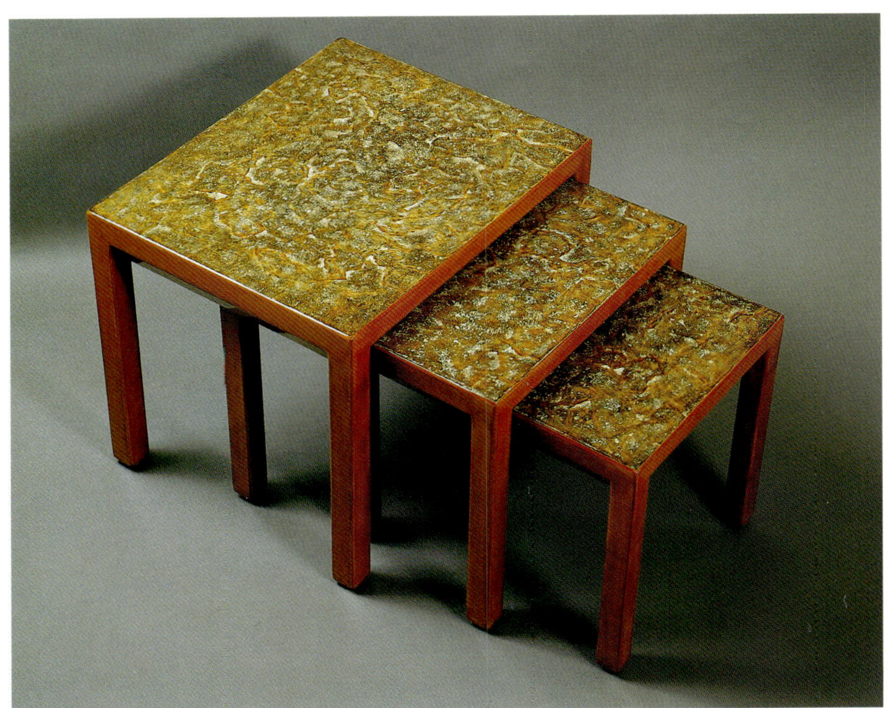

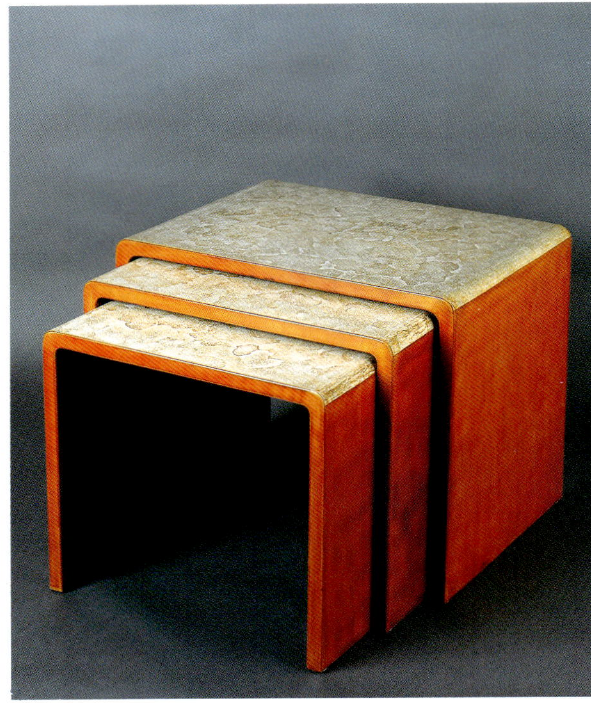

54 **Nest of tables**, *c.* 1925
(*catalogue 408*)

55 **Nest of tables**, *c.* 1925
(*catalogue 407*)

56 **Cupboard** designed by Eugène Printz, made *c.* 1937, with dinanderie panelled doors by Dunand
(*catalogue 550*)

OPPOSITE, ABOVE
57 **Large cabinet** by Ruhlmann lacquered by Dunand to a design by Jean Lambert-Rucki, 1925
(*catalogue 1196*)

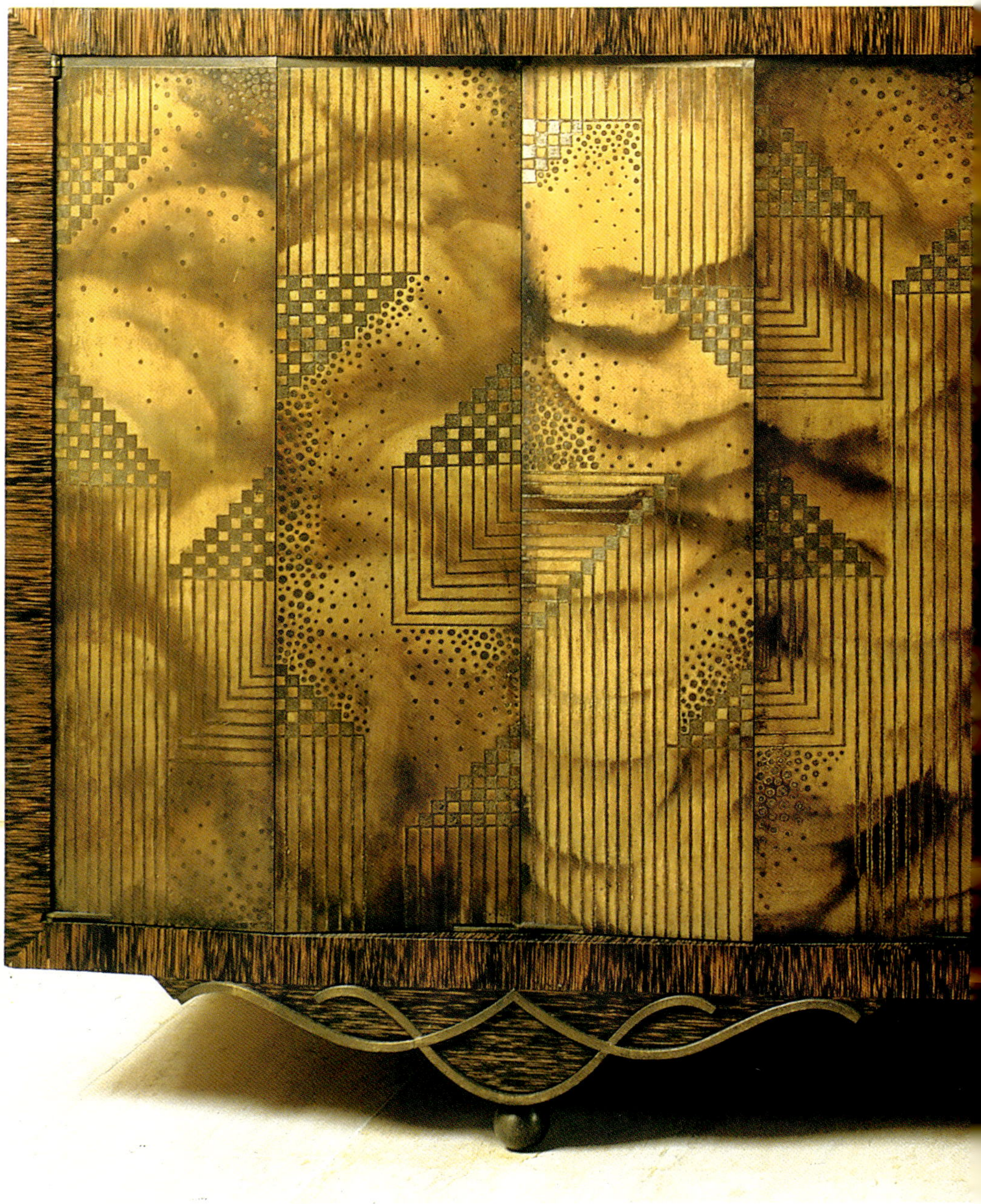

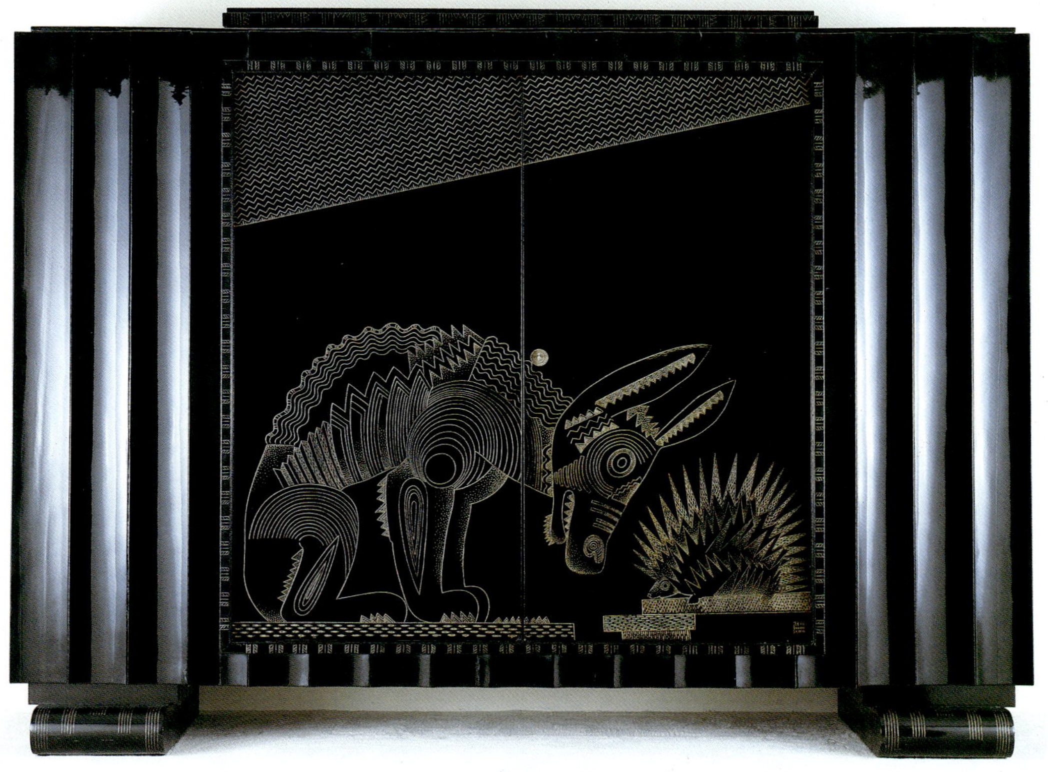

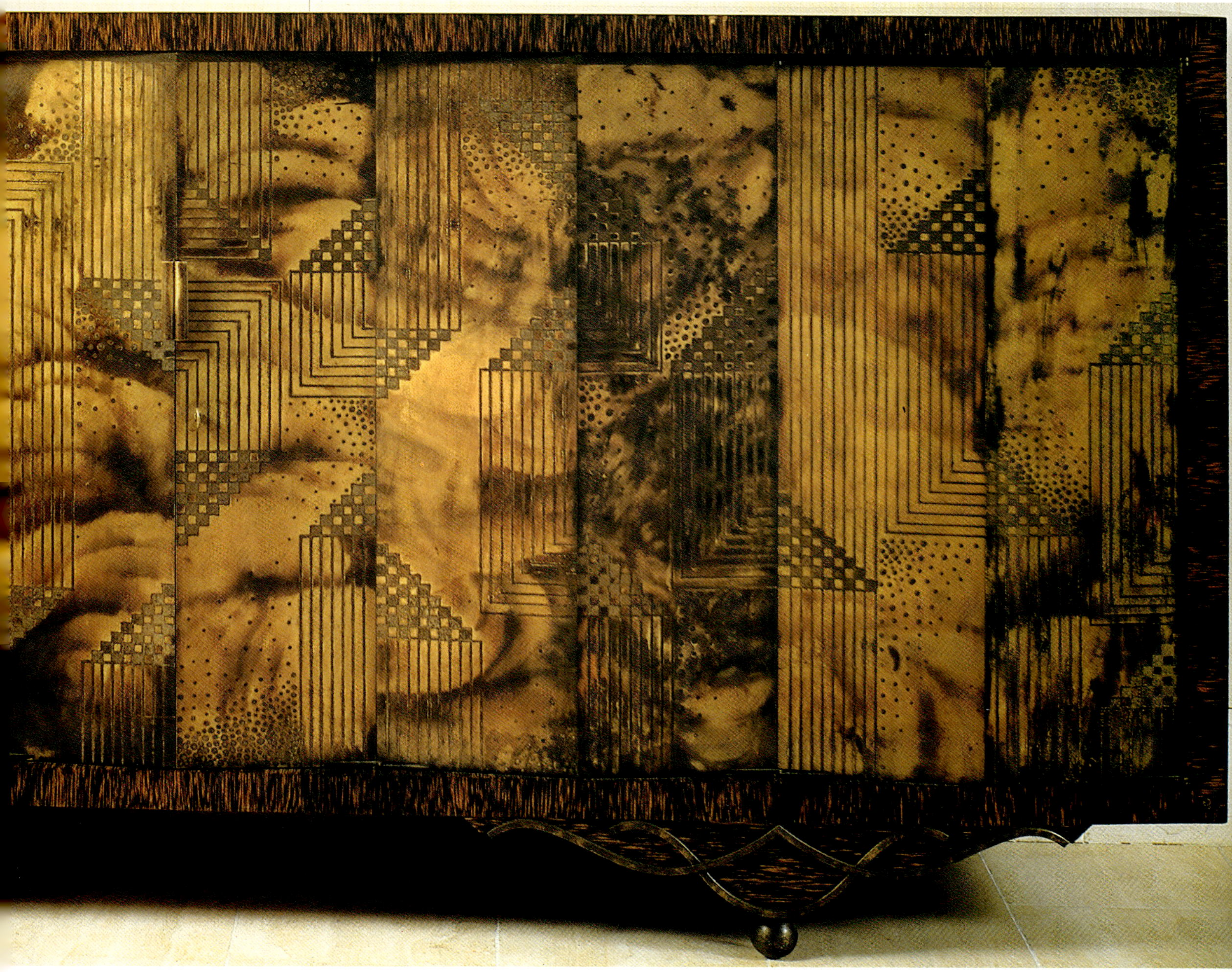

60 **Group of furniture and vases**
(see catalogue numbers 41, 345, 903, 998, 1001)

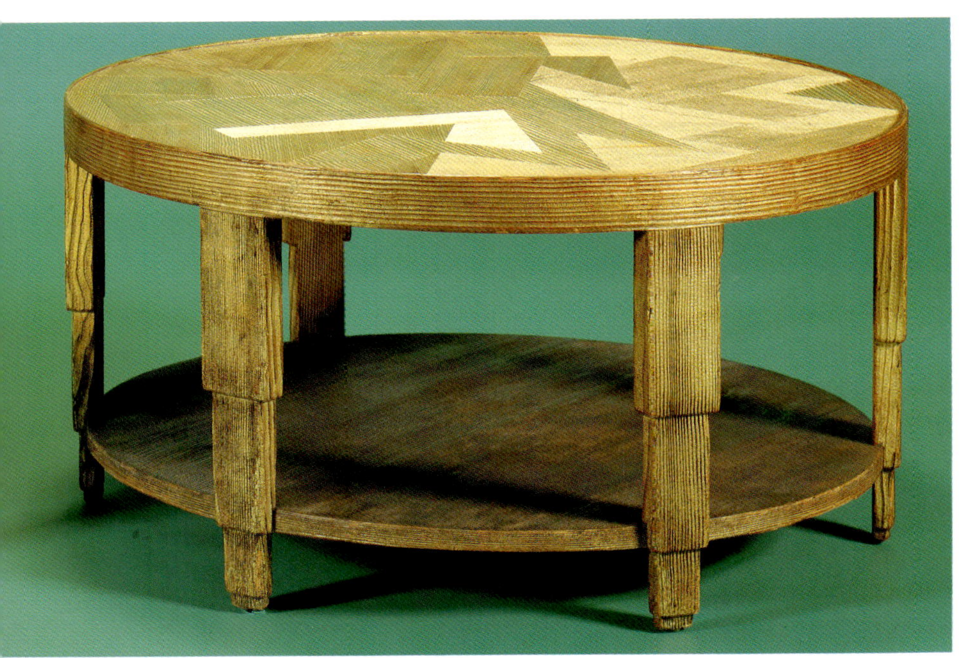

58 **Two-tiered occasional table**, *c.* 1930
(catalogue 459)

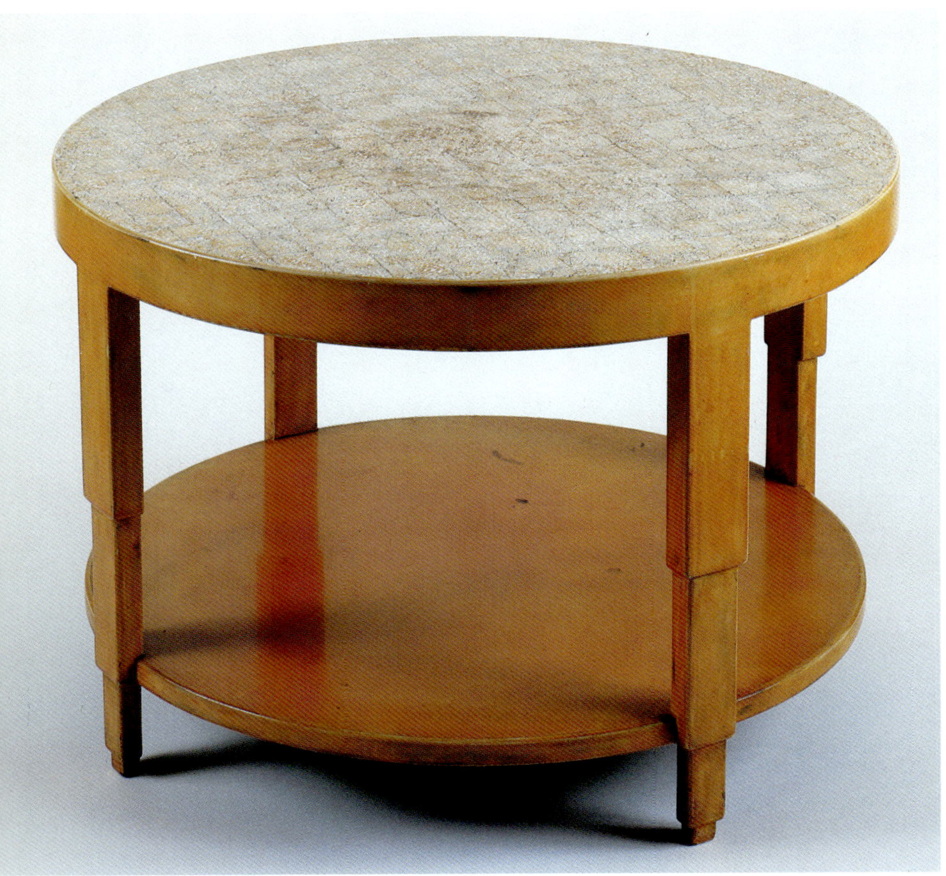

59 **Two-tiered occasional table**, *c.* 1925
(catalogue 458)

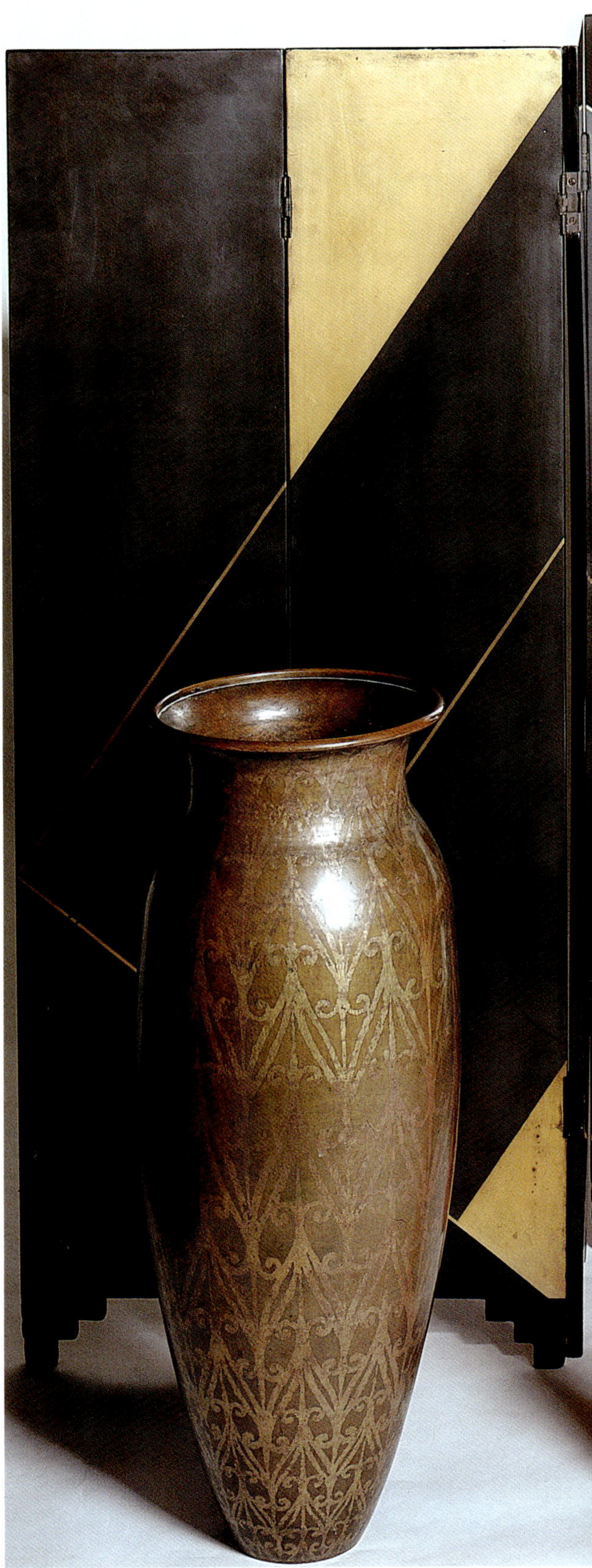

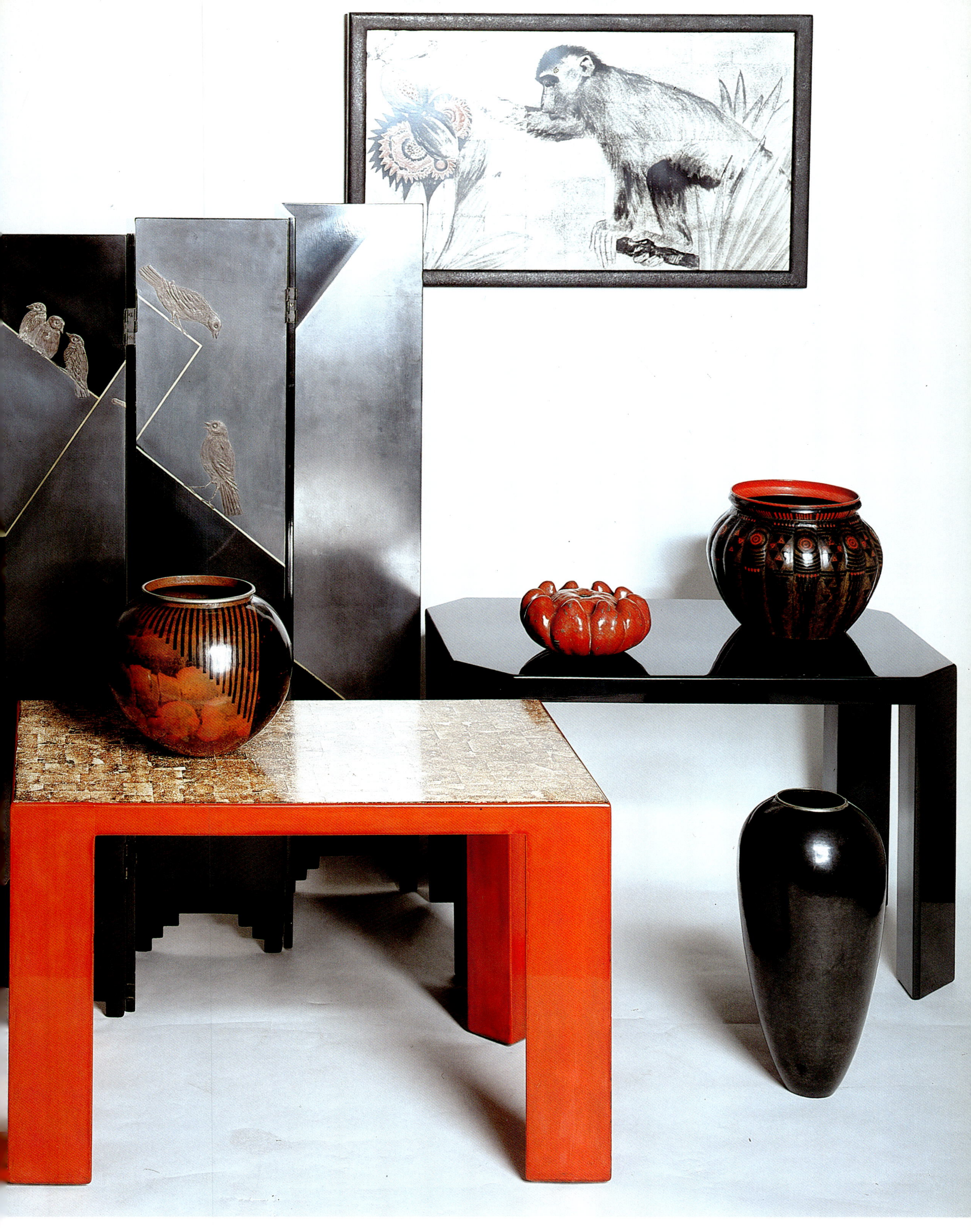

61 **Round occasional table** with brass fittings; lacquered *c.* 1930 by Dunand to a design by Eugène Printz (*catalogue 451*)

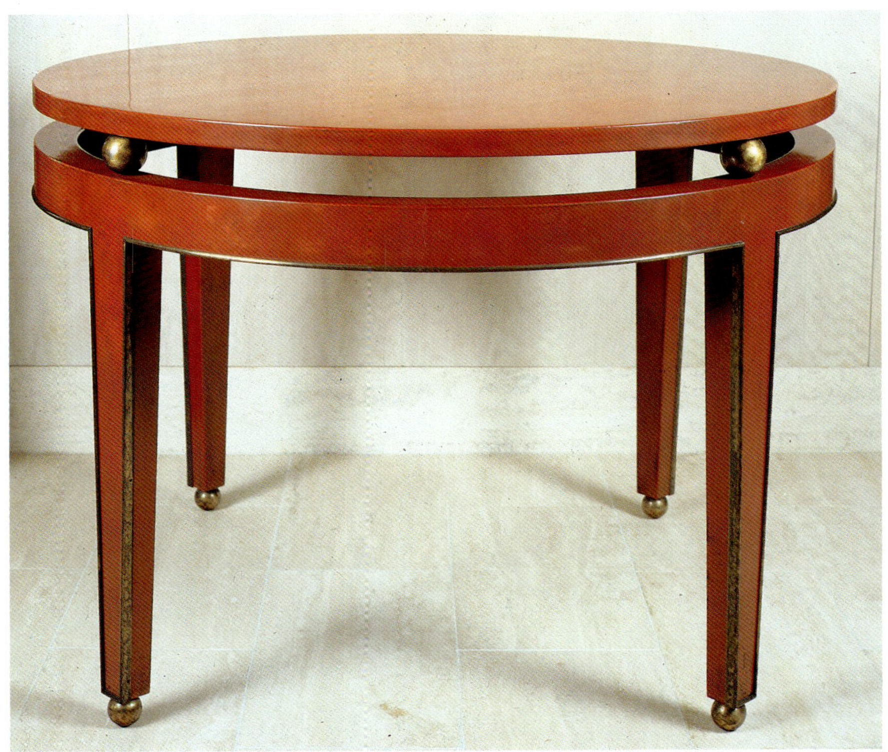

62 **Collector's cabinet**, 1937 (*catalogue 493*)

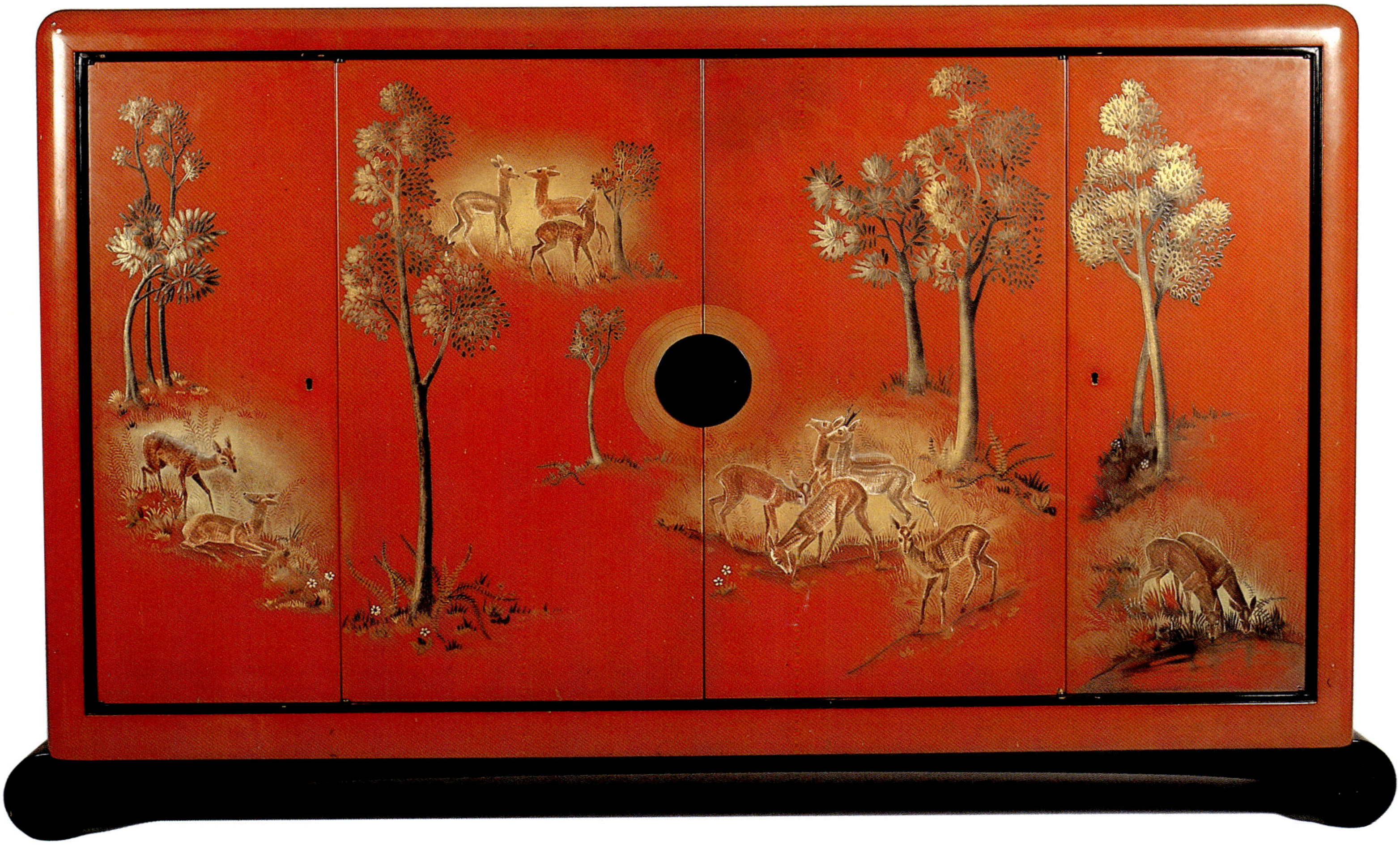

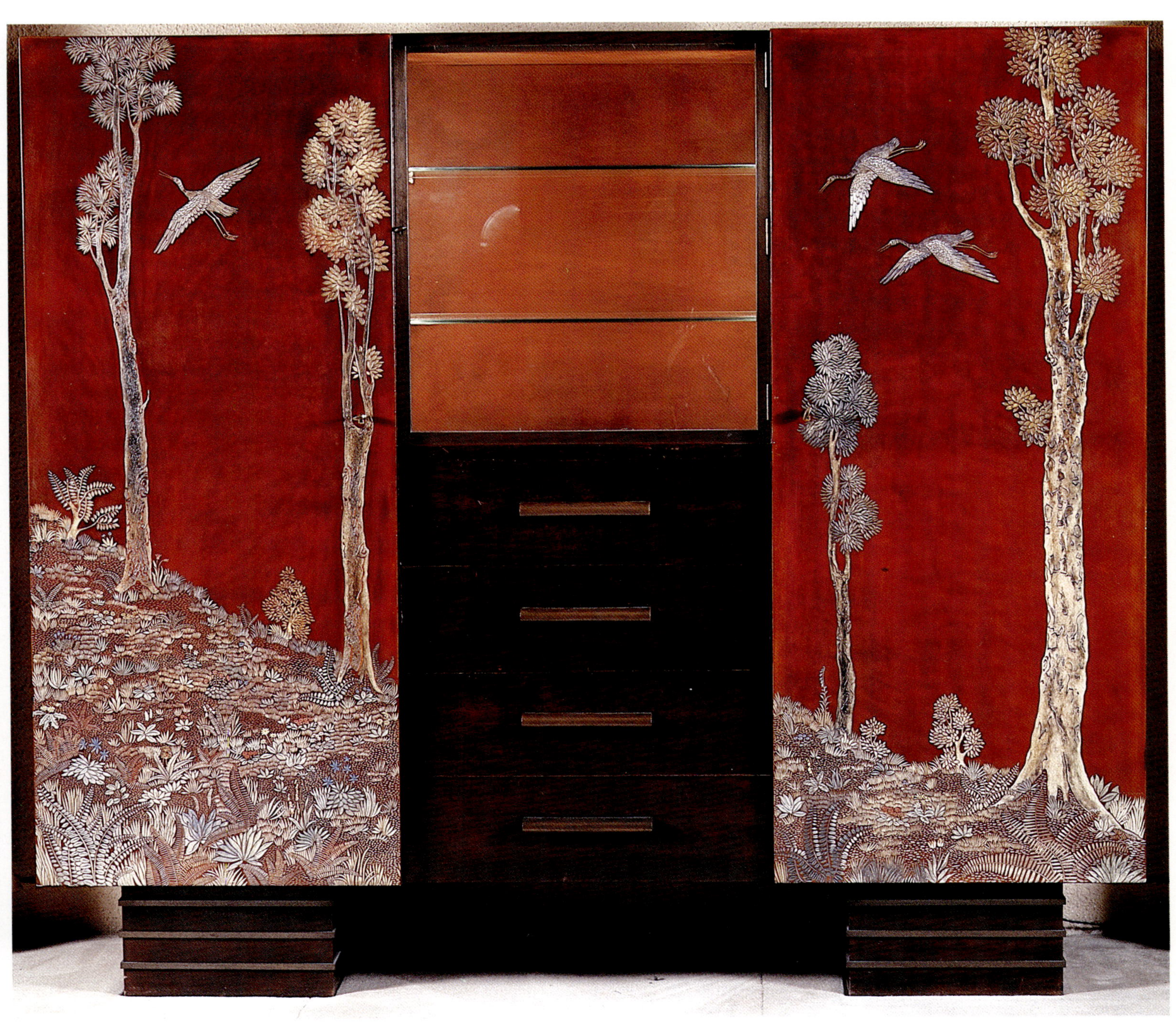

63 **'Stork' cabinet**, 1939
(*catalogue 499*)

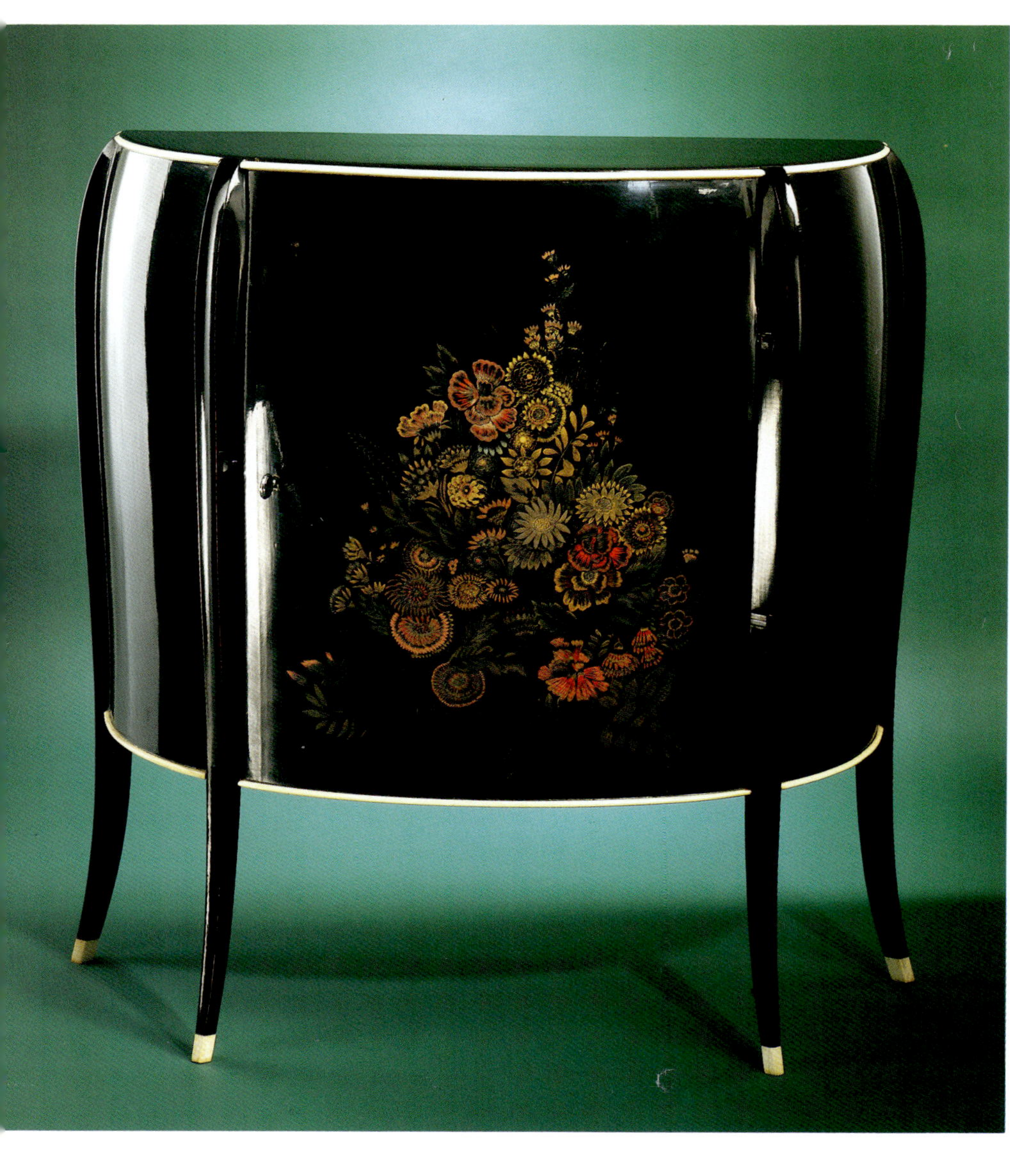

64 **Commode**, *c.* 1935
(*catalogue 556*)

65 **Corbeille bed**, 1932
(*catalogue 515*)

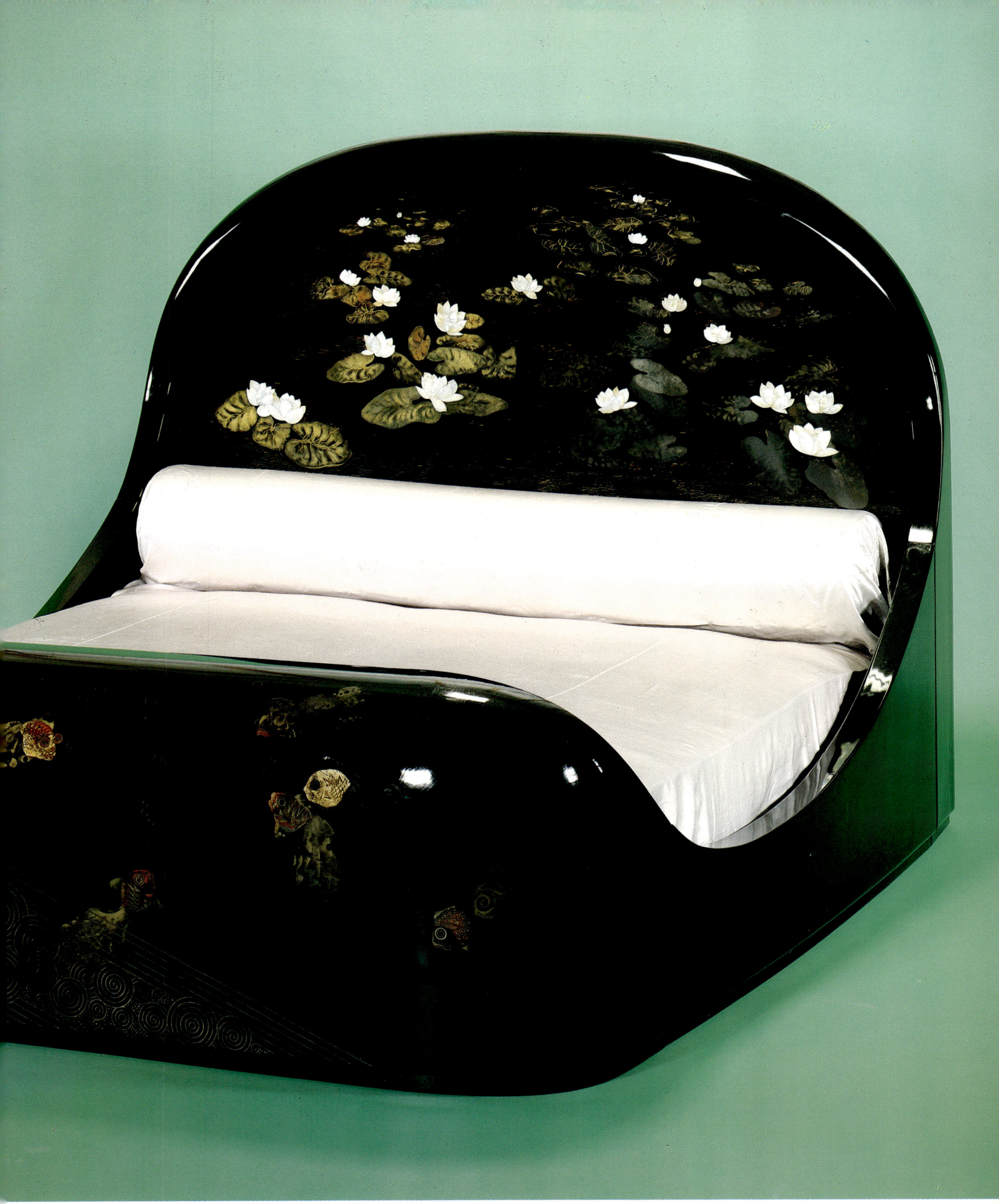

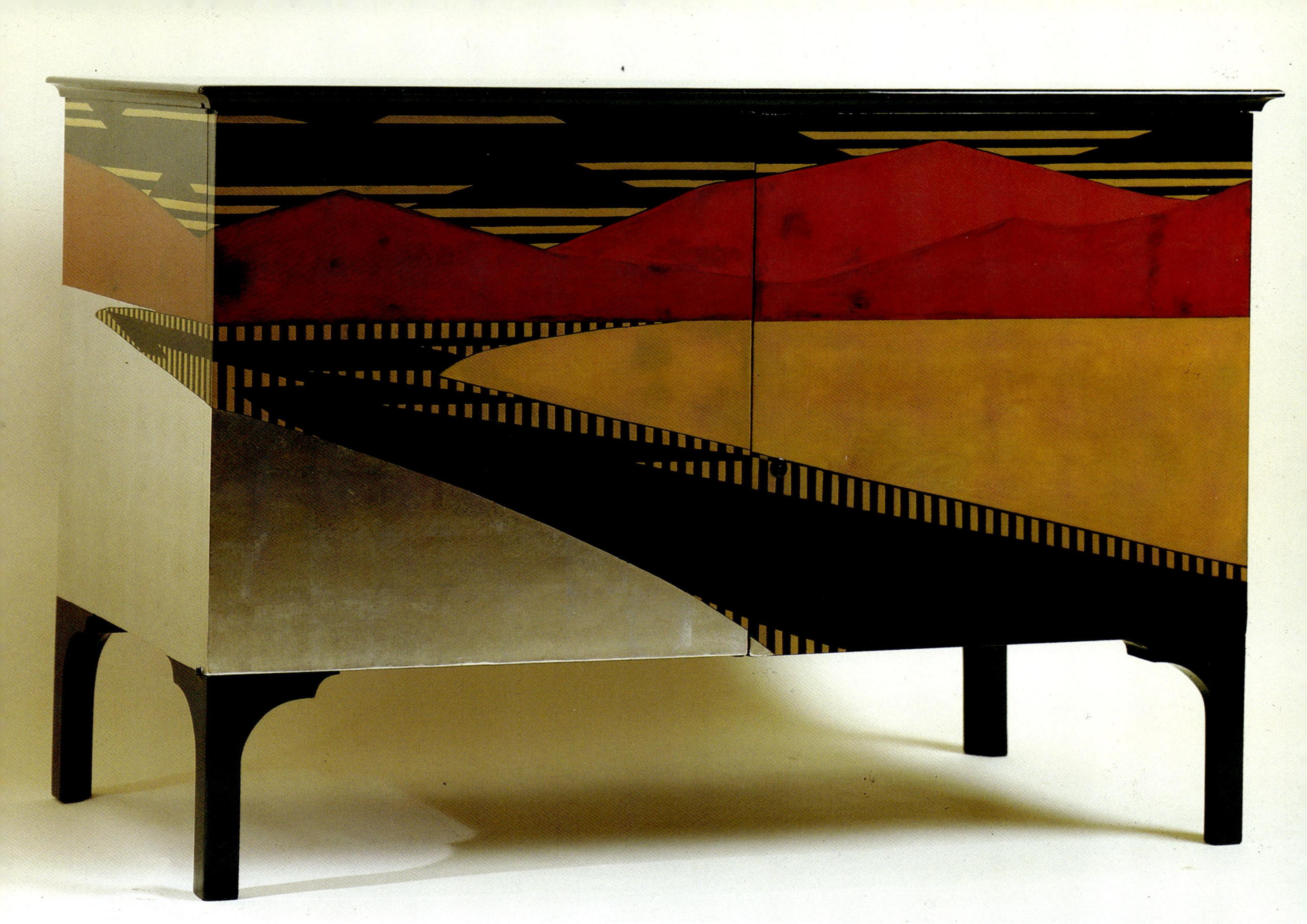

66 **Commode à l'anglaise**, designed by Jean Goulden and made in 1921 (*catalogue 530*)

67 **Telephone table**, c. 1928 (*catalogue 465*)

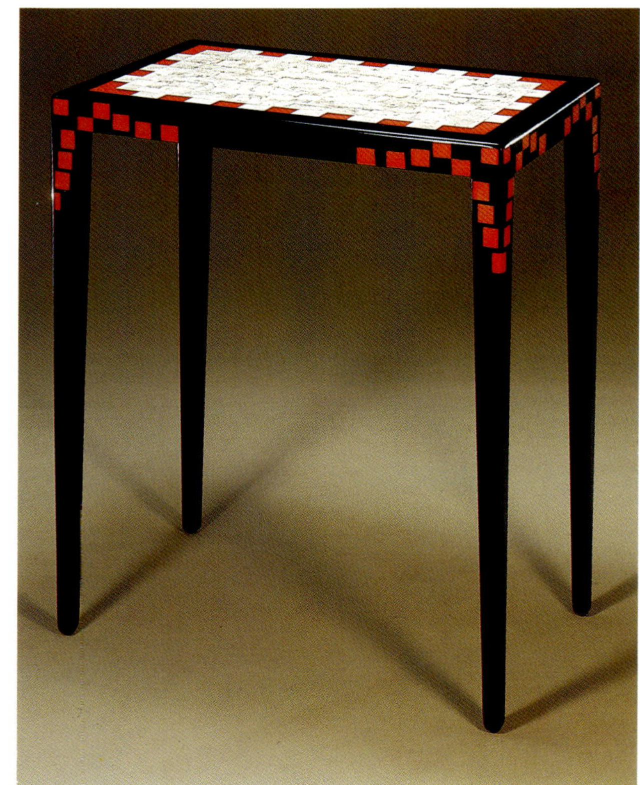

68 **Radio cabinet**, *c.* 1930
(*catalogue 506*)

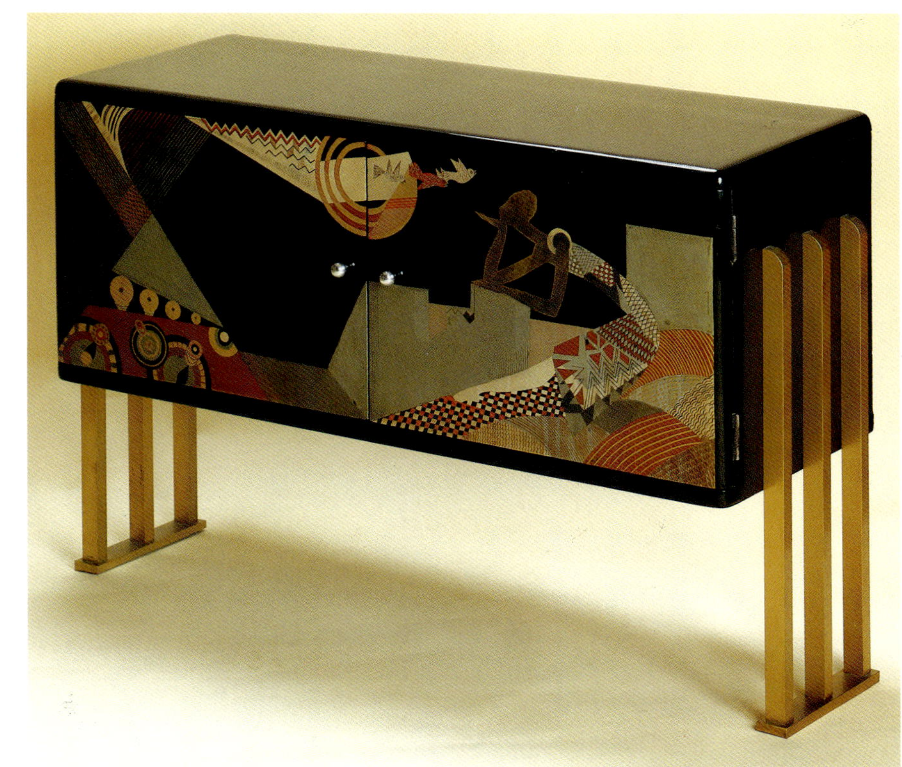

69 **Folding cocktail bar**,
made by Lawrence Rigby, 1928
(*catalogue 523*)

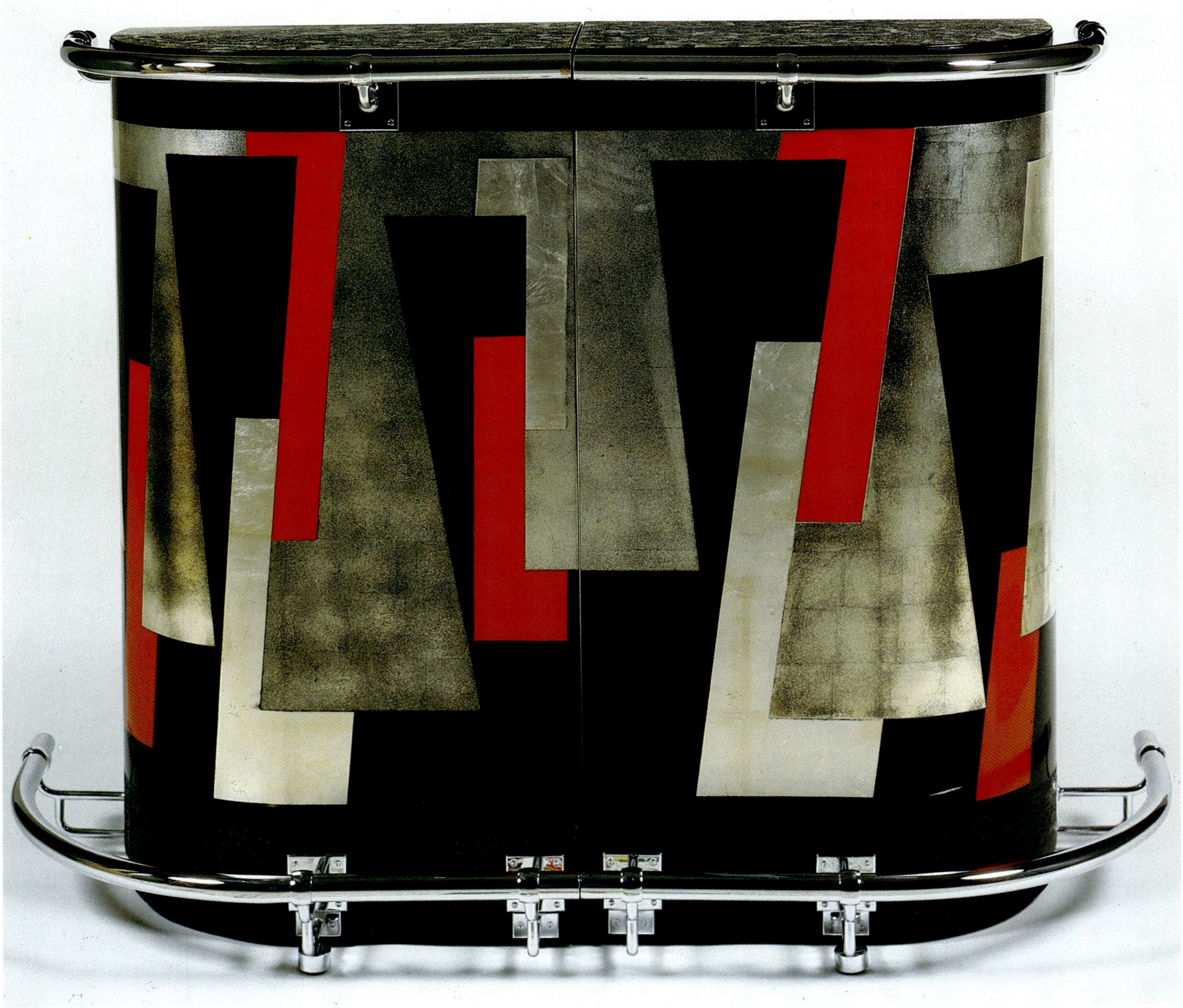

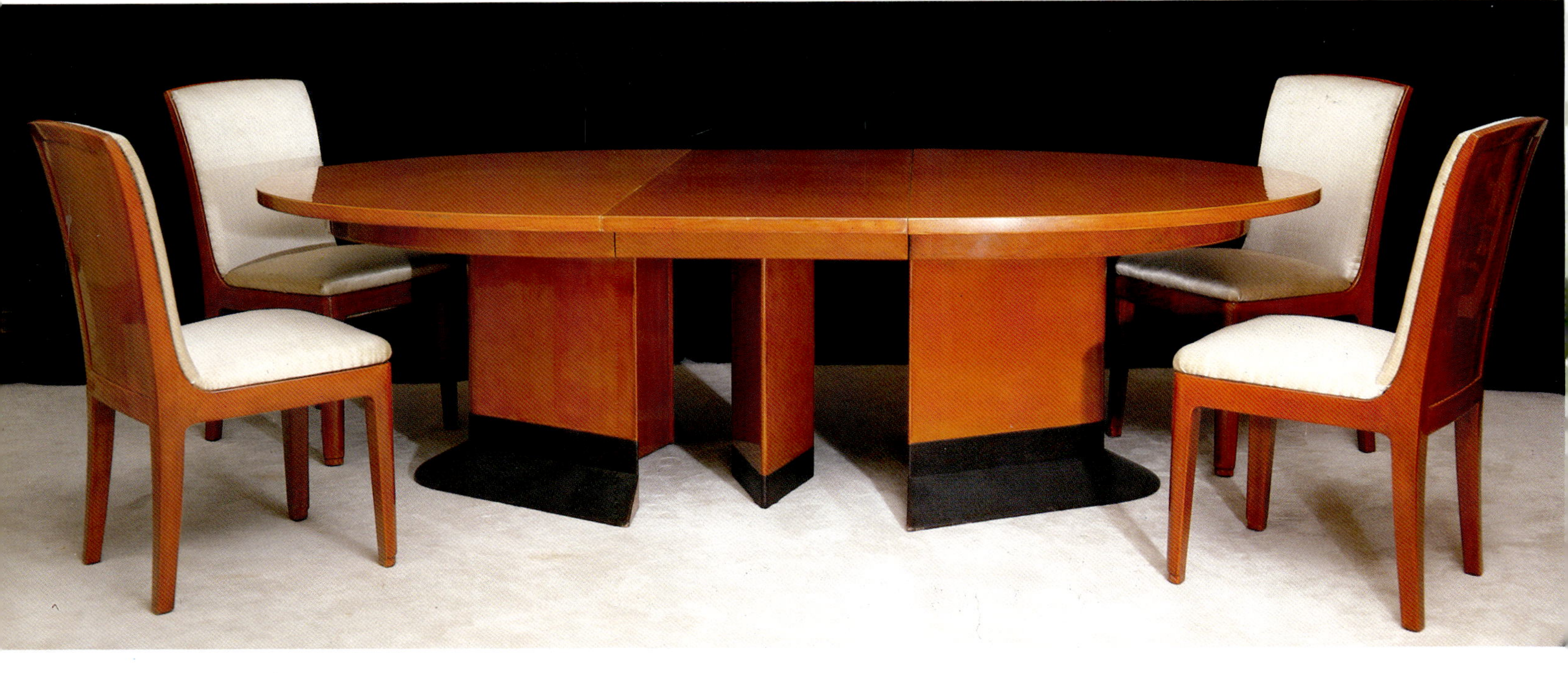

70 **Dining table** (extended) **and chairs** made for the Comte de Polignac, 1929/30 (*catalogue 417*)

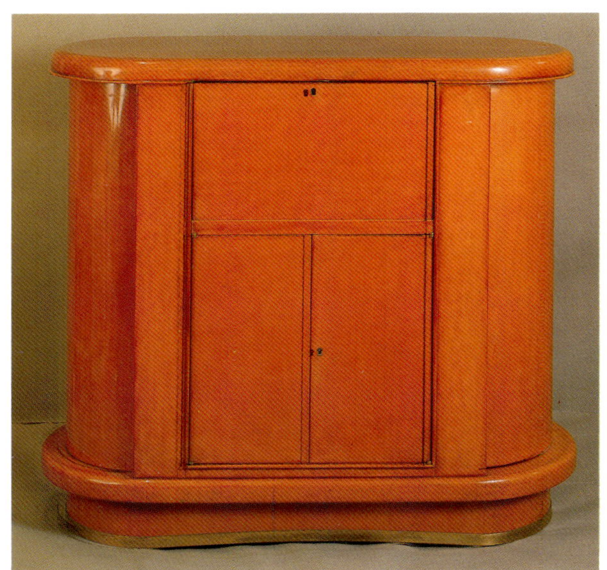

71 **Cocktail bar**, 1937 (*catalogue 524*)

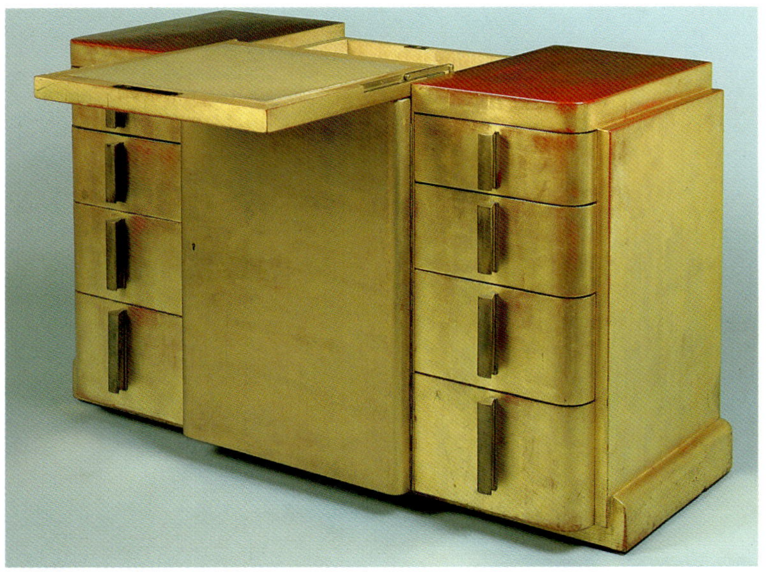

72 **Chest with drawers**, made for Madame Agnès in 1926 (*catalogue 1131*)

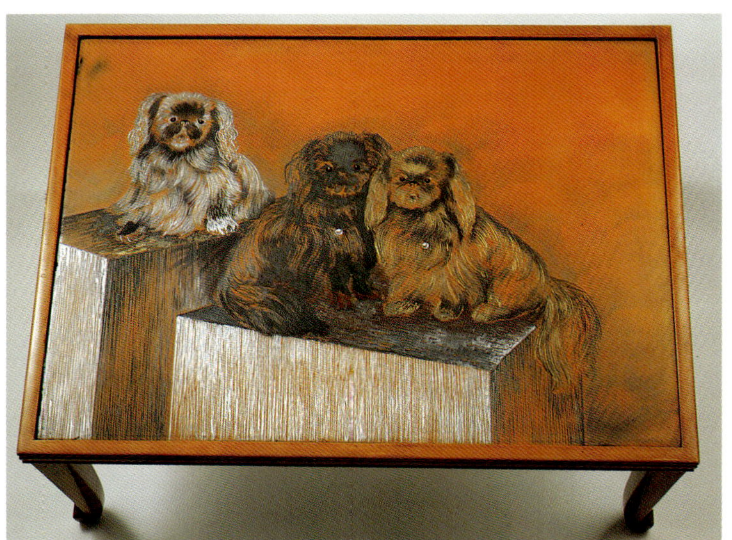

73 **Rectangular occasional table,** *c.* 1928 (*catalogue 439*)

OPPOSITE

74 **Lacquered double door**, *c.* 1925, formerly installed at the entrance to the display room in Dunand's workshops in the Rue Hallé, Paris (*catalogue 561*)

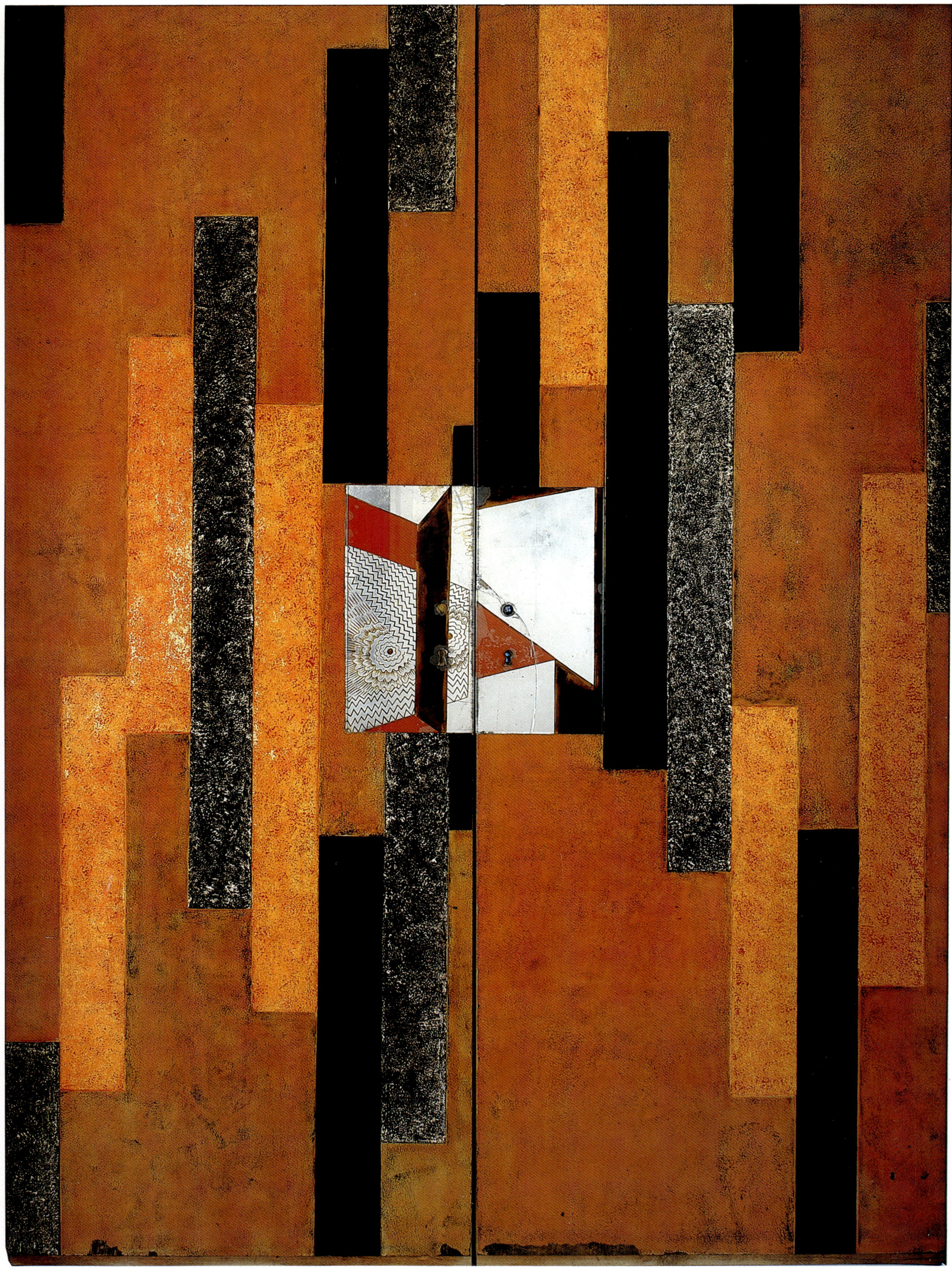

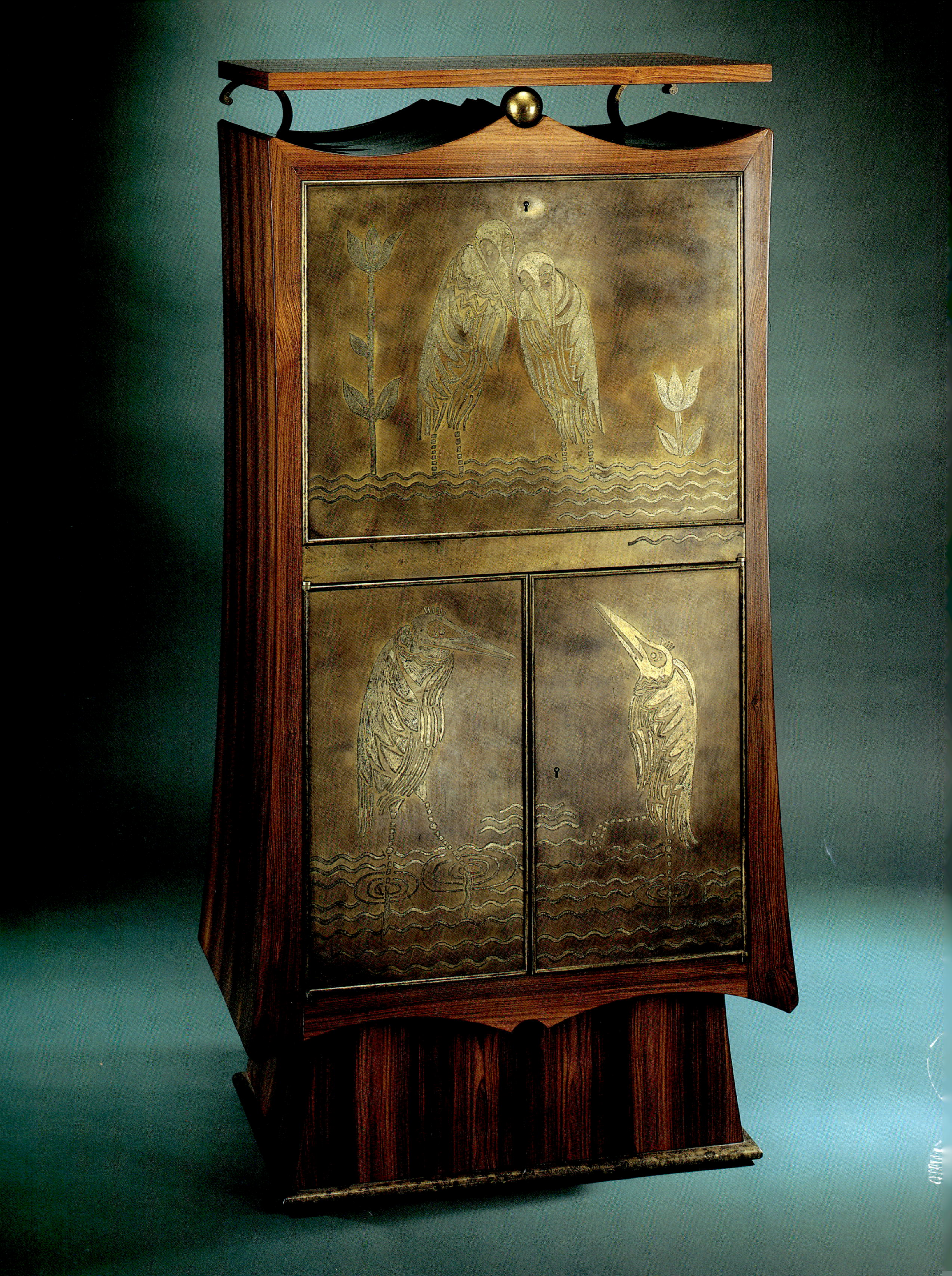

The smoking room for a French Embassy had impressed numerous visitors at the 1925 Exhibition, and subsequently several art lovers, impressed by the aesthetic qualities which the room embodied, placed orders for similar designs, to be adapted to suit their own domestic arrangements. One of the most successful was made for an apartment in the Plaine Monceau in Paris. All the walls were richly clad in wood panelling, with a geometric motif consisting of jagged lines overlapping in shades of matt and shiny silver, while a few touches of colour set off the whole. Some of the engraved motifs even extended across the ceiling to underline the all-enveloping sensation which the design was intended to evoke.

By the same token, the furnishings which Dunand provided for the milliner Madame Agnès in the Rue Saint-Florentin comprised a small boudoir of a refinement that was entirely in keeping with her own designs created for clients. This interior also served as a sort of showcase for Dunand, whose work, by this expedient, became known to all the wealthy customers who visited the salon of Madame Agnès.

Another commission which Dunand had carried out some time earlier was reviewed in the journal *L'Art d'aujourd'hui* in its spring 1927 number. This was designed for the apartment of Madame Henri Labourdette-Debacker and was directly inspired by African statuary, albeit very freely interpreted. Dunand's anthropomorphic chair, reminiscent of those of the Senufo and Korhogo tribes, appeared in many magazine illustrations of the time. In the salon, the chimneypiece was enclosed by three panels with cut-off corners. The frame around the chimney was very simple in form and decorated with a Cubist composition in coloured and eggshell lacquer, in a graphic style of exceptional virtuosity. This extravagant Cubism was marvellously in keeping with the figurative designs on the walls. One of them depicted a child aiming an arrow in the direction of lion cubs which, in fear for their safety, are huddled together. On another panel a little girl cradled an animal that was clearly injured. The overall design was presented against a background of rampant vegetation, its Cubism more restrained than previously, but none the less pervasive. At floor level, surrounded by authentic examples of African furniture, a large vase was conspicuous on account of its heavy black tones. The silver ceiling of *laque arrachée* was lit indirectly, producing a soft light in which the diverse elements blended together.

Dunand's international reputation and his wide-ranging skills led to his appointment as vice-president of the Société des Artistes Décorateurs. He had been offered the presidency, but felt unable to accept it because of his other commitments. The role of vice-president allowed him to take part in all decision-making, without the burden of ensuring its implementation.

Barely six months after the 1925 Exhibition had closed, designers were already eager to demonstrate their enthusiasm for new ideas. The Society's sixteenth Salon was once again a great success. Dunand exhibited a number of mock-antique vases in patinated copper, along with other highly sophisticated pieces in coloured lacquer and eggshell. Additionally, since he was also working on the office interior for Madame Agnès, he exhibited a new portrait of the milliner, an extremely sympathetic likeness showing the sitter wearing a kind of delightfully extravagant African neck ornament.

The exhibition of modern copper and bronze at the Musée Galliéra at the end of June provided further proof of the unrivalled beauty of Dunand's beaten metal vases. He was continuing to assimilate new ideas and still producing surprises with his decorative designs. The majority of his winged vases date from this period, their *appliqué* metal 'wings' seeming to extend the geometrical motifs into space. The ever-increasing size of such vases captivated visitors to exhibitions as much as they impressed art critics, who were at pains to emphasize their beauty and their simplicity and finely balanced forms. 'His silver ornamentation, inlaid into the copper by means of a hammer, has all the restrained elegance of the figures seen on classical pottery,' wrote one critic.

OPPOSITE
75 **Secrétaire**, designed by Eugène Printz, with dinanderie panelled doors by Dunand, *c.* 1935 (*catalogue 551*)

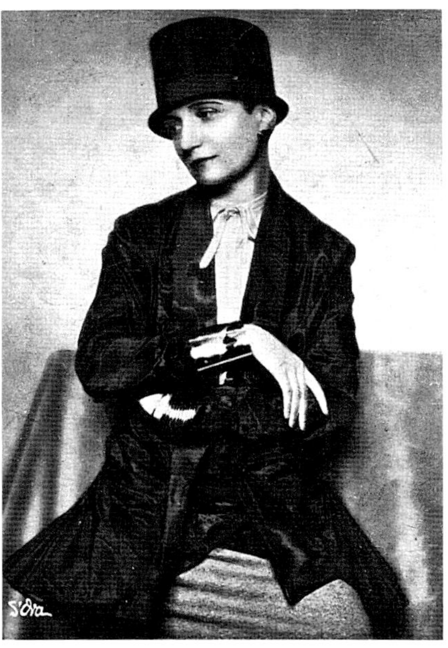

The milliner Madame Agnès photographed by d'Ora in 1926 wearing a hat of her own design and ear-rings and bracelets by Dunand (see cat. no. 736).

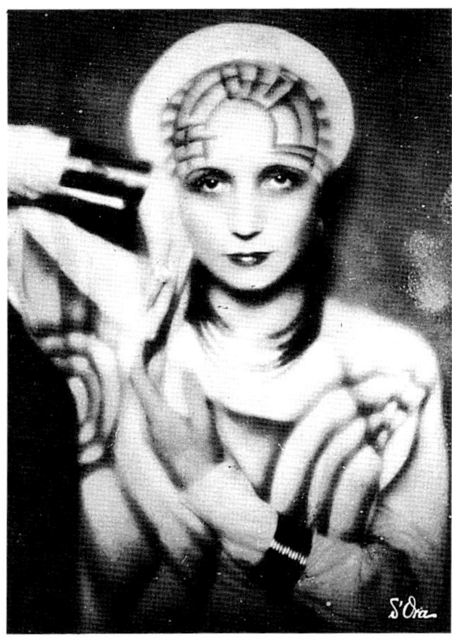

Madame Agnès photographed by d'Ora, 1925 (see cat. no. 732).

In an article published in *L'Illustration* on 1 January 1927, Jacques Baschet asserted that 'Dunand has such a deep understanding of his material that he can bend it at will, drawing from it unsuspected means of expression. He plays with it like a virtuoso, while treating it like a great artist. His style has broadened by becoming simpler. One is astounded by the inventive genius which enters into the ornamentation of his lacquered screens. For here is an art of reflection and of contemplation that leads us back to the art of great craftsmen from the past. They never possessed sufficient learning to be able to express what their thoughts and souls had so long nurtured.'

Dunand's work was already considered a sort of national heritage, and his involvement in the Salon d'Automne gave rise to harsh criticism of those imitators and plagiarists who shamelessly exhibited their work beside Dunand's, copying his forms, his ornamentation and his very materials. Every stand was crammed with *bonbonnières*, cigarette-cases, powder-compacts, vanity bags, matchboxes and jewel-boxes, all in black and red lacquer and highlighted with eggshell. 'That there are trends and fashions which are adopted by people with no creative personality is one thing, but purely and simply to copy what a clever person has invented and even to copy the basic details of a novel formula would deserve the fullest exposure.' Dunand was too modest, however, and was prepared to take a relaxed view of it all, considering, not without reason, that here was the reverse side of success. Leaving his rivals to go on copying his work, he preferred to try his hand at something different, and by so doing to offer his public new surprises and to afford others the material they might need, were they themselves to diversify.

That year Dunand was the subject of a one-man show on the premises of the Brussels jewellers, Wolfers Frères. This combination was all the more interesting in that, quite apart from the fact that Marcel Wolfers and Jean Dunand were friends of long standing, the former also worked in lacquer. For several years he had been combining it with wood for household objects or fancy jewellery. Although the processes each used were completely different, the results were just as spectacular in each case: Dunand favoured ornamentation and formal contrasts, while Wolfers was essentially interested in the effects created by different aspects of various materials, even seeking to emulate the veinings of semiprecious stones and the colours of certain glazes on Chinese and Japanese pottery.

The annual group exhibition at the Galerie Georges Petit once again took place in the main hall, itself more accustomed to the sound of the auctioneer's hammer. This year the exhibition had an air of exotic grandeur, typified by the presence of a large composition by Jouve depicting an elephant (the theme was later used by Dunand on a lacquered panel). In addition to a handful of portraits, including one of Josephine Baker, Dunand's exhibits comprised seventeen screens, all the subject of praise for their imaginative treatment and as examples of good taste. On backgrounds of red or black lacquer, monkeys chased each other or swung from creeper to creeper; elsewhere flocks of birds darted like arrows across silver-streaked skies. On other panels fish swam idly by, tracing luminous paths in the watery depths of a silver sea. Other motifs included rabbits, ducks, sparrows, deer, fantastic beasts, gazelles and dogs, as well as African wildlife, all silhouetted against luxuriant landscapes, while never detracting from neighbouring panels with their resplendent moonlight effects or pounding waves. Dunand's contribution was by far the most significant and most spectacular. It was also the most successful, amusing and witty. It seemed almost as if the other members of the group had suddenly realized they could no longer compete with him. Nonetheless, this meticulous, not to say over-fastidious, execution seems not to have pleased all the critics, some of whom bemoaned the absence of 'stimulating imperfections'.

An exhibition was subsequently staged in New York in a gallery made available by Jacques Seligmann with the aim of introducing Dunand's work to Americans who had not visited Paris. For New York's critics his work epitomized the expression of traditional French taste and refinement. A large vertical panel decorated with exotic fish was widely reproduced in the

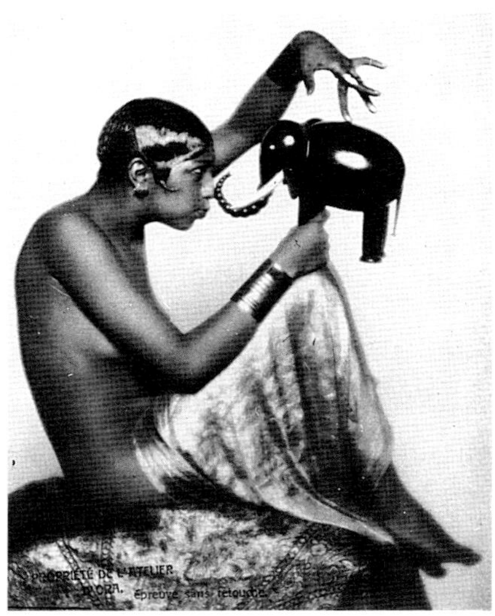

The entertainer Josephine Baker photographed by d'Ora wearing wide bracelets by Dunand, *c.* 1927.

newspapers. The Americans showed their appreciation by inviting Dunand to return for another one-man show.

From 1927 onwards Dunand was president of the dinanderie class at the Exposition Nationale du Travail, an exhibition at which an annual prize was awarded to the 'Best Craftsman in France'.

Appearing with the French delegation at the International Exhibition in Madrid in 1927, Dunand won a first prize. This success was confirmed by the outstanding quality of his stand at the Salon des Artistes Décorateurs in Paris the following June. It was a triumph for lacquer, since not only was the imagination displayed in his decorative work highly appreciated, but also the close link between craftsmanship and art. Benefiting from a pleasant setting, his stand was designed as a small boudoir with arched partitions, open along its longest side. Above the opening a sort of moulding underlined the cross-bar with strips of black lacquered wood in a triangular arrangement resembling organ pipes. This motif was extended to the back of the stand by means of other slats 1 m (3 ft 3 in.) in height.

Around a carpet, woven by Evelyn Wyld to a design by Dunand, were arranged four of his screens. Their decoration reflected the dominant theme of concentric circles and scattered triangles in the carpet's design. The screen on the left showed, panel by panel, migratory birds in flight within large rectangles of silver leaf superimposed on a black-lacquer background. The centrepiece was a large four-panel screen on which were developed two quadrilaterals positioned diagonally and laid out in concentric lines that traced out a multitude of finely etched squares. With its graphic style of design and positioned so as to show off the carpet, it seemed to extend the geometric theme into space. The third screen, to the right, had 'all the solemn humour of a page from a book by Kipling': against the outline of a treeless hill, ibexes advanced warily. At the foot of the screen, and shrouded in darkness, lurked a large tiger, watching their progress in studied anticipation of his next meal. The fourth screen, the smallest, was decorated with a geometric design. On the right-hand wall was a lacquer portrait of Josephine Baker, the skin tones revealing a degree of fantasy and inventiveness.

At the centre stood a low round double-topped table in silver *laque arrachée*, on which stood a vase with a geometric design. On each side was a small armchair with rounded back and a telescopic foot identical in design to the central table, complementing an ensemble to welcome the visitor or prospective purchaser. On the far right, in front of a gondola-backed armchair in shellac, was another small table. Its square top, with cut-off corners, was covered with a splendid eggshell design on a background of black lacquer alternating with red motifs. To the left and right of the entrance, in the angle of intersection, were two large columns with geometric bases, and on each of them was placed a large vase, 92 cm (3 ft) in height. Their necks consisted of a series of recessed bands. Inlaid with patinated silver, the vases were somehow reminiscent of funerary urns.

This interior was at once the most sober and the most subtle that Dunand ever designed. Without being austere or precious, it simply felt perfect and right. It seems to have marked the furthest point of development in Dunand's handling of this type of decorative scheme. What else could he now do but denounce such a useless and vulgar geometric style which had no future, so unsuccessful had attempts been by other interior designers to exploit it? One can understand Dunand's decision to abandon this geometric style and to move more and more in the direction of figurative designs. And one understands how fashions succumb if nothing useful emerges from them. A mere proliferation of triangles and circles could lead only to boredom, and eggshell now figured everywhere, on boxes, screens, footstools, tables and trays. Everyone used it quite shamelessly, including Gaston Suisse, Gérard Sandoz, Jean Fouquet or Raymond Templier. So, too, did Damg-Bui and Nguyen Hop, two artists who had come to Paris from Indo-China to cope with increasing demand, not to mention Dunand's former craftsmen who had set up on their own, having learned their employer's decorative formulas.

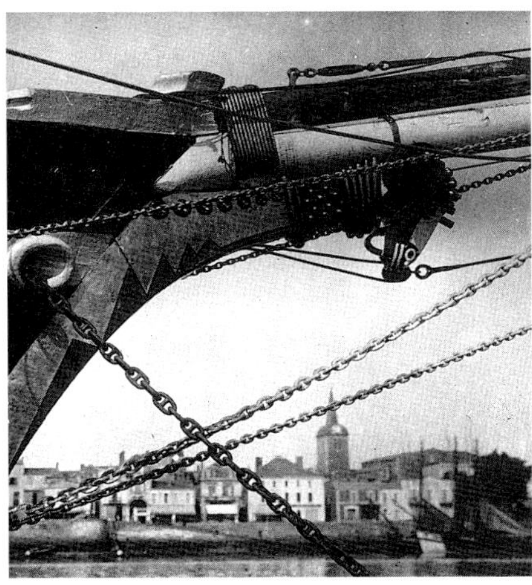

The prow of François-Louis Schmied's boat *Peau-Brune*, moored at Saint-Nazaire, 1927; the carving and lacquer decoration on wood and metal were by Dunand.

Also at this Salon des Artistes Décorateurs, Émile-Jacques Ruhlmann's stand included a most elegant screen of engraved glass, based on designs by Boileau and Cabrière and mounted on a wrought-iron frame made by Jean Prouvé – an original collaboration. To one side of this screen stood a dressing table by Ruhlmann lacquered by Dunand. A sort of eggshell tablecloth appeared to slip from the table in a subtle sliding movement, and on it stood a silvered bronze mirror, contrasting with the overall black-lacquer effect and reflecting the central motif. The dressing table had been designed by Ruhlmann and built in his studio, before being decorated to Dunand's own design in his workshop. A full-scale model of the piece had been made and shown to the client before being finished in lacquer and eggshell.

For Dunand the summer of 1927 was the occasion for a cruise on the yacht *Peau-Brune* that François-Louis Schmied had bought and for which the interior fittings had been designed and partly lacquered by Dunand. Its prow represented a ram's head in wood and metal designed, carved and lacquered in his workshops. Together with several crew members, Schmied, Dunand and Dunand's daughter Alix embarked at Les Sables d'Olonne, near Saint-Nazaire. They sailed around Spain, then along the Mediterranean coast, calling at various ports before arriving at La Ciotat, east of Marseilles. Each port of call and each creek provided a pretext for photography and painting watercolours. Schmied kept a logbook which was published in 1931 with illustrations of the most picturesque locations. Several years later, just before his departure for Algeria and Morocco on 25 January 1933, the by then bankrupt Schmied decided to sell his boat, as he indicated to Dunand on a postcard sent on that date. He had held on to it to the bitter end, in the hope that his luck would turn. Unhappily, the financial crisis which followed the collapse of the New York stock market in 1929, together with Schmied's extravagant expenses and the mismanagement of his affairs, prevented him from ever regaining his former affluence. Having reached his destination, in the region of Marrakech, Schmied wrote in a letter to Dunand, 'It is no good looking elsewhere for heavenly beauty and peace. I vow that, if God grants me life, I shall bring you here ... Your Louis.' He never kept this promise, however, for he died at Tahanaout in 1941 following an illnesss which had all the signs of self-induced poisoning. He had broken with his family and was living on an army pension, selling the occasional painting in an attempt to pay off his debt to Gustave Miklos for their earlier collaborations.

At the end of 1927, Dunand participated, as he had done practically every winter since its inception, in the eleventh annual exhibition of the Artistes Français Contemporains at the Galerie Rouard. At about the same time, examples of his work were shown at the Galerie Moullot in Marseilles, together with pottery by the well-known ceramicist Jean Mayodon; and he also sent numerous pieces to San Francisco for an exhibition of French decorative art sponsored by the French government. His works shown in this exhibition and the reputation which he had acquired in the U.S.A. in well-to-do circles on the East Coast enabled him some months later to win an important interior decoration commission from Templeton Croker, a multi-millionaire from San Francisco.

At the same time, a small panel entitled *St Michael and the Dragon*, together with two double doors and two screens entitled *Crescendo* and *Pianissimo*, depicting the angels being cast out of paradise, were exhibited at the Reinhardt Gallery in New York. They were the work of Séraphin Soudbinine, a sculptor of Russian extraction who had been living in Paris since the early 1920s. This was not Soudbinine's first encounter with Dunand, for they had worked together in 1921, when, in the section of the Salon d'Automne devoted to Russian artists, Soudbinine had entered an *Angel of Sorrows* carved in wood and lacquered by Dunand. The whole of this installation was destined for the music room of Mr and Mrs Solomon R. Guggenheim in their home in Port Washington, Long Island, N.Y. Executed in a shade of duck-egg blue, it was further enlivened by the use of pieces of eggshell, mother-of-pearl and burgaudine with an iridescent sheen.

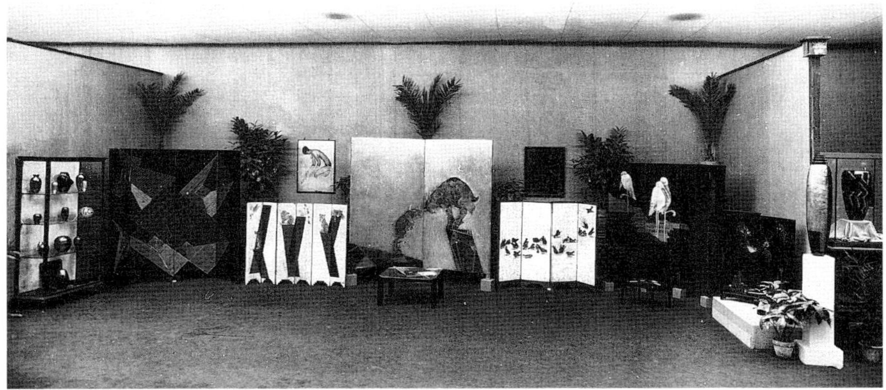

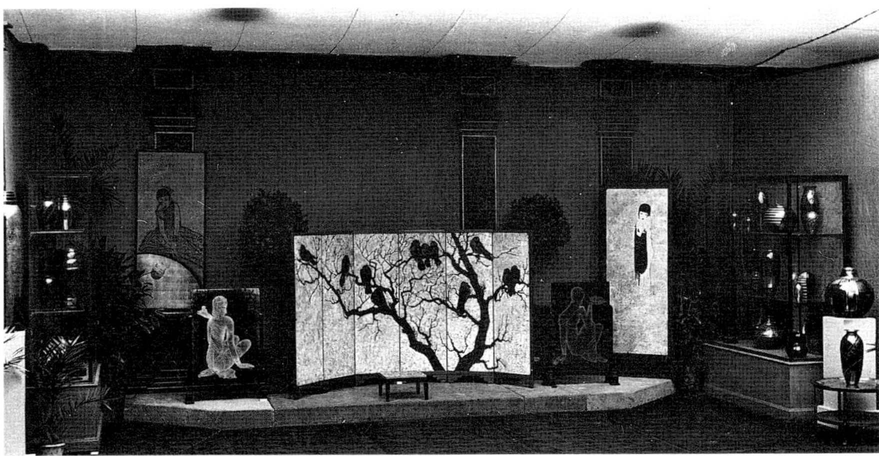

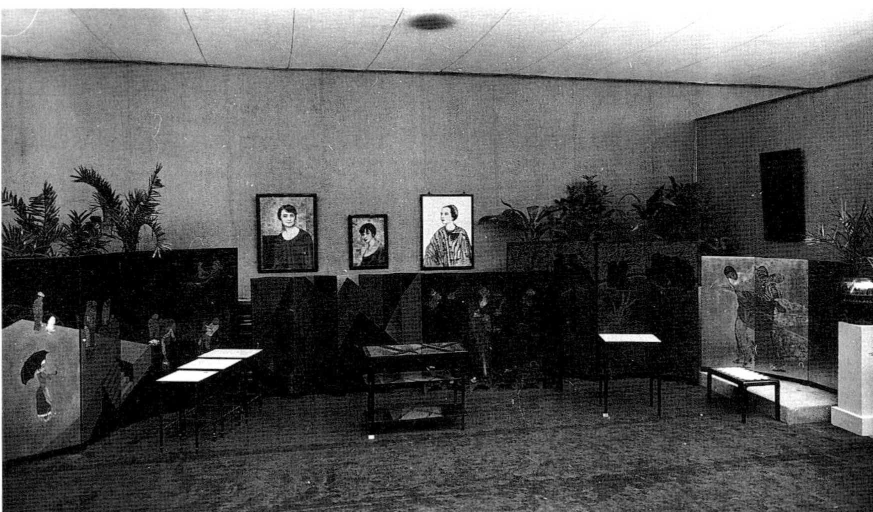

The exhibition at the Galerie Georges Petit, December 1927: three views showing a selection of screens, firescreens, portraits, furniture and vases by Dunand.

Likewise in 1927, Dunand collaborated with a group of French artists on the interior design of the liner *Ile de France*. The main participants were Louis Süe, André Mare, Ruhlmann and Leleu for the murals, Sandoz and Dunand for utilitarian articles, and René Lalique and Henri Navarre for the light fittings and glass sculptures. Although the arrangement was very simple, the opulence of the ornamentation and the extraordinary variety of materials used on this vessel were a foretaste of the splendours that would later be seen on the liners *L'Atlantique* and *Normandie*.

The year ended with the usual group exhibition at the Galerie Georges Petit. Among the works that attracted attention was a lacquered panel entitled *The Mirror*, depicting a young woman seated on the edge of a pool. The industrialist who commissioned the portrait subsequently asked Dunand

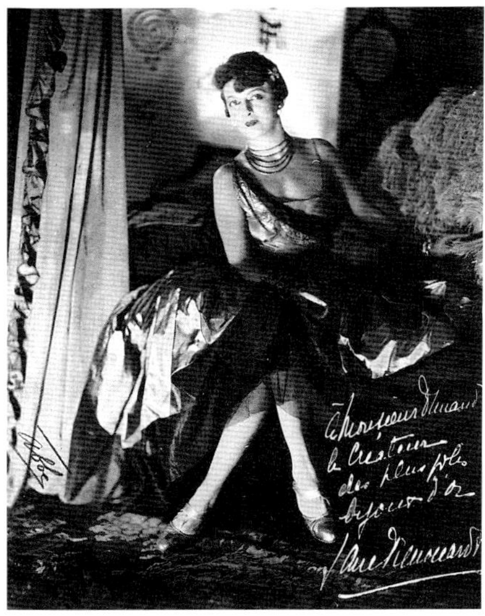

The actress Jane Renouardt, seen wearing necklaces by Dunand in 1927, dedicated this photograph of herself to the artist.

to execute a second version, altering the subject's features from those of his first wife (whom he had since divorced) and substituting a likeness of his equally attractive new partner. What this somewhat bizarre anecdote demonstrates is the great attachment this man felt towards Dunand's lacquer painting. Another lacquered panel showed Josephine Baker, her body covered only by a transparent fabric. Had she not, after all, posed naked in the master's studio, where the artist's son Bernard had the thrill of watching the proceedings, while concealed behind a partition? Since Bernard was the only member of the family able to speak English, he was also responsible for accompanying Josephine Baker by taxi from her apartment in the Avenue Pierre-Ier-de-Serbie to the Rue Hallé. Besides these pieces, rich in anecdotal associations, there were a beautiful cheval-glass and numerous tables and chairs, as well as a handful of other portraits and no fewer than thirteen screens. One of these, showing Breton fishermen silhouetted against a jetty, was based on a sketch by Jean Lambert-Rucki, although the latter's name did not appear in the catalogue. The other screens featured monkeys, rams, fish, ducks, crows, swans, doves, sparrows, herons and frogs, each portrayed with a lively realism.

Despite this clear move away from geometric design, one screen dating from the previous year proved to be the most beautiful of its kind: small in size, with six panels, it was lacquered all over in red and black, and, in its style of composition, it remains the most accomplished example of Dunand's ability to integrate geometrical forms with the decorative aims of the times. Also on this occasion, not having found any buyers for the two large vases he had exhibited at the previous Salon des Artistes Décorateurs, Dunand re-exhibited them, and this time found a buyer, the actress Jane Renouardt.

In the weeks before Christmas, Dunand designed his first poster for a recital by the pianist (and later composer) Dimitri Tiomkin at the Théâtre National de l'Opéra de Paris. Although fascinated by the task, he tried his hand only rarely at graphic work, preferring to leave it to other, more skilled exponents.

On 28 February 1928, Josephine Baker gave her first 'farewell' concert. This was an astute move, repeated, much to her public's delight, on many later occasions. This typically Parisian soirée took place at the Salle Pleyel before a capacity audience. The stage was surrounded by large screens, some gilt, others painted with brightly coloured flowers, while tall black vases completed the decor, their silver geometric motifs highlighted with mother-of-pearl. A jazz group, 'Jacob's Band', opened the proceedings, which included Jean Wiéner and Clément Doucet on two pianos playing popular pieces like Ray Henderson's 'Black Bottom' and Gershwin's 'The Man I Love'. During the interval Josephine planned to auction the special programme designed and illustrated throughout by Dunand, the proceeds to be donated to charity. Inside the programme were several original drawings of the artiste. Her nudity was barely veiled by diaphanous silks painted in lacquer by Dunand. A few ill-mannered whistles halted the auction and put paid to her generous gesture. The result was a bonus for the audience, for the singer did not hestitate for a moment to tell them with typical candour and in her amusing accent, what she thought of the disturbance. All the same, the second half of the evening's entertainment began in an atmosphere of general good humour.

Also in 1928, the directors of the New York store Lord & Taylor decided to hold a major exhibition of French decorative art. The exhibits were intended to create entire rooms, or else to be displayed for sale here and there within the store's various departments. Every branch of the decorative arts was represented, the selection process being operated with greater or lesser success by the organizers. The exhibition was opened by Paul Claudel, the French ambassador to the United States. The twenty-four items which Dunand sent comprised five screens, eighteen vases, a tray and some furniture. The majority of his works benefited from being shown as a group in a small corner room. At the centre was the screen depicting a deer, first

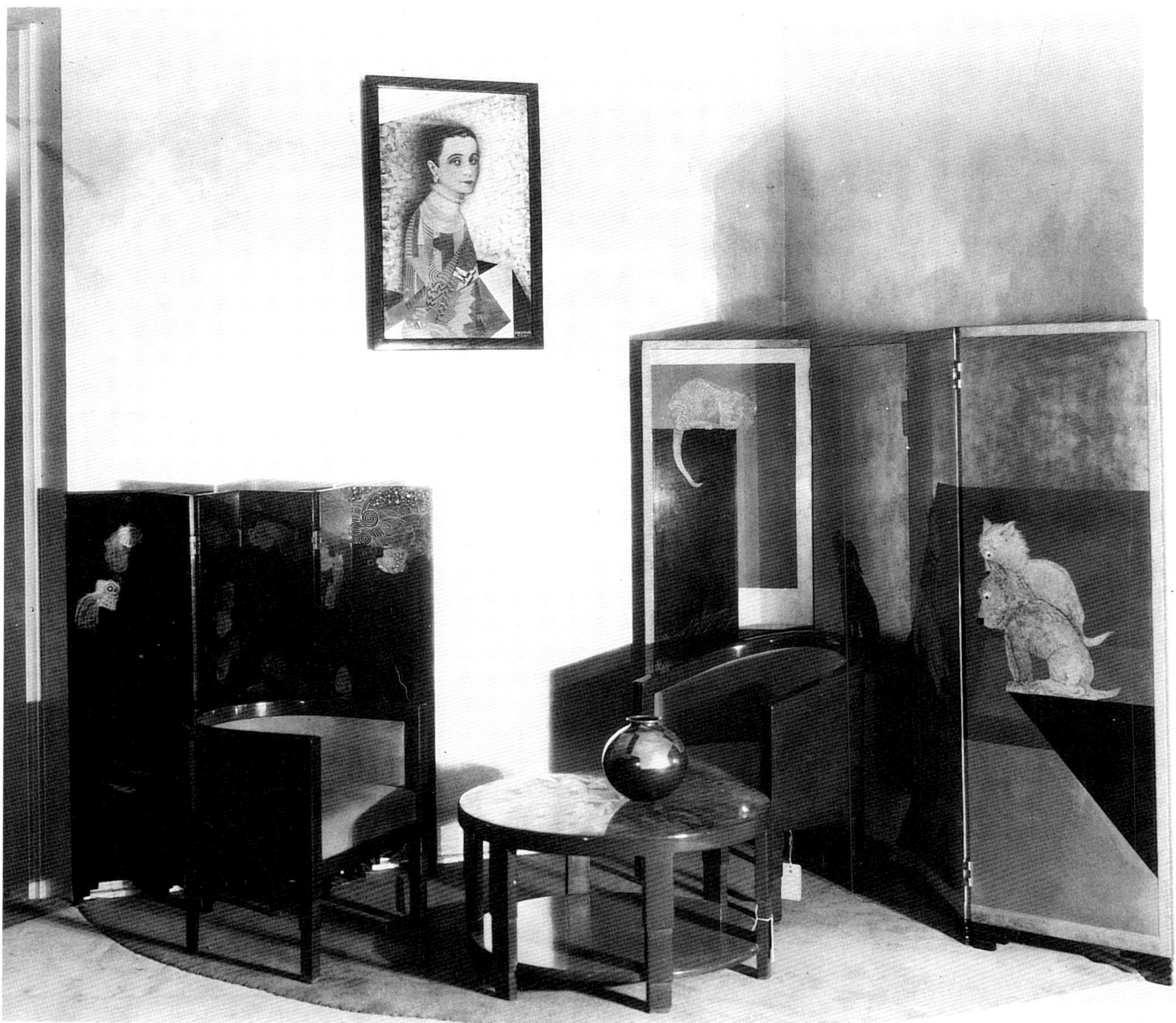

Works by Dunand displayed in the Lord & Taylor exhibition, New York, 1928, included a lacquer portrait of Madame Agnès.

seen at the 1923 Salon; around it was ranged a series of columns, placed in recesses and supporting his lacquered vases with geometric designs. A low couch and a circular twin-pedestal table completed this display. In one corner, a screen decorated with Japanese fish and a vertical panel with the same motif stood in curious contrast with another screen covered with fantastic animals. A low circular red-lacquered table and two armchairs, similar in design to those exhibited at the 1927 Salon des Artistes Décorateurs, stood at the front of a sort of dais. Here and there, vases were dotted around on the tables, while a portrait of Madame Agnès and several firescreens completed the scene.

Planned with the aim of encouraging American artists to adopt a similar creative line, the exhibition sought to convince the public of the desirability of choosing contemporary art in designing their home interiors. It proved a huge success, with some 16,000 visitors, and a considerable number of the pieces displayed were sold. Unfortunately, this success was not universally applauded, least of all by the American trade unions which, through nationalist reaction or real anxiety, fomented and orchestrated a campaign of vilification in the local press. With a somewhat surprising lack of honesty, numerous newspaper articles denounced the 'old-fashioned European style' of the majority of the exhibits, labelling them insipid or even vulgar. Pieces by Helen Johnson Keyes in the *Christian Science Monitor*, by Peter Small in

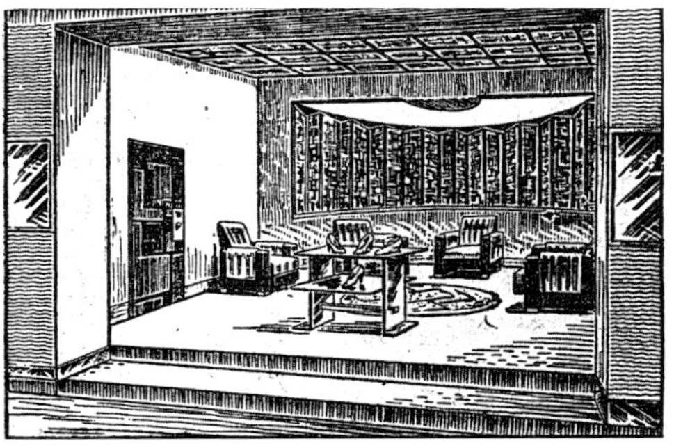

The Bally shoe shop in Paris, 1928, designed by Robert Mallet-Stevens, with an internal door lacquered by Dunand with a geometric design.

Creative Art, and an anonymous article in *The American Architect* of 5 March 1928 all included judgments which posterity has not seen fit to endorse. Ruhlmann was denounced for a dining room showing 'very little taste', despite the inclusion of one of his masterpieces, the famous 'trolley' chest of drawers in Macassar ebony. As for the bedroom by Süe and Mare, critics considered, tongue in cheek, that it was the ideal present for a disagreeable man to offer his 'beautiful but hated mistress'. Nor were the desk by Robert Mallet-Stevens, the chairs upholstered with tapestries by Jean Lurçat, Jacques Lipchitz's sculptures and Chareau's wall lamps in alabaster and metal (nowadays much sought after) exempt from the wholesale carnage. Yet, by an extraordinary stroke of good fortune, Dunand escaped denunciation, perhaps because of his links with the firm of Rodier (which distributed his lacquered fabrics in the United States), or possibly because his work was already known and therefore easier to accept. This exhibition also included a number of works by American artists. Arranged in five rooms on the first floor of the store, they in fact found favour in the eyes of American critics. Some items, however, particularly bedside lamps in the shape of skyscrapers, would have been better suited to stalls at a fun fair. All the same, despite journalistic criticism, the French exhibitors were delighted with the response of the general public.

At about the same time, an exhibition of some 150 portraits of women was held in Paris at the Galerie La Renaissance in the Rue Royale. Works by artists ranging from Ingres to Picasso were shown grouped together, with no attempt at chronological presentation. On this occasion Dunand exhibited a handful of lacquer portraits, but critics considered, not without reason, that he had little to gain from such participation. The stilted appearance and lack of nuance in portraits executed in this medium was all the more apparent when contrasted with the versatility of oil paint. Seen beside Corot's *La Belle Italienne* or Manet's *Madame de Chavannes*, Dunand's portraits had little chance of scoring a major success.

On 3 April 1928, M. Delsol, President of the Paris City Council, and M. Bokanowski, Minister of Trade, opened the new Bally shoe shop in the Boulevard de la Madeleine. The architect, Robert Mallet-Stevens, had designed the façade in an entirely new way, covering it all over with nickel-plated metal plates held in place by regularly spaced bolts. In its general appearance the façade bore a curious resemblance to the armour plating used for hulls of ships, a 'modernist' interpretation which could well shock the observer. In fact, this daring innovation was intended to show off a small and very narrow display window in which Bally shoes were presented as so many treasures.

A bronze door highlighted in gilt gave access to a large room divided towards the back by a tiered landing. The interplay of volumes was further accentuated by the architect's handling of surfaces. The walls were a lightly tinted shade of white, and the plaster had been engraved with a zigzag motif. With their harmonious sense of geometry, Dunand's lacquered doors were scarcely in keeping with Foujita's mawkish compositions; several of these adorned the walls, their detailed brushwork providing a marvellous match with the splendid stained-glass window, based on a design by Le Chevalier and made by Barillet, which was situated at the rear. It resembled a kind of apse, diffusing a subtle radiance with no apparent source of light. The seats were by Francis Jourdain, the materials by Hélène Henry, their modernism matching perfectly the general spirit of the interior. There was a striking contrast between the sober and luminous elegance within and the idea of force and power expressed by the frontage. As a whole, the scheme represented the best possible blend of the art of advertising, use of available space, and handling of colour. There is no doubt that this shop was a significant contribution to the Parisian scene, and one can only regret the firm's later decision to demolish their marvel of urban architecture and to replace it with a banal boutique with large windows better suited to modern retailing.

Plates 76–106

JEWELLERY, BOXES, TRAYS AND OTHER HOUSEHOLD ITEMS

OPPOSITE

76 **Neck-rings** decorated with lacquered geometric motifs, 1927 (*catalogue* 677)

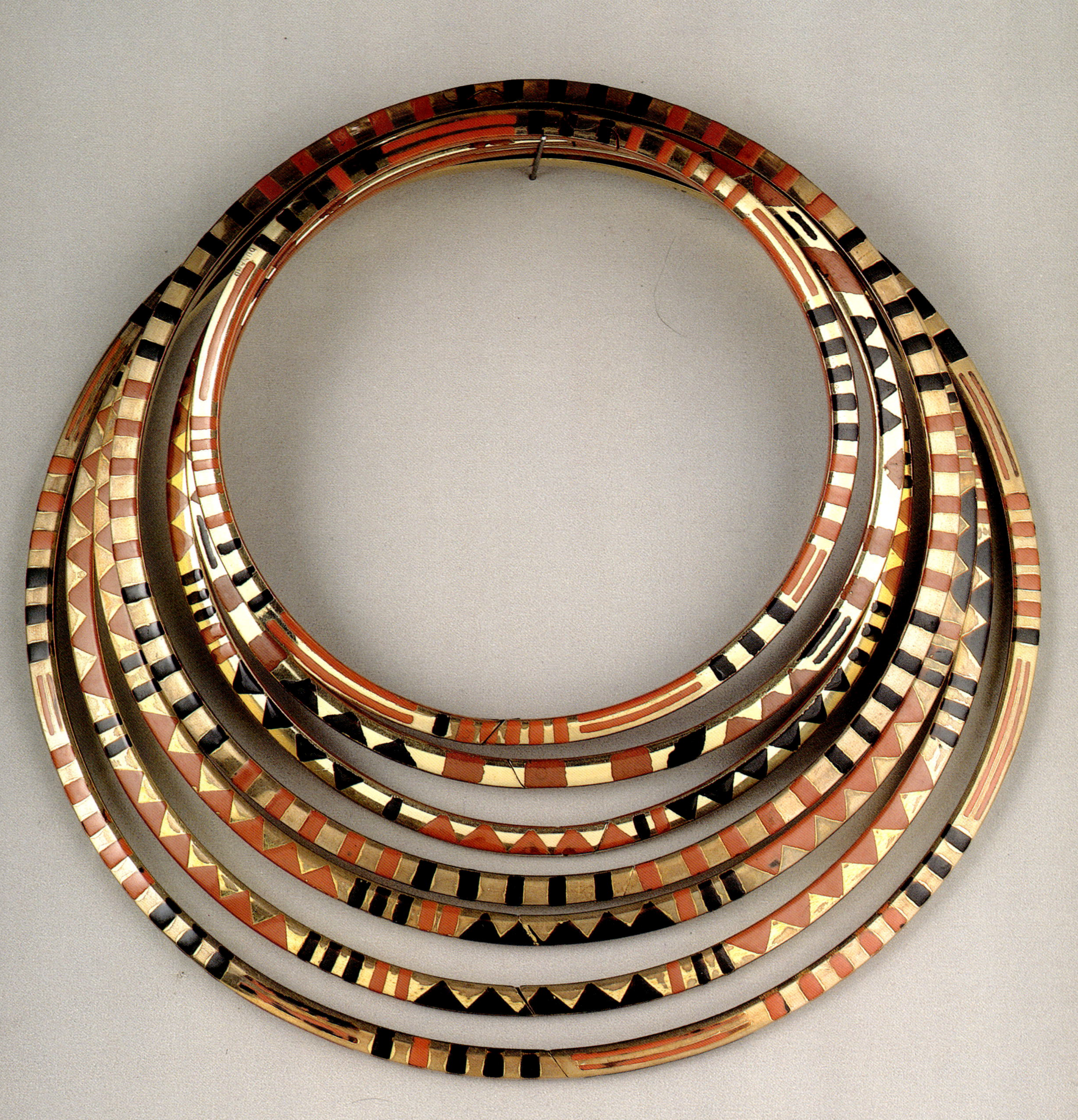

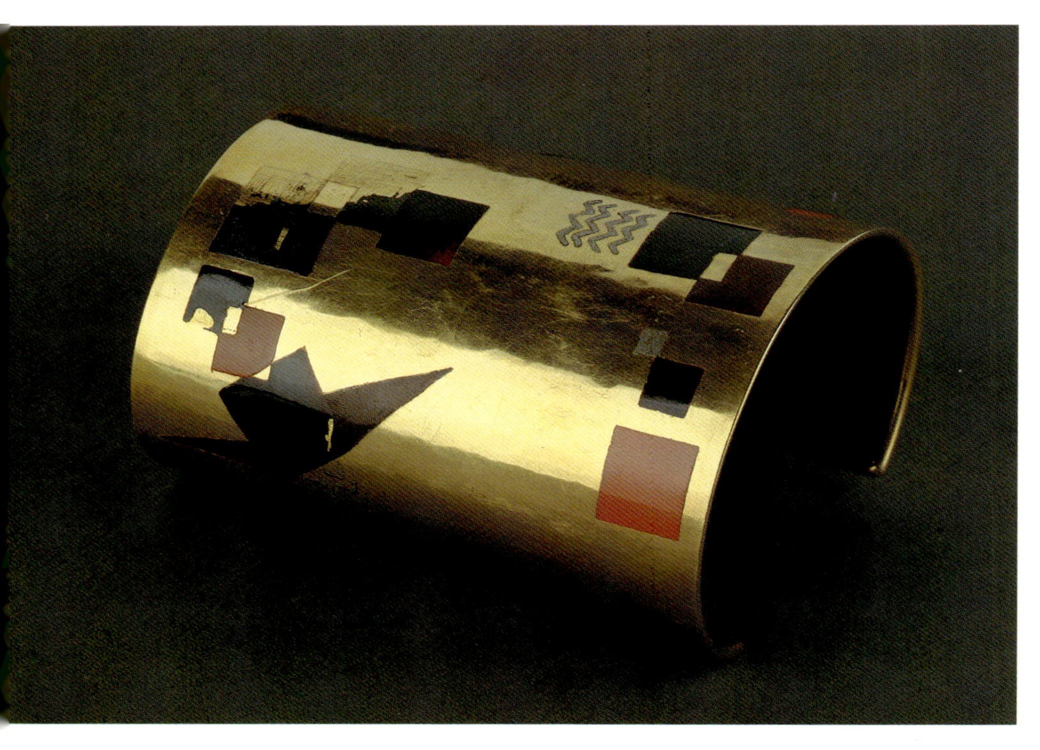

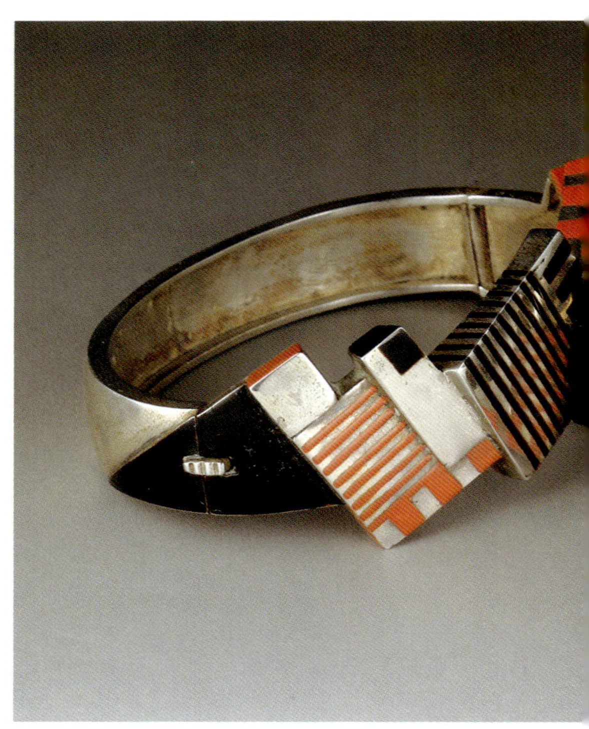

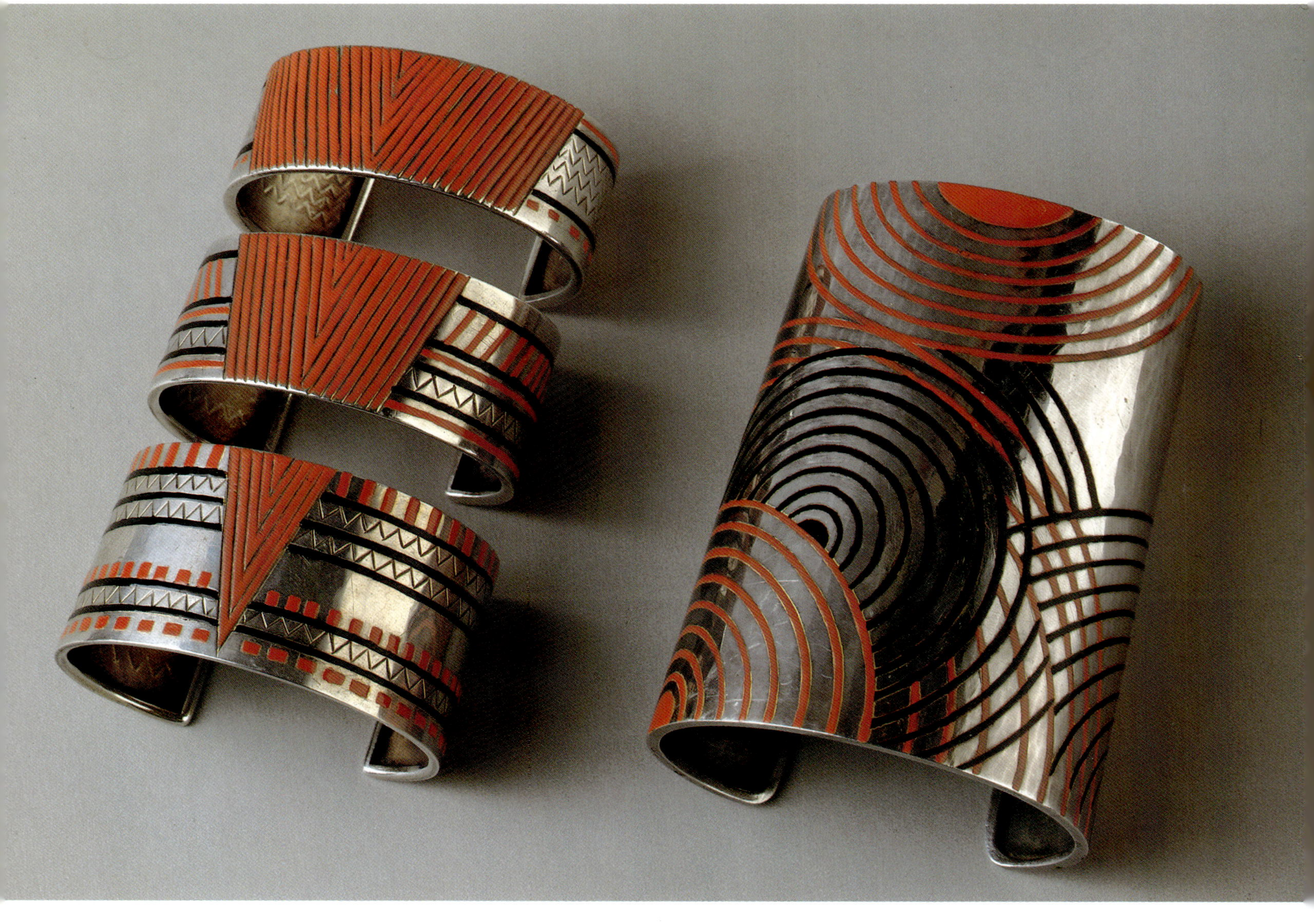

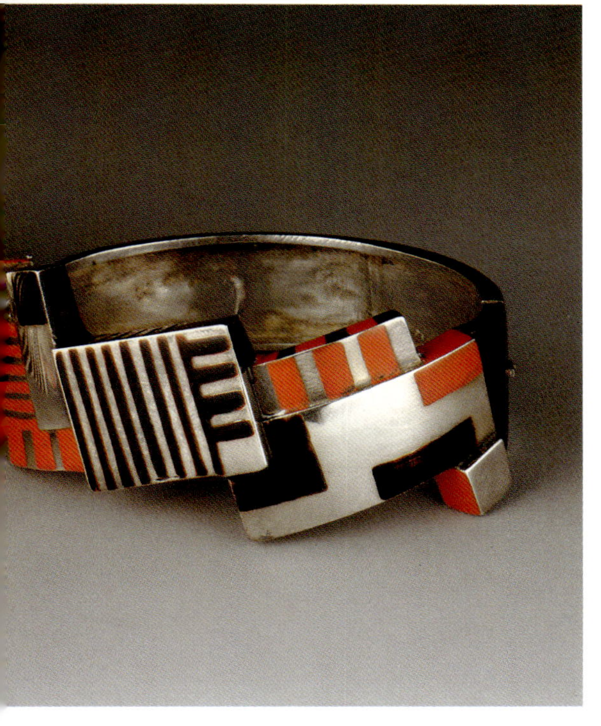

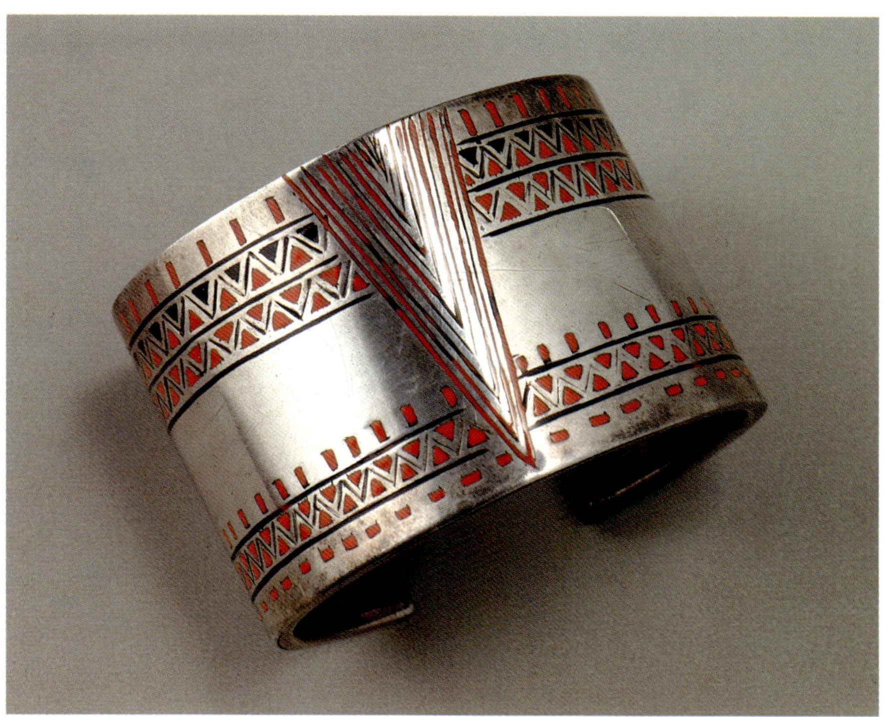

ABOVE LEFT
77 **Wide bracelet,** lacquered oroide, 1928 (*catalogue 684*)

ABOVE
78 **Pair of silver bracelets** with lacquered geometric motifs, *c.* 1924 (*catalogue 679*)

79 **Wide bracelets,** lacquered silver, 1927 (*catalogue 683*)

80 **Wide bracelet**, lacquered silver, *c.* 1925 (*catalogue 681*)

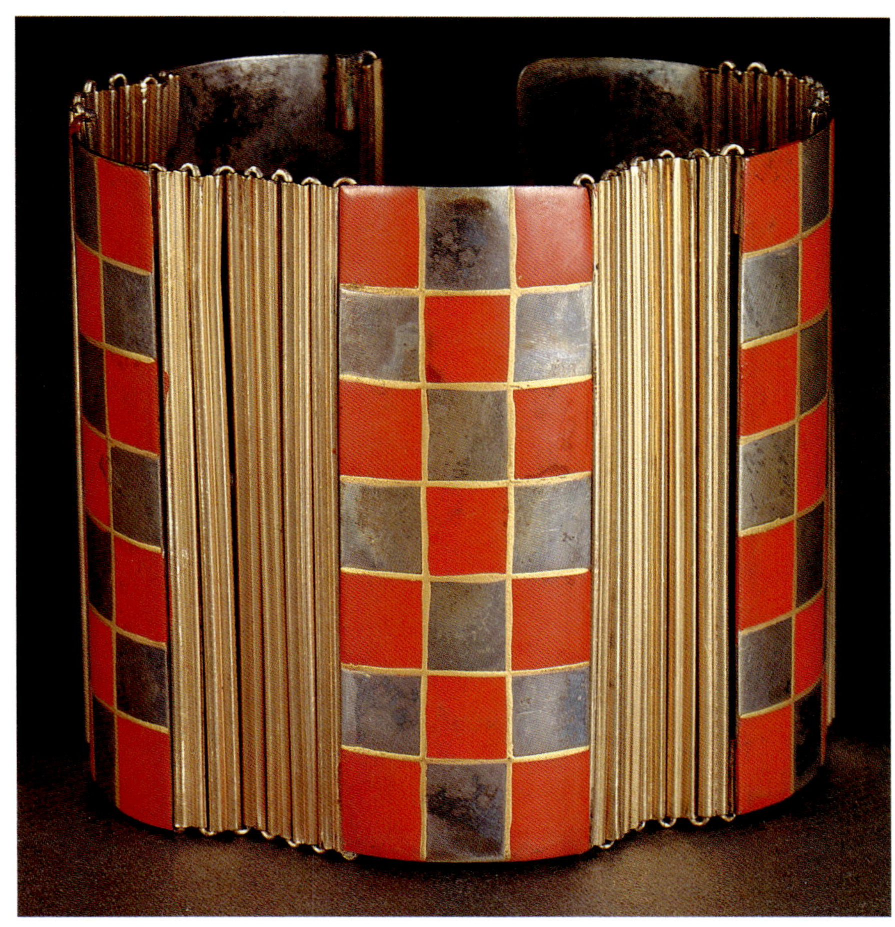

81 **Articulated bracelet**, silver and gilt with lacquered decoration, *c.* 1922 (*catalogue 685*)

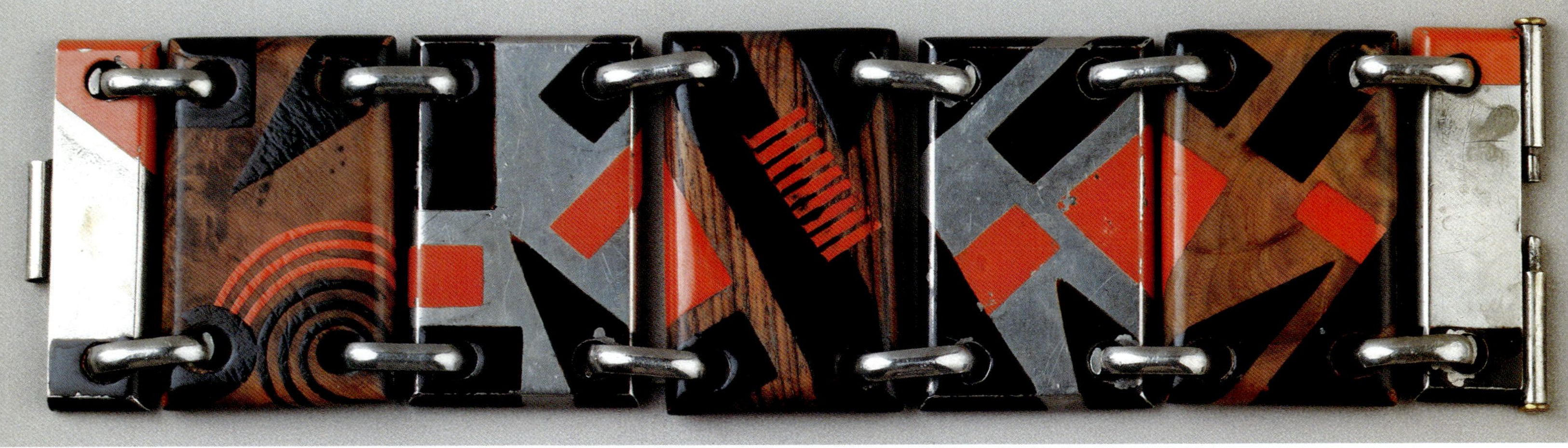

82 **Articulated bracelet** (open), wood and silver with lacquered decoration, *c.* 1930 (*catalogue 686*)

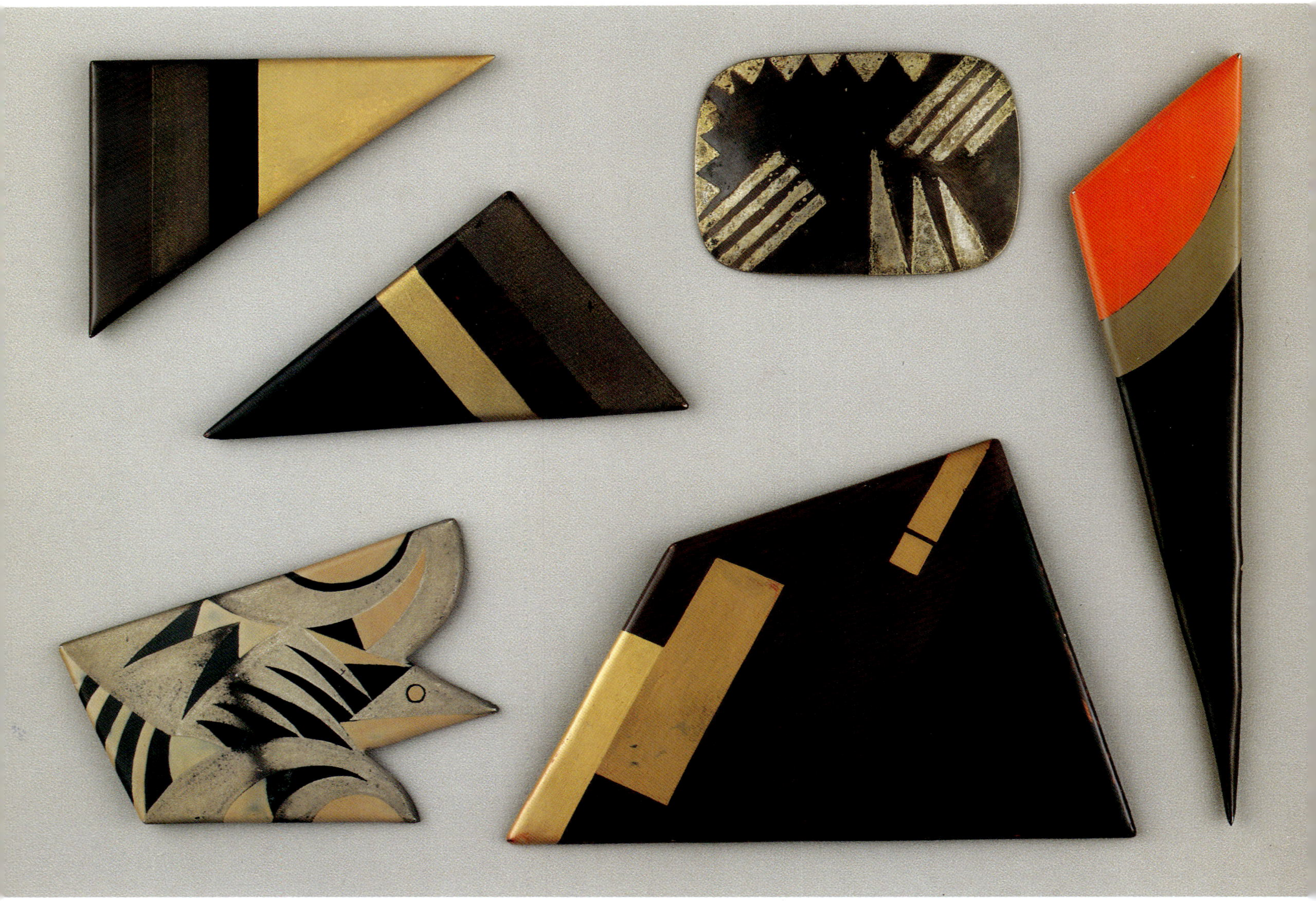

83 **Group of collar ornaments and shoe-buckles**, 1925 (*catalogue 698*)

OPPOSITE

84 **Group of ear-rings and other items**, 1925 (*catalogue 688*)

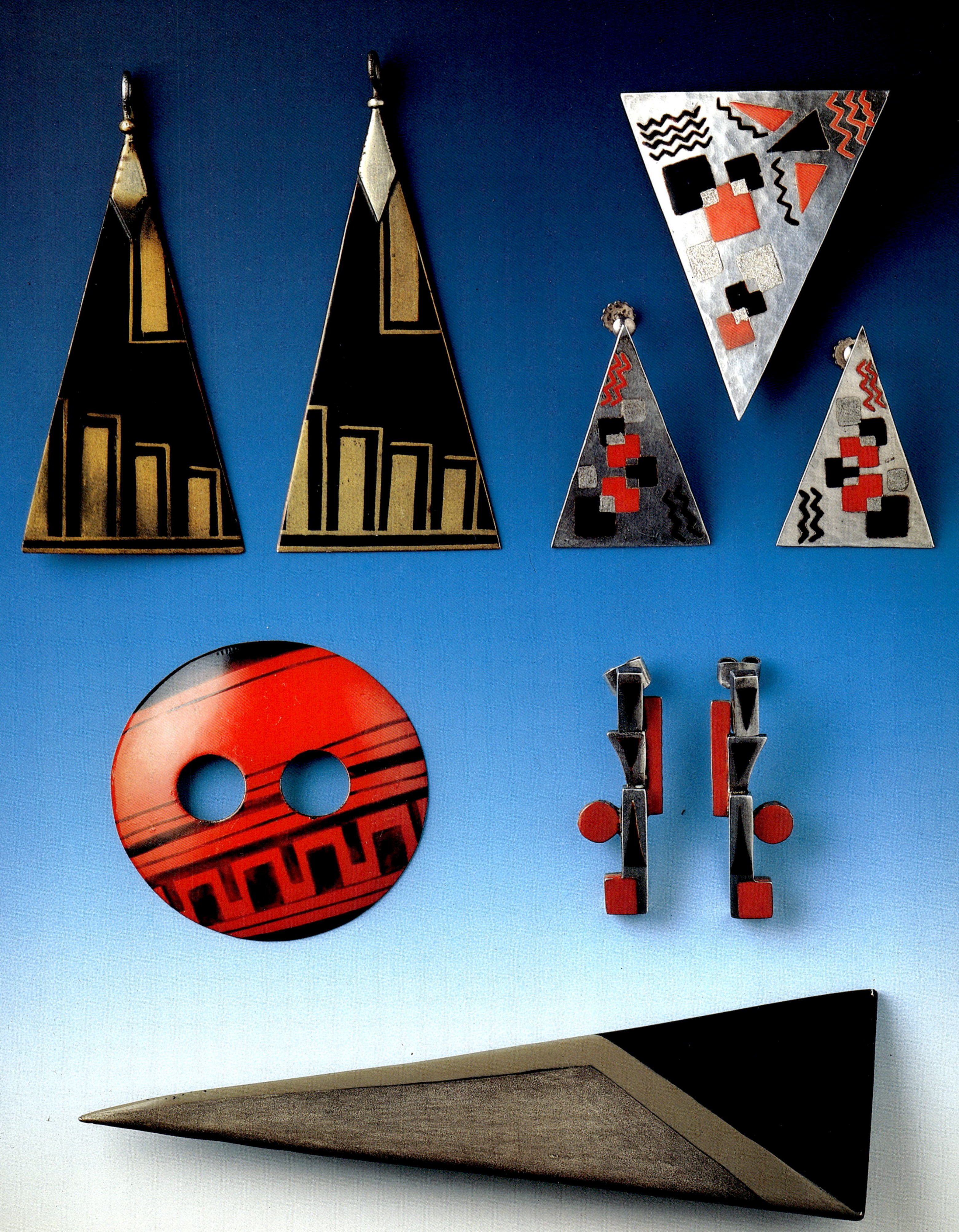

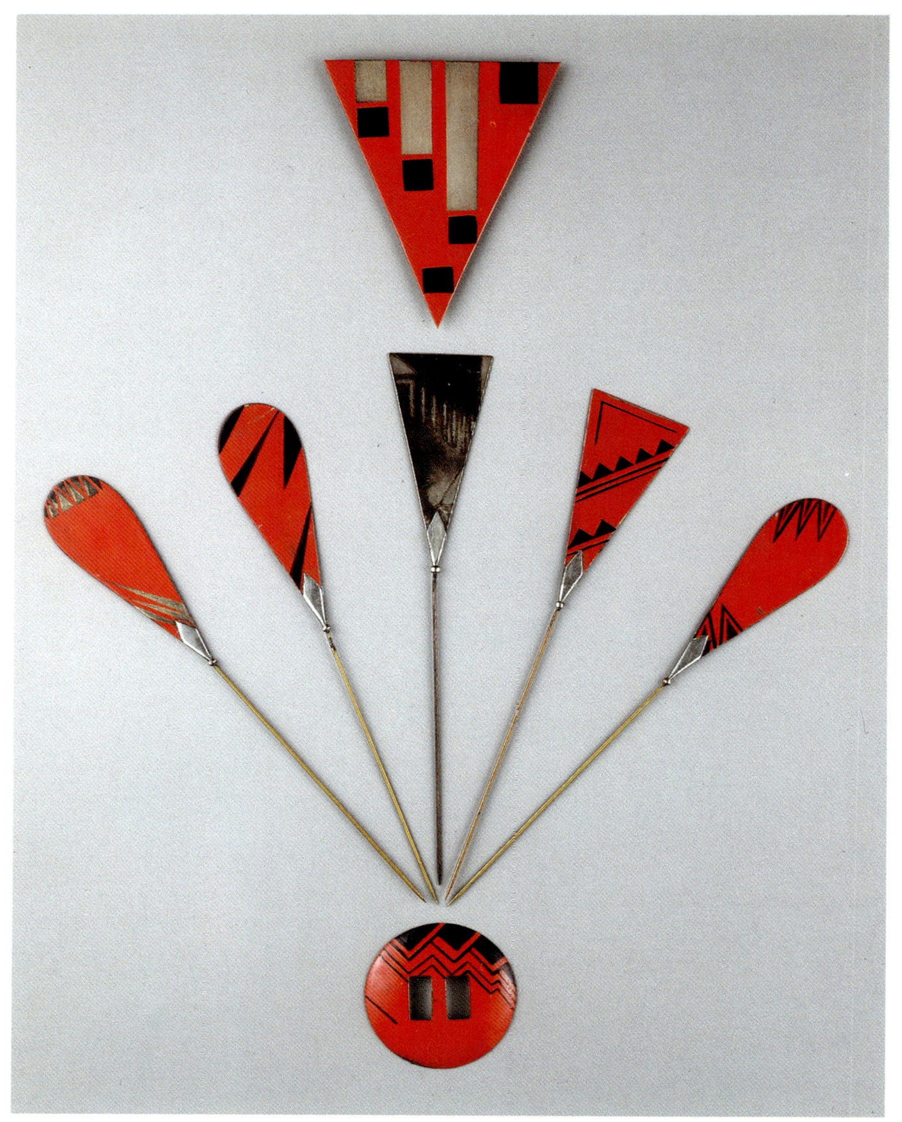

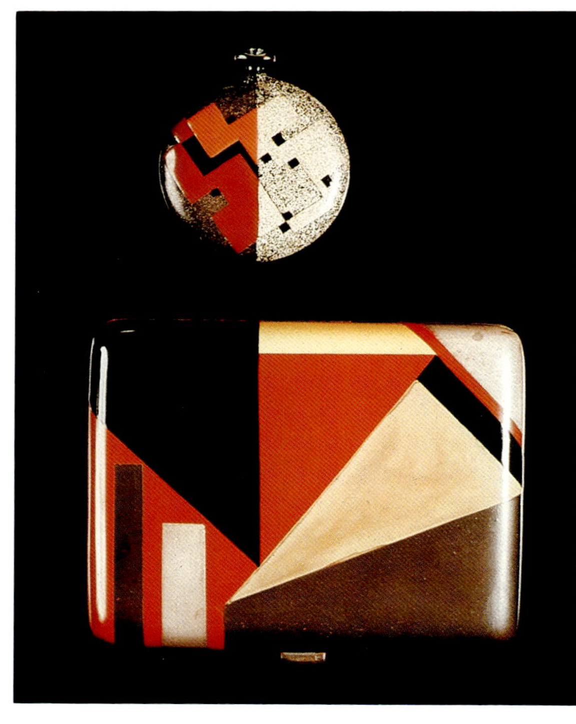

86 **Cigarette-case and watch-case**, *c*. 1925
(*catalogue 727*)

85 **Hatpins and brooch**, 1925
(*catalogue 699*)

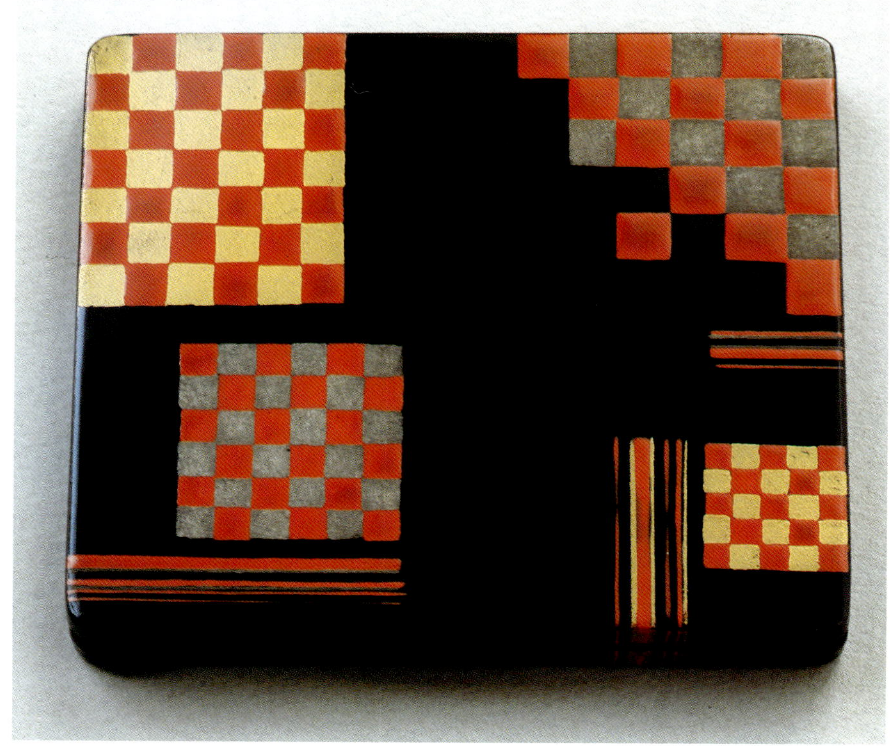

87 **Cigarette-box**, *c*. 1922
(*catalogue 721*)

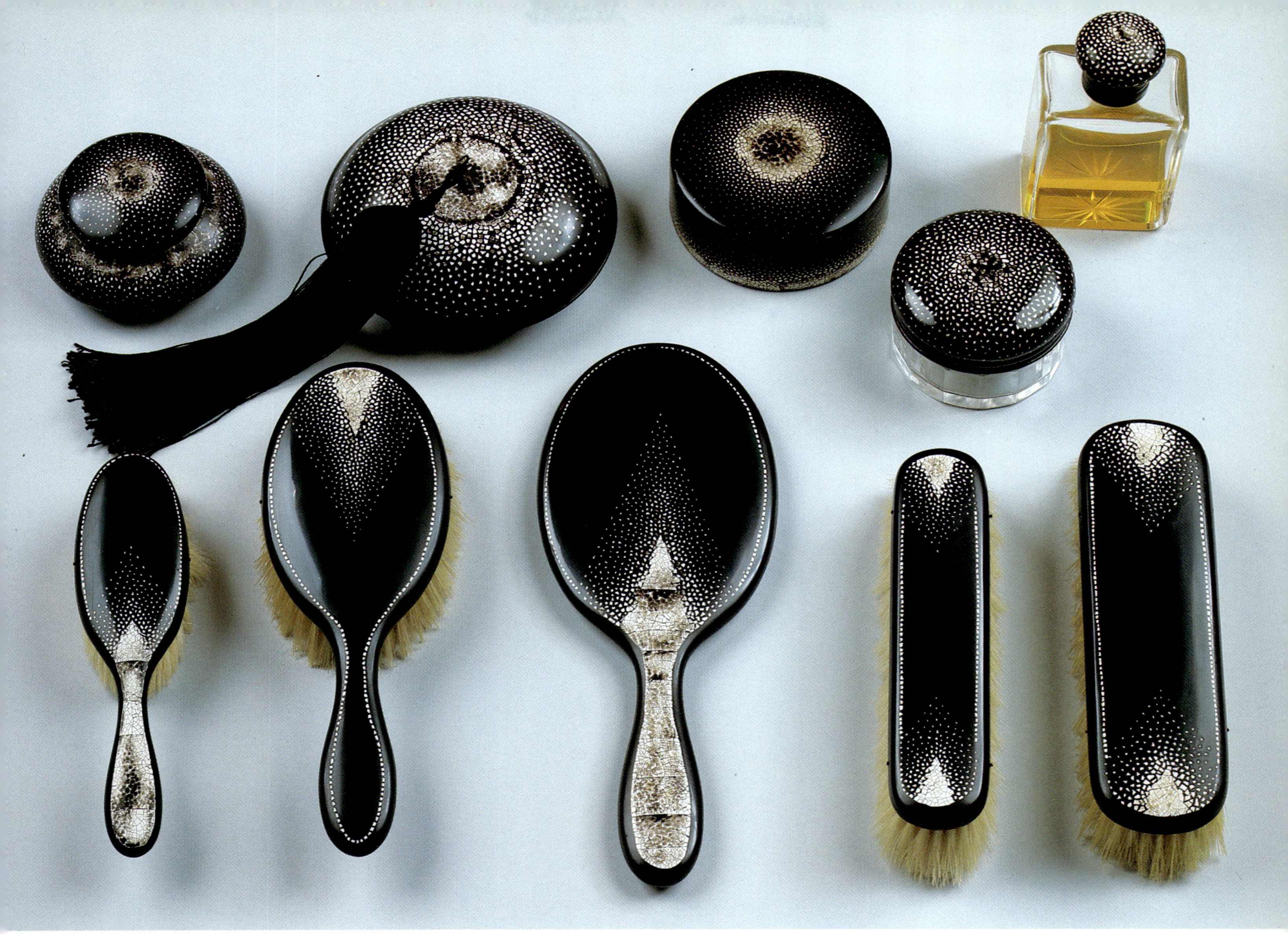

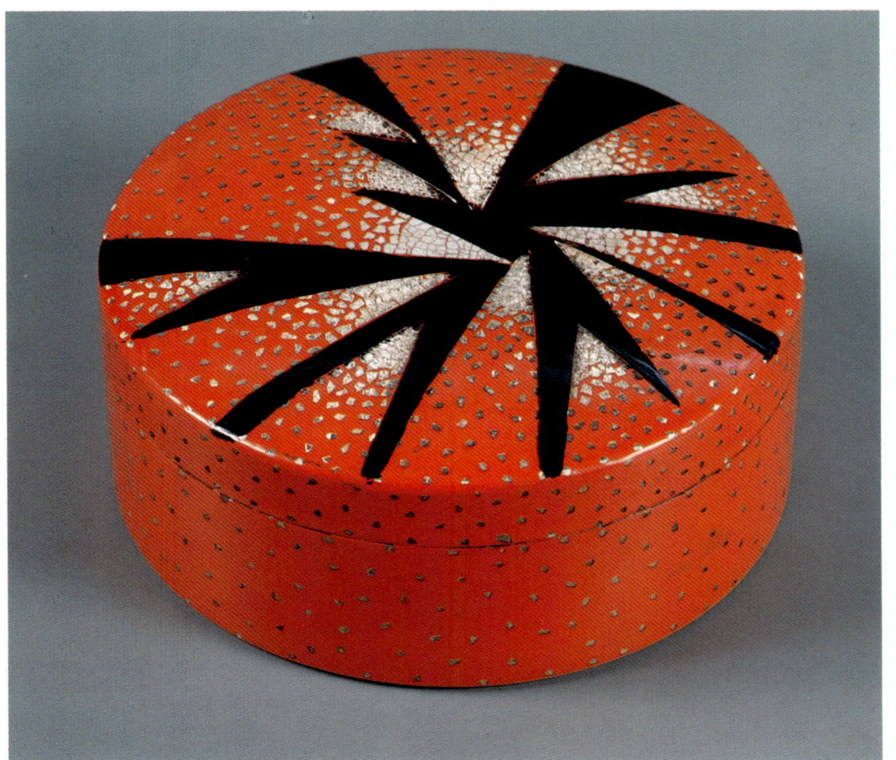

88 **Dressing-table accessories for Madame Dunand**, 1925 (*catalogue 716*)

89 **Powder-box**, 1923 (*catalogue 710*)

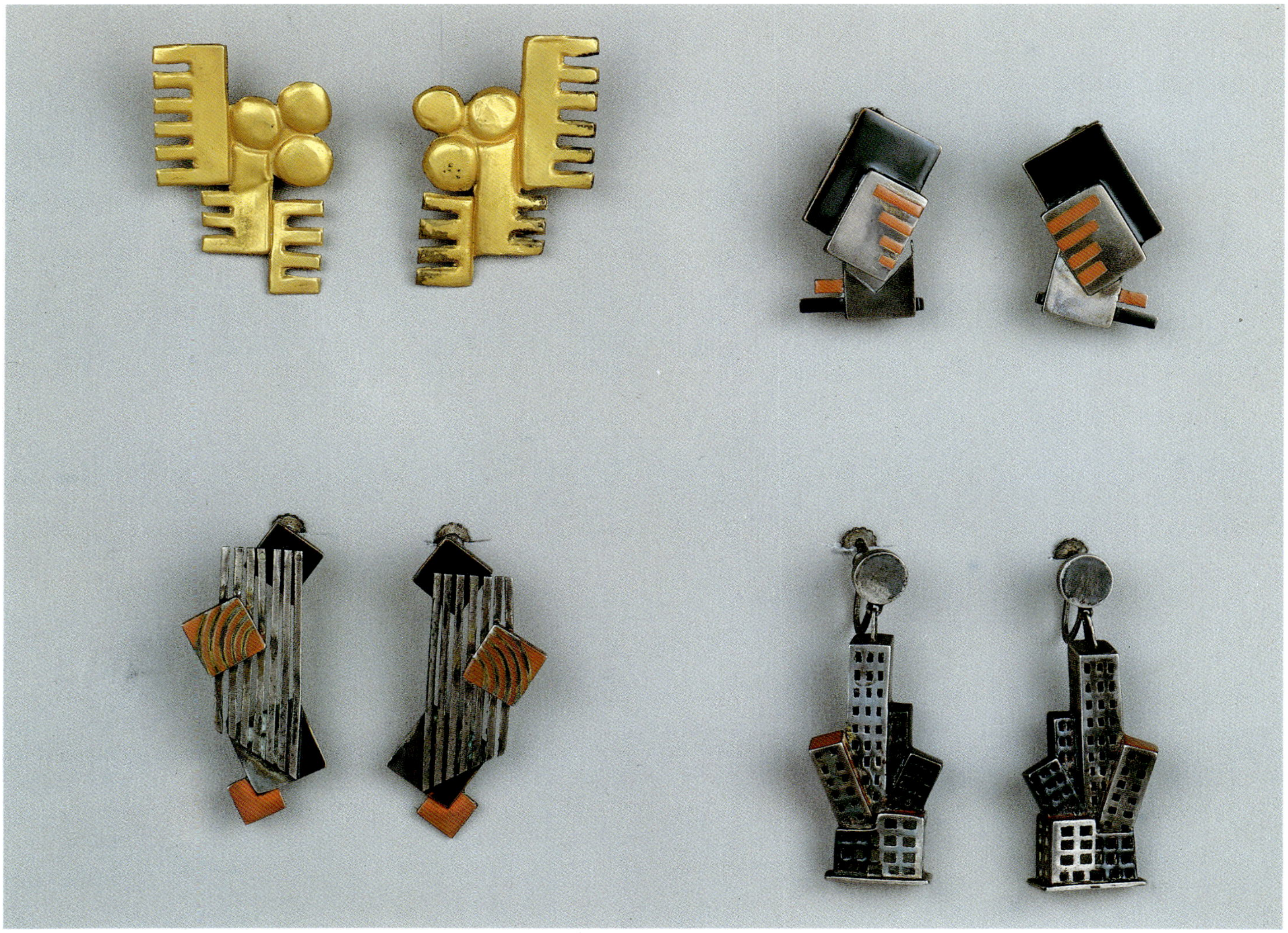

90 **Ear-rings**, *c.* 1922–5
(*catalogue 690*)

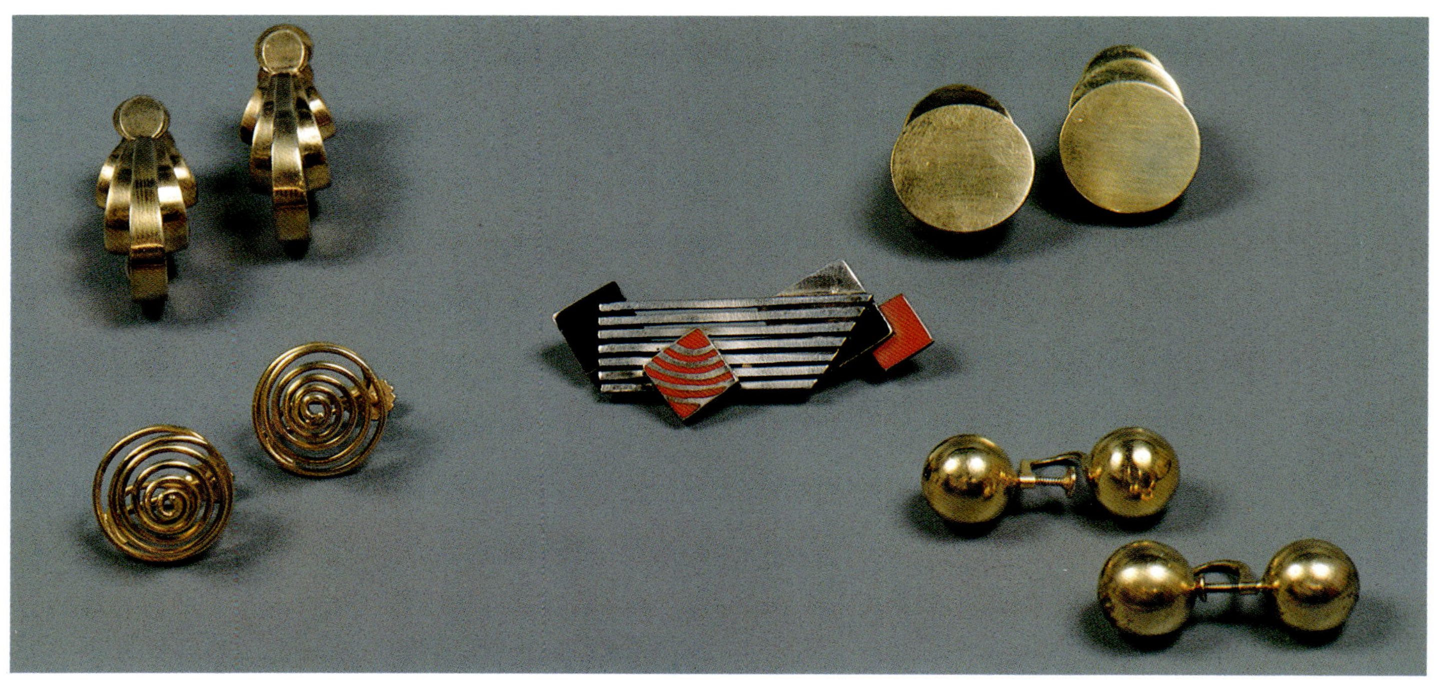

91 **Ear-rings and brooch**, *c.* 1922–5
(*catalogue 687*)

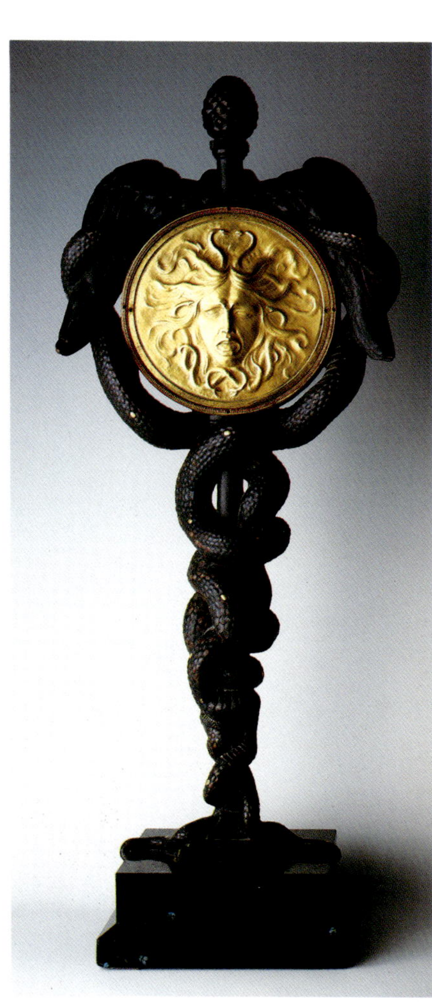

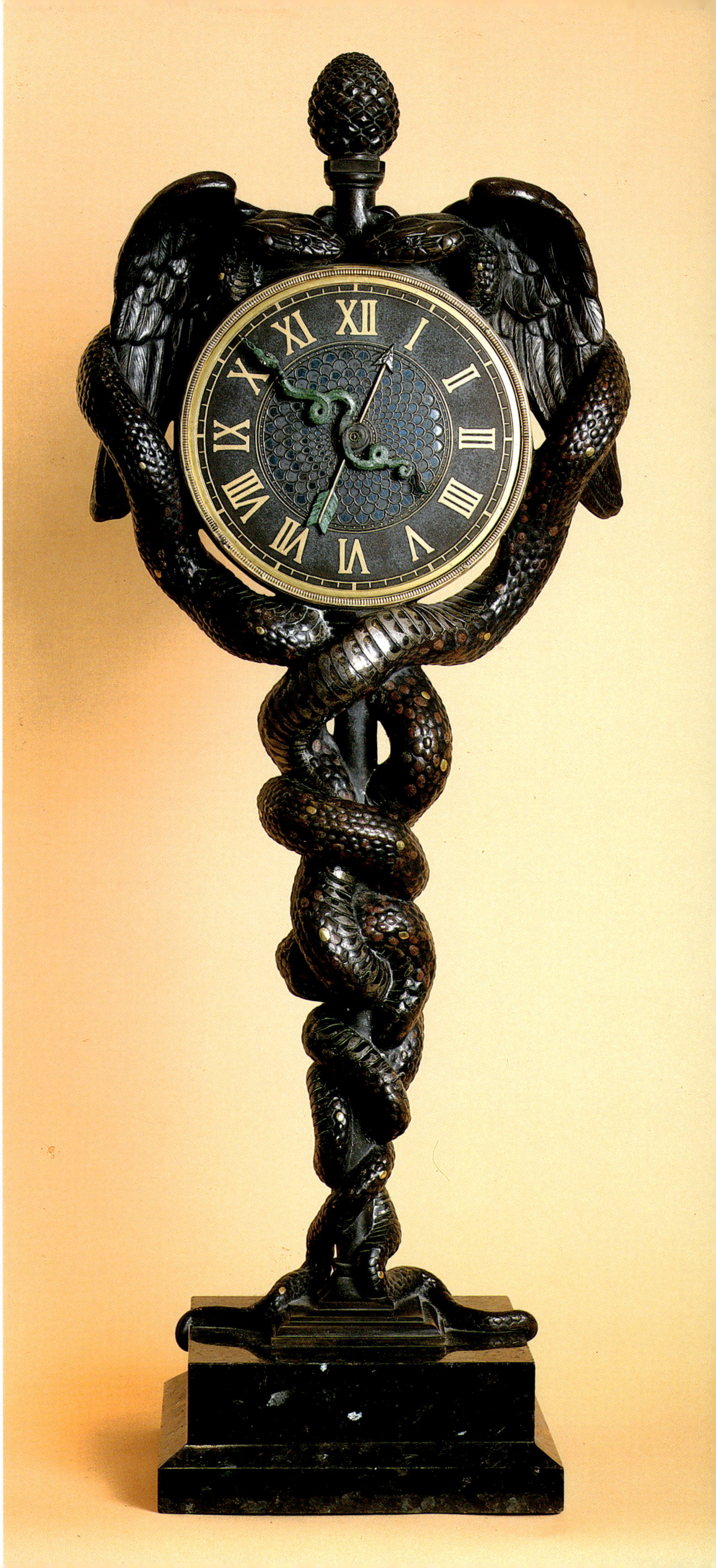

92, 93 **'Caduceus' clock**, 1913, showing Gorgon's head on reverse (*catalogue 649*)

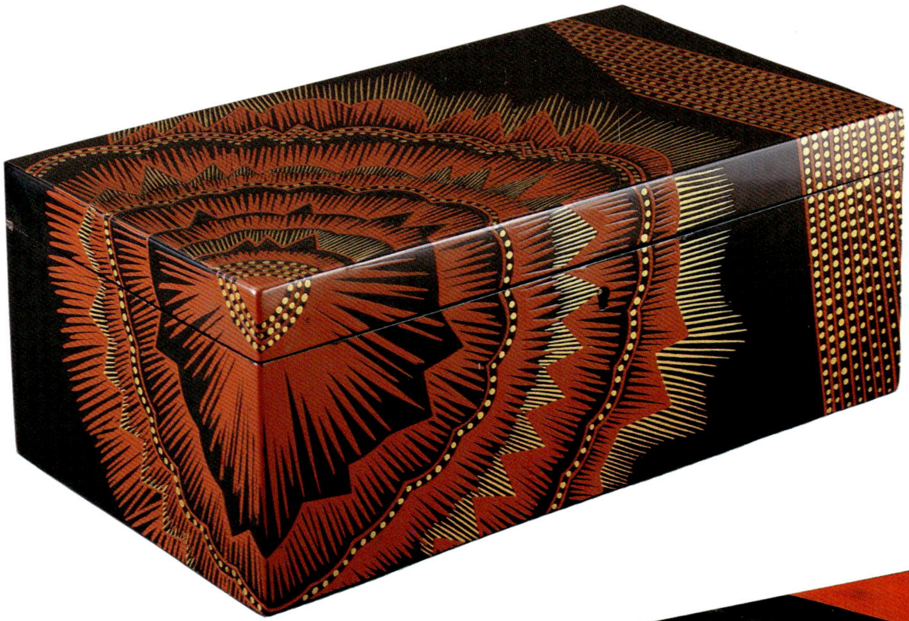

94 **Lacquered box**, 1925
(*catalogue 604*)

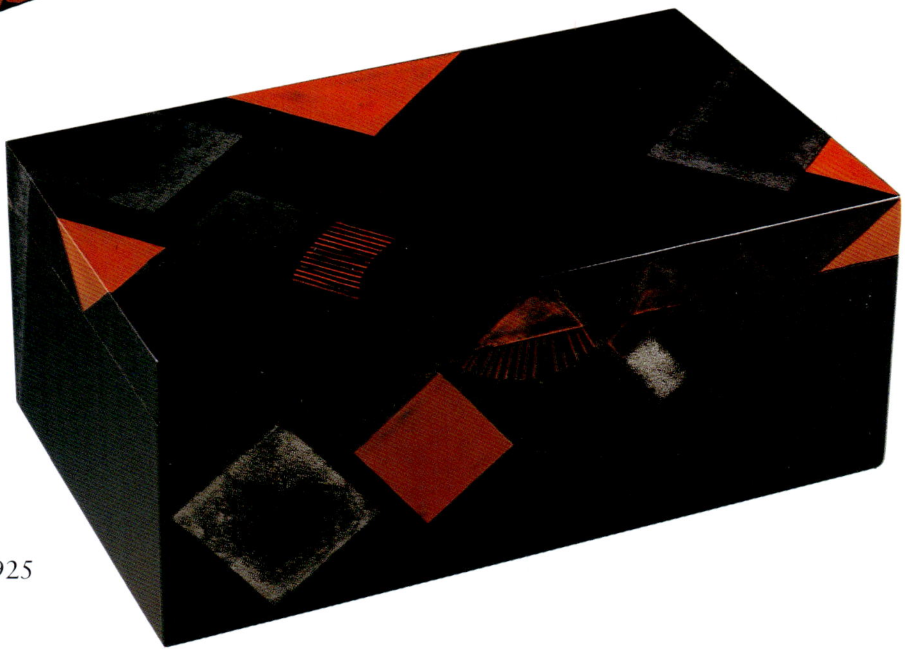

95 **Lacquered box**, *c.* 1925
(*catalogue 603*)

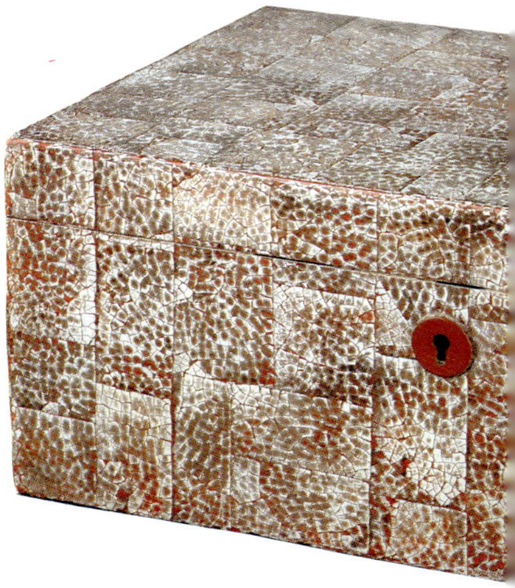

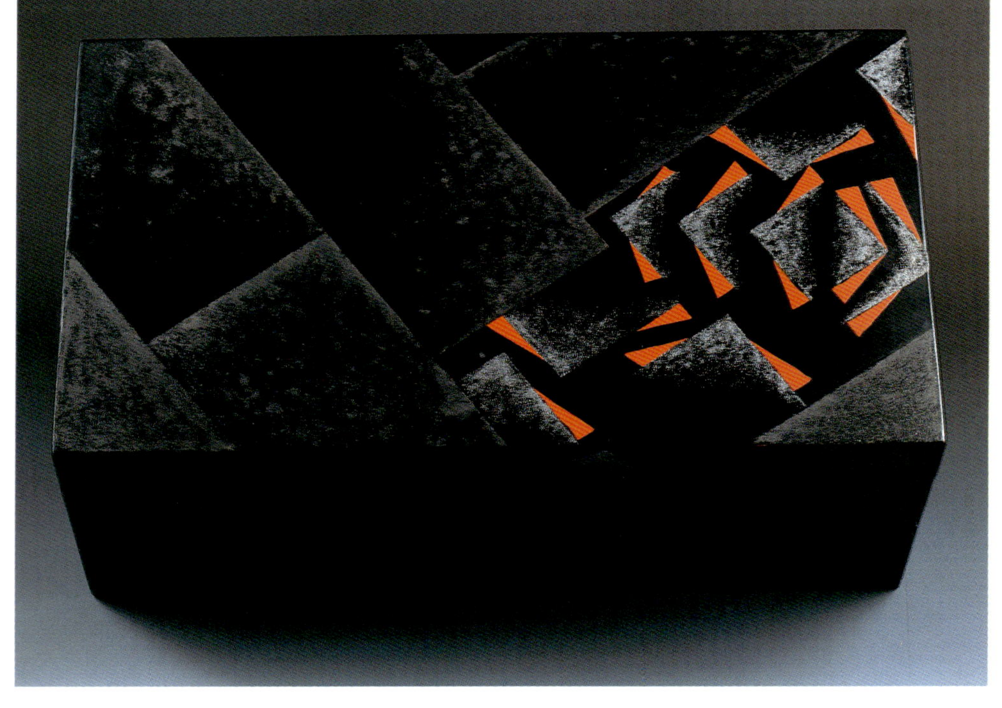

96 **Lacquered box**, *c.* 1925
(*catalogue 601*)

OPPOSITE
99 **Lacquered 'Panther' box**, *c.* 1922
(*catalogue 605*)

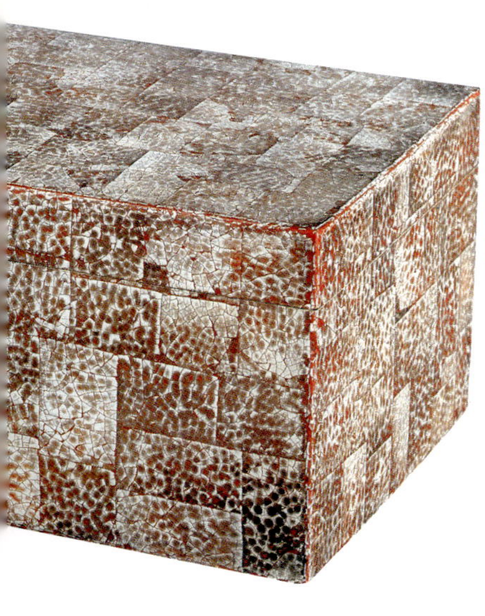

97 **Lacquered box**, *c.* 1922
(*catalogue 600*)

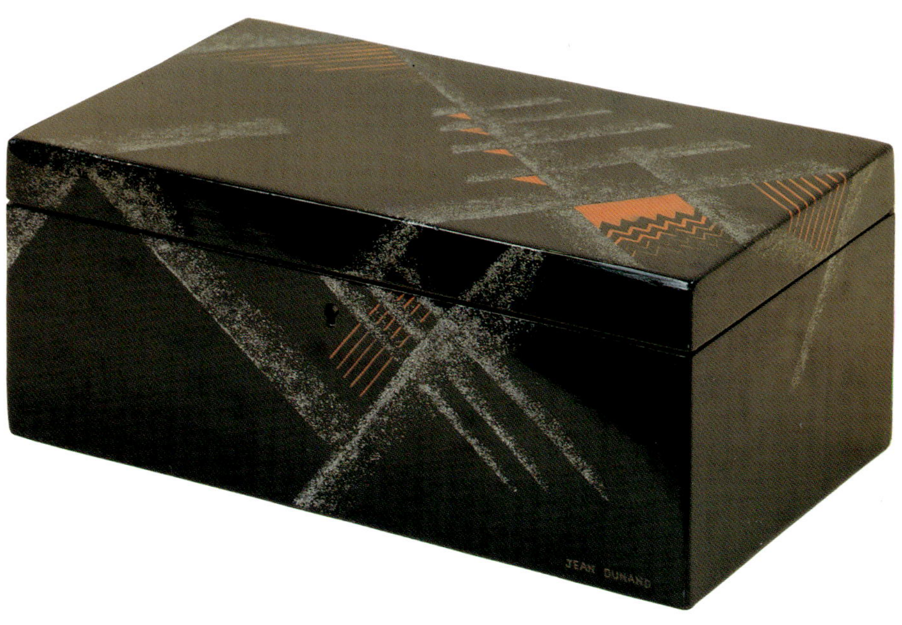

98 **Lacquered box**, *c.* 1925
(*catalogue 602*)

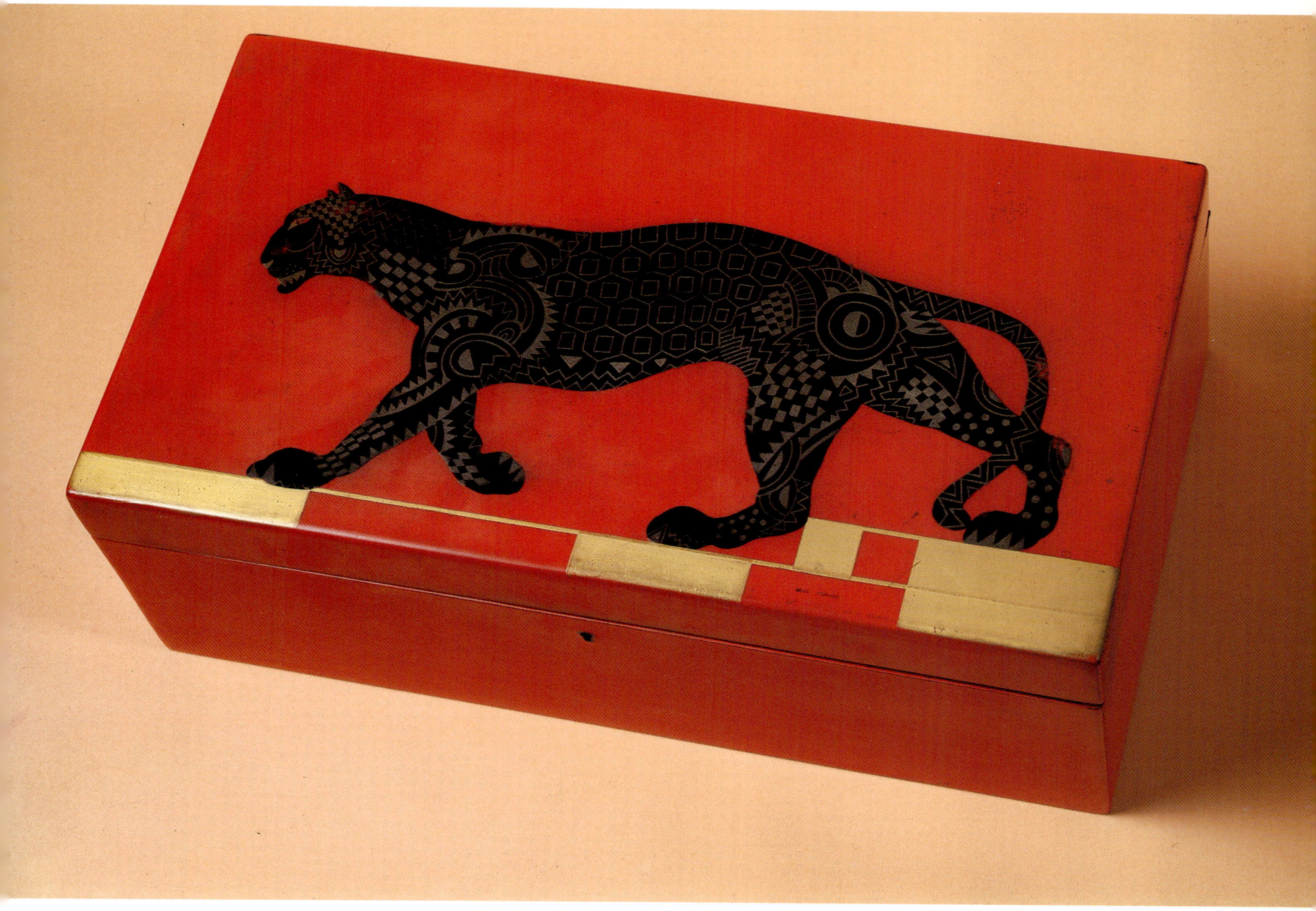

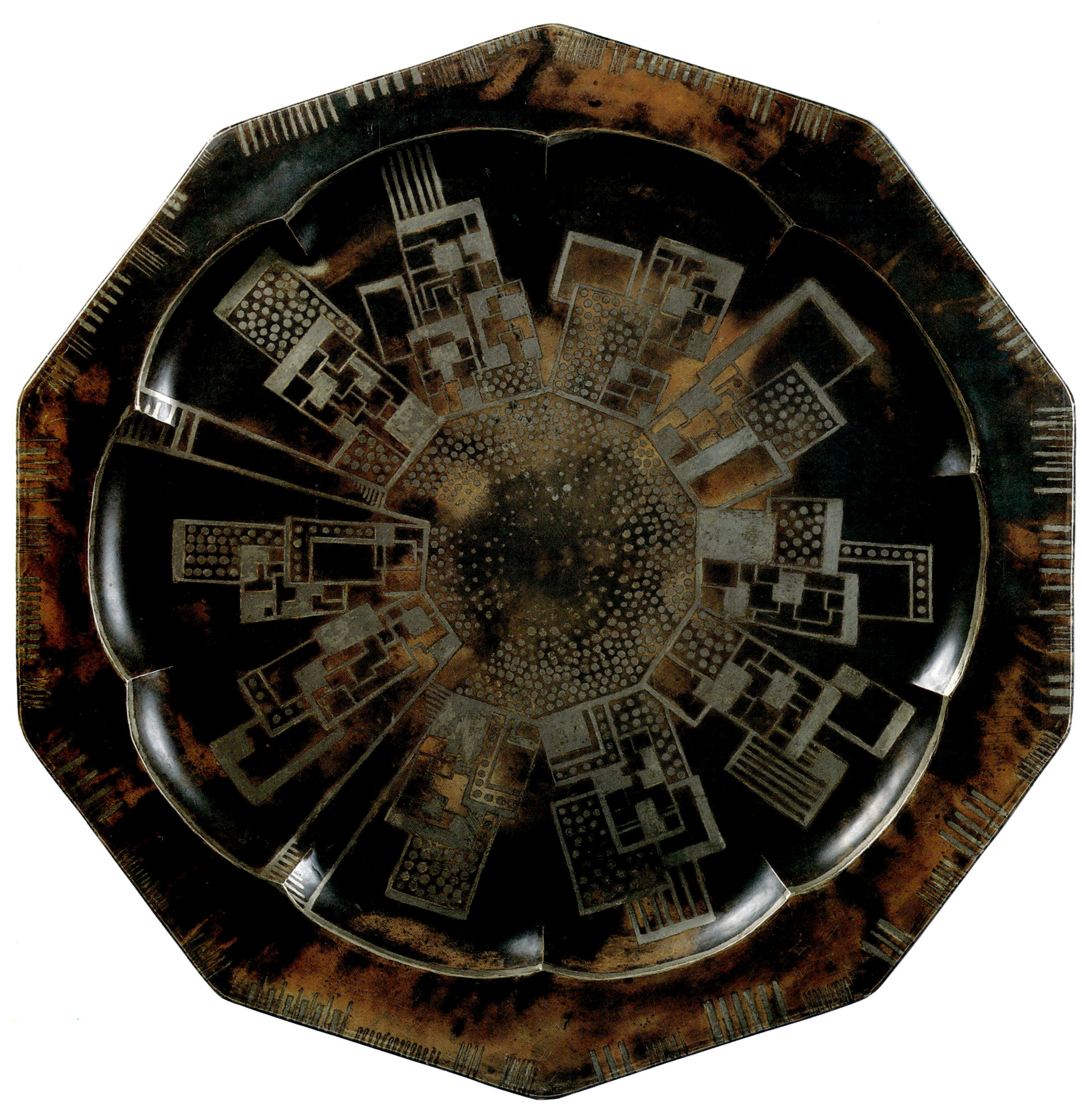

100 **Decagonal dish**, *c.* 1928
(*catalogue 644*)

101 **'Three Snakes' dish**, 1913
(*catalogue 616*)

102 **Circular dish with raised rim**,
c. 1930
(*catalogue 647*)

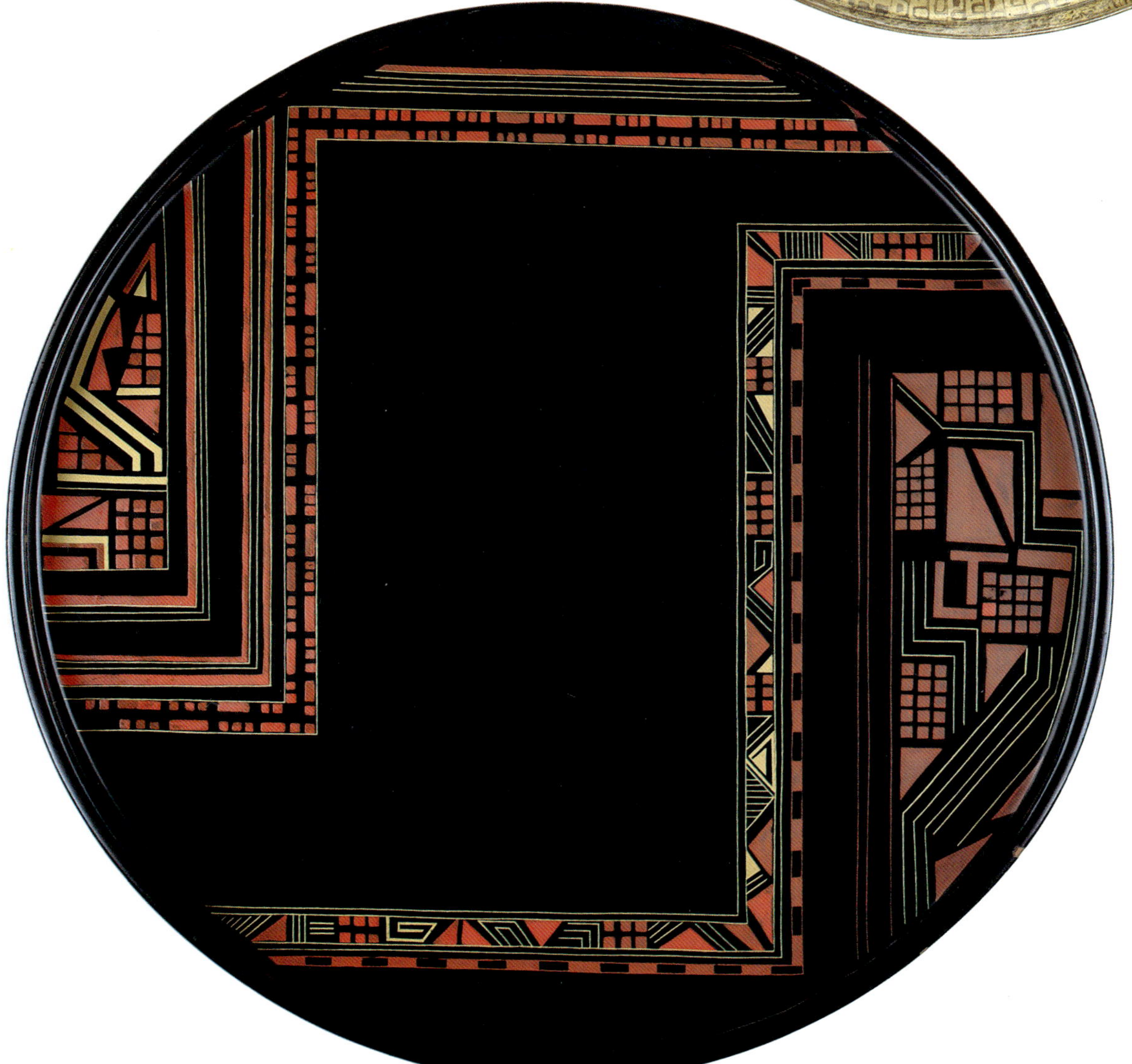

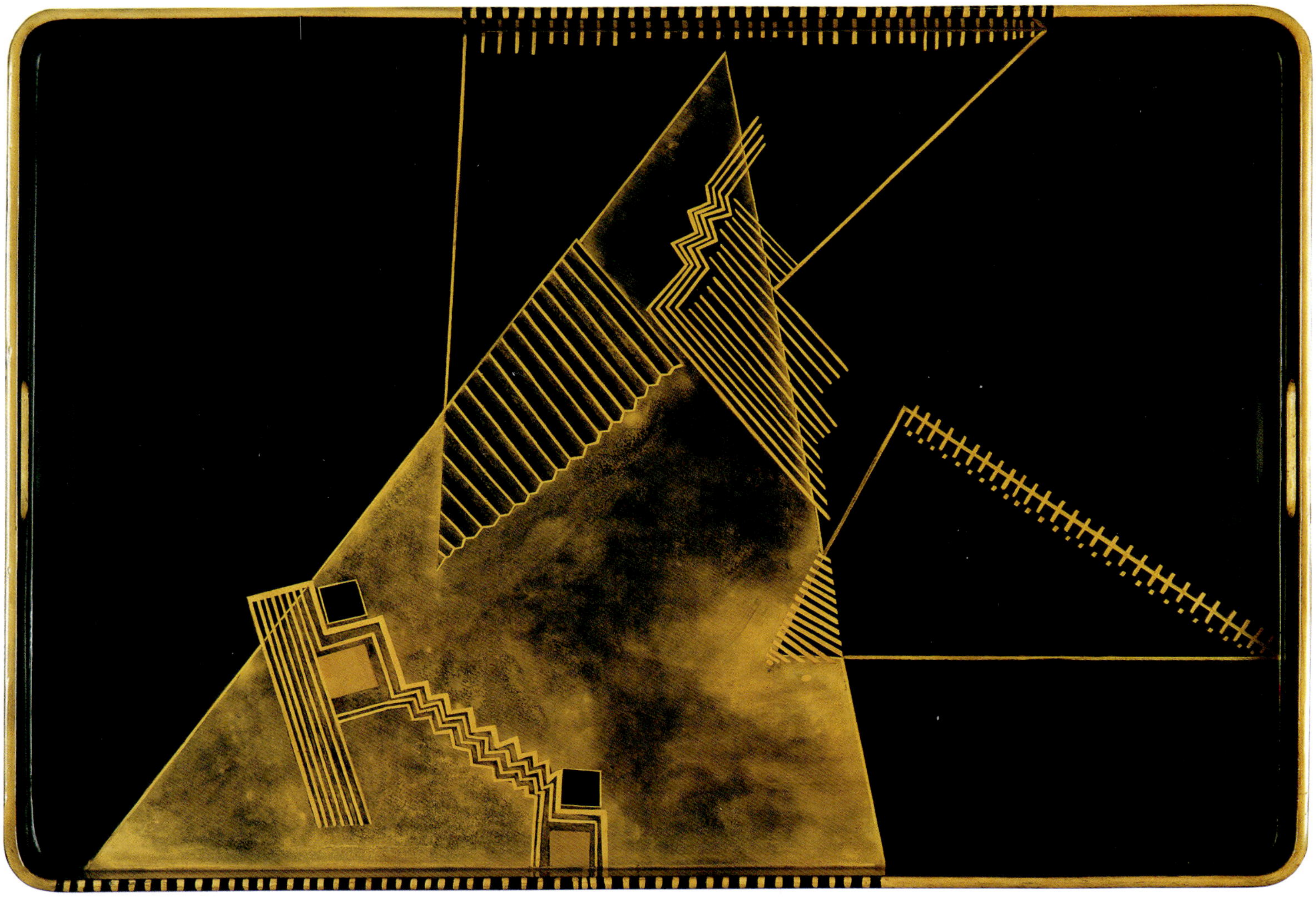

103 **Rectangular dish with raised rim,** *c.* 1930 (*catalogue* 646)

104 **'Mystery' box**, *c.* 1924 (*catalogue* 606)

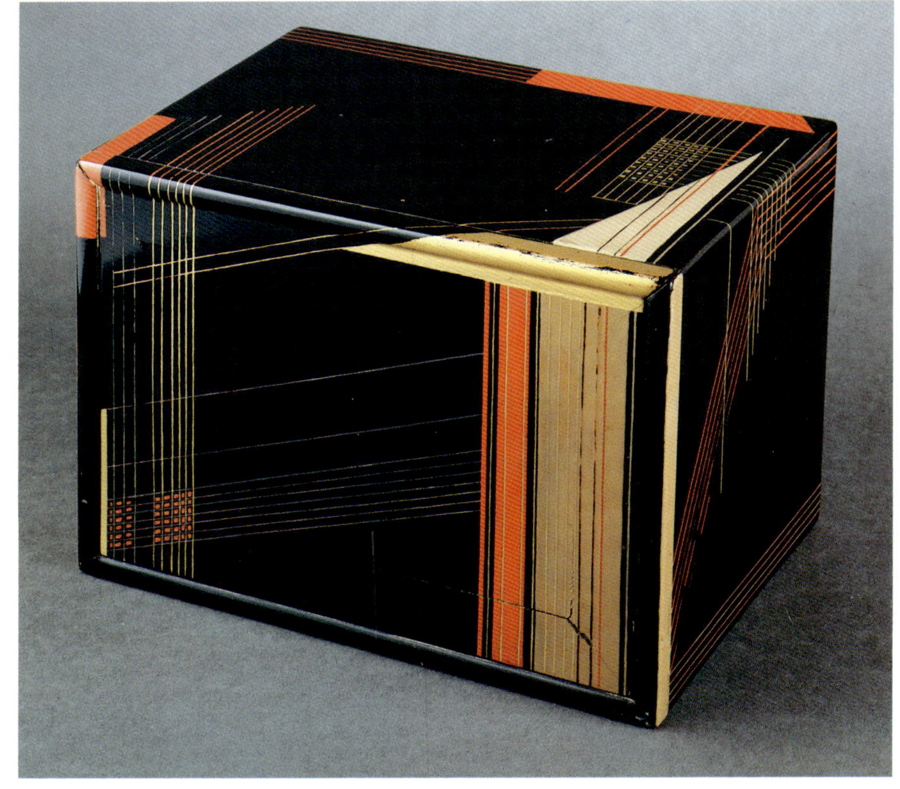

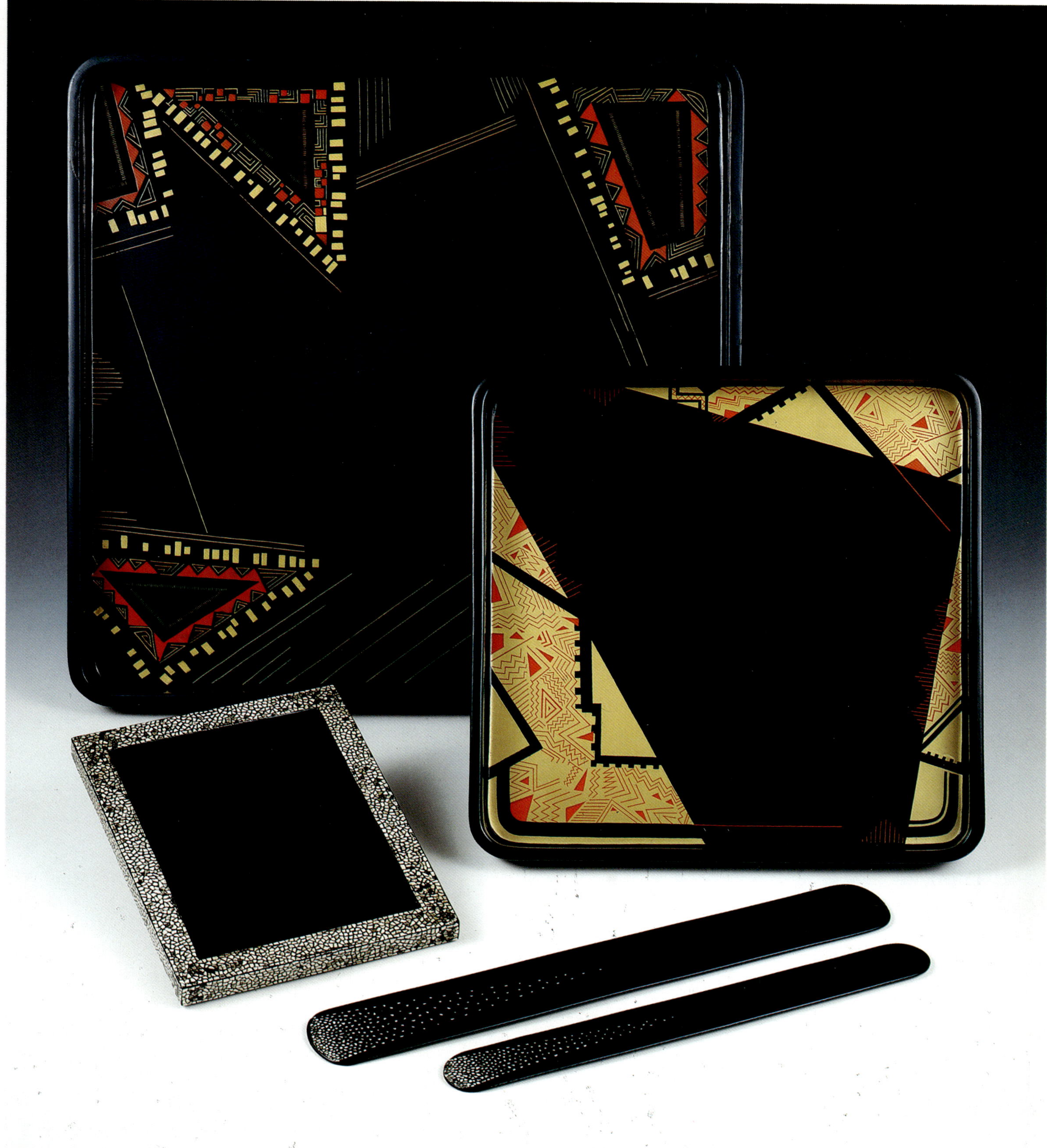

105 **Square trays**, *c.* 1930
(*catalogue 648*)

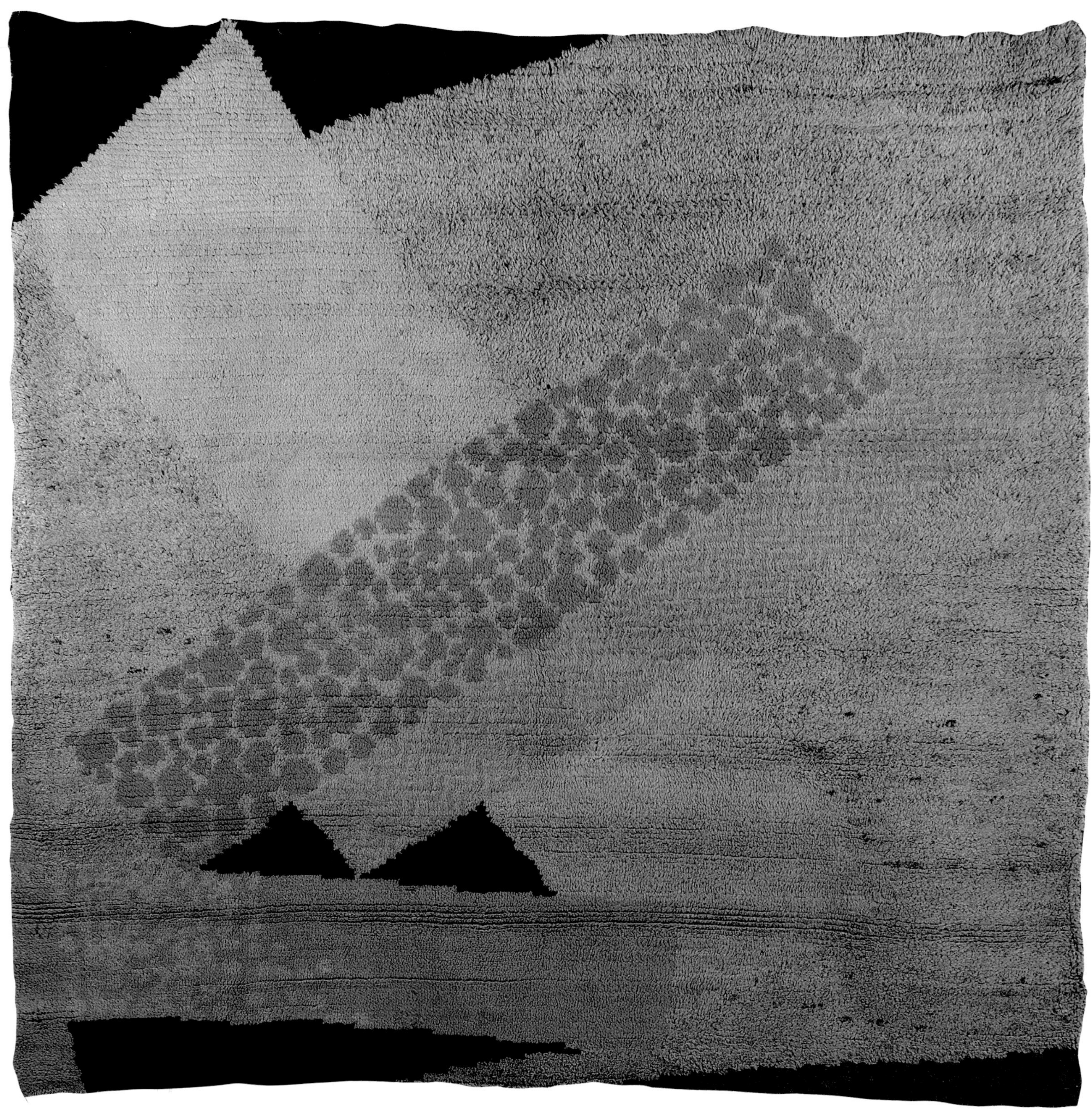

106 **Wool-pile carpet** for Madame Agnès, designed by Dunand and woven in 1927 (*catalogue 754*)

From March to the end of April an exhibition of French art was held in the Greek capital, Athens. Maurice Dufrène was in overall charge of the interior design, and the exhibition proved to be one of the most successful of its period. It brought together the pick of French artists in a number of different categories. By striving to give a sense of homogeneity to collaborations between various artists, art publishers and dealers, the organizers presented all the exhibits in a modern interior together, rather than separately by category (as was the usual practice). Pieces of furniture were placed on the carpets, and individual objects were arranged on the furniture, the walls were covered with paintings, while chandeliers provided the lighting, just as in any normal household. On this occasion Dunand was awarded first prize for an ibex screen and some lacquered vases.

In Paris, however, where his contributions to the Salon des Artistes Décorateurs were relatively unexciting, critics once more protested at less skilled imitators who forced genuinely creative artists in metal and lacquer to withdraw in disillusionment. It was in this dishearteningly *ersatz* environment that Eugène Printz, a newcomer to the world of decorative art, exhibited his furniture, his designs being presented, apparently after much careful study, in a new and wholly personal way. As proof of his ingenuity, he presented a bibliophile's study featuring a walnut desk, the surface area of which could be doubled thanks to the inclusion of a fold-away stand. His new shop, 'Le Studio Printz', in the Rue de Miromesnil, was to be opened a few days later, on 21 June. The ceremony was performed by Paul Léon, government representative for the arts, whose participation marked the official interest now being shown in this artist. The shop design was reminiscent of a strongroom and within its confines the furniture was complemented by a number of vases and screens by Dunand, carpets by Evelyn Wyld, fabrics by Hélène Henry, vases by Jean Sala and paintings by Henry de Waroquier. Although the result was not truly homogeneous, the overall impression was by no means lacking in style and confirmed all the high hopes placed in Printz.

At the Salon des Tuileries Dunand was one of a very few artists, including Bastard, Mayodon and Décorchemont, to bring any lustre to the decorative arts section. Here, a table-cum-bookcase by Dunand, in the form of a cube rotating on a low circular base and with a drawer let into each side, was set off by one of his screens. On the table top stood a vase, a kind of 'flower-pot truncated by a disc diagonally aligned in the manner of Saturn's ring', as Yvanhoé Rambosson later described it in an article in *L'Art ancien et moderne*. This was in fact one of Dunand's 'winged' vases, to use the term which he himself gave them; he went on to produce a number of other, highly elaborate, versions.

Throughout 1928 Dunand continued work on a series of commissions for Templeton Croker's apartment in San Francisco, situated on the top storey of a building overlooking the bay and the city. The entrance hall and main salon were entrusted to Jean-Michel Frank, who created one of his most spectacular designs, worthy of comparison with his Salon des Noailles in the Place des États-Unis, Paris. Dunand had the task of designing the other rooms: the bedroom featured woodwork and furniture in grey *laque arrachée*; the dining room was decorated in gold lacquer, and a breakfast room in black lacquer with a motif of Japanese fish. Dunand even designed a stained-glass window to be made by American glaziers. Jean-Michel Frank travelled to San Francisco to supervise the installation of his own interior designs, which had been executed in Paris, and he also took charge of the installation of Dunand's wood panelling and helped to arrange the latter's furniture.

In September 1928, to mark the sixty-eighth birthday of the Premier, Raymond Poincaré, a reception was held at his country residence at Sampigny, near Bar-le-Duc in eastern France. All his ministers attended, and they presented Mme Poincaré with one of Dunand's vases, a black-lacquer piece with a fish motif. The idea for the gift had come from Louis Barthou, the Minister of Justice, who had commissioned it in an official letter dated 27 July. A letter from Dunand to Dr Amédée Baumgartner, dated 19 September, and now in the Department of Prints and Drawings at the Musée des Arts Décoratifs, includes a sketch in the margin showing his design.

The Salon d'Automne of 1928 would scarcely merit a mention, had it not included a striking piece of furniture by Eugène Printz. Made of palm wood and resting on a gilt-metal cradle, it opened by means of folding doors each of which was covered in copper plates inlaid with silver and executed by Dunand. This was the first in a long series of pieces of furniture which the two artists were to design together, a series continued after Dunand's death by his son Pierre.

Another section of the exhibition included a remarkable collapsible bar fitted with castors; designed by Townley R. Knowles and realized by Lawrence Rigby, this piece incorporated folding stools and featured external decoration by Dunand, who was attracted by the idea and executed several different versions. The one presented on this occasion was decorated with figures by Jean Lambert-Rucki. Executed in red and black lacquer, it was totally different in style from the example produced by the firm of Kirby Beard in Paris. Dunand later made two other models, one of them decorated with Japanese fish, the other with black and silver geometric motifs.

Some time afterwards, while superintending building work on his workshops, Dunand fell from the roof and broke his leg. He was confined to bed for four weeks with his leg in plaster, but his enforced immobility inspired the idea of designing a bedside chest of drawers with a retractable work surface concealed in its top. This accident caused a number of upsets in organizing the eighth annual group exhibition at the Galerie Georges Petit. On this occasion Jouve exhibited a large painting representing a life-and-death struggle between a tiger and a boa constricter. This is without doubt one of the finest of this artist's works. For his part, Dunand presented a screen made up of twelve panels; it was covered in black lacquer engraved and highlighted with silver and depicted a marabou stork gazing pensively at the turbulent waters of a mountain stream. One critic noted that, while Dunand always displayed 'the same technical richness', one could not avoid being struck on this occasion by the brilliance of his new colours which gave 'a magnificence' to his panels and large vases 'with their eurhythmic lines'. It should be added here that Bernard Dunand had been attempting for some time to achieve new lacquer colours, and that he had finally succeeded in fixing the pigmentation of blue and green shades which his father, certain reservations notwithstanding, had decided to adopt. Numerous colour samples were then prepared, and in order to display them a special piece of furniture was made. It opened at the sides, shelves being fixed to the back of each of the two doors. When open, the piece was over 1.50 m (4 ft 6 in.) in length, and the several hundred samples it contained gave a fairly accurate idea of the wide range of possibilities offered by the materials and colours that had been developed in Dunand's workshops.

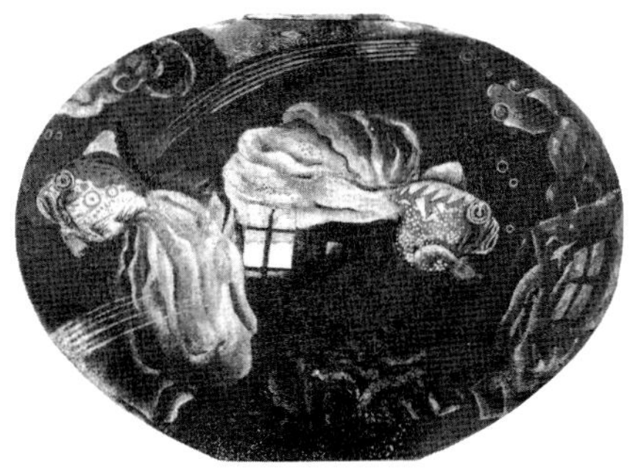

Sketch of the 'Fish' vase (cat. no. 1029) drawn by Dunand in the margin of his letter to Dr Amédée Baumgartner dated 19 September 1928, now in the Musée des Arts Décoratifs, Paris (gift of Félix Marcilhac).

In June 1929, the Galerie La Renaissance put on an exhibition devoted to Jean Dunand. While not strictly a retrospective, the exhibition embraced every aspect of his work to date, with special emphasis on lacquerwork. A catalogue, with an introduction by Léandre Vaillat, listed sixty panels of every shape and description, together with four screens, the collapsible bar with its fish motif, two cabinets displaying dinanderie, a triple-panelled cheval-glass, and numerous carpets based on Dunand's designs and executed by Jacques Dandelot, a friend of Madame Agnès. Dunand was fully aware of the importance of this exhibition, partly because the gallery where it was held was at the forefront of avant-garde aesthetics, but also because he hoped to find new means of artistic expression by applying himself to more imposing objects. He had made a particular point of choosing related pieces, matching them in terms of theme, material and colour. As a result, the pieces selected constituted a cross-section of minor masterpieces. While taking an evident pleasure in deriving stylized forms from nature, he did so with discretion, his

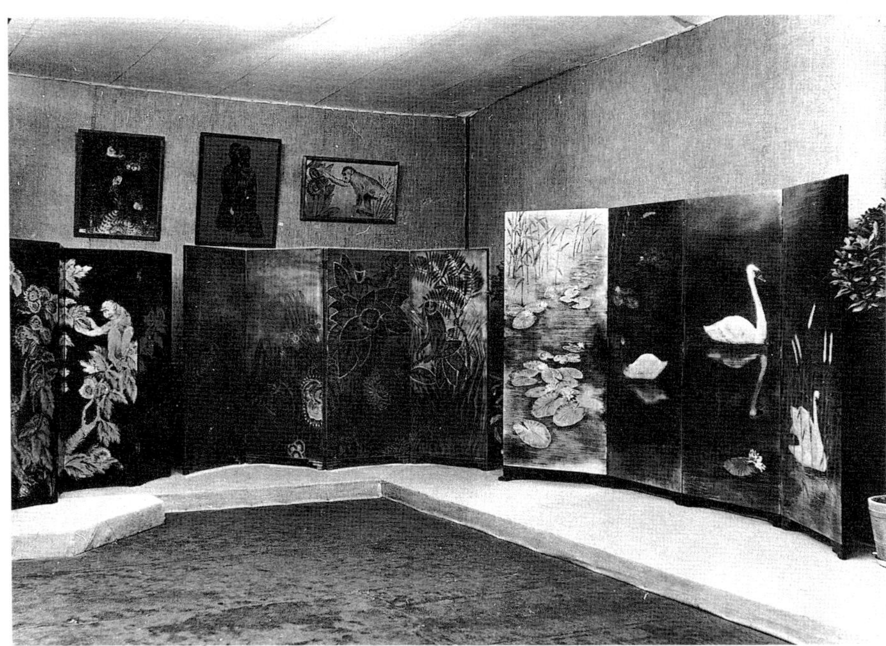

Dunand's stand at the Galerie Georges Petit, December 1928, featuring lacquered screens and panels.

work being in stark contrast with the simplistic decors that characterized the work of his imitators. At the same time, the abstract qualities of his geometric compositions had nothing to do with any supposed Masonic association, as some commentators sought to suggest at the time: his graphic style was entirely in keeping with the richness and exotic qualities of the materials used. A contemporary critic noted: 'Never does Dunand commit the error of treating his themes in a painterly style: his strictly decorative style remains sober and apt.' He knew only too well that the use of lacquer imposes its own special rules and constraints. There was never any question of being simply a painter. The series on gold-, silver-, purple- or black-lacquer backgrounds which he exhibited at the Galerie La Renaissance was typical of his questing spirit and of the sustained effort and the meticulousness which characterize the works of this period, the most prolific of his entire career. His subject matter included a wide variety of human figures, side by side with what Dunand was fond of calling 'fantastic' animals, a term he preferred to 'imaginary'. His monkeys, tigers, leopard, deer and marabou storks and other birds, as well as rabbits and fish, were all depicted in familiar attitudes against a background of charming landscapes in which dream-like imagery and reality merged. Always in search of new techniques, Dunand was never content simply to re-use the wealth of techniques already known to him.

To this harmonious ensemble were added the various carpets. Ingenious in their composition, Dunand's designs harked back essentially to the geometric principle which he had already espoused in decorating plane surfaces, reducing the number of colours used to two or three and highlighting formal contrasts by overlapping simple geometric elements such as circles and areas intersected by squares, or triangles traversed diagonally by straight or wavy lines. Here, too, he avoided the pitfalls of painting, taking care – and with good reason – not to give these lines the illusion of volume and so avoiding unpleasing visual effects, for the visual impression derived from walking on a carpet is not the same as that of seeing it hung on a wall. Once again, Dunand had realized that the graphic style of a carpet design had its own particular rules and that, to be successful, it was not enough to mimic a painting. Furthermore, he designed his carpets to match other elements in a decorative scheme. All were small in size, but were never meant as mere props.

At about this time the daughter of one of African jewellers whom Dunand had met in Geneva in 1896 came to Paris. Her father had kept in touch with Dunand by letter, and so it was entirely to be expected that she would visit him. Because of her striking appearance, Dunand had her sit for him on several occasions.

On the occasion of the International Exhibition held in Barcelona in 1929, Dunand entered a number of large-scale works, including the large chest made for the 1925 Exhibition in collaboration with Ruhlmann. Not having found a buyer, he decided to change the decoration on the door, retaining a sober and geometric style but replacing the puppy and hedgehog design by Lambert-Rucki. In the course of the exhibition the piece was sold to Nadine Oxnard, an American artist living in Paris. It was for her that Serge Rovinski was later to make a whole series of pieces of furniture, constructed around frames built by the Paris cabinet-maker Dennery, and with lacquer decoration by Dunand.

At the Salon des Artistes Décorateurs of 1929 a screen depicting ibexes confronting each other aroused both critical interest and praise, although the other pieces which Dunand exhibited were all equally interesting. These scenes depicting fantastic animals amused visitors to the exhibition, one of whom commented in an article: 'One would not be surprised in the least if this enchanted world sprang to life, if these fish began to swim, this tiger to pounce on its prey, these cobras to raise their flattened heads in a sinuously swaying movement of menace, or this monkey to stretch out its mischievous paw. Indeed, Dunand's realism, based as it is on a form of stylization, does not shock or tire, but always delights the observer, so skilful is he in handling effects and adapting the style of his compositions.'

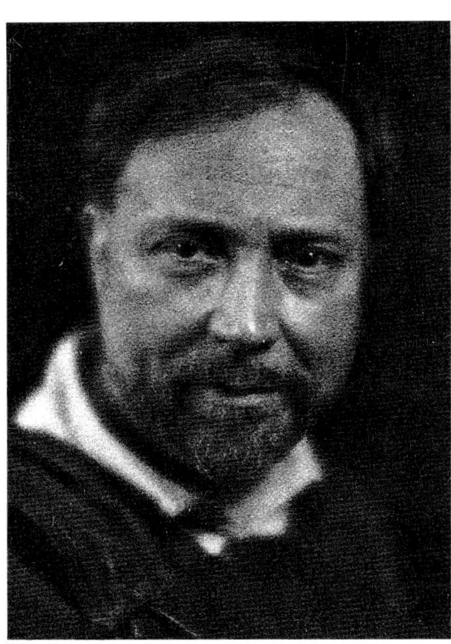

Portrait of Dunand, *c.* 1930.

On 4 August 1929, on the occasion of the election to the Académie Française of Fortunat Strowski, Professor at the Sorbonne and at the Collège de France, another sword by Dunand was presented to the new Academician. The initiative came from the journal *La Renaissance de l'art français*, which had opened a public subscription list. The hilt of the sword was in burnished steel, engraved and inlaid with gold, while its decoration consisted of laurel leaves and its tang was covered with tiny pieces of mother-of-pearl all running in the same direction. The black-lacquer scabbard was similarly inlaid with burgaudine and eggshell.

In the course of an exhibition of religious art held at the Musée Galliéra, Dunand made the acquaintance of certain members of the episcopate who were responsible for the Church's building programme. As a result, he was commissioned to make the altar and communion table for the new church off the Avenue Daumesnil, which was then in the planning stage.

At the beginning of December, Dunand contributed works to an exhibition on animal subjects held in Paris at the Galerie Brandt in the Boulevard Malesherbes. It provided artists and visitors alike with an interesting opportunity to see and compare works on a related theme. As each piece used different materials – bronze or wrought iron obliging the artist to adopt a more restrained stylization – observers could appreciate more readily the flexibility of Dunand's interpretations. By contrast with the works by other artists, Dunand's were always as delectable as they were audacious.

Also in December, the French State purchased a large panel entitled *Forest* exhibited at the Galerie Georges Petit. On a black-lacquer background highlighted with different shades of gold, the design evoked the fear inspired in other animals by the presence of a marauding tiger. This panel would later be shown at the 1931 Exposition Coloniale. On the other screens exhibited at the Galerie Georges Petit the most opulent of decorative flora were brought into play with an inexhaustible ingenuity. Deer made of sheet lead on panels of a species of pine native to Oregon with alternating veins of hard and soft wood contrasted with foxes in a forest of snow-capped fir trees, while swans glided past on a twilit lake. In all, there were seventeen screens and panels, one of which – *Group at Tangiers* (a group of beggars?), executed in gold lacquer – seems to be lost, for we have been unable to discover any trace of its whereabouts. The technique employed on this occasion (fixing the lacquer under glass) would later be used for a whole series of pieces of furniture and radiator covers. Some of these screens were of exceptional elegance, featuring

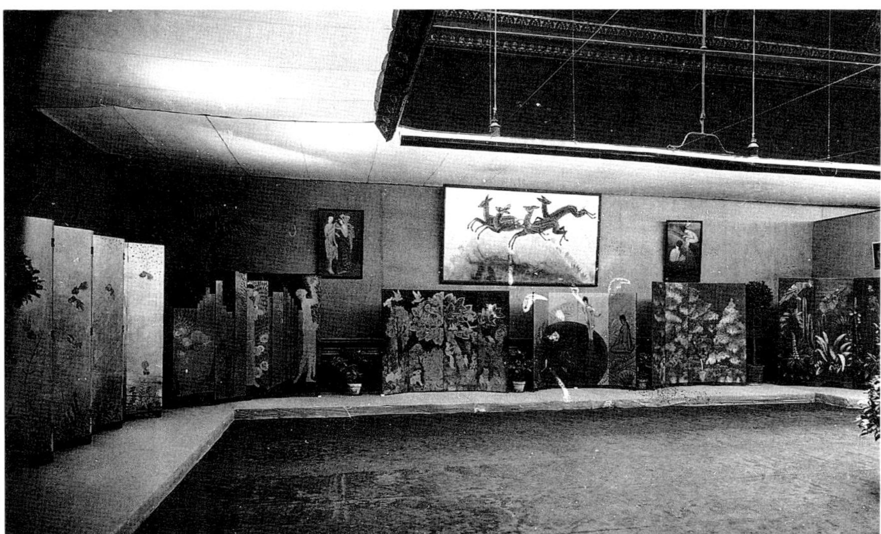

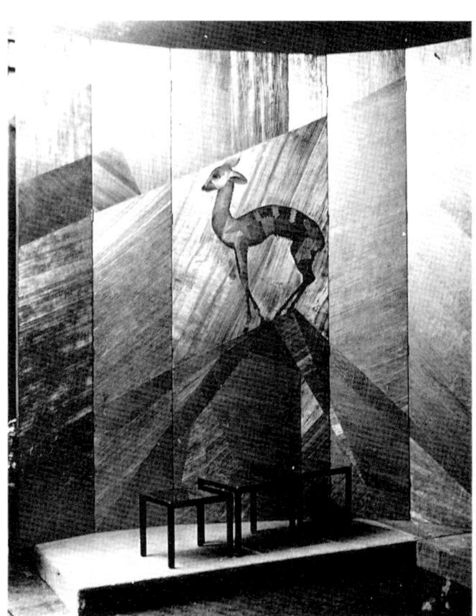

The main exhibition hall at the Galerie Georges Petit, December 1929, and (right) Dunand's screen *Deer* (cat. no. 73).

extremely simple motifs thrown together, as though by chance, with studied casualness, while other screens depicted landscapes, human figures, and entire scenes traced in sweeping stylized lines to produce an effect of rare magnificence.

For a number of months Dunand had been working in parallel on two extremely important commissions. On the one hand, the Compagnie Sud-Atlantique had invited him to undertake part of the interior decoration of their new liner *L'Atlantique*, a vessel designed to serve the major South American ports, while, on the other, he had received an official commission from the government in Paris to fit out part of one of the rooms in the main building that was to house the planned Exposition Coloniale. For such a project, Dunand's compositions had to take account of the different ethnic aspects of France's colonies. A draft outline and a model of the overall scheme having already been accepted in 1929, Dunand had set to work, beginning, once again, by enlarging his studios. Although the room he was asked to decorate was little more than a kind of vestibule, he decided to invest it with such importance that, once installed, it would become the centre of attraction. Two pairs of large vertical panels faced each other, to the left and right of two large openings leading to exhibition area. In addition, two horizontal panels were designed to be placed above these openings. On one side Dunand opted to depict a North African market counterbalanced by an Asian scene, while the opposite side portrayed two scenes of everyday life in Africa. Without abandoning his initial plan, Dunand nevertheless adapted certain aspects in the course of execution, removing some of the anecdotal features.

Dunand first presented this vestibule at the 1930 Salon des Artistes Décorateurs. Executed on a background of crystalline silver lacquer, the tall figures stood out in brown and black *laque arrachée*. Opposite them, and treated in the same shades, were a pottery seller, clearly Moroccan, and, counterbalancing him, two Asian dancers and a man beating a drum. These figures symbolized the French presence in Senegal, Cameroun, Morocco and Indo-China. Above one of the two openings, a tiger could be glimpsed among tall grasses, while above the second opening two ibexes were depicted, their horns interlocked in combat. Between these two walls, with their six panels, was placed a large-scale composition depicting two African elephants. At the entrance to the landing stood two huge vases on wrought-iron supports. On these vases, overlapping concentric circles were scattered fairly freely over a gold-lacquer background. (These two vases are now displayed in the Musée d'Art Moderne de la Ville de Paris.) 'This is a rare and important chapter in the history of contemporary decorative art,' wrote Arsène Alexandre in a magazine article, while a certain Varenne, in *L'Amour de l'art* of 4 August

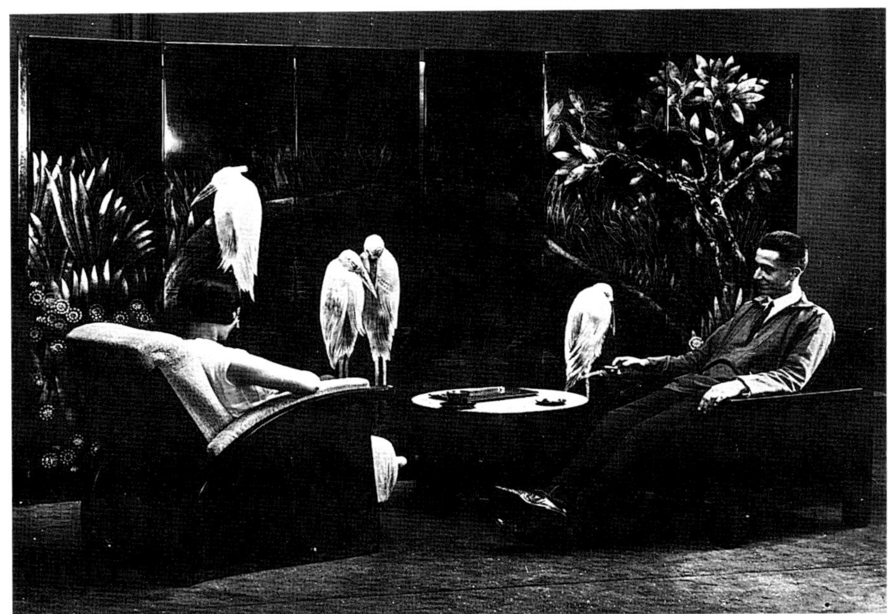

Bernard Dunand and his sister Alix at the Galerie Georges Petit, December 1930; Jean Dunand's screen *Marabou Storks* (cat. no. 59) was one of several shown on this occasion.

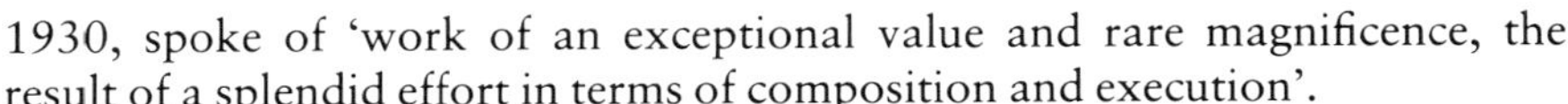

1930, spoke of 'work of an exceptional value and rare magnificence, the result of a splendid effort in terms of composition and execution'.

The two openings were intended to lead into library/reading rooms in the future Colonial Exhibition building, and in his presentation at the Salon des Artistes Décorateurs Dunand took advantage of this plan to have them give access to an alcove on one side and a small boudoir on the other. The alcove, backed by a pleated curtain, was arranged so as to show off a nest of tables and an armchair in silver, pink and gold lacquer. On the other side, the small boudoir made use of wood panelling from the Embassy smoking room previously seen at the 1925 Exhibition. It was described by some critics as a 'Persian boudoir'. The decoration on the panelling consisted of storks in flight against a background of tropical vegetation. To the left, Dunand had arranged a dressing table with side drawers and a chair. Beside it was a three-panel cheval-glass which featured decoration in black, silver and gold lacquer depicting a crouching woman cradling a kitten in her hands.

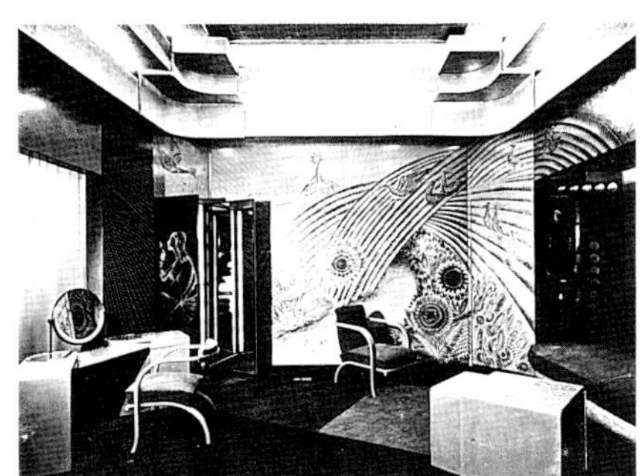

Interior of the boudoir exhibited in 1925 and (below) the dressing table which was included in the scheme; see cat. nos. 1202, 1210.

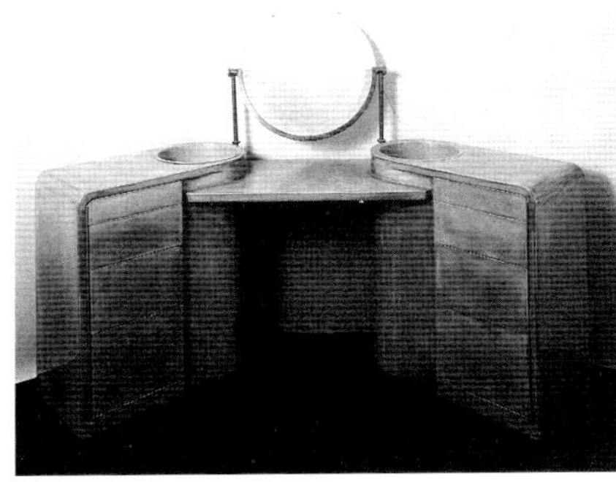

All these figurative compositions revealed the new direction in Dunand's graphic style: he had by now simplified his compositions, investing them with a precision pleasing to the eye and moving towards a type of design that was more direct and more natural, more universal and timeless. Reverting to the method adopted in the 1925 smoking room, Dunand once more incorporated a coffered ceiling with indirect lighting, the silver lacquer having a matt and lightly roughened texture. In the corners, rounded steps allowed light to enter the room from the side, panels of frosted glass being used to soften the illumination. As well as these complete, and wholly successful, groupings, Dunand placed in an adjacent room a large display case containing lacquered vases inlaid with silver complemented by a screen decorated with roe deer.

During the autumn of 1930, Dunand also took part in a group exhibition of contemporary French artists held at the Galerie Rouard, a mixed exhibition combining the work of potters, ceramicists, coppersmiths, glassmakers, fancy-goods makers and goldsmiths. Although Dunand did not enter any pieces specially made for the occasion, he did submit a selection of objects of the greatest refinement.

At the Galerie Georges Petit, the usual group exhibition planned to last four weeks was extended until 6 January 1931. Dunand used the occasion to re-exhibit his *Marabou Storks* screen of 1928, together with another depicting seagulls skimming the waves. In all, he exhibited thirteen screens. Among these was an example as impressive on account of its size as it was for the quality of its execution. It consisted of twelve panels 3 m (10 ft) in height, on which were depicted herons in silver lacquer on a black lacquer background enhanced by inlay work employing mother-of-pearl, eggshell and ivory. The bold composition of this flight of herons by moonlight was matched by the technical perfection of its realization. By now the name of the Dunand was universally associated with lacquerwork and especially with lacquered screens. In one of his plays Henry Bernstein even had his heroine say, 'I'm off to choose a screen by Dunand,' as casually as she might have said, 'I'm off to visit the Eiffel Tower.' Marcel Pagnol used some of Dunand's screens as props, and Bernard Dunand remembers paying visits to various film locations to ensure that the hired screens had been delivered.

Continuing his series of portraits, Dunand presented a likeness of the *couturière* Jenny Sacerdote, its stiffness too far removed from real life, and in striking contrast with his portrait of Jean Guiffrey, which seemed to be emotionally charged in a very individual way. Also shown was a portrait of François-Louis Schmied in Coromandel lacquer: his handsome features stand out against the ram's-head prow of his boat, and one might think Dunand had wanted to give the subject a particular intensity – an intensity that was well served by a more modern approach contrasting strangely with the conventional style of his other portraits.

The Exposition Coloniale (1931)

Dunand's striking contributions to this major exhibition held at Vincennes were the subject of an impressive number of newspaper articles. In addition to the seven pictorial panels forming a vestibule and the two large vases, one on each side of the entrance to the landing that led to the library/reading rooms on the first floor of the Palais Permanent des Colonies, the large *Forest* panel first seen in 1929 was hung in one of the libraries installed by the cabinet-maker Dennery. This magnificent and highly imaginative composition was seen against Brazilian rosewood panelling which enhanced the decorative qualities of Dunand's composition.

The exhibition, under the overall control of Marshal Lyautey, was opened on 17 May by Paul Reynaud, the Minister for the Colonies, and M. Petsch, Under-Secretary of State for the Arts. The Palais Permanent, which subsequently became the Musée des Colonies, was designed by the architects Jaussely and Laprade. The most elegant of all the exhibition buildings, it was constructed on economical lines, using a reinforced-concrete frame and floors, while stone salvaged from the recently demolished city walls was re-used for the infill walls.

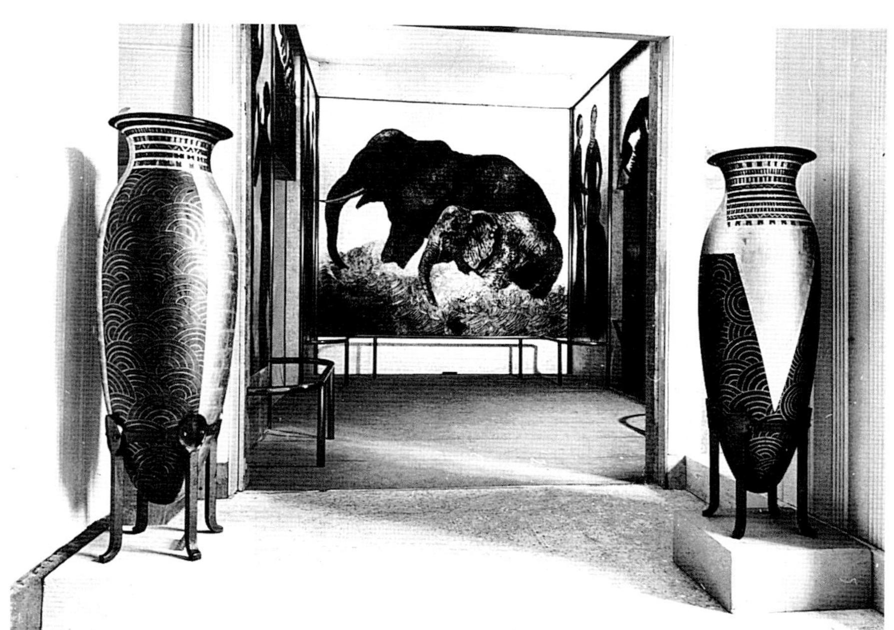

The first-floor vestibule in the Palais Permanent at the Exposition Coloniale, 1931, showing the large panel *The Elephants* (cat. no. 1214) and two monumental vases by Dunand.

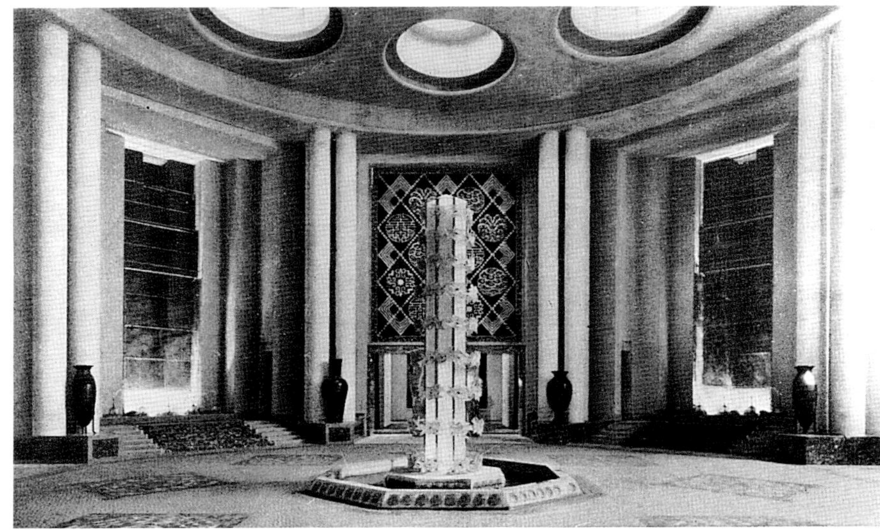

The interior of the Palais Permanent at the Exposition Coloniale showing the fountain by Lalique and four vases by Dunand, each placed in front of paired columns.

The front of the building featured a curtain wall decorated by the sculptor Alfred Janniot with scenes symbolizing the contributions made by the various colonies to the French economy. The building was surrounded by a channel dotted with fountains and enclosed in turn by rectangular flower borders. Supported on each side by groups of leopards designed by Henri Navarre, a metal gate by Jean Prouvé gave access, vis a flight of stairs, to the main entrance where a monumental sculpture by Drivier, *Colonial France*, was a dominant feature. On each side of the spacious vestibule, delimited by grilles by Raymond Subes, was an elliptical room. The one on the right, reserved for Marshal Lyautey, was furnished by Eugène Printz in patawa wood (palm bark from Gabon). It was decorated with painted scenes by Lemaître evocative of Asia. The room on the left, reserved for passing visitors, was furnished by Emile-Jacques Ruhlmann, employing macassar ebony in combination with Sèvres porcelain. Of special note were Ruhlmann's famous 'elephant' armchairs, while Bouquet's paintings evoked an image of Africa. At the far end was the entrance to the banqueting hall, where the decorative scheme by Ducos de la Haille depicted tall symbolic figures that represented an allegory of France extending the dove of peace to the five continents.

Elsewhere in the exhibition, two other panels by Dunand showed African women, in one case pounding millet and in the other leading an ass's foal. Contrary to what Dunand had been told when he accepted the commission, budgetary problems meant that the government could not afford to purchase all the pieces exhibited. Dunand considered, not without reason, that the rightful place for his works was in the future Musée des Colonies, and he preferred to offer them as a gift rather than dismantle the installation, which occupied an area of almost 60 m^2 (70 square yards). Their acceptance by the government was confirmed in a ministerial order dated 28 January 1932. By way of thanks, Dunand was awarded the Grand Prix de l'Exposition Coloniale, and an official plate was presented by the Société d'Encouragement à l'Art et à l'Industrie. It was the least the authorities could do in the circumstances. These panels were taken down and kept in store for many years, but are now on display once more in the former Musée des Colonies (now Musée de l'Art Africain). Their rediscovered magnificence reveals the full extent of Dunand's handsome and generous gesture in this affair.

Nonetheless, Dunand's contribution to the exhibition did not end there. He had entrusted seven of his screens to various exhibitors in the Pavillon de la Métropole, and these, together with a display cabinet of dinanderie, were distributed among various stands with the theme 'Haute Couture'. Among these screens, there were four comprising twelve panels each and measuring 3 m (10 ft) high: they evoked an ambience of tropical forest alive with exotic

Plates 107–145

DINANDERIE: HOLLOW WARE WITH OR WITHOUT LACQUER DECORATION

OPPOSITE

107 **Monumental vase**, 1925
(*catalogue 1199*)

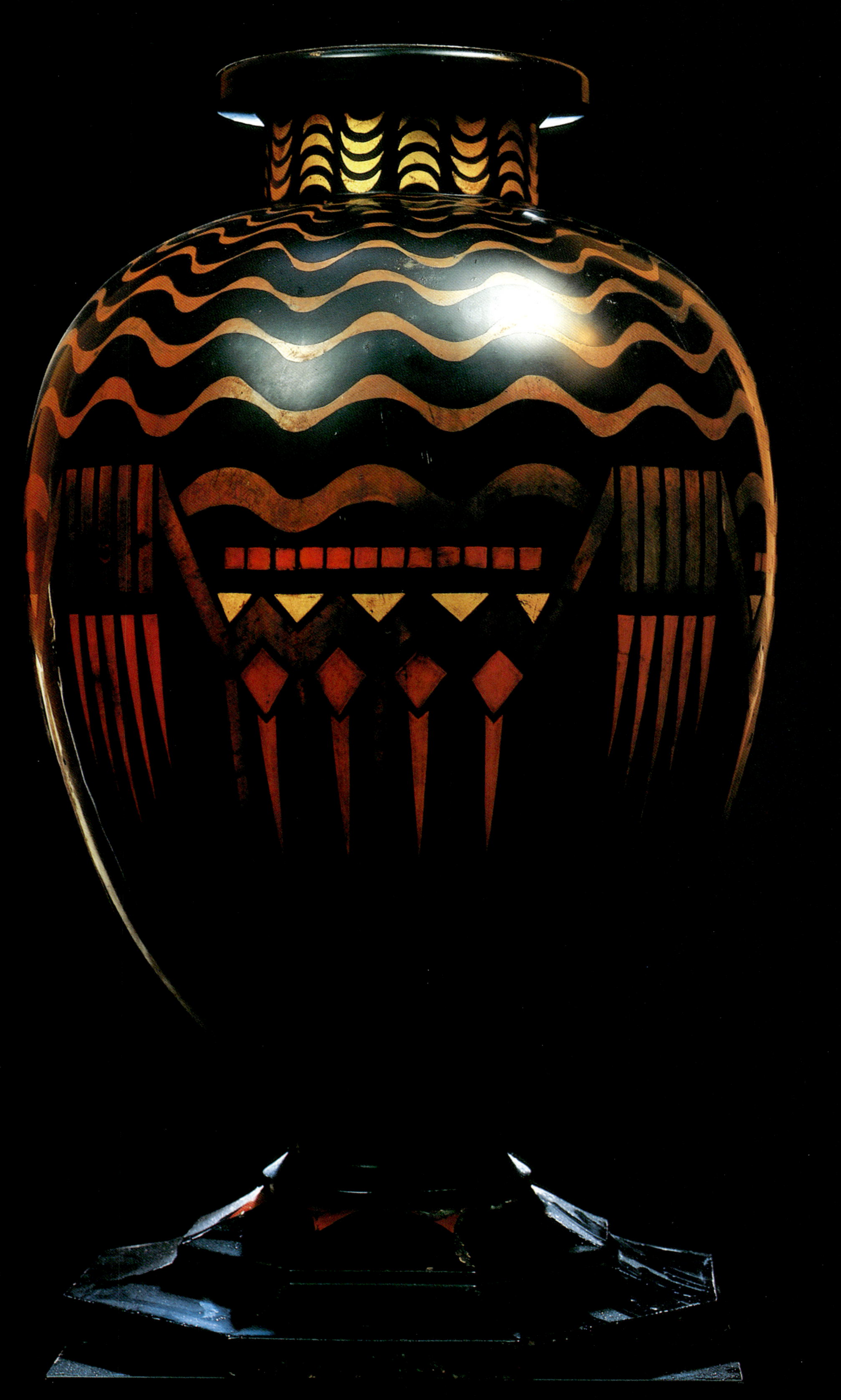

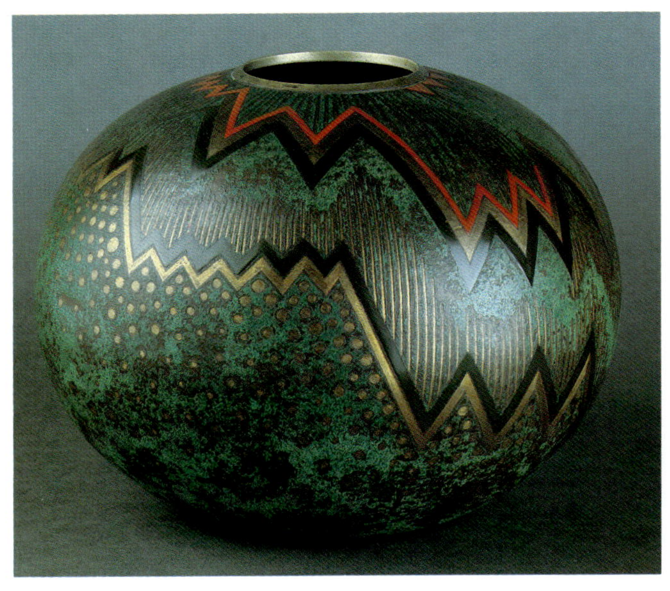
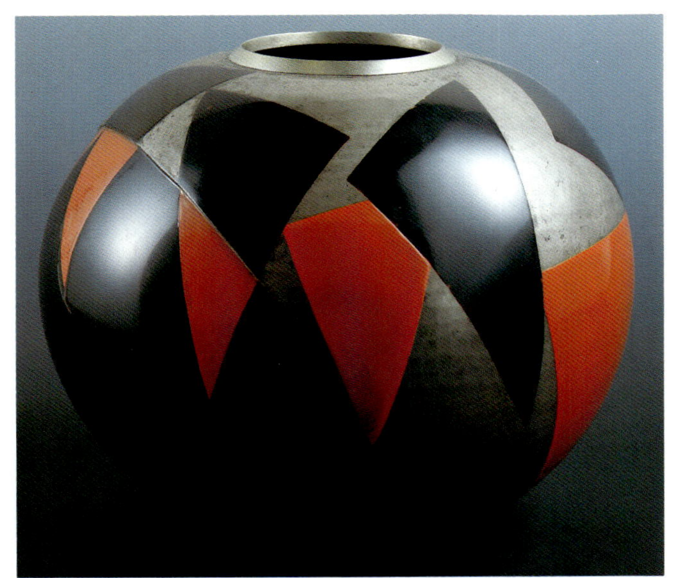
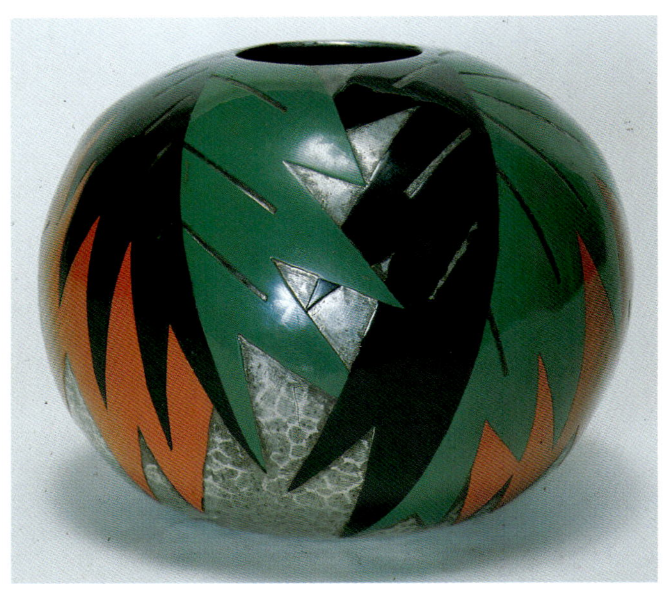
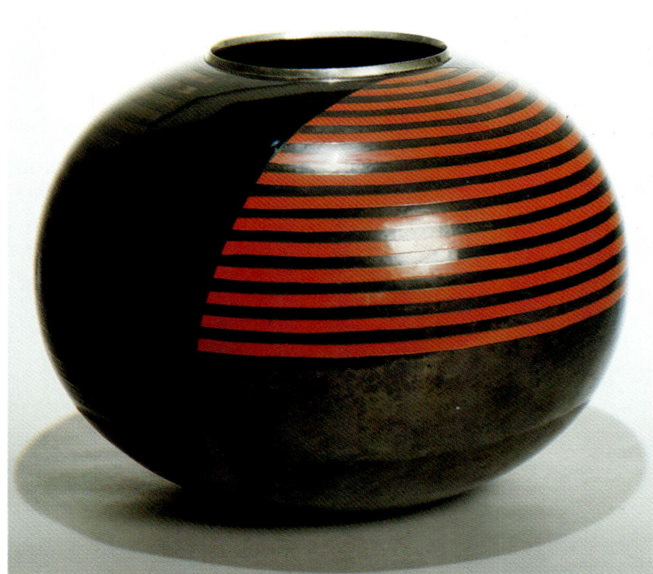
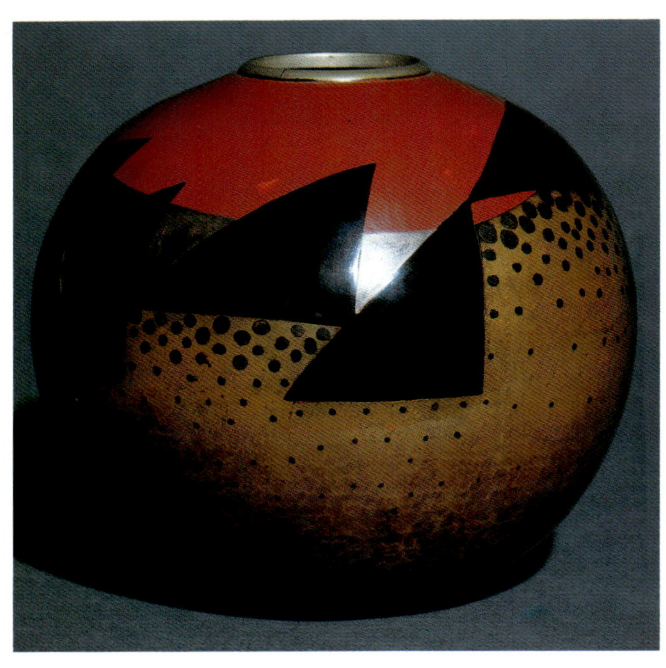
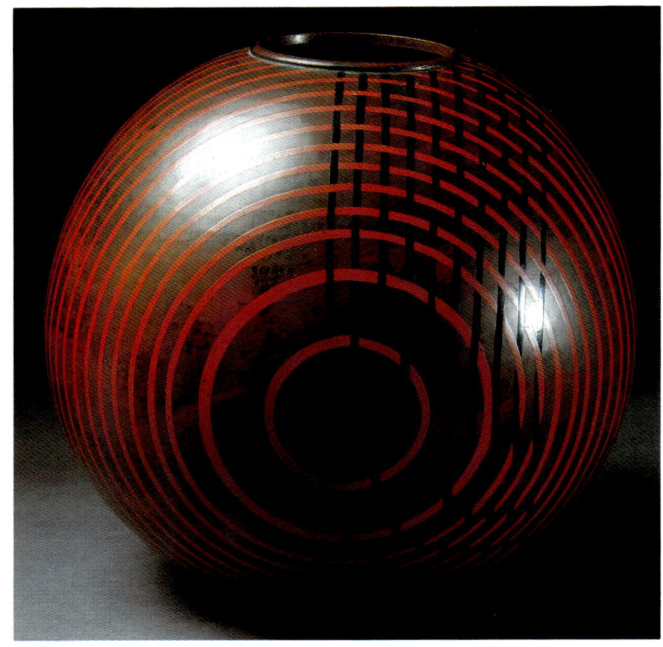

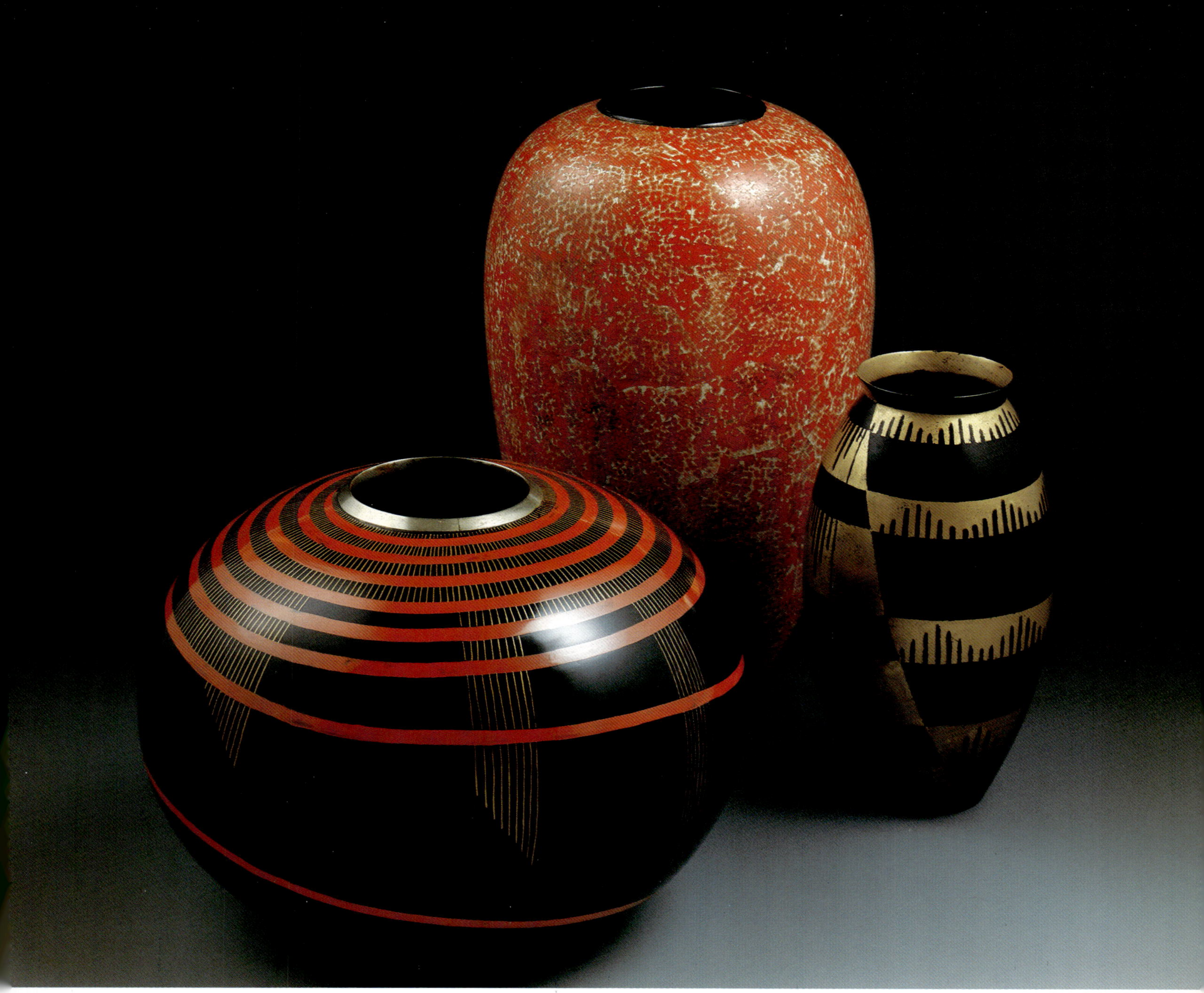

OPPOSITE 108 **Spherical vase**, *c.* 1922–4 (*catalogue 1011*)

109 **Spherical vase**, 1925 (*catalogue 1066*)

110 **Spherical 'Leaf' vase**, *c.* 1926 (*catalogue 1051*)

111 **Spherical vase**, *c.* 1924 (*catalogue 1052*)

112 **Spherical vase**, *c.* 1925 (*catalogue 1069*)

113 **Spherical vase**, *c.* 1930 (*catalogue 1070*)

ABOVE 114 **Group of vases,** 1922/25 (*catalogue 1063*)

RIGHT 115 **Spherical vase,** *c.* 1925 (*catalogue 1024*)

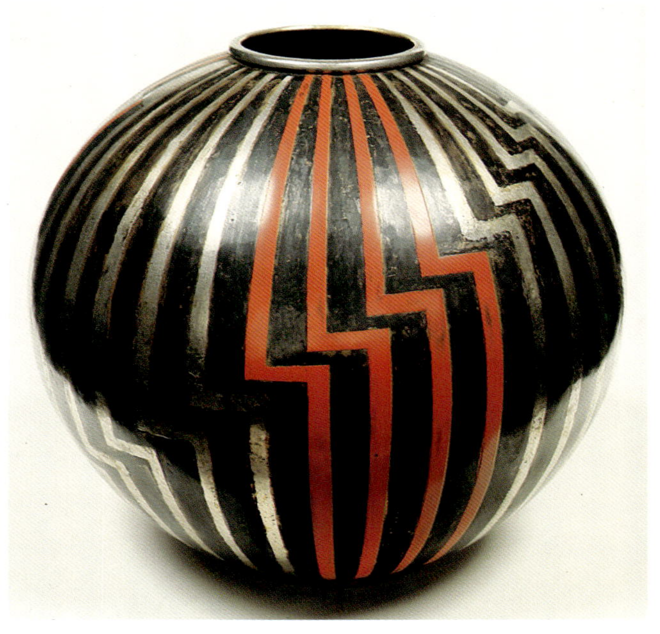

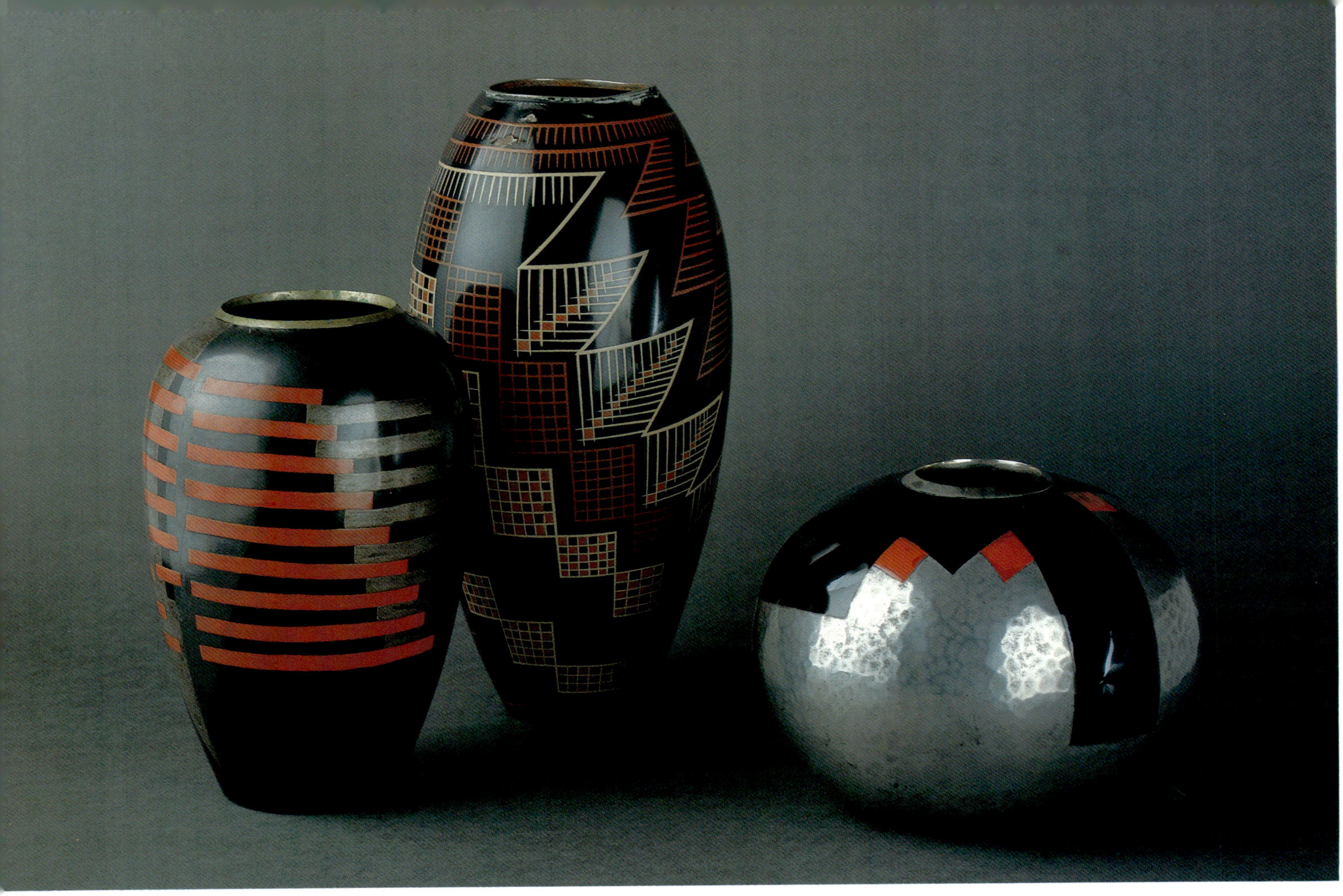

116 **Group of vases,** *c.* 1925
(*catalogue 1025*)

OPPOSITE, ABOVE
118 **Group of vases,** 1925/1920
(*catalogue 1023*)

OPPOSITE, BELOW
119 **Group of vases and**
bonbonnière, *c.* 1925
(*catalogue 1022*)

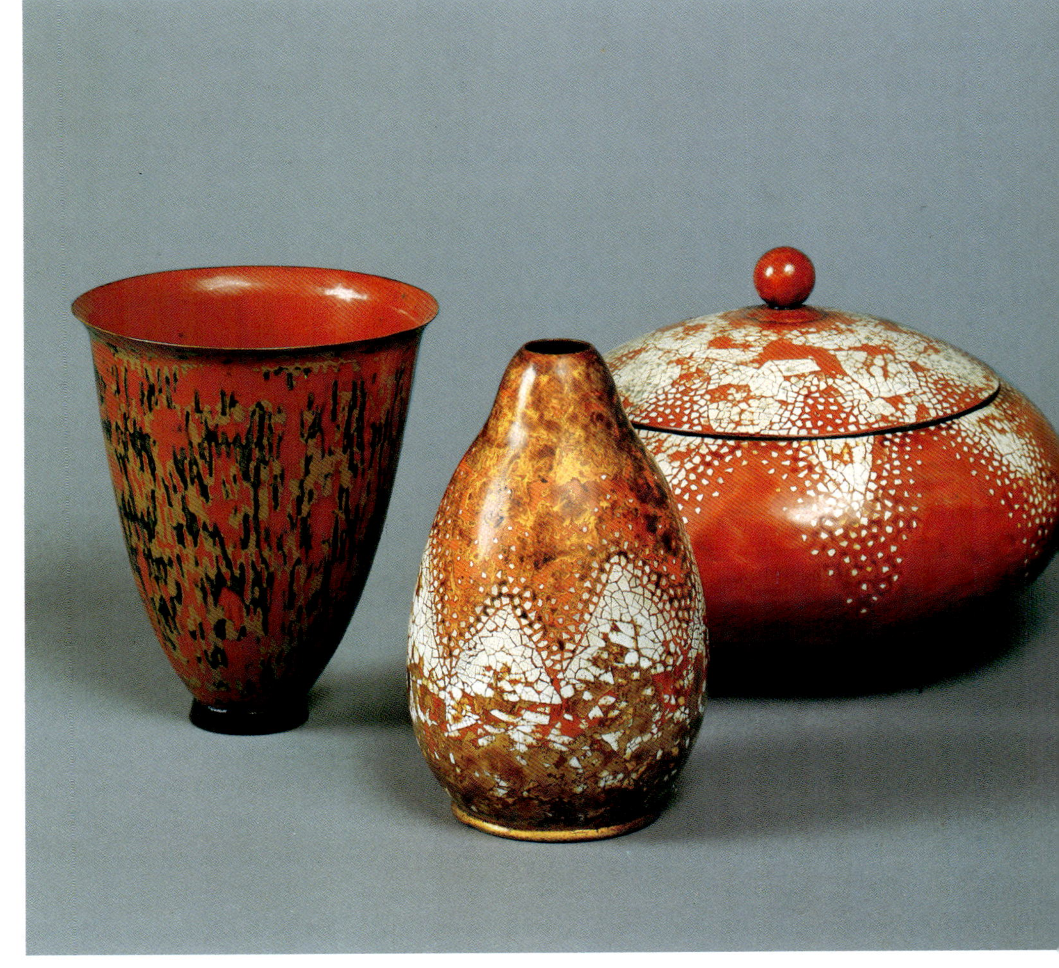

117 **Group of vases and**
bonbonnière, *c.* 1925
(*catalogue 1017*)

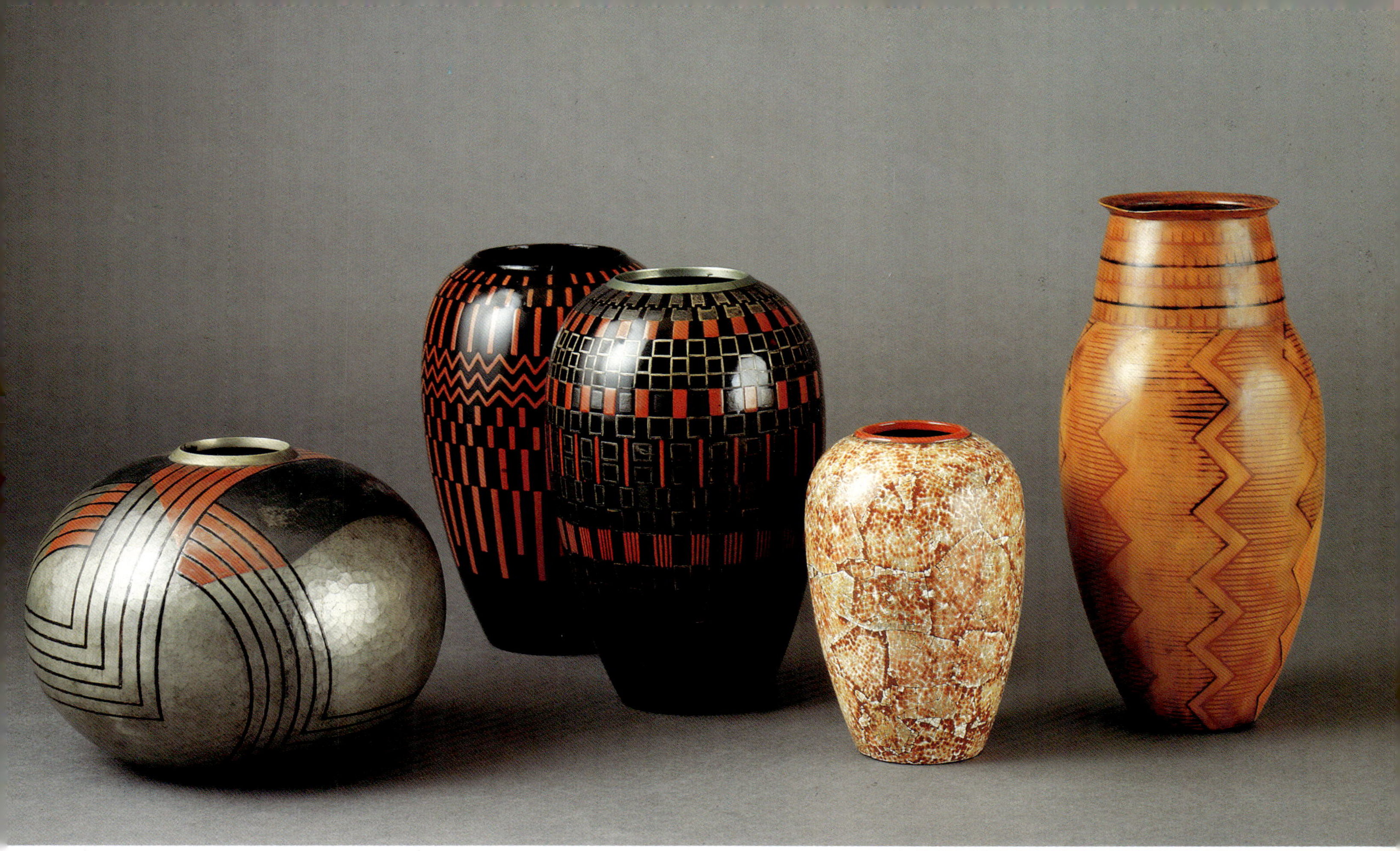

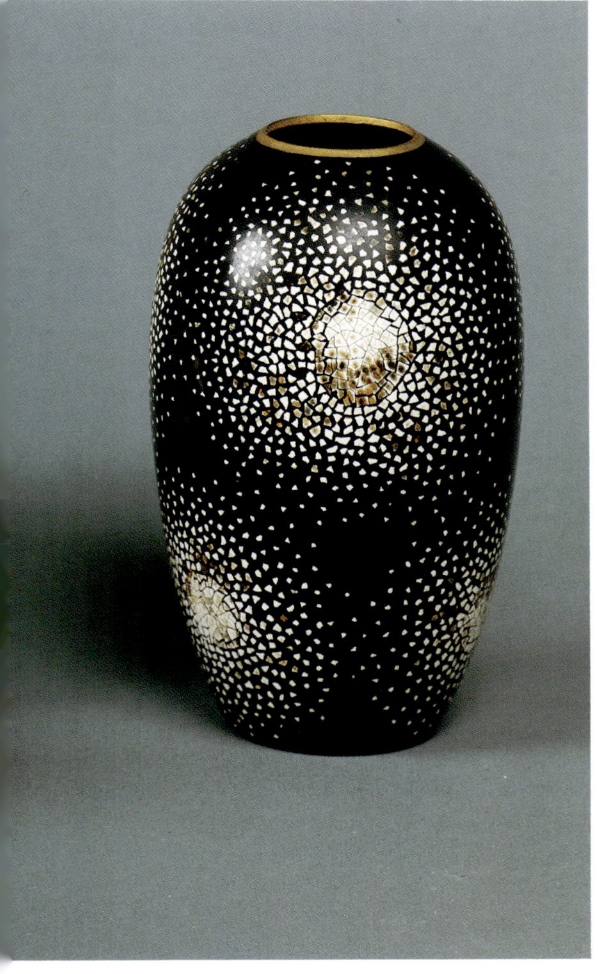

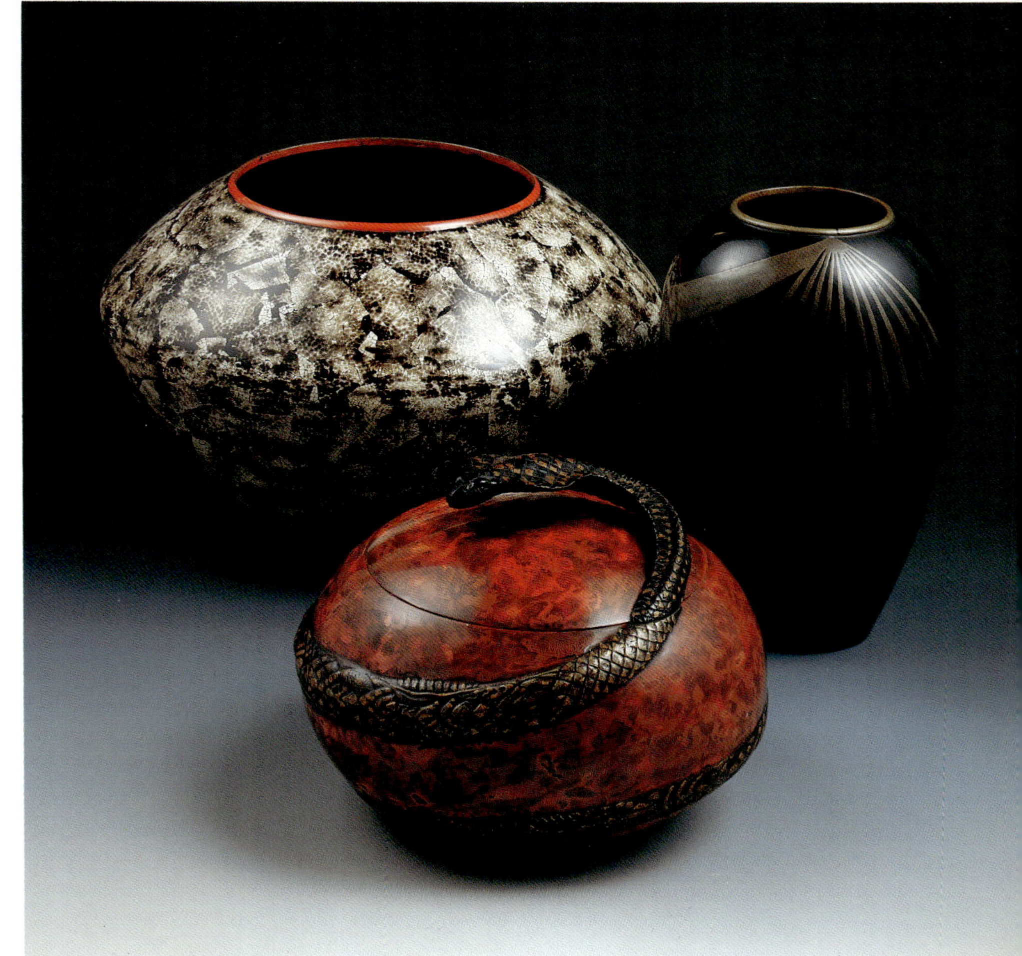

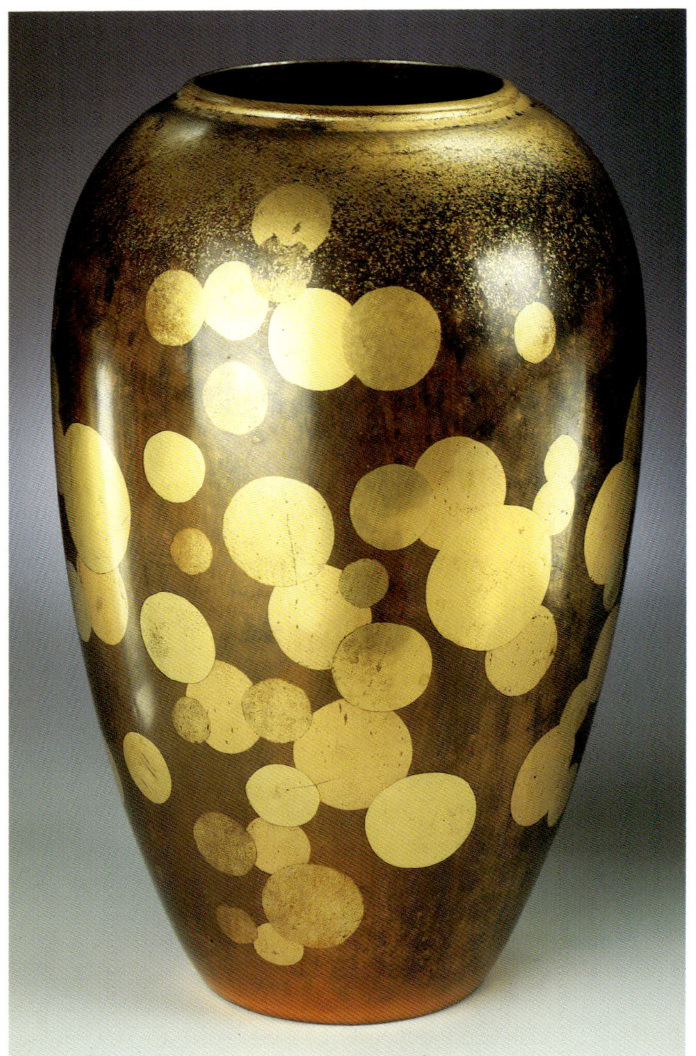

120 **Ovoid vase**, *c.* 1925
(*catalogue 1028*)

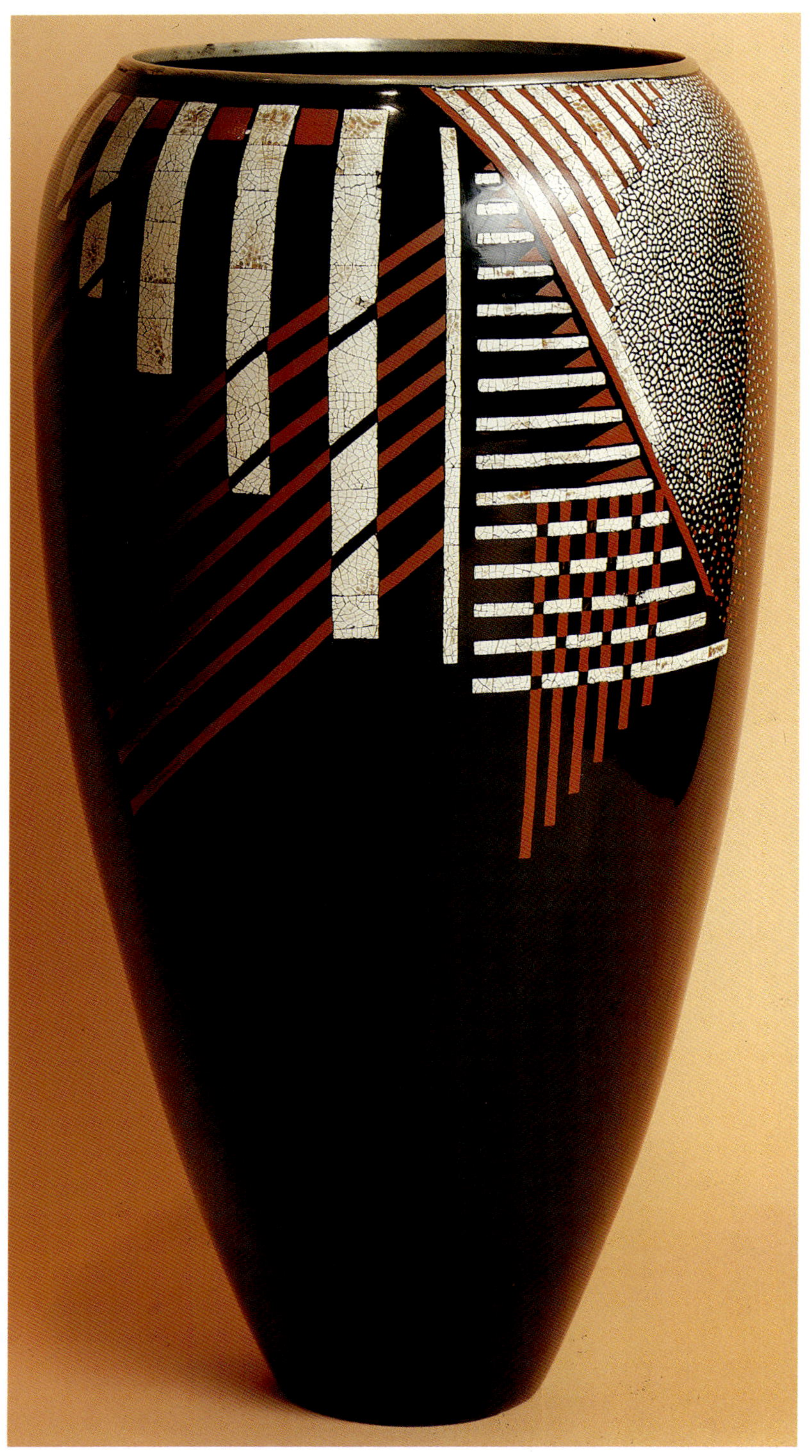

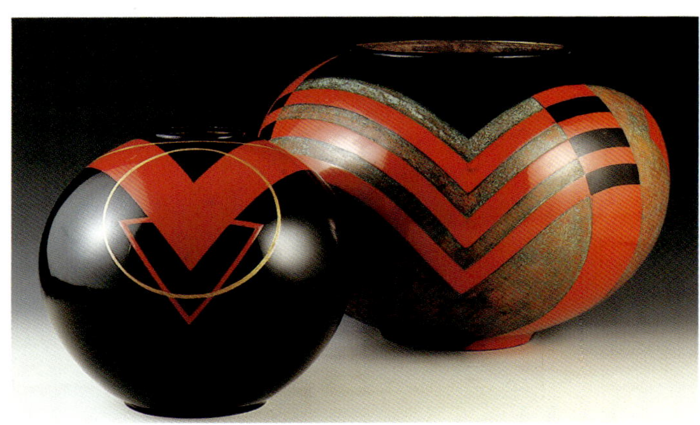

121 **Two spherical vases**, *c.* 1930
(*catalogue 1053*)

122 **Large vase**, 1925
(*catalogue 1054*)

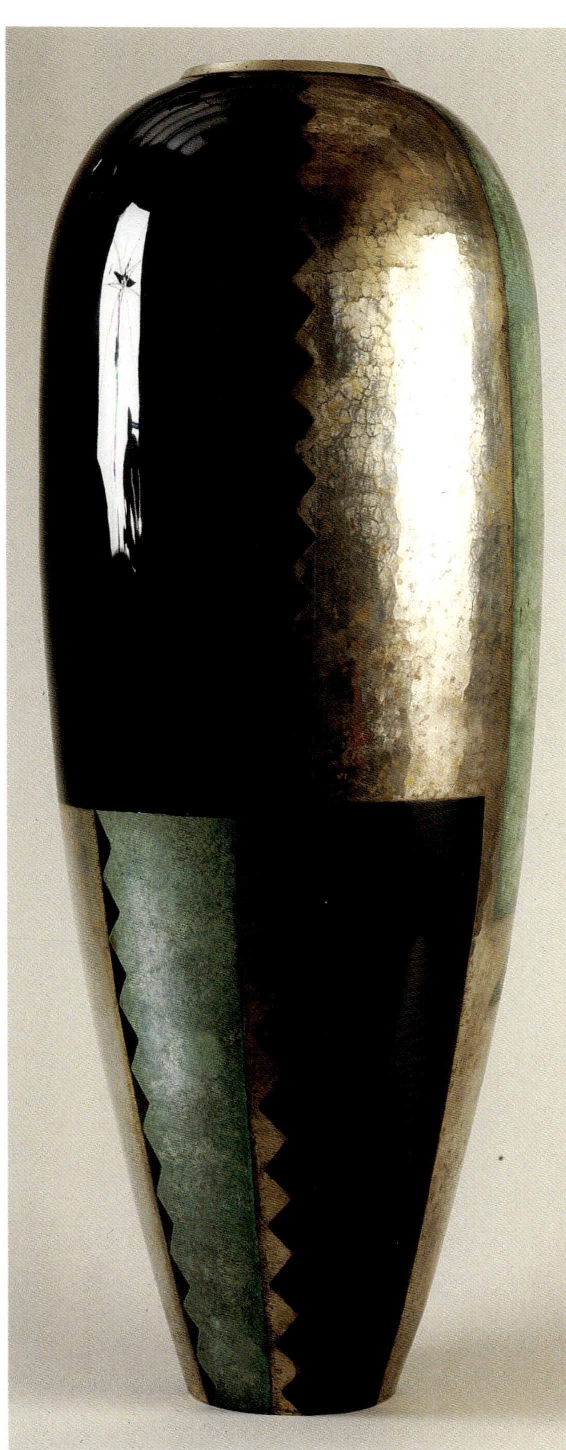

123 **Tall vase**, 1928
(*catalogue 1050*)

BELOW LEFT
124 **Vase with *appliqué* vertical 'wing'**, 1926
(*catalogue 1042*)

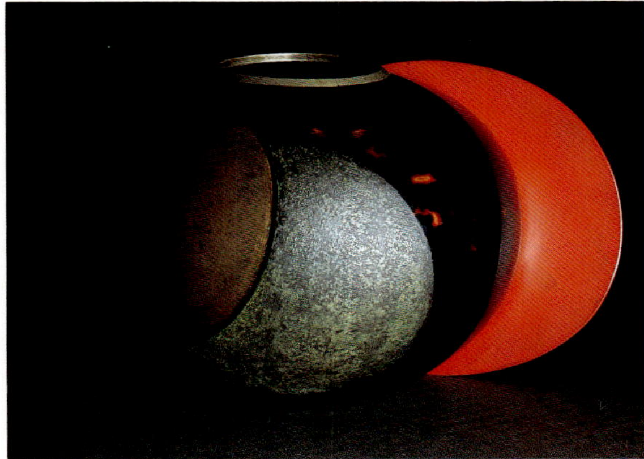

125 **Reflector**, lacquered *c.* 1930
(*catalogue 1056*)

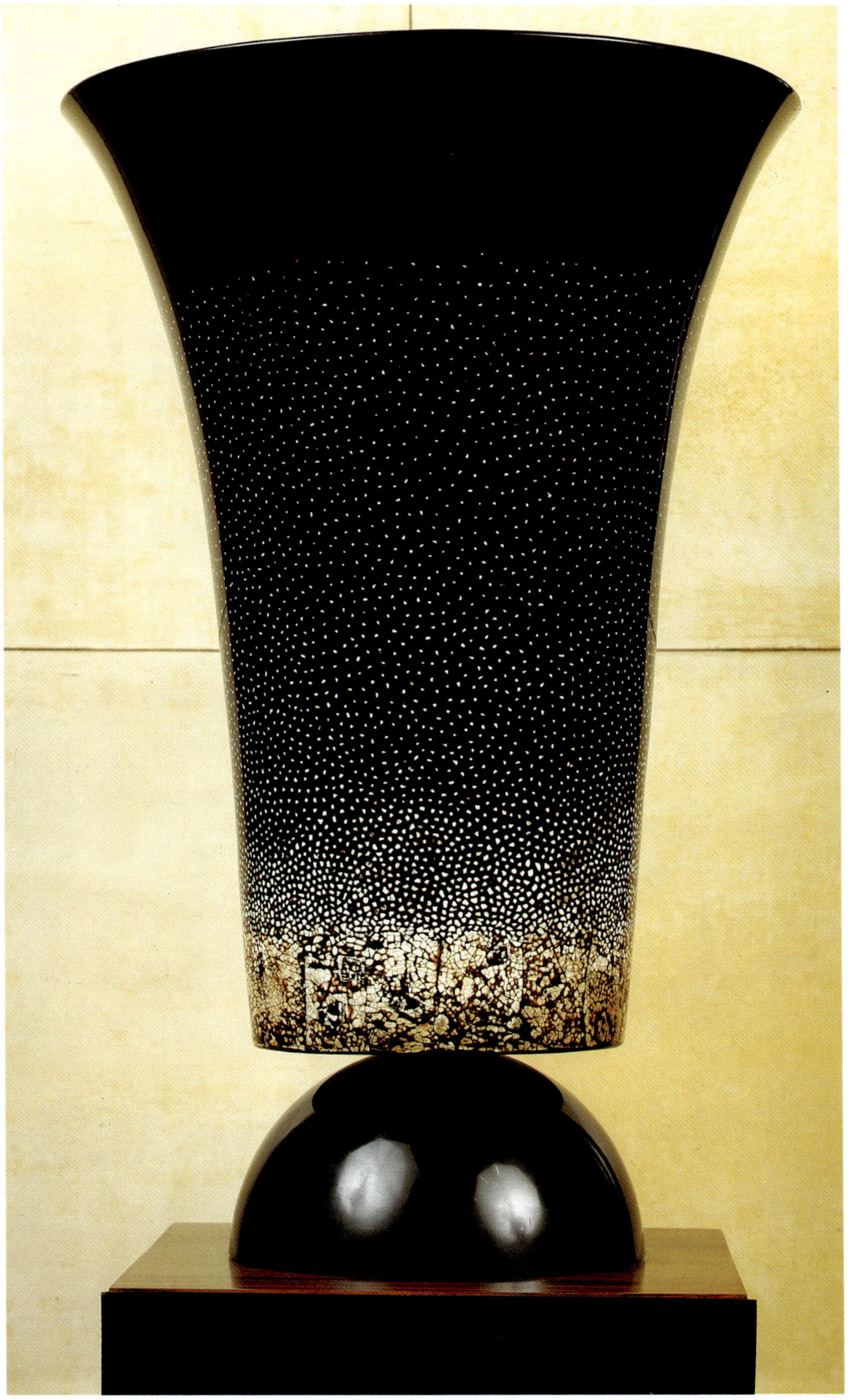

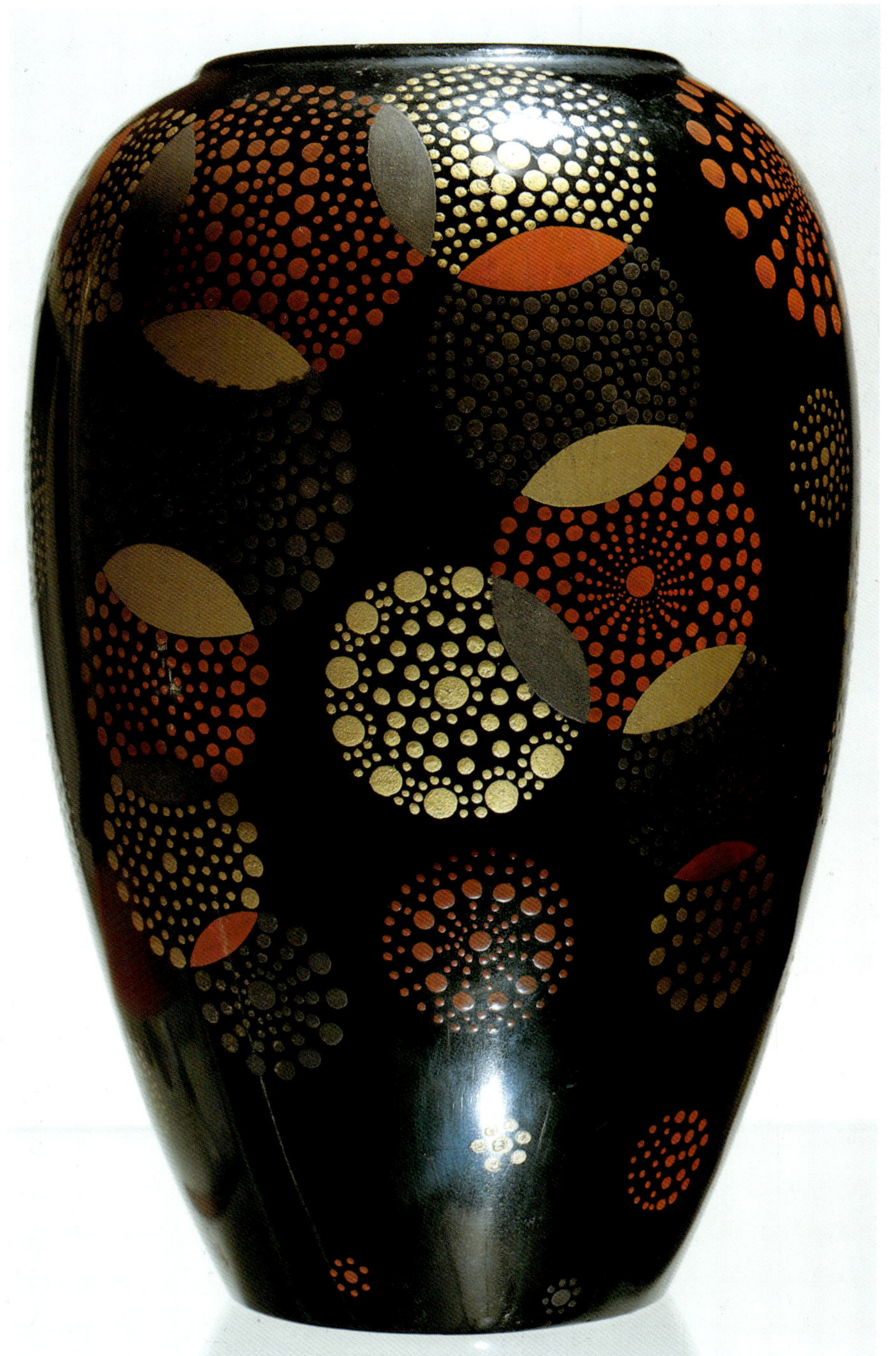

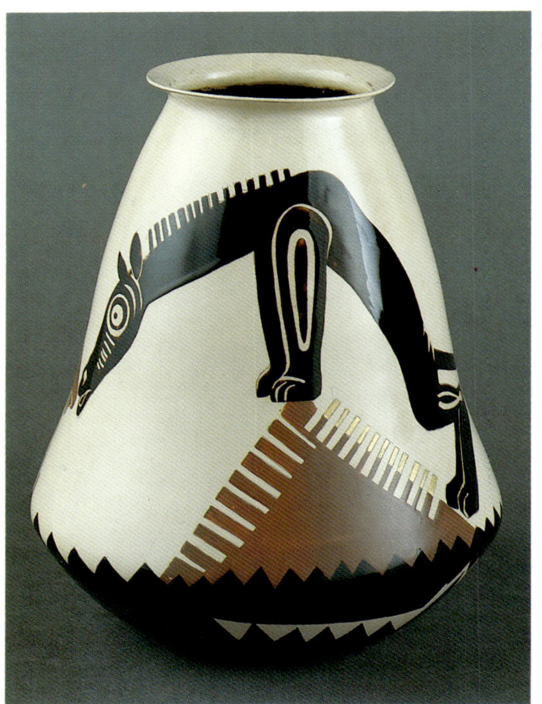

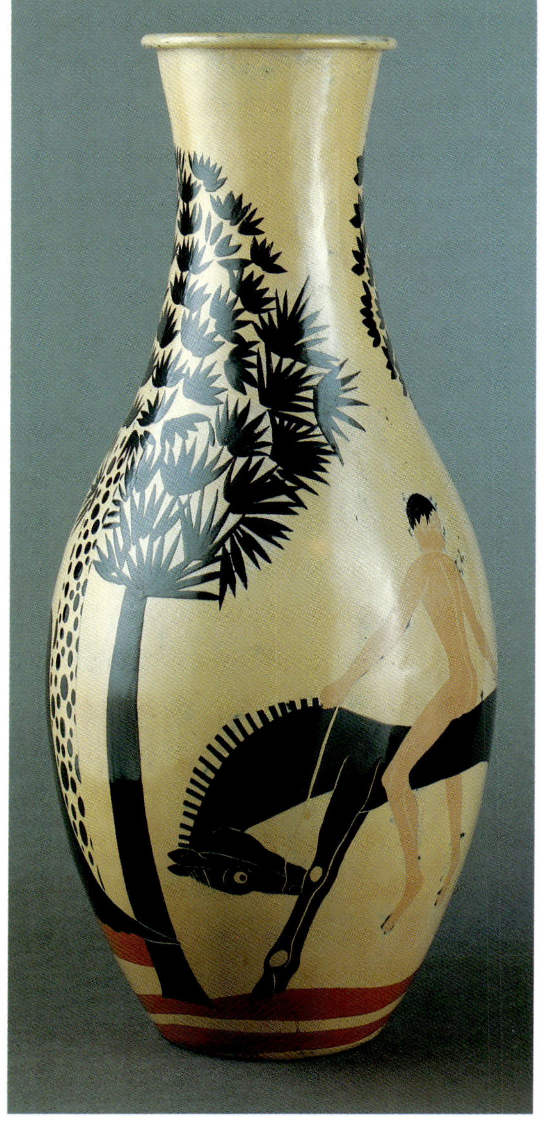

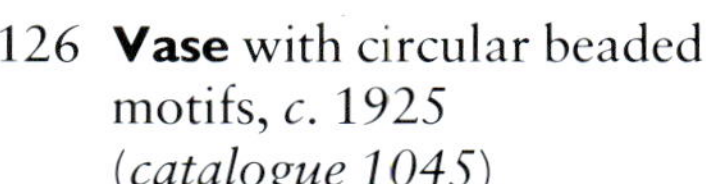

126 **Vase** with circular beaded motifs, *c.* 1925 (*catalogue 1045*)

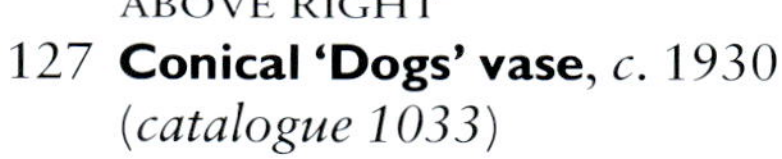

ABOVE RIGHT
127 **Conical 'Dogs' vase**, *c.* 1930 (*catalogue 1033*)

128 **'Horsemen' baluster-shaped vase**, *c.* 1930 (*catalogue 1036*)

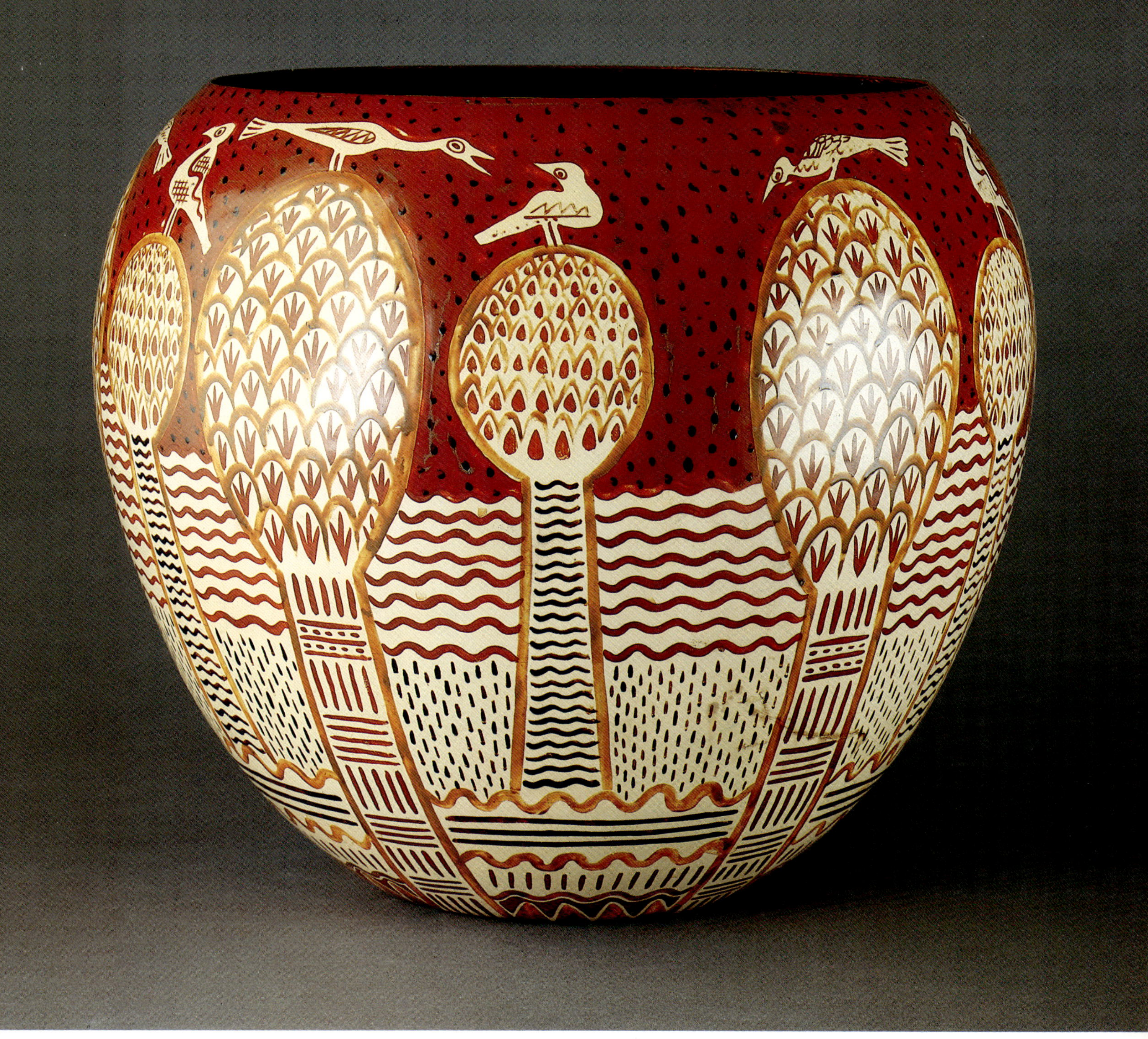

129 **'Birds in Trees' cache-pot,**
c. 1930
(*catalogue 1034*)

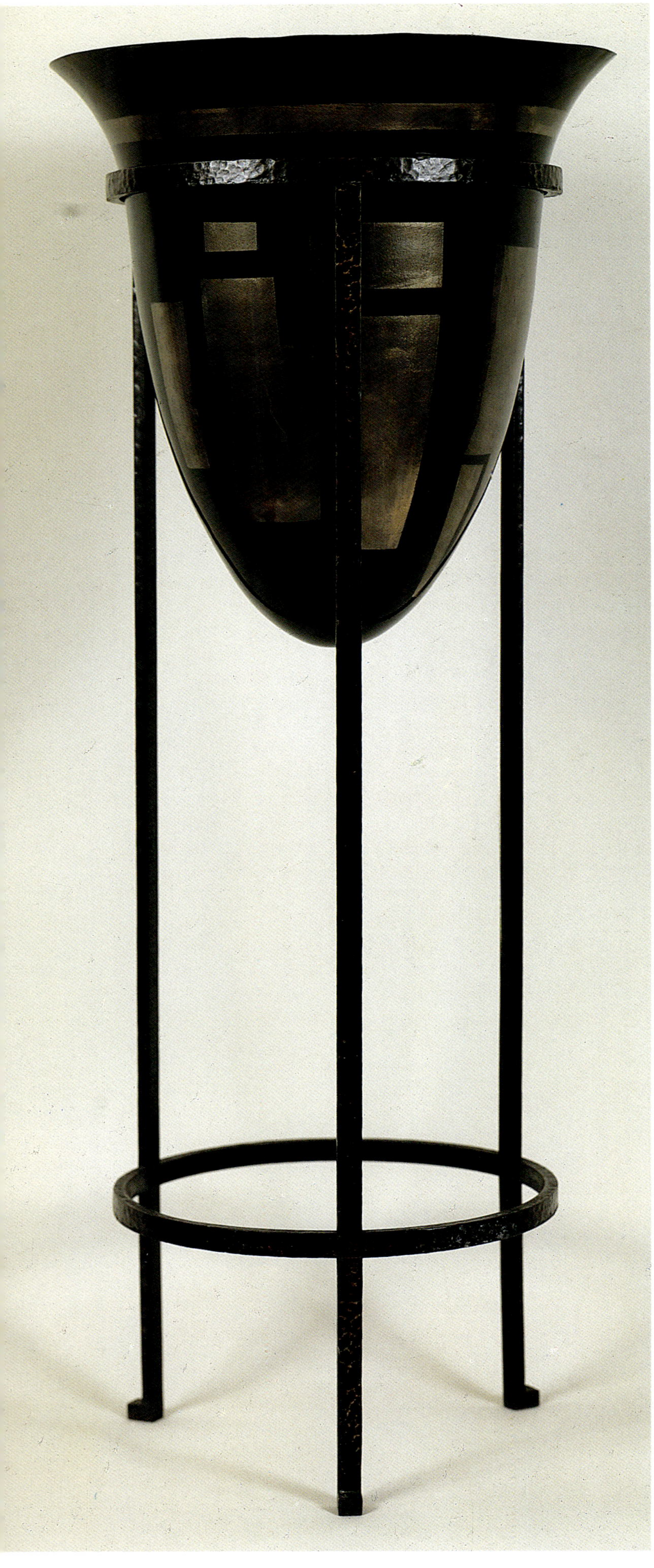

130 **Deep bowl on tripod**, 1923
(*catalogue 1014*)

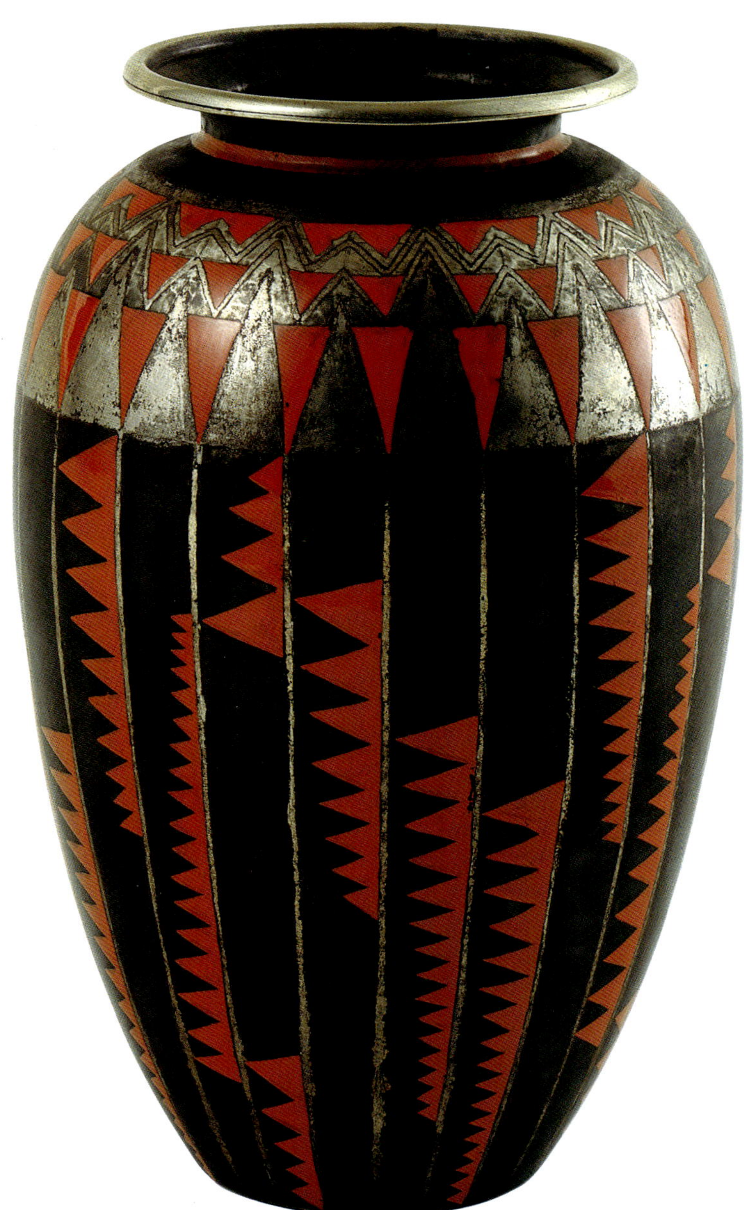

131 **Ovoid vase with everted rim**,
c. 1922
(*catalogue 1003*)

OPPOSITE, ABOVE
132 **Ribbed cache-pot**, *c*. 1920
(*catalogue 1001*)

OPPOSITE, BELOW
133 **Spherical vase**, 1925
(*catalogue 1059*)

134 **Spherical vase**, *c*. 1922–4
(*catalogue 1010*)

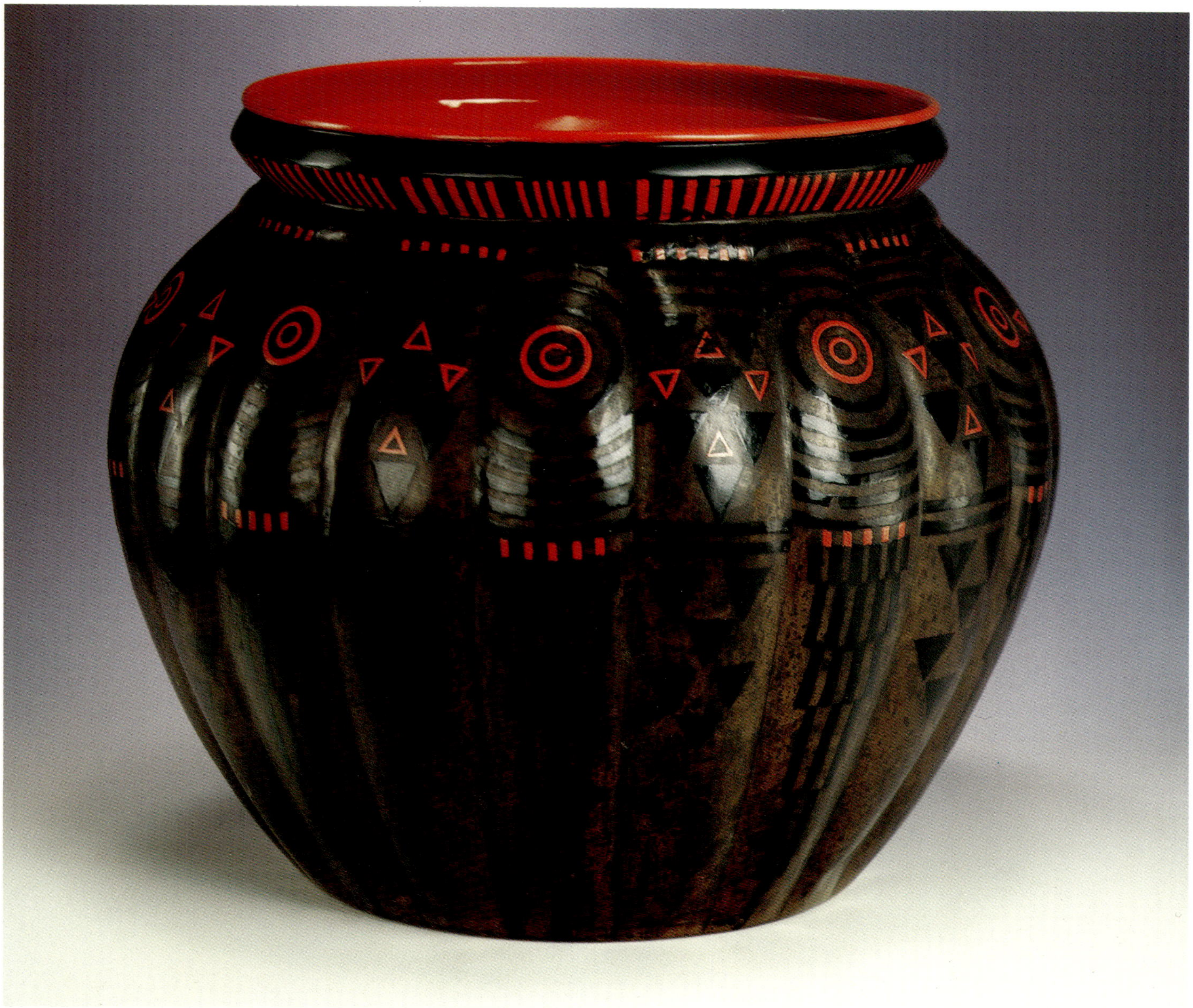

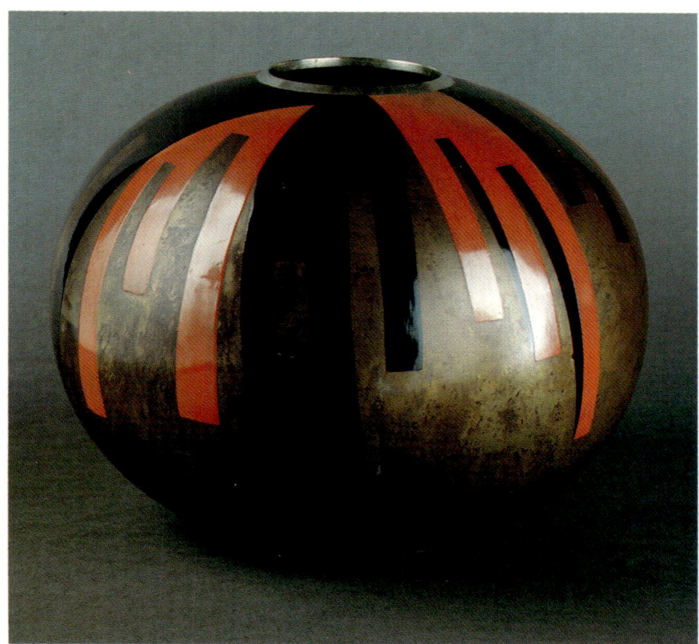

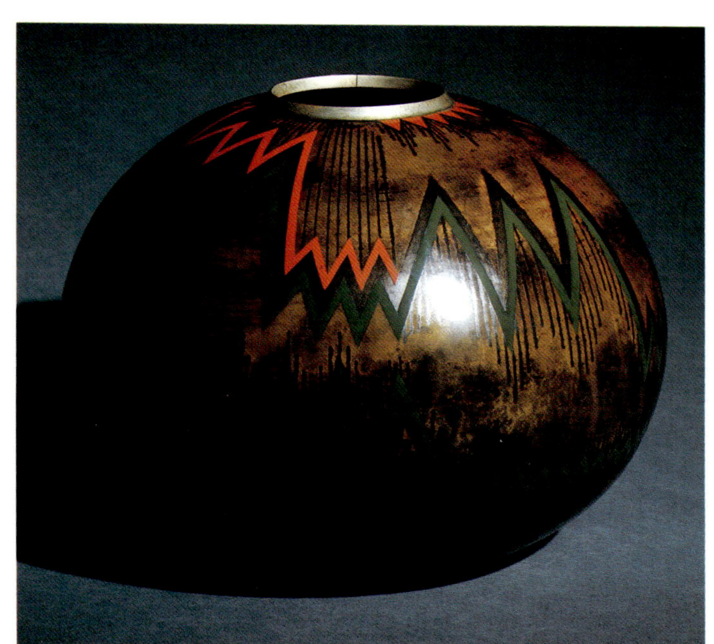

136 **Large cylindrical vase**, 1912
(*catalogue* 907)

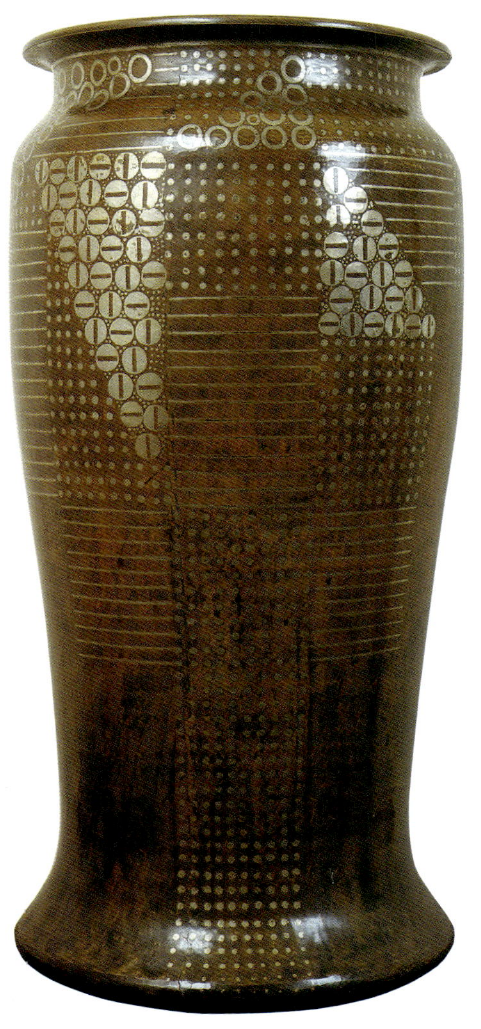

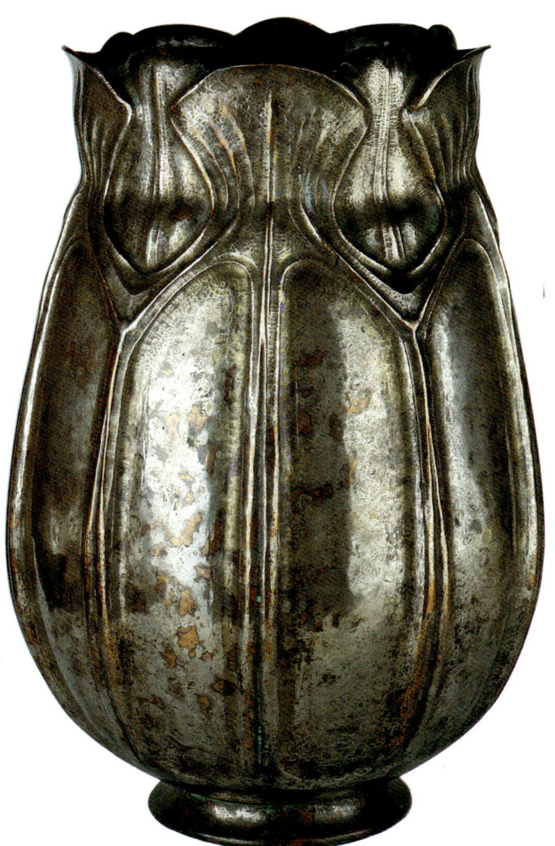

135 **Flower-vase**, 1912
(*catalogue* 904)

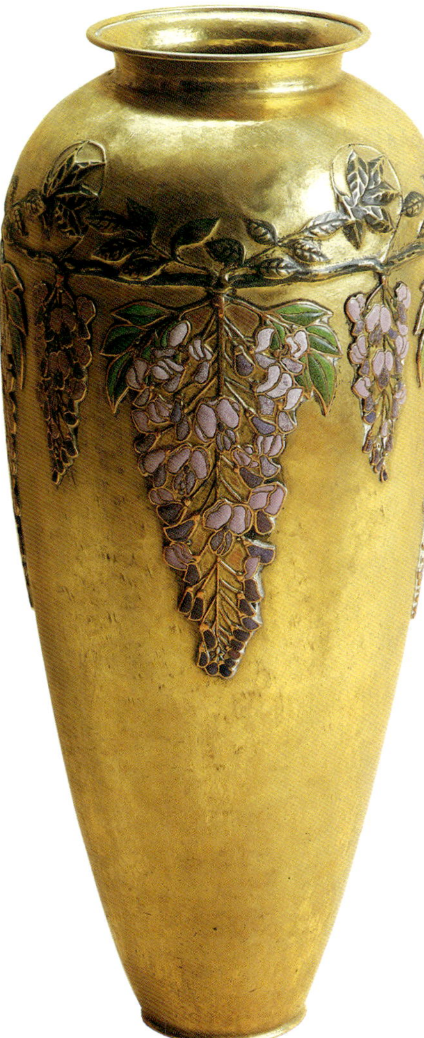

138 **'Wistaria' vase**, 1912
(*catalogue* 932)

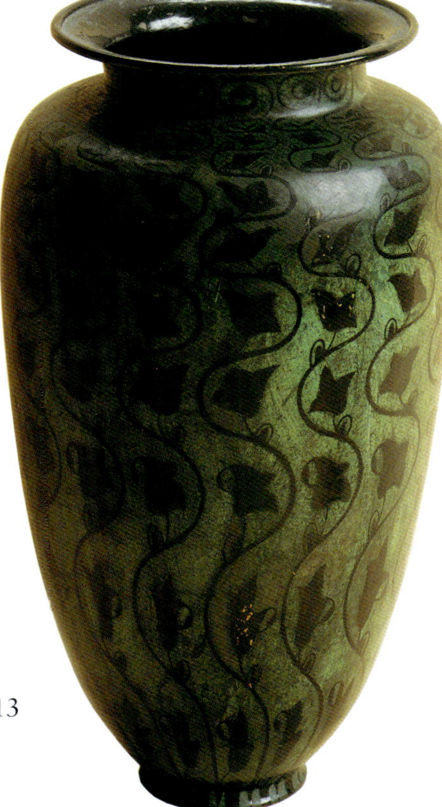

137 **'Ivy' vase**, *c*. 1913
(*catalogue* 939)

OPPOSITE
139 **'Frog' vase**, 1906
(*catalogue* 873)

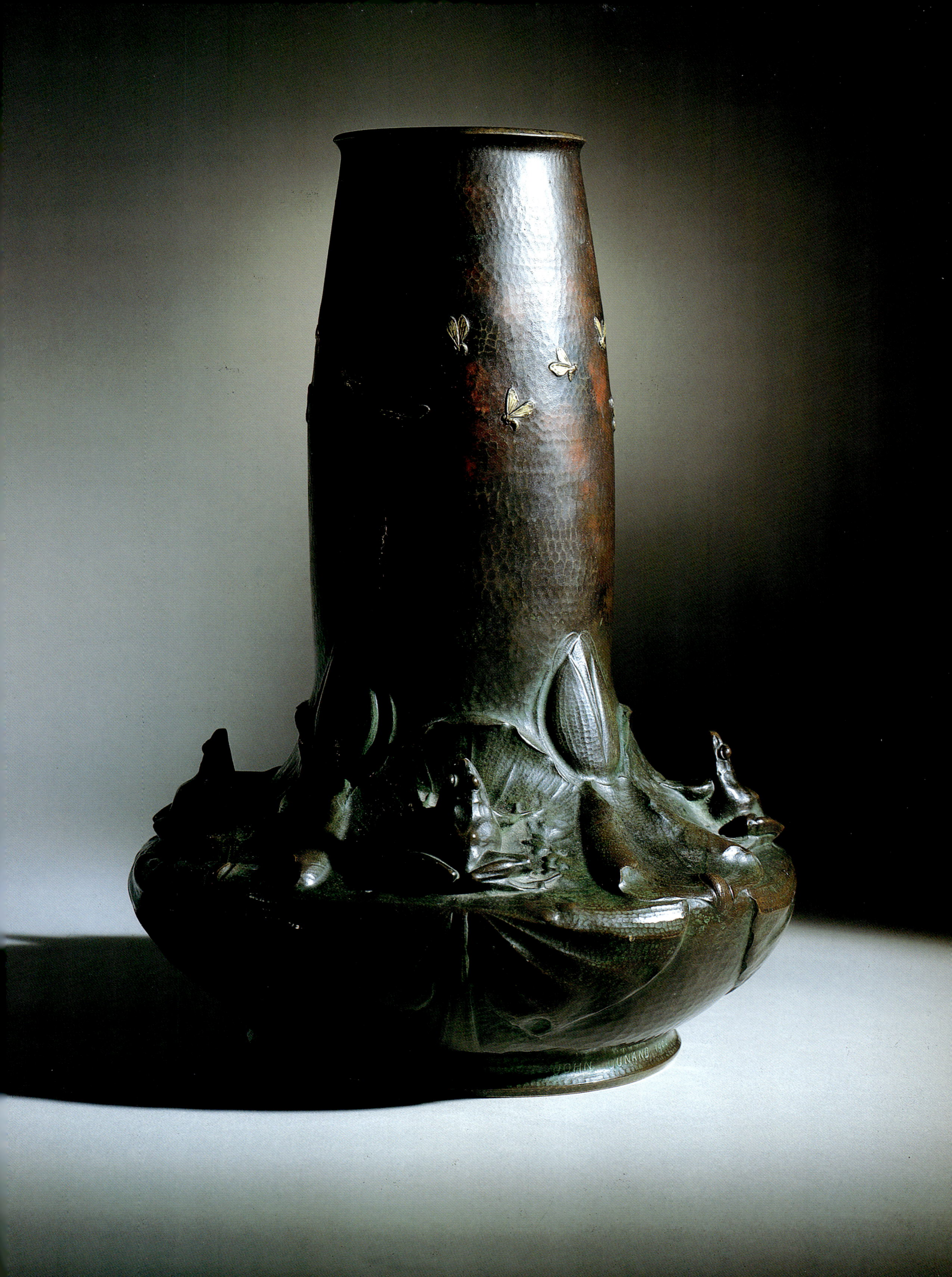

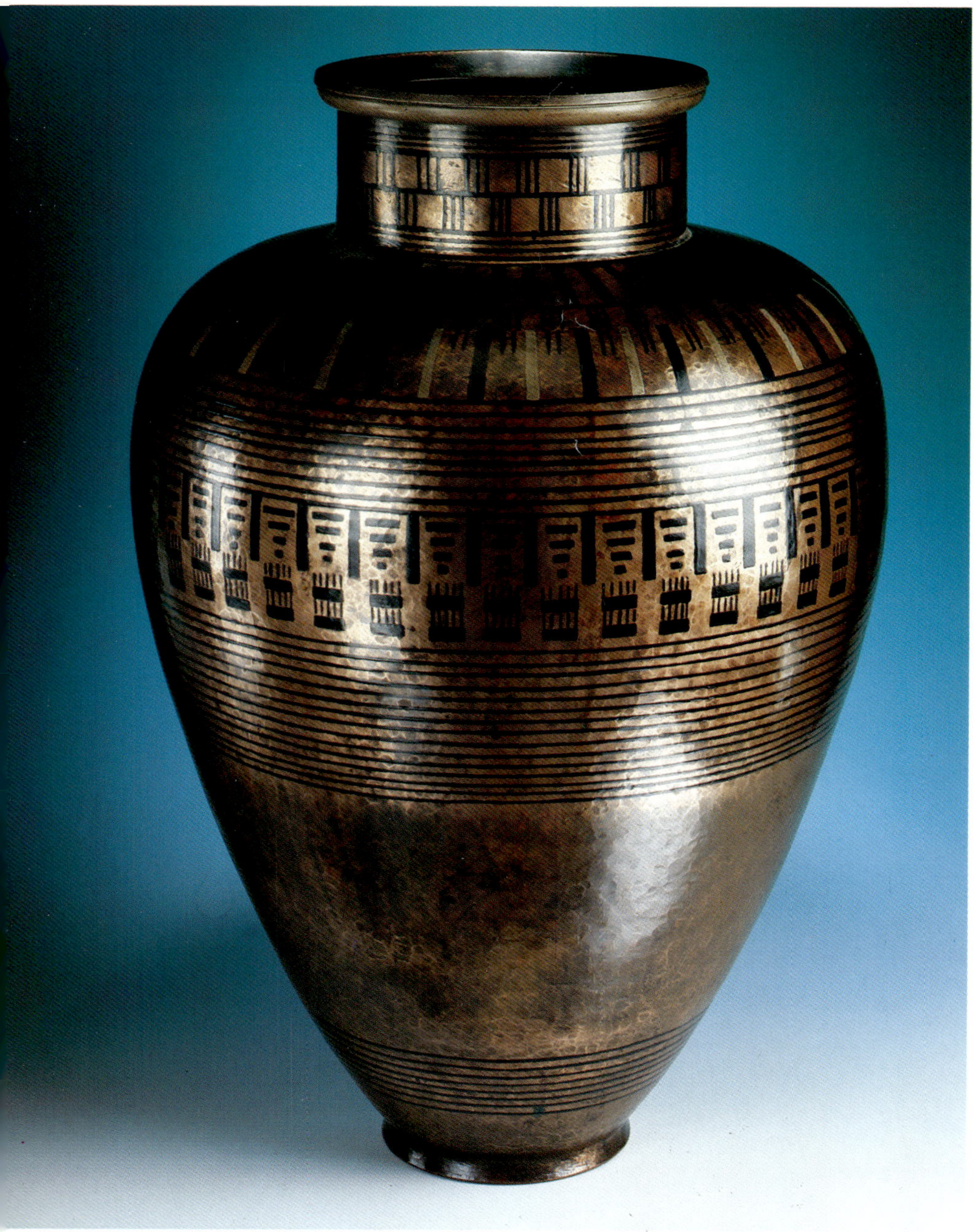

140 **Large urn-shaped vase**, *c.* 1922
(*catalogue 987*)

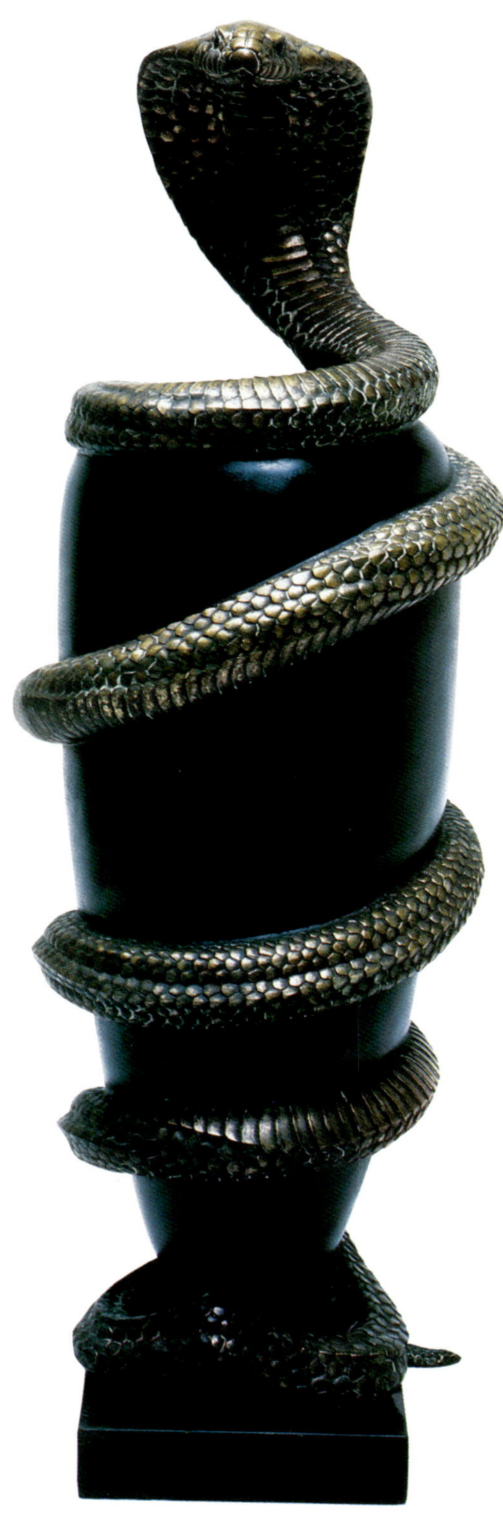

141 **'Coiled Snake' vase**, 1920
(*catalogue 981*)

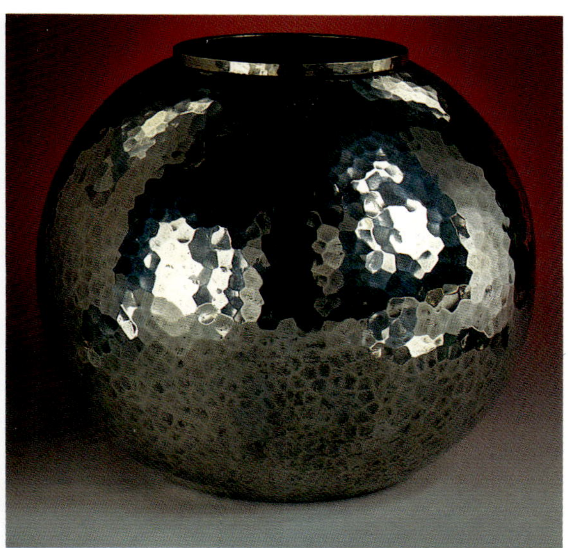

142 **Spherical vase**, *c*. 1922
(*catalogue 982*)

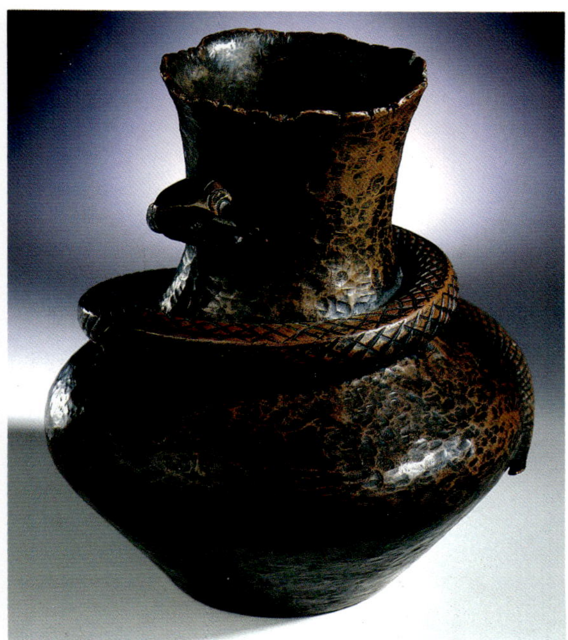

143 **'Snake' vase**, 1907
(*catalogue 876*)

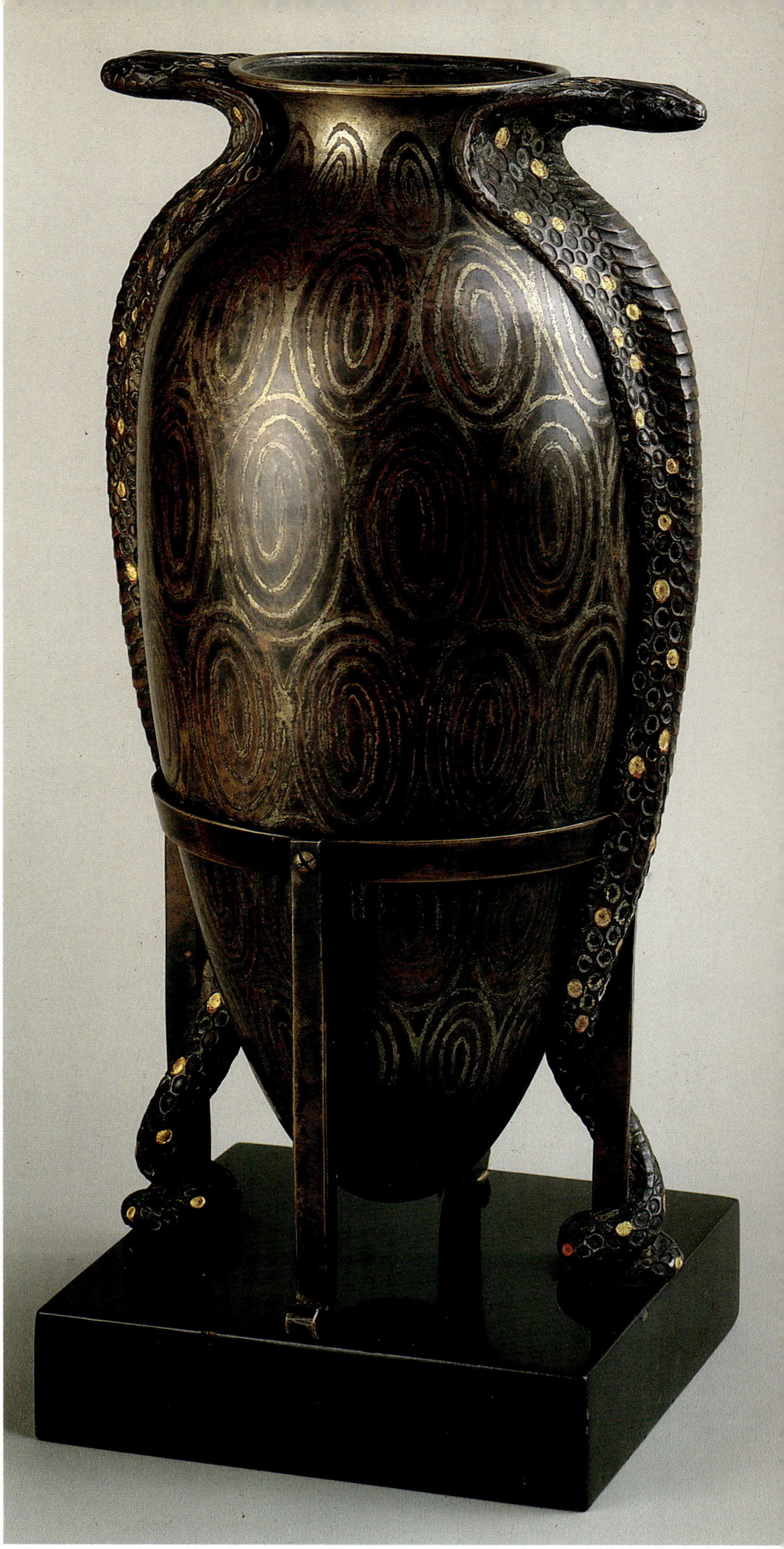

144 **'Snake' vase**, 1913
(*catalogue 936*)

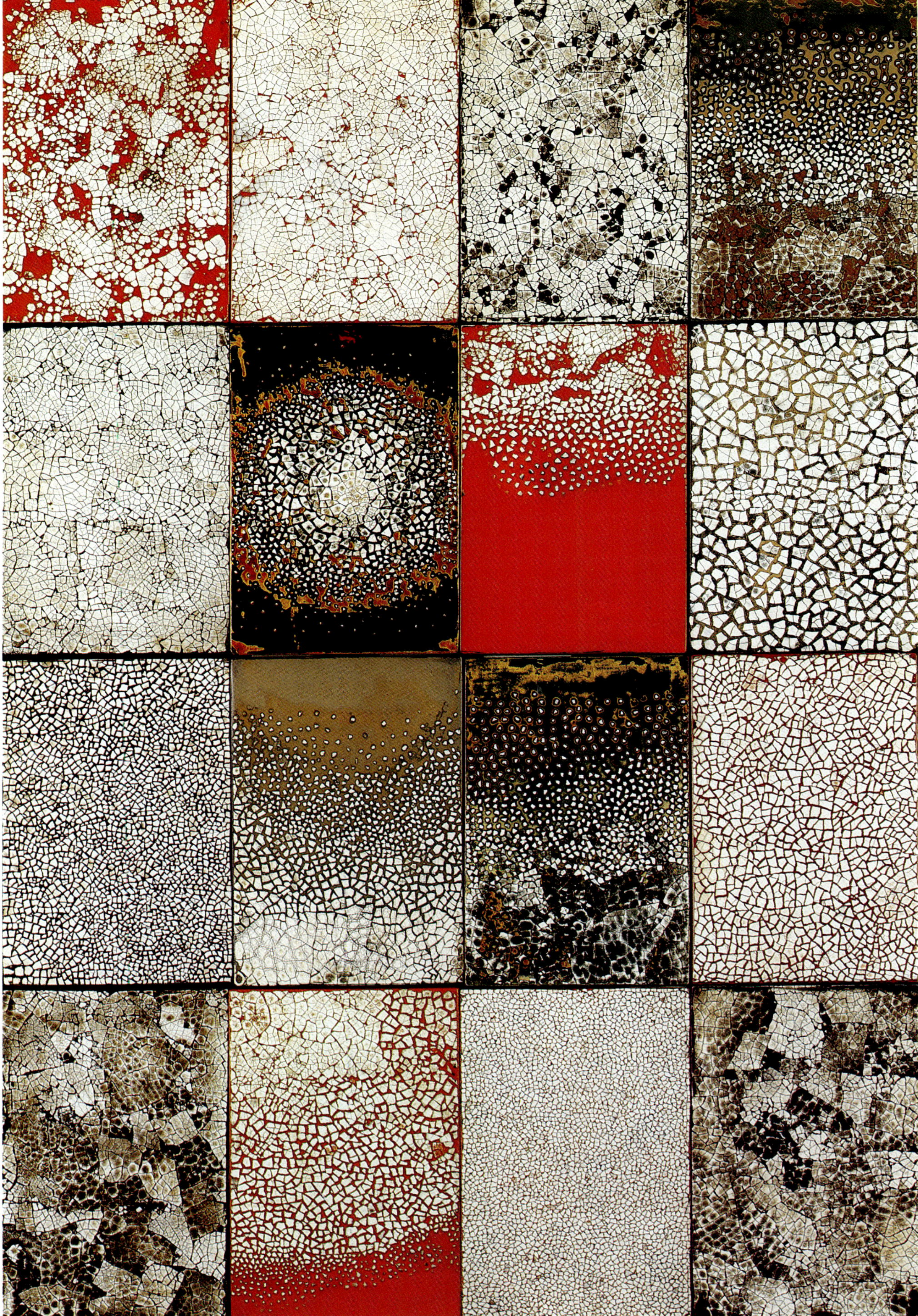

animals and herons, providing a backcloth for fashion models wearing hats by Madame Agnès and dresses by Lanvin and Worth. The three smaller screens depicted seagulls, monkeys and exotic flowers. One of these was placed in the fine arts section, one on the stand of the Société des Artistes Décorateurs and one on that of the Salon d'Automne.

Although Dunand had also designed two posters in a modern and highly audacious graphic style to advertise the exhibition, neither was published. To mark the end of the exhibition, he also designed the cover of the programme that accompanied the official closing ceremony, at which singers such as Damia, Marie Dubas and others performed before a distinguished audience, including government ministers.

The liner 'L'Atlantique'

Following a competition organized among interior designers, under the aegis of the Société d'Encouragement à l'Art et à l'Industrie, the Compagnie Sud-Atlantique decided to entrust all the interior decoration on its new liner to French artists, the work to be under the control of the painter Albert Besnard. The directors of the company gave Dunand an entirely free hand, though draconian deadlines were imposed, and vast penalties were payable in the event of a delay in completing the work. The chosen theme was as grandiose as it was simple: the flora and fauna of tropical countries were to be shown, but without any depiction of the sea, since a study had concluded that representations of waves and boats contributed to sea-sickness among passengers. The aim was once again to foster the decorative arts in France and to give a striking demonstration of their scope and of the use of specialist techniques. And since, in terms of both speed and comfort, the liner would outclass all the other foreign vessels that plied the South American route, it was hoped to provide self-evident proof of French superiority.

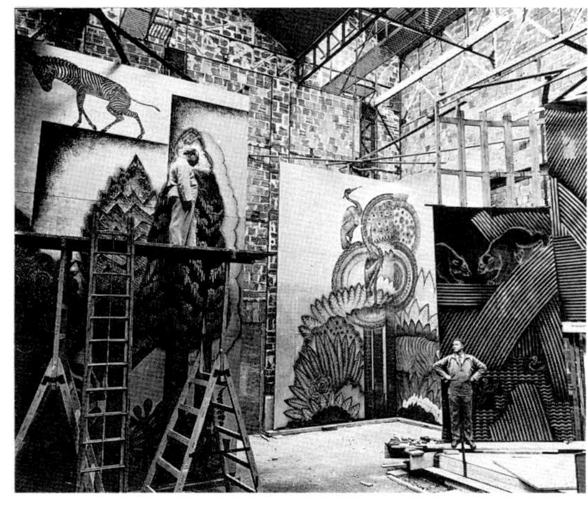

Jean Dunand and his son Bernard in the family workshops during the preparation of the lacquer panels for the dining room of the liner *L'Atlantique*.

The architects Pierre Patout and Raguenet-Maillard were entrusted with the task of fitting out the first-class dining saloon, the two main saloons and a central avenue, 137 m (150 yards) long, lined with luxury boutiques. In size the new liner, weighing 42,500 tons, was in keeping with her owners' ambitions. The ship was 227 m (740 ft) long and nearly 30 m (97 ft) across at its widest point. From the hold to the bridge there was a total of twelve decks, with accommodation for 1,208 passengers. A veritable floating metropolis, the vessel was equipped with the most sophisticated of comforts and the most carefully designed amenities for the long voyage from Bordeaux to Rio de Janeiro, Santos, Montevideo and Buenos Aires. Built at the Penhoët shipyard in Saint-Nazaire, the vessel had been designed in such a way that the exhaust pipes and drive mechanism were located on each side, thus making available a vast open space in between. This unique area was turned to advantage by transforming it into the first-class dining saloon, 32 m long by 24 m wide and 9 m high (104 x 78 x 29 ft). It was situated on the same level as the two side deck terraces, to which direct access was possible through five french windows on each side. A magnificent staircase led to the main saloon. The shop-lined thoroughfare even included a car dealer's showroom displaying several different models. This typically Parisian avenue ended in a large oval-shaped hall designed by Patout and surmounted by a rotunda whose dome, supported by ten columns, each 7 m (23 ft) high, reminiscent of tree-trunks, rose to a height of 9 m (29 ft). The overall impression was one of considerable grandeur.

High up behind these columns was placed a frieze by Dunand. Conforming to the hall's oval plan, it consisted of curved panels, each 4.70 m (15 ft 3 in.) in height. They were finished in black lacquer decorated in gold, depicting all manner of animals among stylized reeds. Polar bears, herons and deer, as well as rams, dogs, wild boar and ducks seemed to pursue one another and conceal themselves among the vegetation. Surrounding the four pilasters and extending above the doors, the composition was calculated, in its simplicity, to hold the passengers' attention, while expressing a real feeling of luxury and sophistication.

OPPOSITE
145 **Samples of decorative lacquer inlaid with eggshell** (cf. pl. 12)

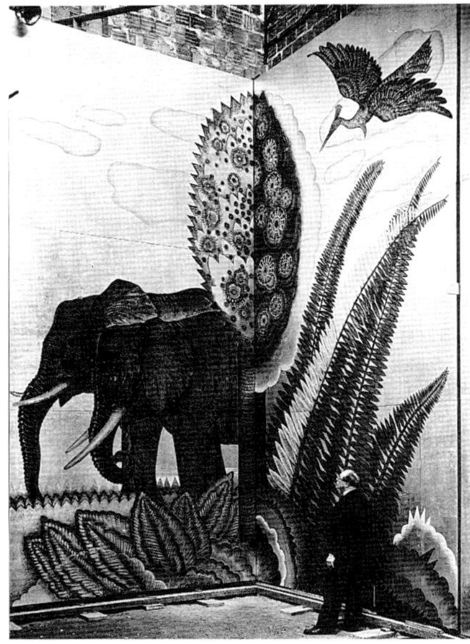

Jean Dunand standing beside the vast decorative panels after their completion in his workshops.

In the dining saloon an even more spectacular impression was created. In each corner Dunand had arranged a series of double panels, 6.50 m (21 ft) in height, on which were depicted groups of animals, different in each case: a zebu and group of gazelles unconcernedly browsing, while on the other side a tiger could be seen, angrily eyeing two elephants. On the panels in the opposite corner, a tiger lay in wait for a zebra. At the far end of the dining saloon, whose coffered ceiling diffused light that was in turn reflected by the lacquered surfaces, Dunand had placed a huge panel depicting a flock of birds, evoking the long seasonal migration between the two hemispheres. The overall effect was grandiose and striking.

In order to be able to execute panels on such a scale, Dunand had been obliged, once again, to extend his workshops in the direction of the Rue Montbrun. He had employed a carpenter and had himself supervised the masonry work. In addition, he had been forced to install the largest wood presses in Paris in order to make his own plywood and bend it to the required shape. To ensure that the panels would not warp in humid surroundings, he braced them with a criss-cross arrangement of poplarwood and tulipwood battens, the whole structure being covered with a veneer of walnut and Gabon mahogany.

Unfortunately, this beautiful vessel caught fire on 5 January 1933 when en route from Pauillac, near Bordeaux, to Le Havre, where she was to be careened. At the time there were only 150 crew on board, half the normal strength. The fire continued to burn for two days off Cherbourg, before the ship could be towed into port on the morning of the 7th; the wreck was sold to salvage companies without any attempt being made to rescue what was left of the interior fittings. All Dunand's lacquerwork was destroyed in the fire, and only a handful of contemporary photographic records survive as evidence of the scale of his enterprise.

In order to replace this liner, the company built the *Pasteur* a few years later. However, the cost of insuring such a vessel during those inflationary times meant that it could not match its predecessor as a prestigious showpiece. The first-class dining saloon was entirely lined with shellac panels by Dunand, but they were left undecorated. In 1939 Dunand and his son Bernard intended to travel on the liner to present an exhibition of their work in Buenos Aires, but the outbreak of the Second World War obliged them to cancel these plans.

The Paris scene in the early 1930s

At the 1931 Salon d'Automne critics contented themselves with registering satisfaction at Dunand's achievements. In an article in the November issue of *Le Cahier*, the writer noted that Dunand had reached 'that moment in his career when he has passed from being a wonderful craftsman to a Master of Arts, in the fullest sense of the word.' Dunand was in full command of the decorative potential of all the various materials he used and of their different applications. Alongside panels depicting delightful bathing girls, he took the opportunity of presenting two of the designs that had served as models for the liner *L'Atlantique*.

In 1932, an illustration by Dunand in the Egyptian style was chosen for the cover of the annual report of the national museums. No doubt we should see here not just an aesthetic decision but also an expression of the government's desire to recompense Dunand for the important gift he had made in the wake of the Exposition Coloniale.

In the same year Dunand and Schmied took part in an exhibition of French art held in the French Residency in Rabat, Morocco. This event led to friendly relations between the two artists and General Catroux, thanks to whom Schmied was able to consider retiring to Morocco the following year. Also, as a direct consequence to this exhibition, Dunand was appointed Commandeur du Ouissan Alaouite on 17 October 1933, by order of the Moroccan government.

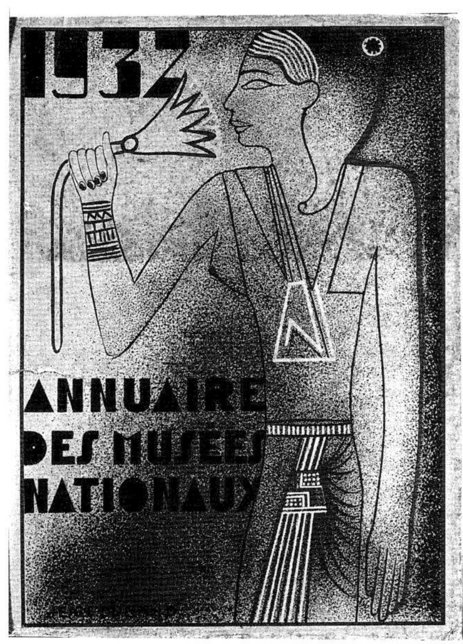

Cover of the annual report of the French National Museums, 1932, designed by Dunand.

At the Salon de la Nationale in April 1932, Dunand exhibited a large screen comprising twelve panels and decorated with stylized flora and fauna symbolizing a forest. Other pieces by him were displayed in a cabinet to one side of the central hall. Besides his own works, Dunand was gratified to see here works by both Claudius Linossier, who had spent some time in his studios in the early 1920s, and Laurent Llaurensou, a Catalan artist from a family of coppersmiths, who had worked for Dunand for a number of years, eventually married one of the latter's secretaries, Mlle Janvier, and set up on his own in Paris. The influence of Dunand's style is so clearly apparent in Llaurensou's work that even today errors of attribution are made. Many years were to pass before he broke free of his mentor and adopted a rather more personal style. It is easy to see from this comparison, however, that Dunand's resolutions of problems associated with ornamentation versus purity of line were always more astute, more natural and more direct than those of his contemporaries. The straightforwardness of his solutions was often lacking in his imitators. Simply knowing how to draw circles and squares and to inlay them with silver was not a guarantee of success in producing dinanderie in the style of Dunand: apart from Linossier and Serrières, few other artists were successful in producing truly original and interesting results.

In May, at the Salon des Artistes Décorateurs, Dunand once again exhibited his *Herons* screen, alongside an occasional table in lacquered wood made by his son Bernard. Even if the piece was not new, its unrivalled excellence could not be overlooked by art critics and visitors to the exhibition. This year the eleventh annual exhibition of the Groupe Dunand-Goulden-Jouve-Schmied took place at the Galerie Georges Petit, exceptionally, in May. Among Dunand's exhibits were some mosaics of his own composition on show for the first time. This novelty was the result of a new passion of his, though it also showed his desire to find new markets for his studio to combat the financial problems provoked by the international economic crisis. In two successive years Dunand and his son Bernard had travelled together to Italy, where they studied at first hand the early Christian mosaics in Ravenna and Venice. On the second occasion they visited glassworks specializing in mosaics, where the secrets of manufacture and colouring are passed on from one generation of craftsmen to the next. With a certain degree of surprise, they learned that the sand used by the Italian glassblowers came from the region around Fontainebleau in France. This sand, one of the richest in silica, had been used by these craftsmen for centuries.

A natural consequence was that the ever-innovative Dunand should try experimenting in this field. Having perfected his technique of lacquering, he had for years been searching for a means of creating exterior decorations capable of resisting the effects of inclement weather. Since lacquer was too fragile and stone took too long to carve, he turned to mosaics, hoping to interest architects in his latest venture.

At this exhibition eight panels utilizing this technique were presented, to critical acclaim. In order to execute them Dunand had sent Bernard back to Italy with the task of choosing specimens. In an interview published in *Art et décoration* in August 1932, the journalist Jean Galloti quoted Dunand as saying, 'You mustn't believe that we can't do what they did in the Middle Ages, it's just that we're no longer asked to do it.' This is the essence of the problem, and Dunand attempted his experiment in the tradition of these earlier master-craftsmen in the hope of reactivating public demand. However, the relatively high cost and the difficult, detailed and lengthy task of making these mosaics militated against their widespread use. In addition, their not inconsiderable weight made it practically impossible for them to be used in interior design. The first four panels which he presented at the Galerie Georges Petit treated religious subjects and were wholly Byzantine in style, proof of the artist's skill in reviving an apparently outmoded tradition. Unfortunately, however, the 'modern' tastes of the contemporary Church seemed once again to be at odds with Dunand's ideas and out of sympathy with the archaizing style of his work. Employing soft colours, Dunand depicted human subjects on glittering gold backgrounds, and one cannot but regret that their strongly traditional character was out of tune with the modern Church's preferred imagery.

By contrast, Dunand's choice of secular themes reveals so fine a sensitivity that one views a Leda at once chaste and erotic or a piquantly modernist marabou stork with all the greater awareness that, if only he had been allowed to handle his sacred subjects with the same freedom, he might have contributed in a very real sense to a new approach to religious art. However, interpretation of traditional Christian iconography is not a matter for improvisation; hence the artist should work within the Roman Catholic Church's own attitudes in order to understand and undertake whatever modification may be necessary in the treatment of such subject matter. Morever, Dunand's Protestant allegiance had hardly prepared him for such a task, and so he owed it to himself to attempt this experiment in the traditional Byzantine style. Even if it was scarcely desirable simply to recreate the magnificence of the original, it is clear that the technique itself was capable of being copied, and that it was sufficient to study the method and put it into practice in order to prove its validity. At this level, Dunand's experiment seems to have been a success, even if it did not lead him to develop the use of mosaics. If sacred art found a gifted interpreter in Dunand, who could invest his subject matter with a noble and grand treatment in marked contrast to the general drabness typical of so much contemporary religious art, it is no less true that in 1932 glass mosaics could not aspire to express anew the sense of wonder and the atmosphere in which the artists who had made the original Byzantine mosaics had worked.

A number of other mosaics followed. Some, bordering on abstraction, were based on sketches by Jean Lambert-Rucki, but they met with no greater success. Dunand soon realized that he risked courting commercial failure. Although fascinated by mosaics, in part as a stylistic exercise, he certainly had no thoughts of abandoning beaten copper and lacquer: twelve new panels and five screens were on show at the Galerie Georges Petit as a reminder to any visitors who might have entertained any doubts.

If Dunand's work attests to the attractions of a medium into which he was able to breathe new life, his friend François-Louis Schmied not only continued his series of illustrations, but also exhibited striking examples of *champlevé* enamel. He attempted to revive an old Limousin practice dating back to the Middle Ages, adapting it to modern techniques, and working on a very large scale. His *Athena* was executed in one piece, while others, like *Tree of Life*, based on designs by Gustave Miklos and almost 5 m (16 ft) high, consisted of several elements. One cannot deny the range of colours and the exceptional quality of these pieces, yet here too there was the question of how they could validly form part of a style of interior design which must of necessity be forward looking.

The Salon des Tuileries of 1932 failed to produce any work of great originality, but the year was notable for an exhibition of modern decorative art at the Musée Galliéra, in which the curator of the museum, M. Clouzot, sought to underline the role of metal in modern furnishings and everyday objects. Metal tables and dinanderie by Dunand, Linossier, Llaurensou and Capron were exhibited side by side with wrought-iron furniture by Pierre Chareau, oxidized brass furniture by Eugène Printz, chromium-plated pieces by Jean-Jacques Adnet, Thonet Frères and the firm of Labométal, and nickel-plated models by Herbst, Ruhlmann and Lalique, each artist combining metal in various ways with lacquered or exotic woods, mirrors, and slabs of pressed or moulded glass. Also on display was work by wrought-iron specialists such as Subes, Brandt, Kiss, Desvallières, Schenck, Poillerat and Prouvé. The Martel brothers, sculptors both, presented their curious compositions which they called '*planisculptures*' (made from sheets of zinc) and there were also works by Carlu for a coffee manufacturer.

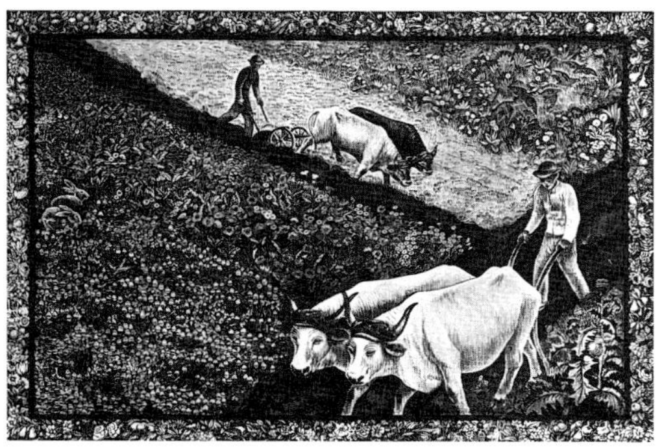

'Eclogue', tapestry design by Dunand for the Gobelins company, 1933 (cat. no. 753).

The museum's curator aimed to show that the renaissance in the applied arts would not have been possible without employing these new materials in furniture, and without new soldering techniques in wrought-iron work. Of course, the use of metals in furniture was nothing new, but the introduction of tubular chromium-plated supports and, at a later date, slabs of glass had given rise to forms and to a style that would have been inconceivable without these new materials. It goes without saying that glass and tubular metal elements impose practical constraints upon the artist just as surely as his aesthetic outlook is modified by their qualities.

Even before the fire that ravaged the liner *L'Atlantique*, Dunand had been engaged in research designed to perfect a new incombustible material with which to make his panels and pieces of furniture. It involved mixing earth or plaster of Paris with lacquer, producing a sort of synthetic material which, once formed and set in moulds, could be lacquered. Its ability to resist a blowlamp meant that, in the case of a fire, valuable time would be gained until help arrived. The arching curves of beds, as well as parts of tables and chairs could thus be formed, without joints or dowels, ready, on being removed from their mould, to receive a coat of paint, after which they could be decorated with lacquer. Dunand summoned the press to his studio and gave a number of spectacular demonstrations. In practice, however, as Bernard Dunand has noted, it is not at all certain whether, had this material been put to the test, it would really have proved to be non-inflammable, but at least it made it possible to produce furniture – under the pretext of providing protection against fire – at a reduced cost and in such a style as to engender, once again, a new aesthetic.

In March 1933, Jean Dunand, François-Louis Schmied and José-Maria Sert received a joint commission to design tapestries for the Gobelins company. Its new director, François Carnot, was more sympathetic to contemporary trends in the decorative arts than his predecessors had been, hence his desire to give the firm a more modern image. Several designs for wall-hangings and tapestries were submitted by Dunand. Consciously designed on a smaller scale than the normal Gobelins wares, his designs were intended to achieve lower production costs and thus be affordable by private individuals. Given the period of general crisis against which this development took place, however, it seems that Carnot's enterprise met with little success.

Between 29 March and 9 April 1933, the twelfth and last Dunand-Goulden-Jouve-Schmied group exhibition took place in Paris, this time at the Galerie Charpentier at 76 Rue Saint-Honoré, the Galerie Georges Petit having ceased to exist in 1932 following its owner's death. For the final show Dunand submitted portraits, together with screens and panels with figurative decoration including women, trees and marine life, as well as geometric designs just as attractive as his earlier works of this type.

In addition to a new portrait of Madame Agnès in profile, there was also a portrait of the *couturière* Madeleine Vionnet, with abundant white hair and wearing a blood-red dress, which contrasted strangely with the general tone of the exhibition. More classical in conception was the portrait of the wife of the well-known *couturier* Jean-Charles Worth, showing a seated figure gazing at herself reflected in a pool, while a portrait entitled *Monsieur la Belle Vie*, as it was listed in the catalogue not without a touch of humour, depicted Johan Colcombet, a silk manufacturer from Saint-Étienne and a keen follower of horse-racing, who was born on the same day as Dunand. By contrast, two panels dealing with sacred subjects – the first a largish piece depicting the Annunciation, the second a bust of the Virgin – were executed in Coromandel lacquer with brightly coloured highlights. Their graphic conception, at once simple and monumental, was entirely in keeping with the current expectations of a new generation of ecclesiastics who hoped that by breathing new life into the more sober and traditional imagery of religious art, they might appeal to man's senses and contribute to his moral uplift. Following this exhibition the French government paid 50,000 francs for Dunand's large four-panel *Forest* screen in black and silver lacquer.

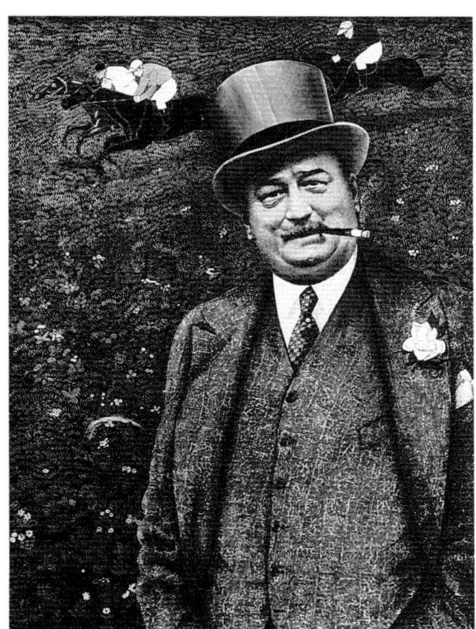

Monsieur la Belle Vie, Dunand's portrait of Johan Colcombet, 1933; see cat. no. 189.

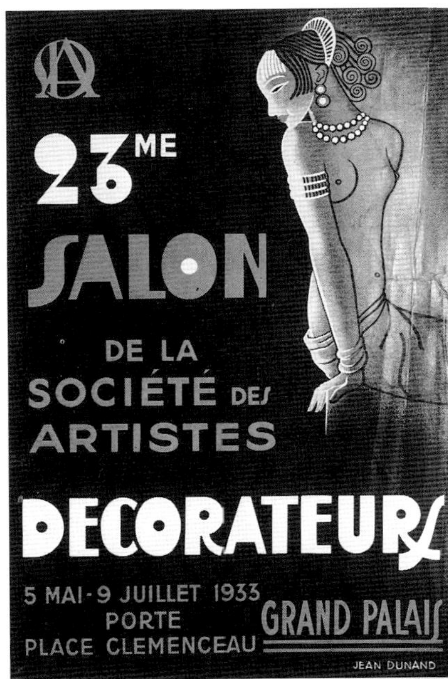

Printed poster for the Salon des Artistes Décorateurs, Paris, 1933, designed by Dunand.

The month of May witnessed the twenty-third Salon des Artistes Décorateurs, the poster for which was designed by Dunand. In spite of the general feeling of economic crisis, the participants made an effort to say something new by offering work which, if less spectacular than before, was no less attractive. Two panels and a two-panel screen by Dunand bespoke the artist's technical mastery. The screen, one of his finest, represented a young man all atremble, offering a mother-of-pearl flower to a smiling girl seated facing him. A simple outline, enhanced with red and gold, was enough to trace these beautiful figures on a black-lacquer background. Executed with extraordinary economy of means and graphic simplicity, this screen represented the culmination of Dunand's stylistic experiments. A number of mosaic panels complemented his lacquerwork, but had nothing new to say.

In July 1933, Dunand, with his friend François-Louis Schmied and his son Bernard, set sail from Amsterdam on the Dutch liner *Stuyvesant*. Leaving his two companions to continue their journey to the Dutch Antilles, Jean Dunand disembarked at Madeira on 1 August. The ship's owners gave them free passage on condition that Schmied and his secretary/assistant Bernard Dunand brought back pictorial material sufficiently evocative to be used in publicizing cruises offered by the company. It was in the course of this voyage that Bernard, inspired by the exotic island scenery, began to prepare his own one-man show. Throughout the voyage he took notes and made sketches, but above all he took many photographs, intending to use these landscapes as the basis for lacquer decoration once he was back in Paris. His feeling for colour and contrast was well rewarded with stimulating visual material.

Earlier in the year, the magazine *L'Illustration* had reproduced in its May issue photographs of the apartment of Madame Yacoubovitch, for which – seemingly flying in the face of the current economic crisis – Dunand had produced gold-lacquered furniture. In July, the same journal showed the interior of a house in Paris occupied by the diplomat Philippe Berthelot and his wife. Although the overall decor, as was usual, combined eighteenth-century French furniture with examples of Far Eastern furniture, the first-floor boudoir was more modern in feeling. As part of the scheme, Jean-Michel Frank had all the walls decorated in a pale-straw shade. Madame Berthelot's room contained a bed designed by Dunand, lacquered in black and featuring stylized Japanese fish, bubbles and shafts of light. Inlaywork in mother-of-pearl and burgaudine depicted water-lilies. On a table beside the bed was a terracotta bas-relief by Gustave Miklos which served to conceal a wireless set. Miklos came to play a fairly prominent role in Dunand's interior designs, either because both men had the same clients, or because François-Louis Schmied, to whom he felt more commitment, had done his utmost to sell his work to those of Dunand's clients and friends whom he counted among his own acquaintances. At all events, Miklos's quest for graphic originality and his handling of different materials were very similar to those of Dunand, either as a result of their temperamental affinity or because they were influenced independently by Lambert-Rucki (with whom Miklos shared a studio). It was, moreover, at Philippe Berthelot's residence that Miklos first introduced Dunand to Jacques Doucet, although the latter had previously corresponded with Dunand. A letter preserved in the family archives describes this meeting, which took place shortly before Doucet's death.

In October 1933, Cardinal Verdier consecrated the new Church of the Holy Ghost in the Rue Cannebière off the Avenue Daumesnil. Clearly Byzantine in inspiration, the church was the work of the architect Tournon. Inside, frescoes by Jean Dupas and Maurice Denis, somewhat affected in style, inspired a mood of reverence and contemplation. The high altar in *repoussé* copper was by Dunand, as was the door of the tabernacle, which depicted the Lamb of God.

At the Salon d'Automne Dunand exhibited another example of a religious theme, his glass mosaic Crucifixion surrounded by a number of representations of the Virgin and Christ, previously shown. There were also two screens, one in silver and grey lacquer depicting swallows perched on telegraph wires, the other, less modern in feeling, portraying a flock of white geese in full flight against a black-lacquer background.

In November Dunand participated in an exhibition on animal themes with the sculptor E. M. Sandoz, who had recently bought the Galerie Brandt in the Boulevard Malesherbes. Dunand's contribution was a screen with wading birds as its main motif. In February 1934, the Muséum National d'Histoire Naturelle in the Jardin des Plantes put on an exhibition of animals in art, thus providing Dunand with a chance to present his latest work in lacquer and eggshell, together with some earlier pieces. Making use of natural materials and colours, one of the earlier screens dating from 1926 depicted black crows in a snow-covered field. In addition to a number of mosaic experiments, including one depicting a marabou stork, Dunand contributed a lacquered panel showing a big cat drinking at a waterhole, described by one critic as a work of 'rare beauty'. Also on view were several snakes cast in bronze.

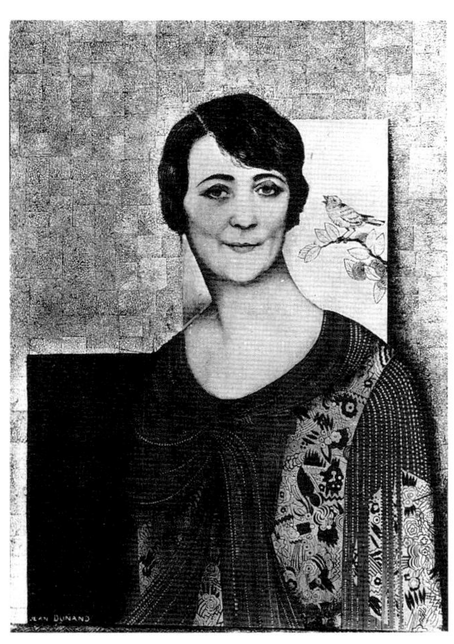

Mme Philippe Berthelot, portrait in lacquer and eggshell (cat. no. 168).

At the Salon des Artistes Décorateurs one of the exhibits was a piece of furniture by Eugène Printz: made of palm wood, it opened by means of ten panels that folded back on each other, five to a side, like the sections of a screen. This curious door, a masterpiece of modernist cabinet-making, was entirely covered with plates of copper with silver inlay forming highly elaborate geometric motifs. Designed by Dunand, the decorative finish precisely matched Printz's architectonic conception. Once again, Dunand presented a number of mosaics (though apparently without much success), together with two large frescoes whose gold-lacquer background provided the setting for a rich display of tropical flora and fauna. He also exhibited a chalice and paten, the former made specially for Father Doncoeur in 1931; the chalice, made of silver and adorned with sapphires, could be taken apart to facilitate storage and transportation.

The Salon des Artistes Français included a piece of furniture stained red with cochineal by Jules Leleu, on which was mounted a lacquered and silver-inlaid copperware plate by Dunand, creating the overall impression of a Printz imitation of such banality that not even Printz himself could take offence. Dunand also decorated various items of furniture which private individuals had had made to their own designs by minor cabinet-makers. Only on rare occasions was Dunand willing to sign such pieces, particularly as it appears that the ornamentation was often dictated by the clients themselves. Hence individual works that are of interest in terms of quality sometimes appear on the market, without necessarily being attributable to Dunand. This was the case with a dining room and salon installed in Paris's 17th *arrondissement*: they were conceived by a private art lover, who also provided the designs for the brass- and copperware. But the same was also true of interior designers such as Alavoine in New York, who, in the manner of Jules Leleu, imagined that they could simply ask other lacquer artists and *dinandiers* to reproduce furniture similar to the original models made by Printz and Dunand.

The year ended with an exhibition of decorative art at the Musée Galliéra. In addition to a variety of contemporary objects, the exhibition included a retrospective of works by Rupert Carabin, a sculptor and cabinet-maker active in the early part of the century, whose carved figures of naked women supporting book-rests and massive tree-trunk cabinets were a source of some amusement; the baroque qualities of Carabin's anthropomorphic chairs were in curious contrast with the stark surroundings of the rest of the exhibition.

The 'Normandie'

The interior decoration of the *Normandie* was already well advanced when its owners, the Compagnie Générale Transatlantique (C.G.T.) decided to end the secrecy that had surrounded the vessel's construction. It was decided to hold a press conference at which plans, models and life-size mock-ups of

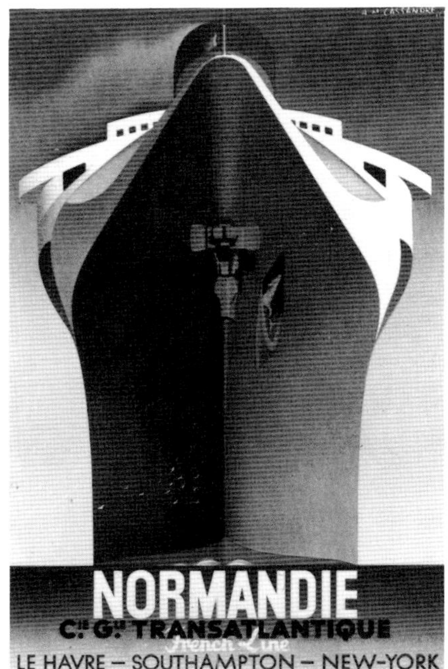

Poster by Cassandre for the liner *Normandie*, 1935.

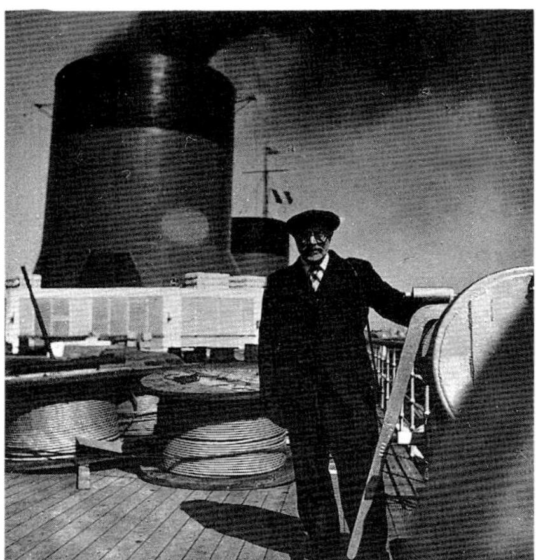

Dunand on deck during the maiden voyage of the *Normandie*.

individual details of this new 'giant of the seas' would be displayed. This highly unusual presentation took place at the company's headquarters in the Rue Auber in Paris, where the collaborative efforts (co-ordinated by the architects Bouwens de Boïjen, Roger Expert, Pierre Patout and Pacon) of the various artists created, according to contemporary reports, 'an impression of grandeur and unity'.

The vessel had been formally named when launched on 29 October 1932 by the wife of the French President, Madame Albert Lebrun. In a manner reminiscent of the building of royal palaces in medieval times, combining with skills of the best master-masons, painters, sculptors and cabinet-makers, every effort had been made to transform the *Normandie* into a showcase of French art. She was the largest and most beautiful liner ever built and in terms of luxurious decor has never been surpassed. Intended to serve the route from Le Havre to New York via Southampton, she won the coveted Blue Riband for the fastest crossing of the North Atlantic on her maiden voyage in May 1935.

Built at the Penhoët shipyard in Saint-Nazaire, the *Normandie* weighed 79,500 tons gross. The ship's overall length was 313.80 m (1,029 ft), with a beam of 35.90 m (118 ft). Her crew numbered 1,345, and she provided accommodation for 848 first-class passengers, 670 in tourist class, and 454 in economy class. Her average speed was 28 knots. Laid up in New York in 1939, she was requisitioned by the U.S. Navy. An early plan to convert her into an aircraft carrier renamed the *Lexington* was abandoned when the United States entered the war against Germany, and instead she was adapted as a troopship and renamed the *Lafayette*. In the course of this refitting work the ship caught fire. For reasons connected as much with military security as with trade-union demands, the authorities had refused to allow French crew members to help with the refitting, and the men who undertook the work were unfortunately not sufficiently acquainted with the ship, with the result that, when fire broke out, they did not know how to handle the situation. Hence, a fire which might have been contained by a crew familiar with operating practices spread quickly and disastrously. One cannot but regret this sad fate of a magnificent vessel which has become part of maritime history.

Dunand, who had known Bouwens de Boïjen since 1914, was entrusted by him and his team of architects with the decor of the entire smoking room and of part of the first-class saloon. The decoration of the saloon was in the hands of Jean Dupas, a former holder of the Premier Prix de Rome and a friend of Roger Expert and of M. Olivier, who had been appointed President of the C.G.T. For his part, Dunand proposed several designs, some of them highly original; being considered not sufficiently traditional, they were all rejected in favour of a rather more sedate scheme. Accordingly, Dunand elected to install five gold-lacquer panels in 'Egyptian' style, based on his own designs, in the smoking room, while a sixth panel, after a design by Dupas, was used on the saloon side of the partition between the saloon and the smoking room.

The overall theme for the smoking room was 'Man's Games and Pleasures': the first of the panels, immediately to the right as one descended the grand ceremonial staircase, depicted 'Fishing', while that on the left was entitled 'Sports'. Both included openings that gave access to the dining-saloon service area. Opposite, to the right and left respectively, were 'Taming the Horse' and 'Grape Harvesting and Dancing'. Resembling a large wall, the partition between the smoking room and the saloon contained two sets of double doors with glazed openings. The theme chosen for the side facing the smoking room was 'Hunting'.

The panels and the firebreak doors were all exactly 6 m (19 ft 6 in.) high. Each panel was 5.80 m (18 ft 9 in.) across, while the double firebreak doors were 8 m (26 ft) wide. Together with the bulkheads in gold lacquer, which completed the installation in the stairwell and the access corridor, the overall design included a total of 1,035 elements. Executed in independent units, they

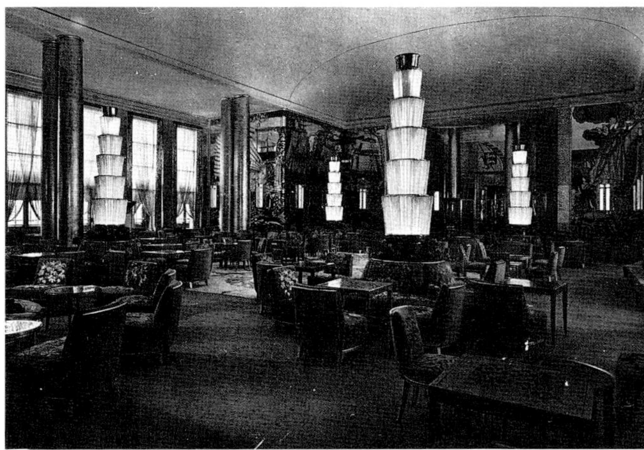

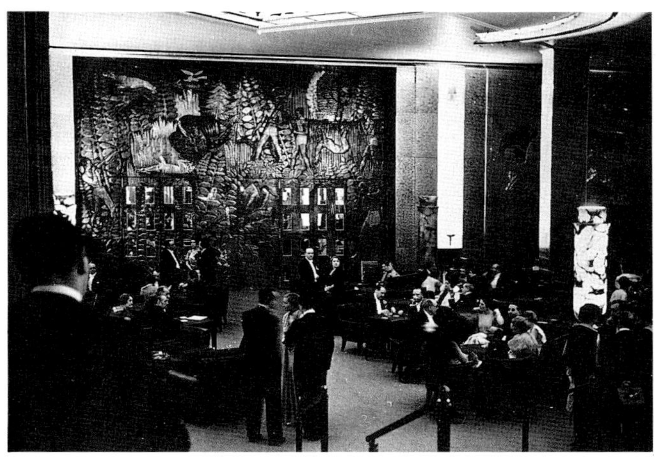

Interior views on the *Normandie*: (above) the first-class saloon with red-lacquered games tables by Dunand, and (right) the Smoking Room looking towards the dividing wall with Dunand's *Hunting* panels.

were fixed in place leaving visible joins so as to allow for the slight movements within the vessel resulting from rolling or pitching. In all, there were 1,200 m^2 (1,400 square yards) of uniform gold-lacquer surfaces, fourteen columns, also lacquered gold, and more than 235 m^2 (275 square yards) of brightly coloured incised lacquer. Reading these figures, and in the knowledge that everything had to be executed by hand, one can gain some impression of the vast amount of work involved. In order to cope with this exceptional workload, the studio of 74 Rue Hallé normally reserved for lacquerwork was used instead to prepare the surfaces to be lacquered, while the metal workshop was similarly re-equipped to enable Kéco to make the necessary brass frames. In this way, craftsmen such as Maurice Charigny, previously a cabinet-maker, and Jean Pascal, an apprentice metalworker, were converted to the idea of using a moulding process. Large and extremely thick glass slabs were bought to ensure that the surfaces were completely flat; and new presses were acquired. The panels to be decorated in low relief were all made to a thickness of 4 cm (1½ in.) using a mixture of hardened plaster and a very fine clay (similar to kaolin) from Indo-China. The resulting compound was white, like plaster, but the material was coloured red or grey in order to conceal the nature of its ingredients. It had the advantage of drying in the open air and of hardening naturally after being placed in a drying room. It was called *sabi* after a kind of Japanese compound of lacquer mixed with sawdust. The material was fire-resistant for up to two hours at temperatures up to 815°C. In addition, it had the enormous advantage of not needing a wooden backing, the use of wood having been excluded in the building specifications.

The production process involved the use of brass corner-brackets, which Bernard Dunand ordered from the Compagnie Française des Métaux, each being squared up and aligned so that, once all the elements were in position, the vertical and horizontal joins would be perfectly straight and true. Four hooks were welded to two cross-bars on the back of each panel to ensure that they could be securely attached to the liner's various bulkheads. Cross-bars welded to the framework of the vessel's interior walls were provided with riveted hooks to which individual panels were attached. Each series of panels contained a maximum of fifteen elements of identical size.

The layout of each of the six panel decorations had been established in advance by means of one-tenth scale models; these were then enlarged to one-third of the intended size before being drawn, full size, in charcoal on the panels themselves. When a design was enlarged, Dunand would almost invariably see the need to make alterations to his original concept, which was no longer entirely pleasing to his eye. For this reason panels corresponding to these intermediate stages and differing in certain respects from the designs as finally executed sometimes come on the market, while others have found their way into the hands of specialist dealers.

Each of the figures was sculpted in very low relief by Dunand after the

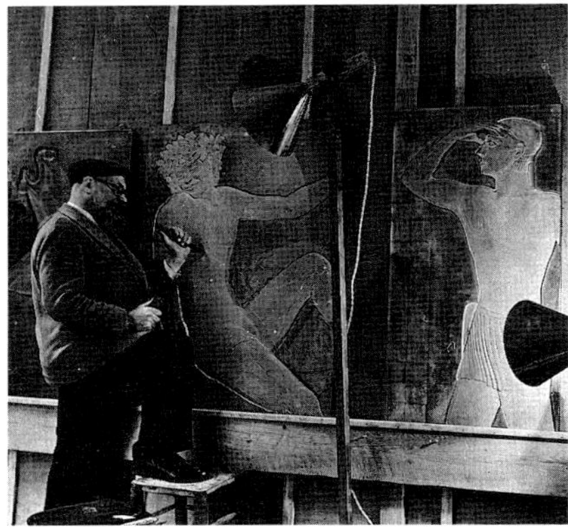

Dunand at work on panels for the Smoking Room on the *Normandie* and (below) special ovens installed in his workshops for the lacquering stage of his bas-relief panels.

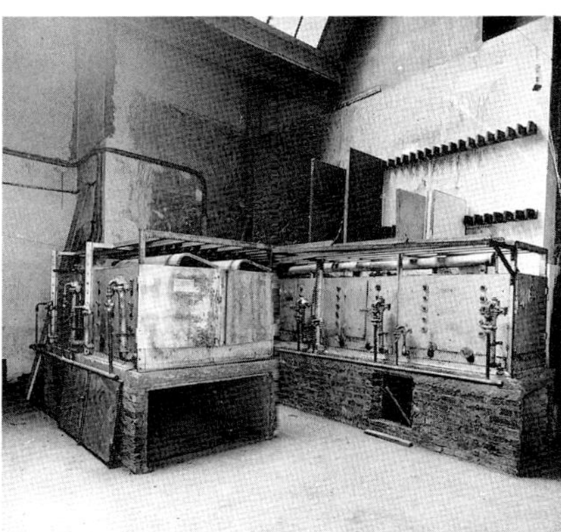

definitive designs had been traced on to the panels placed side by side in the studio. He would go to bed at 2 a.m. and be up again by 6. The results were reminiscent of ancient Egyptian tomb decoration. The illusion of three-dimensionality that Dunand achieved was so strong that he was forced to draw a ruler across the surfaces to prove to disbelieving architects that the decoration was in no way raised. The effect was striking, particularly in the panel depicting the taming of the horse, where the downward emphasis reinforced the impression of movement. In fact, every detail of the decoration was executed by means of a gouge and file, as would have been the case with wood, before the surface was completely covered with gold lacquer.

In order to facilitate the task of sculpting a vertical surface and to work at the correct height, Dunand had a pit dug in the basement of his workshop in the Rue Hallé, a system of pulleys enabling him to raise and lower the panels, so that the surfaces to be worked were always within reach. Anticipating yet a further increase in work, he asked that the pillars supporting the new structure be sunk to a depth of more than 3 m (10 ft) below ground level, so that, should the need arise, a veneer studio could be constructed at this lowest level. This plan, formulated with the future of his son Jean-Louis in mind, was never fulfilled owing to the latter's early death while on military service.

In the course of this excavation work the workmen unearthed remains of the Roman aqueduct of Arcueil, which formerly brought water from thermal springs at Cluny to the centre of Paris. The section of the aqueduct under Dunand's property was some 17 m (55 ft) in length. At a later date, during the Second World War, when Paris was subjected to air-raid alerts and enemy bombardments, Dunand and his family used this subterranean refuge rather than shelter in the nearest Métro station as suggested by the civil defence.

All these complex operations demanded an extraordinary degree of co-ordination to ensure that each individual craftsman completed his work in the time required, using exactly the right materials and tools. Bernard Dunand was responsible for the office administration, linked by a system of bells with the person in charge of each department. At the request of Bouwens de Boïjen, Bernard was made responsible for dealing directly with all the professional bodies involved in the *Normandie* project, including M. Cremer, chief assistant to the architect Roger Expert. During this period more than a hundred craftsmen were employed in the workshops to fulfil this one commission, a figure which gives some indication of the magnitude of the task. Very few artists could have coped with such an undertaking, yet Dunand personally sculpted every detail with a high degree of precision. Thus each strand of the cord that made up the mesh of the fishermen's net was shown in distinct relief. Only when sanding down and lacquering the panels was Dunand prepared to call on his assistants to help.

First, Dunand applied natural lacquer over the entire background, certain of the elements which were to be coloured separately receiving five or six coats. Each of the surfaces was rubbed down before being coated with brightly coloured lacquer or with 24-carat gold leaf, so as to be able to resist the effects of exposure to sea air. The gold leaf was applied only after the final layer of lacquer had been applied, and was added when this was still fresh, in order to fix it while drying. Once the lacquer had dried, the gold was rubbed down with powdered charcoal in order to produce lighter or darker tones as desired.

The main stairwell and the walls of the access corridor were also clad in panels of gold lacquer, uniformly dappled. Mirrored in these lacquered surfaces, Lalique's monumental wall-lamps gave a sense of rhythm to each flight of stairs, their reflections seemingly multiplied to infinity. To underline the luxurious effect and extend the magnificence of this gold lacquerwork into the first-class saloon, Dupas decided to use painted and gilded panels of engraved glass. With their human figures, birds and fantastic animals, their clouds and sailing ships, each of these corner panels created a vast epic poem from classical mythology evoking, in turn, *The Rape of Europa, The Birth of Aphrodite, The Chariot of Thetis* and *The Chariot of Poseidon*. The panels were executed by the mirror manufacturer Jacques Charles Champigneule. The fireproof partition dividing the saloon from the smoking room constituted the fifth decorative panel, executed in gold lacquer by Dunand to a design by Dupas. Around a glittering compass card, it evoked images of dawn and night, of the sea and the sun, and of the winds. The vaulted ceiling was supported by pairs of columns 7 m (23 ft) high, each tapering from a base 86 cm (2 ft 10 in.) in diameter to 74 cm (2 ft 5 in.) at the top. All were covered in uniform gold lacquer. Since each was made in one piece using stucco and the surface was lacquered only once, Dunand had to use a special method to achieve the desired result. Of the fourteen columns in the saloon, only ten were produced in his studio. The other four, which were intended to hide the iron stanchions supporting the upper deck, had to be built, using a special process which Dunand had had to develop, and lacquered *in situ*. In the case of the columns transported from Paris, it was necessary to hold up the local traffic in order to permit their removal via the Rue Dareau. A special method of packing was used to prevent any contact with the lacquered surfaces. Suspended along their axes, the columns arrived at the dockyard without mishap, and they were placed in position with the aid of a winch.

Dunand had them installed one by one, supervising the operation in person, retaining the protective packaging in order to ensure that they would not be damaged before the vessel was launched. The extensive work involved in fitting out the liner, and a slight delay in its completion, meant that some five hundred specialist craftsmen had to sail on her maiden voyage in order to complete the work. Jean Dunand and his friend Johan Colcombet were among those on board. This immense undertaking exhausted Dunand, and he never recovered his health in full. It is no exaggeration to say that the strain contributed to his death a few years later.

In May 1936, during a violent storm in mid-ocean, the central panel of the partition between the smoking room and saloon suffered serious damage. The parts affected were removed when the liner docked in New York, and Dunand was asked to provide replacements. Prescient as ever, he had retained several spare panels, but these were undecorated, and it took several months of work to sculpt and prepare matching replacements. The damaged elements, which had been stored in the warehouses of the C.G.T., were offered for sale at Sotheby's, New York, in the autumn of 1983, their sad state of repair being simply the result of this earlier mishap.

The *Normandie* completed what was to prove her last crossing to New York on 23 August 1939. When war was declared on 3 September, the liner remained in port for fear of being torpedoed by German U-boats. When she was finally taken out of commission in 1941, all the lacquer decorations were removed and packed in crates to be stored in the company's warehouses. Dunand's panels were not returned to France until after the war, when they were altered and remounted in other liners run by the same company. The 'Grape Harvesting' panel, for example, was installed in the liner *Liberté* in 1950, as was a section of the partition depicting 'Hunting'. The former was installed in the smoking room and the latter in the saloon. Both had to be reduced in size because of the difference in the deck heights of the *Normandie* and the *Liberté*. Thus, the lowest sections of the panels were removed, and Pierre Dunand, who supervised the work, had to substitute a new section in the same material, not only adapting the old decorative scheme to suit the reduced height, but altering the composition in such a way that the design appeared as complete as possible.

In 1952 the panel entitled 'Sports' was installed in the departure hall of the C.G.T.'s harbour station of Le Havre. As for the large panel by Dupas and Dunand, this was rehung in 1949 on the liner *Ile de France*, together with the panels 'Fishing' and 'Taming the Horse', the last two with their lower section cut off and adapted by Pierre Dunand so as to conform to the height of the first-class saloon in the new liner.

Several smaller replicas of the smoking-room panels were made by Dunand and offered to his fellow workers and to French and foreign dignitaries who had been connected in whatever way with the *Normandie*. Thus President Lebrun received a copy of 'Taming the Horse', while the Musée de Genève was given the original model for this scene. For his part, Gaston Doumergue received a copy of 'Grape Harvesting and Dancing'. At the same time, several details were reproduced actual size and sold for profit. They included not only the famous horse's head, but also the marabou stork and beater from 'Hunting'.

In December 1935, all these replicas and details were exhibited at the Grand Dépôt at 21/23 Rue Drouot, Paris. Dunand made use of the exhibition, which was held in collaboration with the Métiers d'Art, to show some of his life-size designs for the *Normandie* panels. Such was the success of these pieces that Dunand made numerous copies in order to satisfy public demand. It is impossible to know exactly how many copies were made, but it is no exaggeration to say that some fifty or more were marketed.

In March 1936, an exhibition of sketches and models was put on at the Galerie Charpentier, enabling those who had never seen the famous liner to inspect a reduced-size version of the smoking room and to be made aware of the extraordinary technical and artistic *tour de force* which these lacquered designs represented. In May, an exhibition entitled 'Invitation to a Voyage' was held, at which the public had a further opportunity to admire the *Normandie* in every aspect.

To conclude this extraordinary affair of the *Normandie*, Dunand was proposed, in a recommendation from the Minister of the Merchant Navy to the Arts Minister, for promotion from Officier to Commandeur of the Légion d'Honneur, but this proposal came to nothing.

Exhibitions in 1936 and later

At the twenty-sixth Salon des Artistes Décorateurs held in May 1936 the exhibits included a large panel by Dunand depicting two leopards drinking at a waterhole beside tall grasses. To one side were two cabinets displaying copper and brass vases and bowls, as a reminder that despite various prestigious commissions Dunand was still making more modest objects.

Also in 1936, Dunand was a member of the official delegation of French artists who submitted work to be shown at the Palazzo dell'Arte in Milan as part of the city's sixth Triennale Internationale.

In Paris, an art critic reviewing the Salon d'Automne noted that Bernard Dunand had developed his own lacquering techniques, exhibiting panels with subtle designs which included tall trees with jagged bronze and green leaves, and a mountain village beside the dark waters of a lake over which arched a black and gold sky. Both bore witness to his skill as a colourist, and both had been executed following his voyage to the Antilles. Despite favourable critical comments, however, it appears that at this stage Bernard had no wish to see his career developing along similar lines to his father's. He certainly had plenty to do, supervising and organizing the general running of the workshop, without worrying about questions of personal style.

In the current climate of economic crisis, the élitist atmosphere typical of earlier major international exhibitions had given way to a more practical approach, as the title of the 1937 Exposition Internationale des Arts et Techniques Appliqués à la Vie Moderne indicates. Dunand acted as vice-president of the arts and crafts section and as a member of the jury. Here, for the first time in Paris, an entire section was devoted to lacquer, tortoiseshell and ivory, the latter materials used largely in the fancy-goods industry but perfectly in keeping with those employed by Dunand. Dunand, indeed, was appointed president of this section at the exhibition, which provided him with the opportunity to exhibit for the first time a huge bas-relief panel representing harvesting. Since the organizers of the exhibition were unable to guarantee the cost of commissioning the work, Dunand was obliged to find ways to finance the project himself. Only at the end of the exhibition did the City of Paris put in a bid for this rustic frieze.

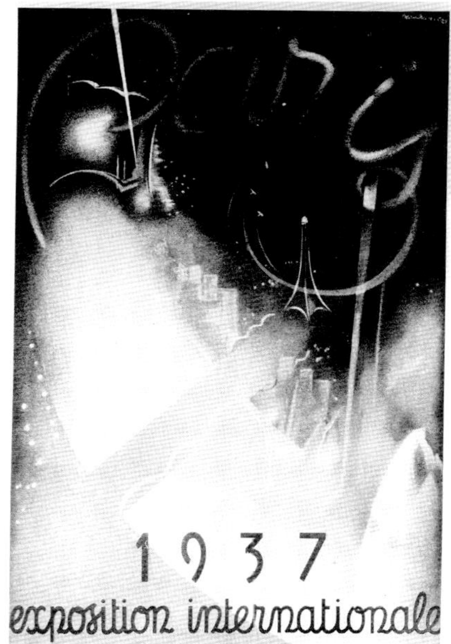

Poster by Paul Beaudoin for the 1937 international exhibition in Paris.

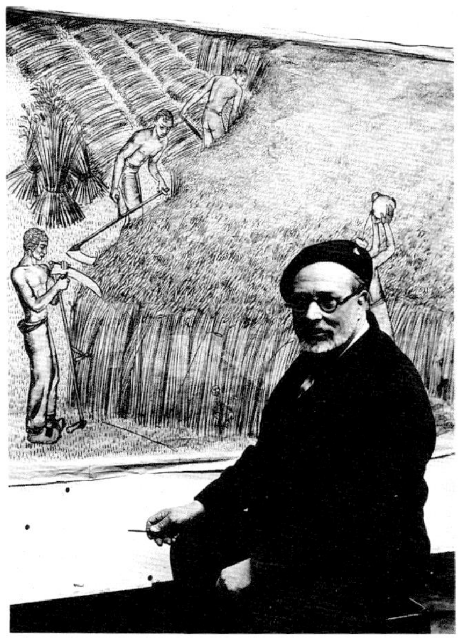

Dunand in his workshop sketching the design for the eighteen-panel mural *The Harvest*, 1936.

For this exhibition, another project, equally huge, was put in hand. It represented the regions of France coming to Paris for the exhibition. In this instance, too, the work was not publicly financed, and Dunand had to appeal to the generosity of various friends. Bernard had the task of going the rounds of the principal donors, with a model of the panel under his arm. Eventually, after the exhibition was over, the town of Sélestat, near Colmar, put in a bid for the work.

Unfortunately for Dunand, the exhibition was badly timed. His large-scale commissions for the *Normandie* had obliged him to enlarge his premises, to buy large quantities of raw materials, and to engage in property investments. In spite of generous loans, he was in a very precarious financial position, especially since he refused to lay off his staff, hoping for new commissions. The replacements for the panels in the smoking room of the *Normandie* had kept the workshop busy for several months, but new orders had to be found. Given this situation, Dunand decided to persuade the exhibition organizers to accept his large panels, hoping that he would succeed in selling them to the organizers in the end.

In spite of numerous financial and technical difficulties, the Société des Artistes Décorateurs decided to repeat its policy of 1925 and construct its own pavilion to house its members' exhibits. The architects Patout, Simon and Chaume were entrusted with the task. Luxury designs – '*haut luxe*', as they were called at the time – were assembled in the first-floor section of a fairly nondescript building. The star attraction here was the Ambassador's Salon, designed by Louis Süe and André Mare and sufficiently sumptuous to represent the official taste of the period, a notable symbol of which was the new Palais de Chaillot at the Paris Trocadéro. Not far from the Ambassador's Salon was a Music Room by Alfred Porteneuve, an interior designer who had taken over Émile-Jacques Ruhlmann's workshop on the latter's death in 1933. His lack of panache and personality meant, however, that the layout and furnishing of this room were in a Far Eastern style lacking in originality. He asked Dunand to make a series of dark-green lacquer facings for the walls, which he hoped would complement the black-lacquer furniture he was planning. A large panel depicting deer in dense undergrowth was intended to complete the overall picture. For all its luxury and skilful workmanship, this joint installation by Porteneuve and Dunand was not well received by the critics, who were growing tired of this type of setting. There is no doubt that, either through lack of preparation or indifference to changing tastes, Dunand had failed to take account of the new 'modernist' trend; having been too absorbed in his work on the *Normandie*, he presumably had no time to react.

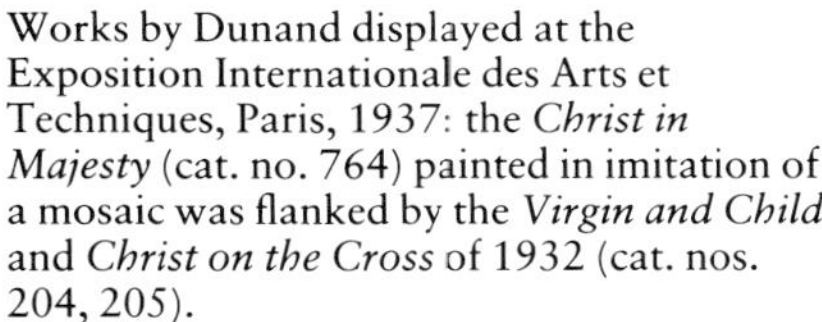

Works by Dunand displayed at the Exposition Internationale des Arts et Techniques, Paris, 1937: the *Christ in Majesty* (cat. no. 764) painted in imitation of a mosaic was flanked by the *Virgin and Child* and *Christ on the Cross* of 1932 (cat. nos. 204, 205).

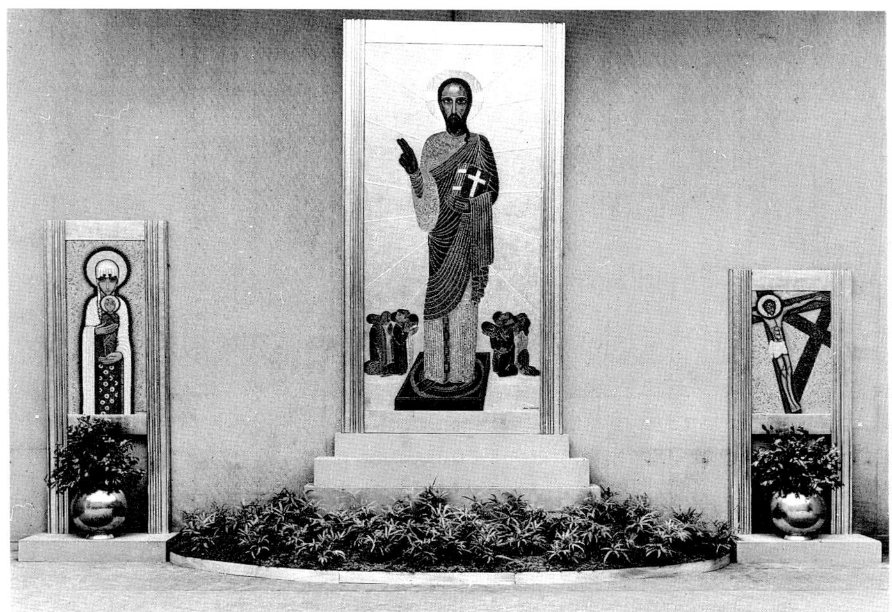

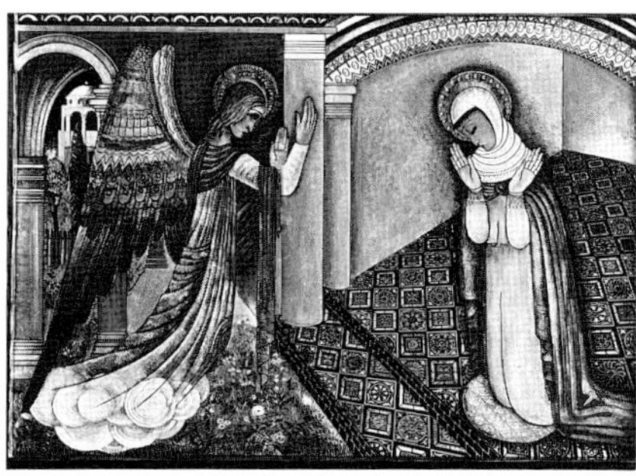

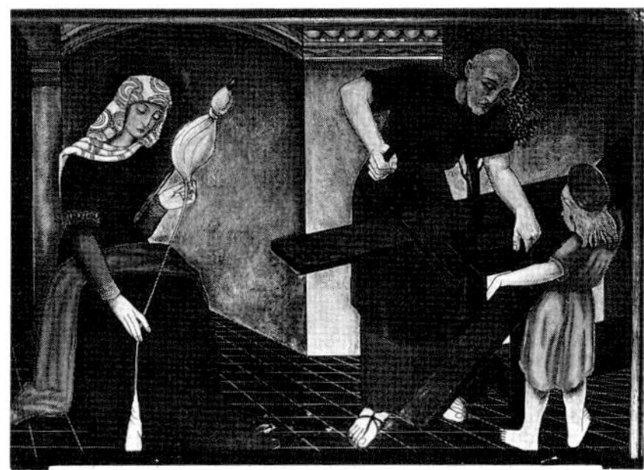

The Annunciation (cat. no. 756) and *Joseph's Workshop* (cat. no. 757), two of Dunand's panels with religious subjects executed in 1933.

The salon was at once luxurious and cold in feeling, but, despite its lack of a clear-cut style, it was not without a certain elegance. The catalogue mentioned that Dunand had had as his principal collaborators his two sons Bernard and Pierre.

A section of the exhibition was devoted to the late Émile-Jacques Ruhlmann and included a cabinet of lacquered dinanderie vases, together with two screens and two large vases by Dunand. Similarly, the Oratory Chapel built by Henri Rapin in the Sèvres porcelain pavilion contained a communion table designed and lacquered by Dunand, the altar being surmounted by a beautiful glass cross by René Lalique. In the section on religious art Dunand once again exhibited his *Annunciation* panel of 1933 and its companion piece, *Joseph's Workshop*. The latter panel was warmly admired by Cardinal Pacelli, then Apostolic Nuncio in Paris, who later became Pope Pius XII. A delegation of French scouts presented this panel to him when he was elected Pope in the spring of 1939. A third exhibit, most moving in its conception, was a monumental mock-up of a projected mosaic, 3 m (10 ft) high, depicting Christ in Majesty surrounded by smaller figures. At ground level, between the panels, Dunand had placed a number of large flowerpot holders in beaten pewter, together with a bowl in classical style on a bronze support.

In the mosaic section of the Pavillon de la Céramique, Dunand exhibited his self-portrait and a number of other panels on sacred and secular themes. A pavilion devoted to the Gobelins tapestry company featured its workshops' latest creations, ordered by François Carnot following his appointment as head of the company. Thus, a large and very spectacular carpet by Louis Süe could be seen alongside a tapestry design by Schmied entitled 'The Imaginary Voyage'. Dunand was represented by his full-size 'Eclogue' tapestry design on canvas, a kind of pastoral poem in praise of ploughing, and a door-hanging which repeated the theme of harvesting. When set beside the highly colourful pieces based on designs by Othon Friesz, Gernez, Chapelain-Midy and Roland Oudot, Dunand's efforts were bound to seem backward-looking and, in spite of their graphic refinement, doomed to failure. The 'Eclogue' canvas was later hung above the entrance to the banqueting hall in the annexe of the civic building in Paris's 14th *arrondissement*.

In parallel with this international exhibition, and with the aim of providing a stylistic introduction to the subject, the Union Centrale des Arts Décoratifs had put on an exhibition in the Pavillon de Marsan entitled 'Décors de la Vie de 1900 à 1925'. It traced the development of furniture and objets d'art through the work of ceramicists, jewellers, fashion designers and glassmakers of the period. Certain of them were still active, and it may well have seemed absurd to compare their past work with current work to be seen elsewhere. Naturally, Dunand's work figured prominently in this exhibition, but the unity of his output was scarcely open to criticism.

The following year, 1938, was relatively uneventful as far as art exhibitions were concerned. The climate of continuing crisis and threat of international conflict were hardly conducive to a blossoming of the arts. Nonetheless, on 16 March, Dunand exhibited a huge lacquered panel, 10 m (32 ft) long, in his studio: it depicted deer at the side of a pond and was destined for the French Embassy in the Turkish capital, Ankara.

In May, such were the scarcity of works of art and the constraints of funding, only a single Salon was held in Paris, combining the usual exhibitions of the Salon de la Nationale and the Salon des Artistes Français. It was held in the Grand Palais, where 'a handful of islands floating in an ocean of mediocrity', as Yvanhoé Rambosson wrote in an article published in *Heures de Paris* on 18 June, represented the only evidence of creative activity. Knowing the enthusiasm of this particular art critic for Dunand's work, one can well imagine that his contributions constituted the principal 'islands' of excellence, more especially his screen decorated in black and gold lacquer representing a 'flotilla of swans on a lake well calculated to delight the dancers'.

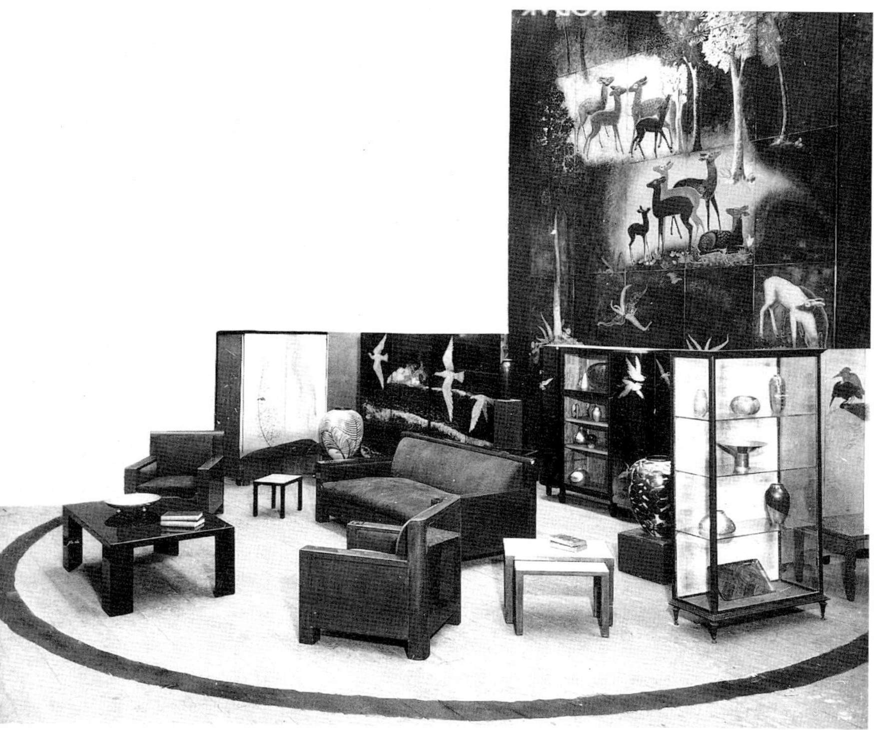

The World's Fair, New York, 1939: display in the lacquer and dinanderie section featuring the panel *Deer in a Clearing* (cat. no. 1224), first shown in Paris in 1937.

In the course of the summer, one of Dunand's large screens owned by the Mobilier National was damaged while being shown in Berlin, and on its return from Germany he was asked to restore it at the expense of the German government.

At the Salon d'Automne critics noted the presence of a screen decorated with figures previously seen in 1933 at the Salon des Artistes Décorateurs, while the annual exhibition of the Salon des Animaliers was an occasion for Dunand to dip into his storeroom to present, alongside his colleagues' work, the strange menagerie which is one of the principal attractions of his oeuvre. In this context, the reader may perhaps be amused to learn that Dunand – who liked to work from life – kept a tame ocelot, native to Central America. It lived in one of the courtyards in his studio complex and over a two-year period spread panic among the chickens kept elsewhere on his premises as a source of eggshells needed for use in lacquerwork.

Having been invited to decorate the French Pavilion (designed by the architects Roger Expert and Pierre Patout) at the New York World's Fair in 1939, Dunand was persuaded to work once again alongside Jean Dupas, although he was scarcely in sympathy with the work of this exponent of neo-classical painting. On 24 March 1939, he held a private showing, by invitation only, in his studio, of *The Epic of the Republic*, a huge curved panel with lacquer decoration based on a design by Dupas; it was intended to be placed in the Hall of Honour in the French Pavilion.

Michel Dufet, a designer of no great originality, was put in charge of the arts and crafts section. He adopted a highly idiosyncratic approach, abandoning the time-honoured system of presenting objects by category, preferring to blend them as if displayed in a private apartment. Scattered throughout the building as a whole, the exhibits produced an extremely lively impression. Thus, a room designed by Jules Leleu, itself an outstanding example of the cabinet-maker's art in ivory, shagreen and gold, contained a superb chest of drawers covered in white shagreen and with incised gold decoration, together with Dunand's large lacquer panel depicting deer that had been shown in Paris in 1937.

The interior space of the pavilion was used to create a large display area, all the most prestigious exhibits being grouped around huge central tables piled high with ceramic tablewares and precious metalwork. A rotunda containing the panel by Dupas and Dunand provided a focal point for the display. Unaffected by events in Europe and their social repercussions, the New York World's Fair proved not only that a taste for luxury was not yet dead in France, but that the country still led the way in the decorative arts.

In parallel with the World's Fair, the cultural service of the French government presented a selection of modern bookbindings in New York at its Fifth Avenue premises, an exhibition in which Schmied and Dunand figured prominently. Made in leather with filigree silver or gold mosaic or inlaid with plates of lacquered ebonite or silver, a number of these bindings were highlighted with mother-of-pearl, powdered burgaudine, eggshell and precious-metal filings. Strikingly original, these bindings added the finishing touch to works as stunning for the quality of their production as for the artistry of their illustrations, which had all been lacquered entirely by hand in Dunand's studios in the manner of Persian miniatures or medieval illuminated manuscripts. Besides these works, which included such titles as *Le Cantique des Cantiques* ('The Song of Solomon'), *Les Climats* and *L'Histoire Charmante de l'Adolescente Sucre d'Amour*, works by Rose Adler, Pierre Legrain, Georges Cretté, Paul Bonnet and Henri Creuzevault provided a marvellous complementary display of French virtuosity in bookbinding.

In May, at the Salon de la Nationale, Dunand exhibited a screen decorated with wading birds, while at the Salon des Artistes Décorateurs, in a boudoir designed by Eugène Printz, a chest made of bubinga wood from Gabon supported by a metal base was placed on a sort of semicircular dais, the base of which was decorated with a long arched frieze with a swan motif. Decorated in black and gold lacquer, this frieze had been designed by Dunand as a kind of stylistic exercise, and although somewhat dull in terms of design, it was perfectly executed.

Wartime in Paris

In spite of the fact that war had recently been declared, a Salon was organized by the City of Paris for the benefit of painters, sculptors and designers. It opened on 18 November 1939 in the Galerie des Animaliers in the Boulevard Malesherbes, by courtesy of the gallery's proprietor, E. M. Sandoz. Some fifty exhibitors took part, none of them members of any particular Salon. Although in no way innovatory, such a wide range of ideas could not fail to charm those Parisians who were still in the capital.

The 1940 Salon took place at the Palais de Chaillot, bringing together 150 exhibitors from various artistic organizations. In spite of the difficult conditions in which all artists and craftsmen – cabinet-makers, lacquer artists, ceramicists, metalworkers or glassmakers – now had to work, participation was general. Regardless of whether artists were dead or remained prisoners-of-war, their next of kin considered it vital that their names should not be forgotten. Dunand exhibited two lacquered screens, one depicting an ass's foal lost on a mountainside, the other in grey on a gold background depicting a deer in relief.

This curious Salon, which was planned to run from 3 to 25 April, was opened by the Minister of Education, Albert Sarraut. Apart from a handful of images of war, as moving as they were sad, most exhibitors sought to avoid the general mood of gloom by evoking picturesque landscapes, the beauty of the human body and magnificent flowers.

At the Pavillon de Marsan, the Union Centrale des Arts Décoratifs devoted its central hall to an evocation of the First World War, drawing on works by Jean-Louis Forain, Roger de la Fresnaye, Luc-Albert Moreau and others. Even if the idea seemed absurd in the circumstances, the exhibition was a fine tribute to the leading artists of the recent past. At the entrance to the exhibition was Dunand's screen, *The Shacks of Argonne*, a work which had been part of the national collection at the Musée des Arts Décoratifs since 1922.

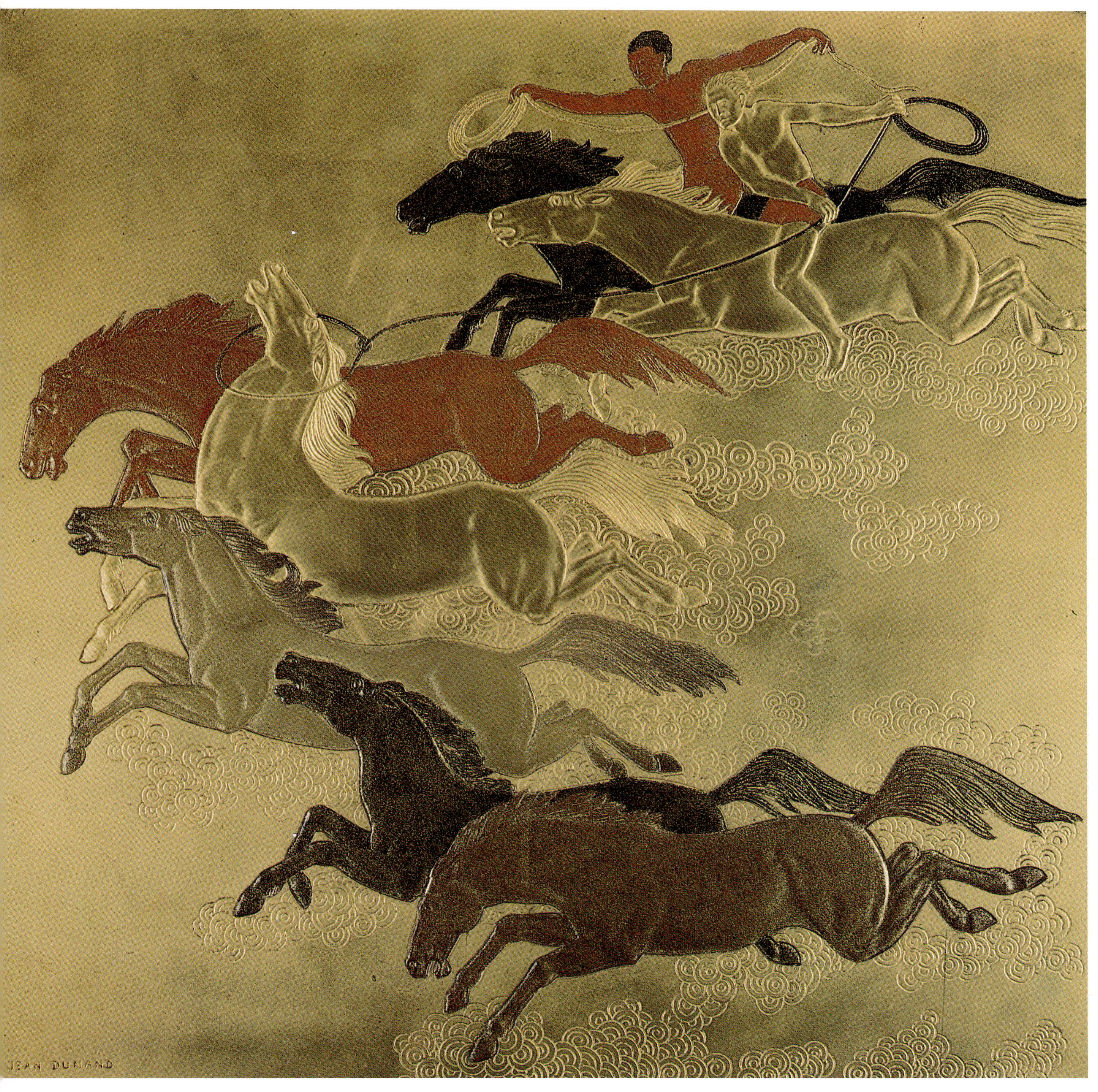

Plates 146–156
DECORATIVE SCHEMES FOR OCEAN LINERS

Plates 146–154
The Normandie (1935)

146 ***Taming the Horse***, reduced-scale copy of the original panel (*catalogue 1090*)

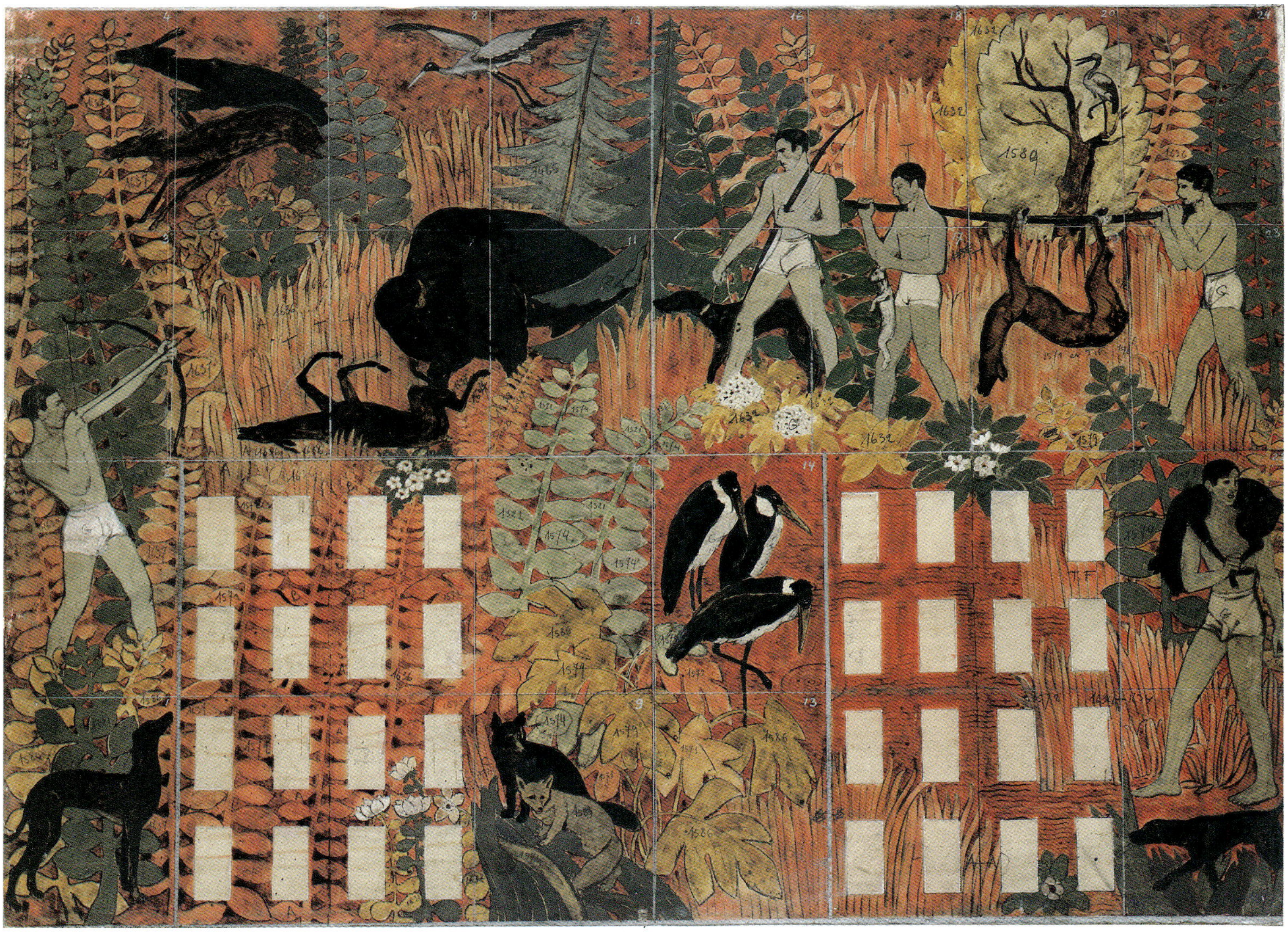

147 ***Hunting***, preparatory sketch for the lacquer panels in the Smoking Room (*catalogue 1106*)

148 ***Marabou Stork***, copy of a motif from the *Hunting* mural (*catalogue 1113*)

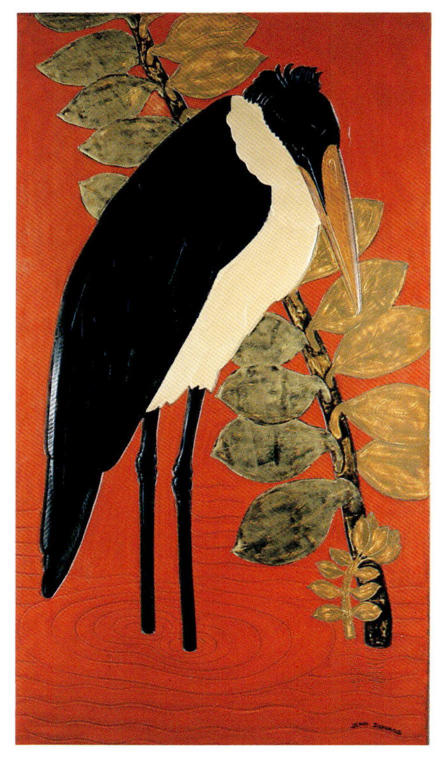

OPPOSITE

149 ***Hunting***, variant of the *Normandie* mural (*catalogue 1111*)

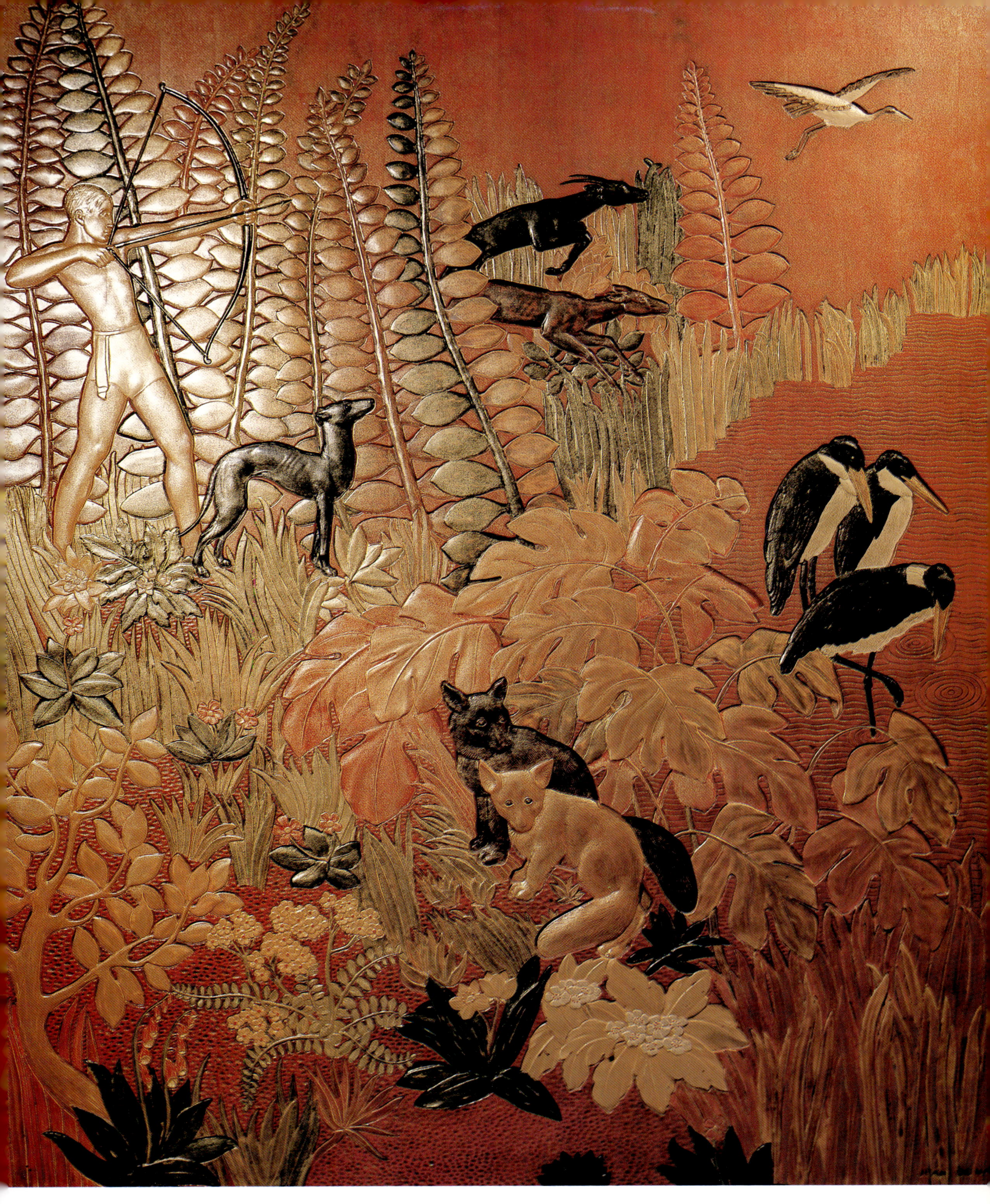

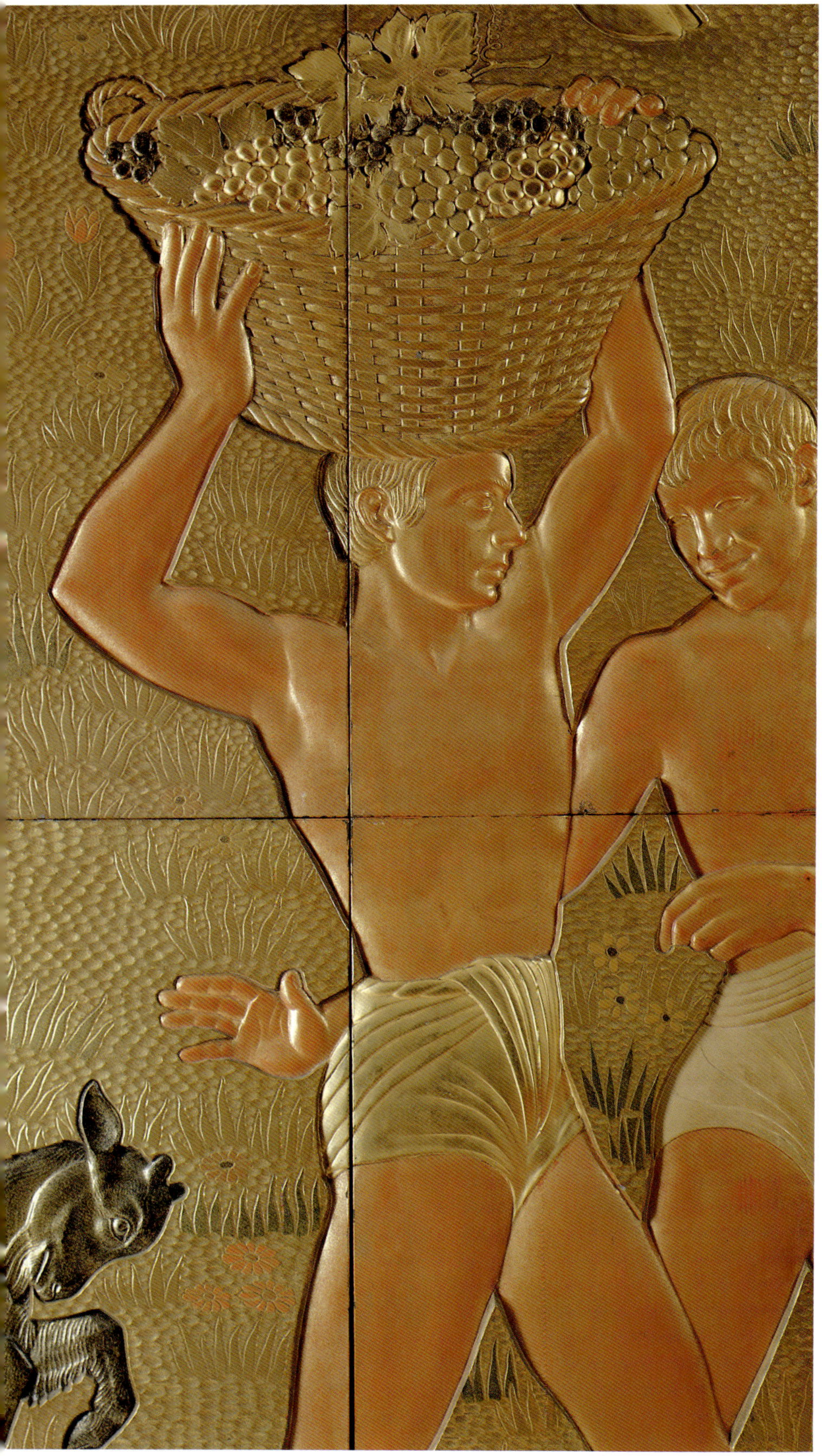

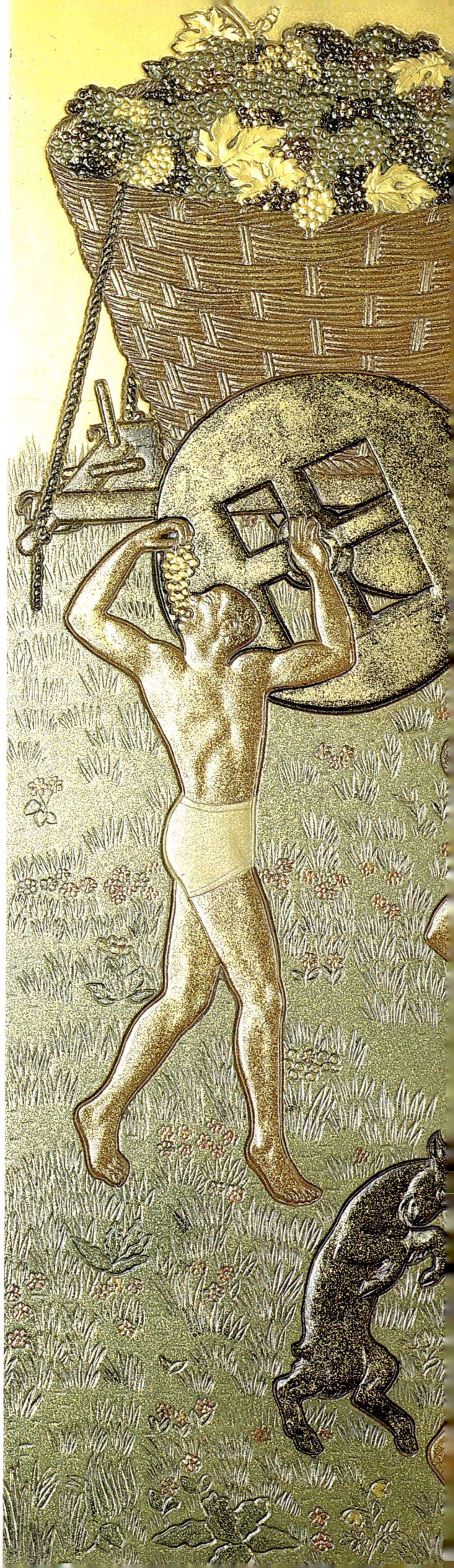

150 ***Grape-pickers***, detail of the *Grape Harvesting* mural (*catalogue 1096*)

151 ***Grape Harvesting***, reduced-scale version of the *Normandie* mural (*catalogue 1099*)

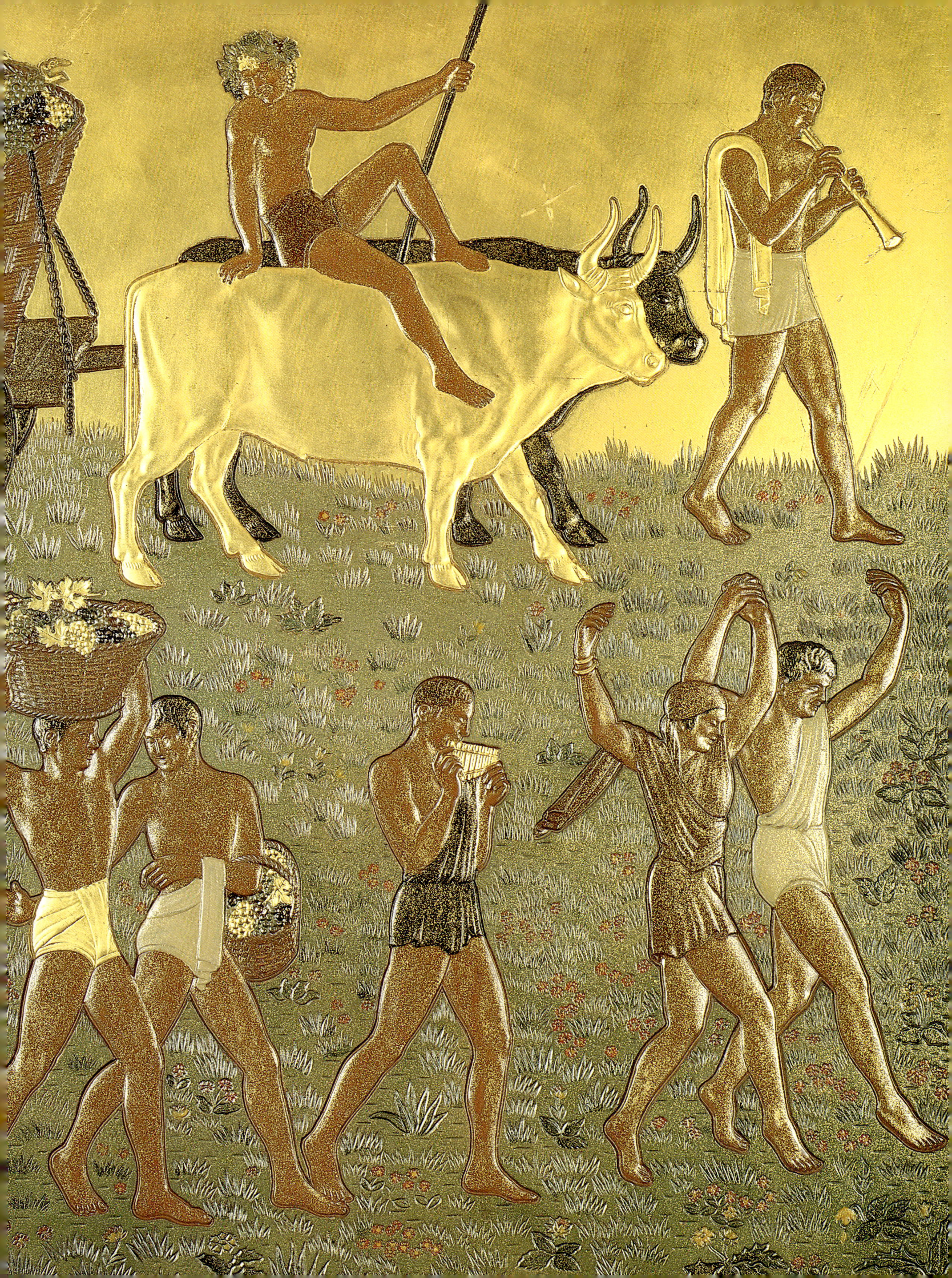

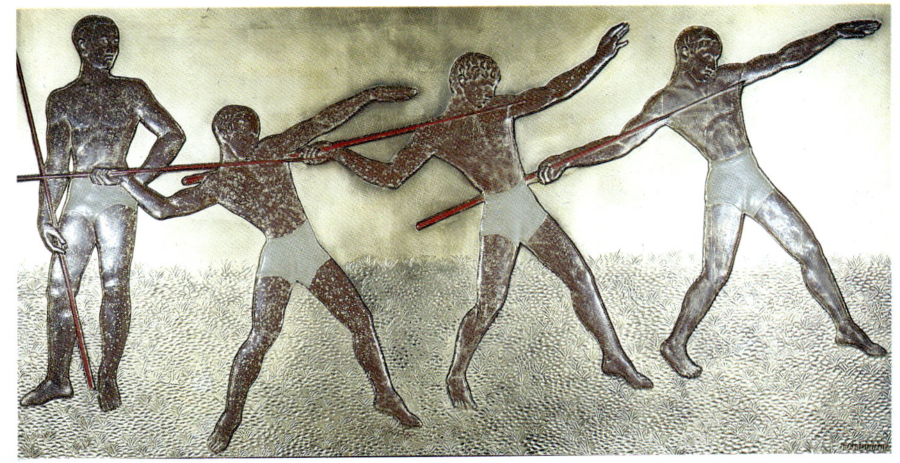

152 ***Javelin Throwers***, variant of the large panel *Sports* (*catalogue 1105*)

153 ***Javelin Throwers***, copy of an unrealized design for a mural (*catalogue 1116*)

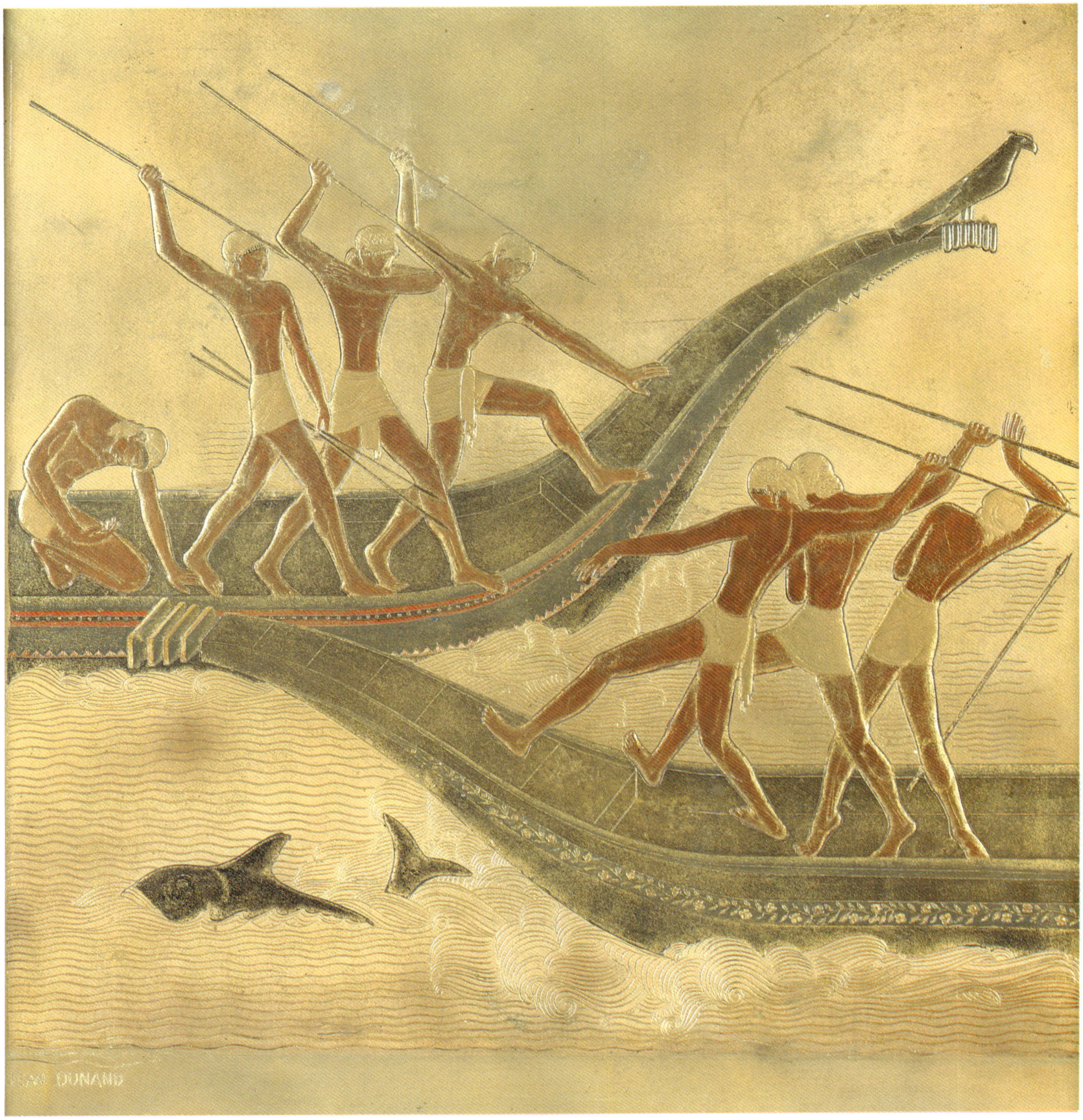

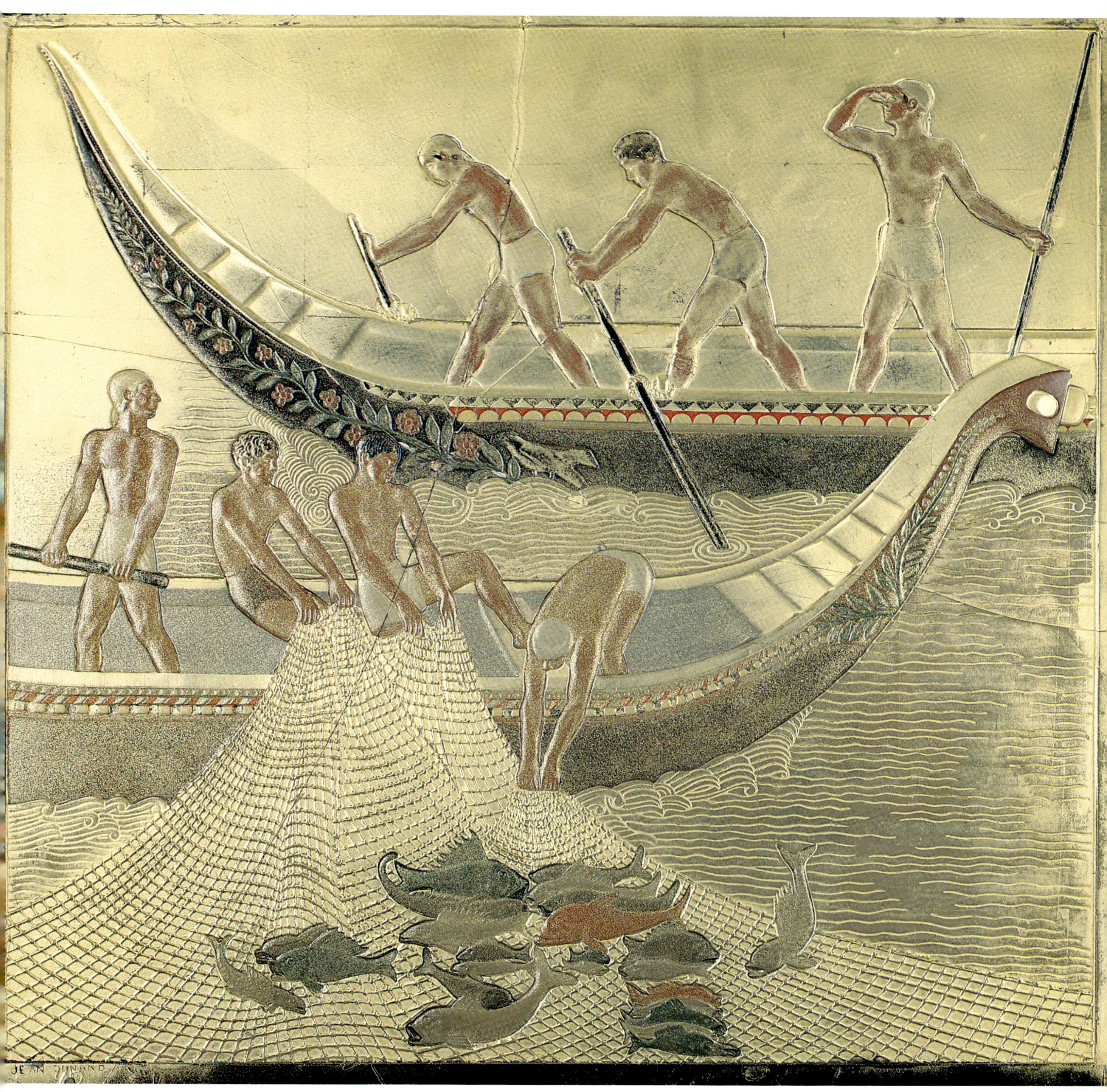

154 ***Fishing***, reduced-scale copy of the panel in the Smoking Room (*catalogue 1102*)

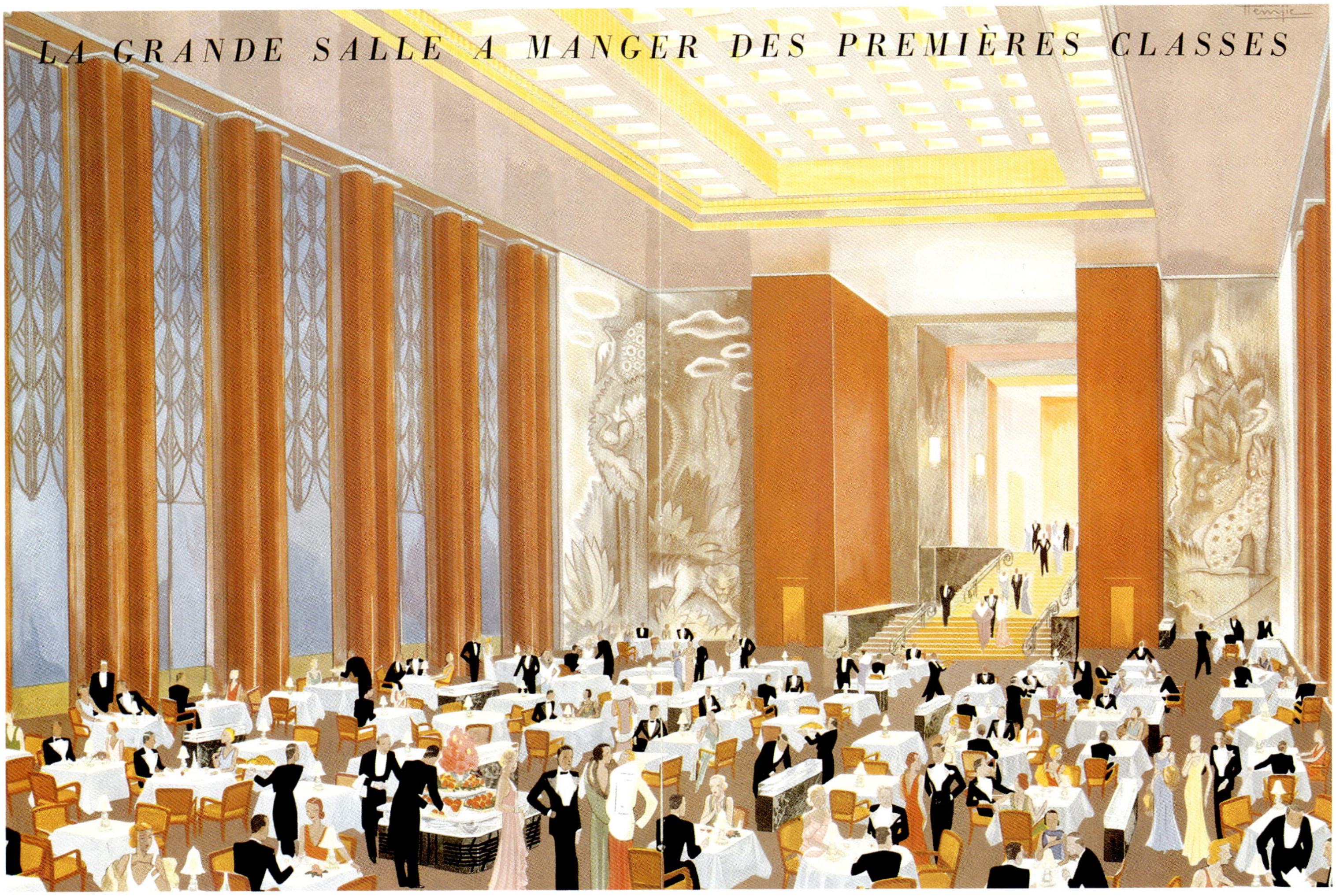

LA GRANDE SALLE A MANGER DES PREMIÈRES CLASSES

155, 156 ***L'Atlantique*** (1931)

Plates from the official brochure, showing the liner's first-class Dining Room and the Oval Saloon

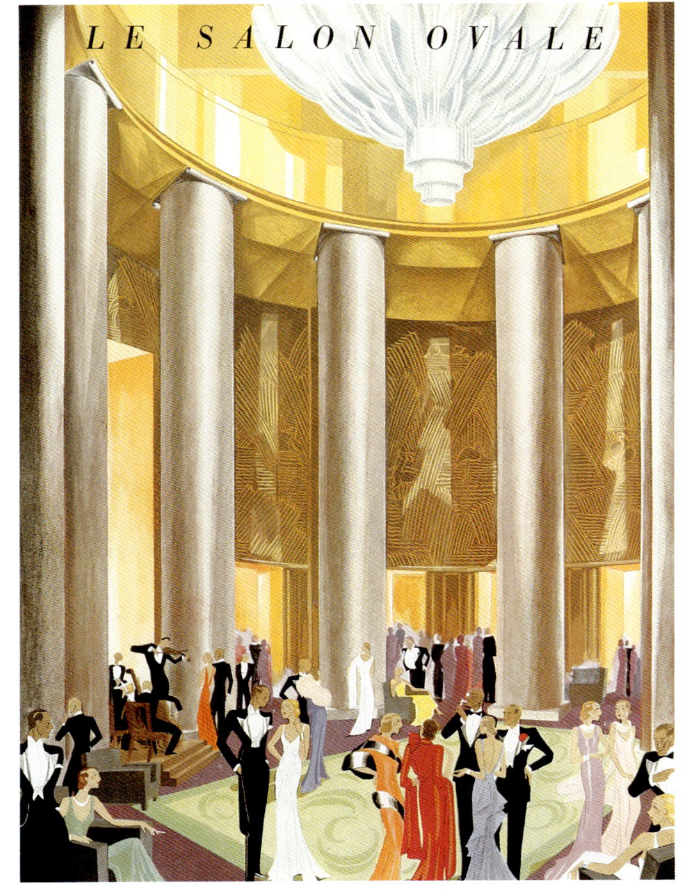

Organized in the record time of seventeen days, the Salon d'Automne opened on 16 November. If anecdotal art inspired by recent events was happily in short supply, decorative art, by contrast, was splendidly represented. The general catalogue drawn up by René Henri noted under Dunand's name, 'Placed at the back ... a most beautiful lacquer screen representing swans and a rectangular table with a drawer lacquered in black and a border of graduated eggshell.'

Following the Franco-German Armistice in 1940, artistic life in Paris seemed to pick up again. Numerous exhibitions were announced as evidence that the situation had returned to 'normal'. One such, held at the Musée Cognacq-Jay in January 1941, was a charity show, at which Dunand offered lacquered metal vases alongside beautiful stoneware pieces by Séraphin Soudbinine and tin-glazed earthenware examples by Jean Mayodon.

During March a kind of retrospective exhibition of works of decorative art produced during the preceding five years was put on at the Pavillon de Marsan. Furniture, tapestries and lacquerwork, as well as glassware, ceramics, ironwork and goldsmith's work were exhibited alongside paintings and sculptures. Dunand exhibited a number of items, together with pieces by his son Bernard, still a prisoner-of-war in Germany.

In April the Salon des Artistes Français included a small piece of furniture by Dunand, lacquered in black and decorated with fish. Even if it conformed to his clients' changing tastes at this time, it is difficult to regard it as a successful piece. Although it was hand-lacquered, its resemblance to a mass-produced dining-room sideboard was scarcely calculated to win admirers. Besides this piece, Dunand exhibited a four-panel screen with similar decoration.

In June came the Salon des Tuileries, held this year in the Palais de Tokyo in the Avenue de New York. Dunand remained loyal to his well-tried formula of sumptuous screens, 'one bronzed and highlighted in silver, evocative of Persian *cloisonné* work, the other gleaming with gold and transporting the viewer into the depths of an autumnal forest with two contented deer'.

In September 1941, Anatole de Monzie began preparations for the 30th Salon des Artistes Décorateurs, due to take place the following year at the Musée des Beaux-Arts de la Ville de Paris, i.e. the Palais de Tokyo. An entire section was to be devoted to works by existing members and by prisoners-of-war, Bernard Dunand's appearing side by side with glass objects by Max Ingrand and the brothers Lardin.

The Palais de Tokyo also provided the setting for the Salon d'Automne, held in October. Because of the height of the exhibition rooms, this building was extremely difficult to heat, and, splendid though the rooms had been in 1937, they were scarcely suited to the prevailing mood of economic gloom. Dunand exhibited a red-lacquer round table and a striking blue-lacquer screen with incised decoration entitled *Hunting*. From this period date a whole series of pieces with simple lines, decorated in the Chinese style with traditional themes of fish or equally traditional scenes of deer in forest clearings. They were not calculated to enhance Dunand's fame and reputation, but intended rather to ensure sales to a less fastidious clientèle, thus enabling him to pay his workmen and maintain his studio. Indeed, it was only by selling this kind of furniture that Dunand managed to balance his books. Also from this period come pieces of furniture finished in light-golden shellac, but otherwise undecorated, and more architectural in form – pieces which were equally easy to make and readily saleable. Most of these items are unsigned, either because Dunand did not design them (some were by Eugène Printz), or because he did not consider them sufficiently worthy.

In November 1941, the 33rd Salon d'Hiver was formally opened. Like the year's other major exhibitions, this was held in the Palais de Tokyo. Since its inception forty-three years earlier, the Salon d'Hiver had provided a link between the principal autumn and spring salons, as well as an occasion to present more modest pieces. In 1941 a special room set aside for portraits became the season's star attraction. Apart from a beautiful portrait of Suzy

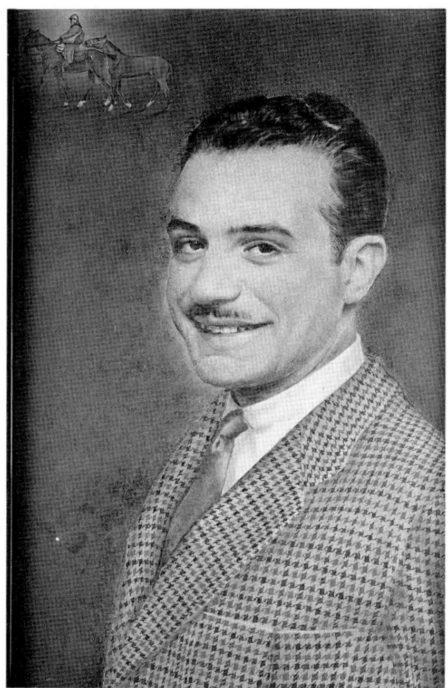

Dunand's lacquer portrait of his son Jean-Louis, painted in 1938 (cat. no. 199).

Solidor which Dunand had painted in lacquer some time previously, there were also portraits of Edith Piaf, Maurice Chevalier, Arletty, Colette and Vincent d'Indy, not to mention Cécile Sorel and Sacha Guitry, all painted by well-known artists. Sacha Guitry was at that time President of the Union des Arts, and on this occasion exhibited a number of paintings and items from his private collection. Among the objects on view were the shoes worn by Little Titch, the crown worn by François-Joseph Talma, the cane carried by Constant Coquelin, and even the candlesticks used to light the stage in Molière's plays. All were touching souvenirs of France's theatrical history rather than objects of any real artistic value.

Although Dunand's contributions to all these exhibitions were successful to a greater or lesser extent, he had difficulty in making ends meet. Fortunately, either out of gratitude for past donations or in the belief that he was acting in the national interest, the Secretary-General of the Ministry of Fine Arts paid 25,000 francs for a black-lacquer bookcase decorated with gilt storks and with a central glazed door, and at the same time settled an earlier account of 3,400 francs for a vase purchased by the City of Paris at the previous Salon d'Automne. Encouraged by this coup, Dunand offered the government, at a relatively derisory price, a whole set of furniture comprising a lady's bureau decorated with fish, a brown-lacquer dressing table with matching stool, a nest of tables in black lacquer and eggshell, an eight-panel screen decorated with fish, a four-panel screen with a hunting motif, a six-panel screen with a floral motif, and a four-panel screen depicting a forest scene. A counter-offer of 276,000 francs was received from the Mobilier National, and this was accepted.

Tired, ill and grief-stricken at the death of his son Jean-Louis, Dunand died on 7 June 1942 at the age of 65. His final creation was a lacquer and eggshell panel, on which he was still working on the eve of his death. Left unfinished, it depicts the church at Estaing in the *département* of Lot.

In their newspaper obituaries many art critics paid a final tribute to Dunand. At the Salon des Artistes Décorateurs, inaugurated by the Archbishop of Paris, the section devoted to religious art contained a small retrospective of Dunand's work, including the panels which the artist had shown in 1937, among them the *Pietà*.

By ministerial order No. 81,478 authorization was given for a commemorative plaque to be affixed to the house at 72 Rue Hallé. It reads: 'Behind these buildings stood the studios of the sculptor, coppersmith and lacquer artist Jean Dunand 1877–1942.' On 6 November 1986, the Mayor of Paris, Jacques Chirac, approved the naming of one of the streets in an area under redevelopment in the 13th *arrondissement* 'Rue Jean Dunand'.

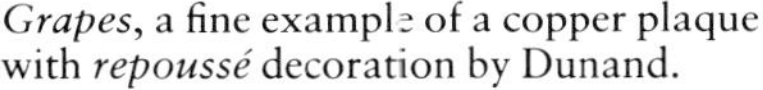

Grapes, a fine example of a copper plaque with *repoussé* decoration by Dunand.

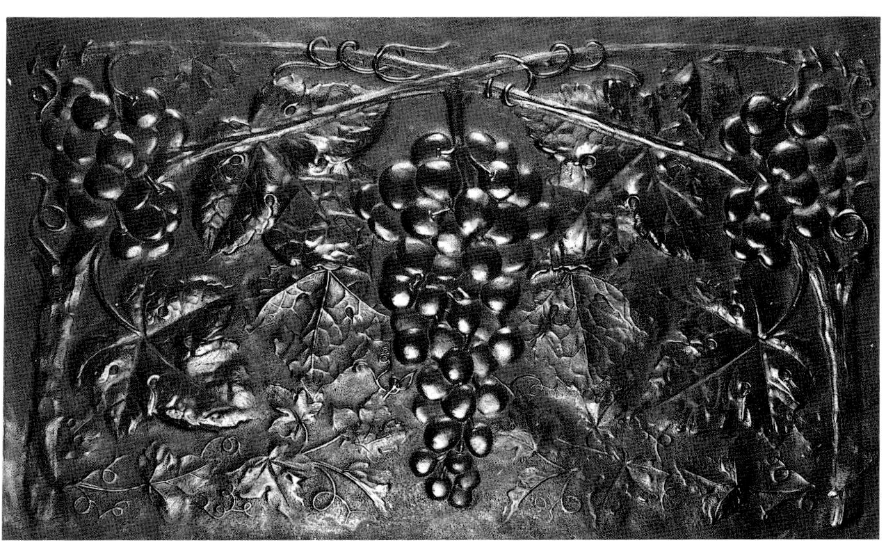

ASPECTS OF JEAN DUNAND'S OEUVRE

Sculpture

As a boy aged fourteen, Dunand first registered in 1891 in the carving and modelling class at the Ecole des Arts Industriels in Geneva. From his earliest years he had been attracted to the idea of drawing and modelling plants and animals, showing an aptitude for handling volumes and the ornamental qualities of his chosen subjects. His father would no doubt have preferred to see him become a craftsman like himself, while at the same time receiving more advanced interdisciplinary training, but his mother wanted to encourage the boy's natural talent and enrolled him in Jules Hugues Salmson's sculpture class. His talents quickly aroused the interest of his teachers, who guided him firmly in the direction of sculpture. At the end of his second year of study Jean was awarded first prize.

Although they lack any distinguishing features, the works of this early period generally reflect the widespread but formative academicism typical of the teaching of the time. The beginnings of a personal style are evident in the allegorical *Switzerland* of 1894. Supported by a tall plinth, a female figure bearing a standard stretches out her hand pointing the way for a young soldier standing beside her, while in her other hand she holds a standard. On the strength of this sculpture, the municipal authorities of Geneva commissioned *Helvetia* from Dunand: a young woman, once again symbolizing Switzerland, extends an olive branch in her right hand as a token of peace, while her left hand rests on a shield bearing the country's coat of arms. *Helvetia* is the most successful and powerful work produced by Dunand during his formative years in Geneva.

Other records show the young Dunand with fellow students. In one photograph he is standing beside his *Bust of a Young Girl*, with the model herself also seen in the group. This work was no doubt an end-of-term study, and it was sufficiently close to Dunand's heart for him to take it with him to Paris. It can be seen, in a photograph taken several years later, on the mantelpiece in a room where he was living in the Rue Michelet.

In another photograph, studies of a male nude allow us to compare Dunand's version with those of other students, and to see that Dunand had already evolved a much more sensitive and elaborate style than that of his fellows. This also appears to have been the piece which won him his end-of-term prize. In this photograph the sculpture by his friend Bocquet appears more rigid and less vibrant, despite its impeccable anatomy, while Dunand's treatment of surfaces is plainly more sensitive.

What these pieces show is that even by this date Dunand had developed his technique sufficiently to create an individual style. No doubt the subject matter is still essentially illustrative and imbued with the characteristic formalism of student work, but a more personal quality was increasingly asserting itself, and his abilities as an ambitious and confident artist were becoming ever more apparent. Following the traditional practice of sculpture studios, he apparently worked together with one of his teachers, a M. Jerdelet, putting the finishing touches to a commemorative bust of a bearded man.

To this period (1896) may be dated Dunand's first meeting with Abdou Faye, a Senegalese artisan who had come to Geneva with an exhibition on African village life. His striking appearance made him an ideal model for the students in the sculpture class at the School of Industrial Art. Dunand made a whole series of statuettes of him in plaster of Paris, which he then coloured before selling them to passers-by on the Pont de l'Arve. A number of busts of Abdou Faye also date from this period, attesting not only to Dunand's feeling for sculptural form but also to his business acumen, for he realized that, in order to sell his work, he needed to offer prospective purchasers pieces that were attractive and pleasing to the eye.

In this same commercial vein he made a plaster vase decorated with vine shoots, a piece which, if lacking in originality, was nonetheless extremely decorative and highly sculptural in quality. Another early commercial venture which combined his talents as a sculptor with his skills as a decorative artist is a model of a bracket clock, together with its support, entered in an interdisciplinary exhibition, the Concours Galland, in June 1897, for which he was awarded a prize of 1,500 Swiss francs. As a result his work was selected by the firm of Henri Sandoz and Paul Nardin and reproduced in bronze for commercial distribution.

His talent having by now been widely recognized, it comes as no surprise that Dunand was awarded a scholarship by the City of Geneva to enable him to continue his training as a sculptor in Paris. As a result, he concentrated exclusively on sculpture from 1897 to 1902, studying under Jean Dampt, a highly fashionable sculptor of the day, who was equally skilled and successful in modelling clay and in stone carving. He taught Dunand all the intricacies of his art, and Dunand worked in turn with clay, marble, wrought iron, ivory and precious metals. The works of this period are all natural and more realistic, seemingly charged with sensuality and life, bespeaking a very real freedom of interpretation. The apprenticeship period was definitely over.

Towards the end of 1899, he modelled a *Bust of a Friend*, Maurice Dieterlin, together with that of a young girl, both works being first exhibited in Paris at the Salon de la Nationale of 1900. Whereas the former still seems somewhat stiff, the latter shows rather more suppleness. Elsewhere, in the Swiss section of the 1900 Exposition Universelle, he exhibited his *Quo Vadis: Figure of an Old Man*. On the strength of the work he presented, Dunand was awarded a gold medal.

The first version of *The Child and Butterfly* also dates from 1900. In form this piece is more precise, revealing a tenderness and beauty in the handling of the subject. A further product of these student years is a striking figure entitled *Vercingetorix*, a sturdily built warrior clad in leather, with a pointed mace resting on one shoulder.

A beautiful standing female nude was modelled at about this time and then sculpted in limestone, and exhibited under the title *The Awakening* in 1904. This major work is proof of Dunand's very real talent, and Dampt was fond of drawing attention of the extraordinary delicacy of its outline and expression.

Aware of the affinity between him and his pupil, Dampt chose Dunand to work with him in an interior scheme for the Comtesse de Béarn, in which task they were joined by Dunand's former schoolfriend, Carl Albert Angst. The work involved the preparation of a full-size model of a room measuring 7 x 5 m (23 x 16 ft), covering the walls with white wood and painted canvases to give an impression of the overall effect. The stucco on the ceiling vault was applied by his usual assistant, Ternois, and Dampt, Angst and Dunand modelled the decorative motifs while the stucco was still soft. Of course, Dampt would touch up his pupils' work, but they were allowed a degree of freedom to depart from the basic model prepared by Dampt. Work on the frieze was carried out in a similar fashion, this time with the help of another of Dampt's pupils, Fraysse. The carved wood panelling was begun by Angst and Dunand and continued *in situ* by a skilled carpenter called Groesser, helped by a wood-carver called Collet. 'I started off the work, and they then copied what I had done,' said Dampt of his pupils. The wrought-iron door plaques were inlaid with copper, and it seems that Dunand worked on these alone under his master's watchful eye. The ivory handles and a pear-wood bust of the Comtesse de Béarn were personally executed by Dampt, who modestly summed up the project by saying in an interview published in *Art et décoration* in 1906: 'With the help of my pupils I succeeded in creating the elements of a very luxurious decor which satisfies the demands of modern living.'

In 1903, guided by his mentor, 'who believes a sculptor should also be a craftsman', Dunand made a tentative move in the direction of the decorative arts, exhibiting a recently completed carved wooden bread-tray at the Salon de la Nationale. Throughout these studies and while executing these collective works, Dunand continued to develop his natural bent. Dampt appears to have realized this before Dunand himself did, noting how adept his students was in applying his skills to the embellishment of everyday objects.

The journey Dunand made to Italy in 1904 provided him with an opportunity to familiarize himself at first hand with classical and Renaissance sculpture and with the sense of proportion and volume that typify antique statuary and with its intrinsic feeling for space.

Back in France, he completed the bust of his cousin Marguerite, a work he had begun as a study in clay during a visit to Switzerland in 1902. Carved in Burgundy stone, the finished sculpture was one which Dunand remained proud of throughout his life, for he captured a mood of charming chasteness well suited to impress the most demanding of critics. The delicacy of detail, the treatment of volume and the articulation of surfaces made this sculpture a most engaging piece. Dunand later made a version in bronze which he exhibited on various occasions in France and elsewhere.

A clay study depicting a bust of a young man which he returned to and completed at this time was a likeness of Sabato Martelli, based on an earlier sketch made in Geneva. Also cast in bronze, this bust reveals a purity of form that harks back to heroic statues of antiquity, even though the piece is only of modest size.

These are the main works of sculpture from Dunand's early years which we have been able to trace, although others undoubtedly did exist. The impression they give is one of a delicacy of taste combined with a scrupulous eye for detail. For Dunand bronze was the sculptural material par excellence. In contrast to what Rodin was doing at this time, he strove to remove all trace of modelling, preferring instead to present a smooth surface devoid of superfluous details. His work, while pure, is powerful and expressive, never resorting to sentimentality. Some years later, after he had abandoned sculpture, Dunand drew the attention of his son Bernard to the work of François Pompon, holding out its expressive power as an example of the finest sculpture of the twentieth century.

In parallel with the formality of the works discussed above, Dunand was capable of treating living, anecdotal subjects with a notable degree of freshness. In 1904, for example, he carved an animal group, *Hen and Chicks*, out of a single piece of walnut. Once again, by carving the wood directly, he revealed both his manual dexterity and his eye for detail, even when treating the most humble of subjects.

However, sculpture would never provide an adequate income, and, in view of the success enjoyed by his decorative pieces, Dunand abandoned sculpture almost completely. In 1931 his projected design for a monumental figure for the liner *L'Atlantique* was not accepted. All the same, he conceived the idea of modelling all the panels for the smoking room of the liner *Normandie* in low relief (see p. 145).

Throughout his career Dunand showed himself to be profoundly concerned with form, whether in the field of sculpture or metalwork. In terms of interior design, his furniture, his decorative schemes and even his carpet designs reflect the approach of an artist who sees everything in a three-dimensional space, rather than in a two-dimensional and decorative way, as was the case with painters of this period, including even the theoreticians of Cubism. The 1925 smoking room, the 1926 office for Madame Agnès and his stand at the Salon des Artistes Décorateurs in 1927 all attest to Dunand's feeling for volume and to his very real understanding of how to handle space. Dampt could be proud of his pupil who, by following his mentor's advice and concentrating on the decorative arts, became one of the present century's undisputed masters in that sphere.

Dinanderie

DINANDERIE – hand-beaten copper- and brassware – takes its name from the town of Dinant, near Liège in Belgium. In the Middle Ages the town specialized in *repoussé* copperwork inlaid with silvered metal. Although familiar to the Persians and Arabs, this process was revived by the Christian craftsmen in the valley of the Meuse, a locality rich in zinc ore. The other component of brass – copper – was imported from the area around Cologne in Germany. Producing ornate or simple tableware such as plates, tankards and ewers, the local trade flourished until cheaper pewter tableware began to compete with it. Mass-produced with the aid of moulds, household objects in this new and less expensive material spread rapidly, to the detriment of skilled work in beaten metal. It must be borne in mind that the entire art of dinanderie consisted of producing an object from a single flat sheet of metal, by beating it into the shape of a vase, plate or jug without recourse to cutting, soldering or adding to it in any way. In other words, this kind of hand-crafted work is quite distinct from wares produced by die-stamping, a mechanical process involving stamping sheet metal with a press or matrix.

Having decided to abandon sculpture, Dunand turned first to dinanderie because in this medium he found the most effective means to express his innate talent. From 1904 onwards he was regularly exhibiting examples of his work. He

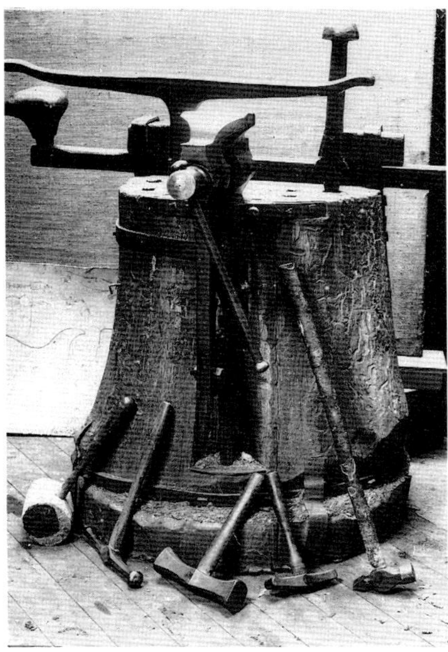

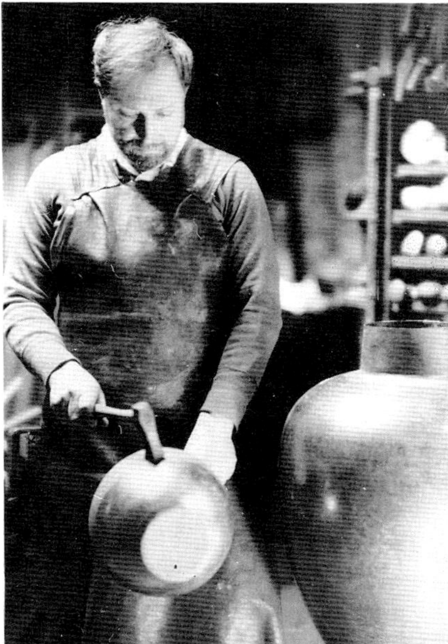

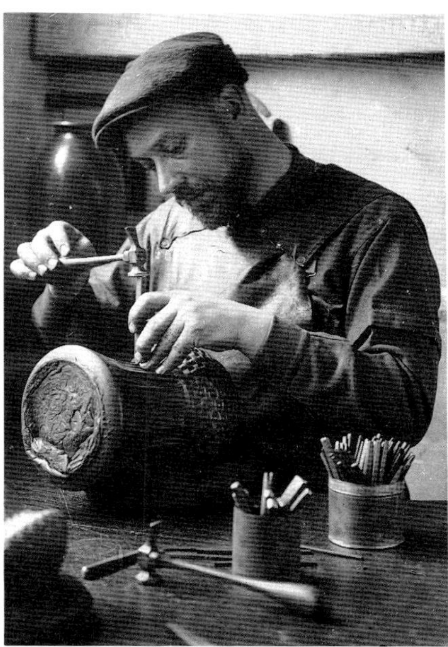

The tools of the dinandier; (centre) Dunand working on a nearly complete metal vase; (right) Dunand chasing the *repoussé* decoration on a vase.

had earlier practised this traditional technique both during his training at the School of Industrial Art in Geneva and in the course of his summer holidays, when he had worked for a Geneva coppersmith called Danhaver. For the purposes of dinanderie, apart from brass and copper, mild steel (an alloy of iron and carbon) may also be used, as may lead, pewter and, very often, 'German silver' (a white alloy of copper, nickel and zinc), the French term for which – *maillechort* – is derived from the names of its inventors, Maillot and Chorier.

Precious metals, especially gold and silver, were traditionally reserved for goldsmith's work (*orfèvrerie*), though Dunand himself did not abide by this distinction, considering himself equally at home with base and precious metals. Since all metals are, in varying degrees, rigid or pliable, hard or porous, malleable or resistant, cohesive, ductile or fusible, a detailed knowledge of their specific properties is required to enable them to be worked together or separately. In addition, Dunand found that certain combinations of metals that differed in appearance and colour allowed him to exploit these qualities for aesthetic ends.

In shaping a piece, the surface area of the metal sheet is of course an important factor, since a tray or dish requires a smaller surface area than a cup, a vase or a jug. Thus Dunand indicated that, for a vase 30 cm (12 in.) high, he would need to start with a sheet of metal 40 cm (15 in.) in diameter. In general, the sheets of copper or brass he used had a gauge of between 1.2 and 1.5 mm (about $\frac{1}{16}$ in.). Such a metal disc, which is the point of departure in any dinanderie, is called a 'blank'.

The first operation, then, consists of shaping the blank with the aid of a boxwood mallet which, while being extremely hard, does not damage the surface of the metal. The process of shaping a hollow object is termed 'raising'. The blank is placed first on a concave block of boxwood, where it is formed into the shape of a shallow dish by being beaten only on what will be the inner surface of the intended object. Such a block may vary in size depending on the desired shape of the piece, and it may be changed as the work proceeds either to accentuate the hollow depression or, conversely, to reduce it. Then, by repeated blows of the mallet the shallow bowl is made deeper until what emerges is a sort of broad-rimmed basin. It is always essential to start at the centre and beat the metal in a regular spiral action. Once the metal has been shaped from the inside, the craftsman proceeds to hammer it from the outside, turning the piece over and placing it on an iron support some 150 cm (5 ft) in length. At one end of this shaft there is a square hole into which is fitted a 'stake-anvil', corresponding in shape to the piece being formed. Some anvils have two horns and are used for smaller pieces. The action of hammering from the outside involves working outwards from the centre, in a spiral movement, using a special hammer. In the course of several such operations the size of the aperture can be gradually reduced until the desired diameter is achieved. Only the top of the vase is subjected to this reduction process.

The effect of the many repeated blows at the earlier stages is to cause the metal gradually to lose its malleability and to become brittle. To avoid the risk of its fracturing while being worked, the metal is annealed by being heated cherry-red with the aid of a blowlamp, thus restoring its natural malleability. Once the piece has cooled, the hammering process continues, until the desired shape and diameter are produced.

Although these operations may seem easy to describe, they demand a great deal of skill, quite apart from the fact that the craftsman must ensure that the metal retains a certain thickness. The final thickness is directly related to the stress to which an object will be subjected in normal use. Certain parts may have to be reinforced, while others may remain very thin since they are not subjected to any special strain. In addition, the heating operation is itself a very delicate one, since heat must be applied gradually and uniformly to those parts which have been most affected by hammering. The best method is to place the whole piece in a coke furnace until it becomes red-hot. Equally, the cooling process must be carried out with care. This consists either of quenching (plunging the piece into cold liquid) if rapid cooling is required, or placing it in a sand-box if slow cooling is preferred.

However regular and precise the hammering, some surface imperfections will inevitably remain, and these, though virtually invisible to the naked eye, can be felt when the metalworker rubs his finger over the surface. It is these palpable irregularities which endow brass- and copperware with a sort of life and suppleness that is lacking in wares produced by die-stamping. In fact, the whole art of dinanderie consists of eliminating traces of hammering as much as possible, while retaining sufficient to enliven the surface imperceptibly. The final planishing is intended to reduce visible traces of hammering or, conversely, to exploit them for decorative effect. To achieve this, a piece will be subjected to a final annealing process, before being plunged into a bath of dilute sulphuric acid. The planishing process is carried out by placing the piece on a steel anvil and striking it with firm, rapid blows at a rate of 200 per minute, the blows overlapping as tightly as possible and describing a spiral. The tool used is a special hammer with a smooth, flat head. This planishing may produce a smooth result or, conversely, a faceted surface, according to the decorative finish desired.

For pieces that were simple in shape or basically spherical, Dunand would sometimes use a lathe with broken mandrels, a sort of convex mould with detachable wooden sections that can be adjusted to suit the size and shape desired. On completion, the interlocking wooden sections can be removed one at a time from inside the piece. However, because the molecular structure of the metal is affected when using this process, the object cannot be engraved or inlaid. Hence this process is only suitable for undecorated pieces. Generally, however, metalworkers consider the resulting shape to be uninteresting, cold and lifeless.

If, despite these reservations, this process is chosen, the work involves hammering the sheet metal until it conforms to the exact shape of the mandrel. Dunand reserved such methods for spherical forms which he then decorated in lacquer with marine backgrounds and coral.

Contrary to all the rules, however, Dunand did – in very rare instances – attach the body of a very tall piece to its base by soldering, joining the two edges by an oxy-acetylene process.

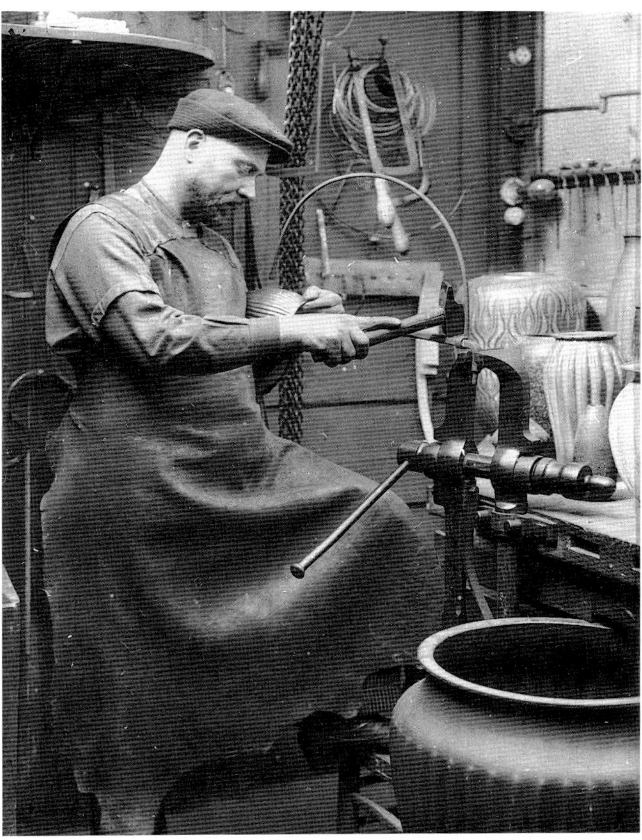

Dunand adding *repoussé* decoration to a metal vase by means of a snarling iron.

Surface ornamentation may be the result of a planishing process in which regular hammering produces splendid faceted or lanceolate effects. It may, however, be the result of treating the surface with acid or heat, which produces a coloured patina or a brown, black or gold bronzing effect. Alternatively, coloured wax may be applied to the surface, though Dunand abandoned this practice when he decided to apply lacquer decoration. In the finest tradition of his craft, however, Dunand preferred *repoussé* decoration and chasing or to inlay the surface with contrasting coloured metals, or, finally, to apply vitrified enamels.

The term *repoussé* (literally 'pushed back') is used to describe relief decoration produced by hammering the metal lightly from behind. Any piece of hollow ware to be decorated in this way must have an opening sufficiently large to allow access to the craftsman's tools. In the case of a narrow opening he will avail himself of a special tool called a snarling iron. This is 60 cm (2 ft) long and consists of two metal arms joined half-way, one of them straight, the other curved. The straight arm is slightly bent at one end, which is fixed in a vice. The other end is inserted into the opening of the piece being worked; at its extremity it forms a right angle extending sideways by 2 cm (¾ in.) and terminating in a small ball. Depending on the work to be done, this ball (or other head) may vary to produce the desired decoration. The other arm is held in such a way that its free end is directly above the place where the head is positioned inside the vase. The craftsman strikes the horizontal arm of the guide at the point where it issues from the jaws of the vice, and thus causes the tool to vibrate along its entire length. The vibrations are amplified and transferred to the head, which acts like a small hammer, striking the inner surface and so pushing the metal outwards by dint of tiny repeated blows. The raised design produced by successive hammerings is poorly defined at first, but can be improved by working over it on the outside. This tooling process is extremely delicate and if care is not exercised the surface of the metal may be perforated. In order to obviate this risk, the piece being tooled may be filled with a sort of cement made of crushed brick, resin and pitch which is heated and poured into the vessel and allowed to cool. When set hard, the filling provides a support for the surface to be worked. In the case of objects made from soft metals such as pewter or lead, a filling of well-packed sand may be used. For his chasing and engraving work, Dunand had a collection of nearly three thousand chisels and other tools, mostly made by himself.

As for inlay work, one method – never used by Dunand – is 'damascening', a delicate technique originating in and used for centuries by sword-makers in Damascus until *c.* 1400. It was later adopted in Spain by goldsmiths in Toledo (then under Moorish rule), notably in the sixteenth century. A fine network of intersecting lines is engraved on mild steel, and threads of precious metal are then applied and beaten with a mallet so that they fill the surface pattern. This technique has the drawback of preventing the craftsman from repairing or polishing the work. As a result, objects produced in this way retain a matt appearance – not always the most desirable effect. For his part, Dunand produced real inlay work by cutting small grooves with a burin in the surface of the metal, then going over the grooves again to give them a dovetailed profile.

Next, threads of silver or gold were inserted into the grooves, after which the two edges of the dovetail were beaten down, closing over the threads and leaving only a finely traced

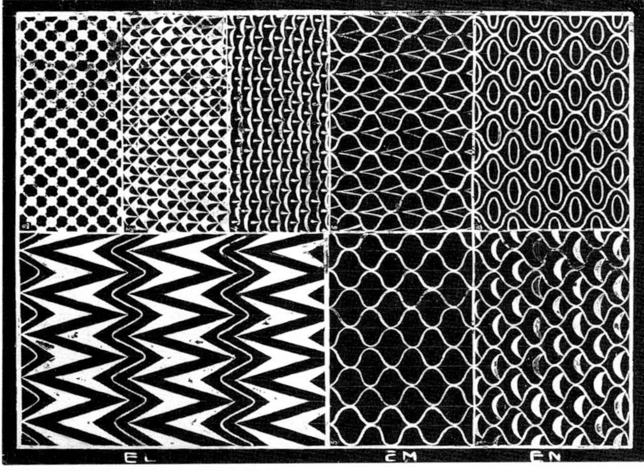

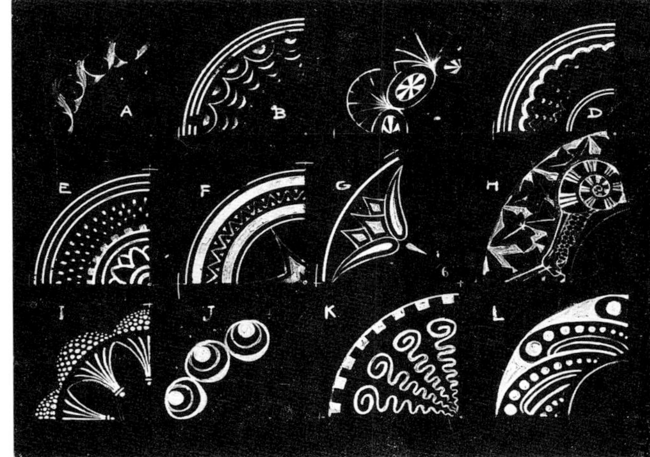

outline which could be left in relief or filed down flush with the surface. Alternatively, they could be polished with the rest of the piece. Once filled in, these grooves blend to form a homogeneous surface. The rules of ornamentation require that, no matter what form it takes, the decoration should never disturb the general line of a vase, but should be integrated with its overall form.

Another technique used by Dunand in his inlay work involved the application of metal filings to a sheet of a different metal having a higher melting point than that of the filings. The filings were heated to melting point by means of a blowlamp, and thus gold or silver might be inlaid on copper, brass or 'German silver' leaving no visible joins.

To begin with, Dunand made only everyday objects in traditional forms: bread-baskets, trays or broad-rimmed bowls with *repoussé* decoration, or simple vases that were pure and massive in form. Ornamentation played only a small part in these early works. He later developed in the direction of more elaborate and less classical pieces with bold decorative motifs in relief. His 'Satin-flower' vase and his bronze 'Frog' vase are good examples of this new direction, first evident in 1906/7.

It goes without saying that, whereas initially Dunand made most pieces himself, he soon acquired numerous assistants. The first of these craftsmen and also the most talented, was Francesco Zambon, the orphan whom Dunand brought back with him from Italy in 1909 and who was nicknamed Kéco. He remained active in the Dunand studios until the 1950s, at which stage he made a number of extremely elaborate pieces for Bernard and Pierre Dunand. Jean Dunand made him follow various outside training courses, and in 1933 he was awarded a medal as 'Best Craftsman in France', when he made a kettle from a single piece of sheet metal, using only a hammer and without soldering or alteration. The subtle shape of the piece gave the impression that several pieces of metal had been attached to each other. From this date onwards Dunand entrusted the decoration of his dinanderie to a handful of skilled craftsmen like Kéco. He even formed a reference collection of decorative motifs comprising several hundred sample plates on which were recorded every imaginable variant of geometric or floral patterns. Executed in white gouache on black paper, they constitute the most beautiful repertory of shapes and decorative elements from this period. Each motif could be adapted, according to size, to suit every kind of vase or tray. The specialist craftsmen whom Dunand had trained needed only to refer to these sources when executing the chosen design.

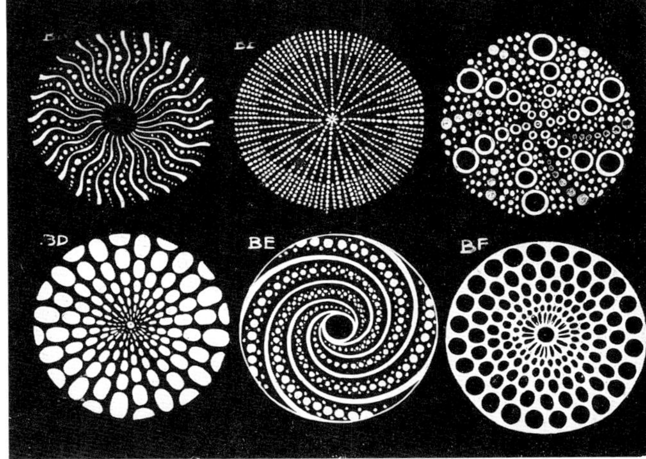

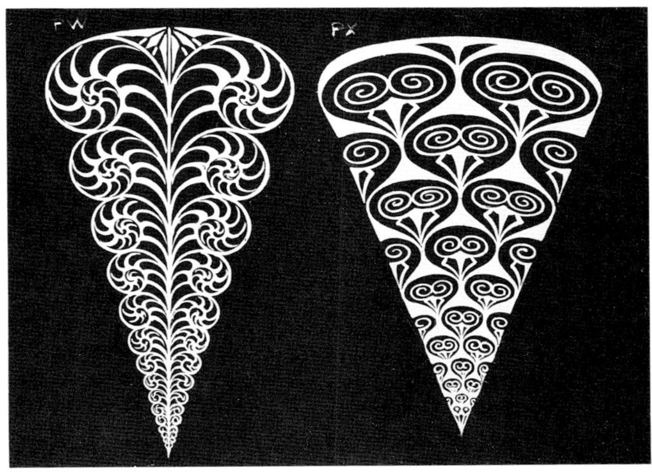

Plates from Dunand's extensive repertory of patterns for inlay decoration on dinanderie objects; for further examples see overleaf.

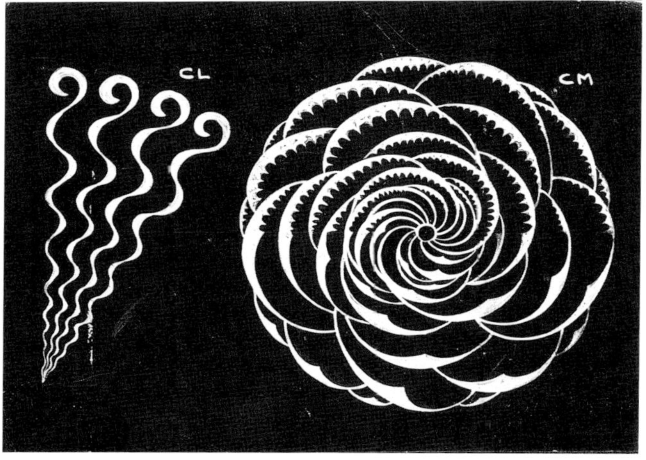

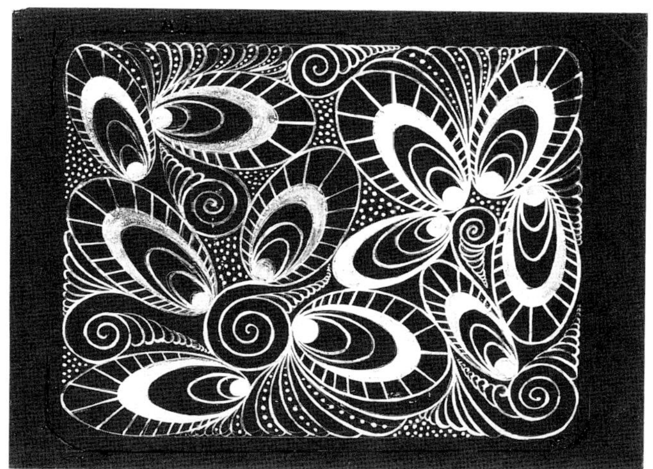

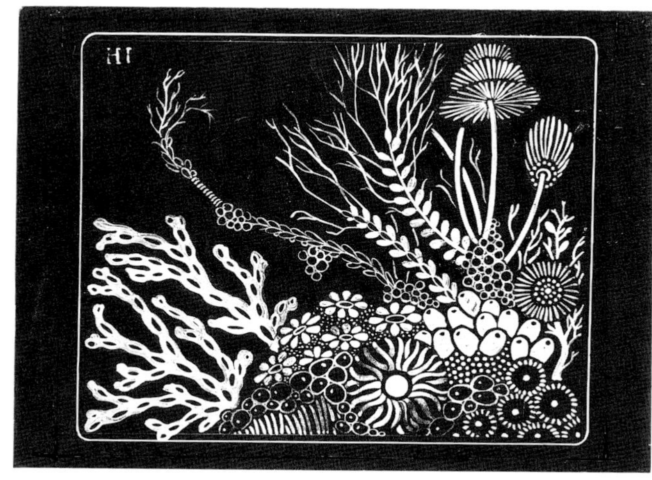

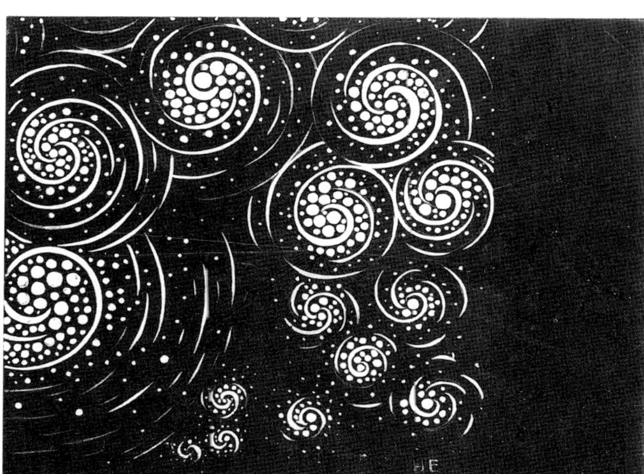

After the war, another of Dunand's specialist craftsmen was responsible for the decoration on the helmet presented to Marshal Foch, as well as for the ornamentation on a number of watch-cases and on the ceremonial swords made for members of the Académie Française. This painstaking work, which required the use of a jeweller's loupe, was executed by a French craftsman named Grunweiser, who later set up in business in Saint-Étienne, returning to Dunand's studio from time to time whenever there was specialized work requiring his skills.

It was not until 1912 that Dunand set up a proper enamelling studio on his premises. He used enamel only sparingly on his vases, the only exception being a series with floral decoration, the garland about the neck being highlighted in each case with opaque coloured enamels. By contrast, we later find him conforming to a fashion that was fairly widespread at the time, producing metal boxes, *bonbonnières* and small caskets. These pieces were made in a neighbouring workshop and enamelled in his own studio using a *champlevé* technique or *en plein sur fond réservé*, i.e. applied directly to the surface. *Champlevé* enamelling involves cutting shallow cells in the surface of the metal, the individual features and details of the composition being outlined by raised ridges delineating the parts to be enamelled in various colours. Since enamelling is a fairly complicated process, and no doubt because he did not wish to appear to be in direct competition with his friend Jean Goulden, who specialized in this technique, Dunand more or less abandoned this type of work shortly after the end of the First World War.

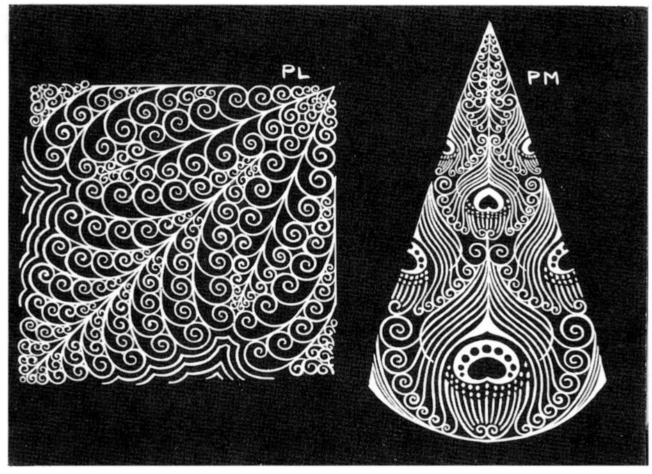
PL
PM

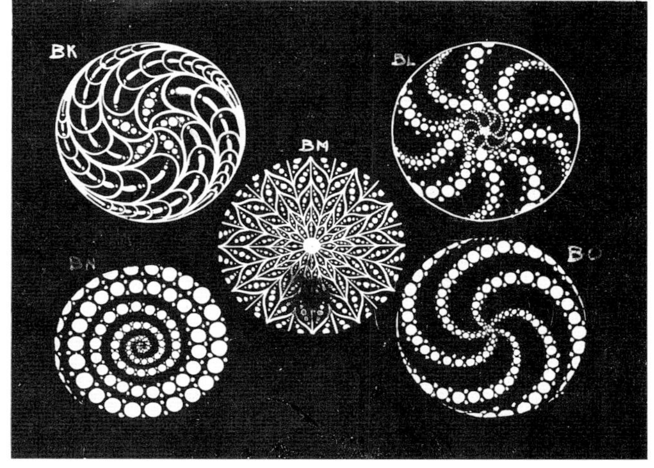
BK
BL
BM
BN
BO

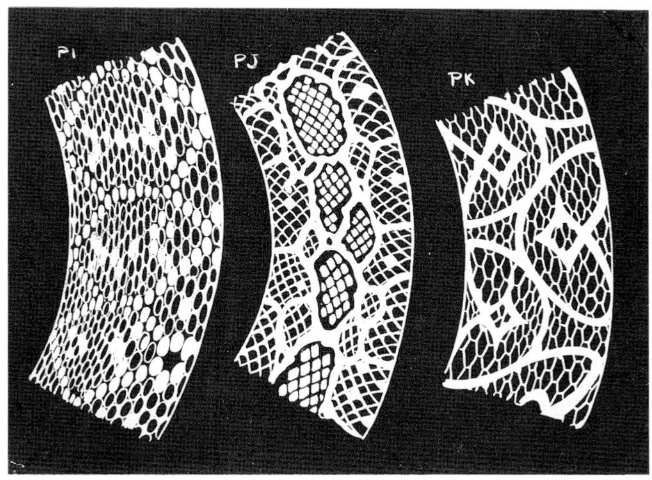
PI
PJ
PK

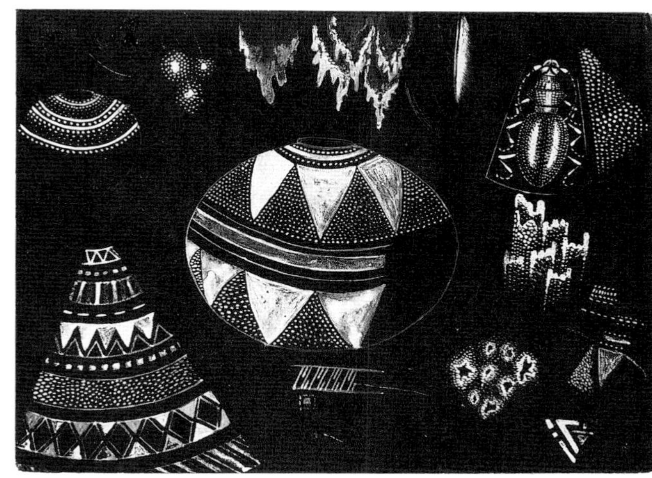

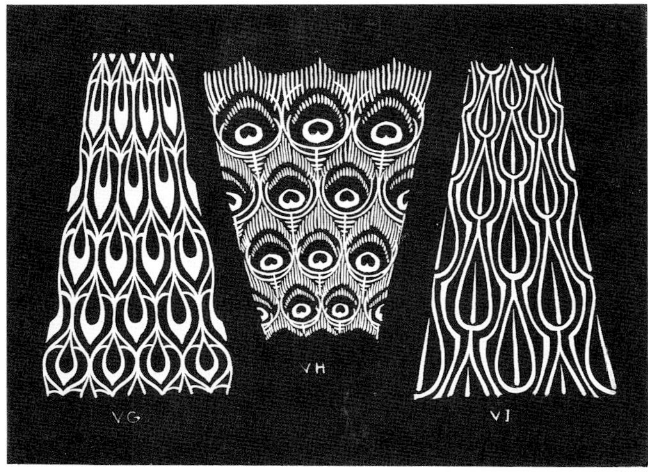
VG
VH
VI

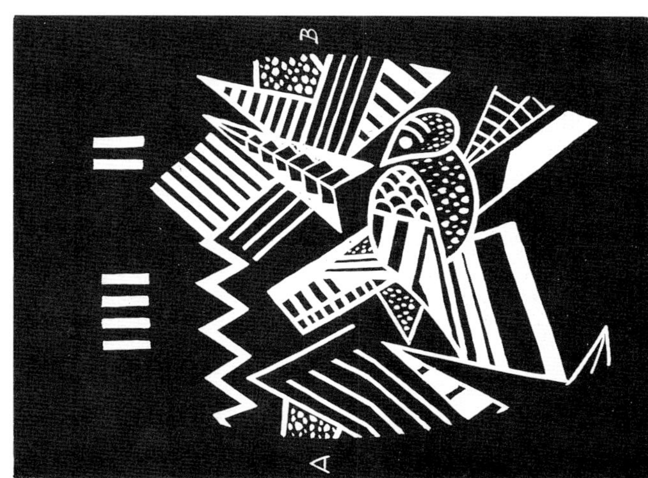
B
A

Lacquer

While studying old Japanese bronzes that had been brought to him for repair, Dunand was struck by the fact that their surfaces bore very thin layers of natural lacquer, resembling a patina. After inviting the lacquer artists then practising in Paris to discuss the subject, he soon realized that in fact they were simply varnishers, and that the secret of oriental lacquerwork had never really been discovered or practised by Western artists. Of course, the early navigators had brought back various chests, panels and other lacquered objects from Japan, and Venice had even maintained trade links with Japan, but no Europeans really knew the secrets of how lacquer was produced. A Jesuit priest, Martin Martinius, had revealed the origins of lacquer in a work dating from 1655, but he had not known how the lacquer was used, nor its exact composition.

Lacquer is in fact an excretion tapped by making incisions in the bark of a tree (see below, p. 171), the sap from which was collected and sold in local markets. Wholesale buyers would store it in wickerwork containers, protected from air and light. This product, known as 'lacquer', was allowed to clarify and was then graded and classified according to density, before being sold to users. In the course of his initiation, every oriental lacquer artist would swear an oath promising never to reveal its composition or uses to anyone.

To overcome this situation and meet the demands of a European public, numerous substitute products were placed on the market in France and elsewhere. The famous Martin Brothers in Paris, varnishers by profession, patented a formula composed of copal-resin, produced by tropical trees and readily available, together with boiled linseed oil and oil of turpentine. This mixture allowed distemper decorations to be coated with a hard, transparent material, which could also be applied to furniture and other objects without producing a yellowing effect. To increase transparency the background was prepared with white lead.

Art historians are generally agreed in acknowledging that, contrary to what may be thought in some Japanese circles, the art of lacquerwork originated in China. It is believed to have been imported into Japan in the sixth century, when the influence of Chinese civilization followed the spread of Buddhism.

On the other hand, it seems undeniable that what had originally been no more than a means of protecting household implements, in other words, an indigenous skill, had become within a century a recognized art form with codified rules. From this point onwards Japanese artists developed lacquering techniques, turning it into a specifically Japanese art. The works thus created, from the simplest and purest examples in the seventh century to the staggering skill of their eighteenth-century successors, provide clear evidence of this development.

Jean Dunand's initiation into the secrets of lacquer dates from his first encounter with the Japanese master-craftsman Seizo Sugawara on 18 February 1912. Sugawara had been a member of the Japanese delegation sent to Paris to represent his country at the Exposition Universale of 1900. The large quantity of lacquered objects and other pieces of furniture exhibited in the Japanese Pavilion enjoyed an enormous success. Evidently attracted by the Parisian atmosphere, Sugawara decided against returning home when the exhibition ended; he settled in Paris, where he opened a studio making traditional lacquers, importing the raw material from Japan. His style moved away from figurative decoration, developing in the direction of exceedingly restrained and increasingly geometric compositions, while using materials of unprecedented opulence. In this way he became one of the first oriental artists to be influenced by the spirit of modern European painting. In 1907 his work aroused the interest of Eileen Gray, a young Anglo-Irish artist who had already worked with lacquer in England. After studying with Sugawara for some time, Eileen Gray set up on her own, opening a small studio in Paris. We must assume, therefore, that Sugawara, like other Japanese lacquer artists, had abandoned the idea of preserving the secrets of his art long before his first meeting with Jean Dunand. As it happened, Dunand's dinanderie interested Sugawara both for its sculptural qualities and for its technical excellence. In an interview published some time later, Dunand explained that, since Sugawara desired to learn more about his methods of metal inlay using heated filings and since he himself wanted to penetrate the mysteries of lacquer, they initiated each other into their respective techniques, exchanging courtesies in their mutual respect and esteem. The family archives contain the school notebook in which Dunand took notes on these earliest lessons, the first of which took place on 16 May 1912; twelve others followed between then and the following July. Considering these notes as a whole, one has the impression that Dunand must already have had his own ideas on the subject, since rather than record any actual revelations, he made notes on working methods, touching on problems of terminology, methodology and formulas for composition or ways of using lacquer. At all events, Dunand's aim was to gain enough practical knowledge to enable him to fix the patinas on his metal vases; certainly he seems to have had no wish at this stage to use lacquer for decorative purposes.

We have to wait until the end of the First World War before Dunand gradually thought of using lacquer as an integral part of his work, this delay being entirely typical of his artistic approach: before putting anything into practice, he would strive patiently to master all its subtleties. This is even more striking when one compares his work over the years with that of Eileen Gray or Sugawara himself, both of whom used lacquer only in relation to coloured materials, while Dunand was the first to commit himself to its use as a 'pictorial substance' suitable for decorating his vases with designs of his own composition. Thus, his earliest pieces of lacquered dinanderie appear in small numbers during the autumn of 1912: here the lacquer is used exclusively as a protective coating, the pieces being otherwise undecorated.

The war then intervened, and a curious combination of circumstances allowed Dunand to extend the field of application for lacquer. In fact, around 1916 Samuel Verneuil, a friend of Dunand's whose brother Jean ran a rickshaw company in Hanoi, contacted Dunand to ask whether he thought that what was then called 'Annamite painting' could profitably be used to protect wooden aeroplane propellers. A member of the air force's testing and research unit at Chalais-Meudon, just outside Paris, Verneuil was looking for a means of protecting propellers which, being made of plywood, regularly shattered in flight when subjected to excessive rain or humidity, as the glue between the layers of wood dissolved under the combined effect of water and speed. No known varnish provided the protection required to counteract these extremely serious drawbacks. Samuel Verneuil therefore decided to speak to Dunand, knowing as he did that the latter used lacquer collected in Indo-China and sent to him by his brother Jean. Experiments had in fact already been carried out in Hanoi in an attempt to prevent artillery shells stored in hangars at military bases there from corroding, and

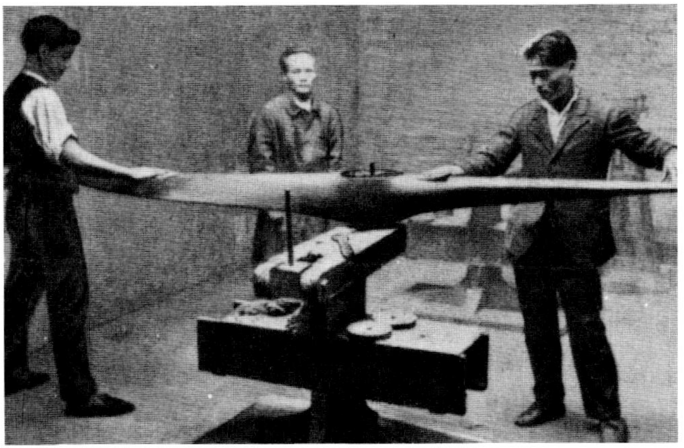

Indo-Chinese craftsmen rubbing down a lacquered aeroplane propeller in the French Army workshops.

since the coachwork of local rickshaws was traditionally protected with lacquer, the two men decided to experiment on aircraft propellers. Dunand provided the tools and the raw materials, and lacquer workmen were recruited from among soldiers of Indo-Chinese origin serving in the French Army. Lacquering of aeroplane propellers began officially at Chalais-Meudon on 1 July 1917. Initial results were encouraging, leading to the foundation of the Société des Laques Indochinoises in the Rue de Silly at Boulogne-sur-Seine. Its purpose was to lacquer propellers, and a former colonial governor named Simoni took charge of the workshop after Samuel Verneuil and Jean Dunand had set it on the right lines. Their success was complete, for not only did lacquered propellers no longer shatter in mid-air, but they lasted longer than propellers which were merely varnished, the lacquer providing much greater resistance to wear than any other protective layer used up to that time.

By contrast, it proved necessary to stop lacquering the canvases used for dirigible balloons since – quite apart from the fact that numerous layers were necessary to give them adequate protection against humidity, thus adding considerably to the balloon's weight – the material became brittle in the long term. The idea was adopted again, however, in protecting the floats of seaplanes, as well as cabin fairings which, when coated and protected in this way, offered less wind-resistance. Lacquer was also used in preparing a sort of waterproof cement, the other ingredients being glutinous rice, oil, lime and sand.

It is necessary at this point to emphasize the distinction between vegetable lacquer proper (see below) and lac (or shellac). The latter is not a by-product but is a secretion of the lac insect which, when dissolved in alcohol, is used as a raw material by cabinet-makers in making French polish.

Interestingly, once the war was over, armaments firms which found themselves in possession of vast stocks of surplus nitrocellulose conducted chemical experiments to find new markets for a product that had formerly served for making explosives. Chemical engineers interested in a by-product of nitrocellulose called collodion found that by mixing resins, plasticizers and dyestuffs they were able to produce a cellulose lacquer. Applied by means of a spray-gun, this cellulose lacquer was to play a crucial role in the automobile industry, reducing from three weeks to twenty-four hours the time required for the bodywork to dry. The oil varnish in use until then was extremely slow to dry and harden. At a slightly later date, in 1927, glycerophthalic lacquer was produced, further reducing the drying time to thirty minutes by evaporating the solvent at high temperatures. As a result, the product was inappropriately termed 'enamel paint'.

Faced with such a multiplicity of competing products, all of which could to some extent be used to imitate natural lacquer, Dunand felt obliged to promote a private bill (No. 5290), which was duly presented in the Chambre des Députés on 28 May 1935 by A. Grisoni. The principal aim of this measure was to restrict the use of the term 'lacquer' to natural vegetable products derived from certain trees (see below), and thus to protect the work of lacquer artists, whose prices were much higher than those of products made with substitutes having a considerably shorter drying time. It was also hoped that the interests of colonial plantations in Indo-China (from where most of the output was exported to China and Japan) would be safeguarded. However, one has only to note the confusion which still surrounds the use of the word 'lacquer' today to understand why the bill presented in 1935 never became law and why none of the hoped for results materialized.

Natural lacquer production

When incisions are made in the bark of certain trees of the genus *Rhus* (*R. succedanea*, native to China, and *R. vernicifera*, native to Japan) or of the species *Succedanea dumoutieri*, which grows in the region of former French Indo-China known until 1946 as Tonkin (now North Vietnam), a resinous sap is exuded which is the raw material used in all natural lacquerwork. Originally growing wild, these trees were later cultivated commercially in plantations. The sap can be gathered from each tree only between its third and eighth years. During this five-year period, it produces a sort of latex resin which resembles liquid cream. At this stage the trees are some 3 to 4 m (10 to 13 ft) high, and incisions must be made in the bark and the latex gathered without exposure to direct sunlight or to rain, since the former would oxidize the latex and the latter would dilute it. The latex – which is an emulsion of gum-lac in a highly concentrated solution of laccic acid – is gathered in river-mussel shells. It is then placed in watertight lacquered wickerwork containers which are hermetically sealed before being shipped to wholesale merchants.

The raw material has to be subjected to long and delicate processes which will determine the quality of the lacquer. First, it has to be filtered carefully through a fine linen gauze in order to remove impurities. It must then be left to stand for several months in lacquered bamboo baskets tightly sealed with sheets of rice-paper. These are stored in dark, well-aired caves so that the lacquer, which has already begun to evaporate, can settle. At this stage the latex has changed from its creamy consistency to an amber-coloured liquid.

As time passes, the product separates out naturally into layers of different density, each corresponding to a different price range, for lacquers are classified by density according to usage. Lacquer obtained in this way by decanting is known as 'natural lacquer'. The uppermost layer which is the least dense, is richest in gum-lac and finest in quality. This lacquer is used by master-lacquerers for the final layers of their work. The lower layers, which become increasingly viscous, are used for undercoats or for other preparations where they are mixed with sawdust, clay, metal filings or various other decorative products. Lacquer adheres to all kinds of materials in addition to wood: not only metals such as copper, silver, pewter, German silver, gold and aluminium, but also stone, cement, glass, leather and paper. If it is to adhere to all these different surfaces, those which are not at all roughly textured must first be sanded to provide a key for the lacquer.

As far as textiles are concerned, lacquer burns most fabrics, the only exception being those made of natural silk, while on substances which can tolerate heat, the lacquer is hardened by firing it in a kiln heated to between 150° and 250°C. Oven-drying involves a process of polymerization. The hardening process begins at 96°, at which temperature laccic acid evaporates. Up to 120° the lacquers remain light in colour, darkening at 180° until they finally assume a burned appearance.

Dunand's kilns were large enough to fire panels measuring 3 x 2 m (10 ft x 6 ft 6 in.), such large areas being typical of his designs, but for small items an ordinary kitchen oven would serve the same purpose. The resulting oxidized lacquers are extremely resistant and hard. This was the process traditionally used by Japanese lacquerers for armour and sword-hilts.

On all other surfaces, the only way to harden the lacquer is to place the piece in a warm, humid atmosphere in which natural fermentation and evaporation of the water content gradually occur. Once hardened, lacquer cannot be attacked by any solvent, and is resistant to all chemical agents, as it is to bacteria. It also makes an excellent electrical insulator and can withstand temperatures up to 400°/450°C, since the process of carbonization only begins at 550°.

Lacquer is, however, an extremely noxious substance and in its liquid state can, in certain individuals, cause a skin condition which, though not serious, is extremely unpleasant and can develop even in the absence of direct contact. Alix Dunand recalls how, as a child, she made this terrible discovery after staying to watch a cask being opened, in spite of the fact that her father had forbidden her to do so. However, the majority of Asian workers are not affected, although some prefer to skirt a lacquer plantation rather than pass through it.

To obtain natural transparent, but coloured, lacquer, the top layer of the decanted mixture has to be churned by hand using a wooden pat. Depending upon the length of the operation and the speed of rotation, a beautiful colour – ranging from light gold to dark brown – will result after ten or twelve days. In order to obviate this long and unpredictable process, Dunand perfected an electrically operated churn which allowed him to obtain results that were practically the same as churning by hand. The device consisted of a sort of propeller blade attached to a motor-driven vertical shaft. Beneath was placed a container of the natural honey-coloured lacquer which forms the basic substance used in lacquer decoration.

Black lacquer is another basic product, and possibly the most beautiful of all. It, too, is obtained by churning natural lacquer, but this time an iron bar is used rather than a wooden pat. The container has to be of stoneware, rather than wickerwork, as used in preparing honey-coloured lacquer. The iron oxide of the metal bar blackens the transparent lacquer on contact with the air.

As for coloured lacquers, these are extremely difficult to obtain. The point of departure is always the highest-quality churned lacquer to which powdered vegetable dyes are added. Red is obtained with vermilion (mercuric sulphide), and green by adding indigo to orpiment (arsenic trisulphide). White is impossible to obtain. One must understand that very few colouring agents are suitable for use with lacquer, since most have the effect of preventing the lacquer from drying or of making it turn black in the course of drying. This last-mentioned disadvantage may not become evident until several months or even years after the work has been finished, hence the extreme care with which the serious lacquer artist uses coloured lacquer. In Dunand's studio, his son Bernard set about the task of perfecting coloured lacquers. He succeeded in varying the tonalities and values in a wholly remarkable way, urged on by his father who was always keen to put these innovations to practical use. As time passed, the attraction of this novelty began to wane and Bernard now admits that natural lacquer should not be worked in too wide a range of colours, for the whole skill of the traditional lacquer artist lies in his evoking a perfect mood with the palette which is naturally at his disposal. Certainly, lacquer is not paint, and it should be applied only in accordance with the specific rules governing its proper use.

In French, the noun *laque* is masculine when applied to an object, such as a large lacquer-decorated panel, and feminine when it refers to the substance itself.

Techniques of lacquerwork

Techniques of manufacture vary according to the object being made. Dunand took extreme care in choosing his wooden panels since they had always to be prepared by special methods in order to resist the effects of humidity.

Simple cupboards were used initially to provide a humid space in which to allow his lacquered pieces to dry, and only after the First World War was he able to fit out a fairly large room where several lacquered screens could be left to dry simultaneously. Having solved the problem of lack of space by adding new premises, he built four drying rooms with the help of his studio workmen. They were a sort of concrete vault on the ground floor of the studio, the only access being through a door which was sealed after the various objects and pieces of furniture had been placed in the room to dry. It was entered from street level, and at regular intervals water ran down the walls to maintain a constant humidity. Since natural lacquer is an enzyme, humid conditions set off a fermentation process, causing the substance to dry out slowly and harden through oxidation.

The panels of Dunand's first screens were made of plywood by outside contractors, and he suffered numerous setbacks, mostly as a result of warping after the panels were placed in the humid drying room. Here, too, as with the aeroplane propellers, the glue would expand when exposed to water, causing the joints to split and spring apart. Accordingly, he decided to open his own carpentry workshop, engaging a full-time carpenter whom he had earlier employed when he acquired the lease of the adjoining premises and was able to enlarge his studio. He bought up materials salvaged from demolition sites, and from now on used casein, a substance which has the advantage of not dissolving in humid conditions, for gluing furniture.

Later, around 1925, when he opened a proper cabinet-maker's workshop, he installed one of the largest wood presses in the Paris region. The sheer size of the works which he was now undertaking virtually forced him to make this move. He also seized the opportunity to install all the machines that he would need in his new enterprise, machines which enabled him to surface the large panels, before planing and bending them. He also acquired bandsaws, circular saws, milled cutters, mortising machines and so on. The wood was sawn up as required, the panels being stored in a large shed and allowed to dry out before being worked.

The types of wood best suited to lacquering should be neither too hard nor too dense, otherwise the initial layers of lacquer will not be able to penetrate the surface. They also need to have as regular a grain as possible, and alternating hard and soft veins should not be too noticeable, while knots and other blemishes must be avoided. Walnut grown in France, lime, tulipwood and mahogany provide the best surfaces.

The plywood that Dunand made in his workshops was generally constructed around a core consisting of a poplar-wood lattice, each slat being cut in a square section, and individual slats being glued to each other to form a continuous sheet. Once it had dried in the press, this sheet was surfaced to correct any play that may still have been left in it. Two or three sheets of veneer were then glued to each side, alternating in such a way that the veins of the wood ran in opposite directions. Dunand recommended that only sheets cut from the same block be used in order to ensure that they had the same network of veins, and that, once glued in place, they would behave in a similar way.

By the same token, lacquered furniture had to be constructed following a special procedure eschewing timber worked across the grain since no matter how it was used this would be liable to warp and hence could not be lacquered. Instead he employed only planks cut with the grain. It was also necessary to ensure that the wood was not jointed either on the surfaces to be lacquered or on the flat surfaces or, again, on the supporting frame of the piece of furniture in question. The joints had to be mitred (in other words, cut at an angle of 45°) and glued together so as to be practically invisible along the edges of the furniture. In this way any possible play resulting from the swelling of the panels would be scarcely perceptible.

To solve certain problems posed by the need to create surfaces larger than could be made out of a single piece of timber, Dunand had the idea of using bevel joints. This consisted of chamfering each of two pieces of wood so that the strips which overlapped were so thin where they joined that the wood had practically no means of swelling. As a result, the panels of screens remained flat and no longer developed cracks. Once the individual sections of a piece of furniture or the panels of a screen had been joined in this way, they had to be rubbed down all over with very fine sandpaper to produce an absolutely smooth and unblemished surfaces for lacquering.

To justify the rellatively high price of his furniture, Dunand would explain to his clients, with some truth, that his pieces were made twice over, first by the cabinet-maker who made them as carefully as if they had been crafted in rosewood, and second by the lacquerer, who worked on them even longer. Certain pieces required as much as two years' work before they could be marketed. Dunand's earliest screens or panels were treated with Coromandel lacquer (see p. 174). To begin with, this was the simplest way for him to work when dealing with large decorated surfaces, while for others he was particularly fond of using layers of uniform lacquer with no decoration.

For each of his screens or panels Dunand would make an oil sketch or other model which he generally drew from nature or with the help of a preliminary rough. He then had assistants in his studio enlarge the design to its intended size in order, finally, to touch it up. Later, when his output began to increase, he contented himself with setting out the idea or outline, while reserving the right to intervene in the course of a piece's execution.

The number of craftsmen varied constantly, depending on the scope and scale of Dunand's commissions at any one time, but it was always necessary to keep the staff occupied during slack periods, even if it meant undertaking work with no potential buyers for pieces begun in this way. The works that Dunand produced were without exception original creations, whether executed by Dunand himself or made by his pupils and employees following his instructions. In his dual capacity as manager and craftsman, he could not, single-handed, ensure that all his projects were properly set up, and so, when orders were heavy, it was entirely natural for him to seek outside help, either from friends or from students at the Ecole des Beaux-Arts or the Ecole des Arts Décoratifs.

In his design studio skilled fellow craftsmen worked on scaling-up his models, tracing outlines or transferring designs; here, too, were kept copies of the motifs used in decorating vases, the design being preserved on paper and subsequently classified, before being transferred to an anthology of models from which it was always possible to draw examples when indicating possible decorative motifs to a client. This also enabled Dunand to keep one or more craftsmen busy while he himself was occupied with other tasks. Pierre Dunand in particular busied himself with these models, while Bernard was given the task of co-ordinating the work of different groups of craftsmen from whom they had to seek extra help.

The actual process of lacquering would begin when a layer of natural lacquer was applied by brush to the prepared surface or ground. Only flat brushes made of Chinese hair could be used (Siberian squirrel, bear and sable being too supple, while horsehair, boar bristle or oxhair would have been too coarse and would inevitably have left brush marks in the lacquer). One must never lose sight of the fact that the consistency of natural lacquer is fairly close to that of liquid honey and that the slightest streak of extra-thick matter will have repercussions for each succeeding layer. These brushes, which were ordered from the Far East, were trimmed like pencils when they became worn; they were made of two blocks of wood with the hair set between them to a width ranging from 1 cm (½ in.) to 6 cm (2½ in.). Although the hair was between 15 and 20 cm (6–8 in.) long, the exposed end protruded only 1 cm (½ in.) beyond the end of the wooden blocks and could be adjusted when trimmed.

The initial layer of natural lacquer is left to dry for five to six days, and is then rubbed down with very fine sandpaper. The next stage is to cover the object being lacquered with a sheet of very fine linen, which both protects the lacquer and serves to hide the pattern of the wood beneath it. This fabric is itself stuck down with natural lacquer and then left to dry, in turn, for five to six days. The surface is now treated with several costs of lacquer mixed with very fine sifted sawdust to fill up the pores in the fabric and remove all trace of unevenness. The sawdust used is obtained from exotic woods and forms a sort of mastic which is applied by means of a horn palette knife. Every layer (and there must be sufficient layers to ensure that the surface is absolutely flat) has to dry in humid conditions for between six and fifteen days; then, when it has hardened, it will be rubbed down with long strips of carborundum and water, the effect being similar to that of the blade of a plane.

The following layers are of clay-based lacquer applied by means of a brush of buffalo hair. The clay from Indo-China (or alternatively kaolin) is applied in layers of increasingly fine texture, and the layers may vary in number from fewer than five to as many as fifteen, each of course being left to dry in a humid atmosphere for six to ten days before being rubbed down with water and emery-paper. After each of these clay-based layers, moreover, a further layer of natural lacquer is added in order to feed and harden the previous ones.

Once these preparatory operations have been completed, the surface of the panel will be completely smooth. Only now are the decorative lacquers applied. Five to six stages will again be necessary, using layers of increasing fineness. Each of

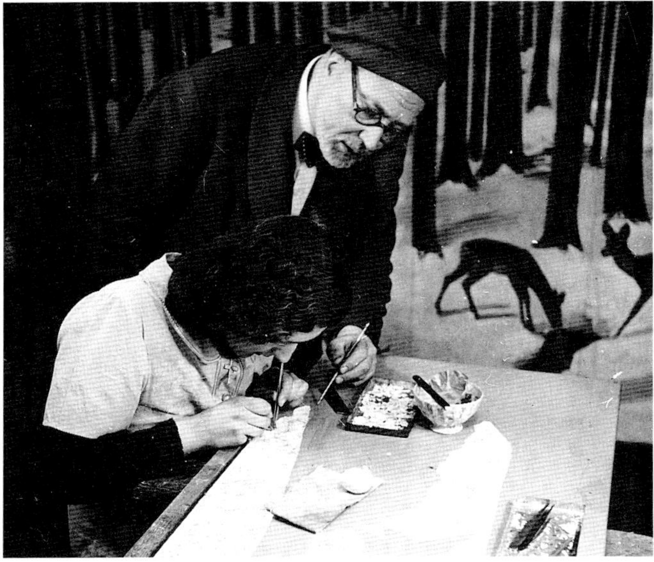

Dunand overseeing the work of applying eggshell decoration in his workshops, 1941.

these must be allowed to dry for a period of between two to four days, and then rubbed down with charcoal. Before being polished, the final layer is dulled, firstly with water and powdered charcoal and secondly with a mixture of oil and extremely fine clay applied with cottonwool. The finishing process is often completed by rubbing powdered ash of stag's horn over the surface with the palm of one's hand. Even when finished, the lacquer will be no more than 3 to 4 mm (⅛ in.) thick, and will have taken a minimum of six months to complete, although it may be necessary to allow as long as nine months in European conditions.

Dunand's work consisted principally of Chinese or Coromandel lacquer on white backgrounds using colour size, since these backgrounds are much more 'tender' than those used for sawdust-based lacquers. They also offer the possibility of recolouring them at a later date, if so desired.

There are countless ways of decorating lacquer, and Dunand used to say that there are as many ways as there are lacquer artists, and that, in the course of his life, any one lacquer artist would use barely a tenth of the methods that he knew or anticipated as possibilities. The simplest method is painted lacquer, the effect being obtained by drawing with an etching needle, the resulting outline being traced over with layers of coloured lacquers; these layers are a decorative motif built up to form a low relief. In order to enrich the effect, gold dust or filings may also be mixed with the final layer of lacquer.

Among the most spectacular techniques, a special place must be reserved for eggshell soaked in lacquer, a technique which Dunand used extensively. He was not of course the first lacquer artist to think of using real eggshell in decorating his furniture, vases and screens. This method had already been used by the Japanese for sword-hilts and scabbards, but there is absolutely no doubt that Dunand was the first to use eggshell to cover large surfaces, to create white areas which could not be achieved with natural lacquers. His use of this unexpected material – what is involved is in fact the shell of hen's or duck's eggs – allowed him to produce a white *craquelure* effect that was both subtle and spectacular. The eggshell is washed and its inner membrane removed, after which it is delicately crushed and the fragments sorted according to size. Each particle is then placed in position with tweezers on a layer of fresh lacquer, and arranged edge to edge like a mosaic in a prescribed pattern. The fragments are then rubbed down to obtain a smooth surface, and soaked in a new layer of lacquer to fill in the cracks. Depending on the effect that is being sought, the covering layer or the lacquer in which the eggshell is soaked may be honey-coloured or black, both of which produce beautiful shadings. Further layers of coloured lacquer may now be applied to these white and finely crackled surfaces, which are then rubbed down to a greater or lesser degree, to produce the desired shading and the necessary degree of transparency.

Another spectacular process, that of *laque arrachée* (literally, 'pulled up'), is less fragile. Used principally for furniture frames and screen supports, as well as for large surfaces on poorer-quality furniture, the method involves applying a wooden spatula to the freshly lacquered surface, pressing it down and raising it quickly so as to produce an effect of wavy granulation, which is then lightly rubbed down to make the surface completely smooth.

Lacquer also lends itself to every kind of inlay work. The inlaid material may either be flush with the surface, as in the case of eggshell or metal filings, or thicker substances may be used, such as powdered mother-of-pearl or 'burgau', the latter a type of nacreous shell with an iridescent appearance. Ivory, carved or in thin plaques, may also be used, but the surface will have to be notched so that the ivory can be wedged more firmly in place before being stuck down with lacquer. Apart from the shells from eggs laid in the Rue Hallé hen-house, raw materials were also supplied by the *pâtissier* in the nearby Place d'Alésia. The shells were sorted according to colour and left to soak, larger pieces first having been set aside. Once the inner membrane had been removed, the pieces of shell were dried and broken up. The shells of hen's eggs are more regular in thickness, which is why they are the preferred kind. Madame Nam, from Annam (now part of Vietnam), was the best *poseuse* (literally, 'positioner') in the studio, carrying out the task of inlaying with great precision. This technique was developed by Dunand to such a pitch of perfection that, having worked for him, many craftsmen from Indo-China returned to Hanoi, where they set up in business on their own and produced articles similar to the ones that Dunand was making. In Paris, meanwhile, the artist Serge Rovinski used Dunand's workshops to make his own screens and furniture. Other artists and firms were less scrupulous and openly lured several of Dunand's craftsmen away to work on their projects.

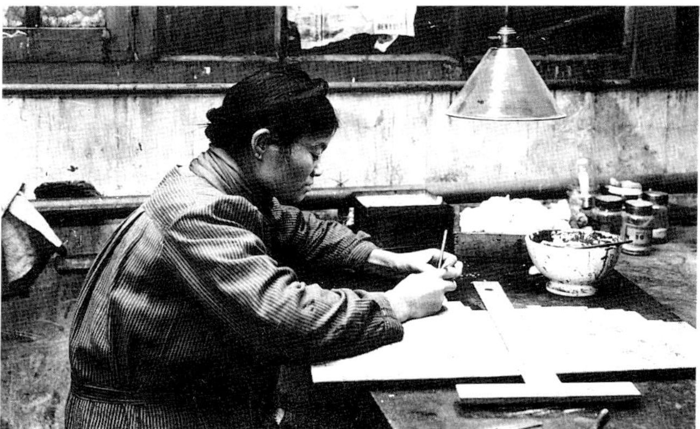

Madame Ho, an Indo-Chinese specialist in the art of applying eggshell decoration, seen at work.

A further technique which deserves to be mentioned here involves the engraving of the lacquered surface. This technique is generally referred to as Coromandel lacquer (after the coastal region in India where such pieces formerly arrived from Honan before being shipped to European destinations). It had been perfected in China and had enjoyed a certain success in Europe in the eighteenth century. The incising process involves using not a chisel, as is the case with wood, but hook-like tools, with which the surface material is removed to reveal the white clay layer beneath. By this method chipping or flaking, which would otherwise occur, can be avoided.

Lacquer, if sufficiently thick, may also be carved, the result being known as Peking lacquer. This technique remained an exclusively Chinese speciality for many years, and requires layers of coloured lacquer from 10 to 15 mm (½ to ⅝ in.) thick. The lacquer is tooled using wooden chisels in such a way as to expose the different coloured layers. It is a very long and delicate process and was never used by Dunand, though he occasionally sculpted motifs in wood and then covered them with coloured lacquer to obtain a similar relief effect.

Gold lacquer involves the use of very fine gold dust or gold leaf; the exact method varies according to whether a matt or glossy finish is preferred. The man in charge of all these gilding operations in Dunand's studios was a highly skilled craftsman named Zuber, who applied only gold dust or gold leaf directly to freshly lacquered surfaces.

Finally, there is the whole range of coloured lacquers – opaque or transparent – which can be applied to flat tints, with clearly defined or shaded contours, or with a clouded effect.

One of the most beautiful qualities possessed by lacquer – and it is this which distinguishes it from imitation products – is the impression of depth which it conveys. The eye sees not just a polished surface, but – because of the presence of superimposed layers – perceives an interplay of light produced by their transparency without it being a simple surface reflection.

Army helmets

When war was declared in 1914, Jean Dunand was still a Swiss national. However, he volunteered to serve with the Red Cross and was posted to the front as an ambulance driver.

At the instigation of the couturier Jean-Philippe Worth, who had converted his salons at 7 Rue de la Paix into an auxiliary hospital, Dunand was transferred there by officials at the War Ministry. He was to remain until January 1918, when he was released from his duties. In his capacity as an ambulance driver, and as laid down by international convention, Dunand was not allowed to carry arms when in charge of his vehicle. On several occasions he was almost taken prisoner when crossing enemy lines with casualties. The auxiliary hospital in the Rue de la Paix specialized in treating head injuries, and in particular injuries which affected the eyes. In fact, Worth had made his gesture to the war effort as a result of the experience of his friend François-Louis Schmied, who had been seriously wounded on 16 December 1914 and, as a result of his injuries, had lost the use of his right eye.

At the beginning of the war, French soldiers had had no protective headgear whatsoever. The sight of men wearing mess-tins on their heads in an attempt to provide themselves with some protection persuaded the authorities to begin

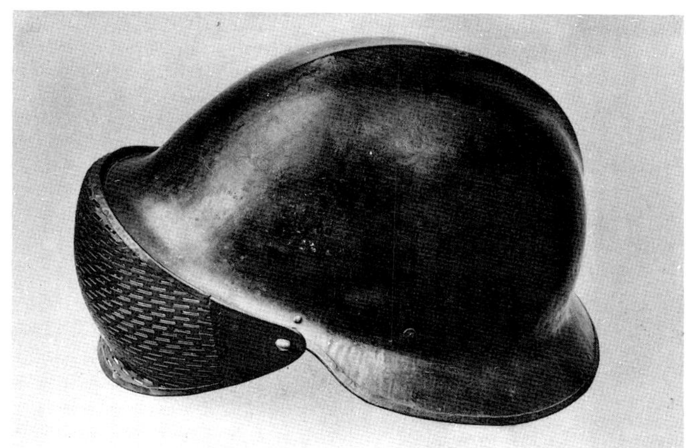

Dunand's army helmet with visor, 1917.

manufacturing sheet-metal hemispheres that could be worn inside forage caps and under a kepi. Later, during 1915, a slightly modified version of the fireman's helmet, known as the 'Adrian Helmet', became standard issue for French soldiers. It was made of tinplate and consisted of three parts, a crown, a visor and a crest assembled and welded in such a way that instead of simply deflecting shrapnel, its surface tended to stop it or cause it to ricochet.

With his understanding of metals, and alerted to the problem because of the injuries suffered by his friend Schmied, Dunand was surprised by the weakness of the tinplate used in making the Adrian Helmet. He could not understand why trenches were dug to protect soldiers' bodies while their heads were left largely exposed, and he felt that the men should be protected at least down to their eyes. Moreover, statistics gathered after over a year of fighting revealed that many more soldiers were injured by small and medium-sized bits of shrapnel than by larger objects or by bullets.

He therefore made a prototype of a helmet with a detachable visor, hammering it out of sheet metal, in the hope of finding a solution that would protect the wearer's eyes and face, and be solid enough to withstand shrapnel. Having fashioned his prototype, he went to consult a number of metallurgists in order to ascertain the best type of steel for the purpose. After deciding on manganese steel, he made contact in early January 1917 with a company manufacturing meters and equipment used in gas-works, and asked for help in organizing industrial production in the event of his receiving a commission to make helmets for the French Army.

On 14 January 1917, he registered his first model, with an explanatory note, at the Patent Office, and ten days later registered a further model (no. 4), together with the model of a 'look-out helmet' with visor (no. 7). On 11 July 1918, three new helmet designs, one of which included a protective visor, were registered at the Patent Office. A commission appointed by the Army Minister conducted a series of trials. Finally, two separate models were submitted to the commission on the same day, 'one of them irritatingly ornamented with flowerets and foliage', patented by Capron and listed as 'a general's helmet', the other one 'magnificently plain and resistant, thanks to the researches of Jean Dunand'.

Dunand's model sat deeper on the wearer's head than did the regulation helmet. Cold-stamped from a single piece of manganese steel, it was sturdier and more effective. In fact, cold-stamping was essential if the metal was to retain its rigidity and resistant qualities, which would be lost if the metal were heated. This type of steel had already been used in

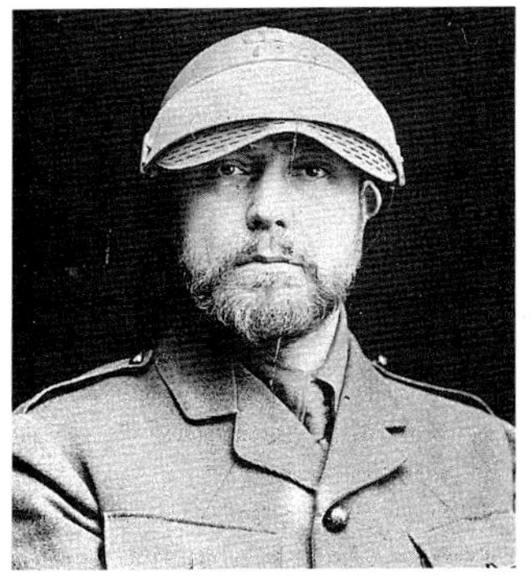

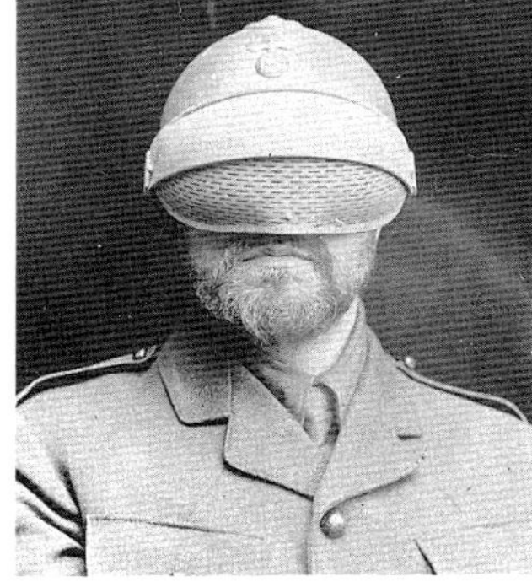

Dunand wearing the army helmet, shown with visor raised and lowered.

England for making helmets, but it had not proved possible to stamp it sufficiently deeply to cover the head, hence the shallower helmets typical of the British armies. By contrast, Dunand had used four successive pressings, using stamping dies of graduated shapes in order to produce a more enveloping helmet which afforded greater protection. At the same time, he had designed a new detachable visor, made out of the same metal, which provided protection for the eyes without in any way reducing the field of vision.

Comparative tests were carried out, and the records kept by the Military Commission demonstrate the clear superiority of Dunand's helmet over all the other models. His helmet received the approval of Generals Desgouttes, Andlauer, Estienne and Colonel A. Weiler. One thousand of these helmets had in any case already been delivered to the Army on 24 January 1917. Tested by combat units shortly before the end of hostilities, they were said to have 'saved the eyesight of numerous soldiers who suffered head wounds', according to written evidence submitted by their commanding officers.

Jean Dunand had received his foreign resident's permit on 3 October 1917; this served as an identity card, residence permit and safe-conduct pass in the war zone, confirming that he had even been invited by the American military authorities to provide them with helmets. An initial meeting took place between 5 and 8 October 1917, and then two more on 29 October 1917 and 12 September 1918, but without agreement being reached on manufacturing a helmet in the United States.

Unfortunately, top-ranking officials in the French Army Supply Corps (who probably had a vested interest in manufacturing the Adrian Helmet) blocked the adoption of Dunand's model, which was inadequately protected by patents which had been registered with undue haste; as a result the design was adopted by the American and Swiss armies, and Dunand had no means of preventing them.

At about the same time, an obvious copy of Dunand's helmet was submitted by a certain Doctor Polack, who had had it made at the same works as the one used by Dunand himself. A few modifications had then been made to its appearance in the hope of being able to conceal the true authorship of the design. The subterfuge was exposed by the Military Commission and Polack's helmet was rejected. In order to compensate Dunand, M. Breton, director of inventions at the Ministry of Munitions, recommended to the commission that the artist be suitably honoured, and he was duly appointed a Chevalier de la Légion d'Honneur on 1 November 1919.

Ironically, early in the Second World War Dunand's son Jean-Louis was killed when hit in the head by shrapnel on 20 June 1940. In a letter written at the time to his eldest son Bernard, then a prisoner-of-war, Dunand mused, 'And to think that for the past twenty years a helmet has been in existence which could have saved the French Army from losses of this order.' Over forty years later, on 7 January 1981, a report in the French daily *Le Monde* confirmed that the French Army was at last to adopt a new all-over one-piece helmet made of manganese steel.

The 'Victory Helmet' for Marshal Foch

Jean Dunand's Victory Helmet, combining his talents as coppersmith and silversmith, was without doubt the most important piece ever made by him. Entirely hammered out of mild steel, it was decorated with inlay work in precious metals and surmounted by a detachable crown of laurel leaves in chased gold (see catalogue no. 673).

Before executing the piece in its entirety, Dunand tried out several details to judge the effect of the ornamentation. For this very exceptional work, he sought the advice of his assistant, Grunweiser, an extremely skilful craftsman whom Dunand had taken on specially and who specialized in steel inlay work. Before the war, Dunand had turned to Grunweiser when making fob watch-cases, whose inlay decoration was carried out with the aid of a jeweller's loupe. And it was also Grunweiser who, at a later date, made the ceremonial swords for newly elected members of the Académie Française. With insufficient work to keep him occupied, Dunand subsequently allowed him to leave for Saint-Etienne, where he worked for the Manufacture Nationale d'Armes et Cycles, specializing in engraving rifle barrels.

The piece, which is now on exhibition at the Musée de l'Armée at Les Invalides in Paris, was presented to Marshal Foch by a group of American admirers as an international gesture in recognition of his wartime achievements against the German armies, but above all to show their respect and admiration for the efficient and competent manner in which he had taken over supreme command of the Allied armies. It must be said that, in view of people's sensitivities at the time, his task could not have been an easy one. At the head of this group of American admirers was Clarence Hungerford Mackay, President of the Commercial Cable Co. and the Postal Telegraph Cable Co. The price agreed was $10,000, which at that time was a considerable sum, but one well calculated to offset the disappointments which Dunand suffered in the affair of cold-stamped manganese-steel helmets for the U.S. Army.

Work on the Victory Helmet was carefully planned down to the smallest detail. Commissioned in April 1919, when Dunand received an advance payment of $2,500, the piece was immediately taken in hand. On 27 October, Marshal Foch's wife wrote a touchingly simple letter setting forth the hat size of her famous husband.

The piece itself is in the shape of the neck and head of a larger-than-life symbolic cockerel, which constitutes the upper part of the helmet, its beak wide open, as if to utter a cry of victory, or perhaps to intimidate the enemy. Head and neck form a single element, the crest being a cockscomb. Overlapping feathers with stylized lateral barbs run down the back of the helmet before arching upwards. At the front, they reveal a triple row of oak leaves and acorns, symbols of a Marshal's rank attached to lateral cockades.

Plates 157–170

WORKS BY JEAN DUNAND IN ASSOCIATION WITH OTHER ARTISTS AND BY BERNARD AND PIERRE DUNAND

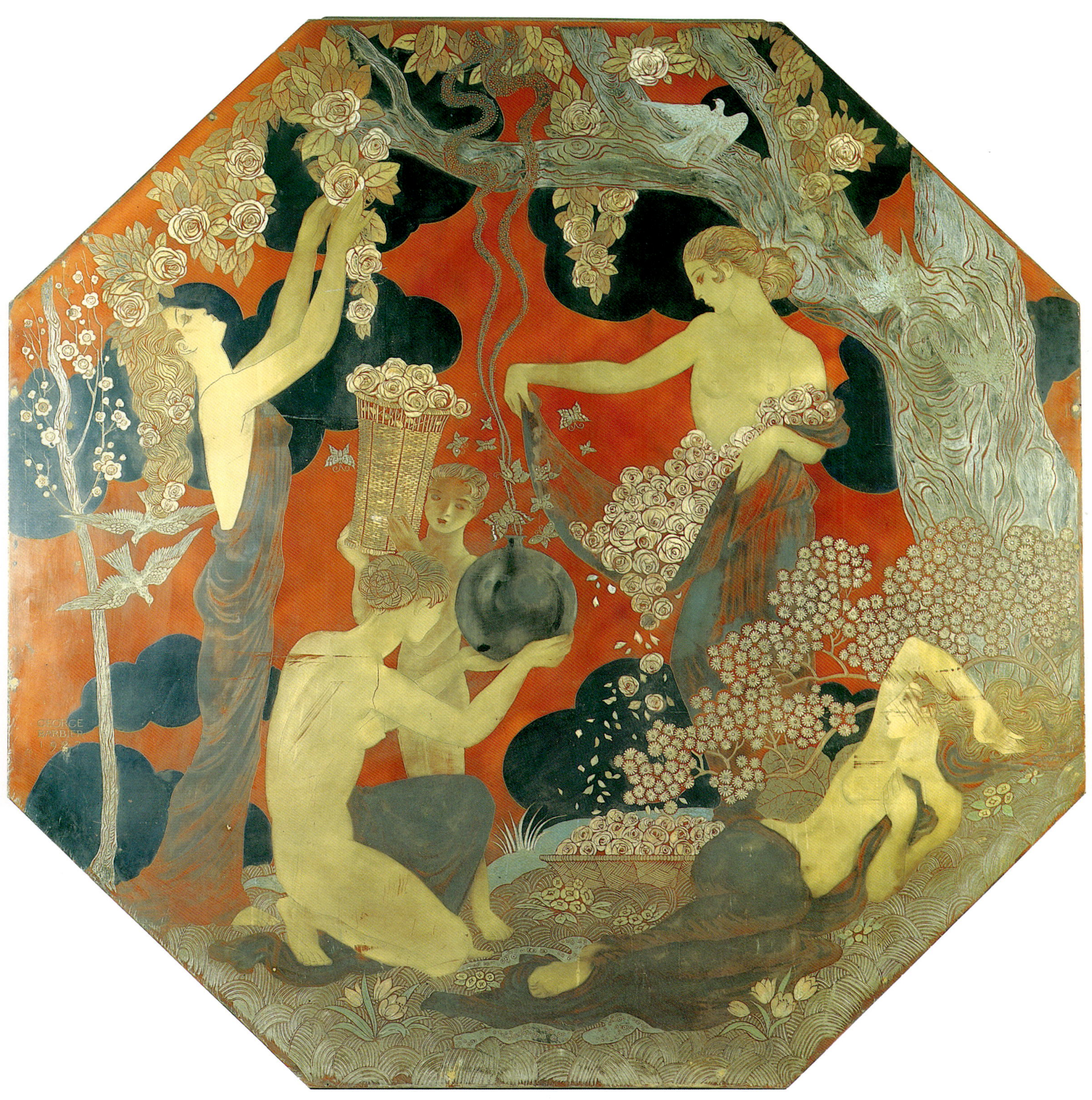

157 ***The Perfumes***, lacquer panel
by Jean Dunand after George Barbier, 1927
(*catalogue 233*)

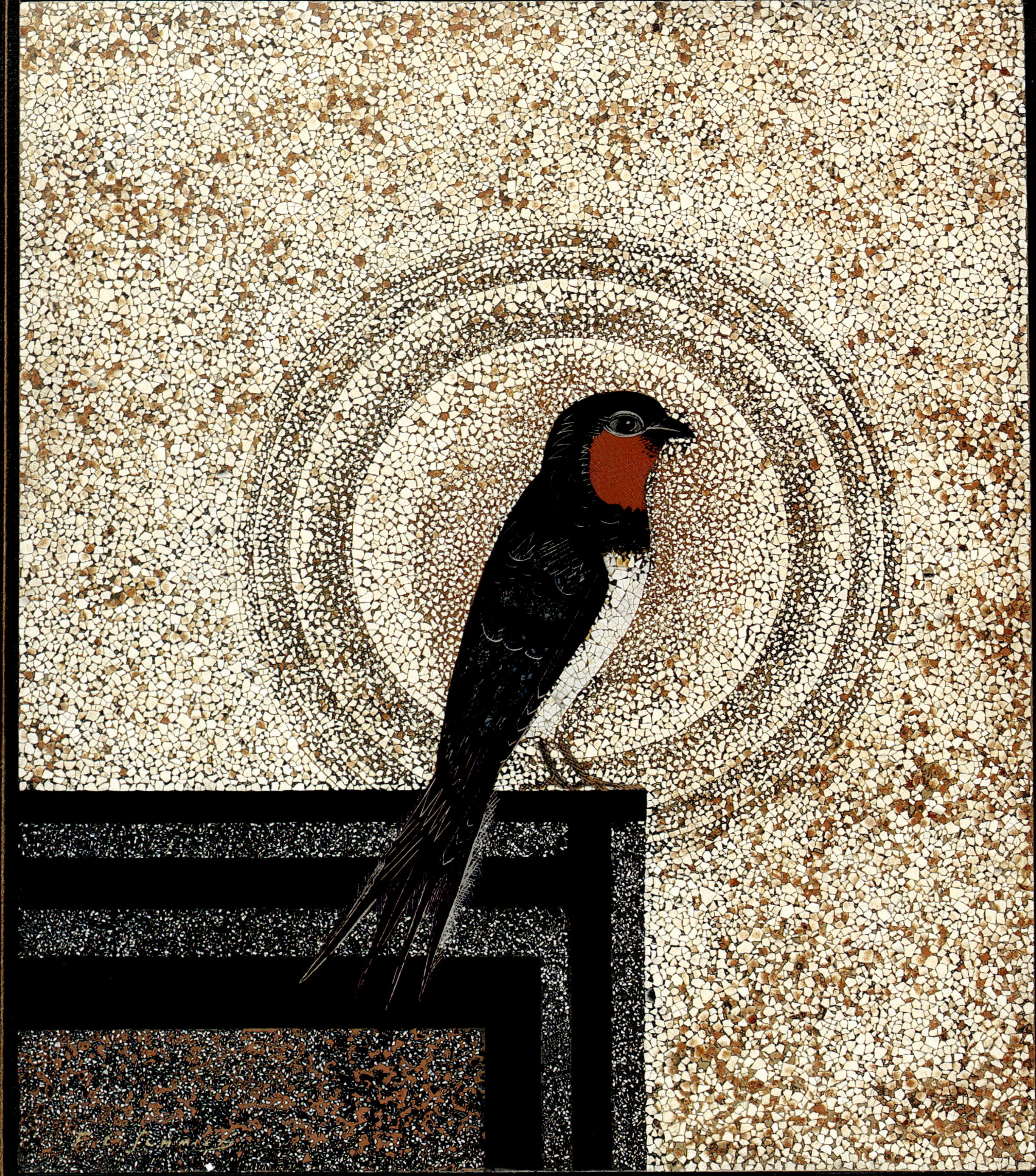
F.L.S.

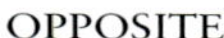
OPPOSITE

158 ***The Nightingale***, inside board by Dunand after François-Louis Schmied for a copy of *Two Tales* by Oscar Wilde, bound by Schmied, 1926 (*catalogue 840*)

159 ***Doves***, binding board by Dunand after a design by François-Louis Schmied, 1925 (*catalogue 836*)

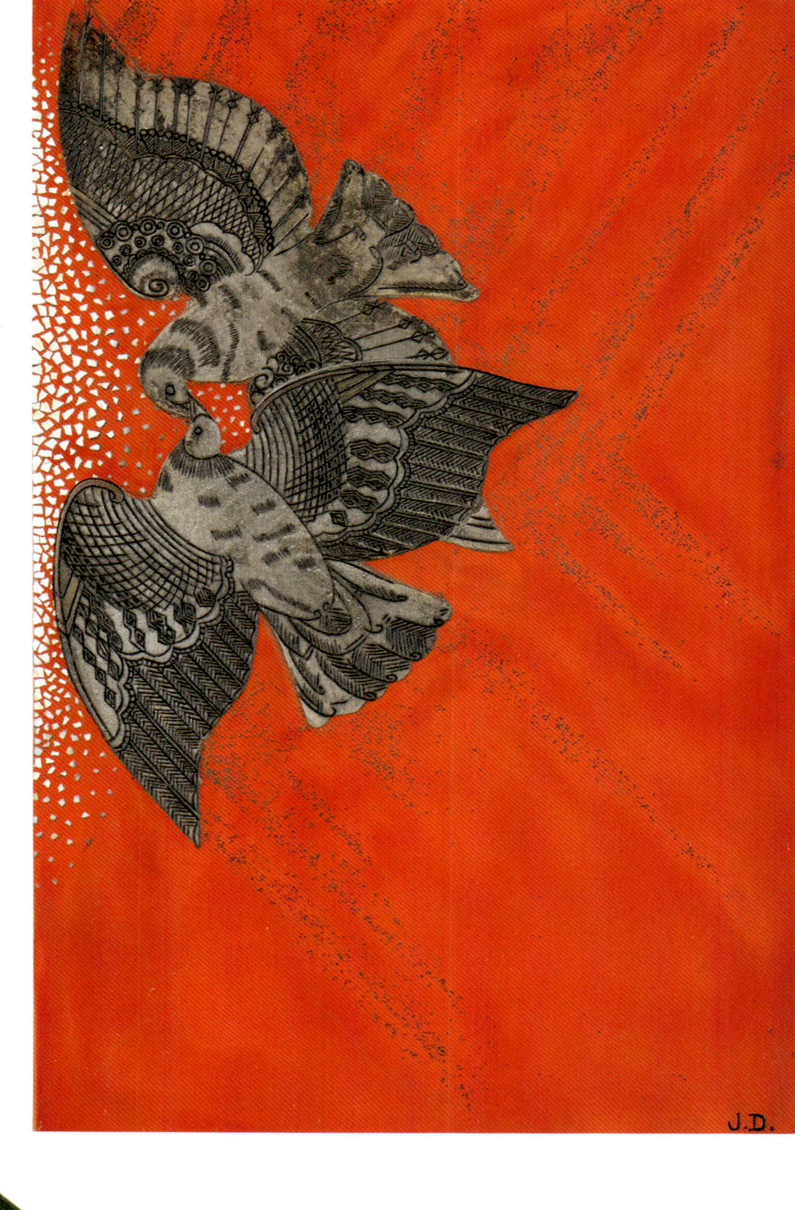

160 ***Flowers and Fruit***, binding designed by François-Louis Schmied for *Le Cantique des Cantiques* (*The Song of Solomon*), 1925 (*catalogue 827*)

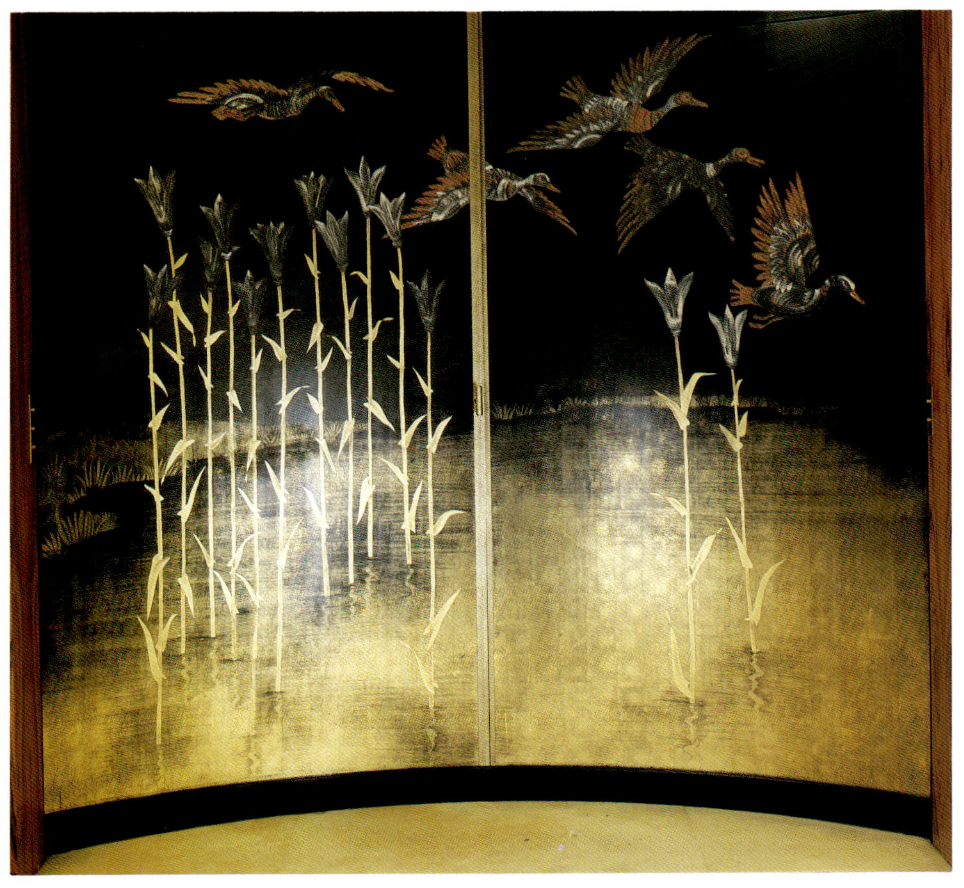

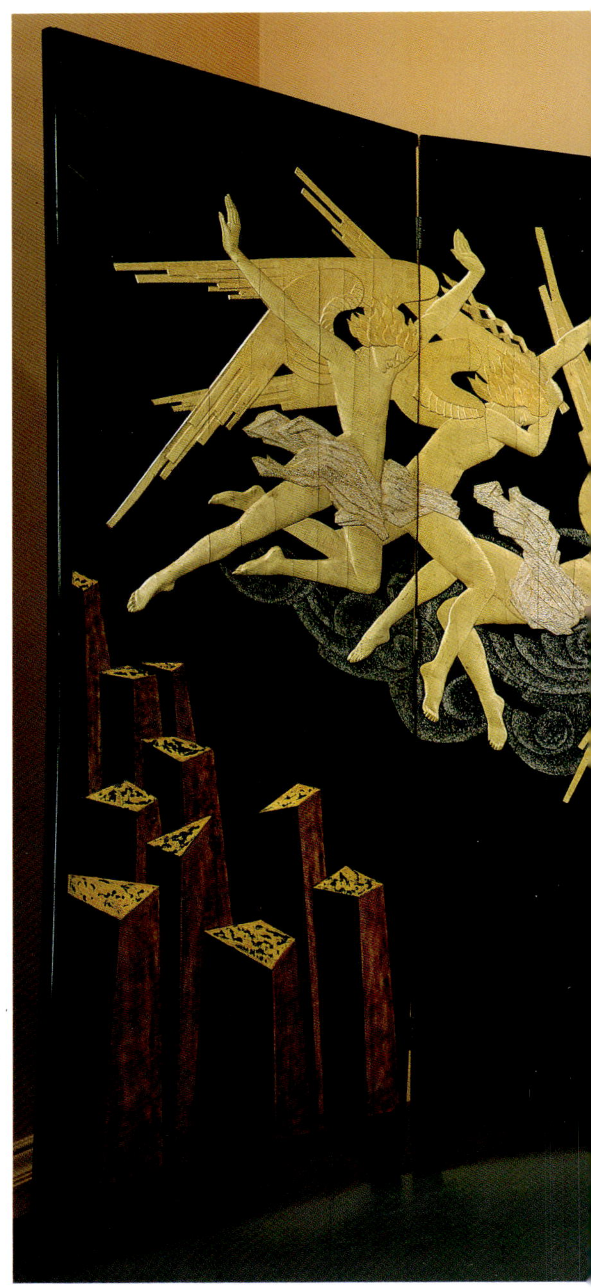

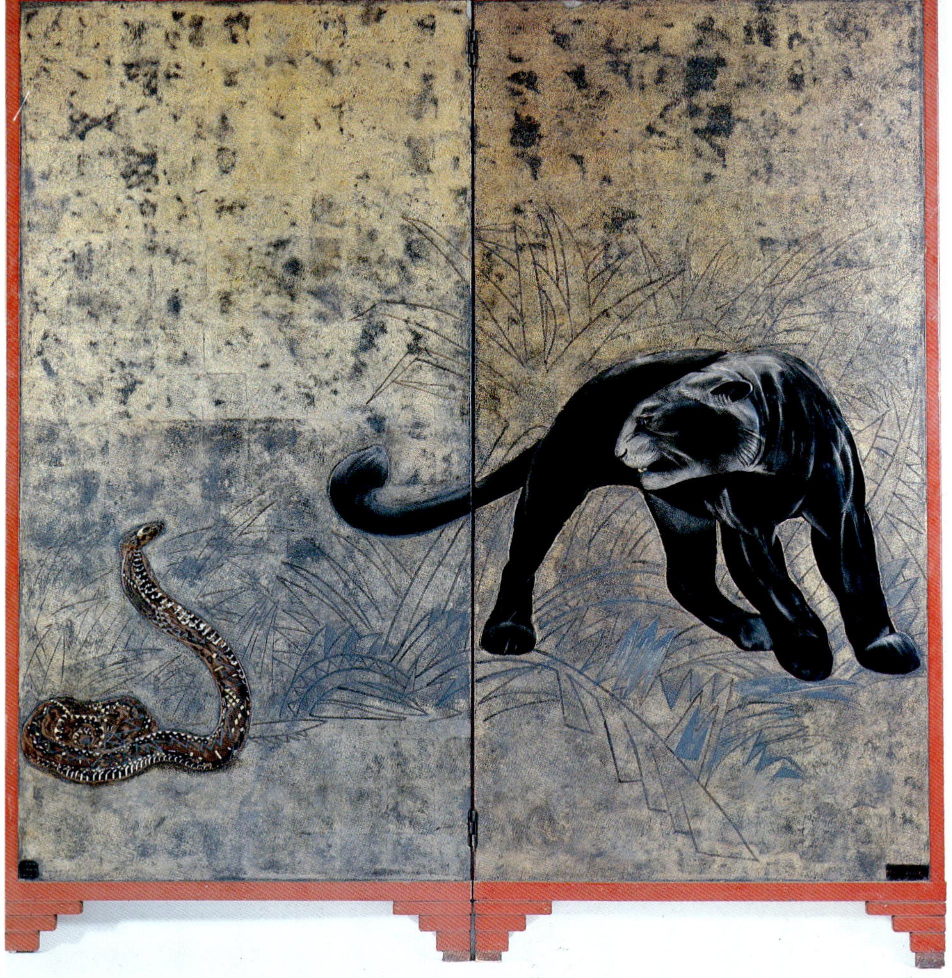

ABOVE LEFT

161 ***Flight of Ducks and Lotus***, two-panel curved screen by Pierre Dunand, *c.* 1945–50 (*catalogue PD11*)

162 ***Leopard and Cobra***, two-panel screen by Jean Dunand after Paul Jouve, *c.* 1922 (*catalogue 2*)

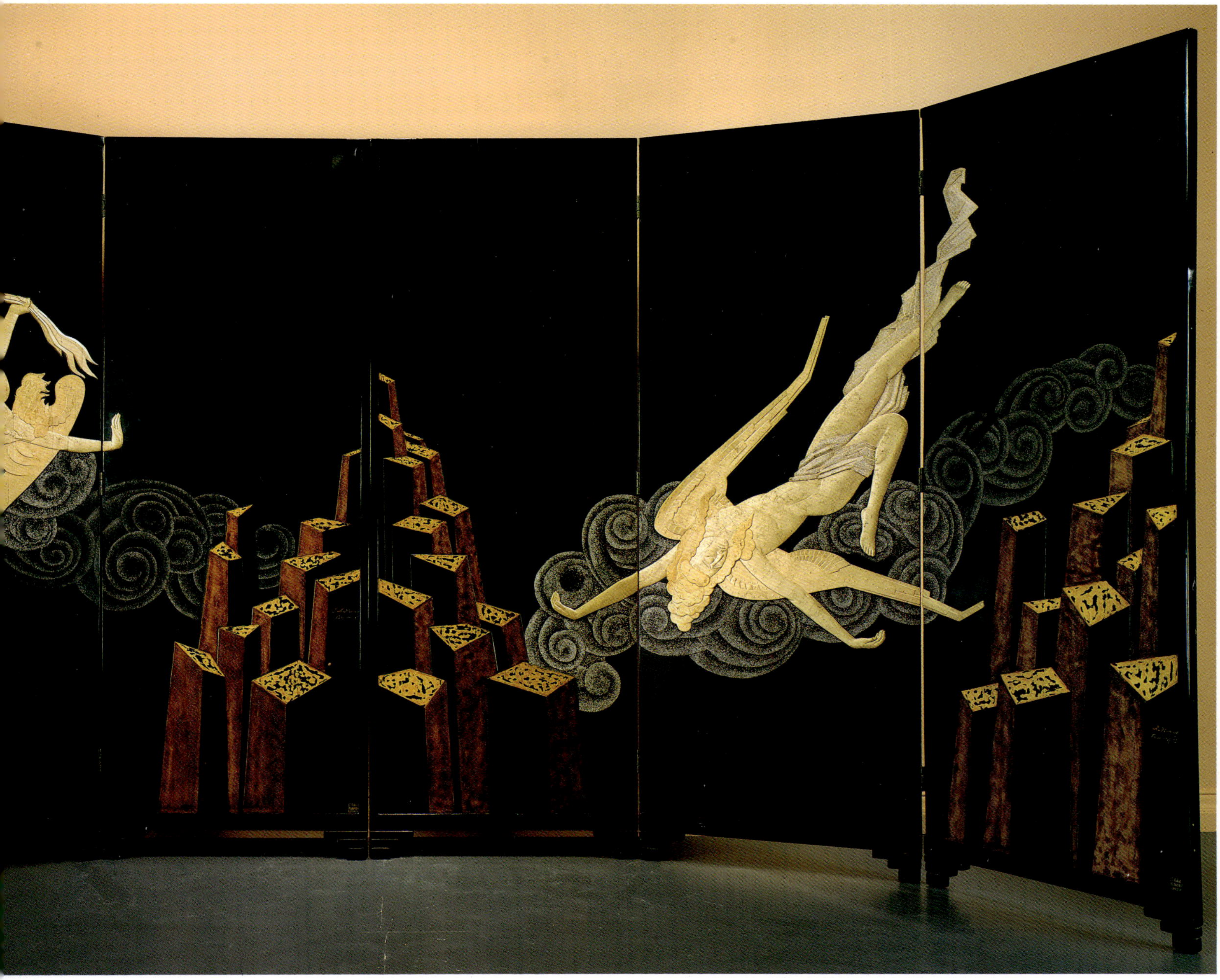

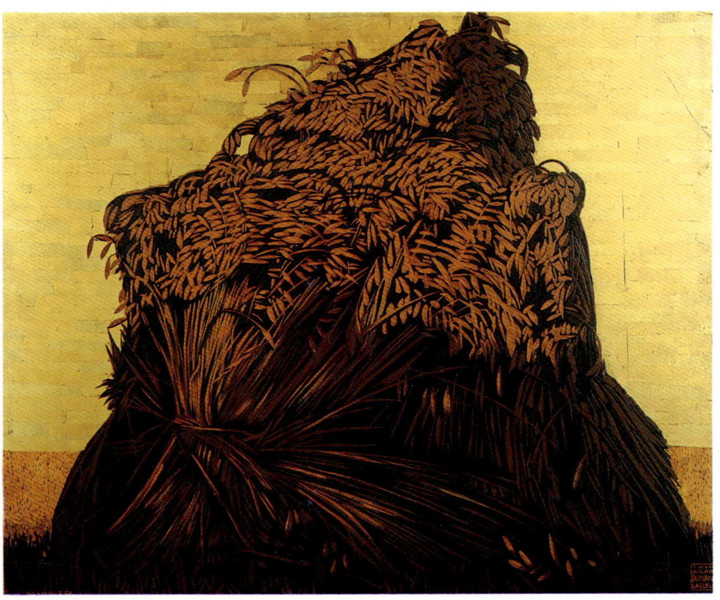

163 ***The Battle of the Angels*** –
'Crescendo' and 'Pianissimo',
two screens carved by Séraphin
Soudbinine and lacquered by Jean
Dunand, 1925/6
(*catalogue 1154, 1155*)

164 ***Sheaves of Wheat***, panel
lacquered by Jean Dunand after
a cartoon by François-Louis
Schmied, 1921
(*catalogue 288*)

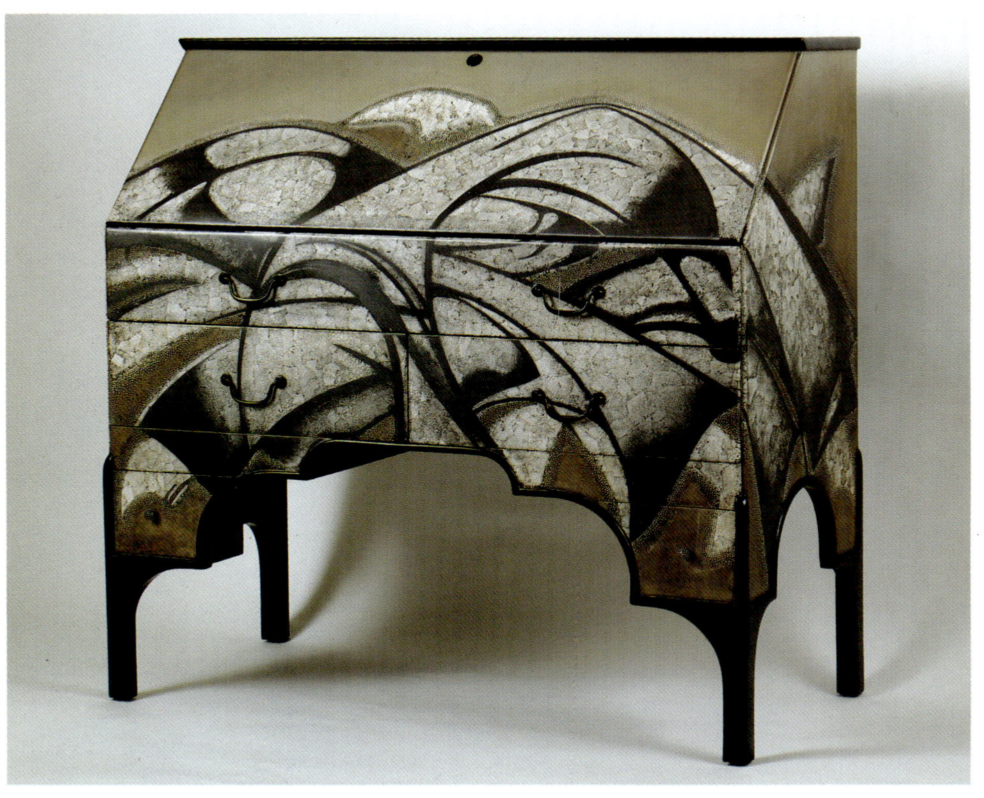

165 ***Bureau de pente*** designed by Jean Goulden and lacquered by Jean Dunand, 1923 (*catalogue 532*)

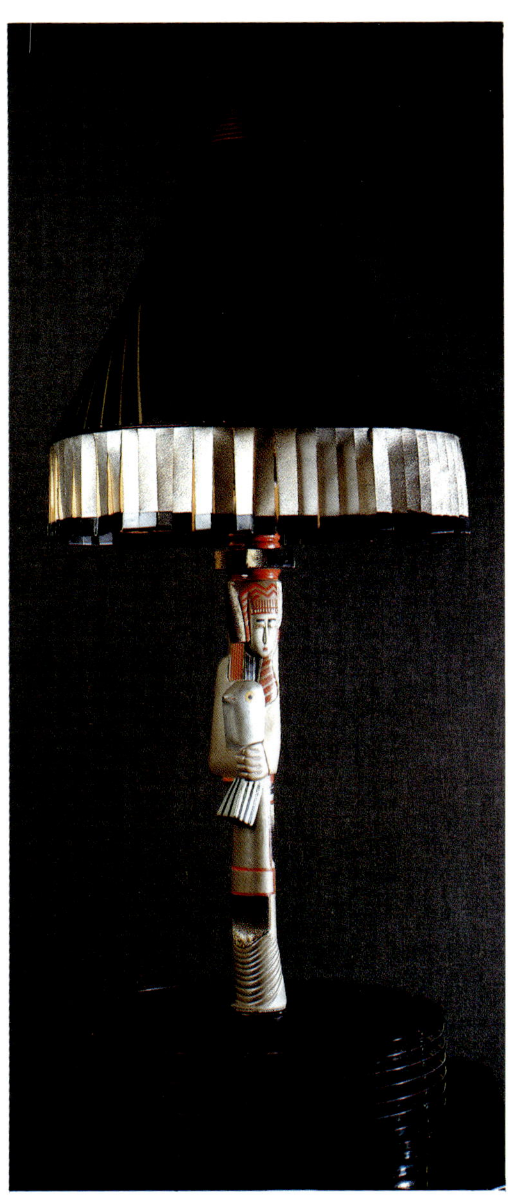

167 **'Standing Figure' table lamp** incorporating figure carved by Jean Lambert-Rucki and lacquered in Dunand's workshops, 1923 (*catalogue 590*)

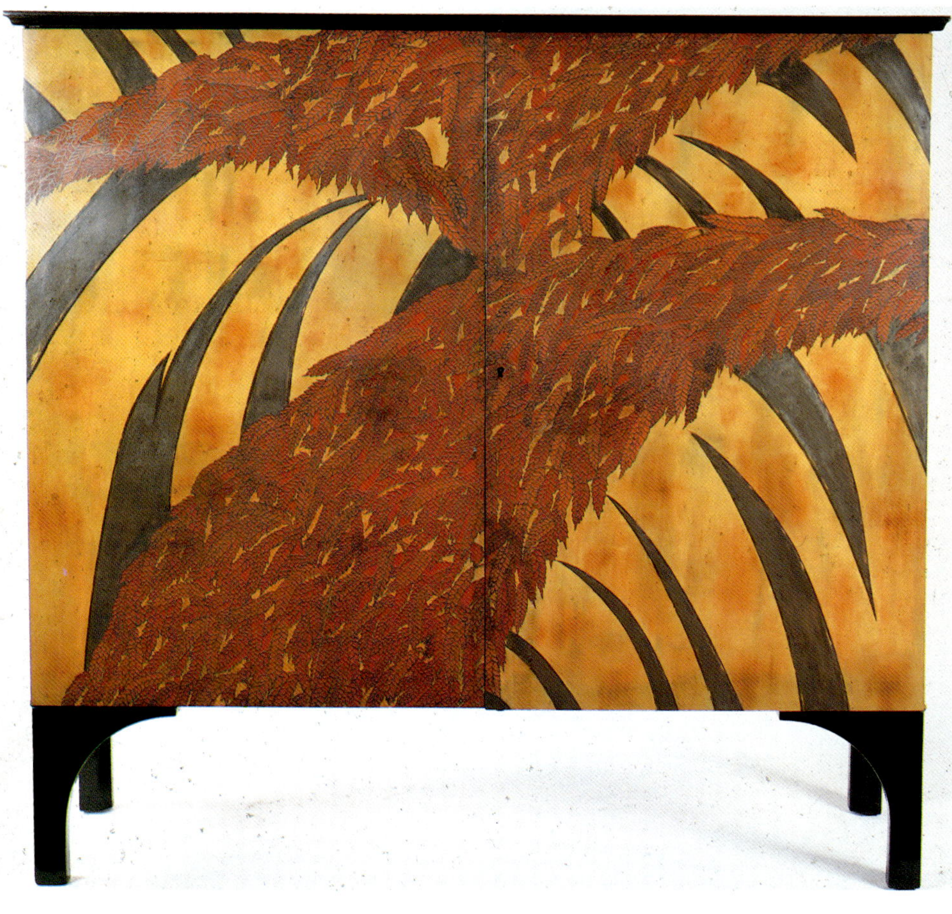

166 **Cabinet** with lacquer decoration by Jean Dunand after Jean Goulden, 1923 (*catalogue 529*)

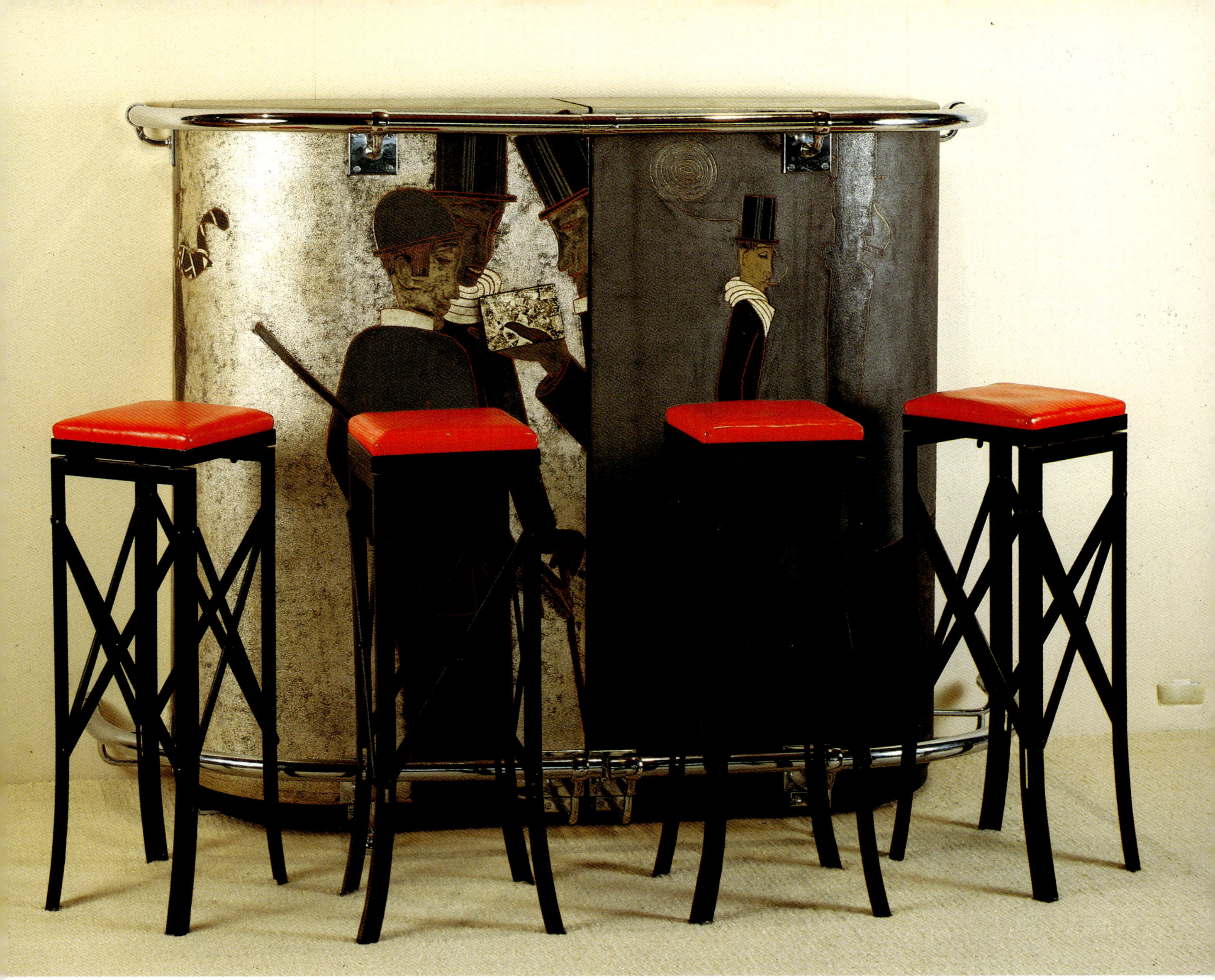

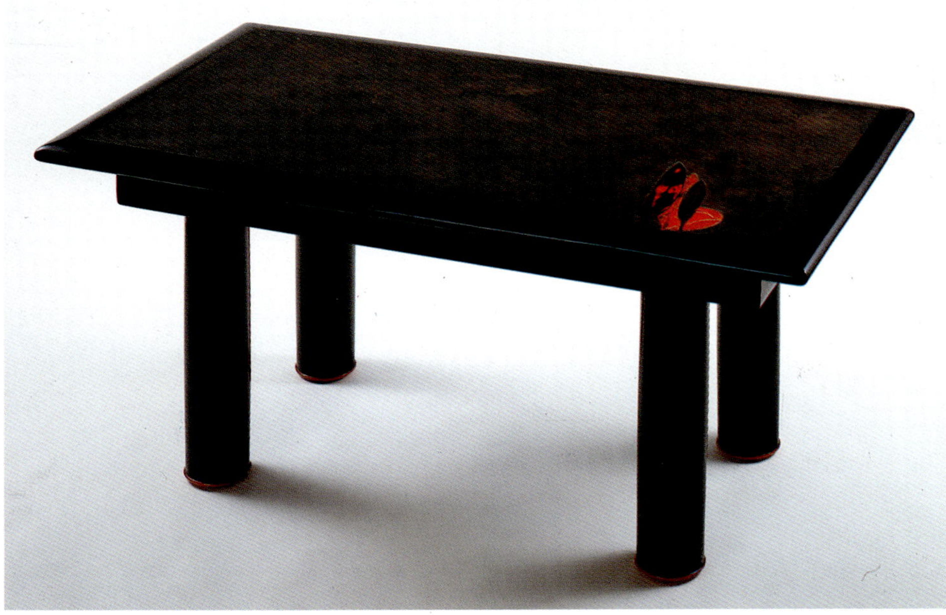

168 **Folding cocktail bar and stools,** the bar with lacquer decoration by Jean Dunand after Jean Lambert-Rucki, 1928 (*catalogue 521*)

169 **Occasional table** with lacquer decoration by Bernard Dunand, 1937 (*catalogue BD4*)

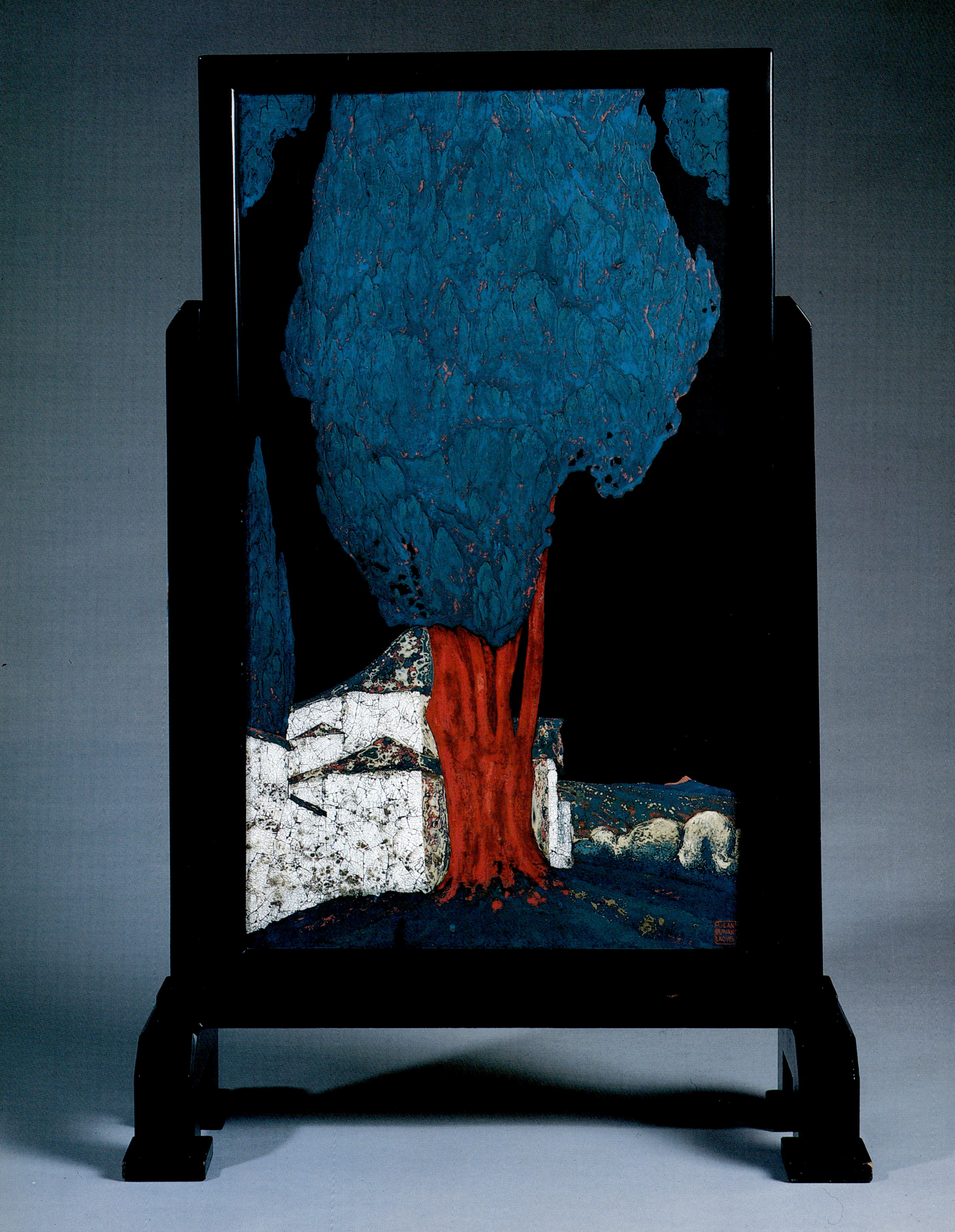

The Victory Helmet also has a fixed visor that repeats the decorative motif of feathers arranged in rows like fish-scales. A chin-strap consisting of two identically decorated bands completes the helmet. With its crown of laurel leaves, the helmet was presented in a large black-lacquer casket. Around the top of the casket is a lacquered frieze inlaid with a motif of exploding shells, while the bottom is decorated by a second frieze, this one depicting barbed wire, the tracery of which forms the words 'Le jour de gloire est arrivé' ('The day of glory has come'). The casket, lined with maplewood, provides a most elegant setting for this masterpiece of metalwork.

The presentation to Marshal Foch took place in New York on 14 December 1921 during an official visit he made to the United States.

Ceremonial swords for members of the Institut de France

In the course of his career, Dunand made four swords for presentation to newly elected members of the Institut de France. Commissioned works, such swords are traditionally paid for out of funds subscribed by a new member's friends and colleagues. A feature common to all Dunand's swords is a finely engraved steel blade inlaid with precious metals.

The hilt-guard is generally made of chased steel, engraved with a number of specific attributes and sometimes embellished with gilt. As for the hilt, this could be made equally well in steel or lacquered with eggshell inlay in the manner of objects made in seventeenth-century Japan. The scabbard habitually had the same decoration, more or less refined.

The first such sword made by Dunand was for Maître Henri-Robert, President of the French Bar, who was elected a member of the Académie Française in 1924. Maître Manuel Fourcade, his successor as president, made the formal presentation, in the name of all his colleagues.

The second sword was commissioned for Georges Lecomte, President of the Société des Gens de Lettres. Subscribers included other writers who were members of his society, as well as friends. Fashioned along similar lines to the Henri-Robert sword, it bore a dedication engraved on the back of the blade. It was exhibited at the Galerie Georges Petit in December 1925, beside the Henri-Robert sword. Richly decorated with mother-of-pearl and burgaudine inlay work, both provided outstanding proof of Dunand's technical versatility. Designed entirely by him, the steel shafts that formed the blades were ordered from hardened steel specialists, and each was decorated with gold and silver inlay work by Grunweiser. They had an astonishingly modern appearance, while at the same time preserving an almost anachronistic quality in their presentation.

The third of Dunand's four ceremonial swords was presented to Paul Landowski in 1926 following his election to the Académie des Beaux-Arts.

The fourth sword was for Fortunat Strowsky, a noted humanist scholar, professor at the Sorbonne and contributor to various art journals. His subscription was opened on the initiative of Madame Charles Pomaret, editor of *La Renaissance de l'art français*, with which Strowsky was associated. The hilt-guard of the sword, in burnished steel, was engraved and inlaid with gold. It was decorated with laurel leaves, a motif repeated on the hilt itself. Its tang was covered with tiny pieces of mother-of-pearl and ended in a sort of button, the 'mechanical' appearance of which gave the sword its modern appearance. It was presented to Strowsky in the summer of 1929, having already been exhibited at the Galerie La Renaissance in the Rue Royale, in Dunand's first large-scale exhibition.

170 **'Cypress' firescreen** designed by and with lacquer decoration after Jean Goulden, 1921 (*catalogue 570*)

Bookbindings

One of the works on display at the first exhibition of the Groupe Dunand-Goulden-Jouve-Schmied at the Galerie Georges Petit in 1921 was Rudyard Kipling's *The Jungle Book*, the illustrations for which had been begun before the war, in 1913. Although the majority of the plates were drawn by Jouve, the *bandeaux* and *culs de lampe* were the work of François-Louis Schmied. Schmied who was also given the task of engraving the plates, since Jouve lacked the necessary skill. It was, so to speak, under the aegis of this magnificent work that the four artists came together, Schmied bringing along Dunand, to whom he was tied by the closest of friendships, while Jouve introduced Goulden, having made the latter's acquaintance while serving with the Eastern army in Salonika.

The success of this first venture encouraged other bibliophiles to entrust Schmied with the task of working on new illustrated editions. Some, such as Dr Baumgartner, also asked him to design the bindings. Instead of using the customary leather, Schmied had the idea of asking Dunand to execute them in lacquer. The motif chosen was frequently borrowed from one of the book's illustrations, then isolated and enlarged to accentuate the decorative aspect of the composition. Dunand – who would never broach a new technique without first understanding the rules – then met Georges Cretté, one of the most skilled bookbinders of the day and the successor to Marius Michel, the undisputed master of the Belle Epoque.

After discussing the matter at length, Dunand decided to use a metal base for his lacquers, since he was unable to work with small wooden panels as boards, these being so thin that they warped when placed in a humid atmosphere during the drying process. For this reason lacquered wood was never included in Dunand's designs, and any such bindings which are represented as being by him are the work of skilful forgers.

To begin with, then, Dunand made use of brass plates as a base for the lacquer. The earliest models were even designed to use the whole of the board's surface. The edges of the plate were not cut on three sides but were bent back by 5 mm (1/4 in.) in order to accommodate the binding board. The narrow borders were carefully turned back to create a groove into which the thick binding board would fit closely on three sides. The board providing the support naturally had to be trimmed or bevelled along its three outer edges so that the metal plate could slide into place without risk of damage. The actual decoration was entirely lacquered and fired, which produced an extremely tough finish. Eventually, Cretté preferred to use simple brass plates glued to the board and secured by clamps, rather than those with edges bent back, since their greater weight rendered the setting less robust.

Dunand later came to regard the use of metal as too restricting, and he therefore tried using sheets of ebonite, a modern plastic substance which, although it cannot be fired in a kiln, is at least unaffected by a humid atmosphere. In addition, the material was commercially available and could be applied directly, its thinness also making it easier to mount. Extremely light and simple to fix in place, the sheets could be recessed into the leather without adding significantly to the weight of the board or imposing undue strain on the binding. This new substance, then, allowed Dunand to give free rein to his imagination, enabling him to soak the cut sheets in lacquer, as well as to treat them with powdered mother-of-pearl and eggshell or precious-metal filings.

More straightforwardly and more traditionally, Dunand also used simple dinanderie plates to decorate the inside boards, principally in the case of plain bindings – in other words, bindings without external decoration; these plates were fixed to the boards with isinglass, using small metal barbs raised in the back of the plate by means of a small chisel. It made no difference whether the metal used was brass, nickel silver, or even silver or gold. Dunand even made plates of silver with hollowed-out designs filled with lacquer in a manner similar to *champlevé* enamelling, decorative motifs being relacquered on to an eggshell ground. Dunand did not, however, wish to compete directly with Jean Goulden, who used a similar technique for his own work; hence he abandoned this method, in which the weight of the boards tended in any case to weaken the joints of the bindings. For his part, Schmied felt that this style corresponded closely to his idea of what fine bindings should be like, and he therefore continued to have the plates made for him in Dunand's studio, mounting them in his own bindery and embellishing them with eggshell, *laque de Chine* and burgaudine.

As for Dunand, his constant search for new ideas led him to experiment with plain leather bindings by applying lacquer on the outside. The leather binding was made separately before being mounted on the book block. Lacquered on both sides and on the spine to obtain uniform tension, the binding was ornamented with inlaid mother-of-pearl and eggshell, the surface of which was then relaquered so as to produce what virtually amounted to relief decoration. Mounting required extreme care and, not having a proper bindery of his own, Dunand preferred to use Schmied's, located at 74b Rue Hallé.

Unfortunately, however much care was taken over this type of binding, its sheer weight was a disadvantage, producing a weaker result. Moreover, the leather would dry out and lose some of its suppleness, thus giving rise to cracks in the lacquer, and with the passage of time these grew to the point where the surface broke up completely. Dissatisfied with this experiment, Dunand soon abandoned the technique and only four or five examples of such bindings survive.

A further experiment which Dunand attempted consisted of fixing small pieces of mother-of-pearl edge to edge to create the appearance of a finely wrought mosaic. The design thus produced would be an accurate representation of one of the book's illustrations. The first such example was made for the binding of *Peau-Brune*, Schmied's account of the cruise that he and Dunand had undertaken around the Mediterranean in 1927. A complete series, to include all the illustrations from the volume, was commissioned by Schmied, but only about ten were ever executed.

A number of sketches supplied by Schmied were in reality the work of Gustave Miklos, although based on drawings by Schmied and photographs taken by him during the cruise. These facts were authenticated by reference to an accounts book, discovered at the home of Madame Gustave Miklos, containing very precise details as well as a description of all these pieces. Two books, *Sucre d'Amour* and *Princesse Boudour*, each published in a limited edition of twenty-five copies, were issued by Schmied with illustrations hand-coloured in Dunand's studio. Although this illuminated work must have attracted some lover of rare books, it led nowhere, and it has to be said that what was involved was not lacquering in the true sense, but fine art work.

The leading bibliophiles of the period wanted to own one or more bindings by the partnership of Dunand and Schmied. One thinks here of Henri Vever, whose collection was by far the most impressive, of Baumgartner, Louis Barthou, Jacques André and many others. Sadly, the economic crisis which began in the early 1930s led to a decline in such patronage, and brought such luxurious experiments to a halt.

Since most of these bindings were intended for works printed by Schmied, with more or less esoteric texts that were not to everyone's taste, these marvels of bibliophilism were completely ignored by art bookshops in the years following the Second World War, as well as by collectors who found them too specialized. This wholly unjustified disaffection was only short-lived, and since the 1970s these books have been restored to favour in the eyes of a new generation of collectors, much to the chagrin of former owners who had earlier sold them off cheaply.

Portraiture

Jean Dunand is without doubt the only lacquer artist of stature to have executed authentic portraits in that medium. It is of course true that for a man like Dunand, who had earlier made a serious study of painting in order to provide the groundwork for his vocation as a sculptor, there was a great temptation to do so. He therefore tried his hand at portraiture all the more enthusiastically in that he continued to wield paint-brushes while elaborating his sketches for lacquer screens and other decorative motifs.

His first essay in this field was a portrait of his wife, a preliminary study for which was shown at the group exhibition held at the Galerie Georges Petit in December 1924. Relatively modest in size, the panel depicted Madame Dunand in three-quarter profile, wearing a sumptuous and colourful cashmere outfit, and around her neck a scarf with a geometric motif complementing the composition's technical complexity. At the same exhibition Angst presented a sculpture of a child, its gold lacquer executed by Dunand in accordance with Angst's design, its manifest dullness contrasting oddly with the boldly drawn portrait of Madame Dunand.

The portrait study's success encouraged Dunand to go one stage further and to paint a definitive version, using coloured lacquers inlaid with gold on a background of eggshell arranged in an irregular mosaic; this was seen the following year at the Galerie Georges Petit, when it appeared alongside portraits of Madame Agnès and Madame Charlotte Revil, both of them noted milliners and fashion designers whom Jean Dunand had got to know at the time of the 1925 Exposition des Arts Décoratifs, when he had supplied them with assertively modernist fashion accessories in copper and lacquered metal. Although these portraits were not commissioned pieces, Dunand was counting on long-term financial benefits by exhibiting them. Each of these famous women was depicted in profile, the one complementing the other, as it were, and both wearing dresses made of fabrics with geometric designs which Dunand had had lacquered by hand in his studios. African-style jewellery in lacquered metal blended with the rest of his sitters' wardrobe.

All the same, in spite of being accurate likenesses, these portraits had a rather self-conscious quality – something rigid and artificial – whereas the portrait of Madame Dunand conveyed an impression of calm tenderness, the artist's intimate knowledge of his subject clearly having inspired him to go beyond the expectations of a purely realistic aesthetic. The faces of the sitters were traced in minute detail by Jean Lambert-Rucki, whose technical precision was well-known. After all, did he not earn his living, when not working for Dunand, by painting extraordinarily realistic bouquets of roses in specialist shops?

Dunand continued to experiment, hoping, as a prudent businessman, to find new markets for lacquer. Without in any way seeking to revolutionize fashionable portraiture, Dunand nonetheless hoped to gain some commercial advantage from his experiments. Astutely, he had realized that one certain means of attracting a new clientèle of wealthy women was by obtaining introductions through their fashionable *couturières*. Exhibited in salons and fashion houses, a portrait of the proprietress could not fail to excite her clients' interest. Thus, the various portraits which Dunand made for Madame Agnès were excellent ambassadors in their originality.

There were also occasions, however, when Dunand adopted a more direct approach to encourage commissions, preparing a sketch of the intended subject, without her knowledge but based on a photographic likeness. He would then present it to her in the hope of being asked to execute a finished work in lacquer and eggshell. Many of these approaches came to nothing, either because the individual concerned did not consider the likeness successful, or because they were deterred by the not inconsiderable cost of commissioning a finished version. It is even said that, in the hope of obtaining a commission to paint a portrait of Maurice Chevalier which he could then use for publicity purposes, Dunand had the idea of first painting Chevalier's mother and offering the portrait to the singer. The latter was not taken in by the ruse, however, and, being a man of legendary thrift, merely accepted his mother's portrait, without commissioning anything further. In fact, the only record is a photograph published in the newspapers, showing Maurice Chevalier seated in an armchair with the portrait of his mother on the wall behind him. History does not record whether this indirect publicity brought Dunand any new orders.

On the practical level, Dunand would paint a portrait of his sitter from life, using colour size or oils, while at the same time availing himself of photographs which he took himself with his Leica. The painting was then copied in the design studio and translated into lacquer and eggshell, thus reducing the number of sittings required. The flesh tones were often executed in white eggshell, in a very fine mosaic that resembled the surface *craquelure* seen on some glazed pottery. Dunand then applied coloured lacquers to this surface, modelling and rubbing them down to achieve the desired shadings and transparencies. This use of photography, with its quality of hyper-realism, transformed Dunand's portrait gallery into one of the most attractive social documents of the day. In their way, these works are at least as interesting as the official portraits proudly displayed by exhibitors at the Salon des Artistes Français and intended, like Dunand's portraits, to capture the essential character of their subjects.

Fashion and jewellery

It was a chance discovery that first led Dunand in the direction of fashion and jewellery. He came across some silk rags that he had used to wipe his brushes and had then been left to dry. The dilute natural lacquer, Dunand noticed, took to certain fabrics very well and, even after it had hardened naturally, they retained their suppleness.

In an article published in the magazine *Vogue* on 1 May 1925, Dunand declared that, despite his observation, only 'the encouragement of a woman of taste and level-headedness, Madame Agnès,' had led him to 'put the discovery to rational use.' This article appeared shortly after he had opened a new studio on 9 March for lacquering fabrics on his own premises in the Rue Hallé. Numerous photographs were published in the newspapers, showing Madame Dunand surrounded by newly created fabrics. The impression might have been given that it was she who had assumed responsibility for this new department, whereas in reality she had simply agreed, out of the kindness of her heart, to appear in this way in order to give the scene a feminine touch. In practice, she never became involved in this new artistic enterprise.

As far as fashion was concerned, Dunand had begun by making some small accessories which he produced by way of amusement, generally for members of his own family. This was the case with his first shoe-buckles and belt-buckles and also with certain lapel-ornaments made to be sewn in place. By the same token, certain of Madame Agnès's hats were decorated with small lacquered motifs or with long red and black hatpins which highlighted their ingenious shapes.

Next, Dunand found a way of exploiting the situation by inviting some of his female relatives to wear examples of his beautiful gold jewellery – a type originally made with only his wife in mind. These parures, at once artless and sophisticated, were in perfect harmony with the latest trends in fashion, whose modern graphic designs were directly inspired by ornamental Cubism. Designers such as Madeleine Vionnet, Jeanne Lanvin, Elsa Schiaparelli, Wormser, Premet, Cheruit and Louise Boulanger, as well as Jean-Philippe Worth, Madame Agnès and Jenny Sacerdote, had their models wear Dunand's novel creations. At the same time as these lacquered gold accessories were growing in number, a greater diversity of styles was developing among fashion designers, the individual personality of each combining with Dunand's creations to produce something new on every occasion.

Madeleine Vionnet and Jean Dunand admired each other greatly. No doubt they shared the bond between successful individualists whose talent is self-evident. Madeleine Vionnet came to Dunand's assistance on several occasions, notably by lending him money and by ensuring commissions that enabled him to acquire the buildings adjacent to his workshops in the Rue Hallé. After his father's death, Bernard Dunand was worried about repaying her when he finally returned from wartime captivity, but was told, 'Think no more about it, as a token of the admiration which I felt for your father, I do not feel the need for this money to be repaid.' When one knows the financial problems which Madeleine Vionnet must have had with the partners in her *maison de couture*, one cannot but be impressed by this act of generosity.

In 1929, Dunand was invited by Boris Lacroix to collaborate on the interior design of Madeleine Vionnet's Paris house, situated in the Square Arnauld in the 16th *arrondissement*. Jean-Michel Frank was also involved in the interior design,

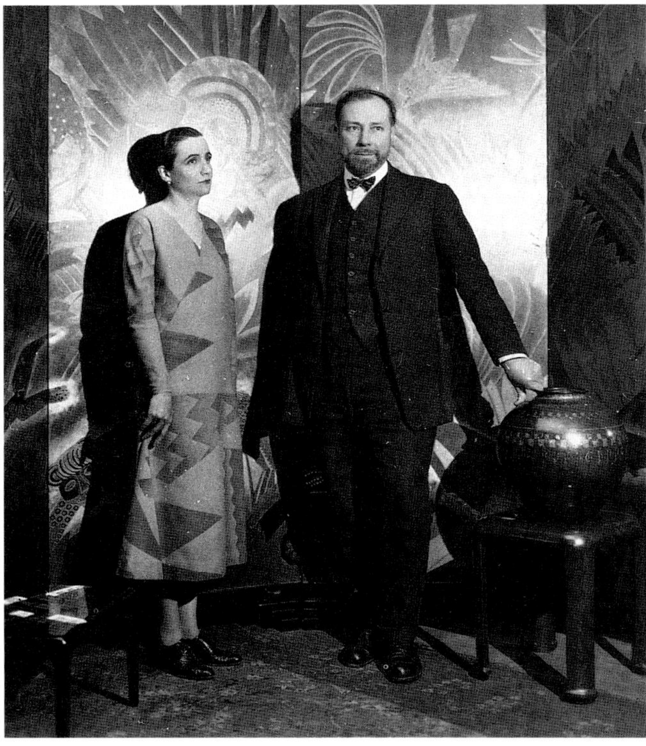

Madame Agnès photographed with Dunand in the Pavillon de la Mode at the Exposition Internationale des Arts Décoratifs et Industriels Modernes, Paris, 1925.

just as he had designed the brown-straw coloured panelling in the library of her former house in the Square Pétrarque, which Madeleine Vionnet had found too large for her taste. She had therefore sold it to a friend, Madame Chaptal, also a *couturière*.

The furniture which Dunand designed for Madeleine Vionnet was extremely original. In addition to a black-lacquer gaming table (with integral chairs), the top of which also featured powdered eggshell, there was an orange-coloured occasional table and a bookcase with rotating sections, also in orange lacquer, the mechanism of which was designed by Boris Lacroix. A panel depicting cheetahs and a *Moonlight* screen completed the ensemble. For her country house Dunand designed a further gaming table in polished oak, sober but impressive in conception. Most of these pieces had been made in collaboration with one of his skilled workmen, Montabré, whose job it was to supervise the execution of the designs in Dunand's workshops.

Through a sort of professional affectation, Dunand set out to rival the boldest creations of other contemporary fashion designers. The craftsman he employed who specialized in lacquering fabrics was called Dunant, spelt with a final 't'.

At the 1925 Exposition des Arts Décoratifs, it was only natural that some of the exhibitors in the clothes section should choose Dunand's parures to adorn the outfits being modelled. He designed each one individually, never repeating the same design. In the majority of cases the motif was 'lacquered' on to a pre-existing gown with the aid of brushes and stencils. Conversely, he did only a very small amount of work for Jean-Charles Worth, who had taken over the business from his uncle Jean-Philippe Worth. Yet here too he undertook the interior design of Worth's house in Neuilly, even going so far as to sand-blast the shutters and lacquer them tortoiseshell-brown. Such was the success and originality of Dunand's compositions that these well-known fashion designers quickly came to see what new ideas he could bring to their world of *haute couture*. Encouraged by Madame Agnès, for whose talents he felt a very real esteem, Dunand allowed himself to be drawn into this feminine atmosphere and, in addition to the usual paraphernalia of powder-compacts, pins and buckles in lacquered metal, he made boxes, étuis, vanity cases and mirrors. Madame Agnès's head seamstress, 'Zette', had special responsibility for selling these accessories to her employer's clientèle. Most of them were made in the Passage Montbrun, not far from the Rue Hallé, by a craftsman called Ariano, whose normal stock-in-trade consisted of Bakelite buttons and small brooches in coloured galalith. Dunand did not personally design all the buckles, but entrusted the work to Mesdemoiselles Lantéron and Godau, both of whom had studied at the Ecole des Arts Décoratifs. They produced designs in Dunand's style, and he then selected those he wished to have executed.

His creations soon became more and more adventurous, including African-style necklaces, slave collars and bracelets to be worn about the dainty neck and wrists of exotic beauties such as Josephine Baker, and sculpted earrings in the shape of skyscrapers or interlocking cogs. The result was an ensemble of unusual jewellery in which the exoticism of a 'Negro' style merged with the discipline of a Cubist conception. In fact, a good part of Dunand's work for Madame Agnès consisted of giving helpful advice and practical suggestions for designing hats which were to be lacquered or decorated with eggshell by Madame Nam in the Rue Hallé workshop, and in return he received introductions to clients who placed orders for screens, portraits or decorative objects. As an example, Dunand's first bracelet was made for Josephine Baker, a commission which the artist received through Madame Agnès.

Dunand's art – the art of a powerful intellect, albeit one which he himself described as somewhat boorish – emerged refreshed and rejuvenated from his dealings with these paragons of elegance, all of whom began to use Dunand's fabrics. Louise Boulanger blended her extravagant sense of colour with the rhythmic qualities of Dunand's graphic style, while Madame Agnès created new shapes for hats, not hesitating to crumple these fabrics and make them up into fantastic shapes, learning from Dunand the joy of seeing matter conform to the artist's creative will. Their collaboration produced the best results of all, some of them wilfully comical, with Dunand even going so far as to wear unusual disguises at fancy-dress balls or creating for her a 'delightful hat-stand screen from which these adorable hats would swing like the severed heads of Amazonian tribesmen, reflected the while in the purest of lacquers'. The designer Paul Poiret was also a frequent visitor to Dunand's studio before the First World War, and Bernard Dunand recalls that when he was a small boy Poiret would tell him stories from the Fables of La Fontaine.

Extending his range of experience still further, Dunand created his own designs by applying dilute lacquer to fabrics by means of a pipette or atomizer and using either geometric masks or, quite frequently, eggshell. At this point he turned to a Lyons fabric manufacturer, Ducharre, to market his designs, later persuading the firm of Rodier to handle exclusive rights in certain other designs which were successfully marketed in the United States, where one of the larger New York stores on Fifth Avenue sold blouses and jumpers in 'kasha jersey' for $110 each.

Crêpe de Chine, shantung, Indian silks and silk velvet were decorated with lacquer, painted by hand. Marthe d'Anville, who owned a high-class lingerie shop in Paris, even entrusted Dunand with an order for several exclusive designs for matching sheets and pyjamas in painted silk muslin.

If the 1925 Exposition des Arts Décoratifs had made it possible to measure the extent to which many artists had evolved by then, it also provided an opportunity for Dunand to see that he had contributed in no small way to the new aesthetic rules and essential characteristics of his time, confirming his role in improving the design of everyday objects. In its turn, this extension into the realm of fashion and ornamentation broadened the range of Dunand's creations and added to his international reputation.

In order to create an ideal setting for his lacquer and eggshell portrait of Madame Agnès, Dunand had the idea in 1926 of designing an office interior in her salon in the Rue Saint-Florentin, an office calculated to impress her clients and, indirectly, to ensure that further commissions would come his way. The room was fairly small and narrow, with a large window on the right as one entered. Since the room was very light, Dunand covered all the walls with gold-lacquer panels, not with the usual uniform and smooth finish, but rough-textured and matt, forming kinds of stripped gold plaques on which the rough surface had been rubbed down in places to reveal an underlay of red. A series of intersecting beams in the corners concealed the electric lights which illuminated the coffered ceiling. This indirect system softened and diffused the artificial lights. For the wall opposite the window Dunand had designed a small triangular niche in which stood an armchair, with a small desk placed in front of it. It too had cut-off corners, and both pieces were lacquered light-brown, with an eggshell top. On the wall behind the chair and desk were fitted shelves and panels in different shades of gold, their radiating motifs picked out in eggshell. Dunand's portrait of Madame Agnès was hung on the right-hand wall, above a fitted cabinet in which fashion accessories were on display. A little further in, also on the right, a lacquered wooden couch with a geometric design recalled the shape of the couch in the 1925 smoking room. On the other side of the room was fixed a three-panel cheval-glass. On the back of the uppermost panel a kneeling woman was seen holding a sheep in her arms. Outlined in gold and lacquered in black, it was in splendid contrast with the wood panelling surrounding it. The second panel, which was revealed by folding back the first, was covered with an elegant geometric motif in shades of amber. On the floor was a red and black wool carpet with a Cubist motif, almost certainly woven by Jacques Dandelot to a design by Dunand. The whole of Madame Agnès's salon was transformed on 25 November to inaugurate this lacquered interior.

Dunand also made a small writing desk and shellac screen for Madame Agnès's private apartment, together with bedroom furniture which, although in extremely refined taste, was left undecorated and did not display any great originality in terms of form.

In decorating his fabrics, Dunand proceeded from geometric figures to animal motifs. Thus, Jeanne Lanvin's pink *crêpe de Chine* was adorned with fantastic fish that stood out in grisaille in the midst of countless round blobs of varying sizes. At the same period, another *couturière* known as 'Renée' was selling blouses whose animal motifs were marked by a highly simplified graphic style that recalled prehistoric cave paintings. At Madame Agnès's, dogs, monkeys, and herons were painted on scarves, shawls, and blouses, together with stylized flowers. In abandoning his geometrical compositions, Dunand appeared to want to transfer to fabrics the entire flora and fauna depicted on his screens.

In 1927 he entrusted to Johan Colcombet in the Place Vendôme the task of making a whole range of fabrics whose subdued graphic style and lively colour combinations recalled the designs for the Ballets Russes, their names evoking some modern orientalist fairy-tale. Gaiety and imagination reigned supreme.

Dunand's final incursion into the extravagant world of fashion took place in Paris during the German Occupation in 1940. Wool and silk being in short supply, Madame Agnès experienced great difficulty in her millinery business. However, while confined to bed recovering from a car accident, she received a visit from Dunand and in the course of their conversation she put to him the imaginative idea of supplying her with long, thin wood shavings lacquered in different colours. Amused by the suggestion, Dunand agreed, thus giving birth to a new line in fashion. Alice Cocéa, Mila Parély and Madame van Parys launched the fashion by wearing those curious hats featuring ribbons of lacquered wood. After all, did these marvellous 'bibis' not withstand the rain far better than all the straw hats of Italy and Panama?

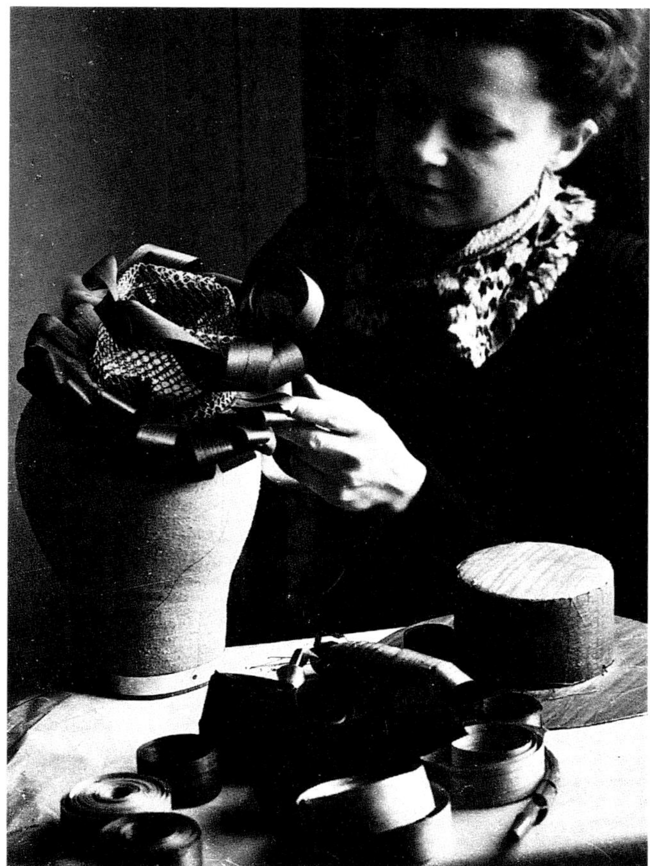

Madame Agnès experimenting with lacquered wood shavings provided by Dunand in 1940, when more luxurious materials for making hats were not obtainable.

Bernard Dunand and his works

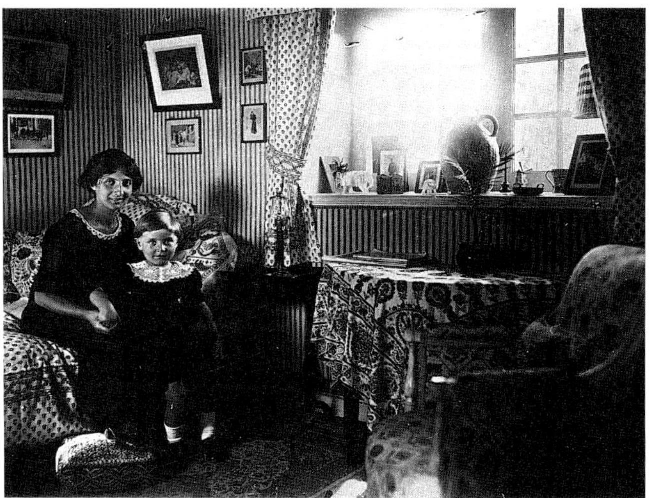

The young Bernard Dunand with his mother at the family home in the Rue d'Alésia, Paris, *c.* 1912.

THE ELDEST of Jean Dunand's sons, Bernard, was born in Paris on 13 June 1908 on the first floor of the building in the Rue Hallé, where his parents lived above the studio. Here the family remained until 1910 when they moved to 48 Rue d'Alésia, a short distance away from the Rue Hallé, thus allowing Jean Dunand to take over the space vacated and to enlarge and develop his workshops.

On his way home from school, the young Bernard Dunand would call in to see his father at work and familiarize himself with the techniques of metalwork. Forge and furnace, anvils and hammers became part of his everyday world. A photograph published in *Miroir* on 12 April 1914 shows the five-year old Bernard watching his father with evident admiration. Only at the age of sixteen, however, did he really begin to work for his father. In the meantime he pursued his studies, completing his fourth year of secondary education at the Ecole Alsacienne before his father finally decided to take him on full-time in 1924, when the preparations were in hand for the major international exhibition of 1925, the Exposition Internationale des Arts Décoratifs et Industriels Modernes. His father instructed him in the techniques of metalwork and lacquering. Bernard recalls, 'Schmied used to say that studying was useless. Examination certificates awarded at the end of your school career didn't exist at that time, and after completing the academic year 1923/24, I remained with my father until war broke out in 1939.'

Jean Dunand's principal assistant Kéco passed on all the subtleties of his art which he himself had learned from the master. Another newspaper article, published after the war, shows Bernard Dunand wearing a metalworker's leather apron, looking very much at ease in front of the family workbench. In fact, he was working at this time with the other craftsmen on simple but exacting tasks for his father. His mother kept numerous examples of Bernard's work from his earliest period. Even today, in the same family tradition Pierre Dunand's grandchildren try their hand at dinanderie from an early age. Whether as a form of amusement, as the preservation of a family tradition, or as a simple test designed to kindle vocational skills, it is something that each of the children have practised at some time or another. Bernard recalls his own youthful experiences thus: 'In fact I trained by watching others at work and asking them for explanations as I went along. I did not take a design course. At one time there was a question of my registering for an evening class given by Eric Bagge at the Ecole des Arts Appliqués, but I already had too much work on, and I very soon had to take over running the workshops and ensuring that my father's artistic wishes were carried out. In other words, I had virtually no free time. In fact, I became a kind of stage manager. To avoid having to run all round the building from one workshop to the next, my father had devised a system of four different bells, so that I could tell from the individual ringing sounds who it was who was calling me.'

In July 1933, Bernard Dunand set off with his godfather François-Louis Schmied on a cruise to the Dutch Antilles and Surinam (Dutch Guiana). Ostensibly accompanying Schmied as secretary because he spoke English, it was in fact a pretext for a free trip for Bernard, at the expense of the Dutch Transatlantic Company, who wanted Schmied to produce suitable pictorial material for their publicity campaign.

Greatly inspired by everything he saw, Bernard Dunand brought back numerous photographs and sketches on which he had carefully noted down, on Schmied's advice, all the effects of colour and composition which he had particularly admired. 'Schmied did not paint any more than I did,' Bernard Dunand recalls, somewhat mischievously, 'but he took an enormous number of photographs. We each photographed separately what interested us most.'

Back in Paris, Bernard Dunand decided to turn the impressions resulting from his journey into lacquered designs. His style was already a very personal one. His graphic style had nothing in common with that developed in his father's studio. Interested in techniques and colour combinations, he

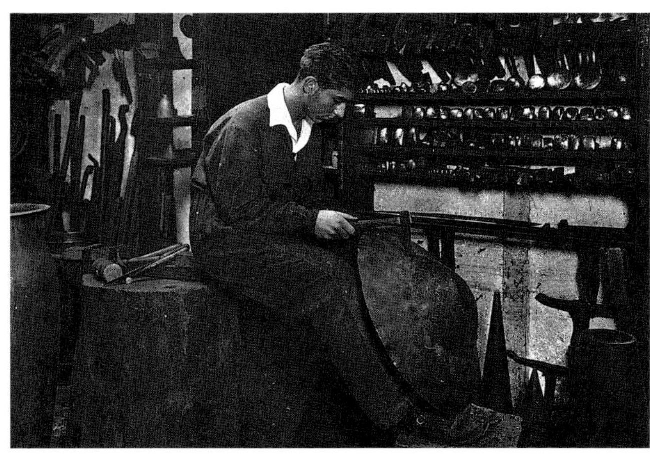

Bernard Dunand at work on a large dish, 1922.

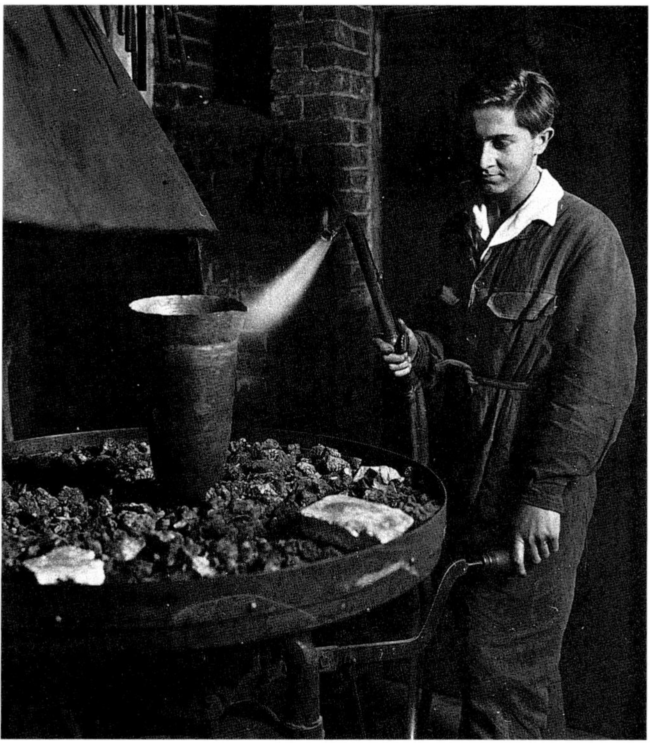

Bernard Dunand heating a metal vase to restore its malleability, *c.* 1924.

sought, unlike his father, to create additional effects by combining lacquers of different colours, overlapping the layers while they were still wet, so that they blended with each other along their edges. Certainly, Bernard Dunand was working in a somewhat experimental fashion, never being really sure what the result would be.

In fact, his altogether spectacular results were calculated to appeal to the eye of a painter rather than to convince a traditional lacquer artist. A large bread-fruit tree whose russet leaves merge with the reddish-brown tones of the landscape is highly characteristic of the colourful effects of this style, which is at once figurative and sensual. He designed his own panels, like a true lacquer artist, but left the craftsmen of Indo-Chinese origin in his father's studio to tackle the preparation of undercoats and supports.

Having completed ten or more panels, he decided to look for a place to show them. The Galerie Charpentier (as successor to the Galerie Georges Petit), which had welcomed Jean Dunand and his group of fellow artists in 1933, now provided Bernard Dunand with a forum. His first private exhibition took place in 1935 and comprised some dozen panels. Georges Huysmans, director of the Société Nationale des Beaux-Arts and Bernard Dunand's former teacher at the Ecole Alsacienne, reported on the event, noting in an article that 'everything here reveals a tolerant and gifted creator, an artist as sure of his technique as he is of his sensibility.' A number of his works were bought by friends and clients of his father, but in spite of their very real qualities, snob-value and a familiar name could not succeed in turning this exhibition into a real artistic event. Any artist who chooses to work in the same field of creative endeavour as his father is inevitably treading on dangerous ground. Even if Bernard Dunand felt reassured by the outcome of his first one-man show, however, he was resolved to continue working with his father. Of course, he did not abandon his own creative ideas, but he did not really want to strike out on his own as an independent artist. His earliest examples of applied art, including vases, tables and panels, appear more as personal variants on the level of form, decoration and colour, variations on the theme of the workshop's traditional products, complementing rather than competing with them.

In fact, Bernard Dunand's greatest pleasure lay in the co-ordination of the different workshops in the Rue Hallé. His sense of organization, his strict discipline and his technical competence found plenty of scope for fulfilment here. By establishing timetables and lists of priorities, he was effectively running his father's collective enterprise, providing tools and necessary materials for one person or going out to obtain supplies for another. He scarcely had time to think of his own endeavours, and devoted himself to his father's creative output right up to the outbreak of the Second World War. Even so, he exhibited regularly at the Société Nationale des Beaux-Arts, the Salon des Artistes Décorateurs and the Salon d'Automne.

For major works such as the liner *L'Atlantique* in 1931 or the *Normandie* in 1934/5, it was he who maintained contact with the various architects, contractors and professional bodies associated with the undertakings. In each case he provided written confirmation of all the arrangements and modifications made to the initial project both by the architect and by Jean Dunand himself. He was in overall charge and saw to it that the studio kept within the time limits for completion imposed by the contract. He also went to Saint-Nazaire to check the progress of work on *L'Atlantique* and to prepare the hanging of the monumental bas-reliefs in the smoking room and first-class saloon, not forgetting the famous columns. Transporting them from workshop to shipyard was an experience in itself, for each had to be handled with great care.

'Between 1920 and 1930 I took an interest in lacquer and in the problems of transparency associated with coloured lacquers, which led me to make experiments in that direction. The necessary pigments were imported from Japan, and I tried to obtain a wider range of colours. I even did some research with a chemist from the Institut Pasteur in an attempt to find a substance which I could rely on in terms of its drying time and colour, since numerous basic pigments, including titanium white, were "spat out" by the lacquer after a period of time.'

In 1931, in the course of the various exhibitions devoted to art and folklore which accompanied the opening of the Exposition Coloniale, Bernard Dunand first met his future wife. Enjoying himself in the company of one of his former school friends from the Ecole Alsacienne at a kind of East Indian dance, he noticed a very attractive young woman whom he finally asked to dance with him. Some time later they decided to live together, and in 1938 they were married. They had two children, Jean-Paul and Huguette.

Passionately interested in techniques and experimentation, Bernard Dunand finally succeeded in perfecting new combinations of coloured transparent lacquer. He exchanged the fruits of his researches, comparing them with those of Japanese lacquer artists with whom he was in correspondence. On one occasion, however, he was the victim of a hoax on the part of a Japanese supplier who claimed to be offering him some new shades of lacquer, whereas they were simply made with a base of chemical products incompatible with the oxidizing process involved when natural lacquer dries.

Bernard Dunand was assisted by the trusty Kéco in making metal vases with an extreme purity of form representing fantastic and exotic fruits, the unusual shapes of which were

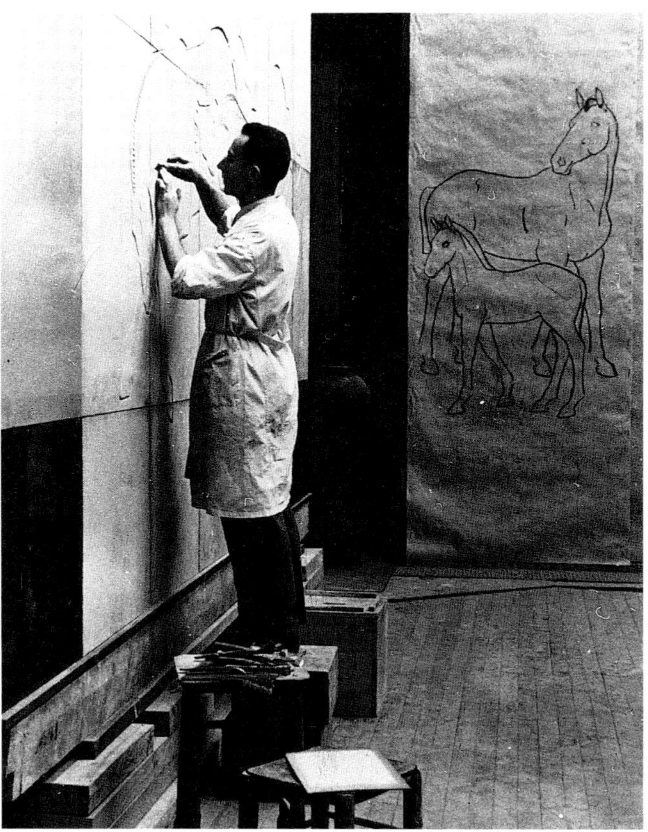

Applying the finishing touches to the bas-relief *Horses*, destined for the Jockey Club of São Paulo, 1952/53.

achieved by clever hammering. The colours and patina were more violent than those of pieces made by Jean Dunand. They seem less traditional, and somehow more modern. Parallel to this development, he asked the Indo-Chinese craftsmen in the workshop to lacquer furniture which he had designed himself and which had been built by his father's cabinet-maker. The resulting works, though few in number, demonstrated a distinctive personal style and remain an interesting testament to his efforts. A red-lacquer console table of great formal purity, forming part of a larger group, creates an impression of extraordinary lightness thanks to a reinforced moulding cut diagonally into the surface, its position and rounded edges making the supports appear non-existent.

Bernard Dunand first exhibited his work in public under his own name at the 1937 Exposition Internationale des Arts et Techniques in Paris. His highly personal pieces earned him a Grand Prix at the exhibition. The French State bought his earliest works, which are now on display at the Mobilier National and the Musée National d'Art Moderne.

This was also the first occasion since they had begun working together that Jean Dunand listed the names of his sons Bernard and Pierre alongside his own, thus confirming their collaborative effort. The Music Room which Ruhlmann's nephew, Porteneuve, presented in this international setting appears therefore to have been designed collectively by Jean, Bernard and Pierre Dunand. It was displayed in the pavilion of the Société des Artistes Décorateurs and enjoyed a modest success, although Porteneuve's furniture designs were far removed from Ruhlmann's *grand style*.

From October 1937 to December 1938 Bernard Dunand was absent from Paris as official representative to the French government in Indo-China, his brief being to establish whether it was possible to exploit commercially the lacquer produced there. The visit also gave him an opportunity to write a report on traditional local arts and crafts.

Only months after his return to Paris in January 1939, Bernard and two of his brothers were called up for military service. Serving in the army, Bernard was taken prisoner in 1940 and spent the rest of the war years in a camp designated Oflag XB at Nienburg an der Weser, south-east of Bremen. The news of the death of his brother Jean-Louis came as a profound shock, and his sense of loss was further compounded by the death of his father, with whom Bernard had exchanged letters on a regular basis during his captivity.

All in all, his enforced absence was a period of profound self-questioning involving a rediscovery of religious beliefs and a reappraisal of his attitude to the use of lacquer in decoration. Bernard put together a series of lectures about his father's achievements as a means of keeping himself usefully occupied while a prisoner. The results reveal a kind of work ethic in which, notwithstanding his specific interest in his father's work, it is possible to detect conclusions slightly different from those he had been advancing for the previous fifteen years. Of all the qualities characteristic of lacquer, the one that presented a real difficulty was not colour but transparency. He now began to regret his earlier experiment in handling lacquer in a painterly manner and he promised himself that he would work in a different way in future. The teachings of his father and of the master-craftsmen of Japan and China had finally impressed upon him the error of his ways. Thanks to this period of self-enquiry, he abandoned his desire to experiment and gave up innovations in favour of a more considered form of expression. In 1949 he published the results of his reflections under the title 'L'Esthétique du Laque' ('The Aesthetics of Lacquerwork'), numbers 3 and 4 in the series *Les Études philosophiques*.

On returning to Paris, he had difficulty, like so many others after the war, in 'getting back into harness'. A year's sabbatical leave from the family studio allowed him to take stock of his situation and to re-establish a relationship with God in his everyday life. Thus it was that he became a Baptist. The great demands which he made of himself led him towards a militant evangelical outlook. He resumed his artistic activities and between 1951 and 1953 made numerous study trips to Italy, Greece and Egypt.

In the course of these years he organized exhibitions of his works in France – in Paris, at the Galerie Guérin in the Rue de la Paix (1947), and in the provinces – as well as abroad, where his works were shown in Abijan (Ivory Coast), Cairo (1951 and 1953), the Dutch East Indies (1954), Brussels (1949), Boston, Mass. (1952), and at the Wildenstein Gallery in New York (1956).

Pierre and Bernard found it difficult to keep the studio going, but refused to accept that the results of their efforts should not allow them to lead normal lives. They went their separate ways, Pierre setting up in business in Montlhéry (south of Paris), having first sold his share of the business, while Bernard retained his part of the workshop and continued to work there. He was appointed to serve on the committee of the Société des Artistes Décorateurs at a time when Jean-Jacques Adnet was its president. Fellow artists such as André Leleu, Jean Royère and Eugène Printz invited him to make various objects for them, including small pieces of lacquered furniture. However, these commissioned works had to be produced quickly and at competitive prices, with the result that instead of using only natural lacquer, he had to work with glycerophthalic lacquers and, later, with polyurethane lacquers, which yielded more spectacular results and were less expensive. Their colours, moreover, were more suited to his experiments.

However, the turnover was scarcely sufficient to feed his family and pay his staff's wages. Accordingly, he set about manufacturing products of a more 'commercial' nature. They were signed 'André Dambrun', an anagram approximating to the letters of his name. These anecdotal panels were presented at the Foire de Paris and the Arts Ménagers by his wife or by his faithful secretary Mademoiselle Alice, both of whom were successful in selling them. As one might expect, these panels depicted flowers and birds in the Chinese style, but there were also various fruits and landscapes with no original features. Alongside this new development, he continued to produce works in a more personal style.

Bernard Dunand continued to receive important commissions similar to those he had received before the war; these included work on the apartment of a Belgian cigarette maker and on that of the textile tycoon Bouchara. With the help of his father's machines and a single cabinet-maker, and in spite of various difficulties, he succeeded in coping easily with the demands of the market.

Taking advantage of his father's reputation and of earlier prestigious orders, Bernard Dunand obtained a number of commissions for public buildings in France and abroad. His most spectacular and important design was for the Jockey Club of São Paulo, conceived in collaboration with the architect Sajous and executed in 1952–3. Once again, he adopted the principle of bas-reliefs in gold lacquer, and, at the specific request of the commissioning body, treated the same theme as had been used for 'Taming the Horse' in the smoking room of the *Normandie*.

No less important, however, were the panels executed for the Chamber of Commerce in Le Havre or those for the board room of the Société Ciba in Paris in 1956. Mention should also be made of panels made for the Société des Laboratoires Sandoz in 1951 and for the Banque de Madagascar in Paris in 1964. In 1966, in collaboration with Max Ingrand, he decorated the great hall of the Société Saint-Gobain in Neuilly, having had a hand in designing the Total oil company's board room, also in Neuilly, the previous year.

Together with Jean Royère, he also undertook work in the Middle East, first in Tehran, where he helped in designing the assembly rooms of the Minister of the Armed Forces commissioned by the Shah in 1962, and then in Beirut, where in 1963 he designed the principal dining room of the Hotel Bristol. The following year he worked on the private residence of King Ibn Saud of Saudi Arabia, and again in Beirut. In 1958, at the invitation of Gaston Louis Vuitton, he had designed a large triptych for the International Society for the Protection of Literary and Artistic Works in Berne, Switzerland; and in 1970 he was involved in the decoration of the newly built palace of President Félix Houphouët-Boigny of the Ivory Coast in Abijan.

Elsewhere, he relived earlier experiences, collaborating in the decoration of the first-class saloon of the liner *Ancerville* (1964) and the first-class cocktail bar on the liner *France* (1965).

Although executed with the help of Jean Dunand's former assistants, who were re-engaged on a part-time basis to work in their old studio in the Rue Hallé, all these works bore Bernard Dunand's signature alone and reflect his own personal style. Comparisons with his father's work are no longer of any relevance here.

In 1952 the journal *Études d'outre-mer* published a special number on the art of lacquerwork. Bernard Dunand contributed a long article, based on past experience and on his professional reflections. The decorative designs, furniture, objets d'art and screens reproduced all bear his distinctive stamp, attesting not only to a highly personal style but also to great technical and aesthetic skill.

Profoundly religious, his works have evolved towards a certain mystical interpretation and are conceived as poems to the greater glory of God. The titles, moreover, are largely evocative of this new outlook and make a total break with his father's tradition.

After having shared with his brothers and sisters the assets derived from the extensive properties patiently built up over the years and inherited from their father, and having distributed among themselves the works still stored in the family studio, Bernard set up in business on his own in Saint-Maur-des-Fossés (near Paris). Here he rebuilt a studio, together with a fairly large drying room and outhouses. Although not as extensive as the Rue Hallé studios, these new premises still permitted him to create a number of larger pieces. He now works almost exclusively with polyurethane lacquers. His work has become much more colourful, new technical developments giving scope for his religious and imaginative creations. Unfortunately, changing tastes and a gradual decline in large-scale commissions have meant that such compositions are now very few in number. In order to remain true to his religious ideals, he has taken to painting more and more small-scale works, all of them with religious themes, though their lyrical abstractionism is not always easy to grasp.

The renewed interest shown by a new generation of collectors and dealers not only in the Art Deco period, in general, but especially in the works of Jean Dunand, is a source of great joy to Bernard Dunand. Not to be left out this revival, he has resumed working in this vein and has made several commissioned pieces manifestly inspired by the art of the period 1925–30. A four-panel screen in which a young woman seems to disappear or to be reflected between its brightly coloured panels is fairly typical of this latest style. Contrary to what some may have feared, such a work is by no means a mere plagiarizing of earlier formulas which may have proved their value in years past; quite the opposite, this return to a past aesthetic is lived and felt by Bernard Dunand as an expression of homage to his father's reputation.

In October 1984, a retrospective exhibition of Bernard Dunand's work was held in the Galerie Hargeline in Paris. For the artist, then aged 77, it was an opportunity to observe and savour the way in which his work, both past and present, sacred and secular, had become the object of sincere admiration on the part of younger generations.

After having been a member of the proficiency panel of the Ecole des Arts Appliqués in Paris, and having served as a committee member of the Société des Artistes Décorateurs (for whom he twice served as Secretary), he has now become a member of the Société des Artistes Français d'Outre-Mer, in addition to enjoying membership of the Société Nationale des Beaux-Arts and the Société du Salon d'Automne. Bernard Dunand is a Chevalier de la Légion d'Honneur, Chevalier de l'Ordre des Arts et Lettres, as well as being a holder of the Croix de Guerre and an officer of the Ordre National du Mérite. In his desire to pay his father a final lasting tribute, he has encouraged the publication of this work devoted to the work of Jean Dunand. To this end, he allowed the present writer free access to the family archives and answered countless questions in two series of extended interviews.

Pierre Dunand and his works

THE SECOND of Jean Dunand's sons, Pierre, was born on 31 May 1914 in his parents' apartment in the Rue d'Alésia; he was their third child. Although he found it extremely difficult 'to be his father's son', more especially because his elder brother had already followed in his father's footsteps, Pierre Dunand very soon became involved in the family's workshop activities.

The workshop reserved for dinanderie fascinated him the most, with its forge and anvils, its sounds and smells. Whenever Pierre went there, Kéco made him feel at home, gradually introducing him to the rudiments of metalwork techniques. His academic studies suffered in consequence and, having failed to gain satisfactory results, he finally devoted himself exclusively to the family workshop. Kéco had grown attached to Pierre, whose decision to leave school at seventeen came as a relief to his family, especially because the young man had just suffered a long bout of pleurisy followed by three months' convalescence, which had meant a complete break from his studies.

This development coincided with work on the liner *Normandie*, which was in full swing, and consequently the workshop was expanding in every direction. The number of craftsmen employed on the premises even passed the hundred mark. Although, strictly speaking, Pierre ws not involved in work for the *Normandie* in the way that his brother Bernard was, he nonetheless bustled about between the various workshops. Because he had no particular artistic training, his principal task was to oversee the making of frames needed for moulding the panels. Varying in size, each series of panels had to be made in its entirety before it could be mounted and sculpted. Many spare panels were made in order to allow for every contingency. It was an onerous task for a young man, particularly, as he himself recalls, since 'Bernard was never there in the morning, and only rarely in the afternoon.' Thanks to the excellent co-ordination that existed among all the members of Dunand's workshops, however, the commission was completed in the required time.

For Pierre Dunand there was no question of private researches, nor of exhibiting work under his own name, for only his father's work counted; this alone was what had to be executed with undivided attention. Later, following completion of his military service, his specific joy was to calculate the cost of each of the techniques practised in the various workshops. For example, he recalls that the price of a portrait was fixed at around 80,000 francs, while the cost per square metre of working in eggshell – a very long and very delicate operation – was set at around 10,000 francs.

Having been more closely involved in the projected designs for Porteneuve's Music Room at the 1937 Exposition Internationale des Arts et Techniques, Pierre was credited, together with his elder brother, when Jean Dunand named them both as joint contributors; all three were mentioned in the exhibition catalogue. At the same time he was continuing to produce panels in the Rue Hallé workshop, overseeing their manufacture and decoration. Strictly speaking, his father did not supervise these formative tasks; rather it was the craftsmen with responsibility for each of the workshops who, on a day-to-day basis, helped in his training. Kéco of course took charge of his dinanderie lessons, but there was also Pascal, a highly skilled craftsman who helped him to acquire not only a knowledge of electricity, when the workshops were being enlarged, but also of plumbing, carpentry and methods of planning. This interdisciplinary training provides the explanation of how, long after the war, Pierre Dunand felt able to set up and run a company to build caravans.

When war broke out in 1939, he was called up to serve in the Navy at Cherbourg, before being transferred to the Navy Ministry in Paris. Assigned to the chauffeuring service, he was free during the mornings and could join his father in the family workshop while Bernard and Jean-Louis were away on active duty. Robert, the youngest of the six children, left Paris to work, under an assumed name, on his future father-in-law's oyster beds at Marennes (Charente Maritime), on the west coast.

Jean Dunand had meanwhile resumed production of visors for manganese steel helmets cold-stamped out of a single sheet of metal, and for this process Pierre Dunand made the necessary tools, including the dies, which were produced in the workshops of the wrought-iron craftsman Raymond Subes. Pierre Dunand was also given responsibility for designing the prototype of a new mess-tin for soldiers serving in the French Army. In fact, the model used by American soldiers was proposed to the general staff and accepted, but an extra compartment was added to the French version for the traditional soup (not part of standard U.S. Army rations). Once again, Jean Dunand received no response from the military authorities, his visor being no more acceptable to the army, it seemed, than his mess-tin.

During this period, following the Paris exodus of May and June 1940 and the ensuing demobilization, Pierre Dunand helped his father with a huge panel, decorated with elephants, for a private bank in the Avenue de Messine. Pierre Dunand was married on 9 September 1940 and Jean Dunand was able to share in the family's joy when on 13 January 1942, Pierre's daughter Danielle was born. This happy event preceded by only a few months Jean Dunand's death, following a short illness, on 7 June.

After a period of indecision, Pierre Dunand resumed his former work. Interior designers who had been friendly with his father passed on orders for a number of pieces. Helped by his father's former assistants, Nguyen Hop, Charigny and Pascal (Kéco having left for a time to work elsewhere), he continued to produce works identical in style to those made by Jean Dunand. There were now only five craftsmen employed by the studio, three of whom were from Indo-China. Jules Leleu came to the workshop to order designs similar to those he had always used: deer, panthers, tropical forests and so on. Pierre Dunand modelled them on his father's sketches, altering them only a little. Leleu, whose clientèle had radically changed during the German Occupation, provided the wooden frames for the screens, folding doors and panels which Pierre Dunand was content simply to lacquer and to decorate; the result was no less striking, however. The lacquering technique, after all, was exactly the same as had been followed during Jean

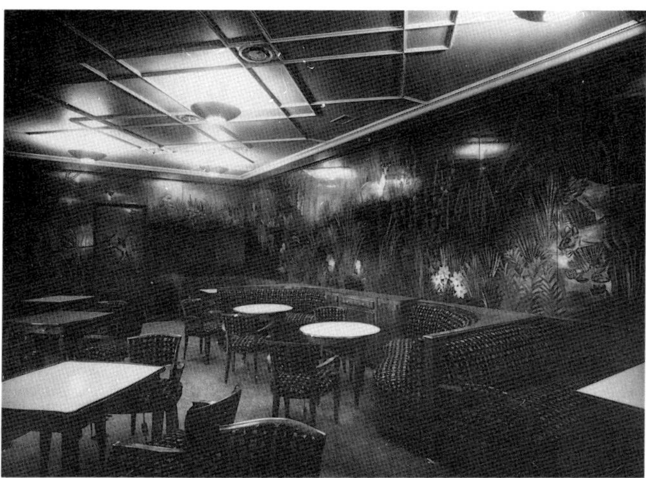

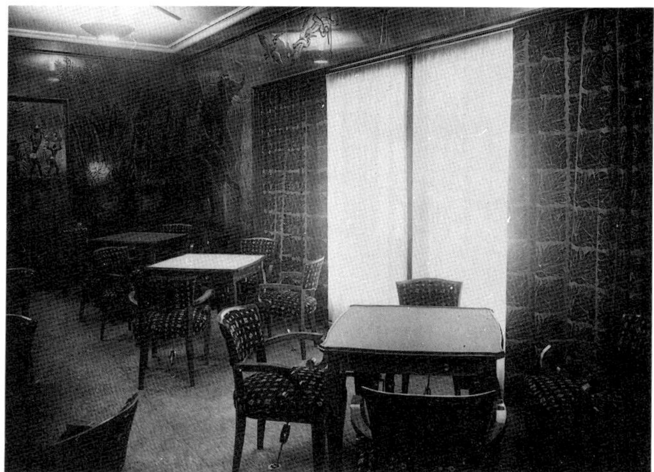

Views of the first-class bridge saloon on the liner *La Marseillaise*, 1949, showing parts of the large-scale mural decoration by Pierre Dunand.

Dunand's lifetime, although Pierre, anxious to achieve a more individual expression, developed a new technique for lacquering his own particular designs. Elsewhere, Eugène Printz had resumed production of top-of-the-range furniture using the wood that he had in stock, and he too passed on orders for dinanderie panels to decorate his doors and so on. Printz also commissioned him to lacquer a number of tables and chests which he himself had designed and which Pierre decorated in uniform shellac or black lacquer.

Throughout the entire Occupation a large-scale plan of Paris on which Jean-Louis had been working before being called up remained in the workshop as testimony to his collaboration on his father's works. It measured 8 m across and 4 m in height (26 x 13 ft). Of all Jean Dunand's sons, Jean-Louis was without doubt the most gifted and brilliant. He had studied architecture, and his father had great hopes of him. But fate willed that neither he nor his father would ucceed in this new venture, for all its exceptional promise.

None of this new work was particularly creative; indeed it was virtually impossible to undertake innovatory work, given the demands of the sons' new clients who wanted works in their father's style. In any case, the family had somehow to make ends meet, especially since Pierre Dunand had to provide for his mother, his wife and his baby daughter.

Like his father, Pierre Dunand did not do any basic lacquering himself, entrusting it instead to the craftsmen whom he employed and who were responsible for preparing the wood, covering it with linen and applying the initial coats of lacquer. He would then apply the final coat, incorporating his chosen design in the fresh lacquer, using his own unique method.

During the German Occupation, there was a shortage of leather, and just as his father had supplied lacquered wood shavings for use in making hats in 1941, so Pierre Dunand began producing shoes made entirely of lacquered wood. He registered a certain number of models, and even took out a patent dated 22 December 1944. Ingenious and bold in shape, these shoes were made in the carpentry workshop in the Rue Hallé with the help of Charigny. Unfortunately, these models, for all the traditional skill that went into making them, were never properly marketed.

Even before Jean Dunand's death in 1942, a project had already been taken in hand for work on a new ocean liner. The vessel, designed by Gaston Falcoz, was to be called the *Maréchal Petain*, and it was planned to include lacquerwork designs in its decor. Because of current economic difficulties, the project was delayed several times, and the liner was finally launched in 1949, but with a different and politically more acceptable name – *La Marseillaise.*

Harking back to his father's earliest plan for a panel based on jungle themes, Pierre Dunand carried out a large-scale scheme in red natural lacquer highlighted in gold. The scenes filled three of the four walls in the first-class bridge saloon. Arranged in a continuous frieze above the wall seats, it allowed for access at each end through two doorways.

For the smoking room, Pierre Bobot, another lacquer artist whose work had gained approval at the 1937 Exhibition, had designed three large panels in synthetic lacquer, showing aerial views of La Ciotat, where the liner was built, Marseilles, the vessel's home port, and the Bay of Along in the Gulf of Tonkin, one of the areas of south-east Asia where the liner was expected to call. The large saloon communicated on one side with the bridge saloon and on the other with a small writing room.

Pierre Dunand's frieze, 9 m (29 ft) in length, comprised a series of animals at a watering hole in some tropical forest, buffalo standing knee-deep in the water, black hunters and porters carrying an antelope and skirting the water's edge, while elsewhere nervous deer moved warily towards the watering place.

Two years later, in 1951, Jules Leleu, who had been commissioned to undertake the interior design of the liner *Maréchal Joffre*, invited Pierre Dunand to design a large panel for this latest ocean-going vessel built for the Compagnie des Messageries Maritimes. One of the elements, lacking in any great originality, depicted the village of Rivesaltes, Joffre's birthplace near Perpignan, in the *département* of Pyrénées Orientales, while a second scene, made up of five sections, took bullfighting as its theme; it was the work of Bernard Dunand. The overall impression was attractive and harmonious, although these new works could not compare with Jean Dunand's pre-war decorative schemes.

The large partition wall, originally designed by Jean Dunand to separate the first-class saloon and the smoking room on the *Normandie* (see p. 144), was modified in 1950 to fit the *Liberté*'s saloon. Instead of two sets of double doors, a single central opening was planned for the *Liberté*. Pierre Dunand had to go back to his father's earliest sketches and replace the two double doors with two decorative panels, extending and completing the vegetation that surrounded the figures of an archer on the left and, on the right, a hunter returning home with a deer draped over his shoulders. The insertion of a large door-opening in the centre of the composition obliged Pierre Dunand to eliminate the four panels depicting a marabou stork and a fox. At the same time, the bottom of the panel had to be modified to allow for the reduction in height to fit the smaller dimensions of the *Liberté* and to restore a proper sense of proportion. The decoration was slightly altered, only plant motifs being re-used, by omitting the dogs present in the original panels.

The 'Grape Harvesting' panel was also rehung on the *Liberté*, but reduced to about half its original height, only a waggon laden with a large basket filled with grapes and drawn by two oxen, together with two human figures, being retained. To achieve this simplification, Pierre Dunand had to modify the composition of the panel, redesigning the whole of its lower section, removing one of the dancers and the arms of others which extended into the upper half of the original design. Similarly, the two panels entitled 'Sports' and 'Fishing', both of which had had small openings cut into them to give access for service personnel on board the *Normandie*, were recut and joined together to produce two complete decorative ensembles (with no openings), each having a single overall theme. Meanwhile, 'The Chariot of Aurora' from the first-class saloon, originally executed by Jean Dunand to a design by Jean Dupas, had been adapted in such a way that the areas corresponding to the two double doors were now filled in, and the overall height was reduced to enable it to be rehung on the liner *Île de France* in 1949.

In an attempt to keep the workshops ticking over, Pierre Dunand made a whole series of vases, modern, not to say abstract in form. They were exhibited in 1952 at the Compagnie des Arts Français, a company run by Jean-Jacques Adnet. Extremely varied in line and made up of sections of beaten and welded metal, they were all lacquered black and red. Kéco had assembled and welded each item, giving concrete expression to Pierre Dunand's designs. The exhibition, unfortunately, had only a limited success.

In its Christmas edition, the journal *Arts industriels* reported on the exhibition, but with no great enthusiasm. Under the heading 'A Vase for Every Flower', the writer sought to ridicule this attempt to produce pure forms, whereas what he had witnessed were the most accomplished results of the application of rules of abstract art and functional form to metallic vases. The similarity between Pierre Dunand's researches and those of the sculptors Hans Arp and Alexandre Noll at this time is plain to see, and even if certain anthropomorphic forms are no more than approximate, nothing about these vases ought to have elicited a smile, for – quite apart from their undeniable sculptural qualities – they represented a final effort on the part of a talented son to renew the image of wares associated with the name of Jean Dunand. This failure to arouse public interest persuaded Pierre Dunand to give up production little by little, although he continued to fulfil a handful of orders for screens.

Having taken the bold decision to make a fresh start, he sold his share in the family workshop and set up in business in Montlhéry to the south of Paris in 1958, building caravans, his own caravan converted for personal use having proved a success. There was in any case during these post-war years a general movement away from domestic luxury and sophistication towards more practical home-making.

Having sought to continue his father's work without daring to change it, Pierre Dunand had come to be regarded as an imitative artist, although in practice he was seeking only to extend a type of artistic expression and style more suited to the pre-war period, while at the same time responding to clients' demands. When he tried to say something new, without making any concessions, by creating bold and extraordinarily modern works, Pierre Dunand found no imitators.

He might have felt bitterness and regret at this turn of events, but, thanks to his love for his father's oeuvre and thanks also to the support of his wife, he retained for himself, as did his other brothers and sisters, these treasures of modern French art. Happily, many screens and panels bear his name and attest to his true personality. Although not the most famous of Jean Dunand's sons, Pierre was the most faithful to his creative style.

CATALOGUE OF WORKS

Author's note

This extensive catalogue of works represents the first attempt to provide a detailed listing of the oeuvre of Jean Dunand in all its varied aspects. While making no claim to being complete, the catalogue does include representative examples of every aspect of Dunand's prolific output, as detailed in the classified list opposite. If it were possible to calculate the number of works produced over the years in Dunand's workshops, the total would have to be reckoned in thousands. Apart from the fact that a realistic limit had to be placed on the number of illustrations to be included in this book, any attempt at a full documentation of so many diverse objects would be doomed to failure because the present whereabouts of numerous works are unknown; indeed, in many instances the present catalogue – the fruits of six years' research – makes use of photographs dating from the time when individual objects were made or first exhibited.

Despite the inevitable gaps, however, some sections can be considered virtually complete. Thus, the decorative screens listed reflect the full range of Dunand's output apart from any possible variants or replicas of original designs. Similarly some preparatory studies for portraits, as well as a few finished works in lacquer not documented or known to me may be absent. The limited output of mosaics as listed is, as far as I have been able to determine from available source material, fully documented. The listing of Dunand's earliest works, the sculptures, is for practical purposes complete, the only possible exceptions being some youthful works from his student days in Geneva which may have been destroyed.

By contrast, the listings of lacquer panels in whatever size or depicting whatever subject cannot be considered exhaustive. These works are now widely dispersed, but the examples included here give a good idea of the range of subject matter in all its variety. The majority of the small lacquered plates for bookbindings, notably those designed by Dunand's friend François-Louis Schmied, are included. The furniture sections can reasonably claim to include at least one representative example of every type or style made by Dunand. Some variants with lacquer decoration in different colours are absent, as also are certain pieces originally commissioned by private clients. In the field of smaller household objects – boxes, caskets, dishes etc., as well as jewellery, fashion accessories and objects of vertu – the range is so vast that inevitably only a representative selection could be included.

In the related areas of fashions, fabrics and other textiles, only the designs emanated from Dunand's workshops, all such items being produced elsewhere; the token examples cited here serve to show the multiple possibilities offered by Dunand's creative ideas and designs. The artist's fertile mind is evident especially in his extensive range of sample shapes and patterns for decoration on metal vases (for a selection see pp. 167–9). It is more than likely that, allowing for the repetition of designs shown in the dinanderie sections, the workshops must have produced several thousand pieces. Those listed are therefore included on the grounds of historical or technical interest, including examples originally chosen to illustrate articles or other publications of particular interest dating from the time of the production of such objects or of their being brought to public notice in, for example, reviews of exhibitions. Interior decorative schemes are dealt with in as complete a manner as circumstances permit, since certain of these remain in private households and the present owners were not willing in every case to allow detailed inspection. A few striking examples therefore had to be omitted.

Dunand's participation in public exhibitions of various kinds – one-man shows, group exhibitions and major national salons, as well as his contributions to special displays at international exhibitions – is well documented throughout his career.

Finally, as an adjunct to the main catalogue listing the wide-ranging oeuvre of Jean Dunand, a selection of works by his sons and collaborators Bernard and Pierre (both of whom went on to develop their own individual styles after their father's death) is included. Though not fully representative of their output, the works listed give some idea of the considerable importance of their individual creative talents.

Each catalogue entry includes basic information, including a brief description of medium and dimensions where known (height before width unless otherwise stated). In addition, listings of major exhibitions (especially the first occasion on which a piece was shown and which provides a firm basis for dating), bibliographical citations, provenance and sales are given, together with cross-references to related entries and an explanatory note wherever appropriate. Black-and-white illustrations appear on the same page as the relevant catalogue entries or on the facing page; references to colour plates appear in the first line of individual entries.

FÉLIX MARCILHAC

Works by Jean Dunand

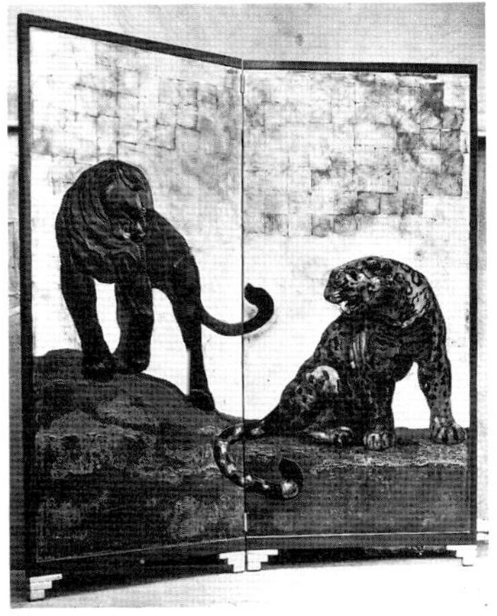
1

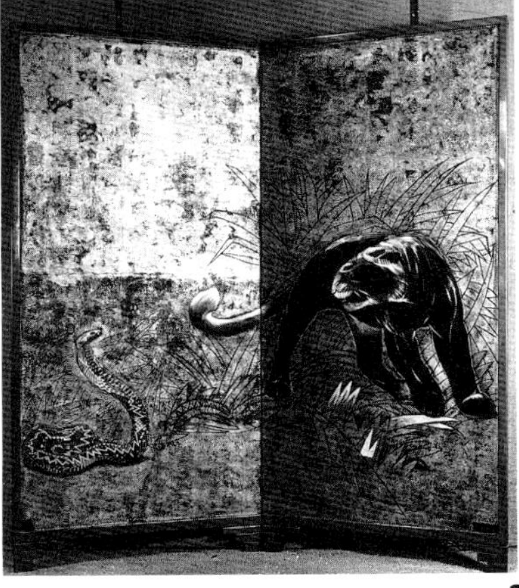
2

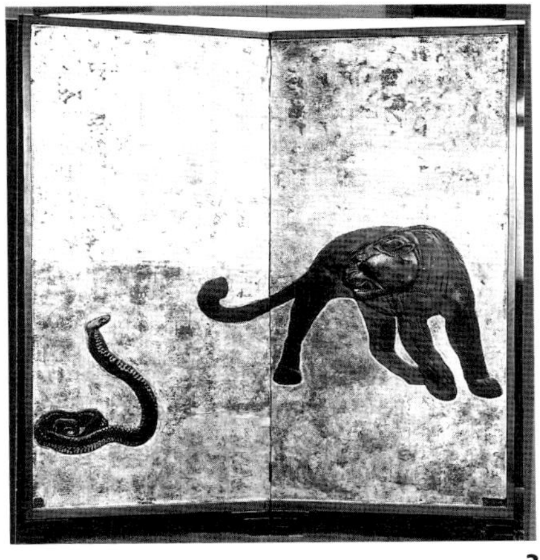
3

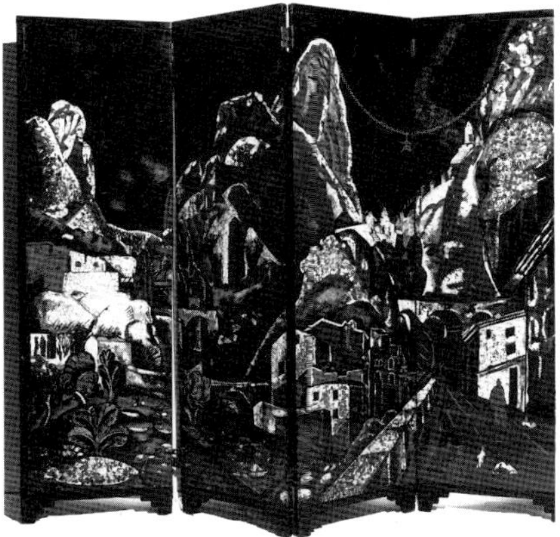
4

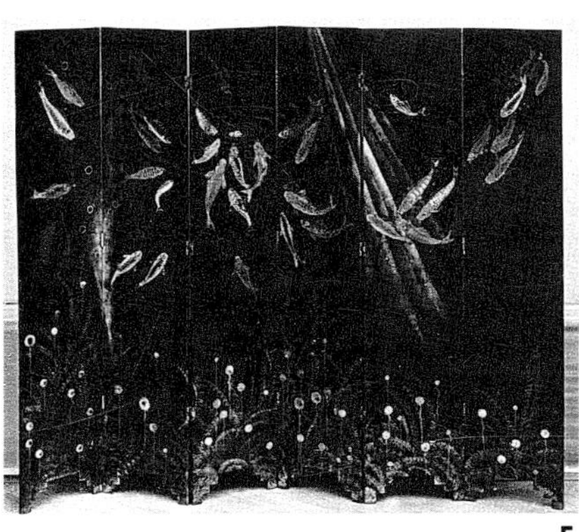
5

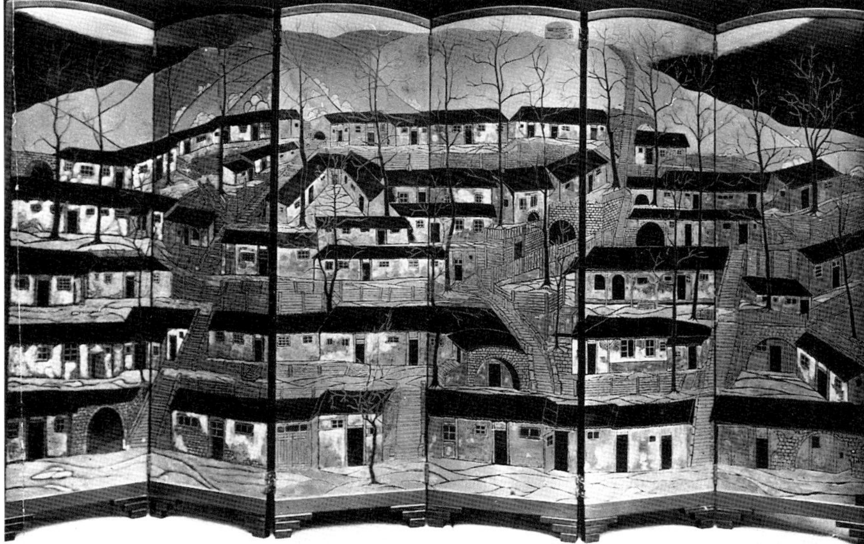
6

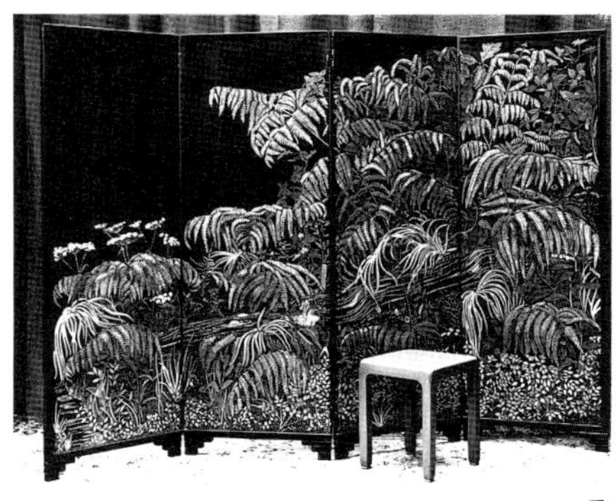
7

DECORATIVE SCREENS

1 Two Jaguars
(two panels)
Black-lacquer relief, after a cartoon by Paul Jouve.
Exh.: Galerie Georges Petit, Paris, 1921, no. 10.

2 Leopard and Cobra *Pl. 162*
(two panels)
Black lacquer and silver *laque arrachée* edged with red lacquer, after a cartoon by Paul Jouve.
Panel size 195 x 90 cm (76¾ x 35½ in.).
Signed *bl* 'Jean Dunand laqueur' and marked *br* 'Paul Jouve'.
Exh.: Galerie Georges Petit, Paris, 1922; Salon des Artistes Décorateurs, Paris, 1923.
Bibl.: *Mobilier et décoration*, February 1926, p. 42; *Conferencia*, 15 April 1926, p. 442; *Good Furniture Magazine*, June 1928, p. 291.
Sold: Christie's (New York), 1 October 1983, lot 215.
For a variant see cat. no. 3.

3 Leopard and Cobra
(two panels)
Black lacquer on a silver ground, after a cartoon by Paul Jouve.
Panel size 195 x 90 cm (76¾ x 35½ in.).
C. 1922, signed.
Variant of the screen (cat. no. 2) exhibited at the Galerie Georges Petit in 1922.

4 Moustiers-Ste Marie
(four panels)
Black and green lacquer inlaid with eggshell, after a cartoon by Henry de Waroquier.
Panel size 190 x 55 cm (74¾ x 21¾ in.).
Signed *br* 'Jean Dunand laqueur' and marked 'Henry de Waroquier N° 646'.
Exh.: Galerie Georges Petit, Paris, 1922.
Formerly in the collection of Félix Marcilhac, Paris; Musée des Beaux-Arts, Le Havre.
Sold: Sotheby's (Monaco), 25 May 1980, lot 103.

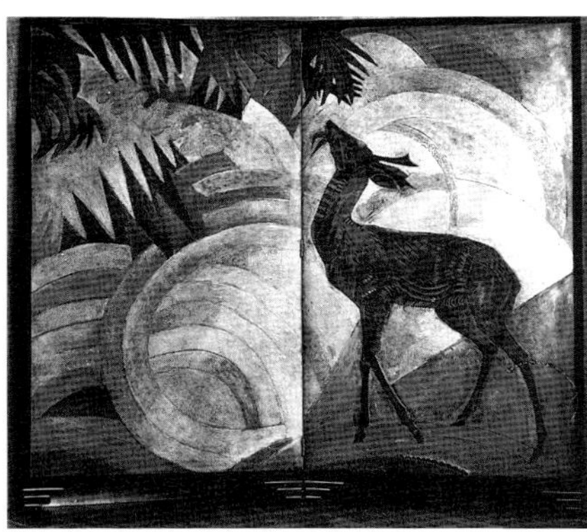
8

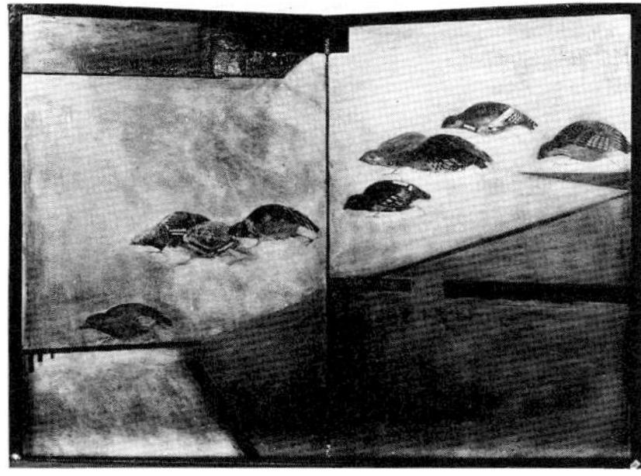
9

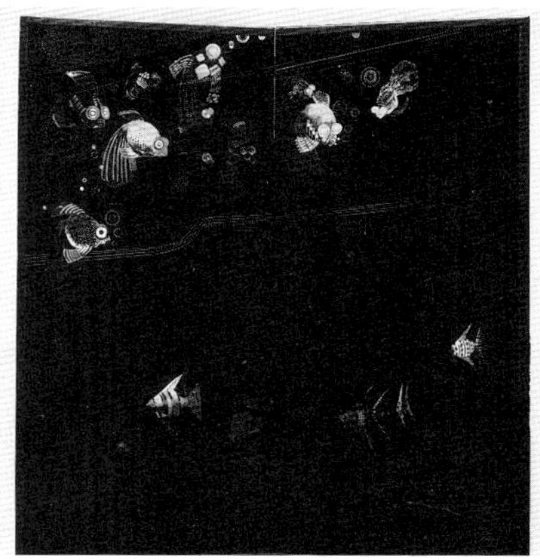
10

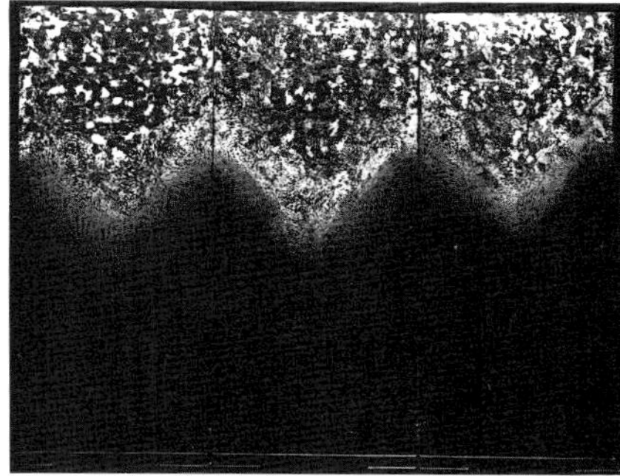
11

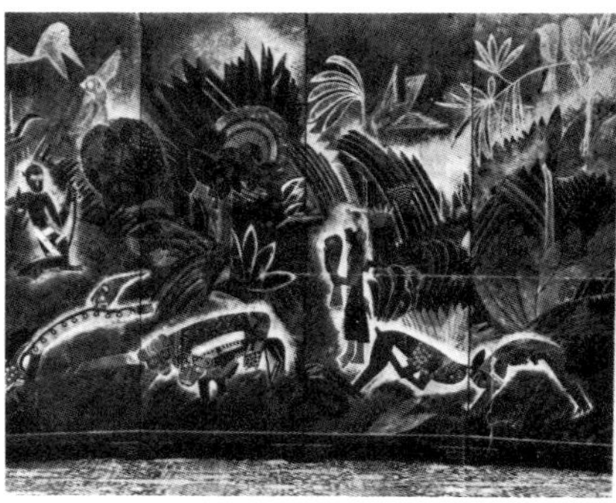
12

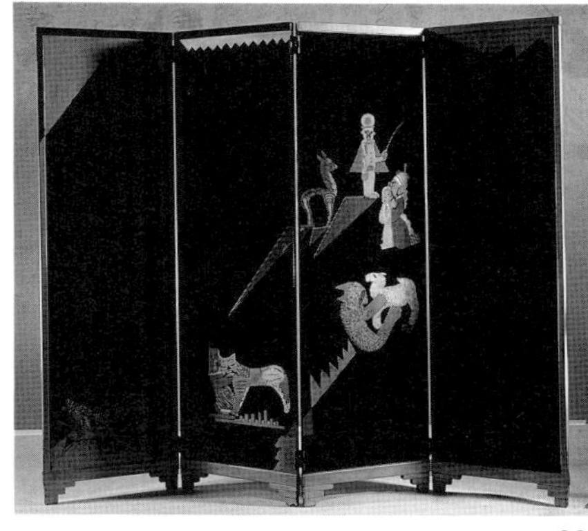
13

5 Fish
(six panels)
Black lacquer.
Signed.
Exh.: Galerie Georges Petit, Paris, 1922.

6 The Shacks
(six panels)
Black lacquer with incised decoration.
Signed.
Exh.: Galerie Georges Petit, Paris, 1922.
Coll.: Musée des Arts Décoratifs, Paris.
The scene depicted is at Côte d'Argonne, near the woods at La Grurie in the Ardennes.

7 Meadowsweet and Ferns
Decorated black lacquer, after a cartoon by Mme Henches.
C. 1922, signed.
Exh.: Salon des Artistes Décorateurs, Paris, 1923.

8 Deer
(two panels)
Silver lacquer and chased lead.
Signed *br* 'Jean Dunand laqueur'.
Exh.: Galerie Georges Petit, Paris, 1923, no. 2; Lord & Taylor, New York, 1928.
Bibl.: Albert Morancé, *Les Arts de la maison* (Winter 1923), pl. xxi; *L'Amour de l'art*, April 1924, unnumbered plate; *Creative Art*, March 1928, pl. xiii.

9 Partridges
(two panels)
Black lacquer and silver lacquer.
Signed.
Exh.: Galerie Georges Petit, Paris, 1923, no. 3.
Bibl.: 'Paris 1925', *The Architectural Review*, July 1925.

10 Fish
(two panels)
Black lacquer.
Signed.
Exh.: Galerie Georges Petit, Paris, 1923, no. 4.
Bibl.: 'Paris 1925', *The Architectural Review*, July 1925.

11 Effect of Matter
(three panels)
Black lacquer and eggshell.
Signed.
Exh.: Galerie Georges Petit, Paris, 1923, no. 5.
Bibl.: *L'Amour de l'art*, April 1924, p. 120.

12 Exotic Forest
(four panels)
Brown lacquer and coloured lacquer, after a cartoon by Jean Lambert-Rucki.
Signed 'Jean Dunand laqueur' and marked 'Jean Lambert-Rucki'.
Exh.: Galerie Georges Petit, Paris, 1923, no. 14.
Bibl.: 'Paris 1925', *The Architectural Review*, July 1925; *L'Art vivant*, 15 November 1925, p. 29.

13 Encounters
(four panels)
Black lacquer, coloured lacquer and eggshell, after a cartoon by Jean Lambert-Rucki.
Panel size 180 x 55 cm (70¾ x 21¾ in.).
Signed 'Jean Dunand laqueur' and marked 'Jean Lambert-Rucki'.
Exh.: Galerie Georges Petit, Paris, 1923, no. 15; Exposition Internationale des Arts Décoratifs, Stand Siegel, Pavillon de la Mode, Paris, 1925; Delorenzo Gallery, New York, 1985 (repr. in catalogue, p. 11).
Coll.: Steven A. Greenberg, New York.
Bibl.: *Vogue*, 1 May 1925; 'Paris 1925', *The Architectural Review*, July 1925; *L'Art vivant*, 15 November 1925, p. 29; *Mobilier et décoration*, February 1926, p. 43; *Jean Dunand – Jean Goulden*, exhibition catalogue (Paris, 1973), repr. p. 12; Yvonne Brunhammer, *Le Style 1925* (Paris, 1978), p. 184.

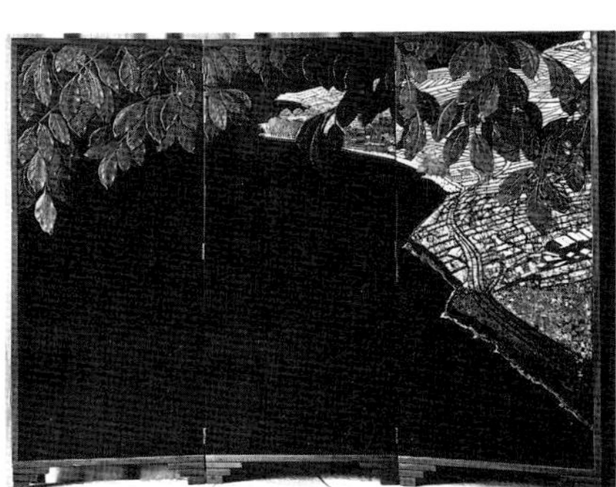
14

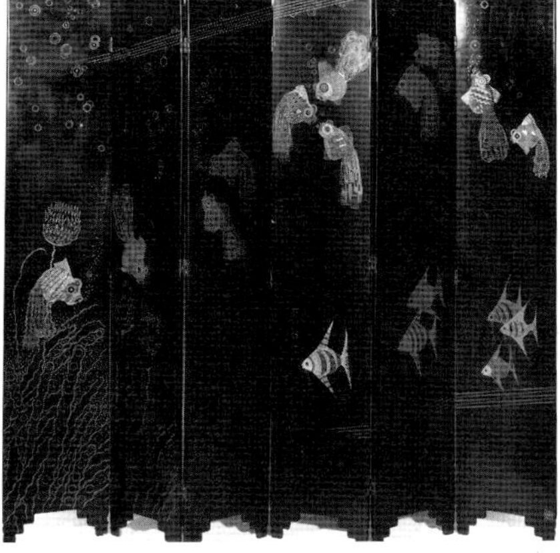
15

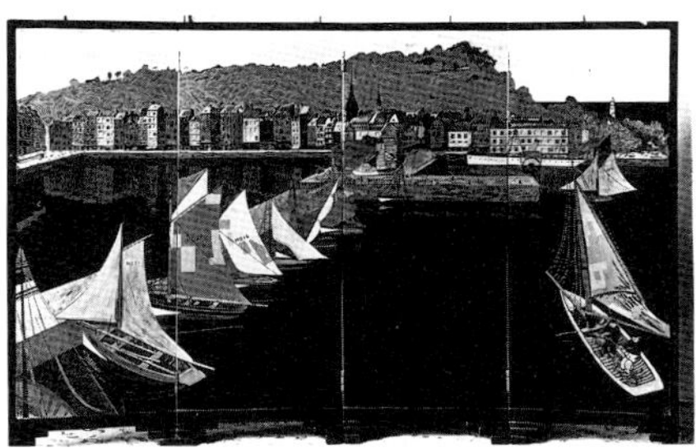
17

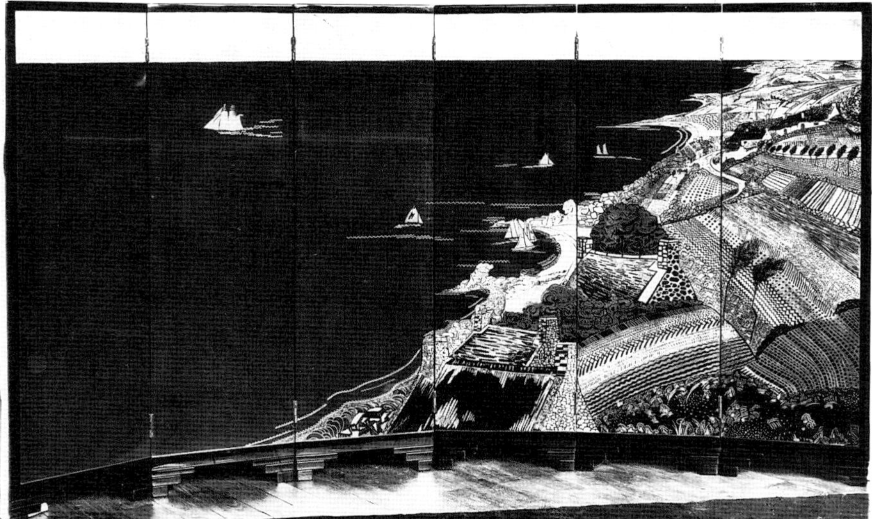
19

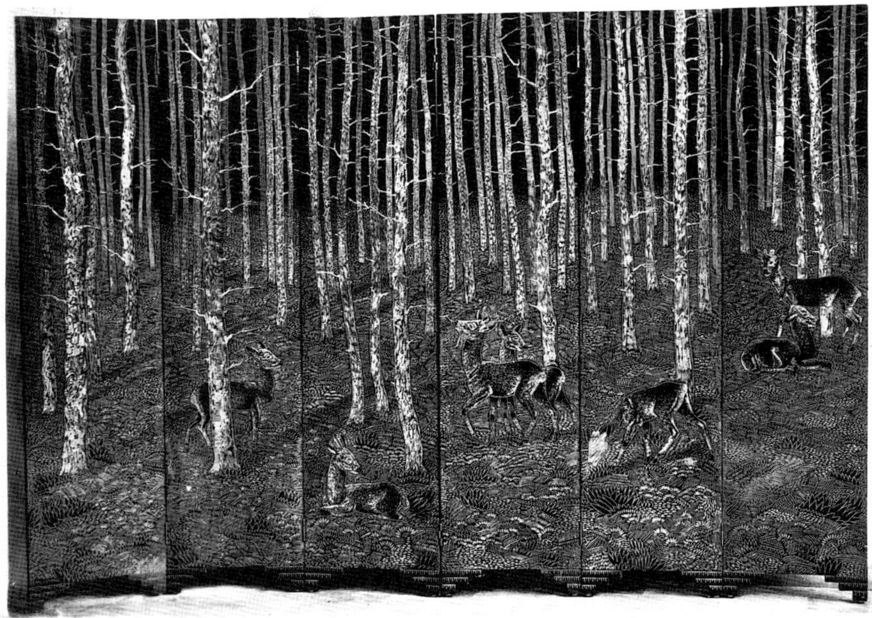
23

14 The Shores of Lake Geneva
(three panels)

Black lacquer, mother-of-pearl and shells, after a cartoon by Ernest Biéler.
Exh.: Galerie Georges Petit, Paris, 1923, no. 18; Salon des Artistes Décorateurs, Paris, 1924.
Bibl.: *Art et décoration*, June 1924, p. 200.

15 Fish
(six panels)

Black lacquer and coloured lacquer.
Panel size 130 x 25 cm (70¾ x 9¾ in.).
Signed 'Jean Dunand laqueur'.
Exh.: Galerie Georges Petit, Paris, 1924, no. 23.
Sold: Laurin, Guilloux, Buffetaud, Tailleur (Paris), 9 December 1976, lot 180.

16 Animals
(two panels)

Black lacquer and silver lacquer, after a cartoon by Jean Lambert-Rucki.
C. 1924, signed.

17 The Port of Honfleur
(four panels)

Black lacquer.
Signed.
Exh.: Galerie Georges Petit, Paris, 1925, no. 1.
Formerly in the collection of the Duchesse de Clermont-Tonnerre.
Bibl.: *Mobilier et décoration*, February 1926, p. 33.

18 Niagara Falls
(three panels)

Black lacquer.
Signed.
Exh.: Galerie Georges Petit, Paris, 1925, no. 3.
Bibl.: *Paris-Times*, 19 September 1926.
See illustration, p. 70.

19 Saint-Gildas
(six panels)

Black lacquer.
Signed.

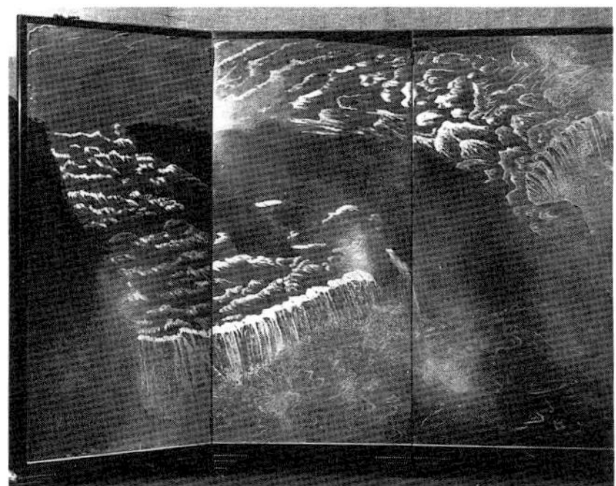
18

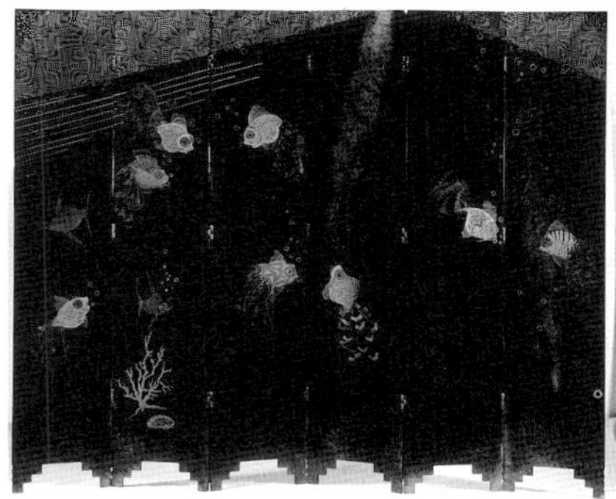
20

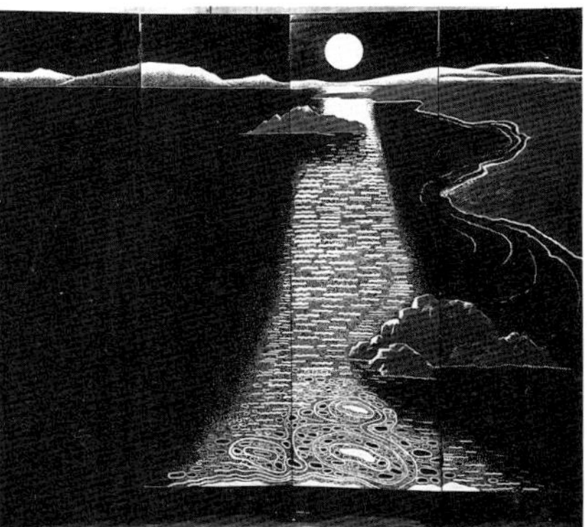
24

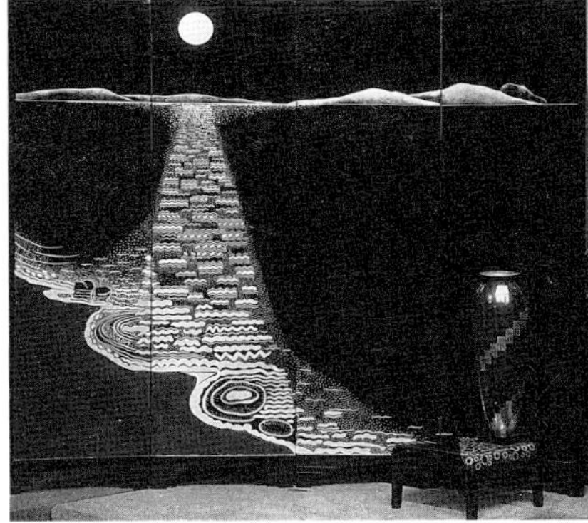
25

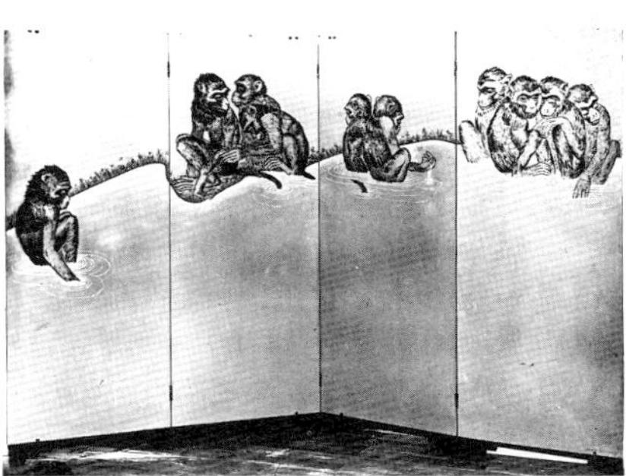
21

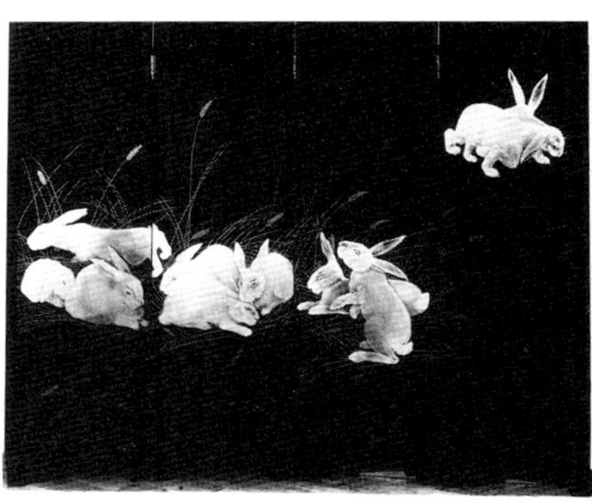
26

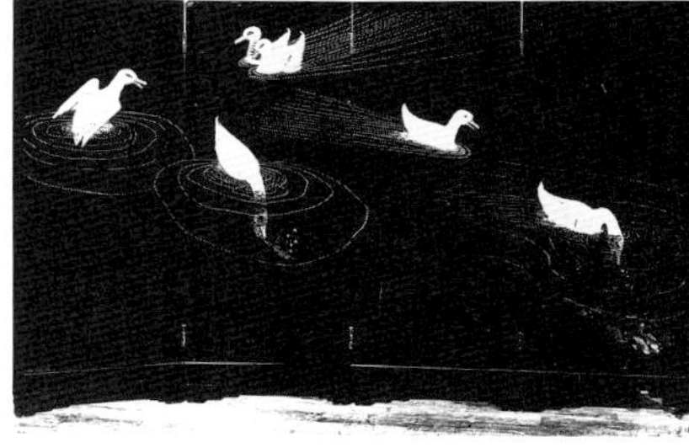
27

Exh.: Galerie Georges Petit, Paris, 1925, no. 4.
Bibl.: 'Une Visite au décorateur Jean Dunand', *La Patrie Suisse*, November 1933; *Etudes d'outre-mer*, December 1952, p. 402.

20 Fish
(six panels)
Black lacquer.
Panel size 125 x 25 cm (49¼ x 9¾ in.).
Signed.
Exh.: Galerie Georges Petit, Paris, 1925, no. 5; Delorenzo Gallery, New York, 1985 (repr. in catalogue, p. 21).
Formerly in the collection of Baron Robert de Rothschild.
Sold: Sotheby's (New York), 1 April 1977, lot 160.

21 Monkeys
(four panels)
Red lacquer.
Signed.
Exh.: Galerie Georges Petit, Paris, 1926, no. 5
A background of vegetation was added and the screen was re-exhibited in 1927 at the Salon des Artistes Décorateurs and at the Galerie Georges Petit (no. 5). See cat. no. 40.

22 Geometric Decor *Pl. 46*
(six panels)
Black and red lacquer highlighted with gold.
Panel size 125 x 25 cm (49¼ x 9¾ in.).
Signed.
Exh.: Galerie Georges Petit, Paris, 1926, no. 6; Galerie du Luxembourg, Paris, 1973, no. 113.
Private collection, Paris.
Bibl.: *Paris 1929* (Paris, 1929), pl. 23; *Jean Dunand – Jean Goulden*, exhibition catalogue (Paris, 1973), repr. on cover and p. 93.

23 Deer
(six panels)
Incised black lacquer.
Signed.
Exh.: Galerie Georges Petit, Paris, 1926, no. 7.
Bibl.: *Good Furniture Magazine*, June 1928, p. 292.

24 Moonlight
(four panels)
Black, red and silver lacquer.
Panel size 170 x 50 cm (67 x 19¾ in.).
Signed *br* 'Jean Dunand laqueur'.
Exh.: Galerie Georges Petit, Paris, 1926, no. 8.
Bibl.: *Mobilier et décoration*, February 1926, p. 37; *L'Illustration*, 15 October 1927, p. 428; 'Une Visite au décorateur Jean Dunand', *La Patrie Suisse*, November 1933.
Sold: Sotheby's (Zurich), 6 May 1975, lot 140.
For a variant see cat. no. 25.

25 Moonlight
(four panels)
Black lacquer and silver lacquer.
Panel size 170 x 47 cm (67 x 18½ in.).
Signed.
Bibl.: Janet Woodbury Adams, *Decorative Folding Screens* (New York and London, 1982), p. 166.
A variant of the screen (cat. no. 24) exhibited at the Galerie Georges Petit in 1926.

26 Rabbits *Pl. 29*
(four panels)
Black, silver and red lacquer inlaid with opals.
Panel size 135 x 40 cm (53¼ x 15¾ in.).
Signed.
Exh.: Galerie Georges Petit, Paris, 1926, no. 9.
Bibl.: *L'Illustration*, 15 October 1927, p. 425.
Sold: Anaf, Le Tonkin (Lyons), December 1979; Christie's (Monaco), 6 December 1987, lot 240.
For a sketch see cat. no. 131.

27 Ducks
(four panels)
Black, silver and red lacquer.
Signed.
Exh.: Galerie Georges Petit, Paris, 1926, no. 11.
Formerly in the Galerie Vallois, Paris.

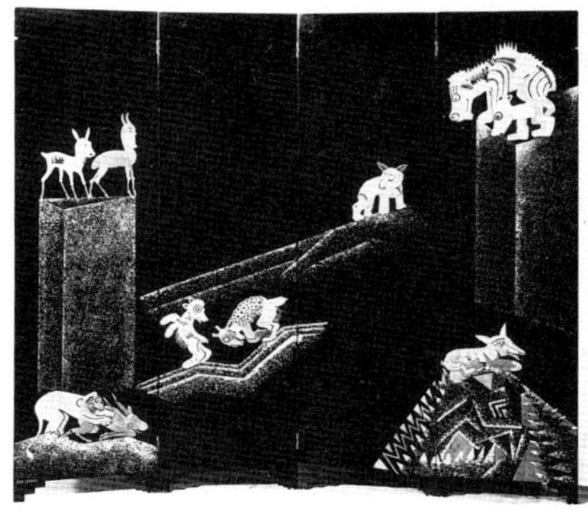

29

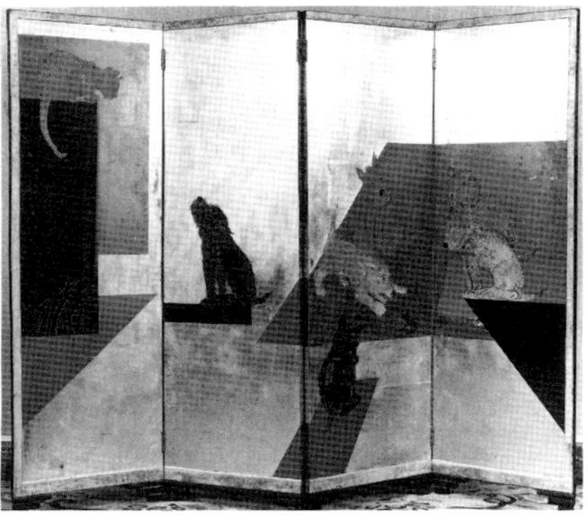

30

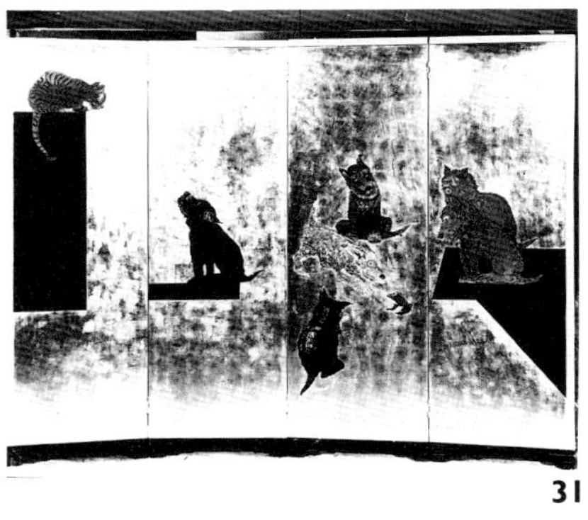

31

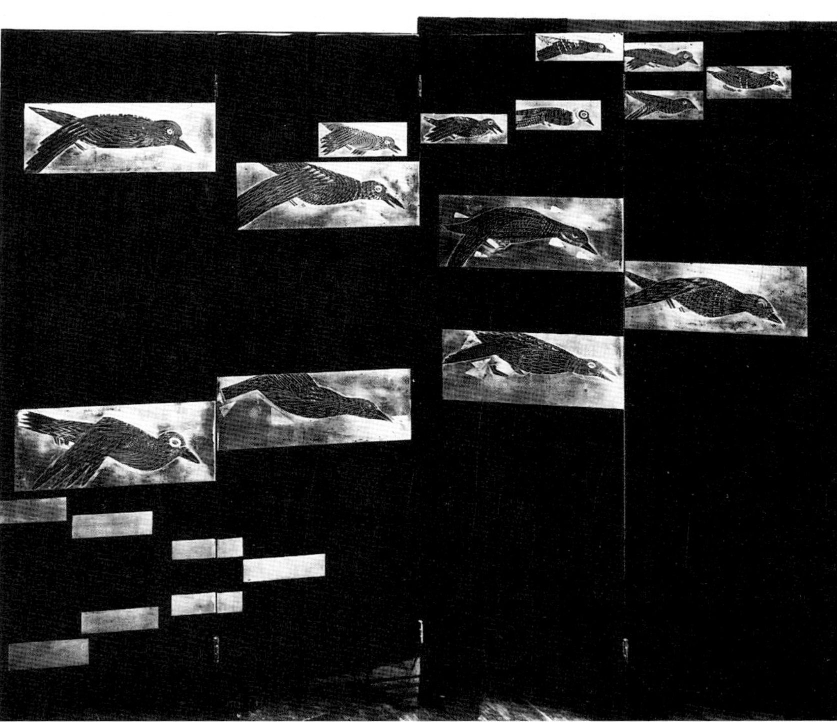

28

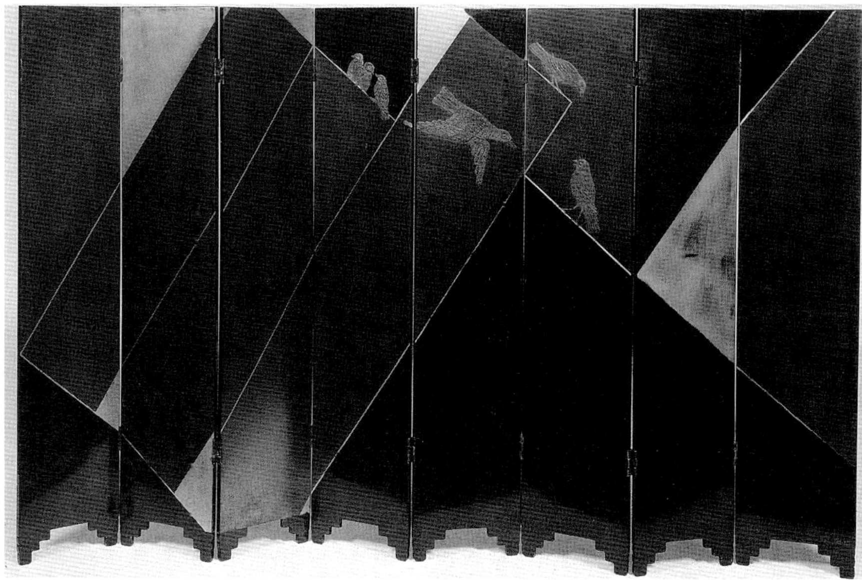

41

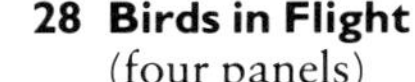

28 Birds in Flight
(four panels)
Black lacquer.
Signed.
Exh.: Galerie Georges Petit, Paris, 1926, no. 13.
Bibl.: *Art et décoration*, June 1927, p. 179.

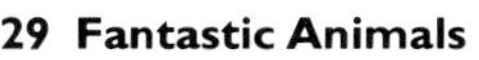

29 Fantastic Animals
(four panels)
Black lacquer.
Signed.
Exh.: Galerie Georges Petit, Paris, 1926, no. 14.
Bibl.: *Good Furniture Magazine*, June 1928, p. 295; 'Une Visite au décorateur Jean Dunand', *La Patrie Suisse*, November 1933.

30 Dogs
(four panels)
Black lacquer and gold lacquer.
Signed.
Exh.: Galerie Georges Petit, Paris, 1926, no. 15; Lord & Taylor, New York, 1928.
Bibl.: *The American Architect*, 5 March 1928, p. 319.
For a variant with a more elaborate geometric design see cat. no. 31.

31 Dogs
(four panels)
Gold, black and coloured lacquer.
Signed.
A variant of the screen (cat. no. 30) exhibited at the Galerie Georges Petit in 1926.

32 Brittany *Pl. 14*
(four panels)
Blue lacquer and eggshell.
Signed.
Exh.: Galerie Georges Petit, Paris, 1926, no. 16.
Private collection, Beauvais.
Bibl.: *L'Art et les artistes*, November 1936, p. 57.
Sold: Laurin, Guilloux, Buffetaud, Tailleur (Paris), 17 June 1977, lot 91.

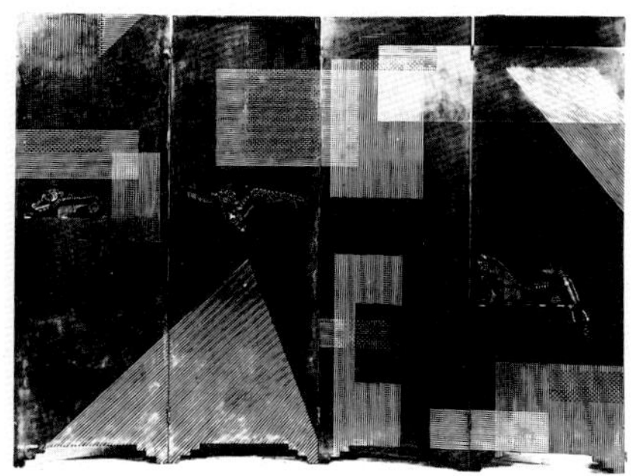
34

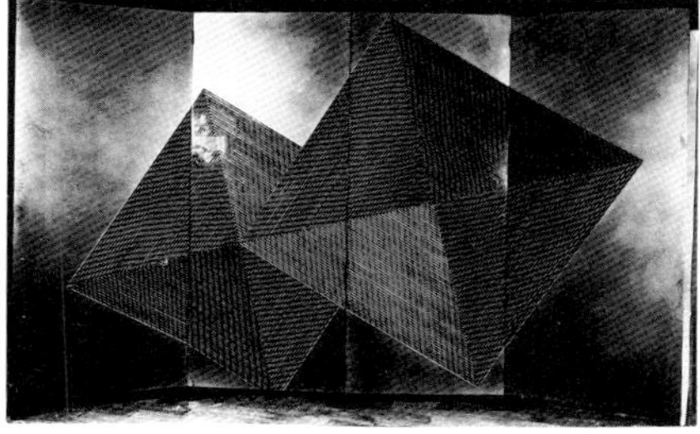
36

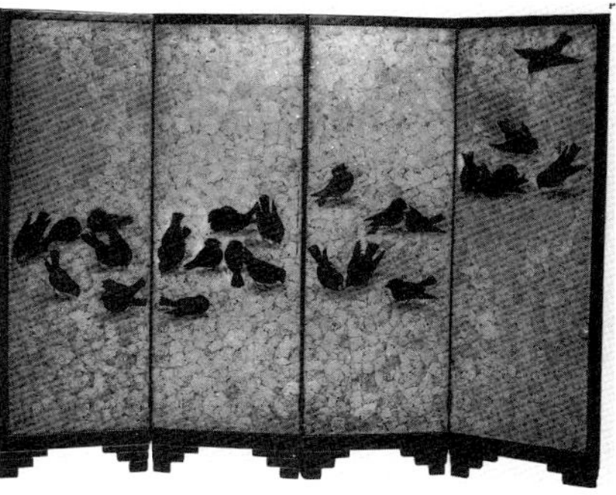
35

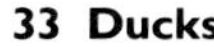

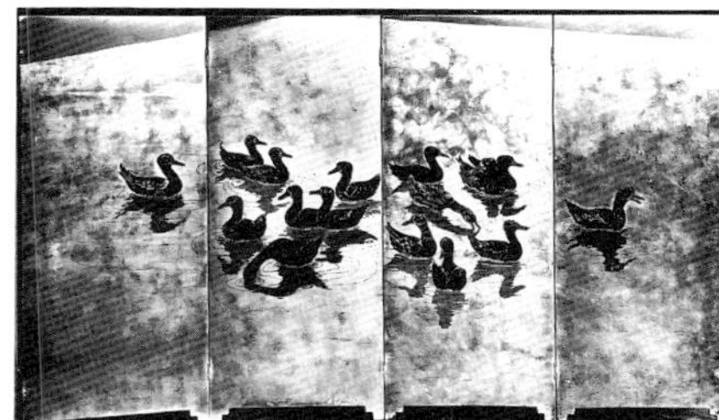
33

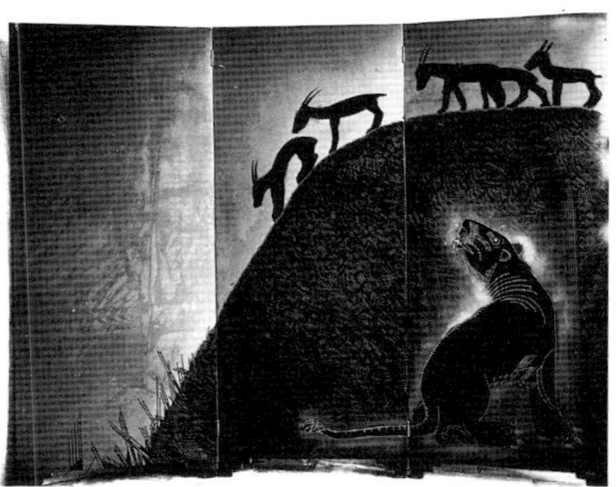
38

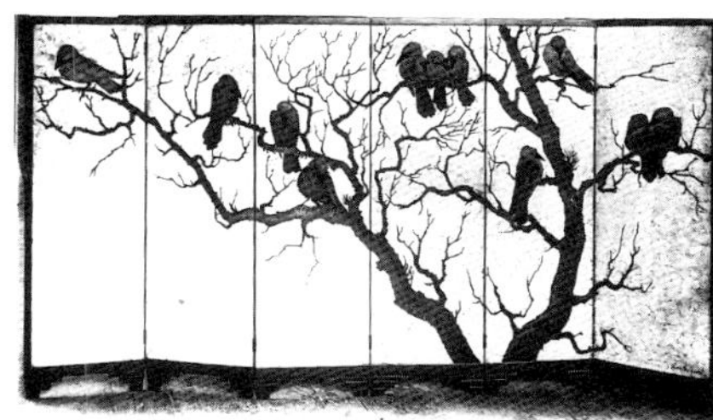
39

33 Ducks
(four panels)
Silver lacquer.
Signed.
Exh.: Galerie Georges Petit, Paris, 1926, no. 17.
Formerly in the collection of Jean-Charles Worth.
Bibl.: *L'Illustration*, May 1927; *Good Furniture Magazine*, June 1928, p. 294.
Sold: Poulain, Lefur (Paris), 19 June 1987.

34 Black Animals *Pl. 39*
(four panels)
Brown shellac and incised black lacquer.
Panel size 160 x 40 cm (63 x 15¾ in.).
Signed.
Exh.: Galerie Georges Petit, Paris, 1926, no. 18.
Private collection, Beverly Hills, Cal.
Bibl.: Pierre Legrain, *Les Objets d'art* (Paris, n.d.), pl. 22; *Building* (New York), March 1930, p. 124.
Sold: Boisgirard (Paris), 22 October 1986, lot 78.

35 Sparrows
(four panels)
Eggshell and lacquer.
Signed.
Exh.: Galerie Georges Petit, Paris, 1926, no. 19.
Bibl.: Armand Dayot, *Les Animaux*, vol. 1 (Paris, 1929), pl. 11.

36 Geometric Decor
(four panels)
Brown lacquer.
Signed.
Exh.: Galerie Georges Petit, Paris, 1926, no. 20; Salon des Artistes Décorateurs, Paris, 1927.
Bibl.: *Art et décoration*, June 1927, p. 179; *Paris 1929* (Paris, 1929), pl. 23.

37 Japanese Fish
(six panels)
Black lacquer and coloured lacquer.
Panel size 170 x 40 cm (67 x 15¾ in.).
Signed.
Exh.: Galerie Georges Petit, Paris, 1926, no. 21.
Coll.: Musée d'Art Moderne de la Ville de Paris.
Bibl.: Jacqueline Lafargue, *Meubles 1920–1937* (Paris, 1986), pp. 40f.

38 Africa
(three panels)
Black lacquer.
Signed.
Exh.: Galerie Georges Petit, Paris, 1926, no. 22; Salon des Artistes Décorateurs, Paris, 1927; Macy's International Exposition of Art in Industries, New York, May 1928.
Bibl.: *La Renaissance de l'art français*, July 1927, p. 344; *Les Échos des industries d'art*, July 1927, p. 23; *Building* (New York), March 1930, p. 123.

39 Crows
(six panels)
Eggshell and lacquer.
Signed.
Exh.: Galerie Georges Petit, Paris, 1926, no. 12; ——, 1927, no. 12; 'Les Animaliers contemporains', Musée d'Histoire Naturelle, Paris, February 1934.
Bibl.: *Sciences et voyages*, 28 March 1935, p. 304.

40 Monkeys
(four panels)
Red lacquer and gold lacquer.
Signed.
Exh.: Salon des Artistes Décorateurs, Paris, 1927; Galerie Georges Petit, Paris, 1927, no. 5; cf. cat. no. 21.

41 Geometric Decor (altered version)
(eight panels)
Black lacquer on a background of lead and gold.
Panel size 125 x 40 cm (49¼ x 15¾ in.).
Signed.
Exh.: Galerie Georges Petit, Paris, 1927, no. 6 (without birds); Salon des Artistes Décorateurs, Paris, 1927.
Sold: Sotheby's (Monaco), 20 March 1981, lot 268.
The piece was modified by the addition of six birds to the original design.

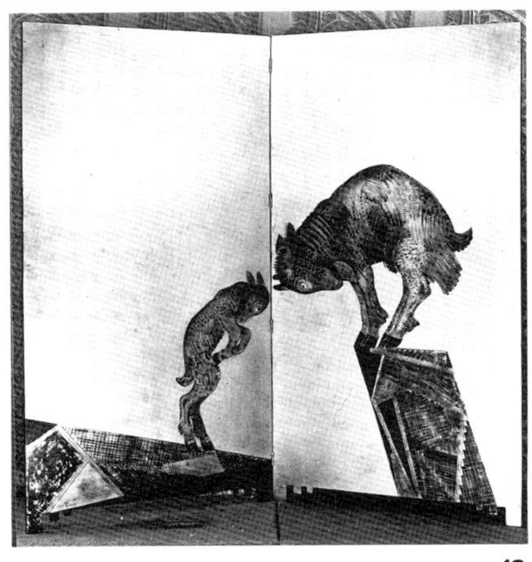
42

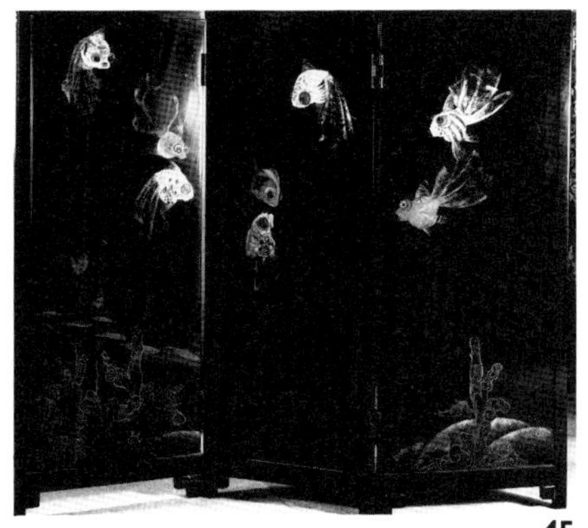
45

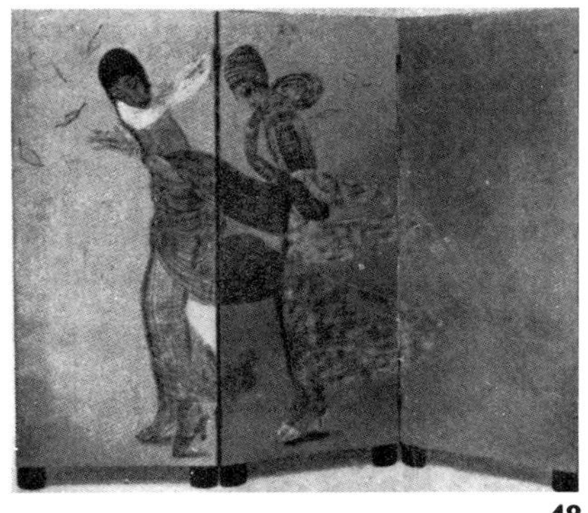
48

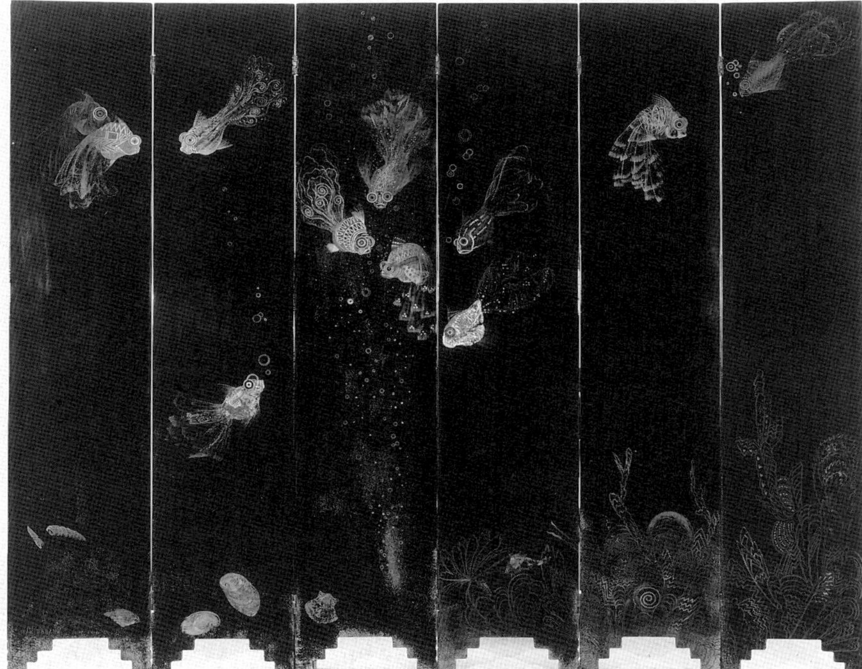
44

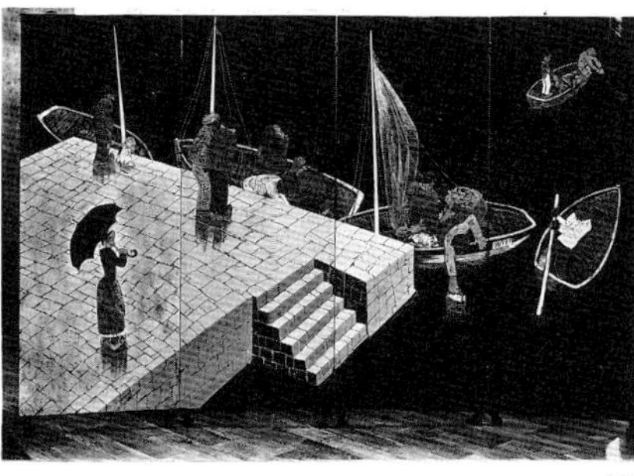
46

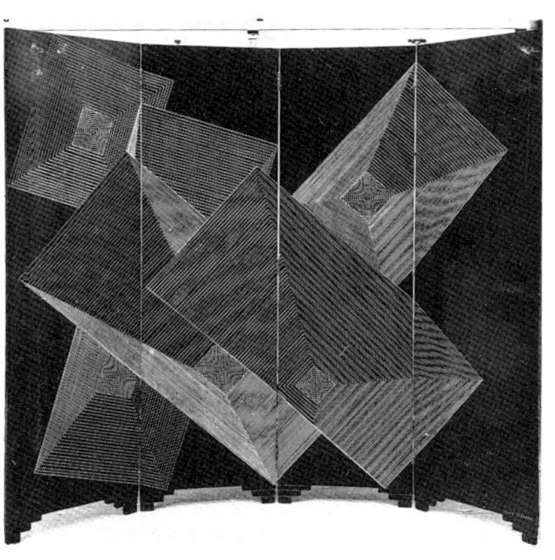
49

42 Rams
(two panels)
Gold lacquer.
Signed.
Exh.: Galerie Georges Petit, Paris, 1927, no. 7.
Bibl.: *La Revue de l'art ancien et moderne*, July 1928, p. 107; *Harper's Bazaar*, April 1928, p. 114.

43 Animals *Pl. 43*
(six panels)
Eggshell, black lacquer and silver lacquer.
Panel size 115 x 25 cm (45¼ x 9¾ in.).
Signed.
Exh.: Galerie Georges Petit, Paris, 1927, no. 8; ——, 1928, no. 7.
Bibl.: *Jean Dunand – Jean Goulden*, exhibition catalogue (Paris, 1973), repr. p. 25.

44 Fish
(six panels)
Black lacquer and coloured lacquer.
Panel size 125 x 25 cm (49¼ x 9¾ in.).
Signed.
Exh.: Salon des Artistes Décorateurs, Paris, 1927; Galerie Georges Petit, Paris, 1927, no. 9.
Sold: Sotheby's (Monaco), 17 March 1985, lot 319.

45 Fish
(three panels)
Black lacquer.
Panel size 105 x 40 cm (41¼ x 15¾ in.).
Signed.
Exh.: Galerie Georges Petit, Paris, 1927 (though not catalogued, this screen can be identified in photographs of the time); Delorenzo Gallery, New York, 1985 (repr. in catalogue, p. 18).
Sold: Laurin, Guilloux, Buffetaud, Tailleur (Paris), 21 March 1980, lot 185.

46 Breton Fishermen
(four panels)
Incised lacquer.
Signed.

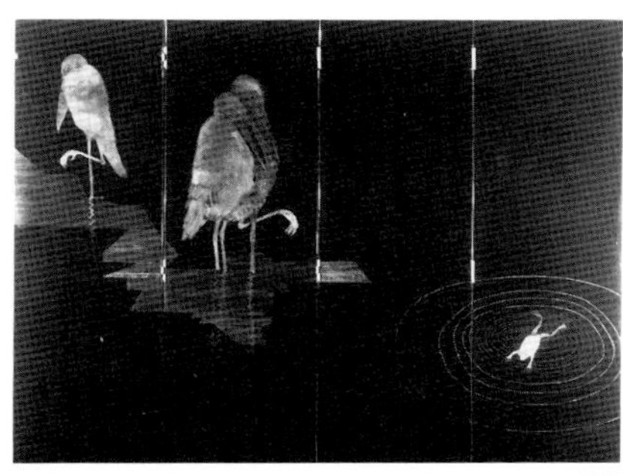

50

51

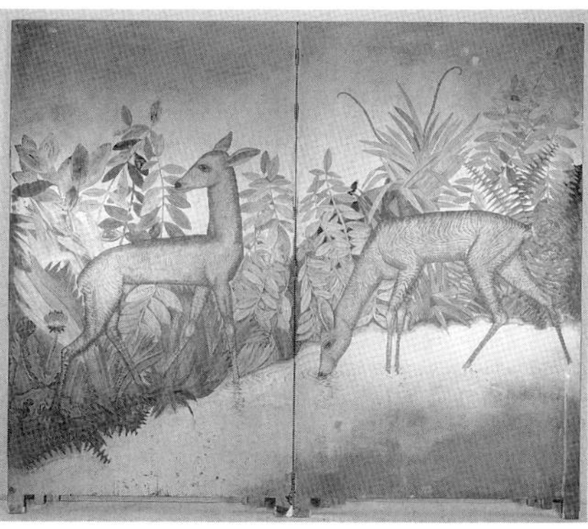

52

Exh.: Salon des Artistes Décorateurs, Paris, 1927; Galerie Georges Petit, Paris, 1927, no. 10.

47 Ducks
(four panels)
Black lacquer and silver lacquer.
Signed.
Exh.: Galerie Georges Petit, Paris, 1927, no. 11.
Bibl.: *Marchal de Genève*, March 1930; *Die Kunst*, 7 April 1933, p. 206; *Etudes d'outre-mer*, Paris, December 1952, p. 402.

48 Autumn
(three panels)
Gold lacquer.
Signed.
Exh.: Galerie Georges Petit, Paris, 1927, no. 16.

49 Geometric Decor
(four panels)
Black lacquer.
Signed.
Exh.: Galerie Georges Petit, Paris, 1927, no. 17.
Bibl.: *Harper's Bazaar*, April 1928, p. 115.

50 Herons and Frog
(four panels)
Black lacquer.
Signed.
Exh.: Galerie Georges Petit, Paris, 1927, no. 18.
For a variant see cat. no. 51.

51 Herons and Frog *Pl. 22*
(four panels)
Black lacquer.
Panel size 170 x 50 cm (67 x 19¾ in.).
C. 1927, signed.
Exh.: Delorenzo Gallery, New York, 1985 (repr. in catalogue, p. 24).
Sold: Champin, Lombrail, Gautier (Enghien), 15 November 1981, lot 155; Christie's (New York), 31 March 1984, lot 372.
Variant of cat. no. 50.

52 Deer
(two panels)
Silver lacquer.
Panel size 180 x 100 cm (70¾ x 39¼ in.).
Signed.
Exh.: Galerie Georges Petit, Paris, 1928, no. 5.

53 Japanese Fish
(four panels)
Black lacquer.
Signed.
Exh.: Galerie Georges Petit, Paris, 1928, no. 6.

54 Carp
(two panels)
Black lacquer and silver lacquer.
Signed.
Exh.: Galerie Georges Petit, Paris, 1928, no. 9.
Bibl.: *Les Échos des industries d'art*, June 1928, p. 32.

55 Water-lilies and Fish
(six panels)
Black lacquer.
Signed.
Exh.: Galerie Georges Petit, Paris, 1928, no. 11.
Bibl.: *Die Kunst*, 7 April 1933, p. 207.

56 Blue Pond
(four panels)
Eggshell and coloured lacquer.
Signed.
Exh.: Galerie Georges Petit, Paris, 1928, no. 12; ——, 1929, no. 3; ——, 1932, no. 23.

57 Monkeys *Pl. 16*
(four panels)
Black lacquer and silver lacquer.
Signed.
Exh.: Galerie Georges Petit, Paris, 1928, no. 13.
Coll.: Claude Ott, Paris.

54

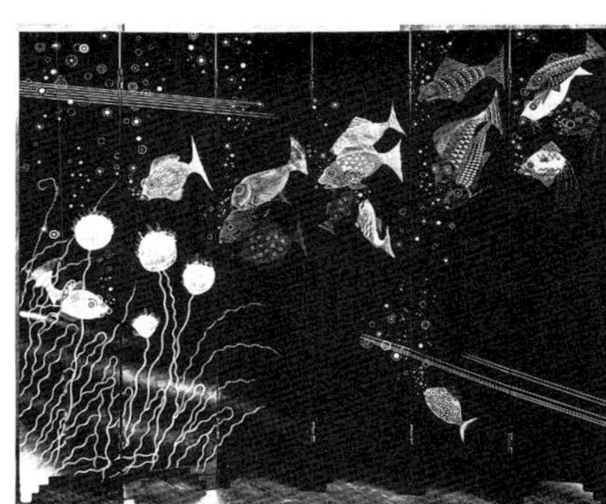

55

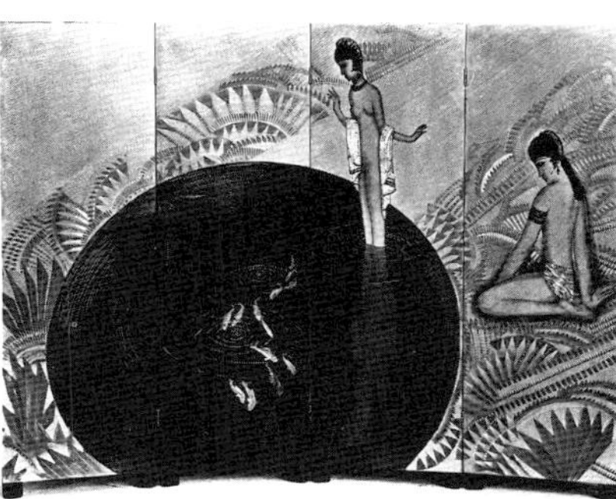

56

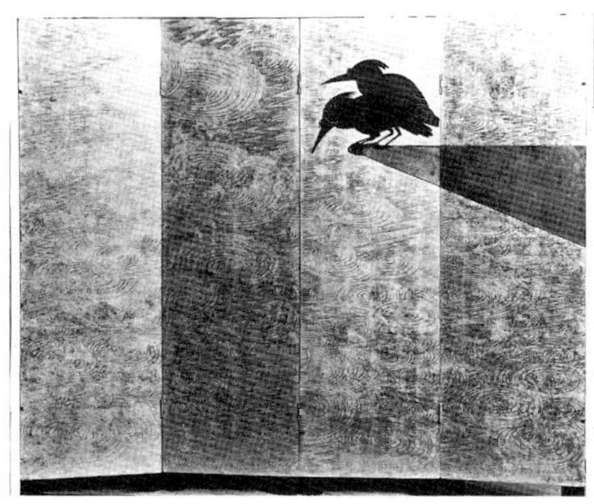
60

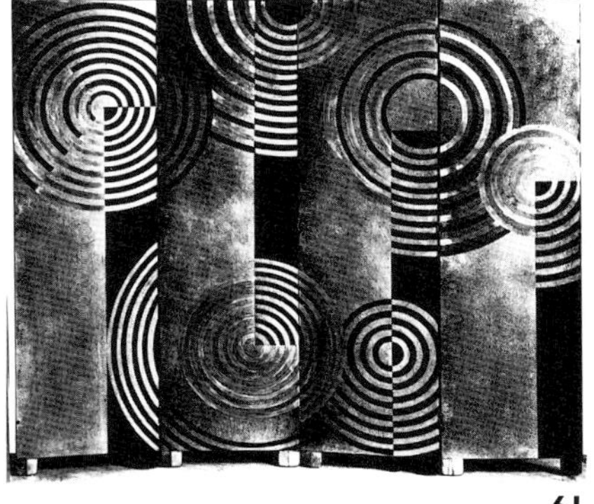
61

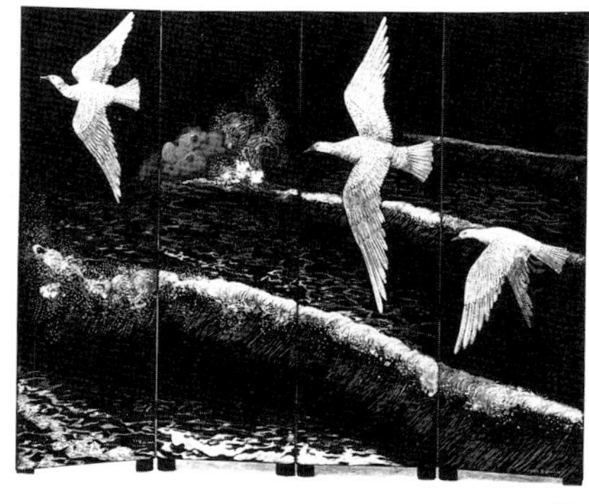
62

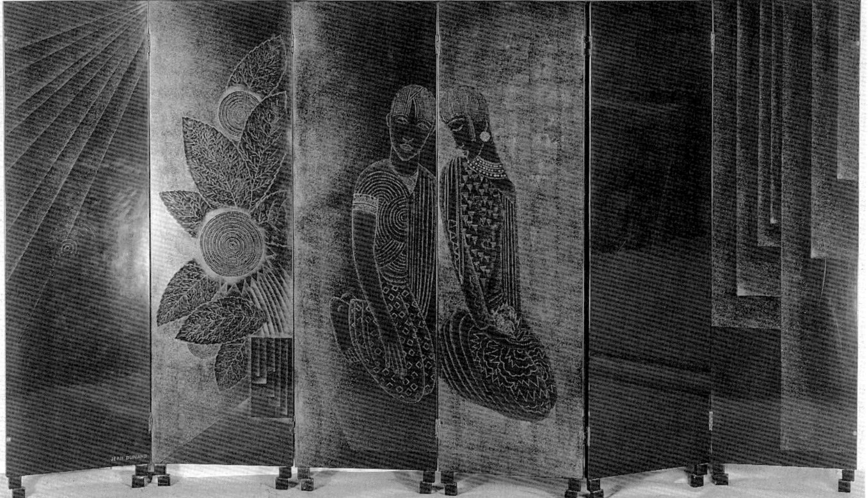
58

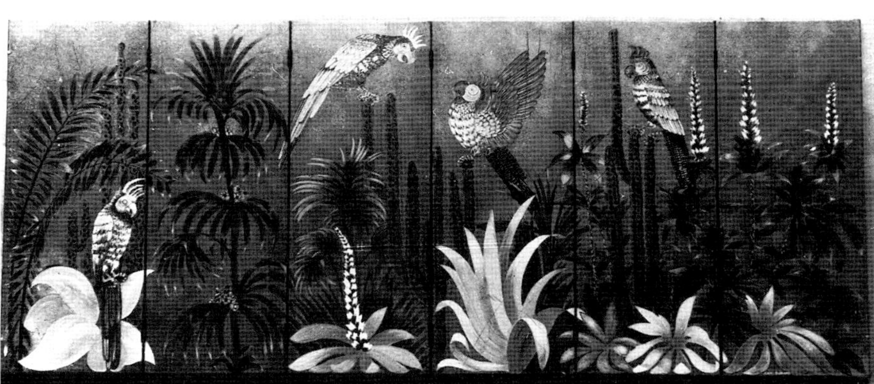
68

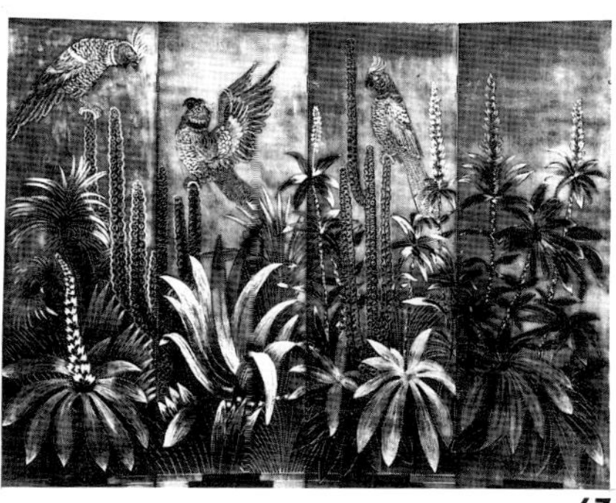
67

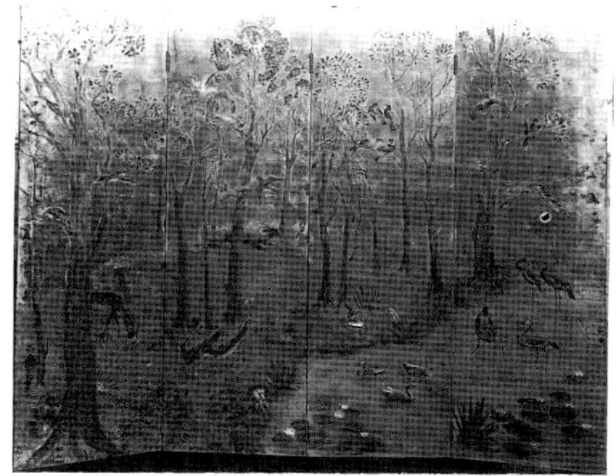
69

58 Two Figures
(six panels)
Black lacquer inlaid with silver and metal filings.
Panel size 140 x 40 cm (55 x 15¾ in.).
Signed.
Exh.: Galerie Georges Petit, Paris, 1928, no. 14; Galerie du Luxembourg, Paris, 1973, no. 111.
Formerly in the collection of Félix Marcilhac, Paris; Private collection, Paris.
Bibl.: *Jean Dunand – Jean Goulden*, exhibition catalogue (Paris, 1973), repr. p. 92.

59 Marabou Storks
(six panels)
Black, gold and silver lacquer.
Signed.
Exh.: Galerie Georges Petit, Paris, 1928, no. 15.

60 Kingfishers
(four panels)
Silver *laque arrachée.*
Panel size 168 x 48 cm (66¼ x 19 in.).
Signed.
Exh.: Galerie Georges Petit, Paris, 1928, no. 17; New York World's Fair, 1939; Galerie du Luxembourg, Paris, 1973, no. 110.
Bibl.: *Comoedia*, 26 December 1928, p. 439.

61 Abstract
(four panels)
Black metal inlaid with silver.
Signed.
Exh.: Galerie Georges Petit, Paris, 1928, no. 18.
Bibl.: *Jean Dunand – Jean Goulden*, exhibition catalogue (Paris, 1973), repr. p. 2.

62 Seagulls
(four panels)
Incised gold lacquer.
Signed.
Exh.: Galerie Georges Petit, Paris, 1929, no. 5; New York World's Fair, 1939.
Bibl.: *Die Kunst*, 7 April 1933, p. 210; *Le Mobilier*, June 1934.

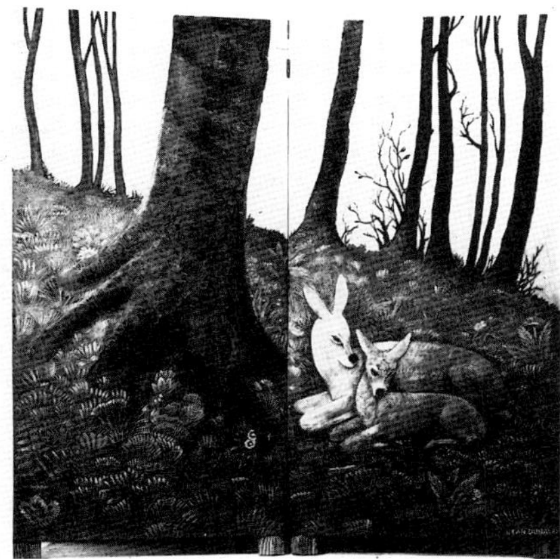
66

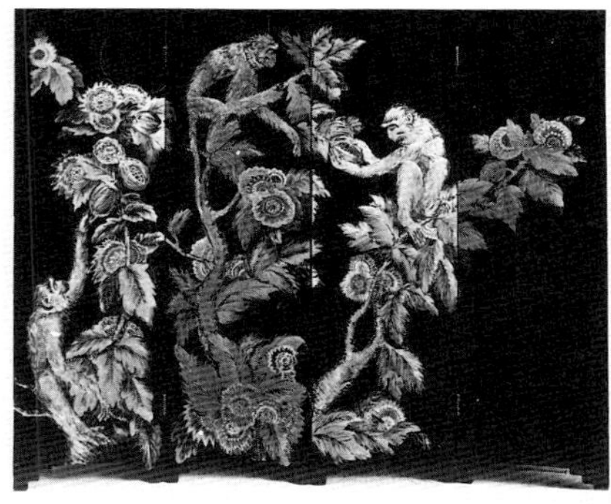
71

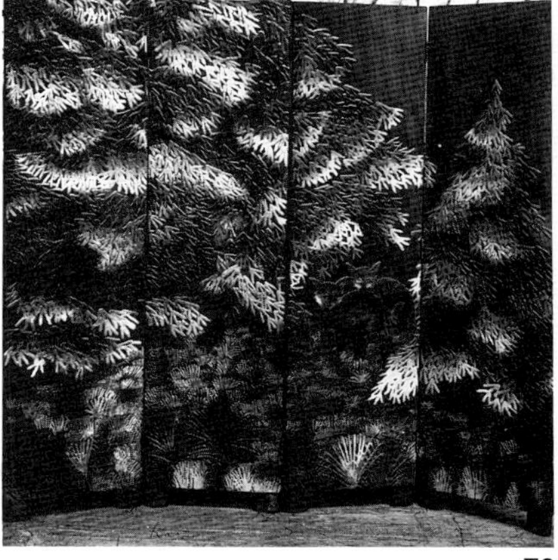
70

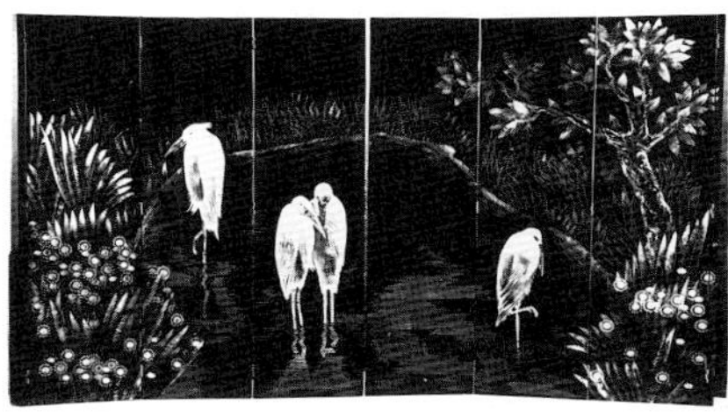
59

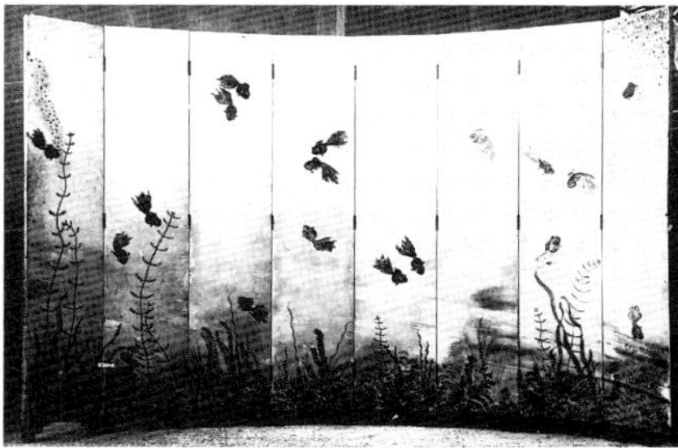
63

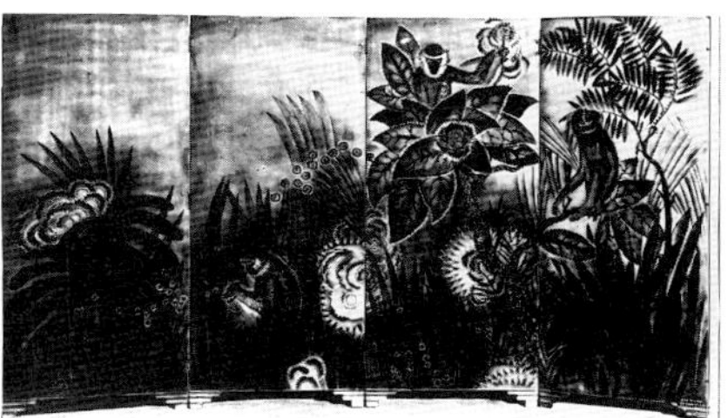
64

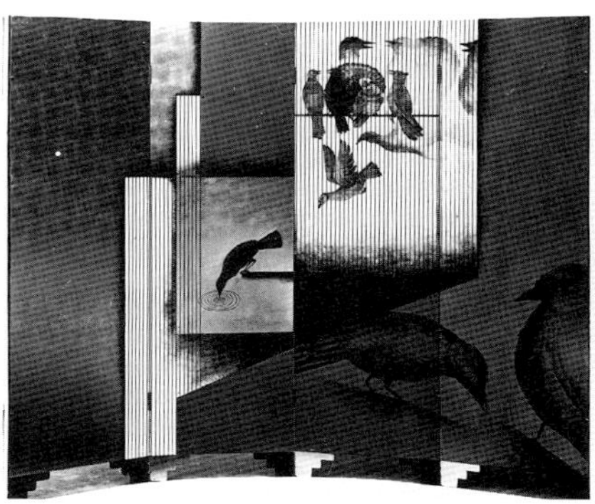
65

63 Fish
(eight panels)
Silver lacquer.
Signed.
Exh.: Galerie Georges Petit, Paris, 1929, no. 7.

64 Monkeys
(four panels)
Light-brown lacquer.
Panel size 180 x 75 cm (70¾ x 29½ in.).
Signed.
Exh.: Galerie Georges Petit, Paris, 1929, no. 9.
Sold: Sotheby's (Monaco), 11 March 1984, lot 210.

65 Birdcage
(four panels)
Grey lacquer and silver lacquer.
Signed.
Exh.: Galerie Georges Petit, Paris, 1929, no. 10; ——, 1930/31, no. 16 (catalogued under the title 'Oiseaux Encagés' ['Caged Birds']).
Bibl.: *Le Cahier*, January 1931, p. 48; *Mobilier et décoration*, June 1931, p. 257.
See also cat. no. 359.

66 Deer
(two panels)
Lead on natural pine.
Panel size 210 x 100 cm (82¾ x 39¼ in.).
Signed.
Exh.: Galerie Georges Petit, Paris, 1929, no. 11; ——, 1930/31, no. 11.
Sold: Laurin, Guilloux, Buffetaud, Tailleur (Paris), 29 May 1974, lot 214.

67 Parrots
(four panels)
Incised brown lacquer.
Panel size 185 x 55 cm (72¾ x 21¾ in.).
Signed.
Exh.: Galerie Georges Petit, Paris, 1929, no. 12; Museo Nacional de Arte Decorative, Buenos Aires, September 1985, no. 99, repr. in catalogue.
Private collection, Buenos Aires.
Sold: Vincent (Paris), 14 February 1973; Libert (Paris), 7 March 1977, repr. on cover of catalogue.
For a six-panel variant, see cat. no. 68.

68 Parrots
(six panels)
Brown lacquer and coloured lacquer.
Panel size 185 x 55 cm (72¾ x 21¾ in.).
C. 1929, signed.
Variant of the four-panel screen (cat. no. 67) exhibited at the Galerie Georges Petit in 1929.

69 Forest
(four panels)
Patinated copper inlaid with silver.
Signed.
Exh.: Galerie Georges Petit, Paris, 1929, no. 13.

70 Foxes
(four panels)
Lacquer on sand-blasted spruce.
Signed.
Exh.: Galerie Georges Petit, Paris, 1929, no. 14; Galerie Charpentier, 1933, no. 8.

71 Monkeys
(four panels)
Silver lacquer and black lacquer.
Signed.
Exh.: Galerie Georges Petit, Paris, 1929, no. 15.

72 Four Figures *Pl. 38*
(four panels)
Gold lacquer and black lacquer.
Signed.
Exh.: Galerie Georges Petit, Paris, 1929, no. 16.
Private collection, Paris.

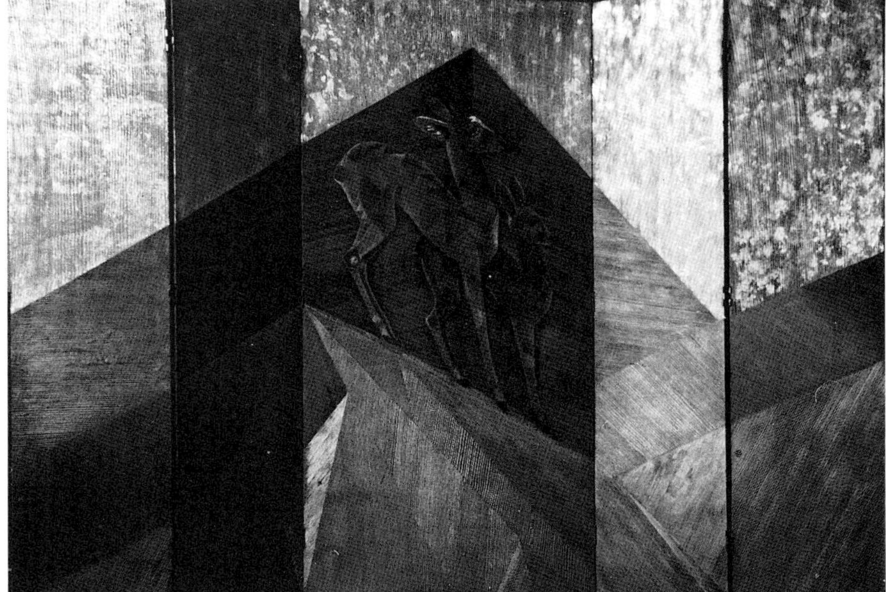

73

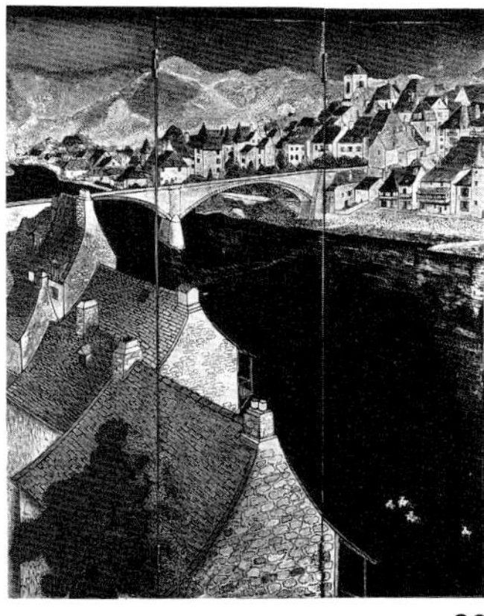

80

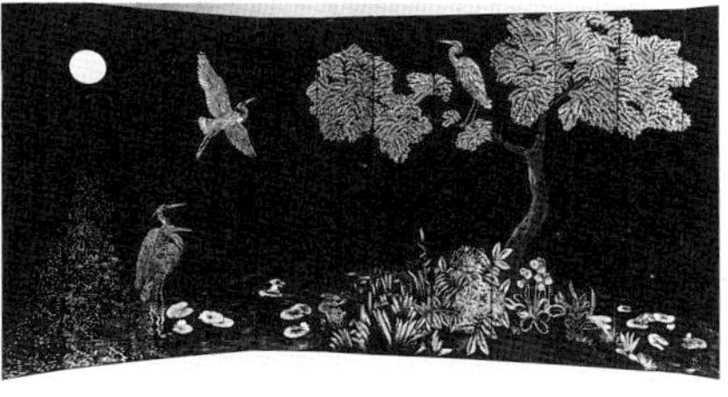

74

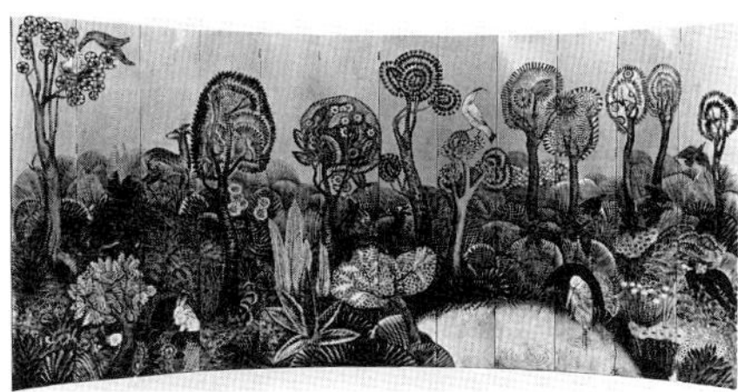

75

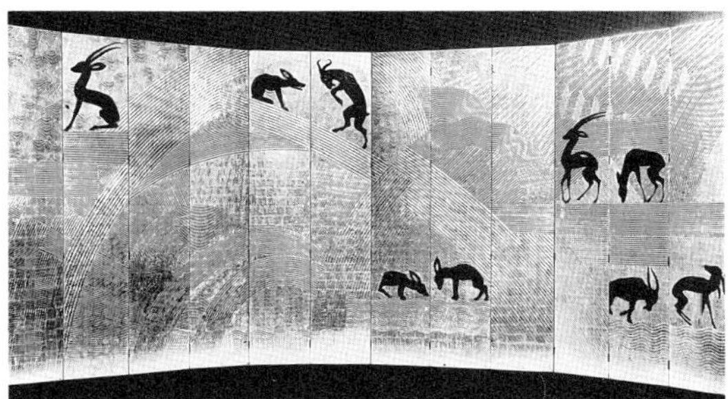

76

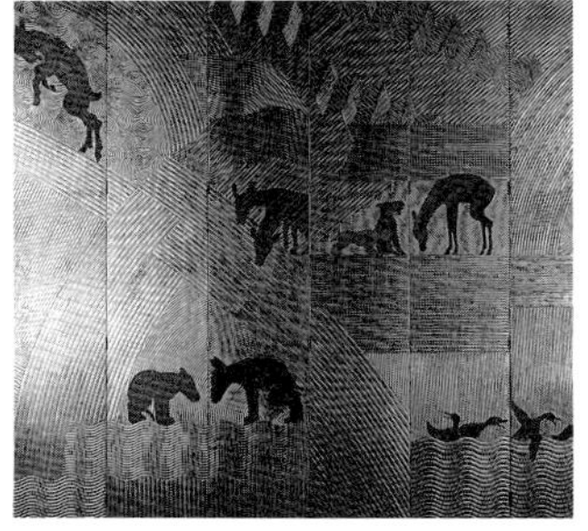

76

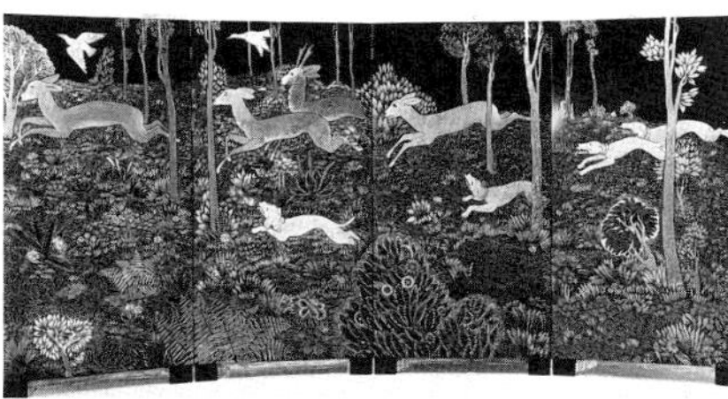

77

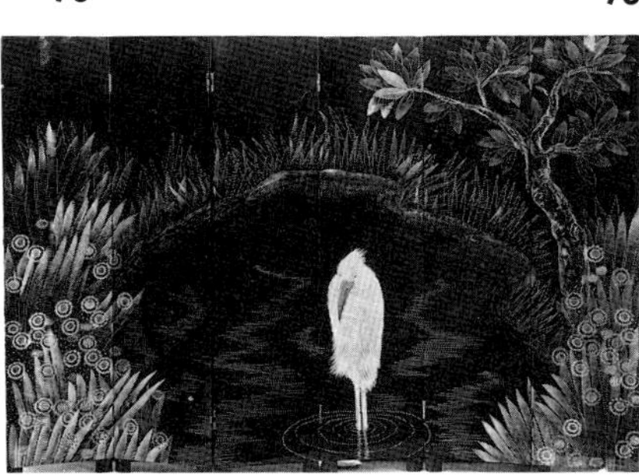

78

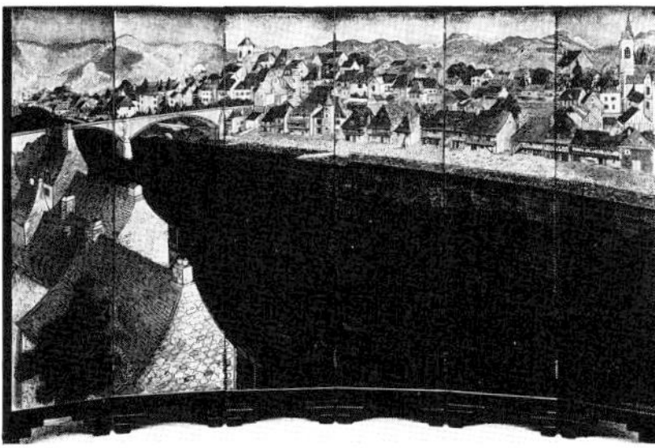

79

73 Deer
(five panels)
Gold lacquer on sand-blasted spruce.
Central panel 225 x 100 cm (88½ x 39¼ in.), others 50 cm (19¾ in.) wide.
Signed.
Exh.: Galerie Georges Petit, Paris, 1929, no. 17.
Bibl.: *L'Illustration*, special number, May 1927; *Mobilier et décoration*, December 1928.
Sold: Sotheby's (Monaco), 23 June 1979, lot 234; ——, 24/25 October 1982, lot 418.

74 Herons *Pl. 30*
(twelve panels)
Incised black lacquer inlaid with mother-of-pearl, eggshell and carved ivory.
Panel size 300 x 50 cm (118 x 19¾ in.).
Signed.
Exh.: Galerie Georges Petit, Paris, 1930/31, no. 5; Salon des Artistes Décorateurs, Paris, 1932.
Private collection.
Bibl.: *Le grand monde*, June 1932, p. 17.

75 Forest
(twelve panels)
Grey frosted lacquer.
Panel size 300 x 50 cm (118 x 19¾ in.).
Signed.
Exh.: Galerie Georges Petit, Paris, 1930/31, no. 6.
Bibl.: *Beaux-Arts*, January 1931.

76 Animals
Silver lacquer and brown lacquer.
Panel size 300 x 55 cm (118 x 21¾ in.).
Signed.
Exh.: Galerie Georges Petit, Paris, 1930/31, no. 7.
The original 12-panel screen was adapted (lacquered gold and made into two 6-panel units). Formerly in the collection of Félix Marcilhac and now in a Los Angeles private collection; sold by Champin, Lombrail, Gautier (Enghien), 22 November 1982, lot 116.

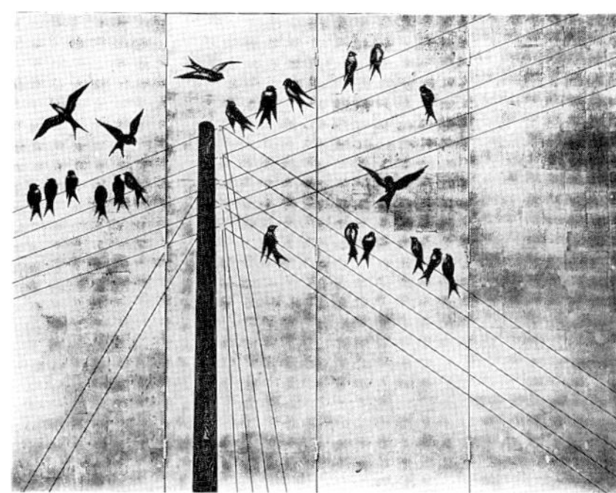
81

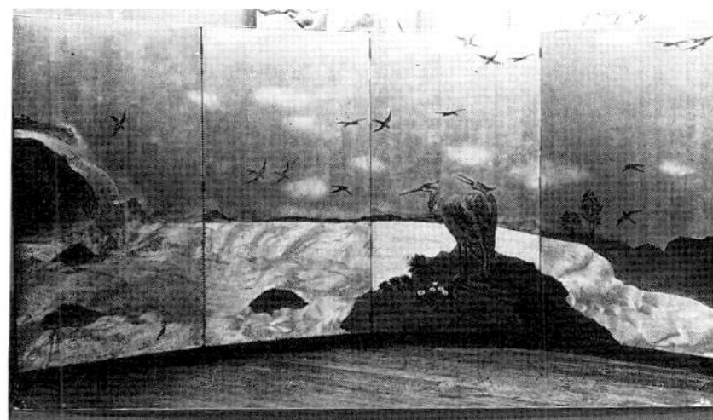
82

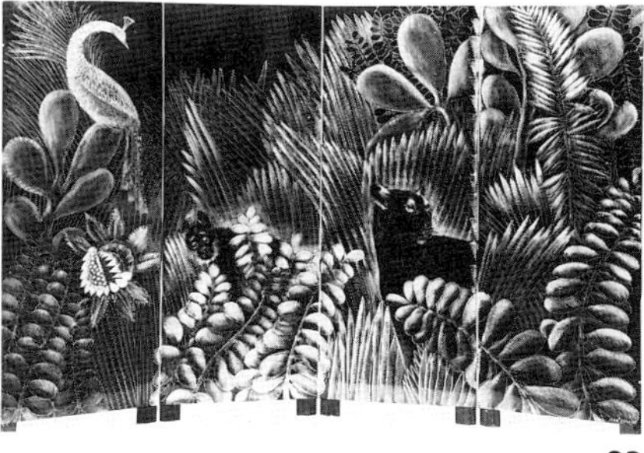
83

77 Hunt
(four panels)
Blue lacquer.
Panel size 198 x 95 cm (78 x 25½ in.).
Signed.
Exh.: Galerie Georges Petit, Paris, 1930/31, no. 8.
Bibl.: *Die Kunst*, 7 April 1933, p. 211; *L'Art et les artistes*, November 1933, p. 59.

78 Marabou Stork
(six panels)
Black lacquer.
Panel size 195 x 60 cm (76¾ x 23½ in.).
Signed.
Exh.: Galerie Georges Petit, Paris, 1930/31, no. 9.

79 Argentat
(six panels)
Incised black lacquer.
Signed.
Exh.: Galerie Georges Petit, Paris 1930/31, no. 10; ——, 1932, no. 22.
Formerly in the collection of Madeleine Granjean.
Bibl.: *Art et décoration*, August 1932, p. 225.
A three-panel version (cat. no. 80) depicts the same subject, using only the left-hand half of the design.

80 Argentat
(three panels)
Incised black lacquer.
Signed.
Bibl.: *Art et décoration*, August 1932, p. 225.
Reduced version of the six-panel screen (cat. no. 79) exhibited at the Galerie Georges Petit in 1930/31.

81 Swallows
(four panels)
Silver lacquer.
Signed.
Exh.: Galerie Georges Petit, Paris, 1930/31, no. 12; ——, 1933, no. 9.
Bibl.: *Le Mobilier*, June 1933.

82 Brook
(four panels)
Incised rose-pink and silver lacquer.
Panel size 200 x 90 cm (78¾ x 35½ in.).
Signed.
Exh.: Galerie Georges Petit, Paris, 1930/31, no. 13; Galerie du Luxembourg, Paris, 1973, no. 112.
Bibl.: *L'Illustration*, 7 December 1940.

83 Jungle
(four panels)
Black, gold and coloured lacquer.
Signed.
Exh.: Galerie Georges Petit, Paris, 1930/31, no. 14.
Bibl.: *Beaux-Arts*, July 1930, p. 16; *Le Cahier*, January 1931, p. 44; *Plaisir de France*, June 1937; *L'Élite de Paris*, 22 July 1937, p. 30; *La Nature*, 15 October 1937, p. 361.

84 Waves and Birds
(four panels)
Black lacquer and silver lacquer.
Signed.
Exh.: Galerie Georges Petit, Paris, 1930/31, no. 17.
Bibl.: *La Nature*, 15 October 1937, repr. on cover and p. 362.

85 Two Figures
(two panels)
Sculpted black lacquer.
Signed.
Exh.: Galerie Georges Petit, Paris, 1932, no. 21; Galerie Charpentier, Paris, 1933, no. 5.
Private collection.
Bibl.: *Bulletin de l'art*, May 1933; *L'Art dans la vie moderne*, Paris, 1937, p. 106; *L'Écho de la France*, 4 June 1944.

86 Swans
(four panels)
Gold lacquer on a black-lacquer ground.
Signed.
Exh.: Galerie Georges Petit, Paris, 1932, no. 24.

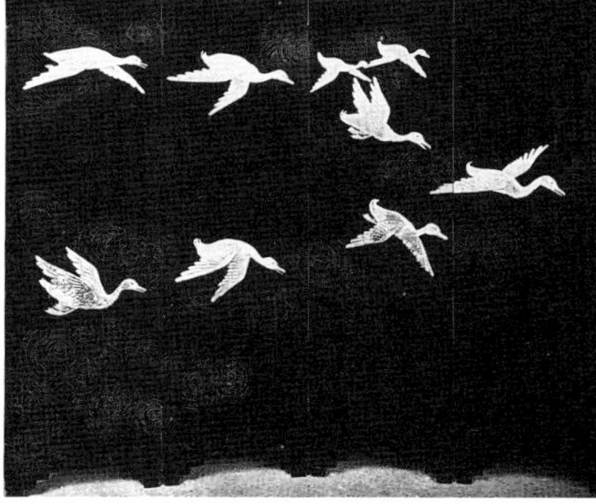
84

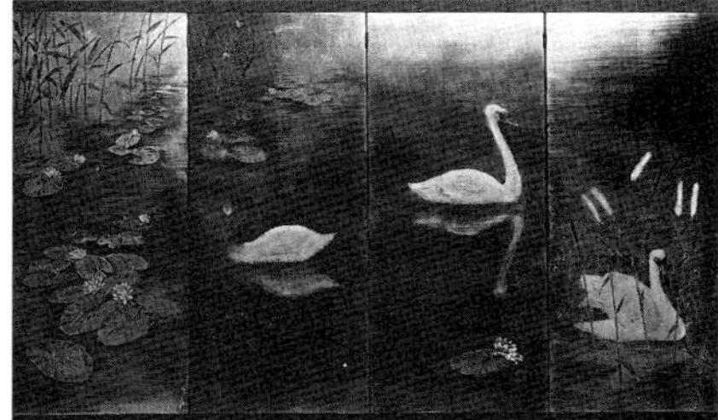
86

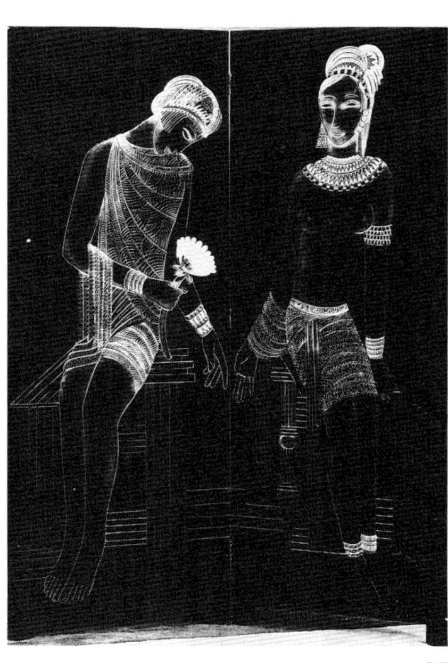
85

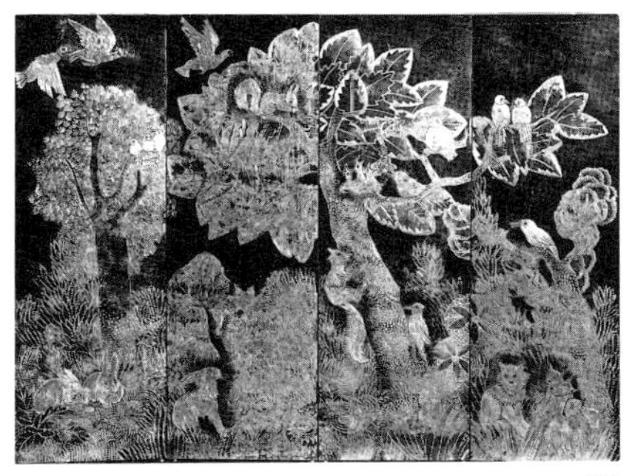

87

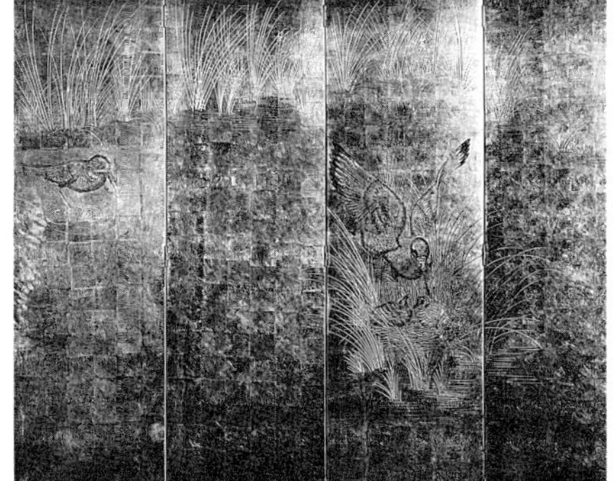

88

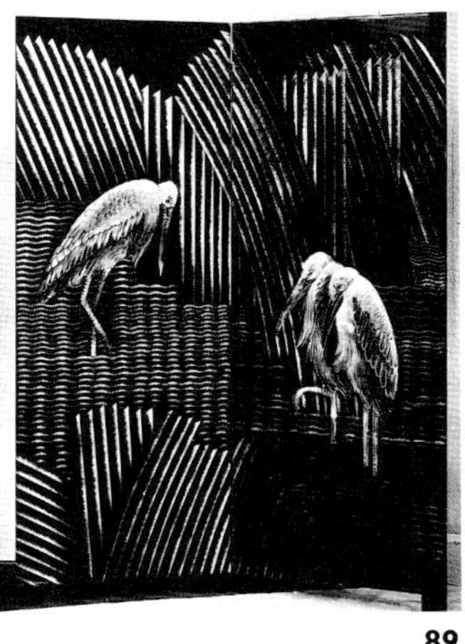

89

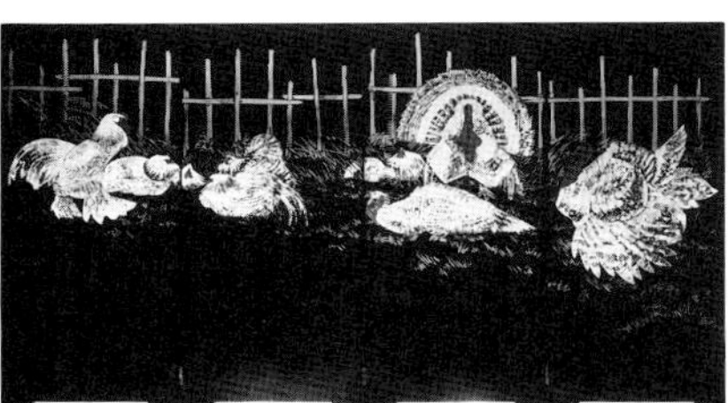

90

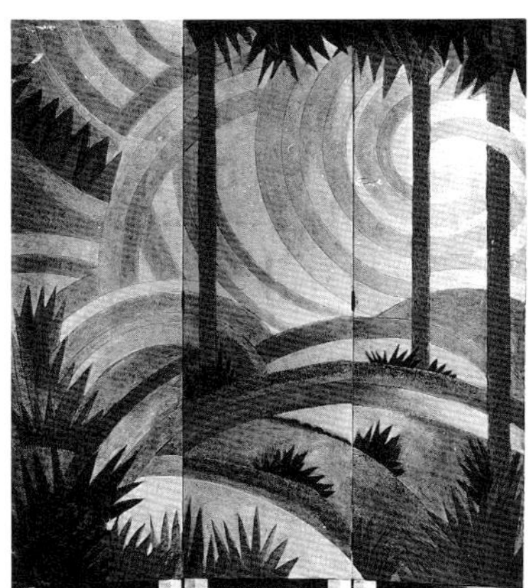

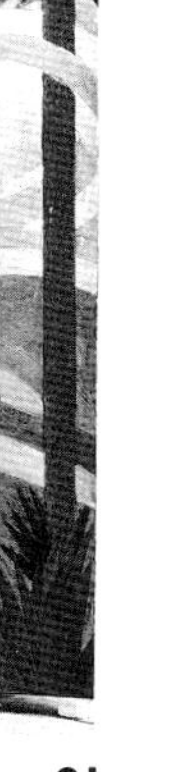

91

92

93

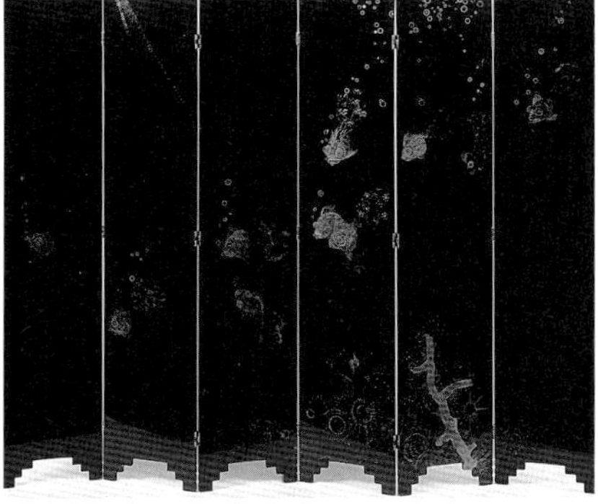

94

98

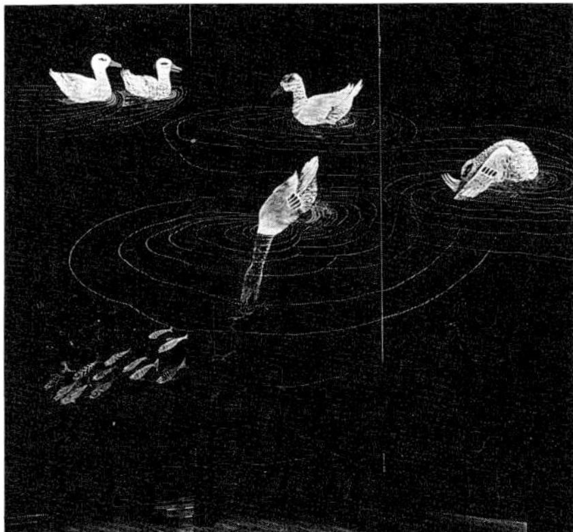

99

87 Forest
(four panels)
Brown lacquer with added metallic particles.
Signed.
Exh.: Galerie Charpentier, Paris, 1933, no. 6.
Coll.: Mobilier National, Paris.

88 Birds
(four panels)
Gold lacquer.
Signed.
Exh.: Galerie Charpentier, Paris, 1933, no. 7.

89 Marabou Storks
(two panels)
Black lacquer and gold lacquer.
Panel size 200 x 80 cm (78¾ x 31½ in.).
Signed.
Exh.: Galerie Charpentier, Paris, 1933, no. 10.
Bibl.: *La Carrosserie*, May 1934, p. 12; *Formal Tempo*, November 1937(?).

90 The Farmyard
(four panels)
Black lacquer and eggshell.
Panel size 170 x 75 cm (67 x 29½ in.).
C. 1922, signed.
Private collection.

91 Geometric Landscape
(three panels)
Silver *laque arrachée* and coloured lacquer.
C. 1923.
Variant of a screen exhibited at the Galerie Georges Petit in 1922; the background remains the same, but the animals depicted on the other screen are omitted.

92 Dogs
(six panels)
Eggshell and silver *laque arrachée*.
Panel size 125 x 30 cm (49¼ x 11¾ in.).
C. 1925, signed.
Exh.: Delorenzo Gallery, New York, 1985 (repr. in catalogue, p. 9).
Private collection, New York.

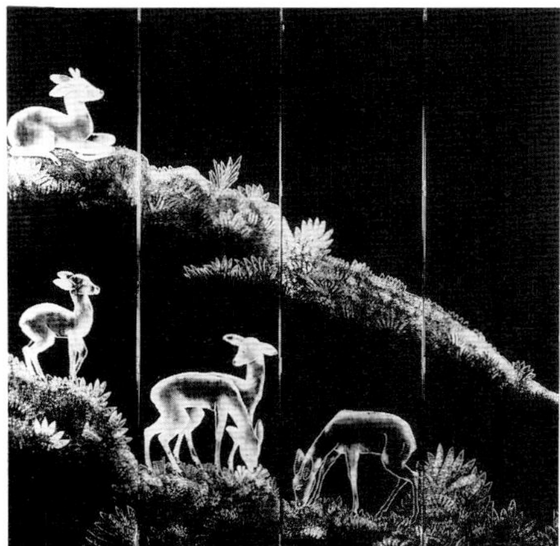

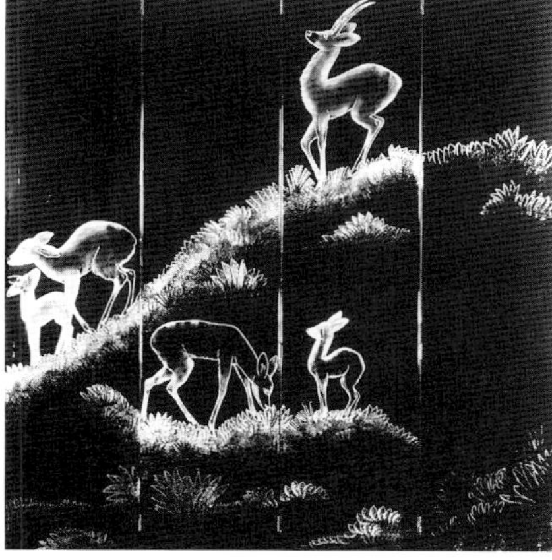

103

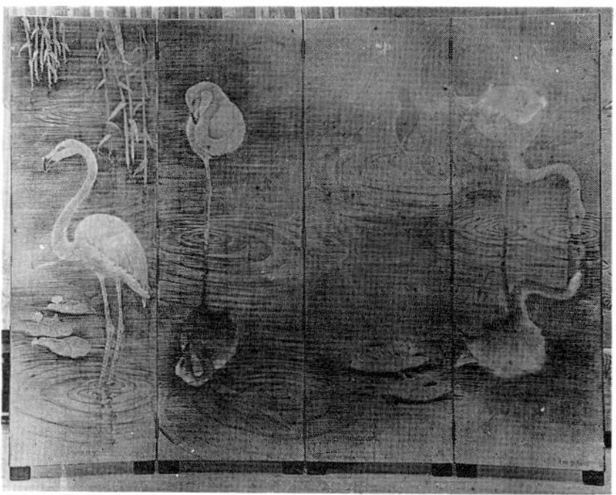

104

93 Geometric *Pl. 47*
(four panels)
Silver lacquer, coloured lacquer and scored brown lacquer.
Panel size 170 x 50 cm (67 x 19¾ in.).
C. 1927, signed.
Exh.: Galerie du Luxembourg, Paris, 1973, no. 107.
Formerly in the collection of Félix Marcilhac, Paris; Private collection, New York.
Bibl.: *Jean Dunand – Jean Goulden*, exhibition catalogue (Paris, 1973), repr. p. 90.

94 Japanese Fish
(six panels)
Black lacquer and coloured lacquer.
C. 1927.

95 Japanese Fish
(four panels)
Black lacquer and coloured lacquer.
Signed.
Bibl.: *Les Échos des industries d'art*, June 1928, p. 32.

96 Sunrise *Pl. 48*
(twelve panels)
Polished and matt gold lacquer.
C. 1930, signed.
Formerly in the collection of Félix Marcilhac, Paris; Private collection, New York.
The reverse side depicts 'Sunset'.

97 Contrasting Forms *Pl. 45*
(double accordion door, each half comprising five panels)
Incised black lacquer and gold lacquer.
C. 1930, signed.
Private collection, Paris.

98 Ducks in Flight
(twelve panels)
Decorated gold lacquer.
C. 1930, signed.

99 Ducks
(three panels)
Decorated black lacquer.
C. 1930, signed.
Bibl.: *Die Kunst*, 7 April 1933, p. 206.

100 Saint-Cernin *Pl. 15*
(six panels)
Incised black lacquer and coloured lacquer.
C. 1935.
Private collection, Paris.

101 Herons and Trout
(six panels)
Black lacquer and gold lacquer.
C. 1935, signed.

102 Snow in the Forest
(four panels)
Eggshell and shellac.
Panel size 175 x 50 cm (68¾ x 19¾ in.).
Signed.
Bibl.: *Beaux-Arts*, 8 May 1936.

103 Deer in the Mountains
(eight panels)
Gold and black lacquer.
Panel size 200 x 40 cm (78¾ x 15¾ in.).
Signed.
Exh.: Delorenzo Gallery, New York, 1985 (repr. in catalogue, p. 31).
Formerly in the collection of the architect Jean Walter.
Bibl.: Ragna Fischer, 'Jean Dunand', *Kunstindustri*, January 1937, p. 9; *L'Art dans la vie moderne* (Paris, 1937), p. 103.

104 Pink Flamingos
(four panels)
Black lacquer and silver lacquer.
C. 1937, signed.

105 Game of Chess
(three panels)
Red lacquer and gold lacquer.
C. 1940, signed.
Private collection, Paris.

106 Deer in the Forest
(four panels)
Brown lacquer and eggshell.
Signed and dated 1942.
Formerly in the collection of Félix Marcilhac, Paris; Private collection, Vienna.

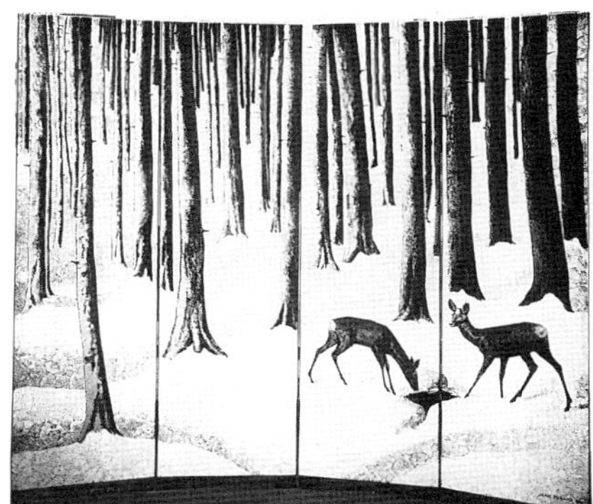

102

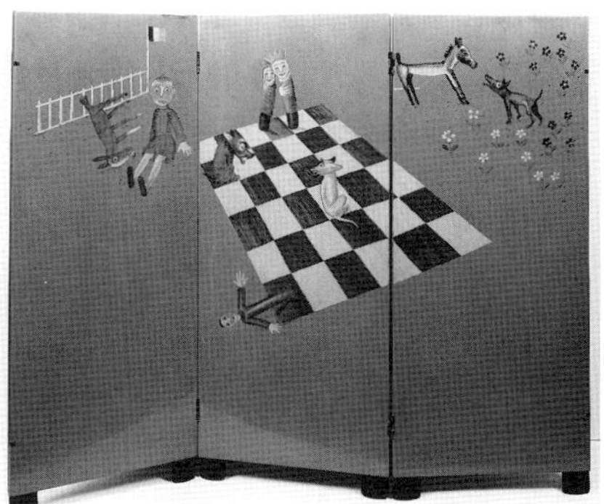

105

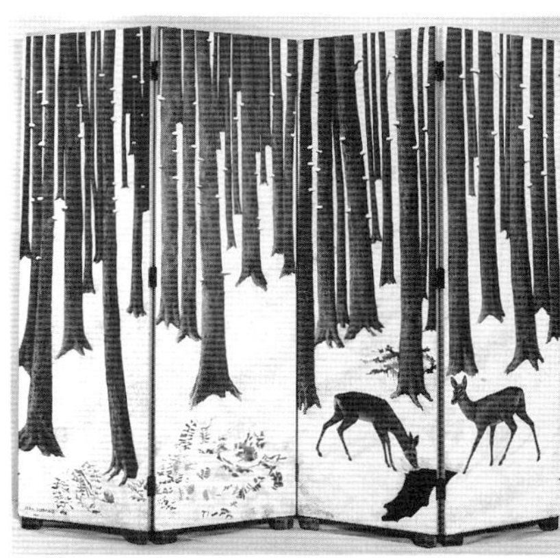

106

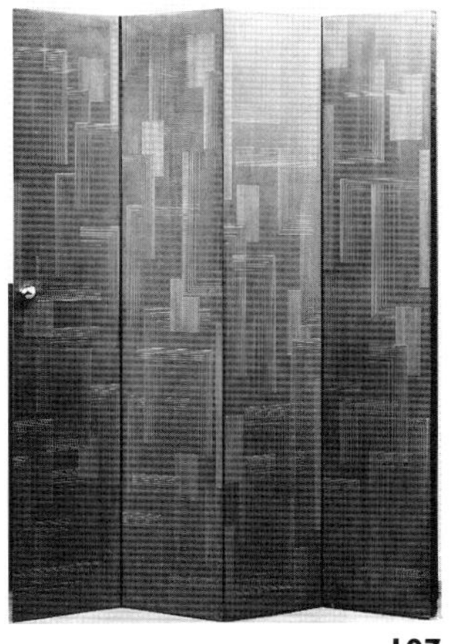

107

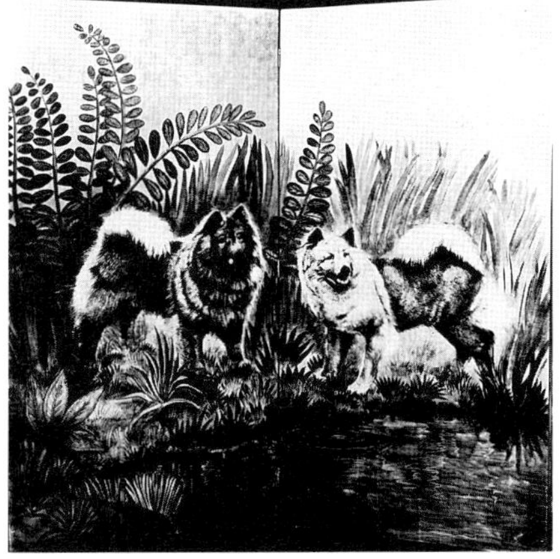

117

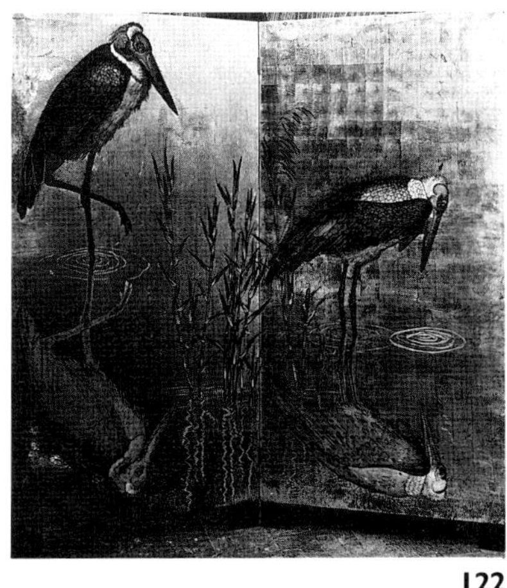

122

112

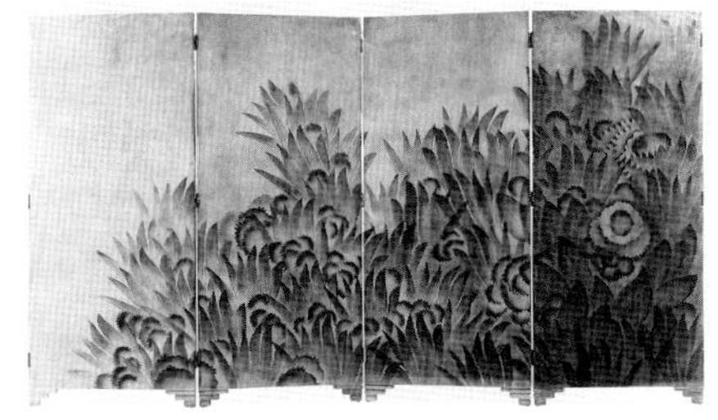

112

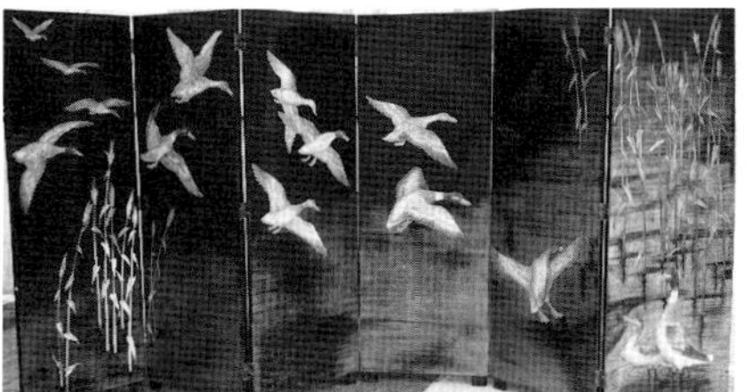

110

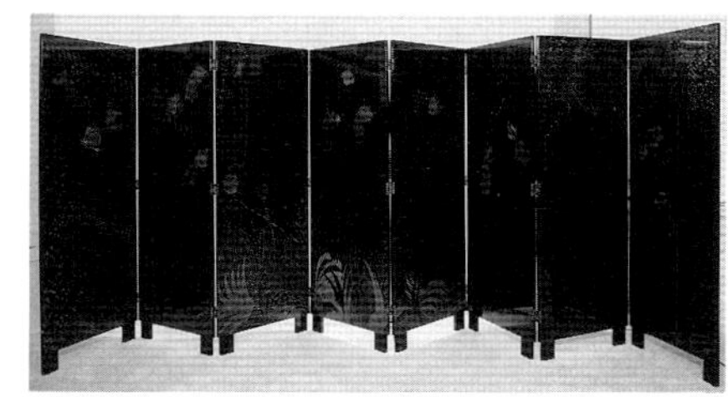

108

115

111

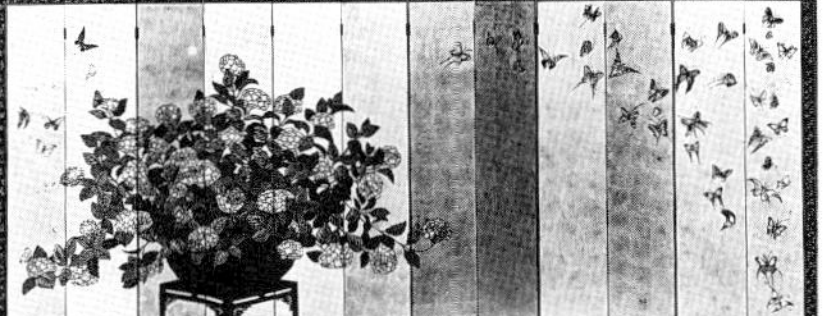

116

118

107 Geometric
(four panels from a double accordion door)
Incised brown lacquer.
Height 199 cm (78¼ in.).
Exh.: Musée des Arts Décoratifs, Paris, 1976, no. 437 (exhibition held to mark the 50th anniversary of the Exposition Internationale des Arts Décoratifs, Paris, 1925).
Formerly in the collection of Robert Mallet-Stevens; Musée des Arts Décoratifs, Paris.

108 Seabed
(eight panels)
Black lacquer, coloured lacquer and mother-of-pearl.
Panel size 165 x 60 cm (65 x 23½ in.).
Signed.
Exh.: Delorenzo Gallery, New York, 1985 (repr. in catalogue, p. 15).
Coll.: Wexler, New York.

109 Grass *Pl. 49*
(four panels)
Light-brown lacquer.
Signed.

110 Ducks
(six panels)
Black lacquer and gold lacquer.
Signed.
Sold: Gallais, Livinec, Pincemin (Rennes), 23 June 1987.

111 Deer in the Forest
Colour size and lacquer, sketch for a screen.

112 Monkeys
(four panels, front and back views)
Clear shellac.
Panel size 175 x 75 cm (68¾ x 29½ in.).
Signed.
Sold: Sotheby's (Monaco), 11 March 1984, lot 210.

113 Plain Gold
(six panels)
Gold lacquer with black-lacquer section.
Panel size 110 x 26 cm (43¼ x 10¼ in.).
Signed.

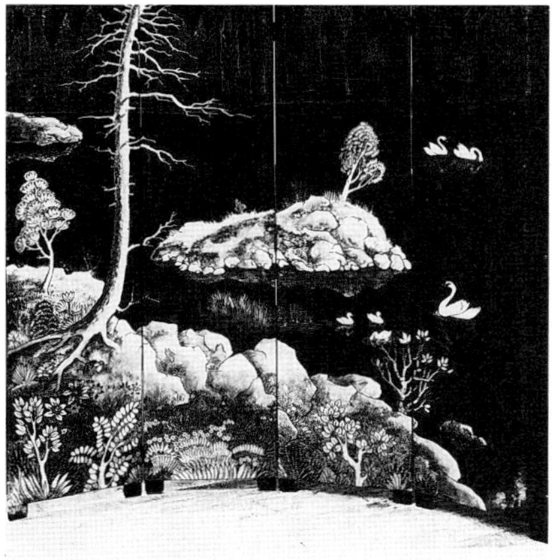
120

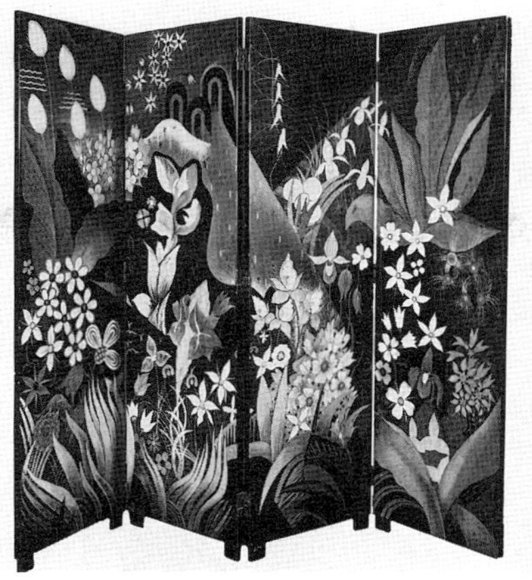
125

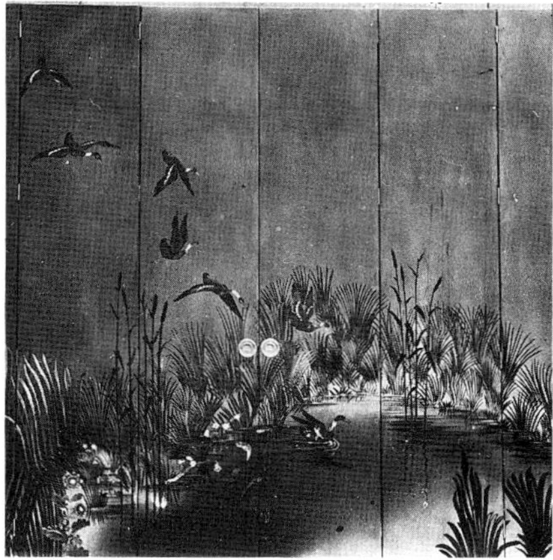
124

Sold: Sotheby's (Monaco), 24/25 October 1982, lot 419.

114 Deer in the Forest
Lacquered pine.
Panel size 190 x 80 cm (74¾ x 31½ in.).
Signed.

115 Seashore by Moonlight
(five panels)
Black lacquer and silver lacquer.
Signed.
Formerly in the collection of Félix Marcilhac, Paris.

116 Hydrangeas
(twelve panels)
Gold lacquer and incised Coromandel lacquer.
Signed.
Formerly in the collection of Jean-Charles Worth.

117 Pomeranians
(two panels)
Natural lacquer.
Signed.
Formerly in the collection of the Princess of Greece.

118 Wading Birds
(two double panels)
Black lacquer and gold lacquer.
Signed.
The reverse is inscribed 'Yvan'.

119 Shepherd-boy in the Mountains
(four panels)
Black lacquer.
Signed.

120 Landscape with Swans
(four panels)
Incised red lacquer.
Panel size 185 x 50 cm (72¾ x 19¾ in.).
Signed.
Private collection.

121 Swans
(four panels)
Black lacquer and gold and silver lacquer.
Signed.

122 Marabou Storks
(two panels)
Black lacquer and gold lacquer.
Signed.

123 Marabou Storks
(four panels)
Black lacquer.
Panel size 188 x 54 cm (74 x 21¼ in.).
Signed.
Formerly in the Lebourgy Collection.
Sold: Ader, Picart, Tajan (Monaco), 15/16 April 1978, lot 255.

124 Ducks
(accordion door, each half comprising three panels)
Shellac.
Signed.

125 Forest
(four panels)
Coloured lacquer and gold lacquer on a black-lacquer ground, after a cartoon by François-Louis Schmied.
Panel size 175 x 55 cm (68¾ x 21¾ in.).
Signed 'Jean Dunand laqueur' and marked 'F. L. Schmied'.
Formerly in the collection of Félix Marcilhac, Paris.
Sold: Ader, Picart, Tajan (Paris), 19 December 1975, lot 35.

126 Seabed
(seven panels)
Four panels in coloured lacquer and three with decorative motifs by Charles Hairon in carved and gilded wood.
Signed.
Bibl.: Émile Bayard, *L'Art appliqué français d'aujourd'hui* (Paris, n.d.), p. 251.

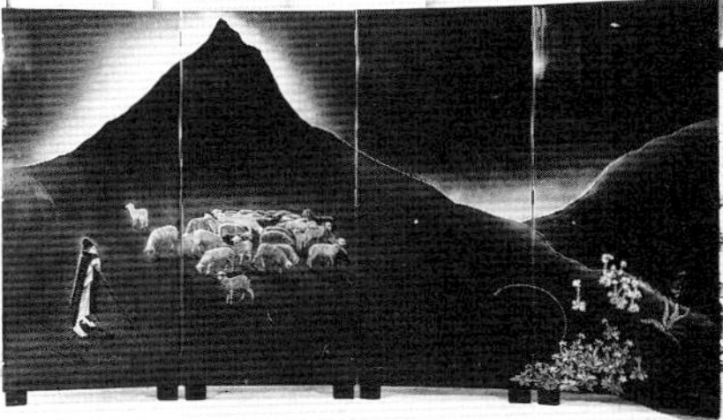
119

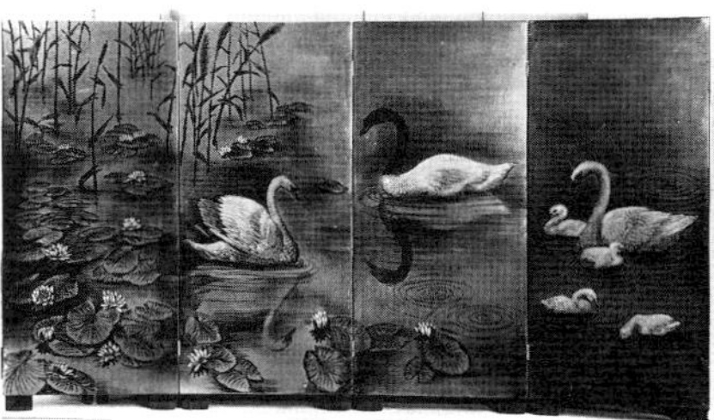
121

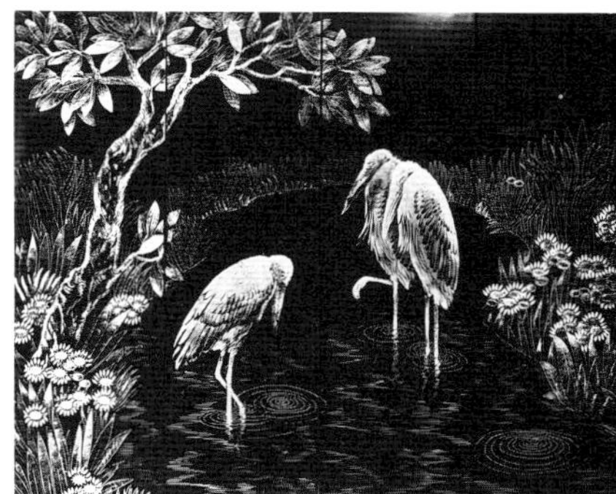
123

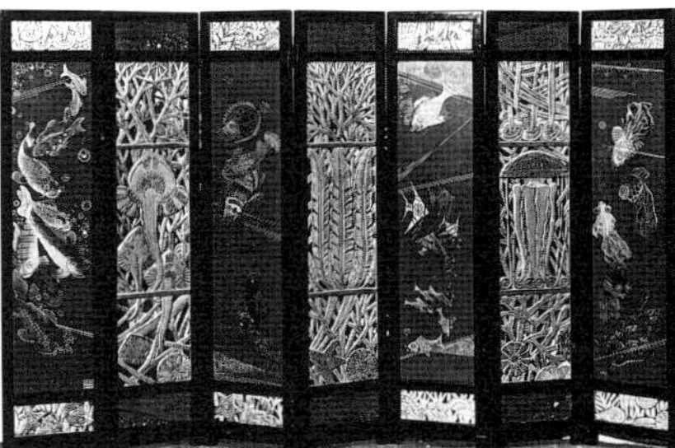
126

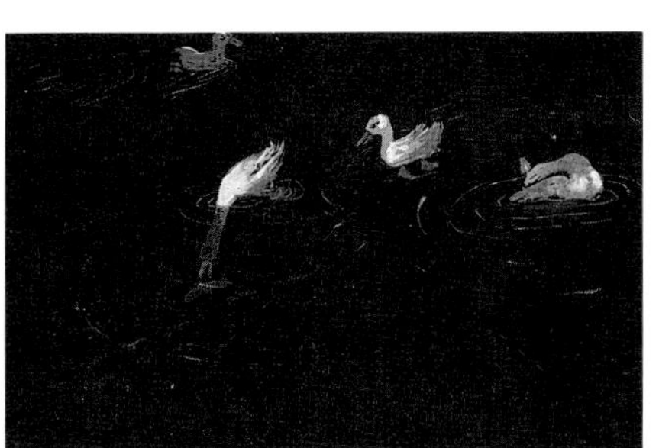

128

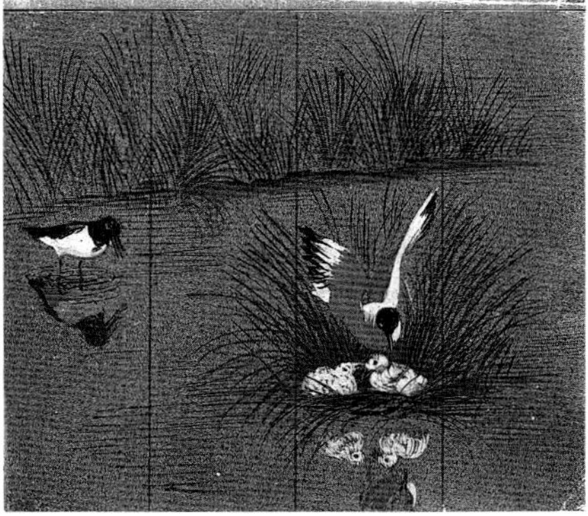

133

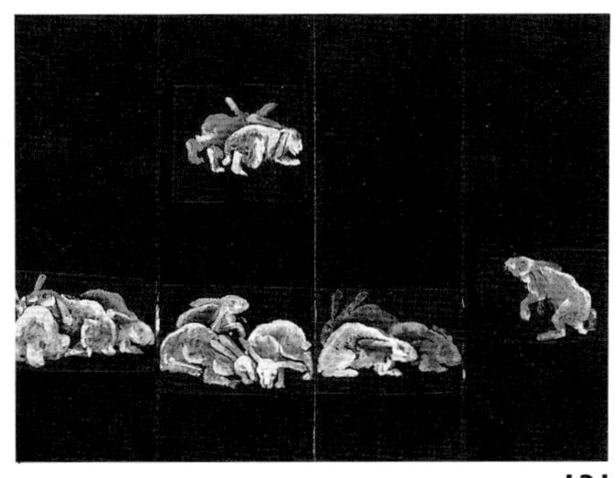

131

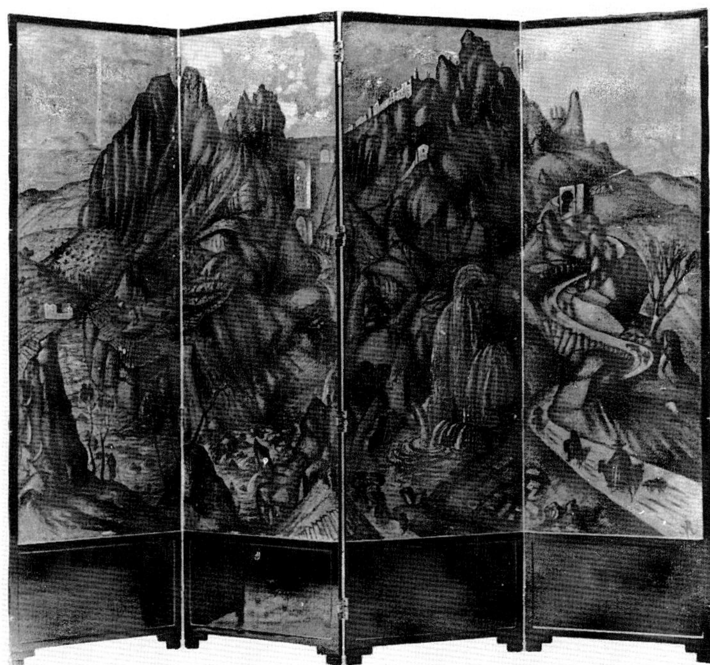

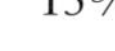

127

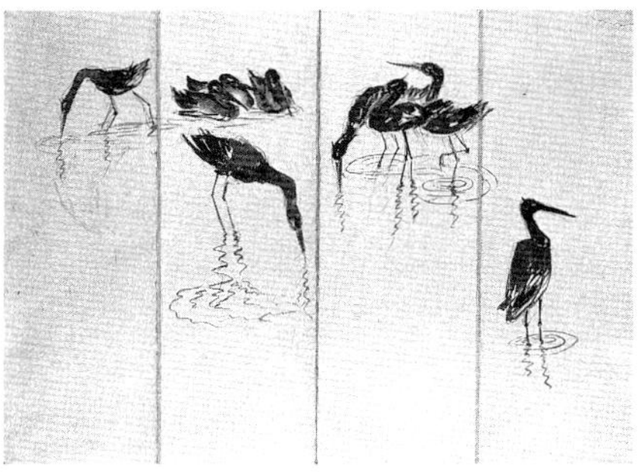

129

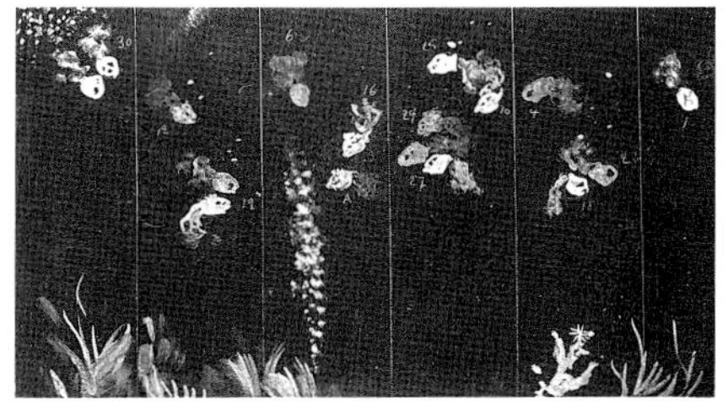

130

132

127 Spanish Landscape
(four panels)
Black lacquer and gold *laque arrachée*, after a cartoon by Serge Rovinski.
Panel size 220 x 60 cm (86½ x 23½ in.).
Signed.
Formerly in the collection of Nadine Oxnard; Félix Marcilhac, Paris.
Sold: Laurin, Guilloux, Buffetaud, Tailleur (Paris), 15 November 1974, lot 150.

128 Ducks
Gouache sketch.
22.5 x 32 cm (8¾ x 12½ in.).

129 Wading Birds
Gouache sketch.
30 x 40 cm (11¾ x 15¾ in.).

130 Fish
Gouache sketch.
8.25 x 28 cm (3¼ x 11 in.).
Sketch for a six-leaf screen with an intended panel size of 140 x 40 cm (55 x 15¾ in.).

131 Rabbits
Sketch in gouache overlaid with cut-outs.
26 x 32 cm (10¼ x 12½ in.).
See also 'Rabbits' screen (cat. no. 26) exhibited at the Galerie Georges Petit in 1926.

132 Leopard Attacking an Antelope
Gouache sketch.
18 x 24 cm (7 x 9½ in.).
Sketch for a four-leaf screen with an intended panel size of 150 x 50 cm (59 x 19¾ in.).

133 Marsh Birds
Gouache sketch.
10 x 36 cm (4 x 14¼ in.).
Sketch for a screen ordered by Valentine Brun, and intended to be executed in incised gold lacquer with a panel size 180 x 56 cm (70¾ x 22 in.).

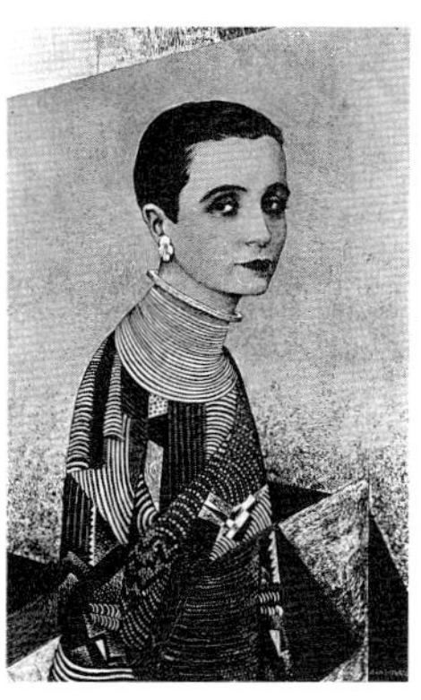
135

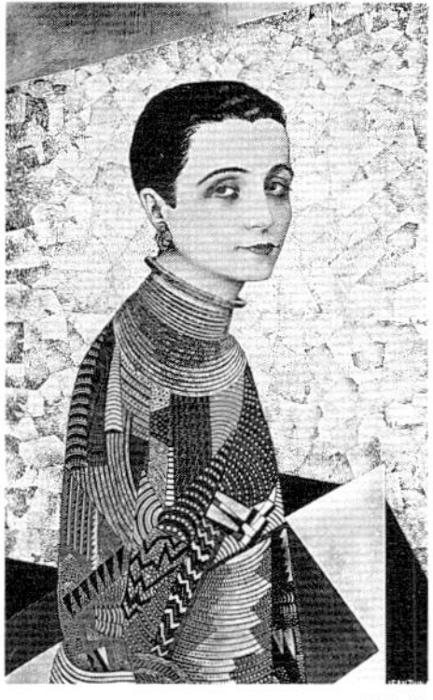
136

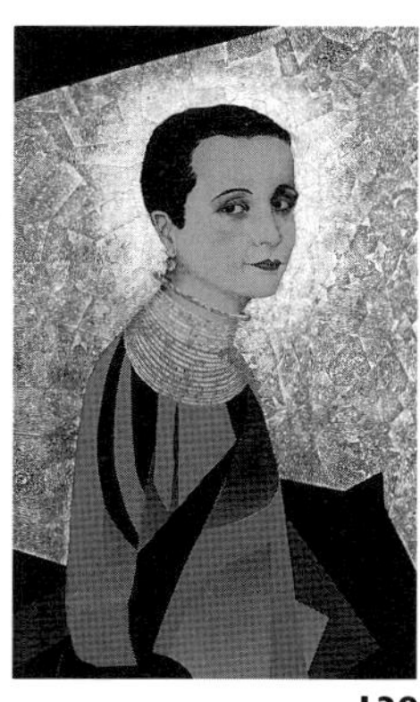
138

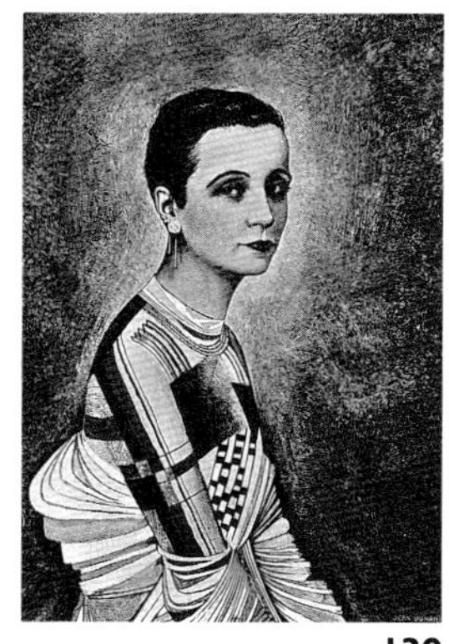
139

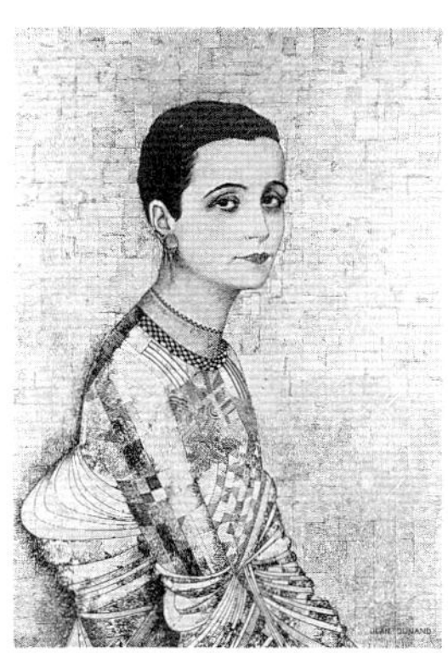
140

PORTRAITS

134 Madame Dunand *Pl. 1*
Gold, silver and coloured lacquer on an eggshell ground.
88 x 63.5 cm (34¾ x 25 in.).
1925, signed.
Exh.: Galerie Georges Petit, Paris, 1925, no. 26; Galerie La Renaissance, Paris, 1928, no. 67; Galerie du Luxembourg, Paris, 1973, no. 100.
Private collection.
Bibl.: *La Science et la vie: la semaine à Paris*, 1 November 1925, p. 381; *Mobilier et décoration*, February 1926; p. 40; *La Nature*, 15 October 1937, p. 362; *Jean Dunand – Jean Goulden*, exhibition catalogue (Paris, 1973), repr, p. 87.

135 Madame Agnès
Study in colour size and varnish.
82 x 51 cm (32¼ x 20 in.).
1925, signed.
Exh.: Galerie Georges Petit, Paris, 1925, no. 27.

136 Madame Agnès
Gold, silver and coloured lacquer on an eggshell ground.
82 x 51 cm (32¼ x 20 in.).
1926, signed.
Exh.: Galerie Georges Petit, Paris, 1926, no. 3.
Bibl.: *L'Officiel de la couture*, November 1926, p. 36; *Arts and Decoration*, October 1927, p. 134; *Jean Dunand – Jean Goulden*, exhibition catalogue (Paris, 1973), repr. p. 24.

137 Madame Agnès *Pl. 2*
Gold, silver and coloured lacquer on an eggshell ground.
82 x 51 cm (32¼ x 20 in.).
1926, signed and dated.
Formerly in the collection of Félix Marcilhac, Paris; Alain Lesieutre, Paris.
A variant of cat. no. 136.

138 Madame Agnès
Gold, silver and coloured lacquer on an eggshell ground.
82 x 51 cm (32¼ x 20 in.).
1926, signed.
Private collection.
Second variant of cat. no. 136.

139 Madame Agnès
Study in colour size and varnish.
80 x 50 cm (31½ x 19¾ in.).
1926, signed.
Private collection.
Third variant of cat. no. 136.

140 Madame Agnès (second version)
Coloured lacquer on an eggshell ground.
1926, signed.
Bibl.: *L'Illustration*, 15 October 1927.

141 Madame Charlotte Revil
Coloured lacquer on an eggshell ground.
80 x 53 cm (31½ x 20¾ in.).
1925, signed.
Exh.: Galerie Georges Petit, Paris, 1925, no. 28.
Bibl.: *Mobilier et décoration* February 1926, p. 41; *Arts and Decoration*, October 1927, p. 134.
A pastel sketch for this portrait was sold by Laurin, Guilloux, Buffetaud, Tailleur (Paris), 9 October 1976, lot 82.

142 Madame Louise Boulanger
Study in colour size and varnish.
80 x 53 cm (31½ x 20¾ in.).
1926, signed.
Bibl.: *L'Officiel de la couture*, November 1926, p. 36; *Arts and Decoration*, October 1927, p. 134.
Sold: Laurin, Guilloux, Buffetaud, Tailleur (Paris), 9 October 1976, lot 84.
The definitive version in coloured lacquer and eggshell was exhibited at the Galerie Georges Petit, Paris, 1926, no. 1.

143 Madame Bourdillon
Study in colour size and varnish.
1926, signed.

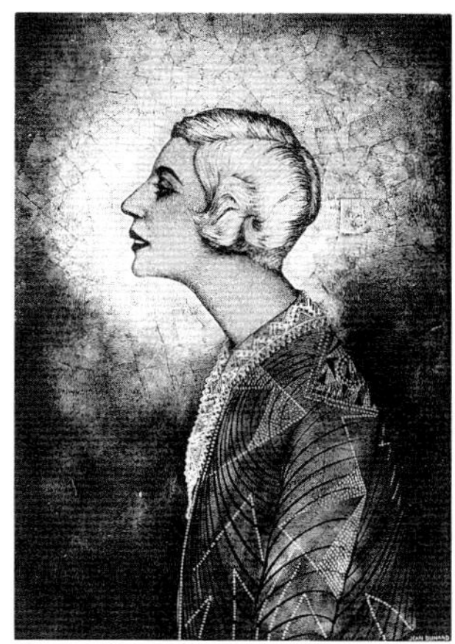
141

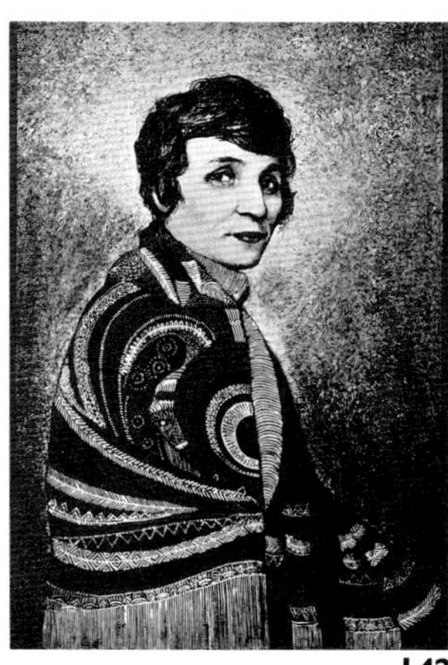
142

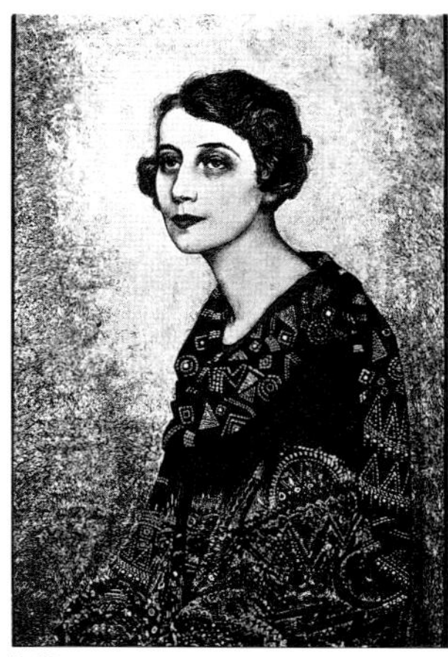
143

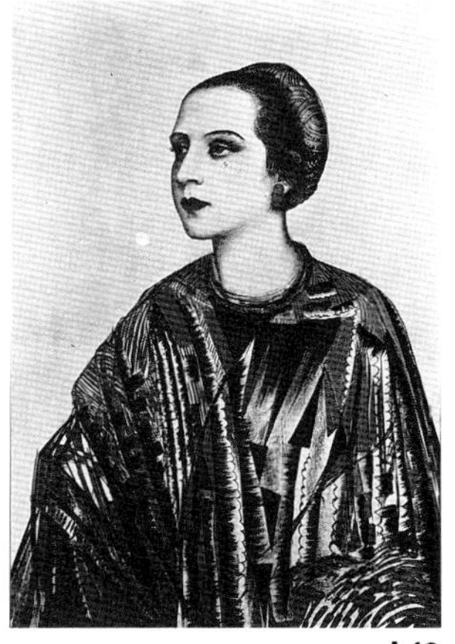

149

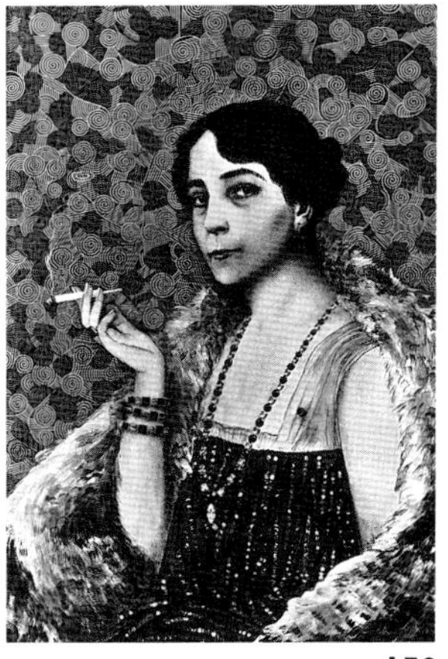

150

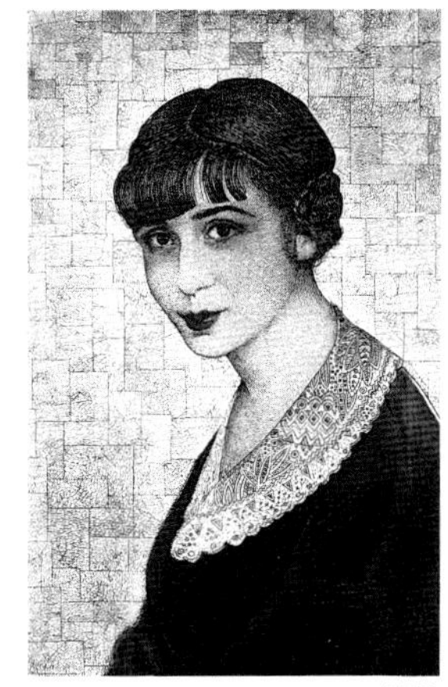

152

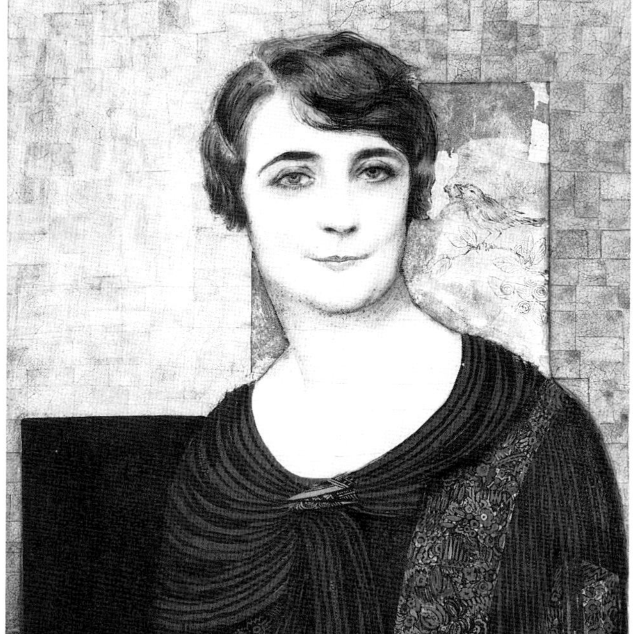

148

144 Madame Bourdillon *Pl. 6*
Gold, silver and coloured lacquer on an eggshell ground.
1926, signed.
Exh.: Galerie Georges Petit, Paris, 1926, no. 2.
Private collection.
Bibl.: *Arts and Decoration*, October 1927, p. 134.

145 Josephine Baker
Silver, gold and black *laque de Chine*.
177 x 69 cm (69¾ x 27½ in.).
1926, signed.
Exh.: Galerie Georges Petit, Paris, 1926, no. 4; 'Portraits et figures de femmes de Ingres à Picasso', Galerie La Renaissance, Paris, June 1928, no. 68; Rosenbach Gallery, New York, 1929, no. 9.
Bibl.: *La Renaissance de l'art français*, July 1928, p. 288; Alastair Duncan, *Art Deco Furniture* (London and New York, 1984), pl. 19.
Coll.: Claude Ott, Paris.
Sold: Christie's (New York), 9/10 December 1988, lot 447.

146 Josephine Baker *Pl. 8*
Study in gold and black lacquer on a silver ground.
82 x 57 cm (32¼ x 22½ in.).
1926.
Private collection.

147 Josephine Baker
Coloured lacquer on a grey lacquer ground.
49 x 33 cm (19¼ x 13 in.).
1927, signed.
Private collection.
The study for this panel, painted in colour size, was sold at auction by Maignan (Paris), 19 May 1972, lot 122.

148 Madame Philippe Berthelot
Study in colour size and varnish.
83 x 37 cm (32¾ x 14½ in.).
1927, signed.
Private collection.
Exh.: Galerie Georges Petit, Paris, 1927, no. 1.

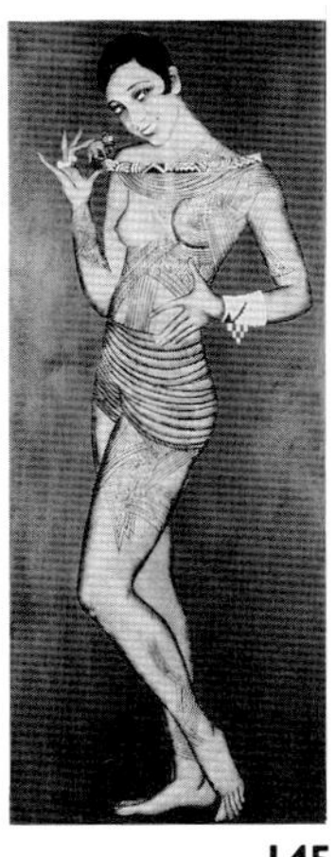
145

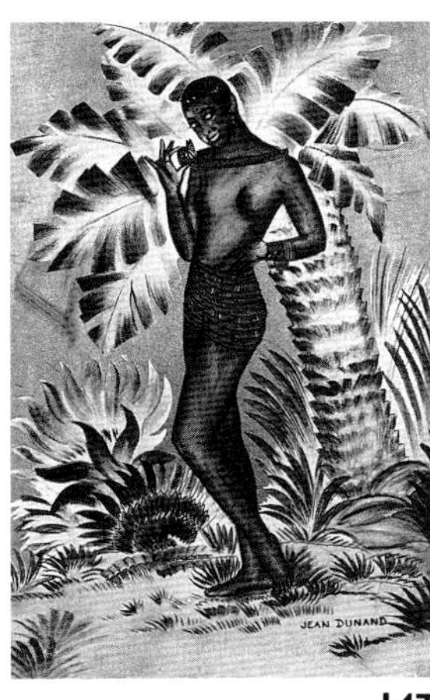
147

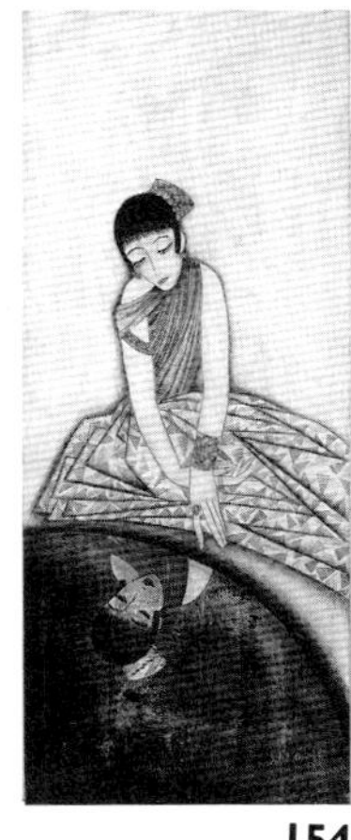
154

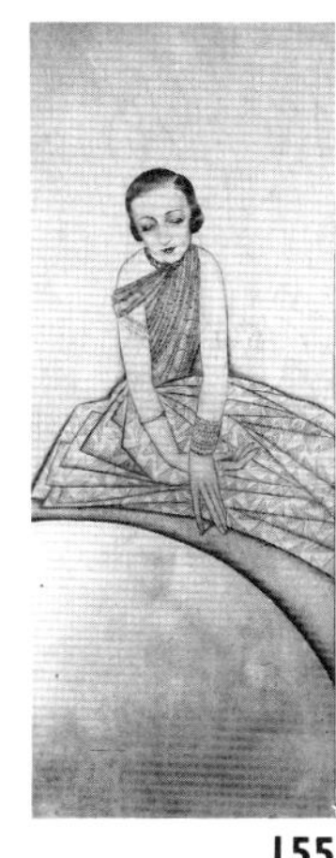
155

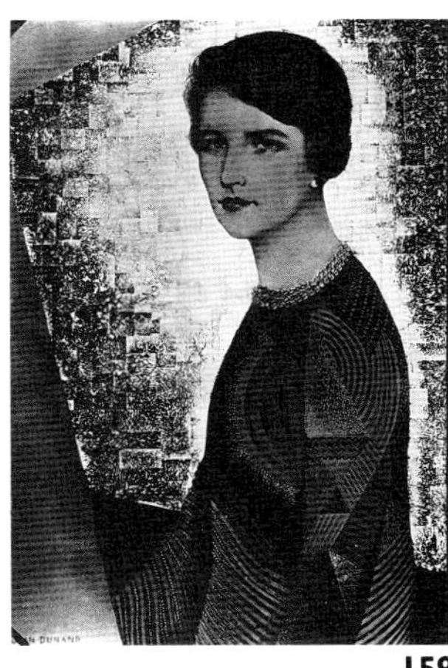
159

149 Madame Fontaine

Study in colour size, silver and varnish.
89 x 61 cm (35 x 24 in.).
1927, signed.
Exh.: Galerie Georges Petit, Paris, 1927, no. 2.
Sold: Sotheby's (Monaco), 26 September 1978, lot 224.

150 Madame Florence Blumenthal

Study in colour size.
78 x 54 cm (30¾ x 21¼ in.).
1927, signed.

151 Madame Florence Blumenthal *Pl. 5*

Coloured lacquer on a gold ground, inlaid with mother-of-pearl and coloured pearls.
78 x 54 cm (30¾ x 21¼ in.).
1927, signed.
Private collection.
Exh.: Galerie Georges Petit, Paris, 1927, no. 3.

152 Mademoiselle Louise Dunand

Coloured lacquer on an eggshell ground.
64 x 42 cm (25¼ x 16½ in.).
1927, signed.
Private collection.
Exh.: Galerie Georges Petit, Paris, 1927, no. 4; Galerie du Luxembourg, Paris, 1973, no. 99.
Bibl.: *Jean Dunand – Jean Goulden*, exhibition catalogue (Paris, 1973), p. 86.
The sitter was the artist's elder daughter, also known as Alix.

153 Josephine Veiled *Pl. 10*

Silver, light-brown and black lacquer.
96 x 56 cm (37¾ x 22 in.).
1927, signed.
Exh.: Galerie Georges Petit, Paris, 1927, no. 24.
Private collection.
Bibl.: *L'Art et les artistes*, November 1936; p. 61.

154 The Mirror (first version)

Black lacquer decoration on light-coloured wood.
143 x 56 cm (56¼ x 22 in.).
1927, signed.
Exh.: Galerie Georges Petit, Paris, 1927, no. 25.
Sold: Sotheby's (Monaco), 9 October 1983, lot 279.
See note to cat. no. 155.

155 The Mirror (second version)

Lacquer decoration on light-coloured wood.
143 x 56 cm (56¼ x 22 in.).
Unsigned.
Formerly in the collection of Karl Lagerfeld.
Sold: Godeau, Solanet, Audap (Paris), 21 November 1975, lot 92, repr. in catalogue, p. 47.
This second version was executed by Dunand at the request of the owner of the 1927 panel who, having been divorced from his first wife and remarried, wanted a portrait of his new wife, identical in size and colour, as a replacement for the earlier work.

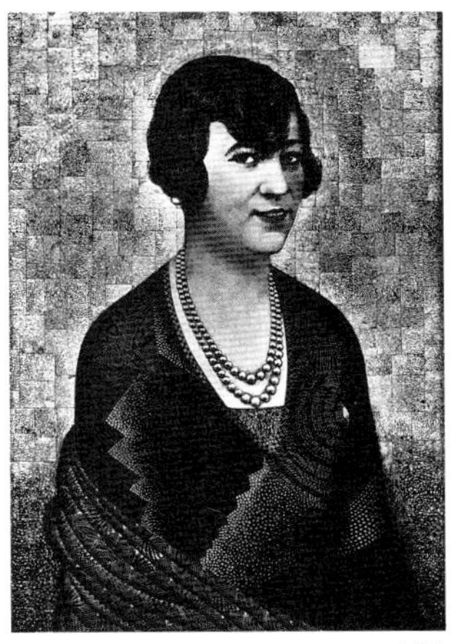

156

156 Madame Rigaud

Coloured lacquer on a squared eggshell ground, with silver beads in relief.
80 x 65 cm (31½ x 25½ in.).
C. 1927, signed.
Exh.: Delorenzo Gallery, New York, 1985 (repr. in catalogue, p. 37).
Sold: Christie's (New York), 31 May 1980, lot 181.

157 Josephine Baker

Study in coloured lacquer and black paint for a lacquer portrait.
88 x 62 cm (34¾ x 24½ in.).
1927.

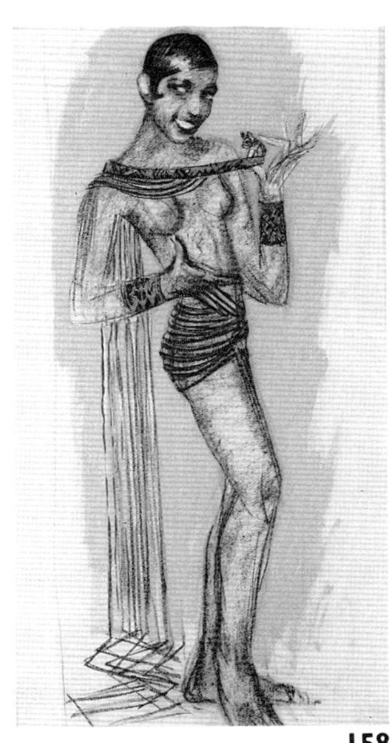
158

158 Josephine Baker

Study in charcoal and gouache for a lacquer portrait.
69 x 37 cm (27¼ x 14½ in.).
Sold: Christie's (New York), 9/10 December 1988, lot 448.

159 Madame Brady

Gold and coloured lacquer on an eggshell ground.
C. 1927, signed.

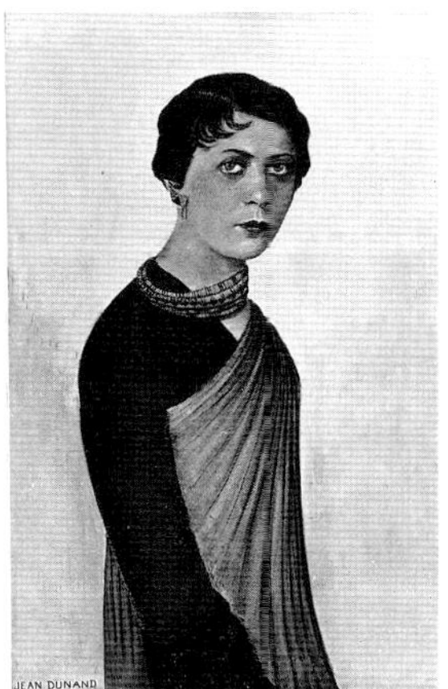

160

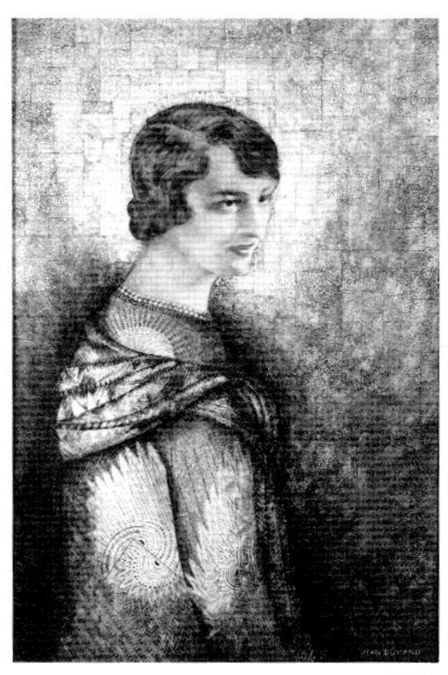

162

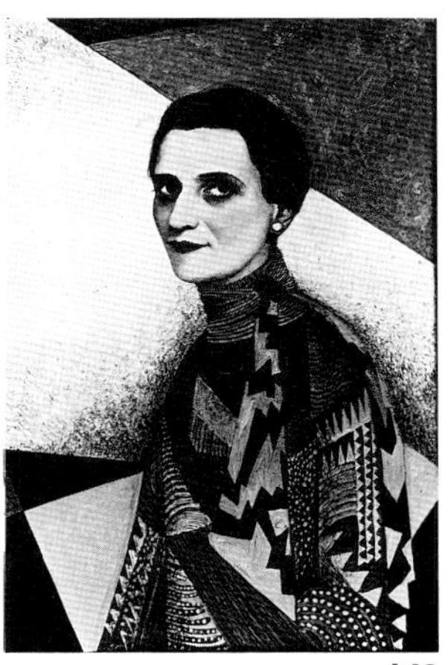

163

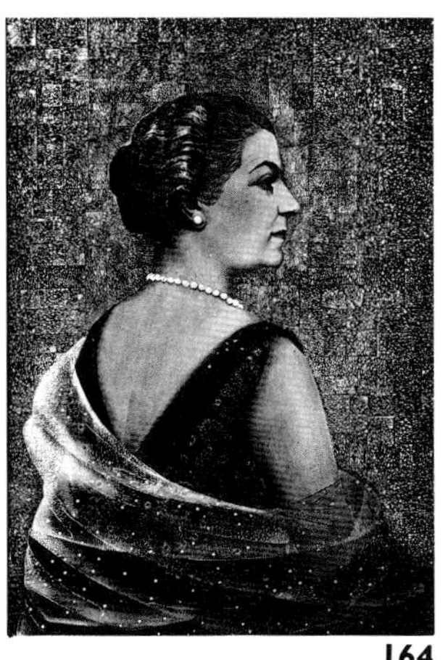

164

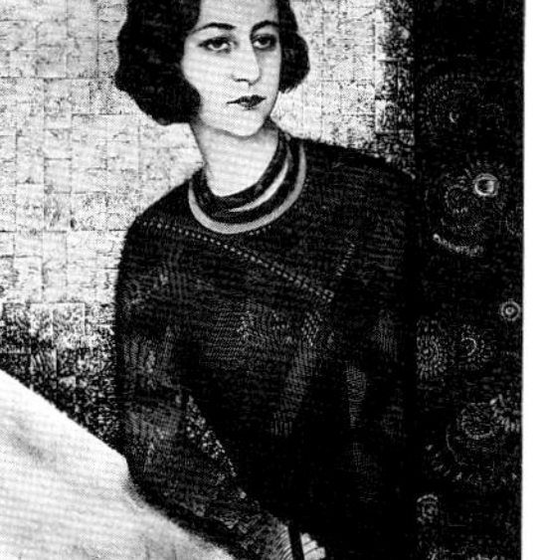

165

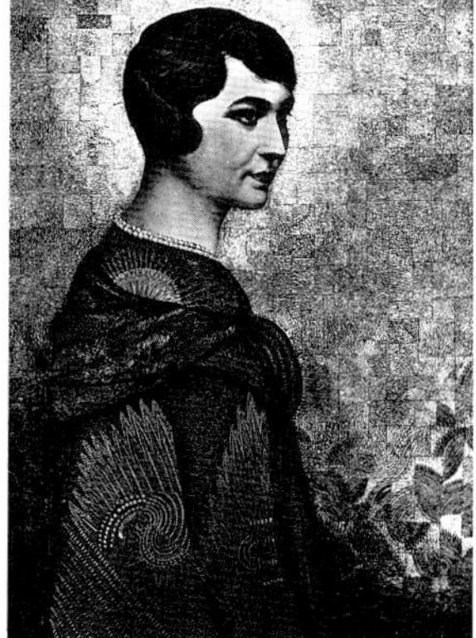

166

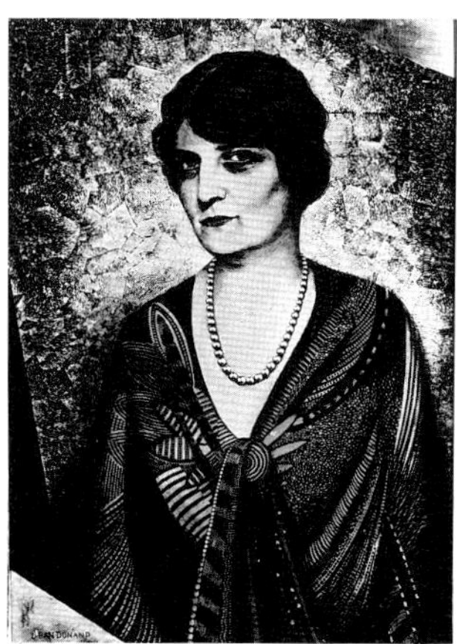

167

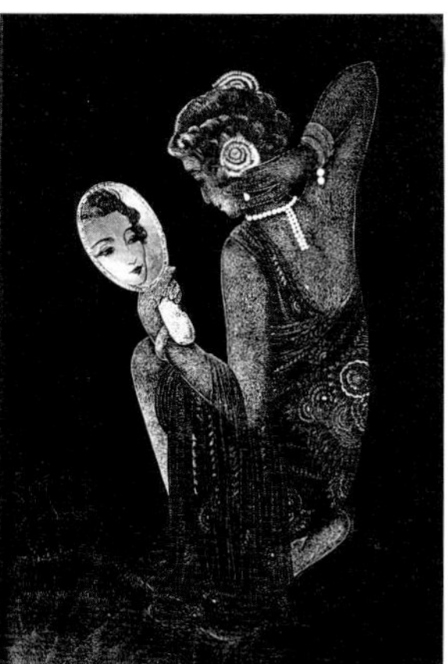

175

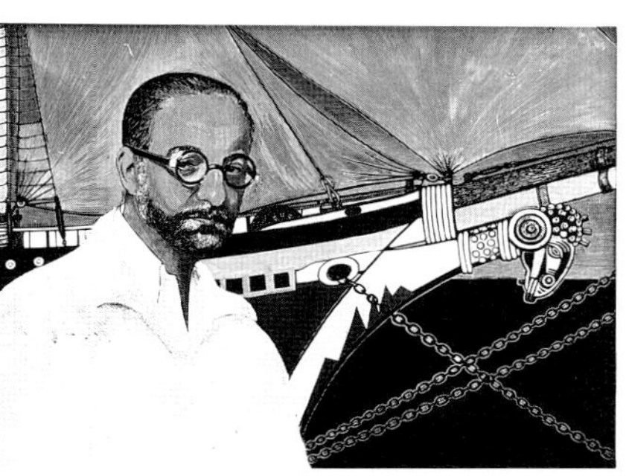

174

160 Madame X
Study in colour size and varnish.
C. 1927, signed.
The sitter is believed to be a French milliner who set up in business in New York in the 1920s.

161 Madame X
Gold and coloured lacquer on an eggshell ground.
C. 1927, signed.
Private collection.

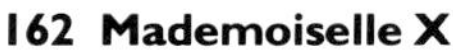

162 Mademoiselle X
Silver, black and coloured lacquer on an eggshell ground.
93 x 63 cm (36½ x 24¾ in.).
C. 1927, signed.
Sold: Sotheby's (Monaco), 24 September 1978, lot 223.

163 Madame Weiss
Study in colour size and varnish.
C. 1927, signed.

164 Madame Henry Dutey
Coloured lacquer on an eggshell ground.
1927, signed.

165 Mademoiselle Shinazi
Silver and coloured lacquer on an eggshell ground.
C. 1927, signed.

166 Comtesse de Guélen
Coloured lacquer on an eggshell ground.
C. 1927, signed.

167 Mrs Guggenheim
Coloured lacquer on an eggshell ground, inlaid with silver beads.
1928, signed.
Exh.: Galerie Georges Petit, Paris, 1928, no. 1.

168 Madame Philippe Berthelot
Coloured lacquer on an eggshell ground; see illustration, p. 143
83 x 37 cm (32¾ x 14½ in.).
1928, signed.
Exh.: Galerie Georges Petit, Paris, 1928, no. 2.

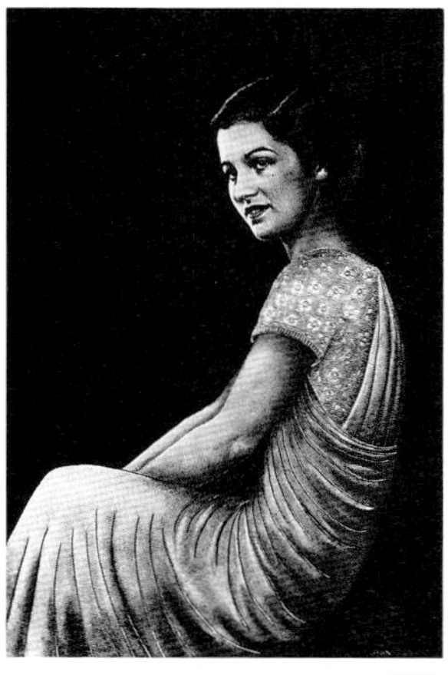

177

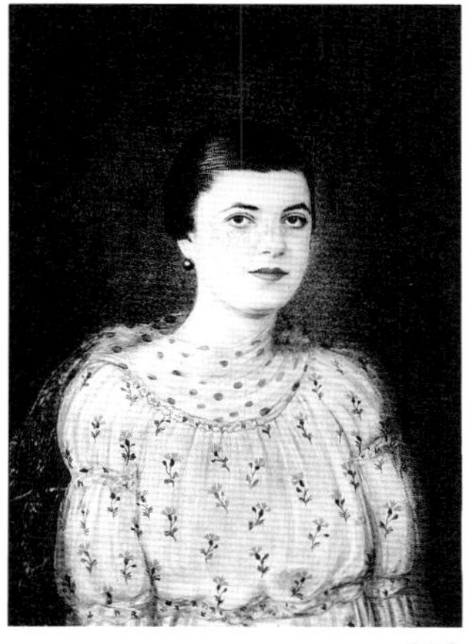

178

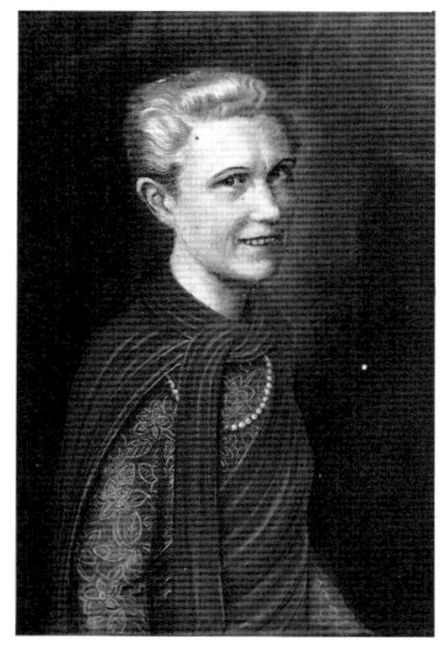

179

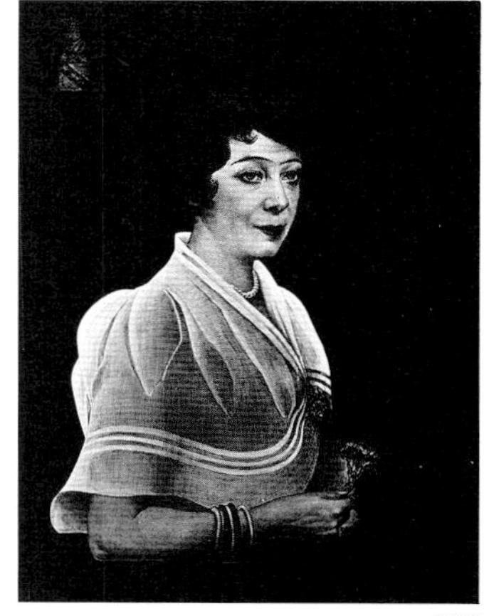

180

169 Madame Paravicini
Study in colour size and varnish.
1928.

170 Madame Paravicini *Pl. 4*
Silver and coloured lacquer on natural wood.
1928, signed.
Private collection.
Exh.: Galerie Georges Petit, Paris, 1928, no. 4.

171 Madame Jenny Sacerdote
Study in colour size and varnish.
210 x 140 cm (82¾ x 55 in.).
1929, signed.
Exh.: Galerie Georges Petit, Paris, 1929, no. 2.

172 Madame Jenny Sacerdote *Pl. 3*
Coloured lacquer with metal inlay on an eggshell ground.
210 x 140 cm (82¾ x 55 in.).
1930, signed.
Exh.: Galerie Georges Petit, Paris, 1930/31, no. 1.
Sold: Sotheby's (Monaco), 5 August 1987, lot 267.
The sitter was a Parisian *couturière*.

173 Monsieur Jean Guiffrey
Brown lacquer.
1930, signed.
Exh.: Galerie Georges Petit, Paris, 1930/31, no. 2.
See illustration, p. 36.

174 Monsieur François-Louis Schmied
Incised Coromandel lacquer.
1930, signed.
Exh.: Galerie Georges Petit, Paris, 1930/31, no. 3.
The sitter – wood-engraver and friend of Dunand – is seen here in front of his boat *Peau-Brune*.

175 Unidentified
Gold and black lacquer.
83 x 55 cm (32¾ x 21¾ in.).
C. 1930, signed.

176 Unidentified *Pl. 7*
Study in colour size and varnish.
83 x 55 cm (32¾ x 21¾ in.).
C. 1930, signed.
Private collection.

177 Mademoiselle Soupault
Study in colour size and varnish.
92 x 63 cm (36¼ x 24¾ in.).
C. 1930, signed.
Sold: Laurin, Guilloux, Buffetaud, Tailleur (Paris), 24 November 1978, lot 69.

178 Portrait of a Young Woman
Study in colour size and varnish.
60 x 45 cm (23½ x 17¾ in.).
Sold: Soissons (Aisne), 9 July 1989.

179 Madame Joubert
Pastel.
70 x 47 cm (27½ x 18½ in.).
C. 1930, signed.
Sold: Boisgirard (Paris), 28 October 1987, lot 193.
The sitter was a Parisian *couturière*.

180 Madame Alex Clavel
Light-brown lacquer.
C. 1930, signed.
Private collection.

181 Monsieur Alex Clavel
Brown lacquer.
1930, signed.
Private collection.

182 Madame Clavel (*mère*)
Brown lacquer.
C. 1930, signed.
Private collection.

183 Madame Clavel (*mère*)
Study in colour size.
C. 1930, signed.
Private collection.

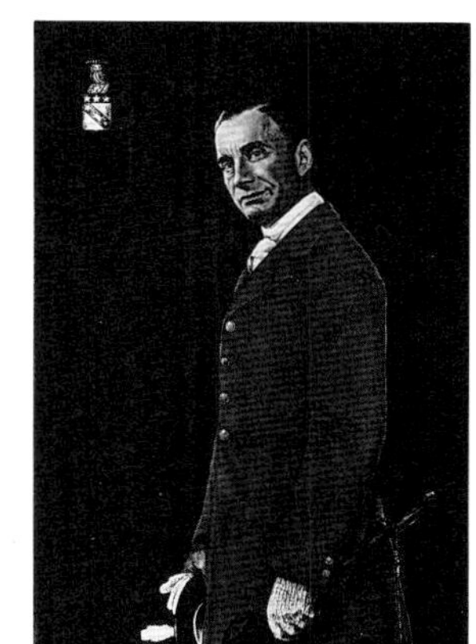
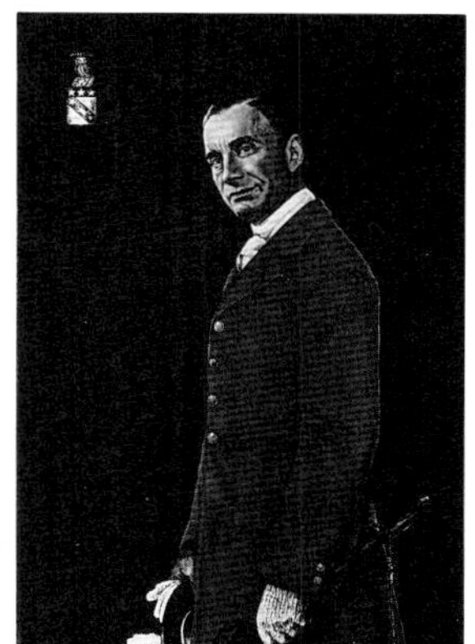

181

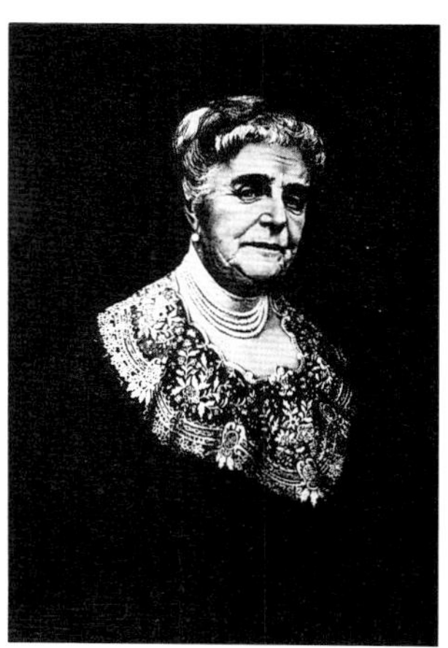

182

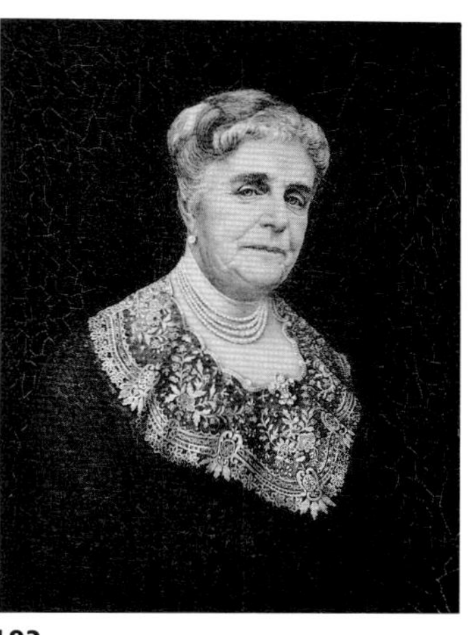

183

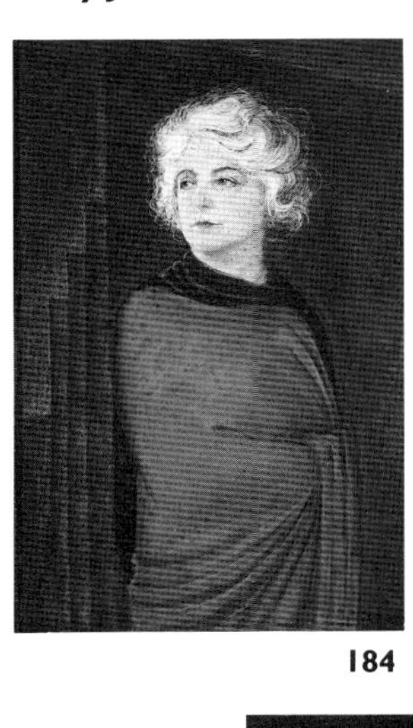
184

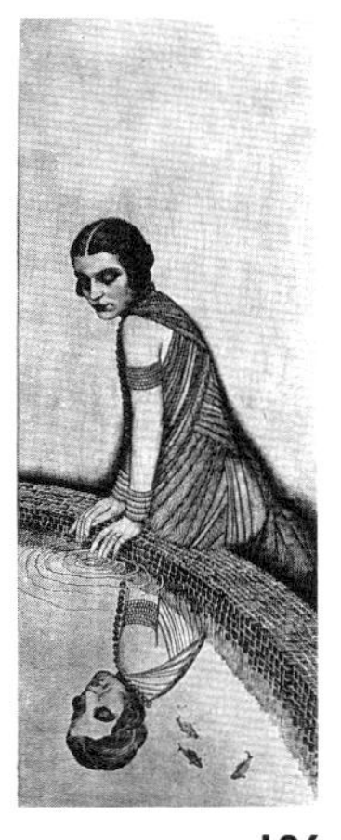
186

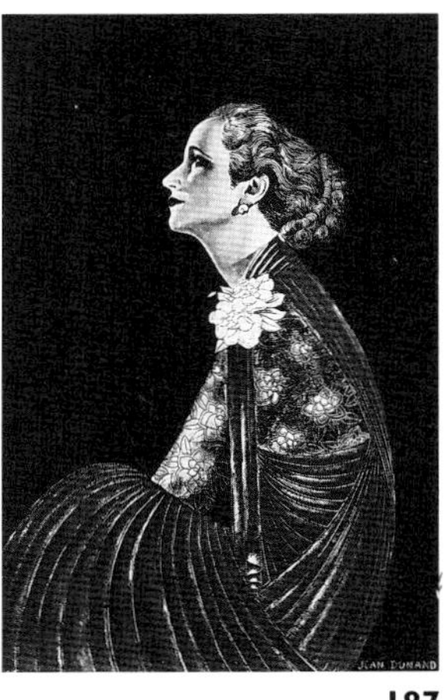
187

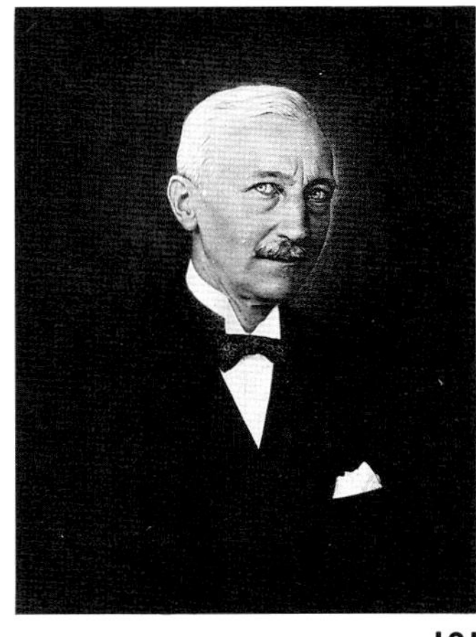
191

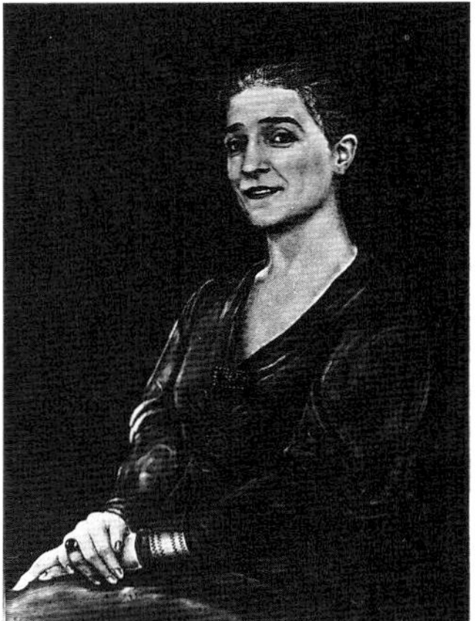
192

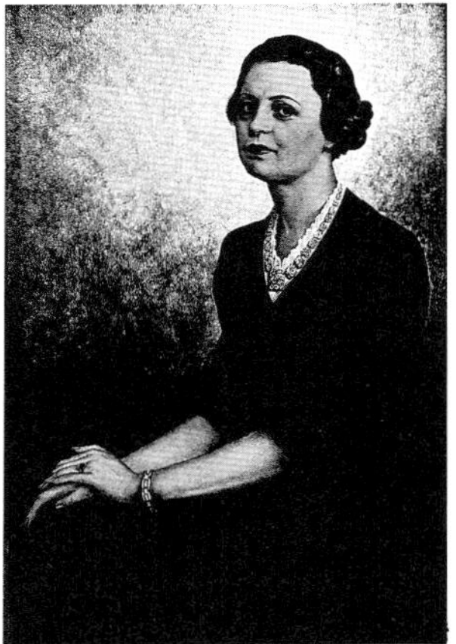
193

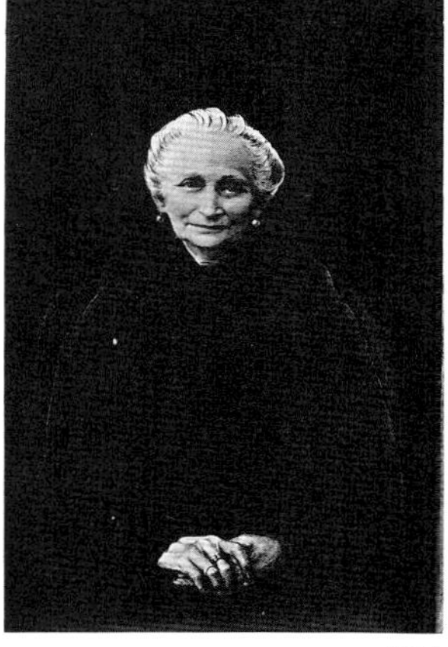
194

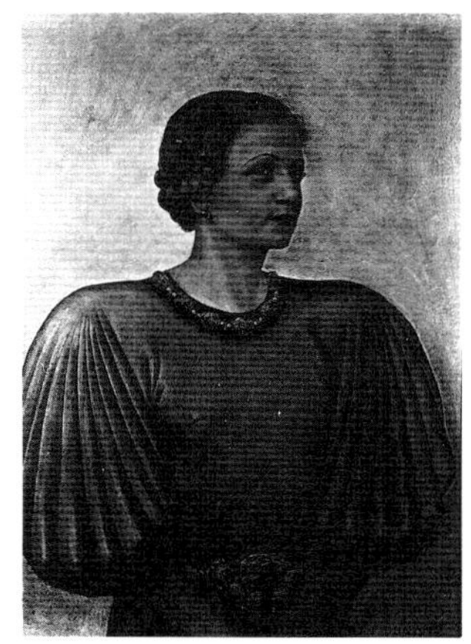
195

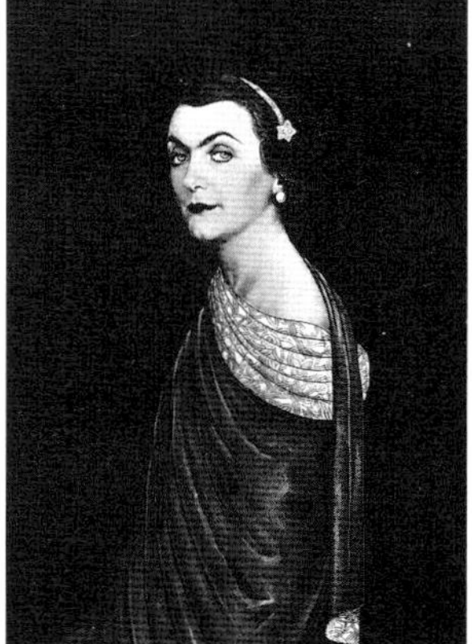
196

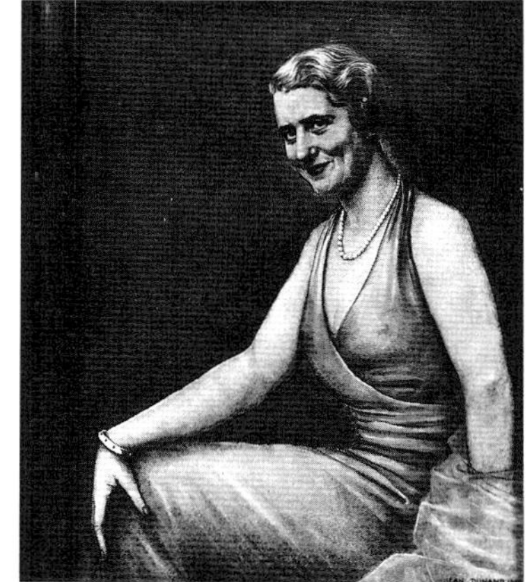
198

184 Madeleine Vionnet
Pastel.
90 x 58 cm (35½ x 22¾ in.).
1932, signed.
Sold: Laurin, Guilloux, Buffetaud, Tailleur (Paris), 9 December 1976, lot 81; Godeau, Solanet, Audap (Paris), 15 May 1985, lot 194, repr. in catalogue, p. 55.

185 Madeleine Vionnet
Brown and red lacquer and eggshell.
90 x 58 cm (35½ x 22¾ in.).
1932, signed.
Exh.: Galerie Charpentier, Paris, 1933, no. 1.
Formerly in the collection of Madeleine Vionnet.
Bibl.: *L'Officiel de la couture*, May 1933, p. 18.

186 Madame Jean-Charles Worth
Silver and black lacquer decoration on natural wood panel.
1932, signed.
Exh.: Galerie Charpentier, Paris, 1933, no. 2.
Private collection.
Sold: Poulain, Lefur (Paris), 19 June 1987.

187 Madame Agnès (third version)
Incised Coromandel lacquer.
83 x 55 cm (32¾ x 21¾ in.).
1932, signed.
Exh.: Galerie Charpentier, Paris, 1933, no. 3.
Bibl.: *L'Officiel de la couture* May 1933, p. 19; *L'Illustration*, special Christmas number, 1934.

188 Madame Agnès *Pl. 11*
Study in colour size and varnish.
83 x 55 cm (32¾ x 21¾ in.).
1932, signed.
Private collection.

189 Monsieur Johan Colcombet
('Monsieur La Belle Vie')
Silver and coloured lacquer on an eggshell ground.
1933, signed.

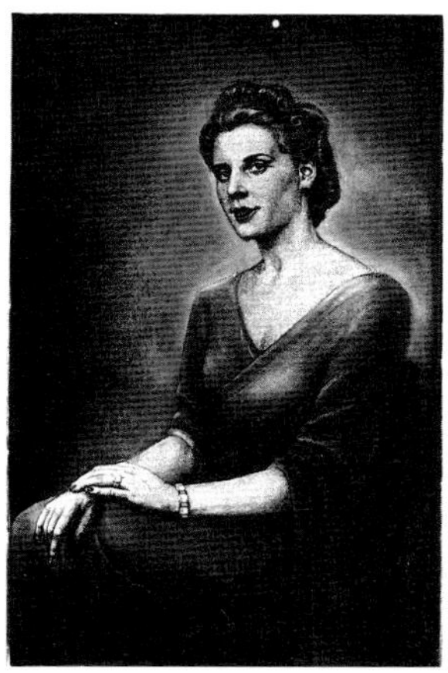
197

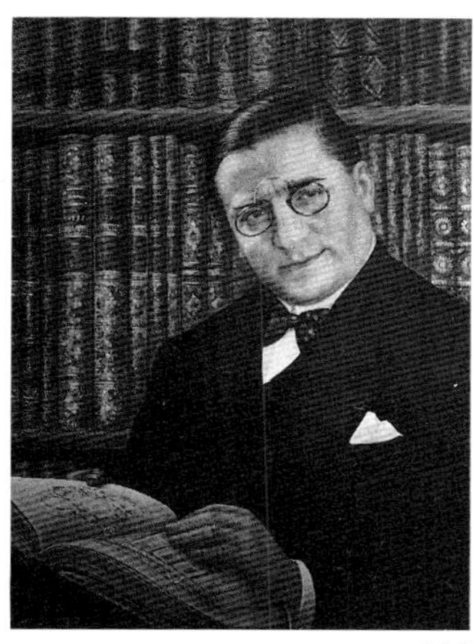
200

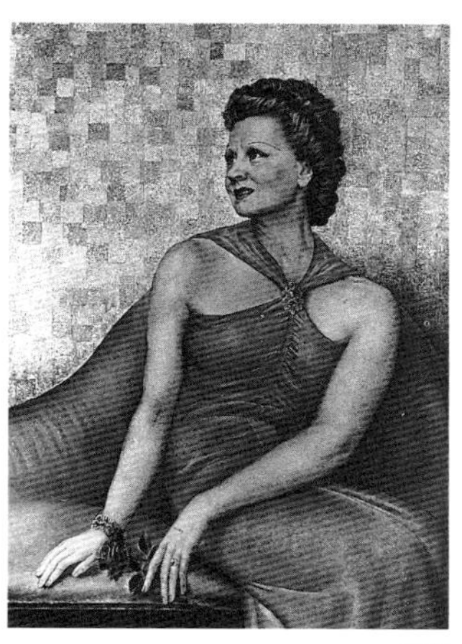
201

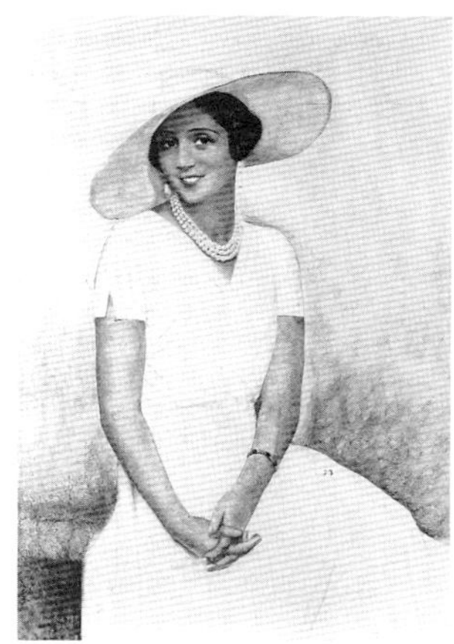
203

Exh.: Galerie Charpentier, Paris, 1933, no. 4.
Colcombet was born on the same day as Jean Dunand.
See illustration, p. 141.

190 Madame Raoul Perrenoud
Study in colour size and varnish.
C. 1936, signed.
57 x 46 cm (22½ x 19¼ in.).

191 Dr Amédée Baumgartner
Study in colour size and varnish.
1936, signed.

192 Madame Octave Raspail
Study in colour size and varnish.
1936, signed.

193 Madame Dervez
Study in colour size and varnish.
C. 1936, signed.

194 Madame Chevalier
Study in colour size and varnish.
C. 1936, signed.

195 Unidentified
Study in colour size and varnish.
C. 1936, signed.

196 Madame Maquinay
Study in colour size and varnish.
C. 1936, signed.

197 Madame Louis Dreyfus
Study in colour size and varnish.
C. 1936, signed.

198 Madame Taillan
Study in colour size and varnish.
1938, signed.

199 Monsieur Jean-Louis Dunand
Study in colour size and varnish.
1938, signed.
See illustration, p. 162.

200 Monsieur Armand-Albert Rateau
Study in colour size and varnish.
1939, signed.

201 Madame Valentine Tessier
Study in colour size and varnish.
C. 1939, signed.

202 Suzy Solidor *Pl. 9*
Brown lacquer and eggshell.
70 x 50 cm (27½ x 19¾ in.).
C. 1939, signed.
Exh.: Salon d'Hiver, Paris, 1941.
Private collection.
Bibl.: *L'Illustration*, 13 December 1941, p. 376.

203 Madame Martinez de Hoze
Study in colour size and varnish.
100 x 68 cm (39¼ x 26¾ in.).
C. 1939, signed.
Private collection.

MOSAICS

204 Virgin and Child
Coloured glass mosaic and gold.
1932, signed.
Exh.: Galerie Georges Petit, Paris, 1932, no. 1; Exposition Internationale des Arts et Techniques, Paris, 1937.

205 Christ on the Cross
Coloured glass mosaic and gold.
1932, signed.
Exh.: Galerie Georges Petit, Paris, 1932, no. 2; Exposition Internationale des Arts et Techniques, Paris, 1937.

206 Virgin
Coloured glass mosaic and *repoussé* gold decorated with gemstones.
1932, signed.
Exh.: Galerie Georges Petit, Paris, 1932, no. 3.

207 Christ in Majesty
Sketch painted for a projected mosaic.
1932, signed.
Exh.: Galerie Georges Petit, Paris, 1932, no. 4.
See also cat. no. 763.

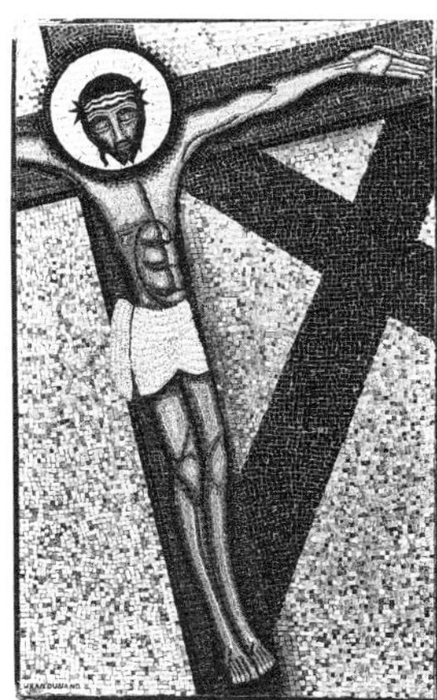
205

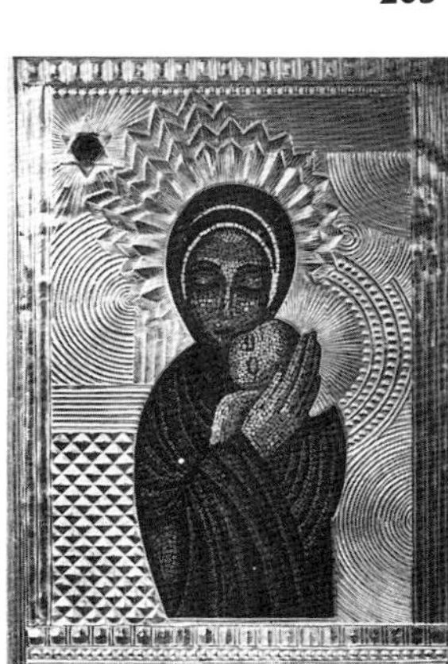
206

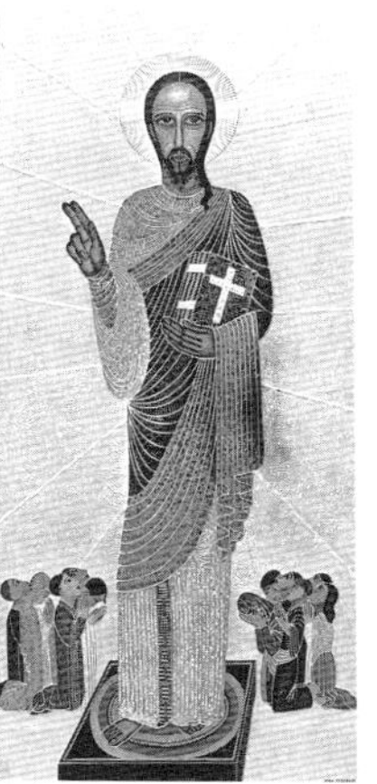
207

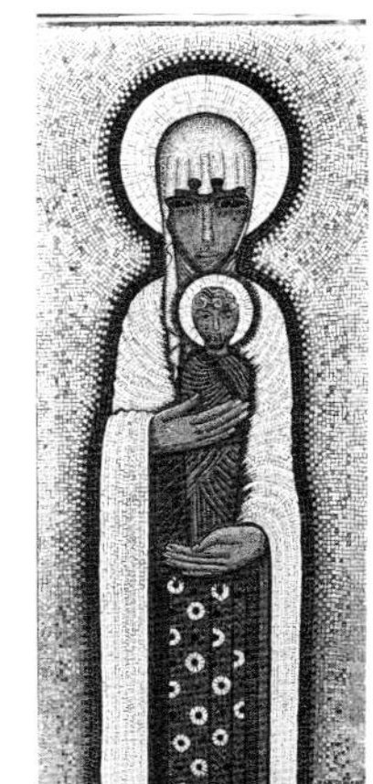
204

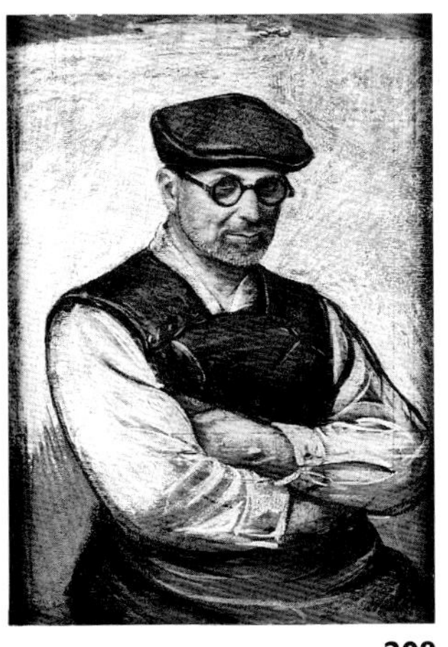
208

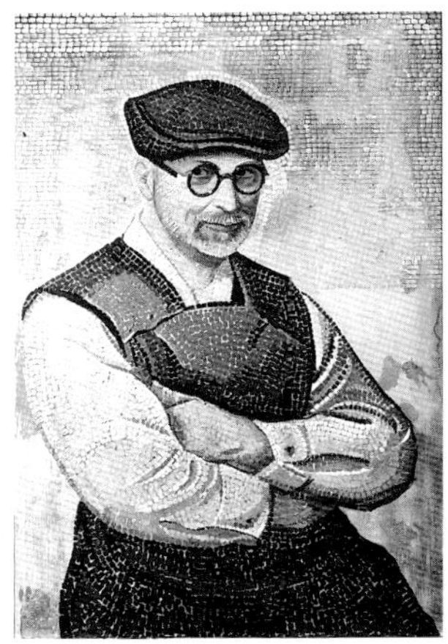
209

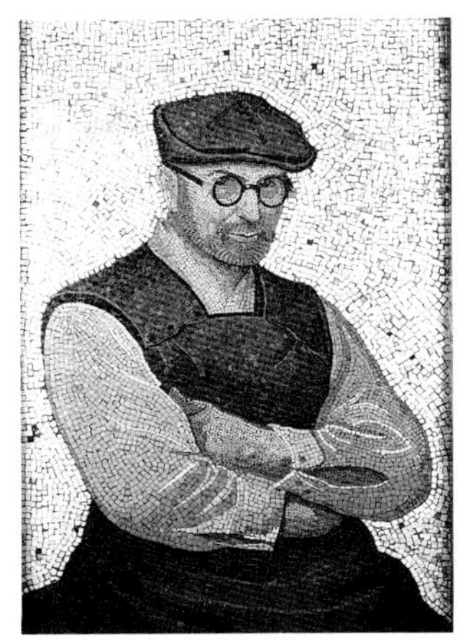
210

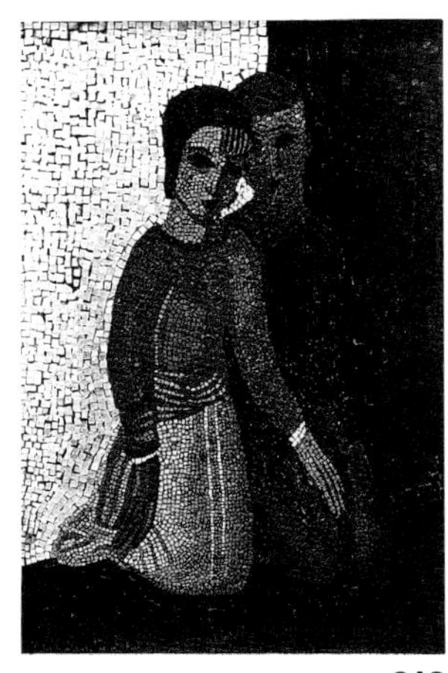
213

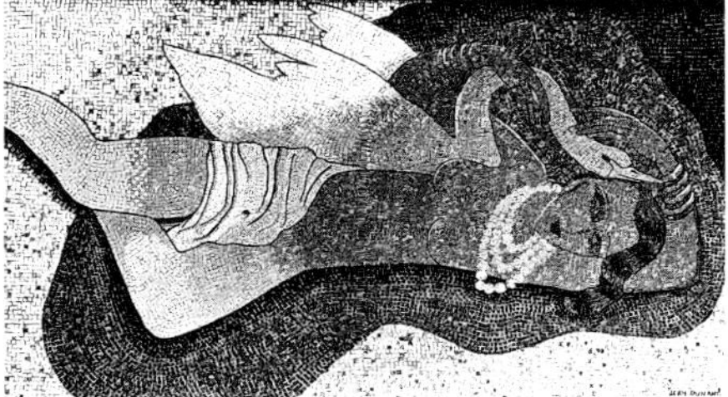
211

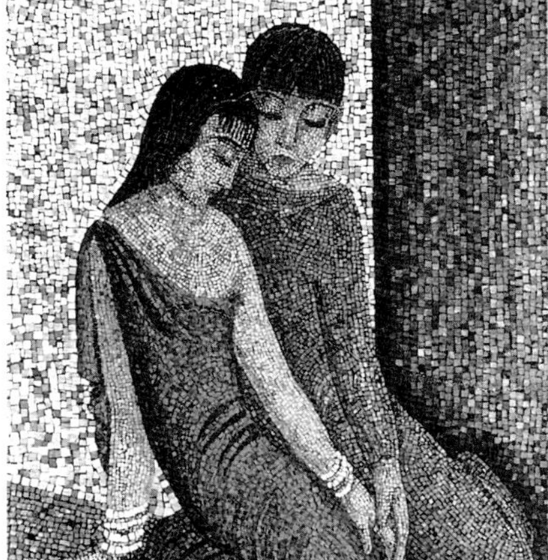

214

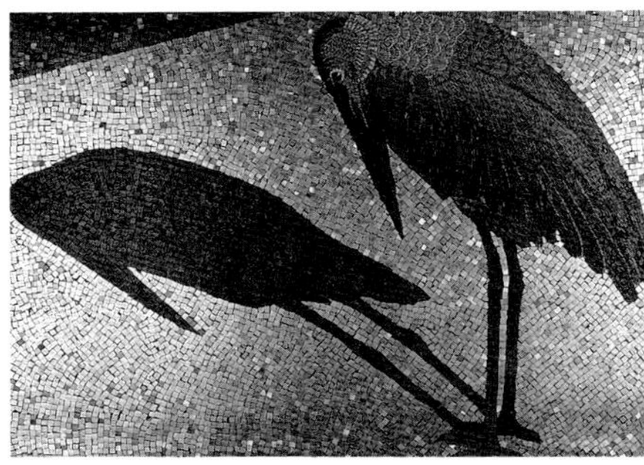
212

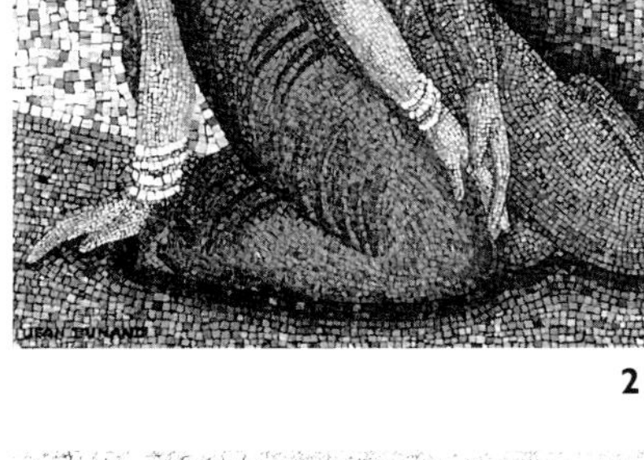

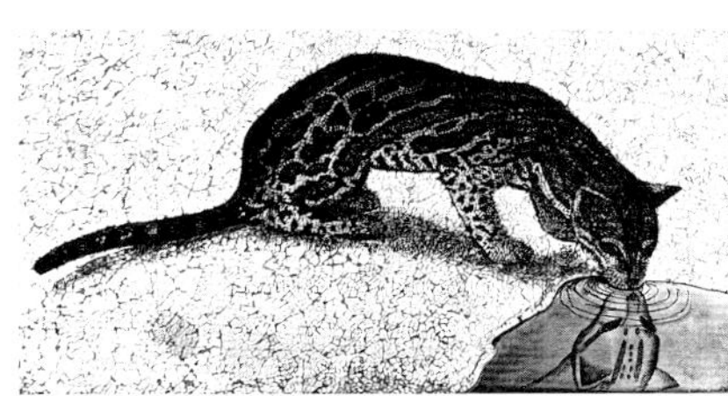
215

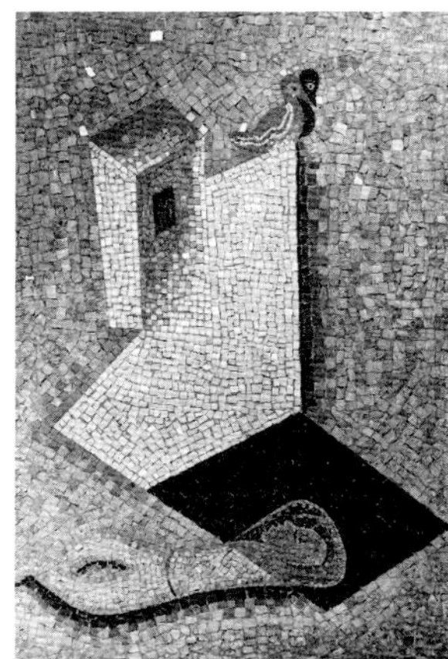
216

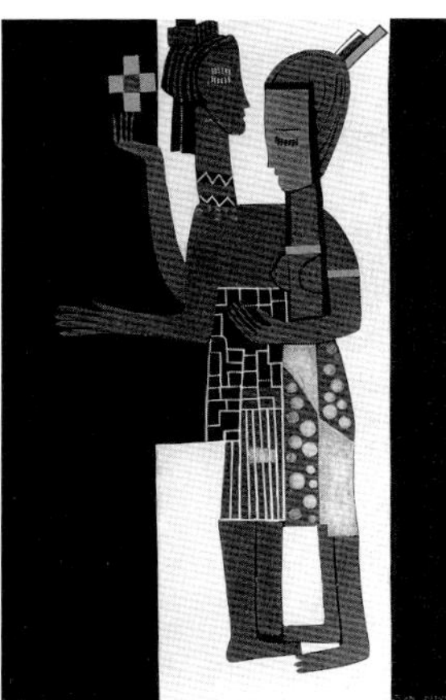
217

208 Portrait of Jean Dunand
Study in pastel.
95 x 65 cm (37½ x 25½ in.).
1932, signed.
Private collection.

209 Portrait of Jean Dunand
Study in colour size and varnish.
95 x 65 cm (37½ x 25½ in.).
1932, signed.
Private collection.

210 Portrait of Jean Dunand
Self-portrait in coloured glass mosaic and gold.
95 x 65 cm (37½ x 25½ in.).
1932, signed.
Exh.: Galerie Georges Petit, Paris, 1932, no. 5.
Private collection.

211 Leda
Coloured glass mosaic and gold.
1932, signed.
Exh.: Galerie Georges Petit, Paris, 1932, no. 6.

212 Marabou Stork
Coloured glass mosaic and gold.
65 x 95 cm (25½ x 37½ in.).
1932, signed.
Exh.: Galerie Georges Petit, Paris, 1932, no. 7; 'Vase, mosaïque et émail' ('Glass, mosaic and enamel'), Palais Galliéra, Paris, 1934.
Bibl.: *L'Art vivant*, July 1934, p. 278.

213 Two Figures
Glass mosaic and gold.
1932, signed.
Exh.: Galerie Georges Petit, Paris, 1932, no. 8.
Bibl.: *Art et décoration*, August 1932; p. 227.

214 Young Women
Glass mosaic and gold.
65 x 48 cm (25½ x 19 in.).
1933, signed.
Sold: Sotheby's (Monaco), 24 September 1978, lot 231.

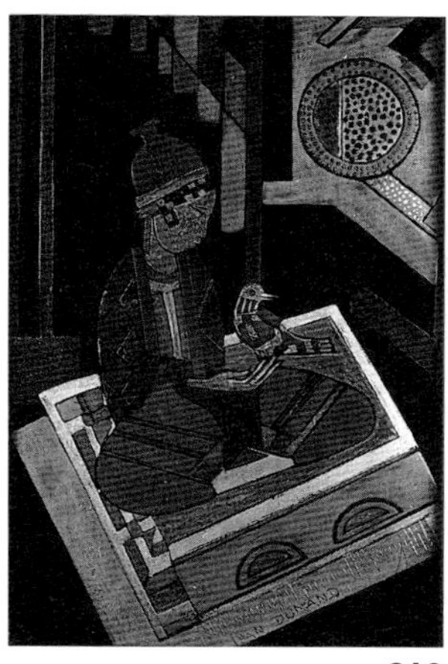
218

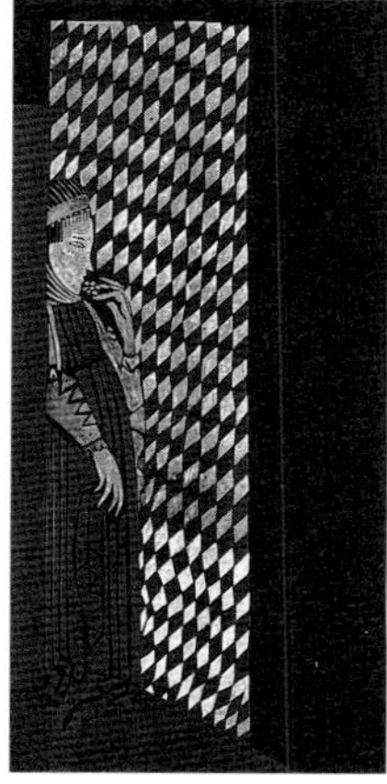
219

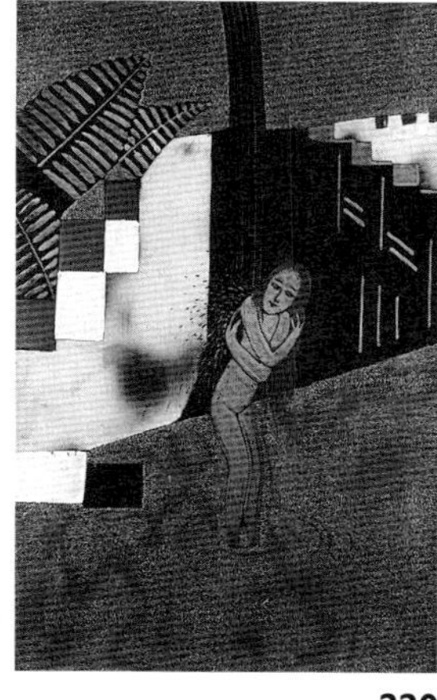
220

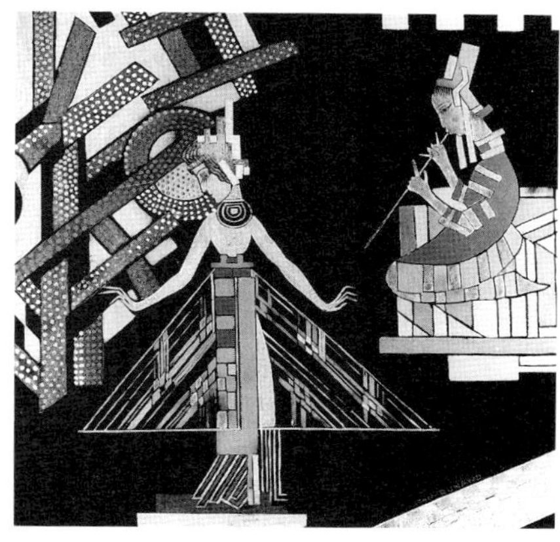
223

215 Panther at a Watering Hole
Glass mosaic on an eggshell ground and silver lacquer on black lacquer.
1933, signed.

216 Siesta
Glass mosaic, after a cartoon by Jean Lambert-Rucki.
C. 1935, signed.
Coll.: Michel Souillac, Paris.
Lambert-Rucki worked in Dunand's workshops both in association with Dunand and on his own account; he too executed several mosaic panels.

PANELS: DESIGNS INCLUDING HUMAN FIGURES
(lacquer on wood unless stated otherwise)

217 Encounter
Black and coloured lacquer.
19 x 13.5 cm (7½ x 5¼ in.).
C. 1923–5, signed.
Formerly in the collection of Félix Marcilhac, Paris; Private collection.

218 Man with a Bird
Black and coloured lacquer.
19 x 13.5 cm (7½ x 5¼ in.).
C. 1923–5, signed.
Exh.: Galerie du Luxembourg, Paris, 1973, no. 92 (repr. in catalogue, p. 84).
Private collection.

219 Middle Age
Black and coloured lacquer highlighted with gold and silver.
19 x 13.5 cm (7½ x 5¼ in.).
C. 1923–5, signed.
Exh.: Galerie du Luxembourg, Paris, 1973, no. 91 (repr. in catalogue, p. 84).
Private collection.

220 Woman Bathing
Black and coloured lacquer.
13.7 x 9.7 cm (5½ x 3¾ in.).
Exh.: Galerie du Luxembourg, Paris, 1973, no. 90 (repr. in catalogue, p. 84).
Private collection.

221 The Book
Black and coloured lacquer highlighted with silver.
18 x 13 cm (7 x 5¼ in.).
C. 1923–5, stamp on back of panel.
Sold: Sotheby's (Monaco), 24/25 October 1982, lot 397.

222 Procession
Red and coloured lacquer, after a cartoon by Jean Lambert-Rucki.
32.5 x 22 cm (12¾ x 8¾ in.).
C. 1923, stamp on back of panel 'Jean Dunand laqueur' (twice).
Sold: Sotheby's (Monaco), 24/25 October 1982, lot 397.
This is a reduced version of a panel for a firescreen (see cat. no. 571) exhibited at the Galerie Georges Petit, Paris, in 1923; the composition was slightly modified when made up and shortened at the base.

223 Oriental Dancer *Pl. 40*
Black and coloured lacquer.
20 x 20 cm (7¾ x 7¾ in.).
C. 1923–5, signed.
Private collection.

224 The Couple *Pl. 42*
Black and coloured lacquer.
17.5 x 12 cm (6¾ x 4¾ in.).
C. 1923–5, signed.
Coll.: M. and Mme Cardinaël, Paris.
Sold: Laurin, Guilloux, Buffetaud, Tailleur (Paris), 1 June 1977, lot 88.

225 Two Figures with Deer *Pl. 37*
Black and coloured lacquer highlighted with gold and inlaid with eggshell, after a cartoon by Jean Lambert-Rucki.
68 x 48 cm (26¾ x 19 in.).
1925, signed *br* 'Jean Dunand laqueur'.
Exh.: Galerie Georges Petit, Paris, 1925, no. 25.
Formerly in the collection of Alain Lesieutre, Paris.
Bibl.: *Mobilier et décoration*, February 1926, p. 39; *Conferencia*, 15 April 1926, p. 441.
Sold: Boscher, Gossart (Paris), 1 December 1980, lot 158.
See also cat. no. 226.

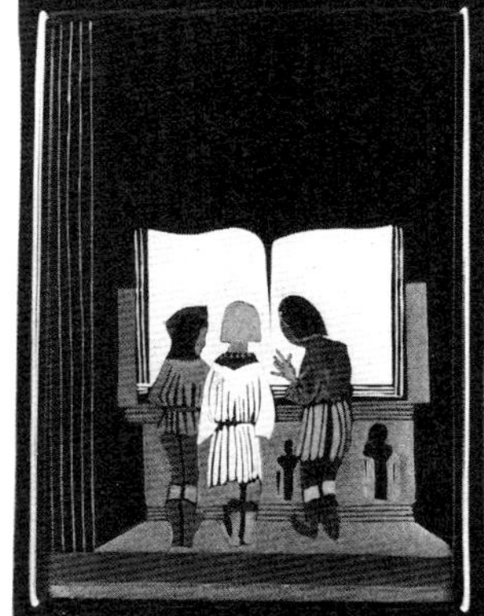
221

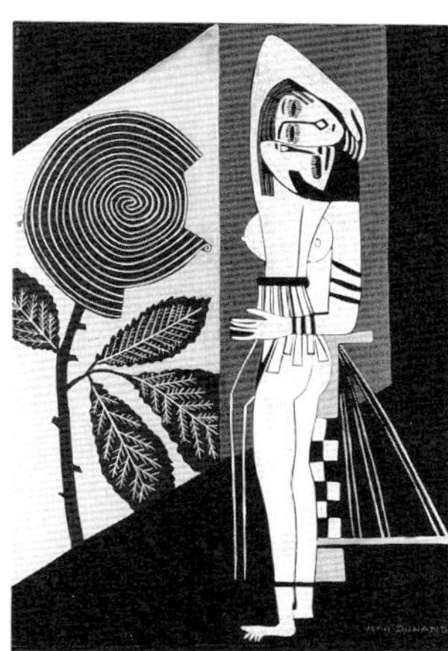
224

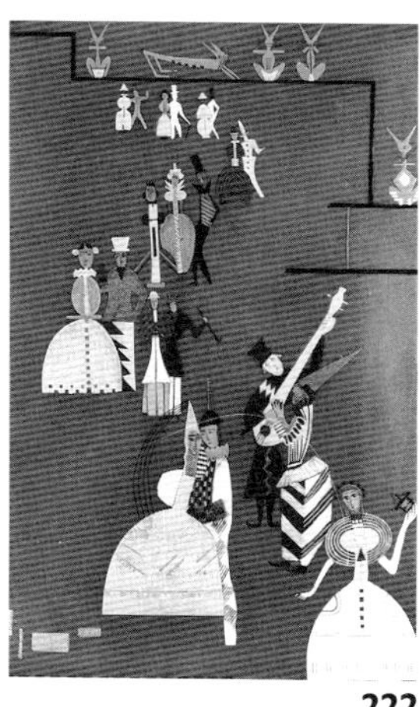
222

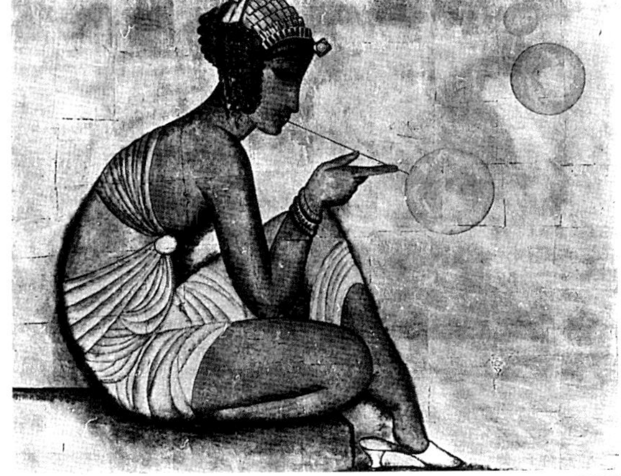
237

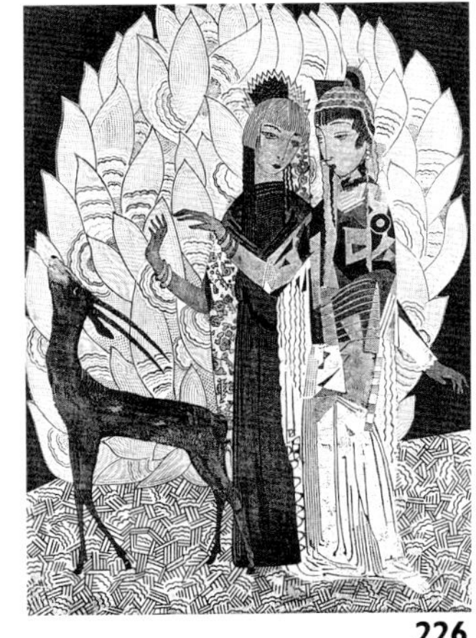
226

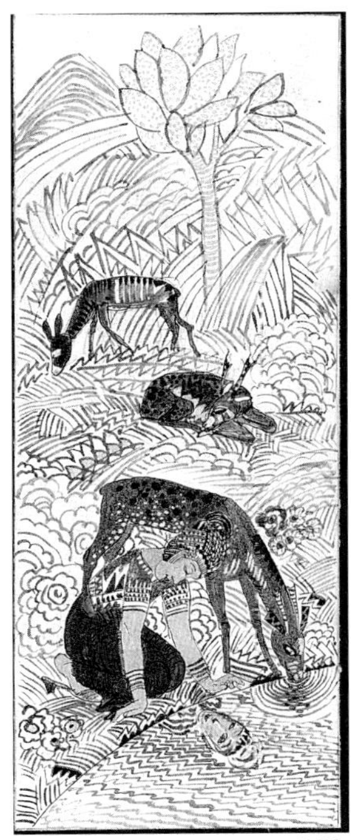
228

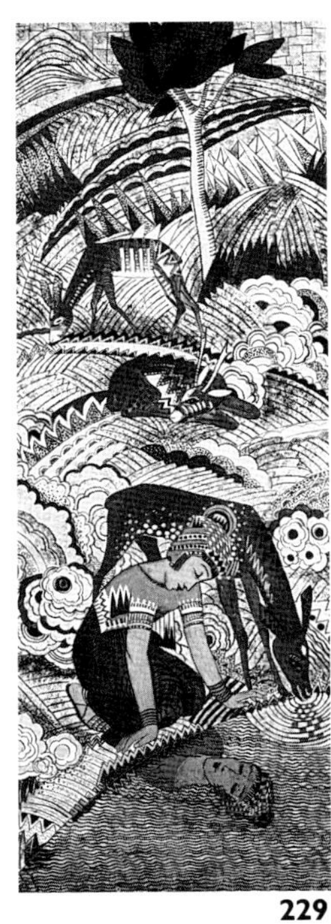
229

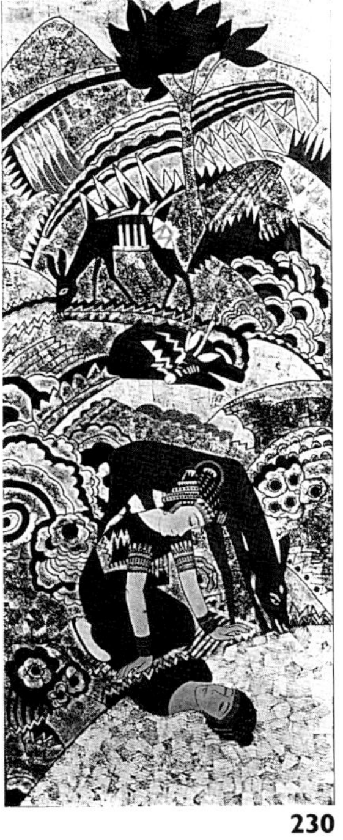
230

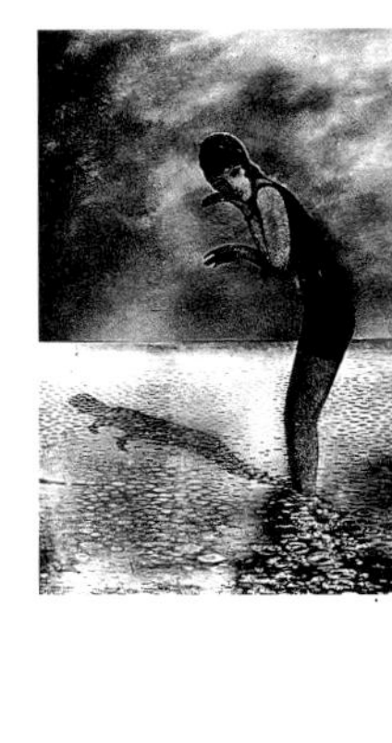
236

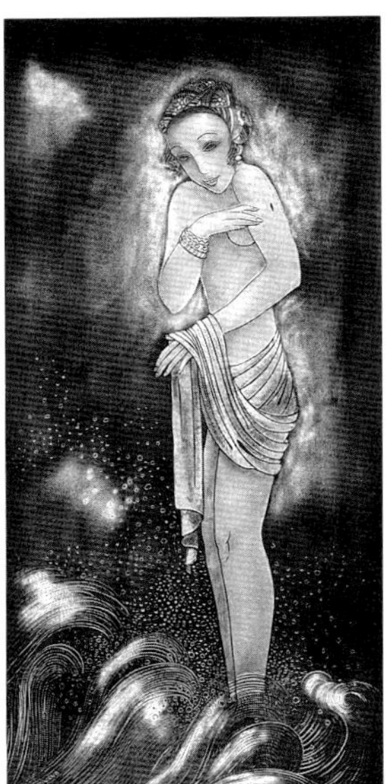
234

235

226 Two Figures with Deer
C. 1926, signed *br.*
The subject is the same as in cat. no. 225, but reversed left to right and painted in different colours; the only record of this work is a colour reproduction published in *Vogue*, 15 October 1927, p. 32.

227 Seated Figure Stroking an Animal *Pl. 44*
Eggshell and coloured lacquer.
57 x 89 cm (22½ x 35 in.).
C. 1924–6, signed.
Exh.: Delorenzo Gallery, New York, 1985.
Bibl.: Delorenzo Gallery catalogue (New York, 1985), repr. p. 10.
Sold: Sotheby's (Monaco), 23 June 1979, lot 266.

228 Figure and Deer by a Fountain
Study for cat. no. 227; gouache on paper, highlighted with silver.
36 x 14 cm (14¼ x 5½ in.).
C. 1924–6.

229 Figure and Deer by a Fountain
Eggshell and coloured lacquer.
185 x 77 cm (72¾ x 30¼ in.).
C. 1924–6, signed.
Sold: Christie's (New York), 26 May 1983, lot 445.

230 Figure and Deer by a Fountain
Eggshell and coloured lacquer.
185 x 77 cm (72¾ x 30¼ in.).
C. 1924–6.
Variant of cat. no. 229.

231 Bathing Woman with Fish
Silver lacquer.
1927, signed.
Exh.: Galerie Georges Petit, Paris, 1927, no. 20.

232 Shepherdess
Light-brown shellac.
C. 1927, signed.
Private collection.

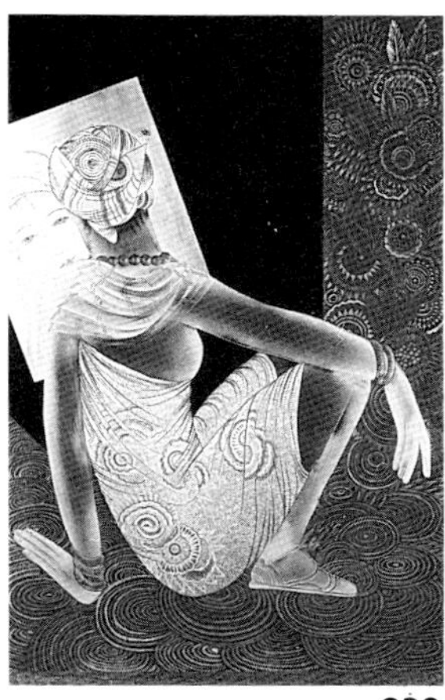
238

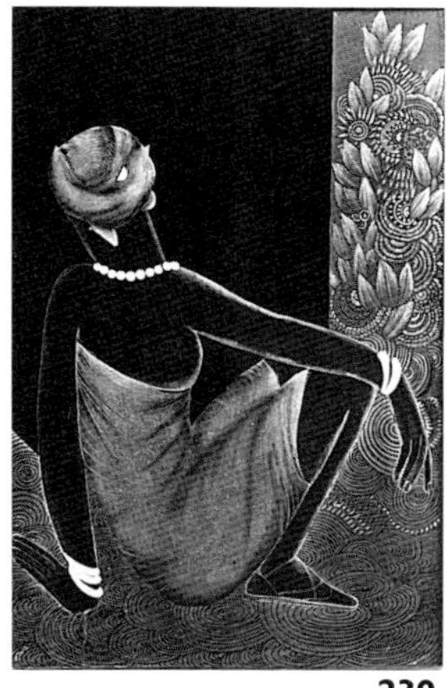
239

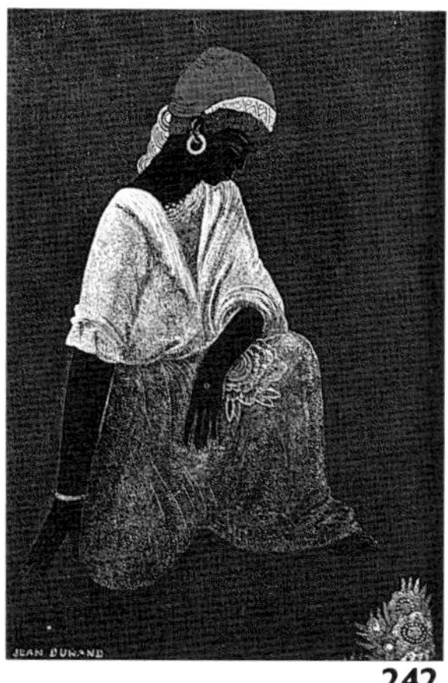

242

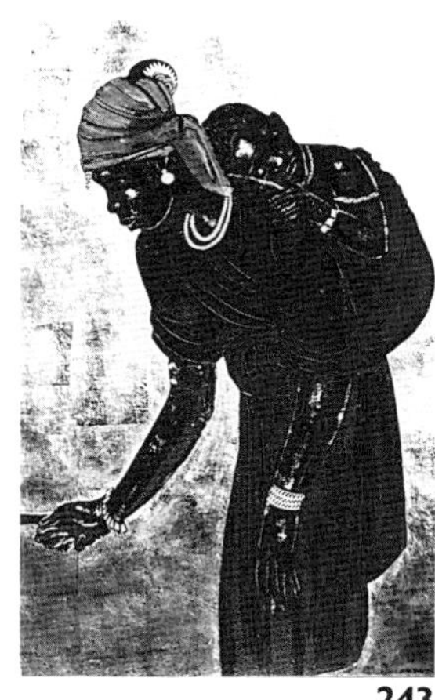
243

233 The Perfumes *Pl. 157*
Incised brown Coromandel lacquer, after a cartoon by George Barbier.
232 x 232 cm (91¼ x 91¼ in.).
Dated '1927' and signed 'Jean Dunand laqueur' and 'George Barbier'.
Coll.: Jean-Claude Brugnot, Paris.
Sold: Rieunier (Paris), 27 June 1986, lot 31.

234 Woman Bathing
Incised brown lacquer highlighted with colour.
58 x 30 cm (22¾ x 11¾ in.).
1928, signed.
Exh.: Galerie La Renaissance, Paris, 1928, no. 29.
Sold: Sotheby's (London), 28 April 1983, lot 183.

235 Woman with Fish
Gold lacquer.
95 x 70 cm (37½ x 27½ in.).
1928, signed.
Exh.: Galerie Georges Petit, Paris, 1928, no. 19.
Private collection.

236 Woman Bathing
Gold lacquer.
1928, signed.
Exh.: Galerie Georges Petit, Paris, 1928, no. 20.

237 Women with Soap Bubbles
Silver lacquer.
1928, signed.
Exh.: Galerie Georges Petit, Paris, 1928, no. 22.

238 Woman and Mirror
Gold and silver lacquer on a black lacquer ground.
98 x 68 cm (38½ x 26¾ in.).
1928, signed.
Exh.: Galerie Georges Petit, Paris, 1928, no. 29; Galerie La Renaissance, Paris, 1929, no. 52; Galerie du Luxembourg, Paris, 1973, no. 103 (repr. in catalogue, p. 88).
Private collection.
See also cat. no. 239.

239 Woman and Mirror
Black lacquer.
98 x 68 cm (38½ x 26¾ in.).
1928, signed.
Variant of cat. no. 238.

240 Prayer *Pl. 36*
Gold and silver lacquer and *laque arrachée*.
58 x 84 cm (22¾ x 33 in.).
1928, signed.
Coll.: M. and Mme Kupperfils, Evreux.

241 Figure Picking Flowers
Study in colour size highlighted with silver.
95 x 70 cm (37½ x 27½ in.).
1928, artist's stamp on back of panel.
Private collection.

242 Figure Picking Flowers
Black and silver lacquer and *laque arrachée*.
95 x 70 cm (37½ x 27½ in.).
C. 1928–30, signed.

243 Negress and Child
Brown *laque arrachée* and silver lacquer.
C. 1928–30, signed.
Private collection.

244 Standing Figure
Black lacquer and *laque arrachée* highlighted with gold and silver.
19 x 13.5 cm (7½ x 5¼ in.).
C. 1928–30, stamp on back of panel.
Coll.: Galerie Vallois, Paris.

245 Woman with Fish
Incised black lacquer.
91.5 x 71 cm (36 x 28 in.).
1929, signed.
Exh.: Galerie La Renaissance, Paris, 1929, no. 3; Rosenbach Gallery, New York, 1929, no. 2.
Sold: Christie's (New York), 4 October 1980, lot 346.

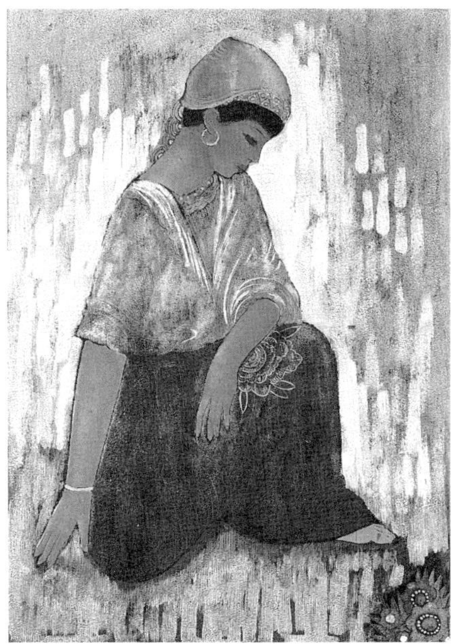

241

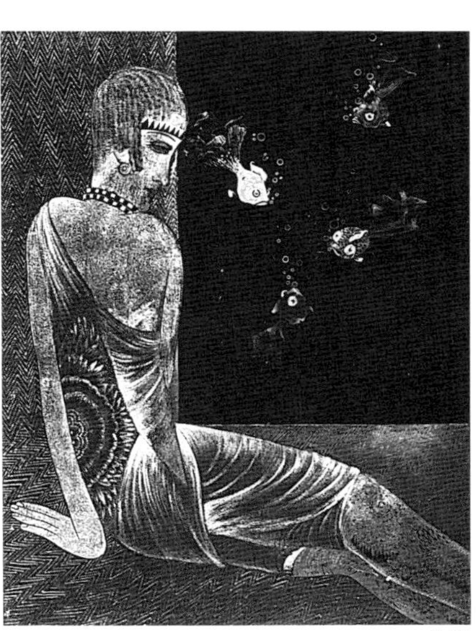
245

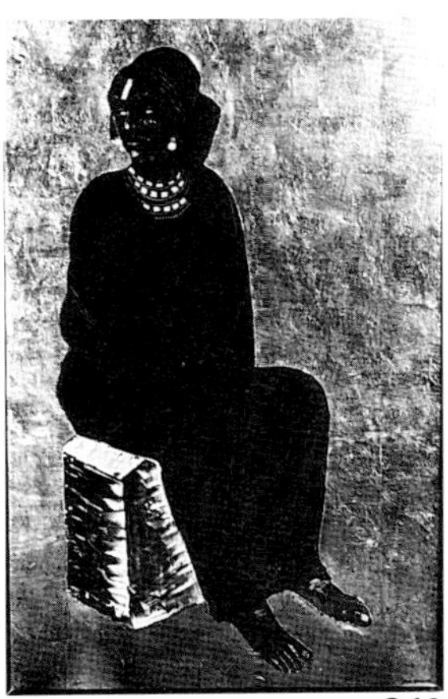
246

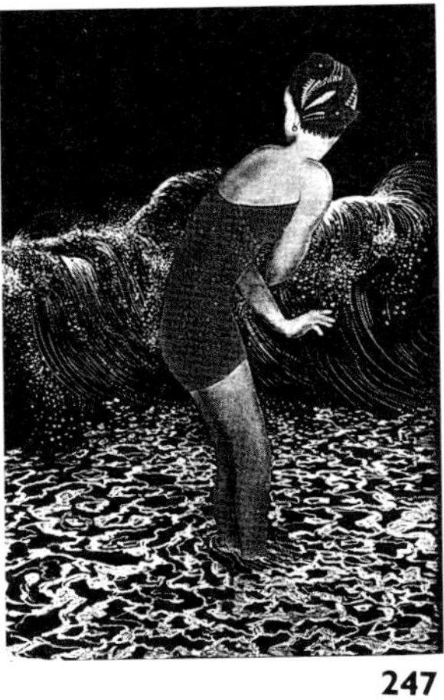
247

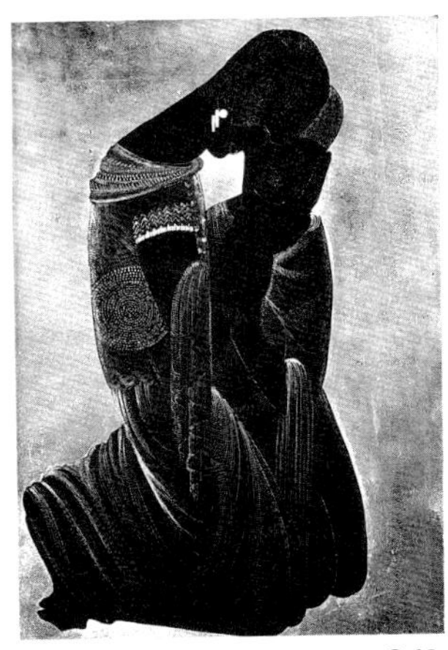
249

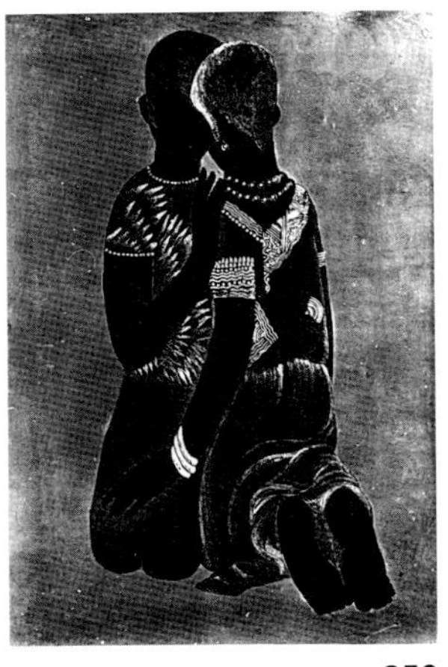
250

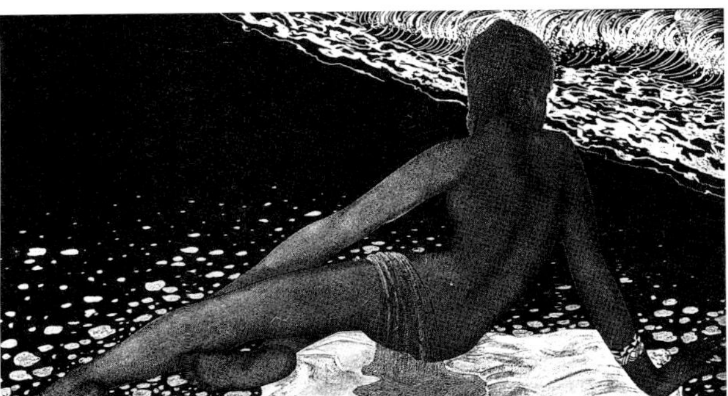
248

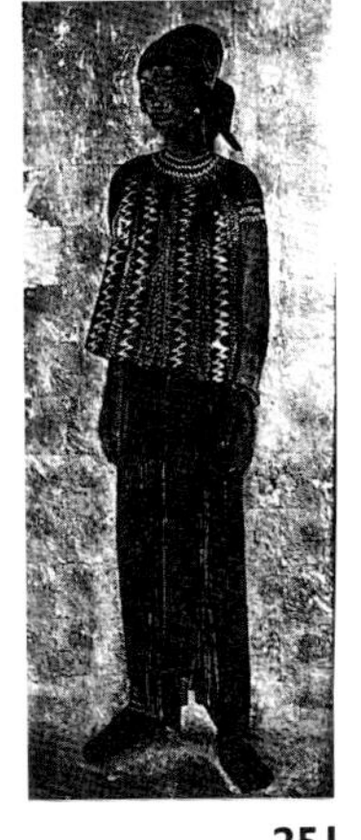
251

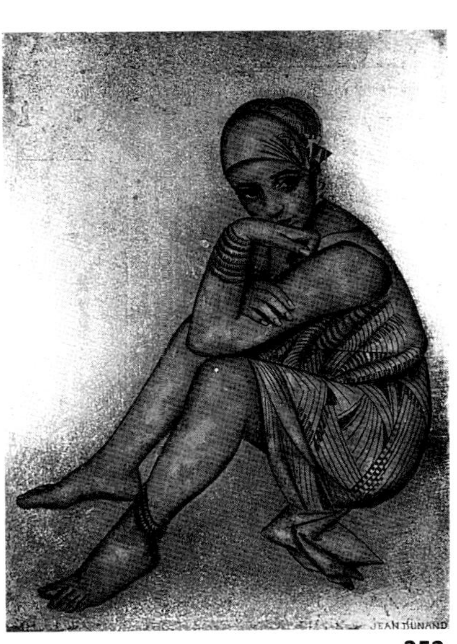

252

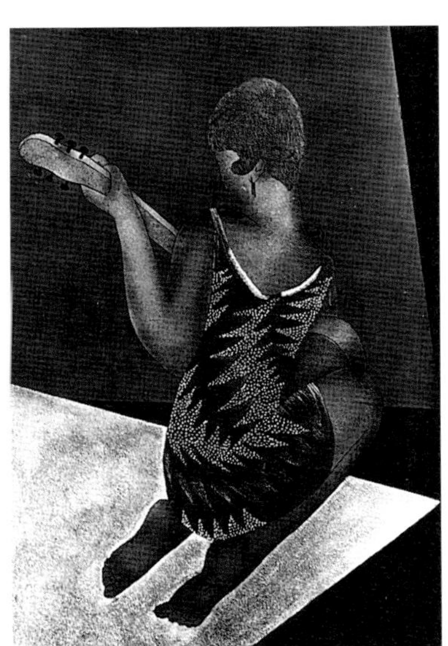
253

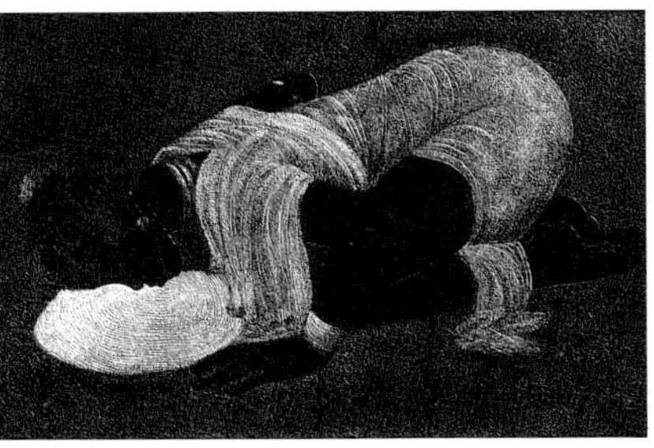
254

246 Seated Female Figure
Brown *laque arrachée* and silver lacquer.
92.5 x 58.5 cm (36½ x 23 in.).
1929, signed.
Exh.: Galerie La Renaissance, Paris, 1929, no. 4; Rosenbach Gallery, New York, 1929, no. 7.
Sold: Christie's (New York), 30 March 1985, lot 326.

247 Woman Bathing
Incised black lacquer.
1929, signed.
Exh.: Galerie La Renaissance, Paris, 1929, no. 5 (repr. in catalogue); Rosenbach Gallery, New York, 1929, no. 15.

248 Reclining Figure
Incised black lacquer.
64 x 99 cm (25¼ x 39 in.).
1929, signed.
Exh.: Galerie La Renaissance, Paris, 1929, no. 6.
Formerly in the collection of Jean-Philippe Worth.
Sold: Gairouard et Besch (Cannes), 5 May 1984.

249 Mother and Child
Black and gold lacquer.
1929, signed.
Exh.: Galerie La Renaissance, Paris, 1929, no. 9; Rosenbach Gallery, New York, 1929, no. 16.
Bibl.: *L'Officiel de la couture*, August 1929, p. 56.

250 Two Kneeling Figures
Grey lacquer.
95 x 70 cm (37½ x 27½ in.).
1929, signed.
Exh.: Galerie La Renaissance, Paris, 1929, no. 12; Galerie du Luxembourg, Paris, 1973, no. 106 (repr. in catalogue, p. 88).
Bibl.: *Art et décoration*, October 1932, p. 230.

251 Laobé Woman Standing
Brown *laque arrachée* on a silver ground.

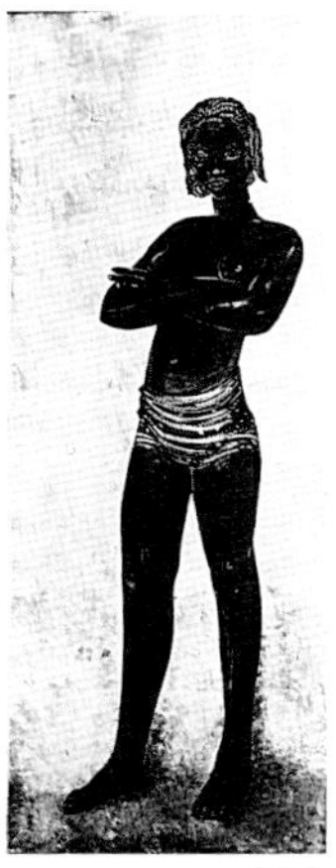
256

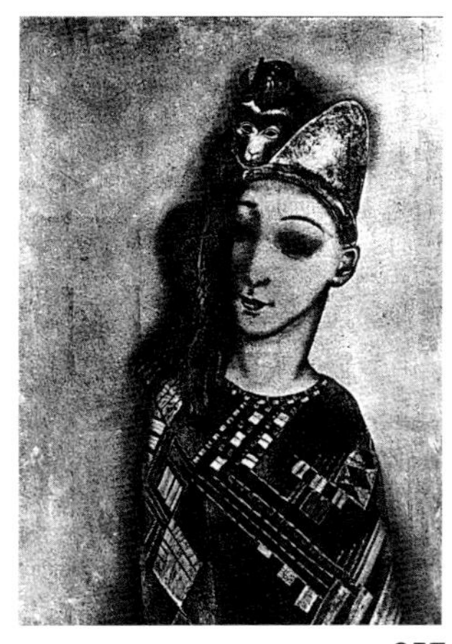
257

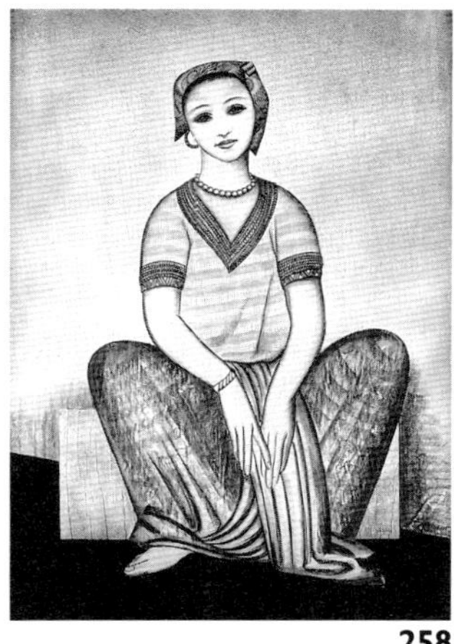
258

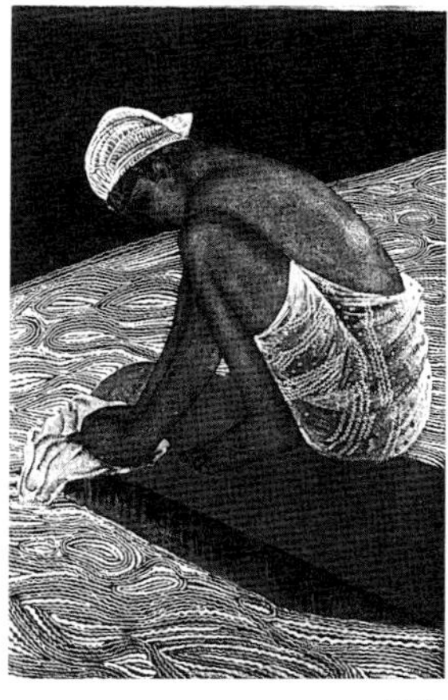
259

135 x 55 cm (52¼ x 21¾ in.).
1929, signed.
Exh.: Galerie La Renaissance, Paris, 1929, no. 14; Galerie du Luxembourg, Paris, 1973, no. 104 (incorrectly titled 'Wolof Woman').
Formerly in the collection of Félix Marcilhac, Paris; Private collection, Vienna.

252 Young Girl
Shellac and gold-dust base.
95 x 68 cm (37½ x 26¾ in.).
1929, signed.
Exh.: Galerie La Renaissance, Paris, 1929, no. 15; Galerie du Luxembourg, Paris, 1973, no. 102 (repr. in catalogue, p. 88).
The sitter was Jean Dunand's second daughter, Suzanne, aged eleven.

253 Woman with Guitar
Laque arrachée on a black lacquer ground.
1929, signed.
Exh.: Galerie La Renaissance, Paris, 1929, no. 16.

254 Prayer
Black and silver lacquer.
58 x 84 cm (22¾ x 33 in.).
1929, signed.
Exh.: Galerie La Renaissance, Paris, 1929, no. 17.
Coll.: M. and Mme Kupperfils, Evreux.

255 Woman Leaning on her Elbows
Incised black lacquer.
1929, signed.
Exh.: Galerie La Renaissance, Paris, 1929, no. 18.

256 Young Nude Negress
Brown *laque arrachée* on a silver ground.
135 x 55 cm (52¼ x 21¾ in.).
1929, signed.
Exh.: Galerie La Renaissance, Paris, 1929, no. 19; Galerie du Luxembourg, Paris, 1973, no. 96 (incorrectly titled 'Nude Wolof Woman').
Formerly in the collection of Félix Marcilhac, Paris; Private collection, Vienna.

257 Monkey and Clown
Laque arrachée.
1929, signed.
Exh.: Galerie La Renaissance, Paris, 1929, no. 22; Rosenbach Gallery, New York, 1929, no. 11.

258 Seated Figure
Shellac and black lacquer.
100 x 65 cm (39¼ x 25½ in.).
1929, signed.
Exh.: Galerie La Renaissance, Paris, 1929, no. 23.
Private collection.

259 Washerwoman
Black lacquer on wood panel.
95 x 70 cm (37½ x 27½ in.).
Exh.: Galerie La Renaissance, Paris, 1929, no. 24.
Coll.: Alain Lesieutre, Paris.

260 Fatou
Black lacquer and silver *laque arrachée.*
1929, signed.
Exh.: Galerie La Renaissance, Paris, 1929, no. 26; Galerie Georges Petit, Paris, 1929, no. 37.

261 Young Wolof Woman
Decorated black lacquer on a silver ground.
1929, signed.
Exh.: Galerie La Renaissance, Paris, 1929, no. 29.

262 Woman with Veil
Brown lacquer and *laque arrachée.*
1929, signed.
Exh.: Galerie La Renaissance, Paris, 1929, no. 31.

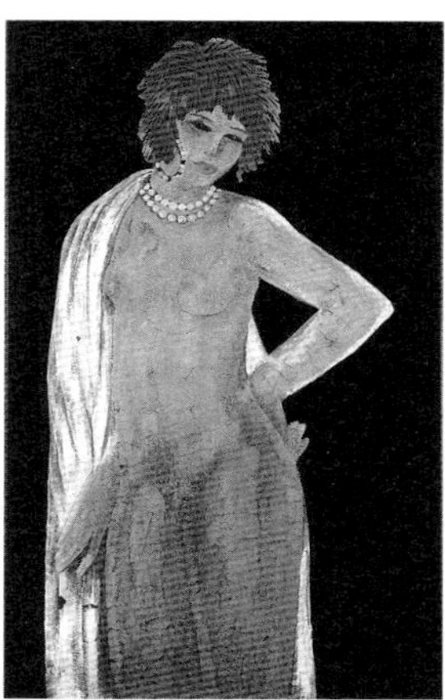
260

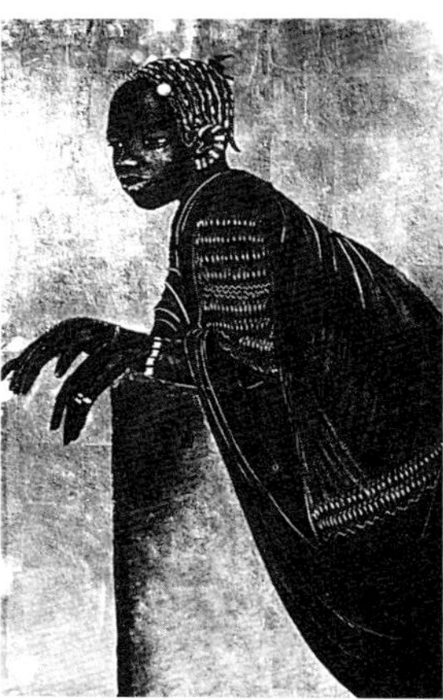
261

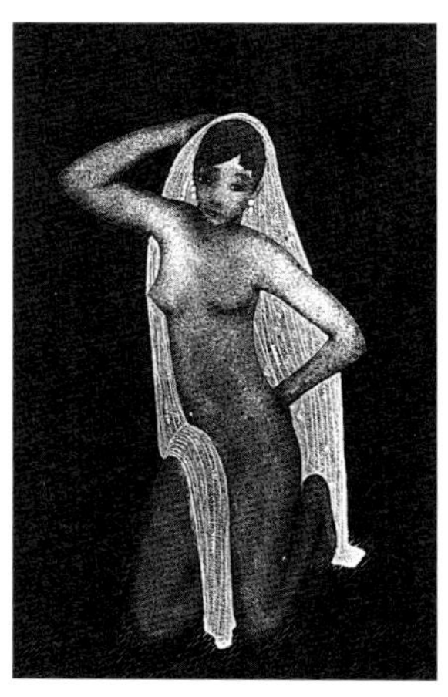
262

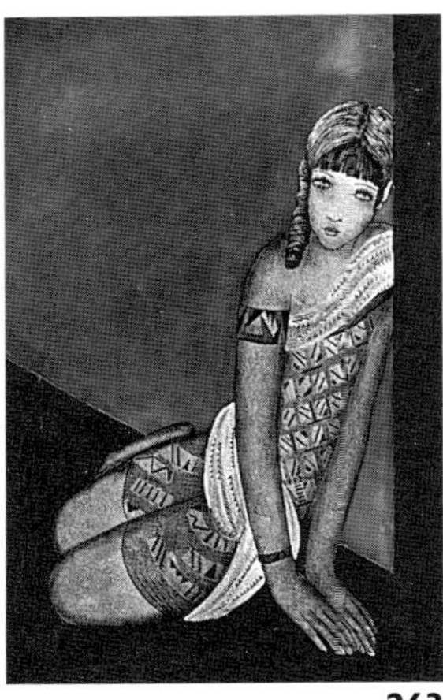
263

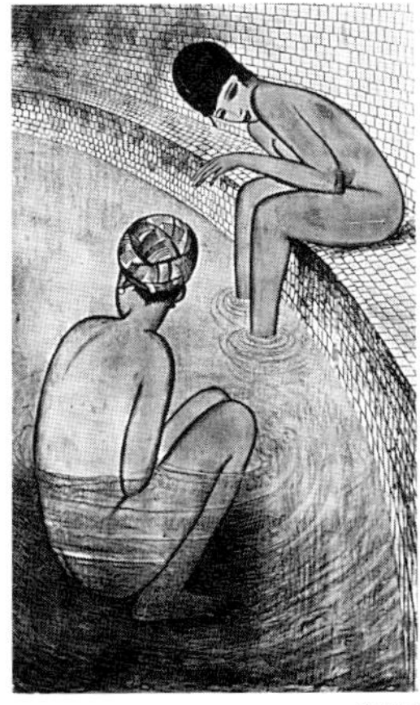
265

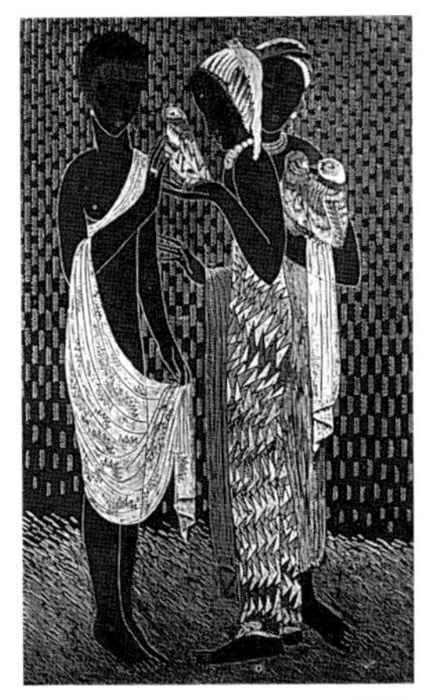
268

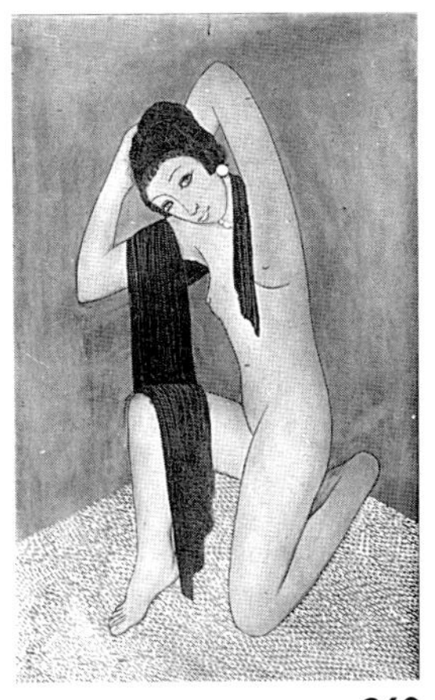
269

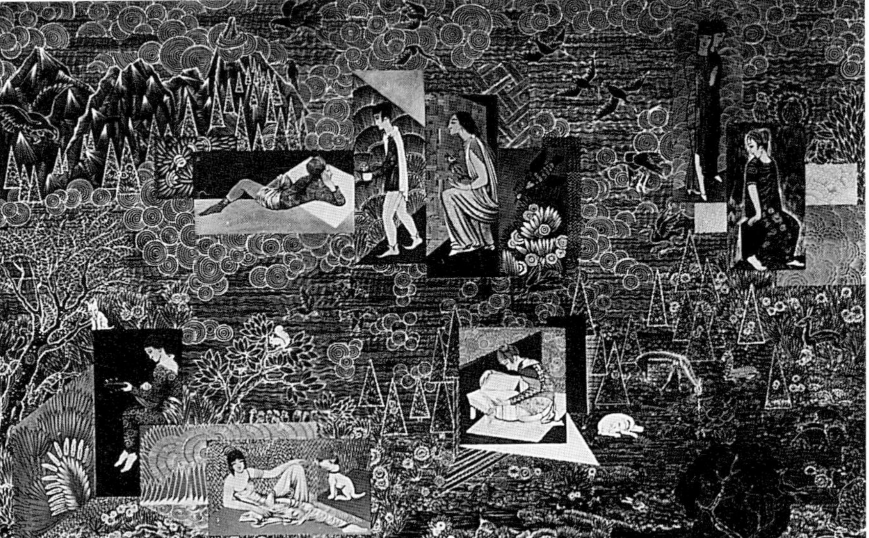
278

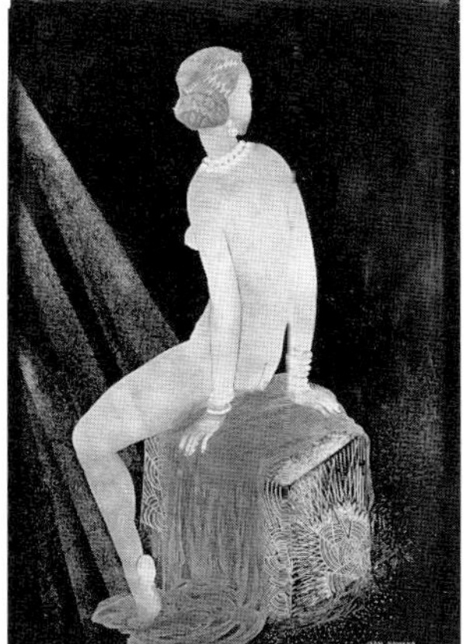
266

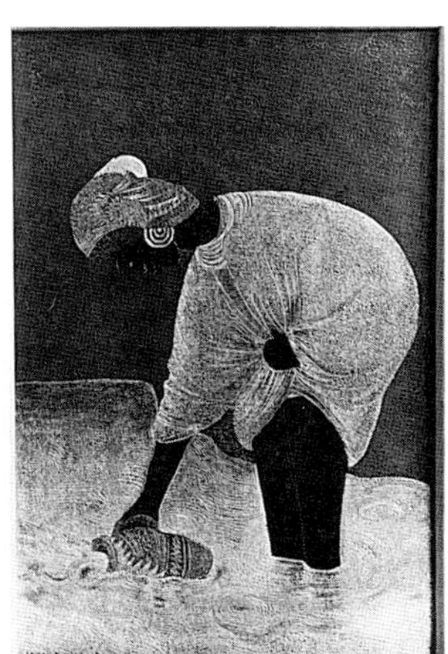
274

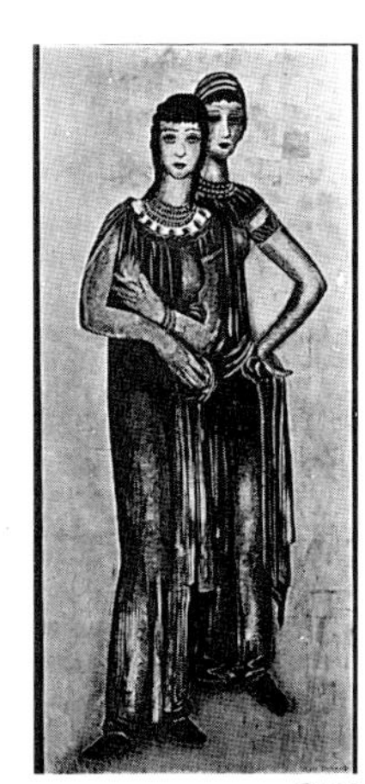
276

263 Young Girl Sitting
Decorated brown lacquer.
1929, signed.
Exh.: Galerie La Renaissance, Paris, 1929, no. 35.

264 Water Carrier
Shellac.
1929, signed.
Exh.: Galerie La Renaissance, Paris, 1929, no. 37.

265 Two Women Bathing
Black and gold lacquer.
1929, signed.
Exh.: Galerie La Renaissance, Paris, 1929, no. 38; Galerie Georges Petit, Paris, 1929, no. 38; Salon d'Automne, Paris, 1931.
Bibl.: *Le Cahier: revue mensuelle des arts et des lettres*, November 1931, p. 71.

266 Nude, Back View
Black and coloured lacquer highlighted with gold and silver.
45 x 32 cm (17¾ x 12½ in.).
1929, signed.
Exh.: Galerie La Renaissance, Paris, 1929, no. 44.
Formerly in the collection of Karl Lagerfeld.
Sold: Godeau, Solanet, Audap (Paris), 21 November 1975, lot 94, repr. in catalogue, p. 49.
For a variant see cat. no. 267.

267 Nude, Back View *Pl. 34*
Black and coloured lacquer highlighted with gold and silver.
44 x 35 cm (17¼ x 13¾ in.).
C. 1929.
Sold: Oger, Dumont (Paris), 4 November 1987, lot 75.
Variant of cat. no. 266.

268 Three Figures
Grey lacquer.
1929, signed.
Exh.: Galerie La Renaissance, Paris, 1929, no. 49; Galerie Georges Petit, Paris, 1929, no. 28.

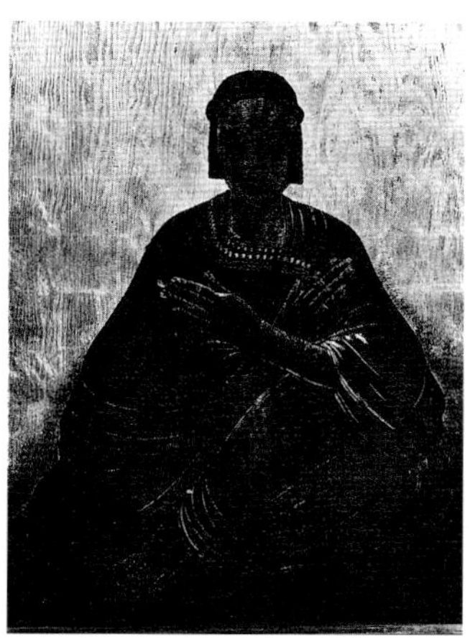
270

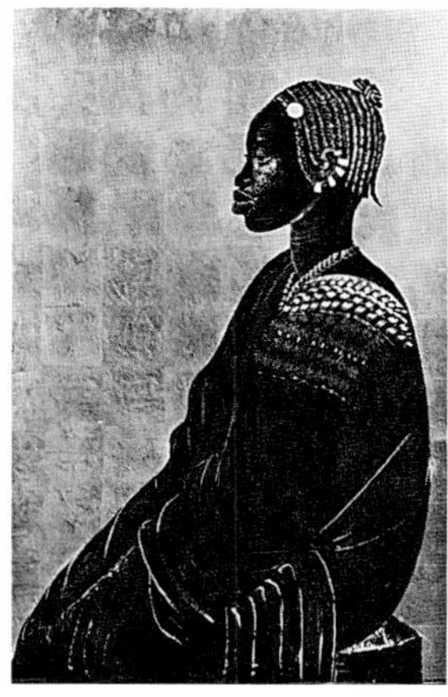
271

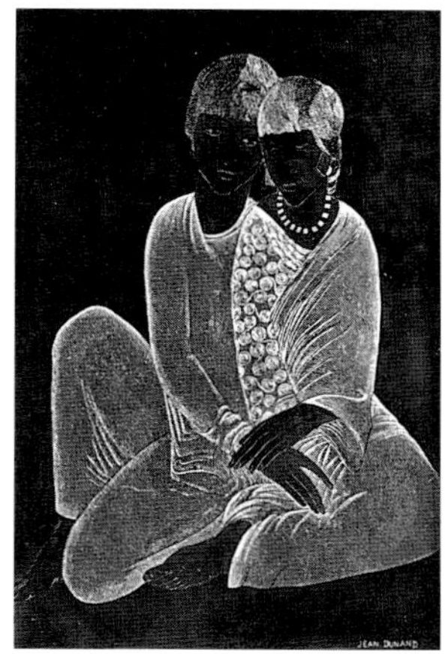

272

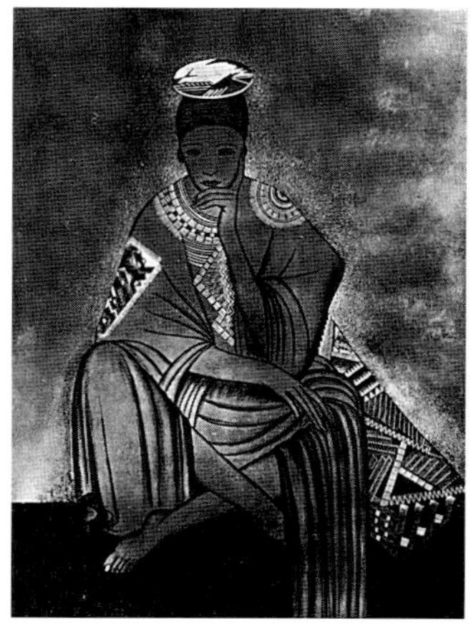
273

269 Nude
Incised black and gold lacquer.
1929, signed.
Exh.: Galerie La Renaissance, Paris, 1929, no. 50.

270 Laobé Woman
Black *laque arrachée* on light-coloured wood.
1929, signed.
Exh.: Galerie La Renaissance, Paris, 1929, no. 54.

271 Daughter of Wolof Chief
Silver and black lacquer.
1929, signed.
Exh.: Galerie La Renaissance, Paris, 1929, no. 55.

272 Two Seated Figures
Decorated black lacquer.
1929, signed.
Exh.: Galerie La Renaissance, Paris, 1929, no. 57.

273 Young Woman Seated
Decorated shellac.
1929, signed.
Exh.: Galerie La Renaissance, Paris, 1929, no. 58.
Bibl.: *Building* (New York), March 1930, p. 122.

274 Water Carrier
Silver and black lacquer.
1929, signed.
Exh.: Galerie La Renaissance, Paris, 1929, no. 60.

275 The Portrait *Pl. 35*
Black lacquer and silver lacquer.
83 x 63 cm (32¾ x 24¾ in.).
1929, signed.
Exh.: Rosenbach Gallery, New York, 1929.
Sold: Christie's (New York), 24 May 1984, lot 323.

276 Two Figures
Grey lacquer.
1930, signed.
Exh.: Galerie Georges Petit, Paris, 1930/31, no. 24.

277 'Miniature' panel
Decorated gold lacquer.
1930, signed.
Like the following four items in the style of Persian miniatures, this panel was executed in 1930. Several were exhibited at the Galerie Georges Petit, but not catalogued.

278 'Miniature' panel
Decorated gold lacquer.
1930, signed.

279 'Miniature' panel
Gold lacquer and silver lacquer.
70 x 52 cm (27½ x 20½ in.).
1930, signed.
Private collection.

280 'Miniature' panel
Grey lacquer and silver lacquer.
1930, signed.
Private collection.

281 'Miniature' panel *Pl. 33*
Silver lacquer and gold lacquer.
1930, signed.
Private collection.

282 Woman Bathing
Incised light-brown shellac.
1930, signed.
Formerly in the collection of Jean-Jacques Dutko, Paris; Private collection.

283 Two Figures
Light-brown lacquer.
1932, signed.
Exh.: Galerie Georges Petit, Paris, 1932, no. 18.

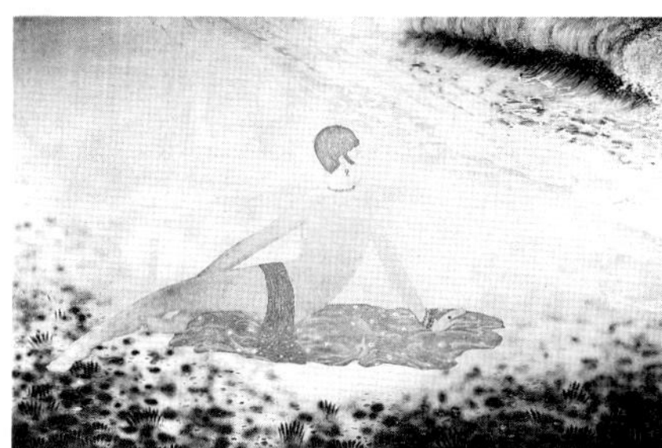
282

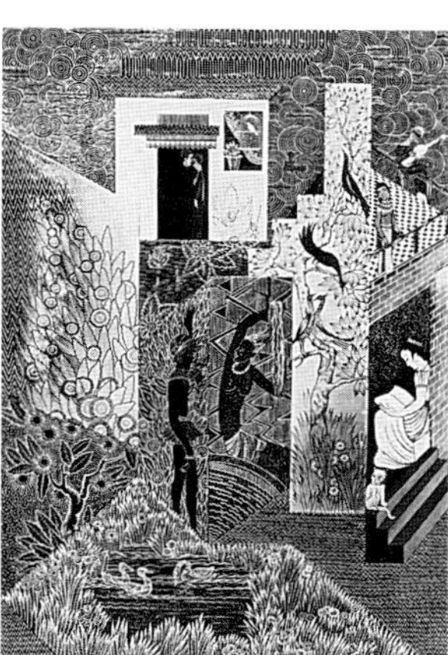
277

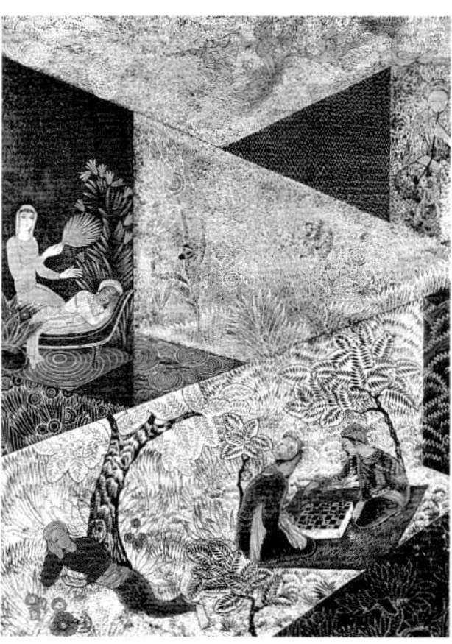
280

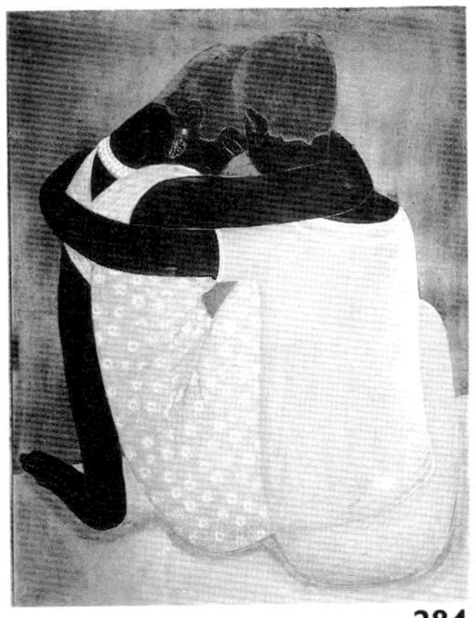

284

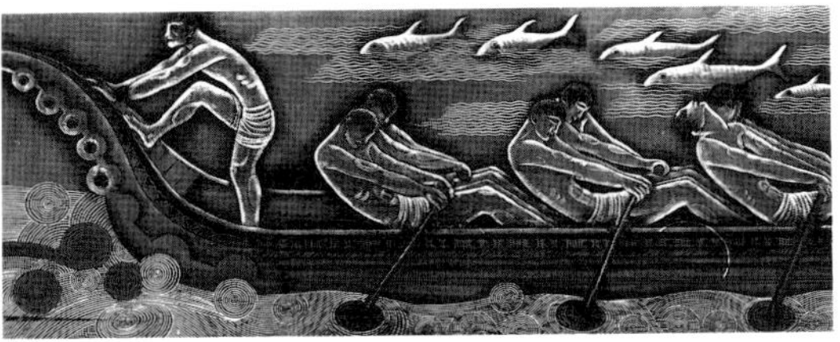

287

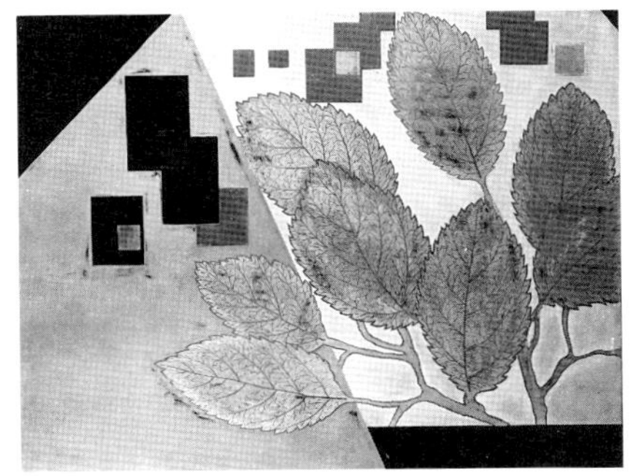

301

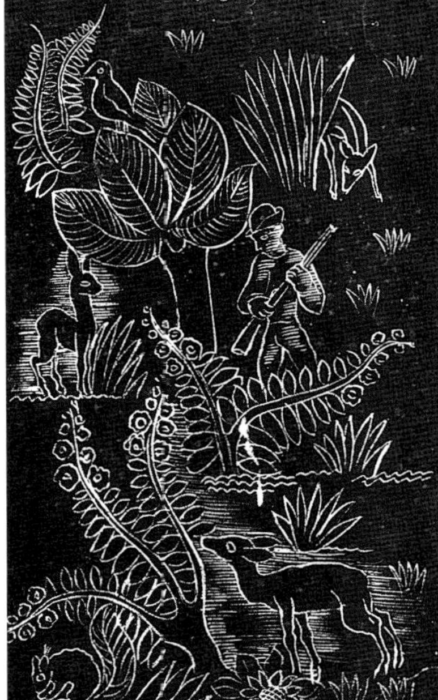

285

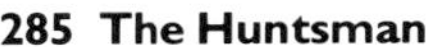

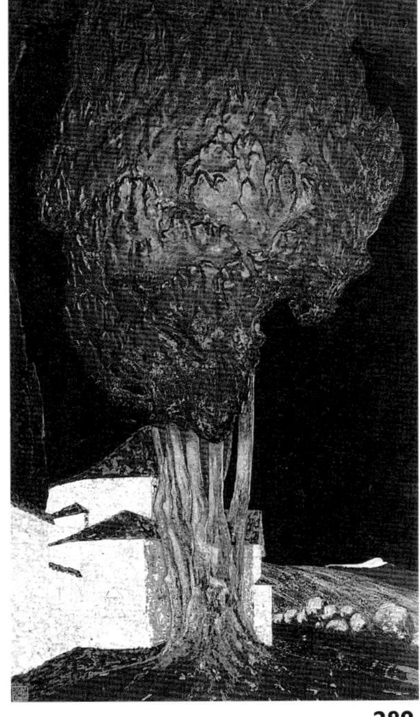

289

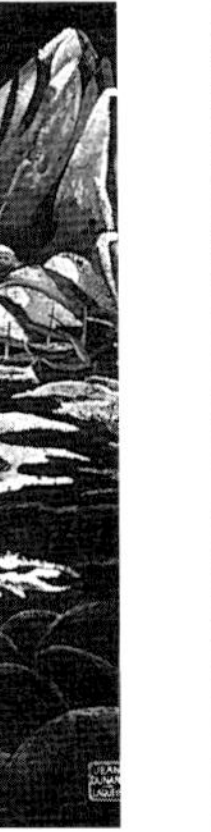

290

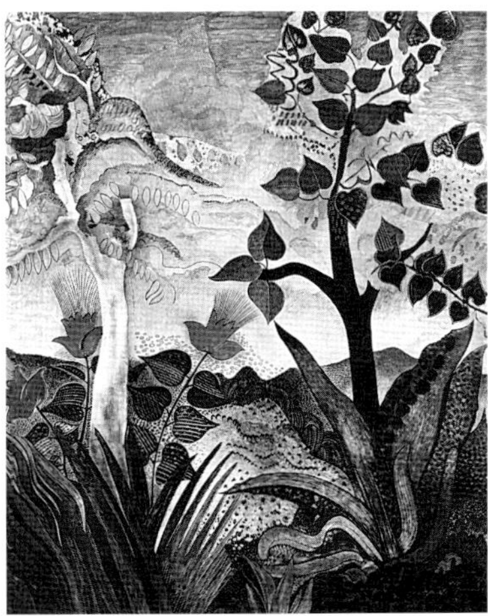

291

284 Two Seated Figures
Black and grey lacquer.
68 x 49 cm (26¾ x 19¼ in.).
1932, signed.
Exh.: Galerie Georges Petit, Paris, 1932, no. 20.
Formerly in the collection of the Rosenbach Gallery, New York.
Sold: Christie's (New York), 24 May 1984, lot 322.

285 The Huntsman
Study in silver gouache on paper tinted with Indian ink.
C. 1935–7.

286 The Apple Picker
Silver design on black lacquer.
C. 1935–7, signed.

287 The Oarsmen
Red lacquer decorated in black and gold.
155 x 365 cm (61 x 143¾ in.).
1937, signed.
Exh.: Galerie du Luxembourg, Paris, 1973, no. 98.
Bibl.: *L'Élite de Paris*, 22 July 1937, p. 29.

PANELS: LANDSCAPE SUBJECTS
(lacquer on wood unless stated otherwise)

288 Sheaves of Wheat *Pl. 164*
Gold and black lacquer, after a cartoon and woodcut by François-Louis Schmied.
1921, signed.
Exh.: Galerie Georges Petit, Paris, 1921, no. 53.
Private collection.

289 Cypress
Coloured lacquer with moulded stucco and eggshell inlay, after a cartoon by Jean Goulden.
250 x 140 cm (98½ x 55 in.).
1921, signed.
Exh.: Galerie Georges Petit, Paris, 1921, no. 6.

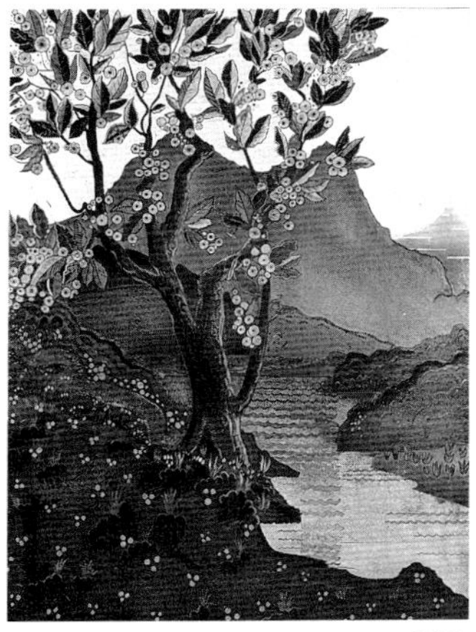
292

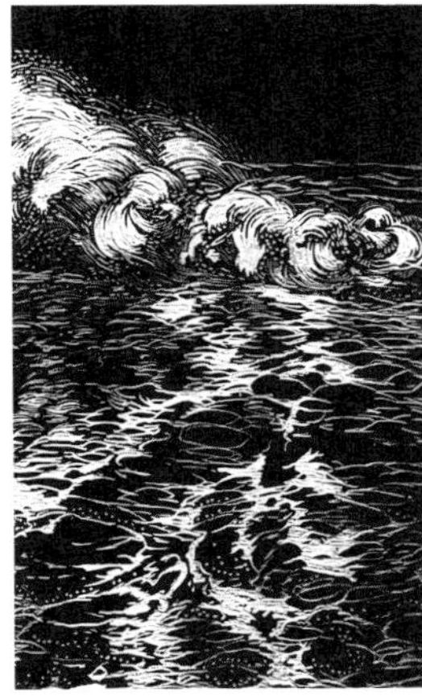
299

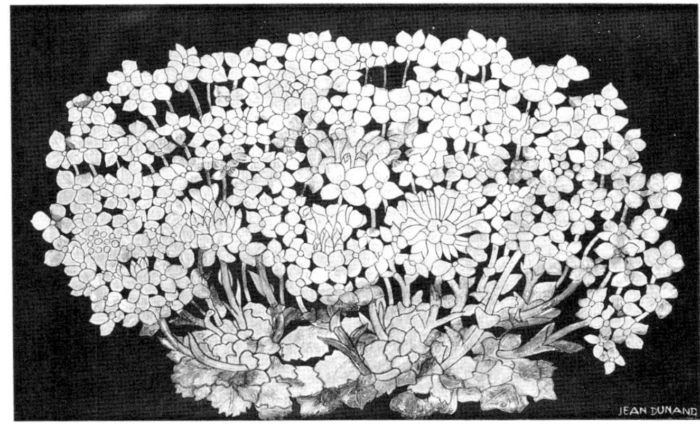

300

Sold: Christie's (Geneva), 16 November 1981, lot 209.
See also cat. no. 570.

290 Sailing Boats
Black and coloured lacquer, after a cartoon by Henry de Waroquier.
Dated 1921 and signed 'Jean Dunand laqueur' and 'Henry de Waroquier'.
Exh.: Galerie Georges Petit, Paris, 1921, no. 11.

291 Landscape
Incised Coromandel lacquer, after a cartoon by François-Louis Schmied.
155 x 125 cm (61 x 49¼ in.).
1922, signed 'Jean Dunand laqueur' and 'F. L. Schmied'.
Exh.: 'Europäische Lackkunst', Museum Bellerive, Zurich, 1976, no. 90.
Formerly in the collections of Charles Henchoz, Geneva, and Félix Marcilhac, Paris; Private collection.
Bibl.: *Europäische Lackkunst*, exhibition catalogue (Zurich, 1976), p. 43.
Sold: Pillias, Gluck (Paris), 30 April 1975, lot 86.

292 The Chestnut Tree
Incised Coromandel lacquer, after a cartoon by François-Louis Schmied.
190 x 130 cm (74¾ x 51¼ in.).
1922, signed.
Exh.: Salon des Artistes Décorateurs, Paris, 1922.
Coll.: Museum of Modern Art, Tokyo.
Sold: Boisgirard (Paris), 28 October 1987, lot 199, repr. on cover of catalogue.

293 Wave
Incised black lacquer.
1925, signed.
Exh.: Galerie Georges Petit, Paris, 1925, no. 19.

294 Saint-Gildas
Incised black lacquer.
1925, signed.
Exh.: Galerie Georges Petit, Paris, 1925, no. 20.

295 Saint-Gildas
Incised black lacquer.
1925, signed.
Exh.: Galerie Georges Petit, Paris, 1925, no. 21.

296 Saint-Gildas
Incised black lacquer.
1925, signed.
Exh.: Galerie Georges Petit, Paris, 1925, no. 22.

297 Saint-Gildas
Incised Coromandel lacquer.
1925, signed.
Exh.: Galerie Georges Petit, Paris, 1925, no. 23.

298 Mountain Landscape *Pl. 13*
Gold lacquer and eggshell.
1925, signed.
Exh.: Galerie Georges Petit, Paris, 1925, no. 24.
Private collection.

299 The Wave
Incised black lacquer.
1925, signed.

300 Flowers
Decorated brown lacquer.
C. 1925, signed.
Private collection.

301 Maple Leaves
Decorated silver lacquer.
88 x 68 cm (34¾ x 26¾ in.).
C. 1925, signed.
Formerly in the collection of Karl Lagerfeld.
Sold: Godeau, Solanet, Audap (Paris), 21 November 1975, lot 96, repr. in catalogue, p. 51.
The present panel was cut from a screen made at an earlier date and then modified.

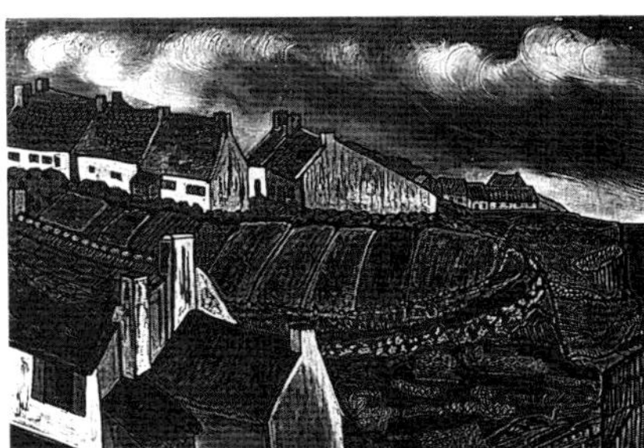
294

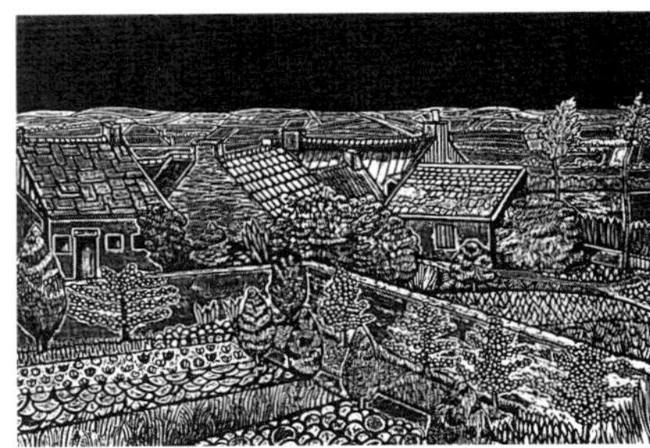
295

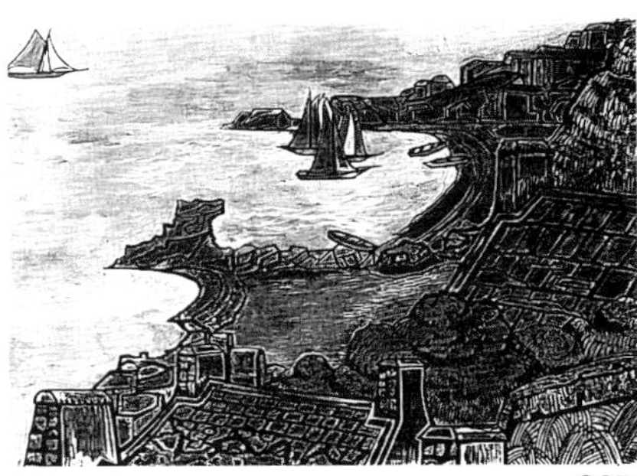
297

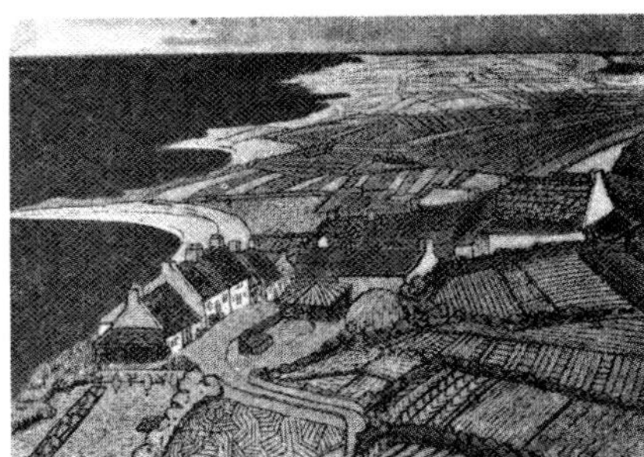
296

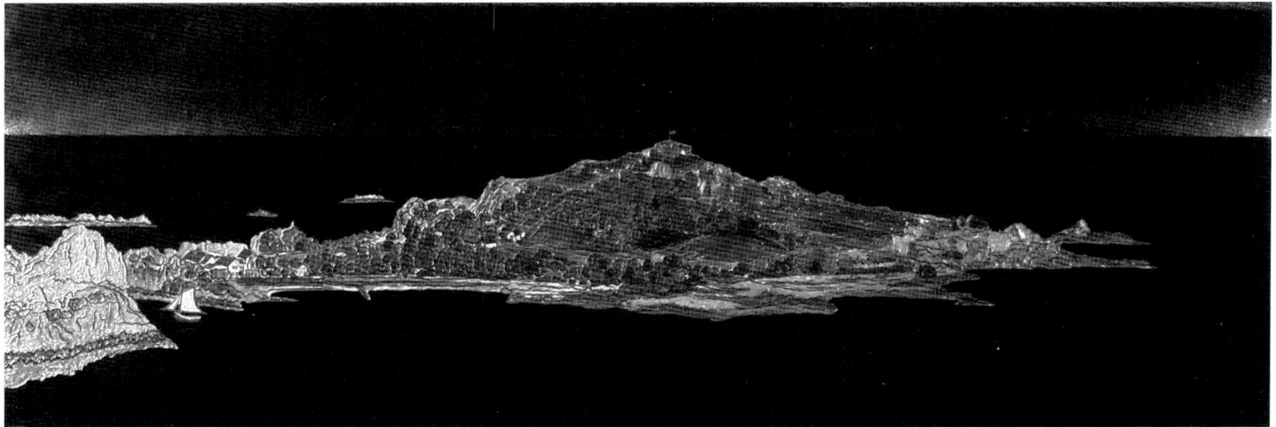

303

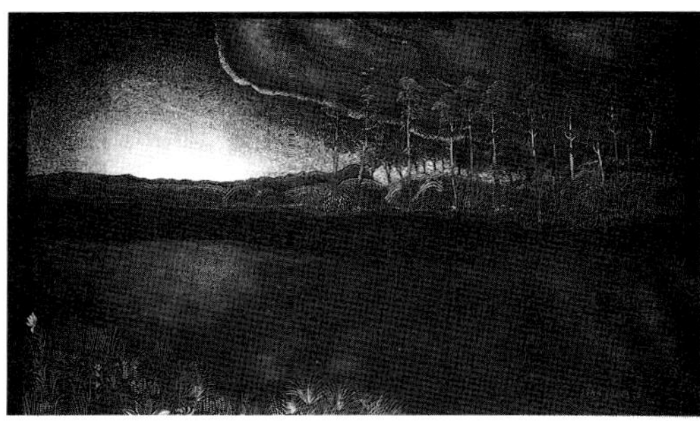

302

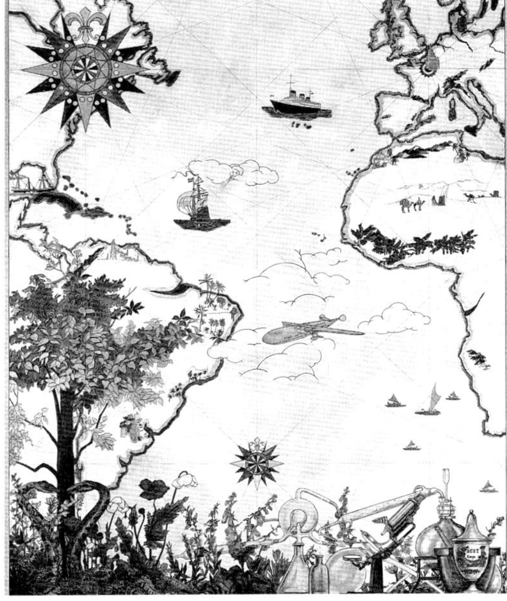

304

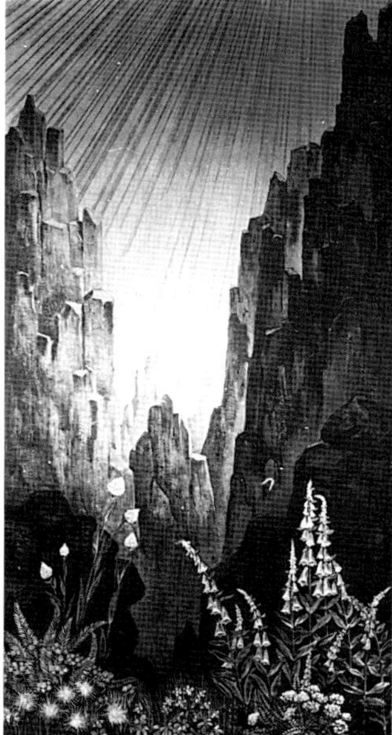

305

306

302 Forest
Incised black lacquer.
1929, signed.
Exh.: Galerie Georges Petit, Paris, 1929, no. 21.
Coll.: Musée National des Arts Africains, Paris.

303 Ile Saint-Riom (Bay of Paimpol, Brittany)
Incised black lacquer.
40 x 115 cm (15¾ x 45¼ in.).
1932, signed.
Exh.: Galerie Georges Petit, Paris, 1932, no. 15.
Coll.: Hervé Aaron, New York.

304 Mappamundi
Decorated gold lacquer, after a cartoon by André Nivard.
C. 1935, signed.
Coll.: Comar, Paris.
Specially commissioned from Dunand for a maker of pharmaceutical products.

305 La Paternelle
Decorated black lacquer.
C. 1935, signed.
Specially commissioned by the La Paternelle insurance company.

306 The Church at Estaing (Lot)
Gold lacquer and eggshell.
1942, signed.
Private collection.
Dunand was working on this unfinished piece on the eve of his death.

PANELS WITH ANIMAL SUBJECTS
(lacquer on wood unless stated otherwise)

307 Panther
Gold and moulded black lacquer, after a cartoon by Paul Jouve.
1921, signed 'Jean Dunand laqueur' and 'Paul Jouve'.

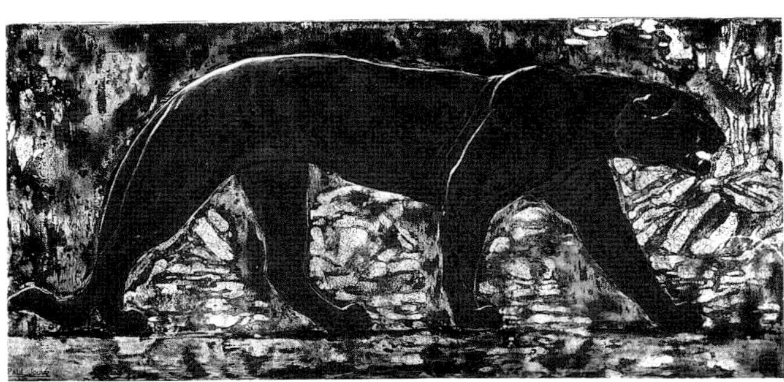
307

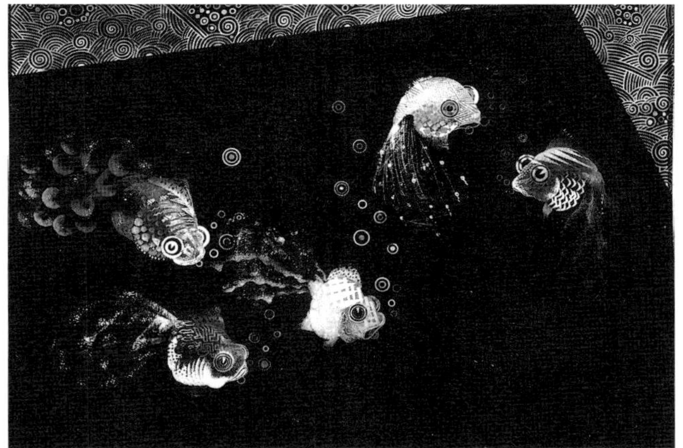
313

Exh.: Galerie Georges Petit, Paris, 1921, no. 9.
Coll.: Metropolitan Museum of Art, New York.

308 Pigeons *Pl. 23*
Coloured lacquer and eggshell.
1923, signed.
Exh.: Galerie Georges Petit, Paris, 1923, no. 12.
Formerly in the Frugès Collection; Private collection.

309 Ermine
Gouache on paper, study for cat. no. 310.
10 x 15 cm (4 x 6 in.).
1923.
Private collection.

310 Ermine
Coloured lacquer and eggshell, after a cartoon by Jean Lambert-Rucki.
1923, signed.
Exh.: Galerie Georges Petit, Paris, 1923, no. 13; ——, 1924, no. 33.
Bibl.: *Mobilier et décoration*, February 1926, p. 34.

311 Fish *Pl. 24*
Red and black lacquer inlaid with eggshell and highlighted with silver.
50 x 70 cm (19¾ x 27½ in.).
1925, signed.
Exh.: Delorenzo Gallery, New York, 1985 (repr. in catalogue, p. 19).
Formerly in the collection of Charles Henchoz, Geneva; Private collection.
Bibl.: *La Science et la vie: la semaine à Paris*, November 1925, p. 380.
Sold: Pillias, Gluck (Paris), 30 April 1975, lot 84.

312 Deer *Pl. 28*
Coloured lacquer on wood panel.
C. 1925, signed.

313 Fish
Black and coloured lacquer.
48.5 x 68 cm (19 x 26¾ in.).
1923, signed.
Exh.: Galerie Devambez, Paris, 1923; Delorenzo Gallery, New York, 1985 (repr. in catalogue, p. 23).
Coll.: Steven A. Greenberg, New York.
Sold: Sotheby's Belgravia (London), 13 October 1978, lot 201; Sotheby's (Monaco), 24/25 October 1982, lot 426.

314 Herons
Shellac and coloured lacquer.
C. 1925, signed.
Formerly in the collection of Mme Martin.

315 Eagle
Black lacquer on plain wood.
140 x 55 cm (55 x 21¾ in.).
C. 1925, signed.
Formerly in the collection of Félix Marcilhac, Paris; Private collection.
Sold: Millon, Jutheau (Paris), 23 November 1983, lot 9.

316 Eagle
Lacquer on plain wood.
140 x 55 cm (55 x 21¾ in.).
C. 1925, signed.
Formerly in the collection of Félix Marcilhac, Paris; Private collection.
Sold: Millon, Jutheau (Paris), 23 November 1983, lot 9.

317 Eagle
Black lacquer on plain wood.
Exh.: Delorenzo Gallery, New York, 1985 (repr. in catalogue, p. 36).
Coll.: Steven A. Greenberg, New York.
Variant of cat. no. 315.

318 Eagle *Pl. 19*
Black lacquer on plain wood.
C. 1925.
Exh.: Delorenzo Gallery, New York, 1985 (repr. in catalogue, p. 36).
Coll.: Steven A. Greenberg, New York.
Variant of cat. no. 316.

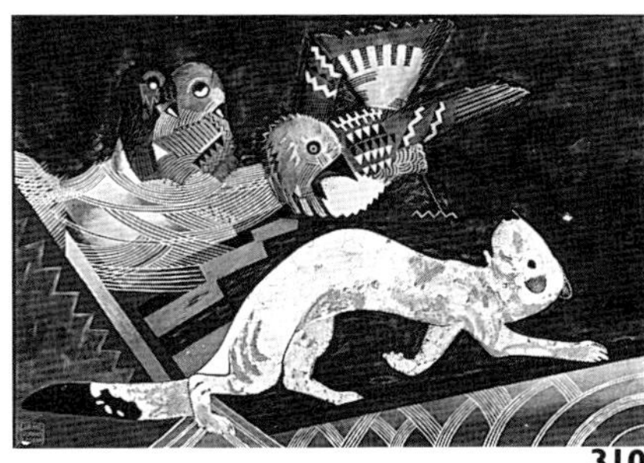
310

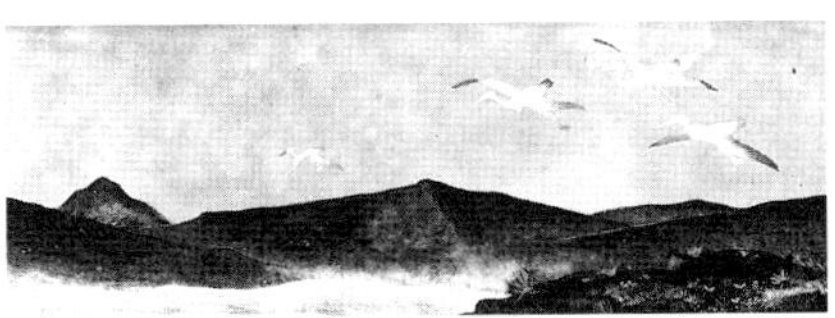
314

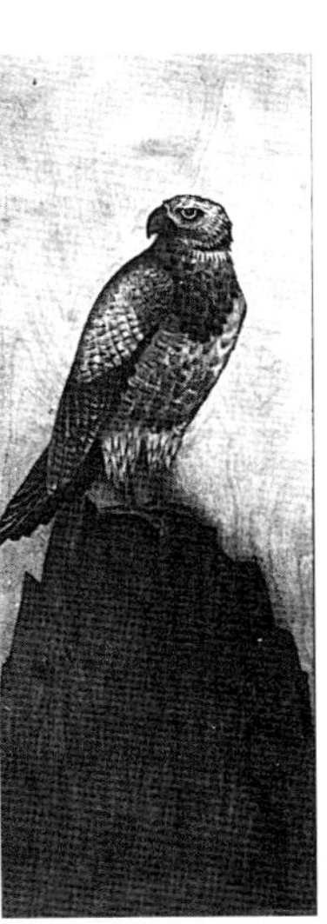
315

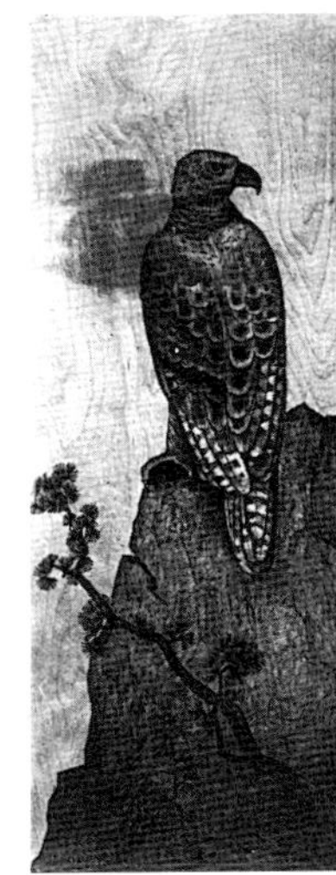
316

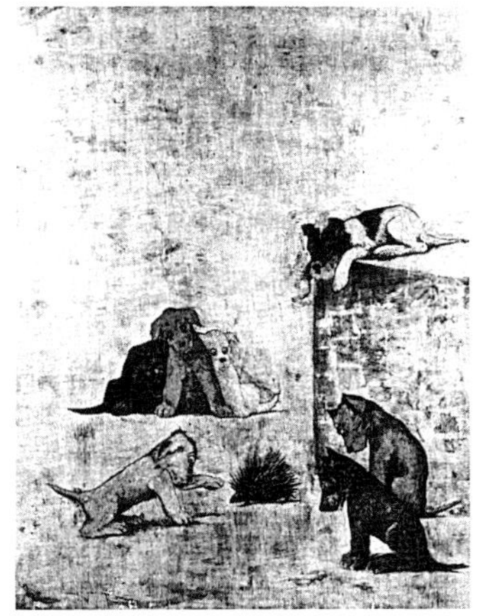
319

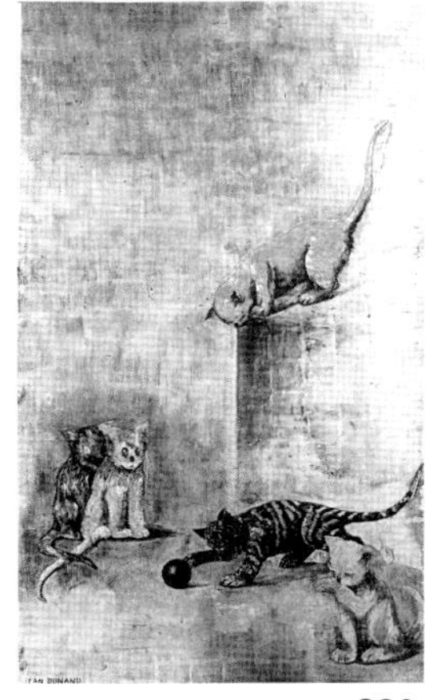
320

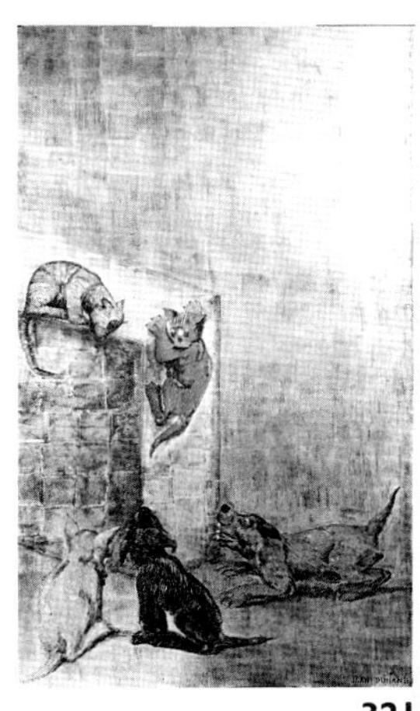
321

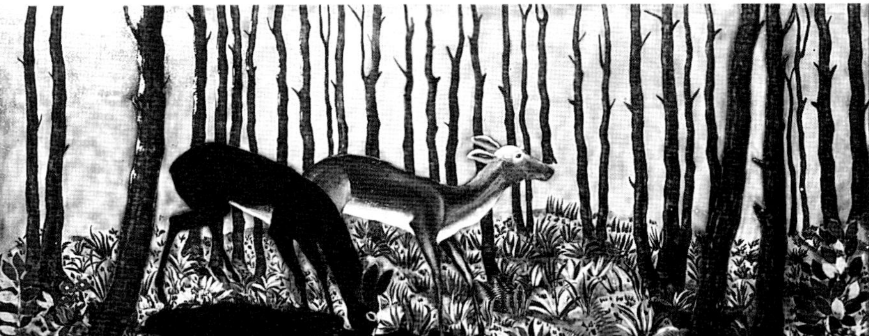
322

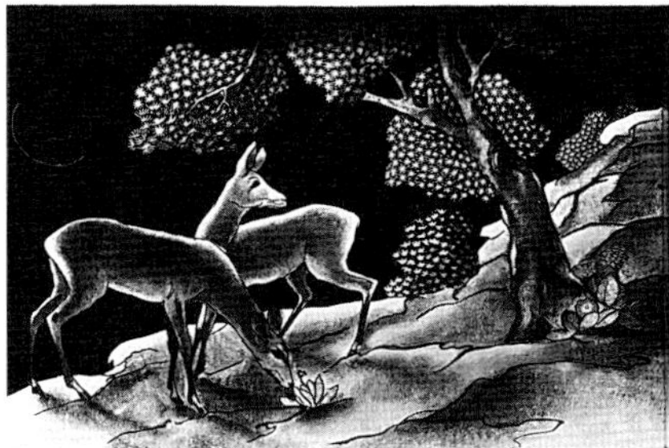
326

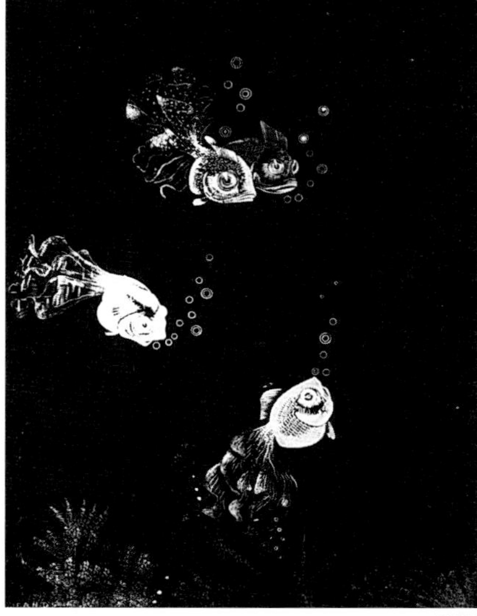
325

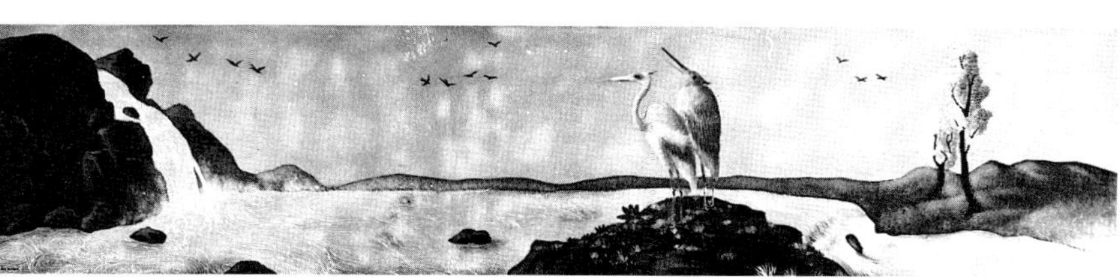
327

334

319 Dogs and Hedgehog
Incised gold lacquer on section of wood panelling.
190 x 155 cm (74¾ x 61 in.).
C. 1925, signed.
Sold: Laurin, Guilloux, Buffetaud, Tailleur (Paris), 10 November 1976, lot 90; Cornette de Saint-Cyr (Paris), 6 March 1981, lot 103.

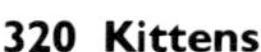

320 Kittens
Incised gold lacquer on section of wood panelling.
Original size 190 x 155 cm (74¾ x 61 in.).
C. 1925, signed.
Sold: Laurin, Guilloux, Buffetaud, Tailleur (Paris), 10 November 1976, lot 90; Cornette de Saint-Cyr (Paris), 6 March 1981, lot 102 (recut to measure 175 x 94 cm (68¾ x 35¾ in.).

321 Dogs and Cats
Incised gold lacquer on section of wood panelling.
Original size 190 x 159 cm (74¾ x 61½ in.).
C. 1925, signed.
Sold: Laurin, Guilloux, Buffetaud, Tailleur (Paris), 10 November 1976, lot 90; Cornette de Saint-Cyr (Paris), 6 March 1981, lot 101 (recut to measure 175 x 92 cm [68¾ x 36¼ in.]).

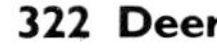

322 Deer
Brown lacquer and *laque arrachée*.
C. 1925, signed.

323 Fish
Two sections of wood panelling, natural lacquer.
Each section 98 x 24 cm (28½ x 9½ in.).
C. 1925, signed.

324 Japanese Fish *Pl. 25*
Black and coloured lacquer highlighted with gold.
75 x 56 cm (29½ x 22 in.).
C. 1925, signed.

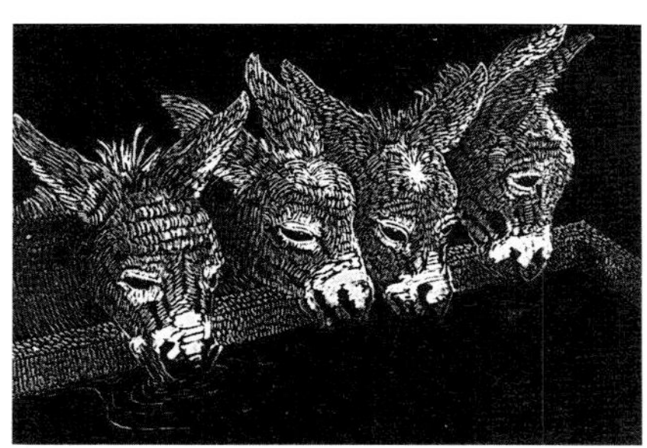
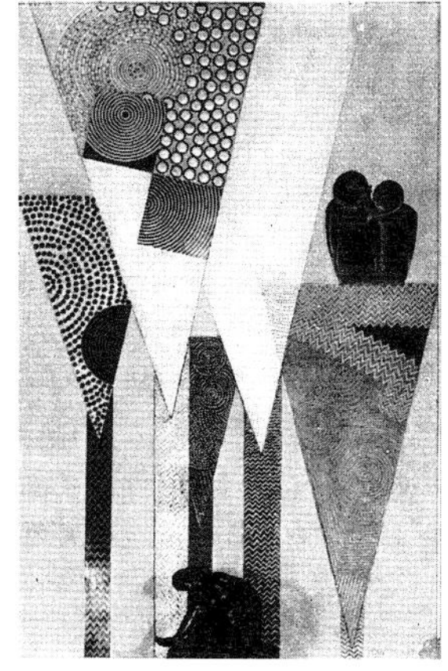
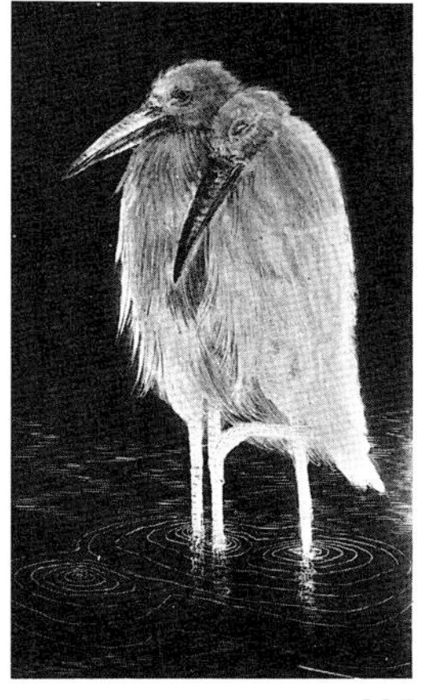
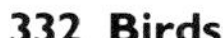

328 332 335

Exh.: Delorenzo Gallery, New York, 1985 (repr. in catalogue, p. 20).
Coll.: Galerie Vallois, Paris.

325 Japanese Fish
Black and coloured lacquer highlighted with gold and silver.
68 x 49 cm ($26^{3}/_{4}$ x $19^{1}/_{4}$ in.).
C. 1925, signed.
Sold: Christie's (Geneva), 13 May 1984, lot 114.

326 Deer
Incised black lacquer.
1926, signed.
Exh.: Galerie Georges Petit, Paris, 1926, no. 24.

327 Dogs
Incised black lacquer.
1926, signed.
Exh.: Galerie Georges Petit, Paris, 1926, no. 25.

328 Donkeys
Incised black lacquer.
56 x 75 cm (22 x $29^{1}/_{2}$ in.).
1926, signed.
Exh.: Galerie Georges Petit, Paris, 1926, no. 26.
Formerly in the collection of Jeanne Fillon.
Sold: Laurin, Guilloux, Buffetaud, Tailleur (Paris), 20 June 1975, lot 203.

329 Eaglets
Incised brown lacquer.
1926, signed.
Exh.: Galerie Georges Petit, Paris, 1926, no. 27.

330 Small Monkey
Shellac.
1927, signed.
Exh.: Galerie Georges Petit, Paris, 1927, no. 22.

331 Monkeys *Pl. 17*
Coloured lacquer on a light-brown shellac ground.
68.5 x 23 cm (27 x 9 in.).
1927, signed.
Exh.: Galerie Georges Petit, Paris, 1927, no. 23; Delorenzo Gallery, New York, 1985 (repr. in catalogue, p. 34).
Coll.: Steven A. Greenberg, New York.

332 Birds
Silver lacquer inlaid with gilt copper.
1927, signed.
Exh.: Salon des Artistes Décorateurs, Paris, 1927.
Bibl.: *Art et décoration*, June 1927, p. 198.

333 Monkey *Pl. 18*
Shellac.
88 x 68 cm ($34^{1}/_{2}$ x $26^{3}/_{4}$ in.).
C. 1927, signed.
Coll.: Félix Marcilhac, Paris.

334 Herons
Incised light-brown lacquer.
C. 1927, signed.
Formerly in the collection of Mme Martin.

335 Two Marabou Storks
Incised black lacquer.
C. 1927, signed.
Bibl.: Armand Dayot, *Les Animaux*, vol. 1 (Paris, 1929), pl. 27.

336 Panther
Transparent light-brown lacquer.
C. 1927, signed.

337 Ducks
Brown lacquer.
C. 1927, signed.
Formerly in the collection of Mme Dubreuil.

338 Fish
Black lacquer.
C. 1927, signed.

339 Panther
Laque arrachée on a silver lacquer ground.
C. 1928, signed.
Formerly in the collection of Jean De Noyer, New York; Hervé Aaron, New York.

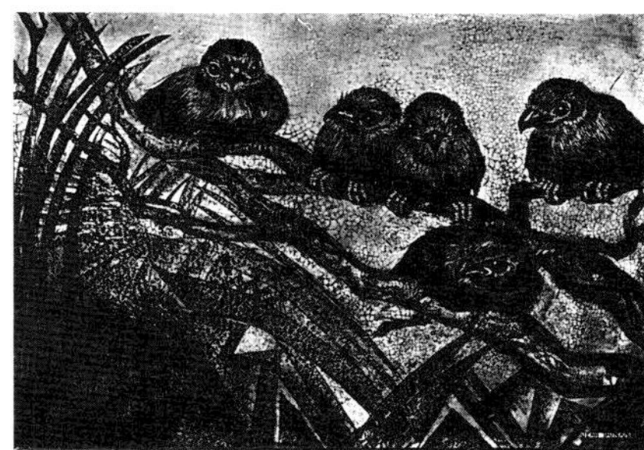
329

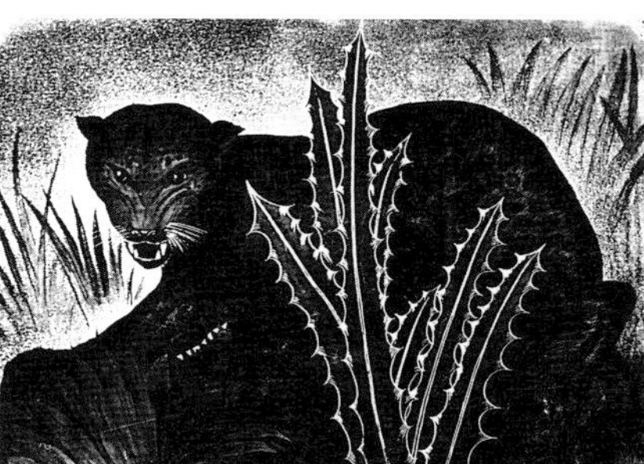
336

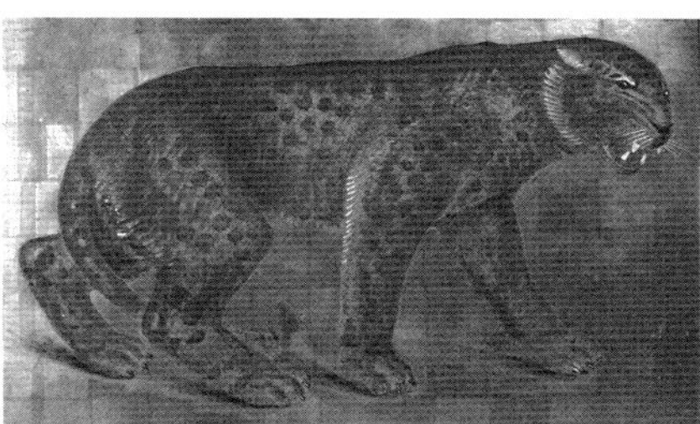
339

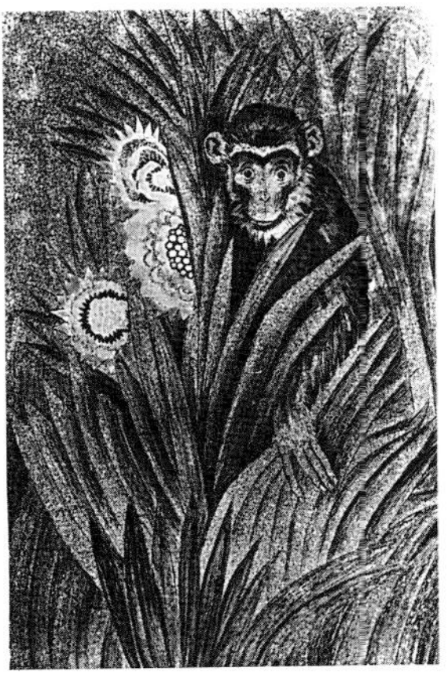

341

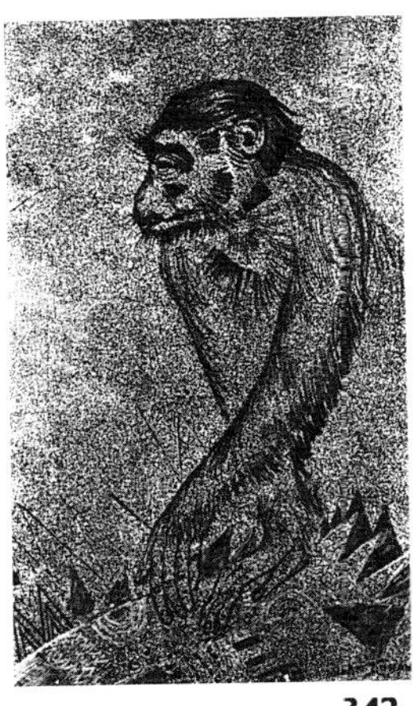

342

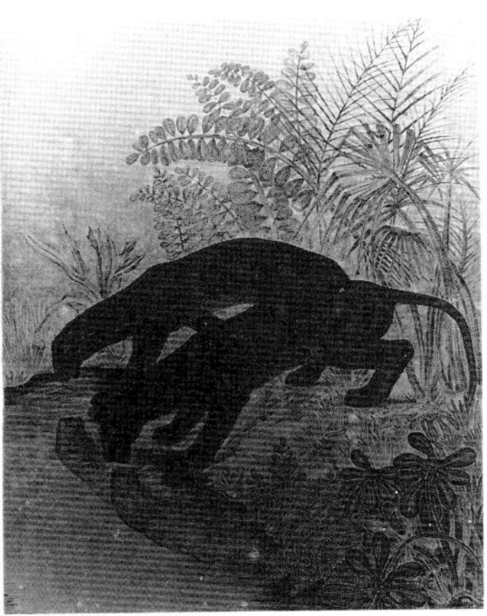

343

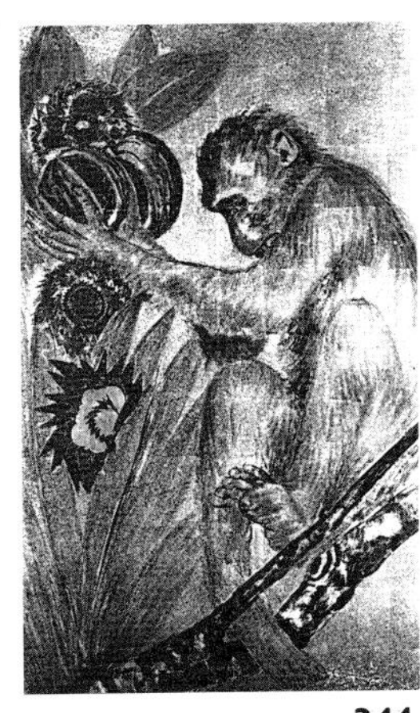

344

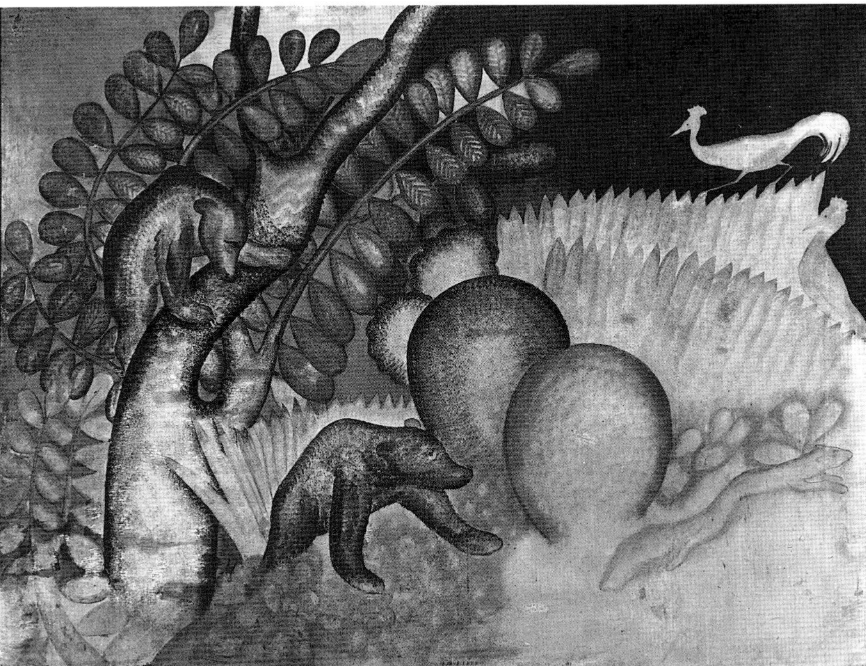

340

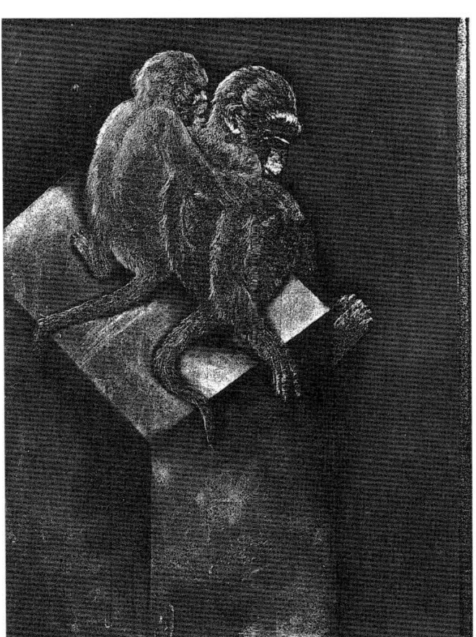

347

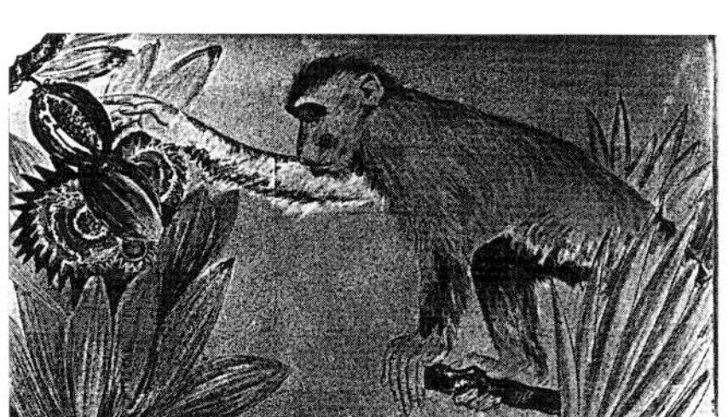

345

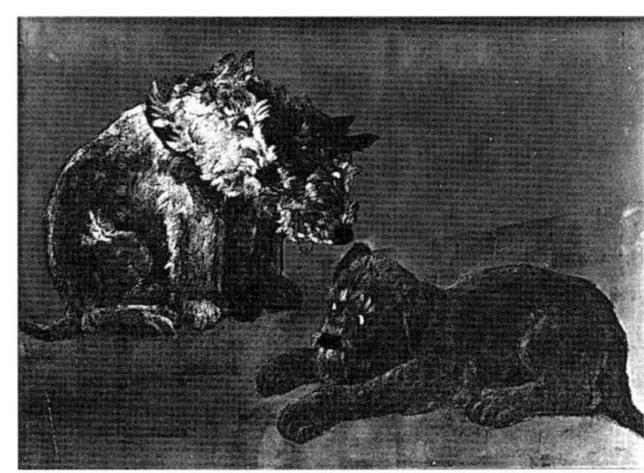

346

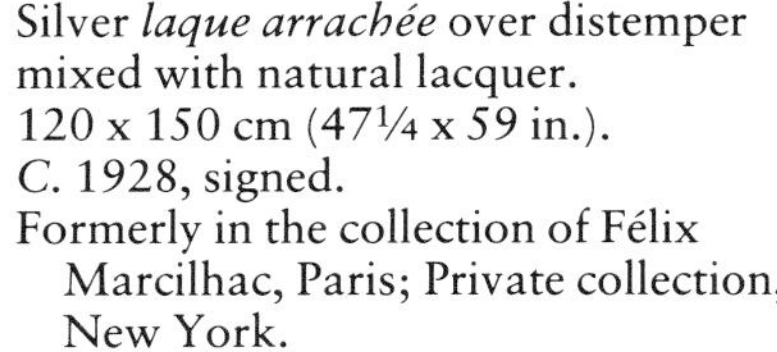

340 Bear Cubs
Silver *laque arrachée* over distemper mixed with natural lacquer.
120 x 150 cm (47¼ x 59 in.).
C. 1928, signed.
Formerly in the collection of Félix Marcilhac, Paris; Private collection, New York.

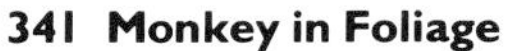

341 Monkey in Foliage
Silver and black lacquer.
92 x 62 cm (36¼ x 24½ in.).
1929, signed.
Exh.: Galerie La Renaissance, Paris, 1929, no. 1 (repr. on cover of catalogue); Rosenbach Gallery, New York, 1929, no. 3.

342 Monkey at the Water's Edge
Gold and black lacquer.
89 x 56 cm (35 x 22 in.).
1929, signed.
Exh.: Galerie La Renaissance, Paris, 1929, no. 2; Rosenbach Gallery, New York, 1929, no. 1.

343 Panthers Slaking their Thirst
Gold and black lacquer.
1929, signed.
Exh.: Galerie La Renaissance, Paris, 1929, no. 8.
Formerly in a private collection, San Francisco, Cal.

344 Monkey and Fruit
Gold and black lacquer.
89 x 56 cm (35 x 22 in.).
1929, signed.
Exh.: Galerie La Renaissance, Paris, 1929, no. 10.
Bibl.: Armand Dayot, *Les Animaux*, vol. 1 (Paris, 1929), pl. 27.

345 Monkey and Fruit
Gold and black lacquer.
56 x 89 cm (22 x 35 in.).
1929, signed.
Exh.: Galerie La Renaissance, Paris, 1929, no. 11.
For a preliminary sketch, see colour plate 60.

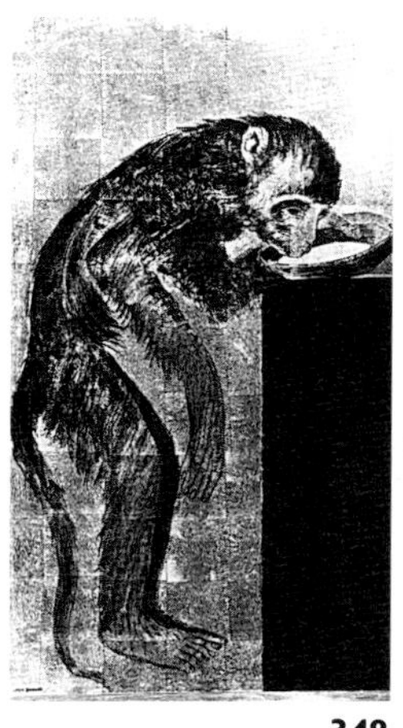
348

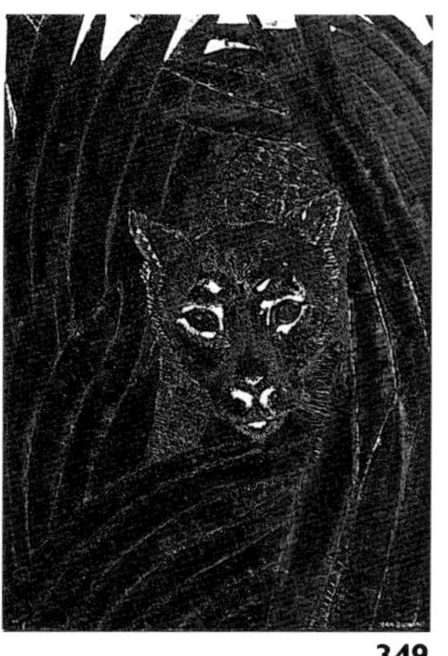
349

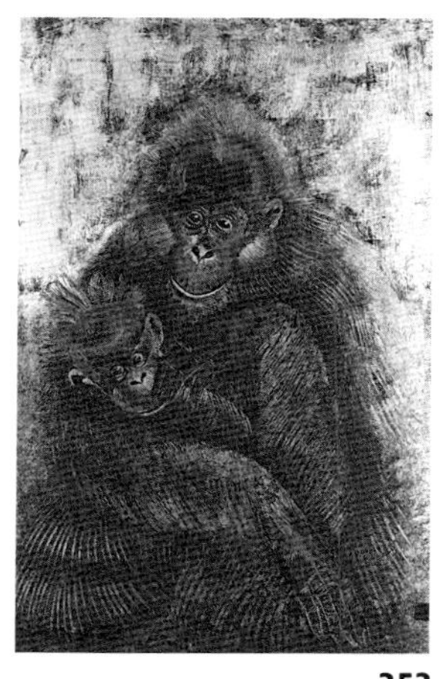
353

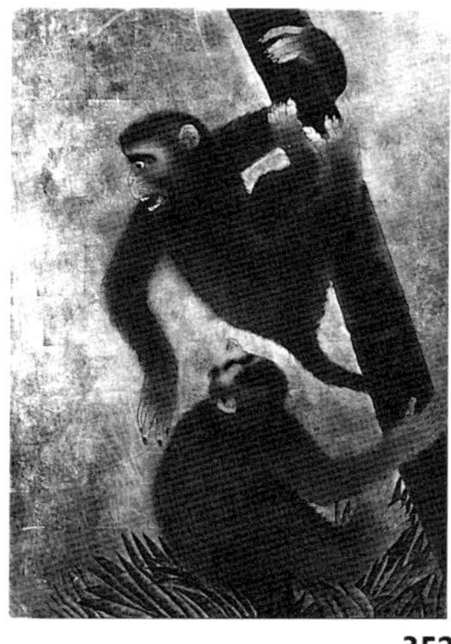
352

346 Three Dogs
Laque arrachée on a gold lacquer ground.
68.5 x 81 cm (27 x 32 in.).
1929, signed.
Exh.: Galerie La Renaissance, Paris, 1929, no. 13; Rosenbach Gallery, New York, 1929, no. 4; Delorenzo Gallery, New York, 1985 (repr. in catalogue, p. 30).
Coll.: John Fleming.

347 Two Monkeys
Silver *laque arrachée* on a red lacquer ground.
73.5 x 54.5 cm (29 x 21½ in.).
1929, signed.
Exh.: Galerie La Renaissance, Paris, 1929, no. 21; 'Europäische Lackkunst', Museum Bellerive, Zurich, 1976, no. 89.
Formerly in the collection of Félix Marcilhac, Paris; Victoria and Albert Museum, London (on loan to the Brighton Art Gallery and Museums).

348 Monkey Drinking
Gold and black lacquer.
89 x 56 cm (35 x 22 in.).
1929, signed.
Exh.: Galerie La Renaissance, Paris, 1929, no. 30; Rosenbach Gallery, New York, 1929, no. 8.

349 Tiger
Laque arrachée.
1929, signed.
Exh.: Galerie La Renaissance, Paris, 1929, no. 39.

350 Pigeons *Pl. 20*
Incised black lacquer.
100 x 66 cm (39¼ x 26 in.).
1929, signed.
Exh.: Galerie La Renaissance, Paris, 1929, no. 40; Galerie Georges Petit, Paris, 1930/31, no. 21.
Sold: Sotheby's (New York), 11/12 May 1984, lot 399.

351 Two Birds
Light-brown lacquer.
1929, signed.
Exh.: Galerie La Renaissance, Paris, 1929, no. 42; Galerie Georges Petit, Paris, 1930/31, no. 23.

352 Monkeys
Brown lacquer on a gold lacquer ground.
1929, signed.
Exh.: Galerie La Renaissance, Paris, 1929, no. 47.

353 Monkeys
Incised lacquer on a gold and silver ground.
92 x 62 cm (36¼ x 24½ in.).
1929, signed.
Exh.: Galerie La Renaissance, Paris, 1929, no. 48; Rosenbach Gallery, New York, 1929, no. 10.
Sold: Laurin, Guilloux, Buffetaud, Tailleur (Paris), 25 November 1977, lot 117.

354 Two Monkeys
Incised lacquer on a gold ground.
75 x 55 cm (29½ x 21¾ in.).
1929, signed.
Exh.: Galerie La Renaissance, Paris, 1929, no. 53.

355 Birds
Decorated brown lacquer on a silver ground.
1929, signed.
Exh.: Galerie La Renaissance, Paris, 1929, no. 56.
Bibl.: *Building* (New York), March 1930, p. 123.

356 Rabbits and Flowers
Gold and brown lacquer.
75 x 55 cm (29½ x 21¾ in.).
1929, signed.
Exh.: Galerie La Renaissance, Paris, 1929, no. 59.
Formerly in the collection of Félix Marcilhac, Paris; Private collection.

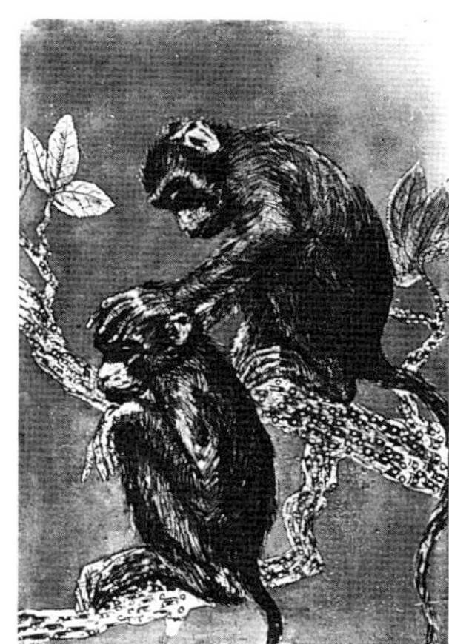
354

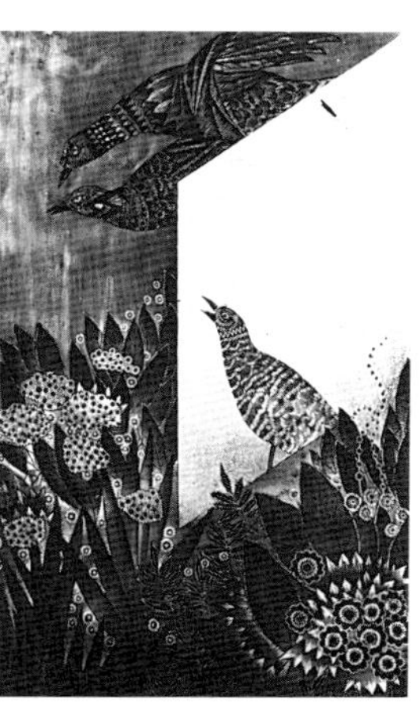
355

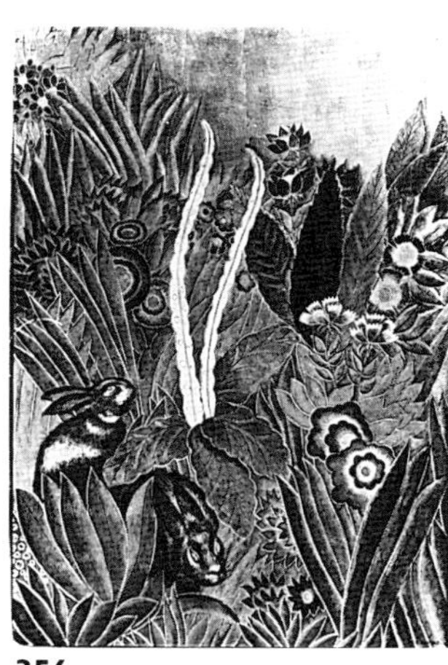
356

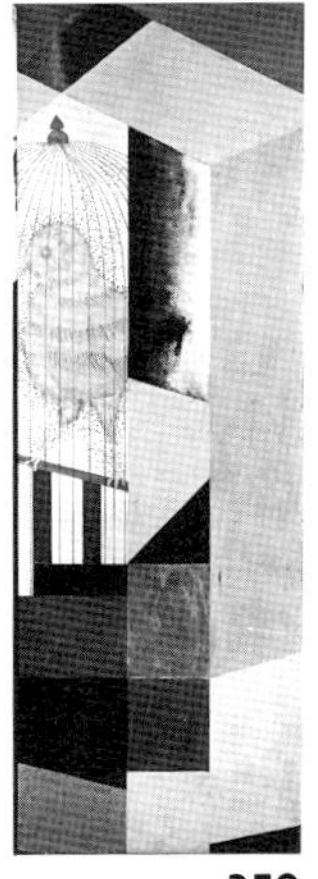

359

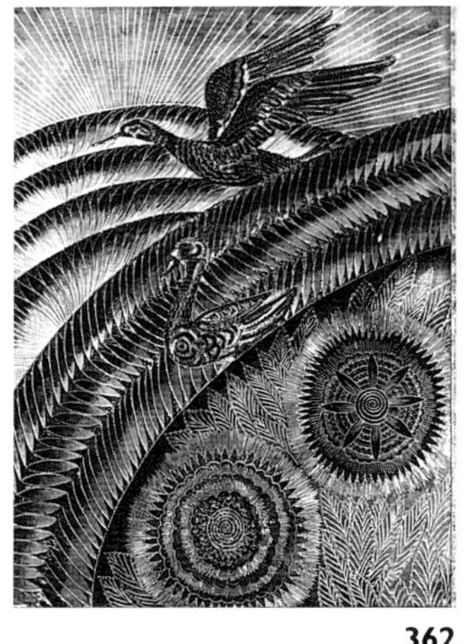

362

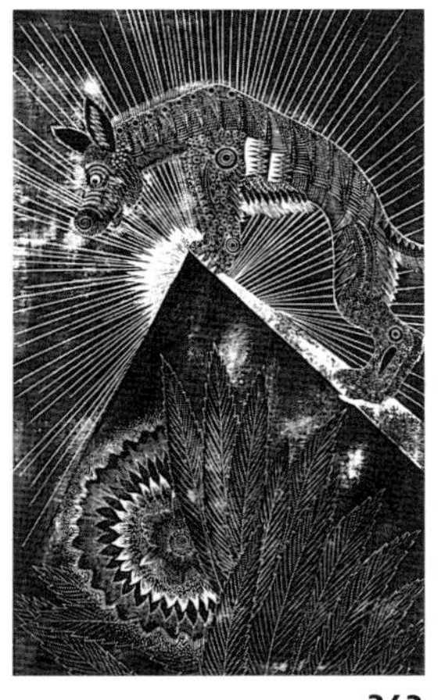

363

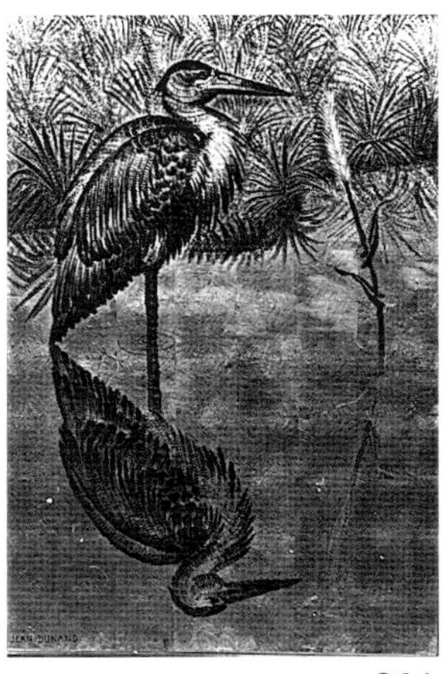

364

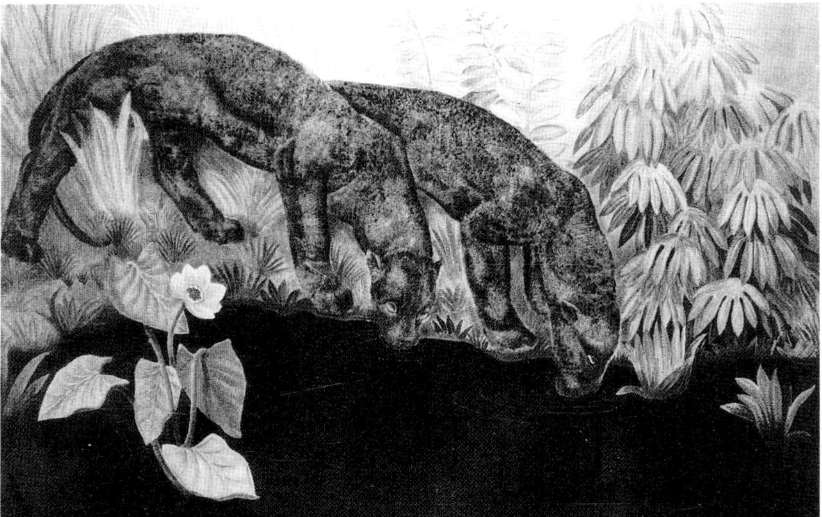

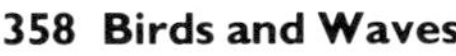

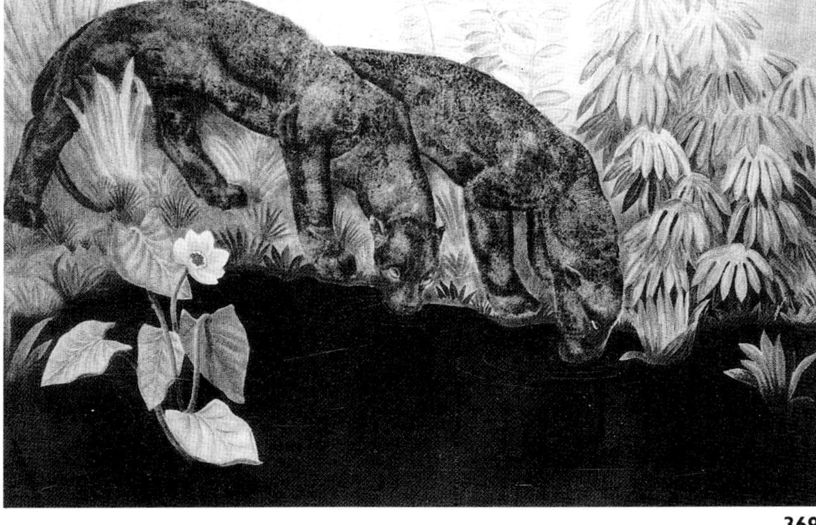

369

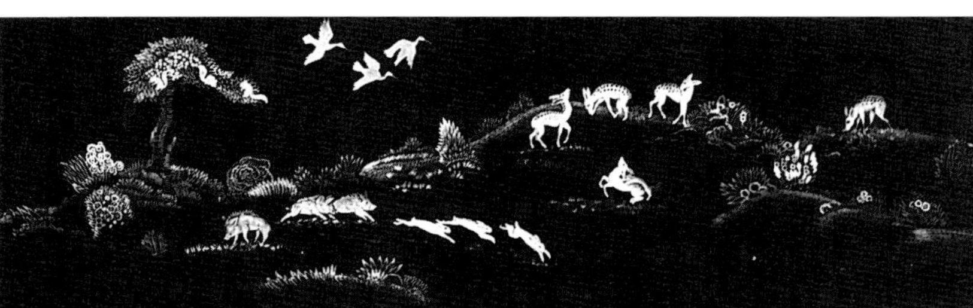

376

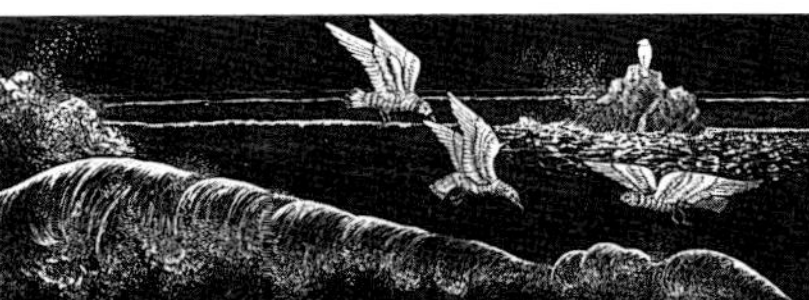

358

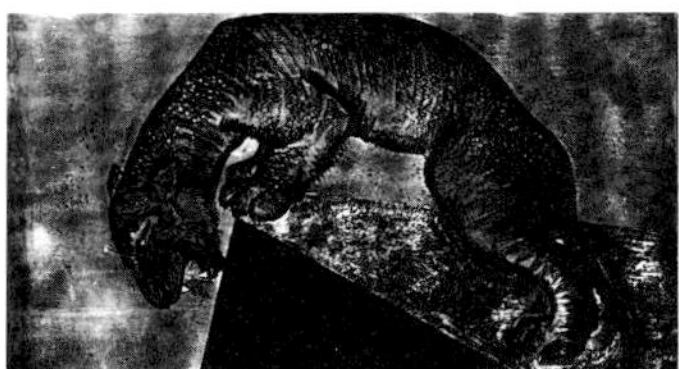

360

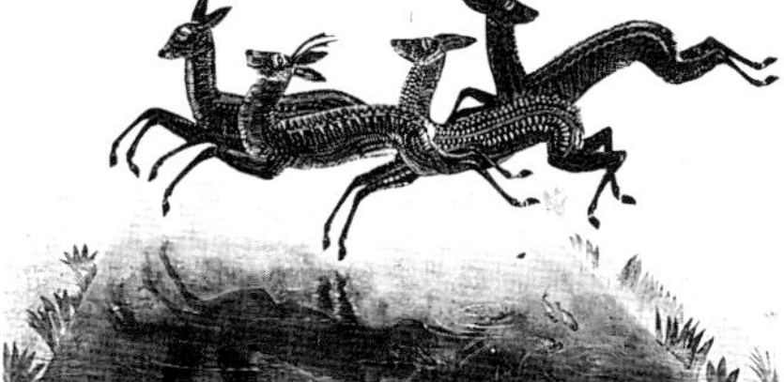

357

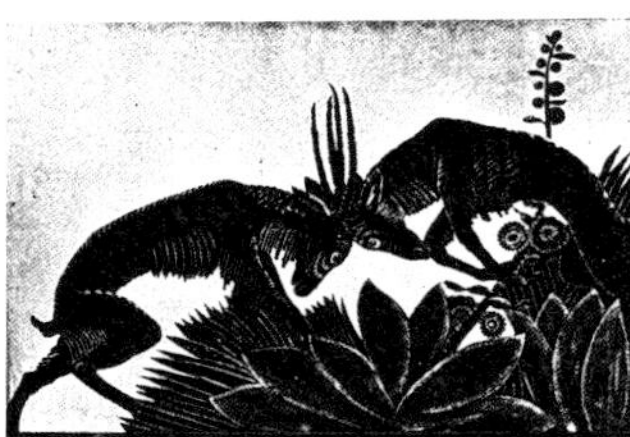

361

357 Deer
Lacquer on a silver ground.
1929, signed.
Exh.: Galerie Georges Petit, Paris, 1929, no. 22.
Bibl.: *Plaisir de France*, July 1939.

358 Birds and Waves
Incised black lacquer.
1929, signed.
Exh.: Galerie Georges Petit, Paris, 1929, no. 33.
Bibl.: *L'Art et les artistes*, November 1936, p. 59.

359 Caged Bird
Grey and black lacquer.
170 x 54 cm (67 x 21¼ in.).
C. 1929.
Formerly in the collection of Karl Lagerfeld.
Sold: Godeau, Solanet, Audap (Paris), 27 November 1975, lot 95.
A variant of a panel of a screen first exhibited in 1929 at the Galerie Georges Petit, Paris (see cat. no. 65).

360 Tiger
Silver lacquer.
1930, signed.
Exh.: Galerie Georges Petit, Paris, 1930/31, no. 18.

361 Goats Fighting
Silver lacquer.
1930, signed.
Exh.: Galerie Georges Petit, Paris 1930/31, no. 19.

362 Birds
Incised black lacquer.
1930, signed.
Exh.: Galerie Georges Petit, Paris, 1930/31, no. 20.

363 Dog
Incised black lacquer.
1930, signed.
Exh.: Galerie Georges Petit, Paris, 1930/31, no. 22.

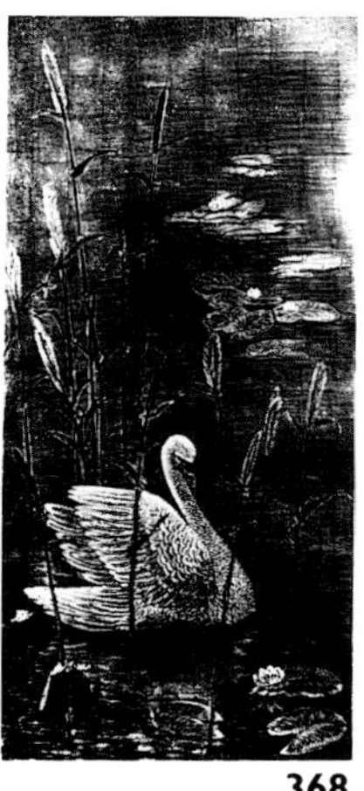
368

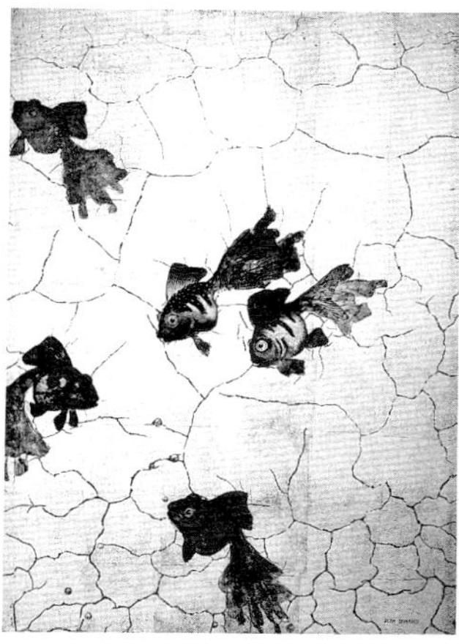
365

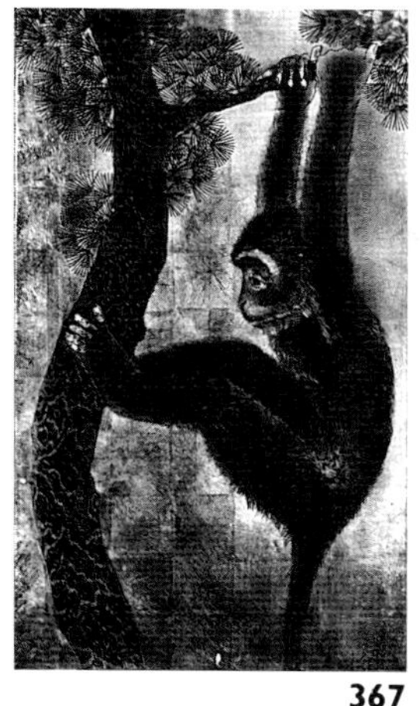
367

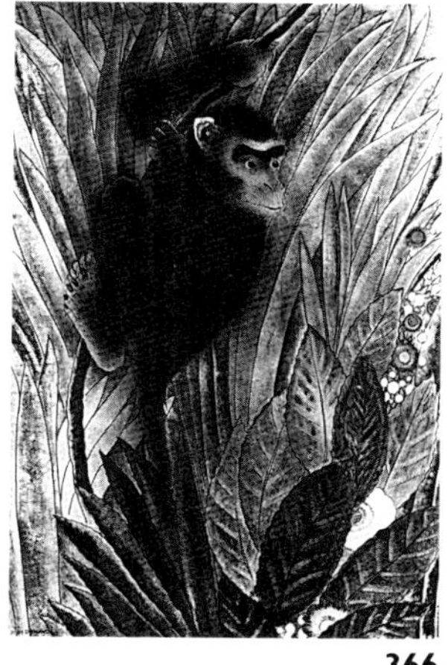
366

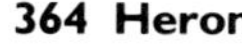

364 Heron
Incised light-brown lacquer.
1930, signed.
Exh.: Galerie Georges Petit, Paris, 1930/31, no. 25.

365 Fish
Lacquer painted on glass, with a silver-leaf backing.
77.5 x 56 cm (30½ x 22 in.).
1930, signed.
Exh.: Delorenzo Gallery, New York, 1985 (repr. in catalogue, p. 22).
Formerly in the collection of Félix Marcilhac, Paris; Steven A. Greenberg, New York.

366 Monkey Hanging from a Liana
Decorated lacquer on a gold ground.
C. 1930, signed.

367 Monkey Hanging from a Tree
Decorated lacquer on a gold ground.
C. 1930, signed.

368 Swan
Gold and black lacquer.
C. 1930, signed.
Formerly in the Lebourgy Collection.

369 Panthers at a Watering Hole
Gold and silver lacquer on a black ground.
130 x 180 cm (51¼ x 70¾ in.).
C. 1930, signed.
Sold: Loiseau, Schmitz (Saint-Germain-en-Laye), 22 May 1981, repr. on catalogue cover.

370 Panthers at a Watering Hole
Preparatory study, gouache on card with trace of squaring.
20 x 38 cm (7¾ x 15 in.).
C. 1930.
Private collection.

371 Buffalo and Panther Fighting
Incised gold lacquer on a black ground.
75 x 150 cm (29½ x 59 in.).
C. 1930, signed.

372 Buffalo and Panther Fighting
Gouache and Indian ink on card with gilt ground.
13.5 x 21 cm (5¼ x 8¼ in.).
C. 1930.
Private collection.

373 The Ford *Pl. 27*
Gold and black lacquer.
80 x 175 cm (31½ x 68¾ in.).
C. 1930, signed.
Exh.: Delorenzo Gallery, New York, 1985 (repr. in catalogue, p. 17).
Coll.: Steven A. Greenberg, New York.
Sold: Laurin, Guilloux, Buffetaud, Tailleur (Paris), 8 June 1978, lot 61c.

374 Herons *Pl. 21*
Gouache and rose-pink silver on cardboard.
33.5 x 24 cm (12¼ x 9½ in.).
C. 1930.
A panel based on this preparatory study was installed in the Paris home of Jacques André, where it is seen *in situ* in a photograph reproduced in *Mobilier et décoration*, May 1932, p. 189.

375 Panther Slaking its Thirst
Decorated black lacquer on a gold ground.
120 x 200 cm (47¼ x 78¾ in.).
C. 1930, signed.
Coll.: Yves Saint Laurent and Pierre Bergé, Marrakech.

376 Forest Animals in the Open
Black lacquer.
C. 1930, signed.

377 Herons
Decorated gold and black lacquer.
C. 1930, signed.

378 Ducks
Preparatory study in gouache and Indian ink.
16 x 14.5 cm (6¼ x 5¾ in.).
C. 1930.
Private collection.

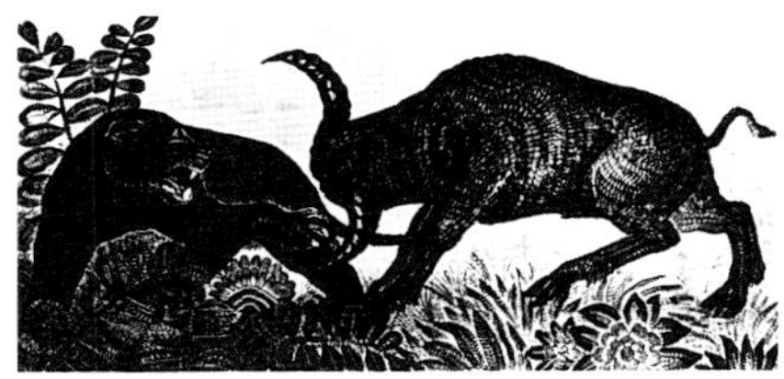
371

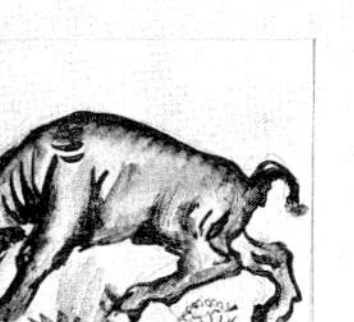
372

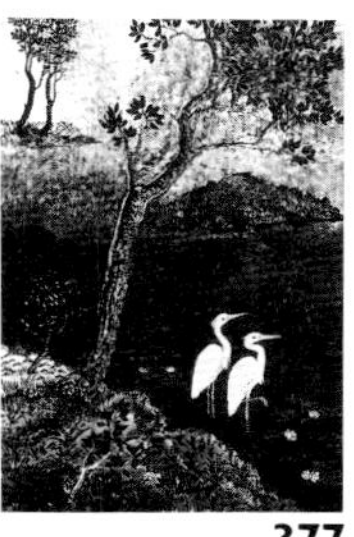
377

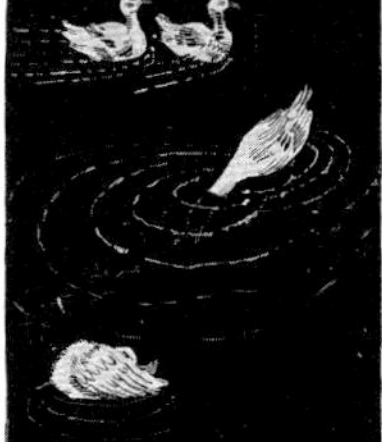
378

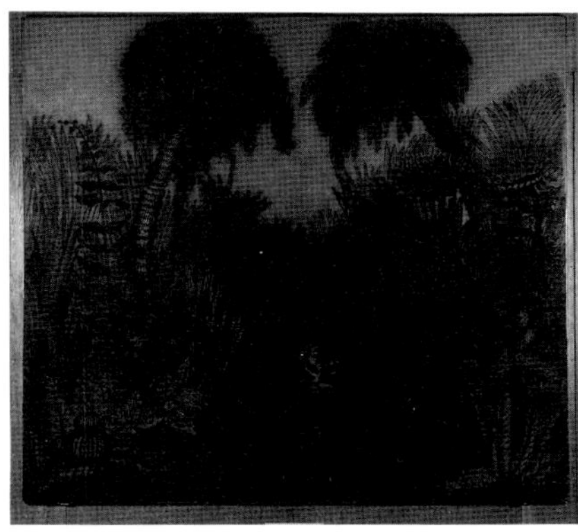
375

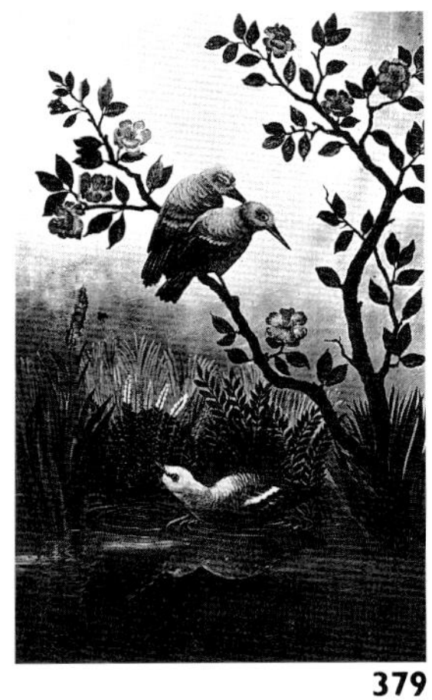
379

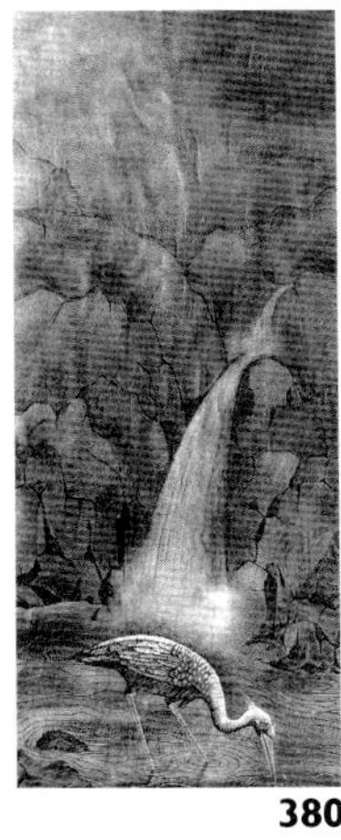
380

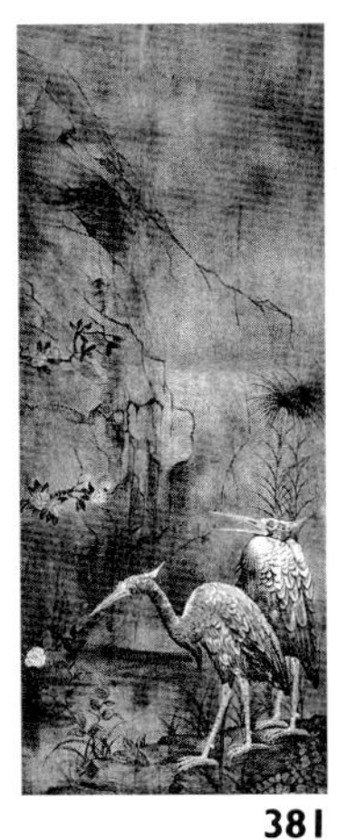
381

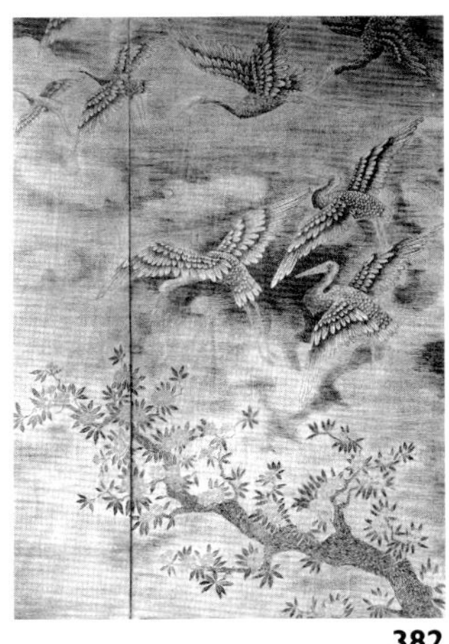
382

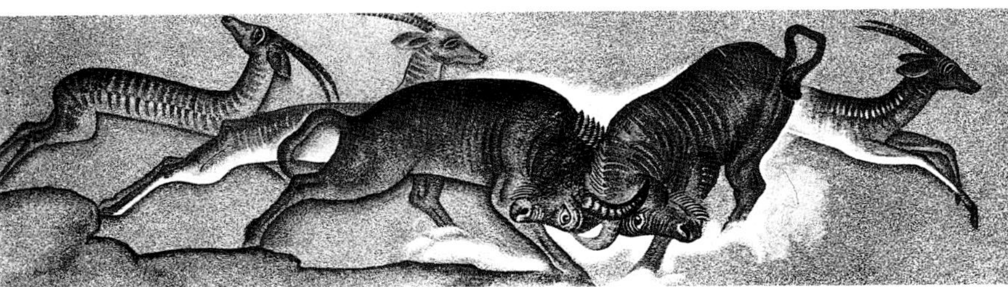
390

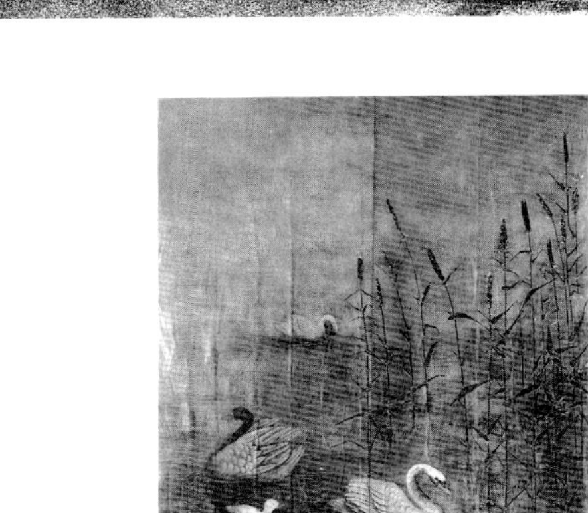

385

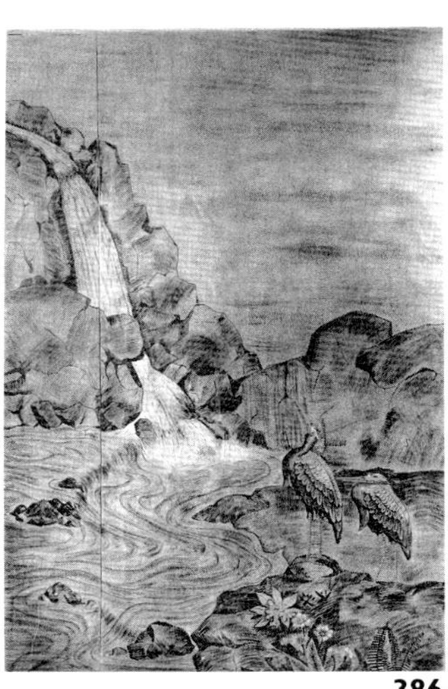
386

387

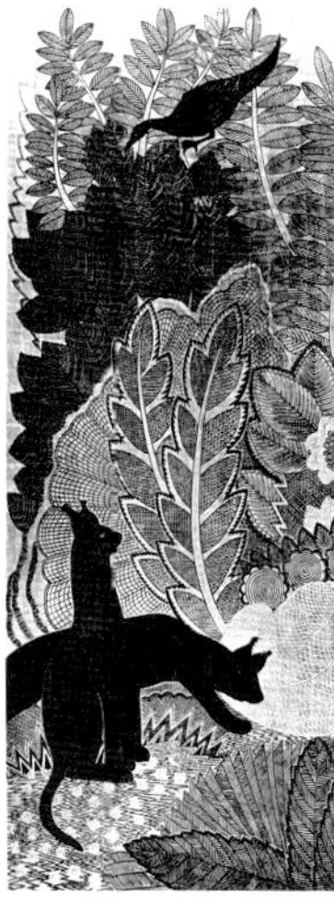
388

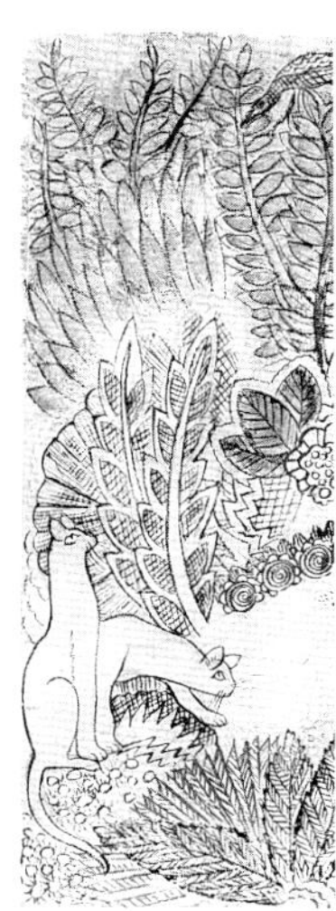
389

379 Water Birds
Gold and brown lacquer.
C. 1930, signed.
Formerly in the collection of Sir Julian Cahn, London.

380 Waterfall and Heron
Black and gold lacquer.
235 x 97 cm (92½ x 38¼ in.).
C. 1930.
Coll.: Claude Ott, Paris.

381 Herons
Black and gold lacquer.
235 x 94 cm (92½ x 37 in.).
C. 1930.
Coll.: Claude Ott, Paris.

382 Storks in Flight
Black and gold lacquer.
290 x 213 cm (114¼ x 83¾ in.).
C. 1930.
Coll.: Claude Ott, Paris.

383 Tree in Blossom
Black and gold lacquer (section of a larger composition).
235 x 35 cm (92½ x 13¾ in.).
C. 1930.
Coll.: Claude Ott, Paris.

384 Herons and Ducks
Gold and black lacquer.
290 x 490 cm (114¼ x 193 in.).
C. 1930.
Coll.: Claude Ott, Paris.

385 White Swan and Black Swan
Black and gold lacquer.
290 x 195 cm (114¼ x 76¾ in.).
C. 1930.
Coll.: Claude Ott, Paris.

386 Herons and Waterfall
Black and gold lacquer.
290 x 195 cm (114¼ x 76¾ in.).
C. 1930.
Coll.: Claude Ott, Paris.

387 Trees
Incised gold lacquer on stucco.
360 x 167 cm (141¾ x 65¾ in.).
1932, signed.

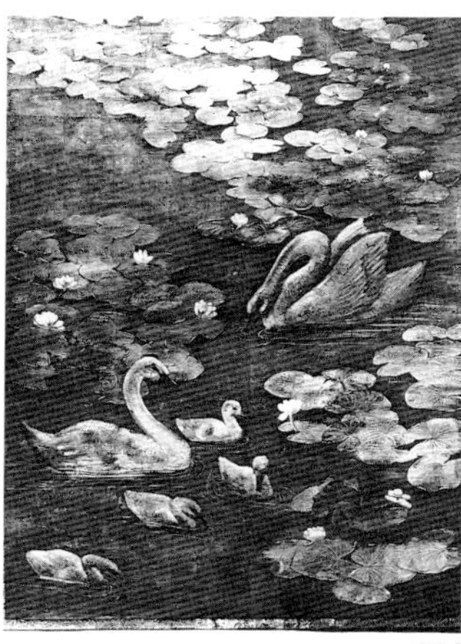
391

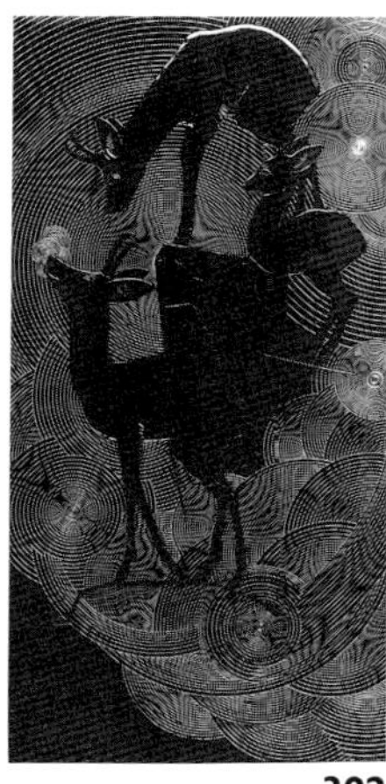
392

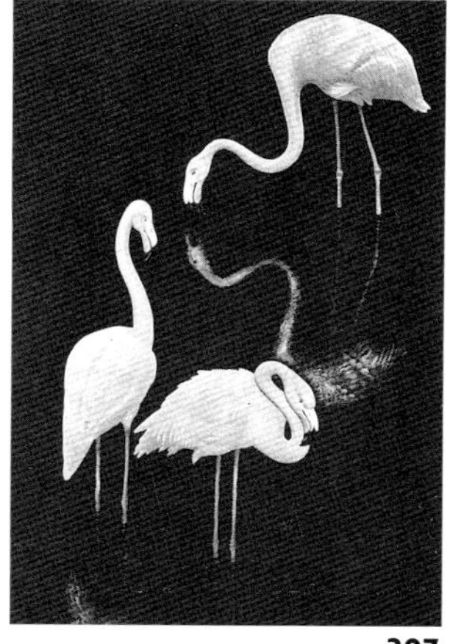
397

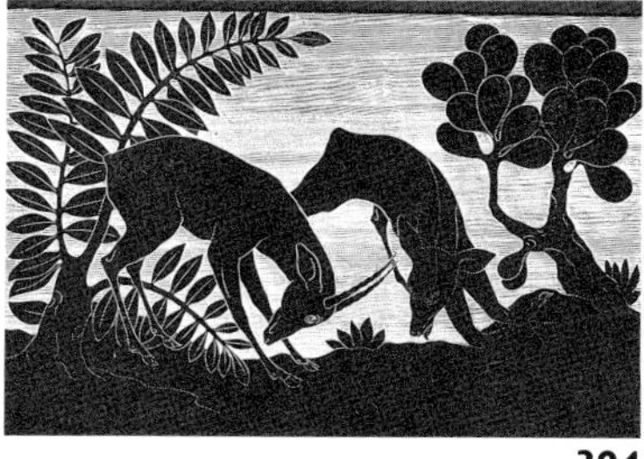
394

Exh.: Galerie Georges Petit, Paris, 1932, no. 9.
Bibl.: *Art et décoration*, April 1932, p. 228.
Sold: Pillias, Morelle, Oger, Maignan (Paris), 24 November 1972, repr. on cover of catalogue.

388 Lynxes
Incised gold lacquer on stucco.
360 x 167 cm (141¾ x 65¾ in.).
1932, signed.
Exh.: Galerie Georges Petit, Paris, 1932, no. 10.
Bibl.: *Art et décoration*, August 1932, p. 229.

389 Lynxes
Gouache, Indian ink and gold; study for a panel to be lacquered by the Coromandel technique and then gilded by roller.
44 x 23 cm (17¼ x 9 in.).
1932.
Private collection.

390 Buffaloes Fighting
Fresco on wood, grey lacquer.
1932, signed.
Exh.: Galerie Georges Petit, Paris, 1932, no. 11.
Bibl.: *Art et décoration*, August 1932, p. 232.

391 Swans
Silver lacquer.
225 x 160 cm (88½ x 63 in.).
1932, signed.
Exh.: Galerie Georges Petit, Paris, 1932, no. 12.

392 Chamois
Sculpted black lacquer.
250 x 110 cm (98½ x 43½ in.).
1932, signed.
Exh.: Galerie Georges Petit, Paris, 1932, no. 13.
Formerly in the collection of Lucien Vallet, Paris.
Bibl.: *Art et décoration*, August 1932, p. 231.

393 Deer
Decorated and incised gold lacquer.
86 x 69 cm (34 x 27¼ in.).
1932, signed.
Exh.: Galerie Georges Petit, Paris, 1932, no. 14.
Sold: Sotheby's (Monaco), 6 October 1985, lot 309.

394 Deer
Black lacquer on a striated gold ground.
1932, signed.
Exh.: Galerie Georges Petit, Paris, 1932, no. 17.

395 Tiger
Matt black lacquer on a silver ground.
1932, signed.
Exh.: Galerie Georges Petit, Paris, 1932, no. 19.

396 Deer *Pl. 26*
Black lacquer on a silver lacquer ground, highlighted with gold.
183 x 102 cm (72 x 40¼ in.).
C. 1932, signed.
Exh.: Delorenzo Gallery, New York, 1985 (repr. in catalogue, p. 16).
Formerly in the collection of Félix Marcilhac, Paris; Steven A. Greenberg, New York.

397 Pink Ibis
Black lacquer on wood panel.
C. 1935, signed.

398 Elephant in the Bush
Brown and black lacquer.
C. 1935, signed.
Panel executed for the Banque de l'A.O.F. (Afrique Occidentale Française).

399 Elephant Hunt
Gouache, gold and Indian ink, study for a lacquer panel.
19 x 25 cm (7½ x 9¾ in.).
C. 1935.
Private collection.

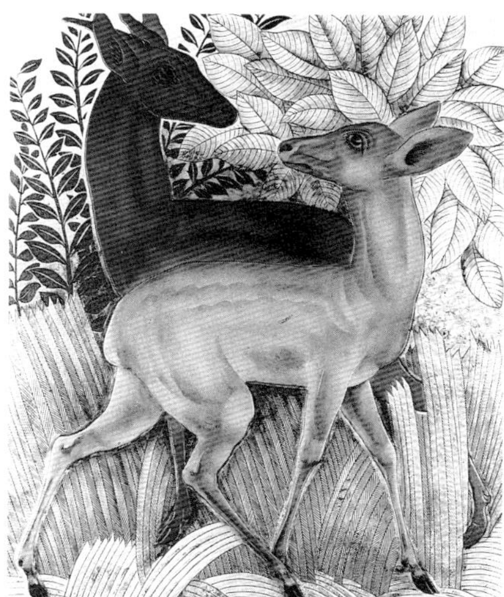

393

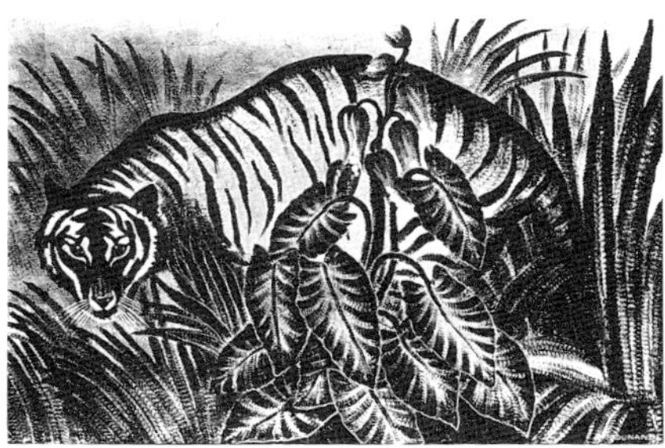
395

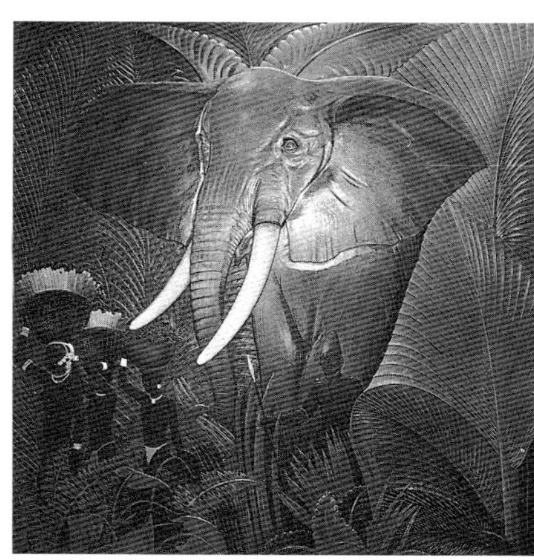
398

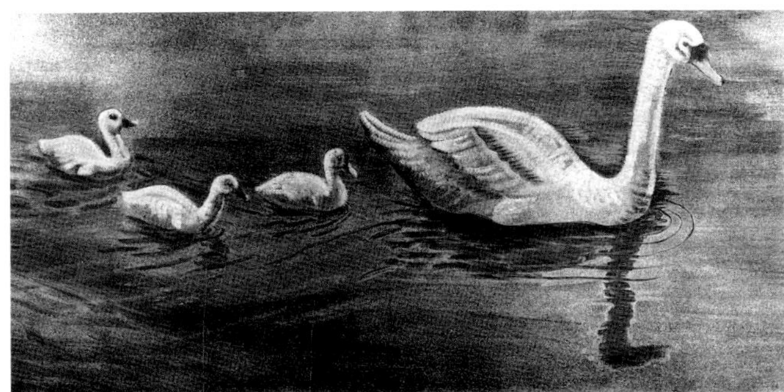

402

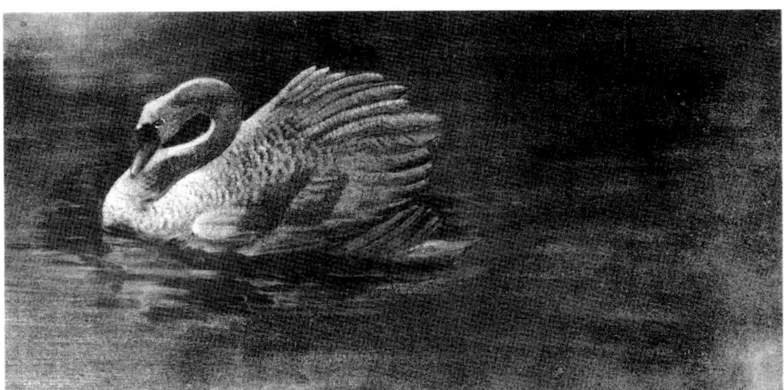

403

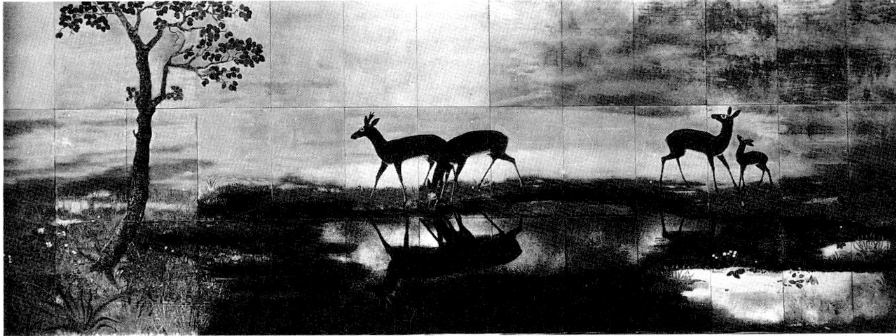

404

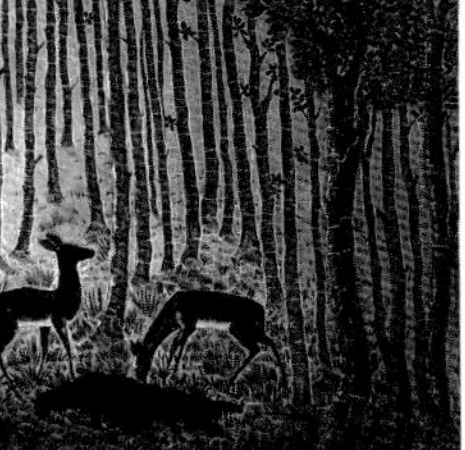

400

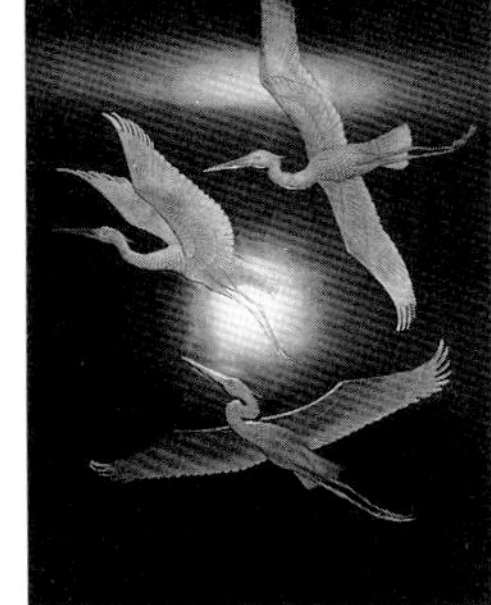

401

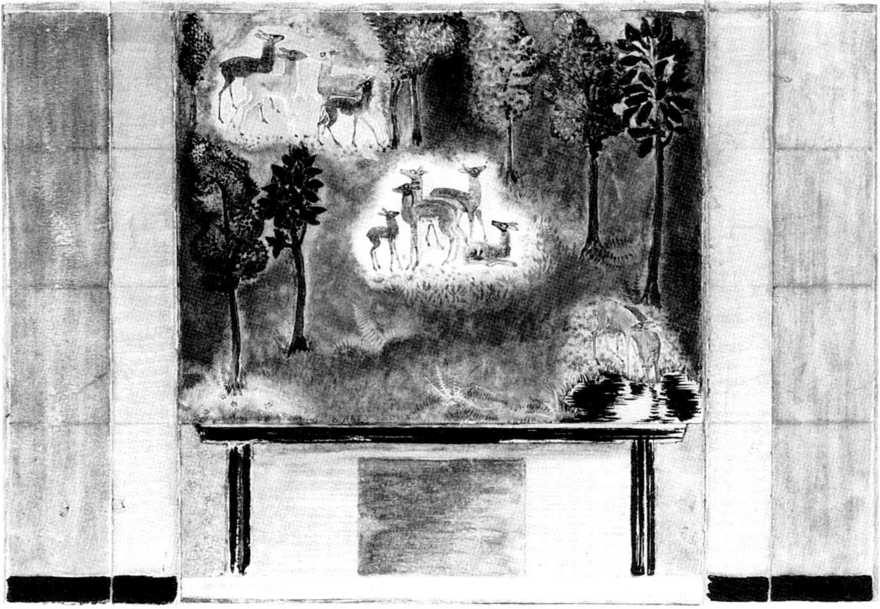

405

400 Deer in Woodland
Decorated brown lacquer.
C. 1935, signed.

401 Storks
Incised black lacquer.
218 x 152 cm (85¾ x 59¾ in.).
1937, signed.
Private collection.

402 Swan and Cygnets
Black and gold lacquer.
1937, signed.
Exh.: Salon des Artistes Décorateurs, Paris, 1939.
Formerly in the collection of Félix Marcilhac, Paris; Hervé Aaron, New York.

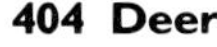

403 Swan
Gold and black lacquer.
1937, signed.
Exh.: Salon des Artistes Décorateurs, Paris, 1939.
Formerly in the collection of Félix Marcilhac, Paris; Hervé Aaron, New York.

404 Deer
Decorated black lacquer.
Length *c.* 10 m (32 ft 6 in.).
C. 1937, signed.
Panel executed for the French Embassy in Ankara.

405 Deer in a Clearing
Gouache, Indian ink and gold on cardboard.
35.5 x 50 cm (14 x 19¾ in.).
1938, signed.
Private collection.
Reduced version of the panel for the Porteneuve Music Room exhibited at the 1937 Exposition Internationale des Arts et Techniques executed for a private client as decoration for the back of an alcove.
See also cat. nos. 1224–1227 and illustration, p. 151.

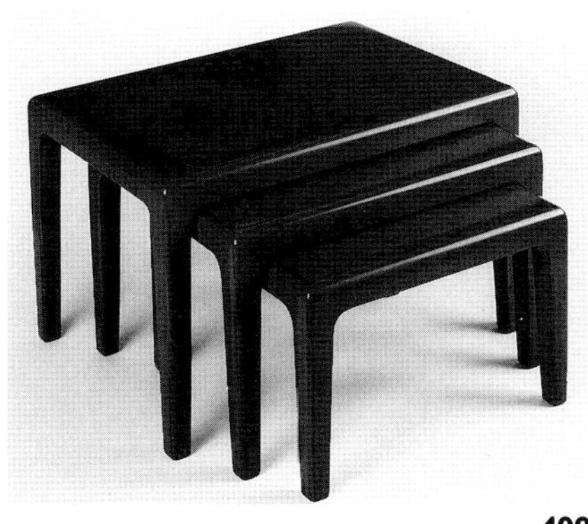
409

410

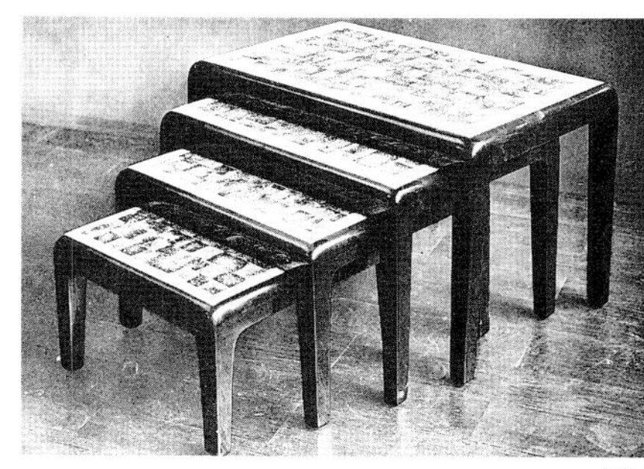
412

FURNITURE: TABLES

406 Nest of three tables
Black lacquer, dinanderie top, copper inlaid with geometric motifs in silvered metal.
Height 44 cm (17¼ in.); top 37.5 x 25 cm (14¾ x 9¾ in.).
C. 1930.
Private collection, Paris.
Sold: Boisgirard (Paris), 25 March 1988, lot 110.

407 Nest of three tables *Pl. 55*
Light-brown shellac, tops inlaid with eggshell mosaic.
Height 60 cm (23½ in.); top 70 x 55 cm (27½ x 21¾ in.).
C. 1925.
Private collection, Paris.

408 Nest of three tables *Pl. 54*
Dark shellac, tops inlaid with eggshell mosaic.
Height 45 cm (17¾ in.); top 40 x 50 cm (15¾ x 19¾ in.).
C. 1925.
Private collection, Paris.

409 Nest of three tables
Red shellac on moulded synthetic base.
Height 40 cm (15¾ in.); top 41.5 x 62.5 cm (16¼ x 24½ in.).
C. 1935.
Private collection.

410 Nest of three tables
Light-brown shellac with radiating design in eggshell.
Coll.: L'Arc en Seine, Paris.

411 Nest of three tables
Black lacquer, tops inlaid with checkered eggshell mosaic.
C. 1935.
Coll.: Mobilier National, Paris.

412 Nest of four tables
Black lacquer, tops inlaid with checkered eggshell mosaic.
C. 1924.
Exh.: Galerie Georges Petit, Paris, 1924.

413 Nest of four tables
Gold lacquer on spruce underframe, tops decorated with geometric design.
1930.
Exh.: Galerie Georges Petit, Paris, 1930/31.
Formerly in the collection of Madame Agnès, Paris; Private collection, Paris.

414 Nest of six tables
Black lacquer.
1930.
Formerly in the collection of the Galerie Vallois, Paris.

415 Nest of four tables
Black lacquer, tops decorated with gold leaf.
1928.
Exh.: Galerie Georges Petit, Paris, 1928, no. 35.

416 Nest of three tables
Black lacquer, tops decorated with geometric eggshell motifs.
1923.
Exh.: Galerie Georges Petit, 1923, no. 7.

417 Dining table and chairs *Pl. 70*
Light-brown shellac within a border of dark-brown lacquer.
Table: height 78 cm (28¼ in.); top 145 x 185 cm (57 x 72¾ in.); extra leaf adds 60 cm (23¼ in.) to length.
Chairs: height 96 cm (37¾ in.).
Designed in 1928 for the Comte de Polignac and made in 1929/30, the table can be extended (the central section having a pedestal support).
Exh.: Delorenzo Gallery, New York, 1985.
Formerly in the collection of the Galerie Vallois, Paris; Private collection, New York.
Sold: Christie's (New York), 31 March 1984, lot 374.
See also cat. no. 477.

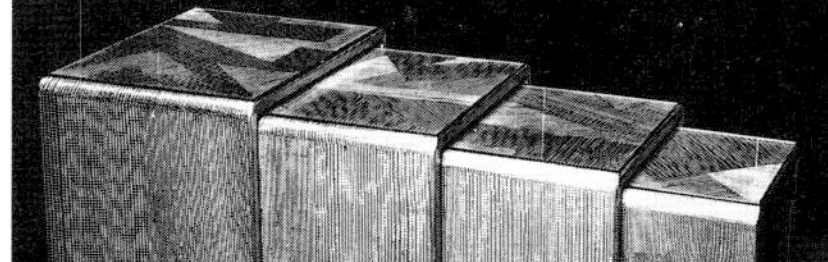
413

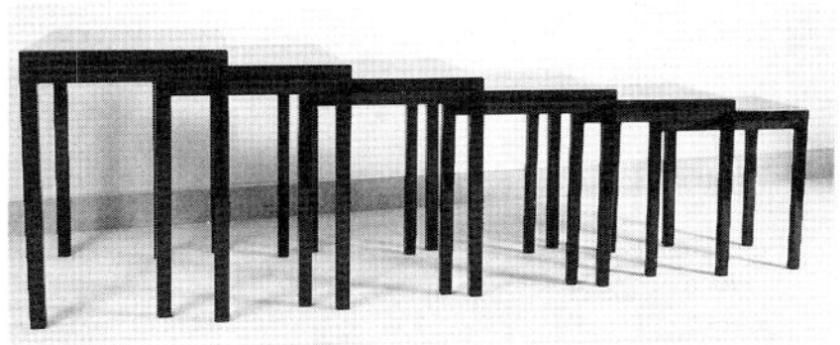
414

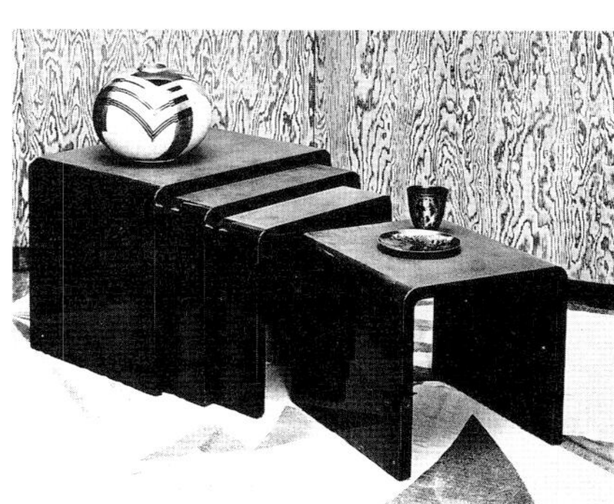
415

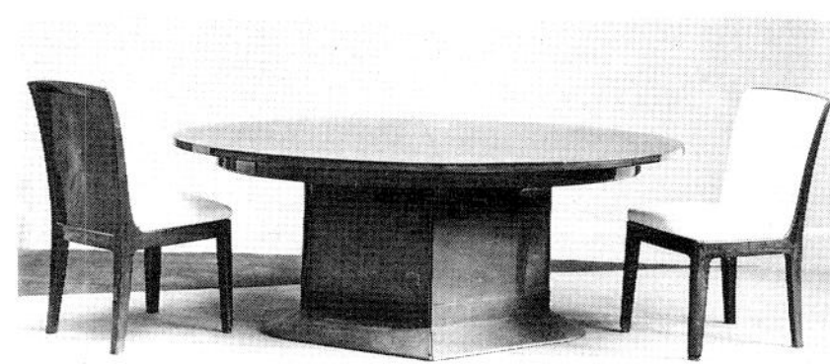
417

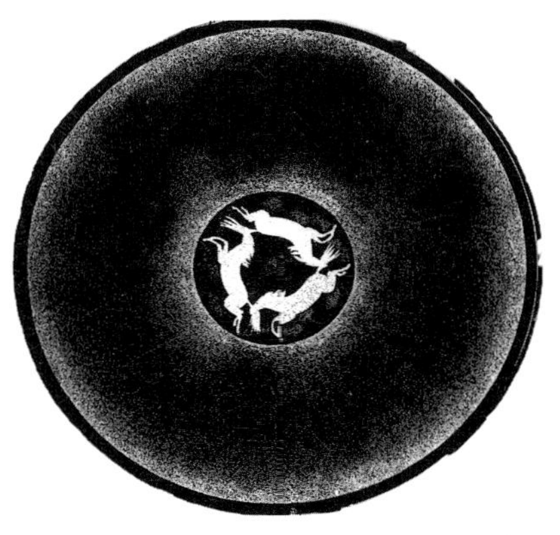

420

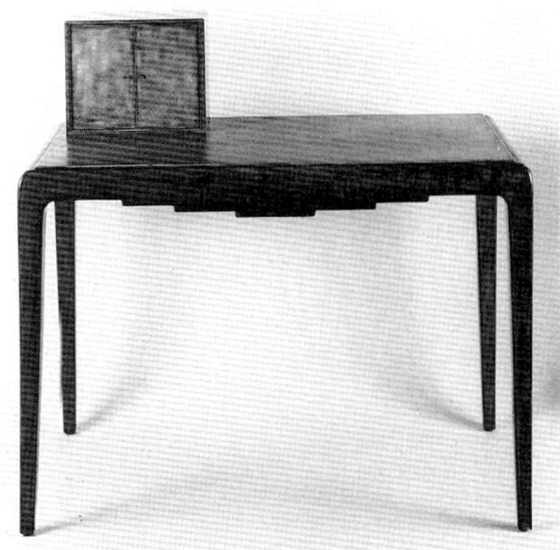

418

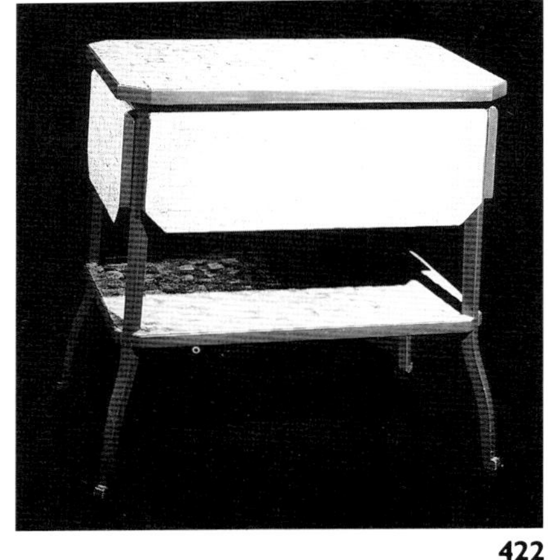

422

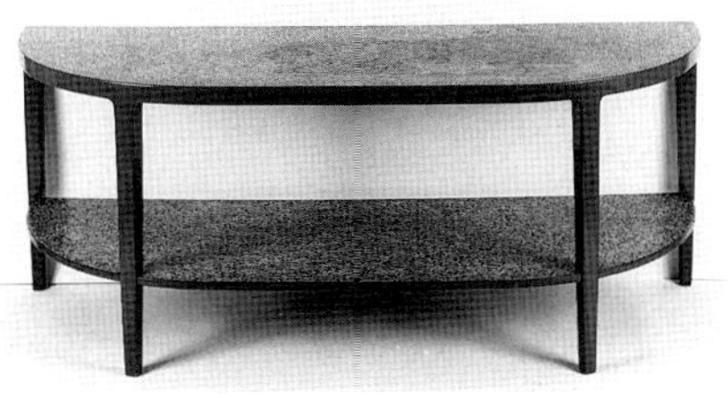

421

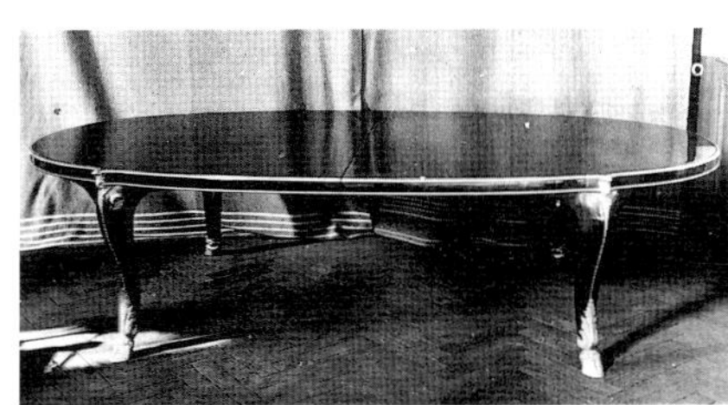

419

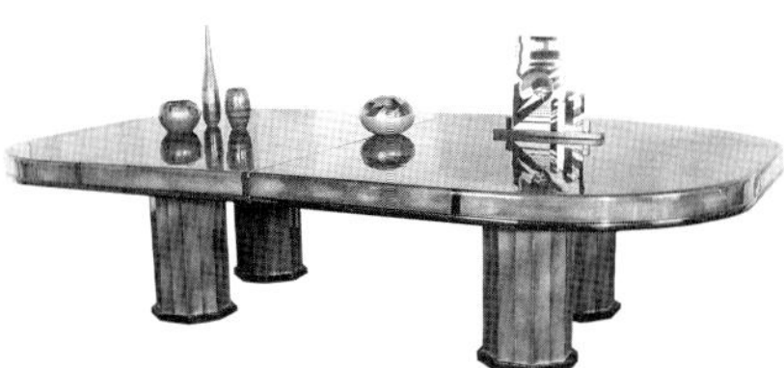

423

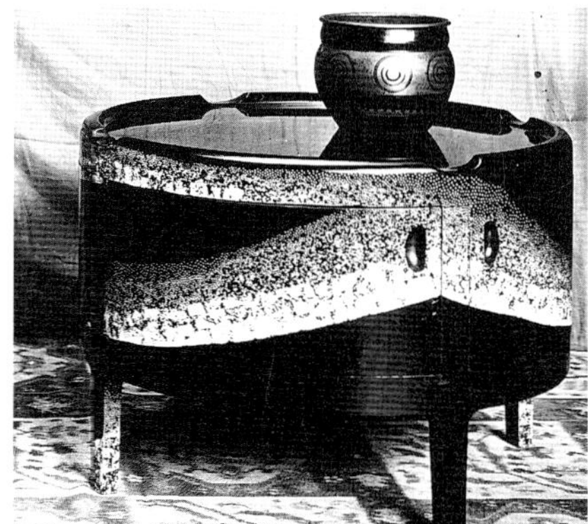

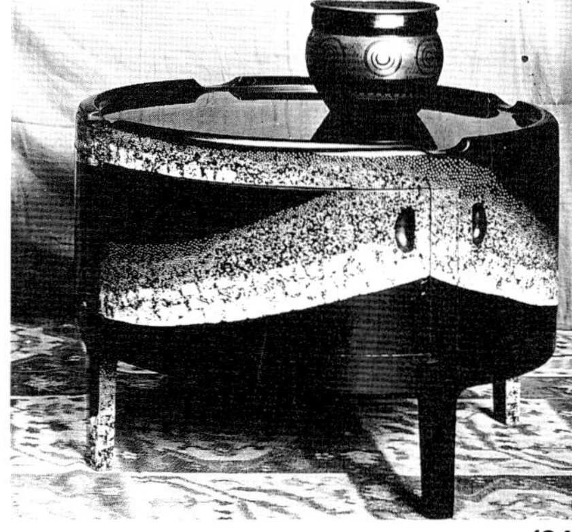

426

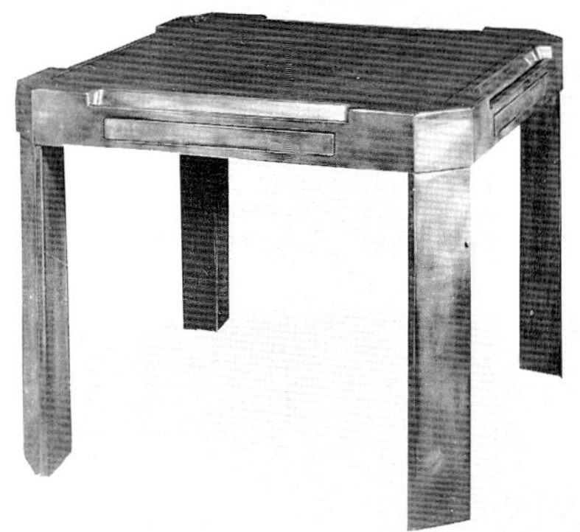

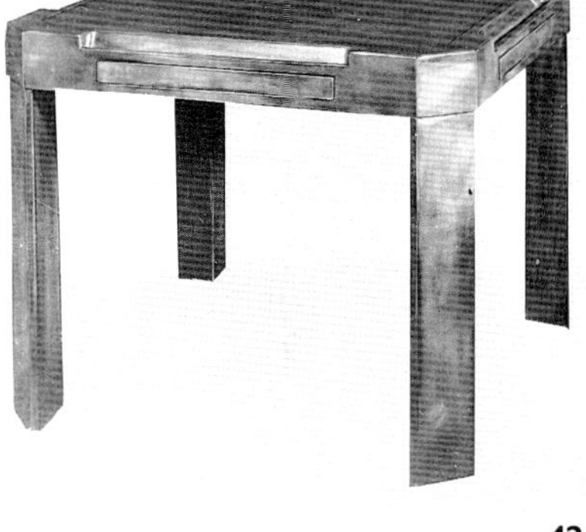

424

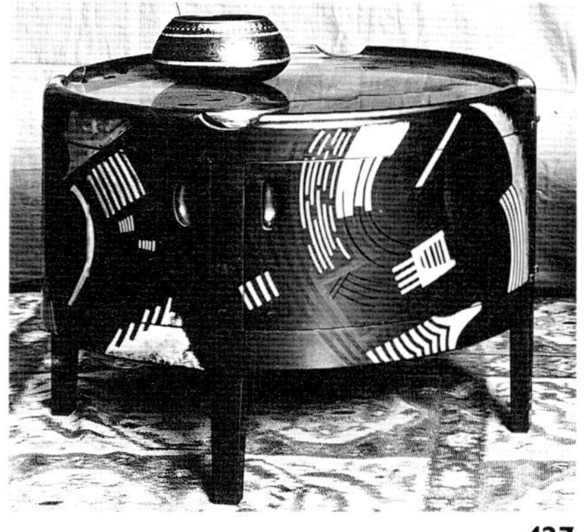

427

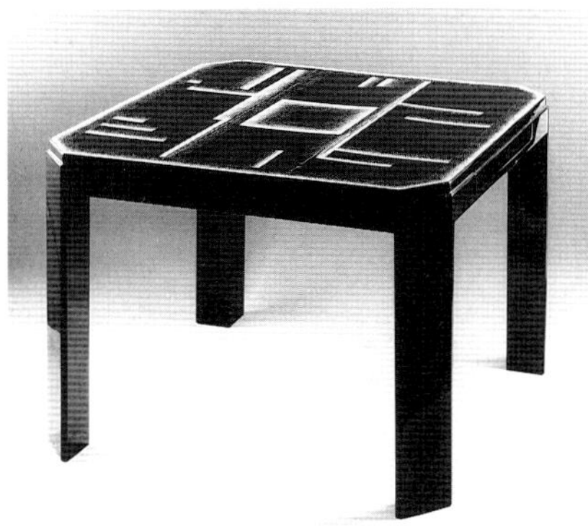

425

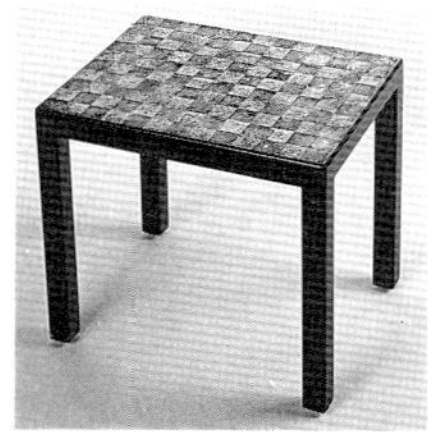

429

418 Lady's writing table with detachable section

Light-brown shellac.
Height 74.5 cm (29¼ in.); top 100 x 59 cm (39¼ x 23¼ in.).
C. 1935.
Private collection.

419 Dining table

Red lacquer, ornamented with gilded chased bronze.
Height 72 cm (28½ in.); top 145 x 270 cm (57 x 106 in.).
Specially designed for Johan Colcombet (see cat. no. 189), in 1930, the table can be extended by 56 cm (22 in.).

420 Round table top

Black lacquer and eggshell, horse motif in the Chinese style.
C. 1925.

421 Dining-room console

Red lacquer, double top decorated with eggshell mosaic.
Height 73 cm (28¾ in.); width 175 cm (68¾ in.); depth 60 cm (23½ in.).
C. 1935.
Private collection.

422 Drop-leaf table

Red shellac, top decorated in eggshell mosaic.
Height 69 cm (27¼ in.); top 70 x 48 cm (27½ x 19 in.).
1923.
Exh.: Galerie du Luxembourg, Paris, 1973, no. 121.
Sold: Christie's (New York), 1 October 1983, lot 219.
A variant of this table was exhibited at the Galerie Georges Petit, Paris, in 1923.

423 Extending dining table

Light-brown shellac edged in black.
Height 73 cm (28¾ in.); top 180 x 300 cm (70¾ x 118 in.).
Lacquered in Dunand's workshops *c.* 1930.
Formerly in the collection of Karl Lagerfeld; Tina and Michael Chow.
Sold: Godeau, Solanet, Audap (Paris), 21 November 1975, lot 114.

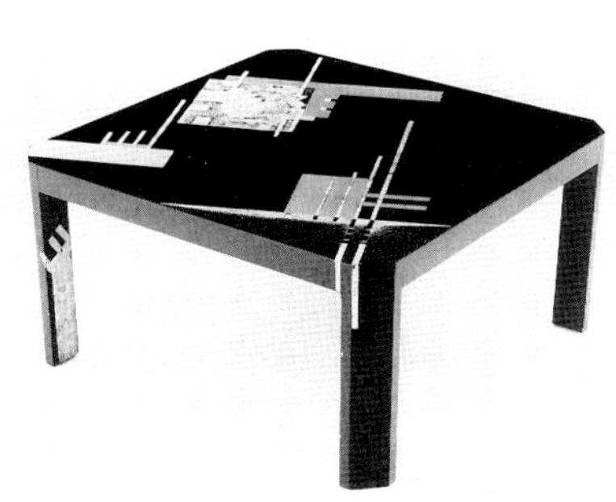
428

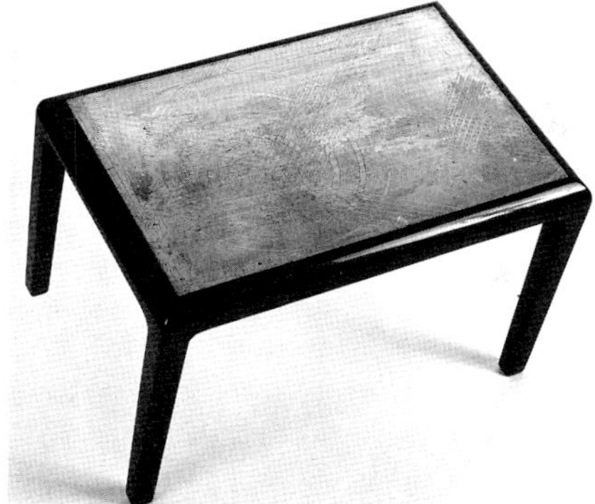
431

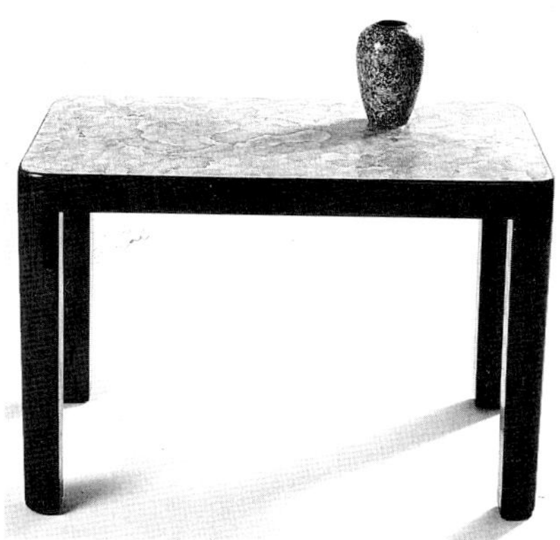
434

424 Mah-jong table
Light-brown shellac.
Height 71 cm (28 in.); top 89 cm (35 in.) square.
1929.
Formerly in the collection of Michel Périnet; L'Arc en Seine, Paris.
Sold: Sotheby's (Monaco), 11 October 1987, lot 300.

425 Games table
Black lacquer with eggshell decoration.
Height 74 cm (29¼ in.); top 90 cm (35½ in.) square.
1929.
Musée des Arts Décoratifs, Paris.

426 Drum table
Black lacquer decorated with eggshell mosaic.
1922.
Exh.: Galerie Georges Petit, Paris, 1922.
Bibl.: *Mobilier et décoration*, February 1926, repr. p. 46.

427 Drum table
Blue lacquer decorated with silver and black geometric motifs.
1922.
Exh.: Galerie Georges Petit, Paris, 1922.

428 Square occasional table
Black lacquer decorated with geometric motifs in eggshell mosaic, highlighted with silver.
Height 38.5 cm (15¼ in.); top 70 cm (27½ in.) square.
1923.
Exh.: Galerie Georges Petit, Paris, 1923, no. 6.
Bibl.: *Mobilier et décoration*, February 1926, p. 42.
Sold: Sotheby's (Monaco), 5 April 1987, lot 264.

429 Rectangular occasional table
Black lacquer, top decorated in eggshell arranged in checkered design.
Height 34 cm (13½ in.); top 40 x 31 cm (15¾ x 12¼ in.).
C. 1925.
Private collection.

430 Rectangular tables
Black lacquer, tops decorated in eggshell mosaic.
C. 1925.
Private collection.

431 Rectangular occasional table
Black lacquer, top covered in copper dinanderie plate decorated with geometric motifs in silvered metal.
Height 38 cm (15 in.); top 53 x 35 cm (20¾ x 13¾ in.).
C. 1925.
Private collection.

432 Rectangular occasional table
Red lacquer, top decorated with eggshell mosaic.
C. 1925.
Formerly in the collection of Félix Marcilhac, Paris; Private collection.

433 Occasional table
Light-brown shellac, voluted underframe edged in brass.
Height 45 cm (17¾ in.).
Formerly in the collection of Félix Marcilhac, Paris; Private collection.

434 Occasional table
Shellac, with rounded underframe.
C. 1923.
Private collection.

435 Rectangular occasional table
Black lacquer, top decorated with eggshell mosaic, underframe with cut-off corners.
Height 45 cm (17¾ in.); top 155 x 75 cm (61 x 29½ in.).
C. 1925.
Private collection.

436 Rectangular occasional table
Orange lacquer, top decorated with eggshell mosaic.
Height 51 cm (20 in.); top 80 x 52 cm (31½ x 20½ in.).
C. 1925.
Coll.: Virginia Museum of Fine Arts, Richmond, Va (gift of Sydney and Frances Lewis).

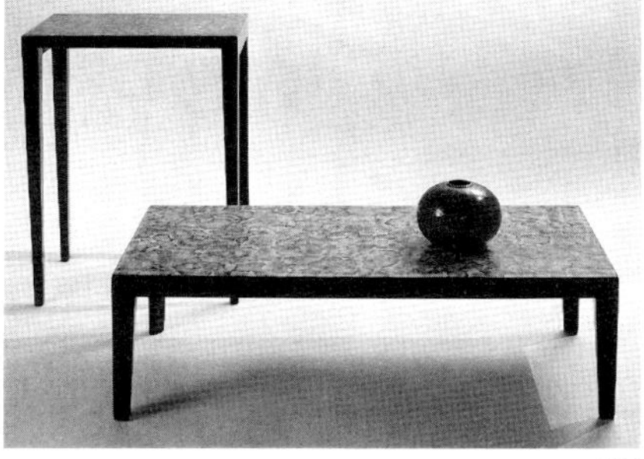
430

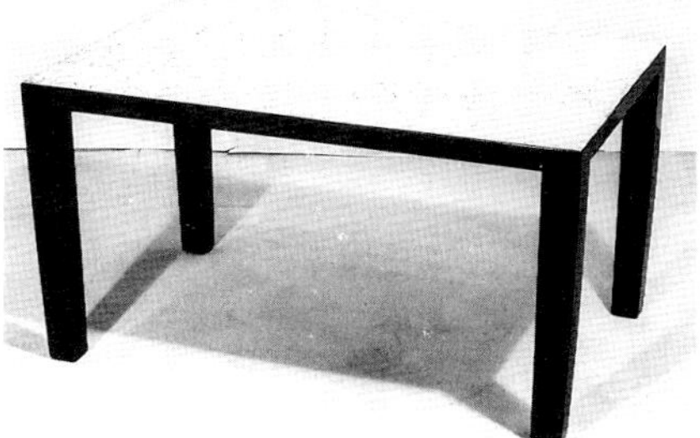
432

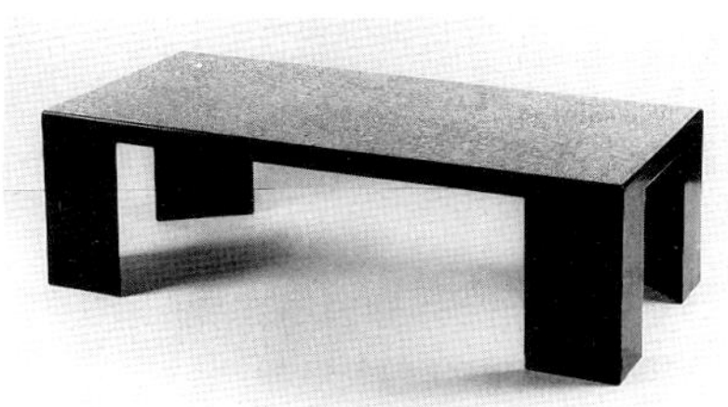
435

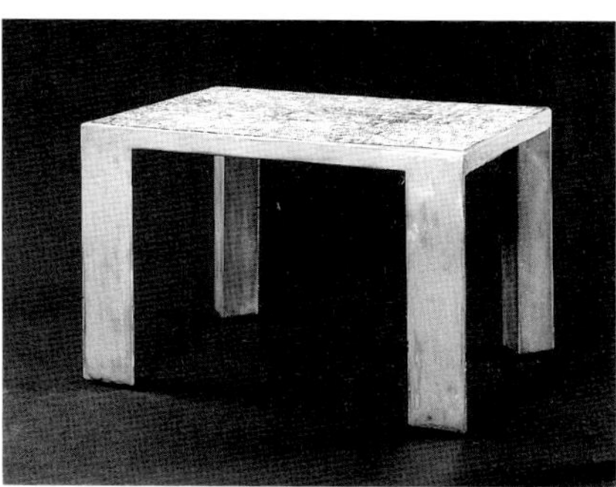
436

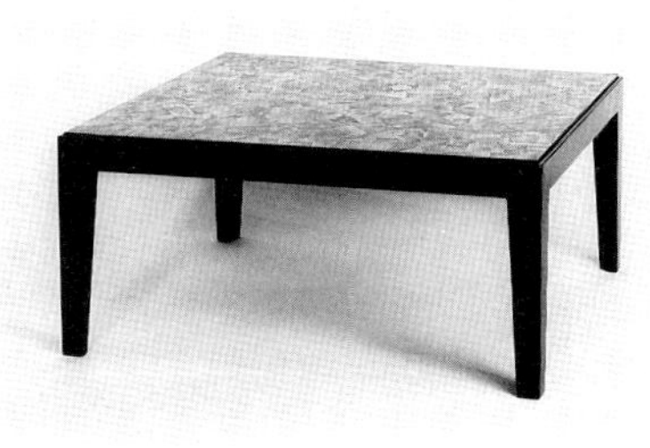

437

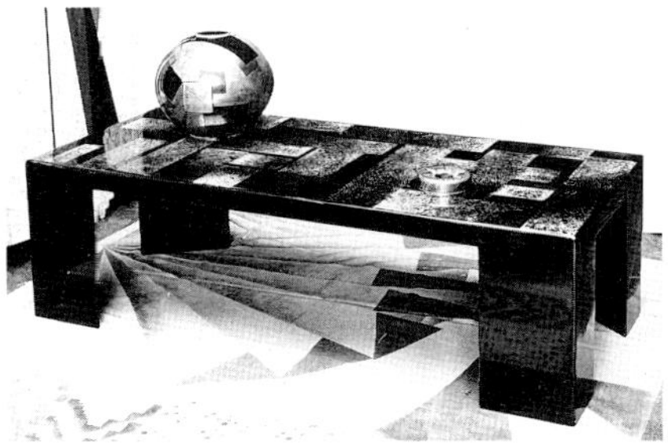

438

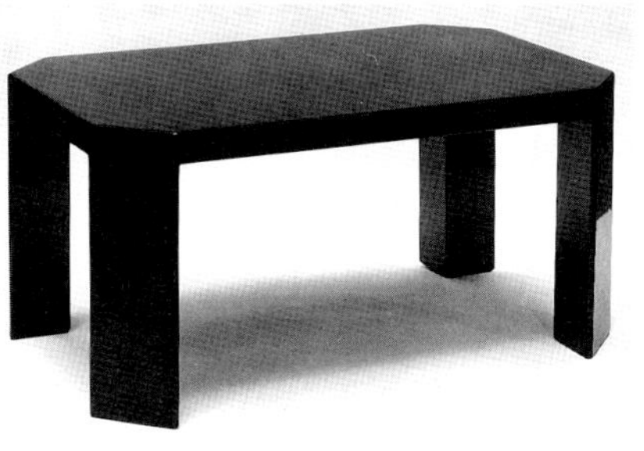

440

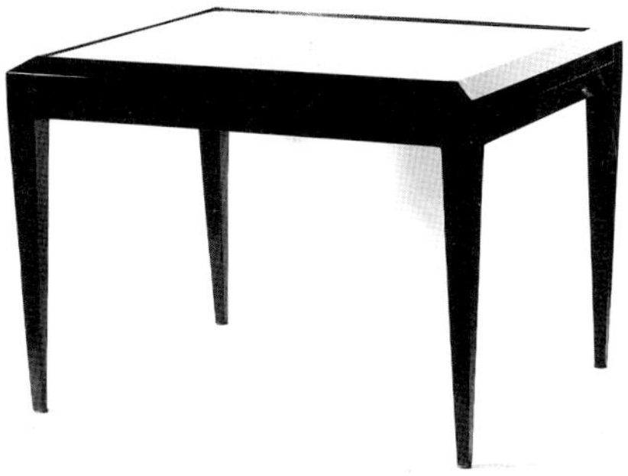

437 Rectangular occasional table
Black lacquer, top decorated with eggshell mosaic.
Height 35 cm (13¾ in.); top 45 x 60 cm (17¾ x 23½ in.).
C. 1925.
Formerly in the collection of Félix Marcilhac, Paris; Private collection.

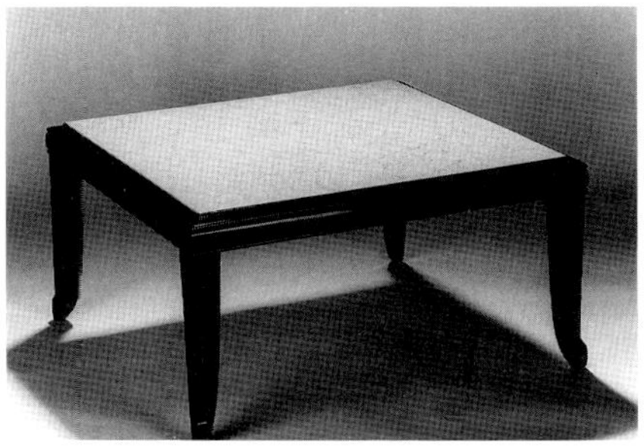

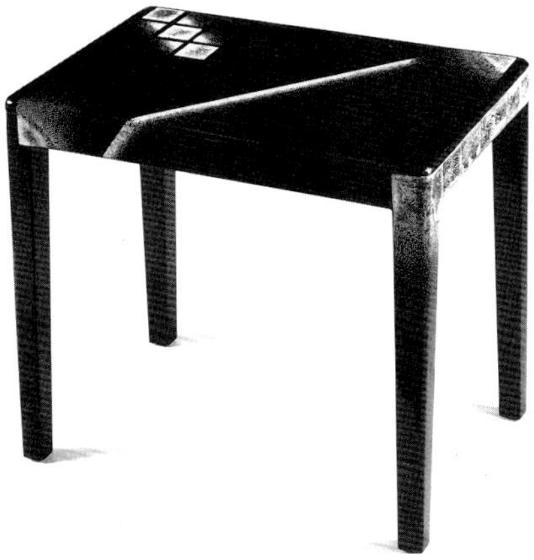

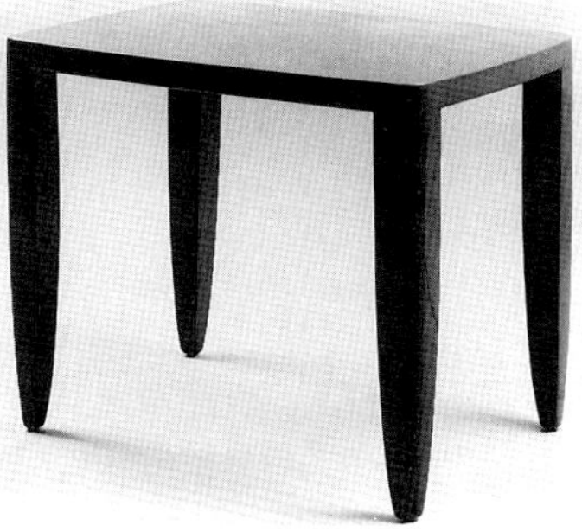

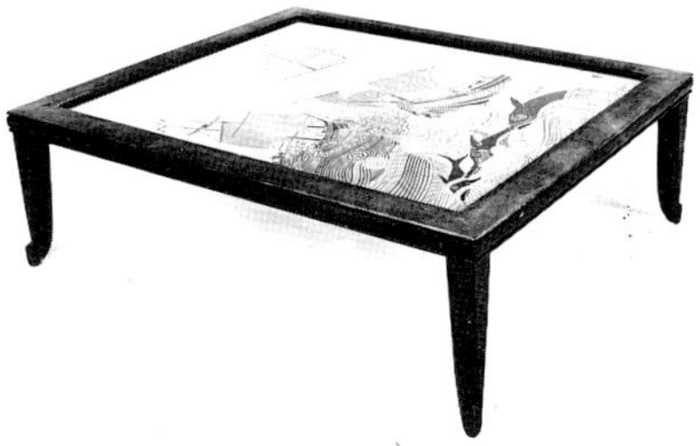

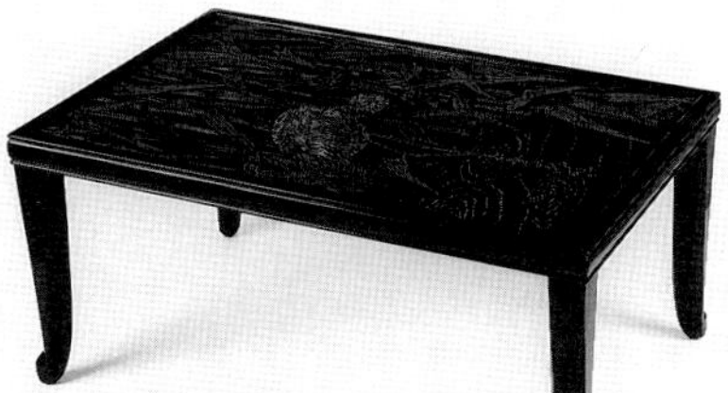

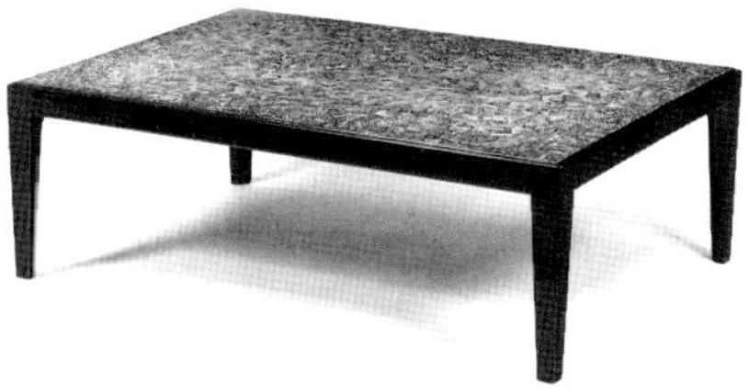

441

444

438 Rectangular occasional table
Black lacquer, top decorated with geometric motifs in eggshell mosaic.
1927.
Exh.: Galerie Georges Petit, Paris, 1927, no. 29.

442

445

439 Rectangular occasional table *Pl. 73*
Light-brown shellac, top incised with black and silver design depicting three pekinese.
C. 1928.
Private collection.

440 Rectangular occasional table
Underframe with cut-off corners.
C. 1928.
Private collection.

443

446

447

441 Rectangular occasional table
Black lacquer, with two sliding flaps. Lacquered in Dunand's workshops in 1929 to a design by Serge Rovinski for Nadine Oxnard.
Formerly in the collection of Félix Marcilhac, Paris.

442 Rectangular occasional table
Black lacquer with geometric design in eggshell.
Height 45 cm (17¾ in.); top 50 x 33 cm (19¾ x 13 in.).
C. 1930.
Coll.: André Bromberg.

443 Rectangular occasional table
Black lacquer, top of table in incised lacquer highlighted in colour with a heron motif.
Height 38 cm (15 in.); top 80 x 50 cm (31½ x 19¾ in.).
C. 1930.
Private collection.

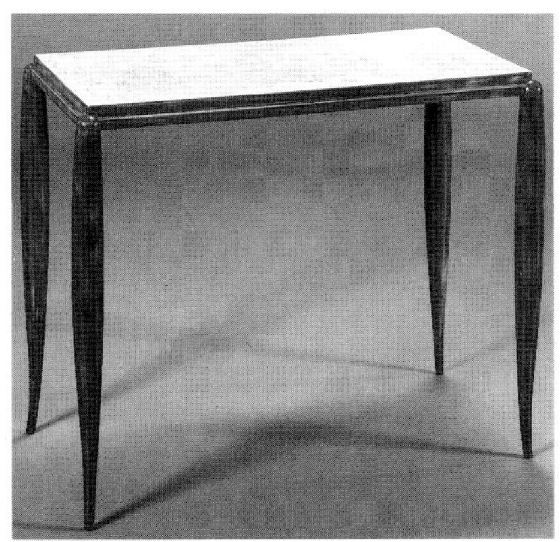
449

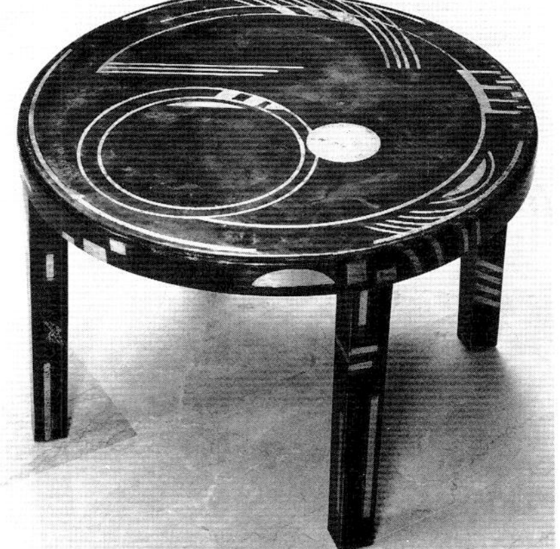
450

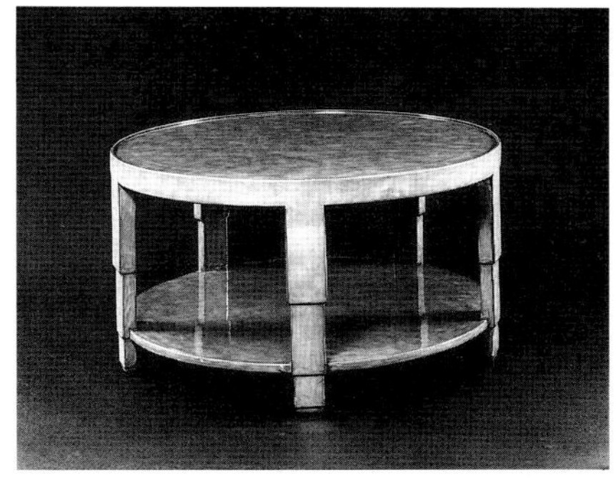
452

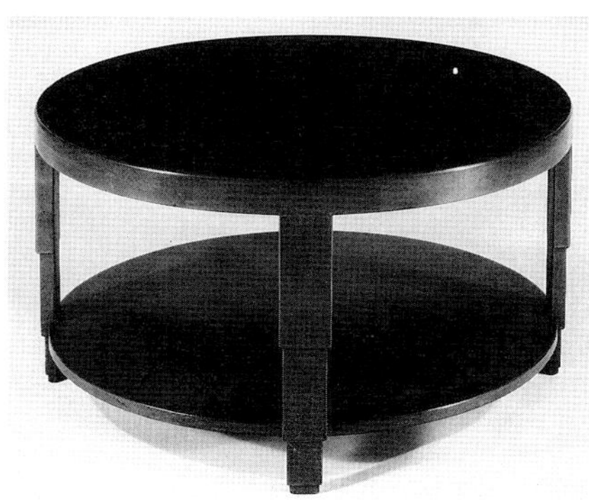
453

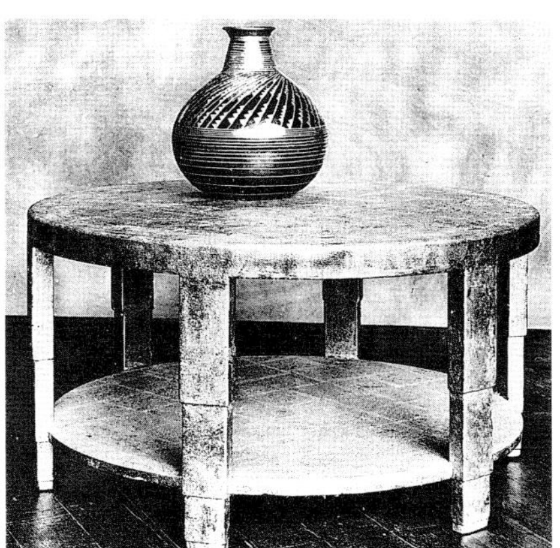
454

444 Rectangular occasional table
Black lacquer, top decorated with eggshell mosaic.
Height 35 cm (13¾ in.); top 40 x 60 cm (15¾ x 23½ in.).
C. 1930.
Formerly in the collection of Félix Marcilhac, Paris; Tina and Michael Chow.
Sold: Christie's (New York), 11 October 1983, lot 217.

445 Rectangular occasional table
Light-brown shellac.
Height 60 cm (23½ in.); top 50 x 75 cm (19¾ x 29½ in.).
C. 1930.
Coll.: M. and Mme Kupperfils, Evreux.

446 Rectangular occasional table
Black lacquer, top decorated with boats and dolphins, after Jean Dupas.
1935.
Private collection.

447 Rectangular occasional table
Black lacquer, top decorated with eggshell mosaic.
Height 71.5 cm (28 in.); top 111 x 61 cm (43¾ x 24 in.).
C. 1935.
Formerly in the collection of Bernard Dunand.
Sold: Boisgirard (Paris), 26 October 1988, lot 122.

448 High table
Black lacquer, top decorated with eggshell mosaic.
Height 70 cm (27½ in.); top 44 x 85 cm (17¼ x 33½ in.).
C. 1935.
Coll.: Mobilier National, Paris.

449 High table
Black shellac, top decorated with eggshell mosaic.
Height 70 cm (27½ in.); top 44 x 85 cm (17¼ x 33½ in.).
C. 1935.
Sold: Sotheby's (Monaco), 25 May 1980, lot 102; Christie's (New York), 17 December 1983, lot 348.

450 Round occasional table
Dinanderie, brass inlaid with geometric motifs in silvered metal.
Height 45 cm (17¾ in.); diameter 64 cm (25¼ in.).
Specially designed for Templeton Croker in 1929.
Formerly in the collection of Sandra Brandt.
Sold: Sotheby's (Monaco), 13 April 1986, lot 313.
See also cat. nos. 469 and 1163–1165.

451 Round occasional table *Pl. 61*
Red lacquer, brass fittings.
Height 73 cm (28¾ in.); diameter 75 cm (29½ in.).
Lacquered in Dunand's workshops *c.* 1930 to a design by Eugène Printz.
Coll.: George Encil.

452 Two-tiered round occasional table
Light-brown shellac.
Height 48.5 cm (19 in.); diameter 80 cm (31½ in.).
C. 1925.
Coll.: Virginia Museum of Fine Arts, Richmond, Va (gift of Sydney and Frances Lewis).

453 Two-tiered round occasional table
Clouded red lacquer.
Height 45 cm (17¾ in.); diameter 80 cm (31½ in.).
C. 1925.
Formerly in the collection of Félix Marcilhac, Paris; Hervé Aaron, New York.
Sold: Blache (Versailles), 20 March 1977, lot 194; Sotheby's (Monaco), 24 September 1978, lot 235.

454 Two-tiered round occasional table
Gold *laque arrachée*.
Height 45 cm (17¾ in.); diameter 80 cm (31½ in.).
C. 1925.

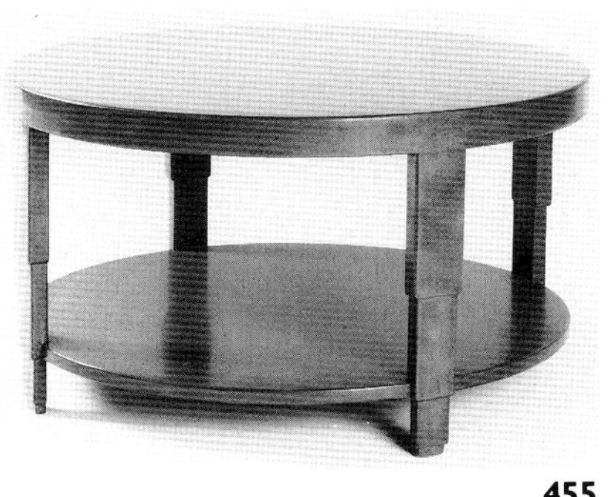
455

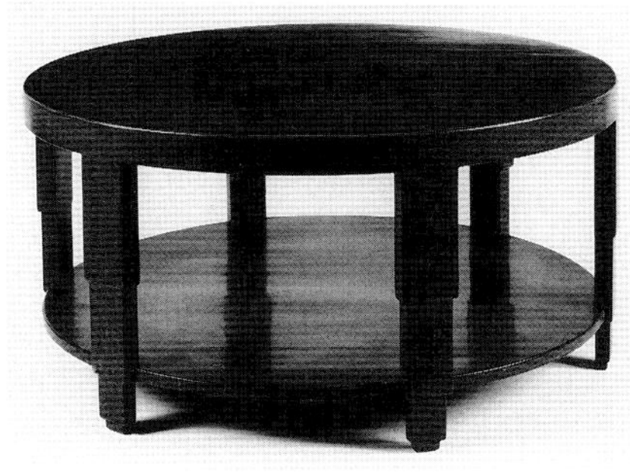
457

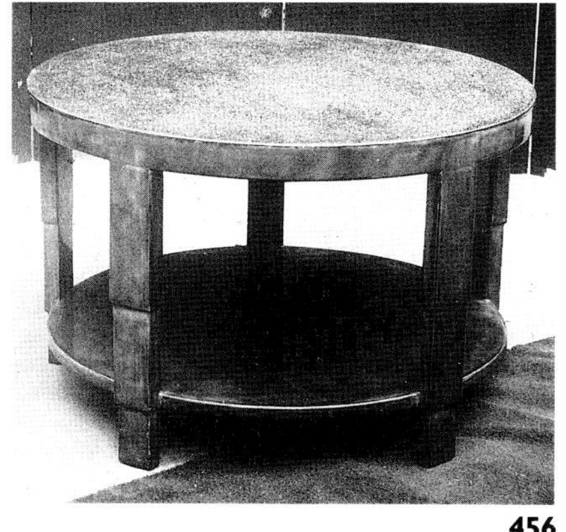
456

455 Two-tiered round occasional table

Red lacquer on black ground.
Height 45 cm (17¾ in.); diameter 80 cm (31½ in.).
C. 1925.
Coll.: Félix Marcilhac, Paris.

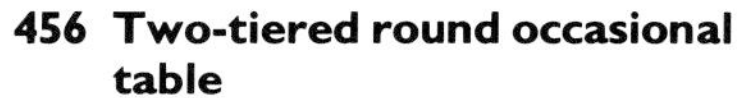
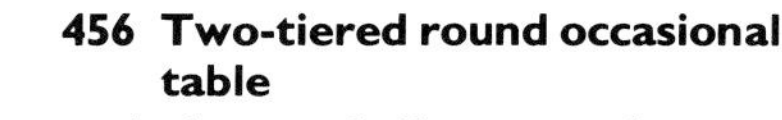

456 Two-tiered round occasional table

Light-brown shellac, top in *laque arrachée*.
Height 45 cm (17¾ in.); diameter 80 cm (31½ in.).
C. 1925.

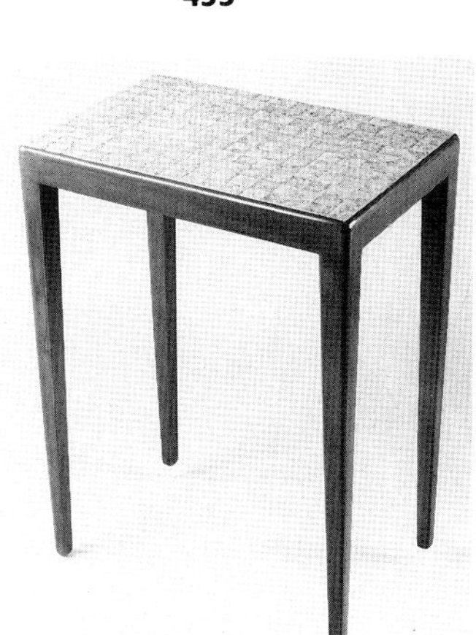
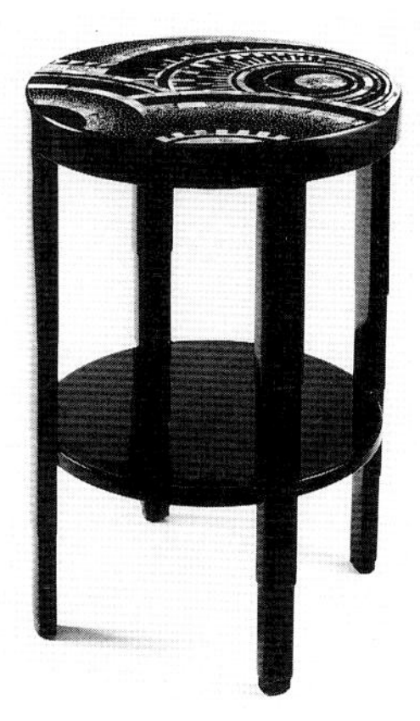

461 460

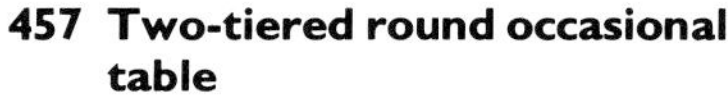

457 Two-tiered round occasional table

Dark-red lacquer.
Height 45 cm (17¾ in.); diameter 90 cm (35½ in.).
C. 1925.
Private collection.

458 Two-tiered round occasional table *Pl. 59*

Light-brown shellac, top decorated in eggshell mosaic.
Height 45 cm (17¾ in.); diameter 65 cm (25½ in.).
C. 1925.
Private collection.

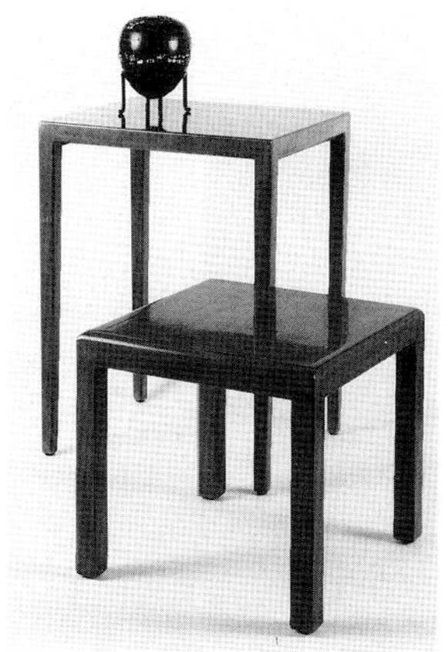
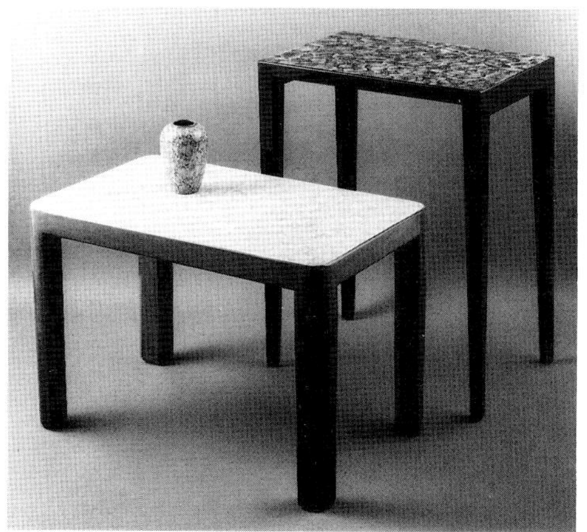

463 462

459 Two-tiered round occasional table *Pl. 58*

Gold lacquer on spruce.
Height 50 cm (19¾ in.); diameter 80 cm (31½ in.).
C. 1930.
Sold: Sotheby's (Monaco), 5 December 1976, lot 197; Christie's (New York), 10 October 1983, lot 216.

460 Two-tiered round occasional table

Black lacquer with radiating design in eggshell.
Height 58 cm (22¾ in.); diameter 40 cm (15¾ in.).
C. 1930.
Coll.: André Bromberg.

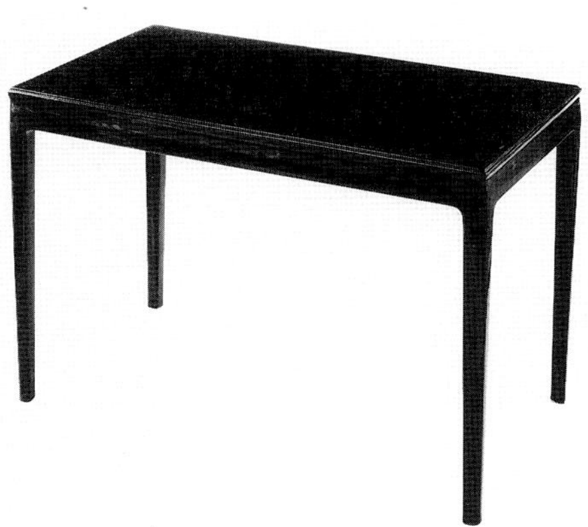
464

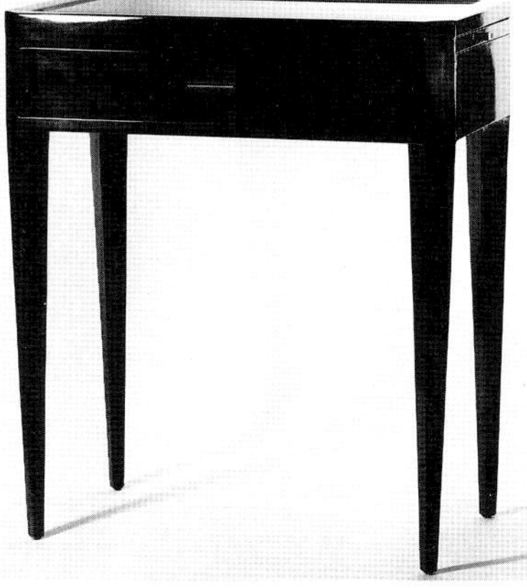
466

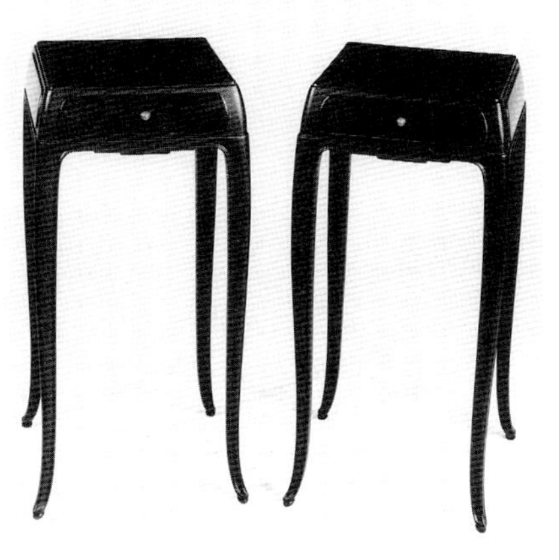

467

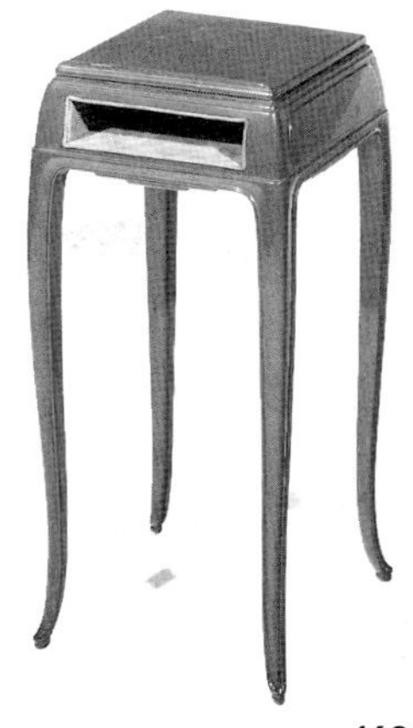

468

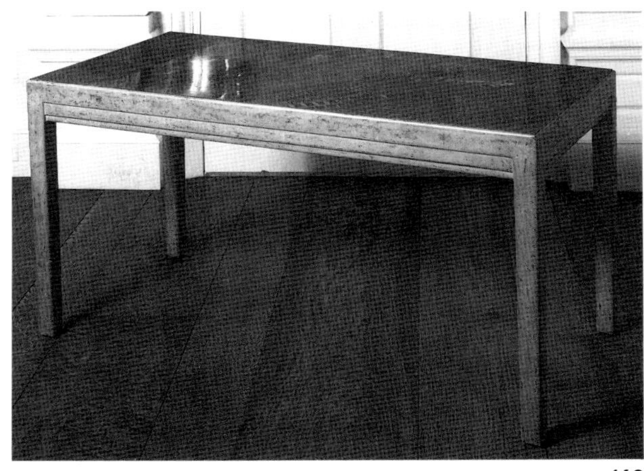

469

461 High telephone table
Red lacquer, top decorated in checkered eggshell design.
Height 70 cm (27½ in.); top 35 x 50 cm (13¾ x 19¾ in.).
C. 1924.
Coll.: Alain Lesieutre, Paris.

462 Tea table and high telephone table
Shellac and black lacquer, table tops decorated in eggshell mosaic.
Tea table: height 45 cm (17¾ in.); top 60 x 30 cm (23½ x 11¾ in.).
Telephone table: height 70 cm (27½ in.); top 35 x 50 cm (13¾ x 19¾ in.).
C. 1925.
Private collection.

463 Square occasional table and high telephone table
Shellac, dinanderie perfume-burner with perforated motifs.
Occasional table: height 45 cm (17¾ in.); top 45 x 45 cm (17¾ x 17¾ in.).
Telephone table: height 70 cm (27½ in.); top 40 x 50 cm (15¾ x 19¾ in.).
C. 1925.

464 Desk table
Rubbed black lacquer on a brown shellac ground.
Height 74.5 cm (29¼ in.); top 100 x 59 cm (39¼ x 23¼ in.).
C. 1928.
Private collection.

465 Telephone table *Pl. 67*
Black lacquer decorated with geometric motifs in red lacquer, top decorated in checkered eggshell design.
Height 70 cm (27½ in.); top 60 x 35 cm (23½ x 13¾ in.).
C. 1925.
Coll.: Virginia Museum of Fine Arts, Richmond, Va (gift of Sydney and Frances Lewis).

466 Dressing table
Black lacquer, grips and handle in red lacquer, folding side flaps, drawer.
Height of table approx. 75 cm (29½ in.); top approx. 50 x 30 cm (19¾ x 11¾ in.).
Lacquered in Dunand's workshops in 1929 to a design by Serge Rovinski for Nadine Oxnard.
Formerly in the collection of Félix Marcilhac, Paris; Private collection.

467 Pair of bedside tables
Black lacquer, grips in red lacquer.
Height 80 cm (31½ in.).
1921.
Exh.: Galerie Georges Petit, Paris, 1921, no. 19.
Coll.: Galerie Vallois, Paris.
Sold: Champin, Lombrail, Gautier (Enghien), 17 April 1983, lot 4.

468 Bedside table
Red lacquer, lined inside with suède, drop-leaf top.
Height 80 cm (31½ in.).
1921.
Exh.: Galerie Georges Petit, Paris, 1921, no. 18.

469 Dessert table
Brushed silver lacquer on black ground, dinanderie top, brass with geometric motifs in silvered metal.
Made for Templeton Croker in 1929.
See also cat. nos. 450 and 1163–1165.

470 Table and tea service
Dinanderie, brass with geometric design in silvered metal, underframe in wrought iron.
Height 55 cm (21¾ in.).
1923.
Coll.: Galerie Vallois, Paris.

471 Low table with cut-off corners
Dark-blue lacquer with decoration in eggshell.
Height 18 cm (7 in.); top 70 x 34 cm (27½ x 13¼ in.).
Exh.: Galerie Georges Petit, Paris, 1924, no. 11.
Formerly in the collection of Baron La Caze.
Sold: Sotheby's (Monaco), 13 April 1986, lot 309.

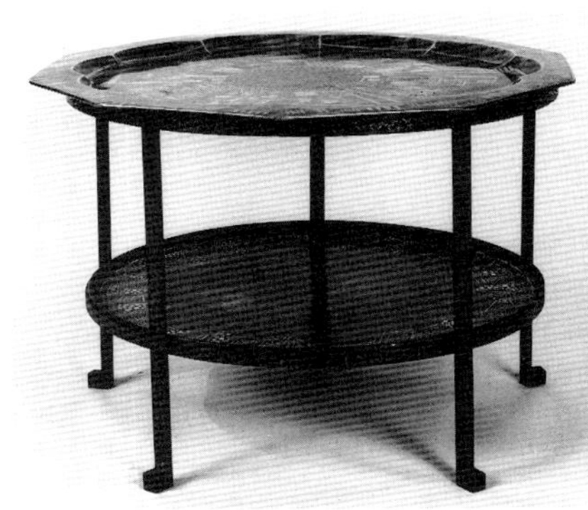

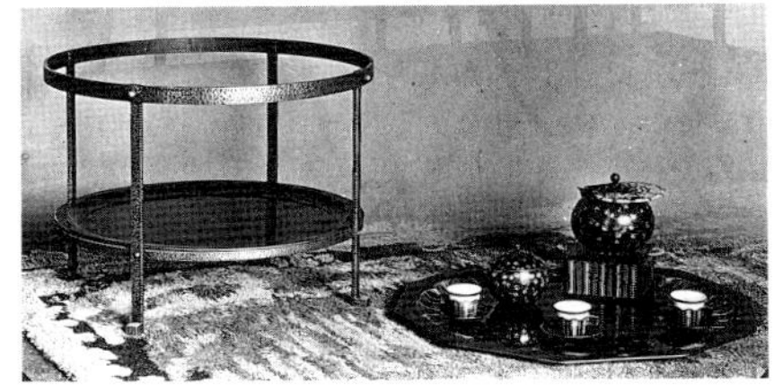

470

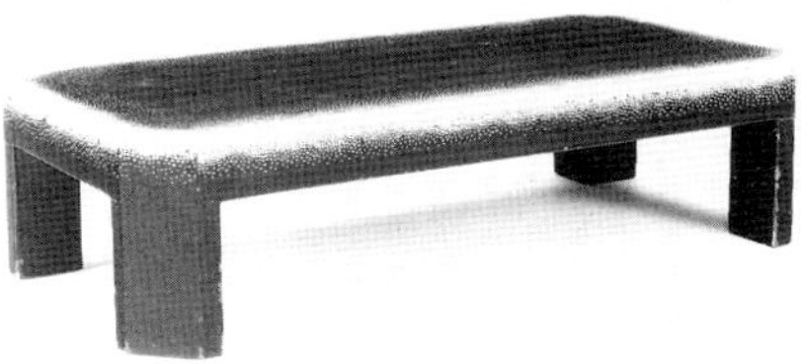

471

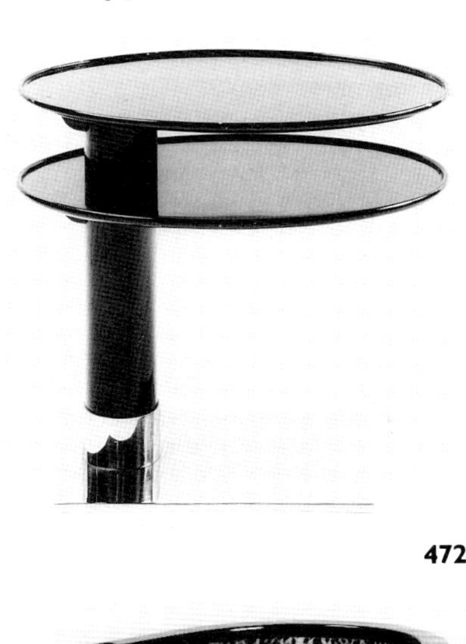

472

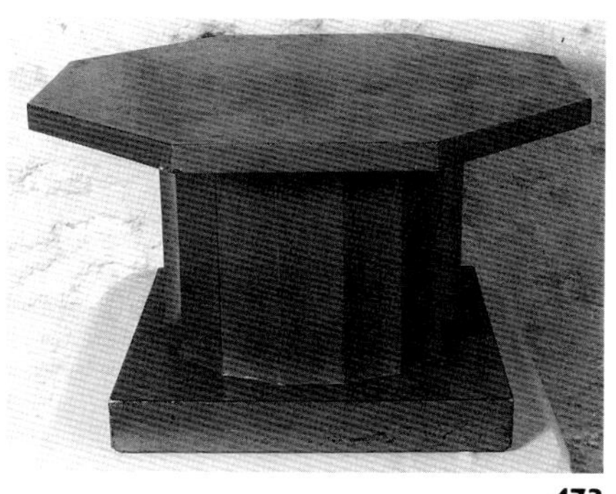

473

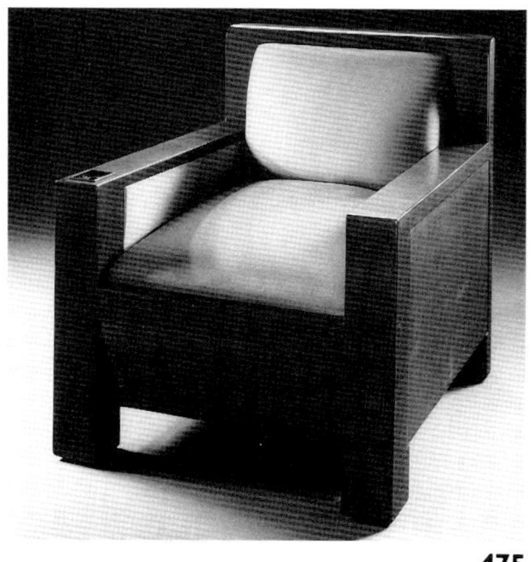

475

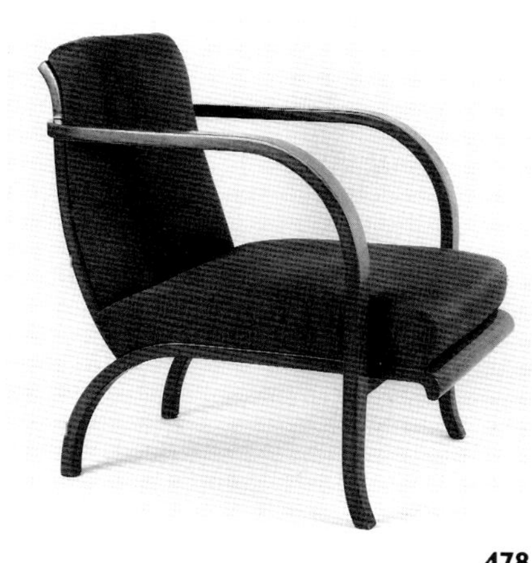

478

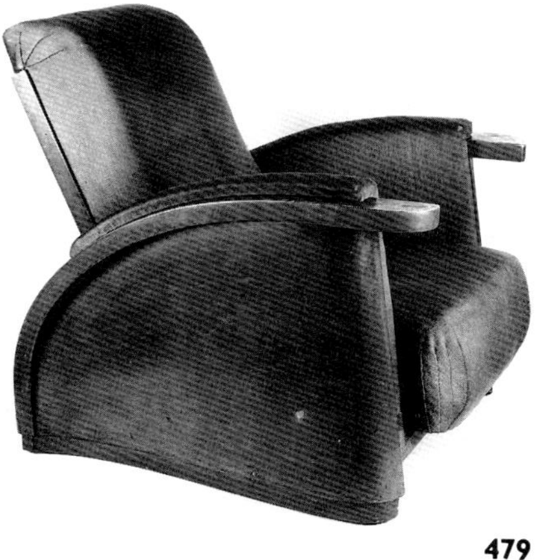

479

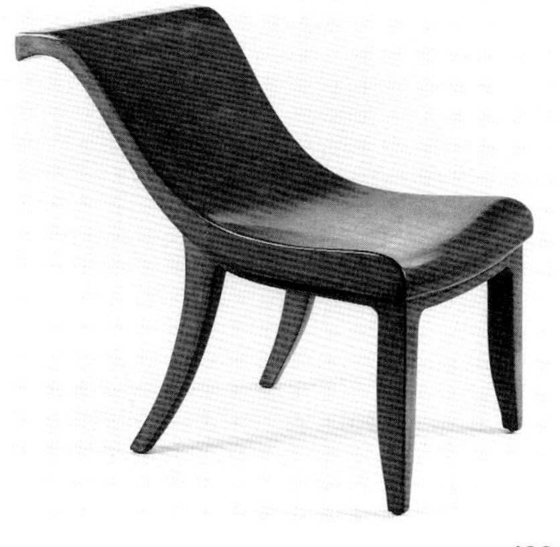

482

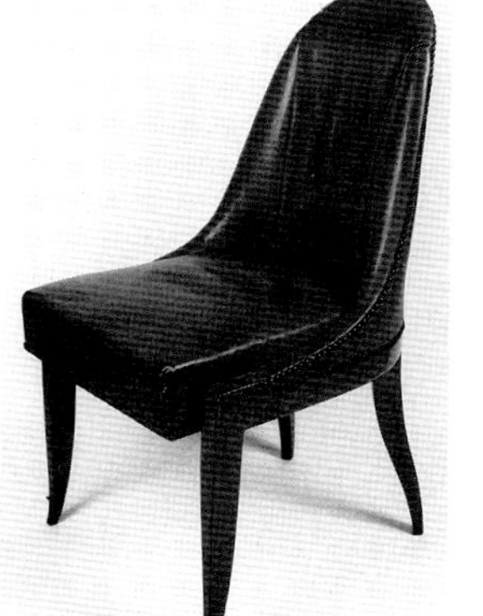

474

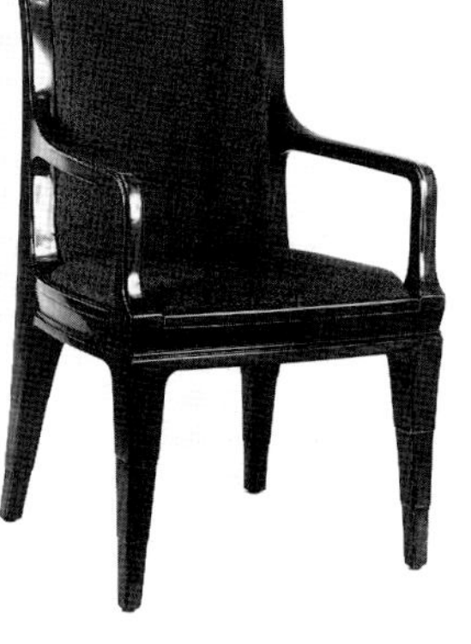

477

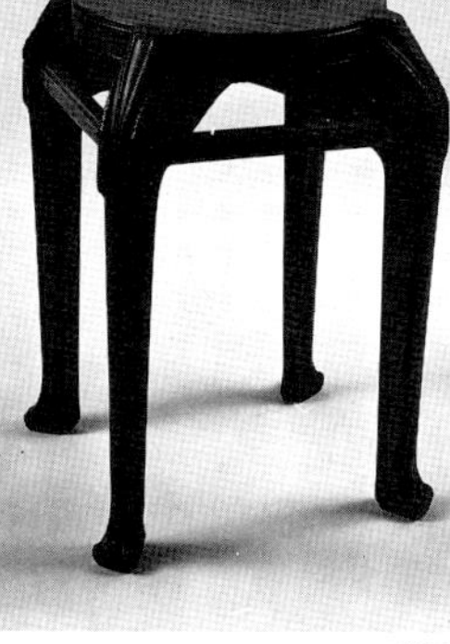

483

476

472 Smoker's table
Black lacquer, underframe in chromium-plated metal.
Height 60 cm (23¾ in.).
Designed by Emile-Jacques Ruhlmann and lacquered in Dunand's workshops C. 1925.
Formerly in the collection of Félix Marcilhac, Paris; M. and Mme Bertrand Maus.

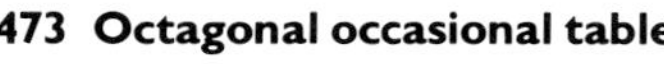

473 Octagonal occasional table
Red lacquer.
Height 55 cm (21¾ in.).
Designed by Emile-Jacques Ruhlmann for Ducharne and lacquered in Dunand's workshops in 1925.
Coll.: Jacques De Vos.
Sold: Gérard de Dianous, Manosque (Basses Alpes), 9 February 1986.

FURNITURE: SEATING

474 Chair
Red lacquer.
Height 95 cm (37½ in.).
Lacquered in Dunand's workshops in 1925 to a design by Émile-Jacques Ruhlmann.
Coll.: Galerie Denise Orsini, Paris.

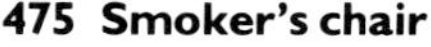

475 Smoker's chair
Red lacquer.
Height 81 cm (31¾ in.); width 71 cm (28 in.).
Specially designed for the Embassy Smoking Room at the 1925 Exposition Internationale des Arts Décoratifs in Paris.
Coll.: Virginia Museum of Fine Arts, Richmond, Va (gift of Sydney and Frances Lewis).
See also cat. nos. 1189–1195.

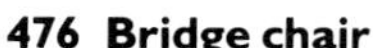

476 Bridge chair
Black lacquer.
Height 65 cm (25½ in.).
1924.
Coll.: M. and Mme Kupperfils, Evreux.

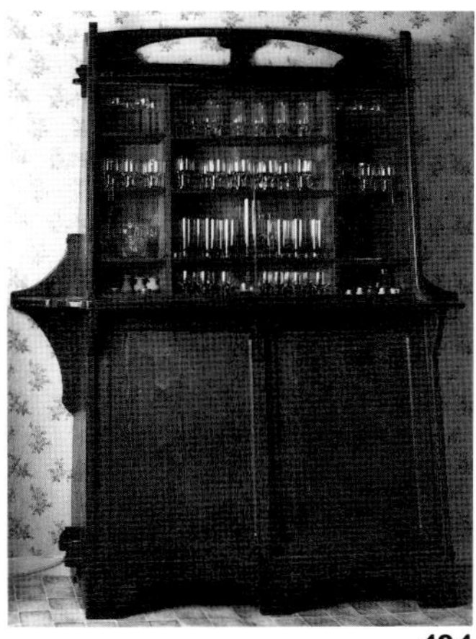
484

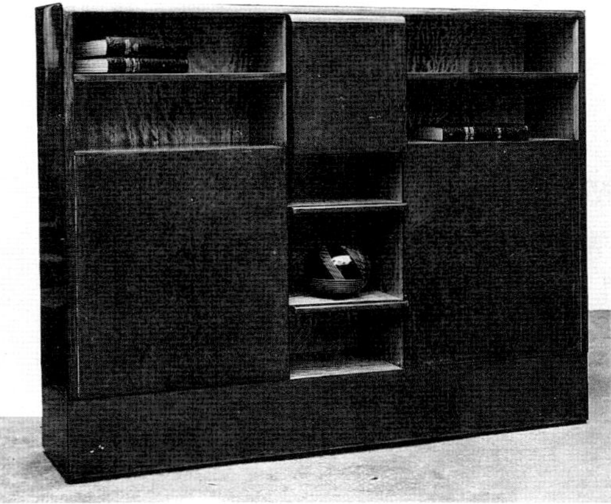
485

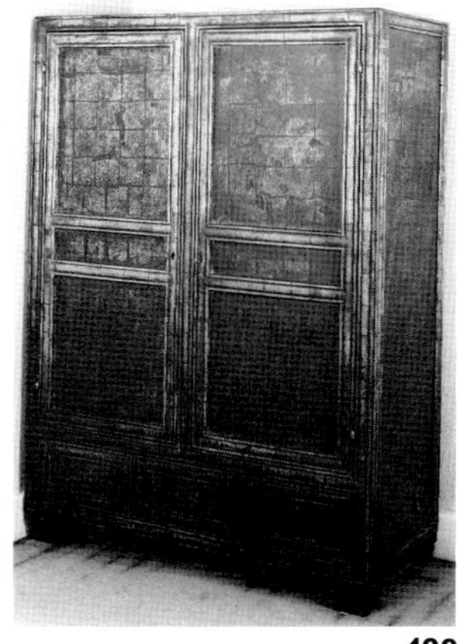
488

477 Dining-room armchair
Shellac.
Height 96 cm (37¾ in.).
Prototype designed in 1928 for the Polignac dining room.
Formerly in the collection of Félix Marcilhac, Paris; Tina and Michael Chow.
See also cat. no. 417.

478 Boudoir armchair
Brown shellac.
Specially designed for the Boudoir exhibited in 1930 at the Salon des Artistes Décorateurs, Paris.
Private collection.
See also cat. nos. 479, 1202–1210.

479 Boudoir armchair
Red shellac.
Specially designed for the Boudoir exhibited in 1930 at the Salon des Artistes Décorateurs, Paris.
Private collection.
See also cat. nos. 478, 1202–1210.

480 Coiffeuse
Black lacquer.
Specially made for Nadine Oxnard to a design by Serge Rovinski and lacquered in Dunand's workshops in 1929.
Coll.: Félix Marcilhac, Paris.

481 Sofa
Black lacquer.
Specially made for Nadine Oxnard to a design by Serge Rovinski and lacquered in Dunand's workshops in 1929.
Formerly in the collection of Félix Marcilhac, Paris; Private collection.

482 Curule chair
Shellac on moulded plastic.
Height 74 cm (29¼ in.); width 45 cm (17¾ in.); depth 75 cm (29½ in.).
1932.
Private collection.

483 Stool
Walnut with carved decoration.
Height 50 cm (19¾ in.).
C. 1910.
Private collection.

MISCELLANEOUS FURNITURE

484 Dresser in pitch pine
Height 235 cm (92¼ in.); width 184 cm (72¼ in.).
C. 1910.
Coll.: M. et Mme J.-P. Ley.

485 Shelf unit
Light-brown lacquer.
1926.
Private collection.

486 Free-standing units (pair) *Pl. 53*
Marble, with fixed decorative glass panels painted on the reverse (*verre églomisé*) with fish motifs in red, brown, gold and black lacquer backed by silver-leaf.
Height 120 cm (47¼ in.); width 58 cm (22¾ in.); depth 30 cm (11¾ in.).
C. 1925.
Exh.: Delorenzo Gallery, New York, 1985 (repr. in catalogue, p. 55).
Formerly in the collection of the Galerie Vallois, Paris; Private collection, New York.

487 Sample cabinet
Light-brown shellac.
Height 160 cm (63 in.).
C. 1925.
Internal shelves arranged in such a way as to display samples of every kind of lacquerwork executed in Dunand's workshops.
Formerly in the collection of Félix Marcilhac, Paris; Private collection.

488 Wardrobe
Silver *laque arrachée* on a red ground.
Height 185 cm (72¾ in.).
1927.
Exh.: Galerie Georges Petit, Paris, 1927, no. 33.
Private collection, Paris.

489 Collector's cabinet
Light-brown shellac.
Height 160 cm (63 in.).
C. 1925.
Private collection, Paris.

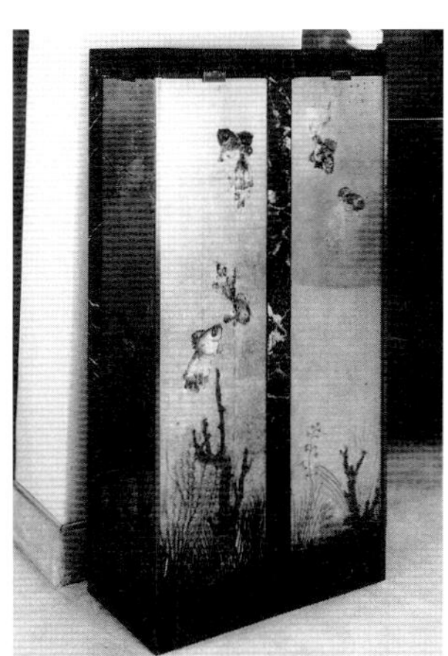

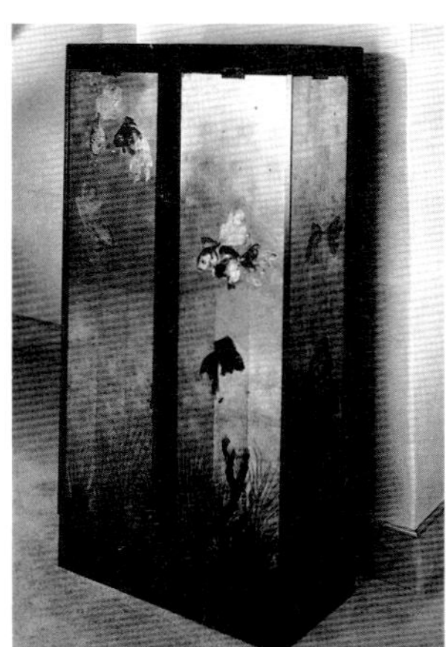
486

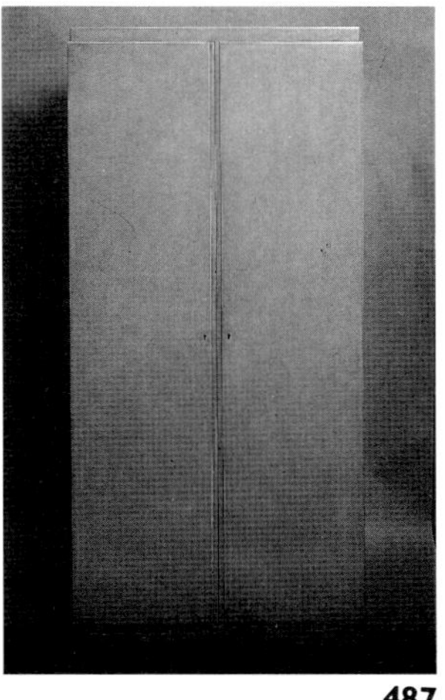
487

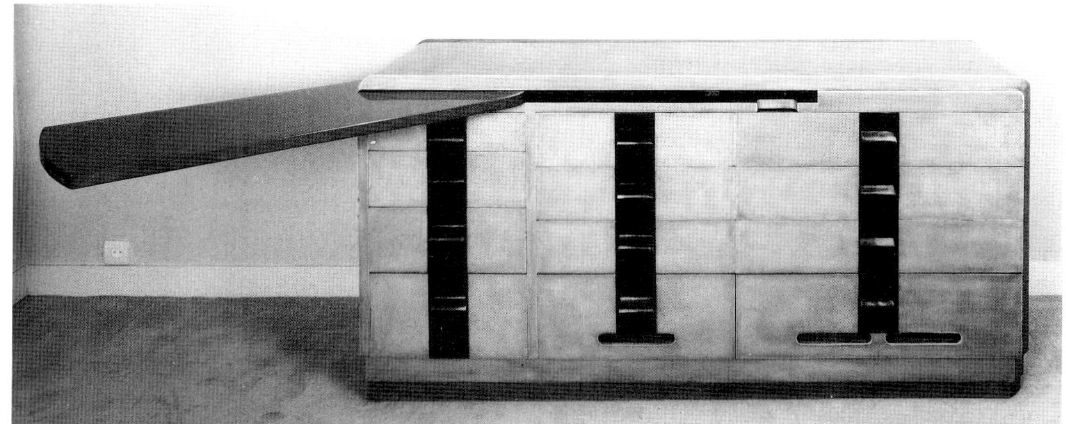

490

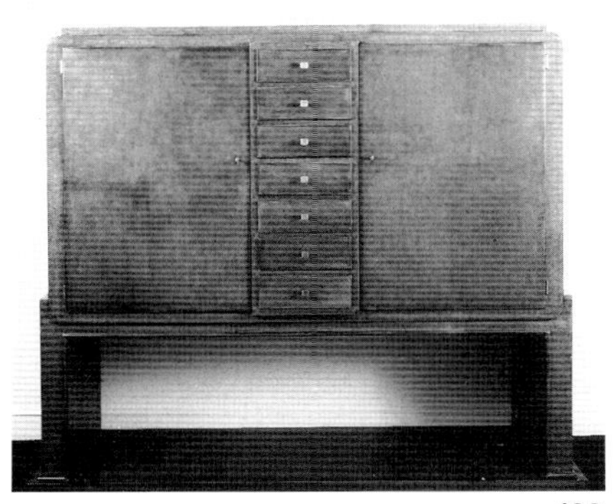

492

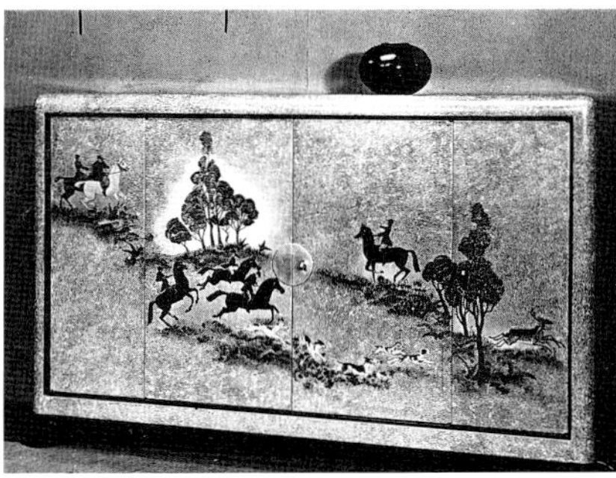

494

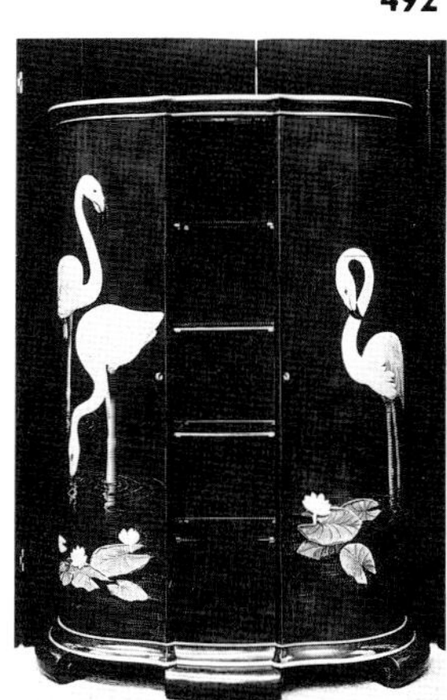

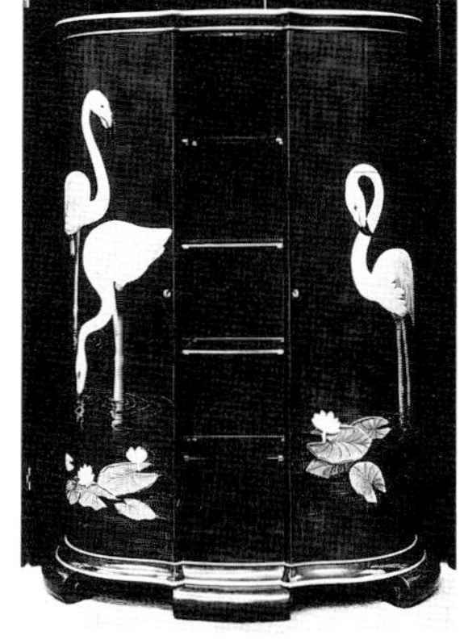

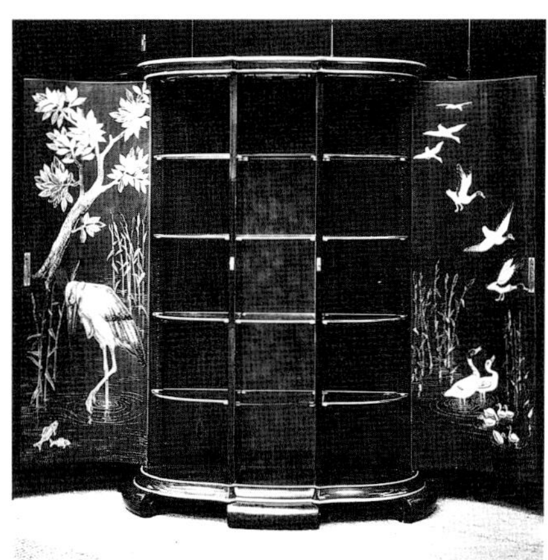

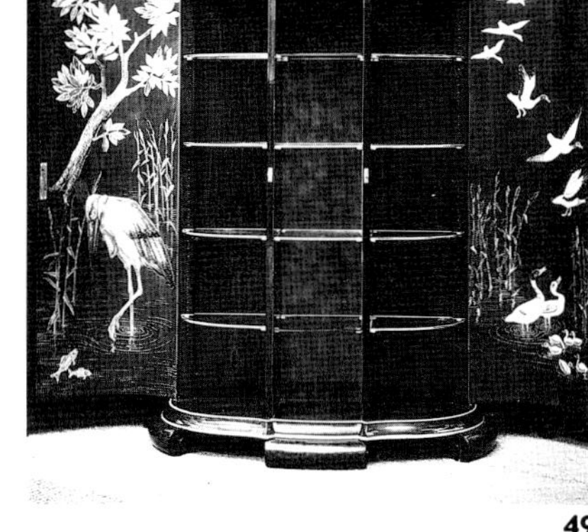

497

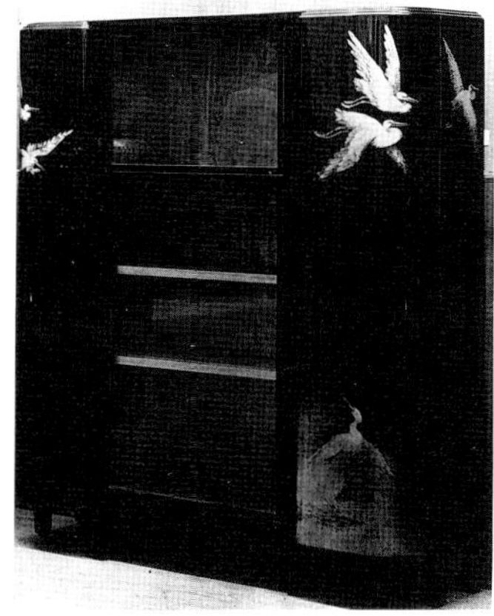

498

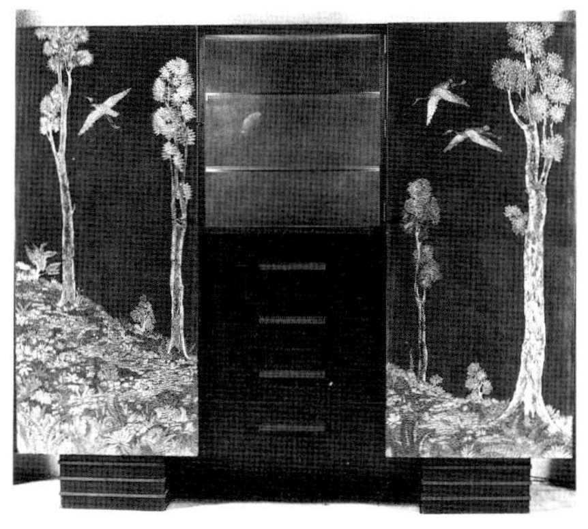

499

490 Chest of drawers with pull-out work surface

Light-brown shellac and black lacquer.
Height 75 cm (29½ in.); width 160 cm (63 in.).
C. 1928.
Private collection, Paris.
Made for Jean Dunand's personal use, this specially designed piece enabled him to continue working when confined to bed.

491 Wardrobe

Red lacquer and shellac.
Height 200 cm (78¾ in.).
C. 1930.
Formerly in the collections of Jacques Denoël and Jean-Marie Rivière; Alain Lesieutre, Paris.
Sold: Christie's (New York), 24 May 1984, lot 137.

492 Collector's cabinet

Shellac.
Height 120 cm (47¼ in.).
C. 1937.
Coll.: M. and Mme Kupperfils, Evreux.

493 Collector's cabinet *Pl. 62*

Red and black lacquer, deer and undergrowth in gold, escutcheon plate with geometric design in black lacquer.
Height 110 cm (43¼ in.); width 200 cm (78¾ in.).
1937.
Coll.: Félix Marcilhac, Paris.

494 Collector's cabinet

Eggshell and coloured lacquer decorated with hunting scenes.
Height 110 cm (43¼ in.); width 200 cm (78¾ in.).
1937.
Private collection, Paris.

495 Display cabinet

Red lacquer.
Height 250 cm (98½ cm); width 185 cm (72¾ in.).
C. 1937.
Private collection.

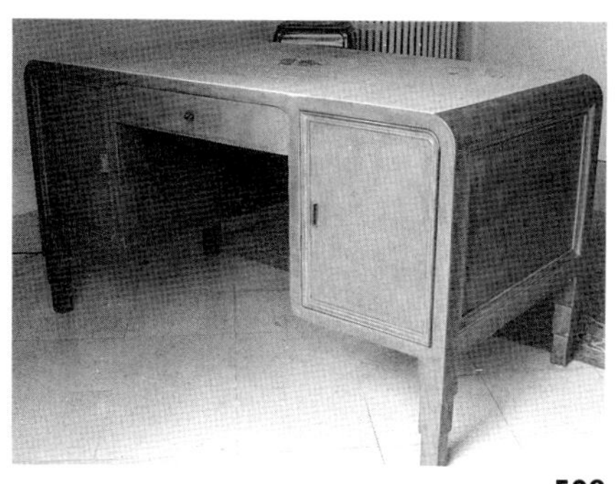
508

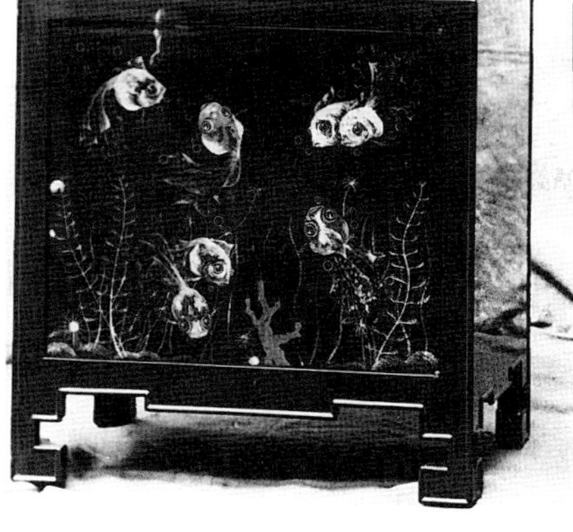
500

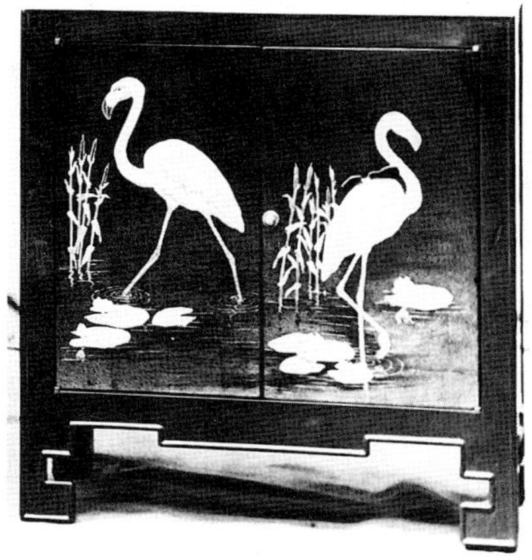
501

496 Cupboard
Shellac, escutcheon plate and metal furnishings in gilt bronze.
Height 90 cm (35½ in.); width 200 cm (78¾ in.); depth 50 cm (19¾ in.).
C. 1937
Exh.: 'Decorative Arts: 1925 Style', Didier Aaron, Inc., New York, November 1979, no. 42.
Formerly in the collections of Félix Marcilhac, Paris, and Didier Aaron, Inc., New York; Private collection, New York.

497 'Heron' display cabinet (with doors closed and open)
Black lacquer, silver decoration.
Height 180 cm (70¾ in.).
1937.
Formerly in the Perrotin Collection.

498 'Stork' bookcase
Black lacquer decorated in gold.
Height 180 cm (70¾ in.).
1939.
Exh.: French Pavilion, New York World's Fair, 1939.
See also cat. no. 1236 and p. 151.

499 'Stork' display cabinet *Pl. 63*
Dark shellac decorated with Coromandel lacquer highlighted in colour.
Height 180 cm (70¾ in.).
1939.
Private collection, Paris.

500, 501 Chinese commodes
Black lacquer decorated with fish in coloured lacquer highlighted with gold.
1939.
Formerly in the collection of René Baschet.

502 Revolving bookcase
Black lacquer.
Height 70 cm (27½ in.).
1927.
Coll.: M. and Mme Kupperfils, Evreux.
Bibl.: *Harper's Bazaar*, April 1928, p. 114.

503 Small free-standing bookcase
Black lacquer with silver stringing, pull-out shelf, red lacquer grip.
Height 60 cm (23½ in.).
Specially designed for Nadine Oxnard in 1928.
Coll.: Félix Marcilhac, Paris.

504 Pedestal table
Pale-green *laque arrachée.*
Height 60 cm (23½ in.).
C. 1930.
Exh.: Delorenzo Gallery, New York, 1985 (repr. in catalogue, p. 58).
Private collection, New York.

505 Radiogram
Black lacquer with silver decoration.
Height 130 cm (51¼ in.).
C. 1937.
Private collection.

506 Radio cabinet *Pl. 68*
Black and coloured lacquer highlighted with gold.
Height 50 cm (19¾ in.); width 80 cm (31½ in.); depth 30 cm (11¾ in.).
C. 1930.
Formerly in the collection of Alain Lesieutre, Paris; Steven A. Greenberg, New York.

507 Lady's writing desk with fitted chair
Blue *laque arrachée.*
Height 75 cm (29½ in.).
1926.
Coll.: M. and Mme Kupperfils, Evreux.
Variant of a piece made for Madame Agnès (cat. no. 1122), with different detailing on drawers.

508 Bureau à caisson
Light-brown shellac with eggshell mosaic top.
Height 74 cm (29¼ in.); top 160 x 70 cm (63 x 27½ in.).
C. 1925.
Private collection.

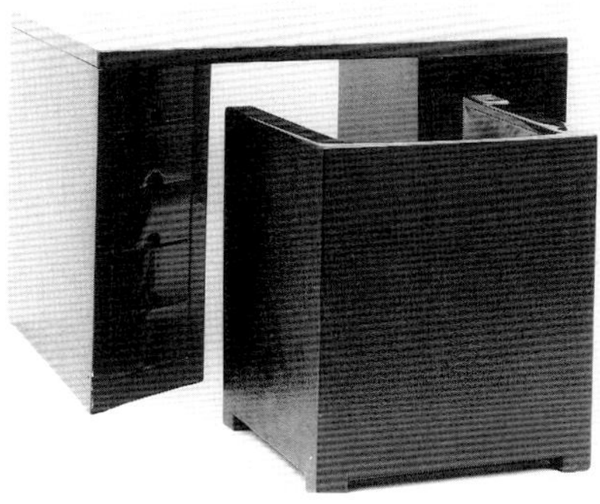
502

507

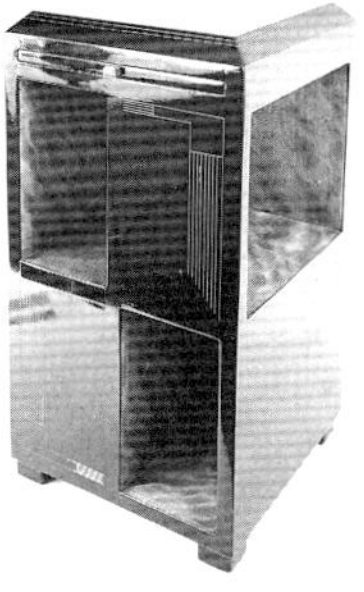

503

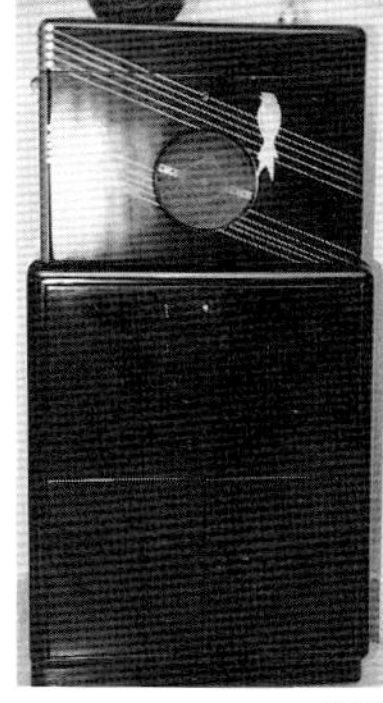
505

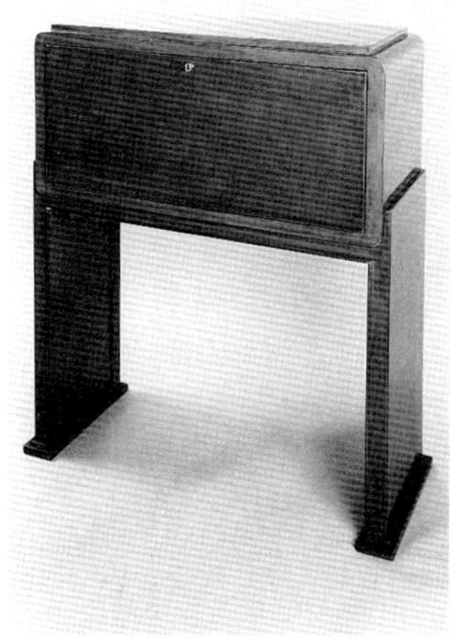

511

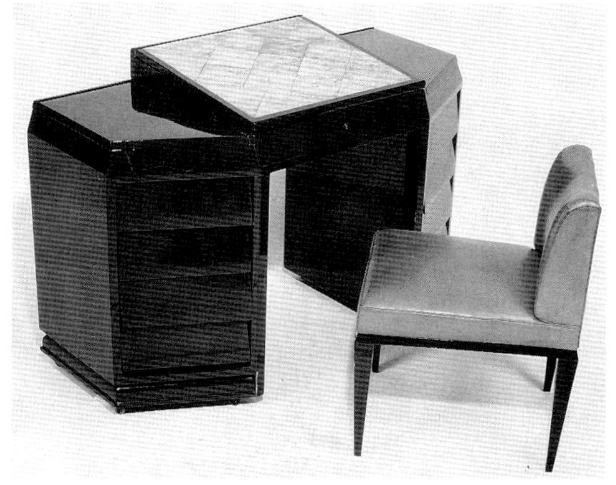

509

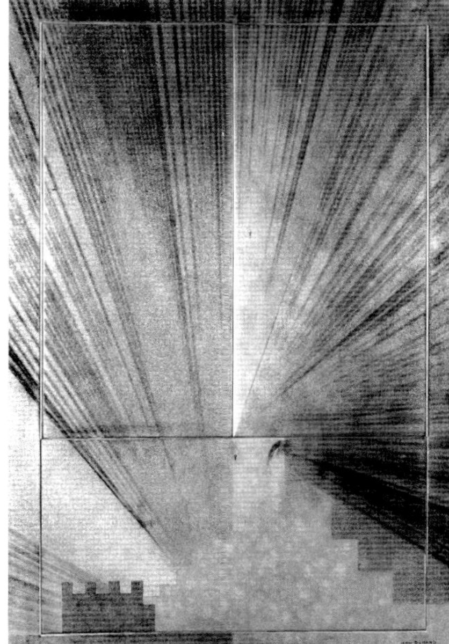

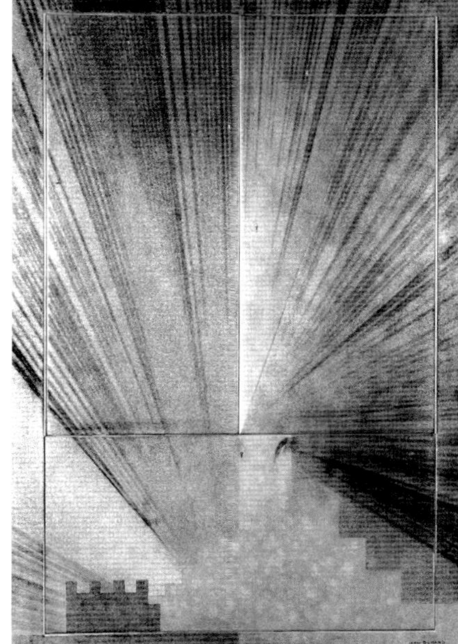

519

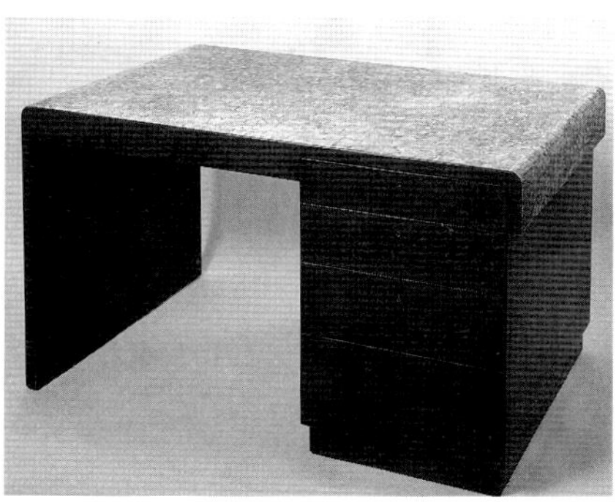

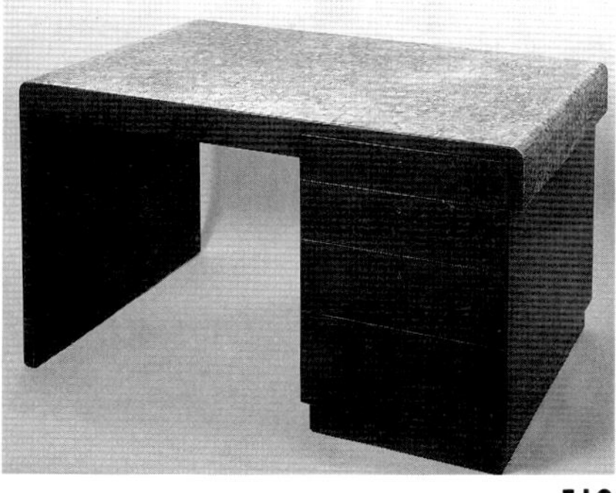

510

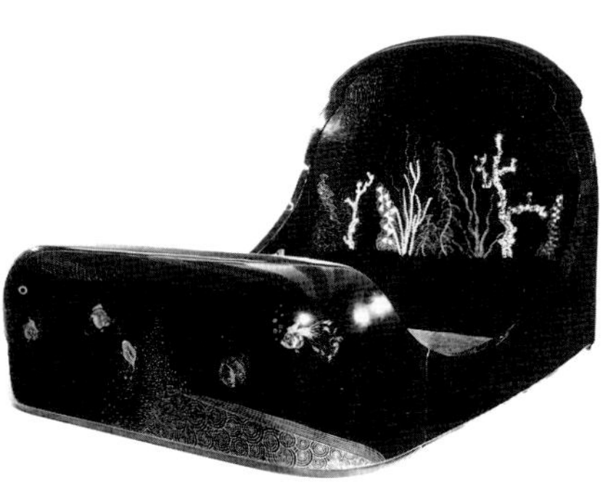

514

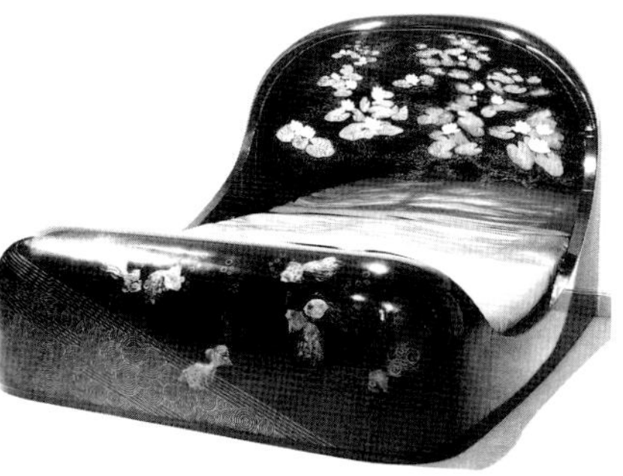

515

509 Lady's writing desk and chair
Dark-maroon lacquer, top sheathed in shagreen.
Height 85 cm (33½ in.); width 120 cm (47¼ in.); depth 70 cm (27½ in.).
Specially designed for Nadine Oxnard by Serge Rovinski and lacquered in Dunand's workshops in 1928.
Formerly in the collection of Félix Marcilhac, Paris, and the Terrin Collection.
Sold: Sotheby's (Monaco), 23 June 1979, lot 264.

510 Desk with drawers
Dark-red lacquer with eggshell mosaic top.
Top 74 cm (29¼ in.); top 120 x 60 cm (47¼ x 23½ in.).
C. 1930.
Private collection.

511 Secrétaire
Light lacquer.
Height 120 cm (47¼ in.).
C. 1937.
Coll.: M. and Mme Kupperfils, Evreux.

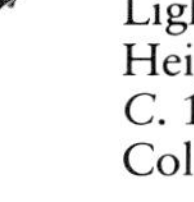

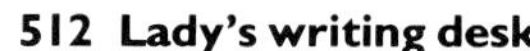

512 Lady's writing desk
Black lacquer with eggshell mosaic top, back decorated with Japanese fish in lacquer highlighted with gold.
C. 1939.
Coll.: Mobilier National, Paris.

513 Moulded bed and chair
Incombustible composite material, reinforced, moulded and lacquered.
1932.
Bibl.: *Sciences et voyages*, 28 March 1935, p. 304.

514 Corbeille bed
Black lacquered composite material inlaid with burgaudine, the depiction of the seabed and fish realized in coloured lacquer.
Maximum height 150 cm (59 in.); width 165 cm (65 in.).
1932.
Coll.: Jean-Jacques Baumé.
Sold: Laurin, Guilloux, Buffetaud, Tailleur (Paris), 2 July 1973, lot 107.

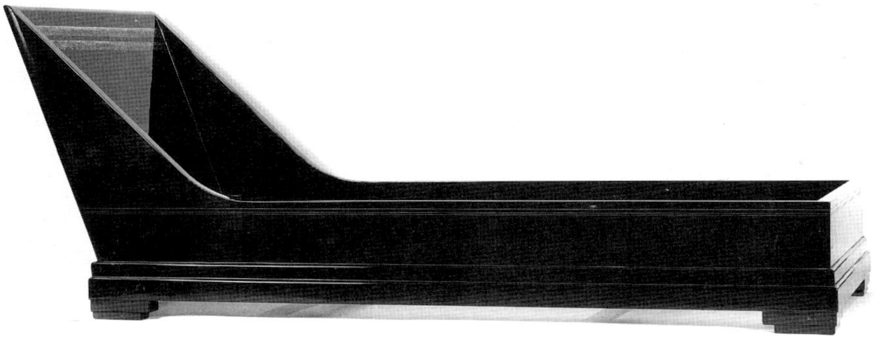
516

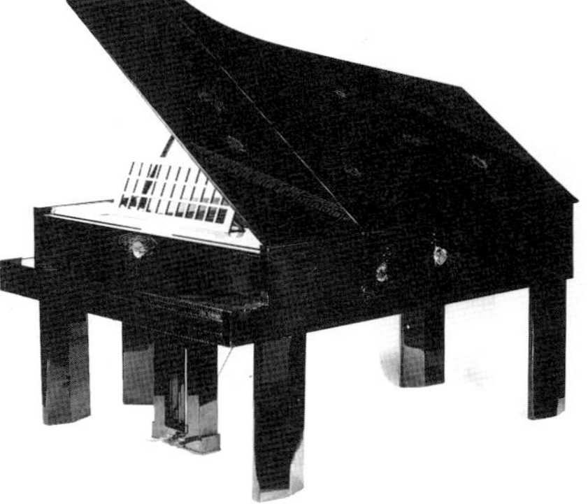
518

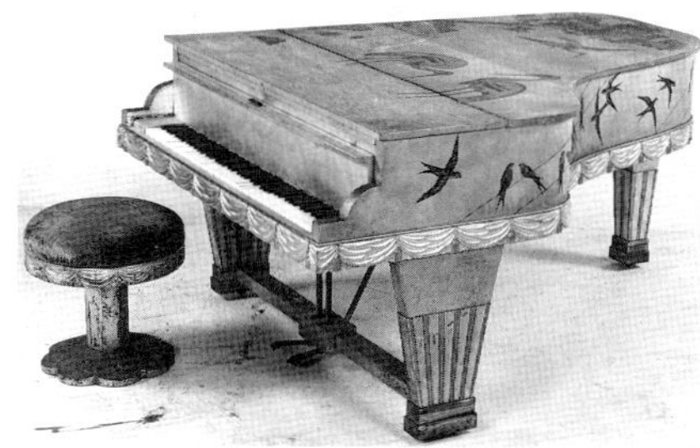
517

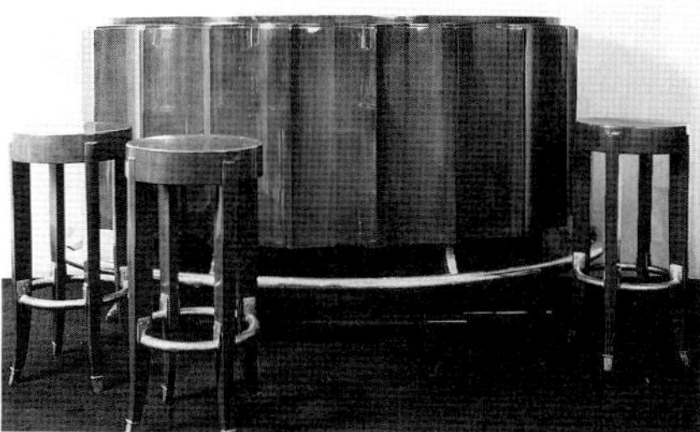
520

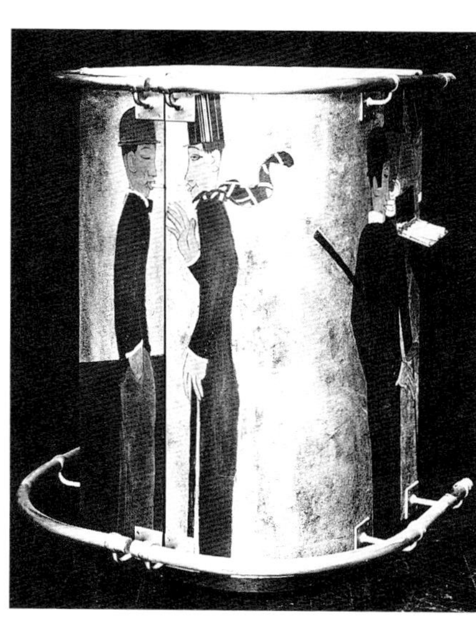
521

515 Corbeille bed *Pl. 65*

Moulded composite material lacquered in black and inlaid with ivory and white mother-of-pearl, the water-lilies and Japanese fish lacquered in colour and highlighted with gold.
Maximum height 150 cm (59 in.); width 165 cm (65 in.).
Specially designed for Mme Philippe Berthelot in 1932.
Exh.: Delorenzo Gallery, New York, 1985 (repr. in catalogue, p. 41).
Formerly in the collections of Jean-Jacques Baumé and the Delorenzo Gallery, New York.
Bibl.: *L'Illustration*, 22 July 1933; Alastair Duncan, *Art Deco Furniture* (London and New York,1984), p. 35.; Dan Klein and Margaret Bishop, *Decorative Art 1890–1980* (Oxford, 1986), p. 160.
Sold: Christie's (New York), 1 October 1983, lot 220.

516 Bateau bed

Black and silver lacquer with silver stringing.
Length 230 cm (90½ in.); width 95 cm (37½ in.).
Specially designed for Nadine Oxnard by Serge Rovinski and lacquered in Dunand's workshops in 1928.
Formerly in the collection of Félix Marcilhac, Paris; Private collection, New York.

517 Piano and stool

Silver and rose-pink lacquer with decoration of herons and swallows.
Built by Erard *c.* 1928 to a design by Walsher.
Coll.: Jacques De Vos.
Sold: Couturier, de Nicolay (Paris), 7 March 1986, lot 79.

518 Baby grand piano

Black lacquer decorated with Japanese fish in coloured lacquer highlighted with gold.
Built by Pleyel *c.* 1930.
Exh.: 'Quant le Mobilier devient Sculpture', *Le Louvre des Antiquaires*, Paris 1981, no. 30.
Formerly in the collection of Alain Lesieutre, Paris; Steven A. Greenberg, New York.
Sold: Champin, Lombrail, Gautier (Enghien), 15 November 1981, lot 154.

519 Front of recessed bar

One of a pair; black and gold lacquer highlighted with coloured lacquer.
Height 155 cm (61 in.); width 100 cm (39¼ in.).
C. 1930.
Formerly in the collections of Félix Marcilhac, Paris, and Karl Lagerfeld; Private collection.
Sold: Godeau; Solanet, Audap (Paris), 20 November 1975, lot 98.

520 Cocktail bar and stools

Red lacquer.
Specially designed for Ducharne by Émile-Jacques Ruhlmann
C. 1925.
Formerly in the collections of Félix Marcilhac, Paris, and Barry Friedman; Private collection, New York.

521 Folding cocktail bar and folding stools *Pl. 168*

Viewed from the side, showing cigarette holder open.
Anthracite-grey and silver *laque arrachée* on natural wood; figures designed by Jean Lambert-Rucki and lacquered in colour; cigarette holder and top inlaid with eggshell.
Height 120 cm (47¼ in.); length (open) 140 cm (55 in.), (closed) 70 cm (27½ in.); depth 90 cm (35½ in.).
Designed by Townley R. Knowles and made in London in 1928 by Lawrence Rigby.
Exh.: Delorenzo Gallery, New York, 1985 (repr. in catalogue, p. 42).
Coll.: Jean-Jacques Baumé.
Bibl.: *Les Échos des industries d'art*, December 1928, p. 22; Alastair Duncan, *Art Deco Furniture* (London and New York, 1984), p. 36.
The stools can be folded away inside the bar.

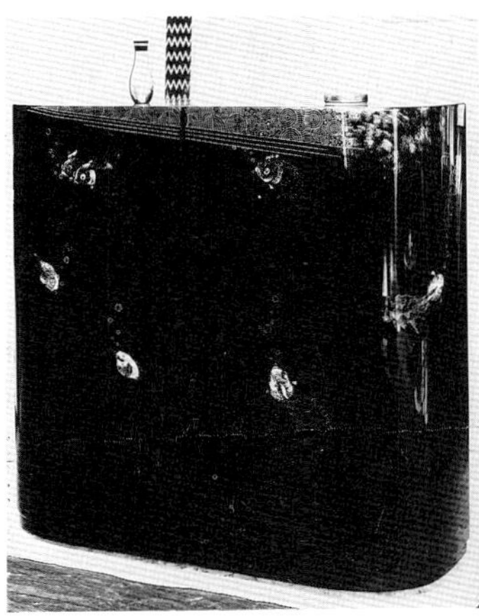

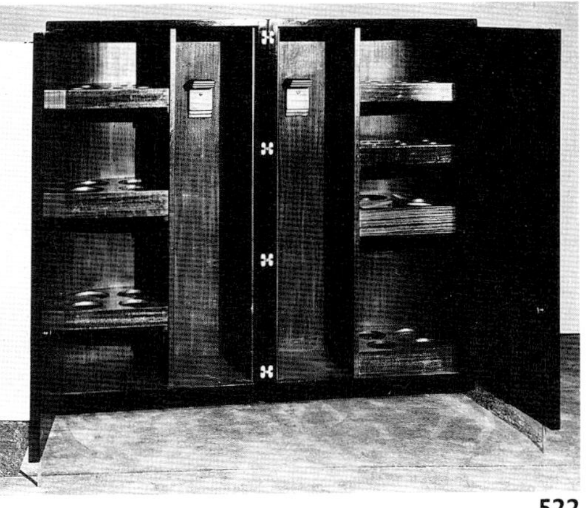

522

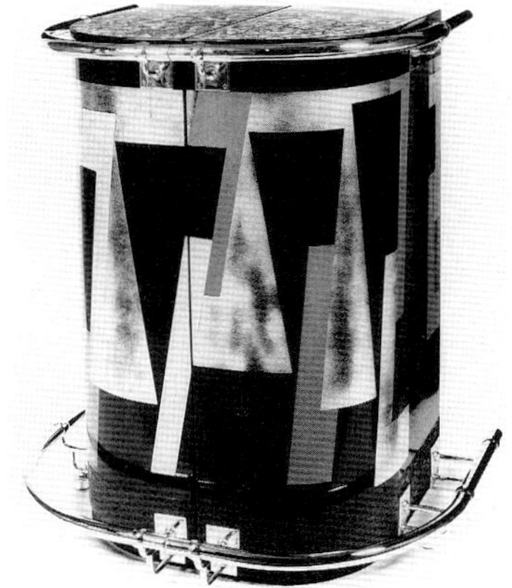

523

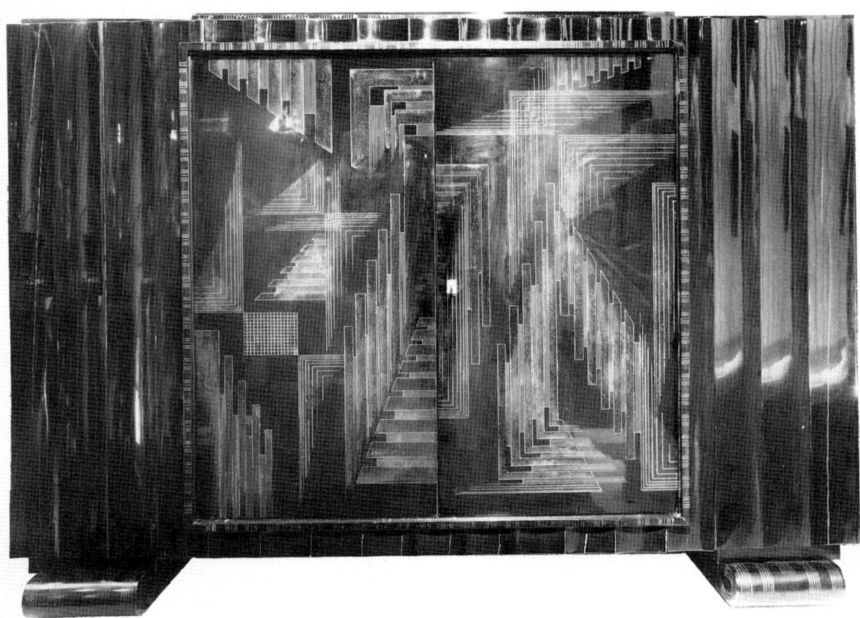

535

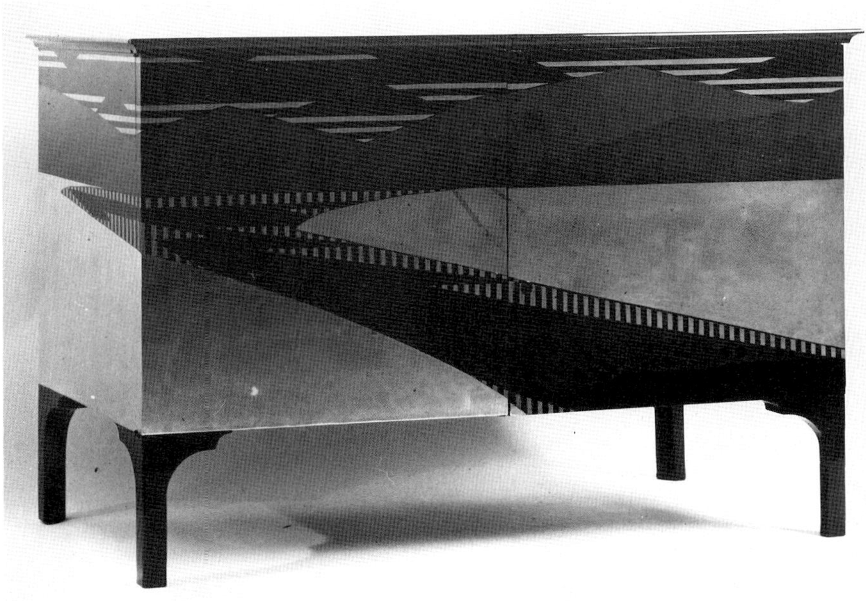

530

522 Folding cocktail bar

Black lacquer, Japanese fish in coloured lacquer highlighted with gold, top in eggshell mosaic.
Height 120 cm (47¼ in.); width (open) 140 cm (55 in.); depth 90 cm (35½ in.).
Made by Lawrence Rigby in 1928.

523 Folding cocktail bar *Pl. 69*

Black lacquer, geometric design in red lacquer, white gold and silver-leaf, top in eggshell mosaic.
Height 120 cm (47¼ in.).; width (open) 140 cm (55 in.); depth 90 cm (35½ in.).
Made by Lawrence Rigby in 1928.
Private collection.
Sold: Boisgirard (Paris), 26 October 1988, lot 121.

524 Cocktail bar *Pl. 71*

Light-brown shellac, folding leaf in eggshell mosaic, revolving side caissons.
Height 110 cm (43¼ in.); top 112 x 48 cm (44 x 19 in.).
1937.
Formerly in the collection of Félix Marcilhac, Paris; Mme K., Italy.

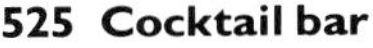

525 Cocktail bar

Similar in form to cat. no. 524, but with full-height doors. The piece is unlacquered.

526 Cocktail cabinet

Light-brown shellac, interior folding leaf in eggshell, pull-out side flap.
Height 120 cm (47¼ in.); top 65 x 45 cm (25½ x 17¾ in.).
C. 1930.
Private collection.

527 Cocktail cabinet

C. 1935.
Formerly in the Rosenbach Collection.

528 Bookcase

Light-brown shellac, animated landscape in brown lacquer after a design by Jean Berque.
Height 120 cm (47¼ in.).
1921.

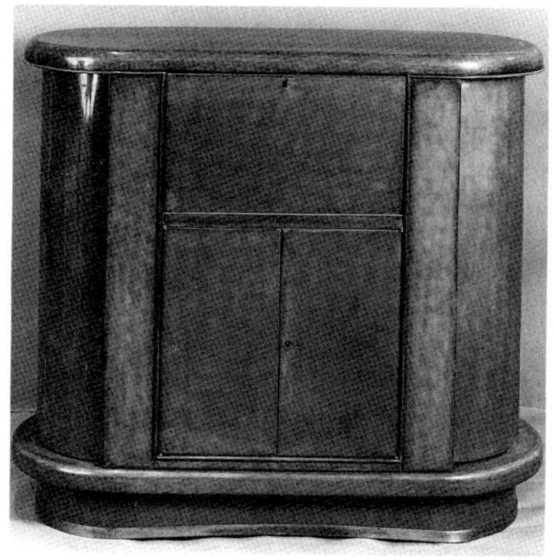
524

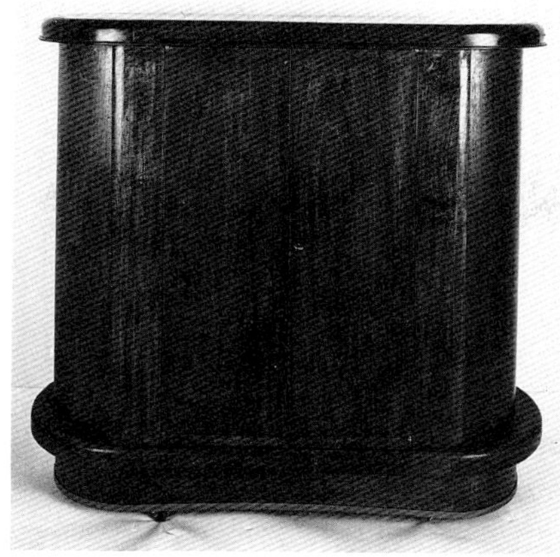
525

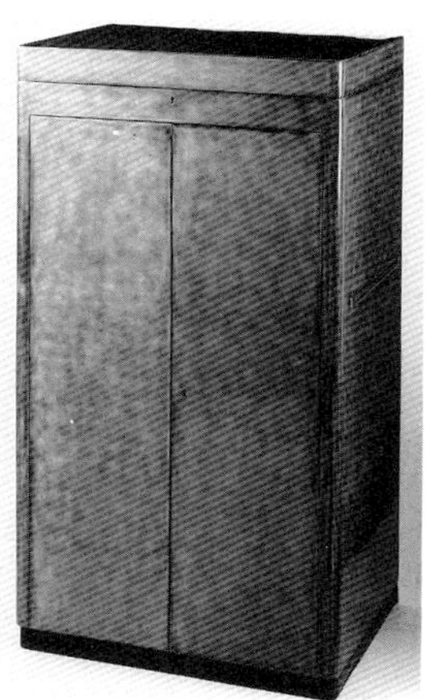
526

Exh.: Galerie Georges Petit, Paris, 1921, no. 15.
Bibl.: *Good Furniture Magazine*, June 1928, p. 292.

529 Cabinet *Pl. 166*
Black lacquer and coloured lacquer, stylized foliage after a design by Jean Goulden.
Height 145 cm (57 in.); width 152 cm (59¾ in.); depth 47 cm (18½ in.).
Designed by Jean Goulden and made in 1923.
Exh.: Galerie Georges Petit, Paris, 1923, no. 35; Delorenzo Gallery, New York, 1985 (repr. in catalogue, p. 53).
Formerly in the collections of Félix Marcilhac, Paris, and Barry Friedman and Lloyd Macklowe; Steven A. Greenberg, New York.
Bibl.: Alastair Duncan, *Art Deco Furniture* (London and New York, 1984), p. 39.
Sold: Champin, Lombrail, Gautier (Enghien), 26 June 1983, lot 39a.

530 Commode à l'anglaise *Pl. 66*
Black lacquer and coloured lacquer, stylized landscape after a design by Jean Goulden, interior lined with bird's-eye maple.
Height 90 cm (35½ in.); top 135 x 63 cm (52¼ x 24¾ in.).
Designed by Jean Goulden and made in 1921.
Exh.: Galerie Georges Petit, Paris, 1921, no. 7; ——, 1923, no. 36.
Coll.: Félix Marcilhac, Paris.

531 Occasional table with drawers and recesses *Pl. 52*
Black lacquer and eggshell.
Height 60 cm (23½ in.); top 100 cm (39¼ in.) square.
Designed by Jean Goulden and made in 1923.
Exh.: Galerie Georges Petit, Paris, 1921, no. 39.
Private collection.
Bibl.: *The Architectural Review*, July 1925.

532 Bureau de pente *Pl. 165*
Silver and black lacquer, eggshell, landscape design picked out in lead.
Height 100 cm (39¼ in.); width 100 cm (39¼ in.); depth 45 cm (1¾ in.).
Designed by Jean Goulden and made in 1923.
Exh.: Galerie Georges Petit, Paris, 1923, no. 38.
Coll.: Félix Marcilhac, Paris.
Bibl.: *The Architectural Review*, July 1925; Lynne Thornton, 'Jean Dunand and his Friends', *Apollo*, October 1973, p. 297.

533 Vitrine
Steel and lacquered wood.
Height 150 cm (59 in.).
Designed by Jean Goulden and made in 1923.
Exh.: Galerie Georges Petit, Paris, 1923, no. 37; ——, 1924, no. 49.

534 Large cabinet
Black lacquer, incised silver decoration after a design by Jean Lambert-Rucki.
Height 200 cm (78¾ in.); width 250 cm (98½ in.).
Designed by Émile-Jacques Ruhlmann and made in 1925.
Exh.: Exposition Internationale des Arts Décoratifs et Industriels Modernes, Paris, 1925 (Hôtel du Collectionneur); Galerie Georges Petit, Paris, 1925, no. 9.
Formerly in the collection of Michael Chow; Steven A. Greenberg, New York.
See also cat. no. 1196 and p. 68.

535 Large cabinet
Identical to cat. no. 534, but with new doors fitted in 1929 for the Barcelona International Exhibition. The incised geometric motif, designed by Émile-Jacques Ruhlmann, is in silver.
Formerly in the collections of Nadine Oxnard, Félix Marcilhac and Michael Chow; Steven A. Greenberg, New York.

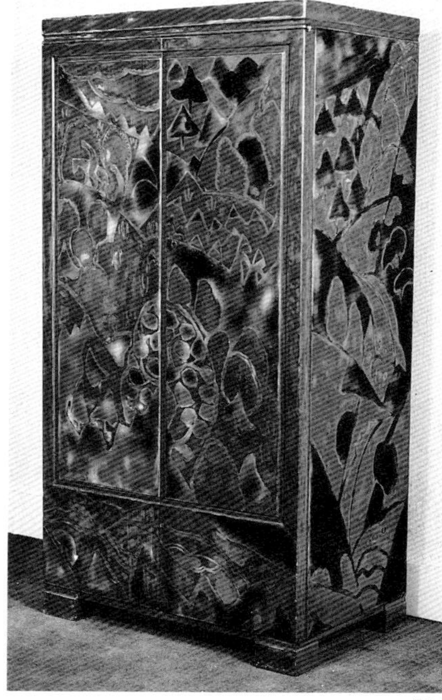
528

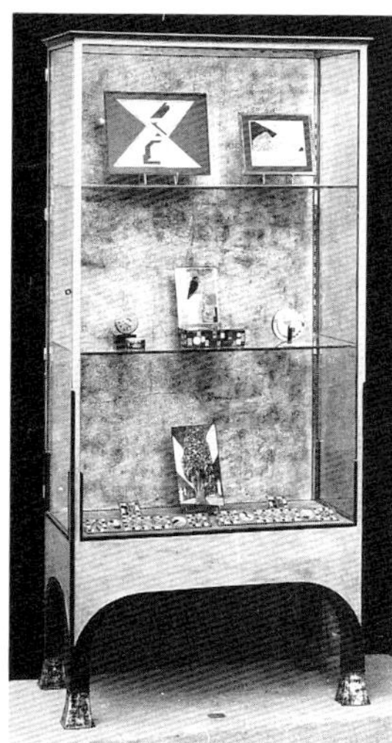
533

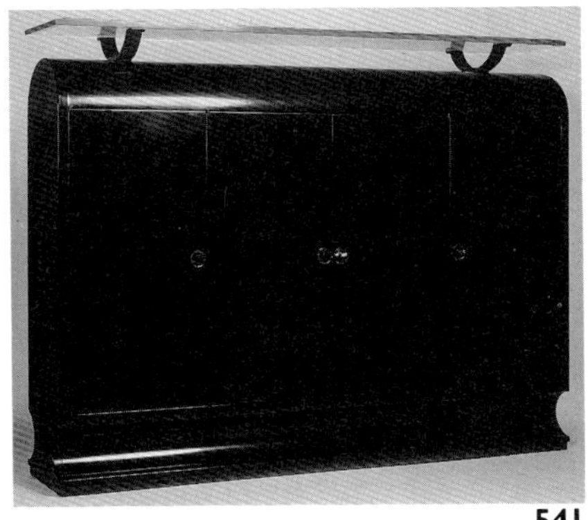
541

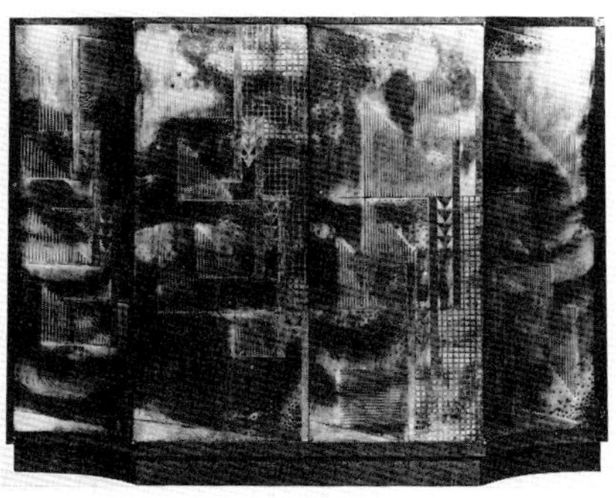
542

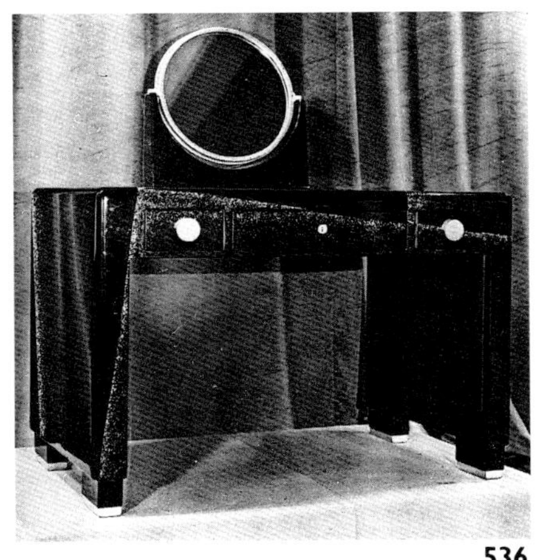
536

548

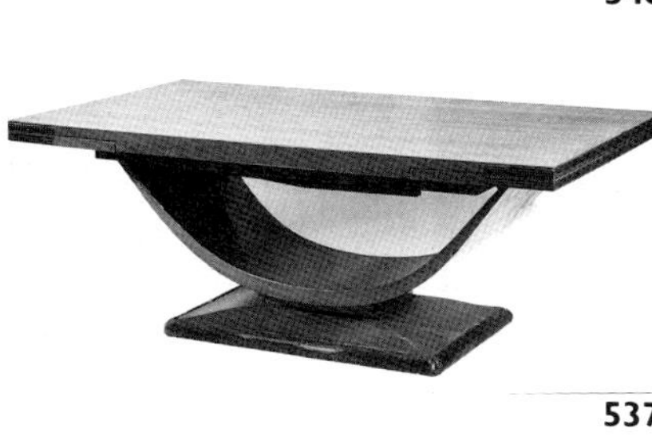
540

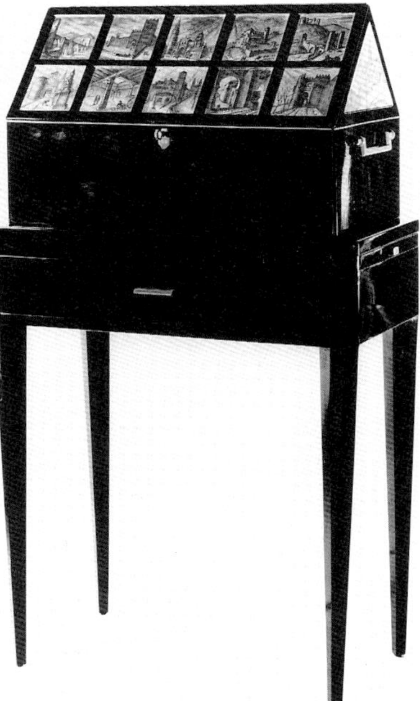
538

537

536 Dressing table and chair

Black lacquer and eggshell; sabots, mirror frame and grips in silvered bronze.
Height 115 cm (45¼ in.); width 100 cm (39¼ in.); depth 60 cm (23¾ in.).
Designed by Émile-Jacques Ruhlmann and made in 1927.
Exh.: Salon des Artistes Décorateurs, Paris, 1927.
Formerly in the collections of M. and Mme d'Estaingville and Michael Chow; Steven A. Greenberg, New York.
Bibl.: *Art et décoration*, June 1927, p. 178; J.-P. Bousquet, *La Laque* (Paris, 1980), p. 48.
Sold: Sotheby's (Monaco), 19 April 1982, lot 193.

537 Dining table

Red lacquer.
Height 74 cm (29¼ in.); top 120 x 200 cm (47¼ x 78¾ in.).
Designed by Émile-Jacques Ruhlmann and made in 1925.
Formerly in the collections of Gueylard and the Galerie Vallois, Paris; Private collection, New York.
Sold: Laurin, Guilloux, Buffetaud; Tailleur (Paris), 10 April 1981, lot 269.

538 Dressing table and chest

Black lacquer, decorated with views of Spanish towns executed in gold *laque arrachée* after a design prepared by Serge Rovinski.
Height 150 cm (59 in.); width 60 cm (23¾ in.).
Specially designed for Nadine Oxnard in 1929.
Formerly in the collection of Félix Marcilhac, Paris.

539 Cabinet

Cochineal, decorated central panel by Dunand.
Designed by Jules Leleu and made in 1934.
Bibl.: *Art et industrie*, June 1934, p. 23.

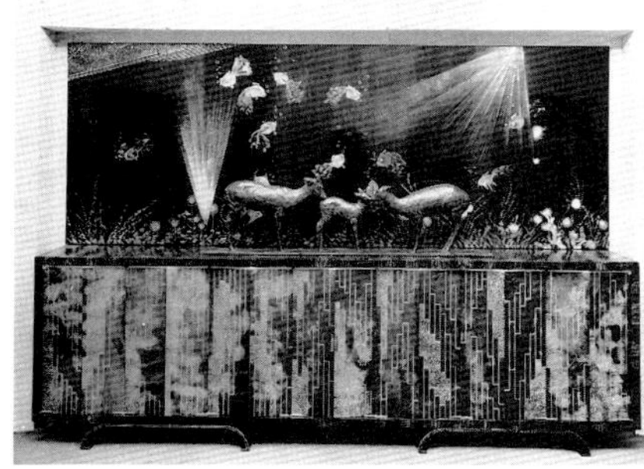

546

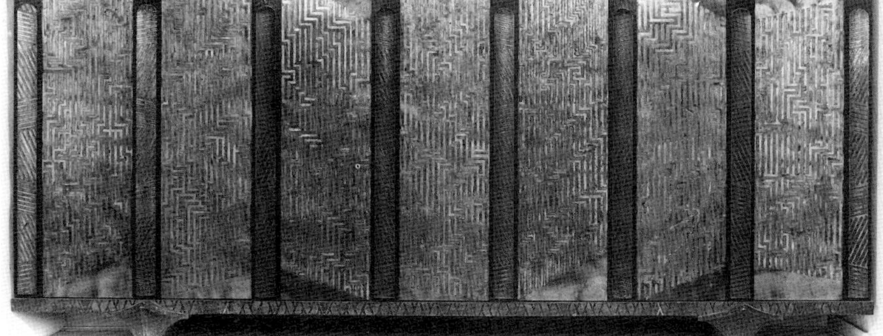

545

540 Large cabinet
Palm wood, folding and sliding doors in dinanderie by Dunand.
Designed by Eugène Printz and made in 1928.
Exh.: Salon d'Automne, Paris, 1928.
Bibl.: *Les Échos des industries d'art*, December 1928, p. 13.

541 Cabinet with glass shelf above
Black lacquer.
Designed by Eugène Printz and made in 1933.
Bibl.: *Mobilier et décoration*, January 1933.
Sold: Sotheby's (Monaco), 19 April 1982, lot 194.

542 Cabinet
Kek wood, with dinanderie doors by Dunand.
Height 125 cm (49¼ in.); width 160 cm (63 in.); depth 30 cm (11¾ in.).
Designed by Eugène Printz and made in 1934.
Sold: Sotheby's (Monaco), 10 February 1981, lot 1464.

543 Cabinet *Pl. 50*
Kek wood, dinanderie doors by Dunand.
Height 125 cm (49¼ in.); width 110 cm (43¼ in.); depth 25 cm (9¾ in.).
Designed by Eugène Printz and made in 1934.
Coll.: Félix Marcilhac, Paris.

544 Secrétaire
Brazilian rosewood, dinanderie doors by Dunand.
Height 125 cm (49¼ in.); width 55 cm (21¾ in.); depth 35 cm (13¾ in.).
Designed by Eugène Printz *c.* 1935.
Coll.: George Encil.

545 Bookcase with revolving sections *Pl. 51*
Palm wood, dinanderie plates designed by Jean Dunand and realized by Pierre Dunand.
Height 150 cm (59 in.); width 300 cm (118 in.); depth 45 cm (17¾ in.).
C. 1937.
Exh.: Musée des Arts Décoratifs, Paris, 1976, no. 729 (exhibition held to mark the 50th anniversary of the 1925 Exposition Internationale des Arts Décoratifs).
Formerly in the collection of Félix Marcilhac, Paris; Virginia Museum of Fine Arts, Richmond, Va (gift of Sydney and Frances Lewis).

546 Enfilade and panel
Palm wood, dinanderie folding doors by Dunand, black lacquer panel, Japanese fish motif by Dunand.
Designed by Eugène Printz and made *c.* 1935.
Formerly in the collection of the Princesse de Faucigny-Lucinge; Private collection.

547 Smoker's table
Gilt oxidized brass and red lacquer.
Designed by Eugène Printz, made *c.* 1937, and lacquered in Dunand's workshops.
Formerly in the collection of the Galerie Vallois, Paris.

548 Cupboard
Gilt oxidized brass and red lacquer.
Designed by Eugène Printz, made *c.* 1937, and lacquered in Dunand's workshops.
Formerly in the collection of the Galerie Vallois, Paris.

549 Cabinet and curved panel
Black lacquer with gilt decoration.
Designed by Eugène Printz, swan motif on panel designed by Dunand.
Exh.: Salon des Artistes Décorateurs, Paris, 1939.
Bibl.: *Le Décor d'aujourd'hui*, June 1939.

550 Cabinet *Pl. 56*
Palm wood with folding and sliding doors in dinanderie by Dunand.
Designed by Eugène Printz and made *c.* 1937.
Coll.: George Encil.

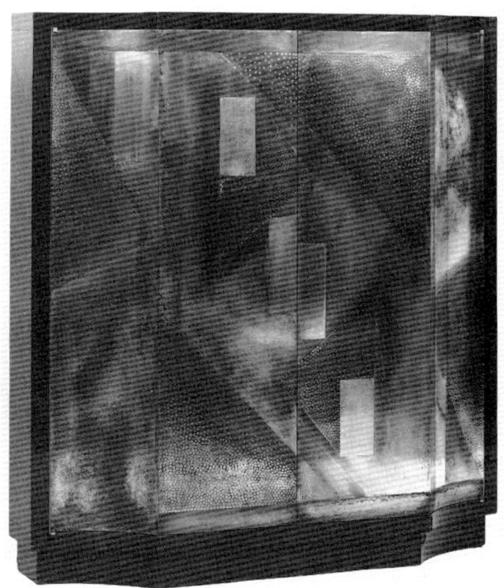

543

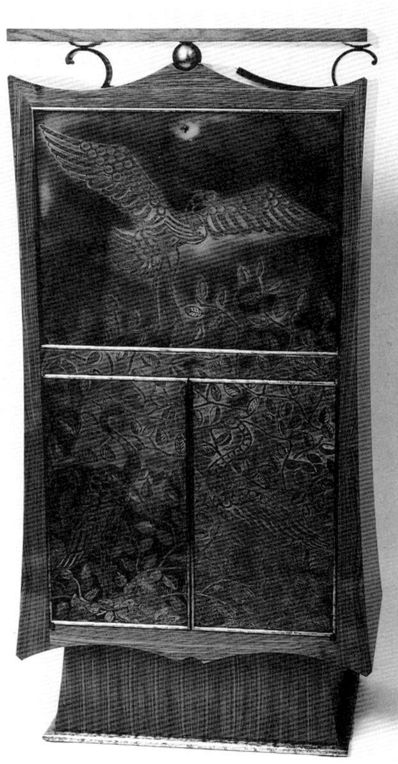

544

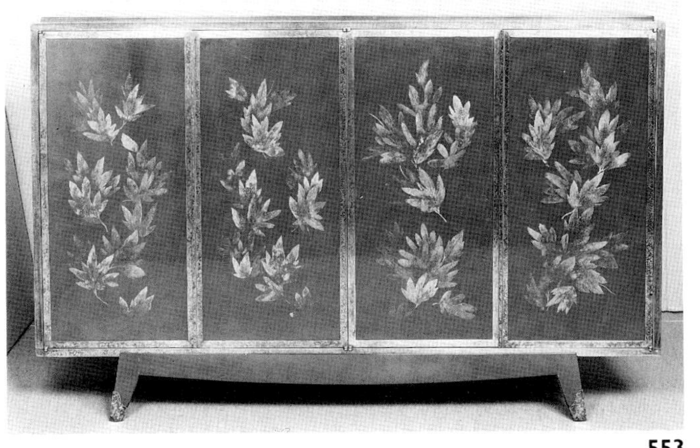
553

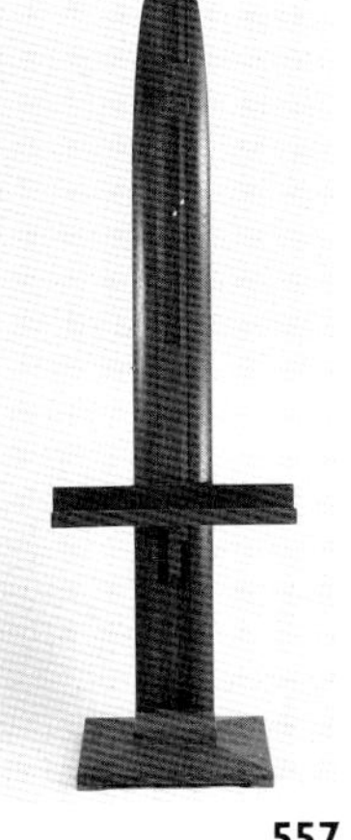
557

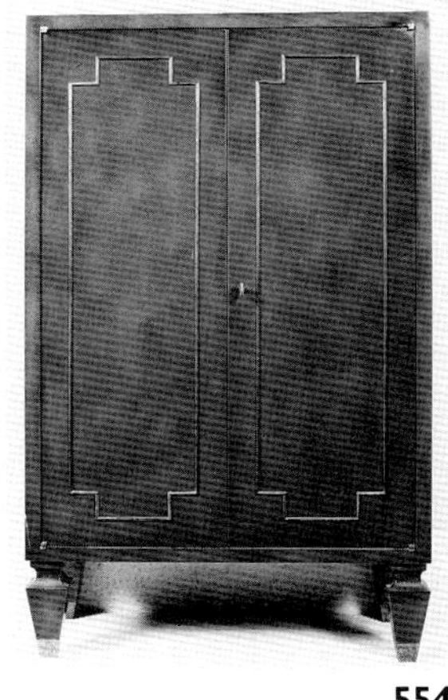
554

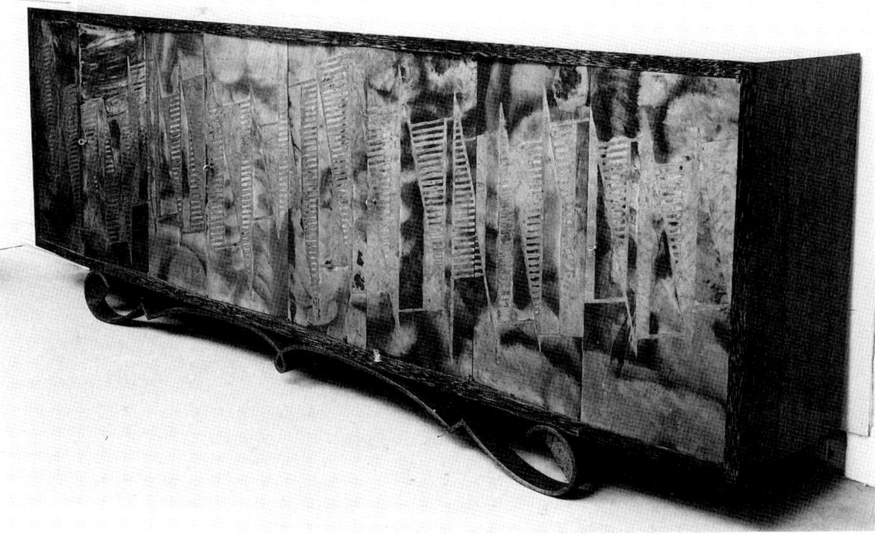
552

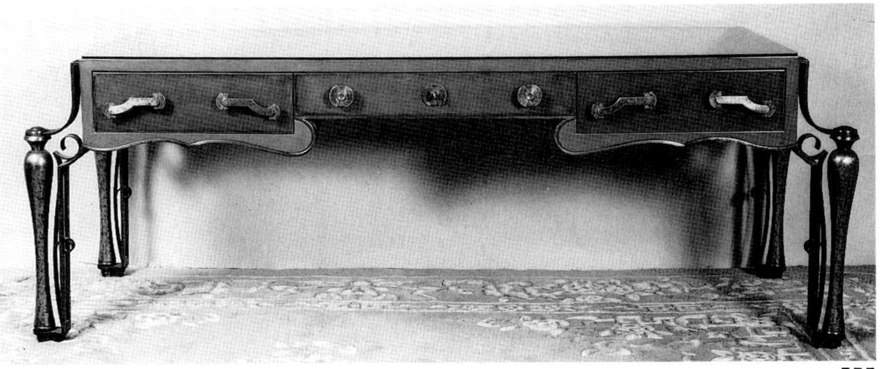
555

551 Secrétaire *Pl. 75*
Brazilian rosewood with dinanderie doors by Dunand.
Height 125 cm (49¼ in.); width 55 cm (21¾ in.); depth 35 cm (13¾ in.).
Designed by Eugène Printz and made *c.* 1935.
Exh.: Delorenzo Gallery, New York, 1985 (repr. in catalogue, p. 57).
Coll.: Delorenzo Gallery, New York.

552 Cupboard
Palm wood with dinanderie doors by Dunand.
Designed by Eugène Printz and made *c.* 1937.
Private collection.

553 Cocktail cabinet
Oxidized metal, gold and red lacquer decoration executed in the family workshops by Pierre Dunand (design by Jean Dunand).
Made *c.* 1945 to a design by Eugène Printz.
Coll.: George Encil.

554 Cabinet
Dark shellac executed in the family workshops by Pierre Dunand (design by Jean Dunand).
Made *c.* 1945 to a design by Eugène Printz.
Coll.: George Encil.

555 Desk
Oxidized brass, red lacquer body executed in Dunand's workshops.
Designed by Eugène Printz and made *c.* 1931.
Coll.: George Encil.

556 Commode *Pl. 64*
Black lacquer decorated with a bouquet of flowers in coloured lacquer.
Height 90 cm (35½ in.); width 90 cm (35½ in); depth 30 cm (11¾ in.).
Designed *c.* 1935 and lacquered in Dunand's workshops.
Exh.: Delorenzo Gallery, New York, 1985 (repr. in catalogue, p. 56).
Formerly in the Yacoubovitch Collection; Jean-Jacques Baumé.

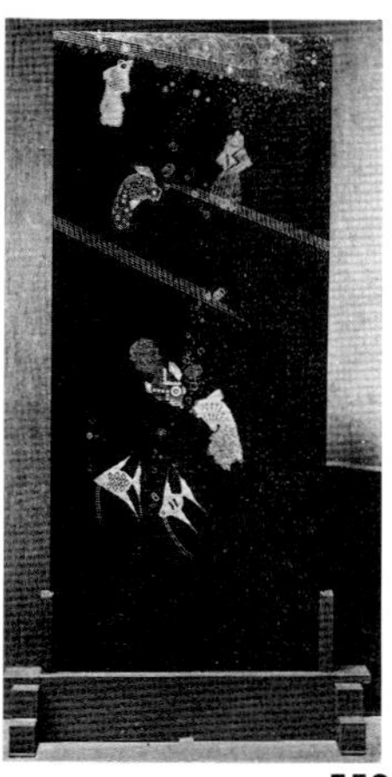
558

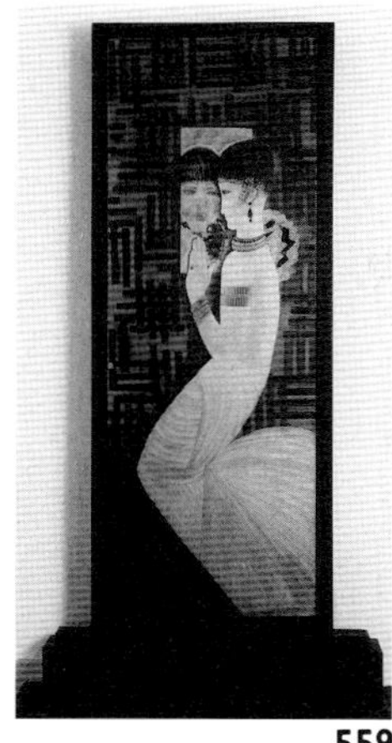
559

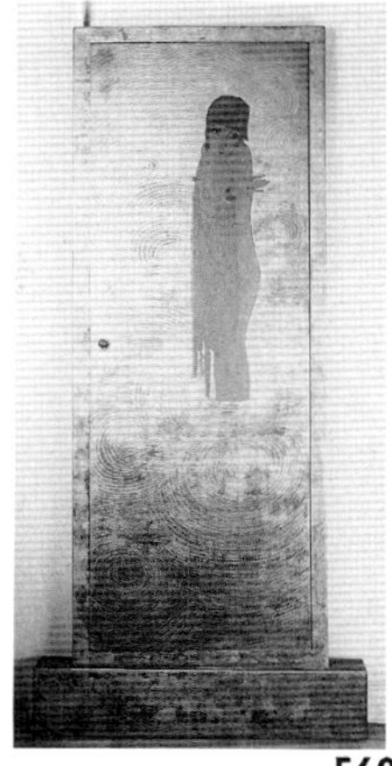
560

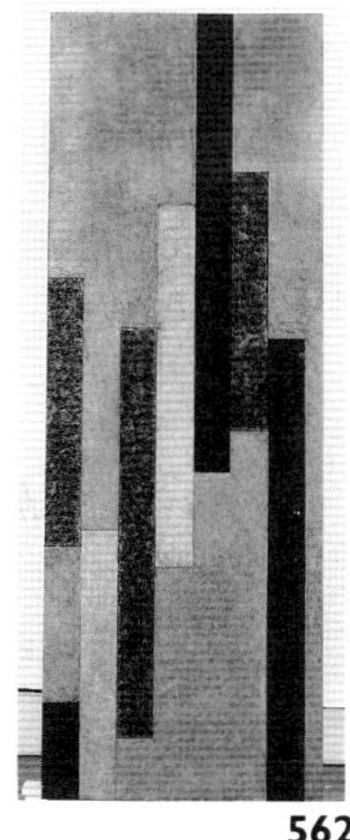
562

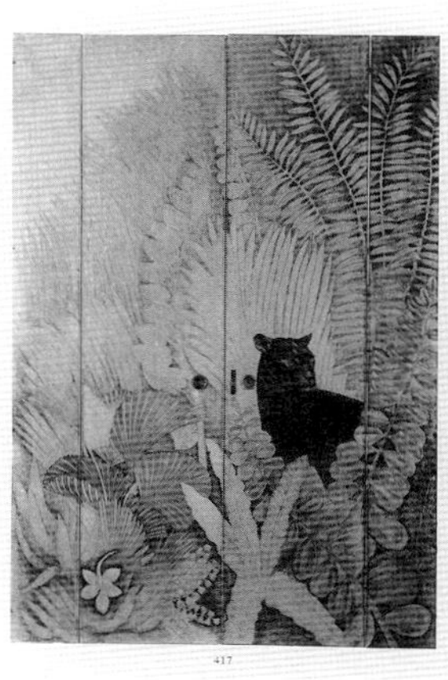
567

Bibl.: Alastair Duncan, *Art Deco Furniture* (1984), pl.15.
Sold: Christie's (New York), 27 May 1982, lot 116.

557 Adjustable easel
Polished oak.
Height 180 cm (70¾ in.).
C. 1930.
Private collection.

558 'Fish' cheval-glass
Black lacquer and coloured lacquer highlighted with gold and silver.
1925.
Exh.: Galerie Georges Petit, Paris, 1925, no. 17.
Bibl.: *Mobilier et décoration*, February 1926, repr. p. 44; *Creative Arts*, 28 March 1926, repr. p. 235; *Le Figaro artistique*, 26 April 1926.

559 'Mirror' cheval-glass
Gold, silver and black lacquer.
Height 180 cm (70¾ in.).
1927.
Exh.: Galerie Georges Petit, Paris, 1927, no. 40.
Formerly in the collection of Robert Walker.

560 'Bathing girl' cheval-glass
Gold and silver *laque arrachée*.
Height 180 cm (70¾ in.).
1927.
Exh.: Galerie Georges Petit, Paris, 1927, no. 39.
Private collection.
Bibl.: *Harper's Bazaar*, April 1928, p. 114.

561 Double door *Pl. 74*
Light-brown shellac, black lacquer and *laque arrachée*, decorated with vertical mouldings, fingerplates in mirror glass, with a design fixed under glass.
Height 200 cm (78¾ in.); total width 150 cm (59 in.).
C. 1925.
Private collection.
This double door formerly gave access to the display room in Dunand's workshops in the Rue Hallé.

562 Section of door
Light-brown shellac, black lacquer and *laque arrachée*, decorated with vertical mouldings.
Height 200 cm (78¾ in.); width: 65 cm (25½ in.).
C. 1925.
Private collection.

563 Folding door *Pl. 41*
Black and coloured lacquer with a design depicting a young woman.
Height 200 cm (78¾ in.).
1926.
Coll.: Manoukian Collection.
A former four-panel screen, two sections of which were adapted by a Parisian interior designer for use as doors.

564 Double door
Black lacquer, fingerplate and handles in silver bronze.
Height 250 cm (100¾ in.).
Designed by Émile-Jacques Ruhlmann in 1927 and made for his offices in the Rue de Lisbonne, Paris.
Sold: Sotheby's (Monaco), 6 March 1983, lot 139.

565 Double door
Coloured and gold *laque arrachée* on a brown shellac ground.
Height 240 cm (94½ in.); width 150 cm (59 in.).
Specially designed for Madame Yacoubovitch in 1929.
Coll.: Jean-Jacques Baumé.
See also cat. no. 1166.

566 Single door
Sketch in gouache and Indian ink for the interior doors for the Bally shoe shop in the Boulevard de la Madeleine, Paris, designed in 1928 in collaboration with Robert Mallet-Stevens.
See also p. 96.

567 Four-leaf folding doors
Black lacquer and coloured lacquer.
Height 256 cm (98½ in.).
C. 1930.
Sold: Sotheby's (Monaco), 24 October 1982, lot 417.

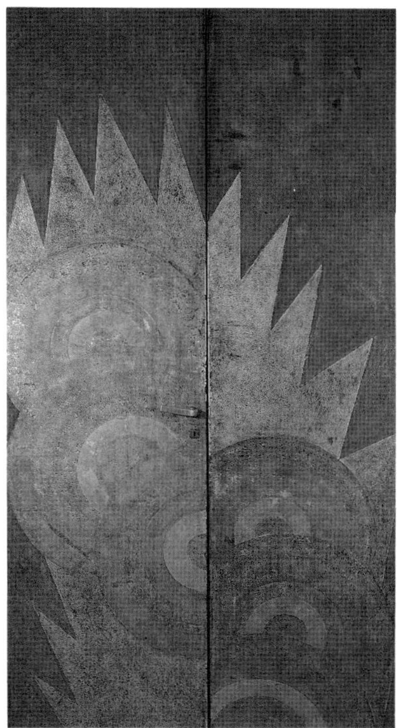

565

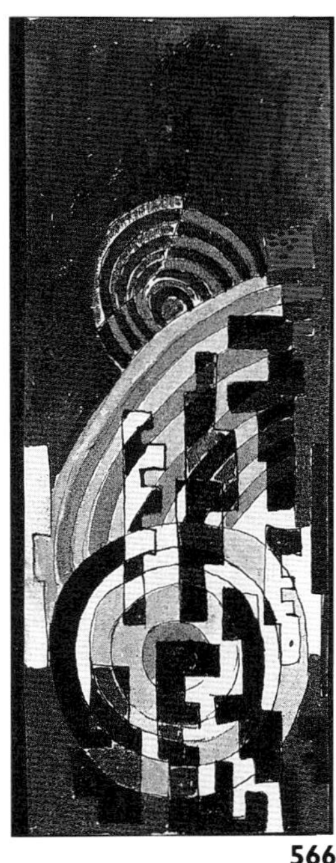
566

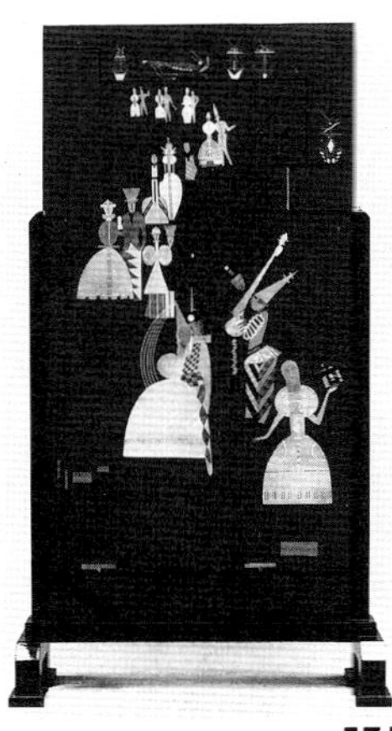
571

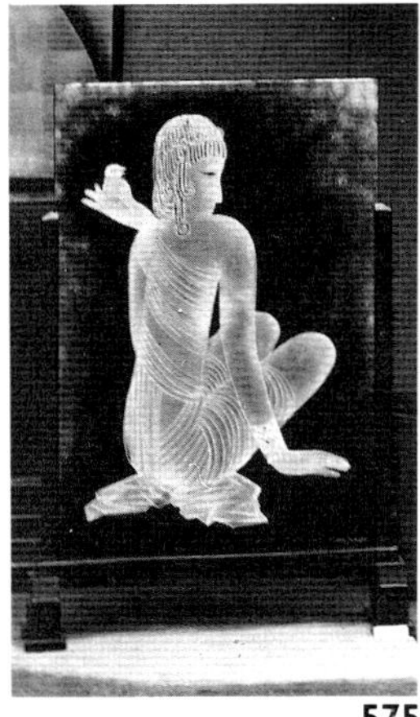
575

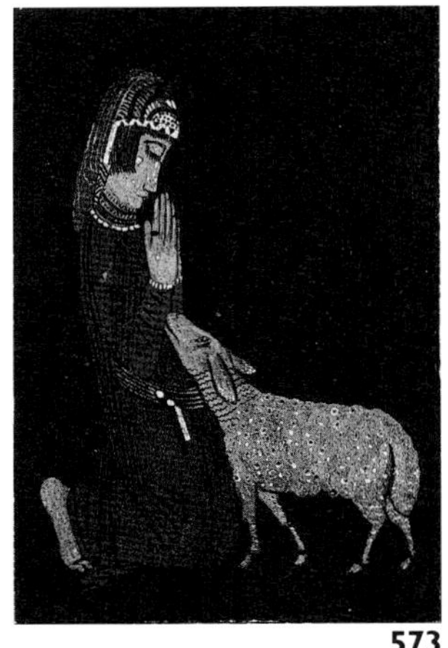
573

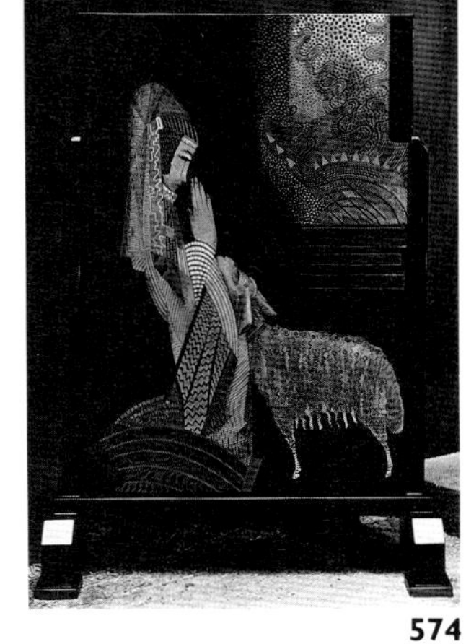
574

568 Accordion door
Dinanderie plaque inlaid with silver.
Specially designed by Eugène Printz *c.* 1935 for La Tour d'Auvergne, Château de Grosbois.
Formerly in the collection of the Galerie Vallois, Paris.

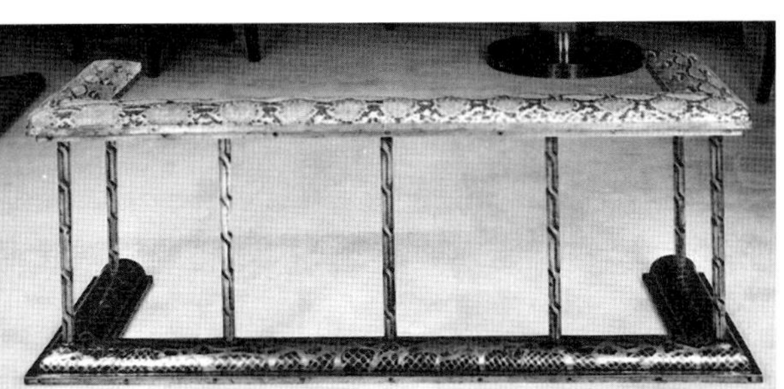
569

HEARTH FURNITURE

569 'Snake' fireguard
Borders in imitation of snakeskin, setting of gilt wrought iron.
1913.
Formerly in the collection of the Galerie Vallois, Paris.

570 'Cypress' firescreen *Pl. 170*
Blue and black lacquer and eggshell.
Height 97 cm (38¼ in.); panel 83 x 50 cm (32¾ x 19¾ in.).
Designed by Jean Goulden and made in 1921.
Private collection.
A large panel with an identical design (cat. no. 289) was exhibited at the Galerie Georges Petit, Paris, in 1921.

571 'Procession' firescreen
Dark shellac and coloured lacquer.
Designed by Jean Lambert-Rucki and made in 1923 (see also cat. no. 222).
Exh.: Galerie Georges Petit, Paris, 1923, no. 16.
Bibl.: *Mobilier et décoration*, February 1926, p. 45; *The Architectural Review*, July 1925.

572 Firescreen
Black lacquer and eggshell mosaic.
Height 104 cm (41 in.).
1924.
Exh.: Galerie Georges Petit, Paris, 1924, no. 30.

573 'Woman and Sheep' firescreen
Study in gouache and Indian ink for cat. no. 574.
Private collection.

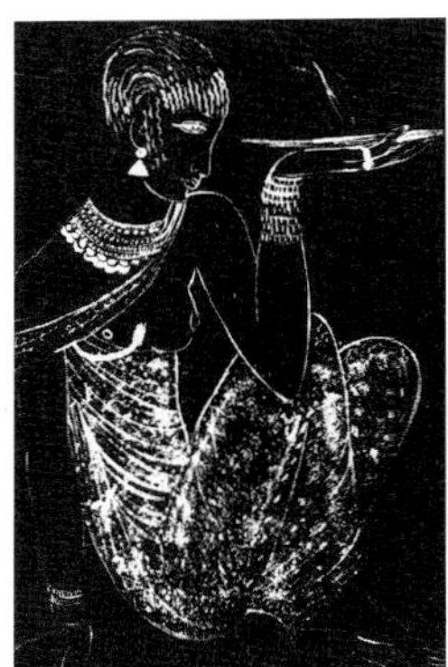

577

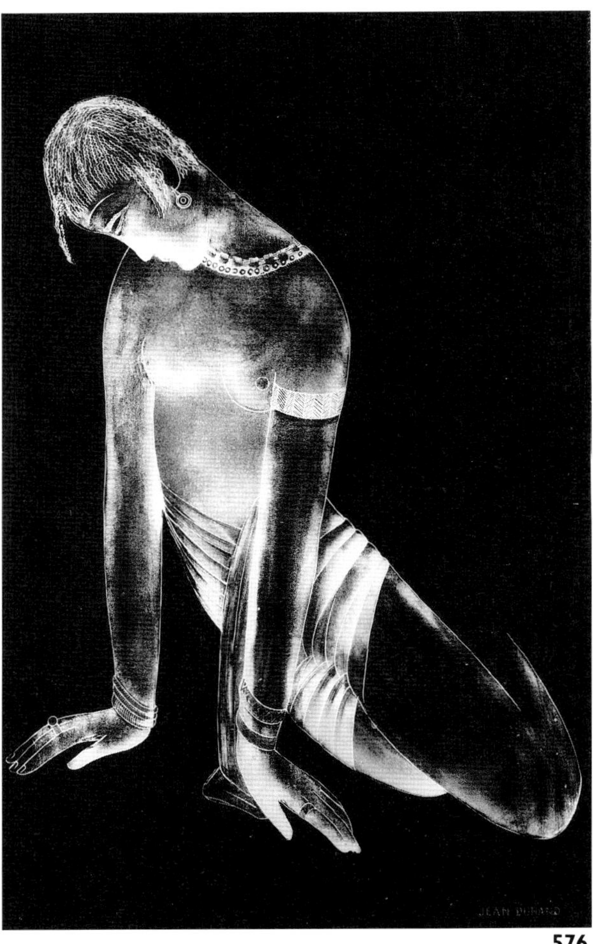
576

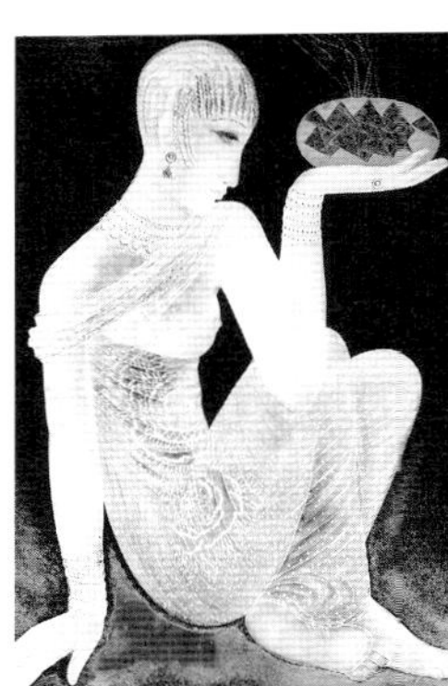
578

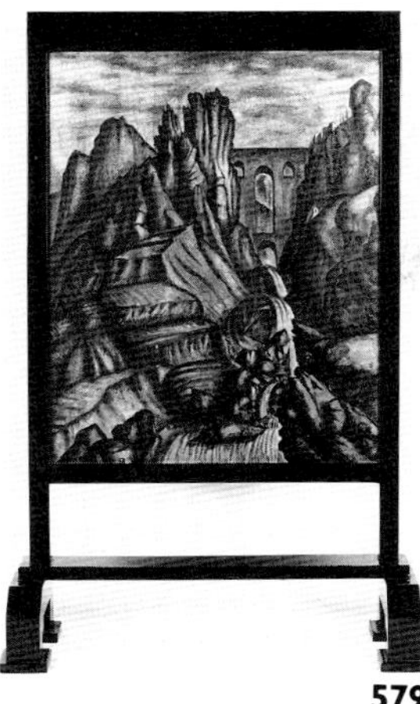

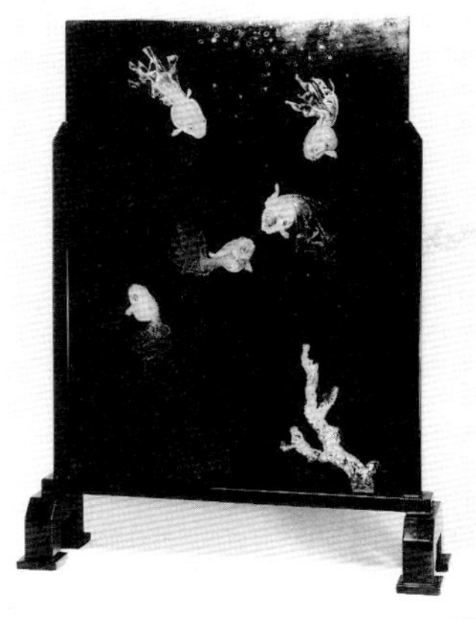

579

583

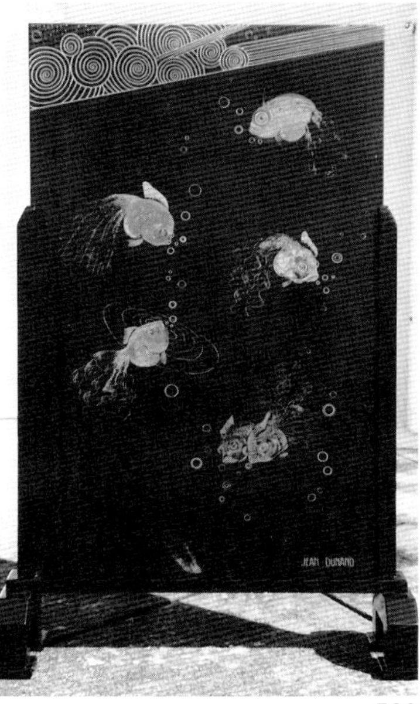

580

574 'Woman and Sheep' firescreen
Black and coloured lacquer.
Height 104 cm (41 in.).
Specially designed for the milliner Madame Agnès in 1926.
Bibl.: *Creative Arts*, 28 March 1926, p. 236.

575 'Woman and Bird' firescreen
Black and gold lacquer.
Height 104 cm (41 in.).
1927.
Exh.: Galerie Georges Petit, Paris, 1927, no. 43.

576 Panel of 'Figure' firescreen
Gold lacquer decoration on a black lacquer ground.
Height 104 cm (41 in.).
1927.
Exh.: Galerie Georges Petit, Paris, 1927, no. 23.
Coll.: Alain Lesieutre, Paris.

577 'Perfume' panel
Study for cat. no. 578 painted on wood.
90 × 72 cm (35½ × 28¼ in.).
1927.
Sold: Sotheby's (Monaco), 25 May 1980, lot 104.

578 Panel of 'Perfume' firescreen
Gold lacquer decoration on a black lacquer ground.
Height 104 cm (41 in.).
1927.
Exh.: Galerie Georges Petit, Paris, 1927, no. 42.
Formerly in the collections of Jean-Charles Worth and Alain Lesieutre, Paris.
Bibl.: *L'Illustration*, 27 May 1933.
Sold: Sotheby's (Monaco), 24 September 1978, lot 229.

579 'Toledo Bridge' firescreen
Black lacquer with decoration executed in gold *laque arrachée* based on a design by Serge Rovinski.
Specially designed for Nadine Oxnard by Serge Rovinski in 1929.
Formerly in the collection of Félix Marcilhac, Paris; Private collection.

580 'Fish' firescreen
Black lacquer with coloured lacquer design highlighted with gold and silver.
1928.
Exh.: Galerie Georges Petit, Paris, 1928, no. 24.
Private collection.

581 'Fish' firescreen
Black lacquer with coloured lacquer design highlighted with gold and silver.
C. 1930.
Formerly in the collection of Félix Marcilhac, Paris; James Stubblebine, New York.

582 'Fish' firescreen
Black lacquer with coloured lacquer design and eggshell support.
Overall height 175 cm (68¾ in.).
C. 1930.
Formerly in the collection of Alain Lesieutre, Paris.
Sold: Sotheby's (Monaco), 24/25 October 1982, lot 425.

583 'Fish and Coral' firescreen
Black lacquer with coloured lacquer design highlighted with gold and silver.
Overall height 104 cm (41 in.); panel height 92 cm (36¼ in.).
1933.
Exh.: 'Quant le Mobilier devient Sculpture', *Le Louvre des Antiquaires*, Paris, 1981, repr. p. 339.
Bibl.: *L'Illustration*, cover of special Christmas number, 1933.
Sold: Christie's (Geneva), 10 May 1982, lot 148.

584 'Grape Harvesting' firescreen
Gold lacquer on moulded stucco.
Overall height 70 cm (27½ in.).
1935.
Exh.: Delorenzo Gallery, New York, 1985 (repr. in catalogue, p. 35).
Assemblage incorporating one of the panels which Dunand executed after 1935 as replicas of the large relief made for the Smoking Room of the liner *Normandie*.
See note to cat. no. 1099.

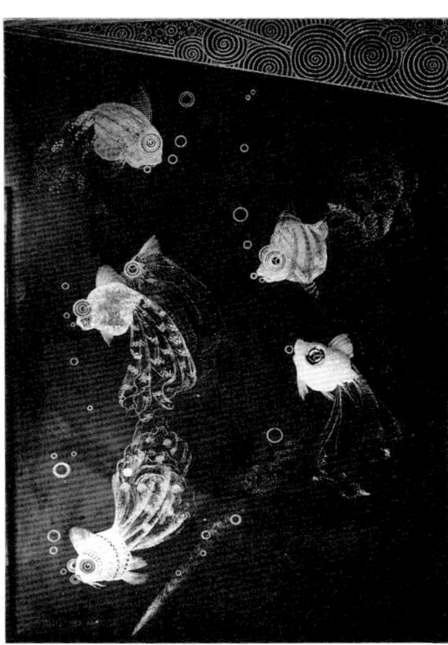

581

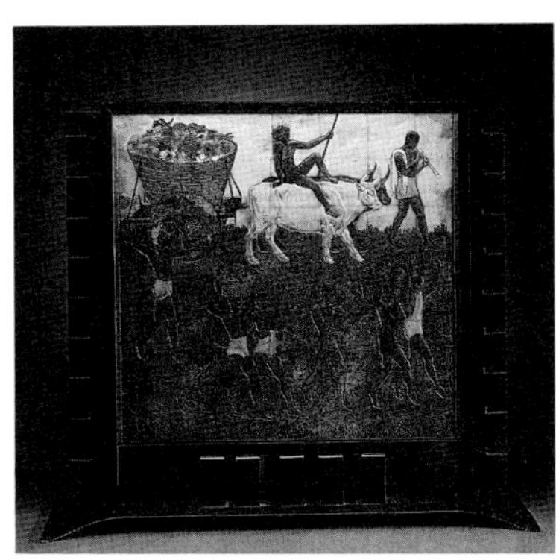

584

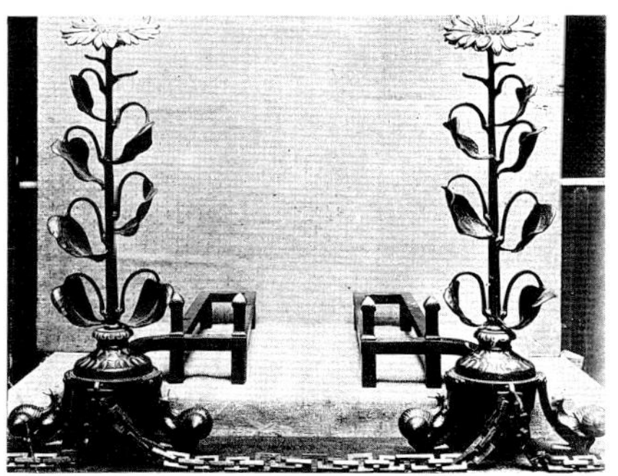
588

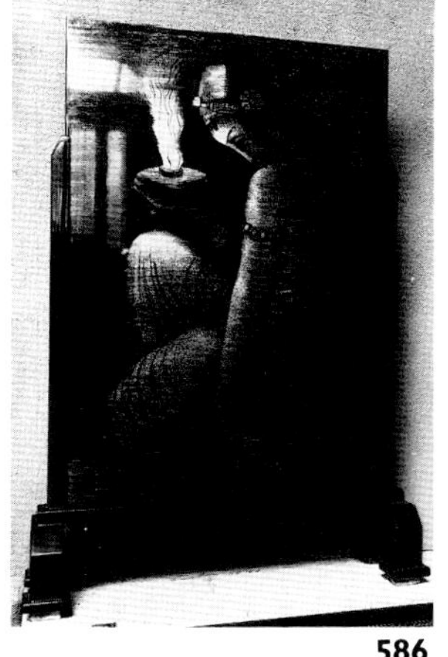
586

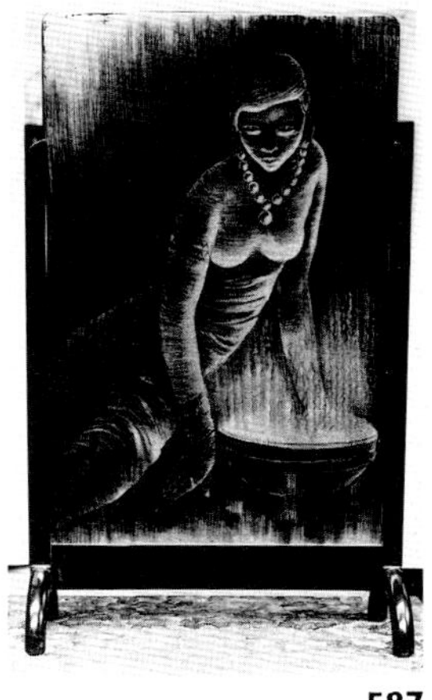
587

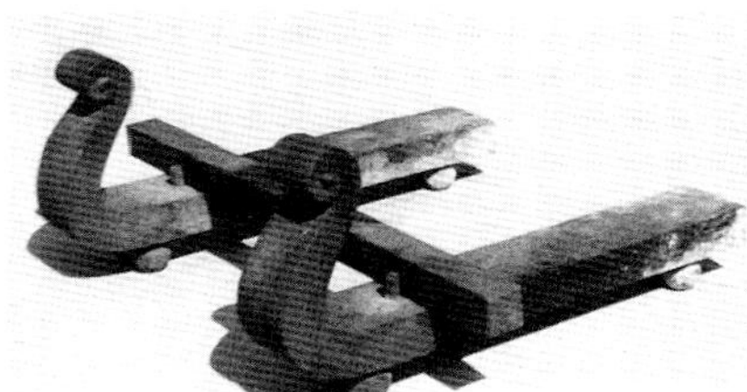
589

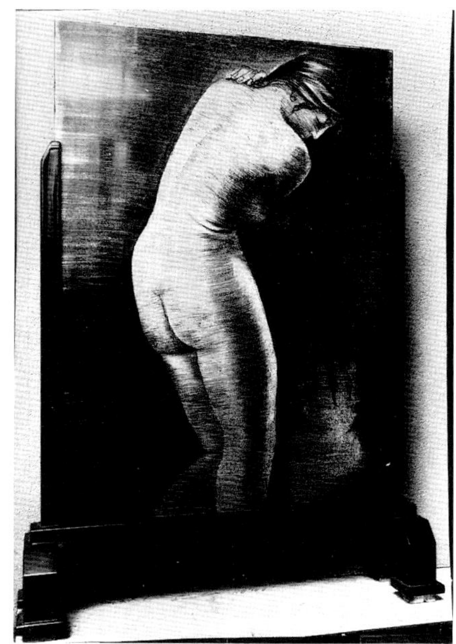
585

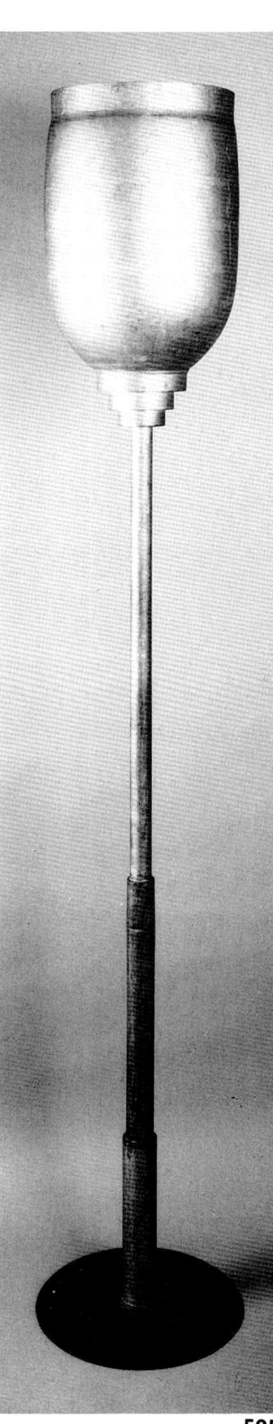
595

585 'Shivery Young Woman' firescreen

Black lacquer with gold design.
Height 104 cm (41 in.).
1939.
Private collection.

586 'Vestal' firescreen

Black lacquer with gold design.
Height 104 cm (41 in.).
1939.
Private collection.

587 'Light' firescreen

Black lacquer with gold design.
1939.

588 'Sunflower' andirons

Wrought iron and *repoussé* copper.
C. 1910.

589 Voluted andirons

Wrought iron.
Length 40 cm (15¾ in.).
C. 1930.
Formerly in the collections of Madeleine Vionnet and Félix Marcilhac, Paris; Private collection.

LIGHTING

590 'Standing Figure' table lamp *Pl. 167*

Carved wooden figure by Jean Lambert-Rucki lacquered in Dunand's workshops, metal base.
Height 110 cm (43¼ in.).
1923.
Exh.: Galerie Georges Petit, Paris, 1923, no. 17; Delorenzo Gallery, New York, 1985 (repr. in catalogue, p. 145).
Formerly in the Labourdette and Couvrat-Desvergnes Collections.
Bibl.: *Mobilier et décoration*, February 1926, p. 38; *Encyclopédie des métiers d'art* (Paris, n.d.), pl. 36; *Jean Dunand – Jean Goulden*, exhibition catalogue, Galerie du Luxembourg (Paris, 1973), repr. p. 12; Yvonne

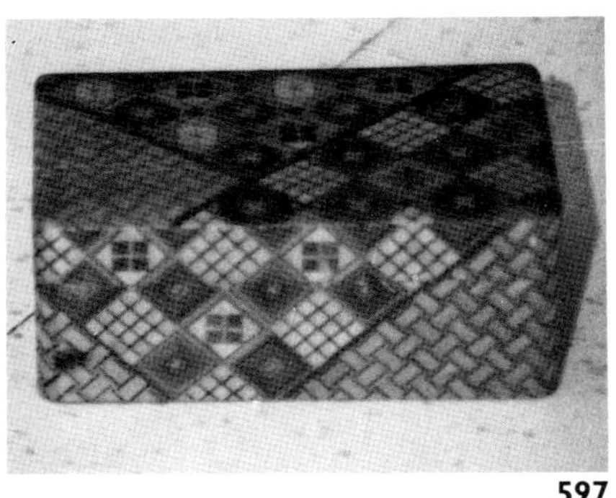
597

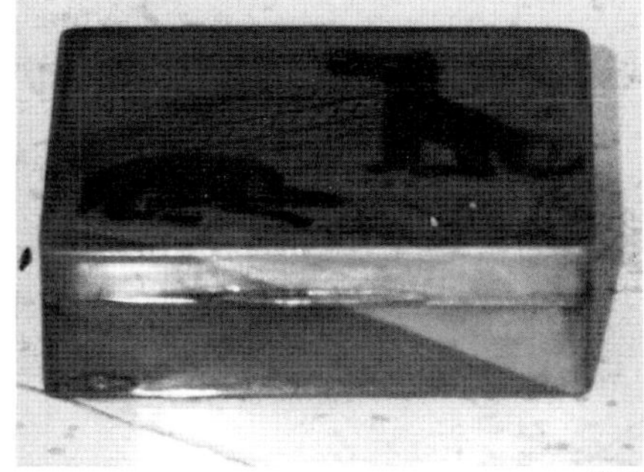
598

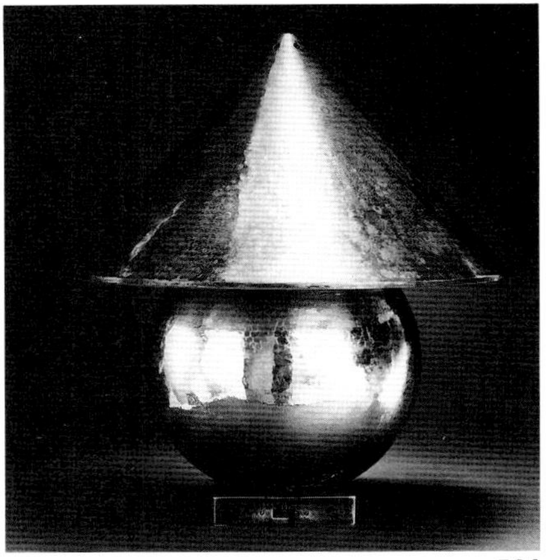
591

Brunhammer, *Le Style 1925* (Paris, 1978), repr. p. 184.
Sold: Sotheby's (New York), 17 November 1984, lot 317.

591 Conical table lamp
Polished pewter base and patinated copper shade.
Overall height 40 cm (15¾ in.).
C. 1925.
Exh.: Delorenzo Gallery, New York, 1985 (repr. in catalogue, p.144).
Coll.: Mr and Mrs Jay Bauer.

592 Conical table lamp
Spherical base in beaten pewter, conical shade in copper inlaid with silver.
Overall height 40 cm (15¾ in.).
C. 1925.
Private collection.

593 'Mushroom' lamp
Made *c.* 1930 and lacquered in Dunand's workshops.
Overall height 95 cm (37½ in.).
Coll.: Pierre Hebey.
Sold: Couturier, de Nicolay (Paris), 23 March 1981, lot 147.

594 'Mushroom' table lamp
Dinanderie shade and patinated metal base.
Height 35 cm (13¾ in.).
1931, designed by Eugène Printz.
Formerly in the Yacoubovitch Collection.
Bibl.: *Art et décoration*, February 1933, p. 65.
Sold: Christie's (New York), 27 May 1982, lot 117.

595 Reflector standard lamp
Hammered and gilt copper and gilt brass.
Height 180 cm (70¾ in.).
C. 1930.
Private collection.

596 'Fish' reflector
Black and coloured lacquer highlighted with gold and silver.
Height 50 cm (19¾ in.).
C. 1930.
Private collection.

LACQUERED CASKETS AND BOXES

597 Japanese box
Lacquered wood in imitation of Japanese inlay work.
1922.

598 'Two Dogs' box
Lacquered wood.
Made in 1923 after a design by Jean Lambert-Rucki.

599 'Three Dogs' box
Black-lacquered wood with a gold and silver lacquered motif after a design by Jean Lambert-Rucki.
1923.
Private collection.

600 Box *Pl. 97*
Red lacquered wood and eggshell mosaic.
C. 1922.
Private collection.

601 Box *Pl. 96*
Black lacquered wood with geometric motifs in red and silver lacquer and in eggshell mosaic.
C. 1925.

602 Box *Pl. 98*
Black lacquered wood with geometric motifs in red and silver lacquer.
C. 1925.
Coll.: M. and Mme Kupperfils, Evreux.

603 Box *Pl. 95*
Black lacquered wood with geometric motifs in red and silver lacquer.
C. 1925.
Private collection.

604 Box *Pl. 94*
Black-lacquered wood with radiating motifs in red and gold lacquer.
1925.
Exh.: Exposition Internationale des Arts Décoratifs et Industriels Modernes, Paris, 1925.
Private collection.

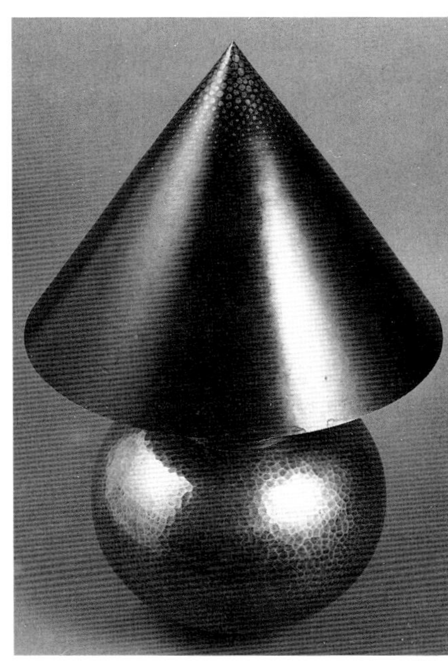
592

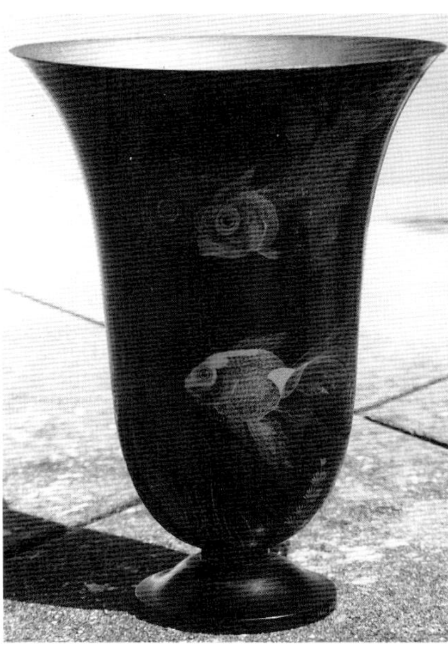
596

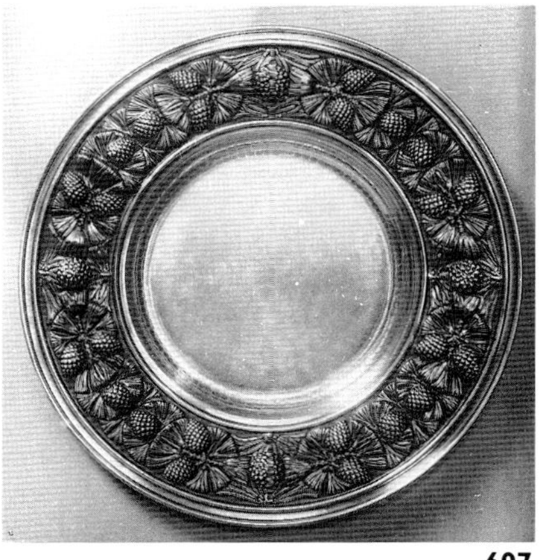
607

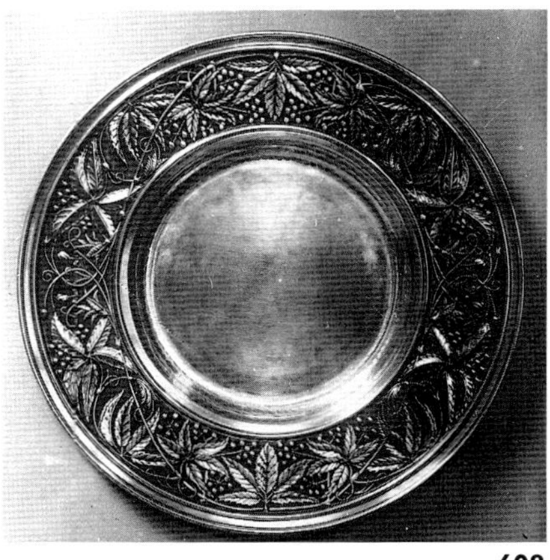
608

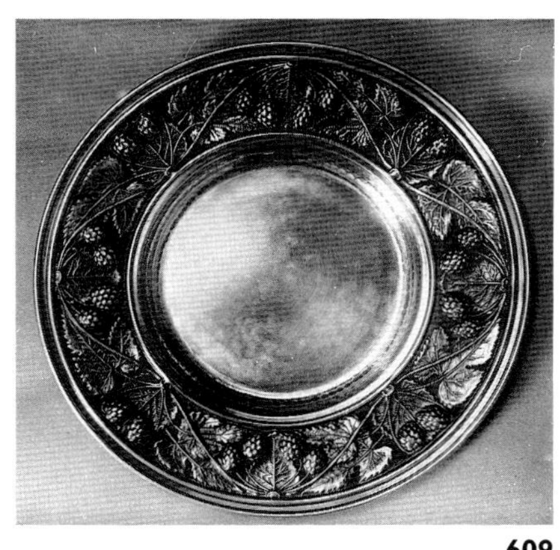
609

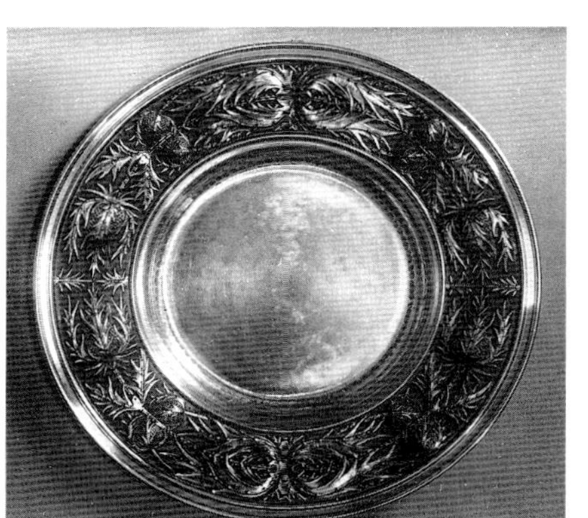
610

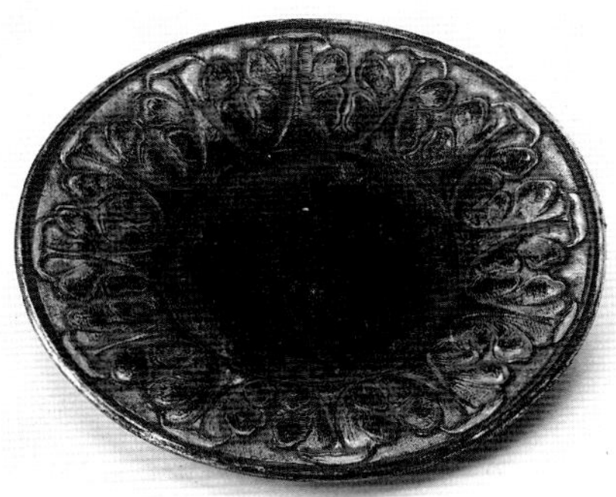
611

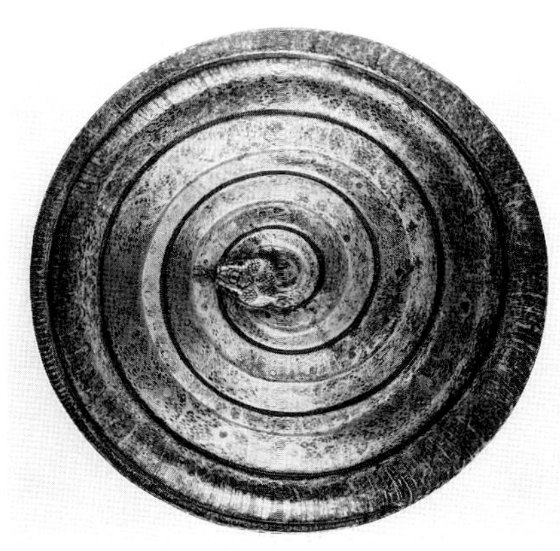
615

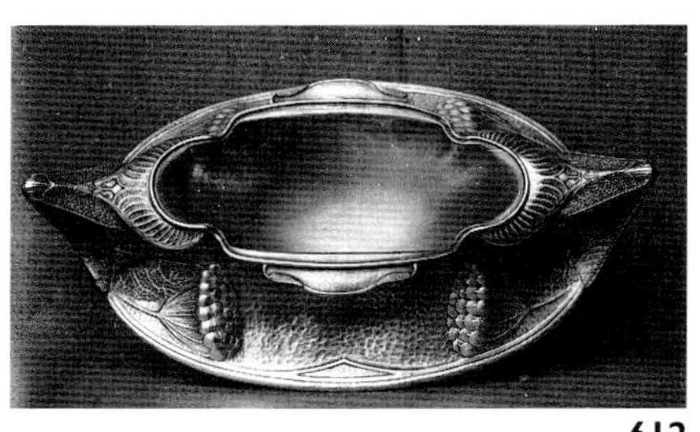
612

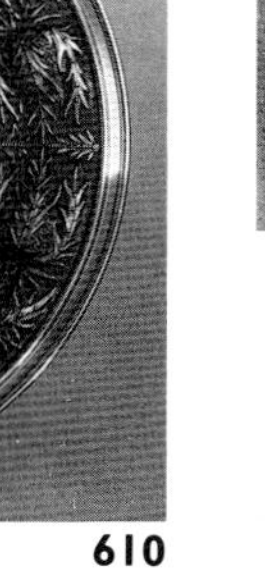

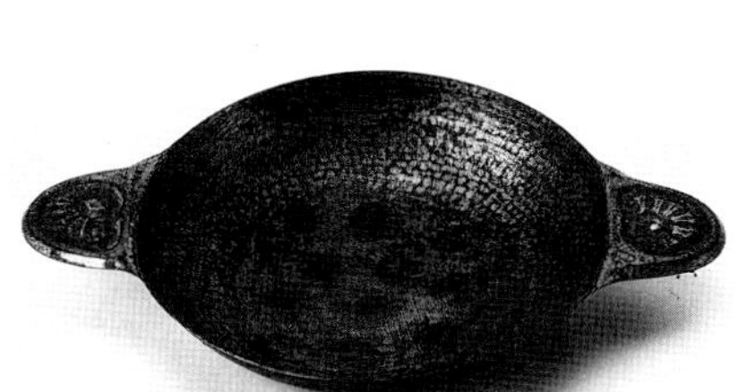
613

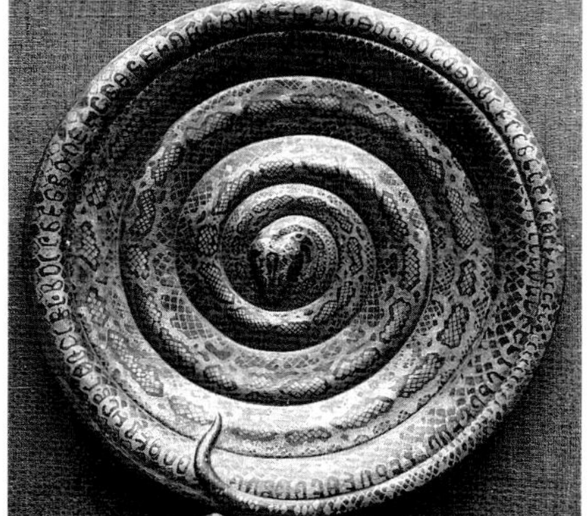
614

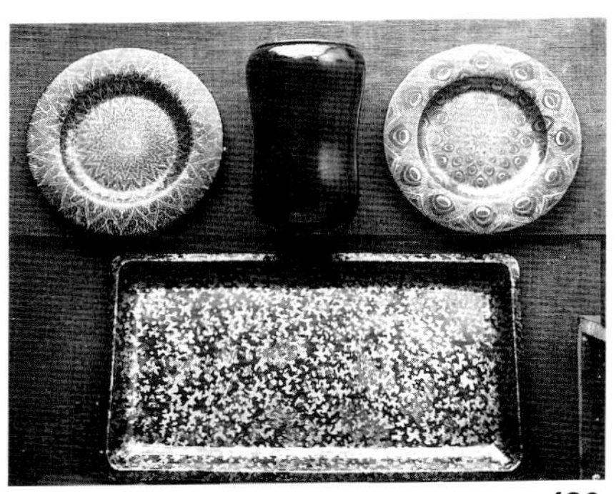
620

605 'Panther' box *Pl. 99*
Red-lacquered wood with black and silver animal design on a gold ground with geometric motifs.
C. 1922.
Exh.: Galerie Georges Petit, Paris, 1922.
Formerly in the collection of Félix Marcilhac, Paris; Private collection, New York.

606 'Mystery' box *Pl. 104*
Red-lacquered wood with geometric motifs, yellow and white gold.
C. 1924.
Private collection.

DISHES AND TRAYS

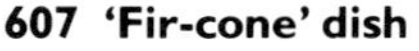

607 'Fir-cone' dish
Silvered *repoussé* copper.
Diameter 39 cm (15½ in.).
1909.
Exh.: Salon de l'Eclectique, Paris, December 1909.

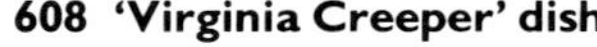

608 'Virginia Creeper' dish
Silvered *repoussé* copper.
Diameter 39 cm (15½ in.).
1909.
Exh.: Salon de l'Eclectique, Paris, December 1909.

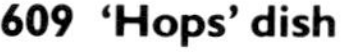

609 'Hops' dish
Silvered *repoussé* copper.
Diameter 39 cm (15½ in.).
1909.
Exh.: Salon de l'Eclectique, Paris, December 1909.
Formerly in the collection of the Musée du Luxembourg, Paris; Musée National d'Art Moderne, Musée d'Orsay, Paris.

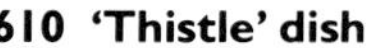

610 'Thistle' dish
Silvered *repoussé* copper.
Diameter 39 cm (15½ in.).
1909.

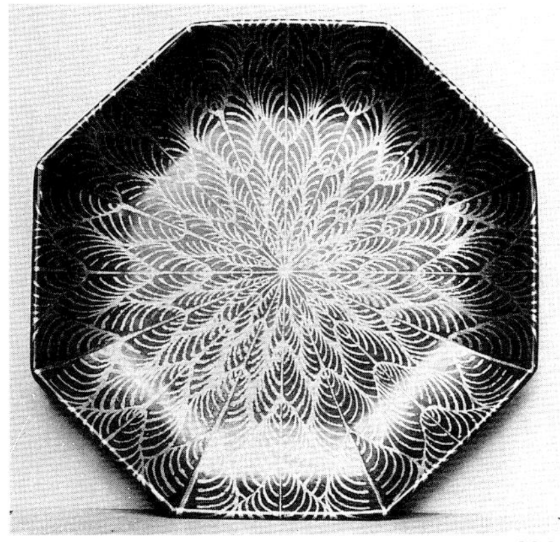
623

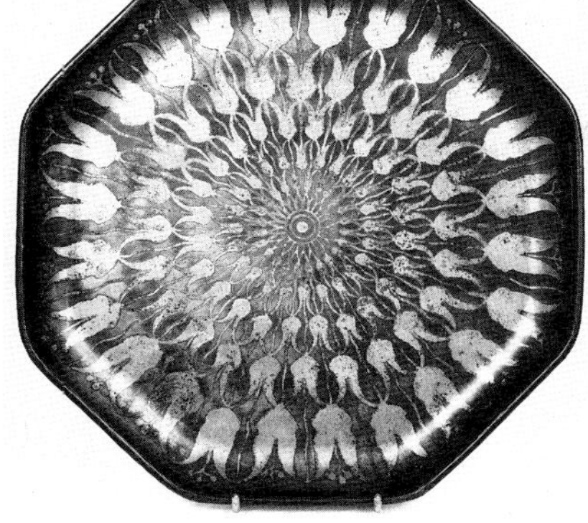
617

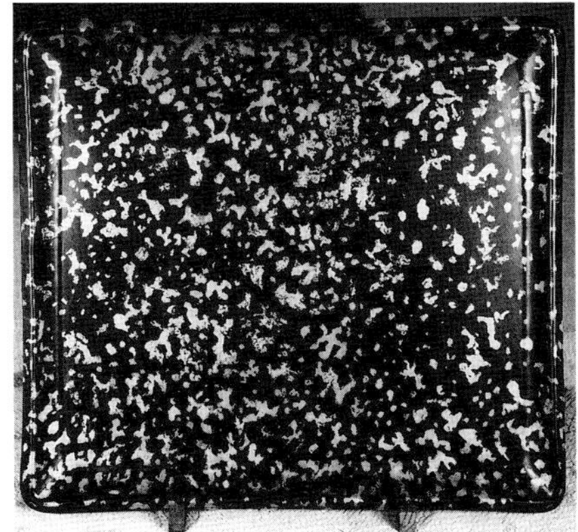
618

Exh.: Salon de l'Eclectique, Paris, December 1909.
Formerly in the collection of the Musée du Luxembourg, Paris; Musée National d'Art Moderne, Musée d'Orsay, Paris.

611 'Lanceolate Leaf' dish
Gilded and patinated *repoussé* metal.
1908.
Exh.: La Cimaise, Paris, 1909.

612 'Umbel' jardinière
Repoussé silver.
1908.
Exh.: Salon de la Nationale, Paris, 1908.
Bibl.: *L'Art décoratif*, January 1909, p. 17.

613 Bowl with handles
Patinated metal, *repoussé* handles with nautilus motifs.
C. 1920.
Private collection.

614 'Snake' dish
Copper with *repoussé* silver inlay work.
1912.
Exh.: Salon de l'Eclectique, Paris, 1912; Salon d'Automne, Paris, 1912; Galerie Manzi, Paris, February 1913.
Bought by the French State in November 1912.

615 'Snake' dish
Variant of cat. no. 614 made in 1913.
Copper with *repoussé* silver inlay work.
Coll.: Yves Saint Laurent and Pierre Bergé, Paris.

616 'Three Snakes' dish *Pl. 101*
Variant of cat. no. 614 made in 1913.
Copper with *repoussé* silver inlay work.
Coll.: Pierre Hebey.

617 Octagonal dish
Patinated nickel silver with silver inlay work.
Diameter 30 cm (11¾ in.).
C. 1912.
Formerly in the collection of Félix Marcilhac, Paris; Private collection.

618 Large square dish
Patinated nickel silver with silver inlay work.
50 x 50 cm (19¾ x 19¾ in.).
C. 1912.
Formerly in the collection of the Galerie Vallois, Paris; Private collection.

619 Two dishes and an ovoid vase
Hammered and patinated brass inlaid with silver.
1912.
Exh.: Salon de la Nationale, Paris, 1912.

620 Vase, rectangular dish and bowls
Hammered and patinated brass inlaid with silver.
1912.
Salon de la Nationale, Paris, 1912.

621 Large dish and vases
Hammered and patinated nickel silver.
C. 1912.

622 Square dishes and rectangular boxes
Hammered and patinated nickel silver inlaid with silver.
C. 1912.
Exh.: Salon de l'Eclectique, Paris, 1912.

623 Octagonal dish
Hammered and patinated nickel silver inlaid with silver.
C. 1912 .

624 Fruit bowl
Hammered and patinated copper inlaid with silver.
C. 1912.
Formerly in the collection of Félix Marcilhac, Paris.

625 Fruit bowl
Hammered and patinated copper inlaid with silver.
C. 1912.
Private collection.

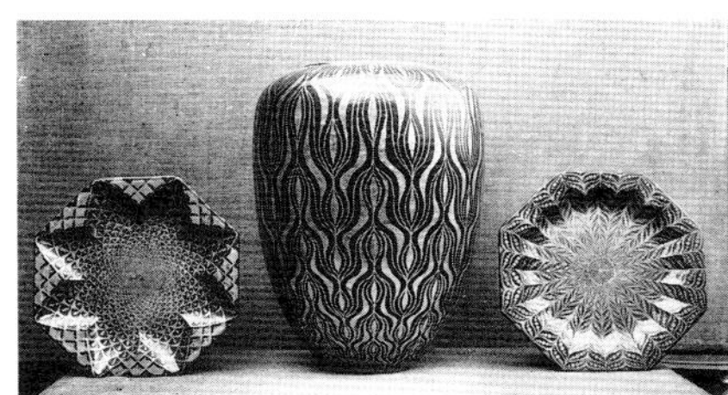
619

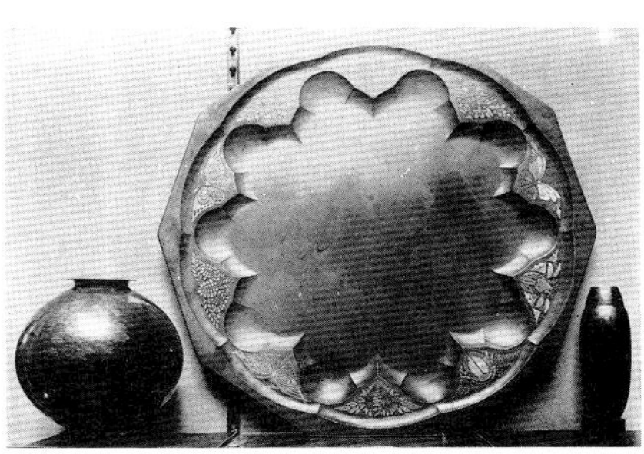
621

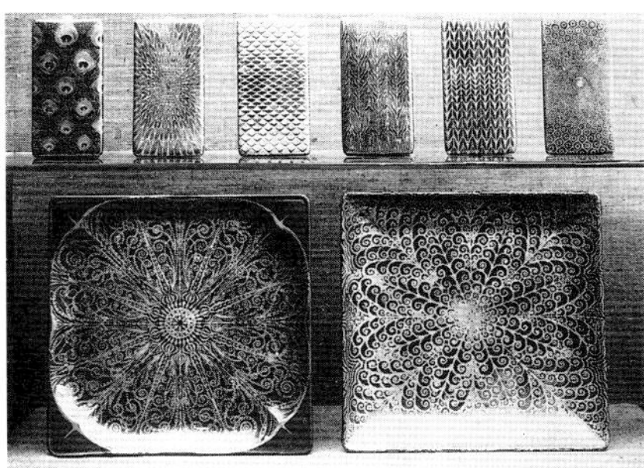
622

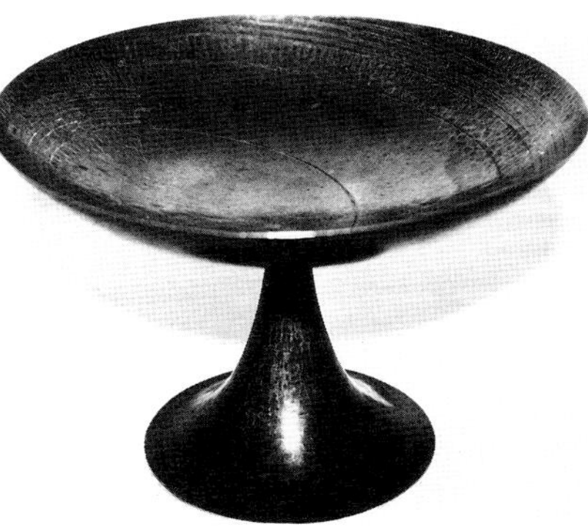
624

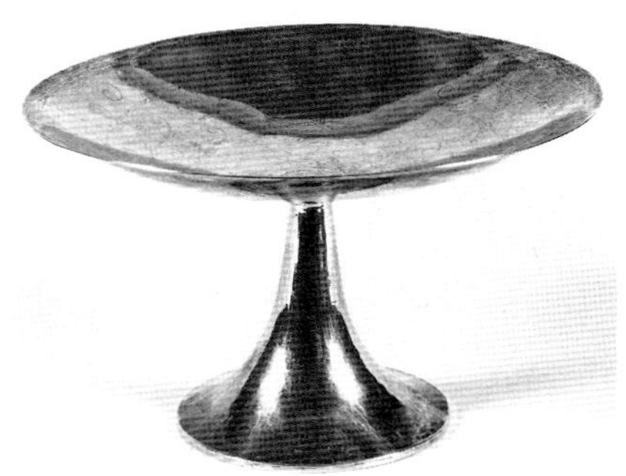
626

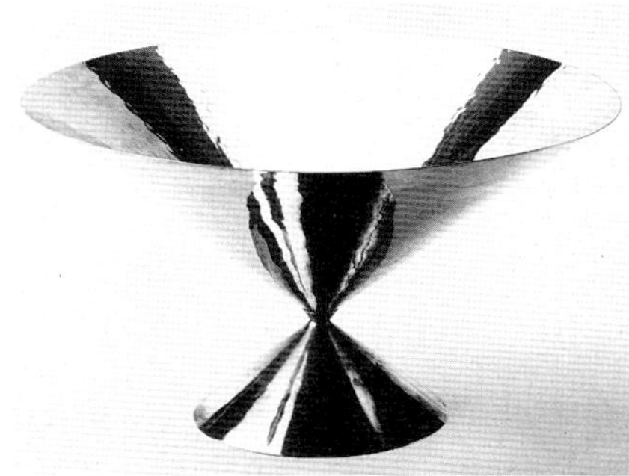
627

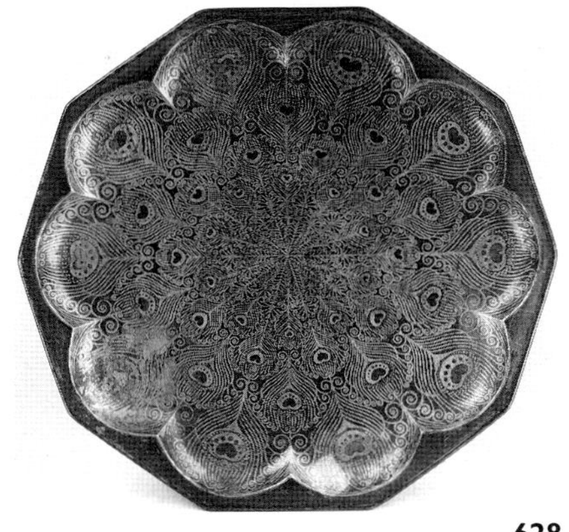
628

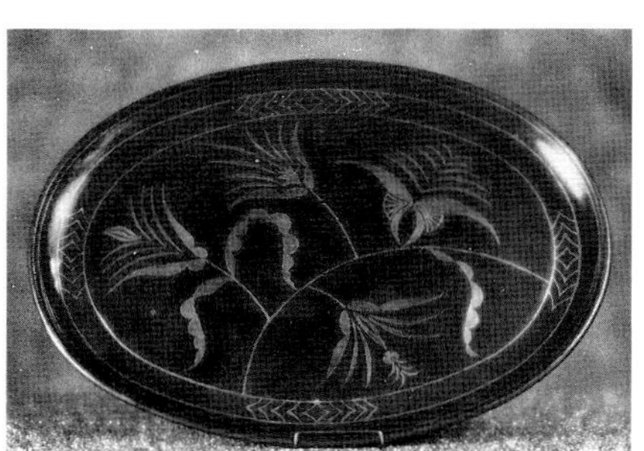
629

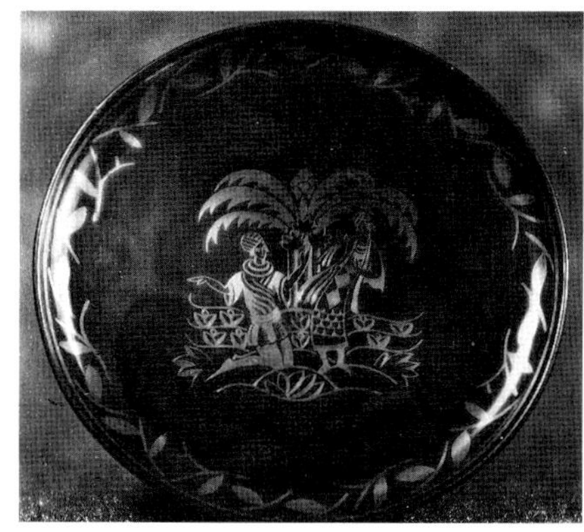
630

632

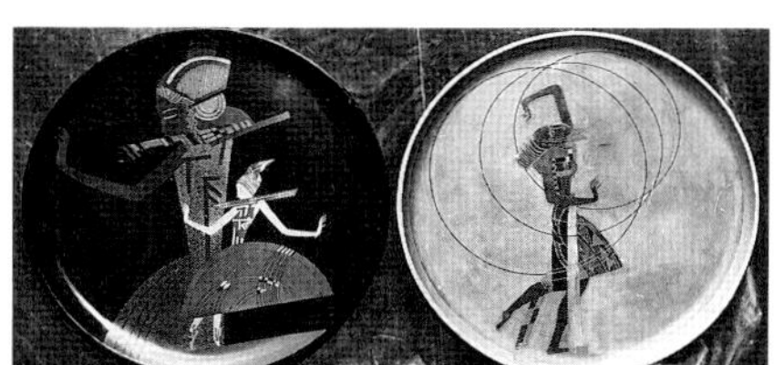
634, 635

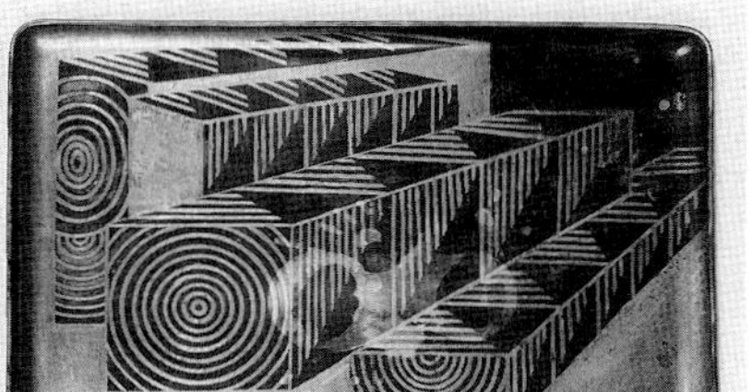
633

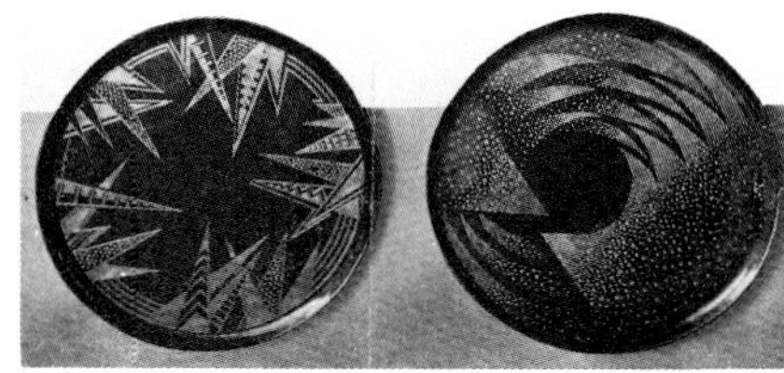
637

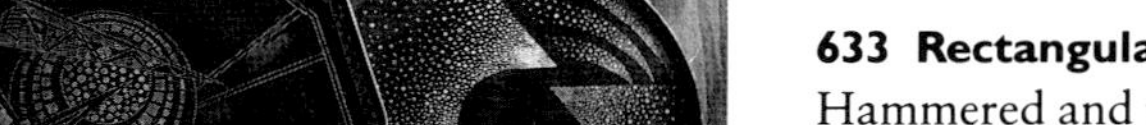
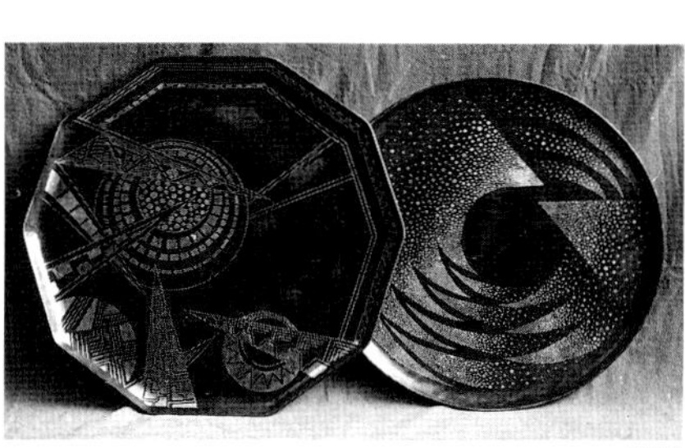
638

626 Fruit bowl
Hammered and patinated copper inlaid with silver.
C. 1912.
Private collection.

627 Dish on stand
Hammered silver.
C. 1914.
Private collection.

628 Decagonal 'Peacock-feather' dish
Brass inlaid with silver.
C. 1914.
Exh.: Salon de l'Eclectique, 1914.
Coll.: Musée d'Orsay, Paris.

629 'Flowers' oval dish
Copper inlaid with silver.
Made *c.* 1925 to a design by Georges Dorignac.

630 'Beneath the Palm Tree' round dish
Copper inlaid with silver.
Made *c.* 1925 to a design by Georges Dorignac.

631 'Fish' rectangular dish
Patinated brass inlaid with silver.
C. 1925.

632 'Three Snakes' bowl
Hammered brass and patinated bronze.
Height 38 cm (15 in.); diameter 67 cm (26½ in.).
1922.
Private collection.

633 Rectangular tray
Hammered and patinated brass inlaid with silver.
53 x 33 cm (20¾ x 13 in.).
C. 1925.
Formerly in the collection of Anne-Sophie Duval; Alain Lesieutre, Paris.

634, 635 'Dancing Figure' trays
Blue lacquered wood and rose-pink lacquered wood.
Diameter 43 cm (17 in.).
Made in 1923 to designs by Jean Lambert-Rucki.

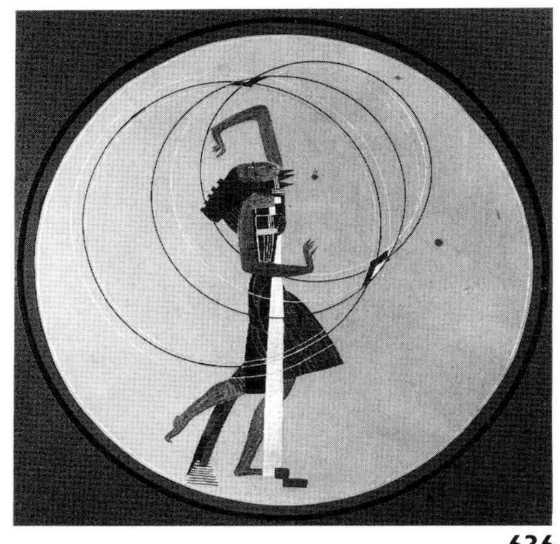
636

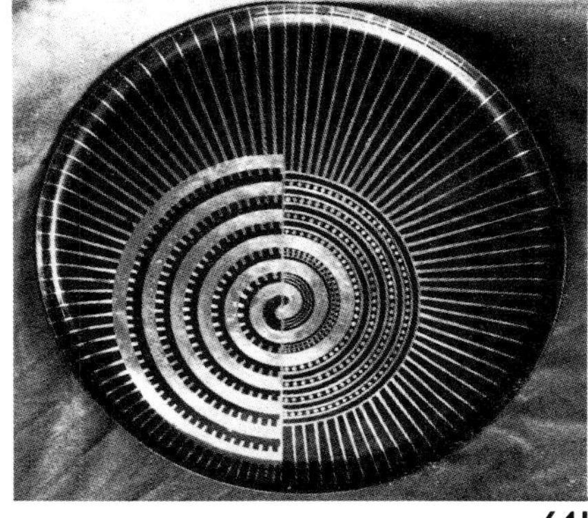
641

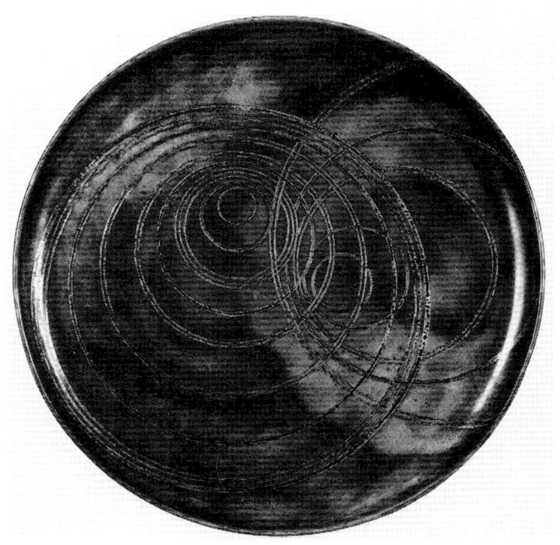
639

Exh.: Galerie Georges Petit, Paris, 1923, nos. 20 and 21.
Bibl.: *Mobilier et décoration*, February 1926, pp. 44–5; *Jean Dunand – Jean Goulden*, exhibition catalogue, Galerie du Luxembourg (Paris, 1973), pp. 3 and 13.

636 'Dancing Figure' tray
Original gouache for cat. no. 635.
Exh.: *Decorative Arts: 1925 Style*, Didier Aaron, Inc., New York, 1979 (repr. on cover of catalogue).
Formerly in the collection of Félix Marcilhac, Paris; Private collection.

637 Circular trays
Hammered and patinated copper inlaid with silver.
C. 1925.
Bibl.: *Les Échos des industries d'art*, August 1928, p. 22.

638 Circular tray and decagonal tray
Hammered and patinated copper inlaid with silver.
1925.
Exh.: Exposition Internationale des Arts Décoratifs et Industriels Modernes, Paris, 1925.
Bibl.: *Mobilier et décoration*, February 1926, p. 36.

639, 640 Circular Trays
Hammered and patinated copper inlaid with silver.
C. 1925.
Sold: Sotheby's (Monaco), 24/25 October 1982, lots 420 and 421.

641 Circular tray
Hammered and patinated copper inlaid with silver.
C. 1925.
Private collection.

642 Geometric design
Original gouache on black paper, study for a dish design.
33 x 31 cm (13 x 12¼ in.).
C. 1922.
Private collection.

643 Decagonal dish
Patinated copper inlaid with silver.
Diameter 61 cm (24 in.).
1925.
Exh.: Exposition Internationale des Arts Décoratifs et Industriels Modernes, Paris, 1925.
Coll.: Musée des Beaux-Arts, Lyons (acquired from the artist in 1926).
Bibl.: *Mobilier et décoration*, February 1926, p. 36.

644 Decagonal dish *Pl. 100*
Patinated copper inlaid with silver.
Diameter 61 cm (24 in.).
C. 1928.
Sold: Boisgirard (Paris), 26 October 1988, lot 124.

645 'Roses and Butterflies' decagonal dish
Patinated copper inlaid with silver.
Diameter 61 cm (24 in.).
C. 1928.
Bibl.: 'Une Visite au décorateur Jean Dunand', *La Patrie Suisse*, November 1933.

646 Rectangular dish with raised rim *Pl. 103*
Black lacquered wood with geometric design in gold.
50 x 35 cm (19¾ x 13¾ in.).
C. 1930.
Formerly in the collections of Félix Marcilhac and Alain Braunstein; Alain Lesieutre, Paris.

647 Circular dish with raised rim *Pl. 102*
Black lacquered wood with design in red lacquer highlighted with gold.
Diameter 37 cm (14½ in.).
C. 1930.
Private collection.

648 Two square trays *Pl. 105*
Black lacquered wood with geometric design in red lacquer highlighted with gold.
C. 1930.
Private collection.

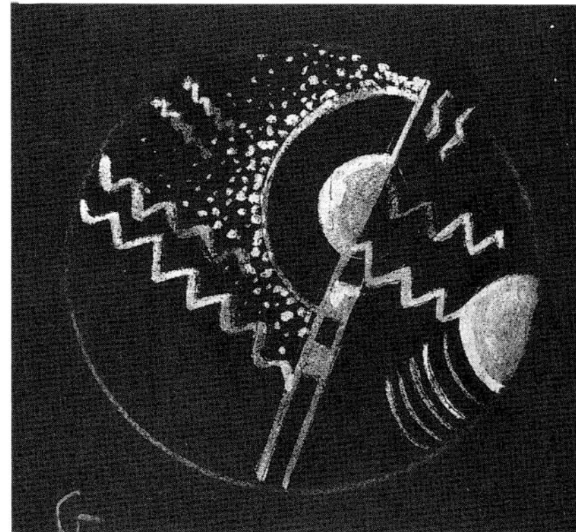
642

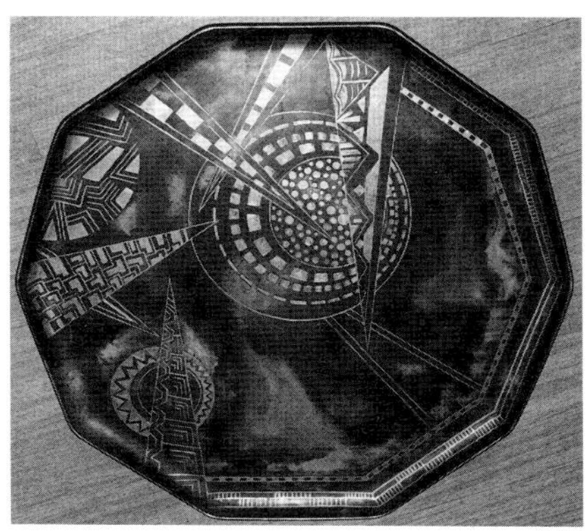
643

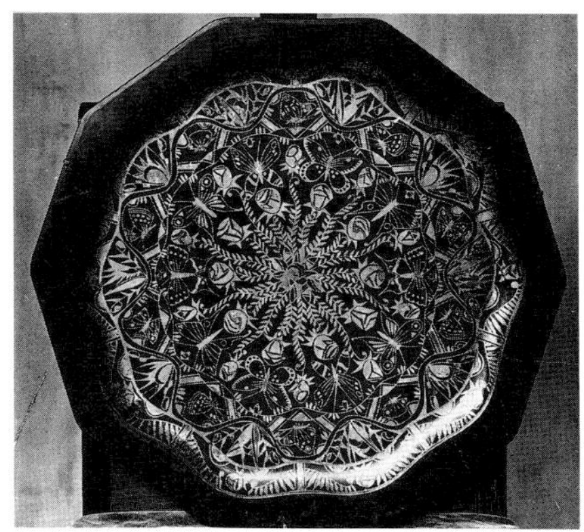
645

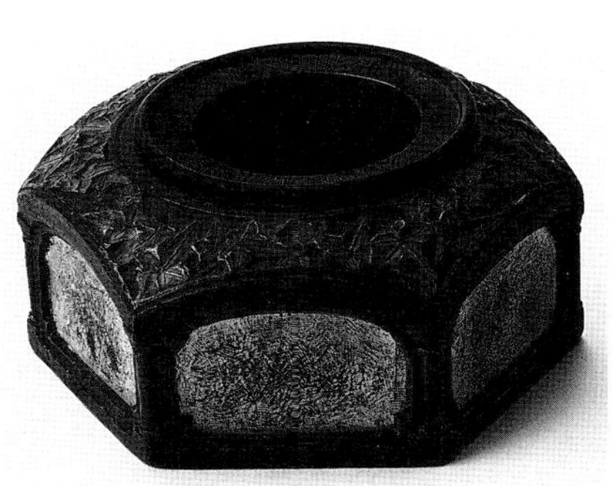

650

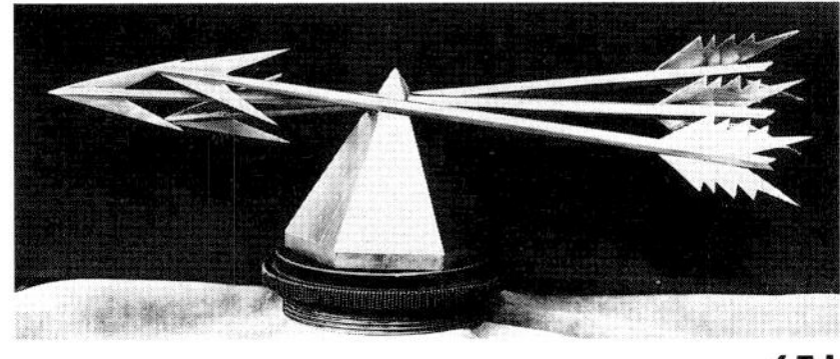

651

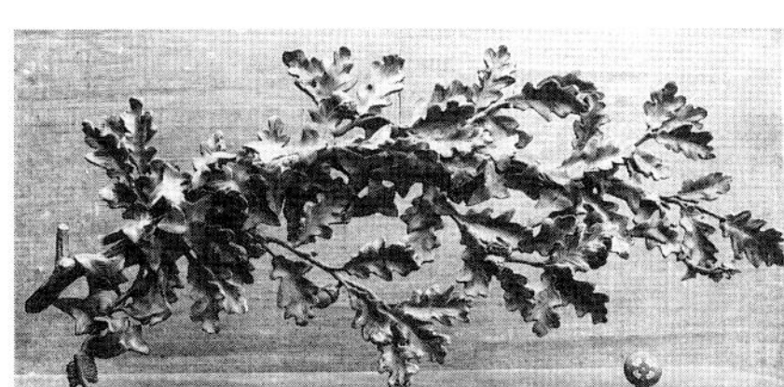

652

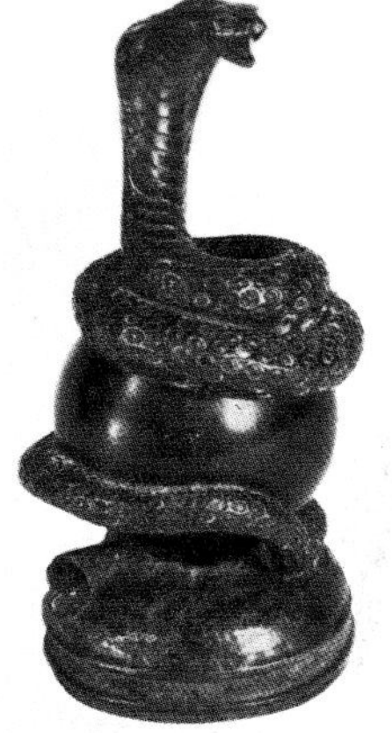

661

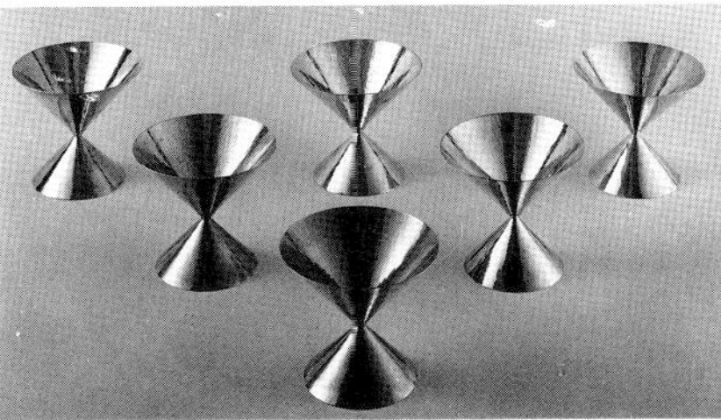

653

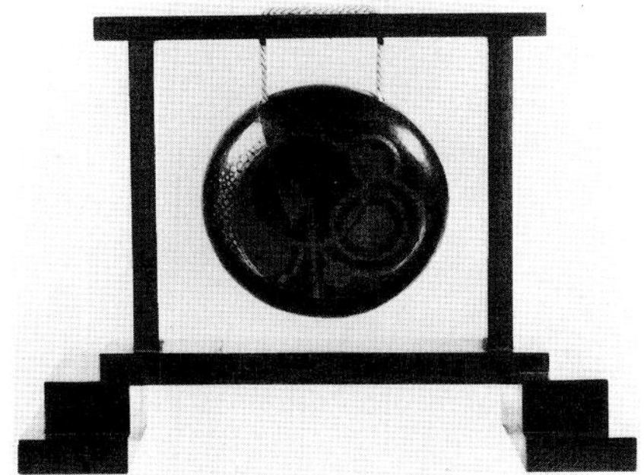

659

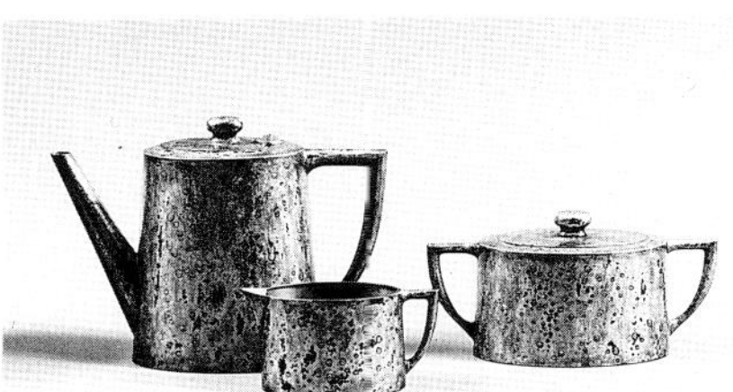

654

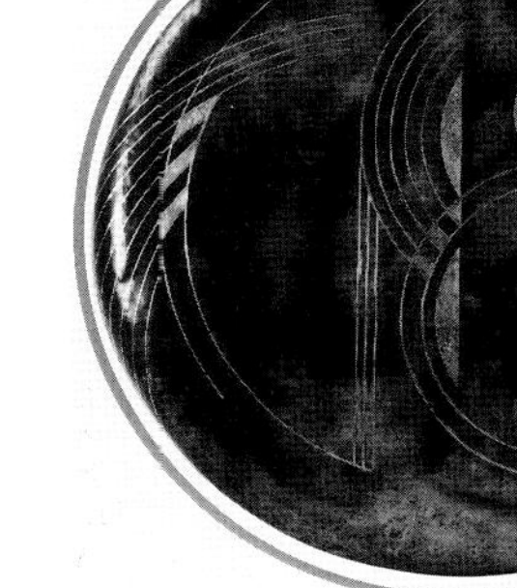

660

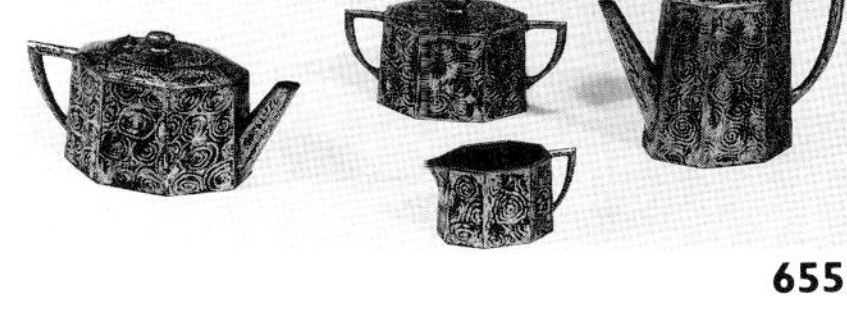

655

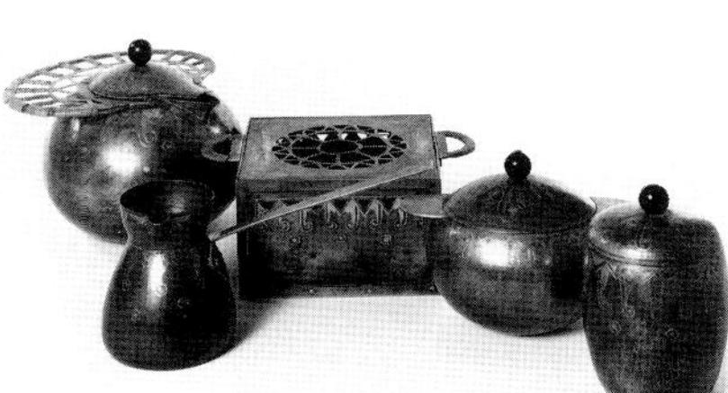

658

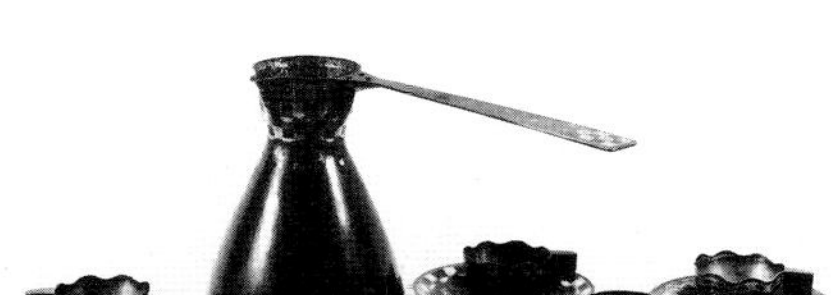

657

656

THE 'CADUCEUS' CLOCK

649 'Caduceus' clock *Pls. 92, 93*
Silver, gold and chased bronze, niello steel face, hands set with rhinestones, Gorgon's head in gilt *repoussé* copper; movement by Patek Philippe of Geneva.
Height 82 cm (32¼ in.).
1913.
Exh.: Salon de la Nationale, Paris, May 1913; Galerie Georges Petit, Paris, 1921.
Formerly in the collection of Jean-Philippe Worth; Félix Marcilhac, Paris.

OTHER HOUSEHOLD ITEMS

650 Inkwell
Gilt chased bronze.
Diameter 12 cm (4¾ in.).
C. 1910.
Sold: Sotheby's (Monaco), 19 April 1982, lot 191.

651 'The Three Arrows' radiator cap
Silvered bronze.
1925.
Exh.: Exposition Internationale des Arts Décoratifs et Industriels Modernes, Paris, 1925.
Bibl.: *L'Art vivant*, 15 November 1925, p. 28.

652 Branch of oak leaves
Repoussé copper.
C. 1913.

653 Cocktail service
Hammer-marked silver.
C. 1914.
Private collection.

654 Three-piece service
Oroide, brushed gold lacquer on a black-lacquer ground.
1924.
Sold: Boisgirard (Paris), 26 October 1988, lot 116.

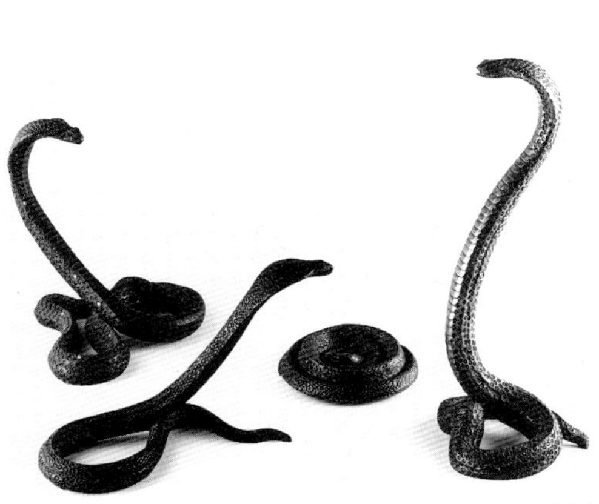

664

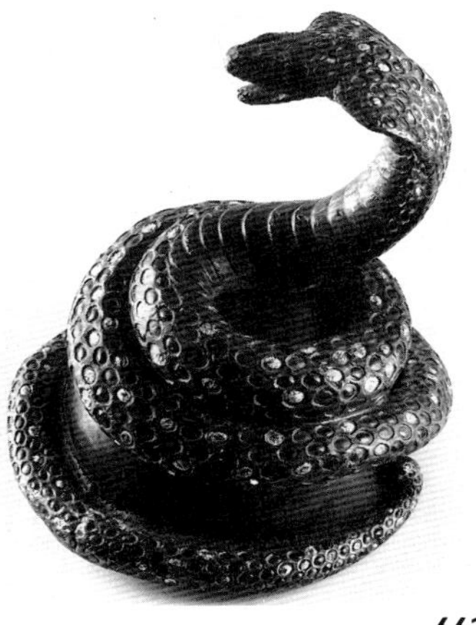

662

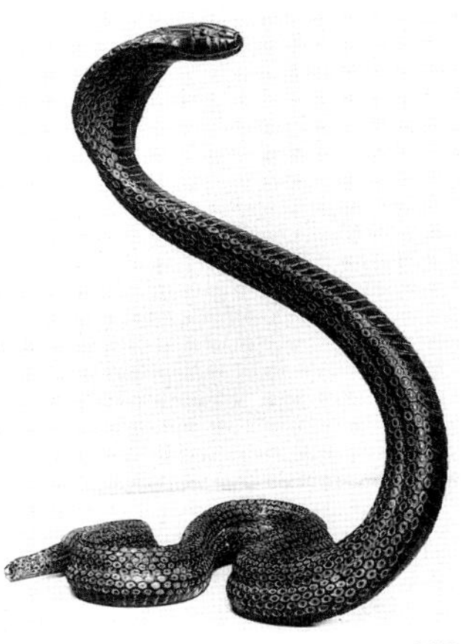

663

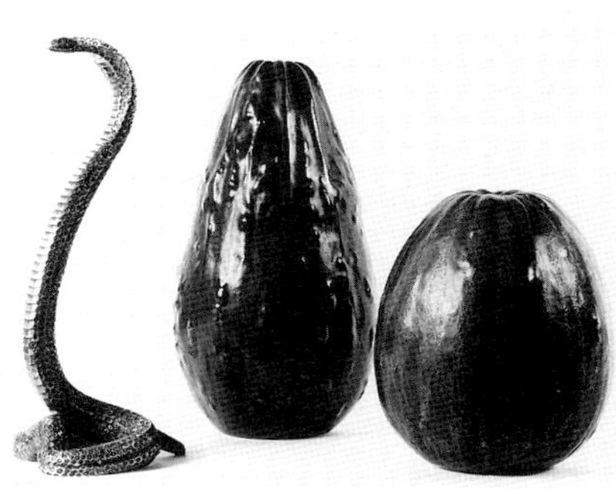

667

655 Four-piece service
Oroide, gold lacquer design on a black-lacquer ground.
1924.
Sold: Laurin, Guilloux, Buffetaud, Tailleur (Paris), 25 November 1972, lot 120.

656 Tea service with warming plate
Patinated nickel silver inlaid with silver, cane handles.
C. 1912.
Bibl.: *Art et décoration*, April 1922, p. 124; *La Nature*, February 1924, p. 84.

657 Turkish coffee service
Patinated nickel silver inlaid with silver.
C. 1912

658 Tea service and Turkish coffee service with warming plate
Patinated nickel silver inlaid with silver, cane handles.
C. 1912.
Sold: Sotheby's (Monaco), 23 June 1979, lot 256.

659 Gong with wooden stand
Hammered and patinated brass inlaid with silver.
Diameter 63 cm (24¾ in.).
C. 1925.
Exh.: Delorenzo Gallery, New York, 1985 (repr. in catalogue, p. 154).
Sold: Sotheby's (Monaco), 23 June 1979, lot 255.

660 Gong
Hammered and patinated brass inlaid with silver.
Diameter 59 cm (23¼ in.).
C. 1925.
Sold: Sotheby's (Monaco), 13 April 1986, lot 312.

661 Rearing Snake
Patinated chased bronze.
Height 16 cm (6¼ in.).
1915.
Sold: Blache (Versailles), 7 March 1976, lot 126.

662 Coiled Snake
Patinated chased lead.
Height 11 cm (4½ in.).
C. 1915.
Sold: Laurin, Guilloux, Buffetaud, Tailleur (Paris), 25 November 1977, lot 114.

663 Rearing Cobra
Patinated chased bronze.
Height 37 cm (14½ in.).
1914.
Bibl.: *Art et décoration*, September/October 1919, p. 118.

664 Snakes Coiled, Rearing and Attacking
Patinated chased bronze.
Height 16 cm (6¼ in.); length 20 cm (7¾ in.); diameter 10 cm (4 in.).
1914.
Coll.: Alain Lesieutre, Paris.

665 Cobra Attacking
Patinated chased bronze.
Height 31 cm (12¼ in.).
1914 .
Coll.: Jean-Marc Maury.

666 Cobra Advancing
Patinated chased bronze.
Height 40 cm (15¾ in.).
1914.
Coll.: Alain Lesieutre, Paris.

667 Hissing Cobra and Gourds
Patinated chased bronze.
Height: snake 26.5 cm (10½ in.); gourds 26 cm (10¼ in.) and 18 cm (7 in.).
1914.
Sold: Champin, Lombrail, Gautier (Enghien), 28 October 1979, lots 159 (snake) and 160, 161 (gourds).

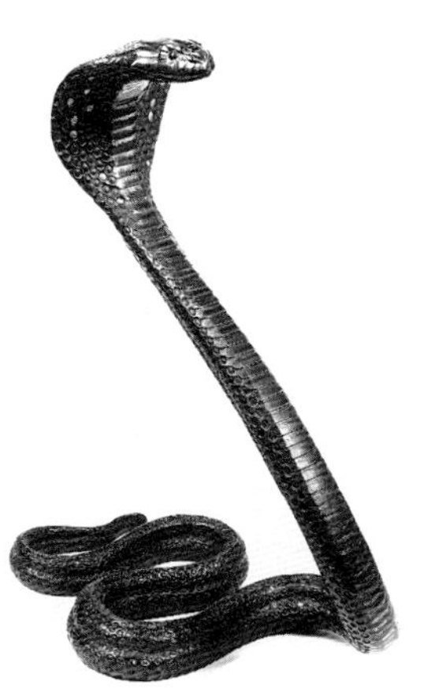

665

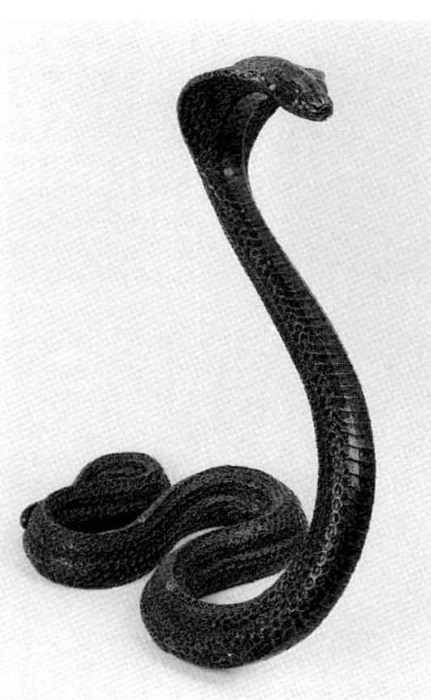

666

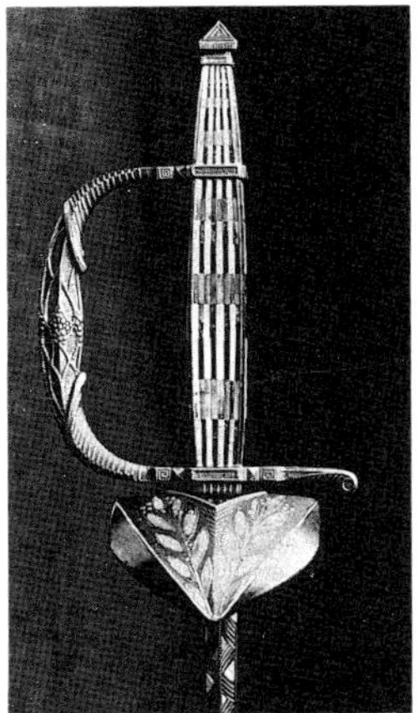
668

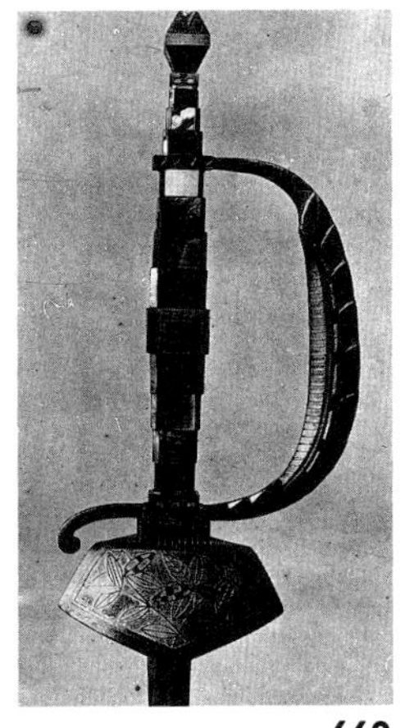
669

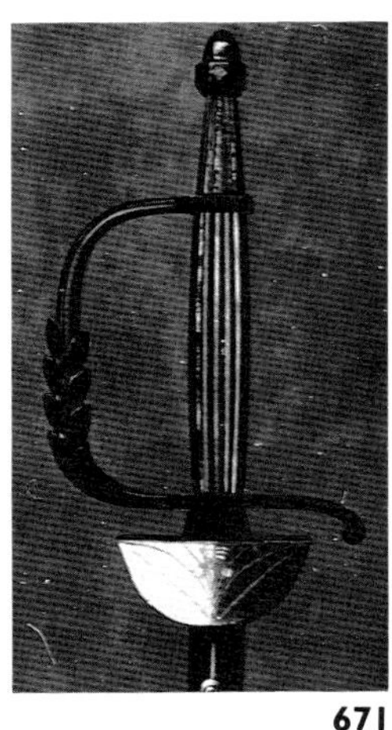
671

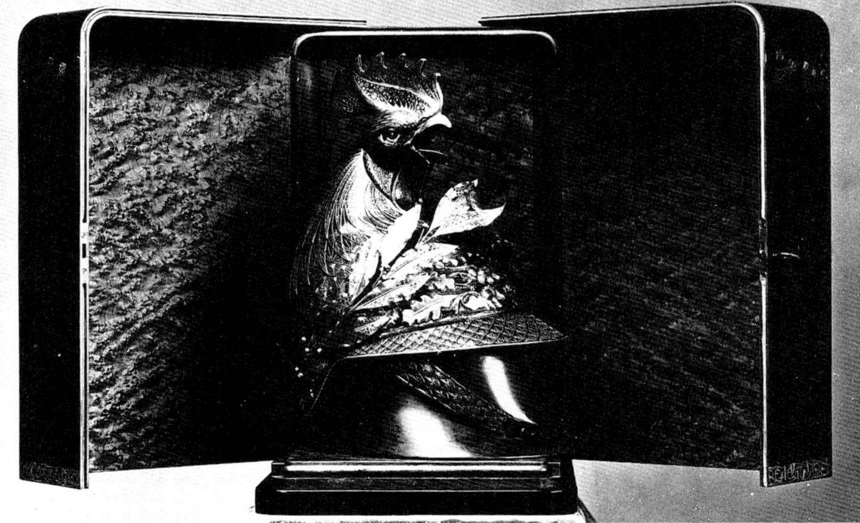
673b

674

CEREMONIAL SWORDS FOR MEMBERS OF THE INSTITUT DE FRANCE (ACADÉMIE FRANÇAISE AND ACADÉMIE DES BEAUX-ARTS)

668 Sword for Maître Henri-Robert
Steel inlaid with gold and silver, black-lacquered scabbard inlaid with white mother-of-pearl.
1924.
Exh.: Galerie Georges Petit, Paris, 1924, no. 14; ——, 1925, no. 36a.

669 Sword for Georges Lecomte
Steel inlaid with gold and silver, black-lacquered scabbard inlaid with eggshell.
1925.
Exh.: Galerie Georges Petit, Paris, 1925, no. 36b.

670 Sword for Paul Landowski
Details not known.
1926.

671 Sword for Fortunat Strowsky
Steel inlaid with gold and silver, black-lacquered scabbard inlaid with burgaudine and eggshell.
1929.

THE 'VICTORY HELMET'

672 Ceremonial helmet for Marshal Foch
Original sketch in white and yellow gouache on black paper.
50 x 35 cm (19¾ x 13¾ in.).
1921.
Private collection.

673 Ceremonial helmet for Marshal Foch
(a) Three-quarter view from the front, (b) helmet seen in its presentation casket, open.
Steel inlaid with silver and gold.
1921.

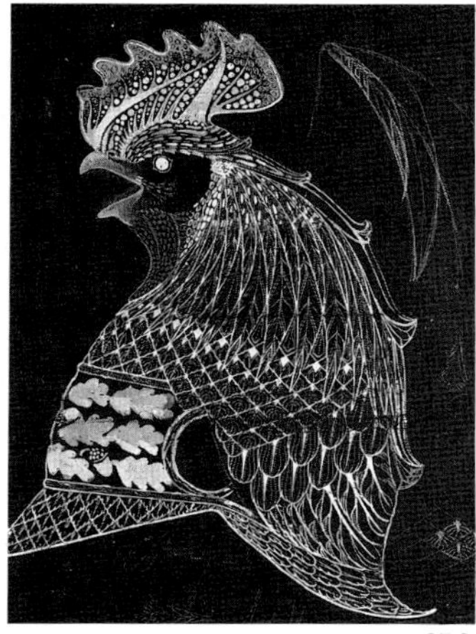
672

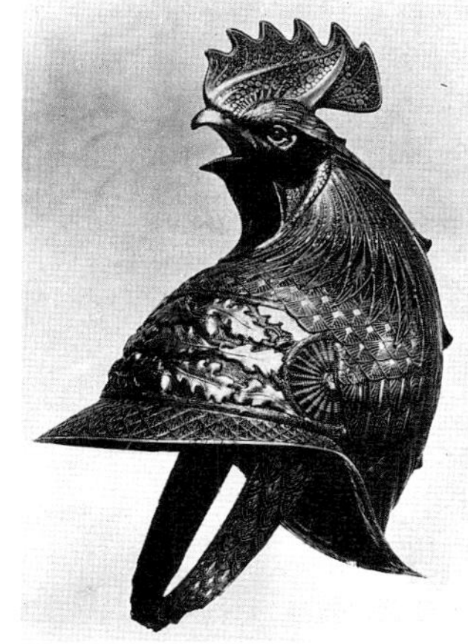
673a

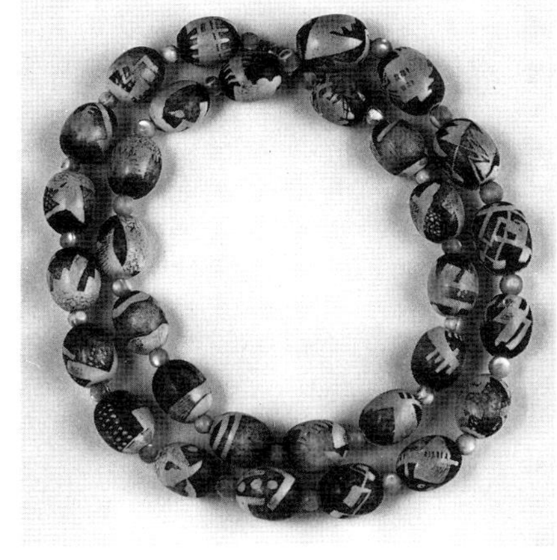
676

Coll.: Musée de l'Armée, Palais des Invalides, Paris (gift of Marshal Foch).
Bibl.: *The Studio*, 15 November 1923, p. 270.
See also p. 35.

674 Presentation casket for ceremonial helmet
Black lacquer inlaid with fragments of shrapnel, maplewood lining.
1921.
Coll.: Musée de l'Armée, Palais des Invalides, Paris (gift of Marshal Foch).

JEWELLERY

675 Chain necklace
Cylindrical links of gilt metal.
C. 1922.

676 Ivory necklace
Ivory beads with lacquered geometric motifs.
C. 1925.
Private collection.

677 Neck rings *Pl. 76*
Oroide decorated with lacquered geometric motifs.
1927.
Private collection.

678 Neck rings
Oroide decorated with lacquered geometric motifs.
1927.
Private collection.

679 Pair of bracelets *Pl. 78*
Silver with lacquered geometric motifs.
C. 1924.
Private collection.

680 Bracelet
Silver with red and black lacquered geometric motifs.
1924.
Private collection.

681 Wide bracelet *Pl. 80*
Silver with lacquered design.
C. 1925.
Coll.: Félix Marcilhac, Paris.

682 Bracelet and pair of matching ear-rings
Silver with black and red lacquered geometric motifs.
C. 1924.
Coll.: Galerie Vallois, Paris.

683 Wide bracelets *Pl. 79*
Silver with lacquered geometric motifs.
Length 12 cm (4¾ in.).
1927.
Formerly in the collection of Madame Agnès; Private collection.

684 Wide bracelet *Pl. 77*
Oroide with lacquered design.
Length 12 cm (4¾ in.).
1928.
Private collection.

685 Articulated bracelet *Pl. 81*
Silver and gilt metal, lacquered design of alternating squares.
Length (open) 16 cm (6¼ in.); height 5 cm (2 in.).
C. 1922.
Private collection.

686 Articulated bracelet *Pl. 82*
Wood and silver with lacquered geometric motifs.
C. 1930.
Private collection.

687 Ear-rings and brooch *Pl. 91*
Silver and gold or silver-gilt.
C. 1922–5.
Sold: Boisgirard (Paris), 16 October 1909, lots 109–113.

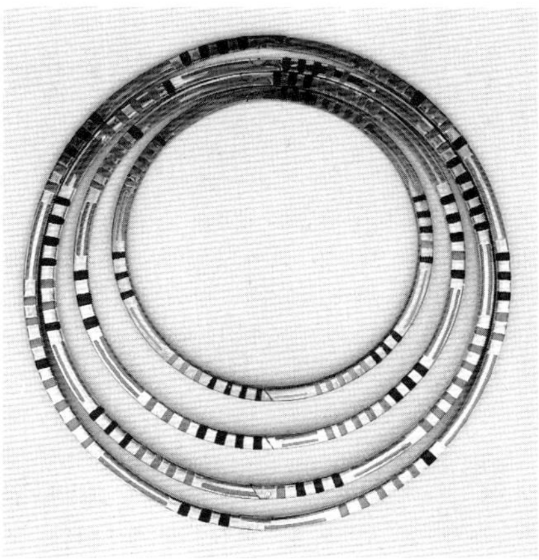
678

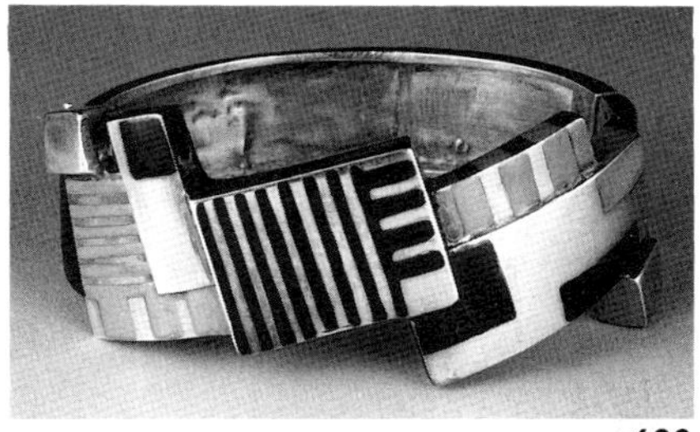
680

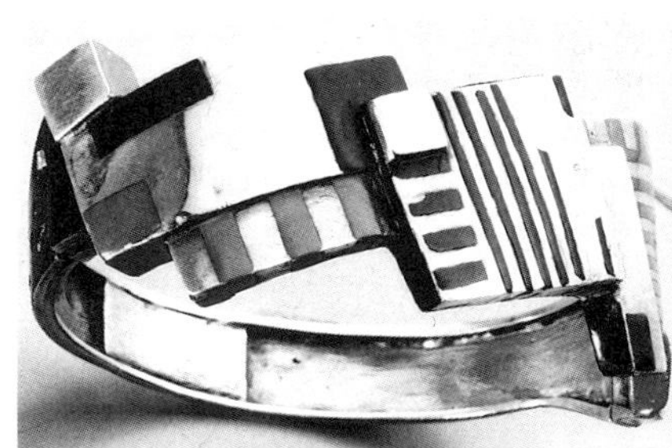

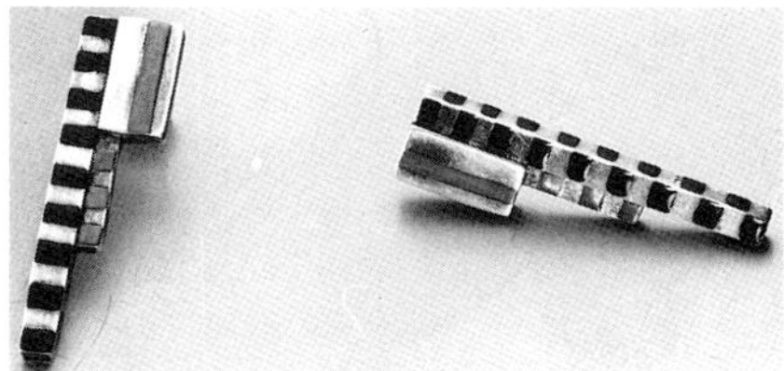
682

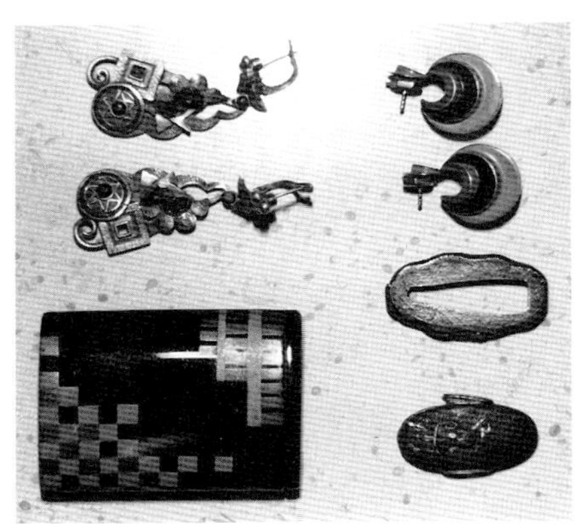

692

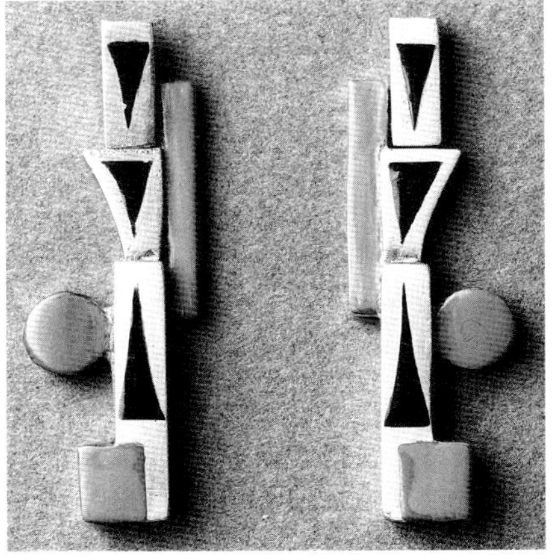

693

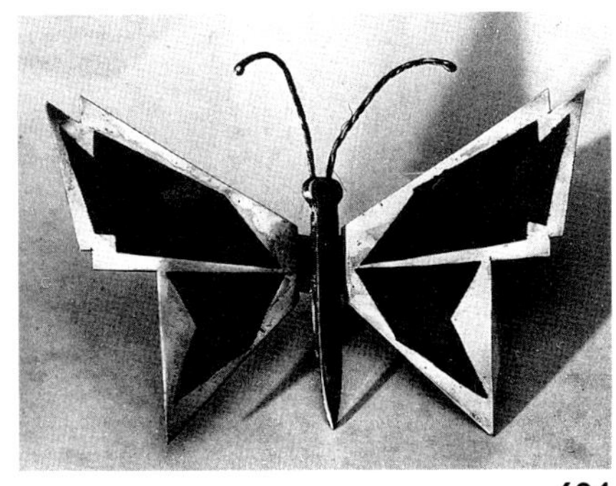

694

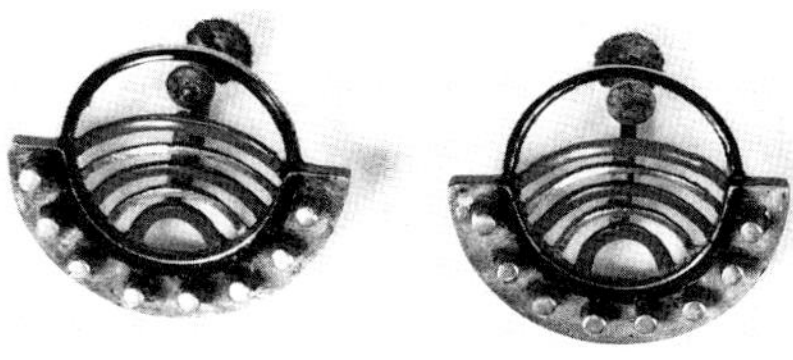

689

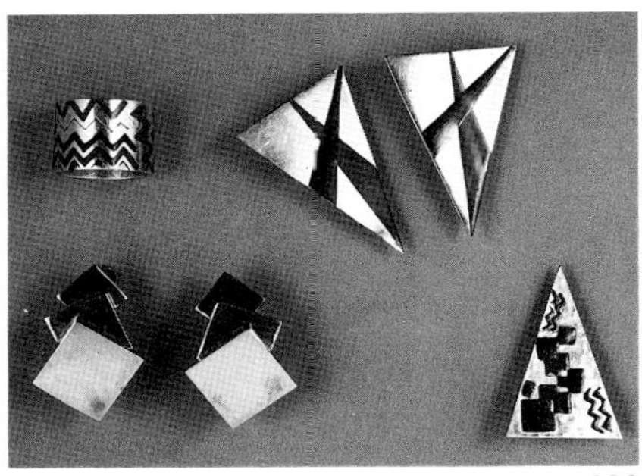

691

697

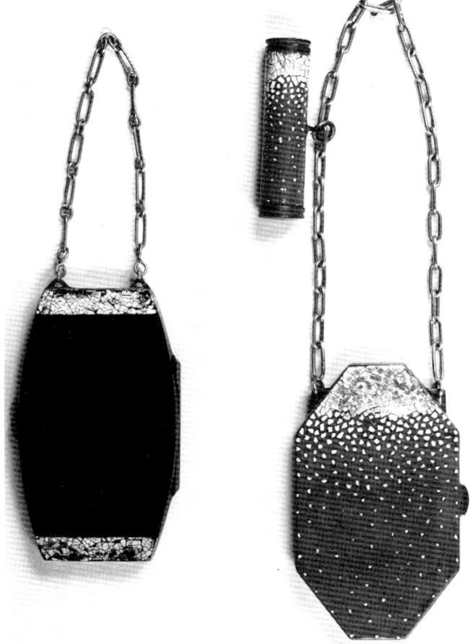

703

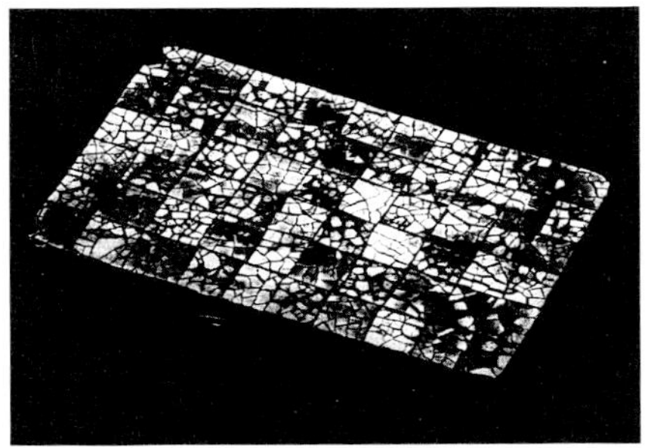

704

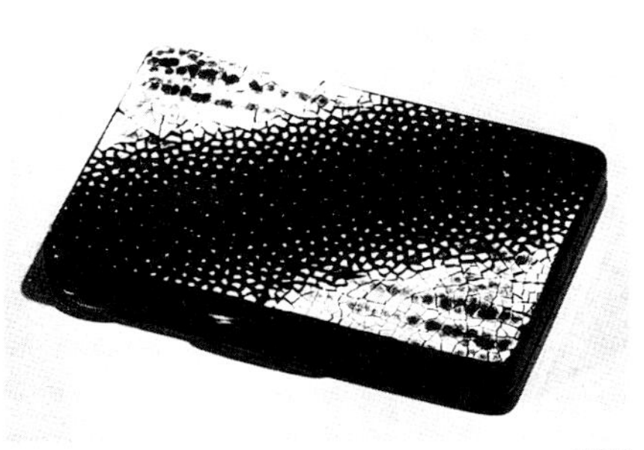

705

695

688 Ear-rings; ear-rings and brooch; handbag ornament; ear-rings; brooch *Pl. 84*

Silver (ear-rings) and other metals, all with lacquer decoration.
C. 1922–5.
Exh.: Delorenzo Gallery, New York, 1985 (repr. in catalogue, p. 159).
Coll.: Delorenzo Gallery, New York.

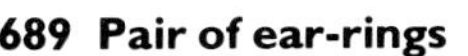

689 Pair of ear-rings

Silver with lacquered design.
C. 1922.
Private collection.

690 Ear-rings *Pl. 90*

Silver with lacquered geometric motifs, and hammered gold.
C. 1922–5.
Private collection.

691 Ring and ear-rings

Silver and silver-gilt with lacquered geometric motifs.
C. 1922–30.
Private collection.

692 Ear-rings and match holder

Gold and oroide with lacquered design.
C. 1925.
Private collection.

693 Pair of ear-rings

Soldered silver with lacquered design.
Length 5 cm (2 in.).
Formerly in the collection of Félix Marcilhac, Paris; Private collection.

694 Butterfly clip

Silvered metal with *champlevé* enamel design.
Length 10 cm (4 in.).
C. 1924.

695 Cubist brooch

Soldered silver with lacquered design.
Length 6 cm (2¼ in.).
C. 1925.
Private collection.
Sold: Boisgirard (Paris), 27 March 1987, lot 89.

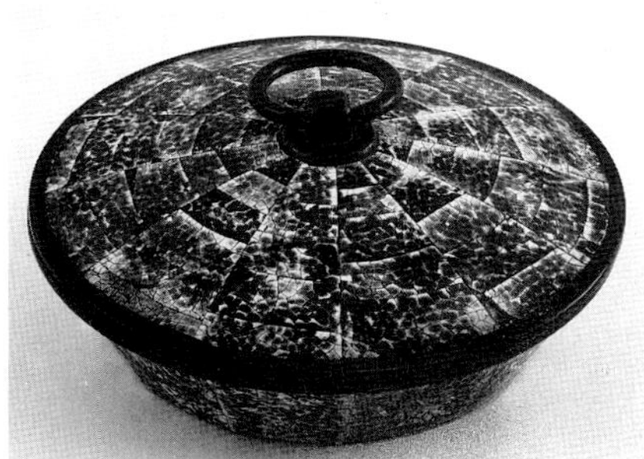

711

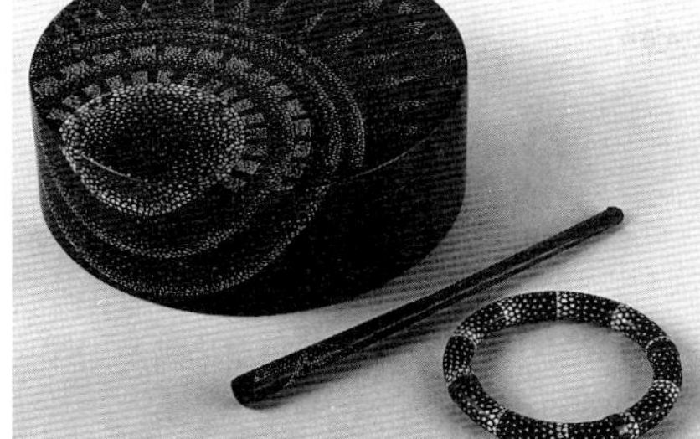

712

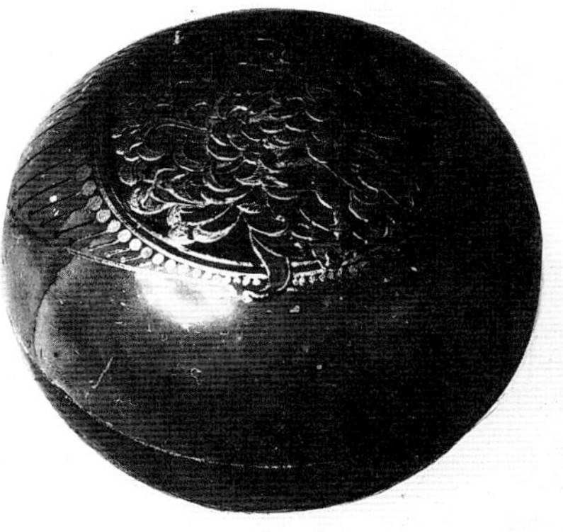

709

696 Brooch and bodice-buckles
Designs in white gouache on black paper.
32 x 49 cm (12¼ x 19¼ in.).
1925.
Private collection.

697 Rose brooches
Silvered metal inlaid with eggshell.
Length 13 cm (5 in.).
C. 1922.
Private collection.
Sold: Boisgirard (Paris), 27 March 1987, lots 87, 88; Sotheby's (Monaco), 24/25 October 1987, lots 413, 414.

698 Collar pins and shoe-buckle *Pl. 83*
Lacquered copper and metal inlaid with silver.
1925.
Coll.: Félix Marcilhac, Paris.

699 Hatpins and brooch *Pl. 85*
Lacquered metal with decorative geometric motifs.
Coll.: Félix Marcilhac, Paris.

OBJECTS OF VERTU

700 Lipstick-case
Lacquered oroide accessories inlaid with eggshell.
1925.

701 Vanity case
Lacquered oroide inlaid with eggshell.
1925.

702 Vanity case
Lacquered oroide inlaid with eggshell.
1925.
Coll.: Félix Marcilhac, Paris.

703 Vanity cases and lipstick-tube
Lacquered oroide inlaid with eggshell.
1925.
Coll.: Félix Marcilhac, Paris.

704 Pillbox
Lacquered oroide inlaid with eggshell.
C. 1924.

705 Pillbox
Lacquered oroide inlaid with eggshell.
C. 1924.

706 Pillbox
Lacquered oroide inlaid with eggshell.
C. 1924.

707 Powder-box and étui
Lacquered oroide inlaid with eggshell.
1923.

708 Compacts and vanity case
Lacquered oroide inlaid with eggshell.
1925.

709 Powder-box
Alabaster, lacquered cover highlighted with gold.
Diameter 12 cm (4¾ in.).
1912.
Sold: Sotheby's (Monaco), 19 April 1982, lot 190.

710 Powder-box *Pl. 89*
Lacquered oroide inlaid with eggshell.
1923.
Private collection.
Sold: Boisgirard (Paris), 26 October 1988, lot 115.

711 Powder-box
Lacquered oroide inlaid with eggshell.
C. 1927.

712 Powder-box, bracelet and cigarette-holder
Oroide and lacquered wood inlaid with eggshell.
C. 1925.

713 Powder-boxes and bonbonnière
Lacquered oroide inlaid with eggshell.
C. 1925.

714 Powder-boxes
Lacquered oroide inlaid with eggshell.
C. 1925.

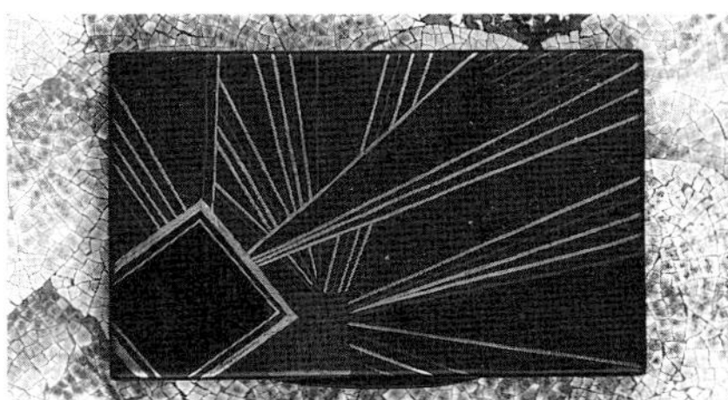

706

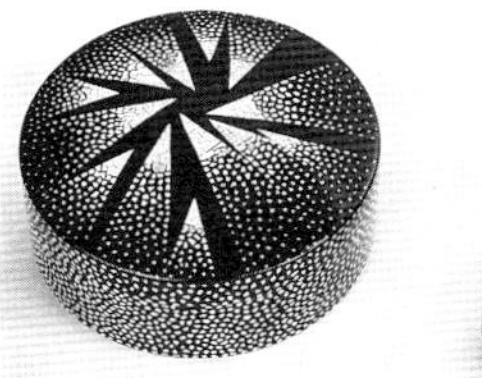

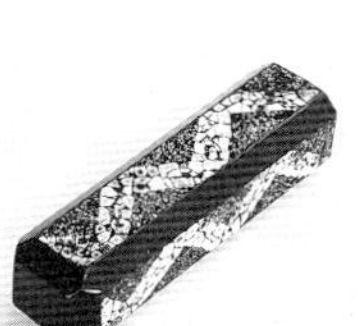

707

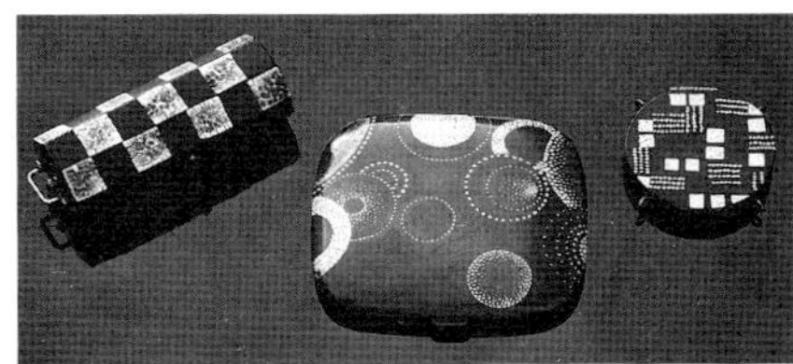

708

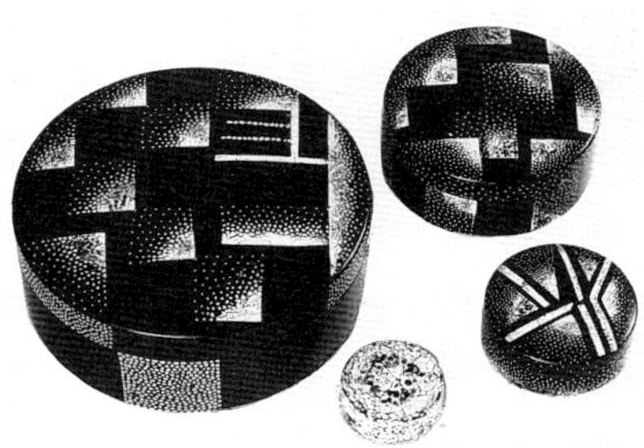

713

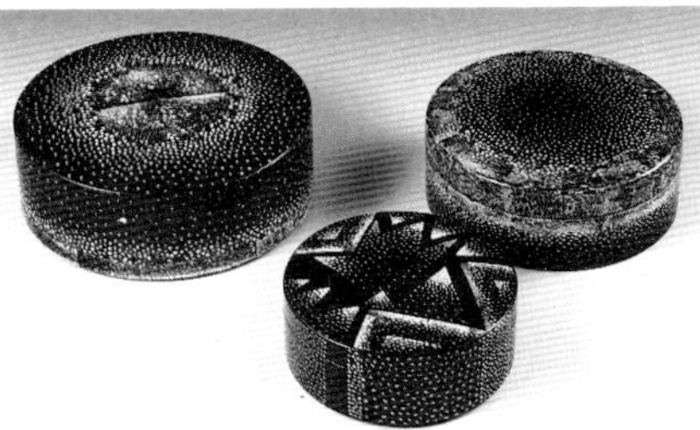

714

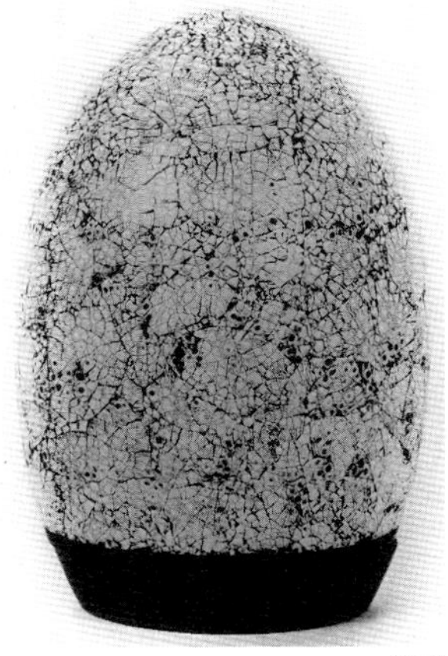
715

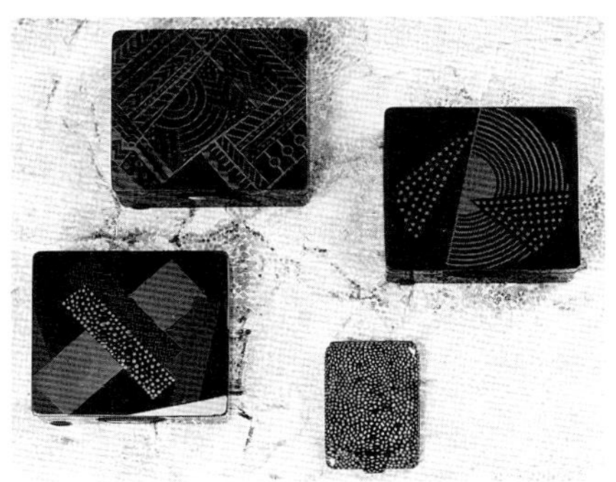
726

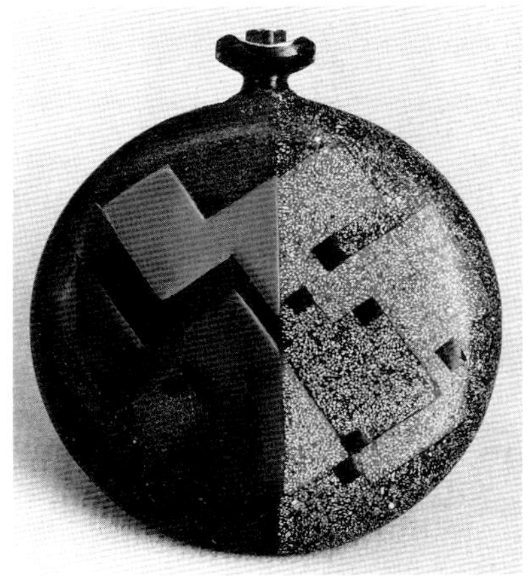
729

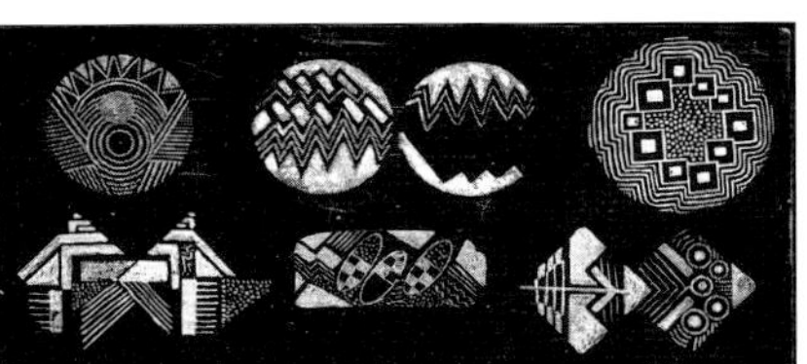
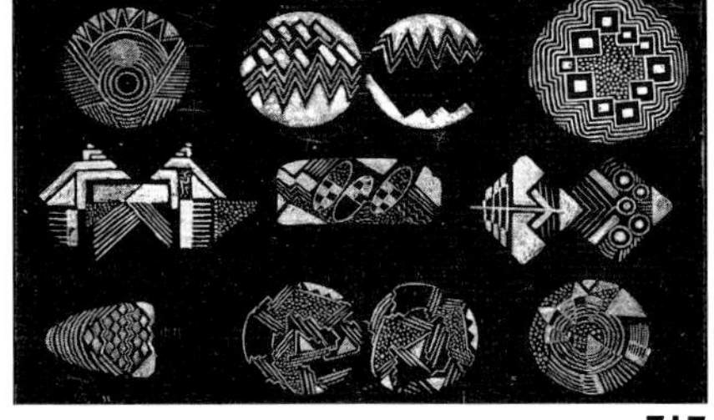
717

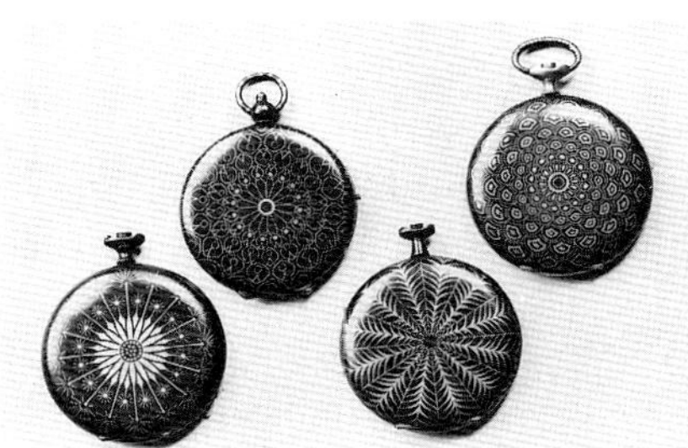
728

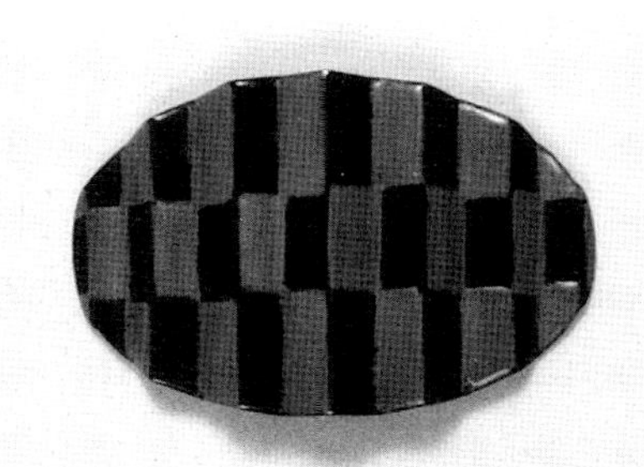
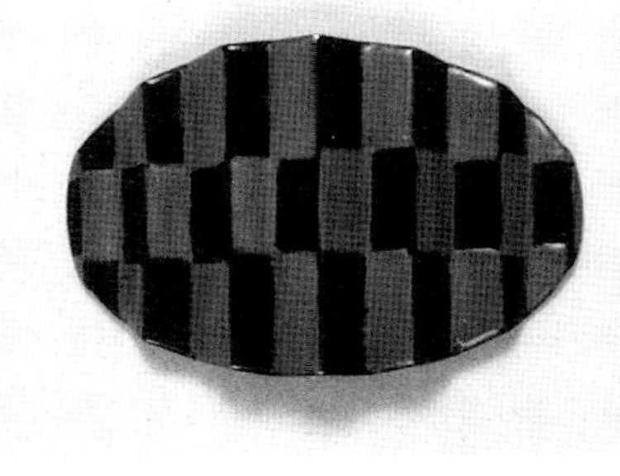

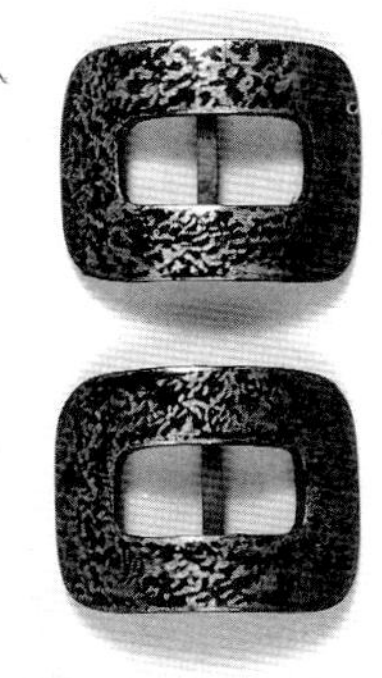
719

722

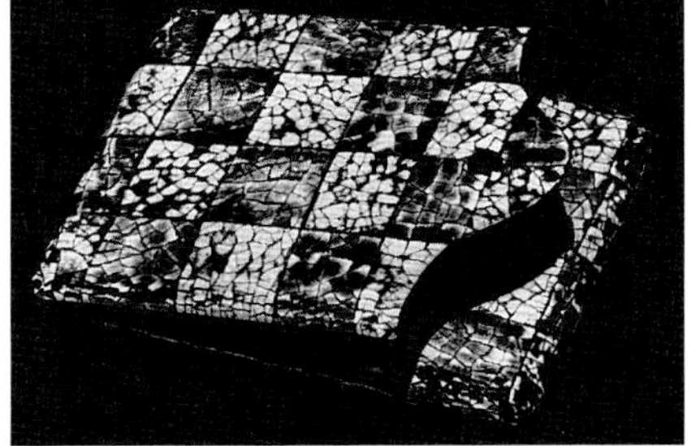
723

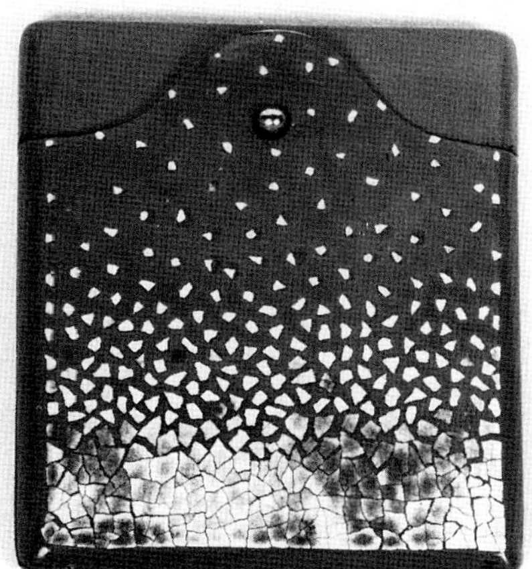
725

715 'Egg' bonbonnière
Lacquered wood inlaid with eggshell.
C. 1925.
Sold: Sotheby's (Monaco), 7 December 1981, lot 266.

716 Dressing-table accessories *Pl. 88*
Lacquered oroide accessories inlaid with eggshell.
Specially designed by Jean Dunand for his wife in 1925.
Private collection.

717 Belt-buckles
Gouache and silver on black paper.
32 x 49 cm (12½ x 19¼ in.).
Studies intended for Madame Agnès and realized in 1927.
Private collection.

718 Belt-buckles
Gouache and silver on black paper.
32 x 49 cm (12½ x 19¼ in.).
Studies intended for Madame Agnès and realized in 1927.
Private collection.

719 Belt-buckles
Dinanderie and lacquered copper inlaid with eggshell.
1927.
Sold: Sotheby's (Monaco), 24/25 December 1982, lots 402, 405.

720 Compact
Lacquered oroide.
C. 1927.
Private collection.

721 Cigarette-box *Pl. 87*
Lacquered oroide.
C. 1922.
Private collection.

722 Cigarette-cases
Lacquered fruit-wood decorated with metal after designs by Jean Lambert-Rucki.
C. 1922.
Exh.: Galerie du Luxembourg, Paris, 1973.
Private collection.

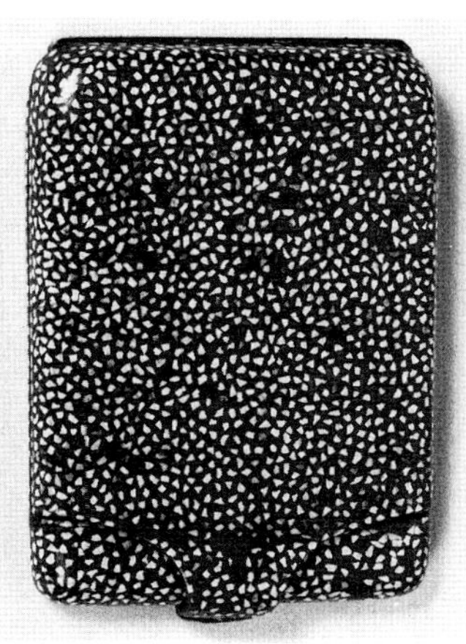
724

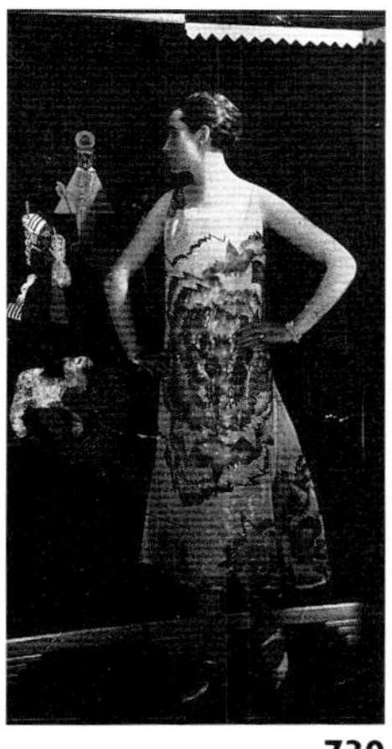
730

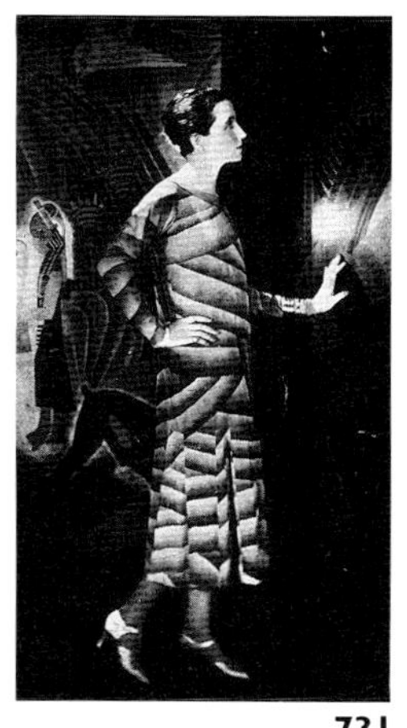
731

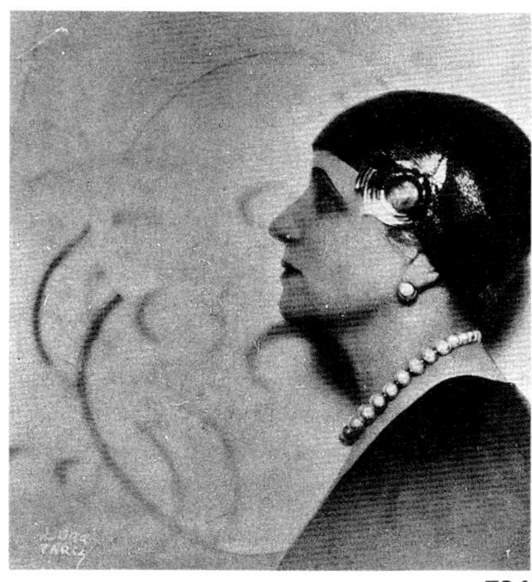
736

723 Étui for book of matches
Lacquered oroide inlaid with eggshell.
1925.

724 Étui for book of matches
Lacquered oroide inlaid with eggshell.
C. 1925.

725 Étui for book of matches
Lacquered oroide inlaid with eggshell.
C. 1925.

726 Cigarette-boxes and étui for book of matches
Lacquered oroide inlaid with eggshell.
C. 1923.
Exh.: Galerie du Luxembourg, Paris, 1973.

727 Cigarette-case and watch-case *Pl. 86*
Lacquered oroide inlaid with eggshell.
C. 1925.
Exh.: Galerie du Luxembourg, Paris, 1973.

728 Watch-cases
Steel inlaid with gold and silver.
C. 1914.
Bibl.: *Les Arts français: le métal repoussé* (Paris, 1918), p. 172.

729 Watch-case
Lacquered oroide inlaid with eggshell.
C. 1925.
Coll.: Félix Marcilhac, Paris.

LADIES' FASHIONS

730 Dress with floral motif
Silver muslin painted with dilute sepia and grey lacquer after a design by Dunand.
Created for Madame Agnès in 1925.
Exh.: Exposition Internationale des Arts Décoratifs et Industriels Modernes, Paris, 1925 (Pavillon de la Mode, *haute couture* stand).
Bibl.: *Vogue*, 1 May 1925.

731 Dress with stripe motif
Crêpe de Chine painted with dilute sepia and coloured lacquer after a design by Dunand.
Created for Madame Agnès in 1925.
Exh.: Exposition Internationale des Arts Décoratifs et Industriels Modernes, Paris, 1925 (Pavillon de la Mode, *haute couture* stand).
Bibl.: *Vogue*, 1 May 1925.

732 Madame Agnès
Photograph by d'Ora, 1925; see p. 90.
Madame Agnès is seen wearing a hat and dress of her own creation decorated with dilute lacquer to a design by Dunand.

733 Designs for hats
Gouache and Indian ink.
C. 1925.
Private collection.

734 Designs for hats
Gouache and Indian ink.
C. 1925.
Private collection.

735 Madame Agnès
Photograph by d'Ora, 1926; see p. 90.
The milliner is seen wearing a hat of her own design, together with oroide cuff ornaments and ear-rings designed by Dunand.
Bibl.: *L'Officiel de la couture*, June 1926, repr. on cover.

736 Madame Agnès
Photograph by d'Ora, 1926.
Madame Agnès is seen wearing a small toque in fine straw lacquered by Jean Dunand, together with an ivory necklace and ear-rings also lacquered by Dunand.

737 Handbag
Morocco leather with a lacquered design.
Made in 1925 at the Michenon leather works to a design by Dunand and distributed by A. Cohn et Cie.
Exh.: Exposition Internationale des Arts Décoratifs et Industriels Modernes, Paris, 1925.

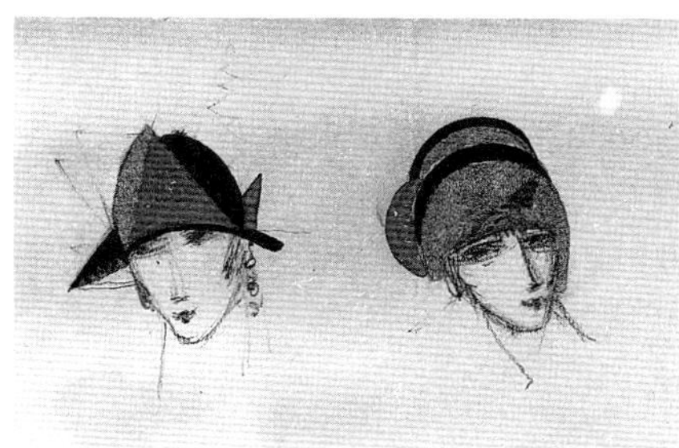
733

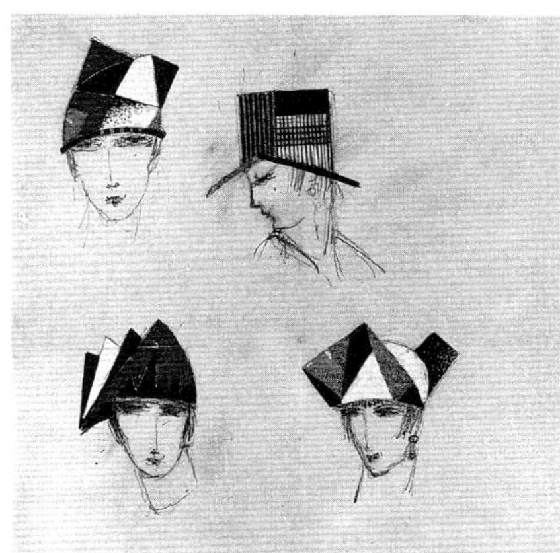
734

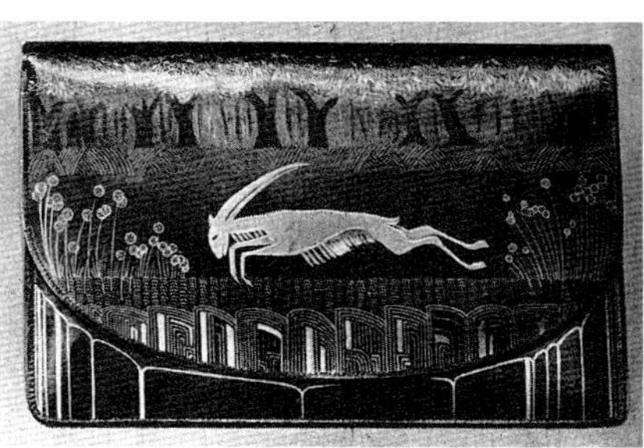
737

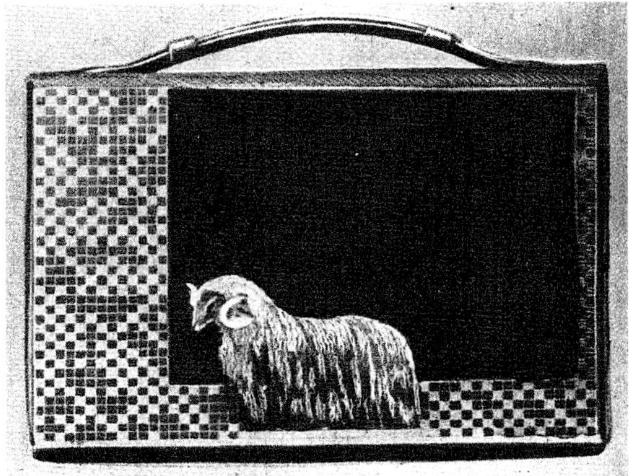
738

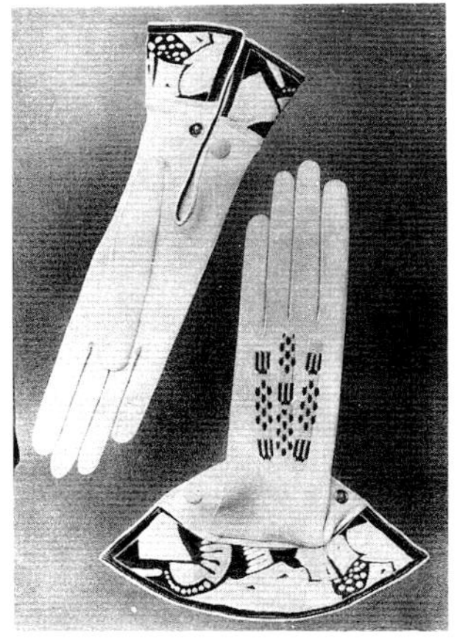
739

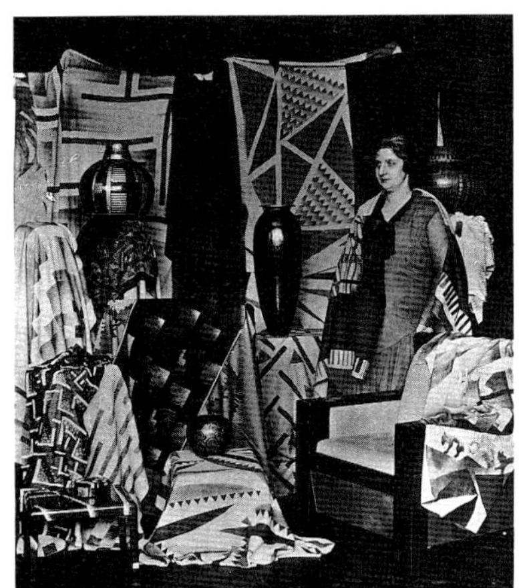
740

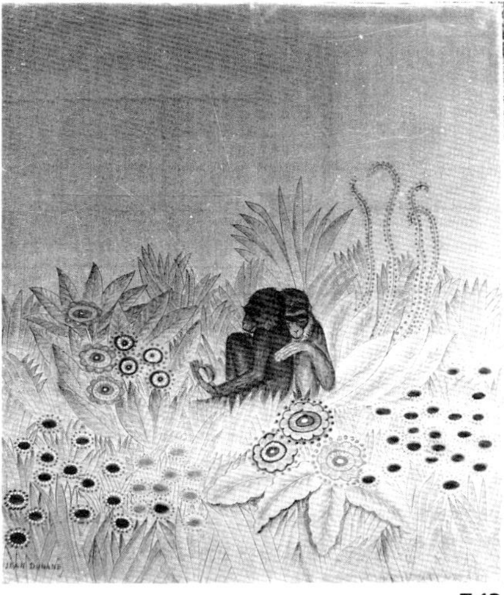
743

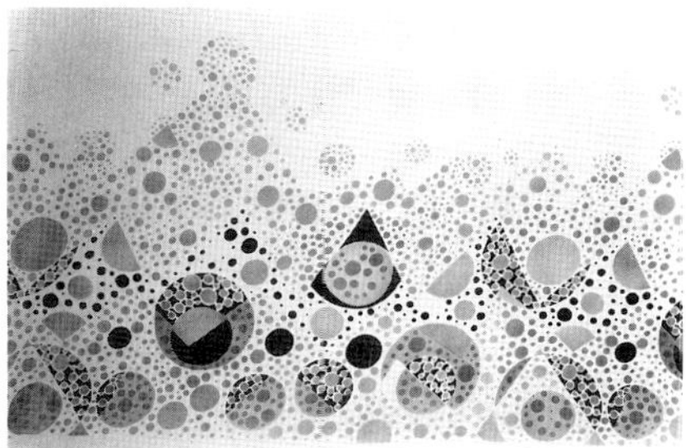
741

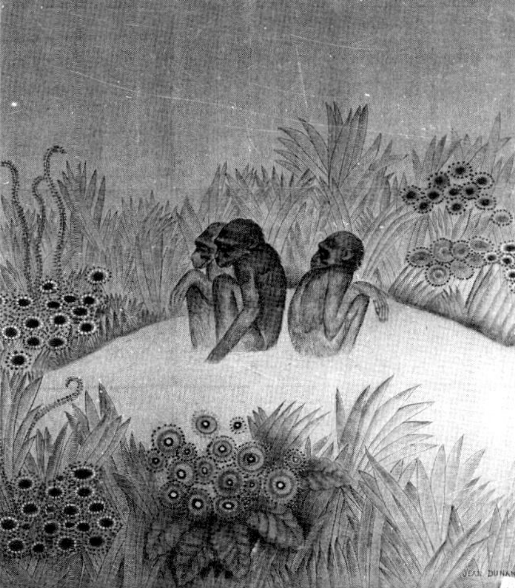
744

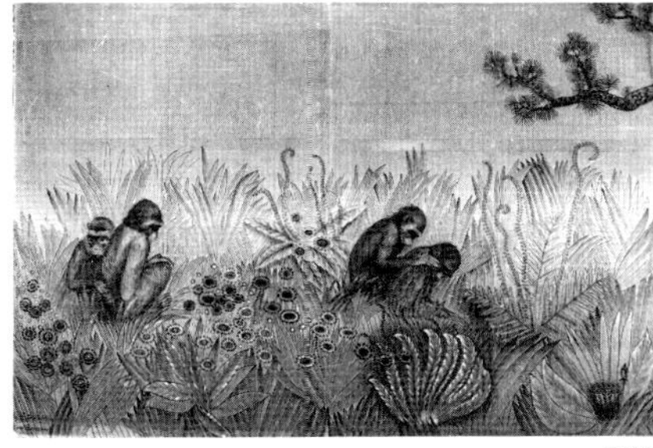
742

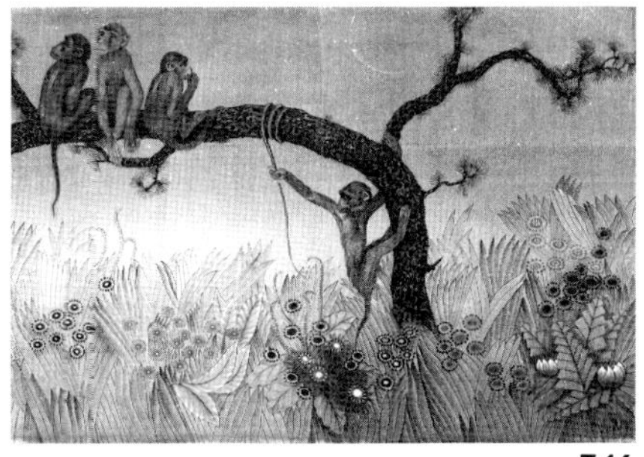
745

746

738 Handbag
Morocco leather with metal flap lacquered to a design by Dunand. Made in 1925 at the Michenon leather works and distributed by A. Cohn et Cie.
Exh.: Exposition Internationale des Arts Décoratifs et Industriels Modernes, Paris, 1925.

739 Pair of gloves
Kid and embroidered leather.
Designed by Dunand and manufactured by Charles Perrin and Henri Jammet in 1925.
Exh.: Exposition Internationale des Arts Décoratifs et Industriels Modernes, Paris, 1925 (Pavillon de la Parure).

TEXTILES DECORATED WITH LACQUER; DESIGNS FOR TAPESTRIES AND A CARPET

740 Madame Jean Dunand
Photograph taken in 1925.
Madame Dunand is seen surrounded by samples of material decorated with designs by her husband, dilute coloured lacquer having been applied to the stencilled outline of the designs.
Bibl.: *Conferencia*, 15 April 1926, p. 445.

741, 742 Silk fabrics
Silk fabrics with stencilled designs, coloured lacquer applied by pipette and paintbrush.
C. 1925.
Private collection.

743–751 Decorated fabrics
Painted with dilute lacquer.
C. 1930.
Formerly in the collection of Anne-Sophie Duval.

743 *Monkeys among Flowers*
744 *Monkeys Bathing*

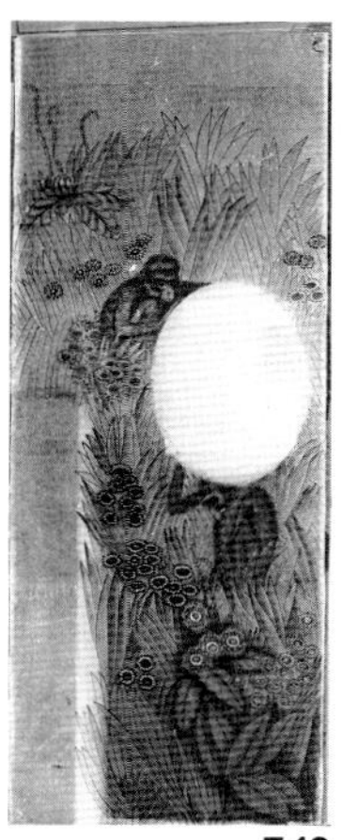
748

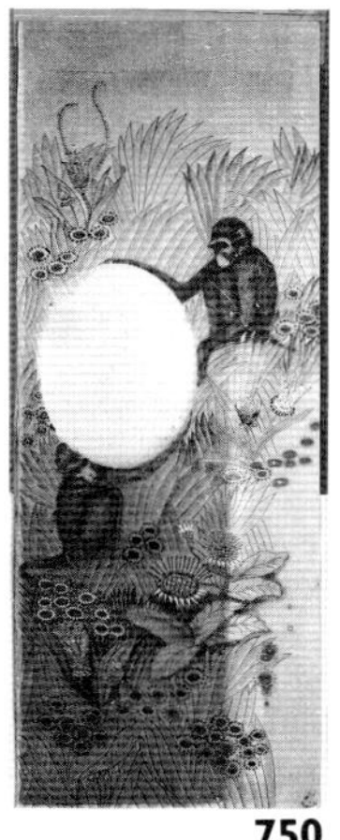
750

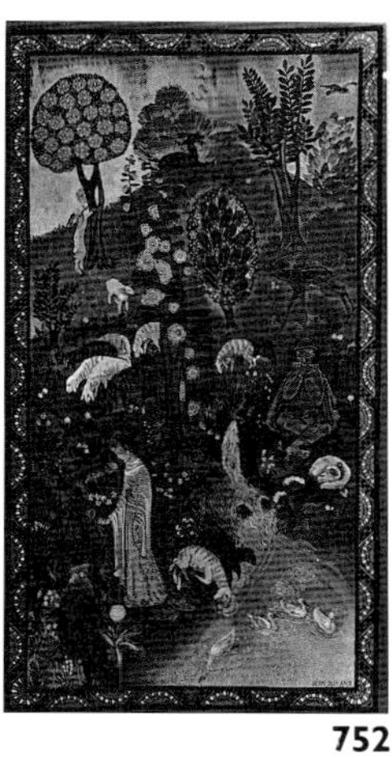
752

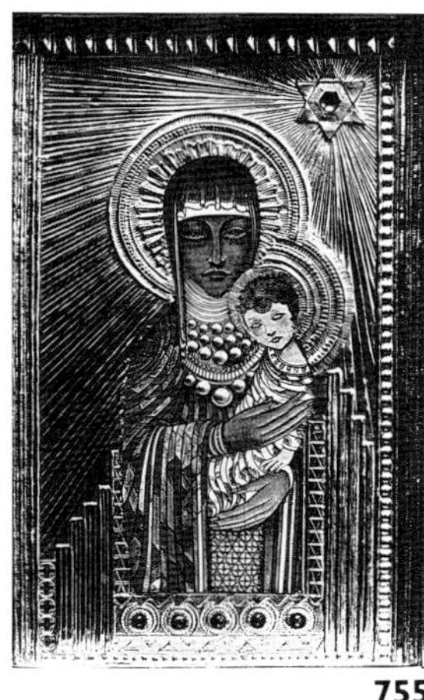
755

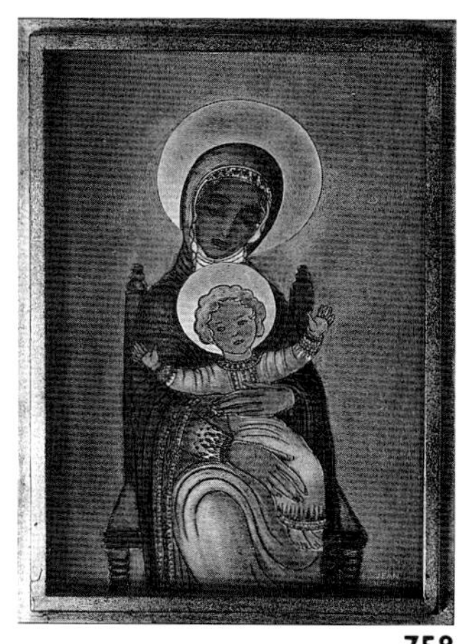
758

745 *Monkeys Grooming Themselves*
746 *Monkeys Playing in a Tree*
747 *Vegetation*
748 *Monkeys*
749 *Monkey Playing with an Insect*
750 *Monkeys*
751 *Monkeys Playing in a Tree*

752 'Pastorale' tapestry design
Tapestry design made in 1932 for the Gobelins Company (manufactured there between 5 July 1932 and 9 September 1933).
200 x 120 cm (78¾ x 47¼ in.).
Exh.: Exposition Internationale des Arts et Techniques Appliqués à la Vie Moderne, Paris, 1937.
Coll.: Mobilier National, Paris.

753 'Eclogue' tapestry design
Tapestry design for the Gobelins Company; see illustration, p. 141.
Full-size study on fabric made in 1933 and exhibited at the Exposition Internationale des Arts et Techniques Appliqués à la Vie Moderne, Paris, 1937.
Coll.: Ville de Paris, currently on display in the banqueting hall in the annexe to the civic building of the 14th *arrondissement*.

754 Carpet *Pl. 106*
Hand-knotted wool pile.
183 x 186 cm (6 ft x 6 ft 1¼ in.).
Specially designed in 1927 for the studio of Madame Agnès.
Exh.: 'Jean Dunand – Jean Goulden', Galerie du Luxembourg, Paris, 1973, no. 135.
Private collection.
Bibl.: *La Renaissance de l'art français*, April 1927; *Art et industrie*, July 1927, p. 15.
Sold: Sotheby's (Monaco), 6 March 1983, lot 143; Champin, Lombrail, Gautier (Enghien), 21 March 1987, lot 35.

MISCELLANEOUS WORKS ON RELIGIOUS THEMES

755 Virgin and Child
Incised Coromandel lacquer.
1933.
Exh.: Salon d'Automne, Paris, 1933 (section on religious art).

756 The Annunciation
Incised Coromandel lacquer; see illustration, p. 150.
1933.
Exh.: Galerie Charpentier, Paris, 1933, no. 11; Salon d'Automne, Paris, 1933 (section on religious art); Salon des Artistes Décorateurs, Paris, 1942 (Dunand retrospective).

757 Joseph's Workshop
Incised Coromandel lacquer; see illustration, p. 150.
1933.
Exh.: Salon d'Automne, Paris, 1933 (section on religious art).
Coll.: Vatican Collection.

758 Virgin
Incised aventurine black lacquer.
43 x 30 cm (17 x 11¾ in.).
1932.
Exh.: Galerie Georges Petit, Paris, 1932, no. 16; Galerie Charpentier, Paris, 1933, no. 12.

759 Chalice for Father Doncoeur
Hammered silver and sapphires.
Height 13 cm (5 in.).
1931.
The underside of the base bears the inscription 'Aimez-vous les uns les autres – 21/25 mai 1931' ('Love one another – 21/25 May 1931').

760 Altar of the Church of the Holy Ghost, Avenue Daumesnil, Paris
Repoussé copper.
1933.

761 Paten
Made in 1933 for the Church of the Holy Ghost, Avenue Daumesnil, Paris.

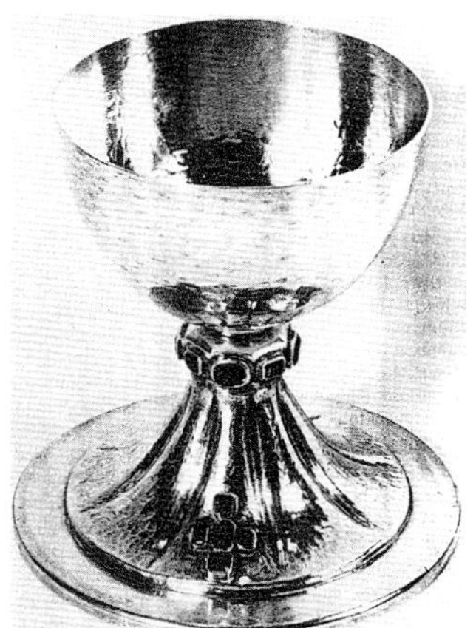
759

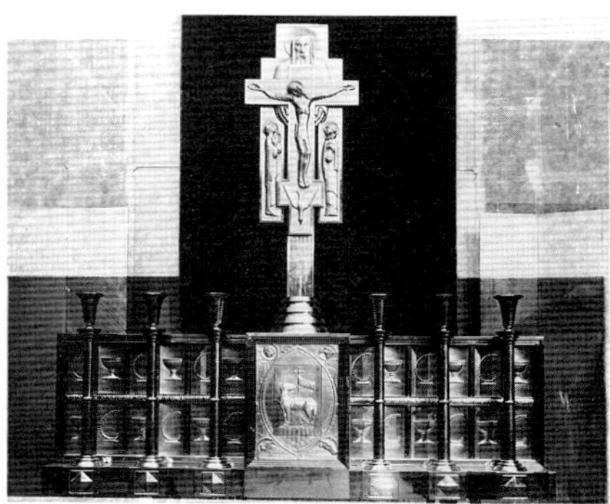
760

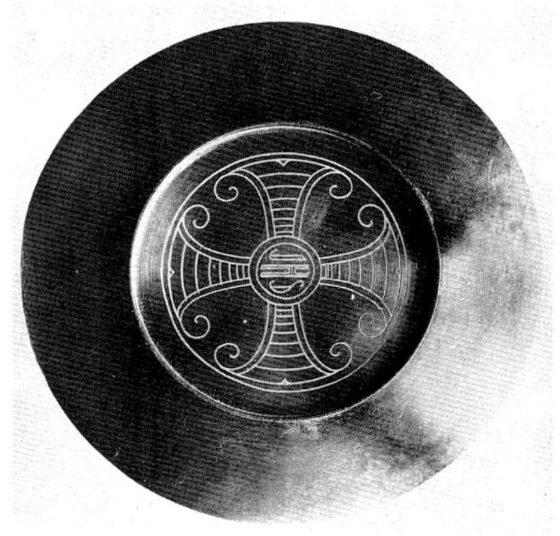
761

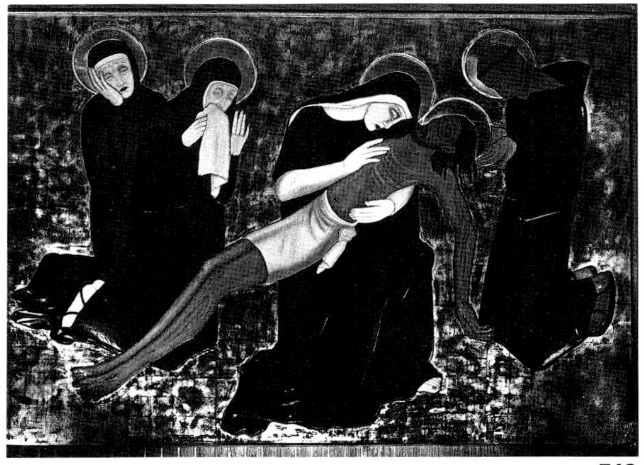
762

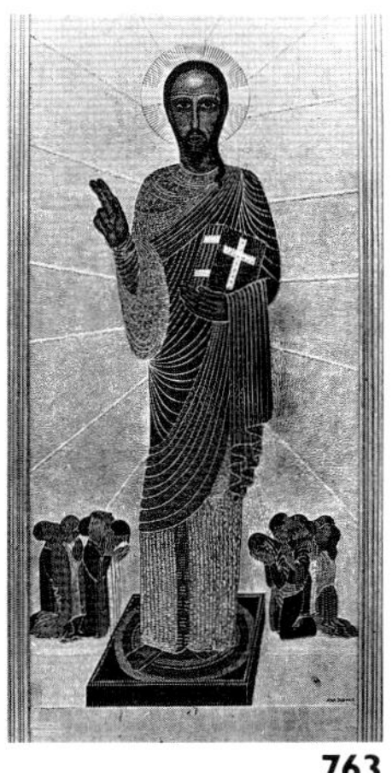
763

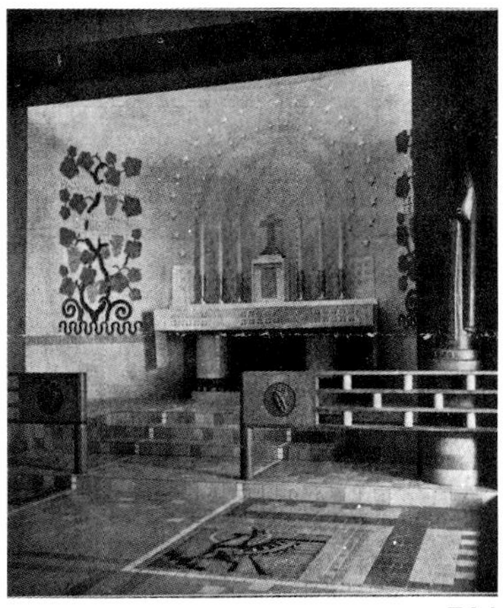
764

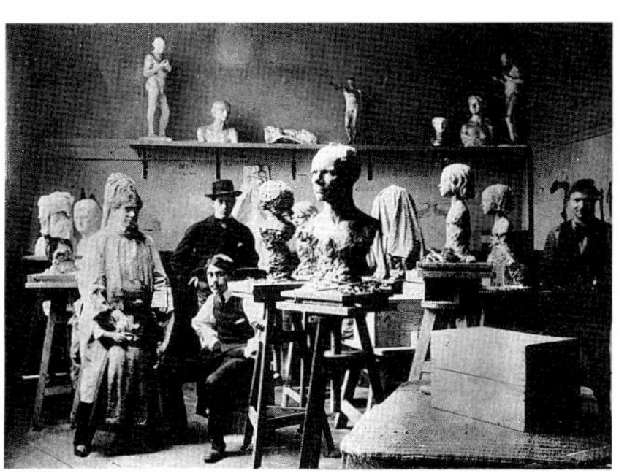
767

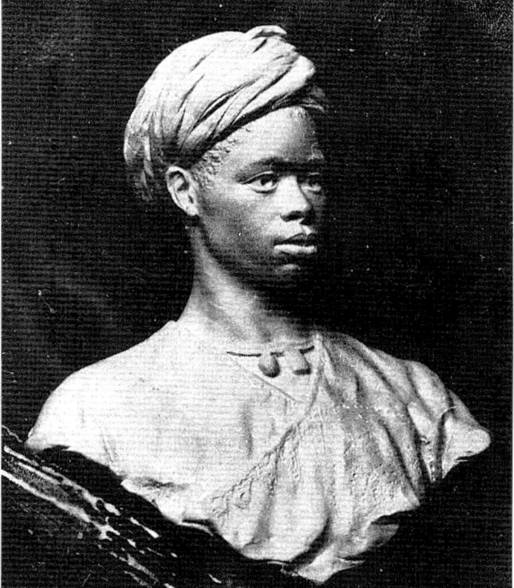
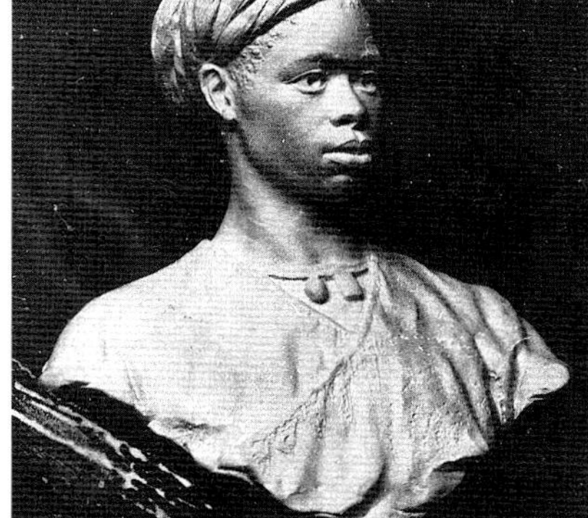
770

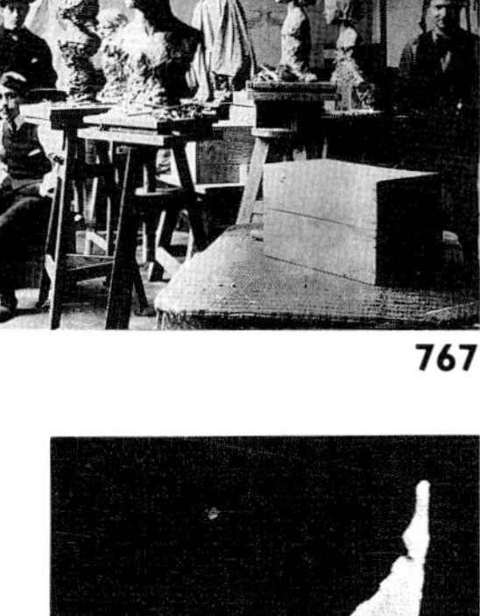
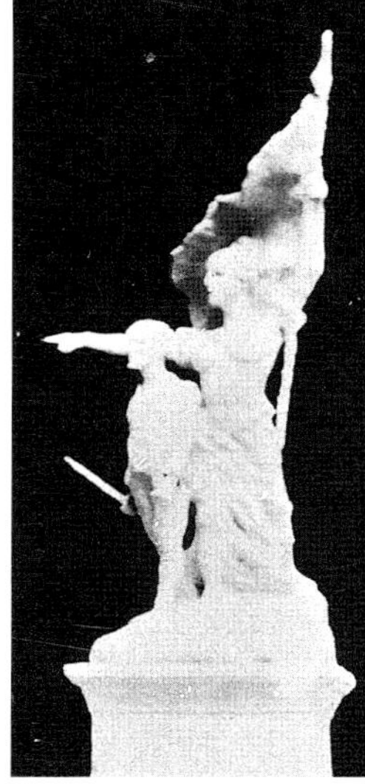
765

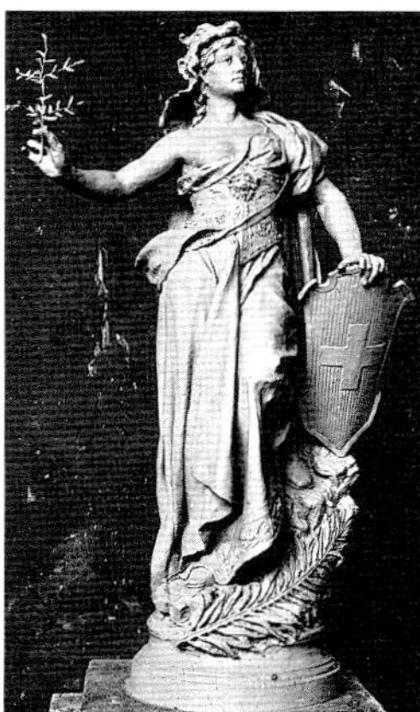
766

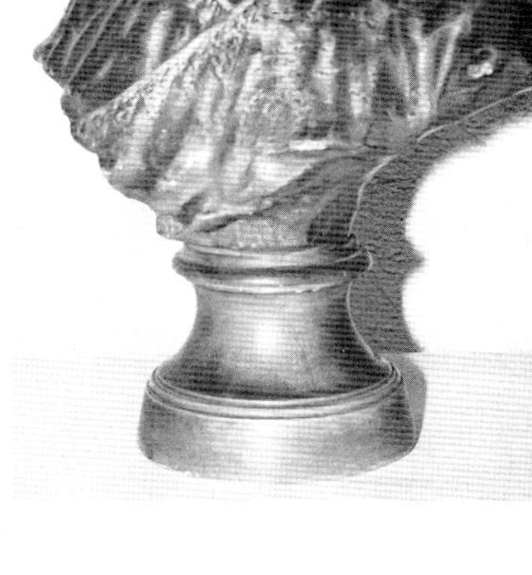
771

762 Pietà

Incised lacquer decorated with gold leaf.
1937.
Exh.: Exposition Internationale des Arts et Techniques Appliqués à la Vie Moderne, Paris, 1937; Salon des Artistes Décorateurs, Paris, 1942 (Dunand retrospective).

763 Christ in Majesty

Fabric painted in imitation of mosaic.
1937.
Exh.: Exposition Internationale des Arts et Techniques Appliqués à la Vie Moderne, Paris, 1937.
This full-size mock-up of a projected mosaic was exhibited in the hope of encouraging an order, but without success; see also cat. no. 207 and p. 149.

764 Communion table

Made in 1937 for the Oratory of the Pavillon de la Céramique at the Exposition Internationale des Arts et Techniques Appliqués à la Vie Moderne, Paris. See also cat. nos. 1224–35. The ceramic high altar, made by the Manufacture Nationale de Céramiques de Sèvres, is surmounted by a large glass crucifix by René Lalique.

SCULPTURE

765 Switzerland

Studio piece in plaster of Paris.
1894.
Created in collaboration with other students in Cagniez's class at the École des Arts Industriels, Geneva; the only surviving evidence of this piece is a poor-quality photograph.

766 Helvetia

Clay.
1895.
Commissioned by the City of Geneva.

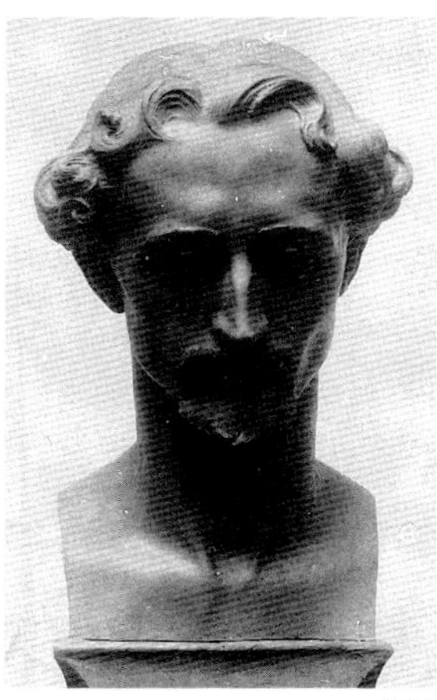
777

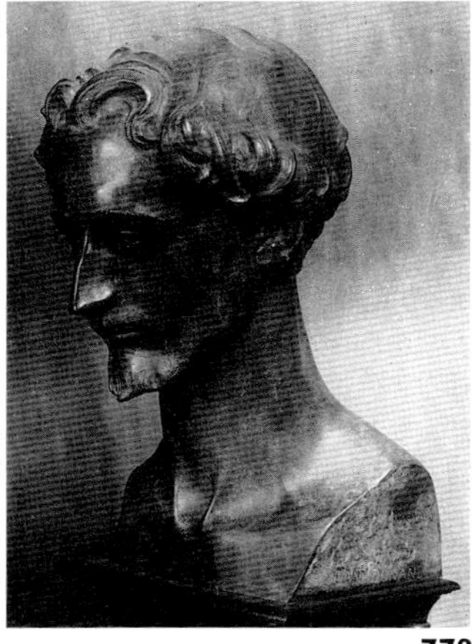
778

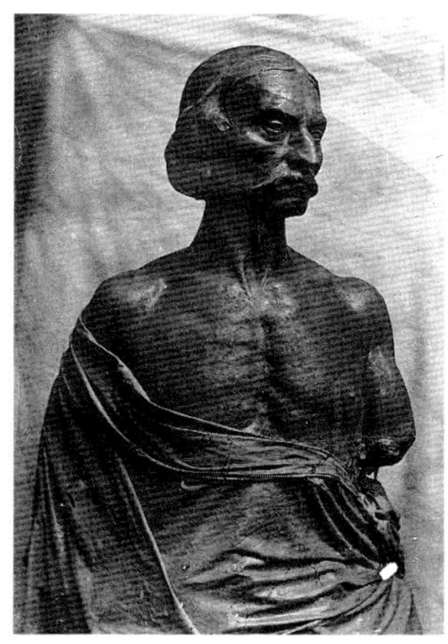
779

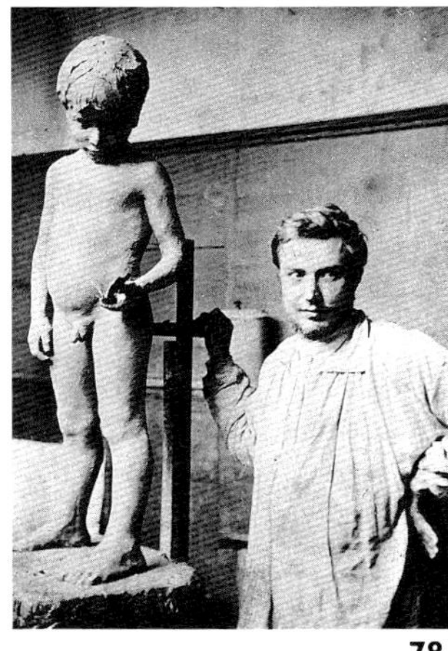
781

767 Bust of a Young Girl
Studio piece in clay.
1895.
Studio photograph, Dunand can be seen standing on the right next to his version of *Bust of a Young Girl.* The model herself can be seen standing on the left.

768 Nude
Studio piece in clay.
1896.
Produced for the end-of-session competition held in Jerdelet's sculpture class at the École des Arts Industriels, Geneva.

769 Bust of a Man
Studio piece in plaster of Paris.
1896.
Probably made in collaboration with one of Dunand's teachers at the École des Arts Industriels, Geneva, for a commemorative monument.

770 Abdou Faye
Hardened plaster.
1896.
Bust of Abdou Faye treated in the manner of a classical Roman sculpture.

771 Abdou Faye
Polychrome hardened plaster.
1896.
Signed 'John Dunand' and entitled 'Abdou Faye'.
Coll.: Galerie Art Nouveau – Art Déco, Geneva.

772 Baluster vase
Study in plaster.
1896.

773 Head of a Woman in Profile
Study in plaster.
1896.

774 Bracket clock and base
Polychrome plaster of Paris.
1896.
With this plaster replica of a clock by Jacquet-Droz in the Musée de l'Horlogerie, Neuchâtel, Switzerland, Dunand won first prize at the interdisciplinary Concours Galland held in Geneva in 1886.

775 Papiers Artistiques Luna (Luna Artistic Papers)
Bronze bas-relief.
18 x 8.5 cm (7 x 3¼ in.).
C. 1900.
Signed, titled and marked 'Vielle et Cie. Lausanne'.
Private collection.

776 Madame Jean-Eugène Dunand
Preliminary study in plaster of Paris.
C. 1900.

777 Maurice Dieterlin or **Bust of a Friend**
Clay.

778 Maurice Dieterlin or **Bust of a Friend**
Trial casting in bronze.
1900.
Exh.: Salon de la Nationale, Paris, 1900 (foreign artists' section).

779 Quo Vadis
Study in clay; see illustration, p. 13.
1900.
Exh.: 1900 Paris Exposition (Swiss section).

780 The Child and Butterfly
Study in clay, first version.
1900.
This first version of the piece was small in scale, the child being depicted with the right elbow bent. The same subject was taken up on a number of subsequent occasions, when the scale of the piece and the position of the child's arms were altered.

781 The Child and Butterfly
Study in clay, second version.
1900.
This second version was larger than the first; the child's right arm is now shown dangling.

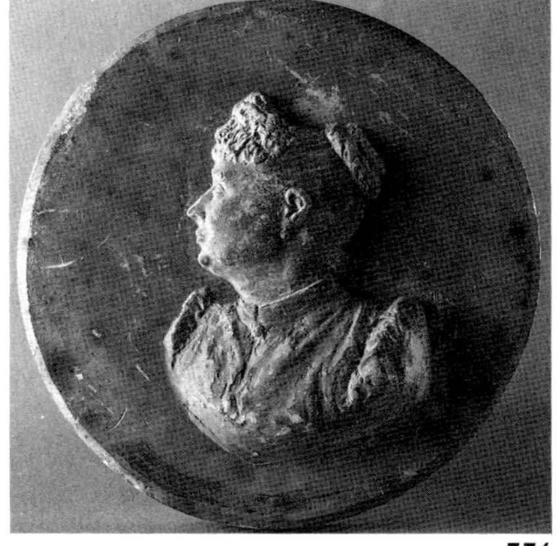
776

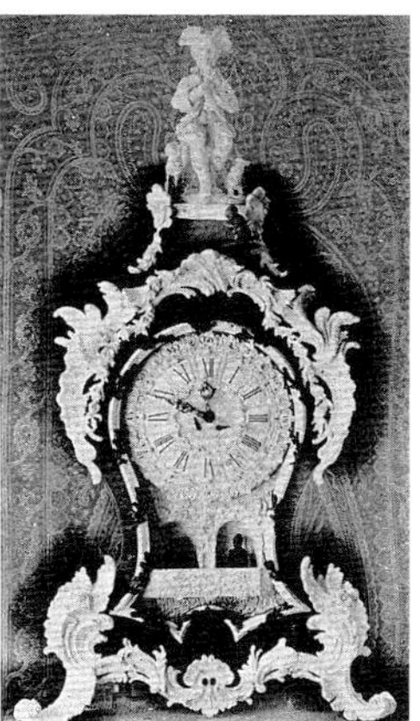

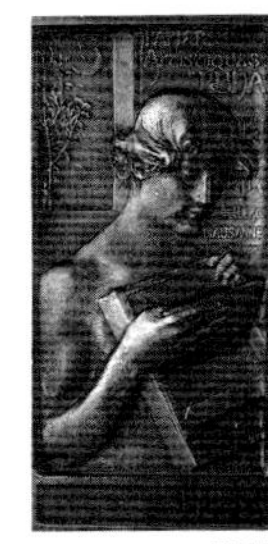
775

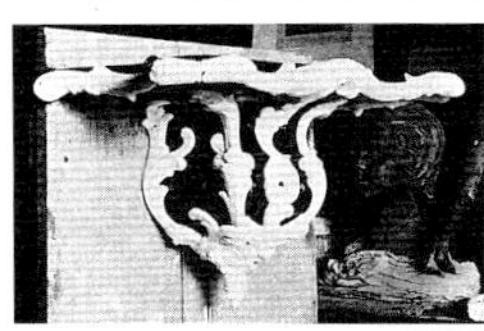
774

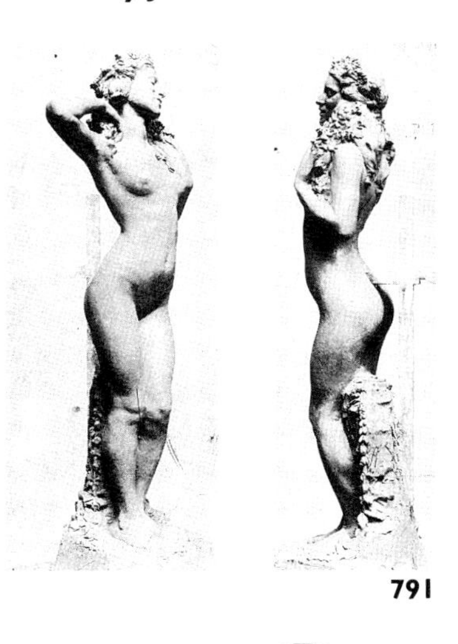
791

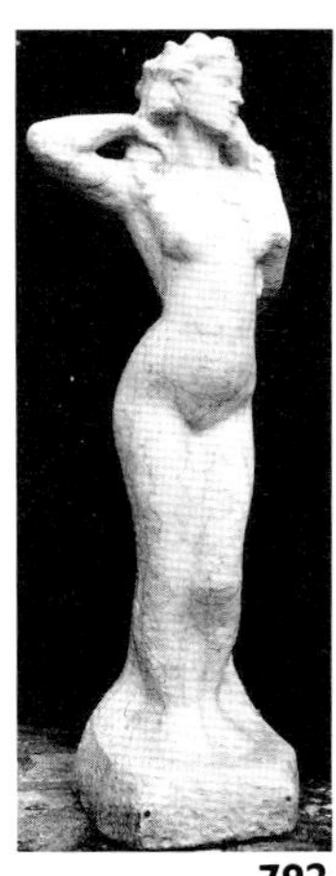
792

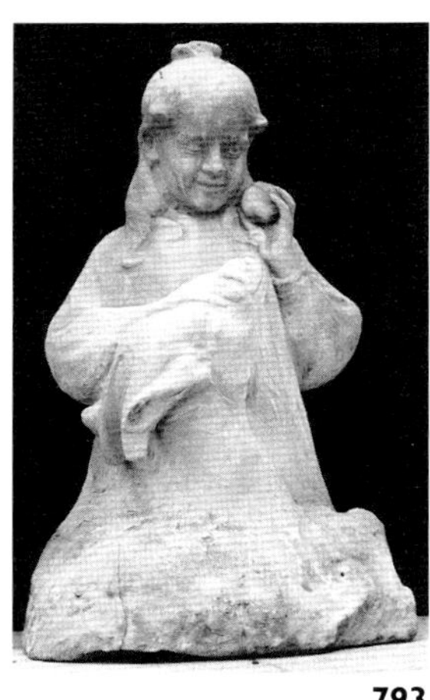
793

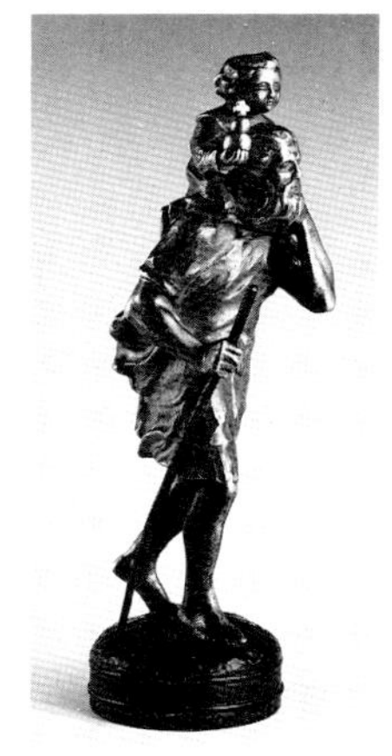
796

788

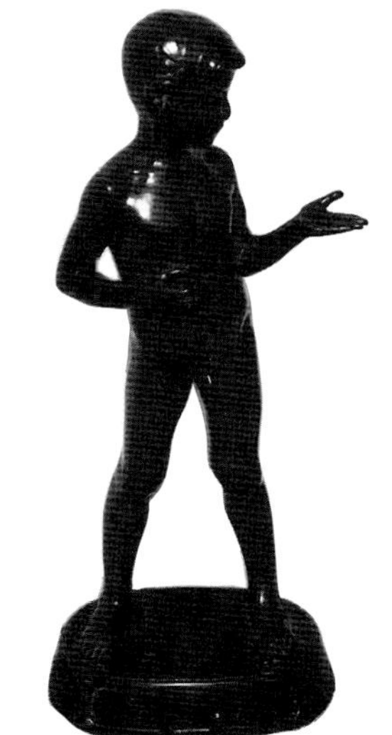
784

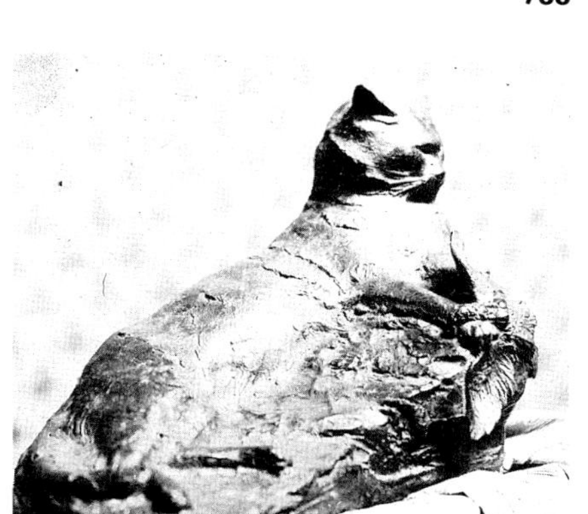
789

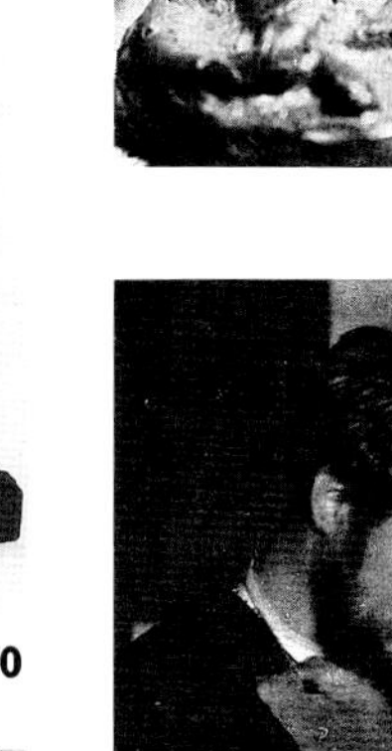
790

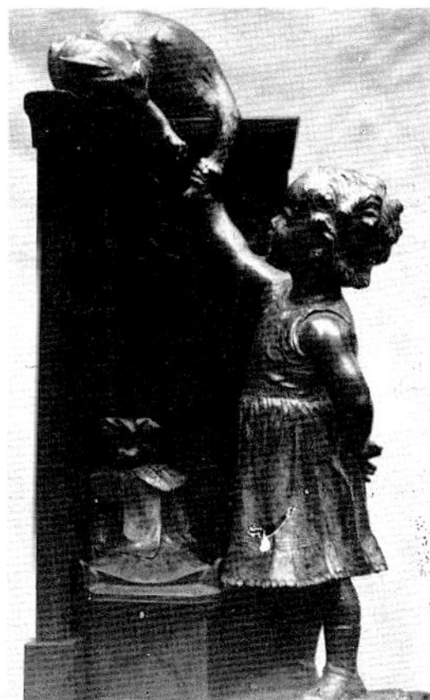
794

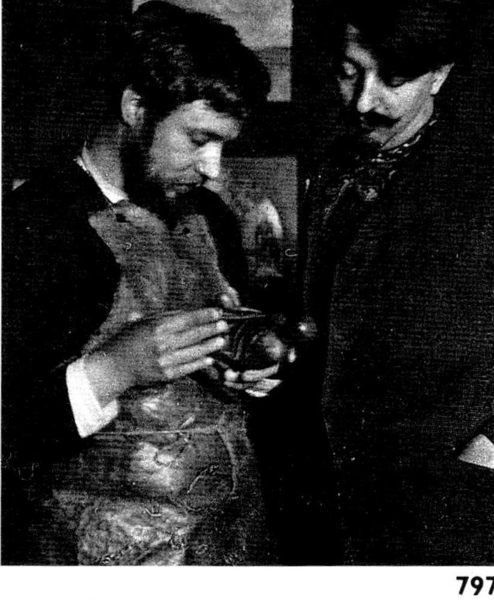
797

782 The Child and Butterfly
Clay, second version.
1900.

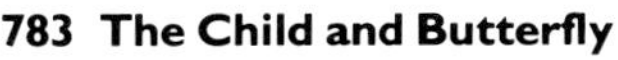

783 The Child and Butterfly
Patinated plaster of Paris; see p. 27.
1900.
Coll.: Musée d'Art et d'Histoire, Geneva.

784 The Child and Butterfly
Trial casting in bronze.
Height 55 cm (21¾ in.).
1900.
Exh.: Salon de la Nationale, Paris, 1901 (foreign artists' section); Association des Artistes Suisses, Paris, 1907, no. 60.
Private collection.
Bibl.: *L'Art décoratif*, January 1909, p. 15.

785 Vercingetorix
Study in clay.
C. 1900.

786 St Eligius
Romanesque stone sculpture.
This headless Romanesque piece was restored by Dunand and Angst *c.* 1901 under the supervision of Jean Dampt in the course of one of their summer visits to Le Gué du Roy in Touraine.

787 Bust of Mademoiselle E. K.
Study in clay.
1901.
Exh.: Salon de la Nationale, Paris, 1901 (foreign artists' section).

788 'Ears of Corn' bread basket
Carved walnut.
1903.
Exh.: Salon de la Nationale, Paris, 1903.

789 The Cat
Study in clay.
1903.
Exh.: Exposition Nationale des Beaux-Arts, Lausanne, 1904.

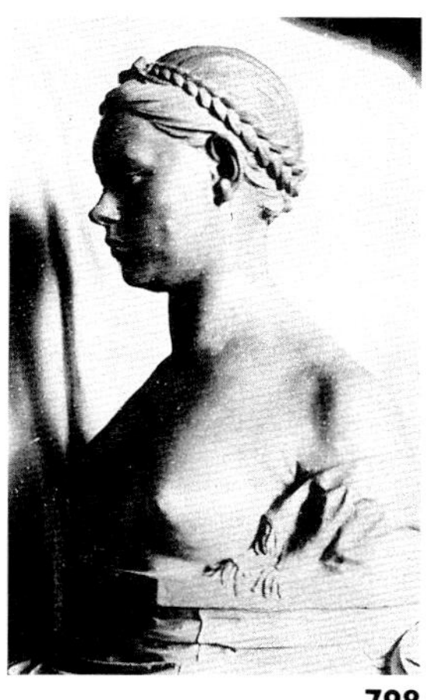
798

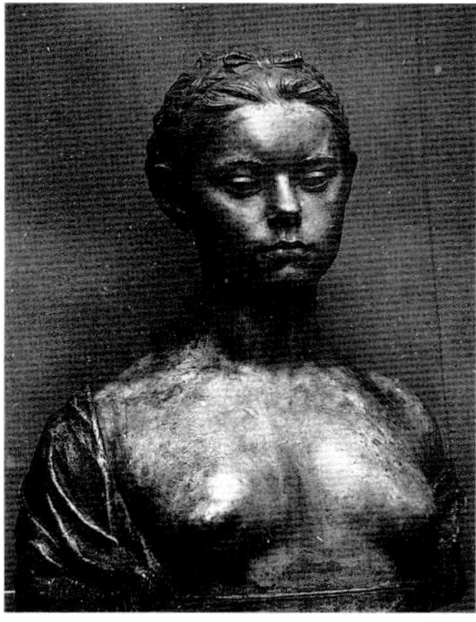
799

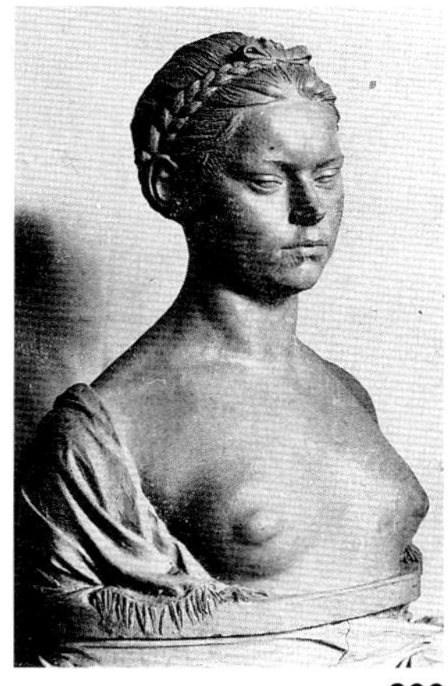
800

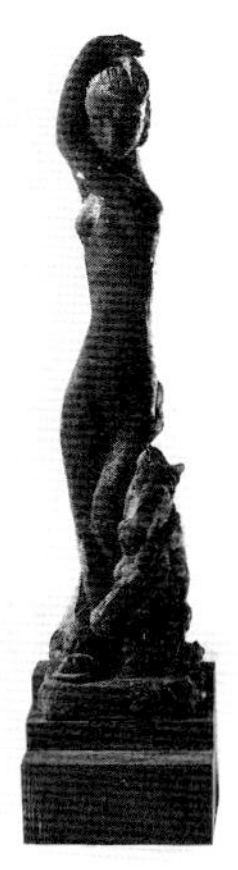
804

790 Hen and Chicks
Carved walnut.
Height 44 cm (17¼ in.).
1904.
Exh.: Salon des Artistes Décorateurs, Petit Palais, Paris, 1904.
Private collection.

791 The Awakening
Clay model, seen from right and left.

792 The Awakening
Marble.
Height 115 cm (45¼ in.).
Exh.: Salon des Artistes Décorateurs, Petit Palais, Paris, 1904.
Private collection.

793 Child and Young Goat
Limestone.
Height 96 cm (37¾ in.).
1905.
Private collection.

794 Young Girl and Cat
Carved wood.
C. 1900–3.

795 Mother and Child
Photograph; see illustration, p. 13.
C. 1900–3.
Dunand, in his rooms in the Rue Michelet (which he left in 1904), is seen working on the statue of a seated female figure whose child is depicted climbing on to her shoulder.

796 St Christopher
Patinated bronze.
Height 23 cm (9 in.).
c. 1900–3.
Private collection.
Originally conceived for a car radiator cap.

797 Kneeling Figure
Clay.
C. 1900–3.
Dunand can be seen in his rooms in the Rue Michelet, showing his friend François-Louis Schmied a statuette which is clearly unfinished.

798 Marguerite
Study in clay.
1902–4.
Begun in 1902, this study for the bust of Dunand's young cousin Marguerite Vachoux (cat. no. 799) was completed in 1904 on his return from Italy.

799 Marguerite
Burgundy stone, finished piece.
1904.
Exh.: Salon des Artistes Décorateurs, Petit Palais, Paris, 1904.
Bibl.: *L'Art décoratif*, January 1909, p. 14.

800 Marguerite
Trial casting in bronze.
1904.

801 Sabato (Martelli)
Clay.

802 Sabato (Martelli)
Trial casting in bronze.
1904.
Exh.: Exposition des Beaux-Arts, Zurich, December 1907.
Coll.: Musée d'Art et d'Histoire, Geneva.
Bibl.: *L'Art décoratif*, January 1909, p. 16.

803 Head of a Child
Plaster cast.
Height 36 cm (14¼ in.).
C. 1914.
Private collection.

804 L'Atlantique
Original wax model.
Height 32 cm (12½ in.).
Private collection.
This piece, intended for the liner *L'Atlantique*, was not used by the shipping company, and the project was never realized.

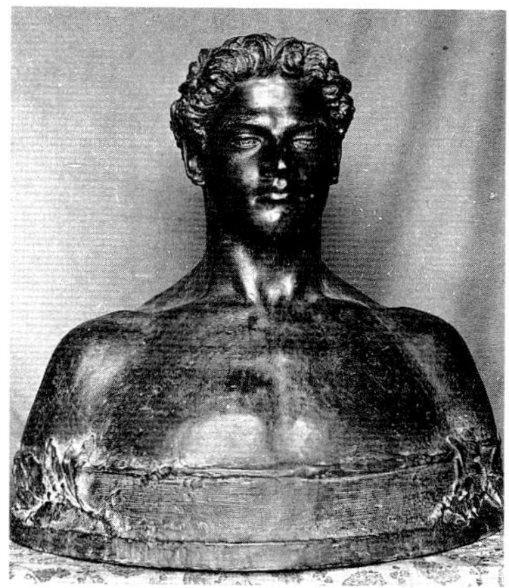
801

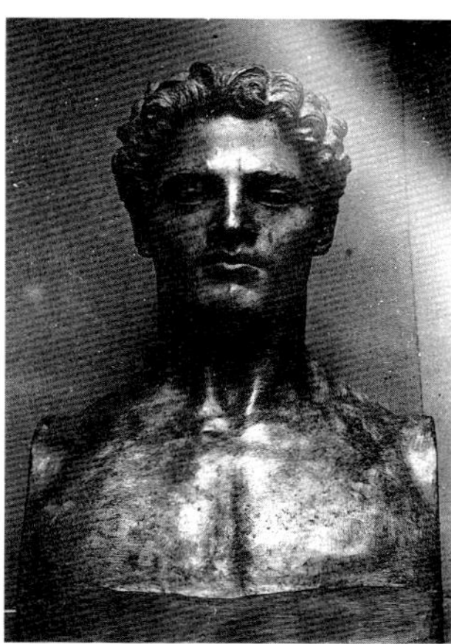
802

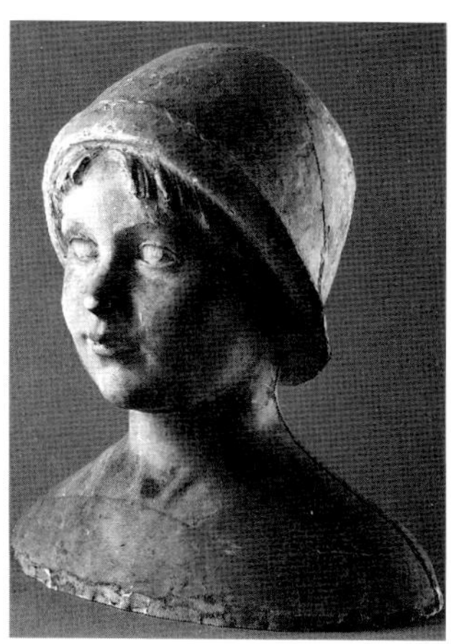
803

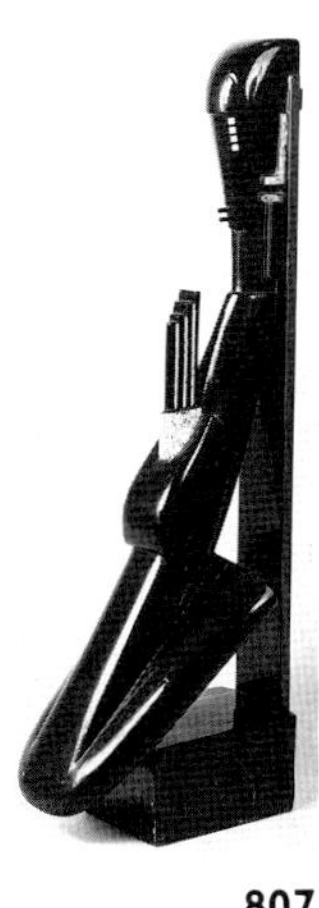
807

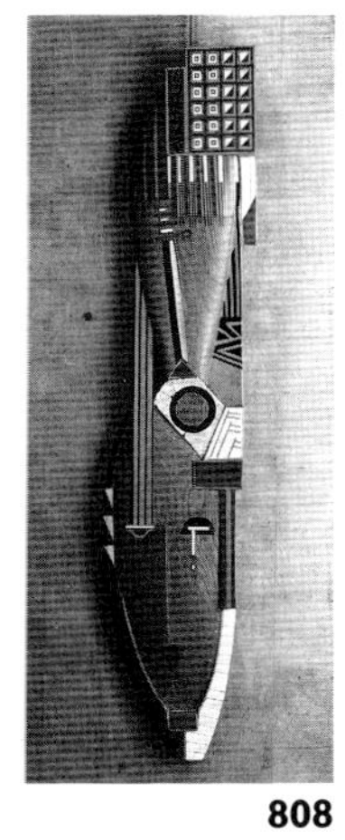
808

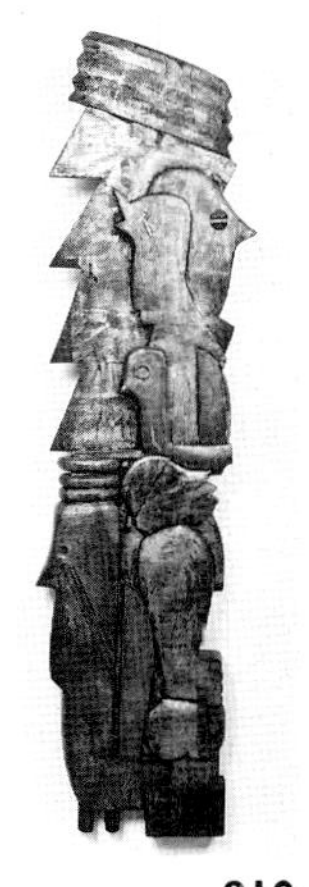
810

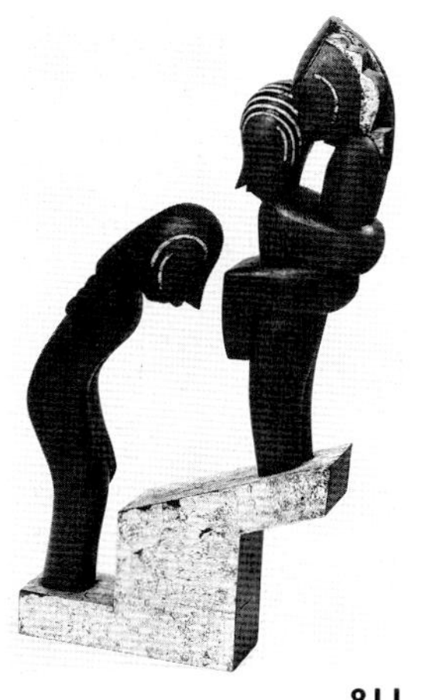
811

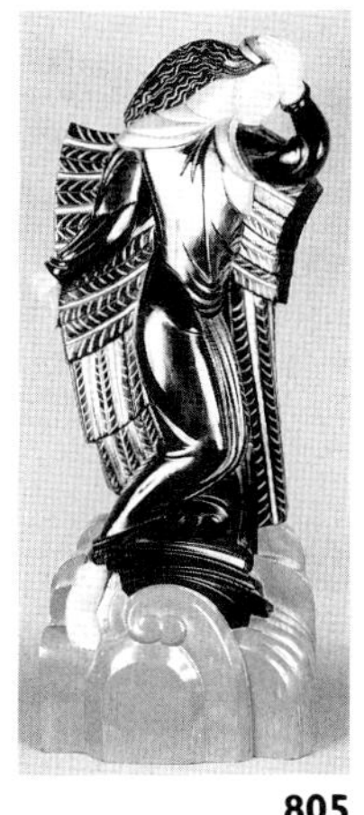
805

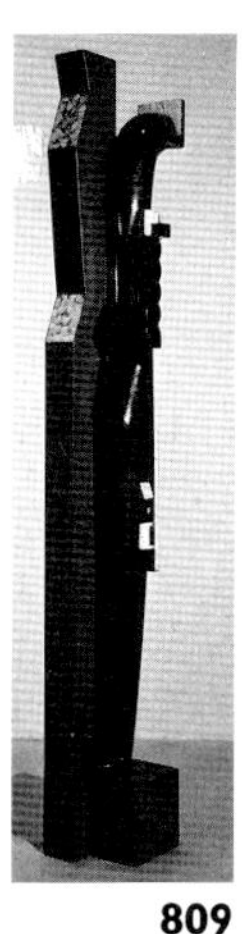
809

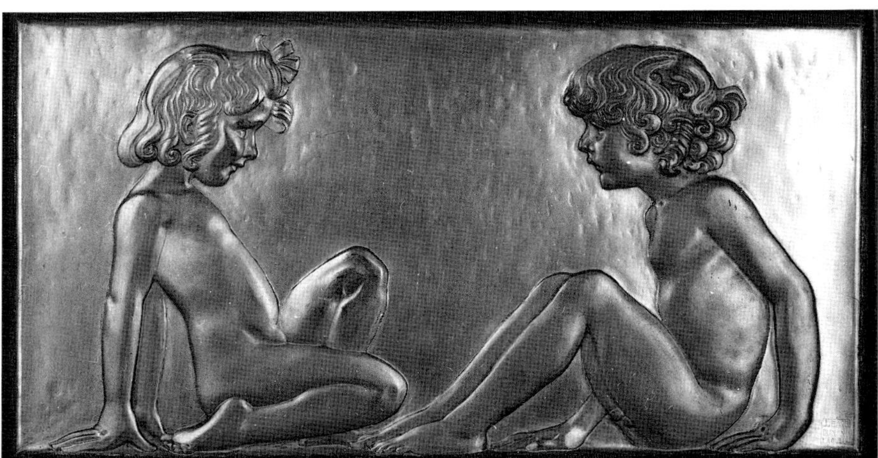
806

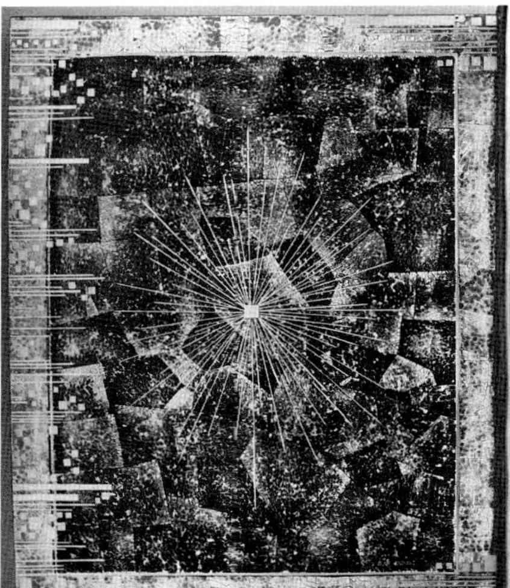
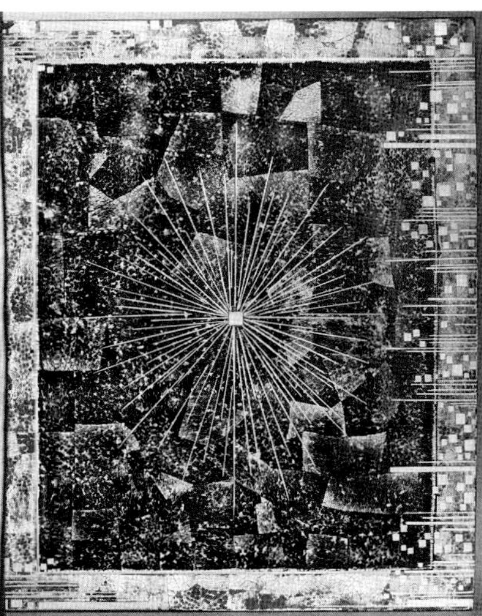
814

SCULPTURES BY OTHER ARTISTS DECORATED BY DUNAND

805 Angel of Sorrows

Wooden statue by Séraphin Soudbinine, lacquered by Dunand.
Height 90 cm (35½ in.).
1921.
Exh.: Salon d'Automne, Paris, 1921 (section for Russian artists).
Coll.: Félix Marcilhac, Paris.

806 Children

Group sculpted by Carl Angst, lacquered in gold by Dunand.
Height 43 cm (17 in.); width 68 cm (26¾ in.).
1923.
Exh.: Galerie Georges Petit, Paris, 1923, no. 19.
Private collection.
Bibl.: *La Science et la vie: la semaine à Paris*, 1 November 1925, p. 384.
The sitters are the twins Suzanne and Jean-Louis Dunand.

807 Prayer

Wooden statue by Jean Lambert-Rucki, lacquered and inlaid with eggshell by Dunand.
Height 94 cm (37 in.).
C. 1927.
Exh.: Galerie du Luxembourg, Paris, 1973, no. 116.
Coll.: Félix Marcilhac, Paris.

808 Two Masks

Oak sculpture by Jean Lambert-Rucki, lacquered and inlaid with eggshell by Dunand.
Height 116 cm (45¾ in.).
C. 1925.
Exh.: Galerie du Luxembourg, Paris, 1973, no. 115.
Coll.: Hélène Rochas.

809 Figure

Wooden sculpture by Jean Lambert-Rucki, lacquered and inlaid with eggshell by Dunand.
Height 192 cm (75½ in.).
C. 1928.

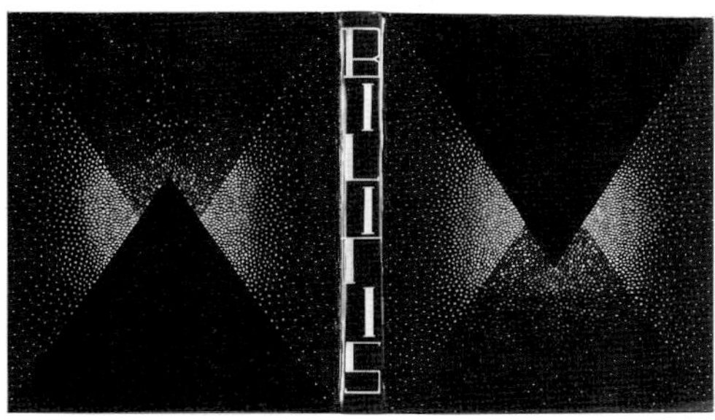

813

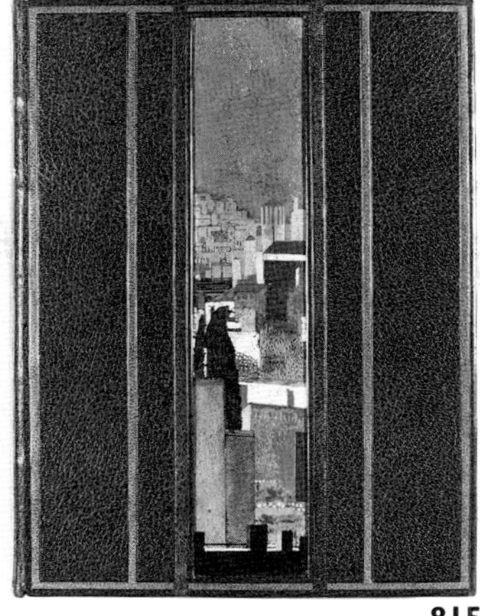

815

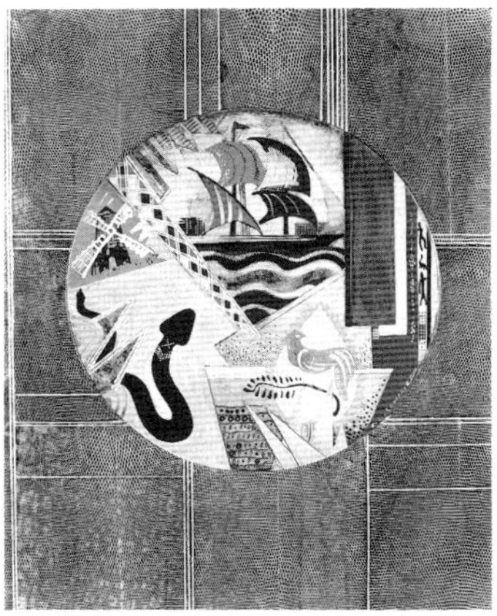

816

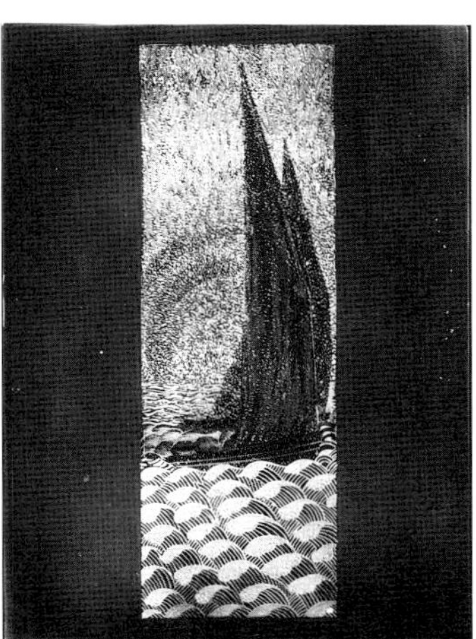

817

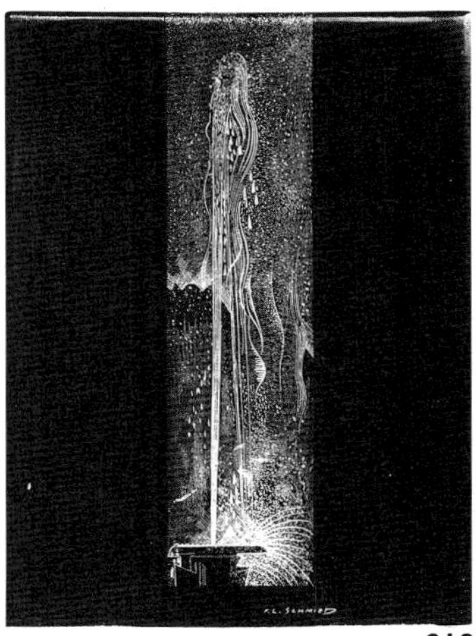

818

Exh.: Galerie du Luxembourg, Paris, 1973, no. 114.
Coll.: Félix Marcilhac, Paris.

810 Men and Birds

Wooden sculpture by Jean Lambert-Rucki, lacquered by Dunand.
Height 152 cm (59¾ in.).
C. 1923.
Exh.: Galerie du Luxembourg, Paris, 1973, no. 160; 'Trois Sculpteurs des années 30: Gargallo, Csaky, Lambert-Rucki', Musée Bourdelle, Paris, 1977, no. 76; Delorenzo Gallery, New York, 1985 (repr. in catalogue, p. 155).
Formerly in the collection of Jacques Mostini; Delorenzo Gallery, New York.

811 Obeisance

Mahogany statue by Jean Lambert-Rucki, lacquered and inlaid with eggshell by Dunand.
C. 1925.
Exh.: 'Jean Lambert-Rucki', Galerie Jacques De Vos, Paris, 1988.
Formerly in the collections of Jacques Mostini, M. and Mme Hombert and in the Dannenberg Collection; Private collection.

BOOKBINDINGS WITH LACQUERED DECORATION BY DUNAND

812 Sacred Elephant

Lacquer on ebonite, executed in 1930 to a design by Paul Jouve; binding by Semet et Plumelle for *Un Pèlerin d'Angkor* by Pierre Loti.
Sold: Delavenne, Lafarge (Paris), 1987, repr. on catalogue cover; Christie's (Geneva), 8 May 1988, lot 69.

813 Triangles

Lacquer on leather inlaid with burgaudine and eggshell, executed in 1922 to a design by Dunand; binding by François-Louis Schmied for *Les Chansons de Bilitis* by Pierre Louÿs.
Coll.: Félix Marcilhac, Paris.

814 Radiances

Inside boards for Schmied's binding of *Les Chansons de Bilitis* (cat. no. 813).
Coll.: Félix Marcilhac, Paris.

815 Oriental Landscape

Lacquer on ebonite inlaid with eggshell, vertical panel executed in 1924 to a design by François-Louis Schmied; binding by Gruel for *Les Climats* by the Comtesse Mathieu de Noailles.
Exh.: Galerie Georges Petit, Paris, 1925, no. 77 (panel only); ——, 1926, no. 86 (finished binding).
Formerly in the collection of André Dubosc; Félix Marcilhac, Paris.

816–820

Decorative panels and boards by Dunand for *Les Climats* by the Comtesse Mathieu de Noailles, all executed in 1924 to designs by François-Louis Schmied; cat. nos. 816, 817 are bindings by Georges Cretté.

816 *Caravel*

Lacquer on copper.
Exh.: 'Books by François-Louis Schmied', Arnold Seligmann Rey, New York, 1927.
Formerly in the collection of Alain Lesieutre; Private collection.

817 *Sailing Boats*

Lacquer on copper.
Exh.: Galerie Georges Petit, Paris, 1924, no. 79 (panel only).
Formerly in the collection of Jacques André; Félix Marcilhac, Paris.

818 *Jet of Water*

Lacquer on copper.
Exh.: Galerie Georges Petit, Paris, 1925, no. 81.
Formerly in the collection of Paul Verdier; Private collection.

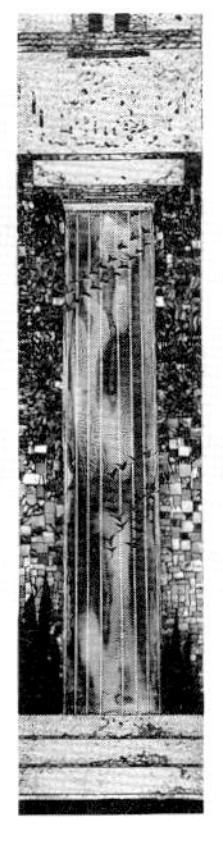

820

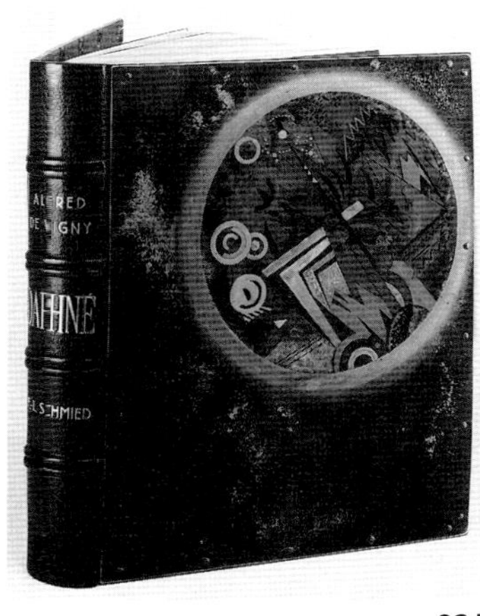

821

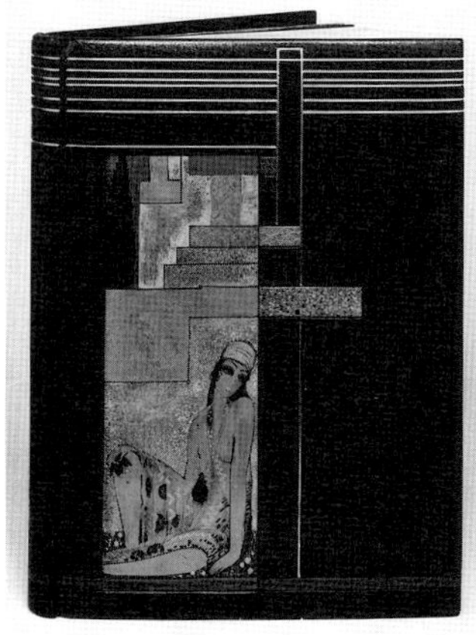

822

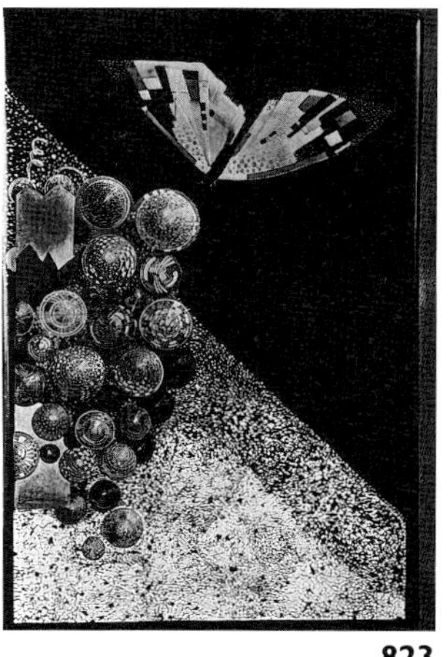

823

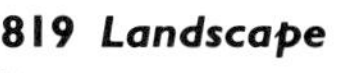

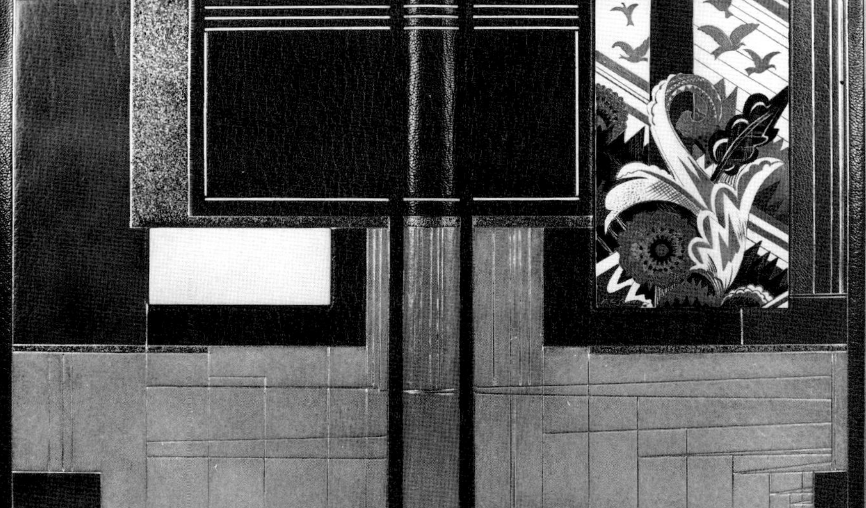

828

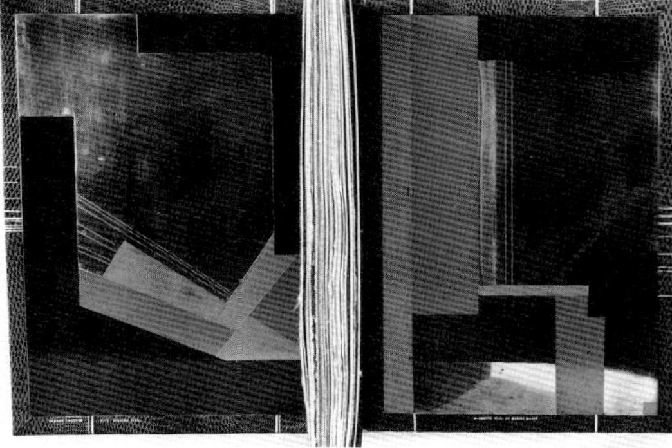

829, 830

824

819 *Landscape*

Lacquer on copper.

820 *Greek Column*

Lacquer on ebonite.
Sold: Pillias, Gluck (Paris), 30 April 1975, lot 83.

821 *Circular Composition*

Lacquer on copper, executed in 1924 to a design by François-Louis Schmied; binding by Georges Cretté for *Daphné* by Alfred de Vigny.
Formerly in the collection of André Bertaut; Private collection.
Sold: Christie's (Geneva), 12 May 1985, lot 66.

822–838

Decorative panels and boards by Dunand for *Le Cantique des Cantiques (The Song of Solomon)*, in the French translation by Ernest Renan, all executed to designs by François-Louis Schmied; cat. nos. 822–830 are bindings by Georges Cretté.

822 *Seated Woman*

Lacquer on ebonite.
1925.
Formerly in the collection of François-Louis Schmied; Félix Marcilhac, Paris.
Sold: Christie's (Geneva), 12 May 1985, lot 11.

823 *Grapes*

Lacquer on copper, inlaid with eggshell.
1924.
Exh.: Galerie Georges Petit, Paris, 1924, no. 87.

824 *King Solomon*

Lacquer on copper.
1924.
Exh.: Galerie Georges Petit, Paris, 1924, no. 84.
Formerly in the collection of Henri Vever; Private collection.
Bibl.: Louis Barthou, 'L'Evolution artistique de la reliure', *L'Illustration*, special Christmas number, 1930.

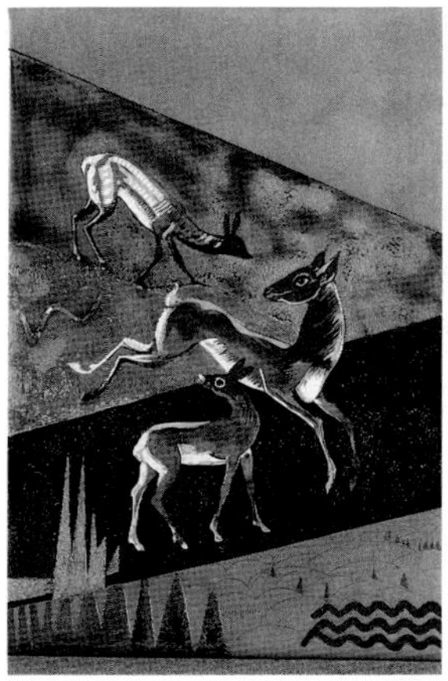
825

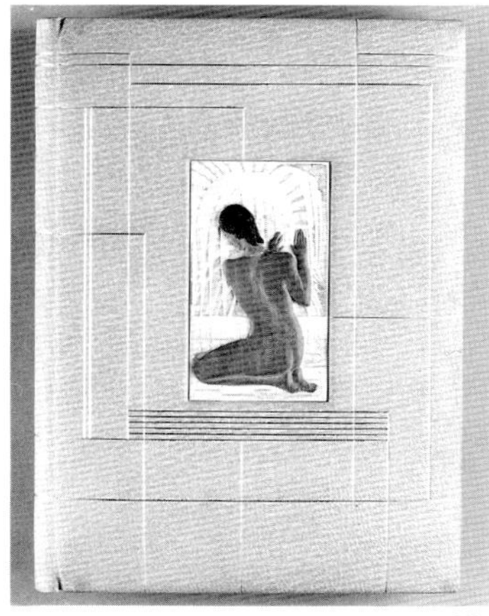
826

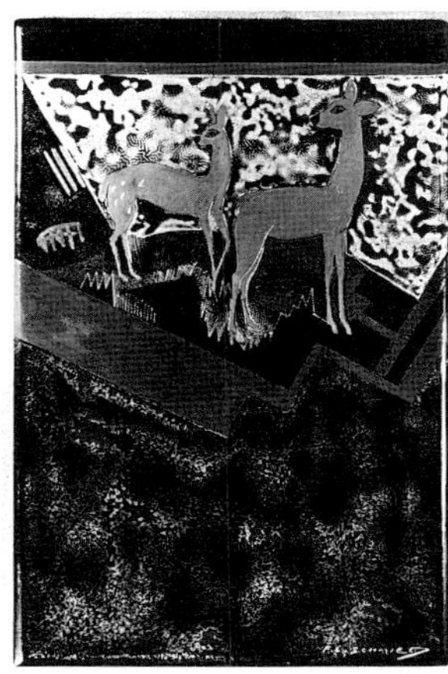
831

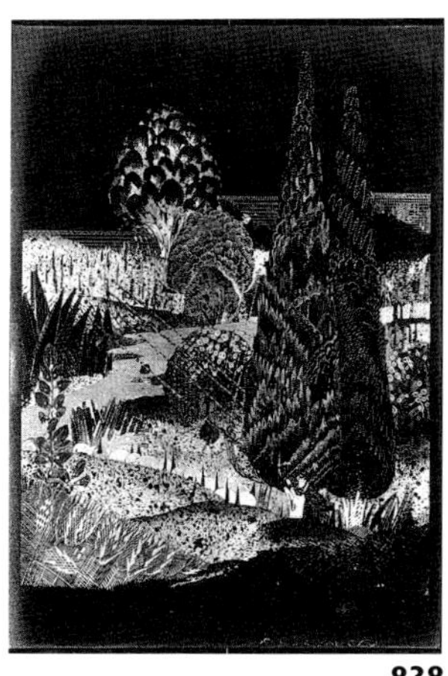
838

825 ***Deer***
Lacquer on copper.
1925.
Exh.: Galerie Georges Petit, Paris, 1925, no. 75.
Formerly in the collection of Jacques André; Félix Marcilhac, Paris.

826 ***Woman Kneeling***
Wood and carved ivory.
1925.
Coll.: Félix Marcilhac, Paris.

827 ***Flowers and Fruit*** *Pl. 160*
Lacquer on copper, inlaid with eggshell.
1925.
Exh.: Galerie Georges Petit, Paris, 1925, no. 78 (panel only).
Private collection.

828 ***Flowers and Doves***
Lacquer on ivory.
1925.
Coll.: Félix Marcilhac, Paris.

829, 830 ***Geometry I and II***
Lacquer on copper (inside boards).
1925.
Coll.: Félix Marcilhac, Paris.

831 ***Deer***
Lacquer on copper.
1924.
Exh.: Galerie Georges Petit, Paris, 1924, no. 89.

832 ***King Solomon***
Lacquer on copper.
1924.
Exh.: Galerie Georges Petit, Paris, 1924, no. 88.

833 ***King Solomon***
Lacquer on copper.
1924.
Exh.: Galerie Georges Petit, Paris, 1924, no. 86.
Formerly in the collection of Pierre Guerquin; private collection.

834 ***Doves***
Lacquer on ebonite, inlaid with eggshell.
1924.
Exh.: Galerie Georges Petit, Paris, 1924, no. 85.
Formerly in the collection of André Bertaut.

835 ***Doves Billing***
Lacquer on ebonite.
1925.
Exh.: Galerie du Luxembourg, Paris, 1973.
Sold: Sotheby's (Monaco), 20 March 1981, lot 267.

836 ***Doves*** *Pl. 159*
Lacquer on ebonite, inlaid with eggshell.
1925.
Coll.: Félix Marcilhac, Paris.

837 ***Butterfly and Grapes***
Lacquer on ebonite.
1925.
Formerly in the collection of the Galerie Vallois, Paris; Private collection.

838 ***Garden***
Lacquer on copper.
1925.
Exh.: Galerie Georges Petit, Paris, 1925, no. 83.
Formerly in the collection of Paul Verdier; Private collection.

839 The Nightingale
Lacquer on ebonite, inlaid with eggshell, executed in 1926 to a design by François-Louis Schmied; binding by Gruel for *Two Tales* by Oscar Wilde.
Exh.: Galerie Georges Petit, Paris, 1926, no. 87; 'Books by François-Louis Schmied', Arnold Seligmann Rey, New York, 1927.
Formerly in the collection of Charles Miguet; Félix Marcilhac, Paris.

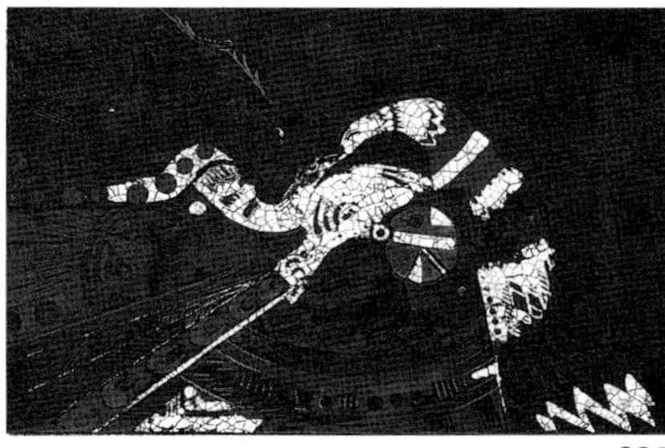
835

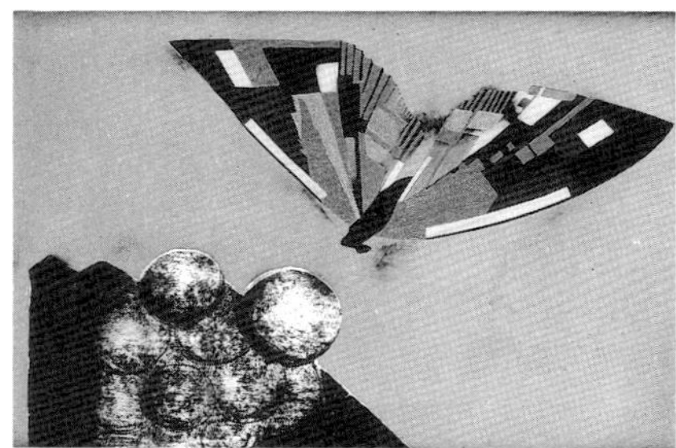
837

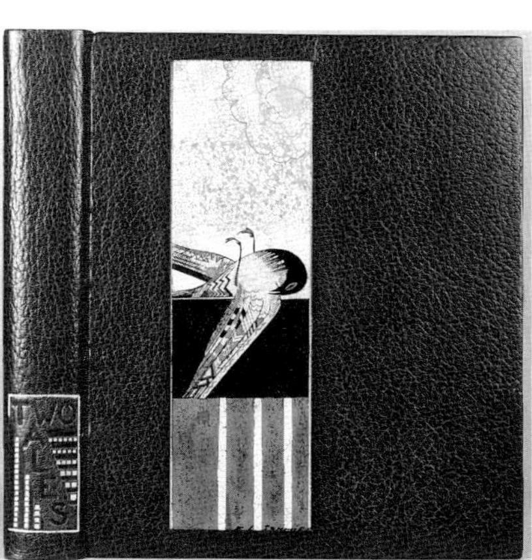

839

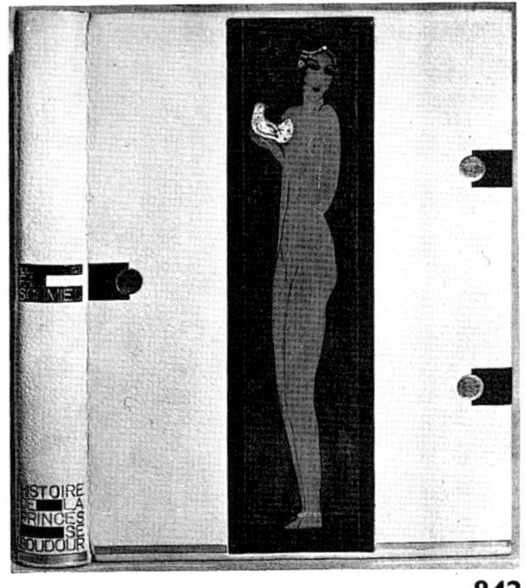

842

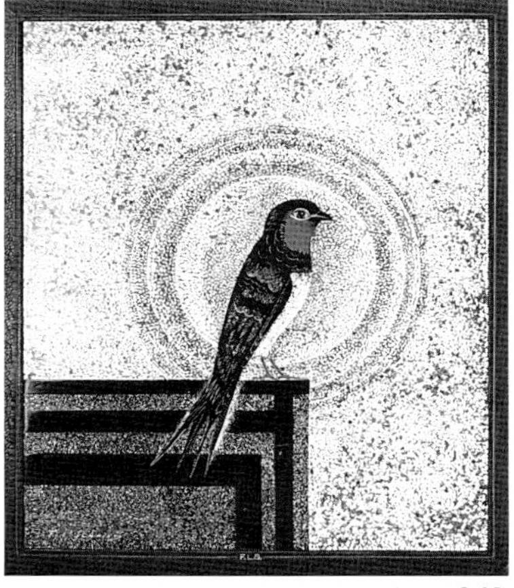

840

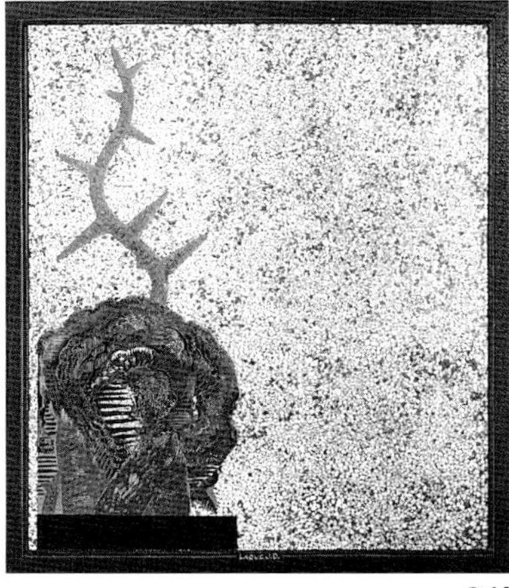

841

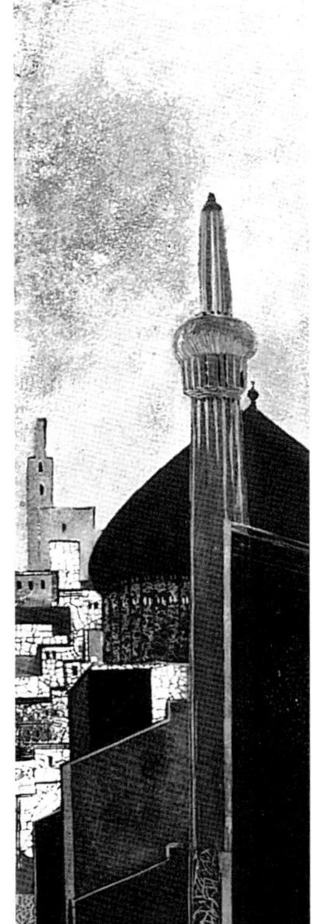

845

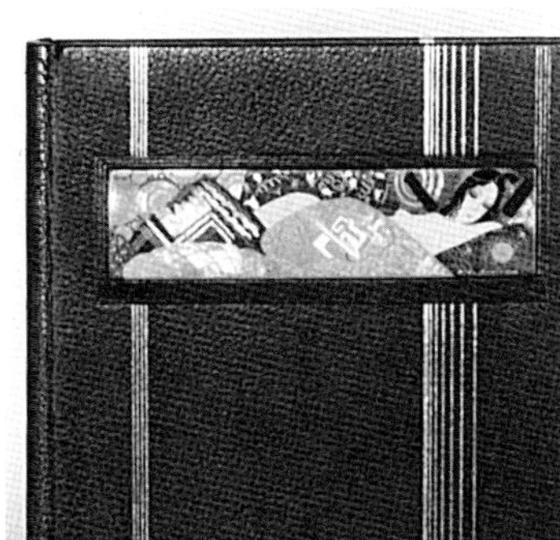

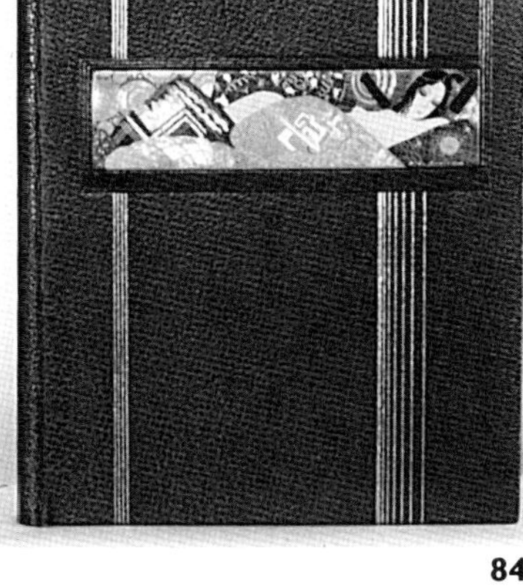

843

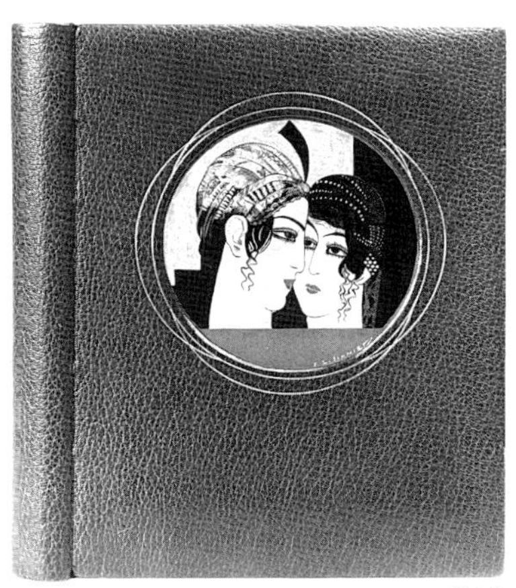

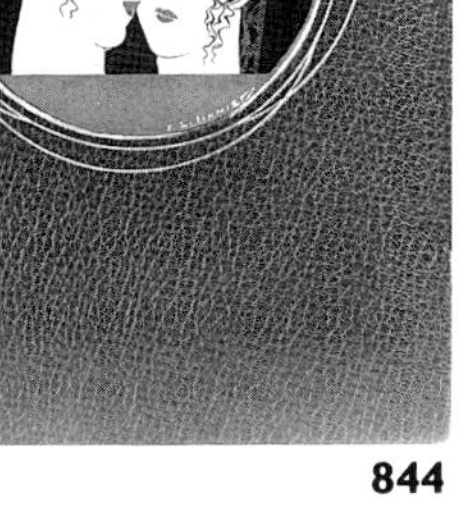

844

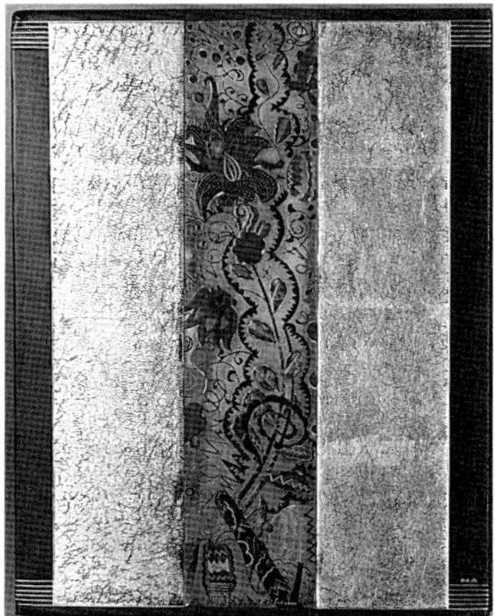

846

840, 841 The Nightingale and Tree *Pl. 158*

Lacquer on brass, inlaid with eggshell, executed in 1926 to designs by François-Louis Schmied; inside boards of a binding by Schmied for *Two Tales* by Oscar Wilde.
Formerly in the collection of François-Louis Schmied; Félix Marcilhac, Paris.

842 Princess Boudour

Lacquer on ebonite inlaid with eggshell, vertical panel executed in 1926 to a design by François-Louis Schmied; binding by Rose Adler for *Histoire de la Princesse Boudour* by Joseph-Charles Mardrus.
Bibl.: Charles Moreau (ed.), *L'Art international d'aujord'hui* (Paris, n.d.), p. 13.

843 Princess Boudour

Lacquer on ebonite, horizontal panel executed in 1926 to a design by François-Louis Schmied; binding by Schmied for *Histoire de la Princesse Boudour* by Joseph-Charles Mardrus.
Formerly in the collection of Henri Vever; Private collection.
Sold: Christie's (Geneva), 13 November 1983, lot 28.

844 Princess Boudour

Lacquer on copper, executed in 1927 to a design by François-Louis Schmied; binding by Gruel for *Histoire charmante de l'adolescente Sucre d'Amour* by Joseph-Charles Mardrus.
Formerly in the collection of the Marquis de Marchena; Private collection.
Sold: Christie's (Geneva), 13 May 1984, lot 51.

845 Oriental Landscape

Lacquer on copper, inlaid with eggshell, vertical panel executed in 1927 to a design by François-Louis Schmied; binding by Schmied for *Histoire charmante de l'adolescente Sucre d'Amour* by Joseph-Charles Mardrus.
Formerly in the collection of Lucien Graux; Private collection.
Sold: Christie's (Geneva), 12 May 1985, lot 49.

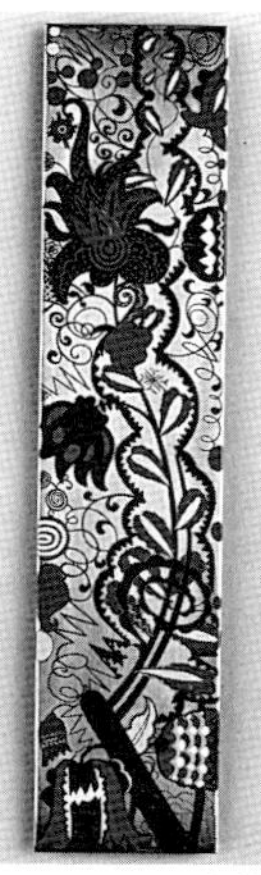
847

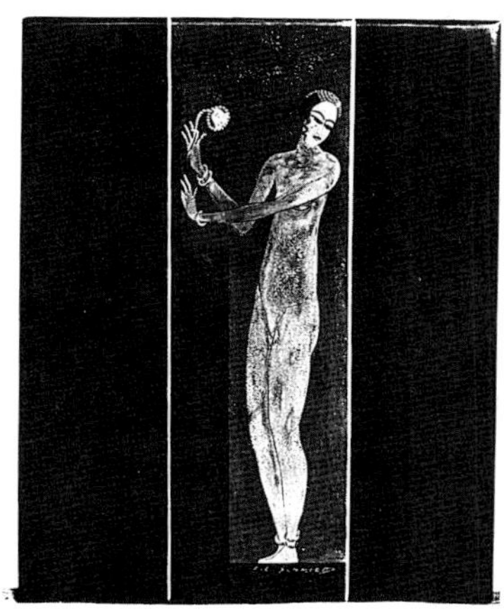
848

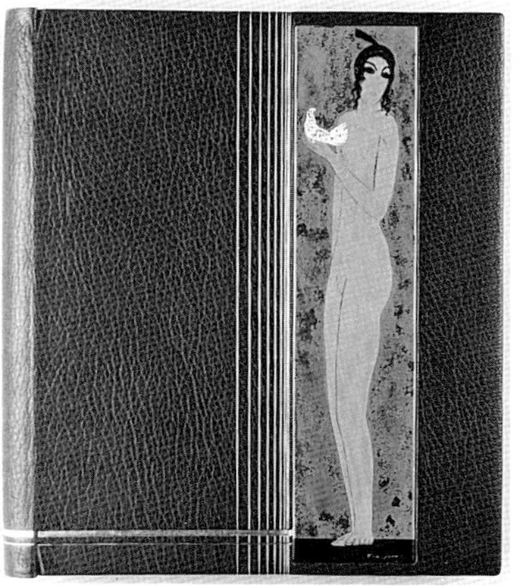
849

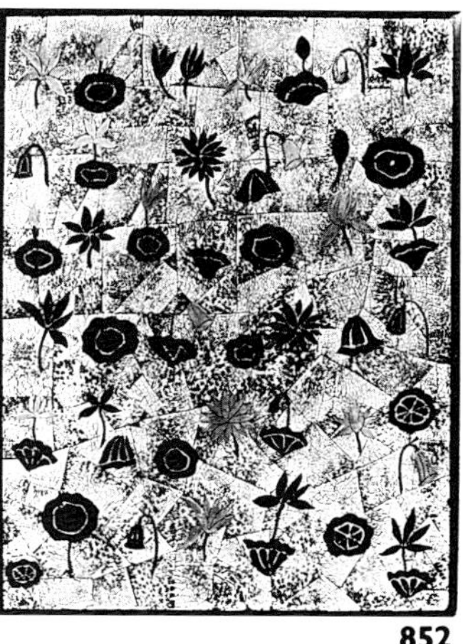
852

846 Flowers
Lacquer on silver, vertical panel executed in 1927 to a design by François-Louis Schmied; inside board of a binding by Schmied for *Histoire charmante de l'adolescente Sucre d'Amour* by Joseph-Charles Mardrus.
Coll.: Félix Marcilhac, Paris.

847 Flowers
Lacquer on silver, vertical panel executed in 1927 to a design by François-Louis Schmied; inside board of binding for *Histoire charmante de l'adolescente Sucre d'Amour* by Joseph-Charles Mardrus.
Coll.: Félix Marcilhac, Paris.

848 Sucre d'Amour
Lacquer on copper, vertical panel executed in 1927 to a design by François-Louis Schmied; inside board of binding for *Histoire charmante de l'adolescente Sucre d'Amour* by Joseph-Charles Mardrus.

849 Sucre d'Amour
Lacquer on ebonite, inlaid with eggshell, vertical panel executed in 1927 to a design by François-Louis Schmied; binding by Schmied for *Histoire charmante de l'adolescente Sucre d'Amour* by Joseph-Charles Mardrus.
Formerly in the collection of Jacques André; Félix Marcilhac, Paris.

850 Sucre d'Amour
Lacquer on copper, inlaid with eggshell, executed in 1927 to a design by François-Louis Schmied; binding by Georges Cretté for *Histoire charmante de l'adolescente Sucre d'Amour* by Joseph-Charles Mardrus.
Formerly in the collection of Félix Boix; Private collection.
Sold: Pierre-Yves Gabus (Geneva), 27 November 1983, lot 420.

851 Landscape with Animals
Lacquer on ivory, panel executed in 1928 to a design by François-Louis Schmied; binding by Georges Cretté for *La Création*, Joseph-Charles Mardrus' translation of the Book of Genesis.
Formerly in the Loucheur Collection; Private collection.
Bibl.: Louis Barthou, 'L'Évolution artistique de la reliure', *L'Illustration*, special Christmas number, 1930.

852 Flowers
Lacquer on copper, inlaid with eggshell, executed in 1928 to a design by François-Louis Schmied; binding for *La Création*, Joseph-Charles Mardrus' translation of the Book of Genesis.

853 The Garden of Eden
Lacquer on copper, inlaid with eggshell, executed in 1928 to a design by François-Louis Schmied; binding for *La Création*, Joseph-Charles Mardrus' translation of the Book of Genesis.

854 Caesar
Lacquer on ebonite, vertical panel executed in 1929 to a design by François-Louis Schmied; binding by Georges Cretté for *Les douze Césars*, J. Estève's translation of Suetonius's *Lives of the Caesars*.
Exh.: Galerie Georges Petit, Paris, 1929, no. 96.
Private collection.

855 Laurel Wreath
Lacquer on ebonite, executed in 1929 to a design by François-Louis Schmied; binding by Georges Cretté for *Les douze Césars*, J. Estève's translation of Suetonius's *Lives of the Caesars*.
Private collection.
Sold: Rabourdin-Chopin de Janvry (Paris), 27 November 1987, lot 70.

856 Python
Lacquer on copper, inlaid with eggshell, executed in 1930 to a design by Paul Jouve; binding by Semet et Plumelle for *La chasse de Kaa (Kaa's Hunting)* by Rudyard Kipling.
Sold: Sotheby's (New York), 20 June 1986, lot 133.

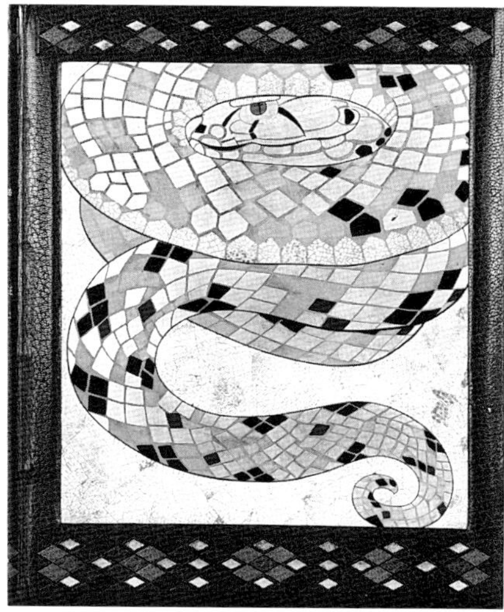
856

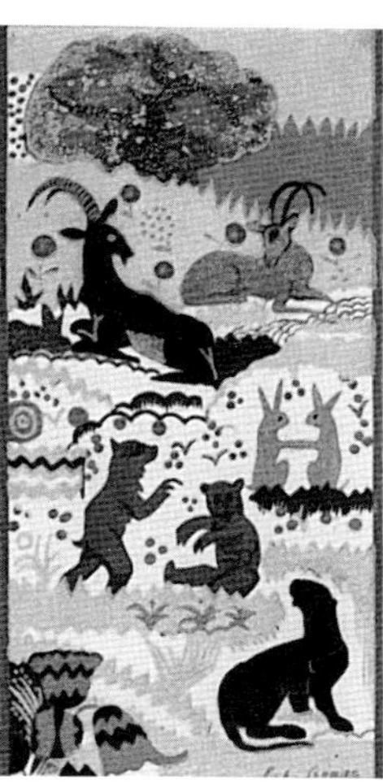
851

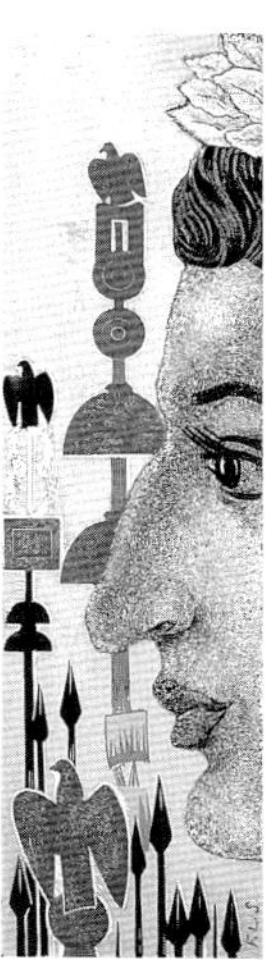
854

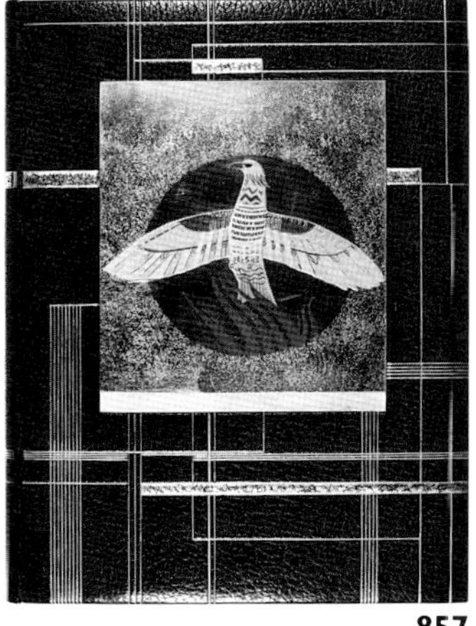
857

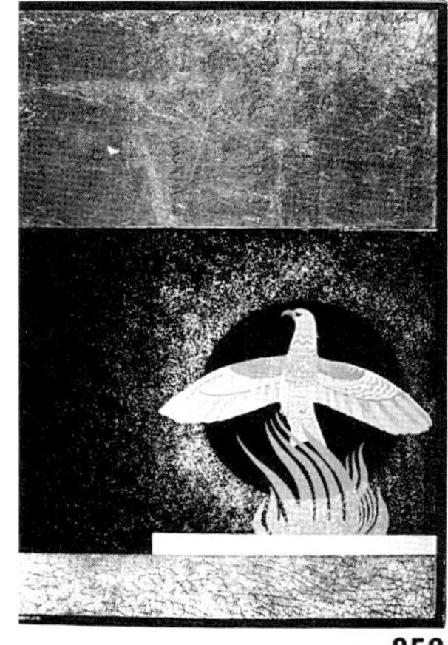
858

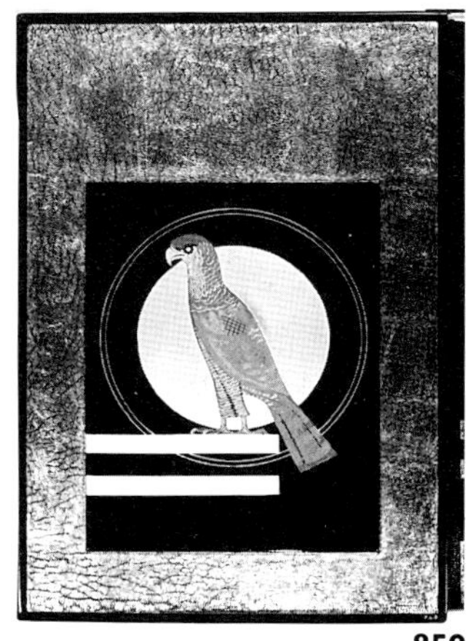
859

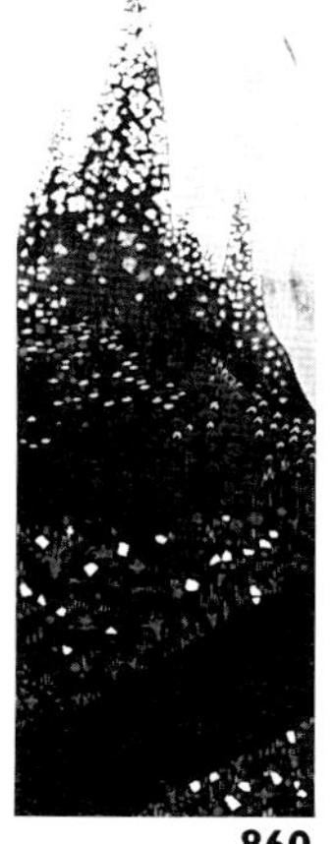
860

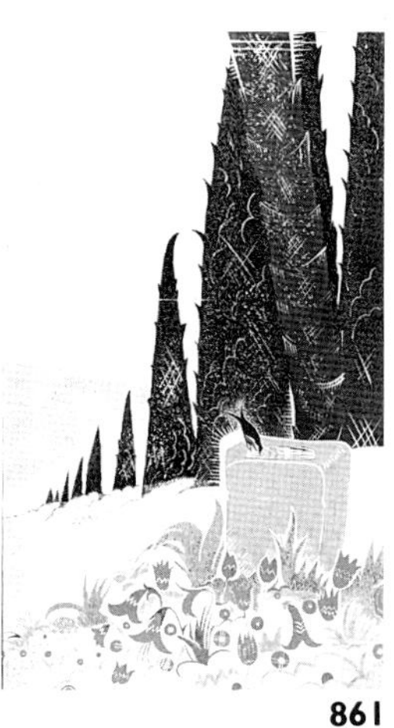
861

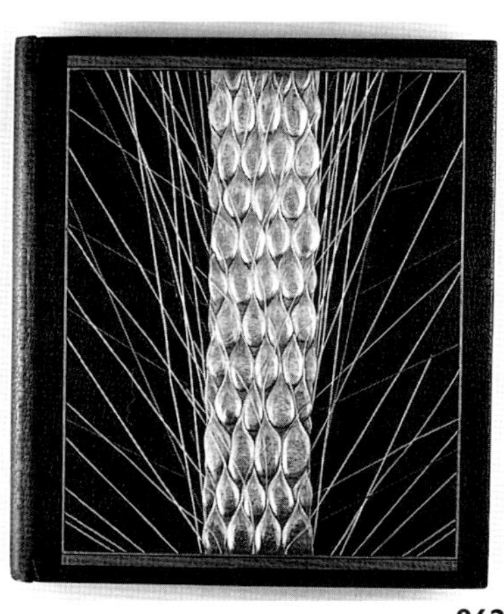
862

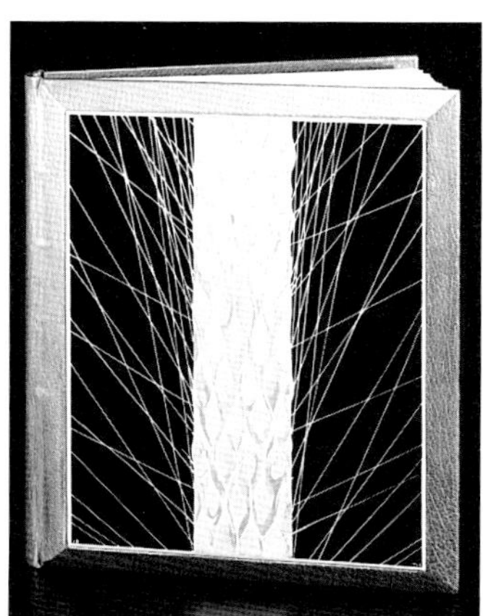
863

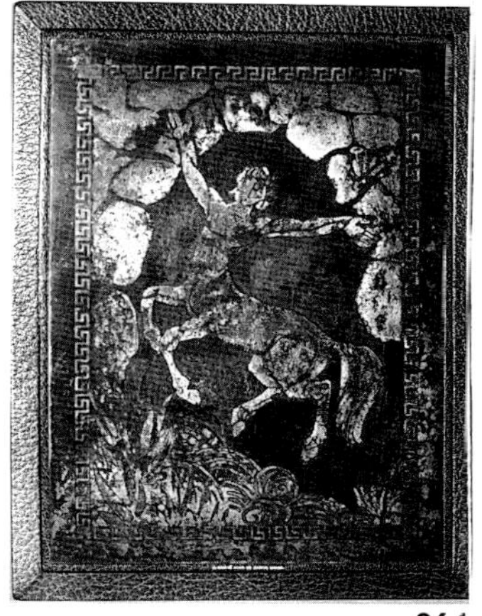
864

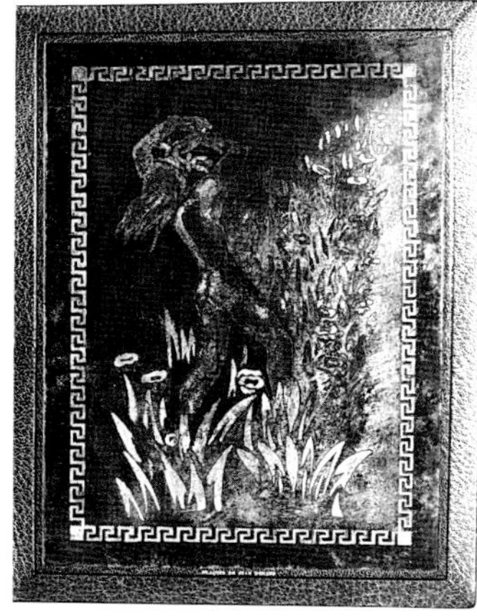
865

857 The Great Winged Simurgh

Lacquer on copper, executed in 1930 to a design by François-Louis Schmied; binding by Georges Cretté for *Le Paradis Musulman*, translated by Joseph-Charles Mardrus.
Formerly in the collection of Jean Borderel; Félix Marcilhac, Paris.
Bibl.: Lynne Thornton, 'Dunand and his Friends', *Apollo*, October 1973, p. 298.

858, 859 The Great Winged Simurgh and **Eagle**

Lacquer on copper, executed in 1930 to designs by François-Louis Schmied; inside boards (front and back) of a binding by Schmied for *Le Paradis Musulman*, translated by Joseph-Charles Mardrus.
Sold: Christie's (Geneva), 11 November 1984, lot 30, both repr. in catalogue.

860 Garden

Lacquer on ebonite, executed in 1930 to a design by François-Louis Schmied; binding by Georges Cretté for *Les Aventures du dernier Abencérage* by René de Chateaubriand.
Sold: Oger, Dumont (Paris), 5 June 1987, repr. on cover of sale catalogue.

861 The Stele

Lacquer on ebonite, executed in 1930 to a design by François-Louis Schmied; binding by René Kieffer for *Les Aventures du dernier Abencérage* by René de Chateaubriand.
Formerly in the collection of René Kieffer; Félix Marcilhac, Paris.

862 Ear of Wheat

Patinated *repoussé* gold, executed in 1930 to a design by François-Louis Schmied; binding by Schmied for *Ruth et Booz*, translated by Joseph-Charles Mardrus.
Coll.: Félix Marcilhac, Paris.

863 Ear of Wheat

Lacquer on copper, executed in 1930 to a design by François-Louis Schmied;

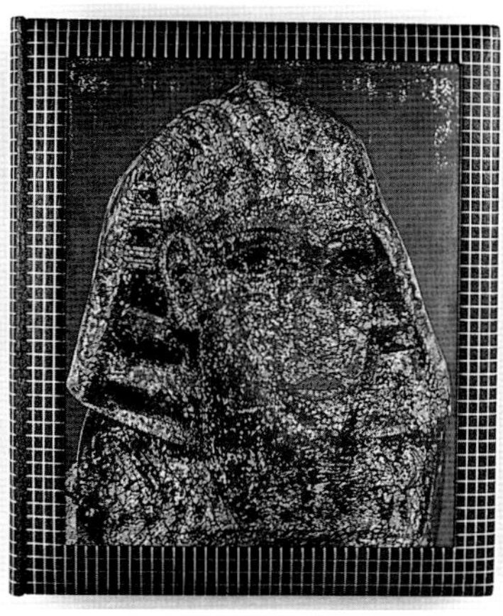

866

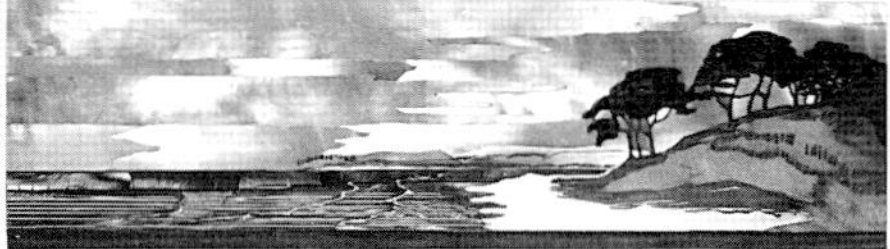

869

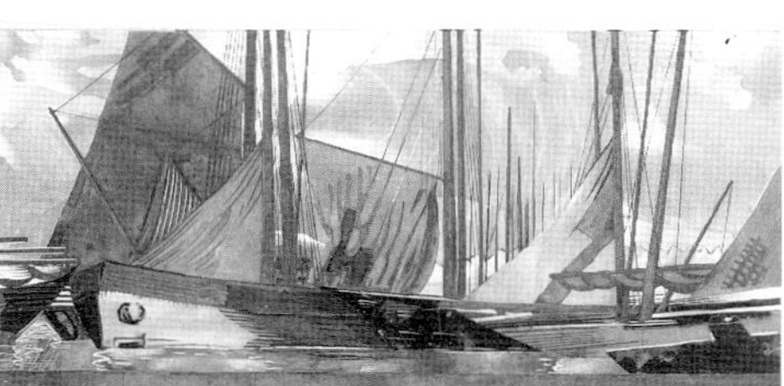

868

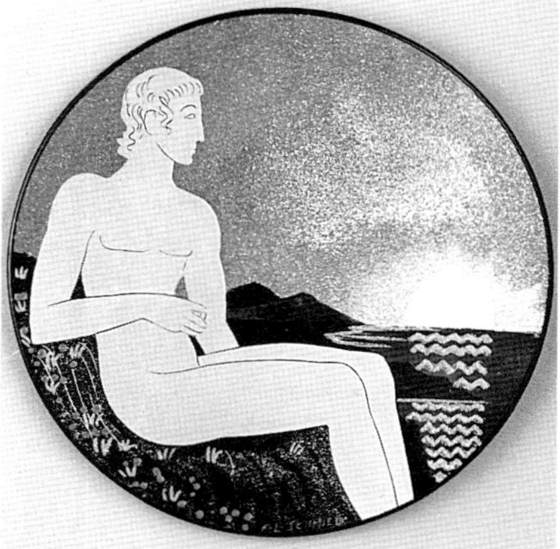

870

binding by Schmied for *Ruth et Booz*, translated by Joseph-Charles Mardrus.
Coll.: Virginia Museum of Fine Arts, Richmond, Va (gift of Sydney and Frances Lewis).

864, 865 The Centaur and **The Bacchante**

Dinanderie inlaid with silver, executed in 1931 to designs by François-Louis Schmied; inside boards (front and back) of a binding by Georges Cretté for *Le Centaure et la bacchante* by Maurice de Guérin.
Formerly in the Baumgartner Collection; Félix Marcilhac, Paris.
Sold: Ferri (Paris), 2 April 1974, lot 168.

866 The Sphinx

Lacquer on ebonite, inlaid with eggshell, executed in 1931 to a design by François-Louis Schmied; binding by Georges Cretté for *Peau-Brune* by François-Louis Schmied.
Coll.: Félix Marcilhac, Paris.

867 View of the Port

Lacquer on ebonite, executed in 1933 to a design by François-Louis Schmied; binding by Georges Cretté for *Paysages méditerranéens* by Paul Morand.
Exh.: Delorenzo Gallery, New York, 1985 (repr. in catalogue, p. 146).
Private collection.
Sold: Christie's (New York), 3 April 1982, lot 116.

868, 869 Sailing Boats in Port and **Seashore**

Lacquer on mother-of-pearl mosaic, executed in 1933 to designs by François-Louis Schmied; panels decorating the inside boards (front and back) of a binding by Georges Cretté for *Paysages méditerranéens* by Paul Morand.
Formerly in the collection of Amedée Baumgartner; Private collection.
Sold: Christie's (Geneva), 11 November 1984, lot 42, both repr. in catalogue.

870 Rising Sun

Lacquer on copper, executed in 1934 to a design by François-Louis Schmied; circular panel decorating binding board for an edition of Homer's *Odyssey* translated by Victor Bérard.
Coll.: Félix Marcilhac, Paris.

871 Geometric Composition

Gouache on maroon paper, design by François-Louis Schmied for a binding (unidentified).
C. 1930.
Private collection.

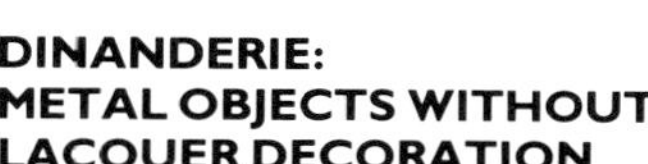

DINANDERIE: METAL OBJECTS WITHOUT LACQUER DECORATION

872 'Satin-flower' vase

Repoussé and chased bronze inlaid with white mother-of-pearl, chased bronze handles.
Height 90 cm (35½ in.).
1906.
Exh.: Association des Artistes Suisses de Paris, 1907.
Bibl.: *La Décoration moderne* (1905/6), pl. 40; Roger de Felice, 'John Dunand', *L'Art décoratif*, January 1909, p. 13.
Coll.: Musée d'Art et d'Histoire, Geneva.

873 'Frog' vase *Pl. 139*

Patinated chased gilt bronze.
Height 31 cm (12¼ in.).
1906.
Exh.: Salon de la Nationale, Paris, 1907.
Bibl.: Roger de Felice, 'John Dunand', *L'Art décoratif*, January 1909, p. 15.
Sold: Christie's (Geneva), 13 November 1983, lot 148.

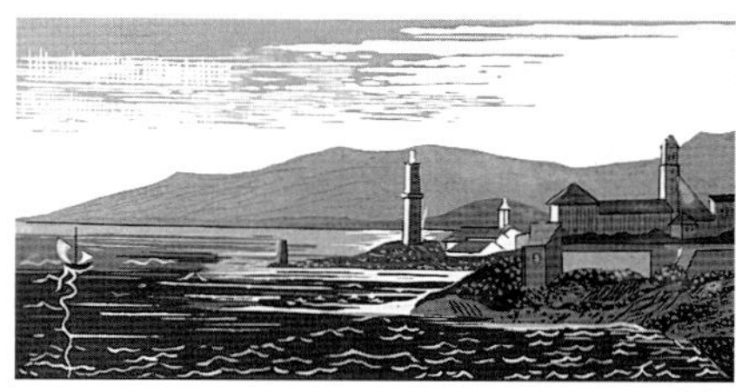

867

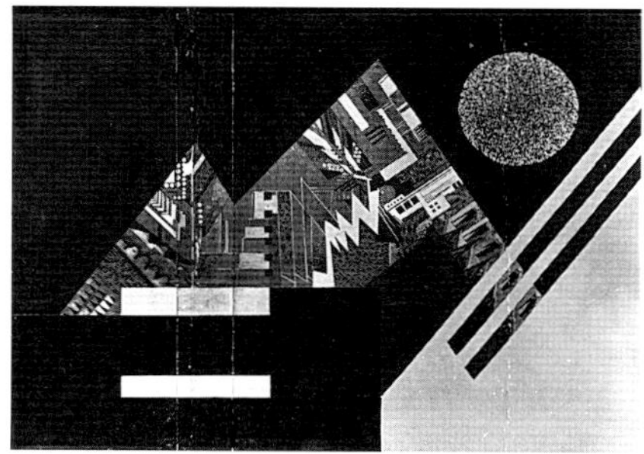

871

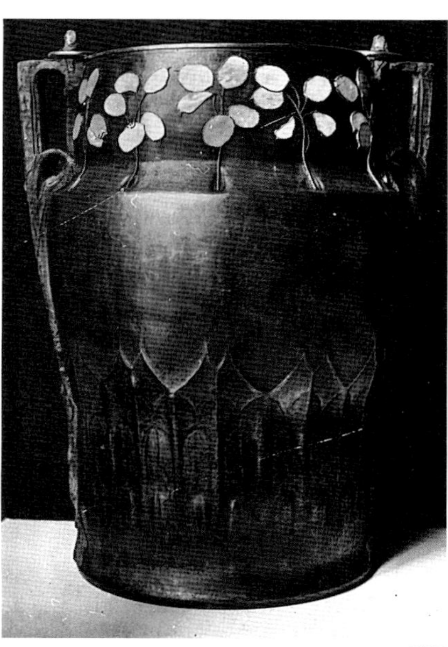

872

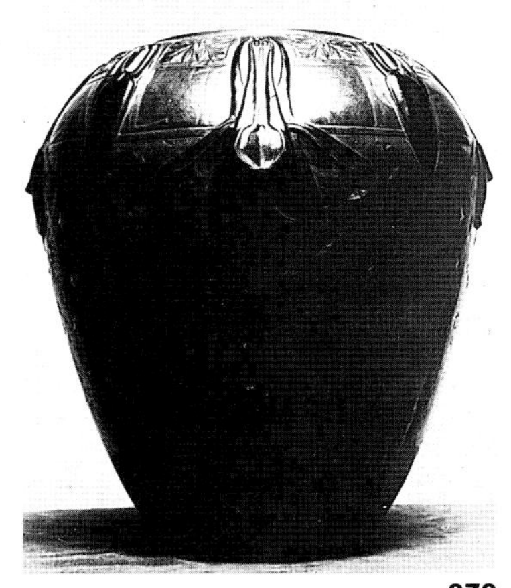

878

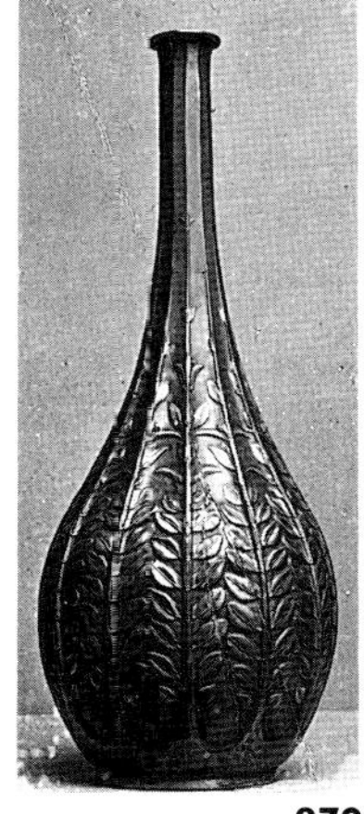

879

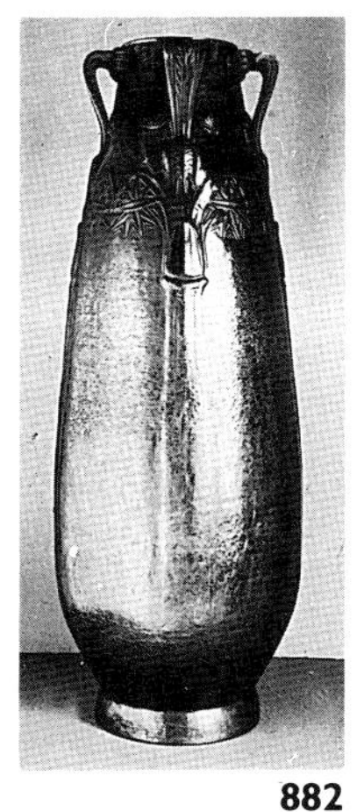

882

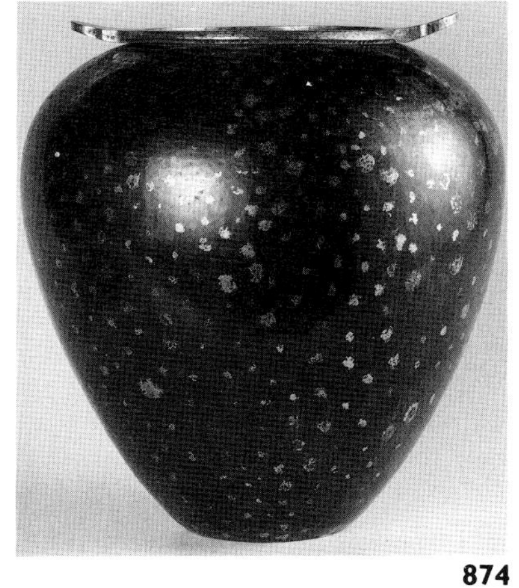

874

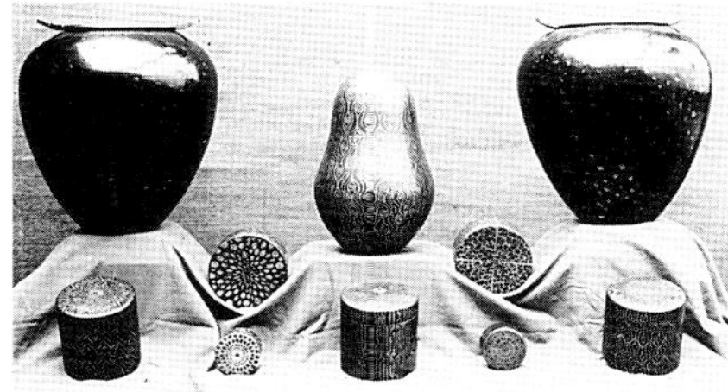

875

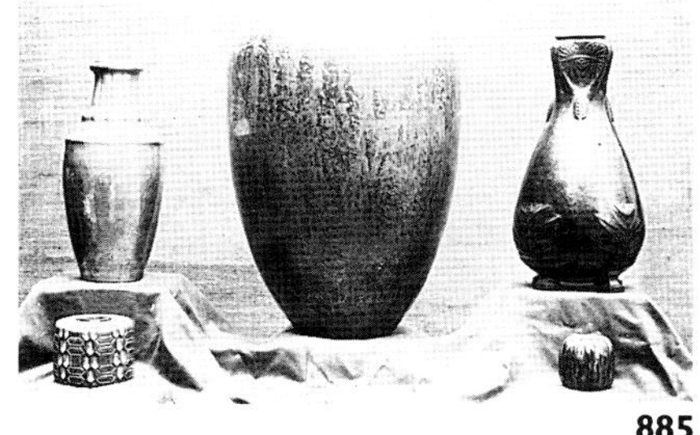

885

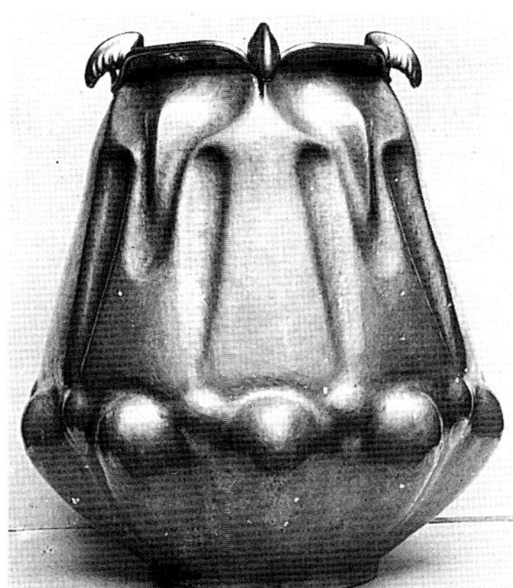

877

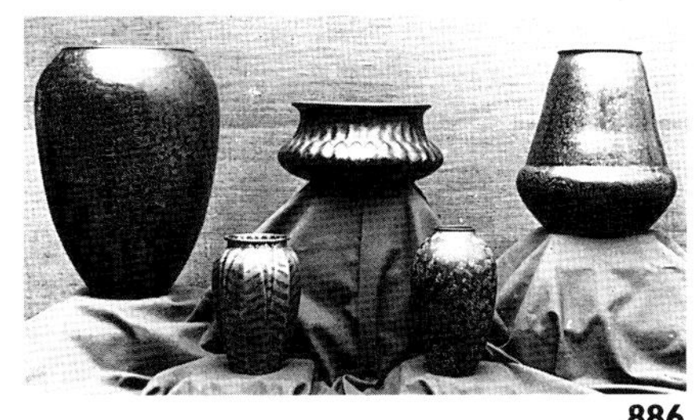

886

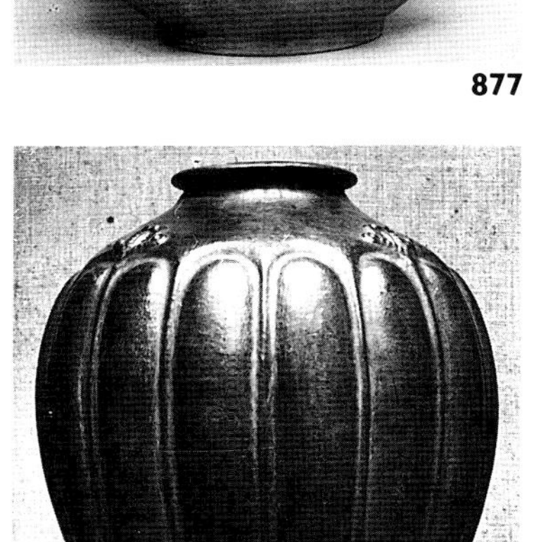

884

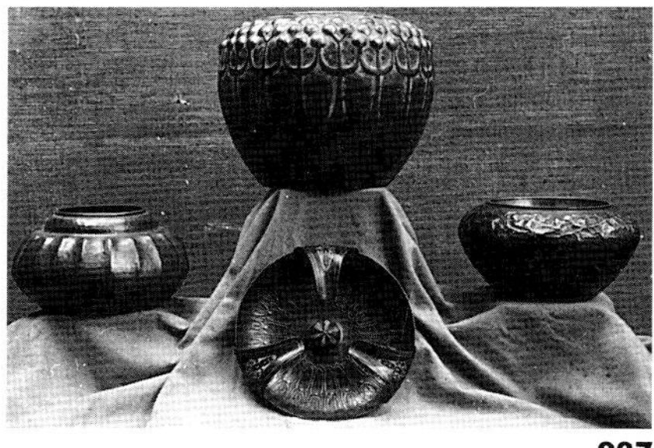

887

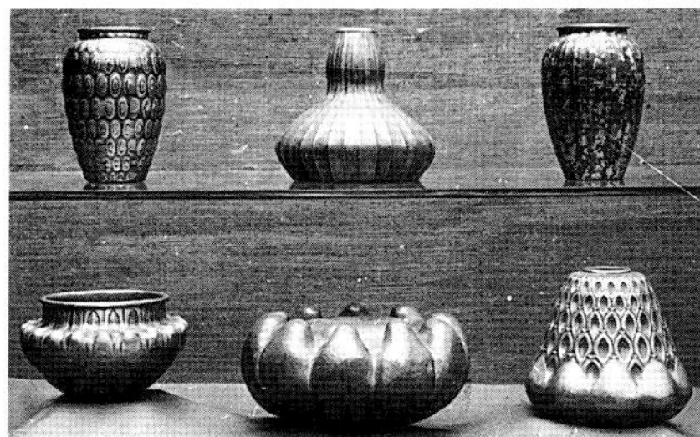

888

874 Collarette vase

Hammer-marked faceted brass flecked with gold, interior cone with gilt-bronze border and projecting handles.
Height 27 cm (10¾ in.).
1907.
Exh.: Salon de la Nationale, Paris, 1907.
Coll.: Alain Lesieutre, Paris.
Bibl.: Jean Monnier, 'Les Vases de M. John Dunand', *Foi et vie*, 16 February 1908, p. 103.

875 Vases and boxes

Various patinated metals inlaid with silver.
Exh.: Salon de la Nationale, Paris, 1907.

876 'Snake' vase *Pl. 143*

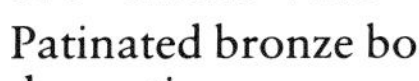

Patinated bronze body with *appliqué* decoration.
Height 16 cm (6¼ in.).
1907.
Exh.: Delorenzo Gallery, New York, 1985 (repr. in catalogue, p. 129).
Coll.: Steven A. Greenberg, New York.

877 Floral vase

Patinated *repoussé* pewter and gilt copper.
1907.
Exh.: Salon de la Nationale, Paris, 1908.
Formerly in the collection of the Musée du Luxembourg, Paris; Musée d'Orsay, Paris.
Bibl.: Roger de Felice, 'John Dunand', *L'Art décoratif*, January 1909, p. 18.

878 'Fuchsia' vase

Repoussé and chased gilt copper.
1907.
Exh.: Salon de la Nationale, Paris, 1908.

879 'Laburnum' vase

Repoussé gilt brass.
1907.
Exh.: Salon de la Nationale, Paris, 1908.
Bibl.: Roger de Felice, 'John Dunand', *L'Art décoratif*, January 1909, p. 16.

880 Lanceolate-leaf cache-pot

Patinated *repoussé* brass.
1907.
Exh.: Salon de la Nationale, Paris, 1908.

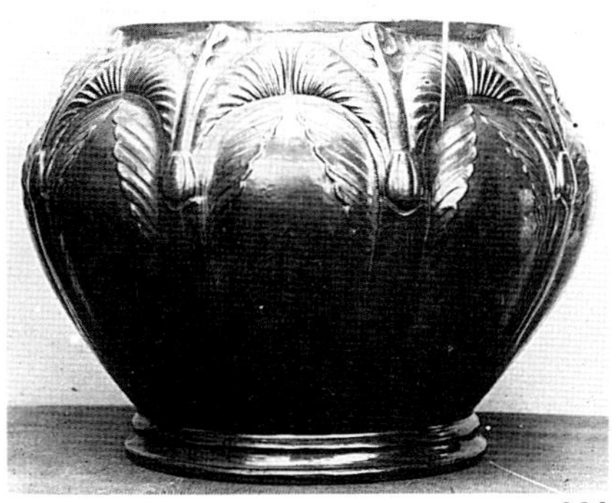
881

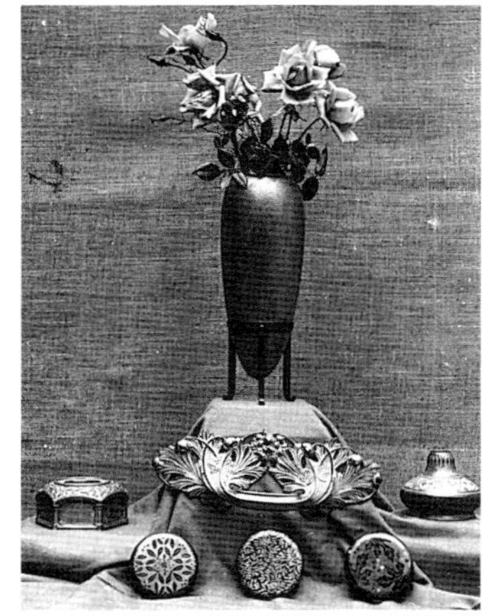

891

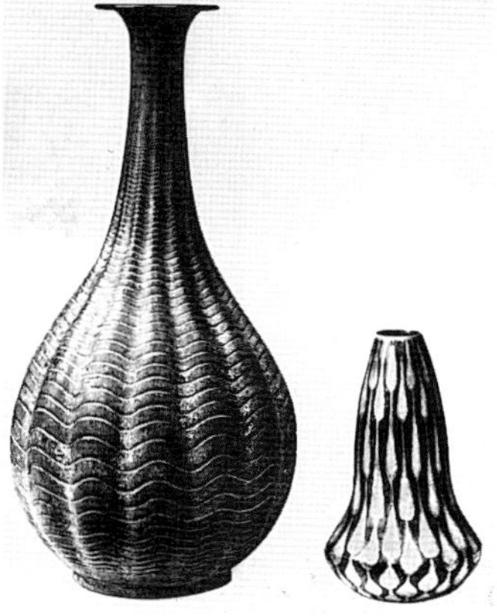
893

Bibl.: Roger de Felice, 'John Dunand', *L'Art décoratif*, January 1909, p. 12.

881 Cache-pot with stylized leaves
Patinated *repoussé* brass.
1907.
Exh.: Salon de la Nationale, Paris, 1908.
Bibl.: Roger de Felice, 'John Dunand', *L'Art décoratif*, January 1909, p. 12.

882 Tall vase with handles
Patinated *repoussé* brass.
1907.
Bibl.: Jean Monnier, 'Les Vases de M. John Dunand', *Foi et vie*, 16 February 1908, p. 103; Roger de Felice, 'John Dunand', *L'Art décoratif*, January 1909, p. 14.

883 Small vase and pot-bellied vase
Small vase in lead and *repoussé* pewter, large vase in faceted gilt brass.
1907.
Exh.: Salon de la Nationale, Paris, 1908.
Bibl.: Roger de Felice, 'John Dunand', *L'Art décoratif*, January 1909, p. 11.

884 Boss-beaded vase
Patinated *repoussé* copper.
1908.
Exh.: Salon de l'Eclectique, Paris, 1909; Galerie Montaigne, Théâtre des Champs-Élysées, Paris, 1913.
Bibl.: Emmanuel de Thubert, 'Jean Dunand', *L'Art et les artistes*, new series, no. 9 (1920), p. 383.

885 Vases and boxes
Various metals patinated and inlaid with silver.
1908.
Exh.: Salon de la Nationale, Paris, 1908.

886 Vases
Various metals patinated and inlaid with silver.
1908.
Exh.: Salon de la Nationale, Paris, 1908.

887 Vases, bowl and cache-pot
Embossed and with patinated finish.
1908.
Exh.: Salon de la Nationale, Paris, 1908.

888 Vases
Embossed and with patinated finish.
C. 1909.
Exh.: No details known.

889 Vases
Various metals inlaid with silver and patinated.
C. 1909.
Exh.: No details known.

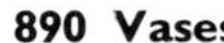

890 Vases
Copper and *repoussé* and chased pewter.
C. 1909.

891 Tripod vase, inkstand, handle and boxes
Patinated copper, pewter, bronze and various metals inlaid with silver.
C. 1910.
Exh.: No details known.

892 Ovoid vase
Patinated brass.
C. 1910.

893 Vases
Bronze and copper inlaid with gold.
C. 1910.

894 Boxes and watch-cases
Patinated *repoussé* copper and steel with niello decoration.
C. 1910.

895 Vases, ashtray and boxes
Various patinated silver-inlaid metals with *repoussé* decoration.
C. 1910.
Exh.: No details known.

896 'Mountain-ash' vase
Repoussé and chased copper with gilt-bronze handles.
Height 90 cm (35½ in.).
1911.
Exh.: Salon de l'Eclectique, Paris, 1911; Villefavart, 1912; Ghent, 1913; Galerie Rosenberg, Paris, 1914.

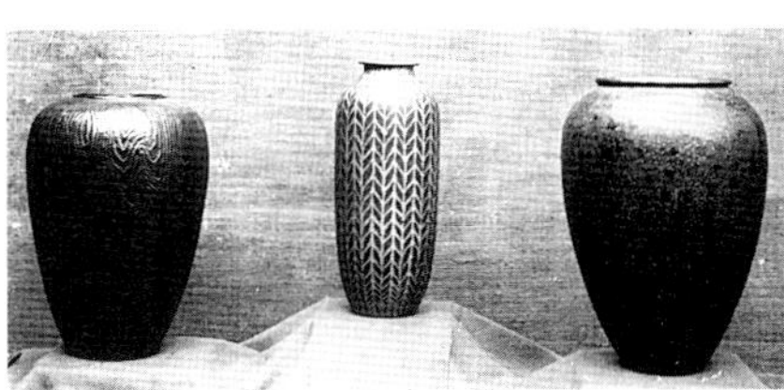
889

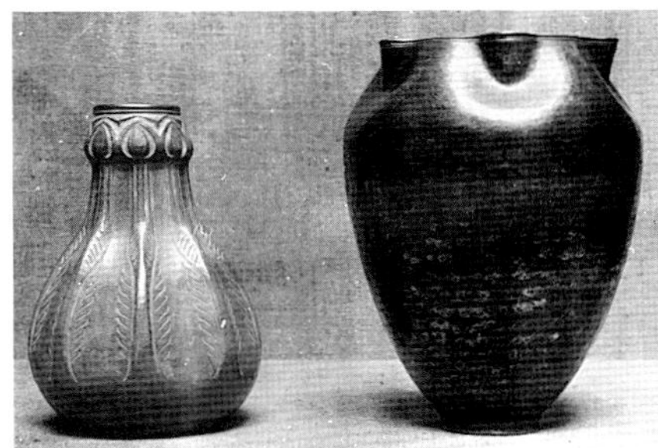
890

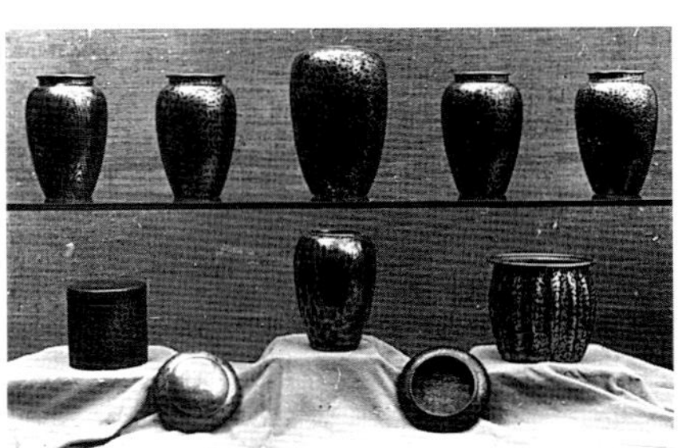
895

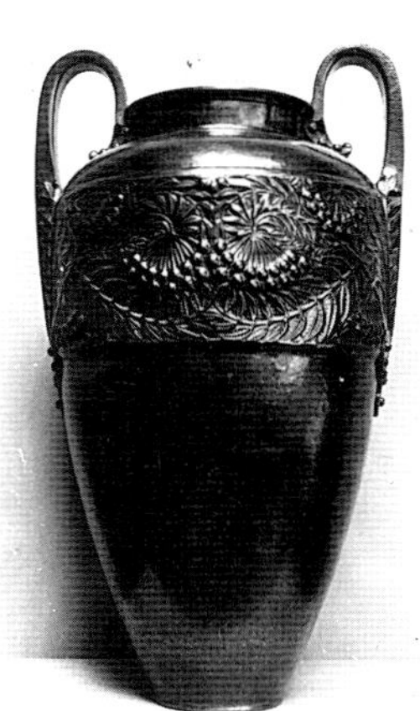
896

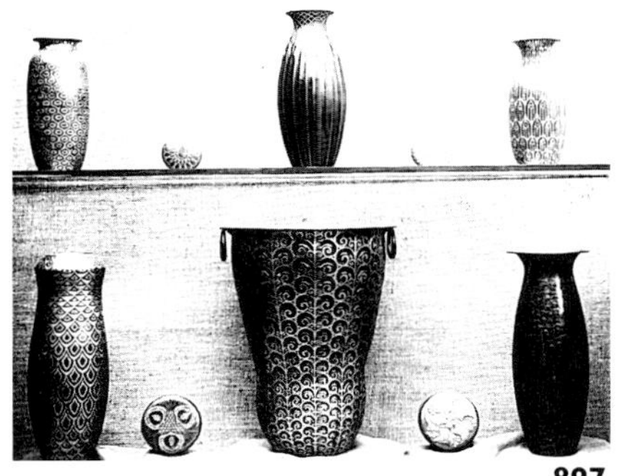
897

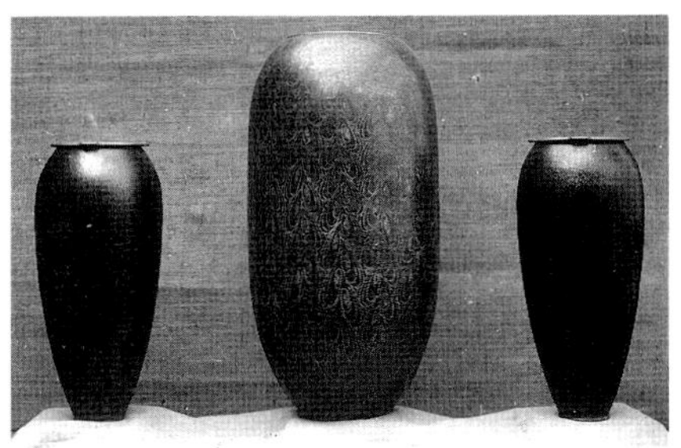
899

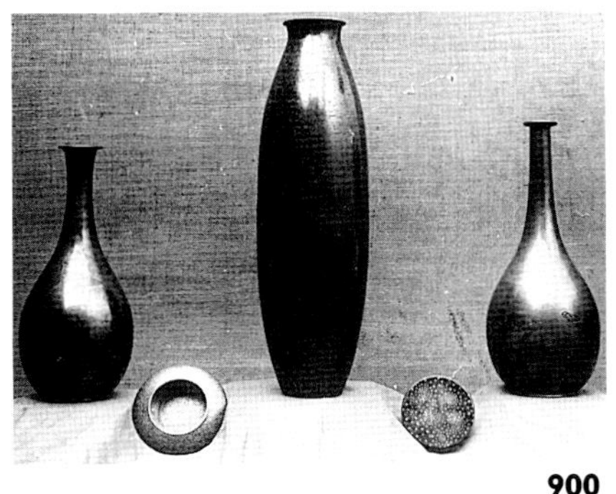
900

908

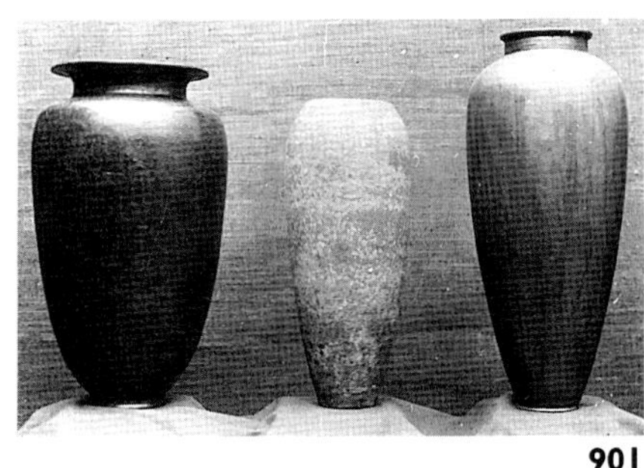
901

905

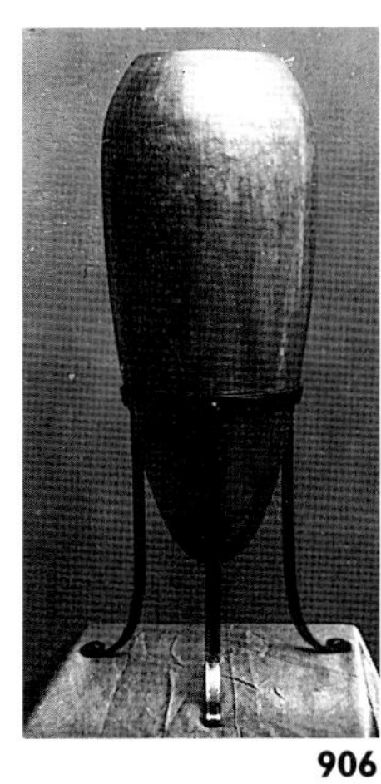
906

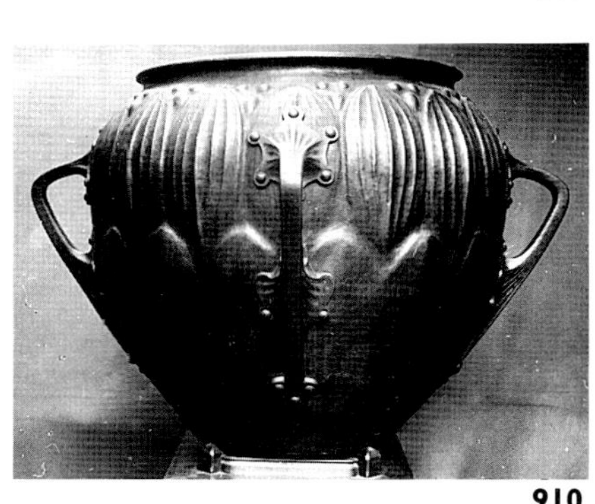
910

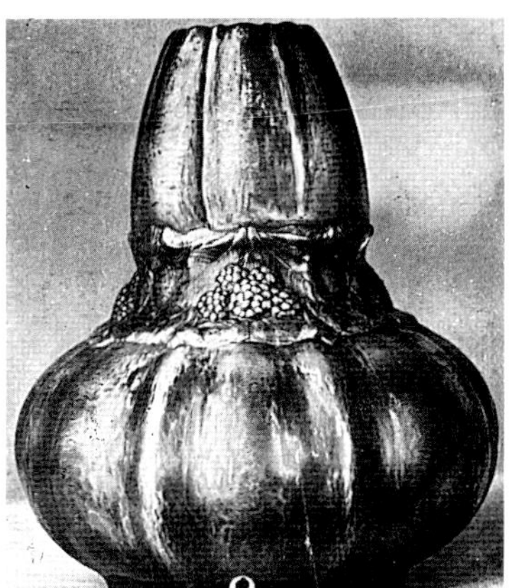
902

897 Vases and boxes
Various metals, including steel inlaid with gold and silver.
1911.
Exh.: Galerie Manzi-Joyant, Paris, 1911; Galerie Rosenberg, Paris, 1914.

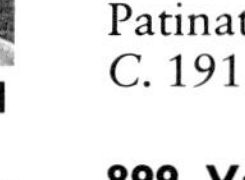
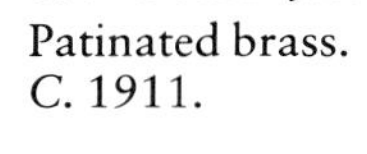

898 Ovoid vase
Patinated brass.
C. 1911.

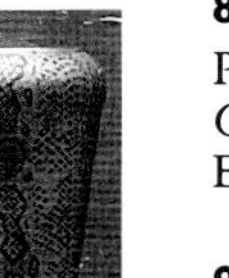

899 Vases
Patinated brass inlaid with silver.
C. 1911.
Exh.: No details known.

900 Bottles, vase and box
Various patinated metals, bottle in gold-lacquered copper.
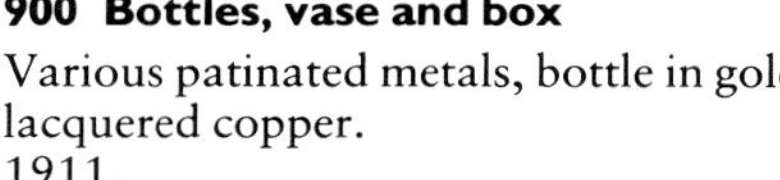
1911.
Exh.: No details known.

901 Vases
Various metals patinated or inlaid.
C. 1911.
Exh.: No details known.

902 'Mulberry' vase
Patinated and *repoussé* copper.
Exh.: Salon de la Nationale, Paris, 1911.

903 Vase
Oxidized brass inlaid with silver.
Height 72 cm (28¼ in.).
C. 1911.
Private collection.
This vase is shown on the far left in colour plate 60.

904 Flower-vase *Pl. 135*
Repoussé and chased nickel silver coated with silver.
Height 60 cm (23½ in.).
1912.
Exh.: Villefavart, 1912; Galerie Montaigne, Théâtre des Champs-Élysées, Paris, 1913; Galerie Rosenberg, Paris, 1914.
Private collection.

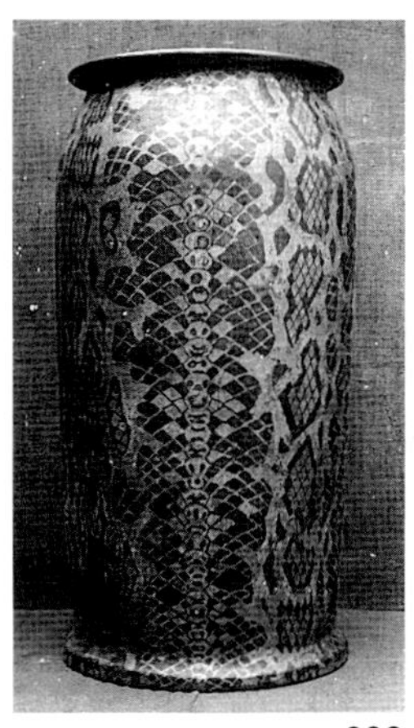
909

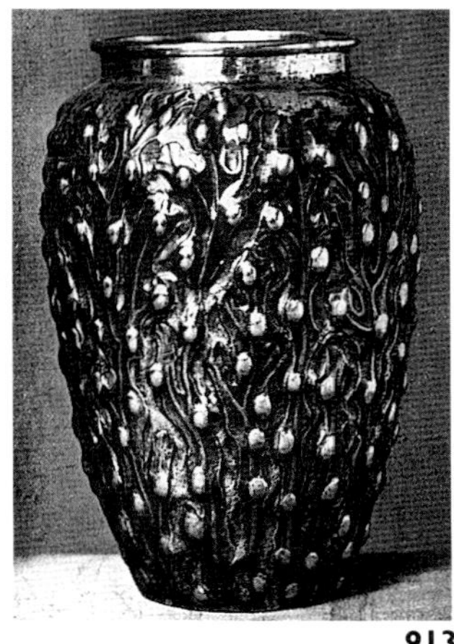
913

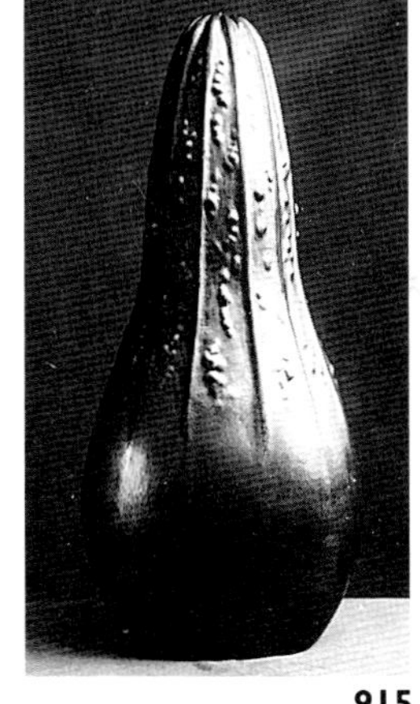
915

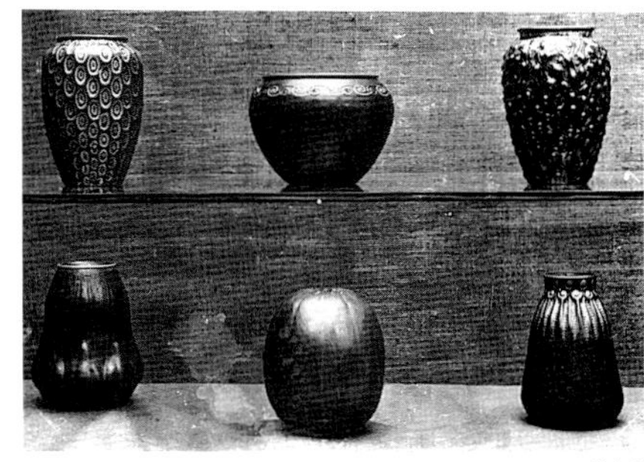
912

905 Vases
Brass and oxidized striated silver with snakeskin volutes.
1912.
Exh.: Excelsior, Paris, 1912; Galerie Manzi-Joyant, Paris, 1913.
Bibl.: M. Testard, 'Le Métal dans l'art moderne', *Nos Loisirs*, 1 July 1922, p. 323.

906 Vase on tripod
Patinated brass vase on wrought-iron tripod.
1912.
Exh.: Excelsior, Paris, 1912.

907 Large cylindrical vase *Pl. 136*
Patinated brass inlaid with silver.
Height 75 cm (29½ in.).
1912.
Exh.: Delorenzo Gallery, New York, 1985 (repr. in catalogue, p. 86).
Formerly in the collection of the Galerie Vallois, Paris; Delorenzo Gallery, New York.
Sold: Perrin, Royère, Lajeunesse (Versailles), 26 February 1984.

908 Large cylindrical vase
Patinated brass inlaid with silver.
Height 76 cm (30 in.).
1912.
Exh.: Grands Magasins du Bon Marché, Paris, 1912; Exhibition of Decorative Art, Neuchâtel, 1912; Galerie Rosenberg, Paris, 1914.

909 Large cylindrical vase
Patinated brass inlaid with silver.
Height 76 cm (30 in.).
1912.
Exh.: Salon d'Automne, Paris, 1912; Ghent, 1913; Kunsthaus, Zurich, 1913.

910 Large cache-pot
Repoussé copper with hammer-marked brass handles.
1912.
Exh.: Exhibition of Decorative Art, Neuchâtel, 1912; Parc de Bagatelle, Paris, 1913.

911 Vases
Patinated bronze, copper and nickel silver studded with gold, wrought-iron tripod.
1912.
Exh.: Excelsior, Paris, 1912.

912 Vases
Various metals, embossed and patinated.
C. 1912.
Exh.: No details known.

913 'Fucus' vase
Patinated *repoussé* copper.
Height 14 cm (5½ in.).
1912.
Exh.: Delorenzo Gallery, New York, 1985 (repr. in catalogue, p. 128).
Coll.: Delorenzo Gallery, New York.

914 Vases, boxes and ashtrays
Various metals inlaid with silver or patinated.
1912.
Exh.: Private exhibition at the home of the Comtesse Greffulhe, Paris, 1912.

915 'Gourd' vase
Hammer-marked and patinated lead.
1912.
Exh.: Salon de l'Eclectique, Paris, 1912.

916 Vases
Copper and nickel silver inlaid with silver or patinated.
1912.
Exh.: Salon de l'Eclectique, Paris, 1912.

917 Vases and bottle
Various metals inlaid with silver, and copper with *repoussé* decoration.
1912.
Exh.: Salon de l'Eclectique, Paris, 1912.

918 Bottles and vase
Hammer-marked pewter, patinated *repoussé* copper and silver.
1912.
Exh.: Salon de l'Eclectique, Paris, 1912.

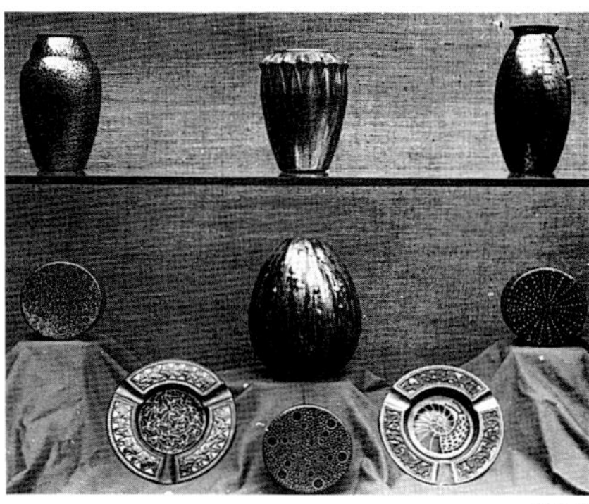
914

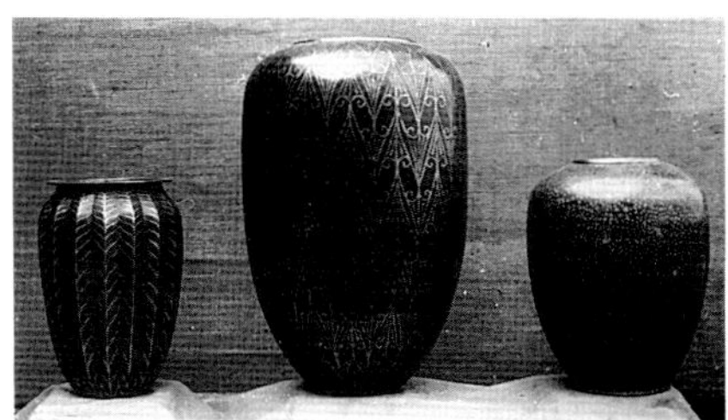
916

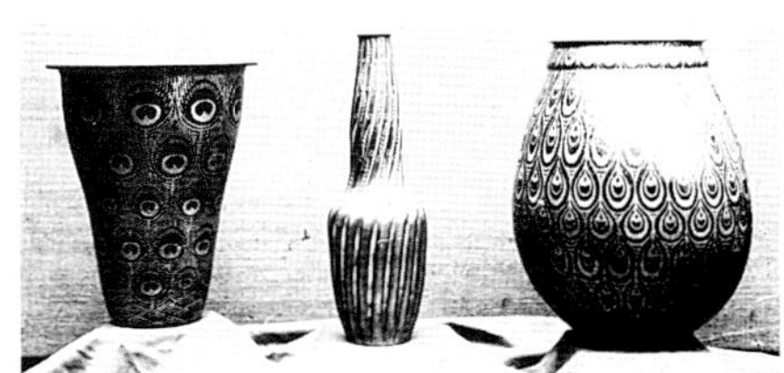
917

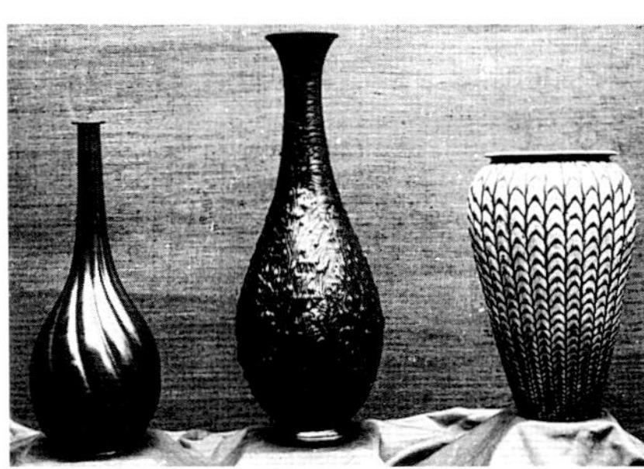
918

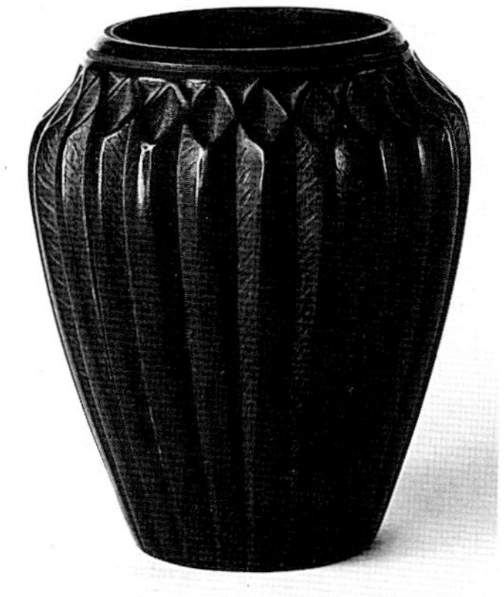

920

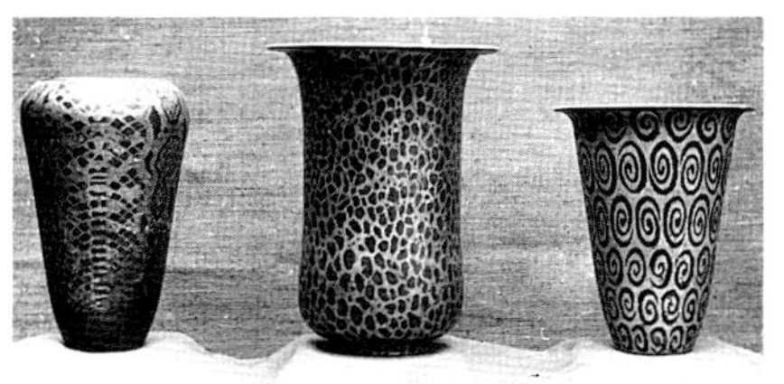

922

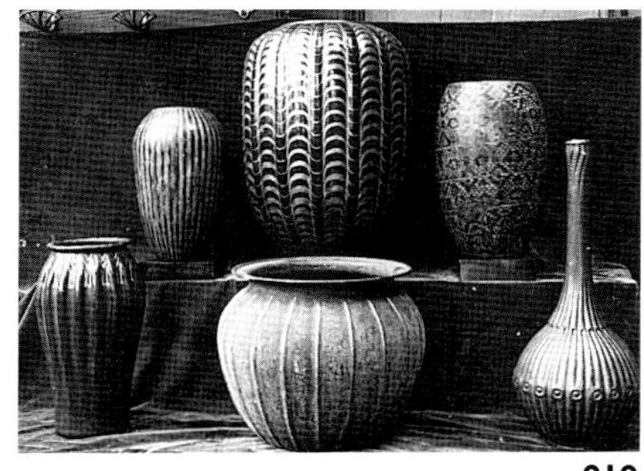

919

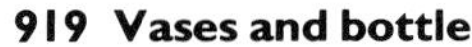

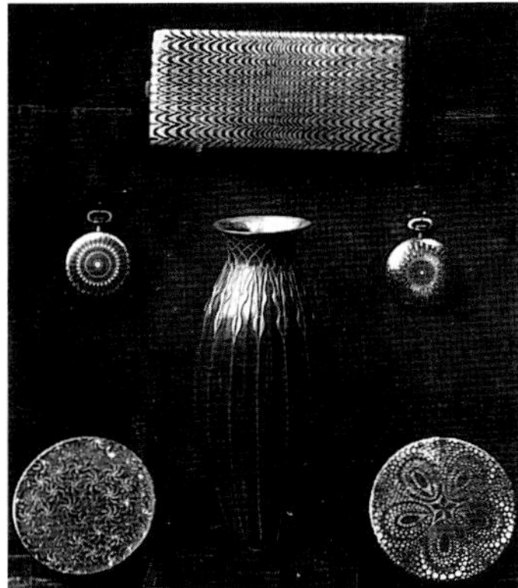

927

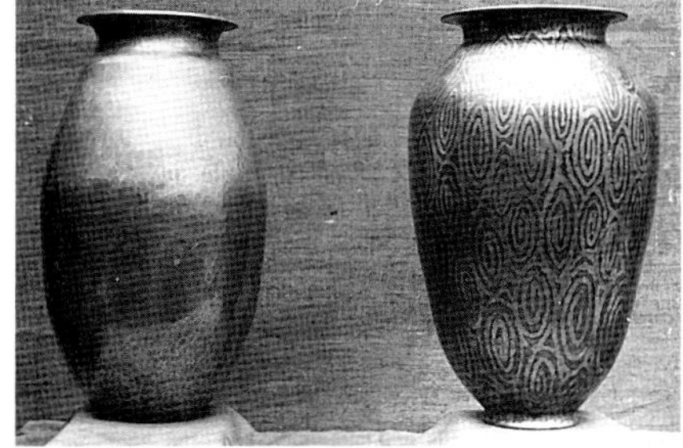

924

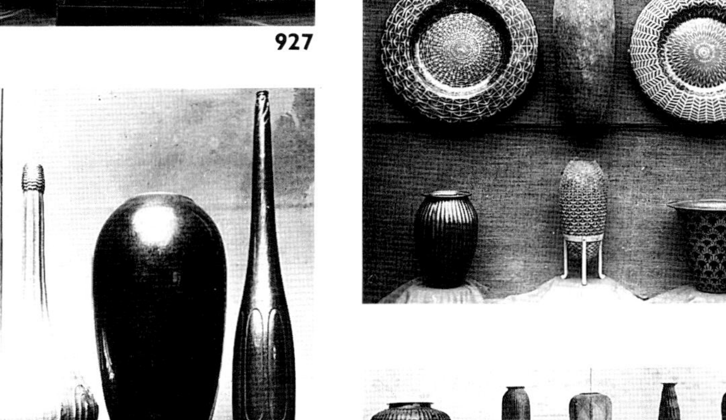

928

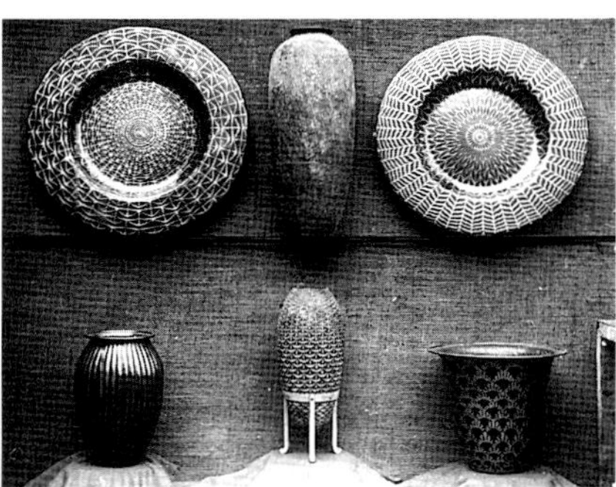

925

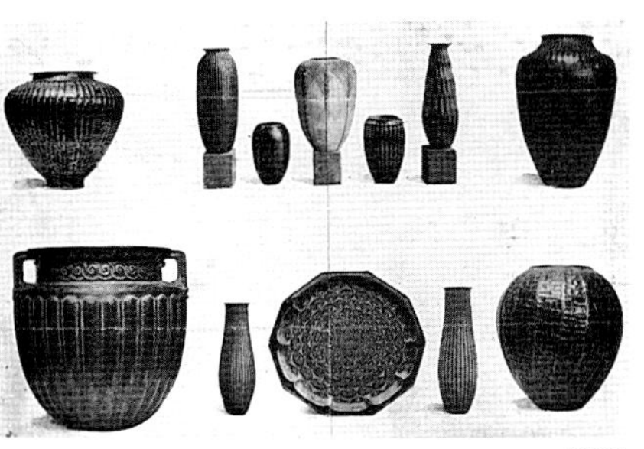

929

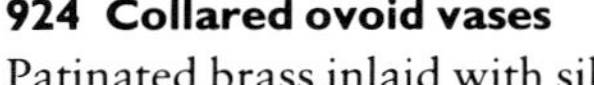

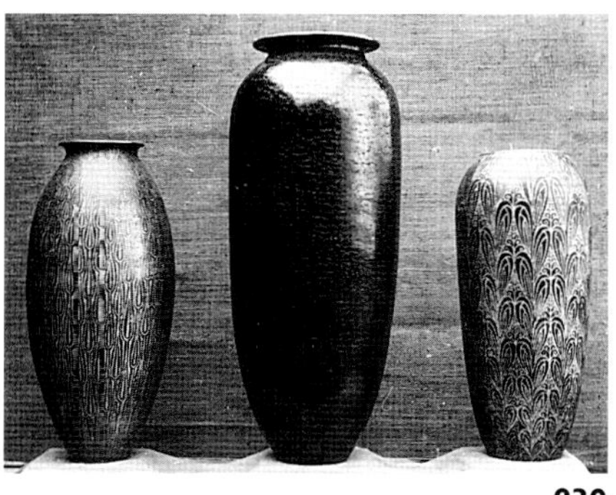

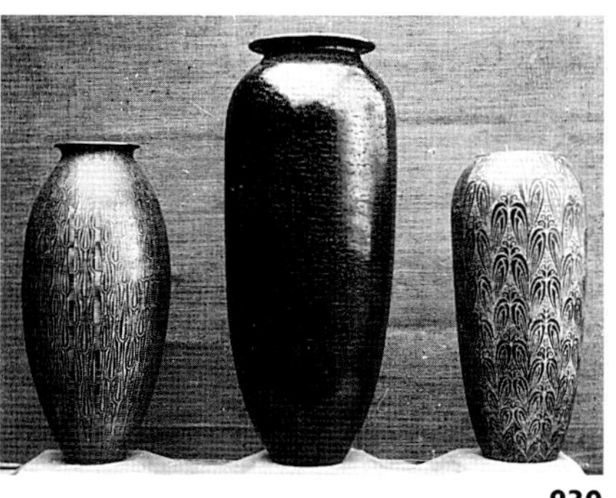

930

919 Vases and bottle
Various metals, including copper with *repoussé* decoration and patinated.
C. 1912.
Bibl.: Rougemont, 'Le métal repoussé et ciselé', *Les Arts français* (Paris, 1918), no. 21, p. 165.

920 Vase with stylized flowers
Pewter with *repoussé* and chased decoration.
C. 1912.

921 Vases, ashtrays and boxes
Various metals with *repoussé* decoration patinated or inlaid with silver.
1912.
Exh.: Private exhibition at the home of the Comtesse Greffulhe, Paris, 1912.
See illustration, p. 29.

922 Vases
Copper inlaid with silver and patinated.
C. 1912.

923 Ovoid vase
Patinated brass inlaid with silver.
1912.
Formerly in the collection of the Galerie Vallois, Paris; Private collection.

924 Collared ovoid vases
Patinated brass inlaid with silver.
C. 1912.

925 Vases and dishes
Silver nickel and patinated copper inlaid with silver.
C. 1912.

926 Large ovoid vase on tripod
Patinated brass with wrought-iron support.
C. 1912.
Coll.: Yves Saint Laurent and Pierre Bergé, Paris.

927 Vase, watch-cases and boxes
Brass, niello steel and patinated nickel silver.
C. 1912.
Exh.: No details known.

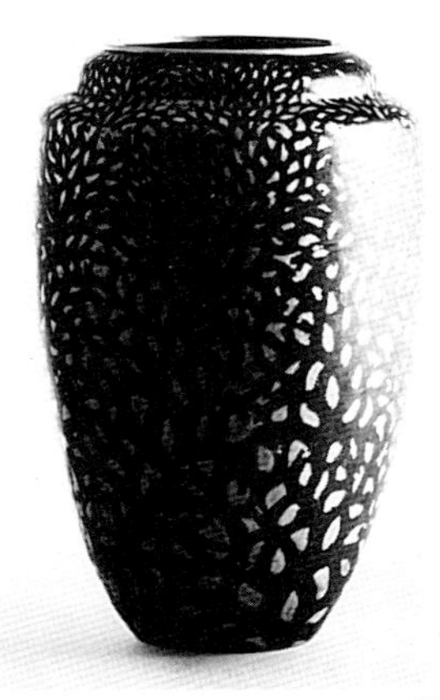
923

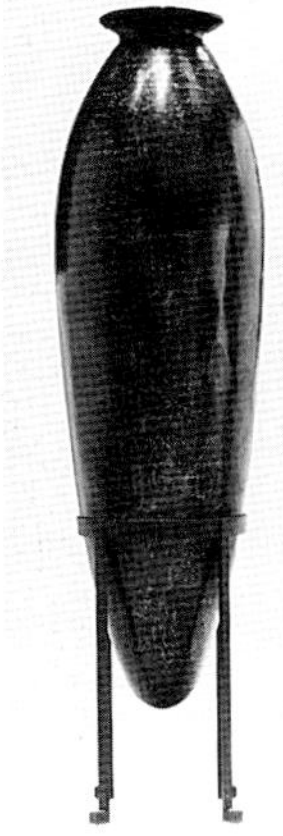
926

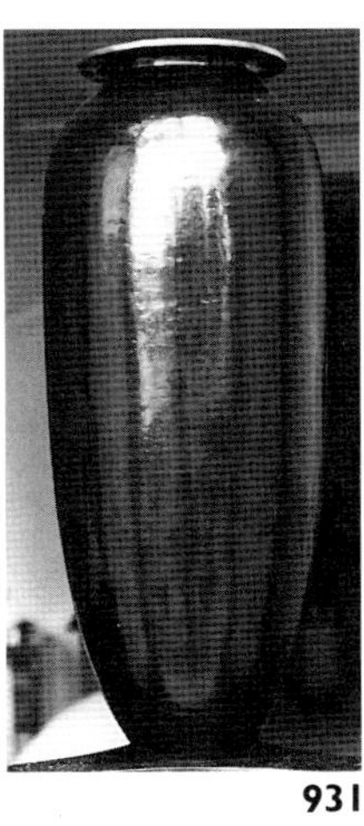
931

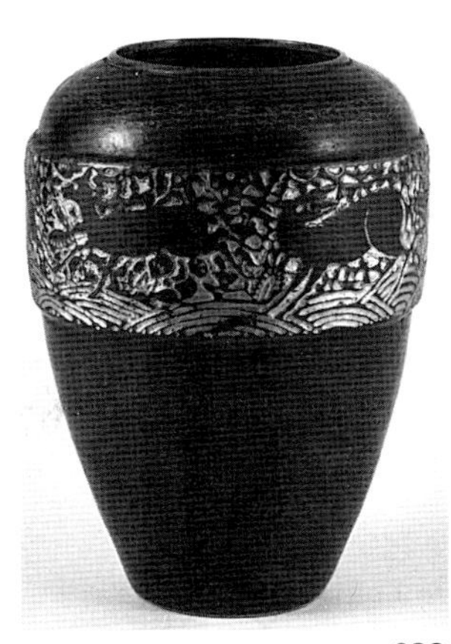
933

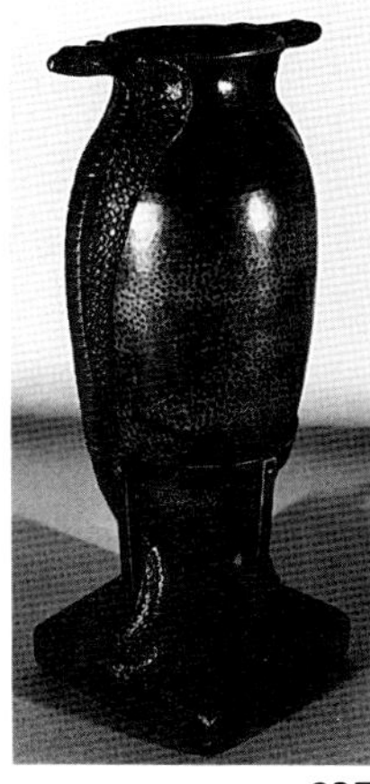
937

928 Bottles and vase
Hammer-marked patinated brass.
C. 1912.

929 Vases and tray
Various hammer-marked metals with patinated *repoussé* decoration.
C. 1912.
Bibl.: André Maurel, 'Arts appliqués: Jean Dunand', *Le Carnet des artistes*, 1 May 1917, p. 14.

930 Vases
Patinated copper inlaid with silver.
C. 1912.

931 Large ovoid vase
Hammer-marked and patinated brass encircled with silver.
Height 67 cm (26½ in.).
C. 1912.
Formerly in the collection of Anne-Sophie Duval; Private collection.

932 'Wistaria' vase *Pl. 138*
Gilt brass with coloured *cloisonné* enamel on *repoussé* and chased ground.
Height 35 cm (13¾ in.).
1912.
Coll.: Alain Lesieutre, Paris.

933 'Deer' vase
Faceted copper with gilt *repoussé* decoration.
C. 1913.
Private collection.

934 'Snake' vase
Patinated brass inlaid with silver, patinated bronze handles with *appliqué* decoration and wrought-iron tripod.
Height 128 cm (50½ in.).
1913.
Exh.: Salon des Artistes Décorateurs, Paris, 1913; Parc de Bagatelle, Paris, 1913; Galerie du Luxembourg, Paris, 1973, no. 6.
Coll.: Hélène Rochas.
Bibl.: *L'Oeuvre*, January 1914, p. 7; Rougemont, 'Le Métal repoussé et ciselé', *Les Arts français* (Paris, 1918), pl. 35; René Chavance, *Les beaux métiers: les hommes et leurs oeuvres*, p. 14; *Jean Dunand – Jean Goulden*, exhibition catalogue (Paris, 1973), repr. p. 57.
See illustration, p. 30.

935 'Snake' vase and **'Snake' paperweight**
Patinated brass inlaid with silver and bronze, and patinated chased lead.
1913.
Exh.: No details known.
Bibl.: M. Testard, 'Le Métal dans l'art moderne', *Nos Loisirs*, 1 July 1922, p. 322.

936 'Snake' vase *Pl. 144*
Patinated brass inlaid with silver, patinated bronze handles flecked with gold, wrought-iron tripod and lacquered wooden plinth.
Height 28 cm (11 in.).
1913.
Private collection.
Variant of cat. no. 935.

937 'Snake' vase
Patinated hammer-marked copper, bronze handles, wrought-iron tripod.
Height 30 cm (11¾ in.).
1913.
Formerly in the collection of Barry Friedman, New York.
Variant of cat. no. 935.

938 Vases
Lead, bronze and various patinated metals with *repoussé* or chased decorations inlaid with silver.
1913.
Exh.: Salon de la Nationale, Paris, 1913.

939 'Ivy' vase *Pl. 137*
Patinated brass with inlay work.
C. 1913.
Coll.: Alain Lesieutre, Paris.

940 Vases and boxes
Brass patinated or inlaid with silver.
1913.
Exh.: Salon de la Nationale, Paris, 1913.

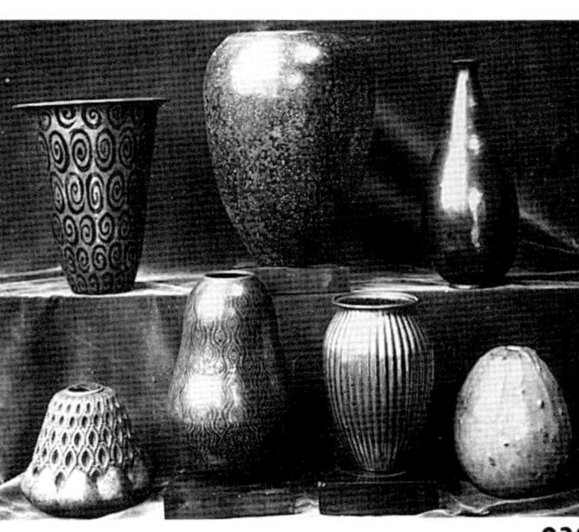
938

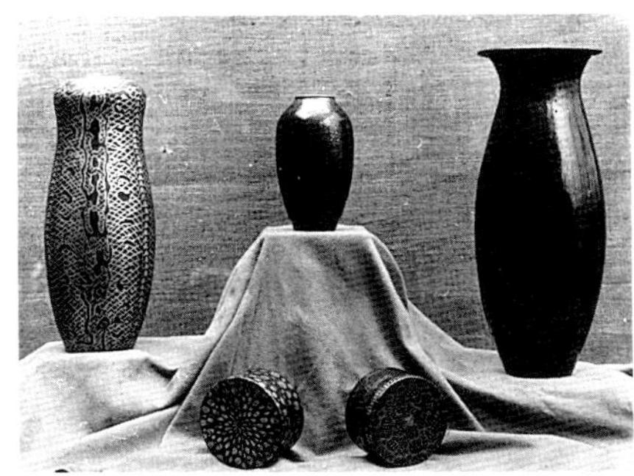
940

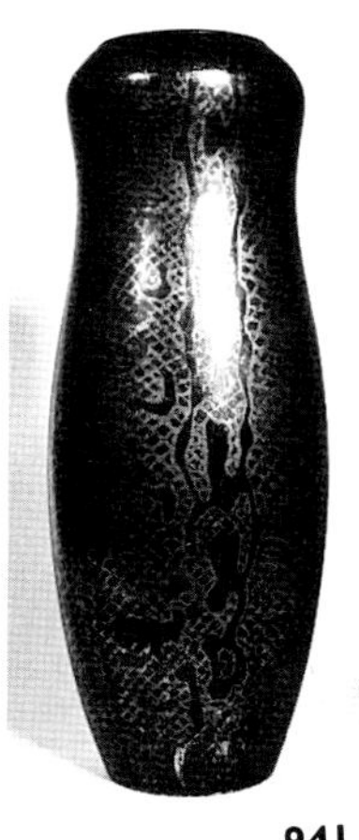
941

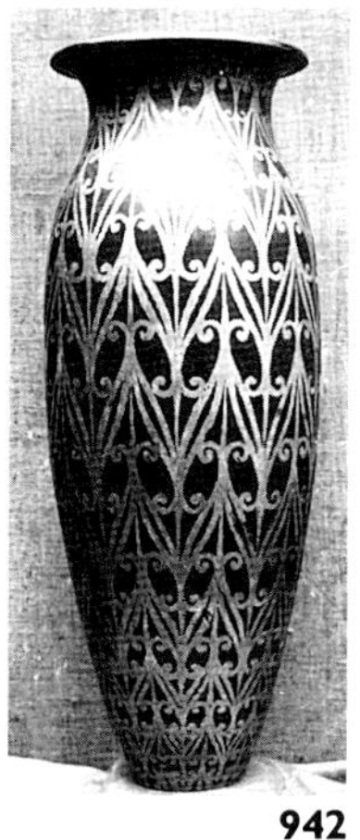
942

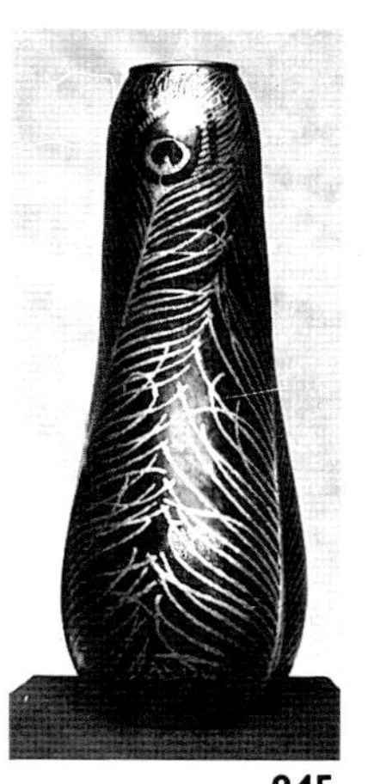
945

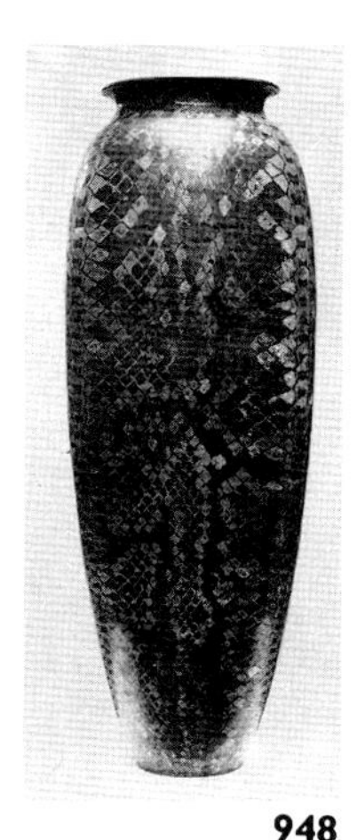
948

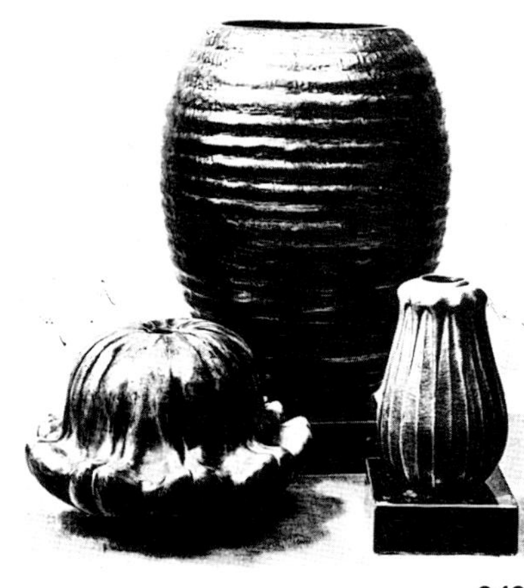
949

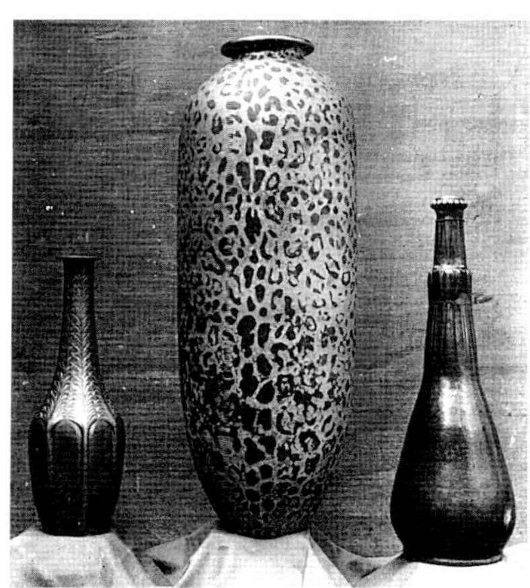
947

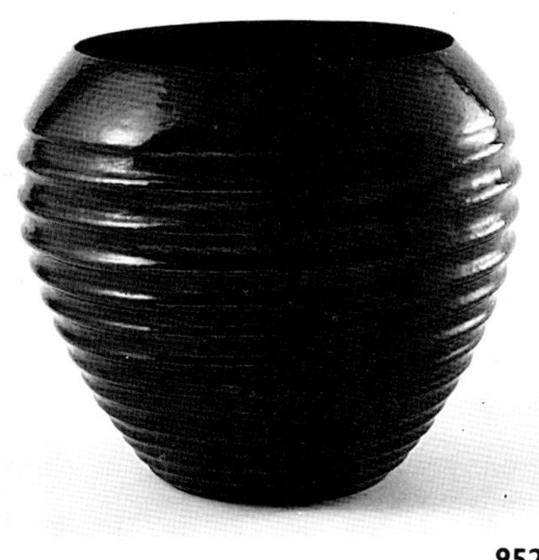
952

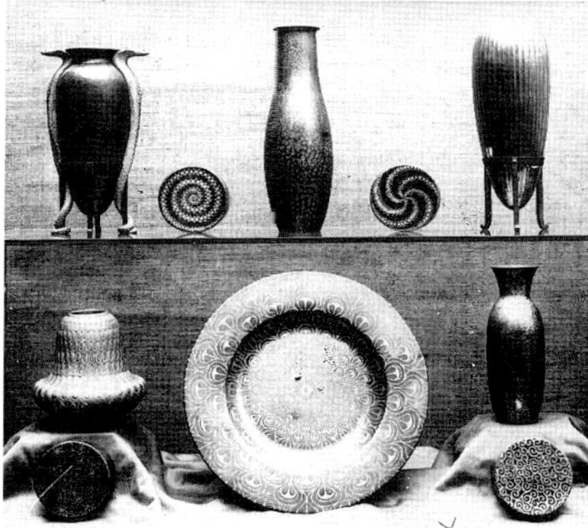
943

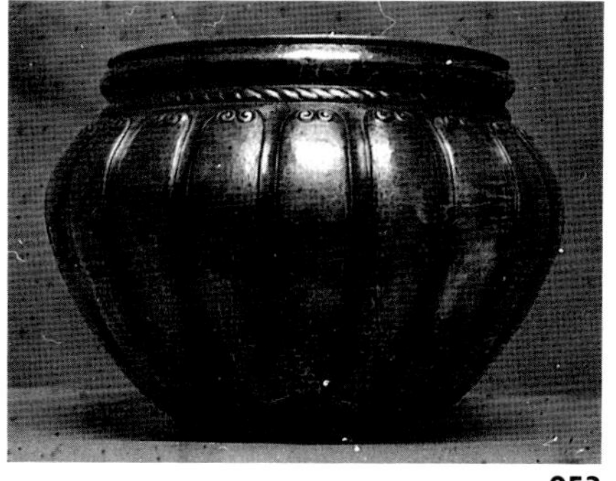
953

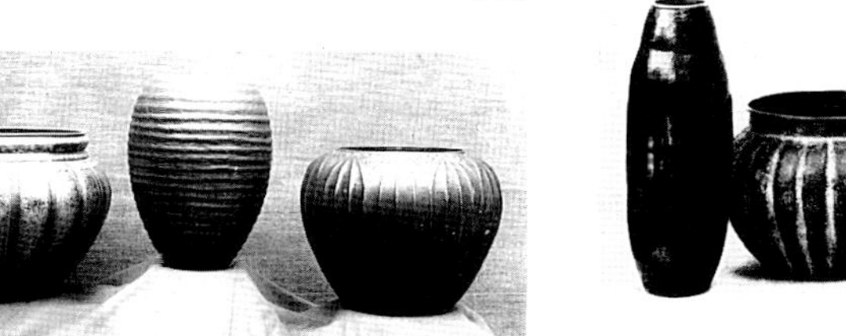
951

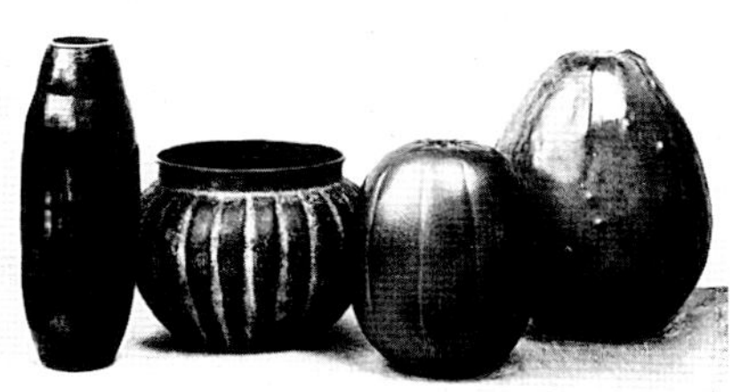
955

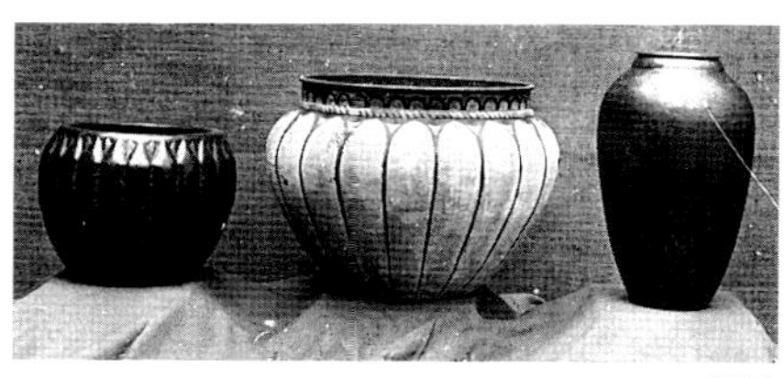
954

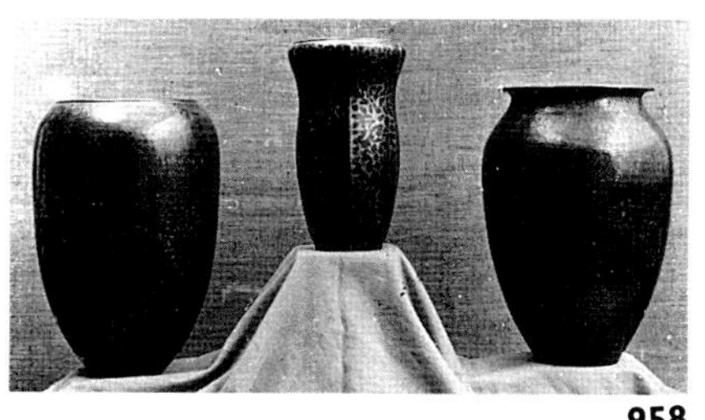
958

941 'Snakeskin' vase
Patinated brass inlaid with silver.
1913.
Exh.: Salon de la Nationale, Paris, 1913.
Formerly in the collection of Félix Marcilhac, Paris; Private collection.

942 Vase with chevron design
Patinated brass inlaid with silver.
1913.
Exh.: Salon de la Nationale, Paris, 1913.

943 Vases, tray and boxes
Lead, bronze and patinated or inlaid brass.
1913.
Exh.: Salon de la Nationale, Paris, 1913.

944 'Fern' vases and bottle
Vases in patinated and *repoussé* brass inlaid with silver, bottle of copper and silver; see illustration, p. 31.
1913.
Exh.: Salon de la Nationale, Paris, 1913; Munich, 1913; exhibition held on board the liner *France*, 1914.

945 'Peacock Feather' vase
Patinated and *repoussé* brass inlaid with silver.
1913.
Coll.: Musée des Arts Décoratifs, Paris.

946 'Ivy' and 'Genista' bottles
Repoussé and chased brass.
1913.
Exh.: Salon de la Nationale, Paris, 1913; exhibition held on board the liner *France*, 1914.

947 Vase and bottles
Vase in patinated brass inlaid with silver, bottles in lead and pewter.
1913 (vase), 1906 (right-hand bottle).
Exh.: Galerie Montaigne, Théâtre des Champs-Élysées, Paris, 1913.
Bibl.: *La Décoration moderne* (1905/6), right-hand vase repr. as pl. 40.

948 'Snakeskin' vase
Patinated brass inlaid with silver.
1913.
Exh.: Kunsthaus, Zurich, 1913.

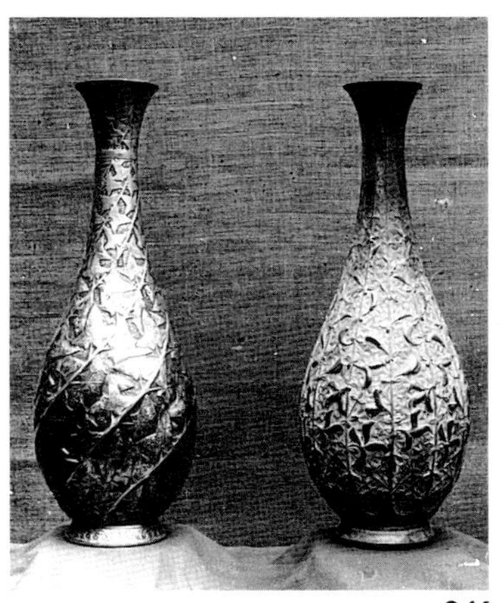
946

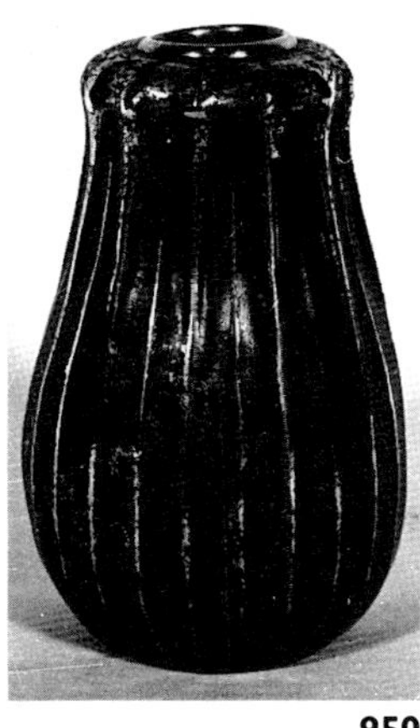
950

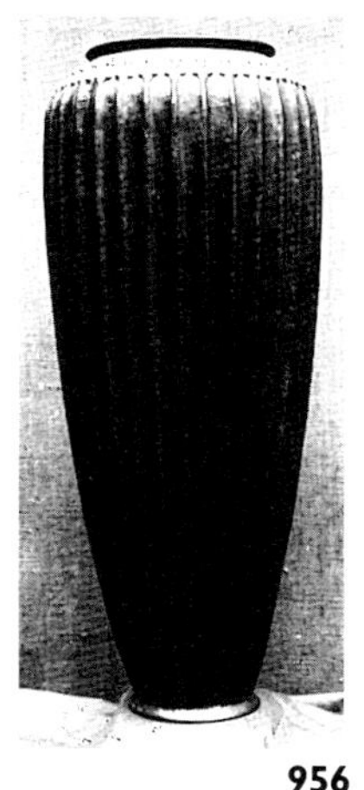
956

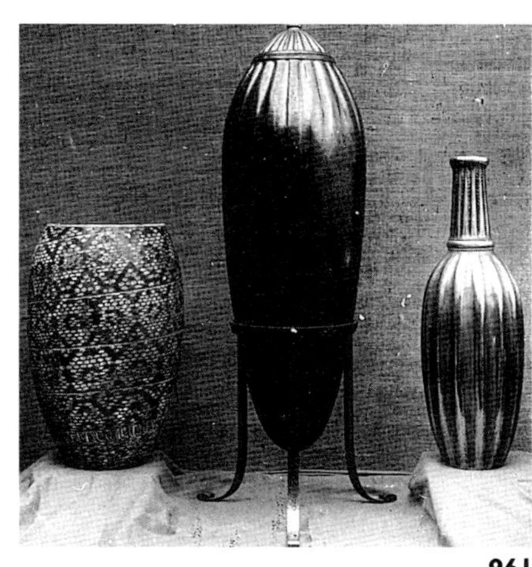
961

949 Vase and gourds
Vase in hammer-marked and patinated pewter with *repoussé* design, copper gourds.
1913.
Bibl.: *Art et décoration*, September 1919, p. 123.

950 'Gourd' vase
Hammer-marked and patinated pewter with *repoussé* design.
Height 15 cm (6 in.).
1913.
Formerly in the collection of Félix Marcilhac, Paris; Private collection.

951 Vase and cache-pots
Patinated copper with *repoussé* and chased design.
1913.
Exh.: No details known.

952 Vase with annular body
Patinated and *repoussé* copper.
1913.
Private collection.

953 Cache-pot
Patinated and *repoussé* copper.
1913.
Exh.: Galerie Montaigne, Théâtre des Champs-Élysées, Paris, 1913.

954 Vases and cache-pot
Patinated and *repoussé* copper.
1913.
Exh.: Galerie Montaigne, Théâtre des Champs-Élysées, Paris, 1913.

955 Vase, cache-pot and gourds
Patinated and *repoussé* brass and copper and patinated bronze.
1913.
Bibl.: *Art et décoration*, September 1919, p. 122.

956 Large fluted vase
Patinated and *repoussé* brass.
Height 90 cm (35½ in.).
1913.
Exh.: Ghent, 1913.
Private collection.

957 Vases and floral bowl
Oxidized brass inlaid with silver and patinated hammer-marked lead.
1913.
Exh.: Salon de la Nationale, Paris, 1913.

958 Vases
Brass, oxidized or patinated, and inlaid with silver.
1913.
Exh.: Salon de la Nationale, Paris, 1913.

959 Vases
Oxidized brass inlaid with silver.
1913.
Exh.: Salon des Artistes Décorateurs, Paris, 1913.

960 Vases, jardinières and boxes
Various metals patinated, oxidized or inlaid with silver.
1913.
Exh.: Salon de la Nationale, Paris, 1913.

961 Vase, bottle and covered urn
Oxidized brass inlaid with silver, patinated and *repoussé* copper and hammer-marked pewter.
1913.
Exh.: Salon de la Nationale, Paris, 1913.

962 Vases, tray, jardinière and boxes
Various metals oxidized, patinated or inlaid with silver; see illustration, p. 30.
1913.
Exh.: Salon des Artistes Décorateurs, Paris, 1913.

963 Vases
Brass oxidized, patinated or inlaid with silver.
1913.
Exh.: No details known.

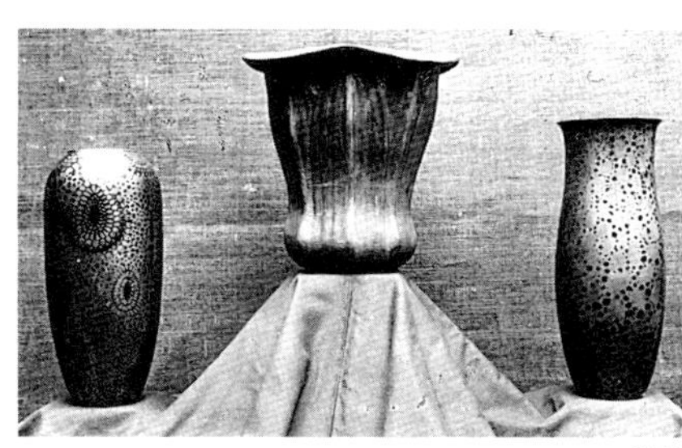
957

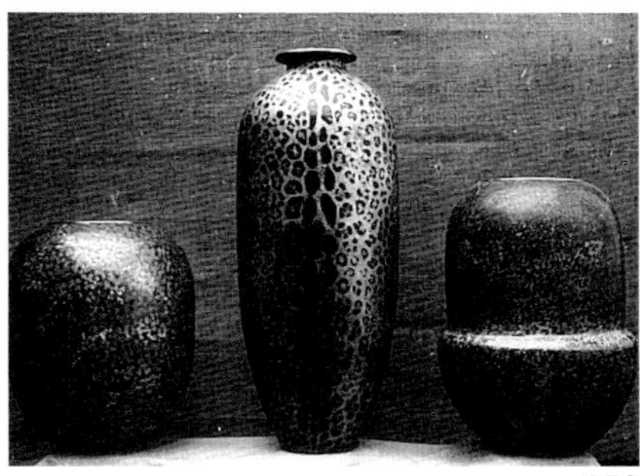
959

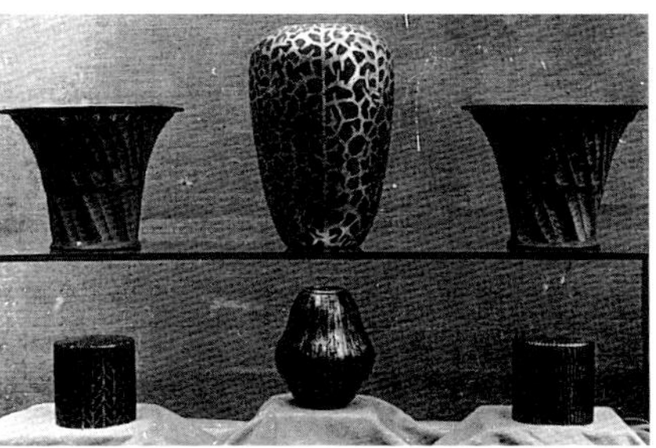
960

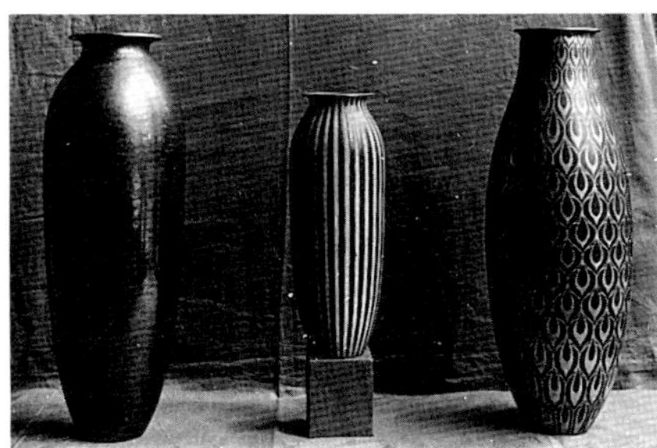
963

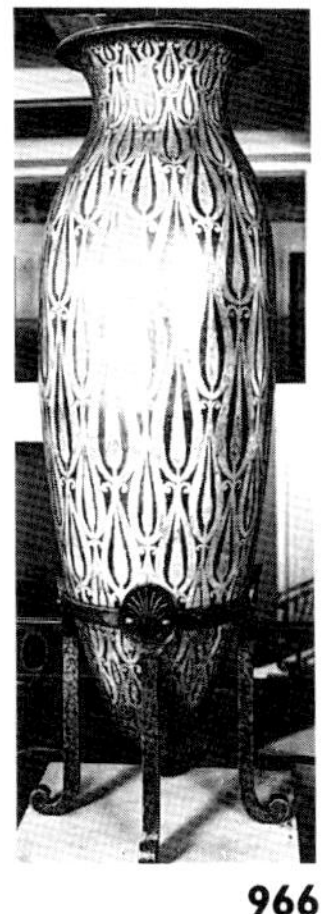

966

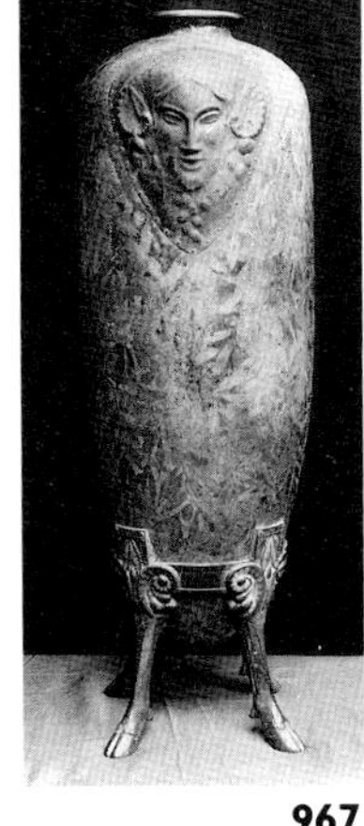

967

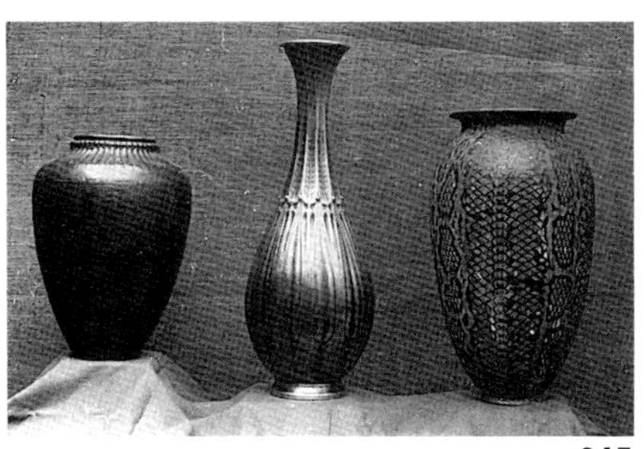

965

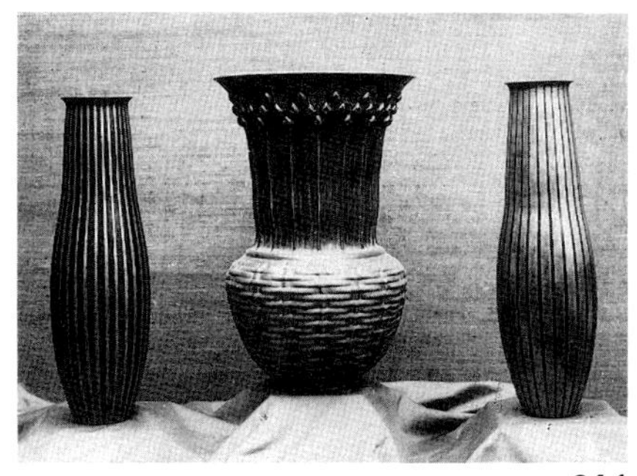

964

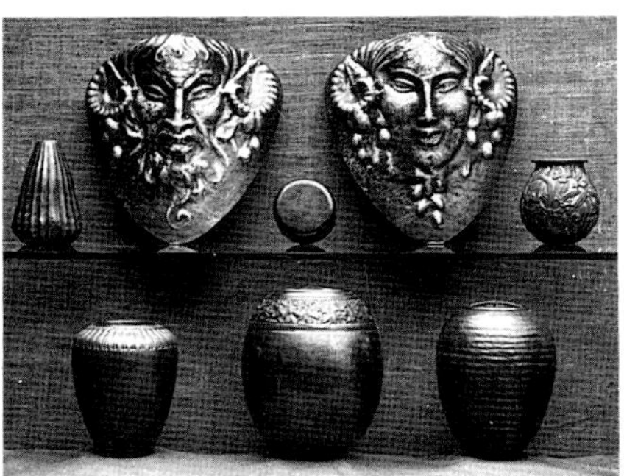

968

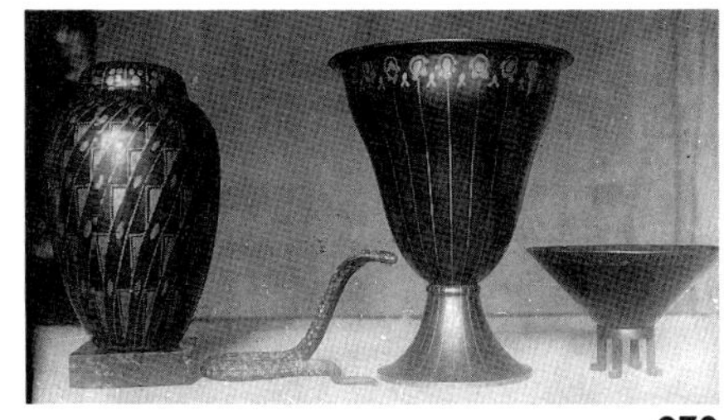

970

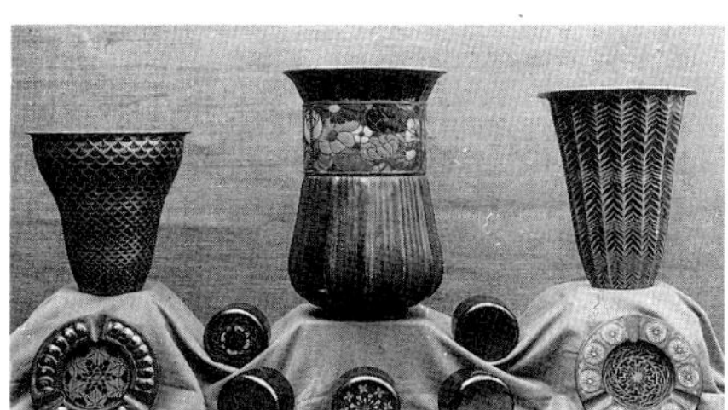

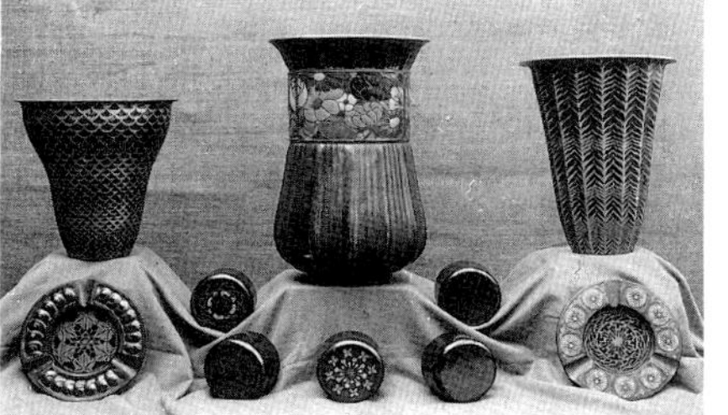

969

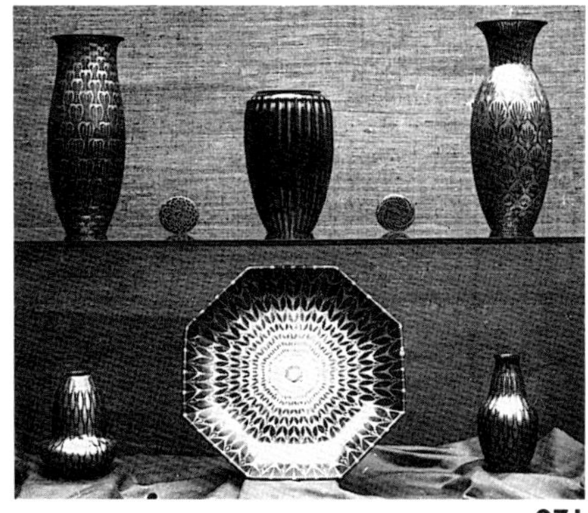

971

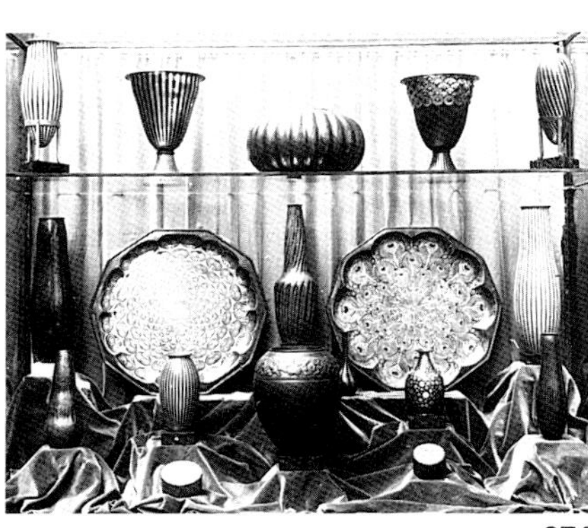

976

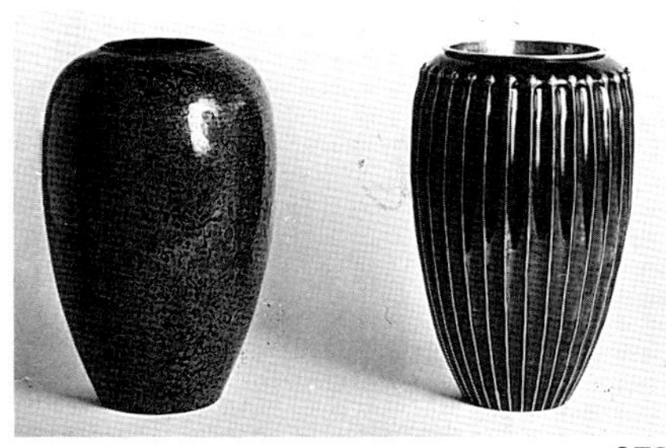

972

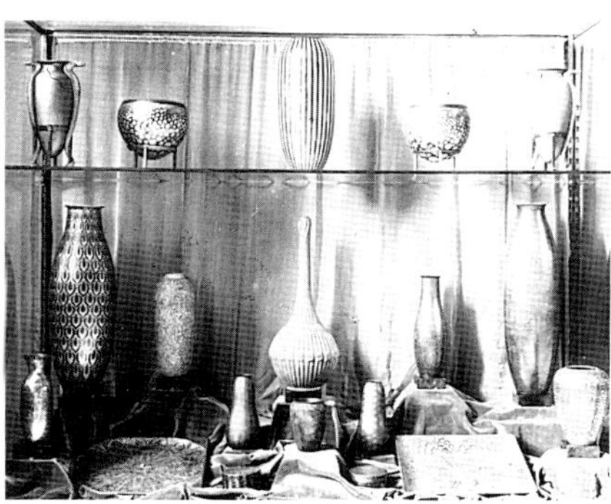

973

964 Vases and large bouquetière
Oxidized copper inlaid with silver and *repoussé* and chased brass.
1913.
Exh.: No details known.
Bibl.: *Art et décoration*, September 1919, p. 118.

965 Vases and bottle
Vases in oxidized and patinated copper inlaid with silver, bottle in patinated *repoussé* copper.
1913.
Exh.: No details known.

966 Monumental vase on tripod
Oxidized copper inlaid with silver; wrought-iron tripod.
1913.
Exh.: Galerie Montaigne, Théâtre des Champs-Élysées, Paris, 1913; Salon des Artistes Décorateurs, Paris, 1922.

967 'Fauns' vase
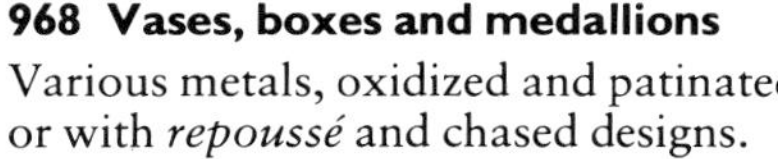
Oxidized and patinated copper inlaid with silver, *appliqué* heads of fauns in chased bronze; tripod in bronze.
1913.
Exh.: Salon des Artistes Décorateurs, Paris, 1913.

968 Vases, boxes and medallions
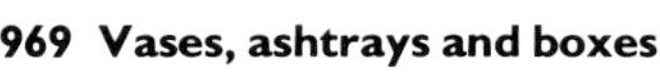
Various metals, oxidized and patinated or with *repoussé* and chased designs.
1913.
Exh.: Salon des Artistes Décorateurs, Paris, 1913.

969 Vases, ashtrays and boxes
Various metals, oxidized, inlaid with silver and patinated or with *repoussé* work in copper, and bronze with *champlevé* enamel decoration.
1913.
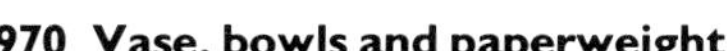
Exh.: Salon d'Automne, Paris, 1913.

970 Vase, bowls and paperweight
Patinated nickel silver and silver, chased bronze.
1914.
Exh.: Salon de la Nationale, Paris, 1914.
Bibl.: *La Nature*, 9 February 1924, the bowl in the centre repr. on p. 81.

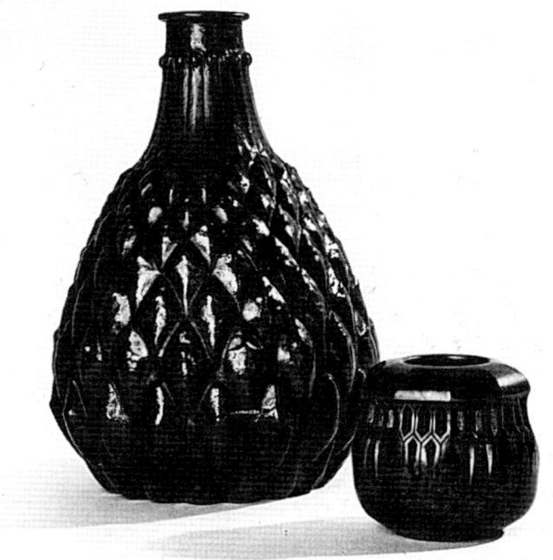

975

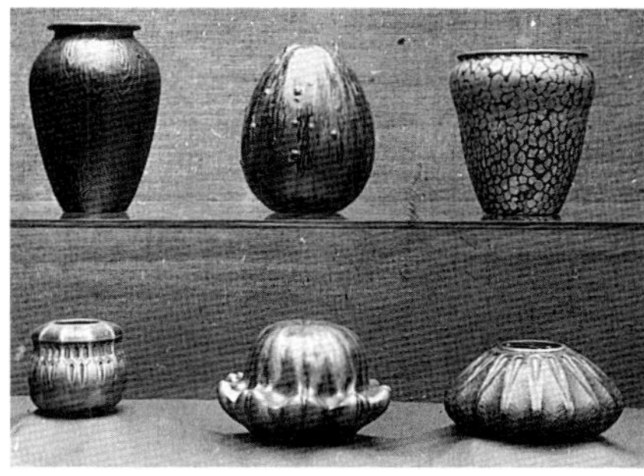

977

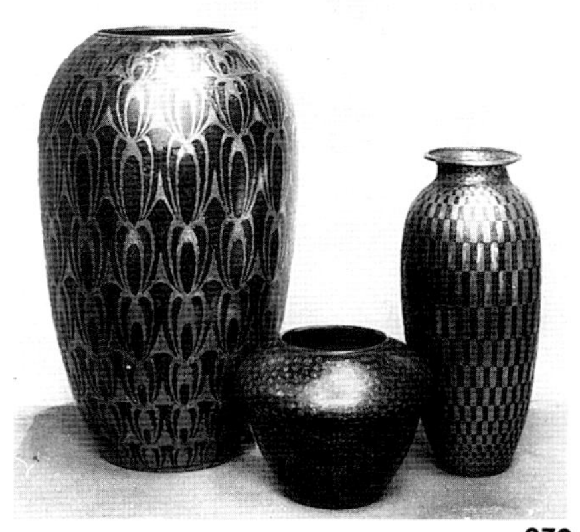

979

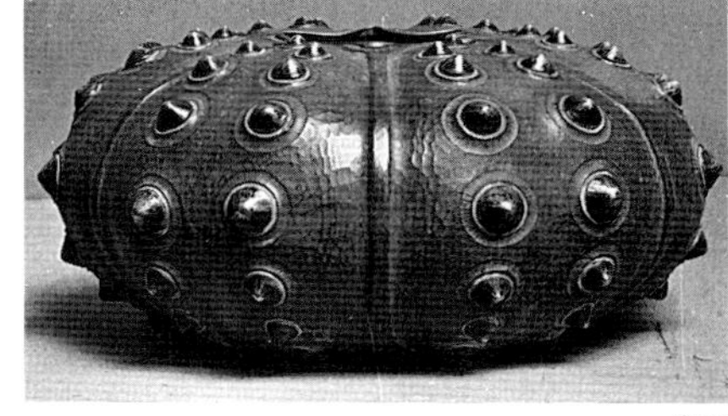

978

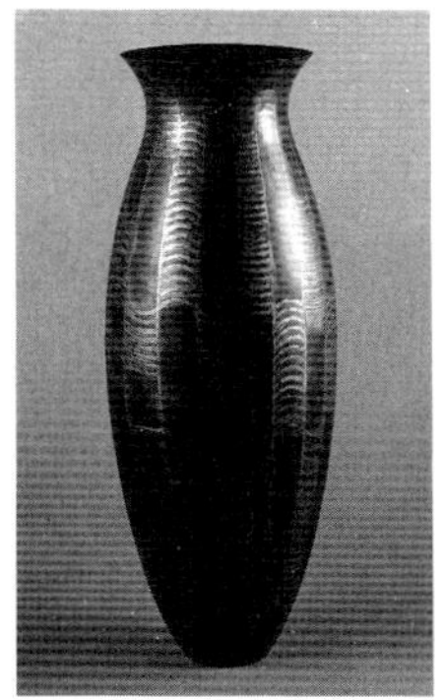

980

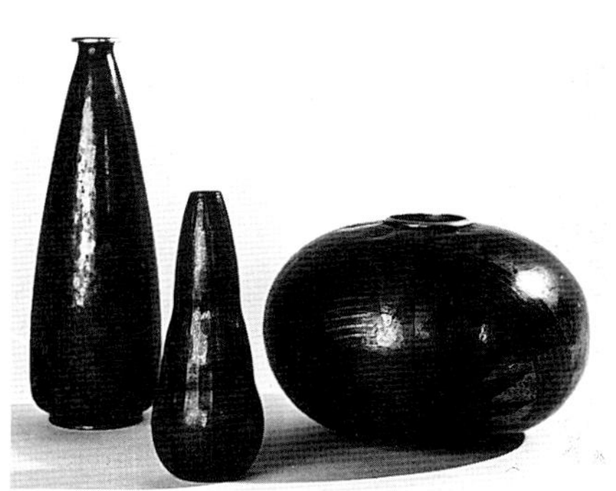

983

971 Vases, trays and boxes
Burnished steel and gold, oxidized copper inlaid with silver, bronze with *champlevé* enamel decoration.
1914.
Exh.: Salon de la Nationale, Paris, 1914.
Bibl.: *L'Oeuvre*, January 1914, p. 9.

972 Vases
Lacquered copper, blued steel inlaid with chased gold flowerets.
C. 1922 (vase on left) and 1914 (vase on right).
Formerly in the collection of Félix Marcilhac, Paris; Alain Lesieutre, Paris.

973 Vases and trays
Various oxidized metals inlaid with silver, *repoussé* copper and hammer-marked pewter.
Exh.: Salon de la Nationale, Paris, 1914.

974 Vases
Patinated copper with *repoussé* and chased designs.
C. 1914.
Bibl.: *L'Oeuvre*, January 1914, p. 8.

975 'Pineapple' vase and small vase
'Pineapple' vase in patinated copper with *repoussé* and chased design, small vase in patinated and chased bronze.
Height of 'Pineapple' vase 28 cm (11 in.); height of small vase 9 cm (3 ½ in.).
1914.
Exh.: Galerie du Luxembourg, Paris, 1973, nos. 3 and 2.
Private collection.
Bibl.: *Jean Dunand – Jean Goulden*, exhibition catalogue (Paris, 1973), repr. p. 56.

976 Bowls, trays, vases and boxes
Various oxidized metals inlaid with silver, *repoussé* copper, and bronze with *champlevé* enamel decoration.
1914.
Exh.: Salon de la Nationale, Paris, 1914.

977 Vases and gourds
Oxidized copper inlaid with silver, *repoussé* copper, hammer-marked and patinated pewter and patinated bronze.
1914.
Exh.: Salon de la Nationale, Paris, 1914.

978 Gourd
Patinated lead with *repoussé* and chased design.
C. 1914.

979 Vases
Oxidized copper inlaid with silver.
C. 1914.
Bibl.: *Art et décoration*, September 1919, p. 125.

980 Vase
Oxidized brass inlaid with silver.
C. 1914.
Private collection.

981 'Coiled Snake' vase *Pl. 141*
Patinated brass, silver and gold patinated and chased bronze.
1920.
Coll.: Yves Saint Laurent and Pierre Bergé, Paris.

982 Spherical vase *Pl. 142*
Hammer-marked pewter.
Height 20 cm (7¾ in.).
C. 1922.
Exh.: Delorenzo Gallery, New York, 1985 (repr. in catalogue, p. 97).
Coll.: Delorenzo Gallery, New York.

983 Spherical vase and conical vases
Spherical vase in oxidized brass inlaid with silver, conical vases in patinated copper.
Height of spherical vase 20 cm (7¾ in.); height of conical vases 35 and 23 cm (13¾ and 9 in.).
C. 1922 (spherical vase) and 1914 (conical vases).
Exh.: Galerie du Luxembourg, Paris, 1973.
Private collection.
Bibl.: *Jean Dunand – Jean Goulden*, exhibition catalogue (Paris, 1973), repr. p. 58.

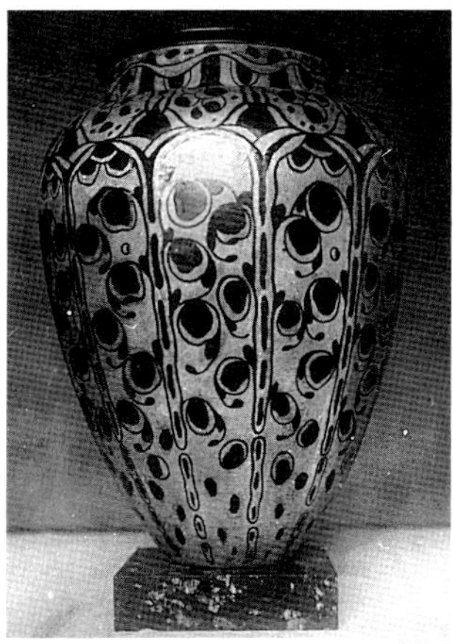
984

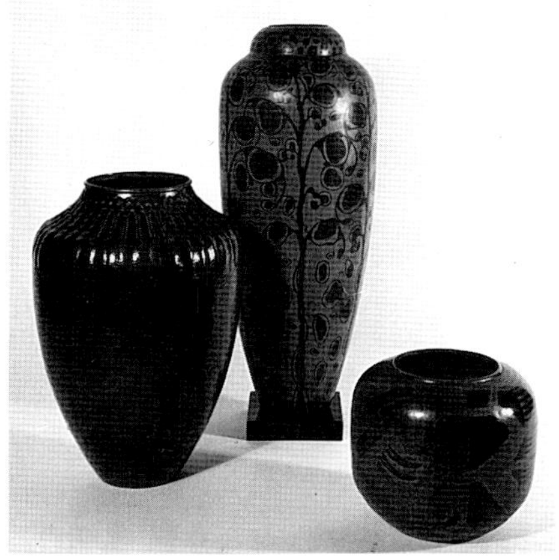
985

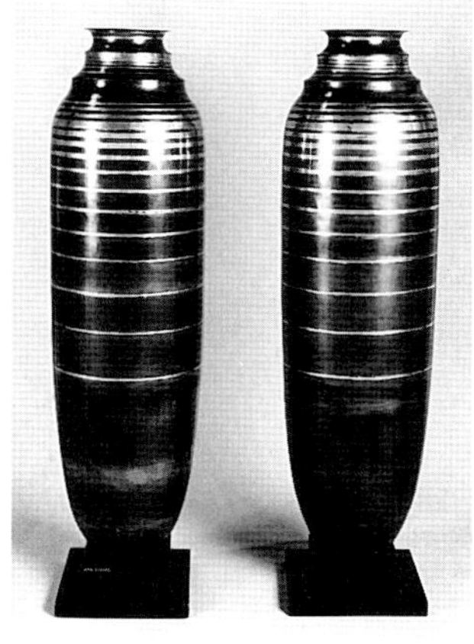
988

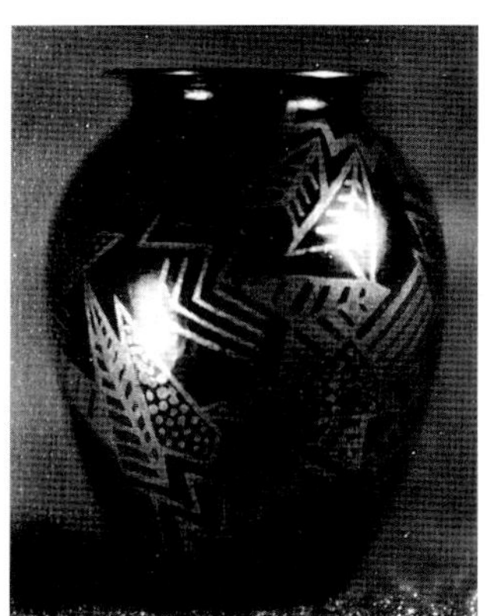
989

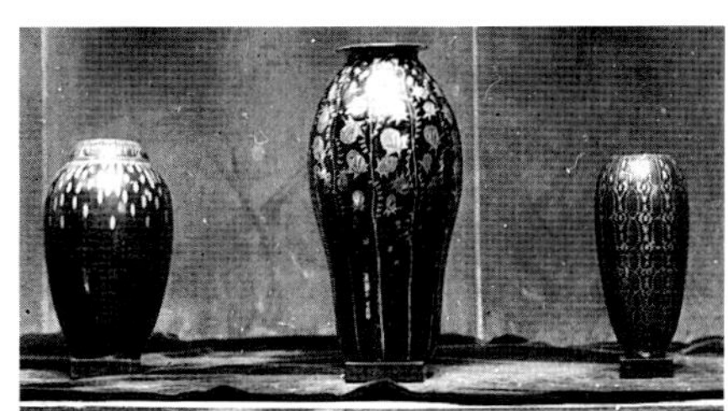
986

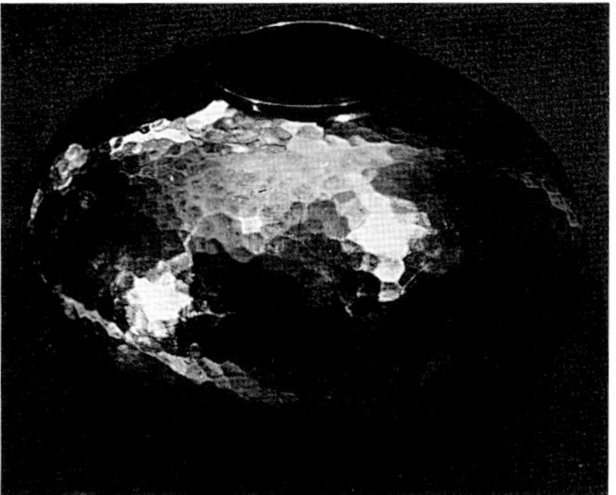
990

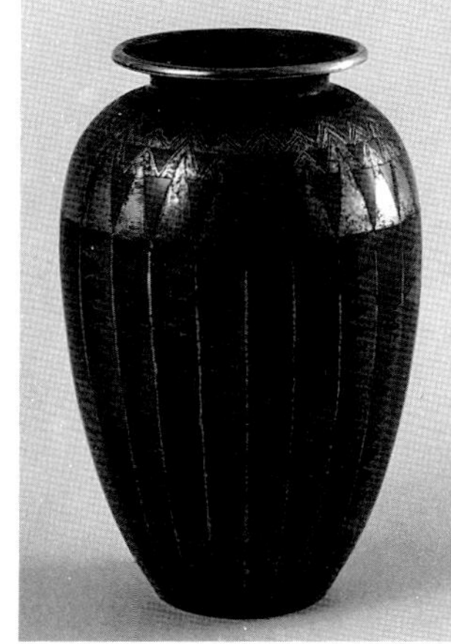
991

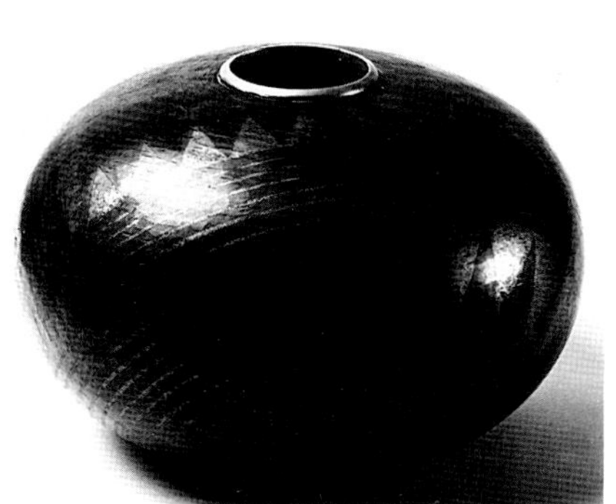
992

984 Vase with stylized leaves
Green and black oxidized brass.
C. 1922.

985 Vases
Patinated copper and green and black oxidized brass, the vase on the right with a lacquered design.
The vase on the left was made before 1914, the others *c.* 1922.
Private collection.

986 Vases
Various oxidized metals inlaid with silver.
C. 1920–5.
Exh.: No details known.

987 Urn-shaped vase *Pl. 140*
Oxidized lacquered brass inlaid with silver.
Height 51 cm (20 in.).
C. 1922.
Exh.: Delorenzo Gallery, New York, 1985 (repr. in catalogue, p. 87).
Coll.: Delorenzo Gallery, New York.

988 Pair of tall vases
Oxidized brass inlaid with silver.
Height 92 cm (36¼ in.).
C. 1922.
Exh.: Delorenzo Gallery, New York, 1985 (one repr. in catalogue, p. 82).
Coll.: Delorenzo Gallery, New York.

989 Vase
Oxidized brass inlaid with silver.
Made *c.* 1925 to a design by Georges Dorignac.

990 Oblate spherical vase
Hammer-marked pewter.
C. 1925.

991 Ovoid vase with flat neck
Oxidized brass inlaid with silver.
C. 1922–5.

992 Oblate spherical vase
Oxidized brass inlaid with silver.
Height 19 cm (7½ in.).
C. 1925.

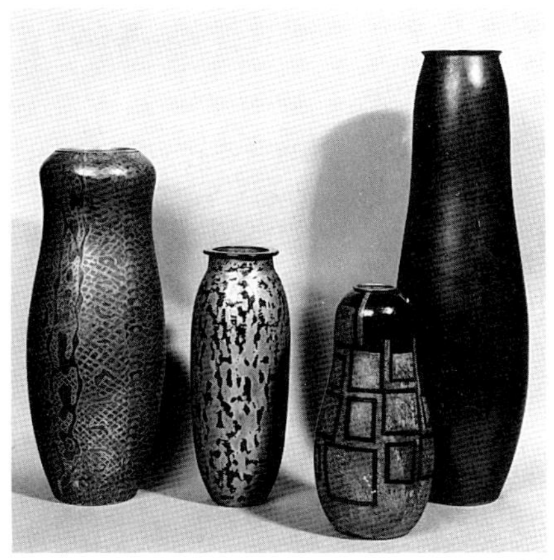
993

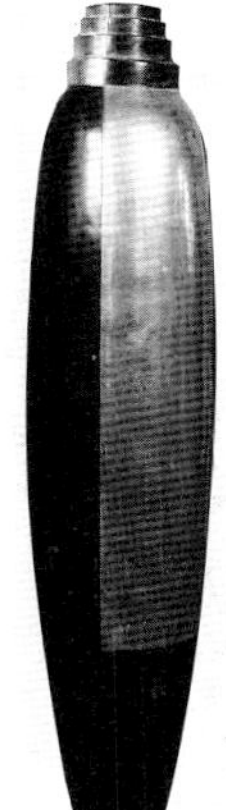
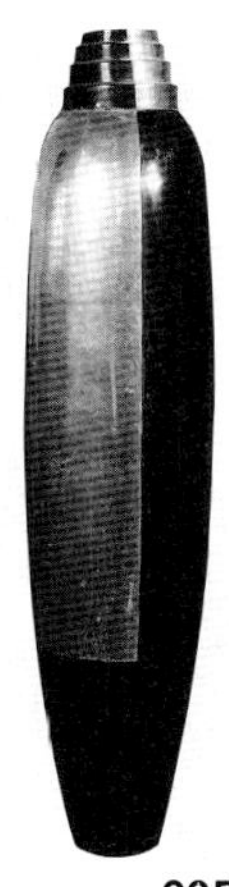
995

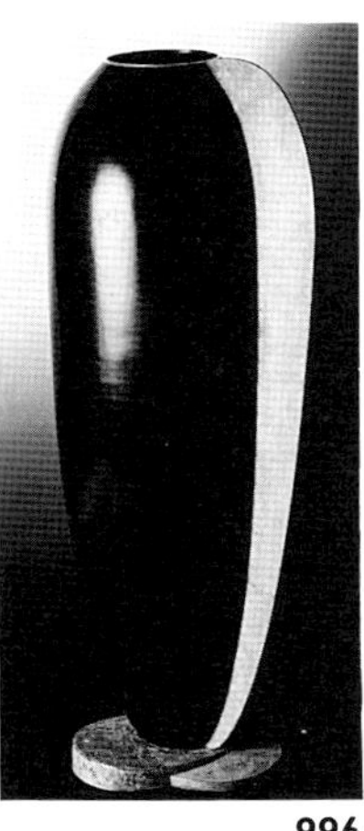
996

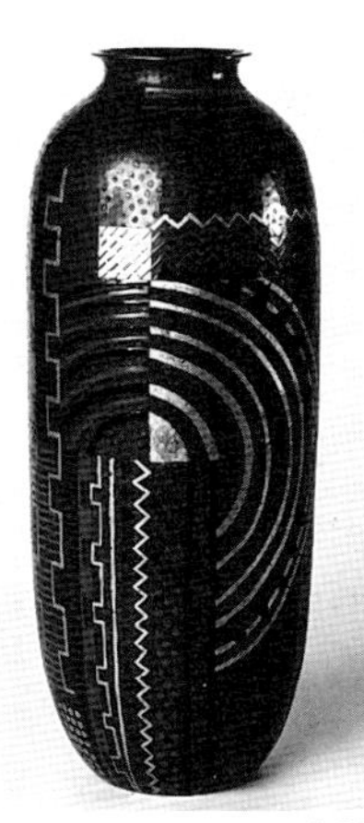
999

Exh.: Galerie du Luxembourg, Paris, 1973.
Private collection.
Bibl.: *Jean Dunand – Jean Goulden*, exhibition catalogue (Paris, 1973), p. 58.

993 Vases
Various oxidized metals inlaid with silver, patinated or lacquered.
Made between 1913 and 1925.
Formerly in the collection of Karl Lagerfeld.
Sold: Godeau, Solanet, Audap (Paris), 21 November 1975, lots 83–6, repr. in catalogue, p. 44.

994 'Wild Boar' vase
Oxidized brass inlaid with silver, mounted on a wrought-iron base; see illustration, p. 66.
1924.
Exh.: Salon de la Nationale, Paris, 1924.
Bibl.: *L'Amour de l'art*, June 1924, p. 190; *Mobilier et décoration*, February 1926, p. 46.

995 Pair of tall vases
Black and silver lacquered nickel silver in the shape of artillery shells.
Height 97 cm (38¼ in.).
1927.
Exh.: Salon des Artistes Décorateurs, Paris, 1927; Galerie Georges Petit, Paris, 1927; Galerie du Luxembourg, Paris, 1973 (repr. in catalogue, p. 73).
Formerly in the collections of Jane Renouardt and Anne-Sophie Duval; Private collection.
Bibl.: *L'Amour de l'art,* July 1927, p. 256.
Sold: Godeau, Solanet, Audap (Paris), 21 November 1921, lot 91, repr. in catalogue, p. 46.

996 Large winged vase
Black oxidized brass, *appliqué* 'wing' and green oxidized plinth.
Height 92 cm (36¼ in.).
1931.
Private collection.
Sold: Boisgirard (Paris), 26 October 1988, lot 118, repr. in catalogue, p. 45.

997 Vases in modern shapes
Oxidized brass.
C. 1935.
Private collection.

DINANDERIE: METAL VASES AND OTHER OBJECTS WITH LACQUER DECORATION

998 Vases
The pewter vase on the left, made in 1924, is decorated with a coloured lacquer design; the other two vases, made in 1913, are of oxidized brass.
Coll.: M. and Mme Kupperfils, Evreux.

999 Cylindrical vase
Hammer-marked copper with a geometric design in coloured lacquer highlighted with gold.
Height 25 cm (9¾ in.).
C. 1920.
Exh.: Galerie du Luxembourg, Paris, 1973, no. 51.
Private collection.
Bibl.: *Jean Dunand – Jean Goulden*, exhibition catalogue (Paris, 1973), repr. p. 70.

1000 Warty gourd
Lead with lacquered and *repoussé* decoration.
Height 27 cm (10¾ in.).
C. 1920.
Private collection.

1001 Cache-pot *Pl. 132*
Oxidized *repoussé* brass with a geometric design in coloured lacquer.
Height 24 cm (9½ in.).
C. 1920.
Exh.: Delorenzo Gallery, New York, 1985 (repr. in catalogue, p. 99).
Coll.: Delorenzo Gallery, New York.
Sold: Sotheby's (Monaco), 9 October 1983, lot 289.

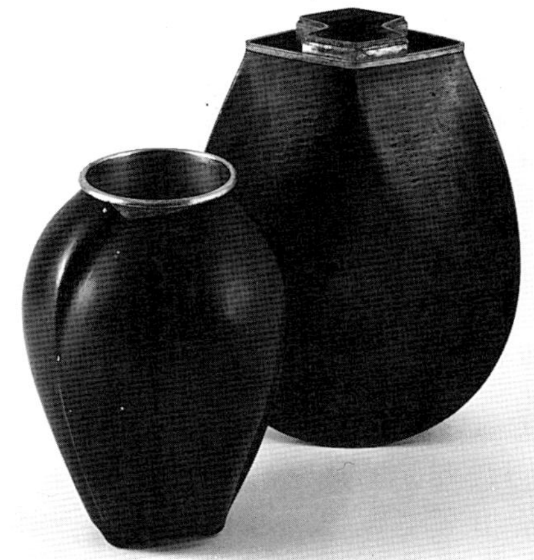
997

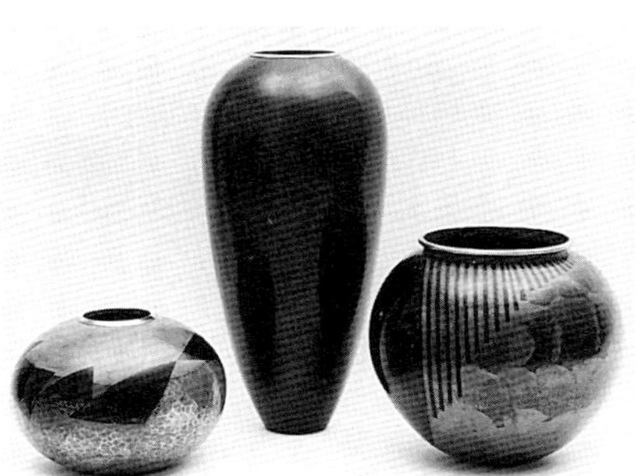
998

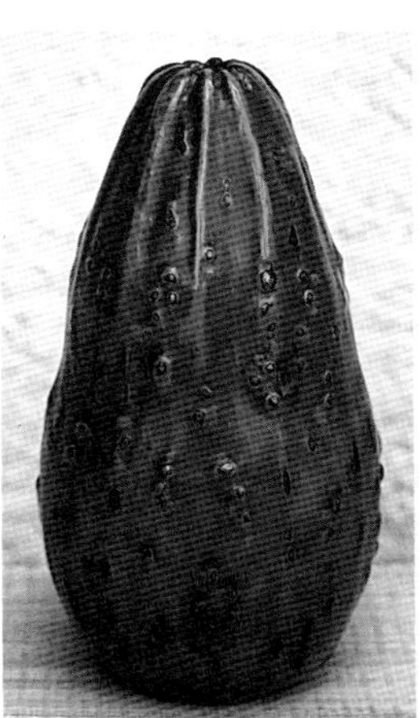
1000

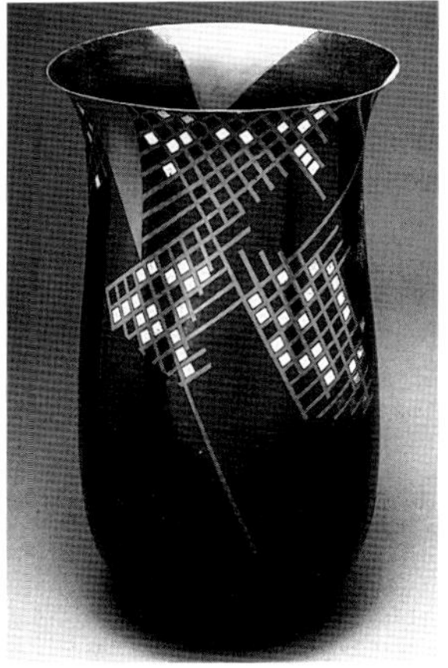

1007

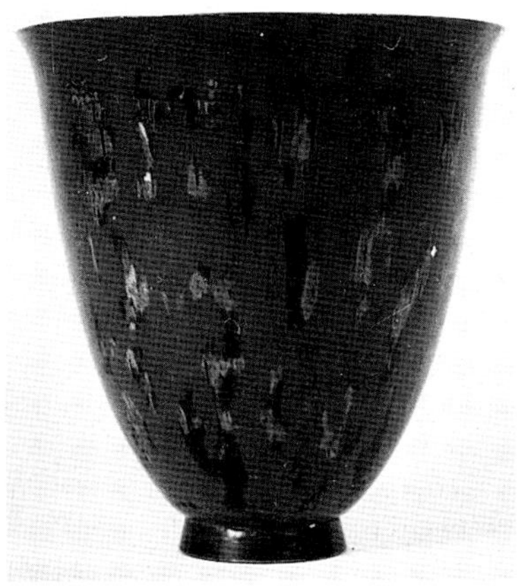

1005

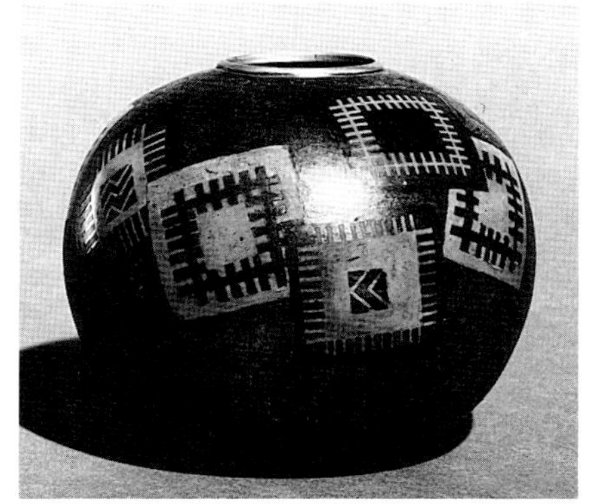

1008

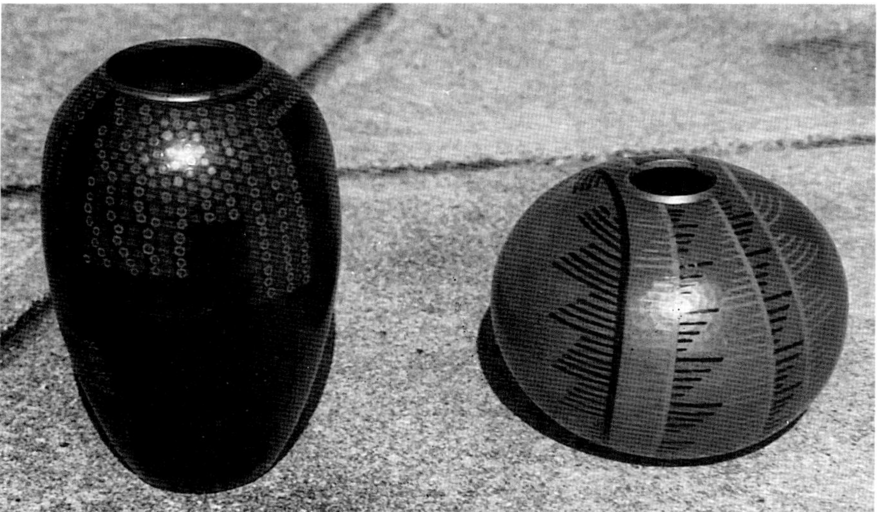

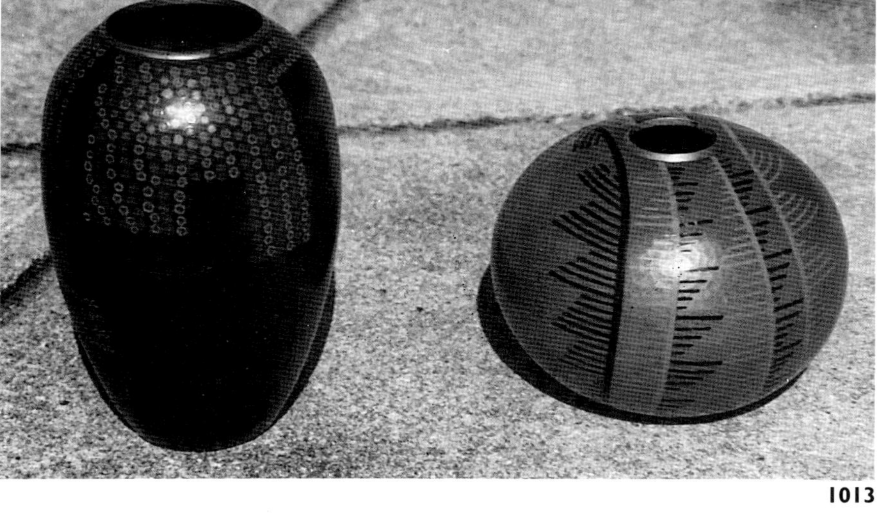

1013

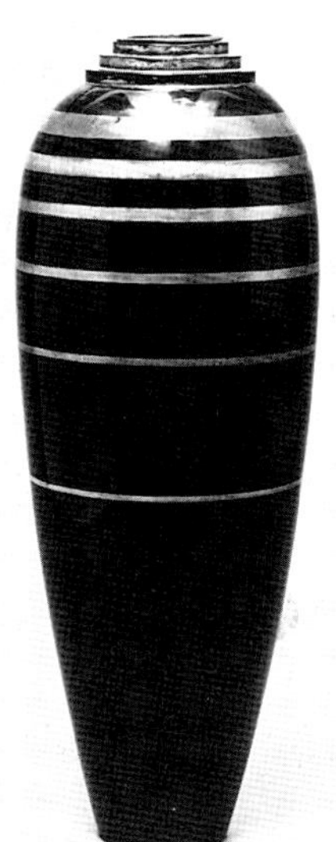

1006

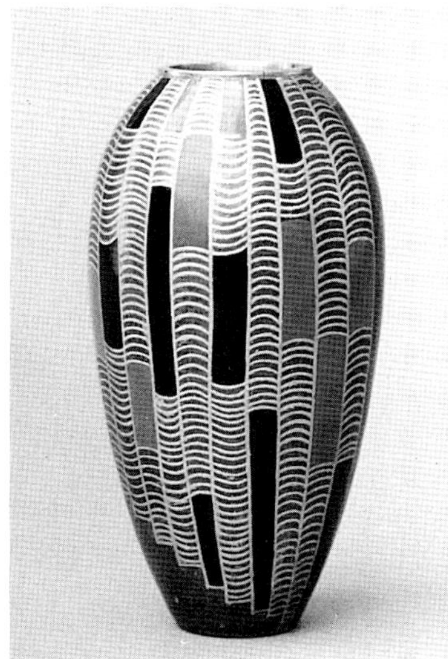

1009

1002 Large vase

Brass with floral design in coloured lacquer.
1922.
Exh.: Salon de la Société des Artistes Français, Paris, 1922.

1003 Ovoid vase with everted rim *Pl. 131*

Oxidized nickel silver with a geometric design in red lacquer.
Height 20 cm (7¾ in.).
C. 1922.
Exh.: Delorenzo Gallery, New York, 1985 (repr. in catalogue, p. 123).
Private collection.

1004 Ovoid vase

Black lacquered nickel silver.
Height 44 cm (17¼ in.).
C. 1922.
Exh.: Delorenzo Gallery, New York, 1985 (repr. in catalogue, p. 77).
Coll.: Delorenzo Gallery, New York.

1005 Small bowl on stand

Copper decorated with brush-marked coloured lacquer highlighted with gold.
Height 12 cm (4¾ in.).
C. 1922.
Formerly in the collection of Félix Marcilhac, Paris; Private collection.

1006 Tall vase

Black lacquered brass in the shape of an artillery shell, with a decoration of circles in white gold.
Height 70 cm (27½ in.).
C. 1922.
Formerly in the Julliac Collection; Tina and Michael Chow.
Sold: Anaf (Lyons), 1 December 1982, lot 51, repr. on cover of the catalogue.

1007 Cornet vase

Oxidized hammered copper with a geometric design in coloured lacquer highlighted with gold.
Height 34 cm (13½ in.).
C. 1922–4.
Sold: Sotheby's (Monaco), 25 June 1981, lot 263; Christie's (New York), 14 June 1986, lot 385.

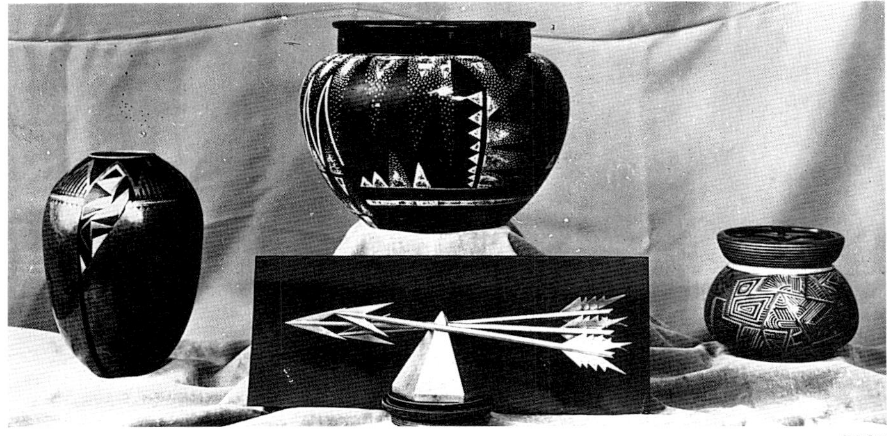

1015

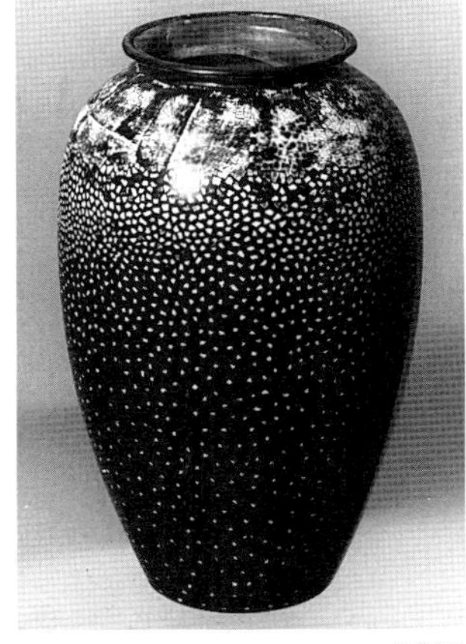

1016

1008 Spherical vase
Nickel silver with roughened surface and a geometric design in red lacquer.
Height 14 cm (5½ in.).
C. 1922–4.
Exh.: Delorenzo Gallery, New York, 1985 (repr. in catalogue, p. 70).
Coll.: Delorenzo Gallery, New York.

1009 Ovoid vase
Copper with a design in red and black lacquer highlighted with gold.
Height 12 cm (4¾ in.).
C. 1922–4.
Exh.: Delorenzo Gallery, New York, 1985 (repr. in catalogue, p. 64).
Coll.: Delorenzo Gallery, New York.
Sold: Sotheby's (Monaco), 10 February 1981, lot 1472.

1010 Spherical vase *Pl. 134*
Oxidized copper with a geometric design in coloured lacquer.
Height 23 cm (9 in.).
C. 1922–4.
Exh.: Delorenzo Gallery, New York, 1985 (repr. in catalogue, p. 72).
Coll.: Jean-Jacques Baumé, Paris.

1011 Spherical vase *Pl. 108*
Green patinated oxidized brass with a geometric design in coloured lacquer highlighted with gold.
Height 23 cm (9 in.).
C. 1922–4.
Private collection.

1012 Long-necked bottle
Black-lacquered brass decorated with red and gold lacquered stringing.
Height 45 cm (17¾ in.).
C. 1922–4.
Private collection.

1013 Vases
Oxidized copper inlaid with silver and decorated with red lacquer; also hammer-marked pewter decorated with a geometric design in coloured lacquer.
C. 1922–4.
Private collection.

1014 Deep bowl on tripod *Pl. 130*
Nickel silver with a lacquered geometric design; wrought-iron tripod.
Height 108 cm (42½ in.).
1923.
Exh.: Galerie Georges Petit, Paris, 1923.
Formerly in the collection of Pierre Hebey; Galerie Vallois, Paris.

1015 Vases, cache-pot and radiator cap
Polished steel and oxidized copper with a geometric design in coloured lacquer inlaid with eggshell.
1925.
Exh.: Exposition Internationale des Arts Décoratifs et Industriels Modernes, Paris, 1925.
Bibl.: *L'Art vivant*, 15 November 1925, p. 28.
See also cat. no. 651.

1016 Ovoid flat-necked vase
Black lacquered nickel silver decorated with an irregular eggshell design.
Height 21 cm (8¼ in.).
C. 1925.
Private collection.

1017 Vases and bonbonnière *Pl. 117*
Brass with a brushed coloured lacquer design and lacquered brass inlaid with eggshell.
Height 10 cm (4 in.); 11 cm (4¼ in.); 14 cm (5½ in.) and 15 cm (6 in.).
C. 1925.
Formerly in the collection of Jeanne Lanvin; Private collections.
Sold: Couturier, de Nicolay (Paris), 14 June 1978, lots 54–7.

1018 Ovoid vase
Brass with red shellac decoration inlaid with eggshell.
Height 15 cm (6 in.).
1925.
Coll.: Musée Saint-Pierre, Lyons.

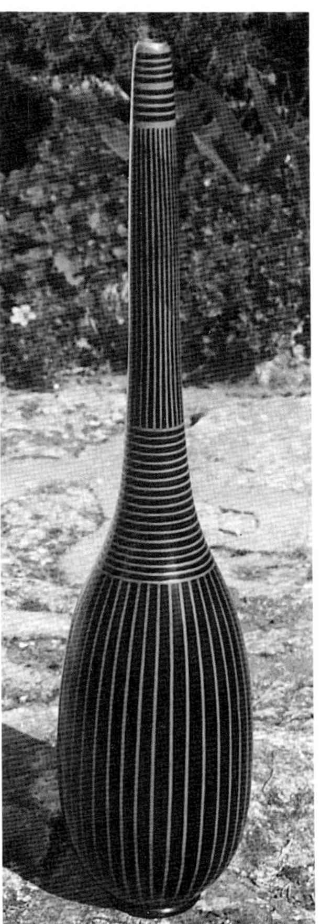

1012

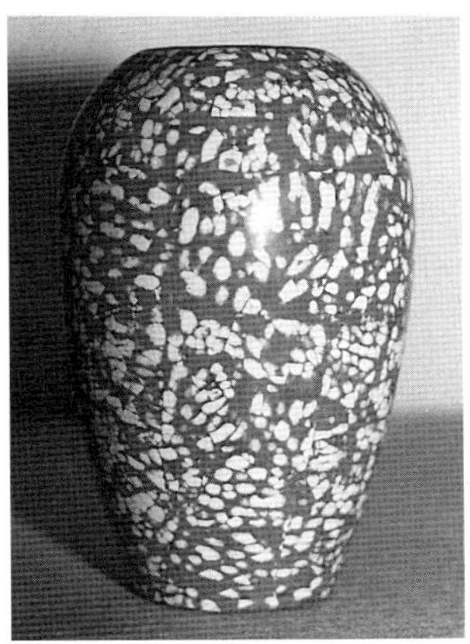

1018

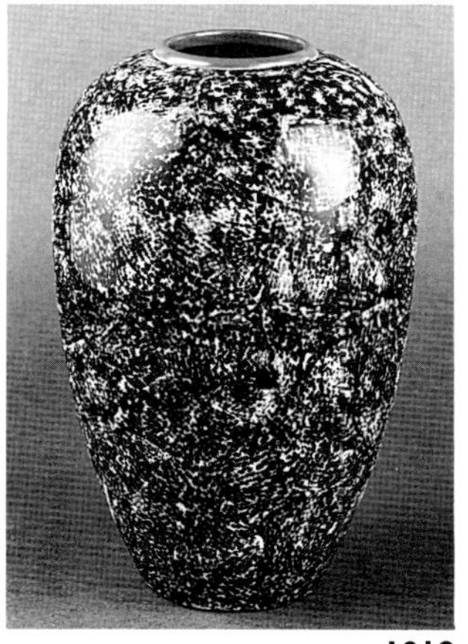
1019

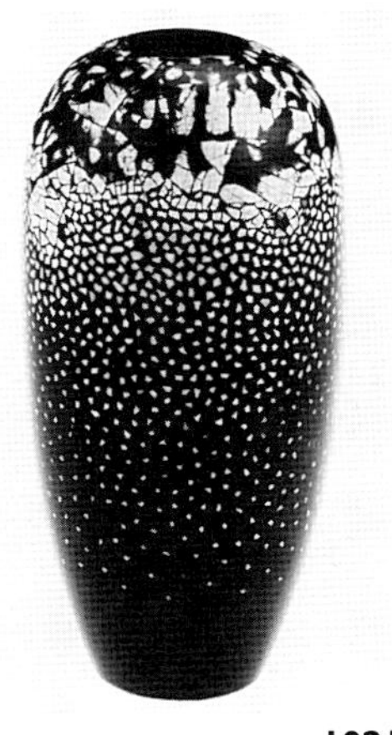
1021

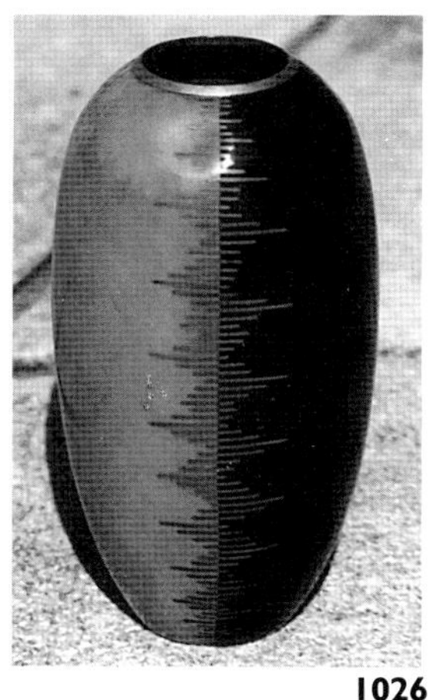
1026

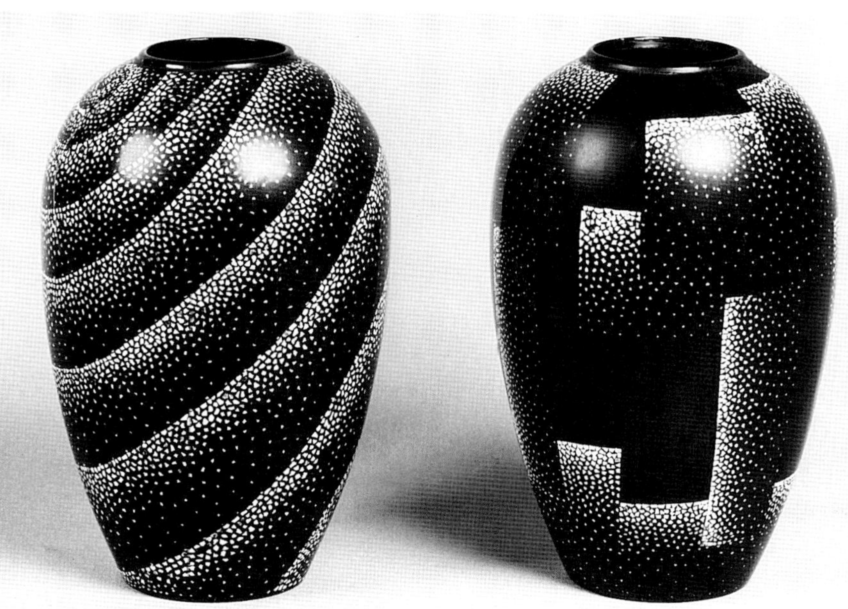
1020

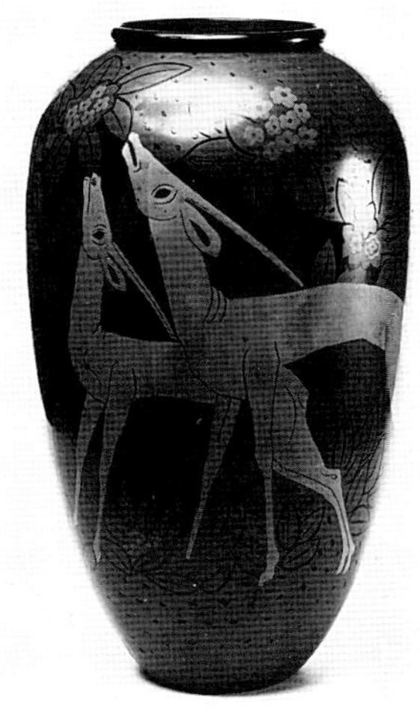

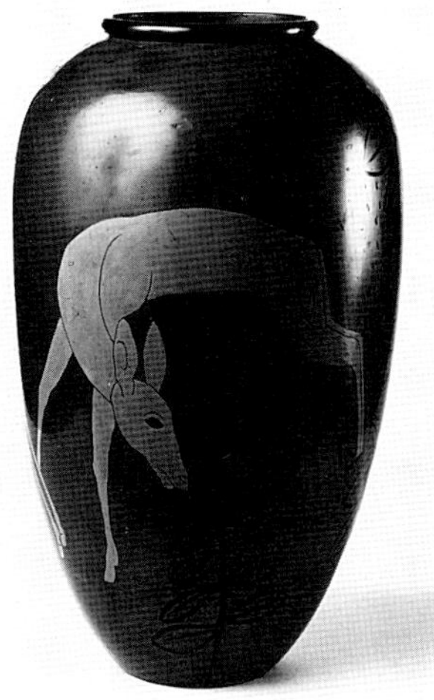
1031

1019 Ovoid vase with lap-jointed neck

Brass with black lacquer design inlaid with eggshell and red lacquer neck.
Height 15 cm (6 in.).
C. 1925.
Exh.: Galerie du Luxembourg, Paris, 1973.
Private collection.
Bibl.: *Jean Dunand – Jean Goulden*, exhibition catalogue (Paris, 1973), p. 71.

1020 Ovoid vases with lap-jointed neck

Brass with black lacquer design inlaid with eggshell.
Height of each vase 19 cm (7½ in.).
C. 1925.
Sold: Ader, Picart, Tajan (Paris), 15 June 1981, lots 181 and 182.

1021 Small ovoid vase

Brass with black lacquer design inlaid with eggshell.
Height 15 cm (6 in.).
C. 1925.
Coll: Virginia Museum of Fine Arts, Richmond, Va (gift of Sydney and Frances Lewis).

1022 Vases and bonbonnière *Pl. 119*

Brass with black lacquer design inlaid with eggshell, anthracite-grey lacquer with silver geometric design, and *repoussé* brass with chased decoration in silver and shaded red lacquer, the snake on the lid in silver patinated bronze.
Height of *bonbonnière* 14 cm (5½ in.).
C. 1925.
Exh.: Galerie du Luxembourg, Paris, 1973, no. 53 (*bonbonnière* only).
Private collection.
Bibl.: *Jean Dunand – Jean Goulden*, exhibition catalogue (Paris, 1973), p. 71 (*bonbonnière* only).

1023 Group of vases *Pl. 118*

Pewter with a geometric design in coloured lacquer; black lacquer with a red lacquer design highlighted with gold; and oxidized copper with a black lacquer zigzag design.

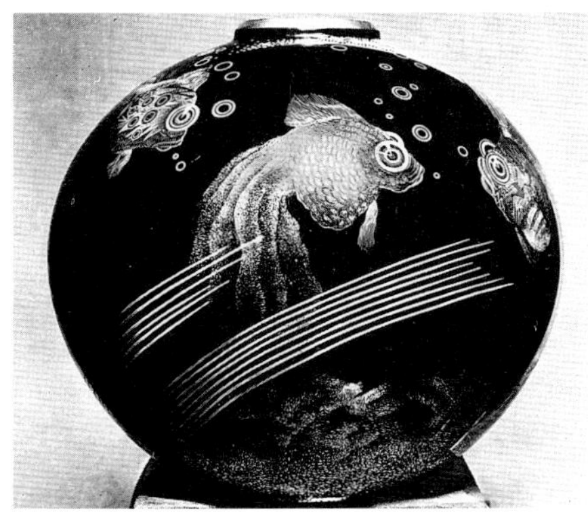

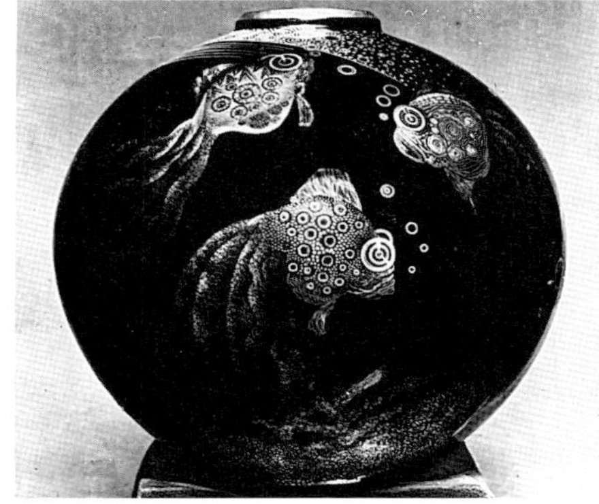

1029

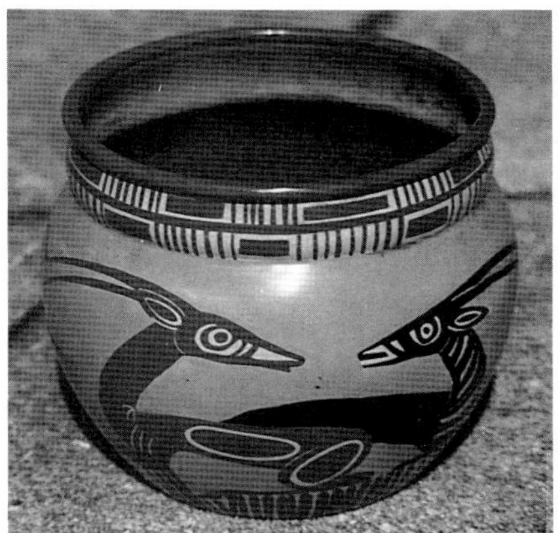

1032

The four vases on the left were made *c.* 1925, the one on the right *c.* 1920.
Bibl.: *Fairchild's International*, June 1929, the vase on the left repr. on p. 32.

1024 Spherical vase *Pl. 115*
Oxidized pewter with a bold geometric design in coloured lacquer.
Height 25 cm (9¾ in.).
C. 1925.
Private collection.
Sold: Boisgirard (Paris), 26 October 1988, lot 120.

1025 Vases *Pl. 116*
Black-lacquered brass with a geometric design in red lacquer highlighted with gold and silver; hammer-marked pewter with a geometric design in coloured lacquer.
C. 1925.
Private collection.

1026 Cylindrical vase
Red and black lacquered brass with gold stringing.
Height 20 cm (7¾ in.).
C. 1925.
Private collection.

1027 Ovoid vase
Red shellac with a geometric design in coloured lacquer.
Height 19 cm (7½ in.).
C. 1925.
Sold: Millon, Jutheau (Paris), 22 March 1985, lot 158.

1028 Ovoid vase *Pl. 120*
Black aventurine lacquered brass with decoration in matt and gloss gold lacquer.
Height 24 cm (9½ in.).
C. 1925.
Exh.: Delorenzo Gallery, New York, 1985 (repr. in catalogue, p. 73).
Sold: Couturier, de Nicolay (Paris), 23 May 1981, lot 39.

1029 Spherical 'Fish' vase
Black-lacquered brass with figurative design in coloured lacquer highlighted with gold; accompanying plinth with dedication.
Height 35 cm (13¾ in.).
1928.
Vase presented to Mme Raymond Poincaré, the wife of the Prime Minister and former President of the French Republic, on the occasion of her husband's 68th birthday. For Dunand's sketch, see illustration, p. 114.

1030 Ovoid vase
Beige-lacquered brass with a figurative design in red and maroon shellac.
C. 1930.
Private collection.

1031 'Deer' vase
Shellac on brass, with figurative design in brown lacquer highlighted with gold.
C. 1930.
Private collection.

1032 'Antelope' cache-pot
Beige-lacquered brass with a figurative design in black and brown lacquer.
C. 1930.
Private collection.

1033 'Dogs' conical vase *Pl. 127*
Beige-lacquered copper with a figurative design in black and brown lacquer highlighted with gold.
C. 1930.
Private collection.

1034 'Birds on Trees' cache-pot *Pl. 129*
Brown and beige lacquer on brass, with figurative design in ochre lacquer.
Height 35 cm (13¾ in.).
C. 1930.
Sold: Boisgirard (Paris), 25 March 1988, lot 108.

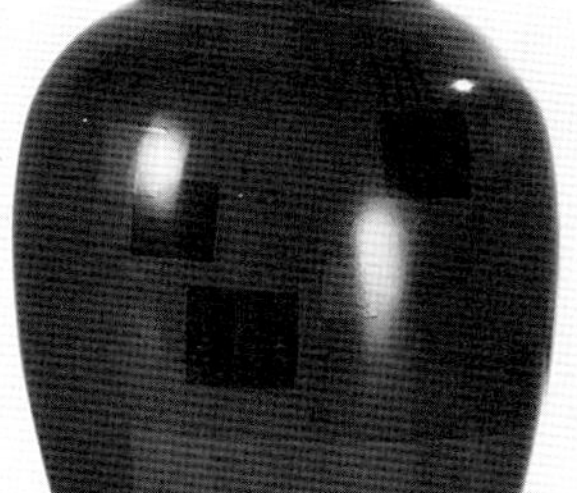

1027

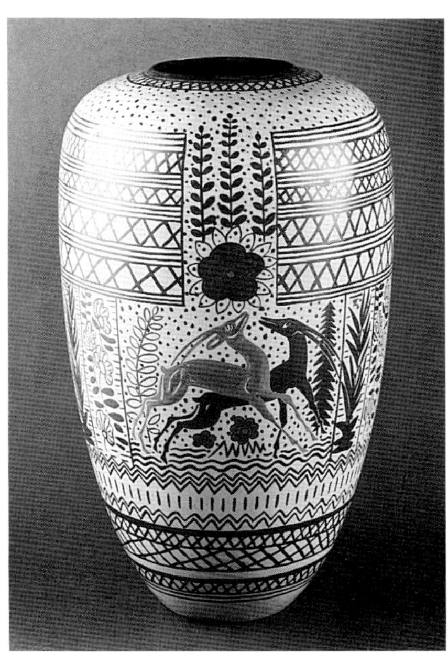

1030

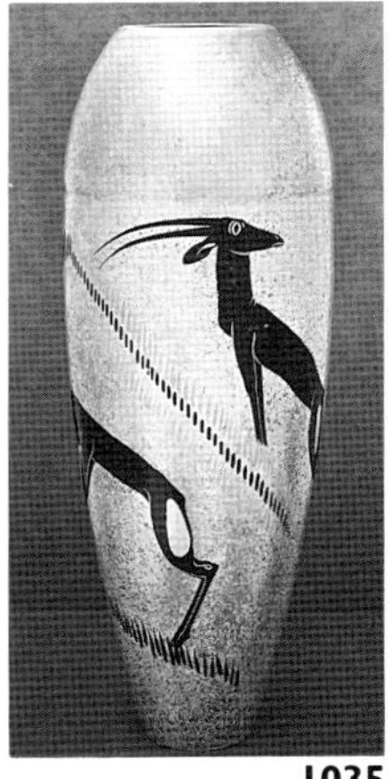
1035

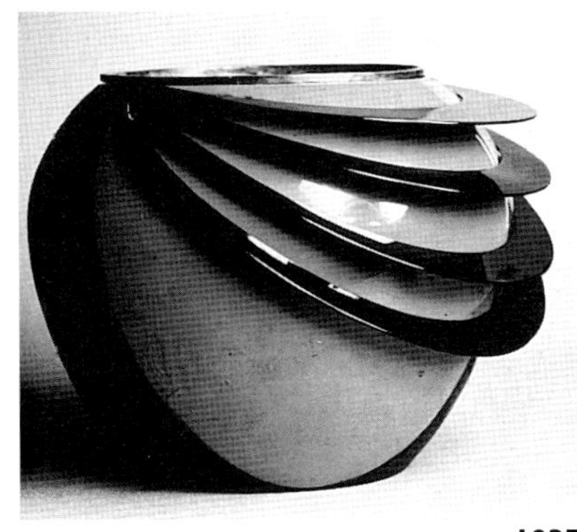
1037

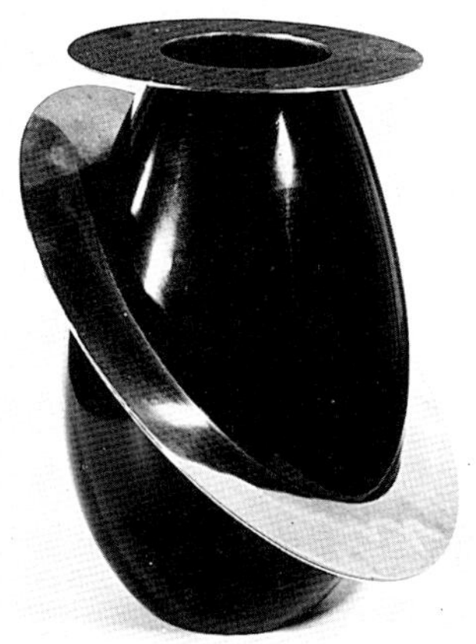
1039

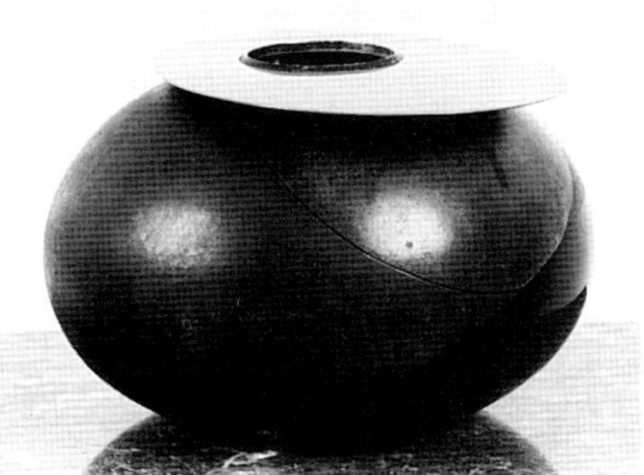
1038

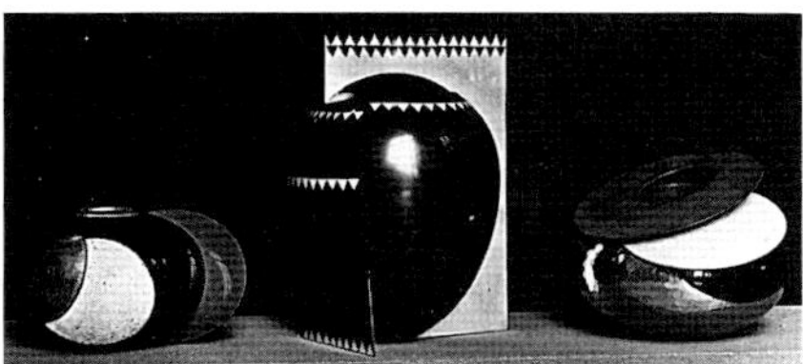
1040

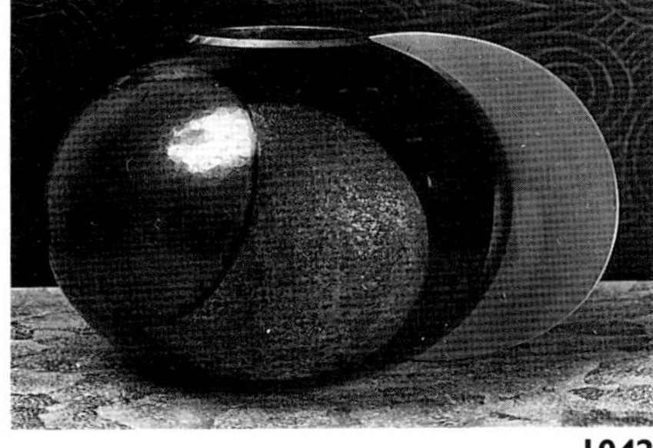
1042

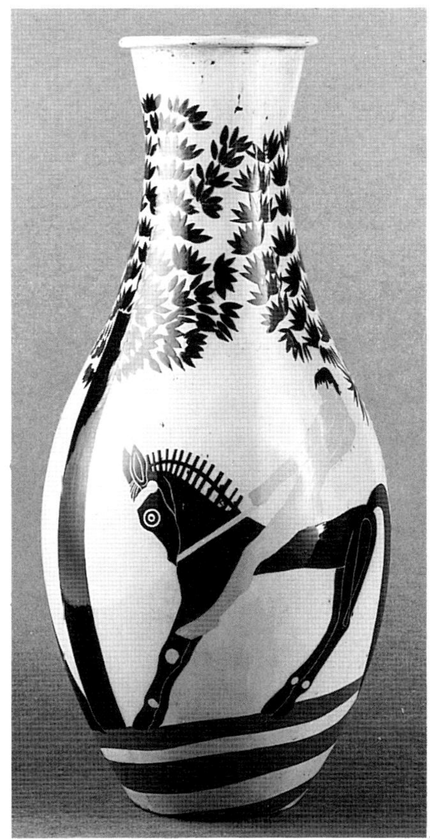
1036

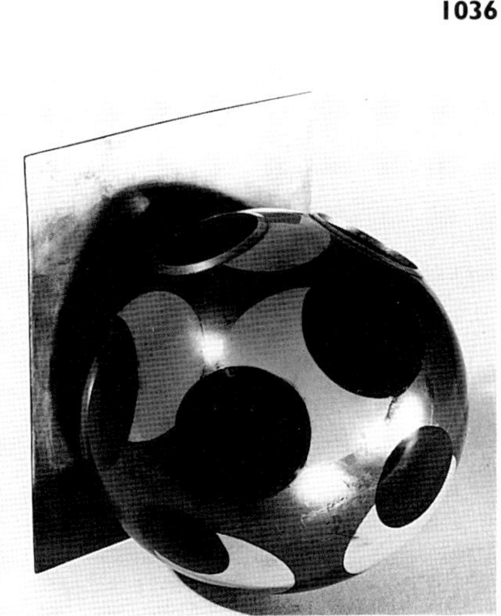
1043

1035 'Antelope' vase

Gold-lacquered brass in the shape of an artillery shell, with roughened oxidized surface and a figurative design in black lacquer.
C. 1930.
Coll.: Galerie Vallois, Paris.

1036 'Horsemen' baluster vase *Pl. 128*

Beige-lacquered brass with a figurative design in black, brown and rose-pink lacquer.
Height 50 cm (19¾ in.).
C. 1930.
Private collection.

1037 Vase

Red-lacquered brass body, with *appliqué* extensions in black-lacquered brass.
Height 23 cm (9 in.).
C. 1925.
Formerly in the Manoukian Collection; Private collection.

1038 Spherical vase with a flat *appliqué* disc

Brass, with black and anthracite-grey lacquer decoration having a roughened surface; the *appliqué* extension in red lacquer.
Height 21 cm (8¼ in.).
1926.
Exh.: Delorenzo Gallery, New York, 1985 (repr. in catalogue, p. 106).
Coll.: Delorenzo Gallery, New York.

1039 Disc vase

Black-lacquered brass with *appliqué* nickel silver discs.
Height 24 cm (9½ in.).
1927.
Private collection.

1040 Winged vases

Pewter and brass in coloured lacquer, *appliqué* discs in red lacquer and black lacquer.
1926.
Exh.: Galerie Georges Petit, Paris, 1926.

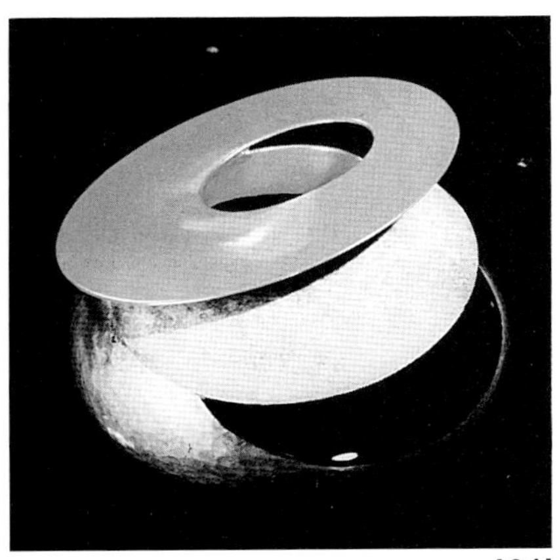

1041

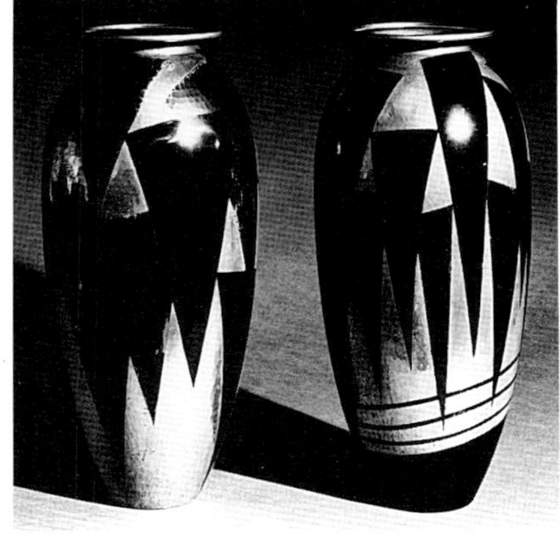

1047

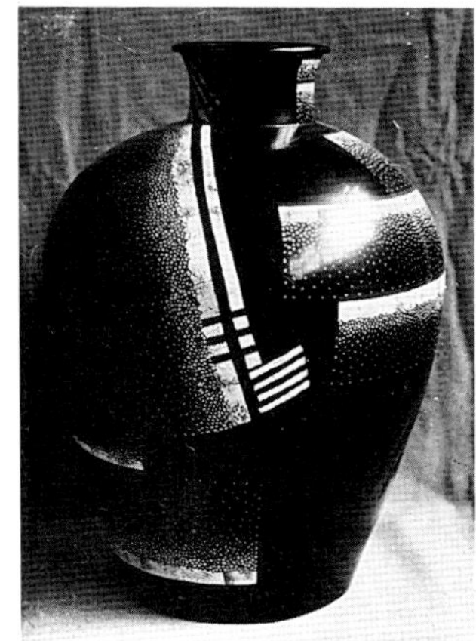

1044

1041 Spherical vase with two discs
Large-faceted hammer-marked pewter, black lacquer, flat disc in red lacquer, diagonal disc oxidized green.
Height 20 cm (7¾ in.).
1926.
Exh.: Galerie Georges Petit, Paris, 1926; Galerie du Luxembourg, Paris, 1973; Rothman's of Pall Mall Ltd, travelling exhibition, Canada, June 1925–May 1926.
Formerly in the collection of the Galerie du Luxembourg; Private collection.
Bibl.: *Jean Dunand – Jean Goulden*, exhibition catalogue (Paris, 1973), p. 9; Rothman's exhibition catalogue, p. 24.
Sold: Godeau, Solanet, Audap (Paris), 26 November 1976, lot 108.

1042 Vase with *appliqué* vertical 'wing' *Pl. 124*
Green oxidized and roughened brass, black and red lacquer.
Height 15 cm (6 in.).
1926.
Exh.: Galerie Georges Petit, Paris, 1926; Galerie du Luxembourg, Paris, 1973, no. 45.
Private collection.
Bibl.: *Jean Dunand – Jean Goulden*, exhibition catalogue (Paris, 1973), p. 68.
Sold: Sotheby's (Monaco), 13 April 1986, lot 308.

1043 Spherical vase
Brass with black, red and anthracite-grey lacquer decoration and nickel silver plaque.
Height 22 cm (8¾ in.); plaque 25 x 20 cm (9¾ x 7¾ in.).
1926.
Private collection.
Sold: Champin, Lombrail, Gautier (Enghien), 26 October 1980, lot 37.

1044 Large bottle
Heavy pottery body lacquered and inlaid with eggshell.
Height 40 cm (15¾ in.).
1925.
Formerly in the collection of Tina and Michael Chow; Private collection.
Bibl.: *Mobilier et décoration*, February 1926, p. 36.

1045 Vase with circular beaded motifs *Pl. 126*
Black lacquer on brass, with a design in red, silver and gold lacquer.
Height 19 cm (7½ in.).
C. 1925.
Coll.: Alain Lesieutre, Paris.
Sold: Champin, Lombrail, Gautier (Enghien), 26 October 1980, lot 36.

1046 Ovoid vase
Oxidized brass with silver inlay and with a geometric design in black and red lacquer.
Height 16 cm (6¼ in.).
C. 1925.
Exh.: Delorenzo Gallery, New York, 1985 (repr. in catalogue, p. 81).
Coll.: Delorenzo Gallery, New York.
Sold: Sotheby's (Monaco), 6 March 1983, lot 140.

1047 Pair of ovoid vases
Nickel silver with a geometric design in black lacquer.
C. 1925.
Exh.: Delorenzo Gallery, New York, 1985 (repr. in catalogue, p. 63).
Coll.: Delorenzo Gallery, New York.

1048 Ovoid vase
Brass with a design in black and red lacquer.
Height 15 cm (6 in.).
C. 1926.
Exh.: Delorenzo Gallery, New York, 1985 (repr. in catalogue, p. 65).
Coll.: Delorenzo Gallery, New York.

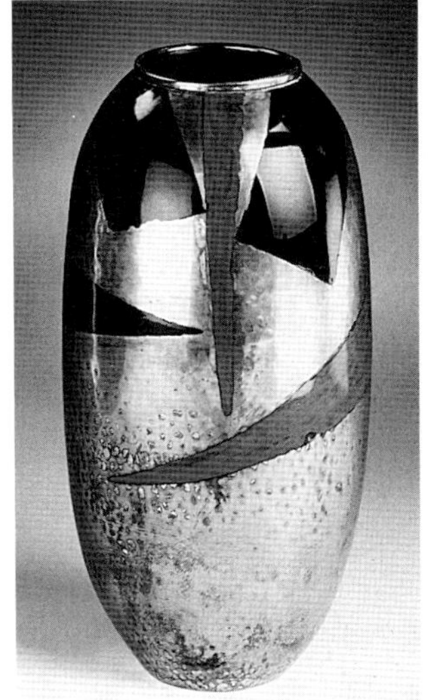

1046

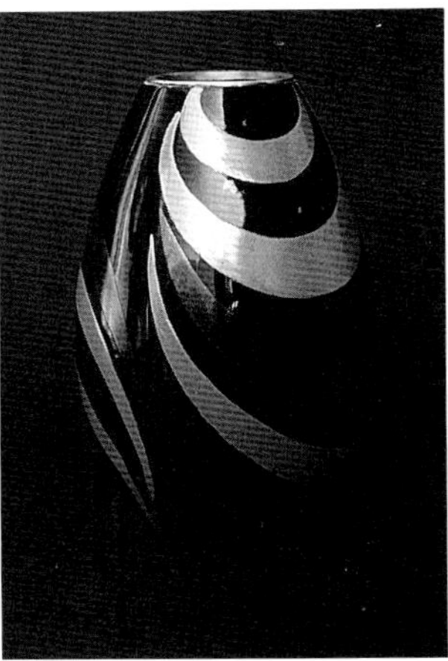

1048

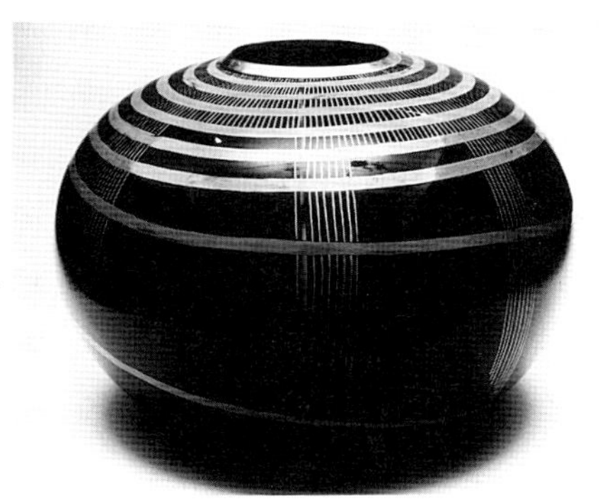

1049

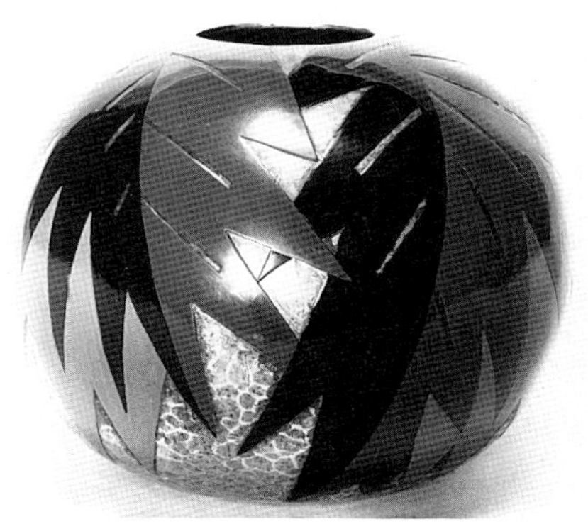

1051

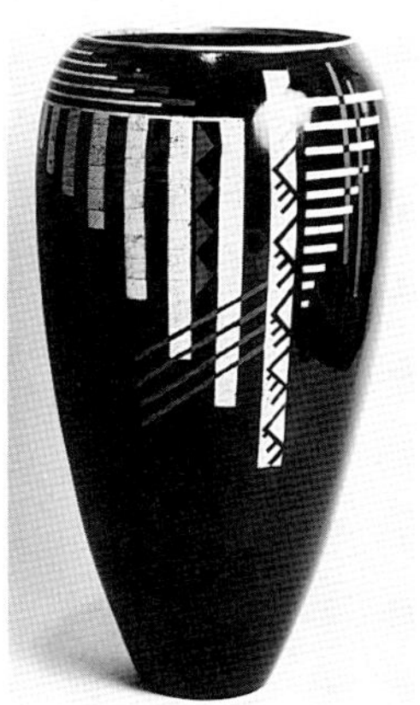

1054

1061

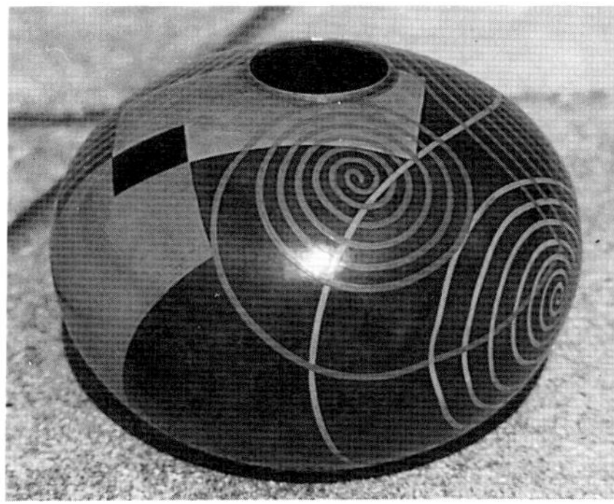

1060

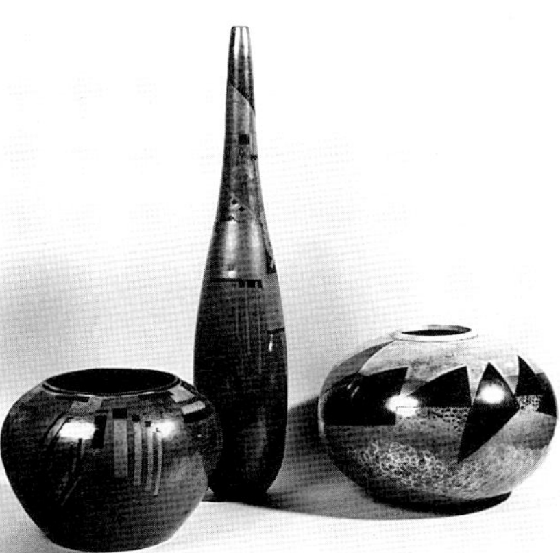

1057

1049 Spherical vase
Black-lacquered brass with unequally spaced concentric rings and vertical stringing in red lacquer highlighted with gold.
Height 15 cm (6 in.).
C. 1922–4.
Private collection.
Sold: Boisgirard (Paris), 26 October 1988, lot 119.

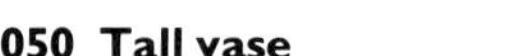

1050 Tall vase *Pl. 123*
Green oxidized and roughened brass with alternating geometric design in black lacquer.
Height 62 cm (24½ in.).
C. 1928.
Formerly in the Frugès Collection and in the collection of Duncan MacLaren; Tina and Michael Chow.
Sold: Sotheby's (Monaco), 24 September 1978, lot 225.

1051 Spherical 'Leaf' vase *Pl. 110*
Hammer-marked pewter with a figurative design in green, red and black lacquer.
Height 13 cm (5¼ in.).
C. 1926.
Sold: Boisgirard (Paris), 22 October 1986, lot 79.

1052 Spherical vase *Pl. 111*
Oxidized brass with a geometric design in grey, black and red lacquer.
Height 32 cm (12½ in.).
C. 1924.
Sold: Christie's (New York), 17 December 1983, lot 349.

1053 Two spherical vases *Pl. 121*
Oxidized brass with a geometric design in coloured lacquer.
Height 25 cm (9¾ in.) and 32 cm (12½ in.).
C. 1930.
Private collection.
Sold: Boisgirard (Paris), 28 October 1987, lots 197 and 196.

1054 Large vase *Pl. 122*
Black-lacquered brass with a geometric design in coloured lacquer inlaid with eggshell.

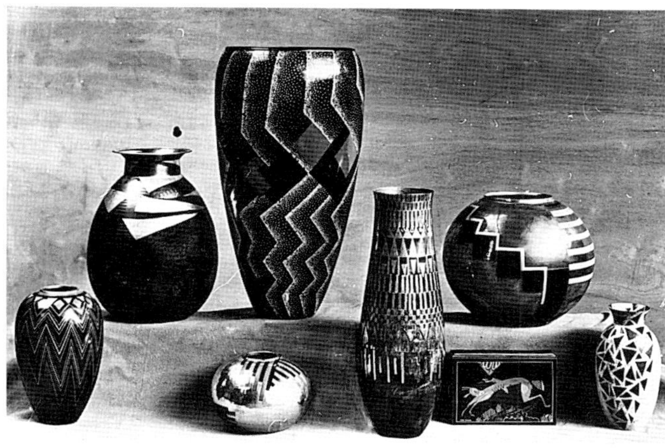
1055

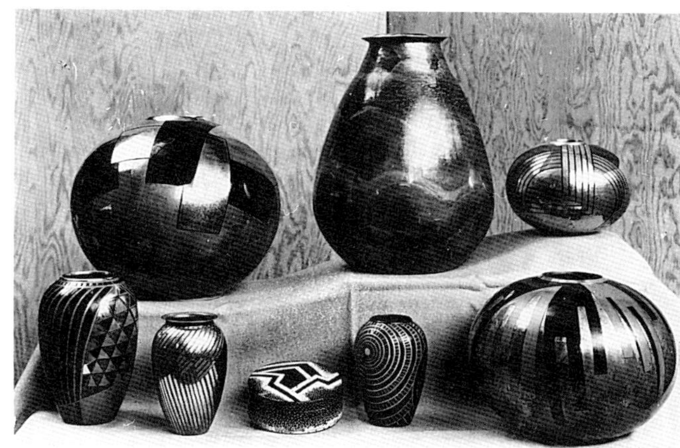
1058

Height 50 cm (19¾ in.).
1925.
Exh.: Galerie Georges Petit, Paris, 1925; Delorenzo Gallery, New York, 1985 (repr. in catalogue, p. 61).
Formerly in the collection of Félix Marcilhac, Paris; Steven A. Greenberg, New York.
Bibl.: *Mobilier et décoration*, February 1926, p. 38.

1055 Vases and box
Various metals, coloured lacquer, eggshell, wood.
1925.
Exh.: Galerie Georges Petit, Paris, 1925.

1056 Reflector *Pl. 125*
Black-lacquered brass inlaid with eggshell.
Height 60 cm (23½ in.).
Lacquered *c.* 1930.
Coll.: Bertrand Maus.

1057 Vases and bottle
Brass and hammer-marked pewter with geometric designs, decoration in coloured lacquer and eggshell.
Height 15 cm (6 in.); 47 cm (18½ in.); 16 cm (6¼ in.).
1923 and 1925.
Formerly in the collection of Karl Lagerfeld; now M. and Mme Kupperfils, Evreux, and private collections.
Sold: Godeau, Solanet, Audap (Paris), 21 November 1975, lots 87, 88 and 89, repr. in catalogue, p. 45.

1058 Vases and box
Various oxidized metals in coloured lacquer and eggshell.
1925.
Exh.: Galerie Georges Petit, Paris, 1925.

1059 Spherical vase *Pl. 133*
Brass with a geometric design in coloured lacquer.
Height 25 cm (9¾ in.).
1925.
Private collection.
Bibl.: *Fairchild's International*, June 1929, p. 32.

1060 Spherical vase
Brass decorated with overlapping circles and squares in coloured lacquer highlighted with gold.
Height 30 cm (11¾ in.).
C. 1925.
Private collection.

1061 Vases, chest and box
Wood, various metals, coloured lacquer and eggshell.
1925.
Exh.: Galerie Georges Petit, Paris, 1925.

1062 Ribbon vase
Oxidized nickel silver with a design of overlaid ribbons in black and red lacquer.
Height 21 cm (8¼ in.).
1939.
Exh.: New York World's Fair, 1939 (French Pavilion, lacquer section); Galerie du Luxembourg, Paris, 1973, no. 36.
Private collection.

1063 Vases *Pl. 114*
Various oxidized metals coloured with lacquer and inlaid with eggshell highlighted with gold.
1922 and 1925.
Private collection.

1064 Spherical vase
Black-lacquered brass decorated with concentric circles in red lacquer and with gold stringing.
Height 25 cm (9¾ in.).
1925.
Exh.: Galerie du Luxembourg, Paris, 1973, no. 52.
Private collection.
Bibl.: *Art et décoration*, July 1932, p. 196; *Jean Dunand – Jean Goulden*, exhibition catalogue (Paris, 1973), p. 70.

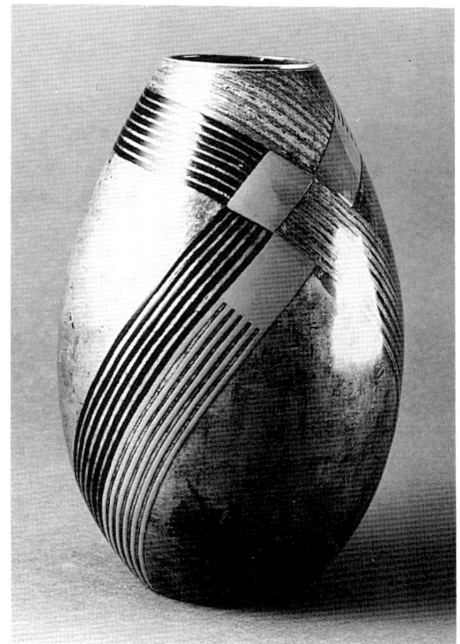
1062

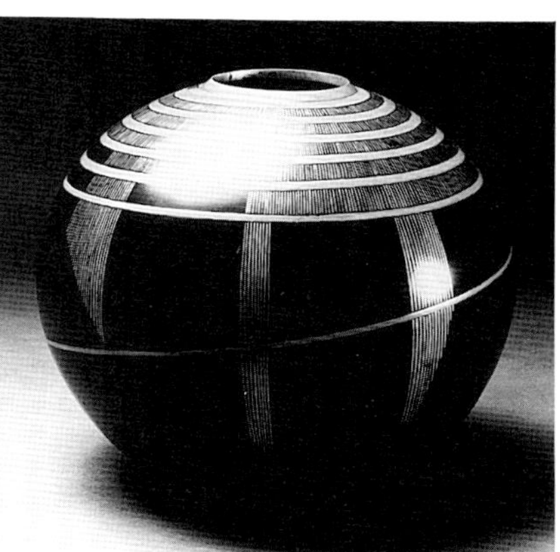
1064

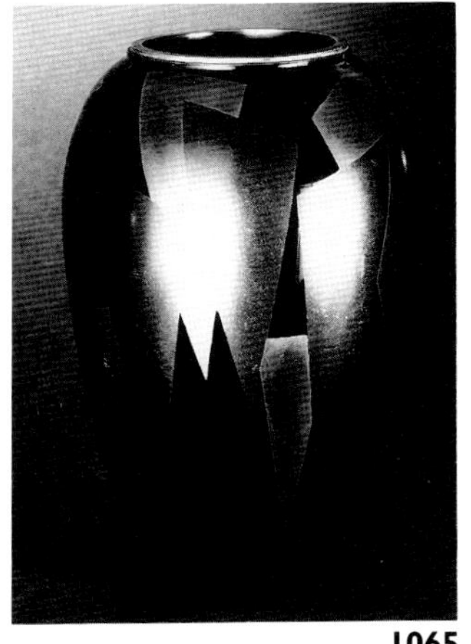

1065

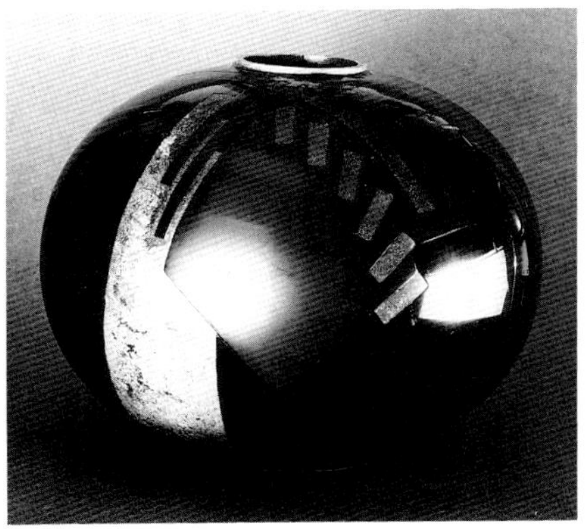

1067

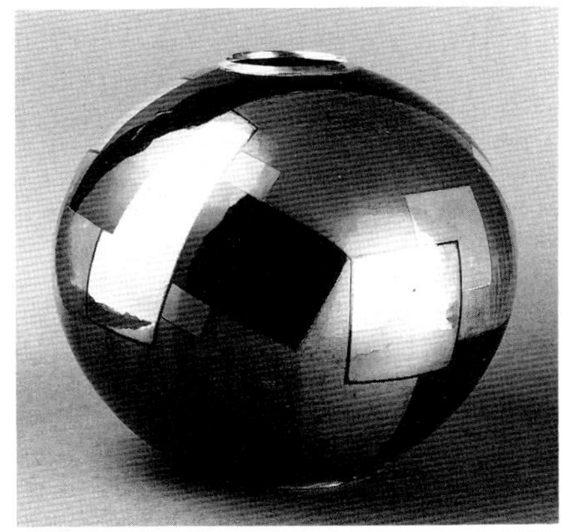

1068

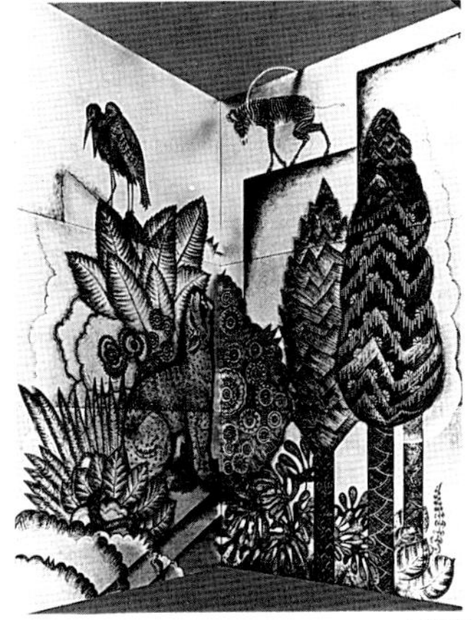

1071

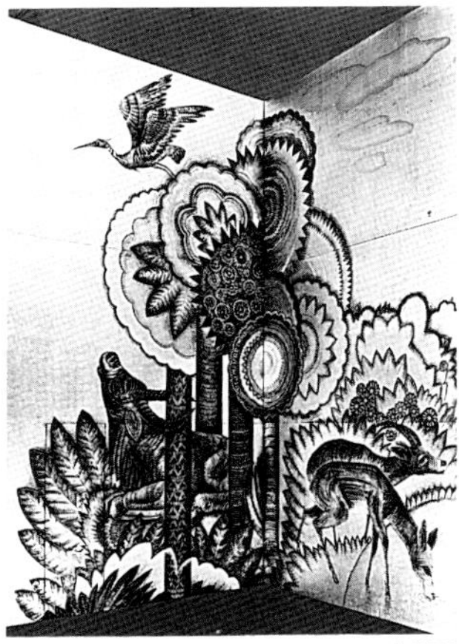

1073

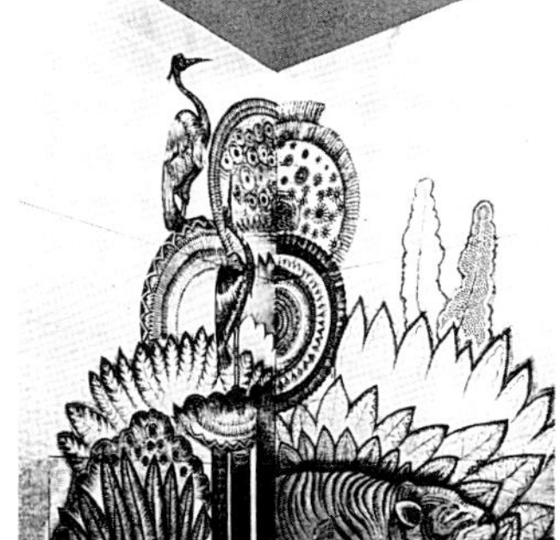

1072

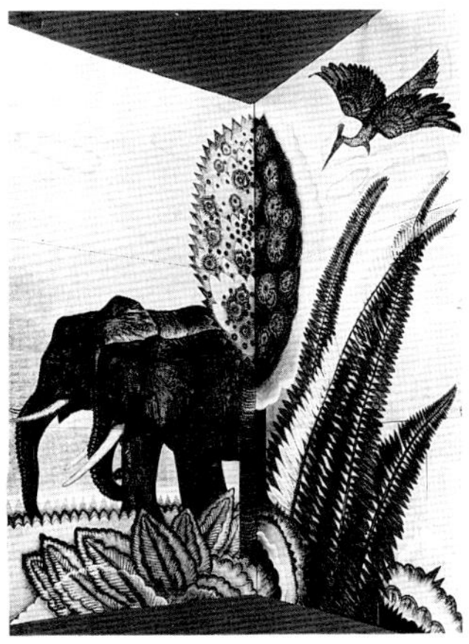

1074

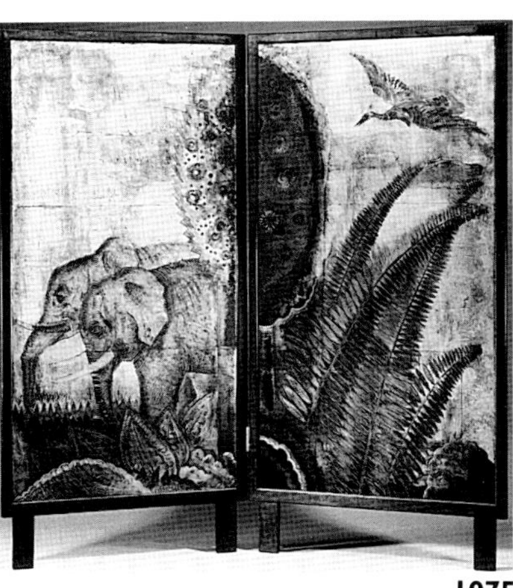

1075

1065 Triangles vase

Brass decorated with overlapping triangles in matt and gloss anthracite-grey lacquer, black-lacquered pewter.
Height 22 cm (8¾ in.).
C. 1927.
Exh.: Galerie du Luxembourg, Paris, 1973, no. 40.
Private collection.
Bibl.: *Jean Dunand – Jean Goulden*, exhibition catalogue (Paris, 1973), p. 65.

1066 Spherical vase *Pl. 109*

Pewter with a bold geometric design in red and black lacquer.
Height 22 cm (8¾ in.).
1925.
Exh.: Galerie du Luxembourg, Paris, 1973, no. 44.
Private collection.
Bibl.: *Jean Dunand – Jean Goulden*, exhibition catalogue (Paris, 1973), p. 67.

1067 Spherical vase

Green oxidized brass with roughened surface, black and anthracite-grey lacquer.
Height 22 cm (8¾ in.).
C. 1925.
Private collection.

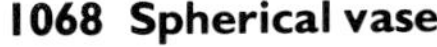

1068 Spherical vase

Brass with a geometric design in silver and with decoration in red and black lacquer.
Height 22 cm (8¾ in.).
C. 1927.
Private collection.
Bibl.: *Fairchild's International*, June 1929, p. 32.

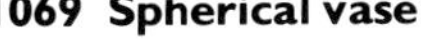

1069 Spherical vase *Pl. 112*

Brass inlaid with silvered metal and with a geometric design in red and black lacquer.
Height 15 cm (6 in.).
C. 1925.
Exh.: Delorenzo Gallery, New York, 1985 (repr. in catalogue, p. 68).
Private collection.

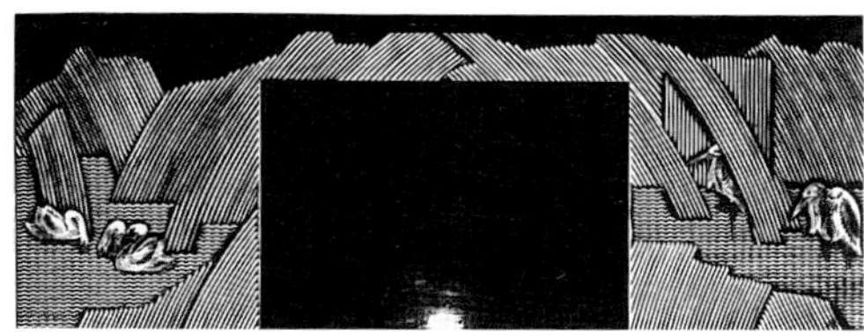
1076

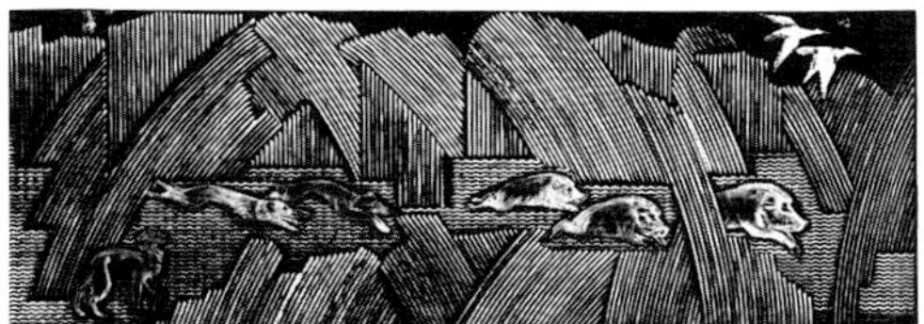
1079

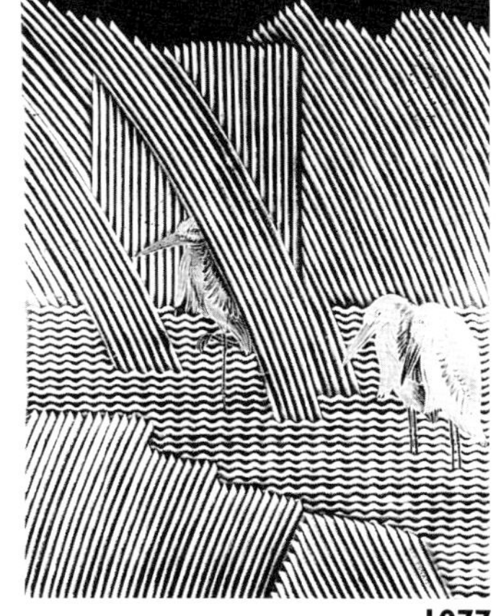
1077

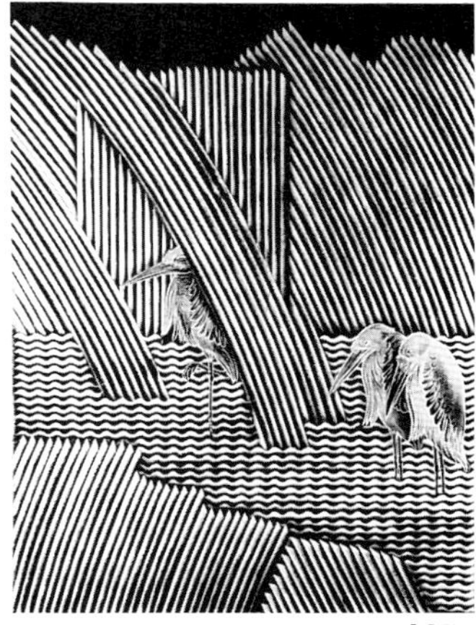
1078

1070 Spherical vase *Pl. 113*
Oxidized brass with a design of alternating concentric circles in red and black lacquer.
Height 25 cm (9¾ in.).
C. 1930.
Private collection.
Bibl.: *Art et décoration*, December 1931, p. 196.

DECORATIVE SCHEMES FOR OCEAN LINERS AND RELATED WORKS

1071–1086
***L'Atlantique* (1931)**
See also colour plates 154, 155.

1071–1074 The Dining Saloon
Double panels decorating the four corners of the Dining Saloon:

1071 *The Panther*
1072 *The Tiger*
1073 *The Buffalo*
1074 *The Elephants*
Each panel decorated in matt brown *laque arrachée* on a silver lacquer ground.
Height 9 m (29 ft 6 in.).
All four panels were first shown in 1930 in Dunand's workshops before installation on the vessel.

1075 *The Elephants*
Preparatory scale-model mounted as a two-panel screen.
Panel size 150 x 73 cm (59 x 29½ in.).
Exh.: Delorenzo Galley, New York, 1985 (repr. in catalogue, p. 14).
Coll.: Steven A. Greenberg, New York.

1076–1086 The Oval Saloon
Decorative frieze consisting of panels executed in black and gold lacquer.

1076 Design for part of the scheme
Scale-model showing the space for the doorway.
Private collection.

1077 *Herons*
Detail of the frieze.

1078 *Herons*
Reduced-size replica of panel.
Private collection.

1079 *Hounds Pursuing Wild Boar*
Detail of the frieze.

1080 *Hounds Pursuing Wild Boar*
Reduced-size replica of panel.
Private collection.

1081 *Bears and Ibexes*
Scale-model for the gold and black lacquer panels (second part).
Private collection.

1082 *Bears and Ibexes*
Gold and incised black lacquer panel.
Detail of the frieze.
Private collection.

1083 *Herons and Deer*
Scale-model for the gold and black lacquer panels (third part).
Private collection.

1084 *Bears*
Detail of the gold and black lacquer panel.

1085 *Bears*
Detail of the gold and black lacquer panel.

1086 *Ibexes Confronting One Another*
Detail of the gold and black lacquer panel.

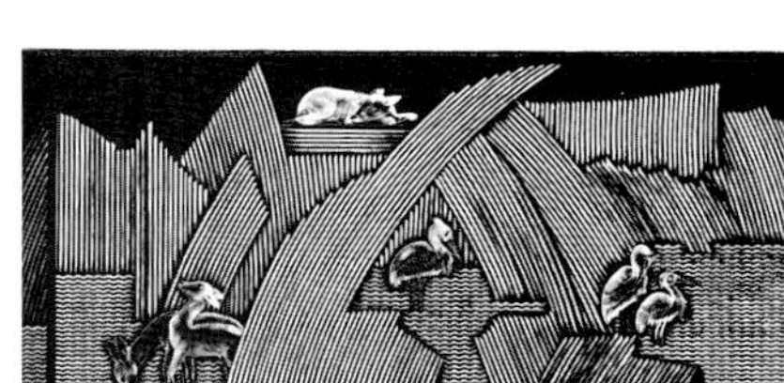
1081

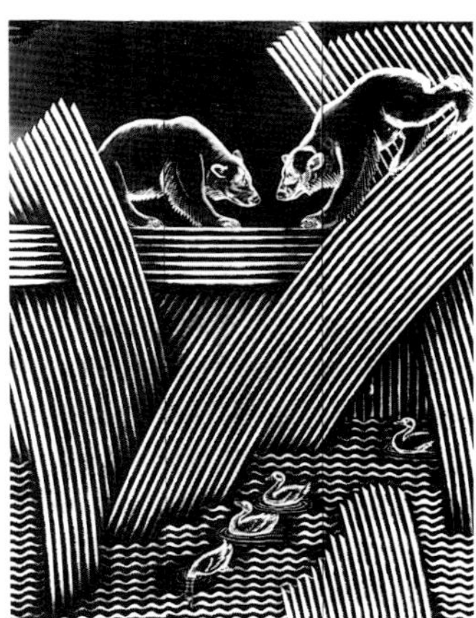
1083

1084

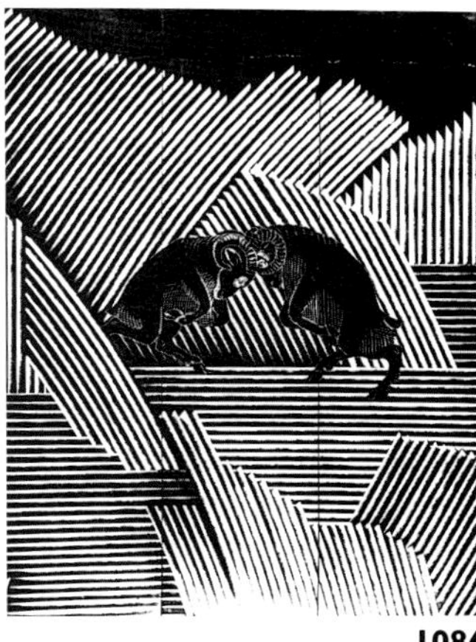
1086

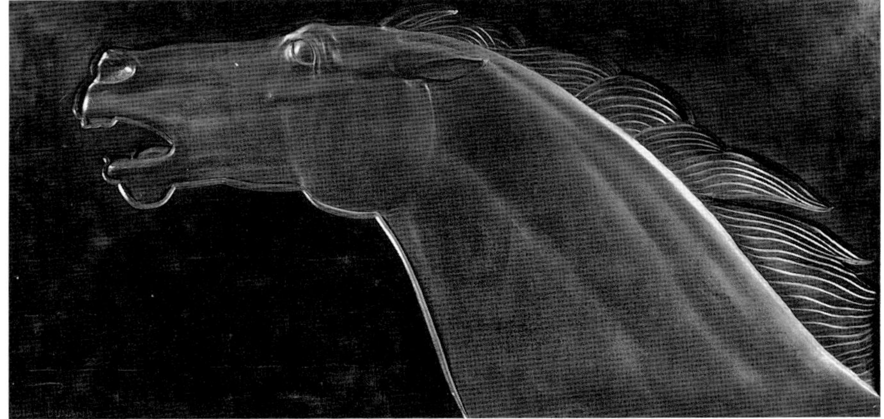

1093

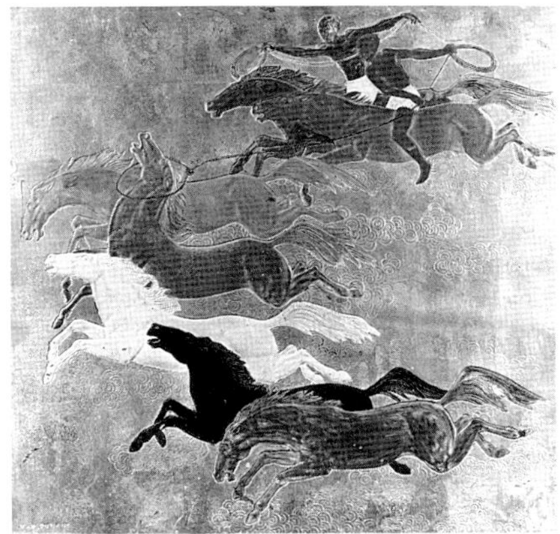

1090

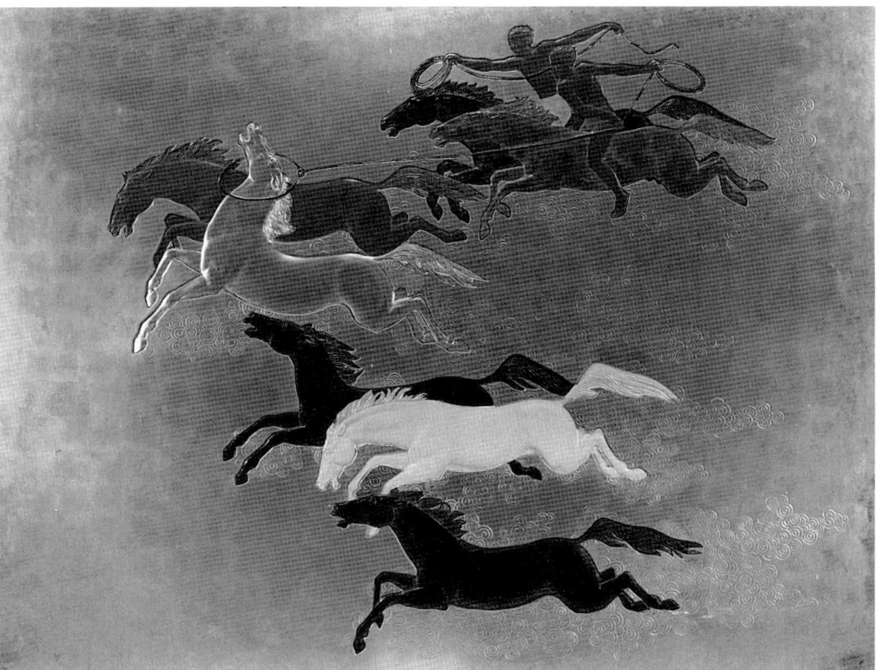

1088

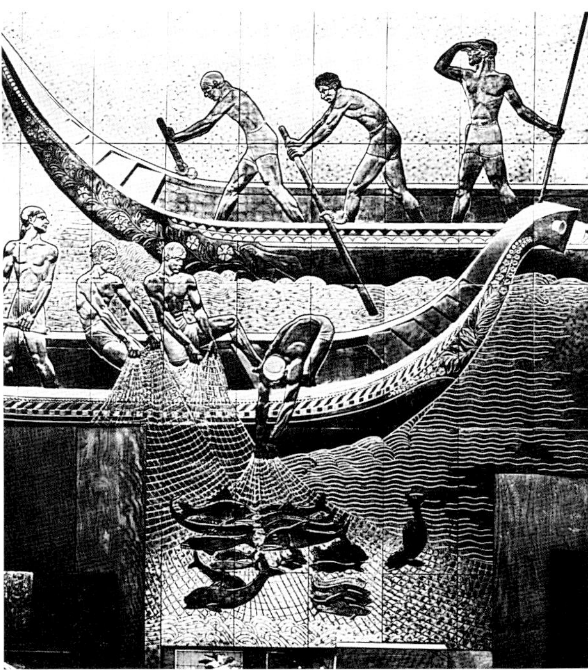

1101

1087–1120
***Normandie* (1935)**
See also colour plates 145–153.

1087–1117 Decorative panels for the Smoking Room (and related works)

1087 *Taming the Horse*
Large mural composed of multiple sculpted gold and coloured lacquer panels.
Coll.: Musée d'Art Moderne de la Ville de Paris.

1088 *Taming the Horse*
150 x 180 cm (59 x 70¾ in.).
Sold: Sotheby's (New York), 11/12 May 1984, lot 398.
Variant of the *Normandie* mural: the horses being pursued are differently positioned from those in the definitive version. Several different versions were made in varying lengths; one, measuring 180 x 250 cm (70¾ x 98½ in.) was specially designed for the apartment of Madame Colette Aboucaya (see cat. no. 1187).

1089 *Taming the Horse*
Coloured lacquer and incised gold lacquer.
Each section 80 x 170 cm (31½ x 67 in.).
Sold: Ader, Picart, Tajan (Paris), 16 October 1974, lot 65.
Another version, in two sections, of the *Normandie* mural: the horses are differently positioned from those in definitive version, and an additional horse has been included in front of the group being pursued.

1090 *Taming the Horse* *Pl. 146*
Coloured lacquer and gold lacquer.
66 x 60 cm (26 x 23½ in.).
Coll.: M. and Mme Jacques Maury.
A reduced-scale version of the mural; this was one of many copies – sometimes lacquered in gold (see cat. no. 1091), sometimes in gold and various colours – made by Dunand. Such copies were either offered to collaborators and well-known figures of the day or sold on a commercial basis.

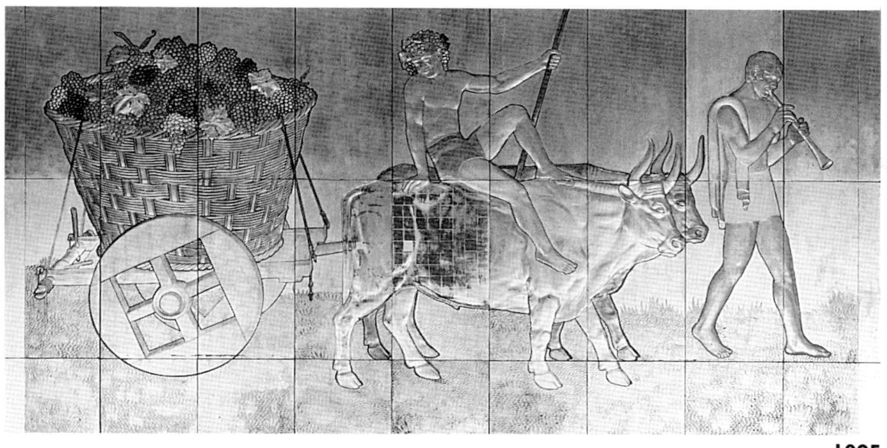
1095

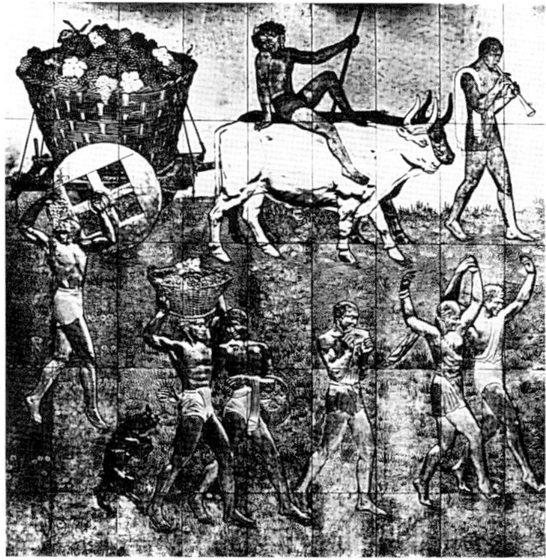
1094

1091 ***Taming the Horse***
Moulded gold lacquer.
66 x 60 cm (26 x 23½ in.).
Private collection.
See note to cat. no. 1090.

1092 ***Head of a Horse***
Incised gold lacquer.
63 x 120 cm (24¾ x 47¼ in.).
Sold: Oger, Dumont (Paris), 13 March 1987, lot 75.
Detail (repeated actual size) of one of the motifs from the mural *Taming the Horse*. See also cat. no. 1093.

1093 ***Head of a Horse***
Incised gold lacquer.
63 x 120 cm (24¾ x 47¼ in.).
Private collection.
Sold: Christie's (New York), 2 October 1981, lot 74.
See note to cat. no. 1092.

1094 ***Grape Harvesting***
Large mural composed of multiple coloured and sculpted gold lacquer panels, seen here mounted in Dunand's workshops on the occasion of their unveiling to the press.

1095 Grape Harvesting
300 x 576 cm (9 ft 10 in x 18 ft 10 in.).
Coll.: Sélestat Municipal Council (Bas Rhin).
Sold: Compagnie Générale Transatlantique (Le Havre), 1 August 1962, lot 31.
Top section of the large panel from the *Normandie* in its revised version by Pierre Dunand, after the lower part was modified in 1949 to enable it to be rehung on the liner *Liberté*.

1096 ***Grape-pickers*** *Pl. 150*
Detail of lower part of the mural *Grape Harvesting*.
Coloured lacquer and incised gold lacquer.
248 x 128 cm (8 ft 1½ in. x 4 ft 2½ in.).
Sold: Champin, Lombrail, Gautier (Enghien), 28 November 1982, lot 113.

1097 ***Grape-picker***
Detail of lower part of the mural *Grape Harvesting*.
Coloured and incised gold lacquer.
248 x 128 cm (8 ft 1½ in. x 4 ft 2½ in.).
Sold: Champin, Lombrail, Gautier (Enghien), 22 November 1982, lot 114.

1098 ***Grape-pickers Dancing***
Detail of lower part of the mural *Grape Harvesting*.
Coloured lacquer and incised gold lacquer.
250 x 190 cm (8 ft 2½ in. x 6 ft 2¾ in.).
Sold: Champin, Lombrail, Gautier (Enghien), 17 April 1983, lot 3.

1099 ***Grape Harvesting*** *Pl. 151*
66 x 61 cm (26 x 24 in.).
Private collection.
Reduced-scale version in coloured lacquer and moulded gold lacquer of the *Normandie* mural. Numerous versions of this scene were made by Dunand, as was also the case with the other panels. Some of them could be mounted for use as occasional tables or as firescreens.

1100 ***Grape Harvesting***
80 x 270 cm (31½ x 106¼ in.).
Sold: Ader, Picart, Tajan (Paris), 16 October 1974, lot 62.
A variant of the large mural *Grape Harvesting* made by placing the upper and lower sections of the definitive version end to end, repositioning the figures and painting over one of the grape-pickers.

1101 ***Fishing***
Coloured lacquer and incised gold lacquer.
Large mural consisting of multiple panels.
Coll.: Musée d'Art Moderne de la Ville de Paris.
The photograph shows the completed mural mounted in Dunand's workshops on the occasion of its unveiling to the press.

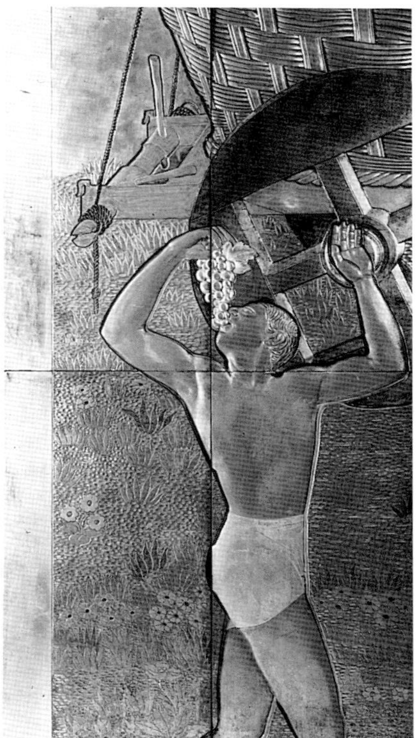
1097

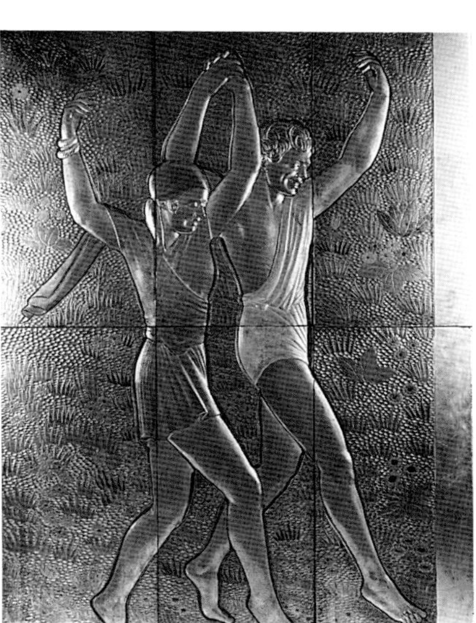
1098

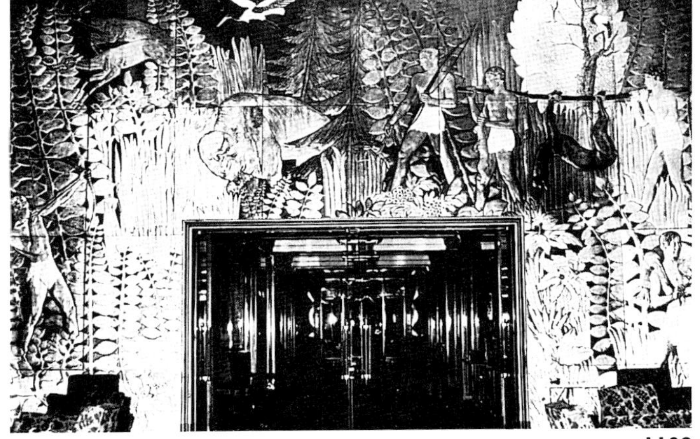

1109

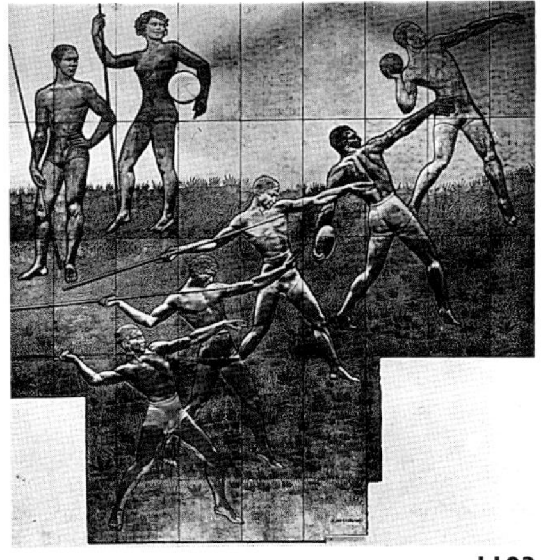

1103

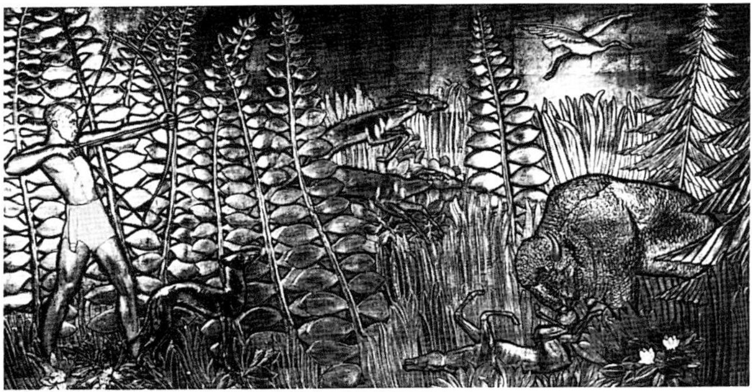

1110

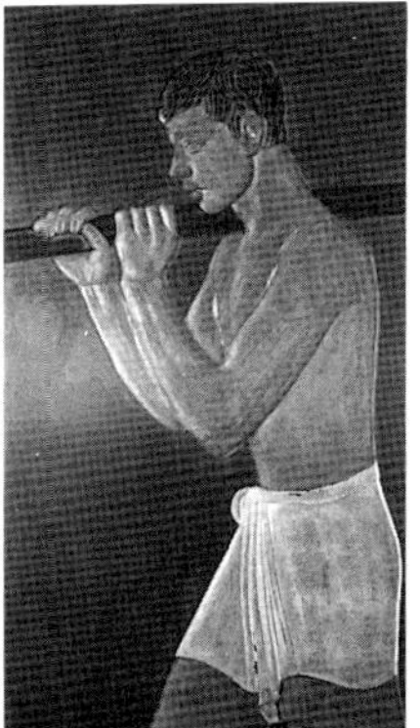

1114

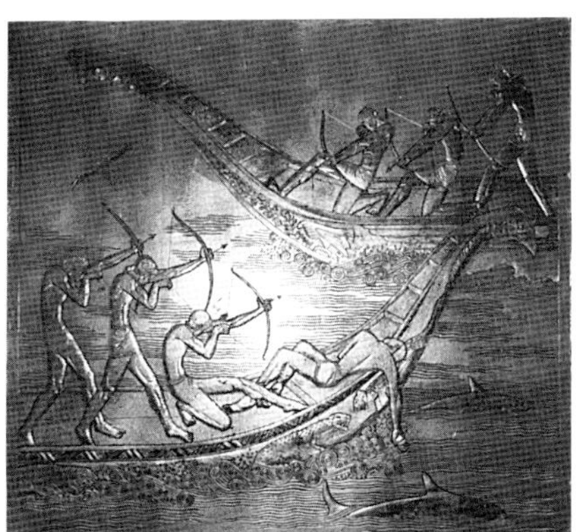

1117

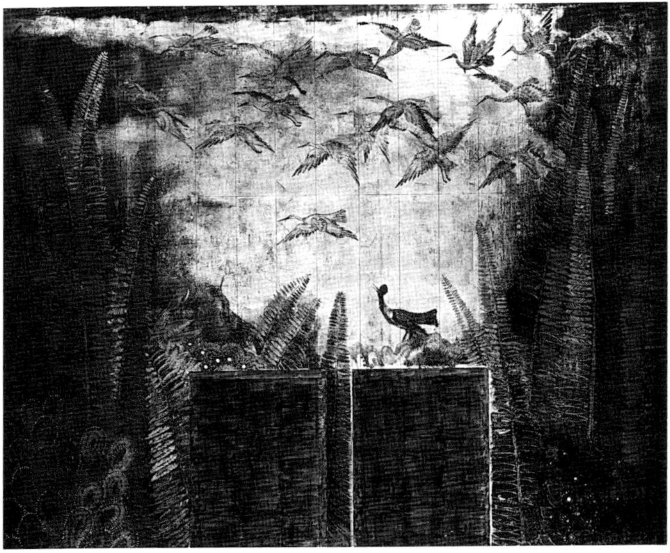

1115

1102 *Fishing* *Pl. 154*
Reduced-scale version of the Smoking Room panel; coloured and moulded gold lacquer.
66 x 61 cm (26 x 24 in.).
Private collection.

1103 *Sports*
Large mural mounted in Dunand's workshops on the occasion of its unveiling to the press.

1104 *Sports*
Large coloured and sculpted gold lacquer mural from the *Normandie* Smoking Room, composed of multiple panels (modified version).
Coll.: Musée d'Art Moderne de la Ville de Paris.

1105 *Javelin Throwers* *Pl. 152*
Coloured and sculpted gold lacquer.
80 x 170 cm (31½ x 67 in.).
Coll.: Félix Marcilhac, Paris.
Variant of cat. no. 1104, with some of the figures repositioned.

1106 *Hunting* *Pl. 147*
Preparatory sketch in gouache and Indian ink showing the method of mounting panels for the partition wall between the Smoking Room and the first-class Saloon.
59 x 79 cm (23¼ x 31 in.).
Private collection.

1107, 1108 *Hunting*
The two sets of double doors in the partition wall between the Smoking Room and the first-class Saloon.
Each set of doors 308 x 180 cm (121¼ x 70¾ in.).
Formerly in the collections of Félix Marcilhac and Lucien Vallet; Jean-Jacques Baumé.
Sold: Compagnie Générale Transatlantique (Le Havre), 1 August 1962, lot 32; Ader, Picart, Tajan (Monaco), 15/16 April 1978, lot 229a, b.

1109 *Hunting*
The *Normandie* lacquer mural composed of multiple panels, seen in its modified version after being redesigned

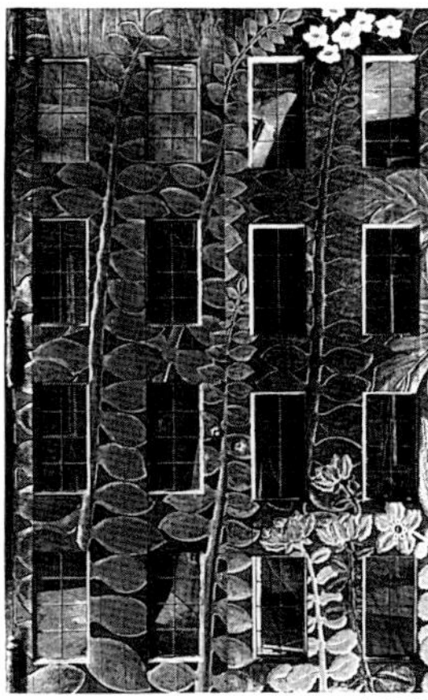
1107

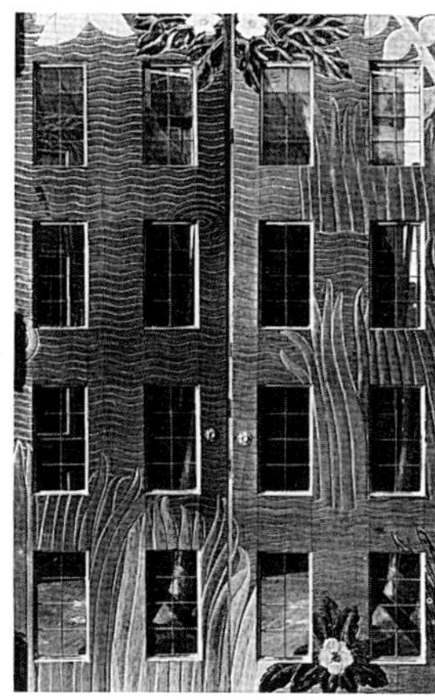
1108

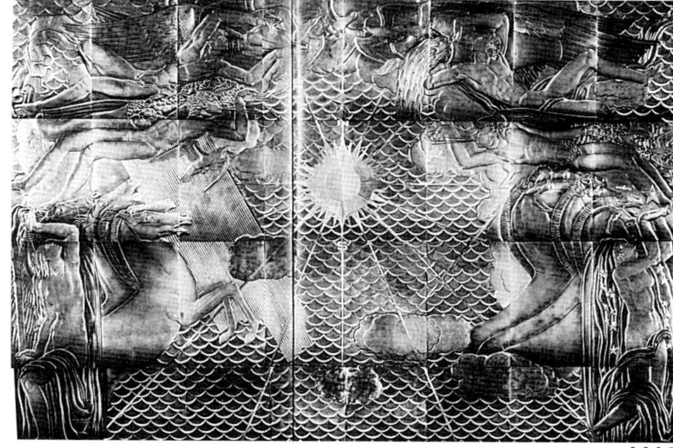
1118

in 1949 by Pierre Dunand and rehung in 24 sections on the liner *Liberté*.
560 x 816 cm (18 ft 4½ x 26 ft 9¼ in.).
Sold: Compagnie Générale Transatlantique (Le Havre), 1 August 1962, lot 32c (ex catalogue).

1110 *Hunting*
Coloured and sculpted gold lacquer.
80 x 150 cm (31½ x 59 in.).
Sold: Couturier, de Nicolay (Paris), 15 December 1976, lot 91.
Variant of the large mural in the *Normandie* Smoking Room; here the horizontal arrangement differs from that of the original version.

1111 *Hunting* *Pl. 149*
Coloured and sculpted gold lacquer.
170 x 142 cm (67 x 56 in.).
Sold: Ader, Picart, Tajan (Paris), 16 October 1974, lot 64.
Variant of the large mural in the *Normandie* Smoking Room; here the vertical arrangement differs from that of the original version.

1112 *Hunting*
Sculpted gold lacquer.
170 x 142 cm (67 x 56 in.).
Formerly in the collection of Félix Marcilhac, Paris; Private collection.
The same composition as cat. no. 1111, but decorated in gold only.

1113 *Marabou Stork* *Pl. 148*
Detail (repeated actual size) of a motif from the coloured and sculpted lacquer mural *Hunting*.
120 x 63 cm (47¼ x 24¾ in.).
Coll.: Alain Braunstein.

1114 *Hunter*
Detail (repeated actual size) of a motif from the coloured and sculpted lacquer mural *Hunting* in the Smoking Room.
129 x 63 cm (47¼ x 24¾ in.).
Private collection.

1115 *Hunting*
Gouache and colour size on wood panel, preliminary study for the partition wall between the Smoking Room and first-class Saloon.
Formerly in the collection of Félix Marcilhac, Paris; Private collection.

1116 *Javelin Throwers* *Pl. 153*
Coloured and moulded gold lacquer.
66 x 61 cm (26 x 24 in.).
Coll.: Alain Lesieutre, Paris.
Reduced-scale replica of the first version of a mural designed for the *Normandie* Smoking Room and intended to be hung opposite the proposed *Archers* mural. Both projects were abandoned. See also cat. no. 1117.

1117 *Archers*
Coloured and moulded gold lacquer.
66 x 61 cm (26 x 24 in.).
Private collection.
Reduced-scale replica of the first version of a mural designed for the *Normandie* Smoking Room. See note to cat. no. 1116.

1118–1120 The first-class Saloon

1118 *The Chariot of Aurora*
Gold and silver lacquer panel, after a cartoon by Jean Dupas, for the partition wall between the Saloon and the Smoking Room.
555 x 805 cm (18 ft 2½ in. x 26 ft 5 in.).
Bibl.: 'Normandie's Sun Rises Again', *The Connoisseur*, October 1984, p. 119.

1119 Games table
Red lacquer and eggshell, intended for the first-class Saloon.
Height 72 cm (28¼ in.); top 71 cm (28 in.) square.
Private collection.

1120 Games table
Red lacquer and eggshell.
Height 70 cm (27½ in.); top 80 cm (31½ in.) square.
Sold: Sotheby's (Monaco), 9 October 1983, lot 288.
Folding version of cat. no. 1119.

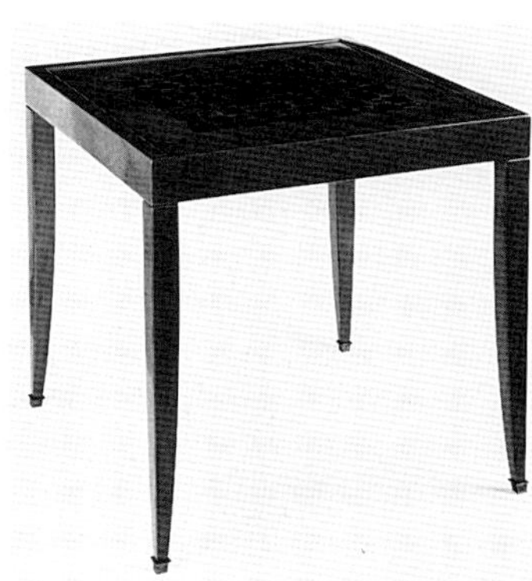
1119

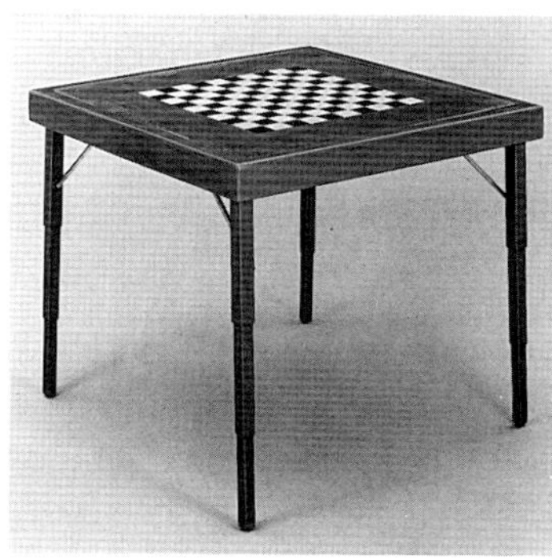
1120

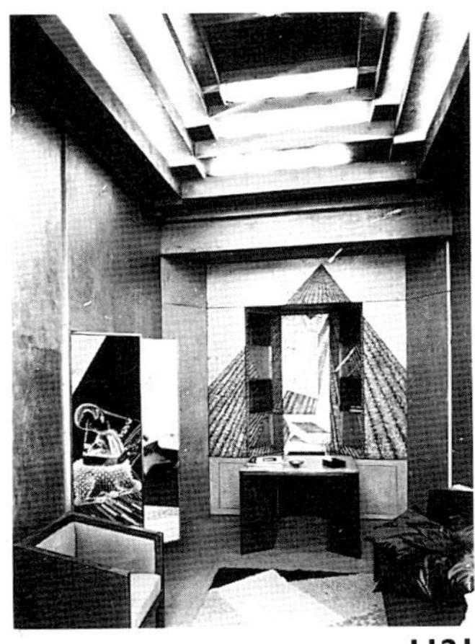
1121

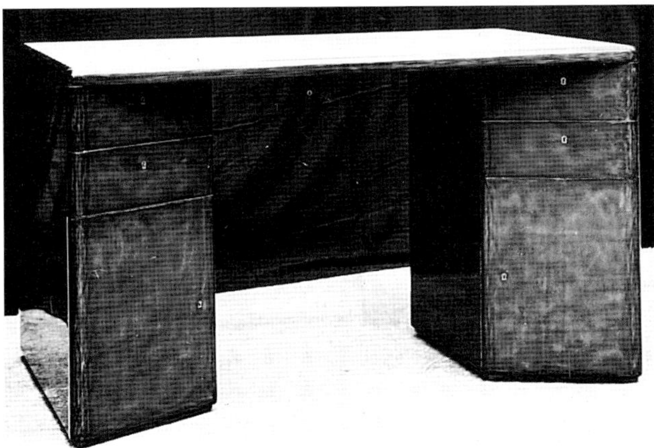
1122

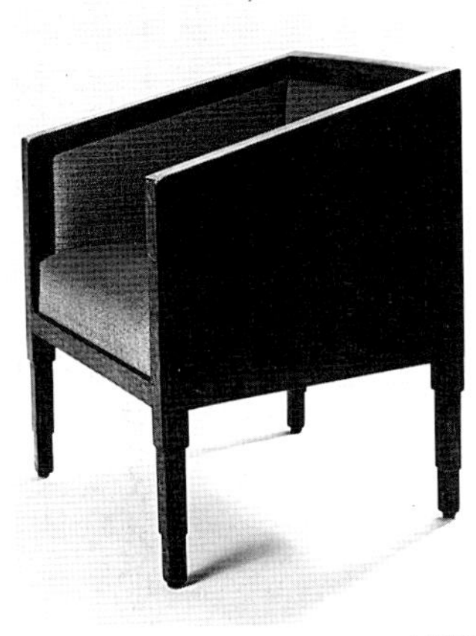
1123

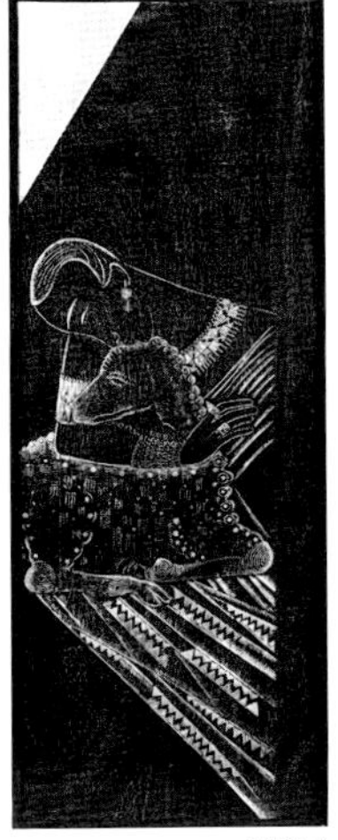
1124

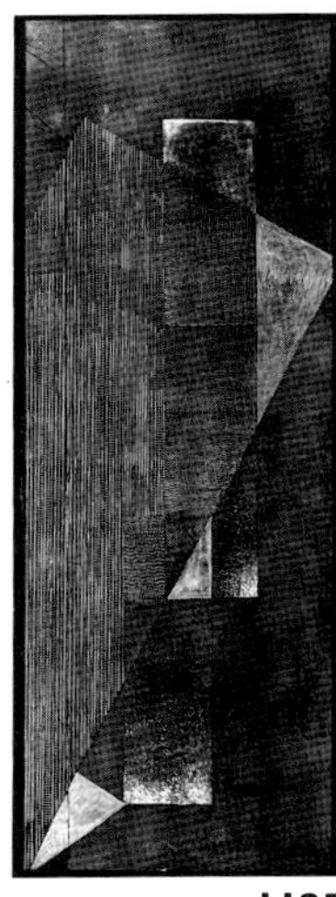
1125

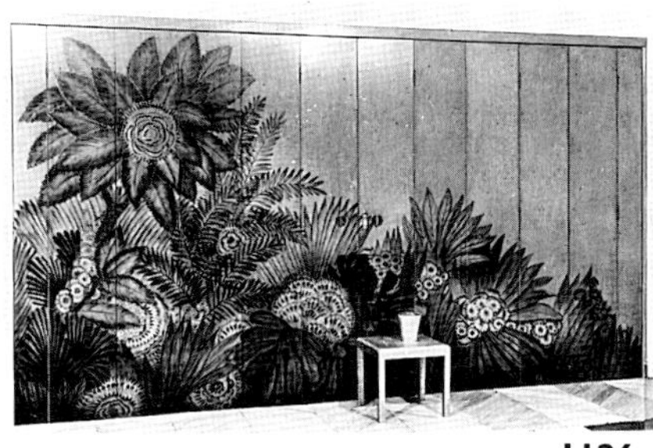
1126a

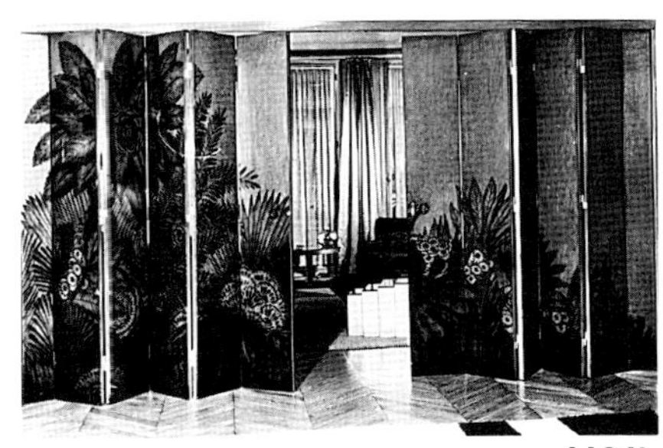
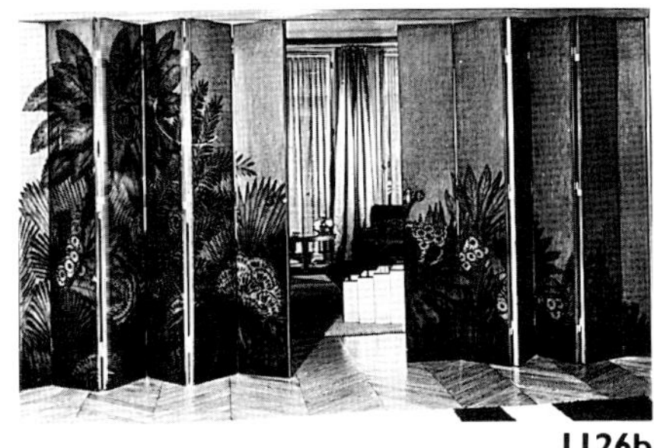
1126b

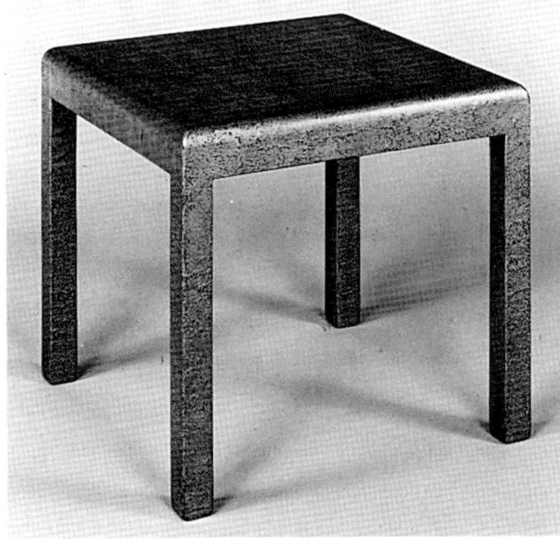
1130

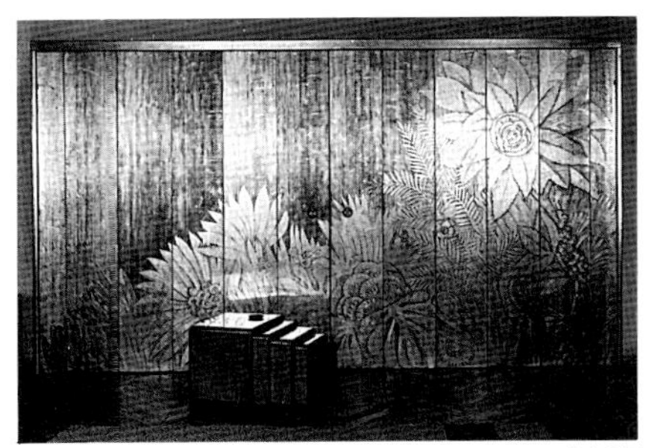
1127

1128

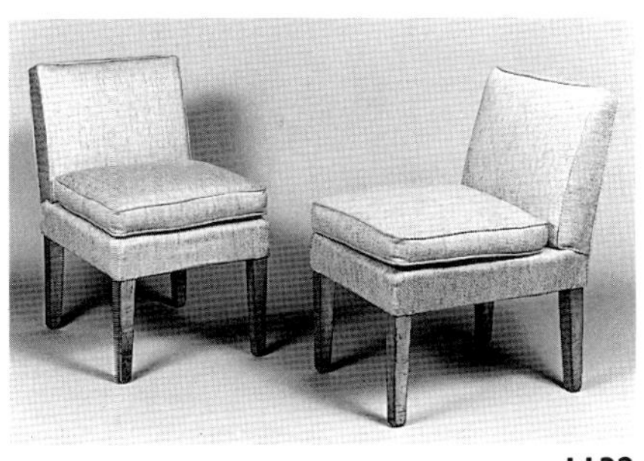
1132

DECORATIVE SCHEMES FOR, AND OTHER WORKS ASSOCIATED WITH PRIVATE CLIENTS AND SPECIAL EVENTS

1121–1132
Madame Agnès (Rittener)
For portraits see cat. nos. 135–140 and 187, 188

Interior decor for Paris apartment/studio (1926)

1121 The Studio
View from the alcove and office.
Bibl.: *L'Art décoratif*, Paris, 1929, p. 53.

1122, 1123 Lady's writing desk and chair
Shellac; eggshell top to desk.
Height of desk 71 cm (28 in.); top 115 x 64 cm (45¼ x 25¼ in.).

1124, 1125 Cheval-glass shutters
Maquettes in coloured lacquer on panels prepared actual size as studies for Madame Agnès's cheval-glass.
Formerly in the collection of Félix Marcilhac, Paris; Jacques De Vos.

1126, 1127 Accordion door
Specially designed for the opening between salon and bedroom, with lacquer decoration on both sides.

1126 View from the salon showing the door (a) closed and (b) partly open; light-brown shellac with decoration in coloured lacquer.

1127 View from the bedroom; gold lacquer with floral design. In front of the closed door is a nest of four tables in matching gold-lacquered spruce.

1128 Bateau bed
Incised gold-lacquered spruce, decorated with a floral design.
Formerly in the collection of Lucien Vallet; Private collection.
Sold: Pillias, Gluck (Paris), 24 November 1972, lot 53; Sotheby's (Monaco), 25 June 1981, lot 265.

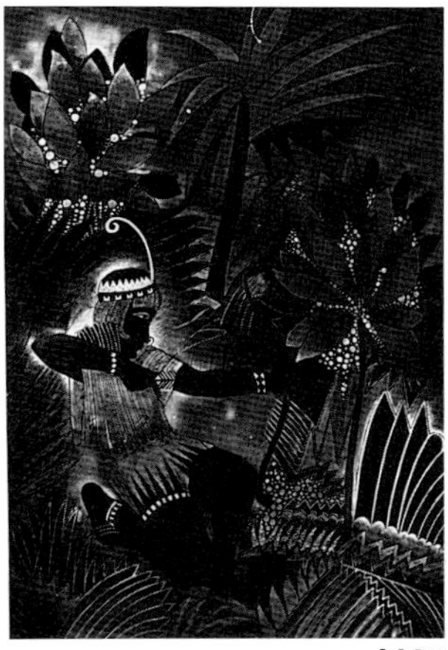
1137

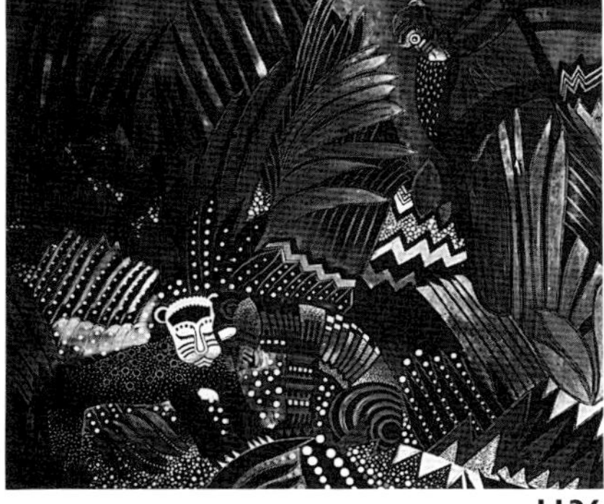
1136

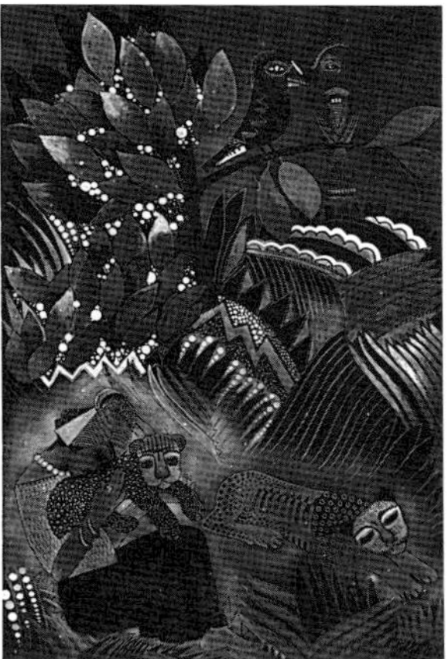
1138

1129 Small six-panel screen
Gold lacquer screen with a frieze of incised flowers.
Panel size 125 x 25 cm (49¼ x 9¾ in.).
Sold: Blache (Versailles), 7 March 1976, lot 195; Sotheby's (Monaco), 9 October 1983, lot 287.

1130 Square occasional table
Gold *laque arrachée* on a brown shellac ground.
Private collection.

1131 Chest with drawers *Pl. 72*
Gold lacquer on a brown shellac ground.
Private collection.
The hinged lid is shown open in the colour plate.

1132 Chauffeuses (pair)
Gold *laque arrachée* on a brown lacquer ground.
Private collection.

1133–1148
Madame Labourdette's 'Salon Moderne' (1926)
See also cat. no. 590.

1133 The Salon
View from the left-hand side, showing the alcove.

1134 General view
The fireplace (cat. no. 1135) and the chimneypiece triptych (cat. nos. 1136–8).

1135 Fireplace
Decoration in coloured and black *laque de Chine* inlaid with eggshell.
Formerly in the collections of Michel Perinet and the Galerie Vallois, Paris; Private collection.

1136–1138 Chimneypiece triptych
Brown and grey *laque arrachée.*

1136 Central panel: *Small Sleeping Lion*
Height 155 cm (61 in.); width 141 cm (55½ in.).

1137, 1138 Left- and right-hand panels: *Young Archer* and *Child with Lion Cubs*
Height 180 cm (70¾ in.); width 122 cm (48 in.) and 120 cm (47 ½ in.) respectively.

1139, 1140 Sections of wood panelling depicting stylized trees
Brown and grey *laque arrachée.*
Height 180 cm (70¾ in.); width 165 cm (65 in.) and 131 cm (51½ in.) respectively.

1141 Section of wood panelling depicting stylized trees
Brown and grey *laque arrachée.*
Height 180 cm (70¾ in.); width 131 cm (51½ in.).
Sold: Sotheby's (Monaco) – (lower part) 24/25 October 1982, lots 424, 424a; (upper part) 13 April 1986, lot 31.

1142 Section of wood panelling depicting stylized trees
Brown and grey *laque arrachée.*
Height 180 cm (70¾ in.); width 168 cm (66¼ in.).

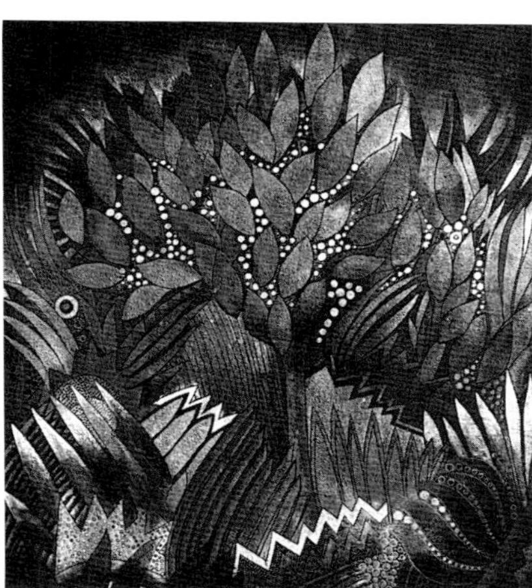
1139

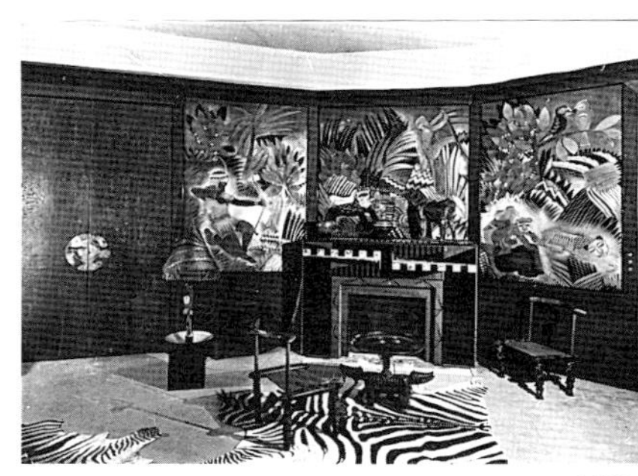
1134

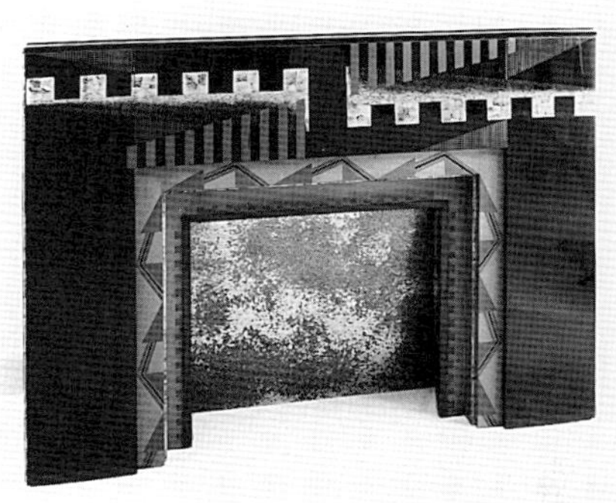
1135

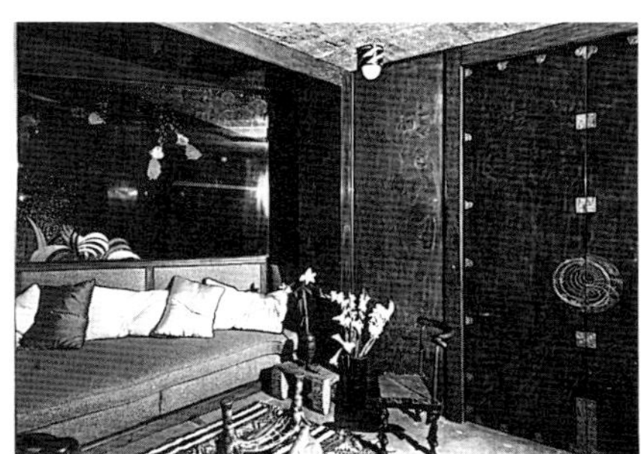
1133

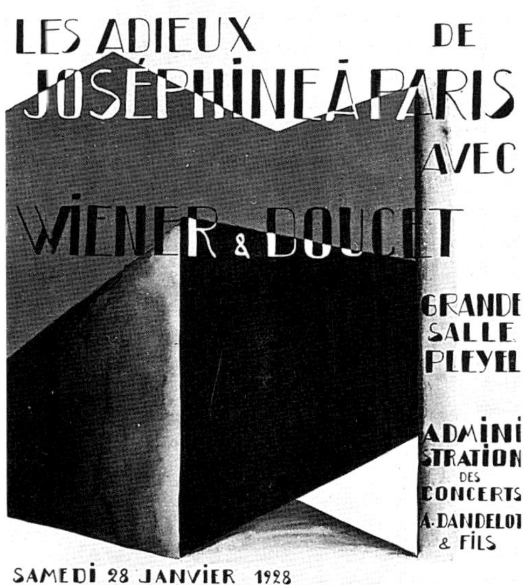

1156

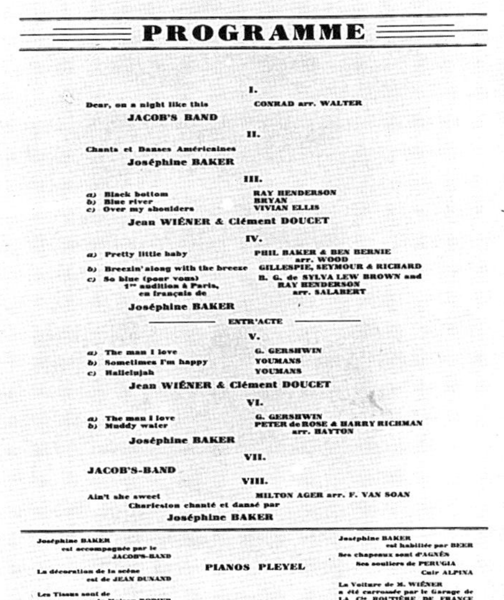

PROGRAMME

I.

Dear, on a night like this — CONRAD arr. WALTER

JACOB'S BAND

II.

Chants et Danses Américaines

Joséphine BAKER

III.

a) Black bottom — RAY HENDERSON
b) Blue river — BRYAN
c) Over my shoulders — VIVIAN ELLIS

Jean WIÉNER & Clément DOUCET

IV.

a) Pretty little baby — PHIL BAKER & BEN BERNIE arr. WOOD
b) Breezin' along with the breeze — GILLESPIE, SEYMOUR & RICHARD
c) So blue (pour vous) 1re audition à Paris, en français de — B. G. de SYLVA LEW BROWN and RAY HENDERSON arr. SALABERT

Joséphine BAKER

ENTR'ACTE

V.

a) The man I love — G. GERSHWIN
b) Sometimes I'm happy — YOUMANS
c) Hallelujah — YOUMANS

Jean WIÉNER & Clément DOUCET

VI.

a) The man I love — G. GERSHWIN
b) Muddy water — PETER de ROSE & HARRY RICHMAN arr. HAYTON

Joséphine BAKER

VII.

JACOB'S-BAND

VIII.

Ain't she sweet — MILTON AGER arr. F. VAN SOAN
Charleston chanté et dansé par

Joséphine BAKER

Joséphine BAKER est accompagnée par le JACOB'S-BAND

La décoration de la scène est de JEAN DUNAND

Les Tissus sont de la Maison RODIER

PIANOS PLEYEL

Joséphine BAKER est habillée par BEER
Ses chapeaux sont d'AGNÈS
Ses souliers de PERUGIA
Cuir ALPINA

La Voiture de M. WIÉNER a été carrossée par le Garage de LA Cie ROUTIÈRE DE FRANCE

1157

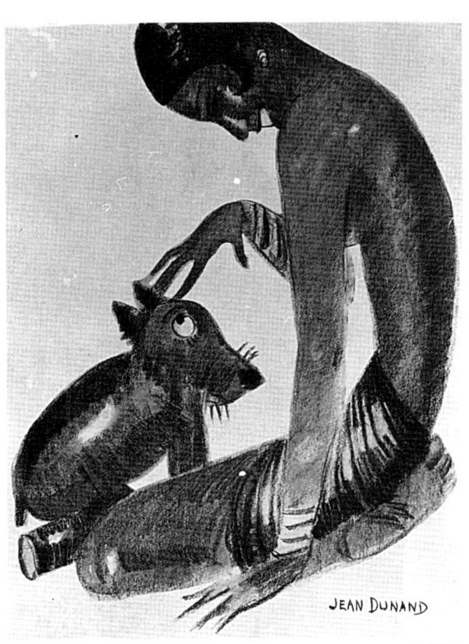

1158

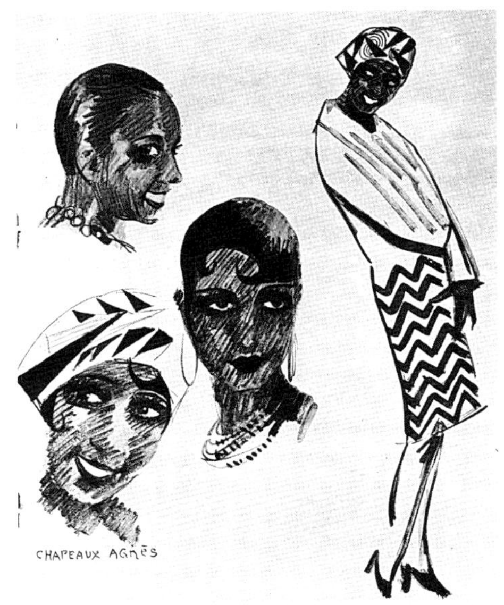

1159

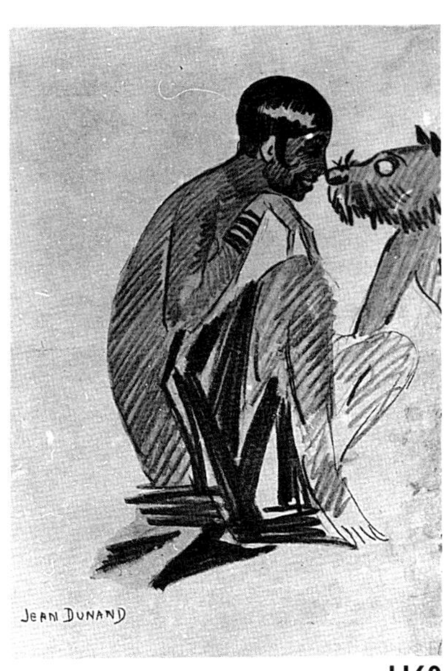

1160

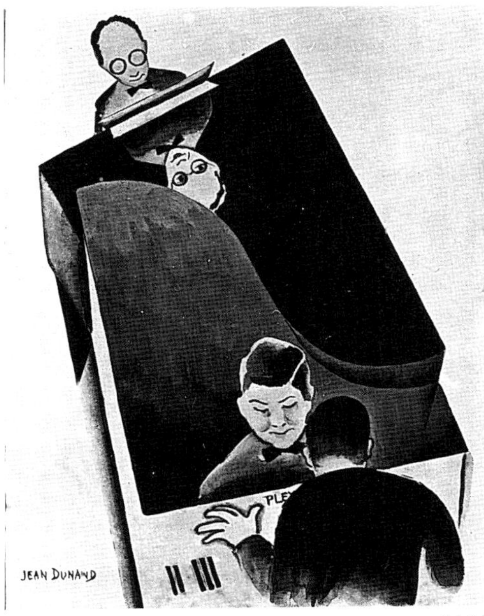

1161

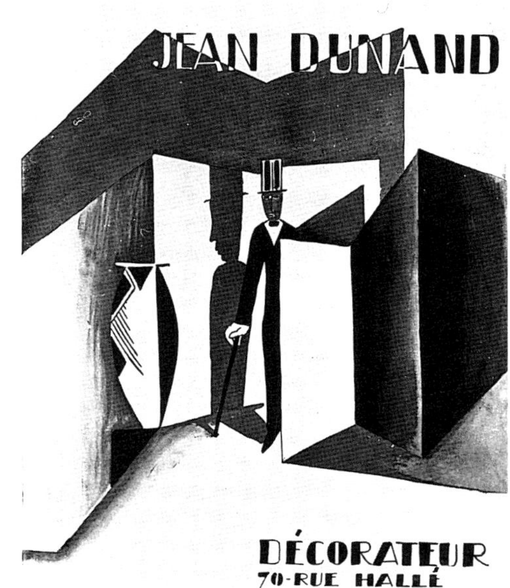

1162

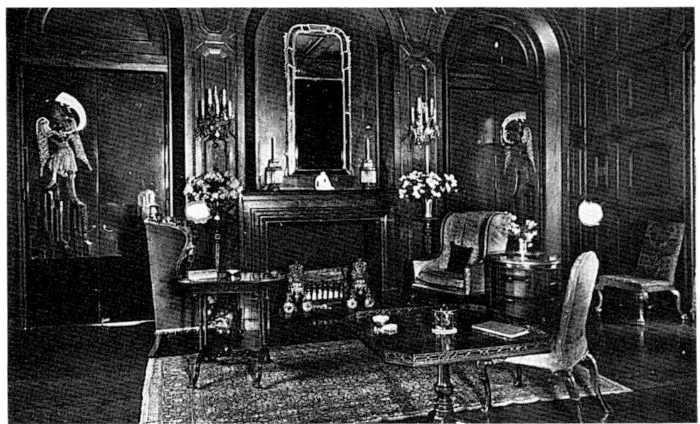

1149

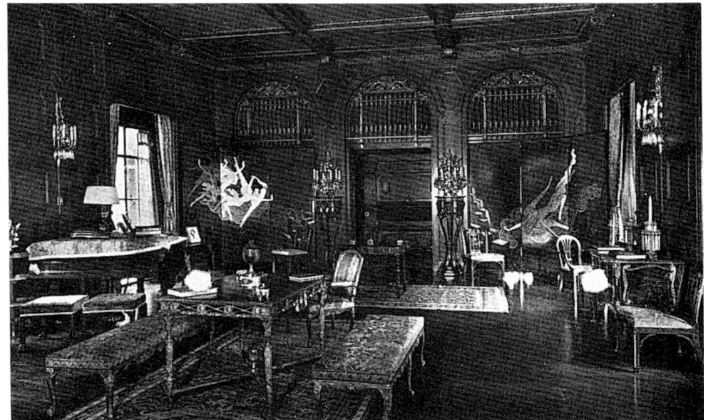

1150

1143, 1144 Sections of wood panelling depicting stylized trees

Brown and grey *laque arrachée*.
Height 180 cm (70¾ in.); width 35 cm (13¾ in.) and 40 cm (15¾ in.) respectively.
Sold: Right-hand panel only, Sotheby's (Monaco), 24/25 October 1982, lot 424b.

1145, 1146 Sections of wood panelling depicting birds, branches and stylized trees

Brown and grey *laque arrachée*.
Height 180 cm (70¾ in.); width 55 cm (21¾ in.) and 58 cm (22¾ in.) respectively.

1147 African-style chair

Black lacquer and coloured lacquer inlaid with eggshell, made in 1924 by Jean Lambert-Rucki and lacquered in Dunand's workshops; see illustration, p. 65.
Bibl.: *Jean Dunand – Jean Goulden*, exhibition catalogue, Galerie du Luxembourg, Paris (1973), p. 5.

1148 Tall vase

Copper inlaid with silver-coloured metal.
Coll.: Jean-Jacques Baumé.

1149–1155

Mr and Mrs Solomon R. Guggenheim: Music Room (1925/26)

1149, 1150 Interior views

Bibl.: *Town and Country*, 15 February 1927.

1151, 1152 Double doors: *Angel Sounding the Last Trump*

Doors carved by Séraphin Soudbinine and decorated in Dunand's workshops: blue and black lacquer with motifs in brown and gold shellac inlaid with eggshell.
Coll.: Metropolitan Museum of Art, New York (gift of Mrs Solomon R. Guggenheim, 1950).

1153 Panel: *St Michael and the Dragon*

Panel carved by Séraphin Soudbinine and entirely lacquered in Dunand's workshops.

1154, 1155 *The Battle of the Angels: Crescendo – Pianissimo* *Pl. 163*

Two three-panel wooden screens carved by Séraphin Soudbinine and decorated in Dunand's workshops: blue and black lacquer with motifs in brown and gold shellac inlaid with eggshell.
Panel size 250 x 90 cm (98½ x 35¼ in.).
Signed 'Séraphin Soudbinine' and 'Jean Dunand laqueur' and dated '1925/6'.
Coll.: Metropolitan Museum of Art, New York (gift of Mrs Solomon R. Guggenheim, 1950).

1156–1162

Josephine Baker

For portraits see cat. nos. 145–147, 153, 157, 158

1156–1162 Programme for farewell concert given in the Salle Pleyel, Paris, on Saturday, 28 January 1928

1156, 1157 Illustration by Dunand for the cover, and details of the concert programme.

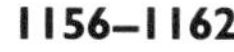

1158–1160 Illustrations by Dunand.

1161 Illustration by Dunand: the pianists Jean Wiéner and Clément Doucet.

1162 Illustration by Dunand after a design by Jean Lambert-Rucki.

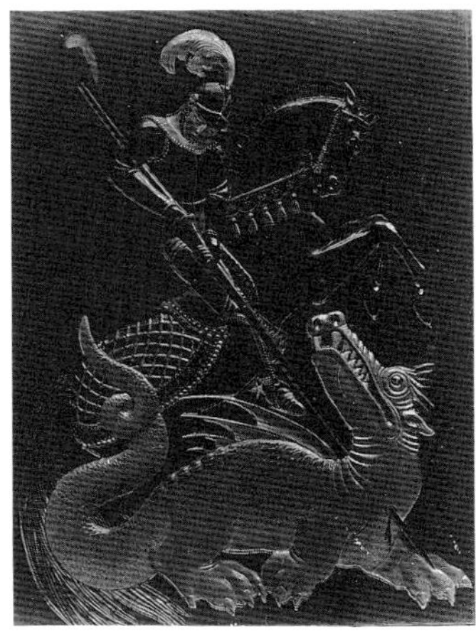

1153

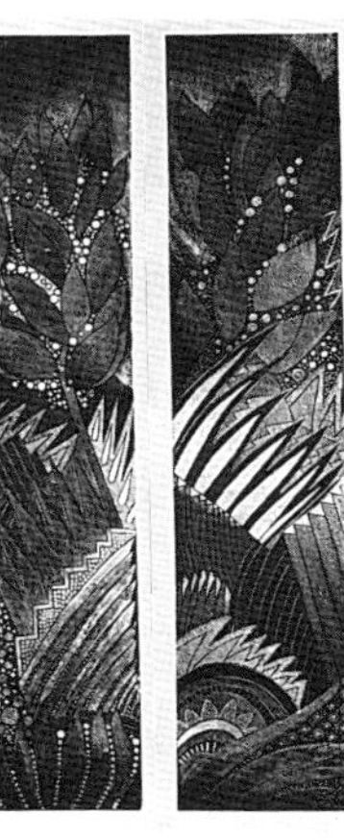

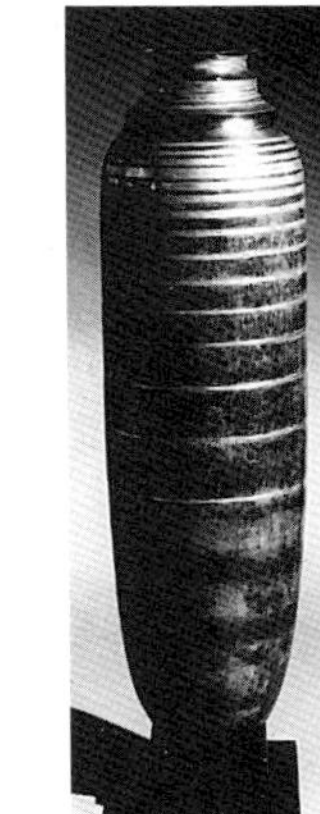

1143, 1144

1148

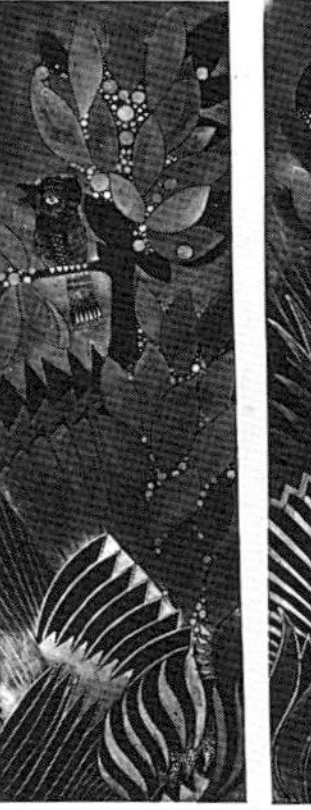

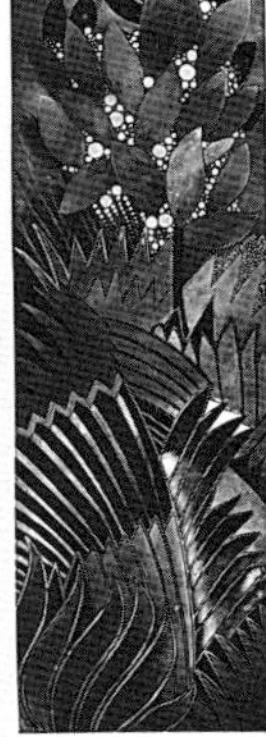

1145, 1146

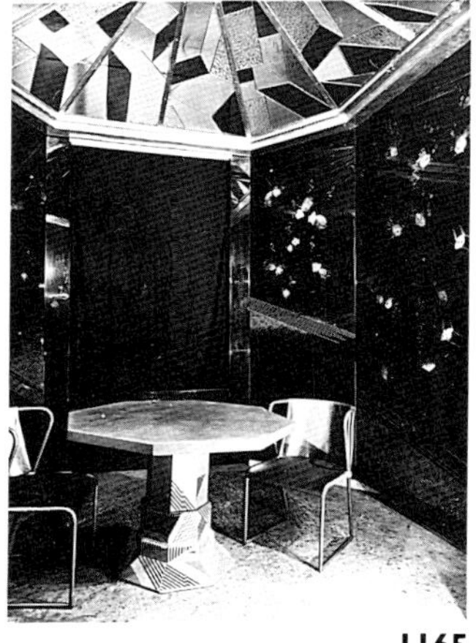

1165

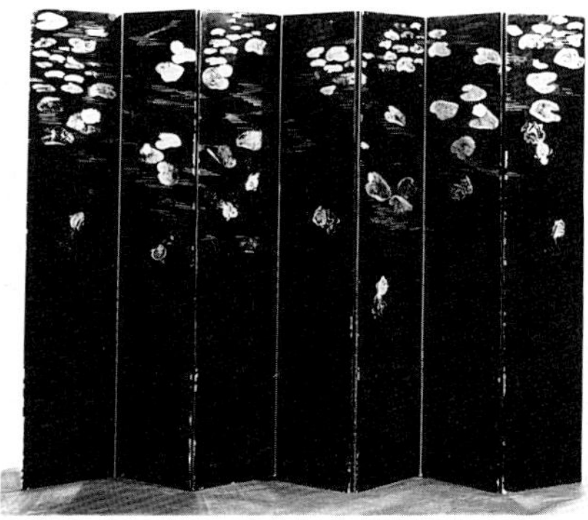

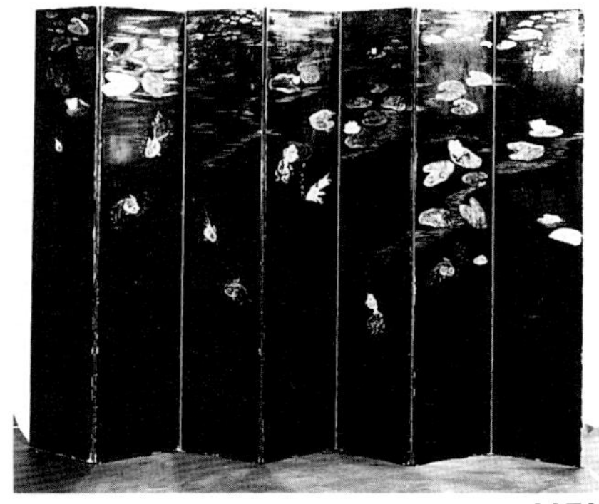

1171

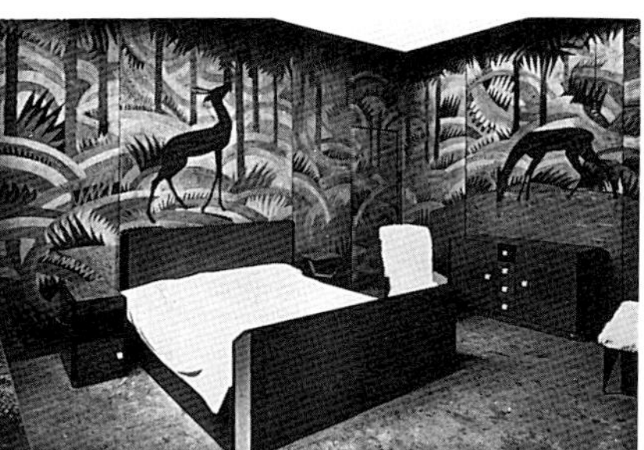

1163

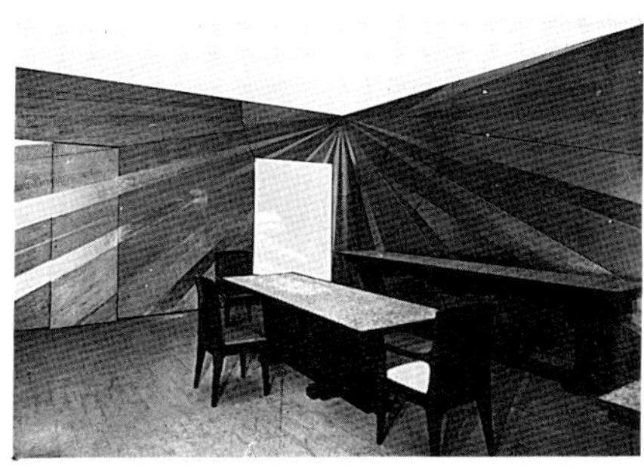

1164

1163–1165

Interior designs for the San Francisco apartment of Templeton Croker (1928)

See also cat. nos. 450, 469

1163 Bedroom

Laque arrachée panelling decorated with deer against a matt rose, white and gold background of rank vegetation; the bedstead, headboards, commode and chairs in brown shellac.

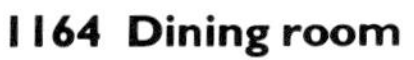

1164 Dining room

Panelling decorated with radiating motifs in gold lacquer, (partly matt), the table, console, chairs and armchairs in brown shellac.

1165 Breakfast room

Panelling decorated with Japanese fish in coloured, black and gold lacquer on a black lacquer ground; table in matt rose, white and gold lacquer; patterned ceiling executed in glass after a design by Dunand.

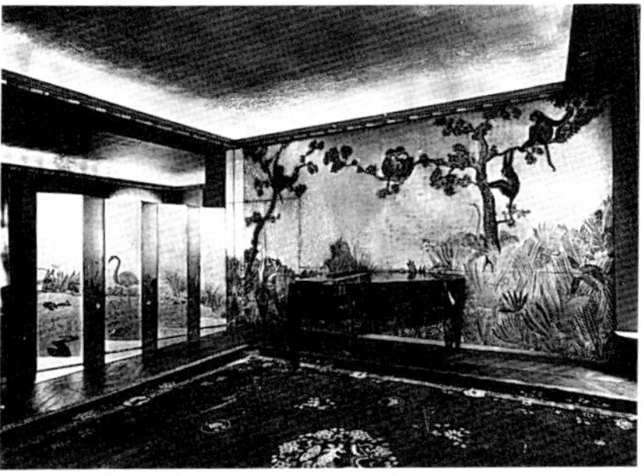

1168

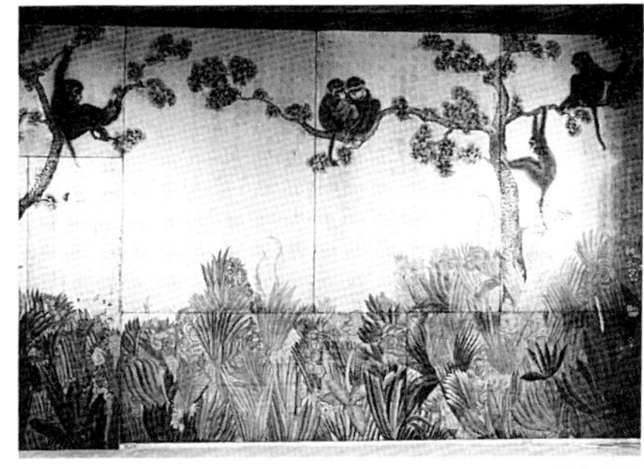

1169

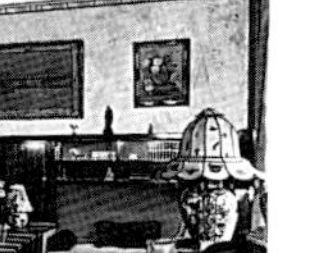

1170

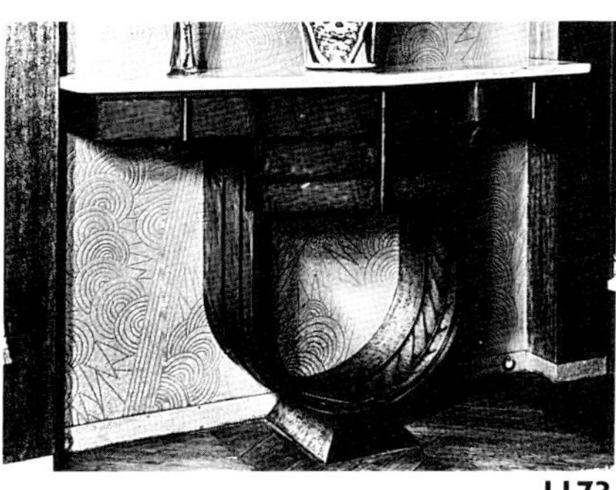

1173

1166–1175

Interior decor for the apartment of Madame Yacoubovitch

1166, 1167 The Boudoir

1166 General view

The photograph shows the alcove panel (cat. no. 1167), divan, nest of tables and double door (cat. no. 565).

1167 Alcove panel: *Deer in the Undergrowth*

Inlaid lead, and black and coloured lacquer on a *laque arrachée* ground. 247 x 242 cm (97¼ x 95½ in.).
Exh.: Delorenzo Gallery, New York, 1985 (repr. in catalogue, p. 33).
Coll.: Steven A. Greenberg, New York.
Bibl.: Dan Klein and Margaret Bishop, *Decorative Art 1880–1980* (Oxford, 1986), p. 158.
Sold: Christie's (New York), 31 March 1984, lot 376.

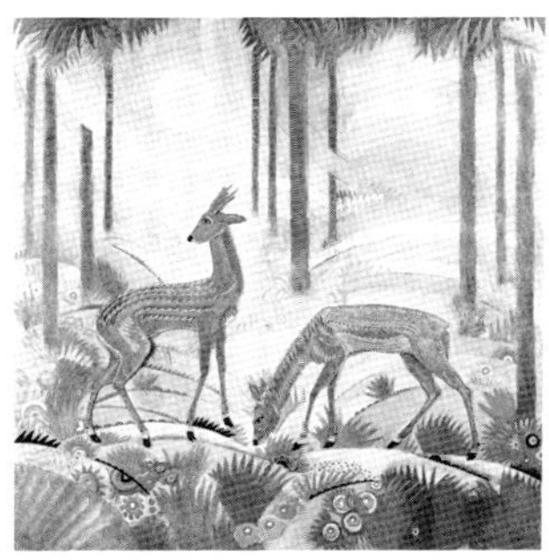

1167

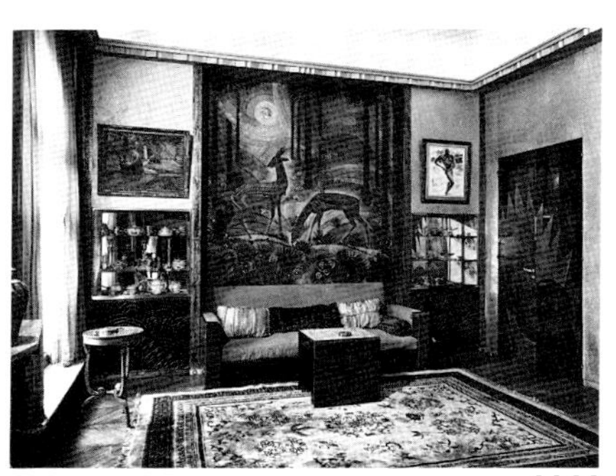

1166

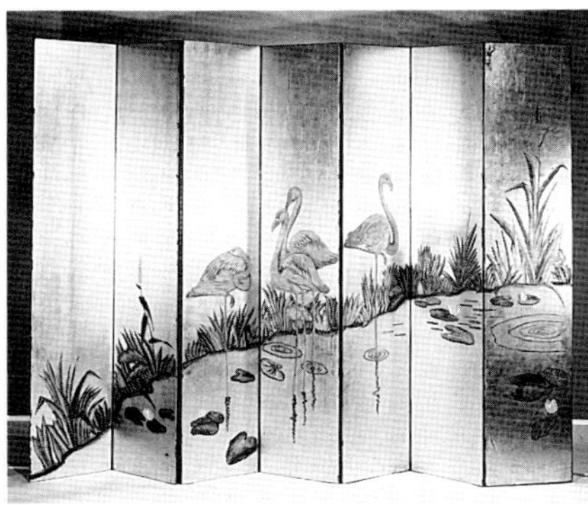

1172

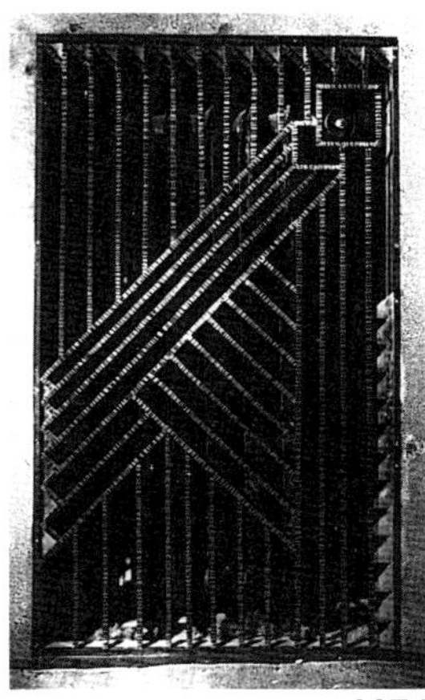

1174

1168–1175 The Salon and the Dining Room

1168 Interior of Salon

Panelling and section of screen (cat. no. 1172).

1169 Decorative panelling in the Salon: *Monkeys Playing in the Trees*

Coloured lacquer on a gold lacquer ground.
Coll.: Jean-Jacques Baumé.

1170 Interior of Dining Room

Wrought-iron table, bookcase, divans and nest of tables, plus section of double-sided screen (cat. no. 1171).

1171, 1172 Double-sided screens (each of seven panels) **dividing Salon and Dining Room**

Underwater scene with fish in gold and black lacquer inlaid with mother-of-pearl; pond scene with flamingos in gold and coloured lacquer inlaid with mother-of-pearl.
Height 200 cm (78¾ in.); total width of each section when open 292 cm (115 in.).
1929.
Exh.: Delorenzo Gallery, New York, 1985 (repr. in catalogue, pp. 12, 13).
Formerly in the collection of Jean-Jacques Baumé; Steven A. Greenberg, New York.
Sold: Christie's (New York), 4 October 1980, lot 338.

1173 Wrought-iron console with marble top

1174 Wrought-iron radiator grille

1175 Decorative panelling: *Flight of Ducks* and *Ducks on a Pond*

Gold and coloured lacquer panelling.
Height 300 cm (9ft 10 in.); total width 522 cm (17 ft 1½ in.).
Exh.: Delorenzo Gallery, New York, 1985 (repr. in catalogue, p. 25).
Formerly in the collection of Jean-Jacques Baumé.
Sold: Christie's (New York), 27 May 1982, lot 136.
See cat. no. 1170 (left background).

1176–1184
Madeleine Vionnet

1176 Games table

Polished oak and stained wood.
1929.
Height 74 cm (29¼ in.); top 80 cm (35½ in.) square.
Formerly in the collection of Félix Marcilhac, Paris; Private collection.

1177 Games table

Black lacquer, checkered design on table top in black lacquer and eggshell; chairs covered in beige leather.
Height 74 cm (29¼ in.); top 90 cm (35½ in.) square.
Specially made for Madeleine Vionnet's library in 1930.
Exh.: Galerie du Luxembourg, Paris, 1973, no. 133.
Coll.: Tina and Michael Chow.
Bibl.: *Jean Dunand – Jean Goulden*, exhibition catalogue, Galerie du Luxembourg (Paris, 1973), pp. 8 and 104.
Sold: Godeau, Solanet, Audap (Paris), 31 May 1985, lot 181.

1178 Panel: *Panthers Slaking their Thirst*

Panel decorated with brown, black and gold *laque arrachée* on a silver (aluminium) ground.
120 x 200 cm (47¼ x 78¾ in.).
Coll.: Gueylard.
Sold: Godeau, Solanet, Audap (Paris), 31 May 1985, lot 153.

1179 Free-standing bookcase with hinged sections

Coral-red lacquer, specially designed by Boris Lacroix and made in 1930 by Dunand.
Height 85 cm (33½ in.); width of each section 65 cm (25½ in.).
Coll.: Félix Marcilhac, Paris.
Sold: Godeau, Solanet, Audap (Paris), 31 May 1985, lot 185.

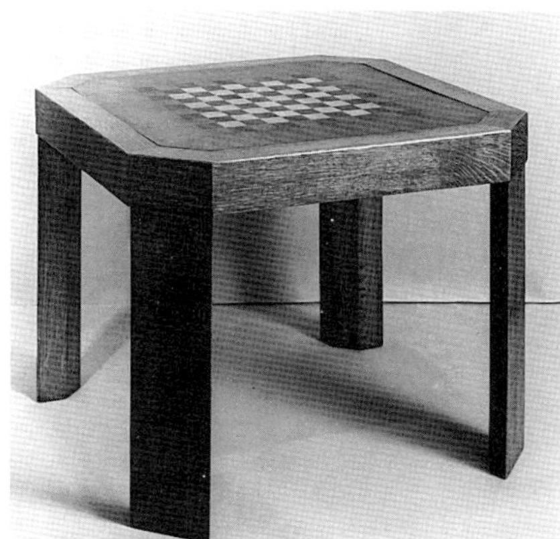

1176

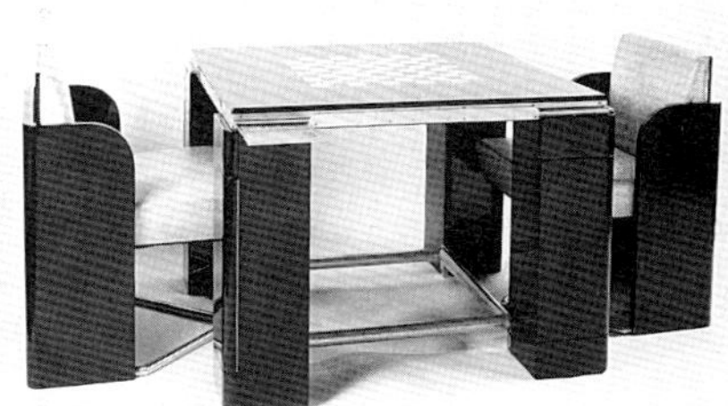

1177

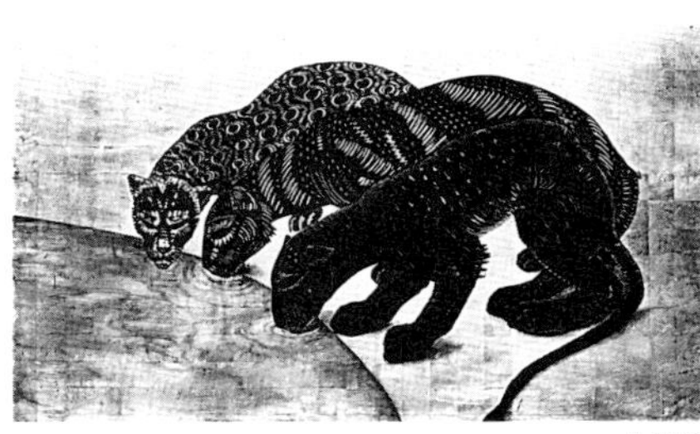

1178

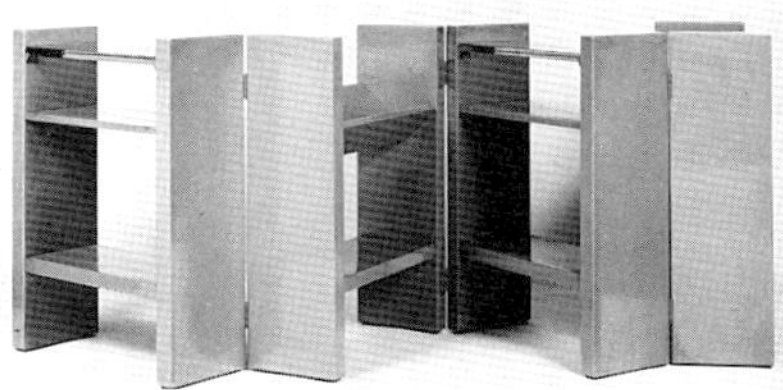

1179

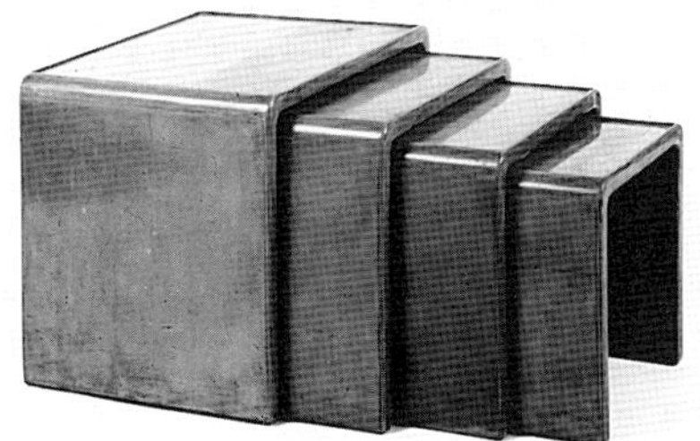
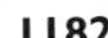

1182

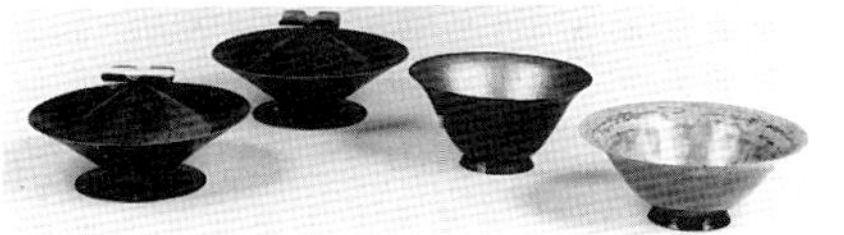

1184

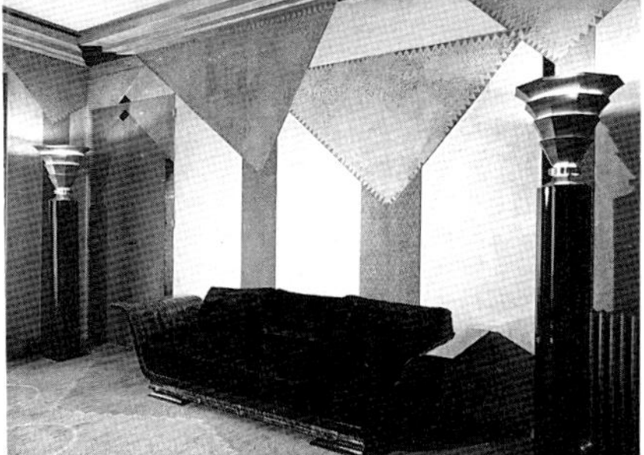

1185

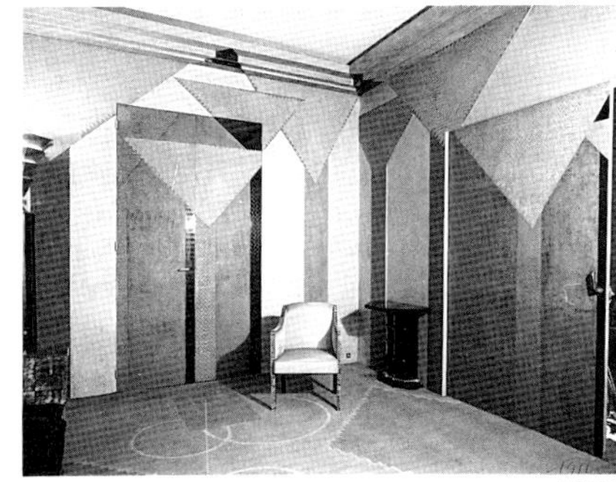

1186

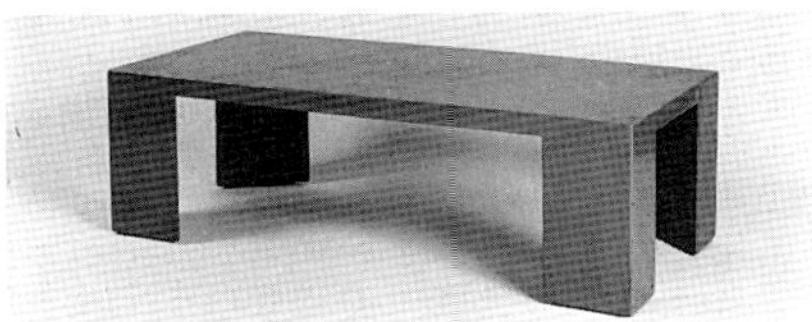

1180

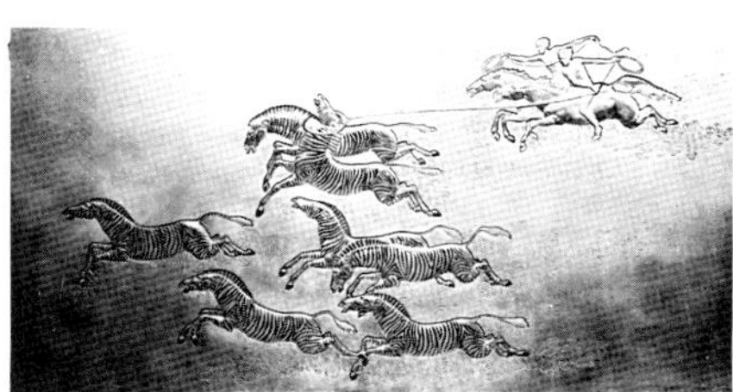
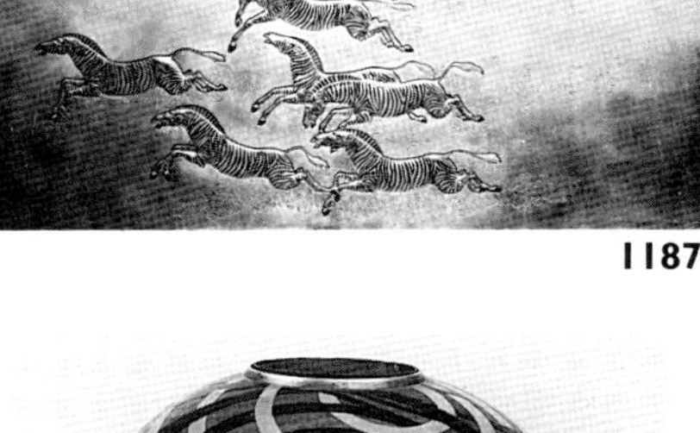

1187

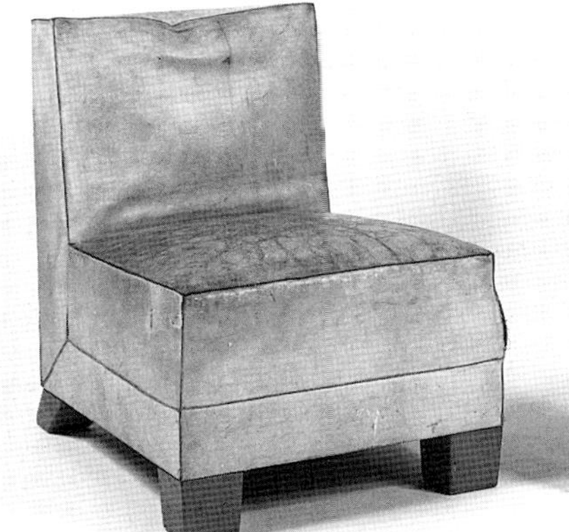

1181

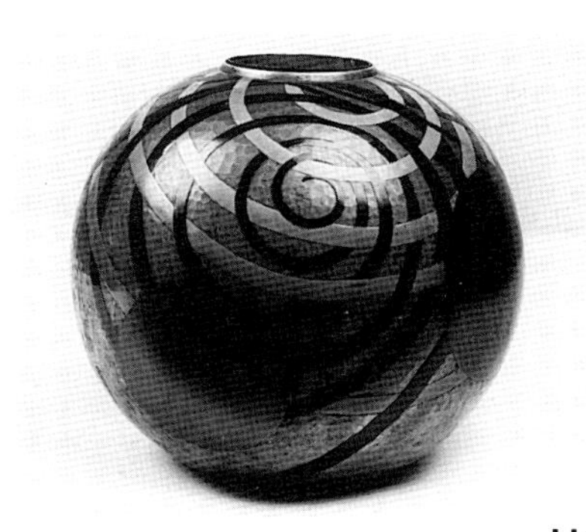

1183

1188

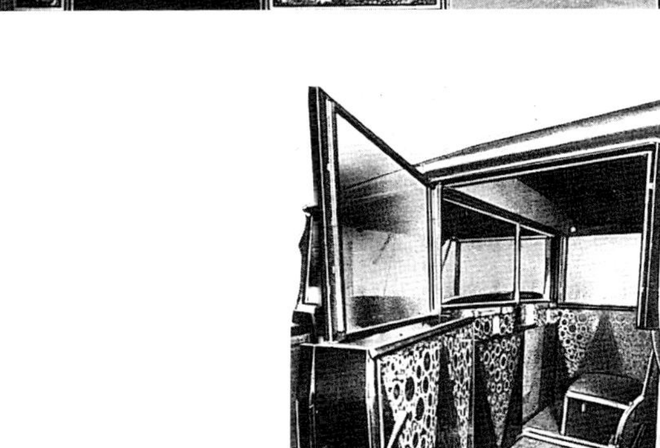

1200

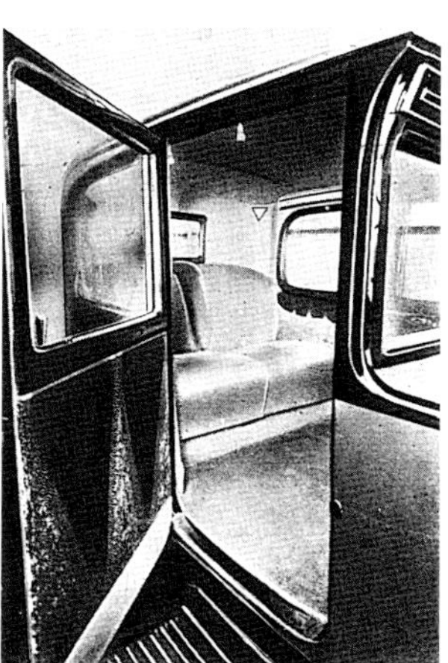

1201

1180 Occasional table

Coral-red lacquer.
Height 40 cm (15¾ in.); top 130 x 58 cm (51¼ x 22¾ in.).
1924.
Sold: Godeau, Solanet, Audap (Paris), 31 May 1985, lot 180.

1181 Chauffeuses (pair)

Coral-red lacquer and beige leather, specially designed by Boris Lacroix and made by Dunand.
Height 72 cm (28¼ in.).
Sold: Godeau, Solanet, Audap (Paris), 31 May 1985, lot 184.

1182 Nest of four tables

Brown shellac.
Height 46 cm (18 in.); top 40 x 54 cm (15¾ x 21¼ in.).
C. 1923.
Sold: Godeau, Solanet, Audap (Paris), 31 May 1985, lot 179.

1183 Spherical vase

Hammer-marked pewter with decoration in black and red lacquer.
Height 30 cm (11¾ in.).
1929.
Sold: Godeau, Solanet, Audap (Paris), 31 May 1985, lot 57.

1184 Ashtrays and small dishes

Dinanderie objects patinated and lacquered on a gold ground.
Sold: Godeau, Solanet, Audap (Paris), 31 May 1985, lots 147–50.

1185–1187

Apartment of Madame Colette Aboucaya (1936)

1185, 1186 The Boudoir

Decor in rose-pink and silver lacquer. The furnishings include a canapé finished in lacquer and shagreen and a black-glass console designed by Gérard Mille.

1187 Panel: *Zebras*

Panel executed in gold and coloured lacquer, the design being based on that of *Taming the Horse* installed in the liner *Normandie* (see cat. no. 1088).

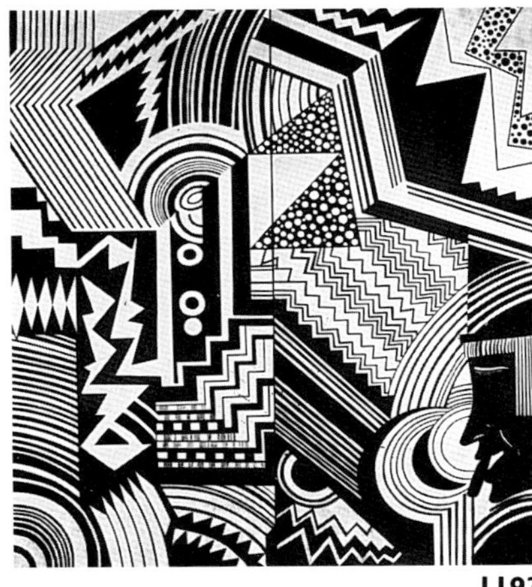
1193

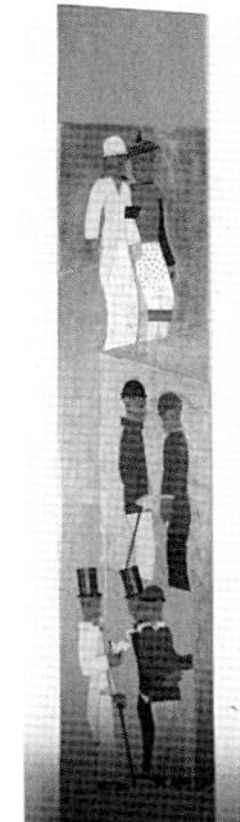
1194

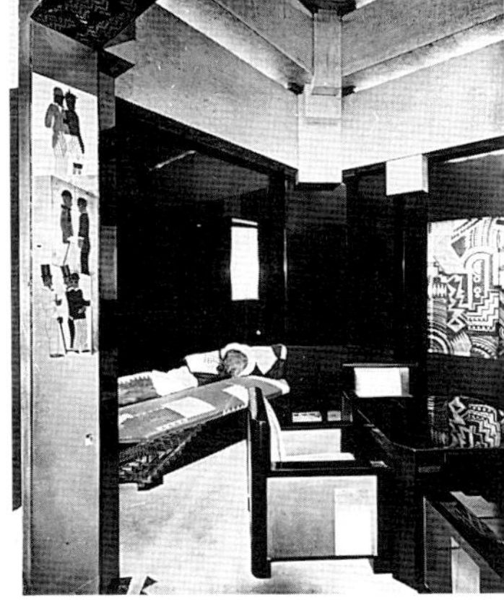
1190

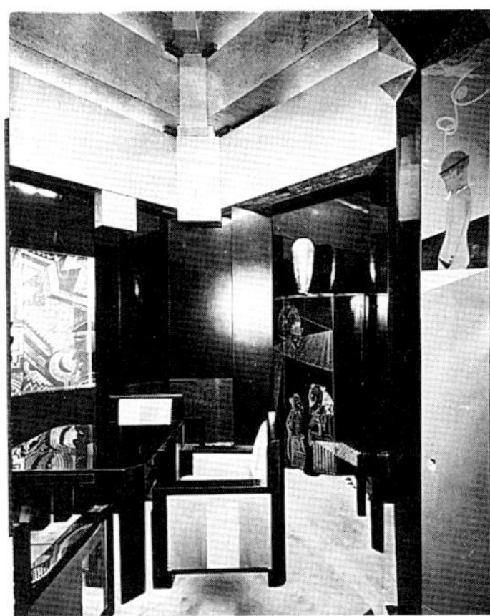
1191

1188 Salon of the Marquise de Brantes
Design (unrealized) for an interior decorative scheme.

EXHIBITION INTERIORS AND DISPLAYS FEATURING WORKS BY DUNAND

1189–1201
The Exposition Internationale des Arts Décoratifs et Industriels Modernes, Paris (1925)

1189–1195 The Smoking Room in the Pavillon de la Société des Artistes Décorateurs (see also cat. no. 475).

1189 Poster for the lacquer display.
For Dunand's poster design, see illustration, p.69.

1190, 1191 Interior
Views to left and right.

1192 The right-hand corner, showing corner armchairs

1193 The twin panels of the lacquered shutter in the middle of the rear wall

1194 Panel: *Bumpkins and Fly-by-Nights*
Lacquer panel by Dunand after a design by Jean Lambert-Rucki.
Private collection.

1195 The ceiling
Bibl.: *Les Echos des industries d'art*, June 1928.

1196 Cabinet *Pl. 57*
Large cabinet by Emile-Jacques Ruhlmann, lacquered by Dunand. The decoration of the doors is in incised black lacquer based on a design by Jean Lambert-Rucki. Ruhlmann's Hôtel du Collectionneur was the centrepiece of the exhibition.
For details of ownership etc., see cat. no. 534.

1197 Four monumental vases
Designs for vases to be placed in the corners of the courtyard of the Pavillon des Arts et Métiers (see also colour plate 107).
Bibl.: *Mobilier et decoration*, May 1925, p. 2.

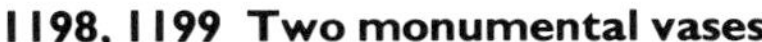

1198, 1199 Two monumental vases
Two of the four vases displayed in the courtyard of the Pavillon des Arts et Métiers.
Dinanderie, gold and coloured lacquer.
Height 100 cm ($39\frac{1}{4}$ in.).
Formerly in the collections of Félix Marcilhac, Paris, and Jeanne Fillon; Yves Saint Laurent and Pierre Bergé, Paris.
See also colour plate 107 and p. 69.

1200, 1201 Automobile interiors
'Saint-Didier' coupé and 'Boule' limousine with bodywork by Henri Binder; decor by Dunand in black *laque de Chine*, eggshell and (in the limousine) mother-of-pearl.

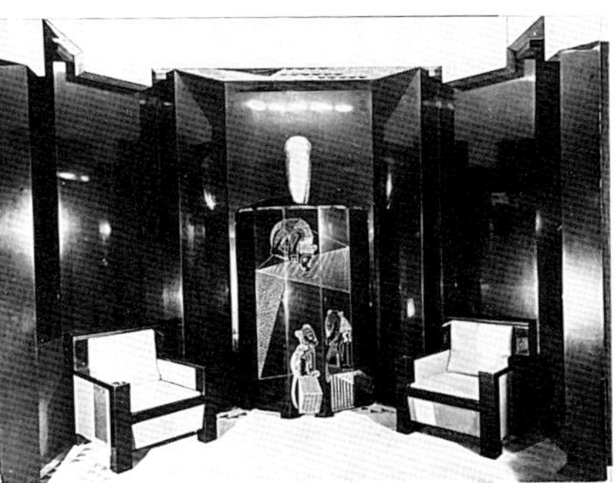
1192

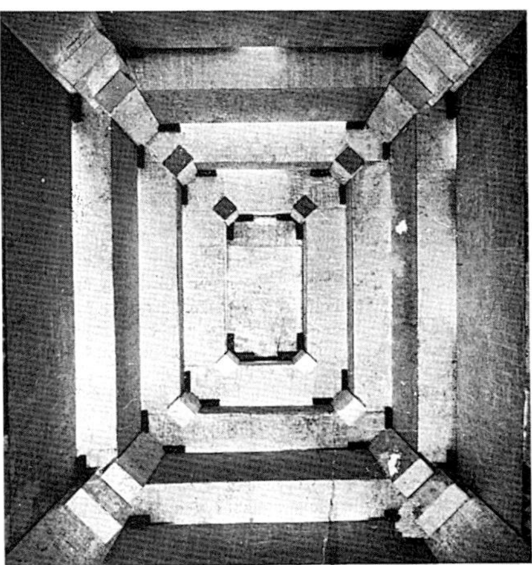
1195

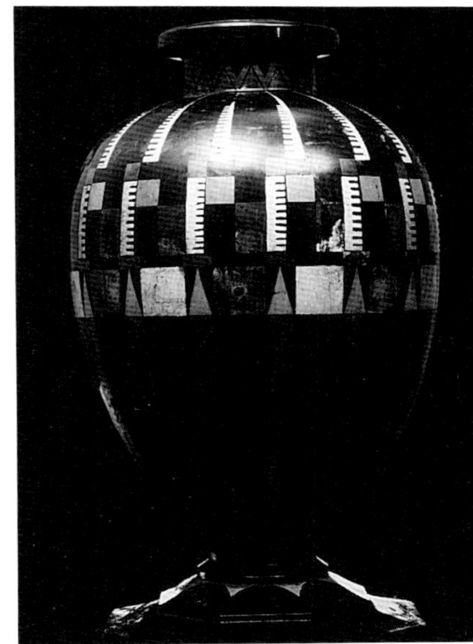
1198

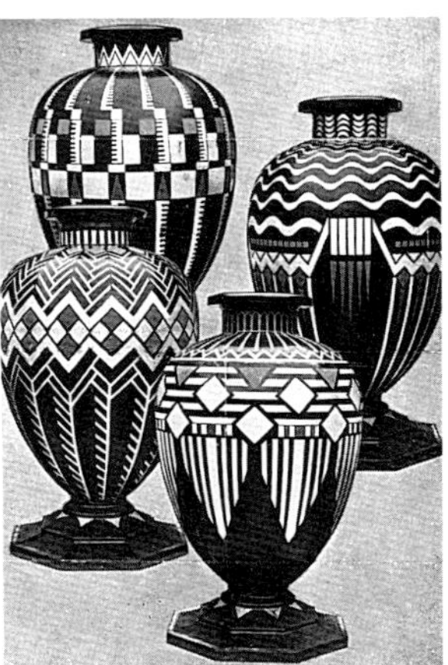
1197

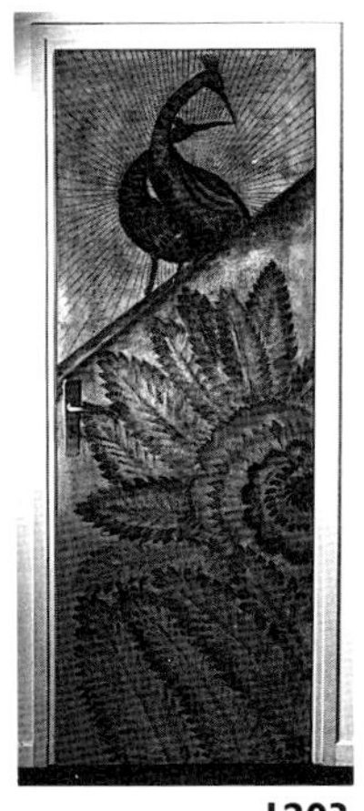
1203

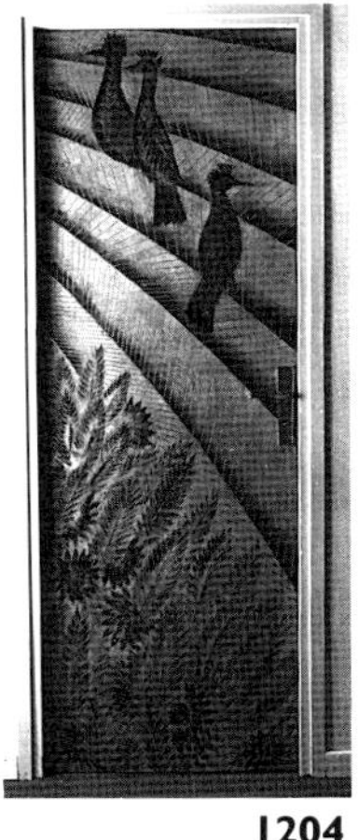
1204

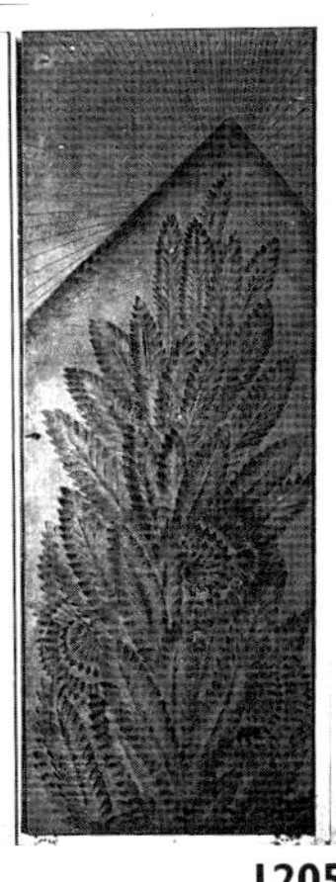
1205

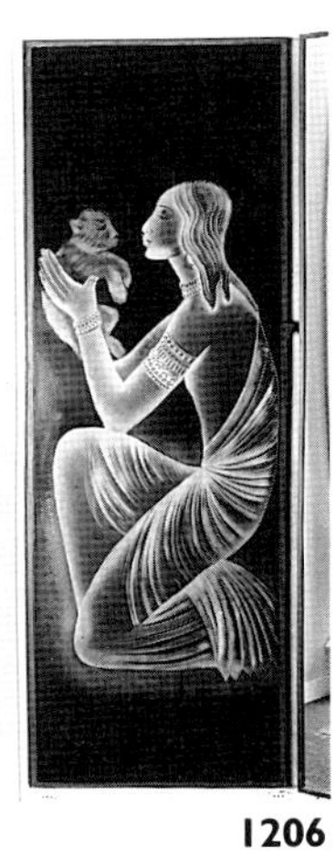
1206

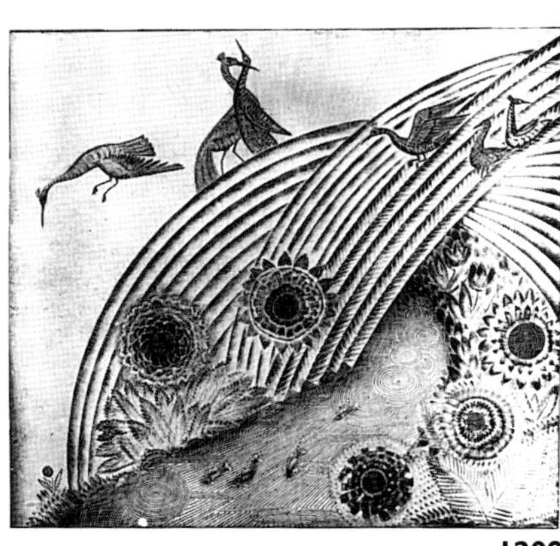
1209

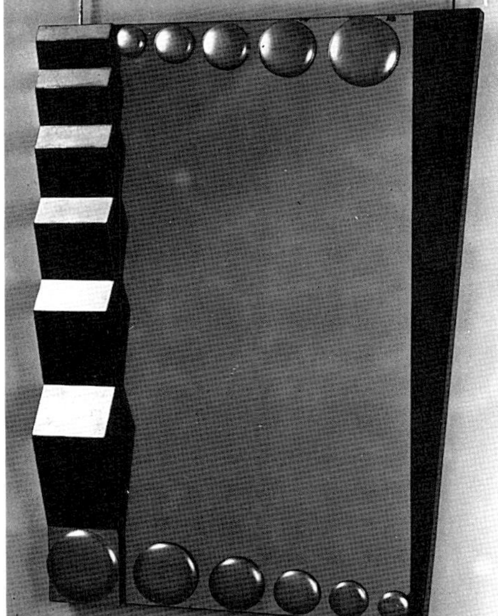
1207

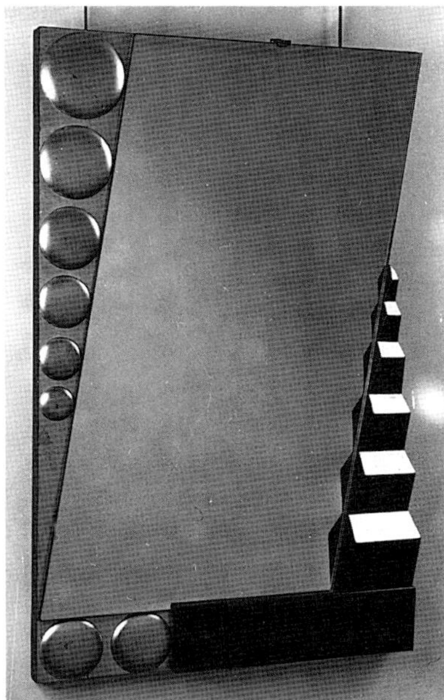
1208

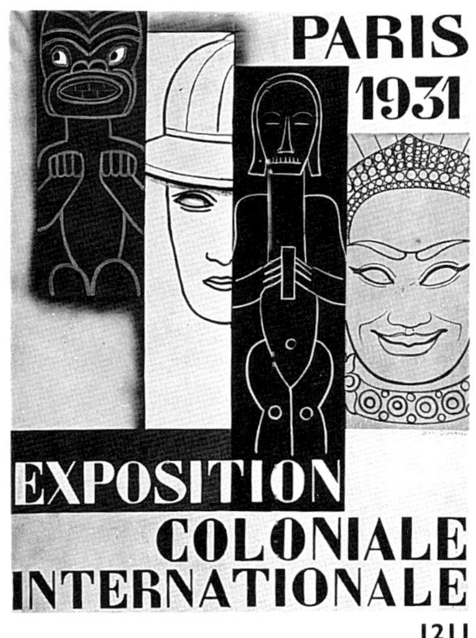

1211

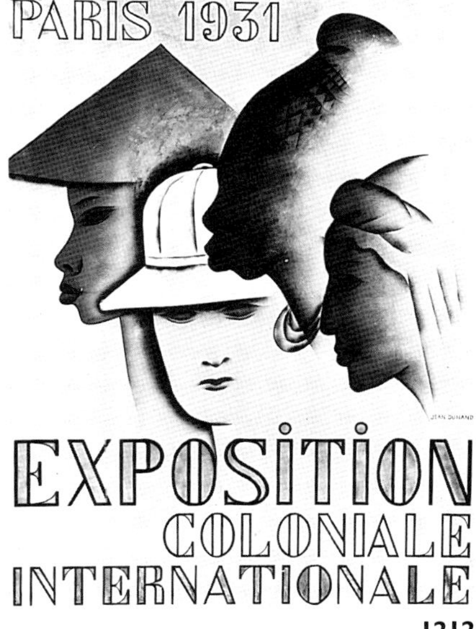

1212

1202–1210

The Boudoir at the Salon des Artistes Décorateurs, Paris (1930)
See also cat. nos. 478, 479.

1202 General view
Interior and furnishings by Dunand; see illustration, p. 118.

1203, 1204 Sections of wood panelling
Panelling decorated with beige frosted lacquer.
Private collection.

1205, 1206 Cheval-glass panels
The decoration is in silver, gold and black lacquer.
Private collection.

1207, 1208 Polyhedral mirrors
Silver and black lacquer.
Height 100 cm (39¼ in.); width 72.5 cm (28½ in.) and 63.5 cm (25 in.) respectively.
Designed by Gustave Miklos.
Coll.: Virginia Museum of Fine Arts, Richmond, Va (gift of Sydney and Frances Lewis).

1209 Central panel
Beige frosted lacquer, with decoration depicting fantastic birds.
Private collection.

1210 Dressing table
Brown shellac, with lacquered-metal mirror frame; see illustration, p. 118.
Height 115 cm (45¼ in.); width 158 cm (62¼ in.).
Formerly in the collection of Robert Walker; Private collection.
Bibl.: *Art et décoration*, 1930, p. 207; *La Renaissance de l'art français* (Paris, 1930), p. 207; *L'Amour de l'art* (Paris, 1930), p. 337.
An identical piece is in the collections of the Mobilier National, Paris.

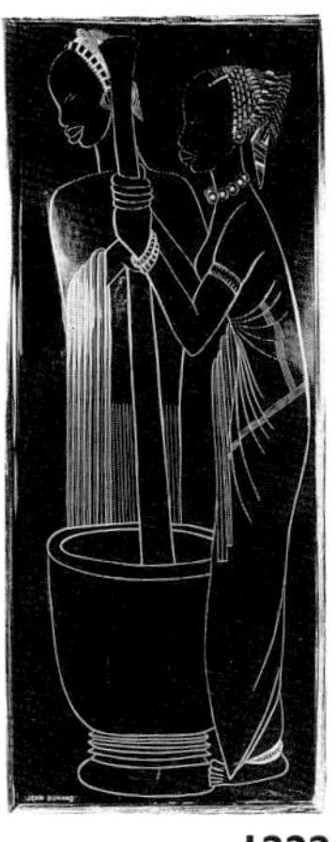

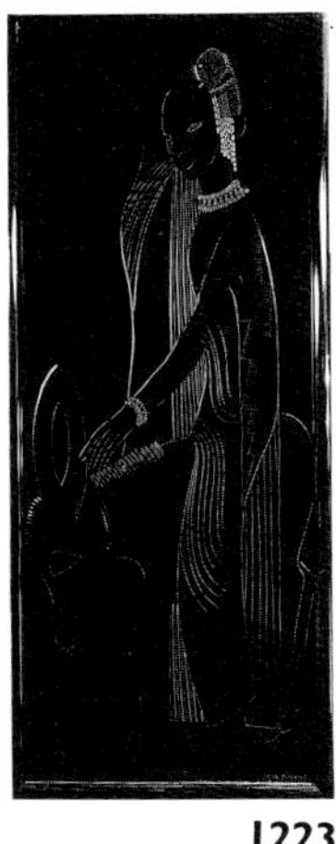

1222 1223

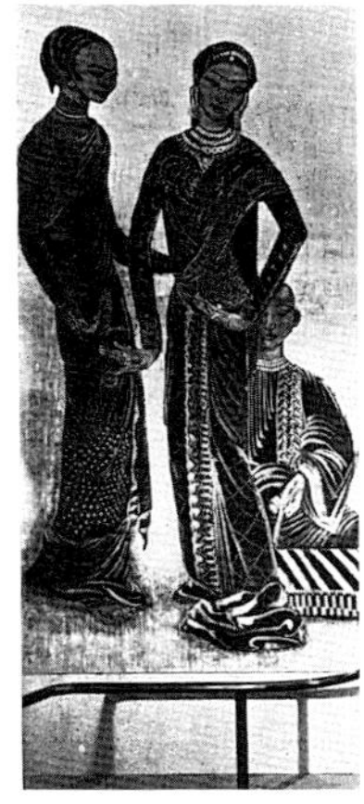

1216

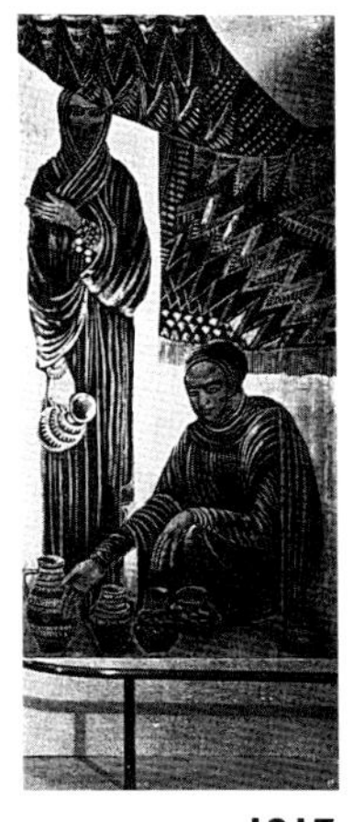

1217

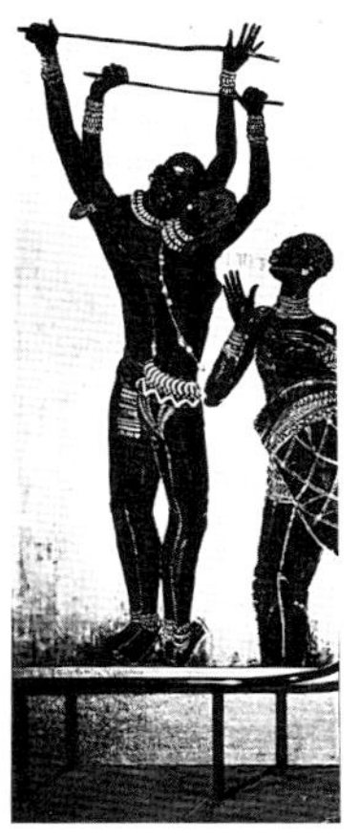

1218

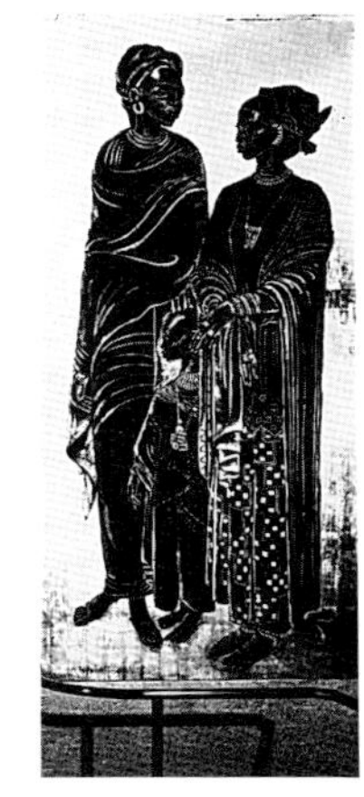

1219

1211–1223

The Exposition Coloniale Internationale, Paris (1931)

1211, 1212 Projected poster designs

Indian ink and wash.
Private collection.

1213 *The Forest* or *Wild Animal at a Watering Place* *Pl. 32*

Large mural decoration in the lecture hall on the first floor of the Palais Permanent.
Incised black Coromandel lacquer highlighted with coloured lacquer.
300 x 330 cm (118 x 130 in.).
Coll.: Musée National des Arts Africains, Paris.
Bibl.: *Beaux-Arts*, 20 January 1930, pp. 16–17; *La Construction moderne*, January 1932, p. 293.

1214 *The Elephants*

Matt brown *laque arrachée* on a silver lacquer (aluminium) ground.
Panel size 300 x 330 cm (118 x 130 in.).
Coll.: Musée National des Arts Africains, Paris.
Bibl.: *La Construction moderne*, January 1932, p. 288; *L'Elite de Paris*, June 1937, p. 31; *Die Dame*, September 1930, p. 21.
See also p. 119.

1215 *The Peoples of Asia and Africa*

Preliminary study (painted on wood) for the panels *The Peoples of Asia and Africa* (cat. nos. 1216–19).
Private collection.
See also p. 120.

1216–1219 Panels: The Peoples of Asia and Africa

Panels in the vestibule of the Palais Permanent.
Matt brown *laque arrachée* on a silver lacquer ground.
Each panel 348 x 180 cm (137 x 70¾ in.).

1216, 1217 *Women of Asia* and *The Pottery Seller* *Pl. 31*

1218, 1219 *Women of Black Africa*

Coll.: Musée National des Arts Africains, Paris.
Bibl.: *Die Dame*, September 1930, p. 20.

1220, 1221 *Ibexes Confronting One Another* and *Tiger Lying in Wait*

Panels in the vestibule of the Palais Permanent.
Each panel 148 x 240 cm (58¼ x 94½ in.).
Coll.: Musée National des Arts Africains, Paris.
Bibl.: *Die Dame*, September 1930, p. 20.

1222, 1223 Panels: *Senegalese Woman Pounding Sorghum* and *Senegalese Woman on her Donkey*

Black lacquer.
Coll.: Musée National des Arts Africains, Paris.

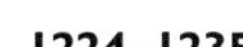

1224–1235

The Exposition Internationale des Arts et Techniques Appliqués à la Vie Moderne, Paris (1937)

1224 Panel: *Deer in a Clearing*

Coloured lacquer panel.
480 x 400 cm (15 ft 9 in. x 13 ft).
Private collection.
Bibl.: *L'Art et les artistes*, June 1939, p. 310.
The panel is shown here mounted in the Music Room by Porteneuve; see p. 149.
See also cat. no. 405 and p. 151.

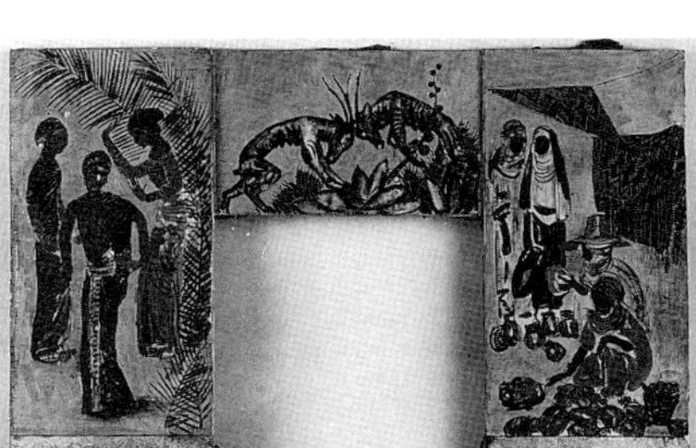

1215

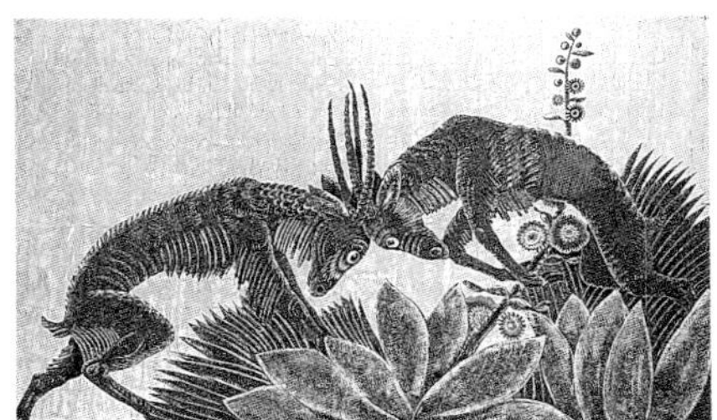

1220

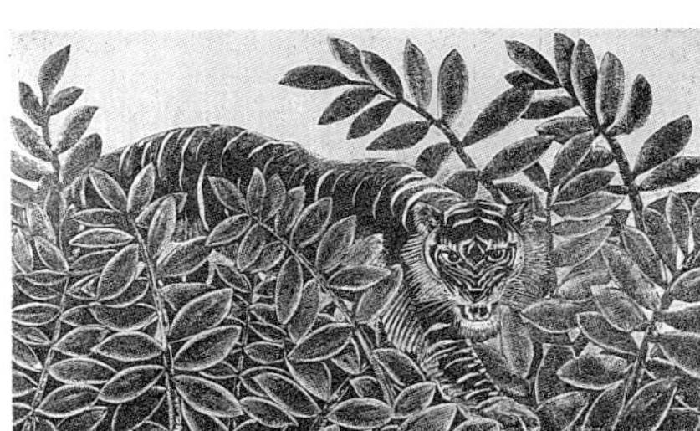

1221

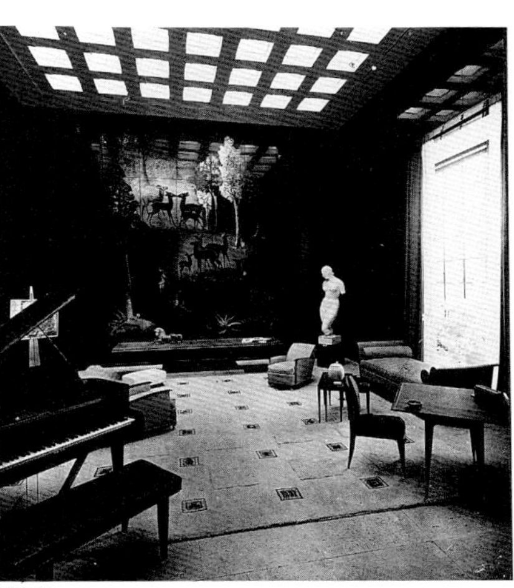

1224

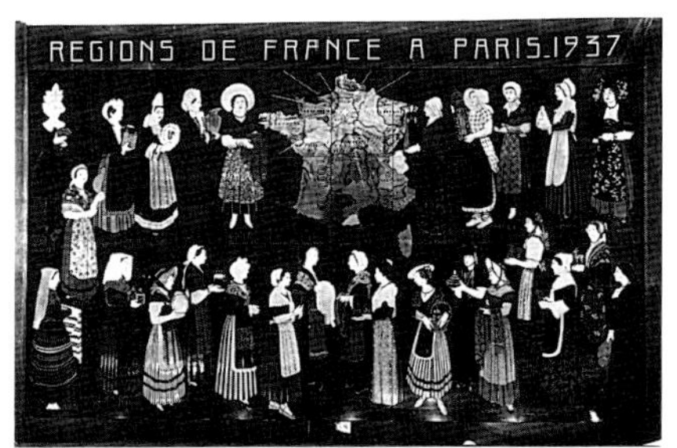

1228

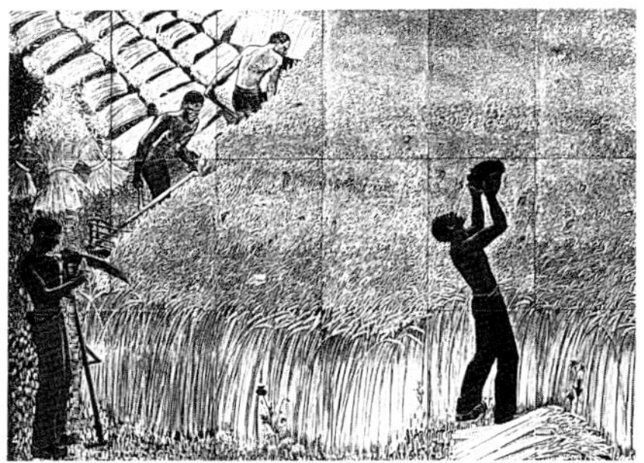
1229

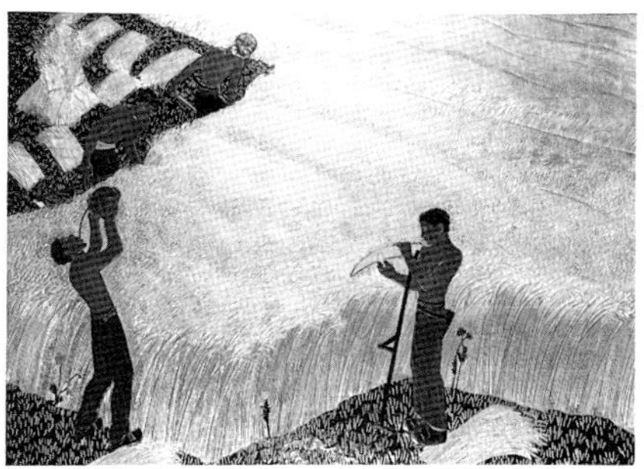
1231

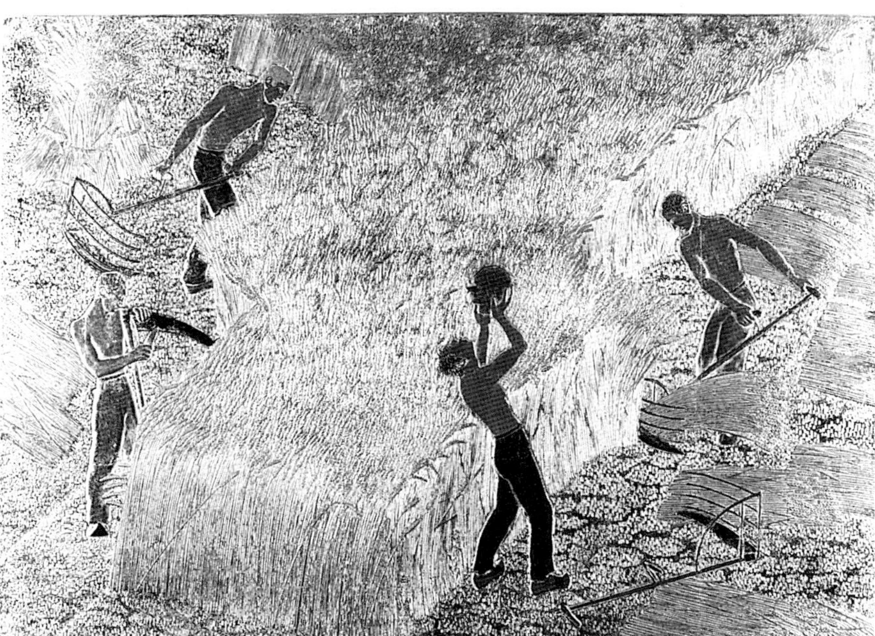
1230

1225

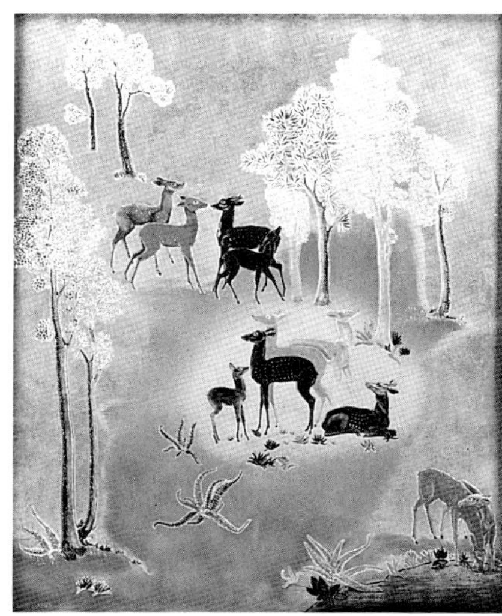
1226

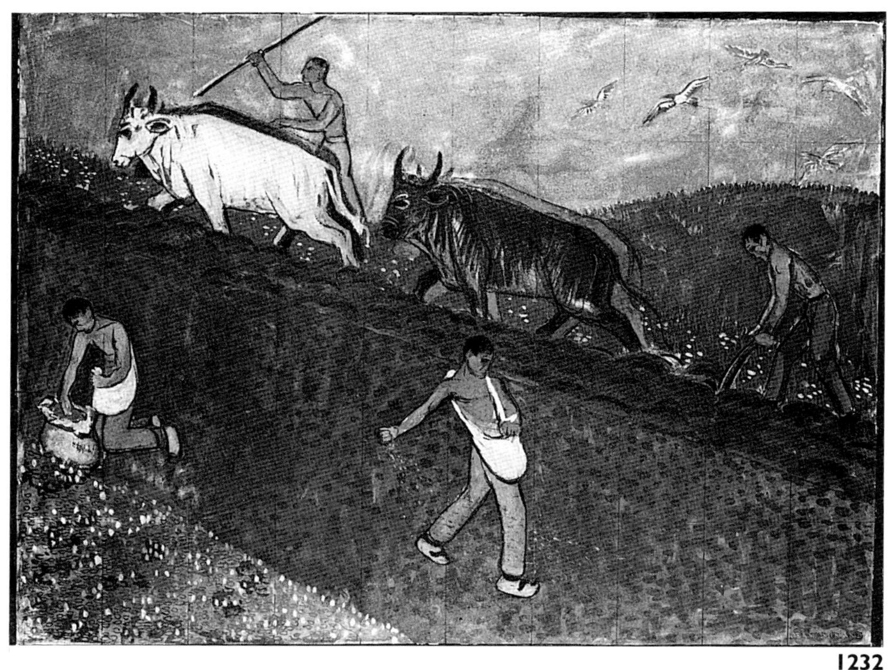
1232

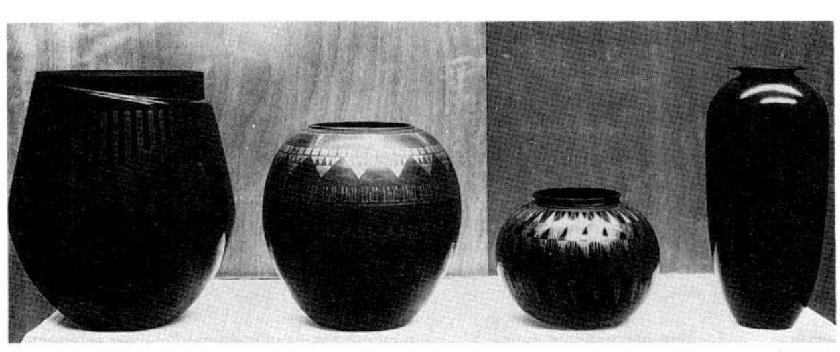
1233

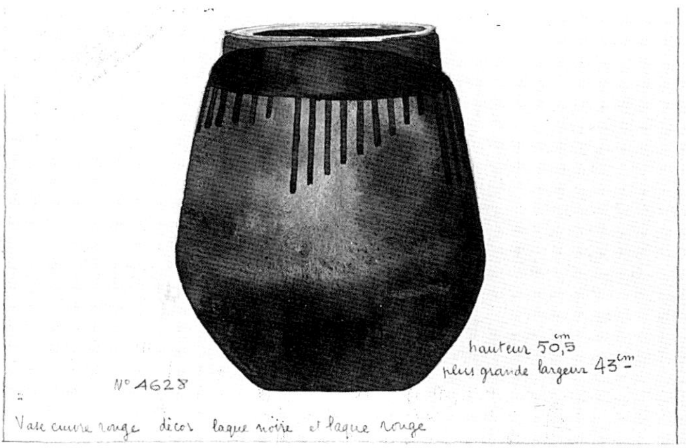

1234

1225 ***Deer in a Clearing***
Reduced-size replica in red, brown and gold lacquer of the panel displayed in Porteneuve's Music Room.
92 x 68 cm (36¼ x 26¾ in.).
Sold: Boisgirard (Paris), 26 October 1988, lot 108.

1226 ***Deer in a Clearing***
Reduced-size replica in red, brown and gold lacquer of the panel displayed in Porteneuve's Music Room.
160 x 130 cm (63 x 51¼ in.).
Sold: Sotheby's (Monaco), 5 April 1987, lot 268.

1227 ***Deer in a Clearing***
Replica in brown, red and gold lacquer of the panel displayed in Porteneuve's Music Room, painted on wood panelling and installed at the home of Monsieur M. in Morocco in 1938.

1228 ***The Regions of France***
Monumental coloured lacquer mural, assemblage of 40 panels (produced in collaboration with Bernard Dunand).
480 x 800 cm (15 ft 9 in. x 26 ft. 3 in.).

1229 ***The Harvest***
Monumental incised gold lacquer mural composed of 18 panels.
360 x 480 cm (11 ft 10 in. x 15 ft 9 in.).
The mural is shown here in Dunand's studio before being assembled for the 1937 exhibition.

1230 ***The Harvest***
Coloured lacquer and incised gold lacquer.
60 x 80 cm (23¾ x 31½ in.).
Formerly in the collection of Félix Marcilhac, Paris; Private collection.
Bibl.: *L'Illustration*, 26 July 1941.
A variant of the large mural displayed at the 1937 exhibition.

1231 ***The Harvest***
Coloured lacquer and incised gold lacquer.
60 x 80 cm (23¾ x 31½ in.).
Formerly in the collection of Félix Marcilhac, Paris; Private collection.
A variant of the large mural displayed at the 1937 exhibition.

1232 ***Ploughing***
Gouache and Indian ink highlighted with gold, study for a tapestry cartoon intended for the Gobelins Company. The full-size cartoon was exhibited on the tapestry stand.
65 x 84 cm (25½ x 33 in.).
Formerly in the collection of Félix Marcilhac, Paris; Alain Lesieutre, Paris.
Sold: Champin, Lombrail, Gautier (Enghien), 15 December 1985, lot 61.

1233 Vases
Lacquered brass, copper and metal vases displayed on Dunand's stand.

1234 Design for a vase
Watercolour and Indian ink wash.
14 x 19 cm (5½ x 7½ in.).
Private collection.
See cat. no. 1235.

1235 Vase
Brass decorated with black lacquer, neck decorated with red lacquer.
Height 50 cm (19¾ in.); diameter 42 cm (16½ in.).
Coll.: Mobilier National, Paris.
The vase was shown as exhibit no. 4628.

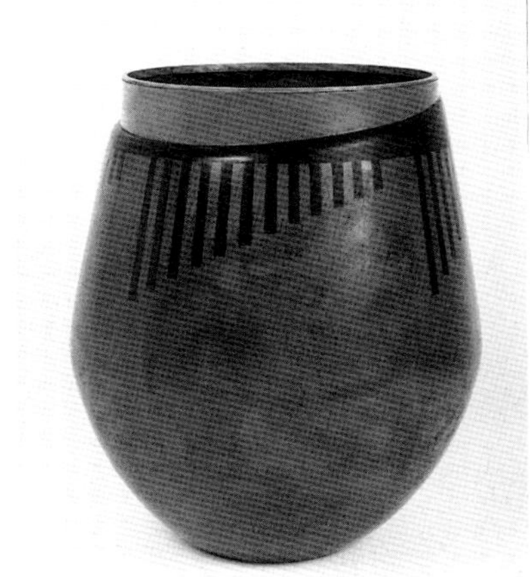
1235

1236
The New York World's Fair (1939)

See also p. 151 and cat. no. 1224.

1236 Panel: *The Epic of the Republic*
Large curved panel in red lacquer by Dunand after a design by Jean Dupas, displayed with sculpture by Paul Landowski.

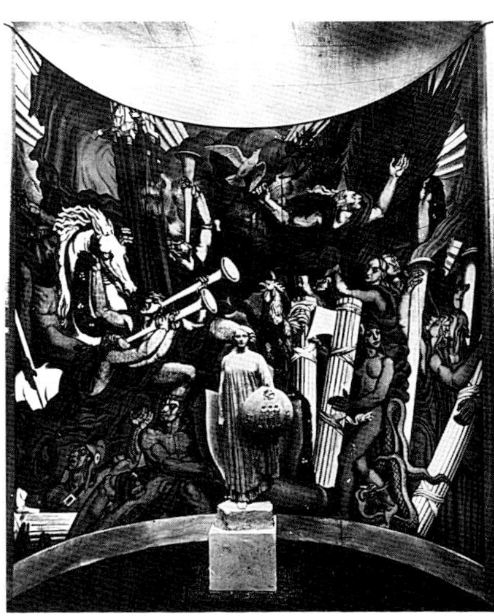
1236

Works by Bernard Dunand

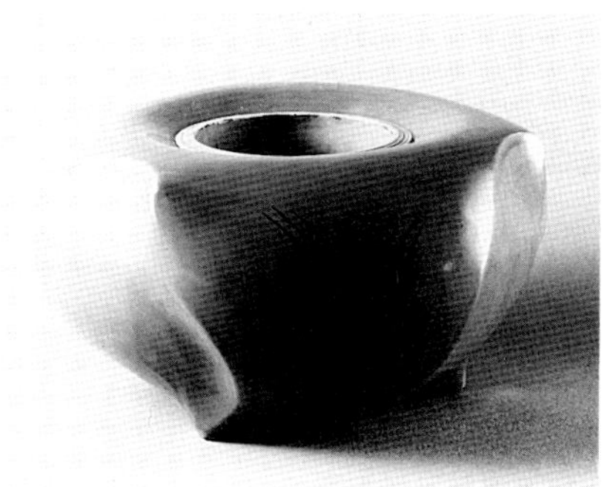
1

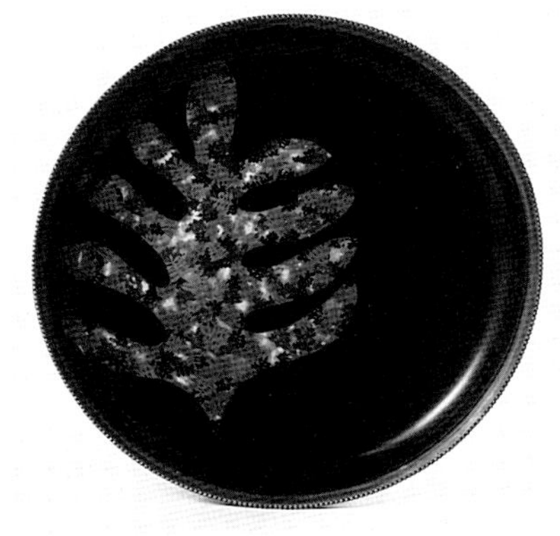
2

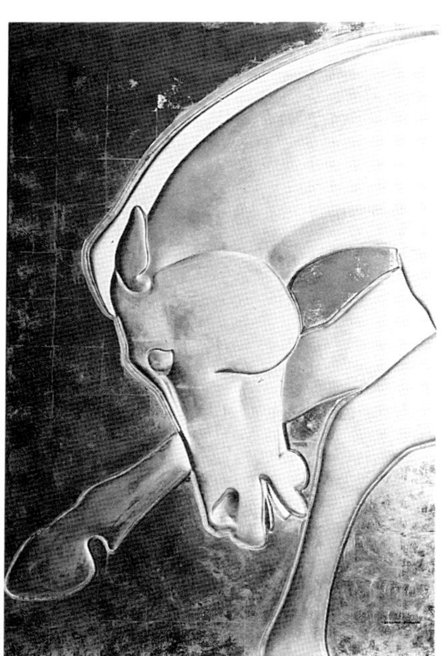
9

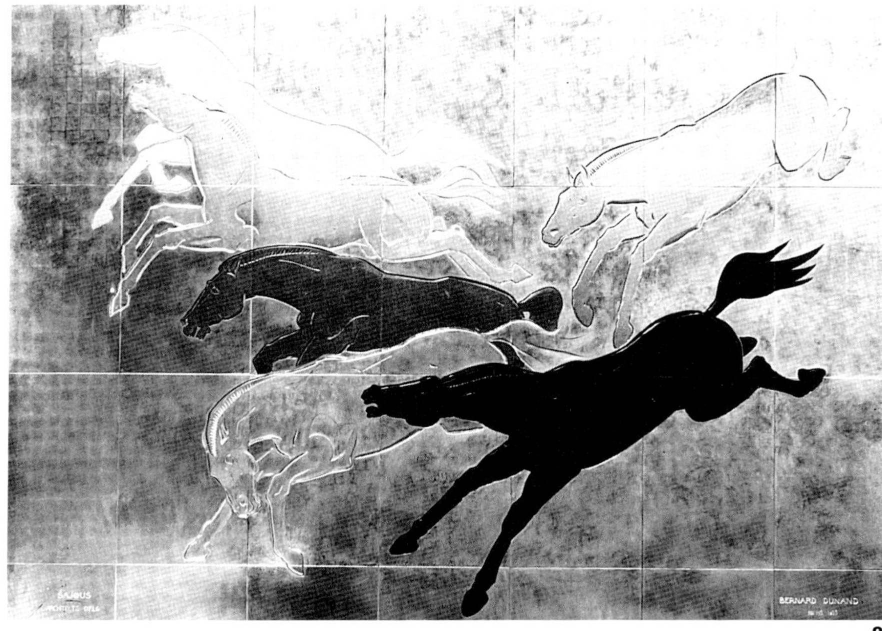

8

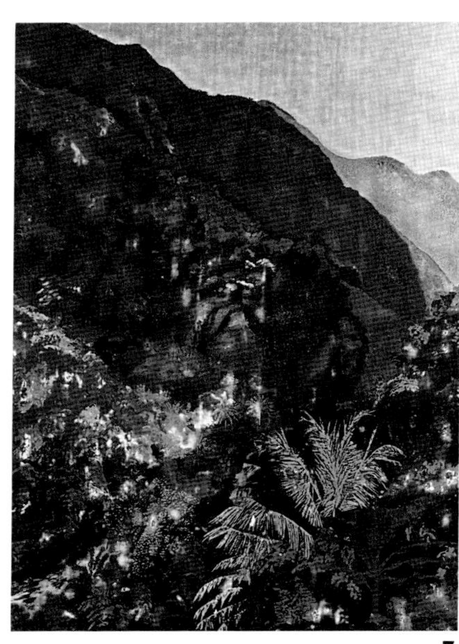
7

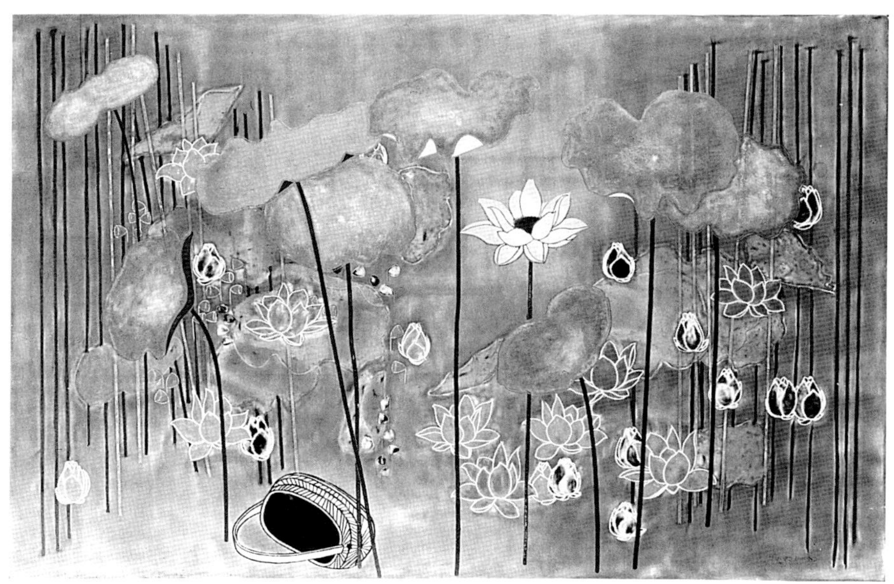
11

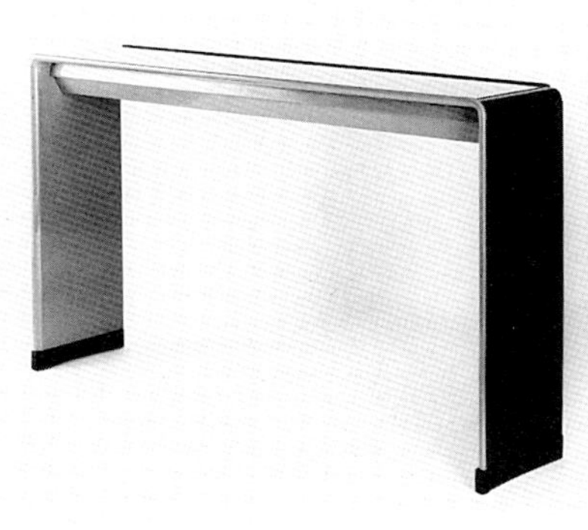

3

5

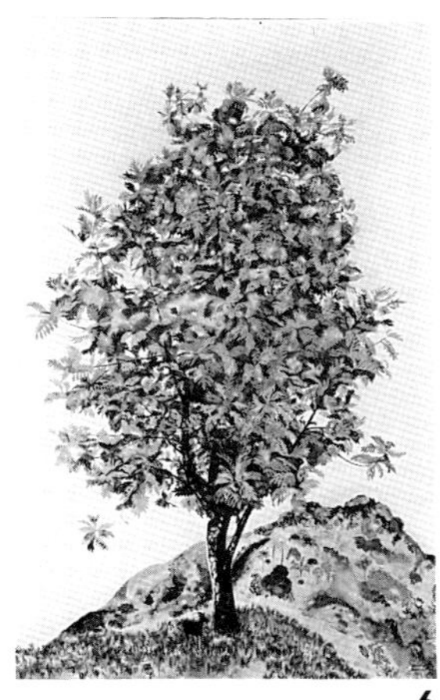

6

DINANDERIE AND FURNITURE

1 Vase with indentations
Orange-red lacquer on brass body.
1937.
Private collection.

2 'Fern-leaf' dish
Black-lacquered brass with coloured lacquered design.
1937.
Private collection.

3 Side-table
Red and black lacquer on wood.
1937.
Private collection.

4 Occasional table *Pl. 169*
Anthracite-grey *laque arrachée* on wood with red lacquer decoration.
1937.
Private collection.

5 Nest of tables
Light-brown shellac on wood.
C. 1960.
Private collection.

PANELS

6 Bread-fruit Tree
Coloured *laque de Chine.*
1935.
Exh.: Galerie Charpentier, Paris, 1935.
Private collection.

7 Landscape in Martinique
Coloured *laque de Chine.*
81 x 68 cm (32 x 26¾ in.).
1935.
Exh.: Galerie Charpentier, Paris, 1935.
Formerly in the Henchoz Collection, Geneva, and in the collection of Félix Marcilhac, Paris; Private collection.
Sold: Pillias, Gluck (Paris), 30 April 1975, lot 87, repr. in catalogue, p. 29.

8 Horses
Bas-relief with lacquer decoration.
422 x 538 cm (13 ft 10 in. x 18 ft 5¾ in.).
1953.
Coll.: Jockey Club of São Paulo.

9 Head of Running Horse
Sculpted gold lacquer (detail of *Horses* bas-relief).
120 x 80 cm (47¼ x 31½ in.).
1953.
Exh.: Wildenstein Gallery, New York, 1956, no. 5.
Formerly in the collection of Félix Marcilhac, Paris; Private collection.

10 The Heart
Coloured *laque de Chine.*
80 x 56 cm (31½ x 22 in.).
1948.
Bibl.: *Plaisir de France*, special Christmas number, 1948.
Sold: Blache (Versailles), 7 March 1976, lot 131.

11 The Basket
Laque de Chine, light-brown, red and black shellac highlighted with gold lacquer.
1949.
Private collection.

12 Mandarin Duck
Shellac and coloured lacquer.
63 x 45 cm (24¾ x 17¾ in.).
1954.
Exh.: Wildenstein Gallery, New York, 1956, no. 11.
Private collection.

13 Bouquet I
Natural *laque de Chine* and coloured lacquer highlighted with gold lacquer.
60 x 48 cm (23½ x 19 in.).
1956.
Exh.: Wildenstein Gallery, New York, 1956, no. 9, repr. on cover of catalogue.

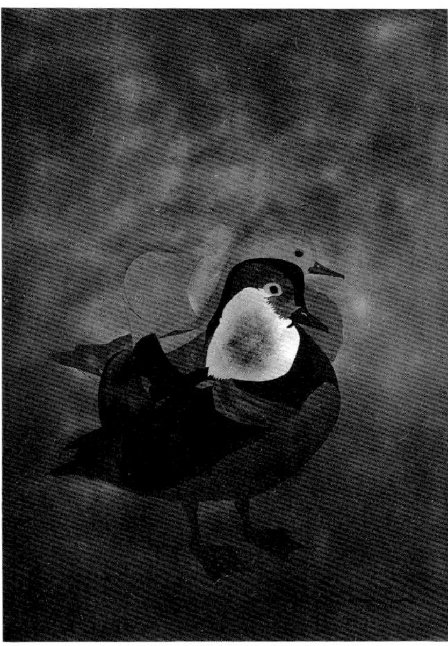

12

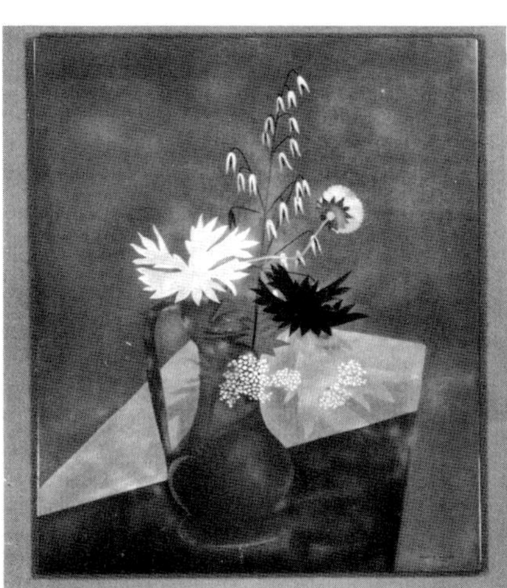

13

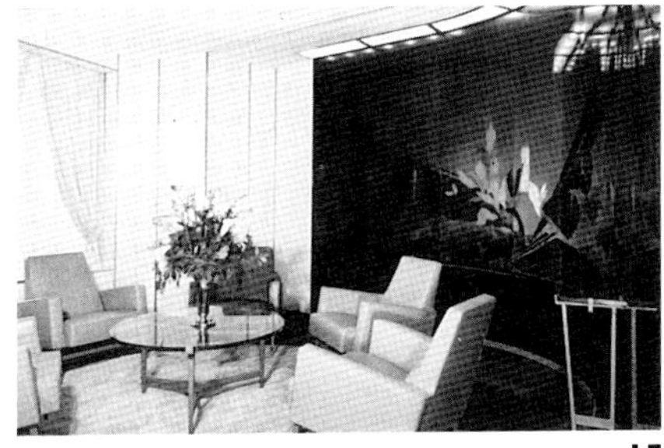
15

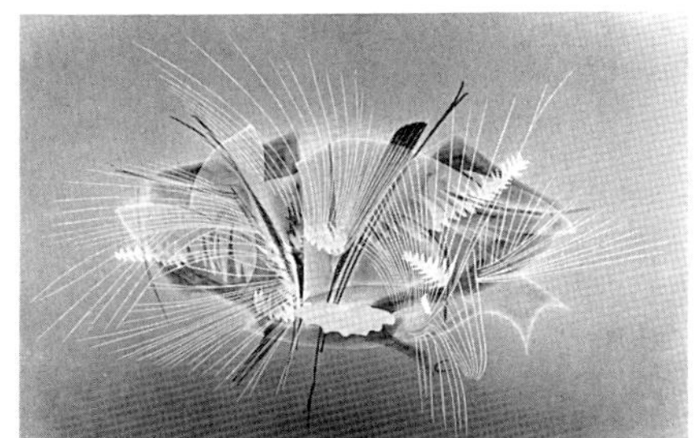
16

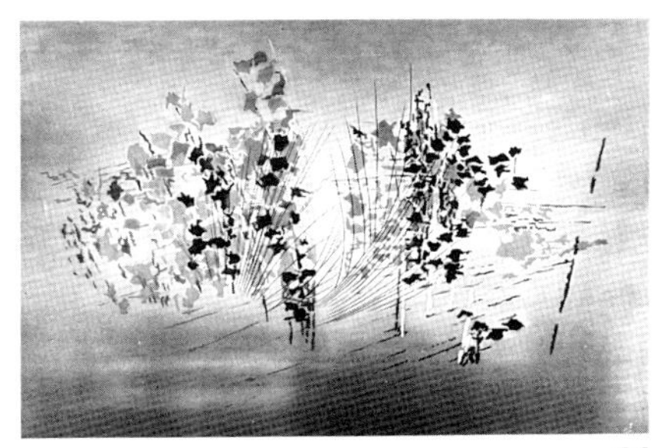
21

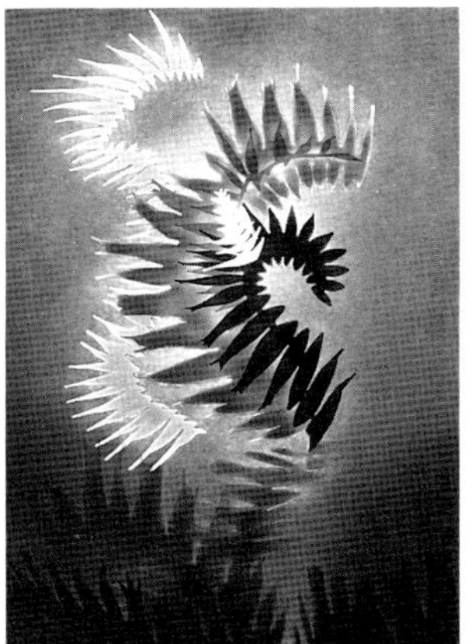
17

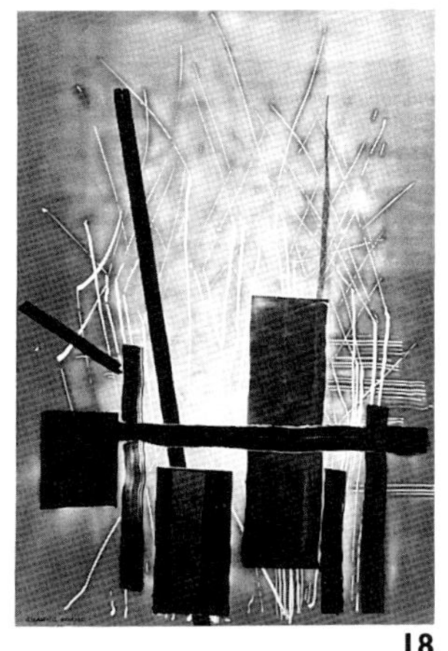
18

14 Leaves
Light-brown shellac.
C. 1952.
Private collection.

15 Composition
Coloured synthetic lacquer.
1965.
Large mural for the first-class cocktail bar of the liner *France*.

16 Counterpoint IV
Coloured synthetic lacquer.
83 x 132 cm (32¾ x 52 in.).
1968.

17 'I will speak of all thy marvellous works'
Coloured synthetic lacquer.
83 x 57 cm (32¾ x 22½ in.).
1969.
Private collection.

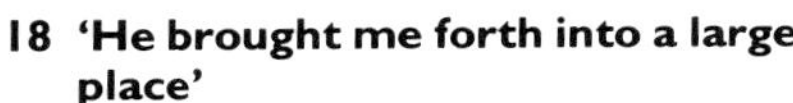

18 'He brought me forth into a large place'
Coloured synthetic lacquer.
80 x 60 cm (31½ x 23½ in.).
1970.
Private collection.

19 The Promise's Perfume
Coloured synthetic lacquer.
80 x 60 cm (31½ x 23½ in.).
1970.
Private collection.

20 As night follows day
Coloured synthetic lacquer.
100 x 70 cm (39¼ x 27½ in.).
Private collection.

21 Ever Closer
Coloured synthetic lacquer.
83 x 132 cm (32¾ x 52 in.).
1970.
Private collection.

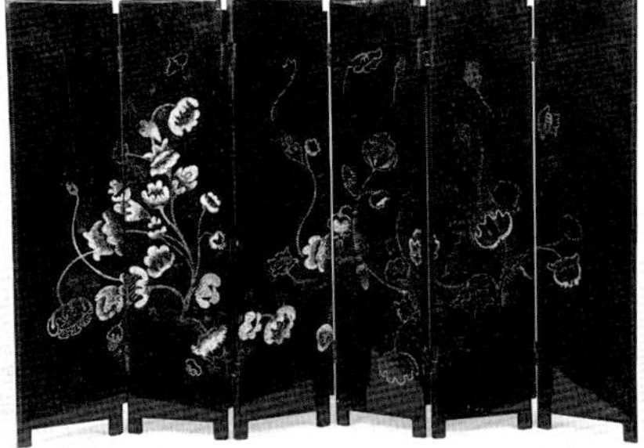
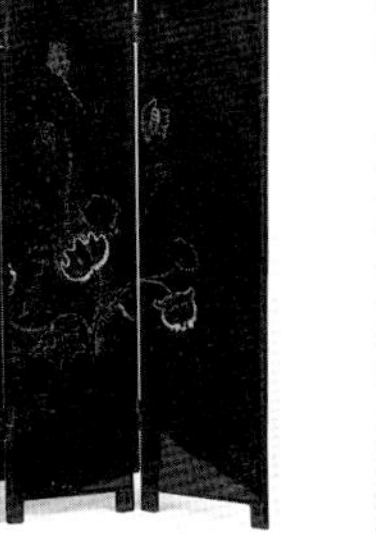
22

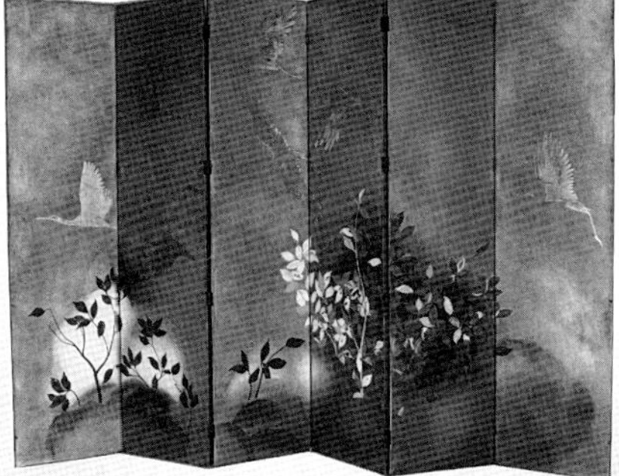
23

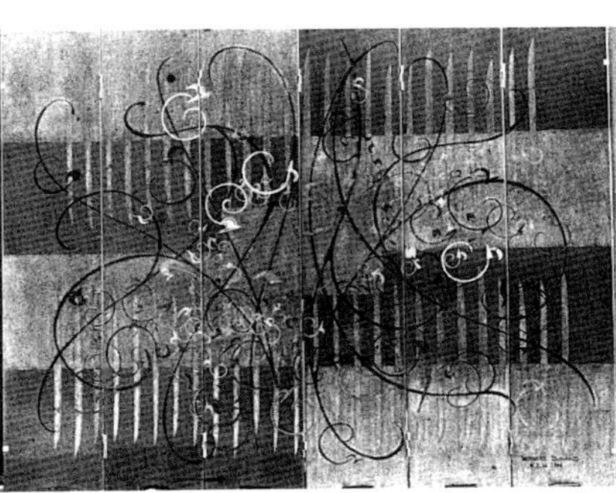
24

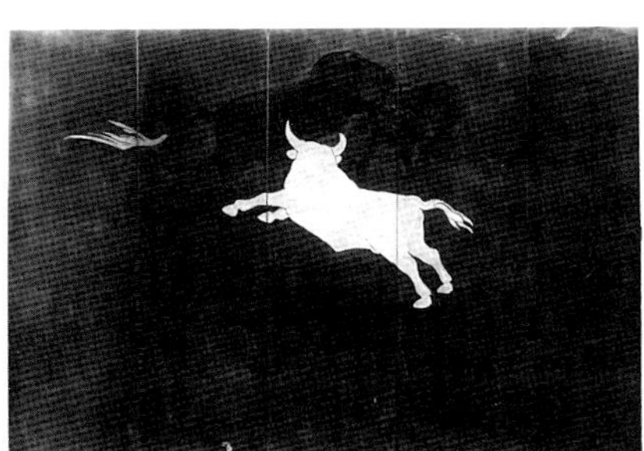
25

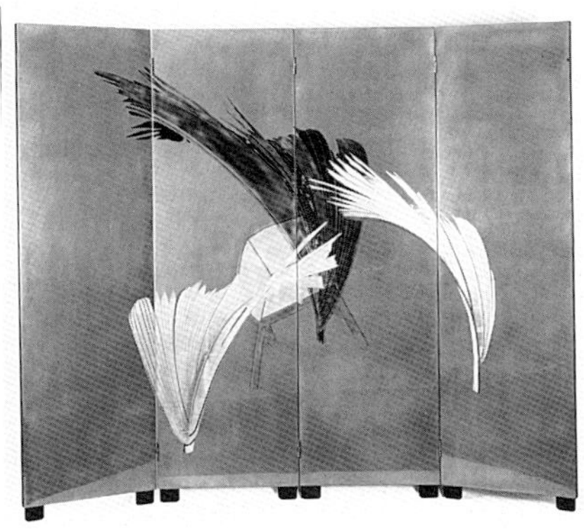
26

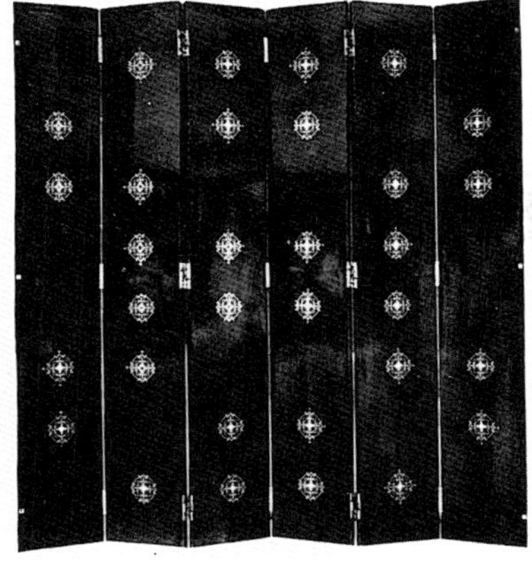
28

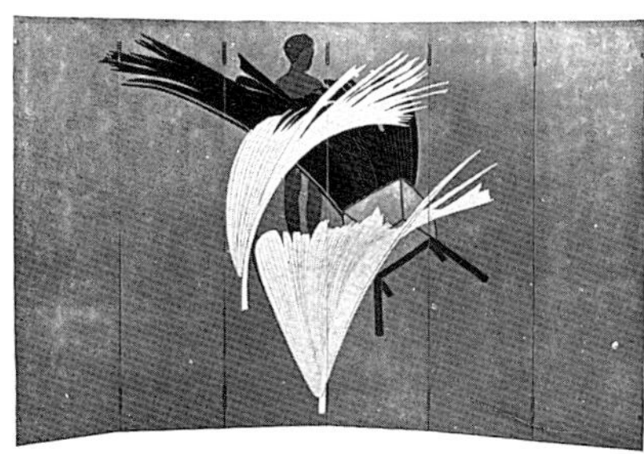
27

DECORATIVE SCREENS

22 Poppy Flowers
(six panels)
Black *laque de Chine* and eggshell.
Panel size 84 x 25 cm (33 x 9¾ in.).
1939.
Coll.: Mobilier National, Paris.

23 Storks on the Wing
(six panels)
Light-brown shellac and gold lacquer.
Panel size 240 x 35 cm (94½ x 13¾ in.).
1939.
Exh.: 'Decorative Arts: 1925 Style', Didier Aaron, Inc., New York, 1979, no. 47.
Formerly in the collections of Félix Marcilhac, Paris, and Hervé Aaron, New York; Private collection.

24 Counterpoint A
(six panels)
Light- and dark-brown shellac and gold lacquer.
Panel size 120 x 25 cm (47¼ x 9¾ in.).
1946.
Private collection.

25 Bulls
(five panels)
Tan *laque de Chine*.
Panel size 190 x 50 cm (74¾ x 19¾ in.).
Painted for the liner *Maréchal Joffre* in 1951.

26 Palm Fronds
(four panels)
Tan *laque de Chine* and gold lacquer.
1952.
Private collection.

27 The Hand-cart
(six panels)
Brownish-red, black and gold lacquer.
1952.
Private collection.
Bibl.: 'L'Art de la laque', *Études d'outre-mer*, December 1952, p. 420.

28 The Circles
(six panels)
Black *laque de Chine* and gold lacquer with red filigree.
1952.
Private collection.
Bibl.: 'L'Art de la laque', *Études d'outre-mer*, December 1952, p. 356.

29 Ears of Wheat
(six panels)
Polished black *laque de Chine*, brown and gold lacquer.
Panel size 125 x 25 cm (49¼ x 9¾ in.).
1952.
Exh.: Museum of the College of Applied Arts, Cairo, 1953.
Private collection.
Bibl.: 'L'Art de la laque', *Études d'outre-mer*, December 1952, p. 420.

30 Vertical Bands
(five panels)
Coloured and gold synthetic lacquer.
1975.
Private collection.

31 Homage to Jean Dunand
(four panels)
Coloured synthetic lacquer.
1975.
Private collection.

32 Homage to Cubism
(four panels)
Black *laque de Chine* ground by Jean Dunand with a design by Jean Dunand executed by Bernard Dunand.
Begun in 1940 and completed in 1985.
Private collection.

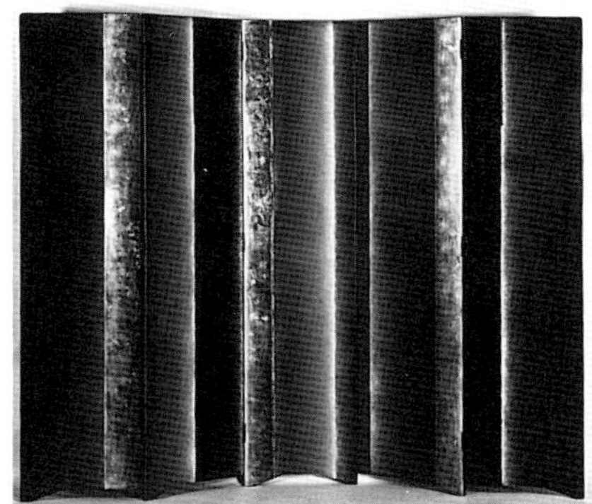
30

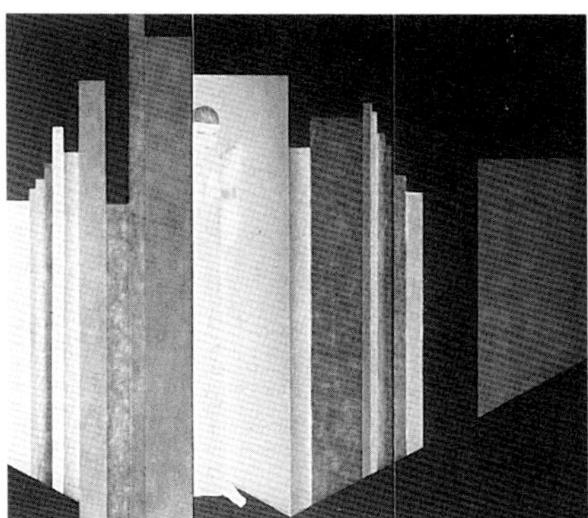
31

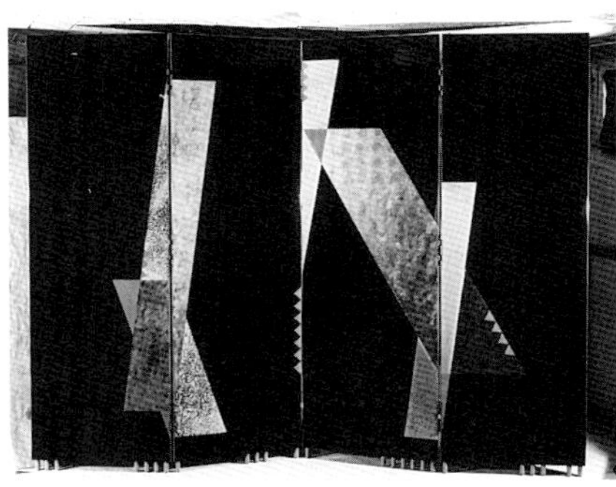
32

Works by Pierre Dunand

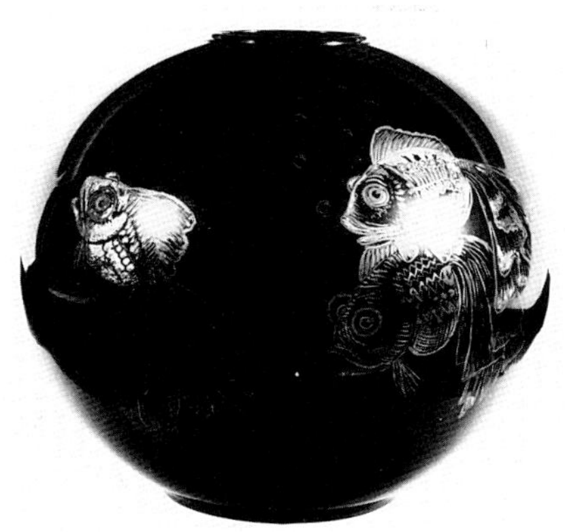

1

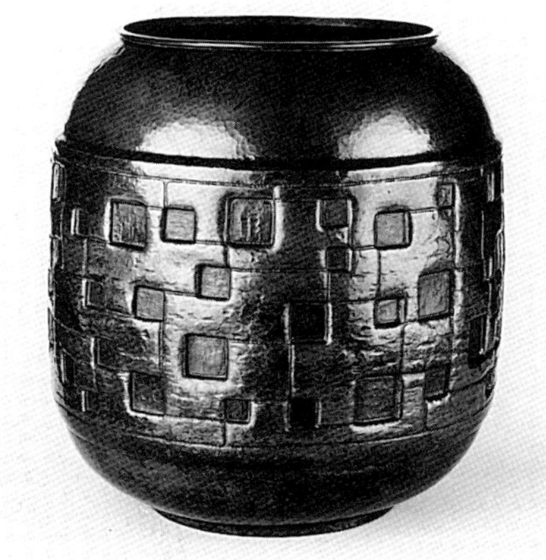

2

3

6

5

4

7

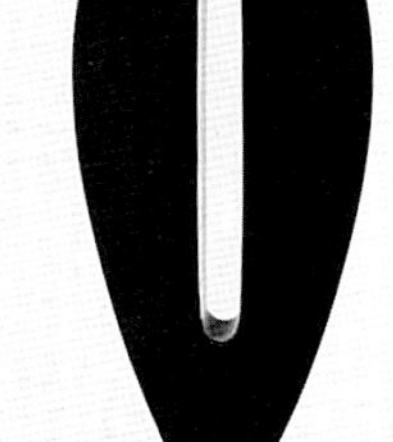

8

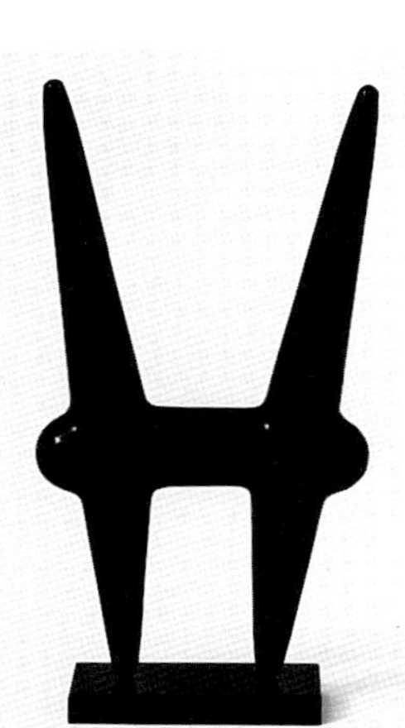

9

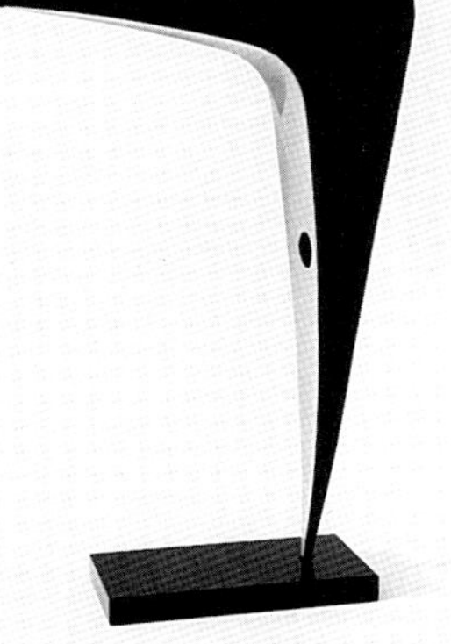

10

VASES

1 Spherical 'Fish' vase
Brass, black *laque de Chine* with a coloured lacquer design highlighted with gold.
Diameter 26 cm (10¼ in.).
Made in 1950 to a design by Jean Dunand.
Formerly in the Leininger Collection; Jean-Claude Brugnot.
Sold: Boisgirard (Paris), 18 April 1986, lot 70.

2 Vase
Oxidized and patinated brass.
Height 35 cm (13¾ in.).
C. 1937.
Private collection.

3 'Double Triangle' vase
Soldered brass, black and red lacquer.
1952.
Private collection.

4 'Mask' vase
Soldered brass, black lacquer.
1952.
Private collection.

5 Anthropomorphic vase
Soldered brass, black lacquer.
1952.
Exh.: Compagnie des Arts Français, Paris, 1952.
Private collection.
Bibl.: *Art et industrie*, December 1952, p. 20.

6 'Two Hearts' vase
Soldered brass, gold and red lacquer.
1952.
Exh.: Compagnie des Arts Français, Paris, 1952.
Private collection.

7 'Fish' vase
Soldered brass, black lacquer.
1952.
Exh.: Compagnie des Arts Français, Paris, 1952.
Private collection.

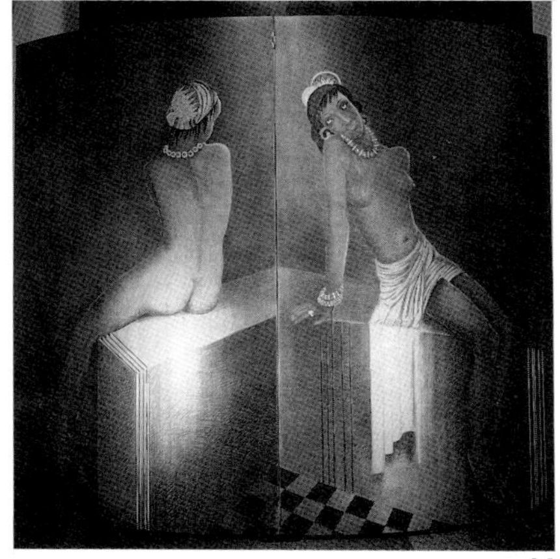
11

12

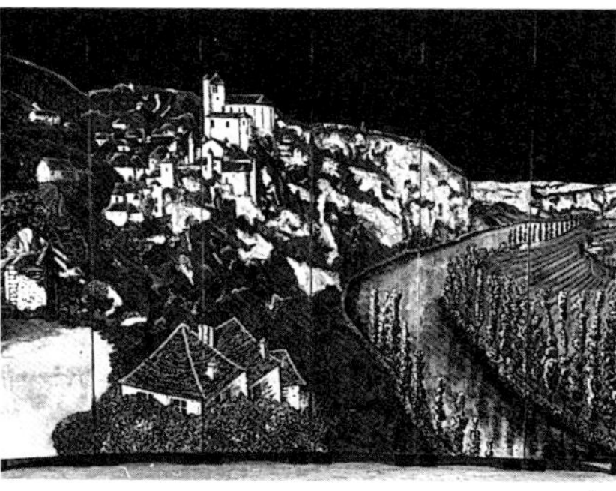
14

8 'Feather' vase
Soldered brass, black lacquer.
1952.
Exh.: Compagnie des Arts Français, Paris, 1952.
Private collection.

9 'Propeller' vase
Soldered brass, black lacquer.
1952.
Exh.: Compagnie des Arts Français, Paris, 1952.
Private collection.
Bibl.: *Art et industrie*, December 1952, p. 21.

10 'Kepi' vase
Soldered brass, red and black lacquer.
1952.
Exh.: Compagnie des Arts Français, Paris, 1952.
Private collection.

DECORATIVE SCREENS

11 Two Figures, One Nude, the Other Draped and **Flight of Ducks and Lotus** *Pl. 161*
(two curved panels, decorated on both sides)
Brown natural and aventurine *laque de Chine* with coloured lacquer decoration.
Panel size 200 x 120 cm (78¾ x 47¼ in.).
C. 1945–50.
Coll.: Félix Marcilhac, Paris.

12 The Rocks
(six panels)
Gold and black *laque de Chine*.
Panel size 170 x 40 cm (67 x 15¾ in.).
C. 1945–50.
Private collection.

13 Fortified Town
(six panels)
Black *laque de Chine* with incised Coromandel lacquer decoration, gold-leaf ground.
Panel size 170 x 40 cm (67 x 15¾ in.).
C. 1945–50.
Private collection.

14 Saint Cirq-Lapopie (Lot)
(six panels)
Black *laque de Chine* with incised Coromandel lacquer decoration, gold-leaf ground.
Panel size 165 x 40 cm (65 x 15¾ in.).
C. 1945–50.
Private collection.

15 Sisteron
(six panels)
Black *laque de Chine* with incised Coromandel lacquer decoration, gold-leaf ground.
Panel size 165 x 40 cm (65 x 15¾ in.).
C. 1945–50.
Private collection.

16 Fantastic Animals
(seven panels)
Gold lacquer with coloured lacquer decoration.
C. 1945–50.
Private collection.

17 The Lake
(four panels)
Black *laque de Chine* with coloured lacquer decoration.
C. 1945–50.
Private collection.

18 The Shepherd Boy
(four panels)
Coloured *laque de Chine*.
C. 1945–50.
Private collection.

19 The Geese
(six panels)
Gold and black *laque de Chine*.
Panel size 165 x 40 cm (65 x 15¾ in.).
C. 1945–50.
Private collection.

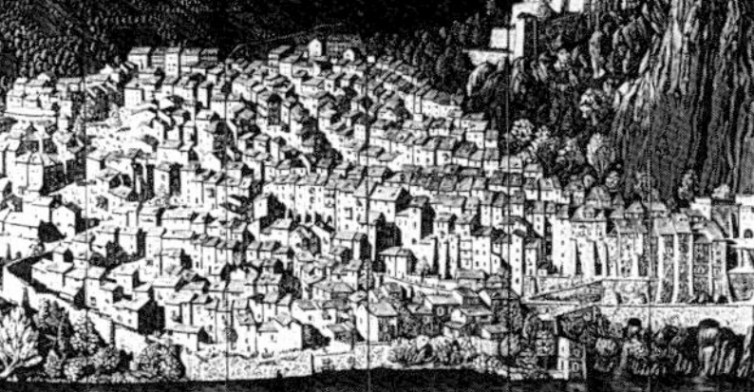
13

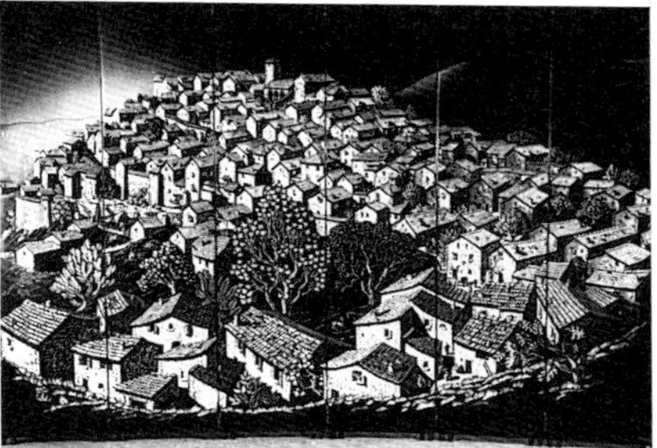
15

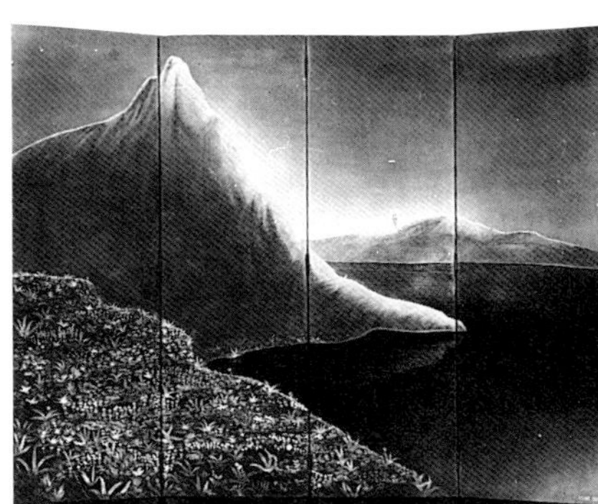
17

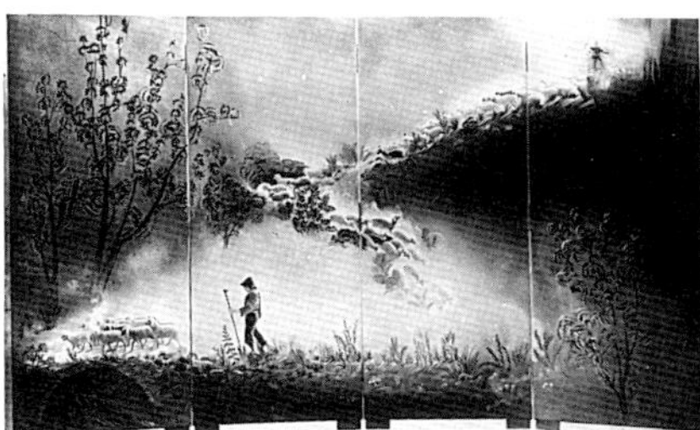
18

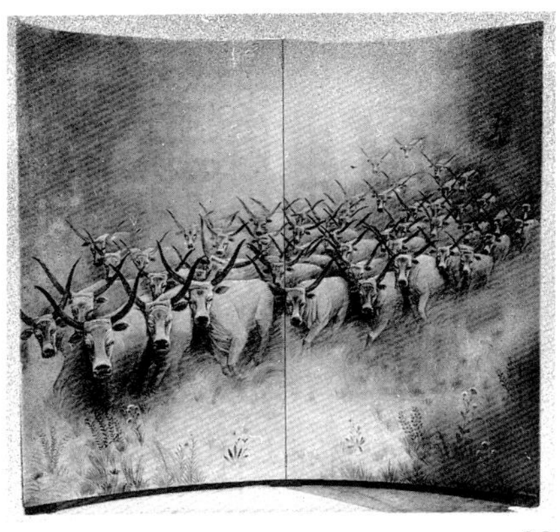

20

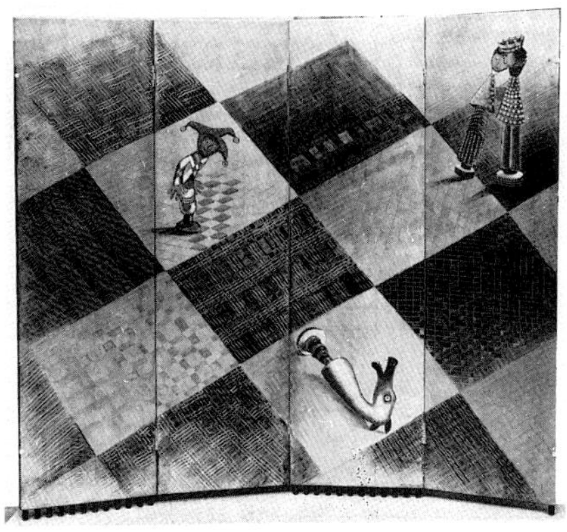

22

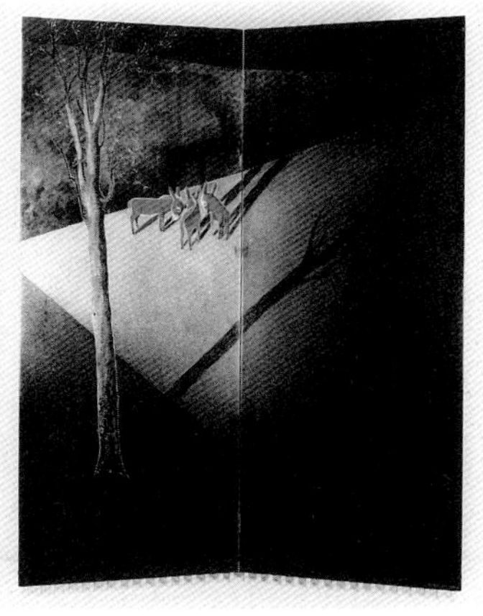

23

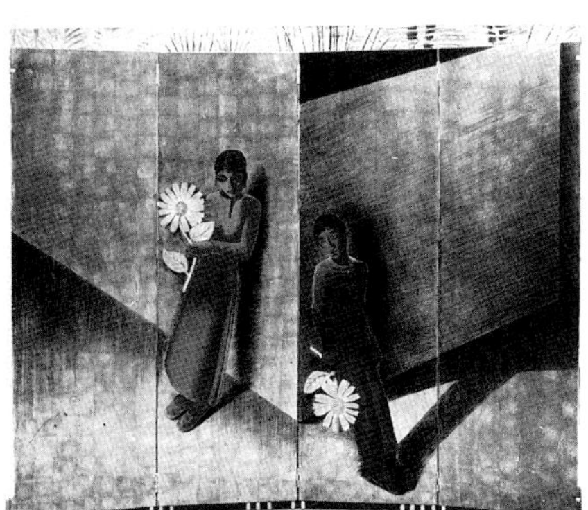

24

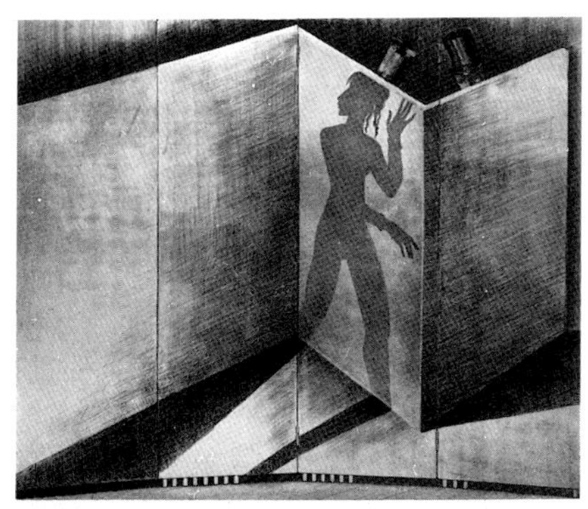

25

26

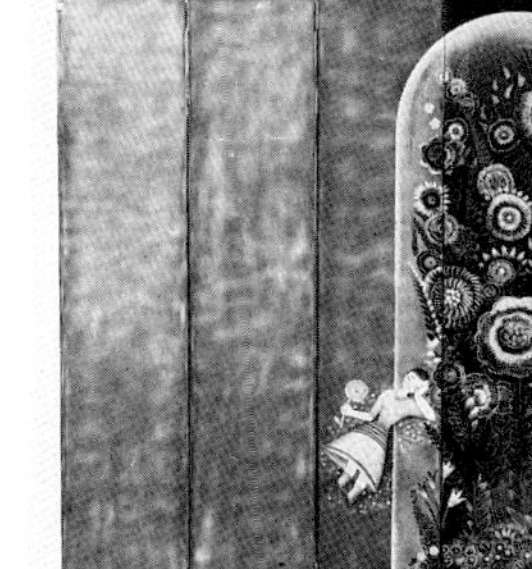

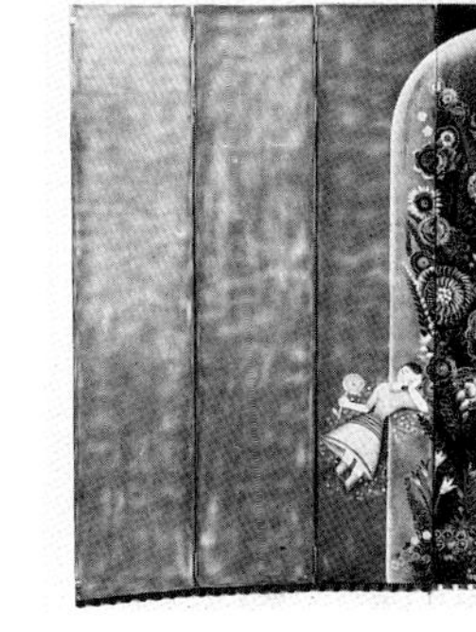

27

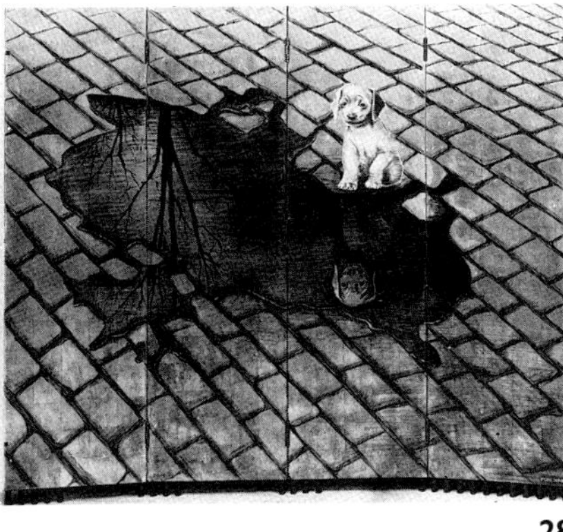

28

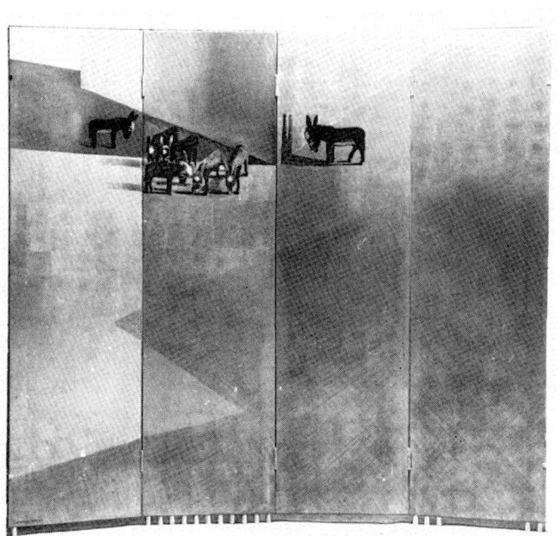

29

20 The Herd of Cattle
(two curved panels)
Brown *laque de Chine* with gold decoration.
Panel size 200 x 120 cm (78¾ x 47¼ in.).
C. 1950–55.
Private collection.

21 The Oyster Bed
(four panels)
Gold and black *laque de Chine.*
C. 1950.
Private collection.

22 Chess
(four panels)
Brownish-red *laque de Chine* with gold decoration.
Panel size 160 x 43 cm (63 x 17 in.).
C. 1950–55.
Private collection.

23 The Ass's Foals
(two panels)
Black *laque de Chine* with gold and red lacquer decoration.
Panel size 200 x 76 cm (78¾ x 30 in.).
C. 1950–55.
Private collection.

24 Rendez-vous
(four panels)
Gold and brown *laque de Chine.*
Panel size 165 x 40 cm (65 x 15¾ in.).
C. 1950–55.
Private collection.

25 Suzanne
(four panels)
Gold and brown *laque de Chine.*
Panel size 165 x 40 cm (65 x 15¾ in.).
C. 1955.
Private collection.

26 Shadow Play
(six panels)
Coloured *laque de Chine.*
C. 1955.
Private collection.

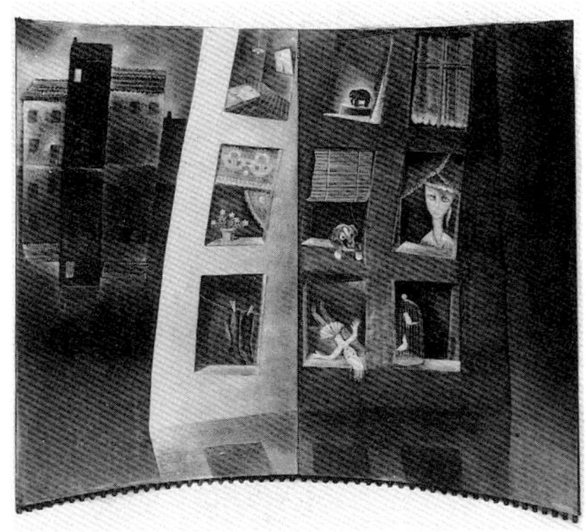
30

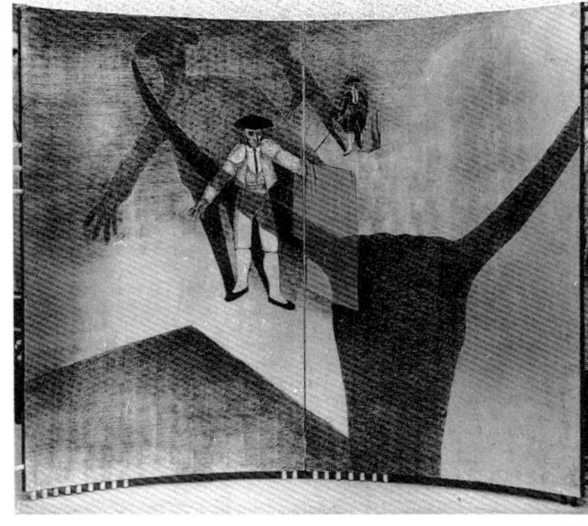
31

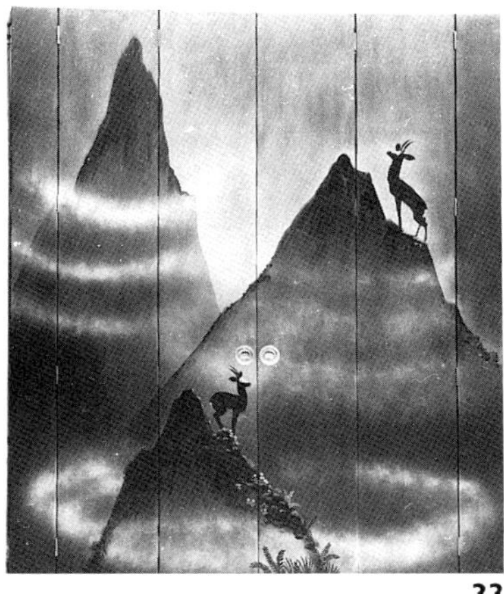
33

27 The Bouquet
(six panels)
Black *laque de Chine* and light-brown shellac with coloured lacquer decoration.
C. 1955.
Private collection.

28 The Puddle of Water
(four panels)
Gold and brown shellac.
C. 1955.
Private collection.

29 The Donkeys
(four panels)
Gold and light-brown shellac with coloured lacquer decoration.
C. 1955.
Private collection.

30 Windows Looking on to a Courtyard
(two curved panels)
Gold and brown *laque de Chine* with coloured lacquer decoration.
Panel size 200 x 120 cm (78¾ x 47¼ in.).
C. 1955.
Private collection.

31 The Bullfight
(two curved panels)
Gold and brown *laque de Chine* with coloured lacquer decoration.
Panel size 200 x 120 cm (78¾ x 47¼ in.).
C. 1955.
Private collection.

32 In the Rain
(two panels)
Gold and brown *laque de Chine*.
C. 1955.
Private collection.

INTERIOR FURNISHINGS

33–40

Accordion doors made for interior decorative schemes by Jules Leleu, c. 1950–55.

33 Chamois
(six panels, double-sided)
Shellac.

34 Deer
(six panels, double-sided)
Gold and black *laque de Chine* with coloured lacquer decoration.

35 Ducks
(six panels, double-sided)
Light-brown shellac with coloured lacquer decoration.

36 The Hunt
(six panels, double-sided)
Light-brown shellac with coloured lacquer decoration.

37 Seabed
(six panels, double-sided)
Light-brown shellac with coloured lacquer decoration.

38 Deer and Undergrowth
(six panels, double-sided)
Light-brown shellac with coloured lacquer decoration.

39 Deer at the Lakeside
(six panels, double-sided)
Light-brown shellac with coloured lacquer decoration.

40 Fish in the Ocean Depths
(six panels, double-sided)
Light-brown shellac with coloured lacquer decoration.

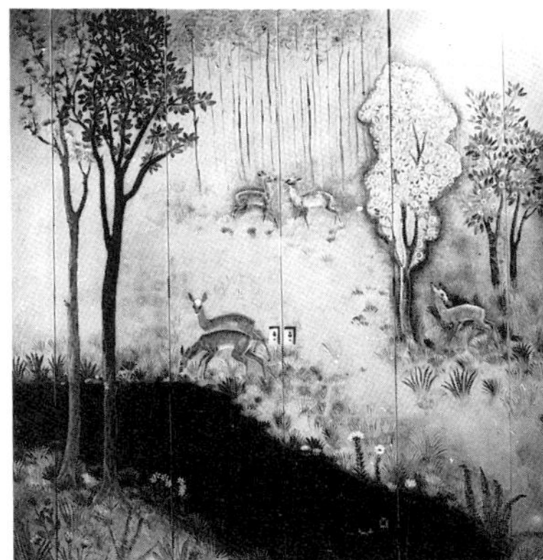
34

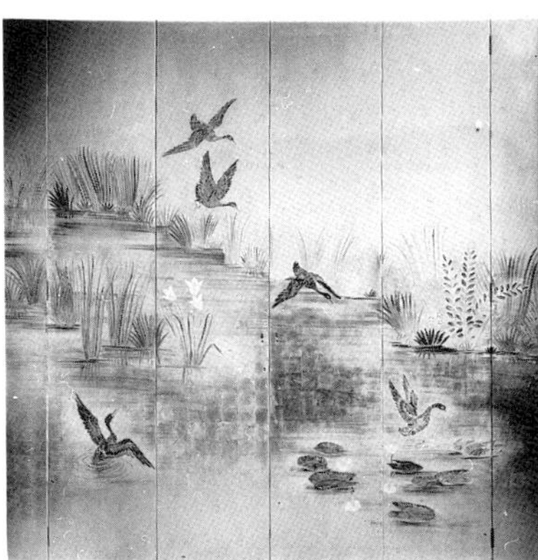
35

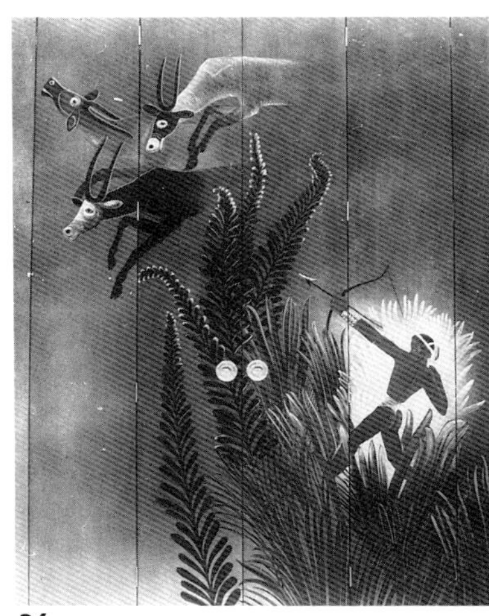
36

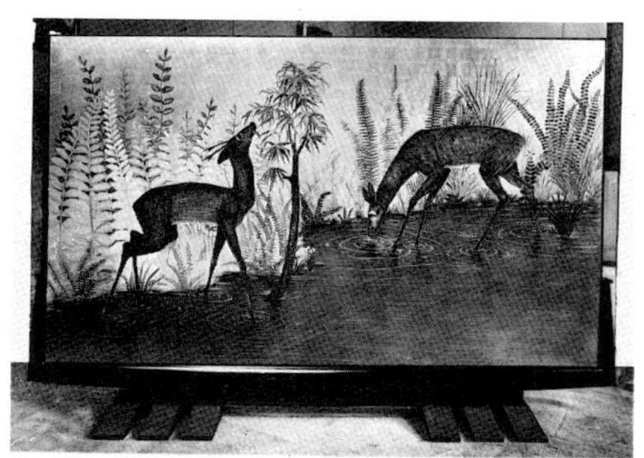
41

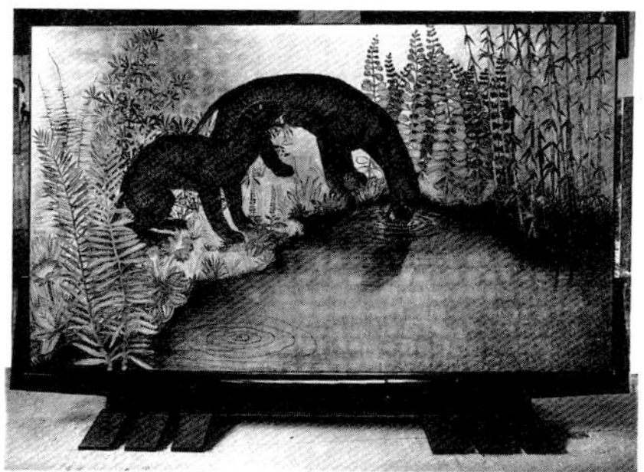
42

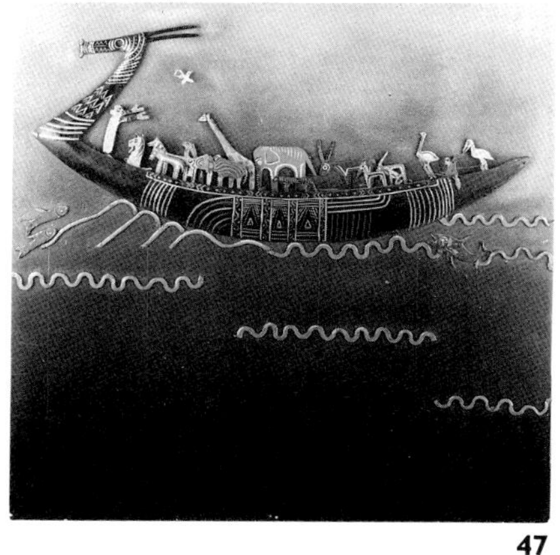
47

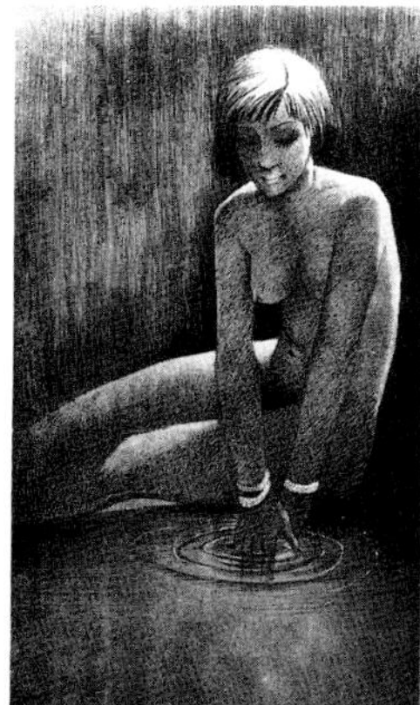
43

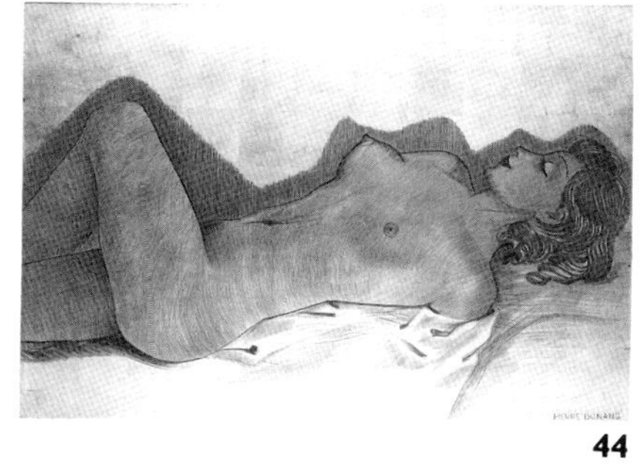
44

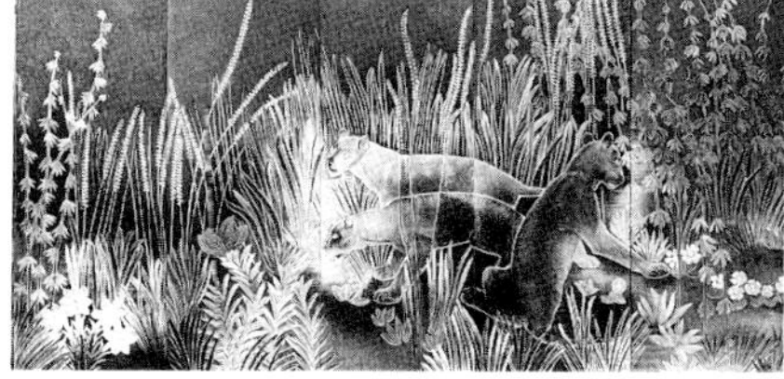
51

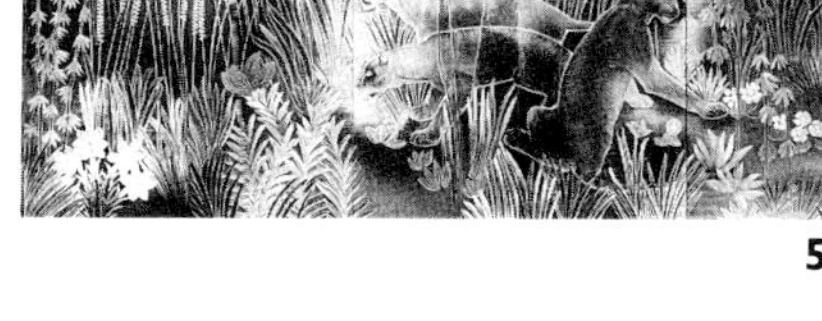
52

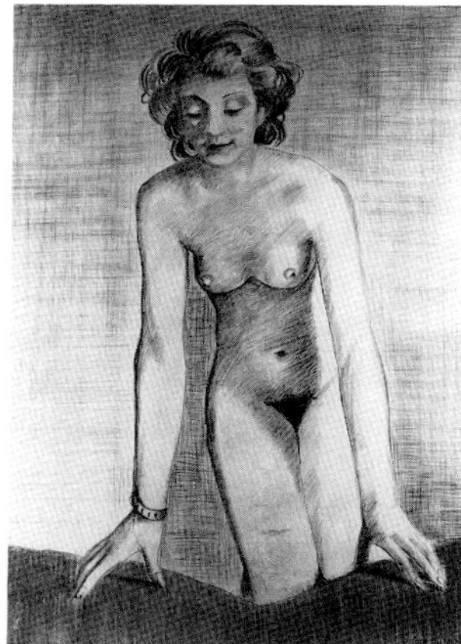
45

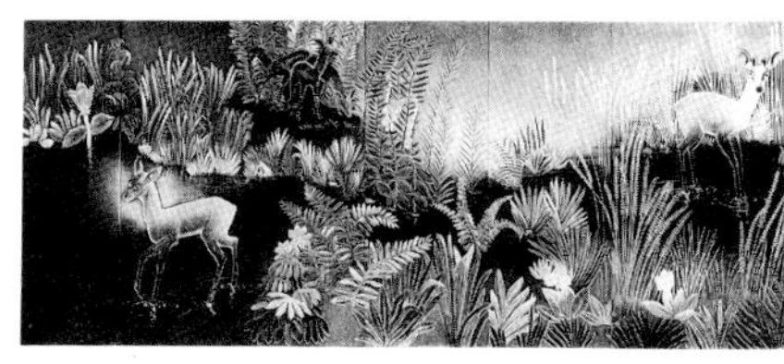

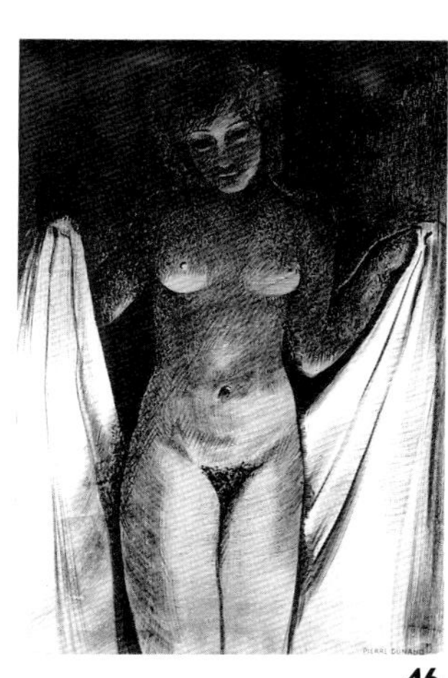
46

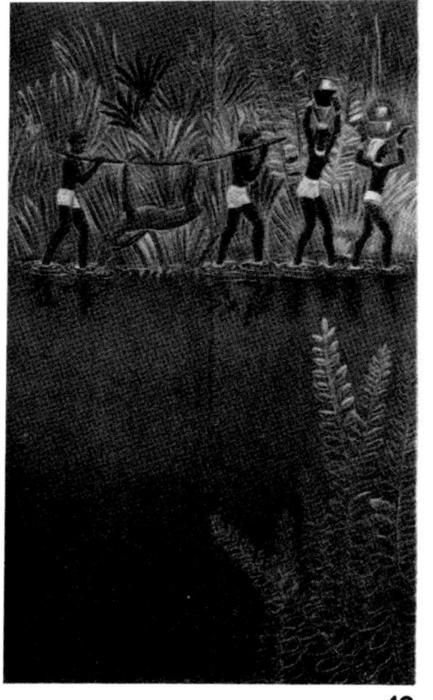
49

41 Deer at a Watering Hole
Black *laque de Chine* firescreen with coloured lacquer decoration.
C. 1945–50.
Private collection.

42 Panthers at a Watering Hole
Black *laque de Chine* firescreen with coloured lacquer decoration.
C. 1945–50.
Private collection.

PANELS

43 Seated Female Nude
Brown and red *laque de Chine* with gold aventurine decoration.
C. 1950.
Private collection.

44 Recumbent Female Nude
Brown and red *laque de Chine* with gold aventurine decoration.
64 x 80 cm (25¼ x 31½ in.).
C. 1950.
Private collection.

45 Standing Female Nude
Brown and red *laque de Chine* with gold aventurine decoration.
84 x 64 cm (33 x 25¼ in.).
C. 1950.
Private collection.

46 Female Nude with Drapery
Brown and red *laque de Chine* with gold aventurine decoration.
80 x 55 cm (31½ x 21¾ in.).
C. 1950.
Private collection.

47 Noah's Ark
Shellac maquette for a mural planned for a café in Nantes.
C. 1950.

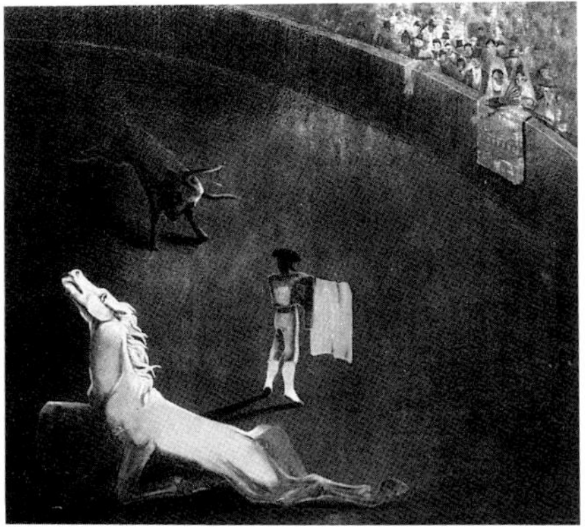
54

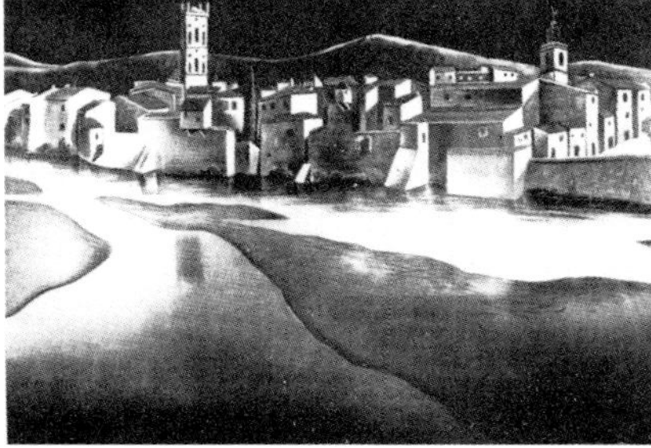
56

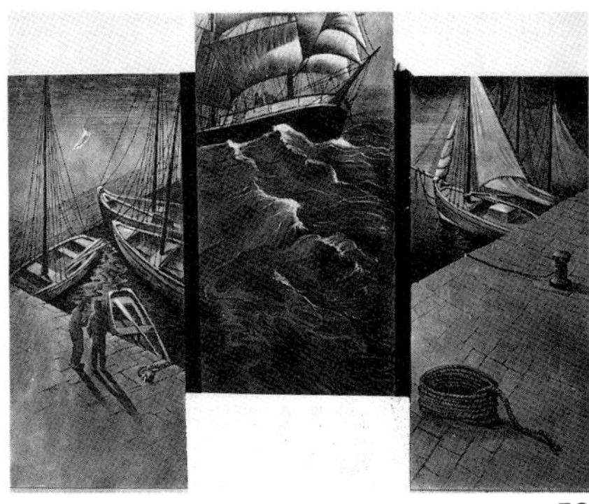
59

48 Charleville, Landscape in the Ardennes
Brown *laque de Chine* with incised Coromandel lacquer decoration.
C. 1950.
Bibl.: 'L'Art de la laque', *Études d'outre-mer*, December 1952, p. 401.

49–52
The liner *La Marseillaise* (1949)
Mural decorations for Jules Lelieu's first-class bridge saloon (see also p. 193).

49 Black Hunters and Antelope Bearers
Shellac with coloured lacquer decoration.
The double doors at the entrance to the bridge saloon.

50 Buffalos and Panther at a Watering Place
Shellac and gold *laque de Chine* with coloured lacquer decoration.
Detail of the mural.

51 Panthers
Shellac with gold lacquer decoration.
Detail of the mural.

52 Deer at a Watering Place
Brown shellac with gold lacquer decoration.
Detail of the mural.

53 Panel: *Black Porters and Elephant*
Gold and brown shellac.
C. 1950.
Private collection.
Sold: D'Anjou (Rouen), 17 March 1985.

54 Panel: *The Kill*
Shellac and gold.
C. 1950–55.

55 Panel: *The Sheep*
Shellac and gold.
C. 1950–55.

56 Rivesaltes
Black *laque de Chine* with gold decoration.
1951.
Mural depicting the village in the *département* of Pyrénées Orientales where Marshal Joffre was born, installed in one of Leleu's saloons on the liner bearing his name.

57 The Bottle in the Sea
Brown shellac with gold decoration.
C. 1950–55.
Private collection.

58 Prancing Horses
Shellac and gold *laque de Chine* with coloured lacquer decoration.
180 x 250 cm (70¾ x 98½ in.).
C. 1950.
Sold: Delorme (Paris), 30 November 1973.

59 The Jetty
Brown shellac with gold decoration.
C. 1950–55.
Fixed panels designed as a mural.

60 The Deer
Gold and black *laque de Chine* with coloured lacquer decoration.
Painted *c.* 1945–50 to a design by Jean Dunand.

61 Panthers at a Watering Hole
Gold and black *laque de Chine* with coloured lacquer decoration.
Painted *c.* 1945–50 to a design by Jean Dunand.

62 Panthers at the Water's Edge
Gold and black *laque de Chine* with decoration in coloured lacquer, executed *c.* 1945–50 to a design by Jean Dunand.

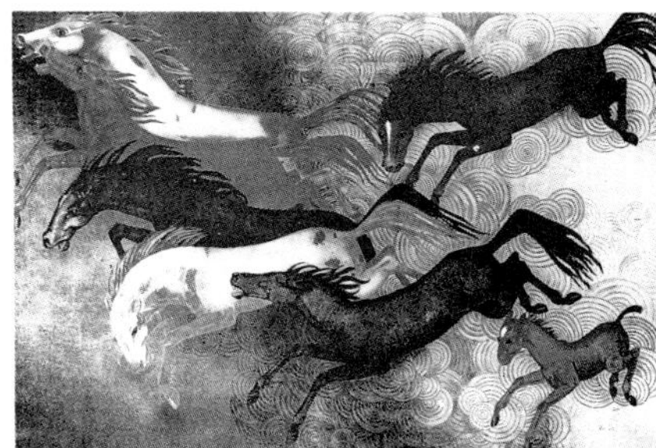
58

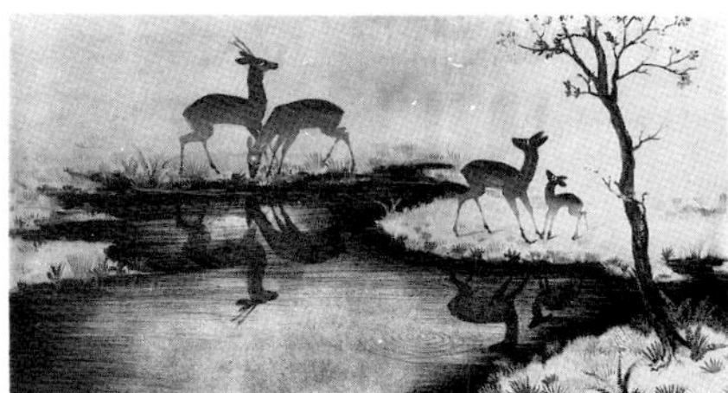
60

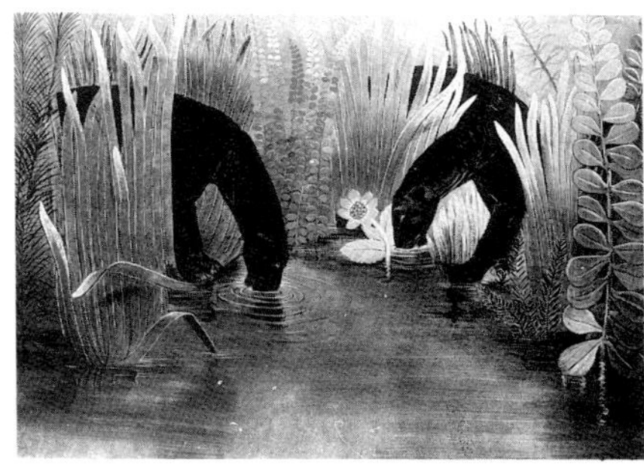
61

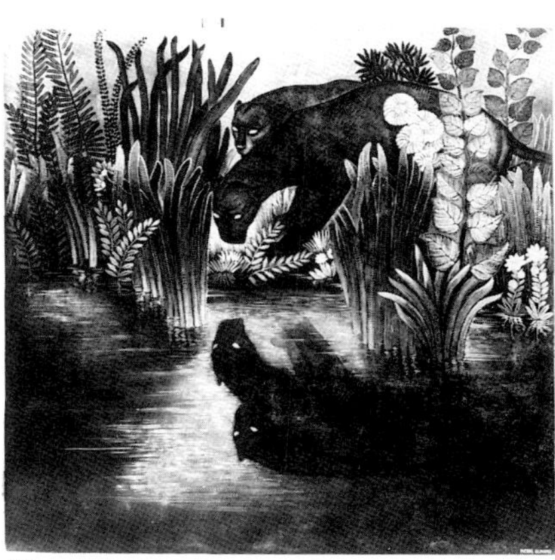
62

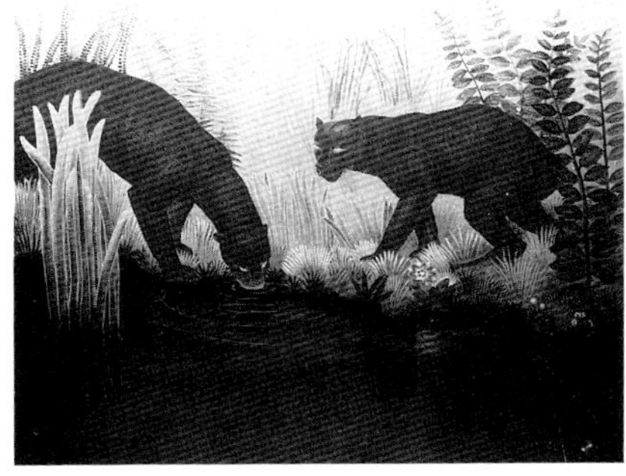

65

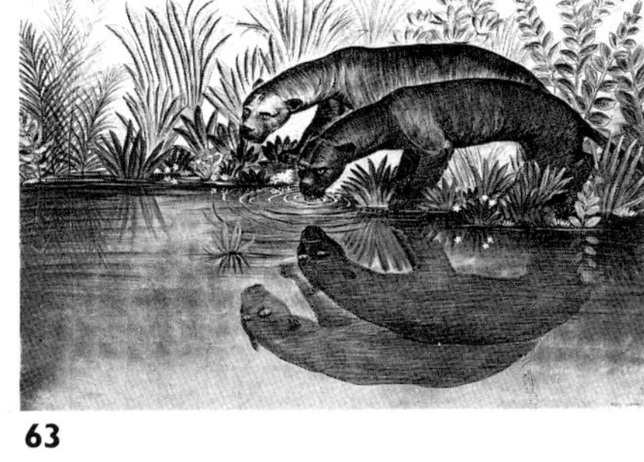

63

64

63 Two Panthers Slaking their Thirst
Gold and black *laque de Chine* with decoration in coloured lacquer, executed *c.* 1945–50 to a design by Jean Dunand. For an identical panel see cat. no. PD 64.

64 Two Panthers Slaking their Thirst
Gold and black *laque de Chine* with decoration in coloured lacquer, executed *c.* 1945–50 to a design by Jean Dunand. Private collection, Montluçon.
The panel, identical in composition to that of cat. no. PD 63, is mounted in conjunction with a dual depiction of a reclining woman in the same pose, but shown nude in one version and draped in the other, the two works being hung side by side. One or other is always obscured by the Pierre Dunand panel, which slides to right or left in front of the paintings.

65 Two Panthers Slaking their Thirst
Gold and black *laque de Chine* with decoration in coloured lacquer, executed *c.* 1945–50 to a design by Jean Dunand. 154 x 190 cm (60½ x 74¾ in.).
Sold: Sotheby's (Monaco), 10 February 1981, lot 1477.

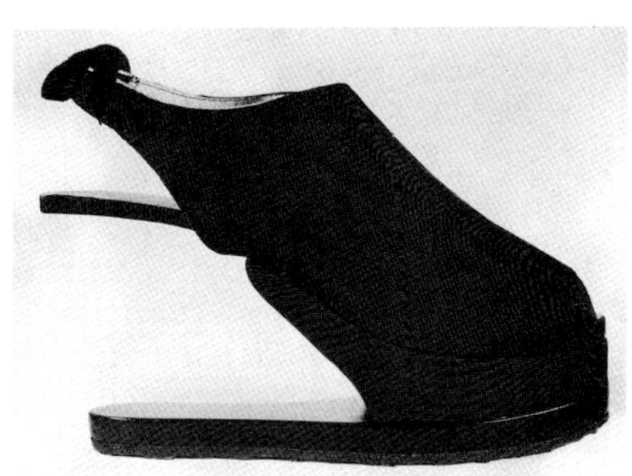

68

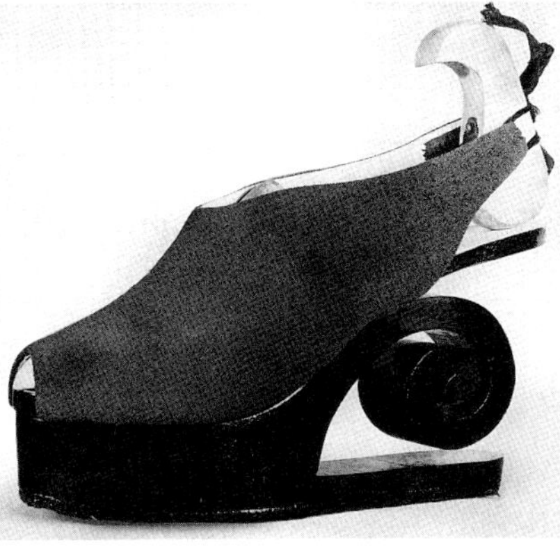

66

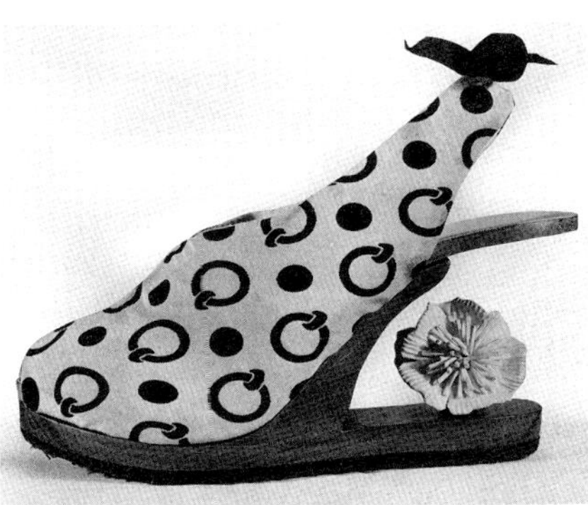

67

LADIES' SHOES (PROTOTYPES)

66 High-heeled shoe
Lacquered wood and fabric.
1944.

67 High-heeled shoe
Lacquered wood and fabric.
1944.

68 High-heeled shoe
Lacquered wood and fabric.
1944.

Bibliography

General books consulted

Adler, Rose, *Reliures*, Paris, n.d.
d'Agnel, Chanoine J. Arnaud, *L'Art religieux moderne*, Grenoble, 1936
Arwas, Victor, *Art Deco*, London/New York, 1976
Battersby, Martin, *The Decorative Thirties*, London, 1971;
——, *The Decorative Twenties*, London, 1969
Bayard, Emile, *L'Art appliqué français d'aujourd'hui*, Paris, n.d., pp. 75, 77, 251;
——, *Le Style moderne*, Paris, 1919
Benton, Tom and Charlotte, and Scharf, Aaron, *Design 1920's – Modernism in the Decorative Arts, Paris 1910–1930*, Milton Keynes, 1975
Bouchet, Léon, *Intérieurs au Salon des Artistes Décorateurs de 1929*, Paris, 1929
Bouilhet, Tony, *L'Orfèvrerie française au XXe. siècle*, Paris, 1941
Bousquet, Jean-Pierre, *La Laque*, Paris, 1980
Broquelet, Alfred, *L'Art appliqué à l'industrie*, Paris, 1909
Brunhammer, Yvonne, *Lo stile 1925*, Milan 1966 (French edition, *Le Style 1925*, Paris, 1978)
Cerri, P., Bosoni, G., and Vragnaz, G., *Il progetto del mobile in Francia 1919–1939*, Bologna, 1986
Chappey, Marcel, *Le XXe. Salon des Artistes Décorateurs*, Paris, 1930
Chavance, René, *Une Ambassade française*, Paris, 1925
Clouzot, Henri, *Le Travail du métal*, Paris, 1921
Dayot, Armand, *Les Animaux* (5 vols.), Paris, 1929–30
Dunand, Bernard, *Sur l'art des laques de Chine*, Marseilles, 1952
Duncan, Alastair, *Art Deco Furniture*, London/New York, 1984
Encyclopédie des arts décoratifs et industriels modernes au XXème siècle (12 vols.), Paris, 1925
Encyclopédie des métiers d'art, vol. I, Paris, n.d., pls. 11–14, 36
Follot, Paul, *Intérieurs français au Salon des Artistes Décorateurs de 1927*, Paris, 1927
Frank, Nino, *Les Années 30*, Paris, 1969
Herbst, René, *25 années – Union des Artistes Modernes (U.A.M.)*, Paris, 1955
Hillier, Bevis, *Art Deco*, London/New York, 1968
Huth, Hans, *Lacquer of the West – The History of Craft and Industry, 1550–1950*, Chicago/London, 1971
Janneau, Guillaume, *L'Art décoratif moderne, formes nouvelles et programmes nouveaux*, Paris, 1925;
——, *Technique du décor intérieur moderne*, Paris, *c.* 1927
Kjellberg, Pierre, *Art-déco. Les maîtres du mobilier*, Paris, 1981
Klein, Dan, *Art Deco*, London/New York, 1974
Lanoux, Armand, *Paris 1925*, Paris, 1957
Legrain, Pierre, *Objets d'art* (L'Art international d'aujourd'hui) Paris, n.d., pls 34, 47
Lejard, André, *Le Meuble*, Paris, 1941
Les Arts de la maison (series of 7 vols.), Paris, 1923–26
Lesieutre, Alain, *The Spirit and the Splendour of Art Deco*, London, 1974/New York, 1975
Lorac-Gerbaud, Andrée, *L'Art du laque*, Paris, 1973
Maenz, Paul, *Art Deco 1920–1940*, Cologne, 1974
Magne, Lucien and Henri-Marcel, *L'Art appliqué aux métiers, décor du métal*, Paris, 1928;
——, *L'Art appliqué aux métiers, décor du mobilier*, Paris, 1928
Marcilhac, Félix, *Art-déco 1925*, Paris, 1984
Menten, Theodore, *The Art Deco Style*, New York, 1972
Mourey, Gabriel, *Histoire générale de l'art français de la Révolution à nos jours*, Paris, 1925
Moussinac, Léon, *Intérieurs* (5 vols.), Paris, 1924;
——, *Le Meuble français moderne*, Paris, 1925
Olmer, Pierre, *Le mobilier français d'aujourd'hui*, Brussels, 1926
Olmer, Pierre, and Bouche-Leclercq, Henri, *L'Art décoratif français 1929*, Paris, 1930
Quenioux, Gaston, *Les Arts décoratifs modernes*, Paris 1925
Rapin, Henri, *Intérieurs présentés au Salon des Artistes Décorateurs de 1930*, Paris, 1930
Répertoire du goût moderne (8 vols.), Paris, 1928
Roche, Antoine, *Paris 1929*, Paris, 1929
Scarlett, Frank, and Townley, Marjorie, *Arts Décoratifs 1925*, London/New York, 1975
Sedeyn, Émile, *Le mobilier* (L'art français depuis vingt ans), Paris, 1921
Selvafolta, Ornella, *Il mobile del novecento – Art Deco*, Novara, 1985
d'Uckerman, P. *L'Art appliqué à l'industrie*, Paris, 1937
Uecker, Wolf, *Art Deco, die Kunst der Zwanziger Jahre*, Munich, 1974
Vaillat, Léandre, *Le Décor de la vie*, Paris, 1919
Verne, Henri, and Chavance, René, *Pour comprendre l'art décoratif moderne en France*, Paris, 1925
Veronesi, Giulia, *Into the Twenties*, London/New York, 1968

Exhibition catalogues

In the course of his career Dunand was a regular contributor to the principal Paris salons, as well as to the group exhibitions at the Galerie Georges Petit

(1921–32) and the Galerie Charpentier (1933) which also featured works by Jean Goulden, Paul Jouve and François-Louis Schmied. Other single or semi-regular occasions when works by Dunand were on public exhibition are noted in the text in the appropriate chronological context and in individual entries in the catalogue of works.

Major exhibitions held since the artist's death include:

Europäische Lackkunst, Museum Bellerive, Zurich, 1976

Jean Dunand, Delorenzo Gallery, New York, May-June 1985

Jean Dunand – Jean Goulden, Galerie du Luxembourg, Paris, May-July 1973

Articles in periodicals, listed by author

Adrianne, Charlotte, 'Jean Dunand and his Influence on the Fashion World', *L'Officiel de la couture*, November 1926, pp. 33–6

Alexandre, Arsène, 'Portraits et figures de femmes de Ingres à Picasso', *La Renaissance*, July 1928, pp. 257–308;

——, 'Une Décoration de Jean Dunand, *La Renaissance*, November 1931, pp. 318–21

Baschet, Jacques, 'Intérieurs modernes', *L'Illustration*, 27 May 1933, pp. 1–2;

——, 'Laques et bronzes', *L'Illustration*, Christmas 1940;

——, 'Les Dinanderies et les laques de Jean Dunand', *L'Illustration*, 15 October 1927, pp. 425–8

Bayer, Patricia, 'Jean Dunand: Premier Craftsman of the Art Deco Style', *Art & Antiques*, May–June 1982, pp. 56–63

Bernard, Oliver P., 'Liners and Lining', *Building*, March 1932, pp. 108–13;

——, 'United Arts of Europe, Paris 1929–1930', *Building*, March 1930, pp. 122–7

Blake, Vernon, 'Modern Decorative Art', *The Architectural Review*, July 1925 (the Paris Exhibition), pp. 24–33

Boyer, Jacques, 'Les Artistes français imitent aujourd'hui les laqueurs japonais', [unidentified journal], *c.* 1923

Brook, Georges, 'La laque végétale d'Indochine', *La Nature*, 15 October 1937

Bushell, S. W., 'M. Jean Dunand's Craftwork', *Visions of Old Russia*, n.d. (*c.* 1926), pp. 235–6

Caël, Jean, 'Une Merveilleuse Industrie: les laques d'extrême-orient en France', *La Semaine à Paris*, 1 November 1925, pp. 379–85

Chavance, René, 'Au Salon d'Automne', *Les Échos des industries d'art*, December 1928, pp. 10–23;

——, 'Le paquebot "L'Atlantique" et les beaux métiers', *Art et décoration*, November 1931, pp. 153–64

Clouzot, Henri, 'Le Salon des Artistes Décorateurs', *La Revue de l'art ancien et moderne*, April 1922, pp. 315–20

Cresswell, Howell S., 'Oriental Lacquers on Modern Furniture', *Good Furniture Magazine*, June 1928, pp. 291–5

Dayot, Magdeleine A., 'Une Visite à Jean Dunand', *L'Art et les artistes*, November 1936, pp. 57–62

Doin, Jeanne, 'Les Salons de 1922', *Gazette des Beaux-Arts*, June 1922, pp. 339–60

Dunand, Bernard, 'Sur l'Esthétique du laque', *Études philosophiques*, July-December 1949, pp. 445–60

Dunand, Pierre, 'Un vase pour chaque fleur', *Art et industrie*, December 1952

Elbaz, Irène, 'Laques de Jean Dunand', *Revue du Louvre*, May 1986, pp. 332–5

F. S., 'Une Présentation nouvelle de tableaux', *Les Échos des industries d'art*, August 1928, p. 22

Felice, Roger de, 'John Dunand', *L'Art décoratif*, January 1909, pp. 11–18

Fischer, Ragna, 'Jean Dunand', *Kunstindustri*, January 1937, pp. 9–11

Frantz, Henri, 'Jean Dampt', *The Magazine of Arts*, n.d. (*c.* 1910), pp. 307–12

Fulter, Jean, 'Le Décor d'un grand paquebot', *Art et industrie*, November 1931, pp. 15–23

Galloti, Jean, 'Quelques oeuvres récentes de Jean Dunand', *Art et décoration*, August 1932, pp. 225–32

Gault, Maxime, 'Désormais les transatlantiques pourront être décorés de panneaux et meubles en laque entièrement incombustibles', *Sciences et vie*, 28 March 1935, pp. 303–4

Gauthier, Maximilien, 'Jean Dunand', *L'Art vivant*, 15 November 1925, pp. 28–9;

——, 'Vingt minutes avec M. Jean Dunand', *La Renaissance politique, littéraire et artistique*, *c.* 1923

Greslet, Henri, 'Les Beaux Laques d'Orient et de France', *La France illustrée*, 17 July 1926, p. 102

Guardia, G. Bruno, 'La Décoration de "L'Atlantique"', *Beaux-Arts*, 25 October 1931; 'La Leçon de l'Atlantique', *Beaux-Arts*, 15 January 1933

Guiffrey, Jean, 'Jean Dunand, Le studio de Madame Agnès, *La Renaissance de l'art français*, April 1927, pp. 175–8

Hay, Yahne de la, 'Jean Dunand, le magicien des reflets', *L'Élite de Paris*, 22 July 1937, pp. 29–31

Henriot, Gabriel, 'Jean Dunand', *Mobilier et décoration*, February 1926, pp. 33–47

Jaloux, Edmond, 'La Maison d'un diplomate', *L'Illustration*, 22 July 1933, pp. 417–20

Janneau, Guillaume, 'Les Directions nouvelles des arts industriels', *Les Échos des industries d'art*, June 1928, pp. 31–4

L. M., 'Le Salon d'Automne', *Le Cahier, revue mensuelle des arts et des lettres*, November 1931, pp. 69–72

Liagre, Christina de, 'Lacquer Perfect', *House and Garden* (U.S.A.), June 1985, pp. 159–66

M. D., 'L'Art de Jean Dunand s'exprime en lignes hardies', *Vogue* (Paris), 1 May 1925

Malglaive, P. de, 'French Ideas of Ship Planning and Decoration', *Journal of the Royal Society of Arts*, 16 April 1937, pp. 500–20

Maurel, André, 'Arts appliqués: Jean Dunand', *Le Carnet des artistes*, 1 May 1917, pp. 14–16
May, Pierre André, 'Les Paravents', *Plaisir de France*, June 1937, pp. 18–21
Merciériondel, M., 'Un Métier d'art, la laque', *Plaisir de France*, July 1937
Mille, Pierre, 'Le Salon de 1918', *Gazette des Beaux-Arts*, April/June 1918, pp. 198–200
Monnier, Jean, 'Les Vases de John Dunand', *Foi et vie*, 16 February 1908 (eleventh year, number 4), pp. 102–6
Monod-Herzen, Ernest, 'L'Art du métal', *Les Arts français* (No. 21), 1918, pp. 175–7
Moreau-Vauthier, Charles, 'Une Salle de l'Hôtel de la Comtesse de Béarn par Jean Dampt', *Art et décoration*, 1906, pp. 109–18
Mouilleseaux, Louis, 'Les Arts, pléiade d'artistes', *Le Cahier*, January 1931, pp. 42–53
Moutard-Uldry, Renée, 'L'Architecture et la décoration' (the French Pavilion at the New York World's Fair), *L'Art et les artistes*, June 1939, pp. 289–314
Nalys, Roger, 'À Bord de l'Atlantique: les panneaux de Jean Dunand', *L'Officiel de la couture*, October 1931, p. 54;
——, 'Les Laques de Dunand à La Renaissance', *L'Officiel de la couture*, August 1929, p. 56;
——, 'Portraits en laque', *L'Officiel de la couture*, May 1933, pp. 18–19
Pascal, [?], 'Verre mosaïque émail à Galliéra', *L'Art vivant*, 1934, p. 278
Patterson, Augusta Owen, 'The Decorative Arts', *Town and Country*, 1 March 1928, pp. 52–3
Pinturicchio, 'Carnet des ateliers: Dunand', *Le Carnet de la Semaine*, 23 November 1919
Plesch, Prof. Dr J., 'Jean Dunand, ein moderner Meister dekorativer Kunst', *Die Kunst*, 7 April 1933, pp. 206–23
Rambosson, Yvanhoé, 'L'Art appliqué aux Salons. Chez les Artistes Décorateurs', *La Revue de l'art*, July 1928, pp. 97–112;
——, 'Le Décor géométrique et les laques dans l'oeuvre de Dunand', *L'Amour de l'art*, July 1923, pp. 613–16;
——, 'Le Pavillon de la Société des Artistes Décorateurs', *Mobilier et décoration*, August 1937;
——, 'Le Salon des Décorateurs', *L'Amour de l'art*, June 1924, pp. 190–4;
——, 'Les Arts appliqués au Salon d'Automne', *Comoedia* (supplement), 1927, pp. 13–32
Roche, Pierre de la, 'Normandie, triomphe de l'art décoratif français', *Art et industrie*, July 1935, pp. 6–12
Rudder, Jean-Luc de, 'Les Laques de Dunand, reflets brillants des arts décos', *L'Estampille*, pp. 60–6
Sanford, Nellie C., 'The Loan Exhibition from the Paris Exposition', *Good Furniture Magazine*, April 1926, p. 187
Sarcey, Liliane, 'Une Visite à l'atelier de M. Jean Dunand', *Conferencia*, No. 9, 15 April 1926, pp. 438–45
Schommer, Pierre, 'Dans la galerie de Jacques Seligmann', *Le Figaro artistique*, 26 April 1926
Sedeyn, Emile, 'Jean Dunand', *Art et décoration*, September/October 1919, pp. 118–26;
——, 'Le onzième Salon des Artistes Décorateurs', *La Renaissance de l'art français*, April 1920, pp. 150–7
Small, Peter, 'The Modern French Decorative Art Exposition' (Lord & Taylor, New York), *Creative Art*, March 1928, pp. xliii-xlv
T. H. [Thomas Hoving], 'Normandie's Sun Rises Again', *The Connoisseur*, October 1984, pp. 118–21
Teall, Gardner, 'Screens and Furniture by Jean Dunand', *Harper's Bazaar*, April 1928, pp. 114–15 and p. 95
Testard, M., 'Le Métal dans l'art moderne', *Nos Loisirs, revue de la femme et du foyer*, July 1922, pp. 322–3
Thornton, Lynne, 'Jean Dunand and his Friends', *Apollo*, October 1973, pp. 294–9
Thubert, Emmanuel de, 'Dans les ateliers de Jean Dunand', *L'Art décoratif*, November 1910, pp. 118–26;
——, 'Jean Dunand', *L'Art et les artistes* (new series, No. 9), 1920, pp. 381–6
Vauxcelles, Louis, 'La Cuisine des salons de peinture', *Le Miroir*, 12 April 1914
Wertz, Léon, Le XVIIe Salon des Artistes Décorateurs, *Art et décoration*, June 1927, pp. 160–200

Other miscellaneous publications including brochures, periodicals and articles (anonymous or authors unknown), listed by title

L'Art d'aujourd'hui (Spring instalment), No. 13 (1927), pls. 17, 18
'L'Art de l'ameublement à l'exposition Les Fumoirs', *La Revue des tabacs*, October 1937, pp. 41–3
'L'Art de vivre', *Vogue* (Paris), September 1961
Art et industrie, September 1928, p. 38; May-June 1935, p. 14
'Les Artistes Décorateurs au Grand-Palais', *Le Grand Monde*, June 1932, pp. 17–18
'L'Atlantique', *L'Illustration*, 19 November 1931, pp. 68–72
'À travers le Salon des Artistes Décorateurs', *La Renaissance*, July 1930, pp. 206–7
'Au Salon des Artistes Décorateurs', *La Renaissance de l'art français*, July 1927, pp. 334–49
'Au Salon, portraits de vedettes', *L'Illustration*, 13 December 1941
Bulletin de l'art français et japonais, September 1927, March 1928 and May 1928
La Carrosserie, May 1934, p. 12
'La Céréale noble: le blé', *L'Illustration*, July 1941
Compagnie des Messageries Maritimes, brochures on the liners *La Marseillaise* (1949) and *Maréchal Joffre* (1951)
Compagnie Générale Transatlantique, brochure on the liner *Normandie* (1935)
'Dunand Screens in the Modern French Spirit', *Art and Decoration*, May 1928, p. 68

'D'une Greffe sur la joue est né le chapeau de bois', *La Semaine*, 26 June 1941

'Les Emménagements', *Journal de la marine marchande*, September 1931, pp. 39–66

Études d'outre-mer, special number on lacquer, December 1952

'Exposition of Modern French Decorative Art', *The American Architect*, 5 March 1928, pp. 317–22

'Expositions, Dunand-Goulden-Jouve-Schmied, Galerie Georges Petit', *Gazette des Beaux-Arts*, 20 January 1930, pp. 16–17

'A Folio of Gift Suggestions from French Designers', *Fairchild's International*, June 1929, pp. 32–7

'Francia', catalogue of the Sixth Triennale in Milan, French section, October 1936

'In Paris You Must Have a Lacquer Portrait', *Art and Decoration*, October 1927, p. 134

'Jean Dunand', *Mobilier et décoration*, No. 7 (1954), biographical index

'Die Lackarbeiten Dunands', *Die Dame*, September 1930, pp. 19–21

'Liou Tse Houa', *La Semaine*, 28 November 1940

'Masterpieces of French Modern Bindings', *Service Culturel Français*, New York 1947

'Le Métal repoussé et ciselé', *Les Arts français* (No. 21), 1918, pp. 165–74

Mobilier et décoration, July 1954

'Modern Decorative Arts from Paris at the Metropolitan Museum of Art', *The American Magazine of Art*, vol. 17 (1926), p. 171

'Le Musée Permanent des Colonies', *La Construction moderne*, 31 January 1932, pp. 278–96

'Normandie', *Architectural Forum*, June 1935, pp. 26–48

'Normandie', *L'Illustration*, 1 June 1935 (special number)

'Normandie, Ambassadeur de France, dans le fumoir les laques de Dunand', *L'Espoir français*, 24 May 1935

'Portrait de Madame Agnès', *L'Illustration*, special Christmas number, 1934

'Le Premier Voyage du Normandie', *L'Atlantique* (special issue of newspaper issued by C.G.T.), June 1935

'Project pour une fête coloniale', *Connoisseur des arts*, May 1981, pp. 82–9

'La Renaissance du métal repoussé', *La Nature*, February 1924, pp. 81–5

'Salle des fastes et la Rotonde d'honneur, centre des arts', *Plaisir de France*, July 1939

'Le Salon des Artistes Décorateurs modernes au Salon des Artistes Français', *Mobilier et décoration d'intérieur*, July 1922, pp. 2–5

The Studio Yearbook of Decorative Art, [1927?], p 136

'Travaux d'orfèvrerie d'artistes de la Suisse occidentale', *L'Oeuvre* (revue mensuelle de l'Association Suisse Romande de l'Art et de l'Industrie [Berne]), January 1914, pp. 6–9

Trouvailles, October-November 1976, p. 54

'Les Vases de Jean Dunand', *La Décoration moderne*, new series, XIIIth year (1905–6), section 'Bronzes, cuivres', pl. 40

'Une Visite au décorateur Jean Dunand', *La Patrie Suisse*, November 1933

Vogue (Paris), 15 October 1927, p. 32.

Acknowledgments

First and foremost among the many individuals who assisted the author in the preparation of this book were the four surviving sons and daughters of Jean Dunand, and especially his sons Bernard and Pierre who were a constant source of inspiration and invaluable first-hand information during the six years that were devoted to detailed research into the life and works of their father.

The documentary material made available by members of the Dunand family was supplemented by information from collectors, both in France and elsewhere, especially Steven A. Greenberg of New York, whose keen and discerning eye has made him one of the most knowledgeable of collectors. I extend my grateful thanks to him and all those listed below: Hervé Aaron, Mme Aboucaya, J.-S. Baumé, A. Blondel, J.P. Bousquet, A. Bromberg, M. and Mme Cardinaël, Michael and Tina Chow, J.J. Colcombet, M. and Mme Dougoud, Jean-Paul Dunand, M. Eidelberg, George Encil, B. Friedman, C. Gaspart, B. Goulden, R. and M. Kupperfils, M. Lambert-Rucki, F. Landowski-Caillet, J.P. Ley, F. and S. Lewis, J. Lhomme, A. Magnol, M. Mathysen, M. and Mme Mouscadet, C. Ott, Mme Perlstein, Mme Pettina, Y. Plantin, M. and Mme Rittener, Lord David Rocksavage, Count and Countess Ghislain de Royère, Yves Saint Laurent and Pierre Bergé, M. Sebert, and Mlle Simon.

Invaluable research was carried out abroad on my behalf by my old friend Professor Martin Eidelberg of New York, and Mme Pettina was particularly helpful in her unstinting efforts to elucidate from official records the history of earlier generations of the Dunand family in the context of changing international boundaries between France and Switzerland and local developments in the Canton of Geneva.

Numerous art galleries specializing in works of the Art Deco period have generously allowed access to their archives and records of past sales, enabling the author to retrace the provenance of certain works and to obtain photographs (see list of credits below). Foremost among these are the Galerie du Luxembourg in Paris and the Delorenzo Gallery in New York, both of which have put on major exhibitions, in 1973 and 1985 respectively, of works by Dunand. Other galleries outside France which have been of great help are Didier Aaron, Inc. of New York and in Geneva the Galerie Art Nouveau-Art Deco and the Galerie des Grandes Époques. Those in Paris whose assistance has been greatly appreciated include especially the Galerie Vallois (Bob and Cheska Vallois). Others are L'Arc en Seine and the following proprietors: Maria de Beyrie, Jean-Claude Brugnot, Thierry Couvrat-Desvergnes, Jacques De Vos, Jean-Jacques Dutko, Anne-Sophie Duval, Alain Lesieutre, Jacques Mostini and Denise A. Orsini.

Aware of the major task facing the author in the preparation of this book, auction houses in France, as well as those with an international organization, such as Christie's and Sotheby's, furnished information concerning sales and supplied photographs of works as and when they appeared on the market. Alastair Duncan of Christie's in New York was the first to reply to the author's enquiries, and even volunteered documentary material known to him, while his colleague Dan Klein in London proved still more enthusiastic. Sylvie Avizou of Sotheby's in Paris was extremely accommodating in her prompt attention to requests for photographs of objects illustrated in sale catalogues. Philippe Garner in London and Barbara E. Deisroth in New York were instrumental in fulfilling almost all similar requests for photographs to be used as illustrations in this book.

The author's fund of documentation was further expanded through the good offices of leading Paris auctioneers, notably: Ader, Picart, Tajan; Boisgirard; Chayette, Calmels; Couturier, de Nicolay; Daussy, de Ricqlès; Delavenne, Lafarge; Delorme; Godeau, Solanet, Audap; Libert, Castor; Millon, Jutheau; Oger, Dumont; Poulain, Lefur; and Rieunier, Bailly-Pommery. Alain Nazare-Aga was also of great help. In the provinces, the following auction houses have made significant contributions: Anaf (Lyons); Champin, Lombrail, Gautier (Enghien); Dianous (Manosque); Gallais, Livinec, Pincemin (Rennes); and Singer, Desbuissons (Lille). One much appreciated item was supplied through the good offices of Thomas and Nancy Hoving. This is a remarkable photomontage showing the complete mural executed in lacquer by Dunand to a design by Jean Dupas for the partition wall between the first-class Saloon and the Smoking Room of the liner *Normandie*; this striking work, the result of juxtaposing photographs of different sections of the overall scheme, was originally reproduced in Thomas Hoving's article in the October 1984 issue of *The Connoisseur*.

With few exceptions requests made to national institutions and museums in France for permission to reproduce photographs of works by Jean Dunand in their collections (as noted in individual catalogue entries) were readily granted. The author wishes to thank the following bodies and their representatives or curators: the Directorate of the Musées de France (Jacques Vilain), the Mobilier National (Mme Anne Lajoix), the Manufacture Nationale de Céramiques de Sèvres and the Manufacture Nationale des Gobelins et de Beauvais (Jean Gouval). Also many museums: Musée des Beaux-Arts de la Ville du Havre; Musée des Beaux-Arts de Lyon; Musée de l'Armée, Paris; Musée d'Art Moderne de la Ville de Paris (Mme Jacqueline Lafargue); Musée des Arts Décoratifs, Paris (Mme

Yvonne Brunhammer); Musée National de la Légion d'Honneur, Paris; Musée National des Arts Africains et Océaniens, Paris; Musée d'Orsay, Paris (Marc Barcou).

Elsewhere valuable help was provided by the following:

ENGLAND: Brighton Art Gallery and Museums, Sussex

SWITZERLAND: Musée d'Art et d'Histoire, Geneva; Musée de l'Horlogerie, Geneva; Musée Cantonal des Beaux-Arts (Palais de Rumine), Lausanne; Museum Bellerive, Zurich (with special thanks to my friend Sigrid Barten).

The massive undertaking of photographing the complete family archives of the sons and daughters of Jean Dunand was carried out at the author's request by Laurent Sully-Jaulmes, who also found time to make vital journeys outside Paris. Similarly, Fred Garcia-Mochales generously provided photographs of works by Dunand taken in French provincial collections while he was involved in preparatory work for an Art Deco exhibition to be held in Tokyo. Many other photographers have also contributed to the illustration material for this book through their fulfilling of orders and requests from the author and publisher or from private collectors who have allowed their works to be included. In addition to acknowledging help from the Photographic Service of the Réunion des Musées Nationaux (M. Ginguay de Beaugendre), thanks are due to: Jean-Pierre Bouret; Davoust & Matet, Vénus Mercenaire; Pascal Faligot; Photo-Flandres; Studio Lourmel; Ph. Sebert.

To all those who have supplied photographs or agreed to their being reproduced, the author wishes to express his sincere thanks. In the absence of any specific mention in the list of photographic credits below, all illustrations are reproduced from material in the author's archives or from private collections. The author is grateful to all those private collectors who have helped in the realization of this project while preferring to remain anonymous. Finally, sincere thanks are due to the staff of Thames and Hudson for their help and encouragement in the planning and preparation of this book.

Photographic credits

Didier Aaron, Inc., New York: cat. 636
Hervé Aaron: cat. 303, 339
Ader, Picart, Tajan: cat. 1020
Anaf: cat. 1006
L'Arc en Seine: cat. 410
Jean-Jacques Baumé: cat. 308 (pl. 23), 521 (pl. 168)
Claude Boisgirard: cat. 1024 (pl. 115)
M. et Mme Cardinaël, Paris: cat. 224 (pl. 42)
Christie's, Geneva: cat. 325, 583, 821, 843, 844, 845, 858, 859, 868, 869
Christie's, New York: cat. 145, 158, 229, 275 (pl. 35), 422, 449, 459 (pl. 58), 867, 1007, 1093
The Connoisseur: cat. 1118
Cornette de St Cyr: cat. 320, 321
Couturier, de Nicolay: cat. 1017 (pl. 117), 1028 (pl. 120)
Daussy, de Ricqlès: cat. 1016
Davoust & Matet, Vénus Mercenaire: cat. 1169
Delorenzo Gallery: cat. 103, 551 (pl. 75), 556 (pl. 64), 591, 688 (pl. 84), 810, 907 (pl. 136), 982 (pl. 142), 988, 1008, 1009, 1028 (pl. 120), 1046, 1047, 1048, 1167
Documentation Photographique de la Réunion des Musées Nationaux, Paris: cat. 608
Dunand family archives: cat. 1166, page 90
Bernard Dunand: cat. BD 8, 24, 25
Pierre Dunand: cat. PD 66, 67, 68
Alastair Duncan: cat. 563 (pl. 41), 1167, page 95
Étude d'Enghien: cat. 1096 (pl. 150), 1097
Pascal Faligot: cat. 665
Barry Friedman: cat. 937
Galerie du Luxembourg: cat. 808, 1177
Galerie Denise Orsini: cat. 474
Galerie Vallois: cat. 324 (pl. 25), 414, 417 (pl. 70), 470 (table), 486 (pl. 52), 1035, 1135
Gallais, Livinec, Pincemin: cat. 110
Claude Gaspart: cat. 931
Godeau, Solanet, Audap: cat. 184, 266, 301, 359, 423, 519, 993, 995, 1057
Goulden: cat. 531 (pl. 52), 570 (pl. 170)
Steven A. Greenberg: cat. 13, 20, 227 (pl. 44), 331 (pl. 17), 365, 373 (pl. 27), 396 (pl. 26), 1075, 1171–2
Metropolitan Museum of Art, New York (gift of Mrs Solomon R. Guggenheim): cat. 1154, 1155 (pl. 163)
Millon, Jutheau: cat. 1027
Mobilier National, Paris: cat. 1235, BD 22
Musée des Arts Décoratifs, Paris: page 114
Musée National des Arts Africains et Océaniens, Paris: cat. 1213 (pl. 32), 1220, 1221
Oger, Dumont: cat. 267 (pl. 33)
Claude Ott: cat. 57 (pl. 16), 380, 381, 382, 385, 386
Pillias, Gluck: cat. 281
Rieunier: cat. 233 (pl. 157)
Yves Saint Laurent and Pierre Bergé: cat. 926, 981 (pl. 141), 1198
Sebert: cat 827 (pl. 160), 1131 (pl. 72), 1132
Sotheby's: cat. 4, 44, 112, 154, 162, 172 (pl. 3), 221, 222, 234, 393, 428, 453, 471, 509, 541, 542, 577, 578, 639, 660, 715, 719, 1088, 1120, 1130, 1226
Virginia Museum of Fine Arts, Richmond (gifts of Sydney and Frances Lewis): cat. 436, 452, 465 (pl. 67), 475, 863, 1021

Index

Page numbers in italics refer to black-and-white illustrations in the text sections; references to the colour plates and to catalogue entries (shown in bold type) are listed by their relevant numbers appearing in the captions and catalogue of works, respectively. For general categories of works see the classified list on p. 199, preceding the catalogue. Specific works by Dunand associated with named individuals (e.g. portraits, private commissions and interior decorative schemes) or with major exhibitions are listed under the names of the persons concerned or the places where exhibitions were held (identified by name of museum, Salon or gallery as appropriate).